MW00990647

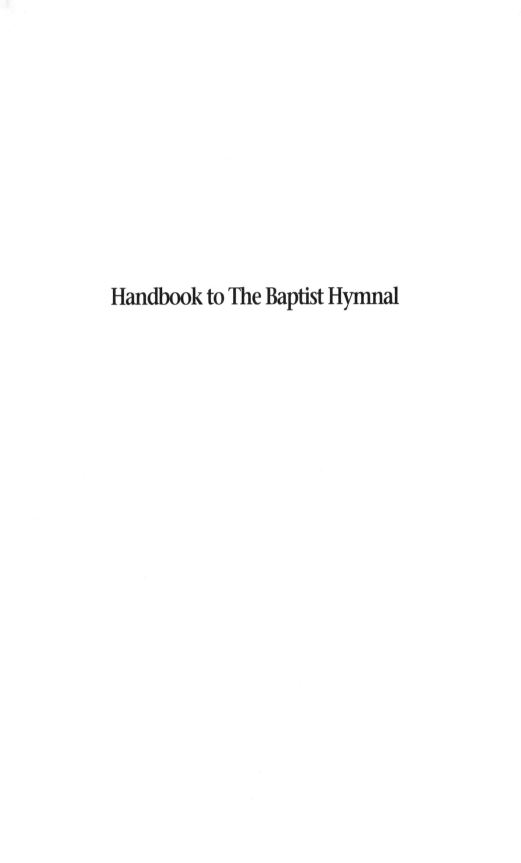

Handbook to The Baptist Hymnal

HANDBOOK
to
THE
BAPTIST
HYMNAL

CHURCH STREET PRESS
NASHVILLE, TENNESSEE

Dewey Decimal Classification Number: 782.27
Subject Heading: HYMNS//COMPOSERS

Church Music Department
The Sunday School Board of the Southern Baptist Convention
127 Ninth Avenue, North
Nashville, Tennessee 37234

Printed in the United States of America

Preface

THE release of *The Baptist Hymnal*, March of 1991, included a rich, "family" resource of supporting editions: organ, piano, choir, orchestra, handbell, and guitar. Both the *Hymnal* and its adjunct editions are constantly updated through a periodical entitled *Worship*. The *Handbook to The Baptist Hymnal* is the latest publication in the "family" resource to *The Baptist Hymnal*.

The basic purpose of the *Handbook* is to illuminate and enrich congregational singing. Thus, the *Handbook* is directed to three audiences: lay persons, college/seminary professors and students, and worship leaders.

To fulfill the basic purpose stated above, it was determined that it's authors should be not only reputable scholars, but, also, practitioners of church music. Fortunately, there exists within the community of scholars associated with Baptist colleges and seminaries stellar hymnologists who are also recognized as outstanding church musicians.

For the lay person, the biographical information on lyricists and composers will bring fresh insight to, and new appreciation of, our rich heritage of hymnody.

Both professors and students alike will find the *Handbook* a rewarding resource, not only for the biographical data on authors and composers whose works are making their first appearance in a hymnbook, but, also, for new data and insights into more familiar hymns.

However illuminating it may be for lay persons, or invaluable for professors and students, it is anticipated that the *Handbook* will be of greatest value to leaders of worship. The leaders of worship always need to be:

- theologically informed in order to faithfully present the truth;
- musically sensitive so as to present the truth in a musically appealing and accessible form;
- evangelically committed so that the declaration of the "good news" is a continuum.

Even as *The Baptist Hymnal* is characterized as a "hymnbook for the people of the Book," so is this volume to be noted as being for the leaders of worship "for the people of the Book."

As such, it is the prayer and aspiration of those whose hearts and minds are encapsulated in its text, that continuing generations will sing with both "spirit and understanding."

Wesley L. Forbis
Editor, *The Baptist Hymnal*

Acknowledgments

*T*HE publishers are indebted to each of the authors for their thorough and scholarly contribution. Given the additional task of locating and corresponding with new writers and composers, their achievement is all the more remarkable.

Following their research of Scriptures appropriate to each musical and responsorial item in *The Baptist Hymnal*, Nolan Howington and James Taulman are to be commended for their painstaking work in identifying Scriptures which undergird each stanza of a given hymn.

Publication of *The Handbook* would not have been possible without the organizational skill and meticulous attention to detail provided by Hugh McElrath. Not only did he designate hymns to the respective authors, receive copy, and provide initial proofing, he also appears as author in his own right, as well as the scribe of word/phrase changes made within selected hymns.

All are indebted to Jere Adams whose gentle, but firm allegiance to deadlines moved the project through to its successful completion.

Editorial Production Staff

Editor
Jere V. Adams

Director, Church Music Department
Wesley L. Forbis

Senior Manager
Mark Blankenship

Textual Editing
Linda Konig, Connie Powell, Leslie Hudson, Susie Collier

Artist Designer
O. Dixon Waters

About the Writers

Hugh T. McElrath is the V. V. Cooke Professor of Church Music at The Southern Baptist Theological Seminary, Louisville, Kentucky. He, a native of Kentucky, and his wife Ruth, a native of Buenos Aires, Argentina, have three children. McElrath attended Murray State University (B.A.), The Southern Baptist Theological Seminary (B.S.M., M.S.M.), and The University of Rochester (Ph.D.). He has also done additional study in Italy, England, and Switzerland.

From 1943-53 he served on staff at various churches throughout North Carolina and Kentucky. He was also Minister of Music at Beechwood Baptist Church in Louisville from 1955-77. In addition to serving churches, McElrath has led music conferences and festivals in the United States, as well as in South America, Europe, Asia, and Africa. He has served as president of the Southern Baptist Church Music Conference and editor of the *Southern Baptist Church Music Journal*.

Among his published works are *How to Use the Hymnal* (1975), *Great Hymns of Praise* (1977), *The History of Our Christian Faith in Hymns* (1987), and numerous articles.

Donald C. Brown was educated at the University of South Carolina (B.A., 1961) and Southwestern Baptist Theological Seminary (M.C.M., 1964; D.M.A., 1973). He served as the president of the Southern Baptist Church Music Conference from 1974-75.

His published works include articles on hymns and hymnody, and *Five Practical Lessons in Song Leading* (1982). He also served as a compiler for *Baptist Hymnal* (1975) and *The Baptist Hymnal* (1991).

With nearly 26 years of service at William Jewell College, Missouri, Brown is presently chairman of the music department and director of church music studies there.

David W. Music received his Bachelor of Arts in Music from California Baptist College (1970). He also attended Southwestern Baptist Theological Seminary, (M.C.M., 1973; D.M.A., 1977) and is now associate professor of church music there.

His honors include Alumnus of the Year, California Baptist College (1988), Outstanding Young Men of America (1983), and the Norman W. Cox Award (1980) presented by the SBC Historical Commission.

Music has published over 100 articles and reviews regarding church music, hymnology, musicology, as well as arrangements and compositions of music for choirs, recorders, and handbells.

Harry Eskew is professor of music history and hymnology and music librarian at New Orleans Baptist Theological Seminary, Louisiana. He has served over 25 years on faculty there.

Eskew was educated at Furman University (B.A. in music, 1958), New Orleans Baptist Theological Seminary (M.S.M., 1960), and Tulane University (Ph.D., 1966). He has also studied at the University of Erlangen, Germany, the University of New Orleans, and Notre Dame Seminary.

Among his published works are entries in *The New Grove Dictionary of Music and Musicians* and the *Encyclopedia of Southern Baptists*. He coauthored *Sing with Understanding: An Introduction to Christian Hymnology* (1980) together with Hugh T. McElrath. Eskew has also written over 300 articles and reviews.

Milburn Price graduated from the University of Mississippi (B.M., 1960). He went on to study at Baylor University (M.M., 1963) and the University of Southern California (D.M.A., 1967). He also took a sabbatical leave to study at Princeton Theological Seminary (1987).

Price has been a recipient of an annual ASCAP Composers Award each year since 1980. He delivered the Northcutt Lecture in Church Music at Baylor University (1987) and presented the Thompson Lecture in Church Music at Furman University (1991).

In addition to his published choral compositions and arrangements, Price and William J. Reynolds wrote *A Survey of Christian Hymnody* (1987).

William J. Reynolds is professor of church music at Southwestern Baptist Theological Seminary and has served there since 1980. He and his wife Mary Lou have two children.

Reynolds served on staff at churches in Oklahoma from 1946 to 1955. He then went to the Church Music Department at the Baptist Sunday School Board (1955-1980), retiring as director. While there he served as chairman of the hymnal committee and general editor for *Baptist Hymnal* (1975) and *The New Broadman Hymnal* (1977).

He was educated at Southwestern Missouri State College (B.A., 1942), Southwestern Baptist Theological Seminary (M.S.M., 1945), North Texas State University (M.M., 1946), and George Peabody College for Teachers (Ed.D., 1961).

Reynolds received the B.B. McKinney Foundation Award (1960). He has composed and arranged over 300 choral anthems, hymn tunes, and children's songs. Among his publications are *Hymns of Our Faith*, *Building an Effective Music Ministry*, and *Companion to Baptist Hymnal*.

Paul A. Richardson is associate professor of church music at The Southern Baptist Theological Seminary and chair of graduate (doctoral) studies in that department.

He graduated summa cum laude from Mars Hill College (B.M., 1973) and also holds degrees from The Southern Baptist Theological Seminary (M.C.M.,1975; D.M.A.,1979). From 1989 to 1990 he served as a visiting scholar to Colgate-Rochester Divinity School at the University of Rochester.

Richardson served as minister of music full-time as well as on an interim basis for churches in North Carolina, Indiana, and Kentucky. He served on the editorial committee for *The Worshiping Church* (1990) and is presently editor of the *Southern Baptist Church Music Journal*.

His published works include *Hymns for Private Devotion* (1986) in addition to numerous articles.

Scotty Wayne Gray became executive vice president at Southwestern Baptist Theological Seminary in January 1990. He had previously served on the music faculty there since 1966. He graduated from the seminary (M.C.M., 1959; D.M.A., 1966) after attending Baylor University (B.M., 1955).

Gray is listed in the *Directory of American Scholars* (1982) and in *Who's Who in American Music* (1983). He has published works in privately circulated mimeographed books and has written articles for *The Hymn*, *Southwestern Journal of Theology*, *Southern Baptist Church Music Journal*, and other periodicals.

Paul G. Hammond graduated from Morehead State University (A.B., 1967) and from The Southern Baptist Theological Seminary (M.C.M.,1970; D.M.A., 1974).

He is presently dean of the Warren M. Angell College of Fine Arts at Oklahoma Baptist University. His articles and reviews have been published in such scholarly journals as *The Hymn*, *American Music*, and the *Southern Baptist Church Music Journal*.

Handbook to The Baptist Hymnal

TABLE OF CONTENTS

HYMNOLOGICAL ESSAYS

Currents and Cross-Currents Impacting Hymnal Formation: The New Baptist Hymnal, Issues and Answers

WESLEY L. FORBIS

SINCE its inception in 1941, the Church Music Department of the Baptist Sunday School Board has been charged with the responsibility of developing music materials for Southern Baptist churches. Of critical importance for congregational music has been the publication of hymnals developed under the leadership of B. B. McKinney (*The Broadman Hymnal,* 1940), Hines Sims (*Baptist Hymnal,* 1956), and William J. Reynolds (*Baptist Hymnal,* 1975). The content of each of those hymnals reflected not only the singing practices/styles of Southern Baptists but also helped to formulate them. Their singular and stellar achievement was to give relevant musical expression to basic beliefs. That those hymnals were successful is substantiated by the statistic that over 89 percent of Southern Baptist churches use one or more of them (Research Dept.).

That same struggle—to provide Southern Baptist congregations a hymnal for the musical expression of basic beliefs—is a continuum; it has confronted the "now" church of yesterday even as it will confront the "now" church of tomorrow.

As the cultural, social, and technological dynamic in which we exist continues to change, even so change must impact the musical and verbal symbols through which the church expresses its "now" faith.

Cultural Currents

One might well describe the twentieth century as a super nova combination of both the Renaissance and the Age of Enlightenment. It would be tempting to discuss its cultural, social, philosophical, and technological matrix. It would be even more tempting to trace and detail the individual phenomena of that matrix as to their discrete influence on the church. Obviously, space does not allow for such perambulations, and, just as obviously, a few more years must pass before so incisive a historical perspective can be formulated. Since historical retrospect is not available, the church must discern the present cultural *Zeitgeist* as best it can and formulate new patterns to fulfill its mission. One can scarcely disagree with William Butler Yeats when he remarked that the center has broken.

How American culture will choose to bind itself together again is a matter of conjecture, although some possible patterns are discernible.

Pluralism, once viewed as a mode of encouraging the examination of competing ideas, now demands more than mere tolerance; it is rapidly becoming society's orthodoxy. It not only requires respect, but demands acceptance of the position that any and all moral and aesthetic classifications, categories, or subsets supersede any value judgment. The paradox of pluralism is that it demands allegiance. The handmaiden of pluralism is the transformation of our value-laden Judeo-Christian religion into a religion-free civil religion.

The consequence may be that the church will find itself to be an isolated, normative subset in a value-free culture. That isolation will only increase as our me-too, Yuppie cultural psyche continues its individual search for its collective self.

Far from being a quiescent volcano whose occasional rumblings are observed and discussed only in the annual conferences of philosophers and then ignored by the church, the dominant forces of pluralism have vented themselves into the cultural wells from which we daily drink: family structures, marketplaces, courtrooms, and classrooms. The more odious evidences have been felt through the drug culture, abortion, gay rights, and pornography.

If those factors are not enough to isolate and blunt the cultural connection of the church, then mix in a healthy dose of technology—quantum physics, microchips, superconductors, lasers, and nuclear weapons—stir with the ladle of biogenetics, sprinkle with impending ecological doom, season with the haunting specter of third-world famine, and heat over the flame of ancient national grudges. The consequence of such a cultural maelstrom is that the church, in its outreach and influence, has suffered an erosion of "connection," i.e., an existential gap between Christ and the contemporary society. That eroded connection is more than the legal winds that leave behind a "naked public square."

To be sure, a de-religionized society is not only inimical to the "Good News," it is also a dangerous place for its advocates. But even more foreboding is the fact that the marginality, the oddity, the scandal of the Christian belief and life becomes increasingly incomprehensible to a lost world. Thus, as the symbols by which Christians objectify their faith simply evaporate, human *voluntas* supplants biblical *veritas*.

With Emerson, the contemporary world cries:
Give me truths,
for I am weary of the surfaces, and
die of inanition (Emerson, 6).

It is imperative, then, that the hymnal serve as proactive stimulus that not only sustains but restores the connection between Christianity and culture. It must communicate through written and musical symbols that can be clearly grasped by a contemporary culture.

This problem is magnified by the very success of the Southern Baptist Convention mission efforts. What was once a regionally (Southern) identifiable convention now includes churches in every state in the United States. Each, whether "out-west" or "up-north," has its own regional and musical distinctives.

The challenge then was to produce a hymnal that carries a common core of hymnody yet was of sufficient diversity to acknowledge and reinforce continuing outreach. The question which each editor confronted was more than simply, "shall I *pass* on the traditional or shall I pass *on* the traditional?" Rather, it was how best to blend and fuse the rich heritage of hymnody with contemporary symbols to produce a nexus for the existential "now."

Diversity of Churches

The task of developing an effective "now" hymnal became more complicated when one looked at the diversity of Southern Baptist churches:

1. More than 60 percent of our churches are less than 200 in membership (15,969);
2. Less than 4500 of our churches have a full-time minister of music or combination staff responsibility;
3. 38.2 percent of our churches are in rural areas (14,347);
4. Approximately 207 new churches are started each year (.6 percent per year for the last five years) [Research Dept.].

The data has expanded meaning as one perceives that congregational singing practices are guided by leaders who range from shape-note singers through ministers who direct their own compositions and from volunteer, part-time, or combination leaders to ministers of music in churches with multiple music staffs.

Demographics

Another element affecting the content of the new hymnbook was that of demographics. For example, when the hymnal was released in 1991, there were over 26,000,000 senior citizens in the United States. They represent the largest population age bracket, and their number will continue to grow well into the 2020s.

A hymnal that does not include hymnic material that helped formulate the Christian growth of our senior citizens would fail to pass on the tradition. To assure that a new hymnal would include materials familiar to this and other age groups, a questionnaire was constructed to ascertain (1) not only the common core of hymnody from the '75 *hymnal* that Baptists wanted included in the new hymnal, but also (2) the hymns most requested from the '56 *hymnal,* the *Broadman* (1940), *Christian Praise* (1964), and the *New Broadman* (1977). At least 30 items from this second group were considered.

Ethnic Concerns

During the last half of the twentieth century, Southern Baptists have witnessed (1) the appointment of the largest number of home missionaries in their history, and (2) the concomitant effort to develop indigenous leaders for (3) an incredible influx of immigrants representing Koreans, Chinese, Vietnamese, Thais, Haitians, Cubans, and other Hispanic subgroups, each of which, while sharing a small core of Western hymnody common to all, nevertheless has brought its own unique musical and worship styles into Southern Baptist congregations.

Could or should the contents of the new hymnal attempt to serve so complex an organizational structure or so diverse a community? Those and related questions required fair and serious consideration, tempered by the fact that it is not within the current assignment of the Church Music Department to produce language hymnals for indigenous groups.

Yet, it was felt that, given the high priority of Southern Baptists for missions, some representative material should be included in the new hymnal; by giving such presence, our interest and support might continue to be sensitized. Dr. Bill O'Brien, a musician, former missionary, and mission board executive, took the lead in the effort to secure appropriate materials, and we are indebted to him for his persistent and sensitive leadership. The criteria for including such material were that it must be (1) in a style indigenous to the nation of its origin, and (2) musically accessible to Southern Baptist congregations. Happily, several selections were strong candidates for inclusion.

Language

We mourn as words lose their original meaning, cringe as idioms are turned inside out, marvel as new words are coined, shudder when forms are contracted or the declension of verbs is ignored. But, whether we mourn or marvel, we recognize that language is not static. Rather, it is a dynamic, changing, evolving form of communication. In the last fifteen years, the questions of language have touched the publication of hymnbooks in these areas: (1) the language which defines and identifies Deity, (2) archaic language, and (3) inclusivity.

Names of Deity

Some major denominations have explored the question of gender of Deity as it relates to hymn texts (most notably the United Methodists).

Contemporary examples fall into two categories: (1) those which would replace masculine references (Lord, Master, King, Father) by genderless referent words, e.g. wind, impulse, rock; and (2) those that would invest God and feminine gender, i.e., Mother God, she, her.

Donald Hughes reflected on this *contretemps* with a delightful satire:

> O worship the thing
> Mysterious below;
> In what terms to sing
> We really don't know.
> The image of Father
> Has now been destroyed,
> So we will preach rather
> The Gospel of Freud (Hughes, no pag.).

The publishers of *The Baptist Hymnal* retained the traditional terms used in the historical Judeo-Christian tradition.

Archaic Language

Too often, unhappily, the God-language of believers is encapsulated by its own tradition. Just as learned professionals whose vocation is so specialized that conversation can occur only with other specialists, so believers through the continued use of archaic speech forms and specialized code words delimit the knowledge of God, thus increasing the existential gap.

At times it would seem that we are intent upon fashioning a new temple veil made from the thread of outmoded words and syntaxes. It requires no more than a cursory review to acknowledge that many hymns we sing, while musically palatable, are nevertheless textually enigmatic and inaccessible to the contemporary experience.

Archaic textual forms appear in discarded verb tenses, consistent use of *Thee, Thou,* and *Thy,* and words whose original meaning is lost, e.g. *awful, bowels,* etc.

Needless to say, one must approach *any* altering of hymn texts with extreme caution not only because the rush to change may create more confusion:

> *God's* craft and power are great
> and armed with cruel hate
> On earth is not his equal (Leaver, 1-2),

but also because it may frustrate the deepest religio-memory of the singer.

To approach the issue with both order and sensitivity, some guidelines were established for the hymnal committee.

1. While hymnic tastes are quite varied among Southern Baptists,

there is, nevertheless, a rather solid core (as revealed by the question-naire) of about 200 plus hymns. Most of those hymns are sung fre-quently enough that the texts have become a part of the worshiper's "spiritual memory bank." It was determined that such texts would remain untouched and left to their own historical destiny.

2. For those hymns that are used infrequently (special ferial days, emphases, etc.) and whose texts are not in the emotive memory bank, judicious changes would be made. Fortunately, Dr. Hugh T. McElrath, a stellar hymnologist, accepted this responsibility. Reference to those changes are included in the *Handbook to The Baptist Hymnal*.

3. New hymns (i.e., new to this compilation) would be carefully reviewed to assure that their texts and poetic imagery would ensure the illumination of the "Good News."

Inclusive Language

The question of Deity gender has been clearly and unequivocally noted earlier. As for horizontal relationships, the publisher has predicat-ed the inclusion of new material on God's call to an unredeemed world:

> There is neither Jew nor Greek, there is neither bond
> nor free, there is neither male nor female: for ye are
> all one in Christ. (Gal. 3:28, KJV)

Interestingly enough, an encouraging number of hymn texts written during the last twenty years indicate that authors have been sensitive to the genderless call of redemption.

Military Language

The stench of Auschwitz, the tragedy of Hiroshima, the slaughter in Cambodia, the guilt of Vietnam, the specter of nuclear war, the genocide in Ethiopia have, "each and all," sensitized a diminishing global com-munity to the horror of war. These events have resulted in protests by a variety of pressure groups (some altruistic and some with vested inter-ests) that the Christian community, which not only hopes and prays for "peace in our time" but also works to achieve it, would be ready to divest itself of any allusion to militaristic language.

As a consequence, several of the more recently published hymnals have dropped such hymns as "Am I A Soldier of the Cross"; others have attempted to "sanitize" such hymns as "Soldiers of Christ, Arise." The publishers of *The Baptist Hymnal* have closely examined such texts, and, reflecting the consensus of the Theology and Doctrine committee, have chosen to view the military references exactly as Paul presented them: the Christian, in *spiritual* warfare with evil, must "put on the whole armour of God."

Cultural/Social References

Among some nineteenth-century hymns, one finds phrases that reflect British imperialism and Western cultural superiority. A flagrant example is the second stanza of "Jesus Shall Reign."

> From North to South the princes meet
> To pay their homage at his feet;
> While Western empires own their Lord,
> And savage tribes attend his word (Watts, no pag.).

I am pleased to report that the Hymnal Plenary Committee voted to delete this stanza in *toto*.

Biblical Terms

Over 2500 unsolicited individual letters and phone calls were received expressing specific concerns for the new hymnal. Several requested the deletion of biblical words felt to be culturally irrelevant or theologically enigmatic, e.g. *sheaves, Ebenezer, remission*.

We are all aware that hymn texts are written on a variety of themes: some are auditory, others intercessory. We also understand that hymns serve a variety of functions: recall, sense of community, etc. We too often forget, however, that one of the most important values of hymnody is that it is didactic. To that end, it is the belief of the editorial group that (1) all hymn texts should "illuminate" the biblical verities from which they are drawn, and (2) that they be enriched by words drawn from the stories, similes, parables, and metaphors of holy writ in new and creative poetic imagery.

It has been the position of this editor that arbitrarily to substitute secondary symbols for raw scriptural words would only increase the existential gap with contemporary society; there will be no "biblical-strip mining" of hymn texts.

Contemporary Worship Practices

Even the most casual observer is aware that the worship practices and musical styles of the contemporary evangelical church are in a state of flux.

Some worship leaders have become spiritual flirts, wooing the process of "group dynamics," having affairs with cozy "sing-a-longs," enjoying brief encounters with Christian-artist concerts, and arranging candle light dinners with multimedia.

In the rush to restore the existential connection—equating "traditional" with "irrelevant or ineffective"—traditional worship forms and hymns have often been discarded.

In contrast to the aforementioned innovations, other churches have retreated into an even more staid, temple-bound tradition in which symbol is substituted for substance.

It would be well if the respective proponents of the two approaches would recognize and embrace the fact that (1) both have theological validity, (2) both have as twin purposes the illumination of the gospel and the spread of the Christian life to a lost world, and that (3) both find meaning through authentic and enthusiastic participation by saint and sinner.

Such polarization of the traditional and the contemporary is common to every generation, but the situation has perhaps never been so intense as now. Whatever the future holds, it can be stated with some degree of certitude that the monochromatic musical fabric of the pre-1950 evangelical church has been shredded and likely will never be mended to its original form.

Renewal Music

Few would have predicted the depth and scope of the conservative response to "the Age of Aquarius." The social crusading of the 60s and 70s—while highly stimulating—proved to be a hollow political disappointment. Yet, during this period were released a myriad of forces that have deeply affected the worship and musical styles of the church.

While student radicals drifted off into religious cults or mysticism, the Christian community sought to renew itself. Just as students had questioned all authority and sought to simplify life in a return to "earth living," so many evangelicals questioned the traditions, doctrines, and effectiveness of the institutionalized church. The result on the one hand was the rapid and varied growth of para-church groups (characterized by a casual and informal approach in worship music styles) and, on the other hand, churches' simplistic approach to worship—often tinged with varying degrees of charismatic spiritual-at-oneness and antirationalism (one musical by-product of this shift has been the genre often referred to as "praise choruses").

> Charles H. Kraft, a professor at Fuller Theological Seminary, writes:
> While I have always enjoyed singing in the church, it wasn't until I freed myself from the exclusive use of the hymnal that I experienced what praise and worship can be. And it is the new music, sung with eyes closed for 10, 15, or 20 minutes at a time, that makes that experience possible.

> We sing hymns so chock-full of rational content and
> information that they are unmemorizable.

> Let's stop being enslaved to the present rationalistic,
> intellect-centered approach to church (Kraft, 8).

Advocates of this genre speak of (1) the need to remove from the worship setting anything—hymnbooks, music, texts (i.e., anything on the physical, conscious level)—that would interfere with (2) addressing God directly, (3) using contemporary language (you/your,I/me), and with (4) the focus being on celebration and praise, a stretto of sustained "Hallelujahs" as it were.

Yet, a close examination of some of the more popular practices and texts reveals that (1) projection screens are substituted for hymnals, (2) the acknowledgment of God is often referential, (3) King James pronouns are used, and (4) the text may be intercessory, supplicatory, or didactic. Perhaps it would be of help if such material were classified under Paul's "spiritual songs" thus leaving room for the various categories.

Advocates of "spiritual songs" would state that their substitution for hymns is requisite to church growth; that failure to use them ensures a dead, cold, traditional worship. On the other hand, others do not choose to use them because the music is simple and the texts often simplistic and because they believe that using them to the exclusion of hymns ensures shallowness in spiritual growth and discipleship.

Perhaps the proponents of each ("hymns" or "spiritual songs") would do well to acknowledge that (1) both have strengths and weaknesses; (2) what we prefer to sing in church, more often than not, is the consequence of our religio-cultural impactment; (3) whether textually and musically popular or traditional, our congregational singing must illuminate both the spiritual and cognitive; (4) fellowship stems from cross-redemption and not musical taste; (5) both can stimulate and evoke that to which we all aspire—congregational participation; and (6) worship must not only reach the lost but must also edify the redeemed.

Yet, one further note of caution is necessary. Those whose advocacy of spiritual songs results in 30 minutes of "praise" (followed by the sermon) would do well to review the worship concepts in Isaiah 6 and note that while *leitourgia* (praise) is a key musical element in worship it is not the only critical element; e.g., consider *koinonia*, *kerygma*, and *diakonia*. This last statement should not be taken as a blanket refutation of "spiritual songs," for the renewal of praise emphasis is of benefit to us all. Yet, psalms, hymns, *and* spiritual songs should be used, not only for cognitive developmental values (i.e., not only for the life to come) but also for the life that is being lived (for leitourgic and eschatological purposes).

It is a curious commentary that one's advocacy of one form over the other might cause us to believe that although we are all New Testament priests, some are more priestly than others. The question might well be asked "can anyone equate depth of commitment and enlightened discipleship with musical taste and practice?"

Contemporary Popular Music

It is hardly necessary to trace or document the pervading influence of the popular music style on congregational singing in evangelical churches. Its presence surrounds us: religious radio stations, television, tapes, compact discs, and Christian artists. One recent statistic indicates that of the money spent on music in Baptist Book Stores, more than 80 percent is spent on tapes of contemporary singers.

While one is always fearful of specifying "the first," it can be generally agreed that the present movement began in the early 1950s when Stuart Hamblen began to write religious song material in a more popular style and Geoffrey Beaumont published his *Twentieth Century Folk Mass*.

The array of contemporary popular composers and performers reflects almost every cultural subset of music: country, rock, jazz, metal, etc. While most of such music is not accessible to congregational singing, because of its performance orientation, some of it has entered into the congregational repertoire.

When selecting content for *The Baptist Hymnal*, the Hymns Recommendation Committee gave thorough consideration to the genre. Among those selected by the committee for inclusion are: "We Shall Behold Him," Dottie Rambo; "My Tribute," Andre Crouch; "Shine, Jesus, Shine," Graham Kendrick; "People Need the Lord," Phill McHugh and Greg Nelson.

Contemporary "Classic" Hymnody

The creative outburst of religious song has not been limited solely to the spiritual songs of charismatic/renewal/popular groups. No little credit must be given to the influence of the Hymn Society of America and Canada and its international counterparts as both the generating sources and conduits for a veritable explosion of twentieth-century classic hymnody.

While faintly reflecting some of the compositional trends of twentieth-century poetry (asymmetrical meter and non-rhyming phrases), most of them are cast in the form of classic hymnody. Many of the texts, reflecting such issues as ecology, ecumenicism, feminism, world hunger, and justice for the oppressed, use strong, pungent, poetic imageries that call the church to proactive actions.

Beyond social issues, however, many of the new texts reflect the same yearning for personal spiritual renewal as is found in the aforementioned spiritual songs.

Among the authors included in *The Baptist Hymnal* are Fred Pratt Green, Brian Wren, Thomas H. Troeger, Margaret Clarkson, Bryan J. Leech, and Carl P. Daw, Jr.

Technology

Technology affects not only how the congregation sings but also what it sings. For years, the staple instrumental support for singing in Baptist churches has been either the organ or piano, or both. That format is rapidly becoming the exception rather than the norm. Most ministers of music now have at their fingertips a dazzling array of technological resources.

Beyond the obvious sound enhancements (orchestral, instruments, handbells) are computers, midis, synthesizers, projection screens, tape decks, and duplicating machines. While one could write at length about the impact of technology on congregational music practices, only three factors will be briefly noted.

1. Projection screens/equipment

Some pastors, convinced that hymnals have only archival value, have opted for music that is either taught by rote or projected on large screens, thus allowing the worshiper to achieve spiritual focus. While there are many attendant problems—copyrights, mechanical problems—churches increasingly have begun to use this approach.

2. Taped accompaniments

The use of tapes for performance groups, a common practice, is now making inroads into support of congregational singing. Certainly, the practice is helpful in missions, storefront and high-rise apartment churches and camps. One fears, however, that the practice will emulate contemporary music with an emphasis on an enveloping sensorial experience rather than on the significance of the text. Here too, the problems of copyrights, mechanical licensing, and securing permissions may delimit both the tune and text repertoire of the church.

3. Copyrights

The third cross-current is not technological but rather a consequent process. To illustrate, in order to feed the demand for the latest "hit" song, an organization called Christian Copyright Licensing, Inc. (one among several) has been formed. Briefly, it charges each church an annual fee, distributes lists of the latest music, records their subsequent use, then, after fees, reimburses the copyright holder. There are both positive and negative features of such a process. On the one hand, it nurtures a continuum of spiritual songs, on the other a church can easily lose its sense of historicity, lineage, and its place in the "great cloud of witnesses" as it were. The problems for the publishers of hymnals are obvious. Inasmuch as hymnbooks have a life of 16-18 years, they cannot stay current with the latest "top 40' list. Nor can hymnals be produced more frequently, for the cost to the church (as well as to a denominational publishing house) becomes prohibitive.

The Baptist Hymnal (1991)

Among the many reasons for the publication of *The Baptist Hymnal* in 1991, one is salient. The decision of the denomination to highlight authentic worship (long awaited) in the years 1990-95 was welcomed by all. The responsibility for leading in this emphasis was assigned to the Church Administration and Church Music Departments of the Baptist Sunday School Board.

That responsibility called for (1) a review of existing worship leadership materials, hymnals, and consultant services; (2) an examination, through forums and questionnaires, of the contemporary practices, trends, wants, and needs of local congregations; and (3) a projection of the new materials needed to support and enrich the emphasis.

It was determined that new materials were needed in three categories.

1. Resource books, textbooks, and church study course books are needed to provide a sound doctrinal basis for worship. Authors have been assigned, and these materials will be released during the 1990-95 period.

2. In addition to providing resource books for theological undergirding, a new periodical (entitled *Worship: Resources for the Church Musician*) released in October, 1990, provides creative approaches to worship, innovative services, service music, and descants.

3. The most significant decision called for the publication of a new hymnal. The available time frame did not permit its preparation and release to coincide with the 1990 beginning of the worship emphasis. It was scheduled for release at PraiSing II, March, 1991 which year, coincidentally, was the fiftieth anniversary of the Church Music Department.

Accompanying the standard hymnal was an array of unique support products that enrich and amplify resources for congregational singing and "authentic worship." Among them are a choir supplement, pianist's edition, organist's edition, orchestra and handbell editions, each of which will have their own unique hymn introductions, tags, descants, and improvisations.

Of particular interest to the minister is the *Handbook to The Baptist Hymnal*, which includes not only hymnological information, metrical and composer/author indices, and first-lines all cross-indexed, but also an expanded scriptural reference for every stanza of every hymn (in short—a concordance).

To assure that the hymnal would represent and include both the unanimity and diversity of singing practices of Southern Baptist churches, four elements were necessary:

1. A position statement of organizing principles;
2. A comprehensive questionnaire distributed to every Baptist church;
3. A representative committee to develop and select materials reflecting the questionnaire data;
4. An editing process capable of responding to the abbreviated time frame.

Space allows only the most brief accounting of each.

Organizing Principles

1. Hymns not only teach theology and illuminate its meaning, they also serve as a vehicle for recall. Thus, each hymn was reviewed line-by-line for theological veracity.
2. The hymnal must be both priestly and prophetic. On the one hand, it must retain the great classic hymns and music that comprise the core of our hymnody, yet, on the other, it must include material that is relevant to the mission of the church of today as well as to that of tomorrow.
3. Recognizing the ethnic and cultural diversity of our convention as well as its mission emphasis, the hymnal includes material from Hispanic, Black, and Asian traditions.
4. In both text and tune, the hymnal must be accessible to and representative of the diversity of Southern Baptist churches. Thus, the pool of material from which the content was to be selected included all major historical periods as well as contemporary materials.
5. Of new texts, only those were considered that affirm that the call to salvation is genderless (Gal. 3:28). To impose that guideline on the more frequently sung traditional texts could violate the historical context in which they were written, distort a specific heritage, and impose forced and artificial poetic structure. Such texts, many of which are staples of congregational singing, will live out their

own historical destiny.
      6. The committee recommended changes in less famil-
iar hymns whose words or phrases are obscure, for
example,

         There is a green hill far away
         without a city wall
      Possible revision:
         There is a green hill far away
         beyond (outside) the city wall.

Questionnaire

With the aid of the BSSB Research Department, a questionnaire was
developed to determine:

1. What hymns should be retained from the '75 hymnal;
2. What material (from whatever source) recommended for inclusion;
3. Organization;
4. Indices;
5. Type and length of responsive readings, and a myriad of related matters.

The questionnaire, distributed to every Baptist church, had an over-
whelming response; its results are reflected in both the "organizing principles" and in the context of the hymnal.

Hymnal Committee

Members of the hymnal committee were drawn from every size
church, every geographical area in the United States, local church members, ministers, ministers of music, volunteer directors, part-time directors, religious education directors, youth directors, children's directors,
professional musicians, college and seminary professors, state music
directors, music evangelists, Christian artists, and denominational workers. Included among these men and women were Blacks, Asians, and His-
panics. Each person was assigned to a subcommittee: Theology/Doctrine,
Design/Organization, Worship Aids, New Materials (including Ethnic),
Music, Hymns Recommendation, and Promotion. The committee roster
totaled 95 in number, and the average attendance for all plenary and
subcommittee meetings was over 95 percent.

Over 4,000 pieces of music were considered in the process. Admitted-
ly, the committee was cumbersome and time consuming. That it was
effective was due to the careful and incessant attention of Dr. Terry York,
staff assistant, who served as process coordinator.

Editing

The production of the hymnal greatly facilitated by the work of Mark Blankenship. His leadership in adapting the Finale computer (music typesetting) program to the project resulted in the first major hymnbook to be published by that process.

Conclusion

It must be stated that at no point were any directives given regarding either content or format of *The Baptist Hymnal*. Both have been selected by the editorial staff to answer not only the traditional and contemporary hymnic needs of churches, but also to affirm and "call to remembrance" the unifying heritage of our Baptist beliefs.

With the complement of its support materials (the *Worship* periodical, etc.) *The Baptist Hymnal* promises to vivify congregational singing and provide a musical bridge across the existential gap of saints and sinners.

Revised and reprinted, with permission, from *Review & Expositor,* Vol. 87, No. 1, Winter 1990. *Review & Expositor* is the faculty journal of the Southern Baptist Theological Seminary, Louisville, Kentucky.

Bibliography

Emerson, Ralph W. *The University Bookman*, 28 (1988): 6.
Hughes, Donald. *The Hymn Society of Great Britain and Ireland Bulletin*, 7, 16 (Summer, 1969).
Kraft, Charles H. "The Hymnal Is Not Enough." *Christianity Today*, 33, 6 (Apr. 7, 1989): 8.
Leaver, Robin. *News of Hymnody*, 9 (January, 1984): 1-2.
Research Department, Baptist Sunday School Board.
Watts, Isaac. "Jesus Shall Reign Where'er the Sun." (1719).

Baptist Hymnody in America

WILLIAM J. REYNOLDS

BAPTIST beginnings in the American colonies, essentially an indigenous movement, were contemporary with Baptist activities in England and not an offshoot or extension of it (McLoughlin, 1:6). Baptists in England, in the early-seventeenth century, were of two kinds. Those called General Baptists were Arminian theologically, believing that Christ died for all persons. The Particular Baptists were Calvinists, believing that Christ died only for those whom God had selected in advance to be saved. Baptist immigrants to the American colonies were from both groups. Most of the churches established in the seventeenth century were in New England, but a few churches appeared in the Middle Colonies toward the end of the century. In 1696 William Screven moved the church he had established at Kittery, Maine, in 1682, to South Carolina to join the Baptists already present in "Charles Towne" (McBeth, 123). By 1700 there were 872 members in 33 Baptist churches in the American colonies (Gardner, 34). Almost one-third of these churches were Particular Baptists.

Congregational singing in England had its beginnings in Particular Baptist churches in the latter part of the seventeenth century, largely through the efforts of Benjamin Keach (1640-1704). General Baptist churches permitted no congregational singing—psalms or hymns—until almost a century later. Most English Baptists who opposed singing in public worship recognized scriptural authority for psalm singing. However, they opposed "promiscuous singing"—the singing of believers and unbelievers together. Also, they opposed the use of "set forms," the metrical versions of the psalms, as being "man made" and unworthy of public worship. These beliefs left only the possibility that an individual might feel inspired to sing a spontaneous song.

Hymn Singing in the Churches

Hymn singing may have existed in Baptist churches in the American colonies in the mid-seventeenth century more generally than in Baptist churches in England. Morgan Edwards reports that psalm singing was practiced in the first Baptist church in Providence, Rhode Island (Edwards, 1867, 314), where the small congregation, organized in 1639 "first met for worship in a grove, unless in wet and stormy weather, when they assembled in private houses" (Benedict, I, 467). Singing was also practiced in the Newport church in Rhode Island, from its beginning (Edwards, 324). In July 1651, John Clarke, pastor of the Newport church, together with John Crandall and Obadiah Holmes, had gone to Lynn, Massachusetts, to conduct a service in the home of William Witter, a member of Clarke's congregation. Two constables, who came to arrest these three for "disturbing the peace," waited until their "prayers, singing, and preaching was over" before they took them to prison in Boston (Benedict, I, 366).

Baptist immigrants who sought fellowship with those of like faith strengthened the Baptist cause, but some brought with them from their mother countries their prejudice against singing in public worship (Benedict, I, 218). This may explain the increased opposition to singing at Providence and Newport churches. English Baptists settled in Delaware from 1675 on. In 1683 Irish Baptists from the county of Tipperary settled near Cohansey, New Jersey. In spite of some opposition, these Irish Baptists practiced psalmody (Edwards, 1885, 52). While Benjamin Keach was advocating congregational singing in his church at Southwark, England, his son Elias arrived in America in 1686. Two years later young Keach became pastor of the Pennepek church in Pennsylvania, which at the time had twelve faithful members. Sharing his father's enthusiasm for singing in public worship, he led his church in this practice, but not without some opposition (Benedict, I, 580).

The early Baptists may have sung from Sternhold's and Hopkins' *Psalter* (1562) or Ainsworth's *Psalter* (1612), which the Separatists knew in Amsterdam, or from one of the editions of the *Anglo-Genevan Psalter*, prepared for the English refugees in Switzerland in 1556 and later. Maring states that among the Baptists in New Jersey, "a book of hymns by Benjamin Keach was the first to be used" (Maring, 26). Keach's *Spiritual Melody, containing near Three Hundred Sacred Hymns* (1691) was published in London, England (Whitley, 369-75). The significance of this collection of original hymns lies in the intent of Keach rather than the quality of his hymn writing. It is also possible that these early Baptists sang from hand-copied metrical versions taken from various sources, in which case only one copy would be needed by a congregation. The pastor or the clerk or the "singing deacon" would "line out" the text, one line at a time, as recorded in the minutes of the Baptist church at Salem: "Concluded that our Brethren John Stow and Abraham Harris parcel out the lines of the Psalms in the future" (Minutes, 1785).

Benson believed that "if the earliest New England Baptists practiced psalm singing at all, they probably, like their neighbors, lined the psalms out of the Bay Psalm Book" (Benson, 196). However, that the Bay Psalm Book should have been found in Baptist hands in New England seems highly improbable—at least until many decades had erased from Baptist minds the memories of the persecution they had suffered at the hands of Boston divines, some of whom were responsible for this psalter. John Cotton, who assisted in preparing it and wrote its preface, opposed the Baptists and engaged in extended controversy with Roger Williams. A law was passed in Massachusetts in 1644, primarily designed to stop the preaching of Baptists (Benedict, I, 360). Imprisonment, harsh fines, and public whippings meted out to faithful Baptist preachers are matters of record. Their only offense was preaching the gospel and worshiping God according to the dictates of their own consciences.

Influence of Welsh Immigrants

In 1701 a group of Welsh Baptists landed in New York, and, after a brief stay at Pennepek, Pennsylvania, settled two years later in New Castle, Delaware, about forty-two miles southwest of Philadelphia. This Welsh Tract church was the principal, if not the sole, means of introducing singing among the Baptists in the middle colonies (Benedict, I, 360). Other Welsh Baptists settled in Pennsylvania, founding the Great Valley church, near Philadelphia, in 1711, and the Montgomery church in 1719. McBeth comments that the Welsh "brought their tradition of great preaching and their love for singing. But most of all, perhaps, the Welsh influenced Baptists in America by their warm and fervent evangelism" (McBeth, 212).

To further affirm their belief in the practice of singing in public worship, the Welsh Tract church in 1716 adopted the Assembly Confession of Faith, prepared in England in 1689, to which Benjamin Keach and his son Elias, in 1697, had added articles on singing psalms and the laying on of hands. Keach's deep conviction in congregational singing is reflected in the following statement, truly a monument in Baptist hymnody:

"We believe that 'acts 16 25 eph 5 19 col 3 16' singing the praises of God, is a holy Ordinance of Christ, and not a part of natural religion, or a moral duty only; but that it is brought under divine institution, it being injoined on the churches of Christ to sing psalms, hymns, and spiritual songs; and that the whole church in their public assemblies, as well as private christians, ought to 'heb 2 12 jam 5 13' sing God's praises according to the best light they have received. Moreover, it was practiced in the great representative church, by 'matt 26 30 mat 14 26' by our Lord Jesus Christ with His disciples after he had instituted and celebrated the sacred ordinance of his Holy Supper, as a commemorative token of redeeming love" (Lumpkin, 351).

Abel Morgan translated Keach's version of this confession into Welsh; and 122 members of the Welsh Tract Church signed the document, the first confession of faith adopted by Baptists in America.

Keach's Confession was adopted by the Philadelphia Association, September 25, 1742, and the following year, the Association ordered a printing of the new edition which was done by Benjamin Franklin. For at least two decades prior to its formal adoption, the confession, which became known as the Philadelphia Confession of Faith, had been the accepted doctrinal standard among the churches of the middle colonies (Lumpkin, 349). This Calvinistic document, with its provision for singing in worship, became widely accepted by early Baptists and was of unusual influence in the South.

Opposition to public singing gradually declined in the early eighteenth century. In churches where the practice had been discontinued, it was restored, and where it had thus far been forbidden, it was instituted for the first time. At the First Church of Newport, during the brief ministry of John Comer, ordained co-pastor in May 1726, congregational singing was restored (Benedict, I, 497). The First Church, Boston, had introduced psalm singing by 1728, and on July 7, 1740, the church voted to "sing that Version of the Psalms done by Dr. Brady & Mr. Tate so long as no objection should be offered against it, & Wn. any should, then this vote to be reconsidered" (Music, 1982, 39). Benson suggests that some Baptist demand in and around Philadelphia may have helped to encourage Benjamin Franklin to reprint Tate's and Brady's *New Version* in 1733 (Benson, 197).

The Hymns of the Great Awakening

Of major significance to hymn singing among Baptists in America was the influence of the Great Awakening from about 1734 to about 1770. Originating within New England Congregationalism, under Jonathan Edwards, this movement received great assistance from the several visits to the colonies of George Whitefield, the great English evangelical preacher. Having witnessed the value of hymn singing in England, he was eager to employ similar methods in the American colonies. He was fond of the psalms and hymns of Isaac Watts, and was largely responsible for their being introduced in the colonies where he preached. General Baptist churches of Arminian background, chiefly in New England, were less affected by this movement than the churches of Calvinistic tendencies. The Separate Baptists, who evolved out of the evangelical movement, became vigorous and enthusiastic hymn singers.

Revival fires spread along the Atlantic seaboard, and the hymns and psalms of Watts became increasingly popular. Watts's *Hymns and Spiritual Songs*, first published in London in 1707, was reprinted in Boston in 1739, in Philadelphia in 1742 (by Benjamin Franklin), and in New York in 1752. These and subsequent editions, combined with reprintings of Watts's *Psalms* (1719), found great favor among Baptist congregations.

The First Baptist Hymnals

The first collection of hymns published for Baptists in the American colonies was Benjamin Wallin's *Evangelical Hymns and Songs* (Boston, 1762), a reprint of an edition published in London in 1750. The first Baptist hymnal compiled and published in the colonies, *Hymns and Spiritual Songs, Collected from the Works of Several Authors* (Newport, Rhode Island, 1766), contained 138 hymns; its compiler is unknown. The book was printed by Samuel Hall, and William Rogers, listed as one of the sellers of the book, was in the first class of graduates of Rhode Island College (now Brown University). A copy of the Newport Collection, in the rare book library at Brown University, bears an inscription by William Rogers to his son, "For use in the Sunday school—2nd Baptist Church in Newport." Hymns were used in public services, in meetings in homes, in family worship, and in private devotions. The singing of hymns also provided a source of comfort and strength in times of distress.

Benedict mentions the practice of hymn singing as he describes the persecution experienced by Baptists in Virginia. Since the Church of England was the "established church" in Virginia, it was unlawful for Baptists and others to preach without a license, which was only rarely granted and then only after much difficulty. On June 4, 1768, John Waller, Lewis Craig, James Childs, and others were arrested for preaching the gospel. The magistrates, who charged them with disturbing the peace, offered to release them if they promised not to preach for one year and one day. This they refused to do, and were sent to jail. "As they were moving on from the court-house to the prison, through the streets of Fredericksburg, they sung the hymn, 'Broad is the road that leads to death,' etc. This had an awful appearance" (Benedict, II, 65). On August 10, 1771, in Goochland, Virginia, Waller, together with James Greenwood and Robert Ware, was arrested for preaching and was jailed. "They were safely lodged in close jail that night about 8 o'clock. Having borrowed a candle of the jailer, and sung the praises of that Redeemer whose cross they bore, and from whose hands they expected a crown in the end—and having returned thanks that it was a prison and not hell they were in—praying for themselves, their friends, their enemies, and persecutors—they laid down to sleep" (Benedict, II, 68).

Hymns for the Ordinances—Baptism and the Lord's Supper

In England, Benjamin Keach successfully introduced hymn singing in his church at Southwark in 1673 by using the scriptural basis that a hymn was sung by Christ and His disciples at the conclusion of the Lord's Supper. Here was an argument for hymn singing that could not be disputed. In America, the first emergence of Baptist distinctives in hymnody came through hymns written for the ordinances. The Newport Collection was divided into three sections: I. On Baptism (16 hymns); II. On the Lord's Supper (74 hymns); III. On Various Occasions (48 hymns). The strong wording of the baptismal hymns supporting immersion, and the large proportion of hymns for the Lord's Supper prompted McCutchan to suggest that this Newport Collection was the "first truly denominational hymnal in America" (McCutchan, 160). In 1791 a small collection, *Baptismal Hymns*, by an unknown compiler, was published in Boston. Another anonymous compilation, *The Boston Collection* (1808), indicated in its preface that it was compiled "principally with a view to accommodate the Baptist churches of Boston and its vicinity, who have long desired such a collection, for the purpose of singing at the administration of baptism."

The Influence of John Rippon

John Rippon, pastor of the Baptist church in Carter Lane, London, published *A Selection of Hymns from the best authors, intended to be an Appendix to Dr. Watts's Psalms and Hymns* (London, 1787). Of the first six thousand copies printed, eight hundred were sent to America (Manley, 190). In September 1791, First Baptist Church, Boston, adopted Rippon's *Selection* (Music, 1982, 43). Its popularity in America encouraged Rippon to publish an American reprint, but before he could do so two unauthorized editions were printed in 1792: one in New York by William Burell, and the other in Elizabethtown by Shepard Kollock. [Between 1802 and 1842, more than 20 printings of various editions of Rippon's *Selection* were published in the United States.] Rippon's *Selection* gave Baptists in the United States early possession of much of the Evangelical hymnody from England and it became a standard for Baptist hymn singing in America as well as a major source of texts for subsequent compilers of both hymnals and tunebooks.

In 1801 Rippon published in London his "arrangement" of Watts's *Psalms and Hymns* based largely on the organizational structure of subjects he had used in his *Selection*. "Rippon's Watts" was printed in Philadelphia in 1820, and became the most popular collection of hymns among the Baptist churches in that area. In 1818 James Winchell, pastor of the First Baptist Church, Boston, published an arrangement of Watts's *Psalms and Hymns*, which was widely used by Baptist churches in New England.

Many collections of hymns that appeared during this time were not intended to replace Watts, for they bore on their title pages the assurance that they were only supplements to his *Psalms and Hymns*. Of these, the most popular among the Baptists in England and America was Rippon's. Other supplemental collections produced by Baptists were *A Selection of*

Evangelical Hymns Supplementary to Dr. Rippon (Burlington, New Jersey, 1807), by William Staughton, pastor of the First Baptist Church, Philadelphia (1805-11); *A Selection of Hymns and Spiritual Songs* (New York, 1809), by William Parkinson, pastor of New York City's First Baptist Church; and *A New Selection of Hymns* (Boston, 1812), by William Collier, pastor of the Baptist church at Charlestown, Massachusetts. John L. Dagg and C. G. Sommers published their version of "Rippon's Watts" in Philadelphia in 1827. Dagg, pastor of the First Baptist Church, Philadelphia, received the support of many Baptist pastors in that city. He later moved to Alabama and Georgia, where he was a highly respected Baptist leader and became president of Mercer University in 1844.

Hymnals Published by Baptist Associations

The role of the association, a volunteer grouping of cooperating Baptist churches in a given vicinity, has had its influence on Baptist hymnody. When such an undertaking would have been impossible for a given church, the association afforded a means of making available a collection of hymns. Such cooperative endeavors led to the denominational publishing that developed in the mid-nineteenth century. The first such organization in America was the Philadelphia Association, established in 1707. The second was the Charleston (South Carolina) Association, established in 1751. By 1800 forty-eight associations had been organized. Thirty of these were located in the South, and six of the eight beyond the Alleghenies were in Kentucky (*Encyclopedia*, 1958).

Philadelphia became a major center of Baptist activity, and in 1788 the Philadelphia Association requested Samuel Jones and Burgis Allison to prepare a hymnal "for the use of the associated churches" (Burrage, 641), which appeared in 1790. The Dover Association (Virginia), by 1830 the largest Baptist association in America, requested Andrew Broaddus to prepare a collection of hymns, and *The Dover Selection* appeared in 1828.

The Emergence of Indigenous Hymns

While Baptist compilers drew heavily on English sources, there was an increasing effort to include indigenous hymns, marking the beginnings of American folk hymnody. One of the earliest collections to do this was *Divine Hymns, or Spiritual Songs* (Norwich, 1784), compiled by Joshua Smith, a Baptist preacher of Brentwood, New Hampshire. Though the indigenous hymns were inferior in literary quality to the borrowed English material, this collection had considerable popularity. Its eleventh edition (1803) was the first hymnal adopted by the First Baptist Church, Portland, Maine (Burrage, 643).

These "spiritual songs" appeared in most subsequent Baptist collections. John Courtney's *Christian Pocket Companion* (Richmond, 1801) contained one hundred and eighty-one hymns and "one hundred and seventy-eight pages of choice Spiritual Songs" (Burrag, 644). A review of this hymnal in a Richmond newspaper stated that the "Spiritual Songs contained in our last publication are comprised in this also with some selected from pamphlets late published in North and South Carolina and in Baltimore" (White, 18). Courtney, pastor of the First Baptist Church, Richmond, for thirty-eight years (1786-1824), and a leader among Virginia Baptists, was fond of hymn singing. However, in spite of the fact that he published three collections of hymns, he would not permit the use of hymn books in his church, preferring to "line out" the hymns to his congregation (White, 37).

Versions that either abused or mutilated these spiritual songs occurred in both manuscripts and in published collections. William Parkinson, who sought to correct this practice in the publication of his *Selection of Hymns and Spiritual Songs* (1809), was quite outspoken on the subject:

"This kind of composition has, for several years past, been greatly abused—Songs have been circulated, not only in Ms. but also in print, which have been so barbarous in language, so unequal in numbers, and so defective in rhyme, as to excite disgust in all persons even of tolerable understanding in these things; which is infinitely worse, so extremely unsound in doctrine, that no discerning Christian can sing or hear them without pain" (Benson, 202).

Tunebooks

Baptist collections of hymns in the eighteenth century consisted only of words, and this practice continued well into the nineteenth century. However, collections of tunes for singing psalms and hymns began to appear, and these were welcomed by Baptists. John Rippon's *A Selection of Psalm and Hymn Tunes* (London, 1791), containing two hundred tunes, did not become widely used in America. Samuel Holyoke's *Christian Harmonist* (Salem, Mass., 1804) appears to be the first American tunebook designed for Baptist churches, and especially those that used John Rippon's *Selection,* Joshua Smith's *Divine Hymns,* and Isaac Watts's *Psalms and Hymns.* While Holyoke was not a Baptist, his tunebook was a commercial venture.

The first composer of music among the Baptists of America was Oliver Holden, a native of Massachusetts (Music, 1980, 46-52). Baptized into the fellowship of the First Baptist Church, Boston, in 1791, he later became leader of the choir. Credited with a number of hymn tunes, he was involved in compiling more than eight tunebooks. His most enduring tune is CORONATION ("All Hail the Power of Jesus' Name"), which first appeared in 1892 in Holden's *Union Harmony.* [Oliver Holden's small pipe organ on which he composed the tune CORONATION is in the Bostonian Society, Old State House, Boston.]

A New Selection of Sacred Music (Baltimore, 1817), was compiled by

Samuel Dyer, the son of an English Baptist minister (Music, 1987, 68-75). The collection included a great variety of psalm and hymn tunes, anthems, odes, and choruses. Metcalf comments that Dyer "called attention to the clear type and letters in his book and notes that this class of music is mostly used 'by candle light' " (Metcalf, 207). Dyer's tunebook went through at least six editions. James Winchell published *Sacred Harmony* (Boston, 1819) to provide tunes appropriate for his "Winchell's Watts."

Baptists sang the hymn tunes of Lowell Mason in the churches in New England and the middle Atlantic states, and his collections of hymn tunes were widely used. However, two collections he designed especially for Baptists failed to receive much acceptance. *Manual of Christian Psalmody* (Boston, 1832), compiled by Mason and David Greene with the assistance of Rufus Babcock, Jr., pastor of the First Baptist Church of Salem, Massachusetts, was a "Baptist edition" of Mason and Greene's *Christian Psalmody* (Boston, 1831). Even less successful was *Union Hymns* (Boston, 1834), also compiled by Mason, Greene, and Babcock.

Hymnal Compilers

Though Baptists seemingly got a late start in the publication of collections of hymns, once this activity had begun, books appeared in almost every state. From the Newport Collection (1766), until well into the fourth decade of the next century, many were busy making compilations. In addition to those previously mentioned should be added the names of Thomas B. Ripley and John Butler of Maine; Benjamin Cleavland and James H. Linsley of Connecticut; Thomas Baldwin, Paul Himes, Jonathan Wilson, William Collier, Gustavus F. Davis, Enoch W. Freeman, Jonathan Howe, and Rufus Babcock, Jr., of Massachusetts; Ebenezer E. Cummins and Edmund Worth of New Hampshire; David Benedict of Rhode Island; John Stanford, Archibald Maclay, James Fenn, and Paris M. Davis of New York; Ebenezer Jayne of New Jersey; Daniel Dodge of Delaware; Lewis Skidmore and Stephen P. Hill of Maryland; Enoch Story, Jr., Lewis Baldwin, William Staughton, and John L. Dagg of Pennsylvania; Eleazer Clay (Richardson, 1990, 1457-59), John Asplund, and Andrew Broaddus of Virginia (Richardson, 1985, 1198-1211). What a noble procession of Baptists, who, recognizing the value of congregational singing, devoted their energies to producing collections of hymns they considered appropriate during this brief period of six decades.

**John Leland: Pastor, Hymn Writer, and
Champion of Religious Liberty**

John Leland, a native of Massachusetts, served as pastor of the Mount Poney Baptist Church, Culpeper County, Virginia (1777-92). An ardent champion of religious liberty, he was a major influence in James Madison's introduction of the First Amendment to the Constitution of the United States guaranteeing religious liberty (McBeth, 273-83). Leland wrote more than twenty hymns and encouraged hymn singing in public services. On a cold, icy day in 1779, while waiting beside a Virginia stream to baptize five converts, he composed a baptismal hymn; the first stanza reads:

> Christians, if your hearts are warm;
> Ice and snow can do no harm;
> If by Jesus you are prized,
> Rise, believe, and be baptized.

Following the election of Thomas Jefferson as president of the United States on March 4, 1801, Leland suggested from his pulpit in the Baptist church in Cheshire, Massachusetts, that a giant cheese be made and presented to the newly elected President. When the 1,600 pound cheese was made, the townspeople gathered for the unusual occasion. Leland led in prayer, and the people joined in singing a hymn to the tune MEAR. By sled, boat and horsecart, Leland and his friends made the five-hundred mile journey to Washington and presented the mammoth cheese to President Jefferson on January 1, 1802. Two days later, on Sunday, Leland addressed both houses of Congress, having been introduced by Jefferson as the preacher of the day (Garrecht, 14).

Campmeeting Songs

Beginning in Logan County, Kentucky, in 1800, the campmeeting movement spread through Tennessee and the Carolinas, into Ohio, Georgia, Virginia, Maryland, Delaware, Pennsylvania, New York, and New England. This spiritual awakening, begun by Presbyterians, soon involved Methodists and Baptists. Many collections were published of songs sung in the meetings. These were welcomed by Baptists, particularly along the western frontier and in the South.

Southern Compilers of Collections of Hymns

Jesse Mercer's *The Cluster of Spiritual Songs, Divine Hymns, and Sacred Poems* (Augusta, 3rd ed., 1810), was the earliest Baptist collection appearing in the South (Brewster, 15). The 1810 edition contained 183 hymns with no music, and by 1835 the collection had grown to nearly 700 hymns. Other "words only" collections were published in South Carolina—Staunton S. Burdett's *Baptist Harmony* (1834), and William Dossey's *Choice* (1820); in Tennessee—Starke Dupuy's *Hymns and Spiritual Songs* (1818) [Music, 1984, 43-47]; in Kentucky—Silas Noel's *Hymn Book* (1814), and Absalom Graves's *Hymns, Psalms, and Spiritual Songs* (1825); and in North Carolina—William P. Biddle's and William J. Newborn's *Baptist Hymn Book* (1825), and John Purify's *Selection of Hymns and Spiritual Songs*

(1826). Hymns by Isaac Watts were most frequently found in these collections, along with hymns by William Cowper, Philip Doddridge, John Fawcett, Joseph Hart, Samuel Medley, John Needham, John Newton, Anne Steele, and Joseph and Samuel Stennett.

In some of these were found quaint hymns of folk tradition emphasizing a strong sectarian message. One of the stanzas of the hymn "You've read the third of Matthew" says:

> John was a baptist preacher,
> When he baptiz'd the Lamb,
> Then Jesus was a baptist,
> And thus the baptists came;
> If you would follow Jesus,
> As christians ought to do,
> You'd come and be immersed
> And be a baptist too (Music, 1984, 46).

Tunebooks

For the folk hymnody in New England in the late-eighteenth century, a vast body of "unwritten music" accumulated; these hymns were "lined out" to the people. Among the backwoods Baptists of New England, the first collection of these tunes appeared (Jackson, 10). Jeremiah Ingalls' *Christian Harmony* is recognized as the first publication of the "Old Baptist" folk melodies. Many of the oblong tunebooks that came later used the shape notation developed by William Smith and William Little in *The Easy Instructor* (1802) The solmization system used the same fournote syllables, *fa, sol, la, mi,* brought by the early English settlers, and which appeared in the 9th edition, 1698, of the Bay Psalm Book, the earliest edition to provide tunes. Only now, different shaped noteheads were used; this method for teaching music reading spread rapidly and became immensely popular.

In the South, Baptist collections of hymns, more than any other factor, prompted tunebook compilers to publish the tunes to which these hymns were being sung and to compose new tunes for others. Of the numerous oblong, shape-note tunebooks that appeared in the South, the two most widely used were William Walker's *The Southern Harmony* (1835) [Eskew, 28-34], and B. F. White's and E. J. King's *The Sacred Harp* (1844) [Cobb, n.pag]. These tunebooks have provided a resource of the religio-folk tunes that have been a rich heritage of Baptists in the South. John Newton's hymn "Amazing grace! how sweet the sound" and the folk tune called NEW BRITAIN (now known as AMAZING GRACE) first appeared together in Walker's *Southern Harmony*. Walker gave Burdett's *Baptist Harmony* (1834) as his source for Newton's hymn. Some of the tunes widely sung among Baptists in the last decade of the twentieth century that can be traced to these Southern tunebooks are BEACH SPRING,

FOUNDATION, HOLY MANNA, KEDRON, LAND OF REST, MORNING SONG, PISGAH, and PROMISED LAND.

The Psalmist and Its Supplement

Samuel Francis Smith, pastor of the First Baptist Church, Newton, Massachusetts, and Baron Stow, pastor of the Baldwin Place Baptist Church, Boston, compiled *The Psalmist*, published in 1843. Since there was a growing need for a more contemporary compilation to replace "Winchell's Watts" and "Rippon's Watts," *The Psalmist* became a unifying force in hymnody, particularly among the Baptists of New England and the middle Atlantic states. But the work of Smith and Stow was not favorably received in the South, for many of the hymns popular in that area had been omitted. In an attempt to remedy this situation, Richard Fuller and Jeremiah B. Jeter published in 1847 a *Supplement to the Psalmist*, adding 1065 hymns. While this supplemental edition was welcomed by urban churches and more educated congregations, it was somewhat advanced for the South and the West. Much more appropriate for popular acceptance in these areas were W. C. Buck's *Baptist Hymn Book* (Louisville, 1842), H. Miller's *New Selection of Psalms, Hymns and Spiritual Songs* (Cincinnati, 1835), and J. M. Peck's *Dupuy's Hymns and Spiritual Songs* (Louisville, 1843) as well as the previously mentioned works of Mercer, Burdett, and others.

The Beginning of Denominational Hymnals
for Southern Baptists

The Southern Baptist Convention was organized in 1845. McBeth points out at least three factors that led to this separation from Baptists in the North: disagreements on methods of organization, problems in home mission work, and the slavery controversy (McBeth, 381). Hymnals used in the churches had been generally compiled and published by individuals. From this time on, however, denominational publishing agencies, both in the North and South, took on greater significance.

The Southern Baptist Publication Society, established in Charleston, South Carolina, in 1847, published *Baptist Psalmody*, compiled by Basil Manly and Basil Manly, Jr. The collection of 1295 hymns was of excellent quality, and the Southern Baptist Convention meeting in Nashville in 1851 voted to recommend it to the churches. It was as favorably accepted in the South as *The Psalmist* was in the North. In 1855 the Society published I. B. Woodbury's *The Casket* and Edwin T. Winkler's *Sacred Lute*.

Basil Manly, Jr., in the preface to his *Baptist Chorals: A Hymn and Tune Book* (1859), provides this information:

> The object of this volume is not to come in competition with hymn books now in circulation, but to render them more useful by supplying tunes adapted

expressly to some of the choicest hymns.... Hymns
have been selected almost exclusively which are to be
found in both the *Baptist Psalmody* and *The Psalmist,* the
two books most extensively used in the Baptist churches in the United States.

Considerably removed from Charleston and Richmond were the less
densely populated and more rural areas of Tennessee and Kentucky.
Among the collections that enjoyed considerable regional popularity
were J. M. D. Cates's *Baptist Companion* (Nashville, 1850?) and *Sacred
Harp* (Nashville, 1867), A. B. Cates's *Baptist Songs, with Music* (Louisville,
1879), and J. R. Grave's *New Baptist Psalmist* (Memphis, 1873). Graves,
the principal leader of the Landmark movement among Southern Baptists and one of the most controversial denominational leaders, pointed
to the theological purity of his collection in the preface:

In this collection there will be found no hymns that
teach the doctrine of baptismal remission or ritual efficacy, no praises to be sung to dead relatives or friends,
nor are children taught to pray to the angels, or desire
to be angels.

The American Baptist Publication Society in Philadelphia published
three significant hymnals for Baptists in the North: *The Baptist Hymn and
Tune Book* (1871), *The Baptist Hymnal* (1883), and *Sursum Corda* (1898).
The first, containing 980 hymns, failed to meet with general acceptance,
largely because of the inferior quality of the tunes. The second collection
was of better quality, and while it shows evidence of the rapidly emerging gospel song, it also reveals the initial influence among Baptists of
Hymns Ancient and Modern (London, 1862), the most significant English
hymnal of the nineteenth century. *Sursum Corda,* compiled by E. H.
Johnson, revealed the compiler's disregard for the emerging gospel song
and his excessive borrowing of Anglican hymns and tunes. This resulted
in a hymnal of highest quality, but one unacceptable to the majority of
Baptist congregations. Its contents, plus the Latin title, were too much
for too many Baptists even in the North.

In 1891 Basil Manly, Jr., then nearing the end of his extraordinary
career, published *The Choice, A New Selection of Approved Hymns for Baptist Churches* (Louisville). Manly's preface written at the close of the century, reveals his concern for the hymnody of Southern Baptists:

For some years it has been apparent that the rage for
novelties in singing, especially in our Sunday Schools,
has been driving out of use the old, precious, standard hymns. They are not memorized as of old. They
are scarcely sung at all. They are not contained in the

nondenominational song books, which in many churches have usurped the places of our old hymn-books. We cannot afford to lose these old hymns. They are full of the Gospel; they breathe the deepest emotions of pious hearts in the noblest strains of poetry; they have been listed and approved by successive generations of those who love the Lord; they are the surviving fittest ones from thousands of inferior productions; they are hallowed by abundant usefulness and tenderest memories. But the young people today are unfamiliar with them, and will seldom hear any of them if the present tendency goes on untouched.

The Gospel Song

Though Manly died shortly after *The Choice* was published, he had felt the initial impact on Southern Baptists of the gospel song—that phenomenon that emerged in the late nineteenth century and continues to the present time. Here was a merging of the influences of folk hymnody, campmeeting songs, singing school songs, and the songs of the Sunday School movement. Sunday School songs, first intended solely for children, were simple in character, popular in musical format, and designed for immediate appeal. Jonathan Howe published in Boston in 1829 the earliest Baptist collection of Sunday School songs.

More significant and influential were later collections by three Baptists—William B. Bradbury, William H. Doane, and Robert Lowry. Bradbury edited or helped compile more than eighty songbook collections between 1841 and 1867, and composed more than one thousand hymn tunes (Shorney, 1). Doane's first compilation in 1862, was the first of forty collections with which he was associated. Following Bradbury's death in 1868, Lowry was invited by Biglow and Main, Bradbury's successor, to serve as music editor. Some of the most popular collections were compiled by Doane and Lowry, and some of the most enduring gospel songs first appeared in the Sunday School collections. By the 1870s many Sunday Schools were including adults as well as children, as indicated in the introductory "Salutation" of Lowry and Doane's *Pure Gold for the Sunday School* (New York, 1871):

> The hymns in this work are not all projected on the plane of childhood. That quiet revolution by which our Sunday Schools for children are passing up to the higher level of Bible Schools for all ages, has not been overlooked.

Aware of this growing activity in the churches, The Sunday School Board at Greenville, South Carolina, published in 1863 *The Little Sunday*

School Hymn Book and also C. J. Elford's *Confederate Sunday School Hymn Book*. In reporting these two collections to the 1866 meeting of the Southern Baptist Convention in Russellville, Kentucky, The Sunday School Board stated that it had been unsuccessful in securing the printing of a collection of Sunday School songs with music, thereby justifying the publication of these two books (*Southern Baptist Convention Annual,* 1866, p. 26.). *Kind Words,* a Sunday School paper for children, established in 1866, frequently contained new songs, and in 1871, The Sunday School Board published *Kind Words in Melody,* consisting of 121 hymns and 59 tunes that had appeared in the Sunday School paper.

The singable Sunday School songs found a warm welcome in those churches where hymn singing of the congregation had declined into a meaningless experience, lacking in vitality and warmth. When educational standards were low and cultural advantages meager, the absence of a traditional hymnody and the freedom and independence of the local congregation provided a fertile climate for the gospel song.

Philip P. Bliss, a Baptist layman, compiled several Sunday School collections for George F. Root in Cincinnati. It was the singing of Bliss in a religious service in Chicago that first impressed evangelist Dwight L. Moody with the power of music in his evangelistic efforts. Moody secured the services of Ira D. Sankey, whose name became synonymous with the gospel song tradition (Wilhoit, 13-19). Lesser-known evangelists and lesser-known song leaders traveled throughout the southern states, and in revivals, tent meetings, campmeetings, and street services, the gospel songs swept through village and hamlet. In many respects the gospel song may be considered a variant expression of American folk hymnody, and nowhere did it receive a more hearty acceptance than among Southern Baptists.

The Twentieth Century

The earliest publishing of gospel song collections by Southern Baptists seems to have occurred at Louisville, Kentucky. The Baptist Book Concern, an independent publishing firm owned by several Baptist leaders in Kentucky, published *Glorious Praise* (1904), compiled by William H. Doane and William J. Kirkpatrick, and Doane's *Song Evangel* (1906). Through the persistent efforts of J. M. Frost, The Baptist Sunday School Board was established at Nashville in 1891, and its first hymnal publication was *The Baptist Hymn and Praise Book* (1904), compiled by Lansing Burrows, pastor of Nashville's First Baptist Church, with a committee of denominational leaders. To the 1905 Southern Baptist Convention meeting in Kansas City, the Board reported that this book was in its second printing, and stated that it considered this hymnal "the very crown of its book publication" (*Southern Baptist Convention Annual,* 1905, p. 207). In 1921 the Board published *Kingdom Songs,* compiled by I. E. Reynolds and

Robert H. Coleman.

In the early decades of this century, the publishing activity of a Baptist layman in Dallas, Texas, was most significant in certain areas of the South. Between 1909 and 1939, Robert H. Coleman published thirty-three collections, ranging from full-sized hymnals to small paperback collections of songs.[A complete listing of Coleman's publications, together with his biography is given in William J. Reynolds' *Companion to Baptist Hymnal* (1976, pp. 285-86).] The most influential of these were *The Modern Hymnal* (1926), and *The American Hymnal* (1933). Sensitive to the hymn-singing practices of the churches, Coleman designed his compilations for popular appeal. His association with George W. Truett, his pastor, and his friendship with B. B. McKinney, destined to become Southern Baptists' most prolific gospel song writer of his day, were tremendous assets. McKinney, on the music faculty at Southwestern Baptist Theological Seminary, Fort Worth, served as Coleman's music editor from 1919 until 1935. While Coleman was no reformer of church music, and proclaimed no high ideals of hymnody, he did include many standard hymns in the two hymnals mentioned above. Southern Baptist congregations, both large and small, first became acquainted with some of these hymns through his books.

During these decades a few voices championed the cause of a higher type of hymnody for Southern Baptists. These crusaders welcomed the appearance of *The New Baptist Hymnal* (1926), published jointly by the publishing agencies of Northern and Southern conventions. While it was used extensively in the North, it had little acceptance in the South. Nonetheless, for at least thirty years it was used in the chapel services at the seminaries at Fort Worth and Louisville, and at several Baptist colleges in the South.

During the first four decades of this century, a wide variety of hymnals could be found in Southern Baptist churches. The publications of many independent publishers—Tabernacle Publishing Company, Hope Publishing Company, Rodeheaver Hall-Mack Company, and Tullar-Meredith Company, as well as Robert H. Coleman—found their way into Southern Baptist churches. The shape-note collections of "convention music" published by James D. Vaughan Company, Stamps-Baxter Music Company, and the Hartford Music company enjoyed great popularity in rural communities in many states. "Fifth-Sunday singings" were a vital part of community life with strong sociological significance.

Southern Baptist Hymnals 1940-1991

The Baptist Sunday School Board, Southern Baptists' publication agency, employed B. B. McKinney as music editor in 1935, with the primary purpose of compiling, manufacturing and publishing hymnals and songbooks. *The Broadman Hymnal* (1940), was McKinney's compilation and became the first hymnal to bring about any degree of unanimity in the congregational singing of Southern Baptists. No purposeful internal organization is evident in the hymnal. Besides the classic English and American hymns of the eighteenth and nineteenth centuries, there are eight short choruses and a concluding section of fourteen choir selections that includes Gounod's "Praise Ye the Father," Stainer's "God So Loved the World," and Handel's "Hallelujah Chorus" (from *Messiah*). McKinney's own contribution is seen in his forty-one original tunes and the twelve tunes that bear his name as arranger. *The Broadman Hymnal* was published in both round- and shape-note editions; the latter helped introduce the hymnal to those churches where shape-note singing was enthusiastically practiced. So extensive was its use that it became, more than any other previous collection, the most generally used hymnal among Southern Baptist churches at that time.

In 1941 The Sunday School Board established within its organization the Church Music Department, with B. B. McKinney as head. In spite of the cordial reception *The Broadman Hymnal* had received, by the early 1950s there was an awareness that a new hymnal was needed. The growing significance of music in the churches, the increasing influence of music education within the curriculum of Southern Baptist seminaries, and the appearance of better trained church music leadership contributed to this concern.

W. Hines Sims, who became head of the Church Music Department in 1952, began plans the following year for a new hymnal. *Baptist Hymnal,* released in 1956, was compiled by Sims, as general editor, with a committee of thirty-seven people. A substantial book, well organized, its contents were well balanced, with a preponderance of nineteenth-century material. Its widespread usage surpassed that of *The Broadman Hymnal* and it became an even greater unifying factor in the singing in the churches.

The church music upheaval of the 1960s, the emphasis on youth in the churches, the new interest in folk music, and the acceptance in church services of new sounds and new songs created a need for a revision of the 1956 hymnal. William J. Reynolds, who became head of the Church Music Department in 1971, requested administrative approval to prepare a new hymnal. A survey of hymn-singing practices was made, and a hymnal committee of sixty-eight persons began work. While the new hymnal drew from many sources and many traditions and encompassed new sounds of the present generation, it remained true to the tradition of its predecessors. *Baptist Hymnal* was released March 13, 1975, its premiere being the climax of PraiSing '75 in Nashville, Tennessee, as 10,000 people sang together from its pages for the first time.

Wesley L. Forbis became head of the Church Music Department in 1980, and by the mid-eighties began discussions concerning a new hymnal. The year of 1991 seemed an appropriate release date for it provided an opportunity to celebrate three significant events—the 300th anniversary of Benjamin Keach's *Spiritual Melody,* published in England in 1691; the 100th anniversary of the establishment of the Baptist Sunday School Board in Nashville, Tennessee, in 1891; and the 50th anniversary of the founding of the Church Music Department at the Baptist Sunday School Board in 1941. Here were distinctive benchmarks in Baptist history.

A hymnal committee of ninety-eight, under Forbis' leadership, forged together this collection, structured on the *Baptist Faith and Message Statement,* adopted by the Southern Baptist Convention in 1963. Forbis believed that the challenge of a new hymnal called for the editor to discover "how best to blend and fuse the rich heritage of hymnody with contemporary symbols to produce a nexus for the existential 'now' " (Forbis, 1990, 77).

With regard to the theological content of the hymnal, every word of every stanza was carefully examined by the appropriate committee. With regard to the language of the hymns, no alterations were made in the core of songs familiar to Southern Baptists. In hymns that are less familiar or infrequently used, some changes were made in archaic language (Forbis, 1991, 8-14). To a common core of hymn tunes sung in the churches, have been added new tunes of the recent decades that enrich the body of congregational songs. These have been chosen wisely and well.

The enthusiastic response given *The Baptist Hymnal* at PraiSing II in Nashville, Tennessee, March 14, 1991, anticipated a like response from the churches who bear the name Southern Baptists and will sing from these pages into the twenty-first century.

> All people that on earth do dwell,
> Sing to the Lord with cheerful voice;
> Him serve with fear, his praise forthtell;
> Come ye before him and rejoice.
>
> Psalm 100
> *Paraphrased by William Kethe, 1561*

Bibliography

Benedict, David. *A General History of the Baptist Denomination in America and Other Parts of the World.* I. Boston: Lincoln and Edmands, 1813.

Benson, Louis F. *The English Hymn.* New York: George H. Doran, 1915.

Brewster, C. Ray. *The Cluster of Jesse Mercer.* Macon: Renaissance Press, 1983.

Burrage, Henry S. *Baptist Hymn Writers and Their Hymns.* Portland: Brown Thurston & Company, 1888.

Cobb, Buell E., Jr. *The Sacred Harp: A Tradition and Its Music.* Athens: The University of Georgia Press, 1989.

Edwards, Morgan. *History of the Baptists in Rhode Island.* 1867.

Edwards, Morgan. *History of the Baptists in Delaware.* 1885.

Encyclopedia of Southern Baptists. II. Nashville: Broadman Press, 1958, 985-86.

Eskew, Harry. "Southern Harmony and Its Era." *The Hymn* (Oct. 1990): 28-34.

Forbis, Wesley L. "Currents and Cross-Currents Impacting Hymnal Formation: The New Baptist Hymnal, Issues and Answers." *Review and Expositor* 87 (Winter 1990): 77.

Forbis, Wesley L. "Congratulations! It's a Hymnal." *The Church Musician* (Apr./May/June, 1991): 8-14.

Gardner, Robert G. *Baptists of Early America: A Statistical History, 1639-1790.* Atlanta: Georgia Baptist Historical Society, 1983.

Garrecht, David. "John Leland: Practicing Politics...Securing Freedom." *Report from the Capital* (Feb. 1991): 14.

Jackson, George Pullen. *The Story of the Sacred Harp 1844-1944.* Nashville: Vanderbilt University Press, 1944.

Lumpkin, William L., ed. *Baptist Confessions of Faith.* Valley Forge: Judson Press, 1959.

Manley, Kenneth Ross. "John Rippon, D. D. (1751-1836) and the Particular Baptists." Diss. Oxford: Regents' Park College, 1967.

Maring, Norman H. *Baptists in New Jersey.* Valley Forge: 1964.

McBeth, H. Leon. *The Baptist Heritage.* Nashville: Broadman Press, 1987.

McCutchan, Robert G. *Hymns in the Lives of Men.* New York: Abingdon-Cokesbury Press, 1945.

McLoughlin, William G. *New England Dissent 1630-1833: The Baptists and the Separation of Church and State.* Cambridge: Harvard University Press, 1971.

Metcalf, Frank J. *American Writers and Compilers of Sacred Music.* New York: Abingdon Press, 1925.

Minutes, First Baptist Church, Salem, NJ, Aug. 20, 1785.

Music, David W. "Music in the First Baptist Church of Boston, Massachusetts, 1665-1820." *The Quarterly Review* (Apr. 1982): 39.

Music, David W. "Oliver Holden (1765-1844): The First Baptist Composer in America." *The Quarterly Review* (Oct. 1980): 46-52.

Music, David W. "Early Baptist Composers and Tunebooks in America." *The Quarterly Review* (Jan. 1987): 68-75.

Music, David W. "Starke Dupuy, Early Baptist Hymnal Compiler." *The Quarterly Review* (Oct. 1984): 43-47.

Richardson, Paul A. "Eleazar Clay's *Hymns and Spiritual Songs* (1793)." *The Virginia Baptist Register* (1990): 1457-59.

Richardson, Paul A. "Andrew Broaddus and Hymnody." *The Virginia Baptist Register* 24 (1985): 1198-1211.

Shorney, George H., Jr. "The History of Hope Publishing Company and Its Divisions and Affiliates." *Dictionary-Handbook to Hymns for the Living Church* (1978): 1.

White, Blanche Sydnor. *First Baptist Church, Richmond, Virginia, 1780-1955.*

Whitley, W.T. "The First Hymnbook in Use." *The Baptist Quarterly* 7. X. (Jul. 1941): 369-75.

Wilhoit, Mel R. " 'Sing Me a Sankey': Ira D. Sankey and Congregational Song." *The Hymn* 42 (Jan. 1991): 13-19.

Baptist Collections of Hymns Published in America

(Because of space limitations only abbreviated titles are used for collections published by or for Baptists. Not included are the many Sunday School collections by Robert Lowry, W. H. Doane and others, nor the collections of splinter groups that developed in the nineteenth century. The listing includes date of publication, title, compiler, and place of publication.)

1762 *Evangelical Hymns and Songs*, Benjamin Wallin [American reprint], Boston, MA.

1766 *Hymns and Spiritual Songs*, (?), Newport, RI.

1773 *Hymns and Spiritual Songs*, (?), Williamsburg, VA.

1782 *A Collection of Hymns* (?), Philip Hughes, Wilmington, DE.

1782 *A Choice Collection of Hymns*, Elhanan Winchester ?, Philadelphia, PA.

1784 *A Choice Collection of Hymns*, Enoch Story, Jr., Philadelphia, PA.

1784 *Divine Hymns, or Spiritual Songs*, Joshua Smith, Norwich, NH.

1786 *Hymns on Different Subjects*, Benjamin Cleavland, Norwich, CT.

1787 *The Works of David Culy*, David Culy, Boston, MA.
1790 *A Selection of Psalms and Hymns*, Samuel Jones and Burgis Allison, Philadelphia, PA.
1790 *A Collection of Sacred Ballads*, Andrew Broaddus and Richard Broaddus, Caroline Co., VA.
1791 *Baptismal Hymns*, (?), Boston, MA.
1792 *A Selection of Hymns* [American Reprint], John Rippon, Elizabeth Town, NJ.
1792 *A Collection of Evangelical Hymns*, John Stanford, NY.
1793 *Hymns and Spiritual Songs*, Eleazer Clay, Richmond, VA.
1793 *A New Collection of Hymns and Spiritual Songs*, John Peak, Windsor.
1796 *Hymns*, Richard Burnham [American reprint], Boston, MA.
1798 *A New Selection of Spiritual Songs*, Andrew Broaddus, Richmond, VA.
1799 *A Collection of Evangelical Hymns*, Andrew Harpending, Mount Holly, NJ.
1801 *The Christian's Pocket Companion*, John Courtney, Richmond, VA.
1801 *Hymns*, Samuel Medley [American reprint], Boston, MA.
1803 *Hymns and Spiritual Songs*, John Courtney, Richmond, VA.
1804 *The Christian Harmonist*, Samuel Holyoke, Salem, MA.
1805 *Hymns*, Elias Smith and Abner Jones, Portland, ME. ?
1807 *A Selection of Free-Grace Hymns*, Ebenezer Baptist Church, New York, NY.
1807 *A Selection of Evangelical Hymns*, William Staughton, Burlington, NJ.
1808 *Hymns and Poems on Various Subjects*, James Fenn, Schenectady, NY.
1808 *Original Hymns and Spiritual Songs*, Lewis Baldwin, Philadelphia, PA.
1808 *A Selection of Hymns and Psalms*, Daniel Dodge, Wilmington, DE.
1808 *The Boston Collection of Sacred and Devotional Hymns*, (?), Boston, MA.
1809 *Hymns and Spiritual Songs*, Ebenezer Jayne, Morristown, NJ.
1809 *A Selection of Hymns and Spiritual Songs*, William Parkinson, New York, NY.
1810 *A New Selection of Hymns* [American Reprint], John Dobell, Morristown, NJ.
1810 *The Cluster of Spiritual Songs* [3rd ed.] Jesse Mercer, Augusta, GA. [Date of 1st ed. unknown]
1811 *Hymns and Spiritual Songs*, Starke Dupuy, Louisville, KY.
1812 *A New Selection of Hymns*, William Collier, Boston, MA.
1813 *The Christian's Duty*, Peter Leibert, Philadelphia, PA.
1814 *A Selection of Hymns on Baptismal Subjects*, (?), Rutland, VA.
1814 *A Hymn Book*, Silas M. Noel, Frankfort, KY.
1815 *A Selection of Hymns and Spiritual Songs*, George C. Sedgwick, Fredericksburg, VA.
1816 *A Selection of Hymns*, Archibald Maclay, New York, NY.
1817 *The Pawtucket Collection of Conference Hymns*, David Benedict, Providence, RI.
1817 *A New Selection of Sacred Music*, Samuel Dyer, Baltimore, MD.
1817 *A Selection of Hymns*, Paul Himes and Jonathan Wilson, Greenfield, MA.
1818 *An Arrangement of the Psalms, Hymns, and Spiritual Songs of Isaac Watts*, James Winchell, Boston, MA.
1819 *Sacred Harmony*, James Winchell, Boston, MA.
1820 *The Psalms and Hymns of Dr. Watts, arranged by Dr. Rippon with Rippon's Selection* [American reprint], Philadelphia, PA.
1820 *The Choice*, William Dossey, Philadelphia, PA.
1821 *A Selection of Hymns*, Thomas B. Ripley, Portland, ME.
1821 *Noel's Selection of Hymns*, Silas Noel and Jeremiah Vardeman, Frankfort, KY.
1822 *Hymns for Conference Meetings*, Howard Malcom, Hudson, NY.
1824 *The Baptist Hymn Book*, James Fenn, Schenectady, NY.
1825 *The Baptist Hymn Book*, William P. Biddle and William J. Newborn, Washington, DC.
1825 *Hymns, Psalms, and Spiritual Songs*, Absalom Graves, Cincinnati, OH.
1825 *The Choice Collection of the Latest Social and Camp Meeting Hymns and Spiritual Songs*, Lewis Skidmore, Baltimore, MD.
1826 *A Selection of Hymns and Spiritual Songs*, John Purifoy, Raleigh, NC.
1826 *The Christian's Pocket-Companion*, John C. Royce, Enfield, VA.
1826 *The Young Christian's Companion*, Gustavus F. Davis, Boston, MA.
1827 *The Harp of Zion*, (?), Pittsburgh, PA.
1827 *The Psalms and Hymn of Dr. Watts, arranged by Dr. Rippon; with Dr. Rippon's Selection*, C. G. Sommers and John L. Dagg, Philadelphia, PA.
1828 *Conference Hymns* [2nd ed.], Daniel Greene, Providence, RI.

1828 *Philadelphia Selection of Sacred Music*, Samuel Dyer, New York, NY.
1828 *The Dover Selection of Spiritual Songs*, Andrew Broaddus, Richmond, VA.
1829 *A Selection of Hymns*, Edmond Richmond, Milford, NY.
1829 *A Selection of Hymns*, Enoch W. Freeman, Exeter, NH.
1829 *The Baptist Songster*, R. Winchell, Wethersfield, CO.
1829 *A Selection of Favorite Conference Hymns*, J. A. Burke, Albany, NY.
1829 *Choice Hymns, for Social and Private Devotion and Lord's Day Schools*, Jonathan Howe, Boston, MA.
1930 *The Revival Harmonist*, (?), Boston, MA.
1830 *The Baptist Conference and Prayer Meeting Hymn Book*, Paris M. Davis, Binghamton, NY.
1830 *A Selection of Hymns*, Cyrenius M. Fuller, Auburn, NY.
1830 *The Psalms and Hymns of Dr. Watts*, John Rippon, Philadelphia, PA.
1831 *The Psalms and Hymns of Dr. Watts, arranged by Dr. Rippon, with Dr. Rippon's Selection*, C. G. Sommers, Boston, MA.
1831 *A Collection of Psalms, Hymns, and Spiritual Songs*, Luke Barker, New York, NY.
1831 *A New Selection of Psalms, Hymns, and Spiritual Songs*, H. Miller, Cincinnati, OH.
1831 *A Selection of Hymns*, John Courtney, Sr., Richmond, VA.
1832 *The Free Will Baptist Hymn Book*, William Lumpkin and Enoch Cobb, New Bern, NC.
1832 *Hymns of Zion*, B.M. Hill, New Haven, CT.
1832 *A Manual of Christian Psalmody*, Rufus Babcock, Boston, MA.
1834 *The Baptist Harmony*, Staunton S. Burdett, Philadelphia, PA.
1834 *Union Hymns*, Rufus Babcock & Lowell Mason, Boston, MA.
1835 *Songs of Zion* [3rd ed.], Wm. C. Manchester, Providence, RI.
1835 *The United Baptist Selection of Psalms, Hymns, and Spiritual Songs*, (?), Nashville, TN.
1835 *The Southern Harmony*, William Walker, New Haven, CT.
1835 *The Conference Manual*, Ebenezer E. Cummings & Edmund Worth, Concord, NH.
1836 *The Virginia Selection*, Andrew Broaddus, Richmond, VA.
1836 *Christian Melodies*, Stephen P. Hill, Baltimore, MD.
1836 *Old School Sonnets*, James Osbourn, Baltimore, MD.
1836 *Select Hymns*, James H. Linsley, Gustavus F. David, Hartford, CT.
1837 *Christian Melodies*, Rev. Mr. Hill, Macon County, NC.
1839 *Revival Hymns*, John Butler, Boston, MA.
1841 *Hymns for the Vestry*, S. S. Cutting, Boston, MA.
1841 *Primitive Hymns*, Benjamin Lloyd, Wetumpka, AL.
1842 *Revival Melodies, or Songs of Zion*, (?), Boston, MA.
1842 *Hymns for Social and Private Worship*, J. B. Hague, ME.?
1842 *The Old Baptist Hymn Book*, R. Knight and J. Tillinghast, Providence, RI.
1842 *The Sabbath School Gleaner*, (?), Philadelphia, PA.
1842 *The Baptist Hymn Book*, William C. Buck, Louisville, KY.
1843 *Dupuy's Hymns and Spiritual Songs*, J. M. Peck, Louisville, KY.
1843 *A Collection of Hymns*, A. A. Guernsey, Strongsville, OH.
1843 *The Psalmist*, Baron Stow & Samuel F. Smith, Boston, MA.
1843 *Hymns for Social Meetings*, A. D. Gillette, Philadelphia, PA.
1844 *The American Baptist Sabbath-School Hymn Book*, J. A. Warne, Philadelphia, PA.
1844 *North Carolina Sonnets*, James Osbourn, Baltimore, MD.
1844 *The Sacred Harp*, B. F. White and E. J. King, Philadelphia, PA.
1845 *Sacred Melodies, designed for Conferences, Concerts, and Sabbath Schools*, Lewis Colby, New York, NY.
1845 *The Evangelical Harp*, Jacob Knapp, Utica, NY.
1846 *Southern and Western Pocket Harmonist*, William Walker, Philadelphia, PA.
1846 *The Companion*, J. M. D. Cates, Nashville, TN.
1847 *Christian Psalmody*, G. B. Utter and E. G. Champlin, New York, NY.
1846 *Free Will Baptist Hymn Book*, Enoch Cobb, New Bern, NC.
1847 *The Supplement to The Psalmist*, Richard Fuller & Jeremiah B. Jeter, Philadelphia, PA.
1847 *A Choice Selection*, Richard Knight, Providence, RI.
1847 *The Christian Psalmist*, Silas W. Leonard, Louisville, KY.
1848 *The Social Psalmist*, Baron Stow and Samuel F. Smith, Boston, MA.
1848 *Ocean Melodies; and Seamen's Companion*, J. H. Hanaford, Boston, MA.
1849 *The Baptist Harp*, George B. Ide and Edgar M. Levy, Philadelphia, PA.

1849 *Conference Hymns*, John Dowling, New York, NY.
1849 *The Manual of the Sacred Choir*, Eli Ball, Richmond, VA.
1849 *The Christian Melodist*, Joseph Banvard, Boston, MA.
1849 *Bethel Hymns*, Elizabeth Sowers, Richmond, VA.
1850 *The Christian Psalmist*, S. W. Leonard, Louisville, KY.
1850 *A Collection of Hymns and Spiritual Songs*. Lemuel Burkitt, Philadelphia, PA.
1850 *Baptist Psalmody*, Basil Manly and Basil Manly, Jr., Charleston, SC.
1850 *Select Hymns*, Committee of the Second Baptist Church, Philadelphia, PA.
1850 *The Baptist Companion*, J.M.D. Cates, Nashville, TN.
1851 *The Southwestern Psalmist*, Sidney Dyer, Louisville, KY.
1854 *The Sabbath School Harp*, (?), Philadelphia, PA.
1854 *Zion's Hymns*, Rufus Hearn, Joseph Bell, Jesse Randolph, [NC?]
1855 *The Sacred Lute*, Edwin T. Winkler, Charleston, SC.
1855 *The Casket*, I. B. Woodbury, Charleston, SC.
1855 *The Social Harp*, John G. McCurry, Philadelphia, PA.
1855 *The Congregational Psalmist*, Jacob R. Scott. Rochester, NY.
1856 *Psalms, Hymns, and Spiritual Songs* [2nd. ed.], Jesse Heath and Elias Hutchins, Richmond, VA.
1857 *The Prayer Meeting Hymn Book*, William Crane, Baltimore, MD.
1857 *Baptist Chorals*, Basil Manly Jr., Richmond, VA.
1857 *The Baptist Hymn and Tune Book*, J. S. Holme, New York, NY.
1858 *The Sabbath Hymn and Tune Book*, [Baptist Edition], New York, NY.
1859 *The Southern Psalmist*, J. R. Graves and J. M. Pendleton, Nashville, TN.
1859 *Church Melodies*, Thomas Hastings and Robert Turnbull, New York, NY.
1859 *The Sabbath Hymn Book*, Francis Wayland, New York, NY.
1858 *Revival Gems*, Joseph Banvard, Boston, MA.
1858 *The Sacred Lyre*, Jonathan Aldrich, Boston, MA.
1858 *The Vestry Harp*, Nehemiah M. Perkins, Boston, MA.
1859 *Melodies of Zion*, H. D. Phinney, Oswego, NY.
1860 *The Psalmist with Music*, B. F. Edmands, Boston, MA.
1860 *Spiritual Songs*, James Inglis, Detroit, MI.
1860 *A Collection of Hymns for Creek Baptists*, Henry F. Buckner, New York, NY.
1861 *A Baptist Hymn Book*, Wilson Thompson, Cincinnati, OH.
1861 *The Union Harp*, Edwin Burnham, Philadelphia, PA.
1862 *Baptismal Harmonies*, Edmund Turney, New York, NY.
1863 *The Athenaeum Collection of Hymns and Tunes*, Horace Waters, New York, NY.
1863 *Choral Harp*, Horace Waters, New York, NY.
1863 *Golden Harp*, Horace Waters, New York, NY.
1863 *The Little Sunday School Hymn Book*, (?), Charleston, SC.
1863 *Confederate Sunday School Hymn Book*, (?), Charleston, SC.
1864 *The Devotional Hymn and Tune Book*, William B. Bradbury, Philadelphia, PA.
1864 *The Sabbath School Gem*, Selma Baptist Sabbath School, Selma, AL.
1865 *The Sunday School Hymn Book*, C. J. Elford, Greenville, SC.
1865 *Revival Hymns*, A. B. Earle, Boston, MA.
1865 *The Baptist Vocalist*, C. A. Worley, Carrollton, IL.
1865 *The Christian Melodist*, Horace Waters, New York, NY.
1866 *Christian Harmony*, William Walker, Philadelphia, PA.
1867 *Zion's Refreshing Showers*, Horace Waters, New York, NY.
1867 *Heavenly Echoes*, Horace Waters, New York, NY.
1867 *Songs for the Sanctuary*, T. S. Griffiths, New York, NY.
1867 *The Sacred Harp*, J. M. D. Cates, Nashville, TN.
1867 *Revival Gems*, Edwin Burnham, Boston, MA.
1868 *Conference and Revival Hymns*, John Dowling, New York, NY.
1868 *Chapel Melodies*, S. J. Vail and Robert Lowry, New York, NY.
1870 *Revival Songs*, Emerson Andrews, Boston, MA.
1870 *Songs of Devotion*, William H. Doane, New York, NY.
1871 *The Baptist Praise Book*, Richard Fuller, and E.M. Levy, New York, NY.
1871 *Baptist Hymn Book*, (?), Philadelphia, PA.
1871 *Baptist Hymn and Tune Book*, John M. Evans, Philadelphia, PA.

1871 *The Service of Songs*, S. L. Caldwell, and A. J. Gordon, Boston, MA.

1871 *Kind Words in Melody*, (?), Greenville, SC.

1872 *The Vestry Hymn and Tune Book*, A. J. Gordon, Boston, MA.

1873 *Heaven in Song*, Henry Clay Fish, New York, NY.

1873 *The New Baptist Psalmist and Tune Book*, J.R. Graves, Memphis, TN.

1873 *The Little Seraph*, J.R. Graves, Memphis, TN.

1874 *Baptismal Chants*, Horace Waters, Yonkers, NY.

1874 *Christian Praise*, Charles D. Bridgman, New York, NY.

1876 *Gospel Music*, Robert Lowry and W. H. Doane, New York, NY.

1877 *A New and Choice Selection of Hymns and Spiritual Songs*, Erasmus D. Thomas, Indianapolis, IN.

1878 *The Calvary Selection*, Charles S. Robinson and Robert S. MacArthur, New York, NY.

1878 *Good Will*, T. M. Towne and J. M. Stillman, Chicago, IL.

1879 *Gospel Hymn and Tune Book*, Robert Lowry and William H. Doane, Philadelphia, PA.

1879 *Baptist Songs with Music*, A.B. Cates, Louisville, KY.

1880 *Manual of Praise*, C. B. Mills, Hillsdale, MI.

1880 *Songs for the Lord's House*, C. D. Bridgman and Henry Camp, New York, NY.

1882 *Harvest Bells*, W. E. Penn and J. M. Hunt, Cincinnati, OH.

1882 *Songs of Praise for Sunday-Schools*, E. H. Johnson, Philadelphia, PA.

1883 *Baptist Hymnal*, A. J. Rowland and William H. Doane, Philadelphia, PA.

1884 *Harvest Bells, No. 2*, W. E. Penn and J. M. Hunt, Cincinnati, OH.

1886 *A Collection of Old and New Songs*, Sanford M. Brown and J.M. Hunt, St. Louis, MO.

1887 *Harvest Bells No. 3*, W. E. Penn and H. N. Lincoln, Cincinnatti, OH.

1887 *Harvest Bells No. 1*, W. E. Penn, Palestine, TX.

1887 *Laudamus*, James R. Kendrick, Boston, MA.

1887 *Hymns of Faith*, Edward K. Glezen, Boston, MA.

1888 *Baptist Chorals*, F. T. Shore and Emma Abbott, Tipton, MO.

1888 *The Students Hymnal*, Thomas J. Morgan and Edward K. Glezen, Boston, MA.

1888 *The Song Gem*, Marion S. Kerby, Temple, TX.

1889 *Harvest Bells Nos. 1, 2, 3 Combined*, [1st ed.], W. E. Penn, St. Louis, MO.

1889 *Select Gems*, Robert Lowry and W. H. Doane, Philadelphia, PA.

1889 *People's Praise Book*, H. M. Sanders and George C. Lorimer, New York, NY.

1889 *Songs of Praise with Tunes*, Lewis W. Mudge, New York, NY.

1889 *Gathered Gems of Gospel Song*, George R. Cairns, Dallas, TX.

1890 *Harvest Bells No. 1, 2, 3*, [2nd ed.], W. E. Penn, St. Louis, MO.

1891 *The Calvary Hymnal*, R. S. MacArthur and Kate S. Chittenden, Boston, MA.

1891 *The Choice*, Basil Manly, Jr., Louisville, KY.

1892 *Soul Songs*, Daniel P. Airhart, R. S. Coward, J. A. Brown, and J. P. Lane, Waco, TX.

1892 *New Laudes Domini*, Charles S. Robinson and Edward Judson, New York, NY.

1893 *The National Hymn Book*, Robert E. Thompson, Philadelphia, PA.

1893 *The Revival Helper*, Charles W. Ray, Chicago, IL.

1894 *Life Songs*, Theron Brown, Boston, MA.

1894 *The Coronation Hymnal*, A. J. Gordon, Boston, MA.

1895 *Bells of Heaven*, John C. F. Kyger, Waco, TX.

1895 *Awakening Melodies*, Marion S. Kerby, Dallas, TX.

1896 *Harvest Bells No. 1, 2, 3 Abridged*, W. E. Penn, Philadelphia, PA.

1896 *Songs of the Kingdom*, William H. Doane, Philadelphia, PA.

1896 *Best Standard Songs for Sunday Schools*, R. H. Pitt and George P. Minor, Richmond, VA.

1897 *In Excelsis*, Robert S. MacArthur, New York, NY.

1898 *Sursum Corda*, E. H. Johnson, Philadelphia, PA.

1898 *The Praise Hymnary*, Thomas J. Morgan, New York, NY.

1898 *The Harp of Glory*, George E. Leonard, Lexington, NC.

1898 *Happy Voices No. 1*, John C. F. Kyger, Waco, TX.

1899 *Select Gems*, Robert Lowry and W. H. Doane, Philadelphia, PA.

1899 *The Revival Harp*, John C. F. Kyger, Waco, TX.

1900 *New Harvest Bells*, Mrs. W. E. Penn, Eureka Springs, AK.

1900 *Sacred Chimes*, John C. F. Kyger and A. Bunyan Little, Waco, TXx.

1901 *The Church Hymnary*, John B. Calvert and E. A. Bedell, New York, NY.

1901 *Zion's Delight*, Charles W. Ray, Philadelphia, PA.

1901 *Hymns for the Living Church*, Charles T. Ives and R. Huntington Woodman, New York, NY.
1901 *Lasting Hymns*, John A. Lee, Cincinnati, OH.
1902 *Hymns Old and New*, Thomas T. Eaton, New York, NY.
1902 *The Chord*, E. M. Stephenson, Philadelphia, PA.
1902 *Endeavor Hymnal*, Howard B. Grose, Boston?, MA.
1903 *National Baptist Hymnal*, R. H. Boyd and William Rosborough, Nashville, TN.
1904 *Glorious Praise*, William H. Doane and W. J. Kirkpatrick, Louisville, KY.
1904 *The Baptist Hymn and Praise Book*, Lansing Burrows, Nashville, TN.
1906 *Lasting Hymns No. 2*, John A. Lee, Glencoe, KY.
1906 *Song Evangel*, William H. Doane, Louisville, KY.
1906 *Praise Book*, Howard B. Grose, Boston, MA.
1907 *Praise and Service*, Chas. H. Gabriel, Philadelphia, PA.
1907 *Church Hymns and Tunes*, Hubert B. Turner, Kerr Boyce Tupper, and William F. Biddle, New York, NY.
1909 *The Evangel*, Robert H. Coleman and W. W. Hamilton, Philadelphia, PA.
1909 *Scripture and Song in Worship*, Francis W. Shepardson and Lester B. Jones, Chicago, IL.
1910 *Heart Praise*, James A. Brown, F. J. Harrell, and James T. Franklin, Fort Worth, TX.
1910 *Fellowship Hymns*, Clarence A. Barbour, New York, NY.
1911 *The New Baptist Praise Book*, Benjamin Shepard and William M. Lawrence, New York, NY.
1911 *The New Evangel*, Robert H. Coleman, Dallas, TX.
1912 *The Greatest Hymns*, John A. Lee, Glencoe, KY.
1913 *The Good Old Songs*, C.H. Cayce, Thornton, AK.
1913 *The World Evangel*, Robert H. Coleman, Dallas, TX.
1915 *Tidings of the Cross*, Woodie W. Smith, S. W. Jones, H.E. Ogden, and H.C. Compton, Dallas, TX.
1915 *The Heart's Offering*, Charles W. Ray, Philadelphia, PA.
1915 *The Herald*, Robert H. Coleman, Dallas, TX.
1916 *Select Gospel Songs*, J.P. Scholfield, E.L. Wolslagel, I.E. Reynolds, Dallas, TX.
1916 *Gloria*, Benjamin Shepard, New York, NY.
1917 *Service Song Book*, Clarence A. Barbour, New York, NY.
1917 *Treasury of Song*, Robert H. Coleman, Dallas, TX.
1918 *Gospel Songs of Hymns*, B.J.W. Graham (?)
1918 *The Popular Hymnal*, Robert H. Coleman, Dallas, TX.
1920 *Songs of Redemption*, W. Plunkett Martin and James W. Jelks, Atlanta, GA.
1921 *Revival Gems*, Samuel W. Beazley, Harvey Cressman, Charles L. Major, and Wiley J. Smith, Philadelphia, PA.
1921 *Victorious Praise*, Robert H. Coleman, Nashville, TN.
1921 *Kingdom Songs*, I.E. Reynolds and Robert H. Coleman, Dallas, TX.
1922 *The Pilot*, Robert H. Coleman, Dallas, TX.
1922 *Living Hymns*, W.E. Chalmers, S. W. Beazley, C.A. Boyd, A.H. Gage and L.H. Koehler, Philadelphia, PA.
1923 *The Chapel Book*, John L. Hill, Nashville, TN.
1923 *Select Songs of Praise*, S.W. Beazley, J.H. Jones, H.E. Cressman, C.L. Major, W.J. Smith, Philadelphia, PA.
1923 *Hosannas*, Robert H. Coleman, Samuel W. Beazley, and William J. Ramsey, Dallas, TX.
1924 *The Baptist Standard Hymnal*, Mrs. A.M. Townsend, Nashville, TN.
1924 *Harvest Hymns*, Robert H. Coleman, Dallas, TX.
1925 *Christian Hymns*, Lincoln Hulley, DeLand, FL.
1925 *Jehovah's Praise*, I.E. Reynolds and B.B. McKinney, Fort Worth, TX.
1925 *The Service Hymnal*, Samuel W. Beazley, Chicago, IL.
1926 *The Modern Hymnal*, Robert H. Coleman, Dallas, TX.
1926 *The New Baptist Hymnal*, (?), Philadelphia, PA, and Nashville, TN.
1927 *Conference Songs*, William H. Main, Philadelphia, PA.
1928 *Gospel Melodies*, Robert H. Coleman, Dallas, TX.
1930 *Majestic Hymns*, Robert H. Coleman, Dallas, TX.
1931 *Service Songs*, Robert H. Coleman, Dallas, TX.
1932 *Praise and Service*, H. Augustine Smith, New York, NY.

1933 *Songs of Faith*, [George W. Card], Nashville, TN.
1933 *The American Hymnal*, Robert H. Coleman, Dallas, TX.
1934 *Pilot Hymns*, Robert H. Coleman, Dallas, TX.
1935 *Hymns for Creative Living*, (?), Philadelphia, PA.
1936 *Leading Hymns*, Robert H. Coleman, Dallas, TX.
1937 *Songs of Victory*, B.B. McKinney, Nashville, TN.
1938 *Precious Hymns*, Robert H. Coleman, Dallas, TX.
1939 *World Revival Hymns*, Robert H. Coleman, Dallas, TX.
1940 *The Broadman Hymnal*, B.B. McKinney, Nashville, TN.
1941 *Christian Worship*, Joint Committee, Philadelphia, PA.
1947 *Voice of Praise*, B.B. McKinney, Nashville, TN.
1950 *Gospel Hymnal*, (?), Chicago, IL.
1956 *Baptist Hymnal*, W. Hines Sims, Nashville, TN.
1956 *North American Hymnal*, Paul Wengel, Forest Park, IL.
1958 *Free Will Baptist Hymnal*, R.N. Hinnant, J.C. Griffin, J.O. Fort, and I.J. Backwelder, Ayden, NC.
1960 *American Baptist Hymnal*, (?), Texarkana, AK-TX.
1961 *Primitive Baptist Hymnal*, Len Dalton and Helen D. Beauchamp, Azle, TX.
1964 *Free Will Baptist Hymnbook*, B.A. Melvin, D. Clark, I.L. Stanley, R.E. Picirilli, and H. Melvin, Nashville, TN.
1964 *Christian Praise*, [William J. Reynolds], Nashville, TN.
1965 *Hymnbook for Christian Living*, Charles Heaton, St. Louis, MO.
1965 *Hymns and Songs of the Spirit*, (?), St. Louis, MO.
1968 *Crusade Hymns*, W. Hines Sims and Bill H. Ichter, Nashville, TN.
1970 *Hymnbook for Christian Worship*, Charles H. Heaton and Edward H. Pruden, Valley Forge, PA.
1975 *Baptist Hymnal*, William J. Reynolds, Nashville, TN.
1977 *The New National Baptist Hymnal*, Ruth Lomax Davis, Nashville, TN.
1977 *The New Broadman Hymnal*, William J. Reynolds, Nashville, TN.
1987 *In Spirit and In Truth*, Steve Butler, Texarkana, AK-TX.
1991 *The Baptist Hymnal*, Wesley L. Forbis, Nashville, TN.

To Sing or Not to Sing:
Seventeenth Century English Baptists
and Congregational Song

Donald C. Brown

(This was an address, delivered by the writer, for a hymnology seminar during PraiSing II, March 1991.)

ALTHOUGH there are varying opinions, most church historians agree Baptists can be traced to English Separatists. Others say there are groups with Baptist beliefs (although not bearing the name) in every era of history "back to the river Jordan." Some scholars believe there is a link with Continental Anabaptists.

During the seventeenth century, there were two principal Baptist groups. One was called General Baptists after their belief that the result of Christ's sacrifice was a General atonement—salvation was available to all. The other group, the Particular Baptists, accepted the Calvinist view of a limited atonement—Christ died for the elect, those predestined to be saved.

General Baptist Views

The oldest work I examined was a 1608 publication by John Smyth, one of the early General Baptist leaders. Smyth, raised an Anglican, was a graduate of Cambridge and, for a time, was a lecturer at Lincoln Cathedral. He was dismissed from that position in 1602 because of "personal preaching." He became a Separatist and around 1607 took his flock to Holland. There he came in contact with Mennonites (Anabaptists).

Smyth's 1608 pamphlet gives some insight into General Baptist views on worship. It is entitled:

> *The Differences of the Churches of the Seperation:*
> *Contayning*
> *A Description of the Leitourgie and*
> *Ministeries of the Visible Church*
> *By John Smyth, 1608*

Three of the six items listed in "The principall contents..." are, I believe, of particular interest to us:

1. "Wee hould that the worship of the new testament

properly so called is spirituall proceeding originally from the hart: & that reading out of a booke (though a lawful eclesiastical action) is no part of spirituall worship, but rather the invention of the man of synn it bee substituted for a part of spirituall worship."

2. "Wee hould that seeing prophesying is a parte of spirituall worship: therefore in time of prophesying it is unlawfull to have the booke as a helpe before the eye."

3. "Wee hould that seeing singing a psalme is a parte of spirituall worship: therefore it is unlawful to have the booke before the eye in time of singinge a psalme."

It is apparent General Baptists were suspicious of the formality and organized liturgies of the Established Church that persecuted them. The phrase, "it is unlawful to have the booke before the eye" reflected their distrust of precomposed songs and prayers. In their view, that would thwart the inspiration of the Holy Spirit. This was the position of the General Baptists throughout the century. The only type of singing permitted was a spontaneously composed solo song.

The views of Smyth were largely adopted by Thomas Grantham (1634-1692), who became one of the most influential leaders of the General Baptists. Grantham, a native of Lincolnshire, published the following book in 1678:

Christianismus Primitivus
or, the
Ancient Christian Religion,
in its
Nature, Certainty, Excellency, and Beauty...
Particularly Considered, Asserted, and Vindicated
from
The Many Abuses Which Have Invaded that
Sacred Profession,
By
Humane Innovations, or Pretended Revelation.

Grantham makes several important assertions and, in the tradition of the times, takes many pages to do so.

He acknowledges the Scriptures suggest we sing, but "the formalities now used ...differ from that which God hath ordained." He believed there were only two ways to approach worship: "either by meer Art, as those do, who only speak what another puts into their mouths, or by the gift of God's Grace and Spirit."

He does not favor precomposed material. He also opposes congregational singing. He believes singing is to be "Edifying, Like as Doctrine is so to be performed ...the Church is to attend (to listen) on him... that they may be taught and admonished by him." At another point he writes, "Now if all speak together, where are the persons that are taught and admonished?" Also, "It is certainly both lawful and very profitable, for one only person to sing the Praises of God at one in Christian Assemblies."

Furthermore, he writes "But that these Psalms are to be sung promiscuously of the whole Congregation, is no way credible." Grantham considered promiscuous singing to be the singing together of believers and unbelievers and, perhaps, the singing together of men and women.

Those who wished to introduce the singing of original hymns found no favor with Grantham.

"Let us consider the practice of those that think themselves more happy, in that they have found out a way to compose Hymns themselves, and set them out, that others may sing the same things with them. Alas, what a groundless practice we have here? The Holy Scripture is a stranger to it... Nor is there any reason that any man's Verses should be introduced in the Church as a part of the Service of God, or that all should be tyed to one Man's Words, Measures, and Tones....

"Surely, this new Device of Singing what is put into mens Mouths by a Reader, makes a fair way for Forms of Prayer to be introduced together with it."

Grantham also stated his opposition to the singing of Psalms "in a rhythmical way," thereby showing his opposition to metrical psalm translations.

Throughout the seventeenth century, most General Baptists accepted the views of Smyth and Grantham. They opposed any type of congregational singing and any precomposed texts. In summary, they permitted only a spontaneously composed solo song. In 1689, the General Baptist Assembly discouraged the admission of congregational Psalmody on the ground it was not safe to admit such carnal formalities.

Particular Baptist Views

Particular (Calvinist) Baptists developed somewhat later than General Baptists. They came from the English Separatist tradition and, although Calvinist in doctrine, not all of them shared Calvin's belief that metrical psalms in the vernacular were suitable to be sung in worship. There was no unanimity of opinion. Some leaned toward the General Baptist position and opposed "conjoined" singing. Some accepted metrical psalms sung by the congregation. Others even favored "hymns of human composure" in addition to the psalms and canticles found in the Bible.

The records of the Broadmead Church in Bristol reveal that by 1671, congregational singing (at least in the form of psalm singing) was regularly practiced, even under the threat of persecution. Informants would tell the sheriff when the little congregation was meeting. Their ministers were often arrested. After the loss of several speakers, they resorted to a rather clever scheme. The meeting place had a lower floor with two lofts, one over the other. The minister was placed in the lower loft so that he could speak and be heard by those above and below. If an informer came, he could hear the speaker but not see him. The stairway to the loft was kept fastened.

The church records (a copy of which is in the library at Regent's Park) describe a poignant incident that occurred on March 14, 1674(5). Informers had brought a constable. The congregation knew he was coming, and, as the records state:

> "We were singing when they came in. Hellier (the informant) commands us all in the king's name ...to depart: which the people not obeying comes to brother Terrill... and commands him... to depart, saying he was a ringleader. But brother Terrill sitting still, and singing with the rest, Hellier lays violent hands on him ...but not beeing able to stir him from the place, he commands the constable to take him, and bring him away ...So they stood for a while, and the people kept singing. (others came but could not move him) ...Then the serjeant... took brother Terrill's hat off the table and put it on his head. But brother Terrill plucked it off again, Because they were still singing."

This went on for sometime until they finally wrote down some names and left.

In 1676, a joint meeting was proposed with another Baptist congregation in Bristol. Some of its members were ready to sing psalms with "others besides the church." A minority "scrupled (objected) to sing in metere as (the Psalms) were translated" and asked permission to keep their hats on or leave while this was happening.

John Bunyan, the author of *Pilgrim's Progress* and, in the opinion of some, a Baptist, argued for congregational singing in his *Solomon's Temple Spiritualized* of 1688. However, he declared only church members should be allowed to sing. Bunyan wrote, "I pray God it be alone by all those that now a days get into churches, in spirit and with understanding."

Particular Baptist Contentiousness

Several Particular Baptists wrote to express their views on congregational singing. Most who favored the practice advocated the use of metrical Psalms. A few supported the addition of "hymns of human composure." By the 1690s, the rhetoric was increasingly bitter and the pamphlet debate escalated. Murdina MacDonald, a Regent's graduate whose excellent doctoral thesis "London Calvinistic Baptists 1689-1727: Tensions Within a Dissenting Community Under Toleration, 1982" examines London Calvinistic Baptists and reports that in the 1690s "the issue of congregational hymn singing polarized the London associational community and sabotaged the attempt to establish a national body, the General Assembly."

Many entered the fray, but the leading protagonists in this drama were Isaac Marlow and Benjamin Keach. Marlow was a Particular Baptist layman, a wealthy jeweler. His 1690 publication, *A Brief Discourse Concerning Singing*, vehemently opposed congregational song. Marlow claimed singing was "an inward spiritual Exercise of the Soul or Mind of Man." It was not *vocal singing*. He believed that "the vocal Singing together, either of David's Psalms, or any humane precomposed Forms, is a corrupting of the pure Worship of Jesus Christ."

Other arguments against singing included:

1. It perverted what was intended as an extraordinary spiritual gift (only the Apostles had the gift) into a standing ordinance.

2. Singing a precomposed hymn confined the operation of the Holy Spirit.

3. Congregational singing corrupted the original practice that was intended to be performed by a single voice.

4. Permitting women to sing was contrary to the New Testament injunction forbidding women to speak in the church.

Benjamin Keach (1640-1704) was originally a General Baptist, but shortly after he arrived in London in 1668 he transferred to the Particular Baptist branch. After his ordination he became pastor of the Horsley-Down church in Southwark. Keach was a prolific writer. As had Bunyan, he had been put in prison for his dissenting beliefs. Keach's *The Child's Instructor or a New and Easy Primer* was declared a "venomous" book and burned before his eyes. In fact, the whole edition was destroyed. After he rewrote it, some copies made their way to New England and became the basis of the famous *New England Primer*.

Keach preceded Bunyan in the writing of allegories, and although not so talented a writer, he rivaled him in popularity and in sales. Hugh Martin wrote: "Keach's *War with the Devil, or the Young Man's Conflict with the Powers of Darkness* of 1673, sold 22 editions in a 100 years, and his later volume, *The Travel of True Godliness,* went on selling for a century and a half." Charles Haddon Spurgeon owned a copy of the latter publication. William Jewell College acquired it when the college purchased Spurgeon's personal collection in 1905 (it was on campus by March of 1906).

Most of Keach's current reputation is associated with his role in the history of English hymnody. Although some claims for him may be unjustified, I believe Hugh Martin is correct when he reports Keach was "the first to introduce the regular singing of hymns into the normal worship of an English congregation." (*Benjamin Keach,* London: Independent Press, 1691, pp. 9-10.)

This was quite an accomplishment and was not done overnight. Writing in 1691 in the Appendix to his *The Breach Repaired in God's Worship,* Keach reported "the Church hath been in this practice near twenty years after Breaking of Bread, and near 14 Years on Thanksgiving-days in a mixt Congregation. And what was done of late in bringing it in after Sermon on Lord's Days, was done by a regular Act of the Church." Keach reported some of the brethren were dissatisfied with the practice, but he felt all would eventually be well if men such as Marlow would not "blow up Coals of Contention amongst us."

In spite of placing the hymn at the end of the service, so that those who objected might leave, a church split did occur. This happened on 17 March 1691, 300 years ago.

Keach's principal treatise in favor of singing was written in 1691 and entitled:

> *The Breach Repaired in God's Worship or*
> *Singing of Psalms, Hymns, and Spiritual Songs, proved to be*
> *an Holy Ordinance of Jesus Christ.*

As the title suggests, the author believed the loss of congregational singing constituted a "Breach" in God's worship. Furthermore, he warned that Baptist opposition to singing was hurting the growth of the Baptized churches. Keach did not ramble so much as Marlow, but he could never be accused of brevity. I will summarize the principal objections to singing and how he sought to refute them.

1. *Singing will lead to instrumental music.* "What a foolish thing to object against this Ordinance because the performance of it under the Law involved instruments."

2. *We do not know how we should sing.* The Scriptures were clear—"They sang an Hymn." There is no other rule, mode, or manner of singing differing from that practiced by Moses and Israel: vocal singing.

3. *But this singing was an extraordinary gift; none has those gifts now; therefore, none must sing in these days.* The apostles had extraordinary gifts of preaching, praying, prophesizing, and interpreting. If we were to follow this absurd conclusion, these activities would all cease.

4. *Only one voice should sing alone.* Keach wrote "It ought to be with United Voices, or to sing together harmoniously." ..."Our Lord Jesus and his Disciples sung a Hymn together." "Should one alone sing in the midst of the Congregation, like a Ballad-Singer?"

5. *We should sing nothing but David's Psalms.* "And as we are not tied up by the Lord in Preaching, to do no more than barely read the Scripture, or quote one Scripture after another, (which would be rather Reading than Preaching) ...so when that which we sing is taken out of God's Word, or is Scripture, absolutely congruous, truly and exactly agreeing thereunto, it may be as truly be called the Word of Christ as our Sermons are, and may be called."

6. *But what ground is there to sing in the church before or after the sermon?* As much, surely, as there is to pray before or after sermon.

7. *What ground is there for the Church to join in singing with unbelievers?* Marlow (*The Controversie of Singing Brought to an End,* London: 1696) argued against singing by a promiscuous assembly of Professors (believers) and profane Men & Women with united Voices together.

Keach stated "the practice of God's Israel of Old revealed the people sang together in a 'mixt multitude.' Also, what ground hath the Church to pray with Unbelievers? Unbelievers joining with them is one thing, and their joining with Unbelievers is another. Besides, what right has the Church to remove Unbelievers from their Assemblies if they know them from others? There may be unbelievers in the Church, and there may be Believers out of the Church.

"Must not the Children have their Bread, because Strangers will get some of it? Have not Unbelievers cause to Praise God? And would you not have any to do this but the Saints? Why allow non-believers to hear Sermon & Prayer but object to their singing hymns?"

8. *Women are forbidden to sing in the church because they are forbidden to speak in the church.*

Keach responded that if this is true, then:

1. "She must not ask a Friend how he or she doth in the Congregation."
2. "She must not be allowed to evidence in case of Church discipline."
3. "If she comes in late, she must not ask what the Text is."
4. "Nor must she say Amen."
5. "Worst of all, she must not give an account of her Conversion, or declare how the Lord was pleased to work upon her Heart."

This is a reasonably advanced view for the time, but Keach, in my opinion, takes a step backward when he cites John Cotton of Boston. Cotton says that women should not be teachers because "the woman is more subject to Error than the Man, and therefore might sooner prove a Seducer." However, the eminent American Puritan believes there are two cases in which a woman may speak:

1. "In way of Subjection, when she is to give account of

her Offence."
2. "In way of Singing forth the Praises of God together with the rest of the Congregation."

Keach writes of the value of "publick Conjunction of Singing Scripture Psalms."

1. "They teach and admonish one another."
2. "Singing teaches us the Unity and Harmony that is and should be among Saints."
3. "Nothing represents the Communion of Saints as well as mutual singing when all at once ...speak the same thing the same moment."

Obviously, Keach is convinced of the efficacy of congregational song, yet he realizes how difficult it is to overcome long-standing opposition to it. Perhaps with a sense of frustration he writes, "Is there any Church that is yet arrived to such a perfection of Knowledge, that they need not the discovery of any Truth but what they have received?"

Bitterness of the Struggle

Keach appealed to people to "love one another though they can't yet agree to sing the Praises of God together." In spite of these fine words, Keach could be contentious. At one point he said of Marlow, I would like to think you are a good man, but you are "strangely beclouded."

Marlow was not one to mince words. He claimed singing would lead churches "to return from whence we came, as a Dog to his Vomit, and as a Sow that was washed, to her wallowing in the Mire." To this Keach replied, "you show too much Gall & Wormwood in your Spirit."

Original Hymns

Keach believed "those who God hath gifted ought to compose hymns." Some would question whether Keach was "gifted," but that didn't stop him from publishing, in 1691, a volume entitled *Spiritual Melody, Containing Near Three Hundred Sacred Hymns*. In a note to the reader, Keach indicates not all of the selections are proper to be sung. When you hear some, you may understand why. Spurgeon is supposed to have said, "the less said about Keach's poetry, the better."

Hymn 12 gave me a start. It is based on Isaiah 42:14 and is entitled, "God as a Travelling Woman." My first thought was that Keach certainly had an advanced view of God. A check with the Oxford Dictionary of the English Language, however, revealed "travelling" once meant "travail." He was speaking of a woman in labor.

1. Like as a woman travailing
      Does cry out in her pain,
   So thou dost say Lord thou wilt do,
      To pour forth wrath amain.
3. A woman when her travel comes
      From crying can't refrain,
   So thou wilt cry from Sions sake
      Like her in grievous pain.
4. A woman in her travel strives
      Her Child for to bring forth.
   So thy deliverance for thy Church
      Wilt work throughout the Earth.

Keach was not a great poet, but his efforts in support of congregational song paved the way for hymnists of greater skill. His vigorous efforts in support of hymn singing truly enabled English Baptists to "repair the breach in God's worship." We owe him much.

The previous hymn, as well as the following hymns, are from the book, *Spiritual Melody, Containing Near Three Hundred Sacred Hymns.* (London: Printed for John Harcock, in Castle-Alley, near the Royal-Exchange in Cornhill, 1691).

Hymn 11—Hosea 5:12
"I WILL BE A MOTH TO EPHRAIM"
Moths secretly do seize and eat,
And spoil fair Garments quite;
So many times thy Judgements are
Hid from most peoples sight.

Hymn 70—1 John 2:20
"BUT YE HAVE AN UNCTION FROM THE HOLY ONE"
Our wounds do stink, and are corrupt,
Hard swellings we do see;
We want a little Oyntment, Lord,
Let us more humble be.

Hymn 104—Hebrew 6:19
"WHICH HOPE WE HAVE"
This World's a Sea, our Soul's a Ship
With raging Tempest Tost;
And if she should her Anchor flip,
She doubtless will be lost.

Repentance like a Bucket is

To pump the water out;
For leaky is our Ship, alas,
Which makes us look about.

Hymn 146—Third Part
"Hell a Bottom Pit"
Here meets them now that Worm that gnaws,
And plucks their Bowels out,
The pit too on them shuts his Jaws,
This dreadful is no doubt.

"A New Song Sing Unto the Lord"
Text: Benjamin Keach, from *A Golden Mine Opened*, 1694
Tune: Forest Green/English Folk Melody
arr. Ralph Vaughan Williams
(Note: This hymn was "spliced together" from texts that appeared at the end of one his sermons. It was first sung in June, 1977, when the Southern Baptist Convention Music Conference met on the campus of William Jewel College.)

A New song sing unto the Lord
For mighty Wonders done,
His right Hand, and his glorious Arm,
Hath our Savlation won.
Let all poor Sinners taste and try (see)
That thou, O Lord, art good;
Nay let them feed, Lord Christ, on thee,
And wash them in thy Blood:

That they with Saints with one accord,
May joy with Holy Mirth,
Before the Great and Glorious Lord,
And shew his Praises forth.
Such souls shall never fall away,
But ever happy be:
Such shall be fed with Christ's own Lambs,
And sing eternally.

Break forth and sing now, all ye Saints,
Lift up God's name on high,
In sacred songs to celebrate
His praise continually:
Exalt the living God above,
Your standing is most sure:
Thy Mercy, Lord, and tender Love,
Will keep our Souls secure.

The Resources:
American Baptist Hymnals

PAUL A. RICHARDSON

(This was an address, delivered by the writer, for a hymnology seminar during PraiSing II, March 1991.)

AS we approach the auspicious occasion of the birth of a new hymnal for Southern Baptists, I have been asked to survey Baptist hymnals produced in America as the resources for what we now publish and sing. What I propose is a sort of genealogy of the new book—a consideration of its forebears. The question might be framed in the words of a carol: "What child is this?"

The answer is not so simple as the biblical begats—Baptists have never been so systematic, no more in their hymnody than in their theology. Further, our denominational hymnic heritage is far more complex and far less predictable than the most intricate genetic study. I doubt that your ancestors or mine lived with the purpose of producing the finest gene pool that would someday give birth to you or me. It is clear that those who went before us in compiling hymnals did not have as their principal goal that in 1991 Southern Baptists might produce the perfect hymnal. What we find is a complex web of individuals, traditions, and hymn collections. If one did not know that this trail of ink was Baptist, one might guess it just by looking, for our hymnic history reflects our nature: it is sometimes proud; it is sometimes curious; it is sometimes perplexing; it is always interesting.

Because we cannot simply follow the house and lineage of the Sunday School Board, at least not until a century ago, we need some means of organizing and classifying this material. I offer two provisional approaches. First is that presented by Wiley Hitchcock in his excellent book, *Music in the United States*. He makes a useful division between what he calls "cultivated" and "vernacular" traditions. In the broader world of music, this allows for symphonies and popular songs to be judged on their own merits. In the realm of hymnody, we can see different purposes for the hymnody of Watts and Wesley and the English Baptists such as Beddome and Steele on one hand, and the songs of the Sunday Schools and revivals on the other. A word of warning: this distinction will not be so simple as we look more closely.

The second means of sorting out this material is by a Pauline taxonomy, that is, "psalms, hymns, and spiritual songs." You will recognize that Paul was an apostle and not a hymnologist. Biblical scholars are not agreed on just what he intended by this enumeration. But the ways in which Baptists have used these terms in the titles of their hymn books reveal something about the different approaches to compiling the collections that are part of our heritage.

The Eighteenth Century

We do not know what the first Baptists in America sang. We presume they brought with them the same collections and the same controversies that had characterized them in England.

The first hymn book to be published in America by Baptists was issued in Boston in 1762. It was based on a collection of hymns by London Baptist pastor Benjamin Wallin. To his texts were added some by Isaac Watts and others by Joseph Stennett. Whether this was a new book or merely a reprint of an English volume is not clear.

Four years later, in 1766, an unknown compiler in Newport, Rhode Island, assembled *Hymns and Spiritual Songs*. The organization of this hymnal may provide some perspective on how these early Baptists selected and used hymns. The book is divided into three sections. The first contains 16 "Hymns for Baptism." That Baptists would sing their distinctive views on this subject is not surprising. The middle section has 75 "Hymns for the Lord's Supper." Again, one is not surprised to find that Baptists would want to present a perspective suited to denominational beliefs, but the sheer number suggests that they placed greater emphasis on this ordinance and practiced it more frequently than do most Baptist churches today. The last part carries the heading, "Hymns and Spiritual Songs," clustering without distinction a variety of texts totaling 47. I would propose that this book may have been a Baptist supplement to a more "standard" collection, perhaps some anthology of Watts. Such an arrangement would have drawn its "psalms" and most of its "hymns" from the larger collection, while adding in this unique supplement texts relating to the ordinances and a small number of other favorite "hymns and spiritual songs."

In the years before 1800, nearly thirty collections were produced in America by Baptists. Some are anonymous. Some are the products of such interesting figures as Elhanan Winchester, a Baptist Calvinist Universalist! He may, in one person, have embodied the range of diversity that has always characterized Baptist theology and hymnody.

As exemplars of this early development, let me cite two collections from 1790. The first was *A Selection of Psalms and Hymns Done Under the Appointment of the Philadelphian Association*. This book, as the title relates, was commissioned by the Philadelphia Association, at that time the largest and most influential such body of Baptists in this country. It was a book intended primarily for worship, but it included a section of texts meant for private use. All of its psalms were Watts' versions. It also included some of his hymns, as well as those by Cennick, Hart, Steele, and Robinson, among others. It shows clear evidence of the influence of Rippon's *Selection*. Hitchcock might label this a "cultivated" collection, containing, as Paul would list them, mostly "psalms and hymns," with a few "spiritual songs."

A contrasting book was the *Collection of Sacred Ballads*, compiled in Virginia by Richard and Andrew Broaddus. It is a much smaller volume, but with 107 texts. It was designed for social singing, that is, fellowship and exhortation, though its preface notes that it does contain "a few select hymns," so that it could be used for worship. In Hitchcock's terms, this is a "vernacular" book. In Paul's language, it is mostly "spiritual songs," with a few "hymns." "Psalms" would seem to be absent. Yet in a small book that is decidedly "vernacular" in outlook are these texts: "Am I a Soldier of the Cross," "Come, Thou Fount of Every Blessing," "How Tedious and Tasteless the Hours," and "Love Divine, All Loves Excelling"—all "cultivated" hymns.

These two books are illustrative not just because they show different types of literature and their intermixing. Rather, they show different purposes. The "Philadelphia Collection" was intended primarily for worship. The Broadduses' book was meant mainly for less formal situations. The difference had little to do with music—both of them are text-only collections. The issue was not good versus bad or right versus wrong, but the appropriateness of the selected materials to a particular exercise of the Christian life. If we use this perspective for examining our heritage, we will understand both it and our present better. The work of the church is both cultivated and vernacular. Its life requires psalms and hymns and spiritual songs.

One other of these early collections merits mention here: Eleazar Clay's *Hymns and Spiritual Songs*, published in Richmond, in 1793. The compiler and collection are both interesting in a number of ways. For our purposes today I would note that this was the first hymn book assembled by a Baptist in America to include "Amazing Grace," currently Southern Baptists' favorite hymn, according to research conducted for the 1991 book.

The Nineteenth Century

At the beginning of the nineteenth century, the core of Baptist hymnody for worship seems to have been the psalms and hymns of Watts. Baptists performed significant service by preparing editions of, and supplements to, his work. Among American Baptists who contributed in this way were William Staughton, James Winchell, Charles G. Sommers, and John L. Dagg.

The rule of the day, beyond the core provided by Watts, was the editing and publication of local collections. There can hardly be said to have been a hymn book with common use beyond a fairly limited area. Certainly compilers might have wished that their work would sell widely and become something of a standard collection for Baptists—indeed, this was often stated in the prefaces—but there were no books of national or even regional dominance before the 1840s.

There were many "local" collections of importance. Among the leading ones in the South were Jesse Mercer's *Cluster* (Augusta, 1813), Silas Noel's *A Hymn Book* (Frankfort, 1814), Starke Dupuy's *Hymns and Spiritual Songs* ([place of 1st ed. unknown], 1818), William Dossey's *The Choice* (Philadelphia, 1820), John Purify's *A Selection of Hymns and Spiritual Songs* (Raleigh, 1823), Andrew Broaddus' *The Dover Selection of Spiritual Songs* (Richmond, 1828), and Staunton Burdett's *The Baptist Harmony* (Philadelphia, 1834).

Our survey is entering the time when Baptists began to issue influential shape note tune books. These may have done more than the text-only collections to begin to standardize the repertory of Baptists in the rural South. You will recognize the Baptist compilers and their books: William Walker, *The Southern Harmony* (New Haven, 1835); B. F. White and E. J. King, *The Sacred Harp* (Philadelphia, 1845); John G. McCurry, *The Social Harp* (Philadelphia, 1855).

In the 1840s there came renewed and more effective attempts at the development of collections for wide use by Baptists. One of these was William C. Buck's *Baptist Hymn Book* (Louisville, 1842). It showed sensitivity to the tastes of the South and West, while being built around the now traditional core of standard ("cultivated") hymnody. Its acceptance, however, was limited principally to churches in the South and West.

In 1843, the American Baptist Publication and Sunday School Society gave its imprimatur to *The Psalmist*. This book, published in Boston, was edited by Samuel F. Smith, the author of "My Country, 'Tis of Thee" and numerous other hymns now faded from use, and Baron Stow, like Smith, a Massachusetts minister. It was widely accepted, particularly in the North, and held its place in the churches and in the market until after the Civil War. *The Psalmist* set a new standard for "cultivated" books by Baptists. Its limited success in the South can be attributed to at least three factors. First, it omitted several texts that were regional favorites—texts that were in the Southern "vernacular," but not in that of the North. Second, it was edited in ways that left it open to challenge. Stanzas were omitted and words changed in a manner that offended purists—or at least gave opponents some literary basis for objection. The denominational press of the period is replete with editorials and letters to the editor about such issues (Measels, no pag.). Third, it was a Yankee book. The omissions noted earlier exacerbated this perspective in an era in which regional animosity was growing rapidly.

In an attempt at reconciliation (and protection of market share), a subsequent edition (1847) added a supplement, edited by Richard Fuller and J. B. Jeter, both Southern pastors, that had Southern favorites. The preface to the supplement noted that these selections were primarily for social worship. Among the additions were: "Amazing Grace," "How Firm a Foundation," "How Sweet the Name of Jesus Sounds," and "The God of Abram Praise."

Lest we be tempted to think that these Yankees were just too high church, we take note of *The Social Psalmist*, issued by the same editors in 1848. This was, as stated in its subtitle, "A New Selection of Hymns for Conference Meetings and Family Worship." The distinction, again, was more one of function than of theology, poetry, or music.

It was in this period that Southern Baptists emerged as a denomination and as a force in the production of hymnals. (Please refer to the list of Southern Baptist hymnals at the conclusion of this address.) *The Baptist Psalmody* was edited by Basil Manly, Sr., and Basil Manly, Jr., and was published in Charleston in 1850 by the Southern Baptist Publication Society. The SBPS was not an agency with the close ties to the convention of the Foreign or Domestic Mission Boards, but, rather, an organization parallel to the main body, much in the manner of Southern Seminary at its beginning.

This was a highly significant book. It existed on the same plane as *The Psalmist* and exceeded it in editorial standards. This first Southern Baptist hymnal was, as its subtitle states, "A Selection of Hymns for the Worship of God," and was, clearly, a "cultivated" book. It contained principally "psalms" and "hymns," but also had many of what we might identify as "spiritual songs," those less-formal hymns that had been omitted from *The Psalmist*. It was a large book. With apologies to the copywriter of the promotional material for *The Baptist Hymnal* (1991), *The Baptist Psalmody* remains "the largest, most comprehensive hymnal ever produced by Southern Baptists." Its acceptance was by no means universal, however, even among Southern churches. But it is with this book that we can speak, for the first time, of some measure of Southern Baptist identity in a hymnal. Though the book was not commissioned by the Convention, it received its endorsement in 1851.

As the first Southern Baptist hymnal, *The Baptist Psalmody* was, obviously, the first in this new family to include many texts. Among those that we can trace "all the way back" are: "Praise the Lord! Ye Heavens, Adore Him," "Blest Be the Tie," "When I Survey the Wondrous Cross," "Just As I Am," "Go to Dark Gethsemane," and "On Jordan's Stormy Banks."

It may at first seem easy to dismiss this "cultivated" book as the product of what has come to be known as the Charleston tradition—as though that made it somehow suspect. Note, please, that the same publishing body soon released *The Sacred Lute* (1855). Just as Baptists in the North had produced two books for two types of church assemblies, so had Baptists in the South. The distinction continued to be neither theological nor educational, but functional, with regional differences based on familiarity and sociology having lesser influence. Those "cultivated" varieties, the "psalms" and "hymns," were considered, both in the South and the North, to be better suited to the worship of God, while the "vernacular" "spiritual songs" were provided for prayer meetings, revivals, and social singing.

The Psalmist and *The Social Psalmist* established a firm foothold in the North. *The Baptist Psalmody* and *The Sacred Lute* provided parallels in the South. Though local collections continued to be produced throughout the country, the dominance of these leading books and the disruption of the Civil War meant that it was more than twenty years before other "major" Baptist collections were issued.

In 1871 three new hymnals were produced in an effort to establish a new common worship resource for Baptists. All were produced in the North. We must recall that the economic resources of the South had been decimated, that one of the casualties had been the publication arm of the SBC, and that the American Baptist Publication Society had continued to provide literature for Baptists North and South. The three new contenders were *The Service of Song for Baptist Churches* (Boston and New York), *The Baptist Hymn and Tune Book* (Philadelphia), and *The Baptist Praise Book* (New York). The three seem to have divided the market, though the Philadelphia book was apparently the most successful. None of these were widely accepted in the South.

Two other developments of this period demand notice. The more important was the burgeoning popularity of Sunday School and gospel songs. Time will not permit here a tracing of the streams influencing their development. Among the leading producers were Baptists William Bradbury, Robert Lowry, Philip P. Bliss, William Howard Doane, and George C. Stebbins. Though all were Baptists, not one was from the South. Southern Baptists eventually became leading consumers of this stream of "vernacular" "spiritual song," but they were not, in its formative period, producers. Once more, we must be careful about generalizing from what we know of these persons and their work. Robert Lowry, for example—he of "Shall We Gather at the River" and "Low in the Grave He Lay"—was a professor of literature who also composed and published chants for use at baptismal services.

One of the unique streams, theologically, that emerged in Southern Baptist life during this time was Landmarkism. Two of its leaders, J. M. Pendleton and J. R. Graves, edited hymnals. The remarkable thing about these hymnals is that they are unremarkable. They contain "cultivated" and "vernacular" traditions in roughly the same proportions as the collections of the more orthodox. The same authors predominated, with little evidence of new hymns from the movement. In neither *The Southern Psalmist* (Nashville, 1859) nor *The New Baptist Psalmist* (Memphis, 1873) are there hymns about the true church or other of their landmarks. In fact, among the 16 communion hymns in *The Southern Psalmist*, one finds not a single text about closed communion, but rather these lines:

> All who bear the Savior's name,
> Here their common faith proclaim;
> Though diverse in tongue or rite,
> Here, one body we unite;
> Breaking thus one mystic bread,
> Members of one common head.
> *(hymn 511, st. 2, by Josiah Conder)*

The only text in the section on the church that might be read to endorse some sort of succession is a widely-published hymn by Doddridge.

In 1883, the American Baptist Publication Society released *The Baptist Hymnal.* Its editors were E. H. Johnson and William Howard Doane. Their employment was a shrewd move by the publishers, for these two men were, respectively, the leading figures in "cultivated" and "vernacular" hymnody among Baptists. Their cooperation and the balance sought within the book remain worthy models for a diverse people. That this book was intended for sale in the South as well as the North is indicated by the presence of five distinguished Southerners on the consulting committee. Among these were Basil Manly, Jr., and E. T. Winkler, the editors of the two collections that the Southern Baptist Publication Society had produced.

Other hymnals continued to be issued. Some weighed more heavily on the "vernacular" side. Others, such as Johnson's *Sursum Corda* (Philadelphia, 1898) incorporated in large numbers the works of the Oxford movement in an attempt to make Baptist hymnody more "cultivated."

The Twentieth Century

You will recall that one of the anniversaries celebrated in 1991 was the hundredth birthday of the present Sunday School Board. In its fourteenth year, the fourth of the present century, it issued its first hymnal, *The Baptist Hymn and Praise Book* (Nashville). Its editor, Lansing Burrows, began his preface by stating that his goal was to prepare "a book of praise to Almighty God ...not to gather in convenient form a number of pleasing songs." That smacks of "cultivation." On the other hand, he wrote that he sought to restore texts of long and valued use in combination with tunes known in the churches served by the Board. He noted that the collections used heretofore had been produced in areas of the country where these pairings were not known. That is decidedly a "vernacular" approach. Further, he continued, the book had drawn from more recent styles of thought and expression, "with careful heed to the truthful interpretation of our doctrinal belief."

As the first major hymnal issued by a Southern Baptist Convention agency in a half century, *The Baptist Hymn and Praise Book* marked the official entry into our repertory of many hymns, both "cultivated" and "vernacular." Among these were: "A Mighty Fortress Is Our God," "Holy, Holy, Holy, Lord God Almighty" "Jesus, the Very Thought of Thee," and "My God, How Wonderful Thou Art" (not seen again until 1991); but also "Come, Every Soul By Sin Oppressed," "Softly and Tenderly Jesus Is Calling," "Jesus Saves," and "There's Sunshine in My Soul Today." Many more well-known items of varied styles made their Southern Baptist debuts in this collection.

Where had Southern Baptist churches gotten their hymnals between *The Baptist Psalmody* and *The Baptist Hymn and Praise Book*? Some churches, mostly eastern or urban, purchased Baptist hymnals published in the North. Others used hymnals produced by nondenominational publishers. But most Southern Baptist churches, I suspect, turned to commercial song books, limited in size, scope, and expense. These decidedly "vernacular" collections were not designed primarily for worship, but for revivals, Sunday Schools, and social and family devotions. Their heavy emphasis on this single style of "spiritual songs," to the neglect largely of "hymns" and entirely of "psalms," helped to distort the balanced approach to congregational song that so many of the earlier compilers had strived to attain.

The next Southern Baptist hymnal was published not by the Sunday School Board, but by the Home Mission Board. *Songs of Redemption* (Atlanta, 1920) was edited by Plunkett Martin and James Jelks and was the work of "a committee of the evangelistic singers of the department of evangelism of the Home Mission Board." We would expect such a book to have a strong "vernacular" flavor, and it did. In this hymnal, Southern Baptists were introduced to "Jesus Is All the World to Me," "Higher Ground," "'Tis So Sweet to Trust in Jesus," and "In the Garden." But this was also the first printing for us of "Faith of Our Fathers" and "Break Thou the Bread of Life."

The Sunday School Board's next book, *Kingdom Songs*, was edited by I. E. Reynolds and Robert H. Coleman. Here, again, we would expect a "vernacular" book. But, while many gospel songs, such as "Faith Is the Victory" and "When Upon Life's Billows You Are Tempest Tossed," were introduced here, so were the standard hymns "O Master, Let Me Walk with Thee" and "O Zion, Haste."

Robert H. Coleman deserves his own notice here. A Dallas Baptist layman, Coleman published more than thirty books, which had no official Baptist ties until Broadman purchased his copyrights in 1945. Nevertheless, his collections were widely used by Baptist churches, especially in the South and Southwest. Many Southern Baptist churches that had existed for decades on a diet of small gospel song books became acclimated to the idea of a larger book through *The Modern Hymnal* (1926) or *The American Hymnal* (1933).

If *The Modern Hymnal* was the "vernacular" collection of 1926, its "cultivated" counterpart was *New Baptist Hymnal*. This was a joint publication of the Northern and Southern Baptist publishing houses and was the heir to the 1883 *Baptist Hymnal*. It listed among its guiding principles: (1) "to include the standard hymns which through the years have proved their worth and are in general use in the ordinary worship of the churches;" and also (2) "to select from the very best of modern gospel songs those deserving a place in permanent hymnology." This book was both a success and a failure in the South. It was a failure in terms of sales, because it was not bought by a large number of churches across the Convention. It was a success because it did find a place in seminary and college chapels and in some significant urban and progressive congregations, so that its influence was felt in later books, especially in the 1956 *Baptist Hymnal*.

The expectation—if anyone had it—that *New Baptist Hymnal* might become a standard for Southern Baptist churches was unrealistic. There was *no* standard Southern Baptist hymnal at this time and no tradition of a single common book among the churches. Further, there was nothing like the awareness of denominational identity that we have come to accept as the norm. Indeed, the Cooperative Program was in its infancy, and the *Baptist Faith and Message* statement (the first document of its kind) was new. The ties that bound Southern Baptists were much looser, based on common interests and shared beliefs, but with little compulsion for conformity. We should not be surprised that the hymnals in the pews varied so widely.

New Baptist Hymnal introduced Southern Baptists to much "cultivated" hymnody that continues to flourish even in those congregations that sing mostly "vernacular" music. A sampling includes "Stand Up, Stand Up for Jesus," "Lead On, O King Eternal," "Joyful, Joyful, We Adore Thee," "O Come, All Ye Faithful," and "The Church's One Foundation." And where would generations of G.A.'s have been without "We've a Story to Tell to the Nations?"

You may have noticed that I have not recently mentioned the categories of "psalms, hymns, and spiritual songs." By this time, Baptist practice in publication and use had altered the formula. Through much of our history we have struggled to keep a balance from book to book and situation to situation between "cultivated" and "vernacular." But, a hundred years or so ago, the debate became one between hymns and gospel songs.

With the issue framed in those terms, we lost sight of the psalms.

This is a particularly ironic situation for us. We are a people who love and attempt to live by the Bible, according to the best light given to each of us. Why have we quit singing from its hymn book? We may have different understandings about what the "hymn" and "spiritual song" categories mean, either in the first century or today. But "psalms" is pretty plain, isn't it? Why did we cease following that biblical mandate?

I would suggest that the first book to have any claim to be a common collection for Southern Baptists was *The Broadman Hymnal*. Its subtitle cast a wide net: "Great Standard Hymns and Choice Gospel Songs New and Old, for Use in all Religious Services, such as the Worship Hour, Sunday School, Young People's Meetings, Assemblies, and Evangelistic Services." What is even more remarkable, it was used in all those ways. Though it said hymnal in the title, it was a hymnal in the tradition (might I say, the family line) of the Coleman hymnals. It did contain some standard hymns, as had Coleman's books, but it was first and foremost a substantial book of gospel songs. But it even had, as B. B. McKinney would have said, "an-thems." What it also had was the peculiar genius of McKinney—not just his genius for composing gospel songs (and he, better than anyone else, knew the meaning of "vernacular" in Southern Baptist life)—but his genius for promoting a musical identity that matched Southern Baptists' rapidly growing denominational identity. It was clearly a "vernacular" book, lacking such characteristics—seen in many of the earlier Baptist hymnals—as a clear plan of organization. It gave Southern Baptists for the first time "Heavenly Sunlight," "Tell Me the Story of Jesus," and "Near to the Heart of God", but also "The First Noel the Angel Did Say."

The second common hymnal of Southern Baptists, and the first to bring into some balance the "cultivated" and "vernacular" traditions, was *Baptist Hymnal* of 1956. Its "vernacular" family tree can be traced back through *The Broadman Hymnal*, the Coleman books, and the wide variety of gospel song collections that had found currency in our churches. The "cultivated" genealogy drew on the inheritance of *New Baptist Hymnal*, the 1883 *Baptist Hymnal*, and *The Baptist Psalmody*. You will realize by now that neither of these lines is "pure," for overlap and sharing have always existed to one degree or another. It is my perception that the 1956 *Baptist Hymnal* achieved greater success as a common hymnal for Southern Baptists than any other collection. By the end of its twenty-year life span, it was exceptional to find another book when one entered a Southern Baptist church for worship.

The reasons for its success, I would suggest, were at least three. First, it did provide a balance between the "cultivated" and "vernacular" traditions in a way attempted, but not achieved, before. Second, it was made available at a time of unparalleled cohesiveness and cooperation in denominational life. The broad appreciation of denominational publishing, promotion, and service to the churches was at its peak. Third, related to the second, this hymnal was the work not of one person, not even one genius like McKinney, but of a large and representative committee.

Not only did this book claim both of the broad traditions, it added to both. Southern Baptists were introduced in this hymnal to "Praise to the Lord, the Almighty" as well as "Great Is Thy Faithfulness"; to "God of Grace and God of Glory" and "There's a Glad New Song"; to "In Christ There Is No East or West" as well as "Grace Greater than Our Sin."

The 1975 *Baptist Hymnal* followed in this hybrid line. It continued to include gospel songs in greater numbers than did the collections of other major denominations. It added standard hymns long in other traditions, but new to Southern Baptists. In selecting from both old and new sources, it enlarged the range of "cultivated" and "vernacular" traditions. To the long-standing "vernacular" tradition of gospel songs, it added "Turn Your Eyes upon Jesus" and "Victory in Jesus." It recaptured some of Baptists' own "vernacular" tradition in "What Wondrous Love Is This." It borrowed from the wealth of black spirituals. It introduced songs of John Peterson and Ralph Carmichael and the Gaithers. From classic hymnody it gave us for the first time "O Come, O Come, Emmanuel" and "Praise the Lord Who Reigns Above." It drew from the searches of The Hymn Society and from the beginnings of the "hymnic explosion," being one of the first American hymnals to include texts of Fred Pratt Green. It also provided an opportunity for the use of a large number of texts and tunes in many styles by contemporary Baptists.

Yet, if my impressions are correct, this hymnal, though accepted widely, never achieved the status of its predecessor in becoming the common book for Southern Baptists. I attribute this to at least three causes. First, the seventies and eighties were times of unparalleled change, both in church and in society, and of expanding cultural diversity. There were now, even in the formerly insular South, many more approaches to worship, evangelism, and ministry. Second, there was a proliferation of materials from other sources to serve every growing edge of the church and its musical expression. No one competitor threatened the Board's market, but many more options were available for every taste, style, and tradition. Third, these were the times in which denominational identity began to ebb. You will find *Baptist Hymnal* (1975) in churches all across whatever spectrum you choose to propose; but you will also find other collections in numerous churches across that spectrum.

We are led back to the question with which I began: "What child is this?" Where does *The Baptist Hymnal* (1991) get its genes? I perceive that it continues to combine "cultivated" and "vernacular" family traits. There are new hymns of Brian Wren and Thomas Troeger and Jane Parker Huber. There are songs from the new "vernacular" traditions that my colleague Donald Hustad calls "teeny hymns" and "star-kissed" songs. The new hymnal has "hymns" of many types and "spiritual songs" of many more, but, alas, few "psalms."

What kind of life will this child have? Whom will it serve, and what will it pass on to its heirs? That depends on many things, not all of them hymnological. Sociology, politics, and economics will all be influential—so will our ability to grasp the broader vision of varied hymnic function that many of our forebears articulated well. That would enable us to understand the roles of "psalms, hymns, and spiritual songs" from both "cultivated" and "vernacular" traditions. Such a perspective would enhance not only our ability to see beyond hymnological distinctions, real and artificial, but to have ministries that enable diverse individuals and congregations to worship and educate and minister and proclaim. In that way we would own the heritage proclaimed by one of the fine contemporary hymns newly added to our legacy:

> So has the Church, in liturgy and song,
> In faith and love, through centuries of wrong,
> Borne witness to the truth in every tongue...
>
> And may God give us faith to sing always:
> Alleluia! *(Green, 51-52).*

Bibliography

Green, Fred Pratt. "When, in Our Music, God Is Glorified." *The Hymns and Ballads of Fred Pratt Green*. Carol Stream: Hope Publishing Company, 1982.
Hitchcock, H. Wiley. *Music in the United States: A Historical Introduction*. 3rd ed. Englewood Cliffs: Prentice-Hall, 1988.
Measels, Donald Clark. "A Catalog of Source Readings in Southern Baptist Church Music: 1828-1890." Diss. The Southern Baptist Theological Seminary, 1986.

Non-Southern Baptist Convention Hymnals Cited

- 1762 *Evangelical Hymns and Songs....* Boston.
- 1766 *Hymns and Spiritual Songs, Collected from the Works of Several Authors.* Newport.
- 1790 *A Selection of Psalms and Hymns Done under the Appointment of the Philadelphian Association.* Samuel Jones and Burgis Allison. Philadelphia.
- 1790 *Collection of Sacred Ballads.* Richard Broaddus and Andrew Broaddus. [n.p.].
- 1793 *Hymns and Spiritual Songs, Selected from Several Approved Authors.* Eleazar Clay. Richmond.
- 1807 *A Selection of Hymns...* [Rippon, with additions]. William Staughton. Philadelphia.
- 1819 *An Arrangement of the Psalms, Hymns, and Spiritual Songs of The Rev. Isaac Watts, to Which Is Added a Supplement....* James Winchell. Boston.
- 1827 *The Psalms and Hymns of Dr. Watts, Arranged by Dr. Rippon; with Dr. Rippon's Selection... Corrected and Improved.* C. G. Sommers and John L. Dagg. Philadelphia.
- 1813 *The Cluster of Spiritual Songs, Divine Hymns, and Sacred Poems; Being Chiefly a Collection.* Jesse Mercer. Augusta.
- 1814 *A Hymn Book, Containing a Copious Selection of Hymns and Spiritual Songs, from the Best Authors.* Silas M. Noel. Frankfort, KY.

- 1818 *Hymns and Spiritual Songs, Original and Selected.* Starke Dupuy. [n.p.]
- 1820 *The Choice.* William Dossey. Philadelphia.
- 1823 *A Selection of Hymns and Spiritual Songs.* John Purify. Raleigh.
- 1828 *The Dover Selection of Spiritual Songs.* Andrew Broaddus, Richmond.
- 1834 *The Baptist Harmony; Being a Selection of Choice Hymns and Spiritual Songs for Social Worship.* Staunton S. Burdett. Philadelphia.
- 1835 *The Southern Harmony and Musical Companion.* William Walker. New Haven, CT.
- 1844 *The Sacred Harp, A Collection of Psalm and Hymn Tunes, Odes, and Anthems; Selected from the Most Eminent Authors.* B. F. White and E. J. King. Philadelphia.
- 1855 *The Social Harp; A Collection of Tunes, Odes, Anthems, and Set Pieces Selected from Various Authors.* John G. McCurry. Philadelphia.
- 1842 *The Baptist Hymn Book.* Wm. C. Buck. Louisville.
- 1843 *The Psalmist: A New Collection of Hymns for the Use of the Baptist Churches.* Baron Stow and S. F. Smith. Boston.
- 1847 *The Psalmist, With a Supplement.* Richard Fuller and J. B. Jeter. Boston.
- 1848 *The Social Psalmist.* Baron Stow and S. F. Smith. Boston.
- 1871 *The Service of Song for Baptist Churches.* S. L. Caldwell and A. J. Gordon. Boston and New York.
- 1871 *The Baptist Hymn and Tune Book, for Public Worship.* Music adapted and arranged by John M. Evans. Philadelphia.
- 1871 *The Baptist Praise Book.* Richard Fuller, E. M. Levy, S. D. Phelps, H. C. Fish, Thomas Armitage, E. T. Winkler, W. W. Everts, Geo. C. Lorimer, and Basil Manly, Jr., J. P. Holbrook, special musical editor. New York.
- 1859 *The Southern Psalmist.* J. R. Graves and J. M. Pendleton. Nashville.
- 1873 *The New Baptist Psalmist and Tune Book, for Churches and Sunday-Schools.* J. R. Graves. Memphis.
- 1883 *The Baptist Hymnal, for Use in the Church and Home.* W. Howard Doane, musical editor; E. H. Johnson, associate editor. Philadelphia.
- 1898 *Sursum Corda: A Book of Praise.* E. H. Johnson, editor; E. E. Ayre, associate editor. Philadelphia.
- 1926 *The Modern Hymnal.* Robert H. Coleman. Dallas.
- 1933 *The American Hymnal.* Robert H. Coleman. Dallas.

HYMNS AND TUNES

A Child of the King—See *My Father is rich in houses and lands*

A mighty fortress is our God 8

Both text and tune of Martin Luther's great "Battle Hymn of the Reformation" are believed to have first been published in Joseph Klug's *Geistliche Lieder* (Wittenberg, 1529), but no copies of that first edition now exist. Markus Jenny made an exhaustive analysis of this hymn *(Jahrbuch für Liturgik and Hymnologie*, 1964) showing that the first three stanzas correspond to the three strophes of Psalm 46 as separated by the sign *Selah.* Jenny contends that stanza four is unrelated to the psalm and must be regarded as an addition to it. Jenny's analysis and evaluation is summarized by Fred D. Gealy in *Companion to the Hymnal: A Handbook to the 1964 Methodist Hymnal* (Nashville, 1970, p. 66). Luther's hymn gained immediate popularity over Germany. Haeussler observed that "In many communities it was the entering wedge for the Reformation, as in Schweinfurt, Franconia, where a Catholic congregation sang the hymn in church and children sang it on the streets in spite of prohibitions by the priests." The first translation into English by Miles Coverdale was in use within ten years after the publication of the German original beginning "Oure God is a defence and towre" (*Goostly Psalms and Spiritual Songs*, 1539). Julian describes the history of this hymn in translation. Before 1900 over 80 translations in 53 languages had been made. In England, Thomas Carlyle's translation, "A safe stronghold our God's still" is in common use. In America, the preferred translation is that of Frederick H. Hedge, first published in *Hymns for the Church of Christ* (Boston, 1953). The first American Baptist collection to include this hymn appears to have been *Baptist Hymnal* by W. H. Doane and E. H. Johnson (Philadel-

phia, 1883). It entered for the first time into a Southern Baptist collection in *The New Baptist Hymnal* (Nashville, 1926, No. 37).

The form of the tune EIN' FESTE BURG in common use today is based on the version of J. S. Bach, who composed a cantata (BWV 80) based on it. The original rhythmic version is given below. Other composers who have used this melody include Mendelssohn, in his Fifth Symphony; Meyerbeer, in his opera *Les Huguenots*; and Wagner, in his *Kaisermarsch*. This text and tune came into a Southern Baptist collection first in *The Baptist Hymn and Tune Book* (Nashville, 1904, No. 58).   *H.E.*

A parting hymn we sing 375

This hymn text by Aaron R. Wolfe was one of the eight of his hymns published in Thomas Hastings' *Church Melodies* (1858) under the initials "A.R.W." According to Wolfe, this text was intended for use as a fitting conclusion to the observance of the Lord's Supper. Its first publication in a Southern Baptist hymnal was in *Baptist Hymn and Praise Book* (Nashville, 1904, No. 503), where it appeared with the DENNIS tune.

DENNIS—See hymn 387, Blest be the tie. *M.P.*

A pilgrim was I 422

John W. Peterson and Alfred B. Smith wrote both the words and music together, as described by Peterson:

"In 1958 I resided in Montrose, Pennsylvania. There I was working with Alfred B. Smith and serving as editor of Singspiration, Inc. One morning I was sitting at the piano improvising and Al walked in. As I continued to play, a melody took shape. Soon Al and I were each adding phrases until we had completed the entire song. Rarely have I collaborated with others in such a way in the writing of a song, but in this instance it was a successful effort for God has greatly used the song.

"It was a great favorite during the second Billy Graham London Crusade. Cliff Barrows reported that if he failed to use it on a given night he would get notes sent up to the platform from the crowd. It was first published in *John Peterson's Folio of Favorites*, August 1, 1958" (Reynolds, 1976, 25).

The text of this song is a free elaboration on Psalm 23 in the form of a Christian testimony. The musical idiom has been described as "western;" it was published later in Peterson's *Western Style Songs* (Grand Rapids, 1963, Vol. 2). Its first publication in a Southern Baptist hymnal was in *Baptist Hymnal* (Nashville, 1975, No. 228), where the three stanzas with refrain and coda appeared. The name GOODNESS was given the tune in the 1975 hymnal. *H.E.*

A purple robe 154

This hymn on Christ's passion was written in 1968 by Timothy Dudley-Smith for *Youth Praise 2* (1969). The worshipper becomes part of the drama as the final verse of each stanza summarizes each scene of the passion narrative. *The Baptist Hymnal* (1991) is the first Southern Baptist publication to include this hymn.

SERENITY—See hymn 480, Immortal Love, forever full. *P.H.*

A ruler once came to Jesus 322

In August, 1877, George Stebbins was assisting evangelist George F. Pentecost in a revival in Worcester, Massachusetts. Dr. Pentecost quoted the words of Jesus to Nicodemus, "Verily, verily, I say unto thee...Ye must be born again" (John 3: 3-7). These words impressed Stebbins as being suitable for a chorus to a hymn, and he asked Rev. W. T. Sleeper to write the verses. The hymn and tune first appeared in *Gospel Hymns No. 3* (1878).

BORN AGAIN was the name given this tune in *Baptist Hymnal* (1956). *The Modern Hymnal* (Nashville, 1926, No. 284) was the first Southern Baptist collection to contain this gospel song. *P.H.*

A wonderful Savior is Jesus my Lord 340

The text by Fanny Crosby and the tune by William J. Kirkpatrick were first published in *The Finest of the Wheat No. 1*, compiled by George D. Elderkin, R. R. McCabe, John R. Sweney, and Kirkpatrick (Chicago, 1890, No. 49). In that same year they also appeared in *Songs of Saving Power*, compiled by John McPhail (Chicago).

KIRKPATRICK was the name assigned to this tune in *Baptist Hymnal* (1956). The first appearance of both text and tune in a Southern Baptist compilation was in *Songs of Faith* (Nashville, 1933, No. 60). *M.P.*

Abide with me 63

The opening lines of this hymn by Henry F. Lyte are based upon Luke 24:29. Two versions exist concerning its origin. In a letter published in *The Spectator* (Oct. 3, 1925), H. T. Bindley claimed that Lyte wrote the hymn in 1820 following a visit to a dying friend, William Augustus Le Hunte. A copy of the hymn purportedly was given to Le Hunt's brother. The other story of the hymn's origin is provided by the author's daughter, Anna Maria Maxwell Hogg, in the preface to Lyte's *Remains*. Describing the day of September 4, 1847, when Lyte preached his final sermon to his congregation at Lower Brixham, in Devonshire, England (having resigned because of failing health), she wrote: "In the evening of the same day he placed in the hands of a near and dear relative the little hymn, 'Abide with Me,' with the air of his own composing, adapted to the words."

In an article in the *London Times* (Nov. 1, 1947), Walter Maxwell-Lyte, great-grandson of the author, offered additional information. The Le Hunte manuscript was a copy (rather than an autograph) which seemed to have been written in 1847. Further, a letter from Lyte to Julia Bolton (who later married Lyte's youngest son) dated August 25, 1847, contained the hymn text, described by Lyte as "my latest effusion." The date of the letter would place the origin of the hymn earlier than the September 4, 1847 date claimed by Lyte's daughter.

The hymn was first published in Lyte's *Remains* (London, 1850). Its first publication in the United States was in *Hymns for the Church of Christ* (Boston, 1853), a Unitarian hymnal. Its first appearance in a Southern Baptist hymnal was in *The Baptist Hymn and Praise Book* (Nashville, 1904, No. 352).

EVENTIDE was written by William H. Monk as a setting for "Abide with me: fast falls the eventide." Like the text with which it is identified, there are two stories concerning the tune's origin. The most commonly accepted one is that Monk composed it in a few minutes following a meeting of the committee compiling *Hymns Ancient and Modern* (London, 1861) when it was decided that there was no suitable tune for that text. Monk's widow has provided the other version, having reportedly said that the tune was written "in her company out-of-doors at a time of great sorrow, after they had stood for some time watching the glory of the setting sun." *M.P.*

According to Thy gracious Word 372

This text by James Montgomery was first published in the author's *Christian Psalmist* (1825), where it appeared in six stanzas of four lines each. The heading which accompanied it, "This do in remembrance of Me" (Luke 22:19; 1 Cor. 11:24), suggests the text's emphasis upon the Lord's Supper, with which it has been associated through the years. The earliest publication of this text in this country is listed in the *Dictionary of American Hymnology* as *A Collection of Psalms and Hymns for Christian Worship* (Boston, 1830). It was included in the first Southern Baptist hymnal, *The Baptist Psalmody* (Charleston, 1850, No. 925). In *The Baptist Hymnal* (1991), only the first four of Montgomery's original six stanzas appear.

AVON—See hymn 145, Alas, and did my Savior bleed. *M.P.*

Alas, and did my Savior bleed 139, 145

This hymn was published in July, 1707, in Isaac Watts' *Hymns and Spiritual Songs*. The collection had three books: I. *Collected from the Scriptures*; II. *Composed on Divine Subjects*; and III. *Prepared for the Lord's Supper*. "Alas, and did my Savior bleed" was in Book II under the heading "Godly Sorrow

Arising from the Sufferings of Christ." The second stanza of the original six has seldom been used:

Thy body slain, sweet Jesus, Thine,
And bathed in its own blood,
While all exposed to wrath divine
The glorious sufferer stood?

In later editions the hymn was printed with this stanza bracketed to indicate it could be omitted. The last line of stanza one originally appeared as "For such a worm as I." It is usually altered to read "For such an one as I" or "For sinners such as I." The original stanza five has been restored in *The Baptist Hymnal* (1991) as stanza four. Many Christians, including Fanny Crosby, have testified to the influence of this hymn in their conversion experience. The hymn is found in the very first hymn collection to be published by Southern Baptists, *The Baptist Psalmody* (Charleston, 1850, No. 434).

AVON (used with hymn 145) has also been called MARTYRDOM, FENWICK, DRUMCLOG, INVERNESS, and ALL SAINTS. The tune is the work of Hugh Wilson who probably got his inspiration from a Scottish ballad. In the late 18th century, Wilson issued the tune in leaflet form for use in music classes. In this version it was in common (4/4) time. In 1825, however, it appeared in triple time in R. A. Smith's *Sacred Music Sung in St. George's Church* (Edinburgh, 1825, 2nd ed.). Wilson, Smith, and Scottish folk music all played parts in the shaping of this tune.

Perhaps the hymn titled "At the Cross" could be described as a camp-meeting version of Watts' "Alas, and Did My Savior Bleed." The catchy refrain and tune are of that type. Ralph E. Hudson was responsible for the refrain which was added or adapted when he composed HUDSON. The present version of the tune was first published by Hudson in 1885 in *Songs of Peace, Love, and Joy* (Alliance, 1885, No. 81).

The difference in the music used for the stanza and that used for the refrain implies they were not composed as a unit. Reynolds suggests the refrain was already in existence and was borrowed by Hudson to complete the hymn setting:

"Further evidence supports this possibility by the fact that this refrain melody appears as a separate tune in *Glad Hallelujahs*, edited by J. R. Sweeney and William J. Kirkpatrick (Philadelphia, 1887, No. 123). It is set to Charles Wesley's "O How Happy Are They Who the Saviour Obey," with a da capo refrain using the text, "At the cross, at the cross where I first saw the light." The tune is said to be "arranged by E. E. Nickerson." The same treatment is used for this refrain melody in the *Emory Hymnal* (Philadelphia, 1887, No. 98), with original stanzas provided by R. Kelso Carter and the same refrain text as above" (1964, pp. 6-7).

The first appearance of Hudson's "At the Cross" tune in a Southern Baptist collection was *The Baptist Hymn and Praise Book* (Nashville, 1904, No. 113). *D.B.*

All creatures of our God and King 27

Francis of Assisi was known as a lover of all of God's creatures. This paraphrase of his "Canticle of the Sun" invites many elements of creation to join in praising the Creator. The text was written in 1225 during an unusually hot summer when Francis was ill and losing his sight. The straw hut provided by Clare (a friend who founded an order for nuns similar to the Franciscans) was invaded by a swarm of field mice. During his final illness, Francis added a stanza giving thanks for "our Sister, the death of the body."

This paean of praise is thought to be the oldest religious poem in the Italian language. Popular devotional poetry known as *laudi spirituali* began in this period and evolved eventually into the 16th-century oratorio. These songs in dialogue form were dramatized in that part of the church known as the *oratorio*. The paraphrase included here was made by William Henry Draper for a children's Whitsuntide festival at Leeds, England, some time between 1899 and 1919. It was first published in Draper's *Hymns of the Spirit* (1926). The first United States publication was in *The Oxford American Hymnal for Schools* (1930). Howard Robbins translated the poem more literally as "Most High, Omnipotent, Good Lord" in 1939. "All Creatures of Our God and King" was first published by Southern Baptists in *Baptist Hymnal* (Nashville, 1956, No. 3).

Lasst uns Erfreuen was derived from a folk tune popular among Roman Catholics in 17th-century Germany. The name comes from the Easter hymn with which it appears in *Geistliche Kirchengesang* (1623). The tune's modern revival came in *The English Hymnal* (1906) set to "Ye Watchers and Ye Holy Ones" and harmonized by Ralph Vaughan Williams. Without the fermatas, the tune may be sung in canon. Antiphonal singing is also a natural outgrowth of the "alleluia" refrain.   *P.H.*

All day long 463

The introduction of this African-American hymn to Southern Baptists has been traced to a Texas revival meeting in the mid-1960s. Jerry L. Spencer, the evangelist at this revival, relates in a letter to Harry Eskew dated April 20, 1991, perhaps the earliest account of the singing of this song in a Southern Baptist congregation: a small rural church in Sulphur Springs, Texas. The church's pastor, Bill Sutton, himself the son of a Baptist minister, was a product of the Mid-South. Sutton admitted that he was at that time prejudiced against African-Americans owing to an earlier unpleasant experience. These repressed hostile feelings were

to rise to the surface during the course of the revival.

To promote attendance at the 1965 revival, Spencer spoke in several county schools, including a class of fourth-graders at a recently integrated school. He taught them songs and invited them to sing at the revival. Only two little Black girls accepted the invitation and came. Spencer narrates the events which followed:

"I asked the pastor, Bill, 'Are we going to ask these girls to sing or tell them they are not allowed to be here?'

"Well, you have put me into a terrible situation. This church has never had a Black in attendance; but it's your problem; you let them sing!'

"I asked the little fourth-grade girls if they wanted to sing something I had taught them or something of their own choosing."

"If it's all right, we'd like to sing 'All Day Long I've Been with Jesus.'"

"I've never heard that song, but I'm sure it will be just fine. Now who will play for you?"

"No, sir, we can't sing with no instrument. We'll sing—just the two of us."

"Those little bright-eyed ladies stood like two old pros, faced each other, smiled like this was the happiest night of their life, and as they began to sing in beautiful harmony, you could have heard a pin drop. By the time they had finished, faces in the congregation were wet with tears; and surely we had "moved up one step higher." The girls curtsied, said 'Thank you,' and went to the back and sat with their older sister who had brought them.

"The housekeeper in the home where I was staying knew the song the girls had sung. She learned it from her grandmother in 1904. She said that it had come from slave days and was a true Negro spiritual.

"In 1975 I sang the song in a conference

at Baylor University. Jack Taylor heard it and began spreading it around. Its popularity in the white community has soared since then.

"The original version that I heard goes:
All dá long I been wif Jesus.
It have been a' glorious dá-á-áe.
I done moved up one step higher,
And I'm walkin' on the King's highway.
oo-ow-oo——

I got to go and make it right,
So I can testify tonight.
I'm walking down the King's highway.
oo-ow-oo——."

Stanzas two and three have been added by Hugh Warner. The tune ALL DAY LONG encompasses only the first four notes of the major scale. The first and third phrases of this tune bear a strong resemblance to Eduardo J. Lango's setting of "When He Calls Me I Will Answer" (copyright 1939 by Herbert G. Tovey), a hymn widely sung in African-American worship.

The Baptist Hymnal (1991) is the first Southern Baptist collection to include this hymn. *H.E.*

All glory, laud, and honor 126

"Gloria, laus, et honor" is the first line of a Latin hymn of 78 lines which is generally attributed to Theodulph of Orleans. Legend has it that the hymn was written about 820 A.D. while Theodulph was imprisoned in Angers for suspected disloyalty to the Emperor, Louis the Pious. During a Palm Sunday processional which passed the prison, the Emperor paused briefly and heard Theodulph singing this hymn. Charmed by what he heard, Louis forgave the writer, restored his church offices to him, and ordered that the new hymn should thenceforth be sung every Palm Sunday. Unfortunately, the earliest known source for this tale, Clichtoveus' *Elucidatorium* (1516), dates from nearly seven centuries after the supposed event and there are serious reasons to doubt the truth of the legend.

John Mason Neale made two translations of "Gloria, laus, et honor." The first, "Glory, and Honour, and Laud Be to Thee," appeared in his *Mediaeval Hymns* (1851). His second effort, "Glory, and Laud, and Honour," was published in Part II of *The Hymnal Noted* (1854). In the first edition of *Hymns Ancient and Modern* (London, 1861), the nine stanzas of the second version were reduced to six (which now appear as three double-stanzas) and altered to their present form.

In its Latin version, "Gloria, laus, et honor" was sung to a plainsong melody (*Liber Usualis*, 1961, p. 586). The present tune, ST. THEODULPH, was composed by Melchior Teschner and published in a pamphlet, "Ein andachtiges Gebet" (Leipzig, 1615), as one of two settings for Valerius Herberger's hymn "Valet will ich dir geben." The tune was first linked with Theodulph's text and given its present name in *Hymns Ancient and Modern* (1861).

The first Baptist collection to include this text and tune, albeit in a form slightly different from the present one, was *New Baptist Hymnal* (Nashville, 1926, No. 142), a joint production of the American Baptist Publication Society and Southern Baptist Sunday School Board. *D.M.*

All hail the power of Jesus' name! 200, 201, 202

This ecumenically popular hymn exists in many versions. Edward Perronet published the first stanza in Augustus Toplady's *Gospel Magazine* (November, 1779) with the MILES LANE tune of his close friend William Shrubsole. The complete text appeared in the April, 1780, issue of the same magazine with the heading "On the Resurrection, the Lord Is King."

Modern usage combines Perronet's original with alterations by Baptist minister John Rippon and emendations by later editors. In *The Baptist Hymnal* (1991), Perronet's first stanza remains intact with the change of only one word. The second stanza reflects Rippon's transposition of words necessitated by his address of the stanza to "Converted Jews." The original words are: "Ye seed of Israel's *chosen race*/Ye ransom'd of the fall." The third stanza is essentially Rippon's and retains only five words from Perronet's original. Stanza four is entirely by John Rippon. Basil Manly's *Baptist Psalmody* (Charleston, 1850, No. 239) was the first Southern Baptist hymnal to contain this hymn, using five stanzas.

CORONATION is the oldest American tune in modern hymnody to be used continually. Oliver Holden composed this as a fuging tune, in which the bass and tenor are given a duet on the third phrase, "Bring forth the royal diadem." It was first printed in Holden's *Union Harmony* (Boston, 1793). The name CORONATION was derived from the refrain "Crown Him Lord of all." The tune first appeared in a Southern Baptist hymnal in *The Baptist Hymn and Praise Book* (Nashville, 1904, No. 137).

DIADEM was written by a 19-year-old British hatmaker, James Ellor, in 1838. This florid tune was intended for the text "All hail the power of Jesus' name" and takes its name from the "royal diadem" of the first stanza. Although this tune is found in Reynolds and McKinney's *Jehovah's Praise* (Ft. Worth, 1925, No. 44) and in Coleman's *The Modern Hymnal* (Dallas, 1926, No. 214), the first "official" Southern Baptist collection to include it was *The Broadman Hymnal* (Nashville, 1940, No. 255).

MILES LANE, by William Shrubsole, was originally printed with stanza one of "All Hail the Power of Jesus' Name" in a supplement to Augustus Toplady's *Gospel Magazine* in November, 1779. Shrubsole was 19 years old when he wrote the tune and, as with CORONATION, MILES LANE was a fuging tune. Individual parts sang each "Crown him" before concluding with a harmonized finale. The tune name and attribution of Perronet's authorship was given by Stephen Addington, the pastor of Miles Lane Meeting House, London, in his *Collection of Psalm Tunes* (1780). Ralph Vaughan Williams, in the *Manchester Guardian* (1943), makes reference to Edward Elgar as having pronounced MILES LANE the finest tune in English hymnody. *P.H.*

All my life I had a longing 539

Clara Tear Williams wrote the text in 1881, the same year Ralph E. Hudson wrote SATISFIED. Hudson copyrighted both tune and text in 1881, but evidently they were not published until 1884 when Hudson's *Gems of Gospel Songs* was produced. Its appearance in a Baptist hymnal came after William J. Reynolds heard Dean Wilder, formerly of the Hale-Wilder duo and since 1975, Director of Vocal Studies at William Jewell College, sing the hymn at the Southern Baptist Church Music Conference in Dallas in 1974. A few hymns were needed to complete *Baptist Hymnal* (1975). Reynolds was so impressed with the selection and with its performance, he decided to include it in the hymnal. Consequently *Baptist Hymnal* (Nashville, 1975, No. 344) was the initial inclusion of this hymn in a Southern Baptist collection. *D.B.*

All on the altar 326

"All on the Altar" was written by B. B. McKinney in 1936 after he became editor of music at the Southern Baptist Sunday School Board. He wrote it to appeal to Christian young people. Possibly more suitable as a soprano-alto duet in the form originally published in *The Broadman Hymnal* (Nashville, 1940, No. 83), it was given a congregational quality in the setting for *The Baptist Hymnal* (1991). In its appearance in *The Broadman Hymnal*, the hymn bore this subheading: "Dedicated to young people, B. B. McK."

ALTAR, for obvious reasons, is the name selected by *The Baptist Hymnal* (1991) committee for B. B. McKinney's tune to "All on the Altar." H.T.M.

All people that on earth do dwell 5

This metrical version of Psalm 100 is generally considered to be the work of William Kethe. It appeared in 1561 as one of 25 psalms he wrote for the *Anglo-Genevan Psalter,* the book of praise used by English-speaking Protestant refugees in Geneva. In the same year it also appeared back in London in Day's *Psalter* when some of the refugees had returned from exile after the cessation of persecution. It was included in the later versions of the *English Psalter* (Sternhold and Hopkins, from 1564) and in the *Scottish Psalter* (1564-6). In the latter book, the third verse of stanza one read: *Him serve with mirth,* thus changing from Kethe's: *Him serve with fear,* to be closer to the King James translation from the Hebrew: *Serve the Lord with gladness.*

However, throughout its over-four-century history, this hymn has undergone only minor alterations, such as in the third verse of stanza two, the substitution of "flock" for "folck" owing to a printing error. Kethe's words antedate by more than a century the familiar doxology by Thomas Ken, "Praise God from whom all blessings flow" to which OLD HUNDREDTH is most often sung. "All People That on Earth Do Dwell" is by far the oldest set of English words to be used with this venerable tune. As such, Kethe's hymn

ranks as one of the oldest in continuous use among English-speaking Christians.

"All People That on Earth Do Dwell" is not found in any hymnal used by Southern Baptists before *The New Evangel,* compiled by Robert H. Coleman and J. Fred Scholfield (Dallas, 1911, No. 326). It was included in all later Southern Baptist collections, however, including *The Modern Hymnal* (Dallas, 1926, No. 483) and *The Broadman Hymnal* (Nashville, 1940, No. 3).

OLD HUNDREDTH first appeared in the enlarged edition of the French *Genevan Psalter* (1551) where it was set to Psalm 134. The first half of the tune contains phrases which may have existed in plainsong and folk song for centuries. The latter part of the tune and its overall form is the work of Louis Bourgeois, John Calvin's musical collaborator in the formation of the *Genevan Psalter*.

The name of the tune refers to the English psalm by William Kethe with which it was associated. The term "old" was later applied to those tunes which were used in connection with the "old version" of the *Psalter,* also known as Sternhold and Hopkins from the names of its two principal translators.

OLD HUNDREDTH is the only tune which has been preserved intact throughout the entire history of metrical psalmody and modern hymnody and thus ranks as the most venerable of all hymn tunes in current use. H.T.M.

All praise to Thee 229

F. Bland Tucker wrote this paraphrase of Philippians 2:5-11 in 1938, while serving on the committee that was preparing *The Hymnal 1940* (New York, 1943). He had been attracted to the tune SINE NOMINE, by Ralph Vaughan Williams, to which was set William Walsham How's "For All the Saints, Who from Their Labors Rest," and desired to produce words that could have more general use. Tucker's text first appeared in *The Hymnal 1940*, but it was set there to ENGLEBERG, by Charles Villiers Stanford, rather than to SINE NOMINE.

This text entered Southern Baptist hymnody in *Baptist Hymnal* (Nashville, 1975, No. 43). In that publication, an error from *The Methodist Hymnal* (Nashville, 1966) was inadvertently repeated: The word "high" was omitted from the second line of stanza four. The omission recurs in the first printing of *The Baptist Hymnal* (1991).

SINE NOMINE—See hymn 355, "For All the Saints."   *P.A.R.*

All praise to you, my God, this night 449

This hymn was written, probably in the early 1670s, by Thomas Ken. It was first published with his "Awake, My Soul, and with the Sun" in "A Morning and Evening Hymn, Formerly made by a Reverend Bishop," a London pamphlet of 1692 issued without the author's permission by Richard Smith. Its first printing with Ken's approval was by Charles Brome in "Three Hymns. In the following year, Ken issued a new edition of his *A Manual of Prayers for the Use of the Scholars of Winchester College And All other Devout Christians. To Which Is Added Three Hymns for Morning, Evening, and Midnight; not in former Editions: By the Same Author. Newly Revised.* Its title reflects the inclusion (for the first time) of this hymn, his morning text, and his midnight hymn "Lord, Now My Sleep Does Me Forsake" (later, "My God, I Now from Sleep Awake"). Each of these concluded with his now-famous doxology, "Praise God, from Whom All Blessings Flow." That these hymns may have existed as early as the 1670s is deduced from the 1674 edition of the *Manual*, which directs the scholars to "Be sure to sing the Morning and Evening Hymn in your chamber devoutly."

The various early publications of this text differ in several lines and in the number of stanzas. Two opening lines are known: "All praise to thee;" and "Glory to thee." Ken's final version of 1709 begins "All praise to thee" and has 11 stanzas plus the doxology. The stanzas in *The Baptist Hymnal* are revisions of the original first, second, and fourth, as prepared for *Psalter Hymnal* (Grand Rapids, 1987). The early versions of the complete text may be seen in John Julian's *A Dictionary of Hymnology* (reprint, Grand Rapids, 1985).

With the opening line, "Glory to thee, my God, this night," five stanzas of this text appeared in *The Baptist Psalmody* (Charleston, 1850, No. 1141), the first hymnal produced by Southern Baptists. In that printing the first three stanzas are like the original, but the other two bear little resemblance to any of Ken's work.

TALLIS' CANON was composed by noted English composer Thomas Tallis. It was one of nine tunes appended by printer John Day to the psalm paraphrases of Anglican Archbishop Matthew Parker in *The Whole Psalter, translated into English Metre* (London, *c.* 1567). There it sets Parker's versification of Psalm 67. For this book, Tallis provided a tune in each of the eight church modes plus the one now know as TALLIS' ORDINAL. A table of tunes describes each, saying for this one that "The eyghte goeth milde: in modest pace."

The name of the tune reflects its composer and its structure. It is best known by as many as 10 other names, including EVENING HYMN, which reflects its long association with Ken's text. The original had the melody in the tenor, a second voice in canon, and two other parts to complete the harmony. It repeated each phrase, suiting it to the eight-line stanzas of Parker's text. The repetitions were eliminated in Thomas

Ravenscroft's *The Whole Booke of Psalmes* (London, 1621).   *P.A.R.*

All That Thrills My Soul—See *Who can cheer the heart like Jesus*

All the way my Savior leads me 62

This is one of the most enduring of Fanny J. Crosby's many hymns. The words came to the blind poet as she reflected on God's goodness. A friend wrote out the text for her and sent it to Robert Lowry. Lowry wrote the tune ALL THE WAY. The result of their collaboration was first published in a collection by Lowry and W. H. Doane entitled *Brightest and Best* (Chicago, 1875, No. 64). The Scripture reference given was Deuteronomy 32:12, "The Lord alone did lead him."

This text with the Robert Lowry ALL THE WAY tune is first found in a Southern Baptist collection in *The Baptist Hymn and Praise Book* (Nashville, 1904, No. 264). *D.B., H.T.M.*

All things bright and beautiful 46

This text, by Mrs. Cecil Frances Alexander, was first published in her *Hymns for Little Children* (1848). It is one of several hymns which she wrote to interpret phrases of the Apostles' Creed in language that children could understand. This text was written to explain the meaning of the phrase, "Maker of heaven and earth," and is based upon Genesis 1:31. The original version had seven stanzas of four lines each. In the present version, four of the original seven stanzas are combined into two eight-line stanzas.

This hymn was first published by Southern Baptists in 1926, when it appeared in two hymnals, the *New Baptist Hymnal* (Nashvile, No. 400, with the SPOHR tune) and *The Modern Hymnal* (Nashville, No. 64, with the GREYSTONE tune).

SPOHR (also called CRUCIFIXION, JERUSALEM, SIMPSON, and THE INNER LIFE) was adapted from a solo in Louis Spohr's oratorio *Des Heilands letze Stunden*, first performed in Kassel on Good Friday, 1835. In the English version (entitled *Calvary*) prepared by Edward Taylor, there is a solo, "Though all thy friends prove faithless," sung by Mary. The melody of this solo was arranged as an anthem by James Simpson setting the text "As pants the hart." The popularity of this anthem led to the further adaptation of the opening section as a hymn tune which has carried, among its several tune names, the name of the original composer.   *M.P.*

All to Jesus I surrender 275

William J. Reynolds (*Companion to Baptist Hymnal*) has quoted this hymn's author, Judson W. Van DeVenter's account, stating that it was written "in memory of the time when, after a long struggle, I had surrendered and dedicated my life to active Christian service. The song was written while I was conducting a meeting at East Palestine, Ohio, and in the home of George Sebring, who later founded the city of Sebring, Florida. The Sebring camp meeting at Sebring, Ohio, was also founded by him."

SURRENDER was composed by Winfield S. Weeden for this text, being first published in *Gospel Songs of Grace and Glory*, compiled by Weeden, Van DeVenter, and Leonard Weaver (Philadelphia, 1896, No. 83). Of its original five stanzas, the present version uses stanzas 1, 3, and 4. The original soprano-tenor duet of the stanzas (as in *The Broadman Hymnal*, 1940, No. 82) was altered in *Baptist Hymnal* (1956) to provide for four-part singing throughout.   *H.E.*

All to Thee-See *I have heard the voice of Jesus*

Alleluia 223

This praise chorus with only four notes in the melody and three chords in the harmony was first heard in the 1970s. The multiple claims made to its authorship became the subject of litigation. The result was its attribution to Jerry Sinclair, who wrote it while working in an evangelistic street ministry in Lawton, Oklahoma, and the assignment of copyright to Manna Music. Additional stanzas may be improvised from four-syllable phrases, with these repeated eight times or alternated with "Alleluia," as was the early oral tradition.

Baptist Hymnal (Nashville, 1975, No. 422) was the first Southern Baptist collection to include this song.

The tune name ALLELUIA is taken from the common title and general theme of the hymn.   *P.A.R.*

Alleluia, alleluia! Give thanks 170

This song was composed by Donald E. Fishel. According to the composer, it was written spontaneously during a prayer time in the summer of 1971. *The Baptist Hymnal* (1991) marks its first appearance in a Southern Baptist hymnal.

ALLELUIA NO.1 is the name assigned to the tune.   *D.M.*

Alleluia, Alleluia! The majesty and glory of Your name 37

This extended chorus is adapted from the 1979 anthem of the same name (Word Music, 1979) by the composer Tom Fettke and author Linda Lee Johnson. The text is based on Psalm 8:9. *The Baptist Hymnal* (1991) is the first Southern Baptist collection to include it.

SOLI DEO GLORIA is adapted from Tom Fettke's anthem of the same name. The music builds melodically, harmonically, and rhythmically to a majestic climax and then subsides again. The hymn tune name is from the Latin, meaning "to God alone the glory." This is the phrase that the great com-

poser J.S. Bach regularly inscribed at the end of his scores of sacred music.   *S.W.G.*

Almighty Father, hear our prayer 656

The source of the text of this prayer response is not known. Its first appearance in a Southern Baptist collection was in *The Baptist Hymn and Praise Book* (Nashville, 1904, No. 585).   *H.T.M.*

ALMIGHTY FATHER is drawn from the penultimate number of the first part of Mendelssohn's oratorio *Elijah* which was first performed at Birmingham, England, on August 26, 1846. In the oratorio it is the people's response to Elijah's prayer for rain. The words of entreaty are: "Open the heavens and send us relief: Help, help thy servant now, O God" and "Then hear from heav'n and forgive the sin; Help, send thy servant, help, O God."   *S.W.G.*

Am I a soldier of the cross 481

Based on 1 Corinthians 16:13, this hymn is appended to Sermon 31, "Holy Fortitude, or Remedies against Fear" in Isaac Watts' *Sermons* (1721-24, Vol. III). *The Baptist Hymnal* (1991) omits stanzas five and six of the original six stanzas.

> Thy saints, in all this glorious war
>   Shall conquer, though they die;
> They view the triumph from afar
>   And seize it with their eye.

> When that illustrious day shall rise,
>   And all thy armies shine
> In robes of victory through the skies,
>   The glory shall be thine.

The first Southern Baptist collection, *The Baptist Psalmody* (Charleston, 1850, No. 641) included this hymn.

ARLINGTON—See hymn 353, Our God has built with living stones.   *D.B.*

Amazing grace! how sweet the sound 330

John Newton's hymn first appeared in *Olney Hymns* (London, 1779, No. 53) in six four-line stanzas entitled "Faith's Review and Expectation." Included in Book I, which contained hymns based on "select passages of Scriptures," the hymn was based on 1 Chronicles 17:16, 17. The first four stanzas of the present version are unaltered from the original. The first American publication seems to have been in *The Psalms of David with Hymns and Spiritual Songs* (New York, 1789), published for the Dutch Reformed Church in North America.

By 1825, John Newton's hymn had appeared in more than 25 hymn collections, which is a measure of its growing popularity. The fifth stanza of the present version, beginning "When we've been there ten thousand years," is not Newton's. It appears as a final stanza with the anonymous hymn "Jerusalem, My Happy Home" in numerous early American collections, e.g. *A Collection of Sacred Ballads*, compiled by Richard and Andrew Broaddus (Caroline County, VA, 1790). In E. O. Excell's *Coronation Hymns* (Chicago, 1910, No. 282), the first three stanzas of Newton's hymn appear with this anonymous stanza as the fourth and final stanza. Excell's version appeared in Robert H. Coleman's *The New Evangel* (Dallas, 1911, No. 281), and was included in all Coleman's subsequent collections.

NEW BRITAIN, an early American melody of unknown origin, has borne such names as ST. MARY'S, GALLAHER, HARMONY GROVE, SYMPHONY, SOLON, REDEMPTION, and AMAZING GRACE. The earliest appearance of the tune has been identified by Warren Steel as being in *Columbian Harmony,* or *Pilgrim's Musical Companion* (Cincinnati, 1829), compiled by Benjamin Shaw and Charles H. Spilman and registered as a copyright in Kentucky. The tune was used twice, as ST. MARY'S and GALLAHER. Both are variants of AMAZING GRACE. Neither of these tunes was set to John Newton's text. In 1831, the tune appeared in James P. Carrell and David L. Clayton's *Virginia Harmony,* but not with Newton's text.

The "wedding" of Newton's text to this tune can be credited to William Walker of Spartanburg, South Carolina, in his *Southern Harmony* of 1835. Following this, most southern oblong shape-note tunebooks used the tune with Newton's hymn. The transfer of the tune from the "oblong" to the "upright" collections in the south may have been the work of Rigdon M. McIntosh in the several collections he published in the latter part of the 19th century. McIntosh was the leading musician in the Methodist Episcopal Church, South. The present form of the tune is credited to E. O. Excell, who included it in his *Make His Praise Glorious* (Chicago, 1900, No. 235).   *W.J.R.*

Amen 650, 651

This Hebrew word has long been used in both Hebrew and Christian worship, most often as a congregational assent to prayer (Deut. 27:16ff; 1 Cor. 14:16). Amens became choral in the Middle Ages.

DANISH, although extensively used in Denmark's churches, is from an unknown source.

DRESDEN may have been composed by Johann Gottlieb Naumann (Apr. 17, 1741 - Oct. 23, 1801) at Dresden, where he served in various capacities until receiving a lifetime contract as Oberkapellmeister in 1786. He was a prominent musician on the European scene in the late 18th century. The Amen appeared in the Zittau choir book and was later used prominently by Mendelssohn in the "Reformation" Symphony and by Wagner in the opera *Parsifal.*   *P.H.*

Amen (Threefold 1) 652

The composer and source of this "Amen" setting are unknown. Its first appearance in a Southern Baptist collection was in *The Broadman Hymnal* (Nashville, 1940, No. 501). *M.P.*

Amen (Threefold 2) 653

This threefold Amen was composed by Richard Ham to meet a need for a choral prayer response in the worship of First Baptist Church, Richmond, Kentucky, where he has been the minister of music since 1983. *The Baptist Hymnal* (1991) is the first collection in which this response has appeared. *H.T.M.*

Amen (Threefold 3) 654

This threefold Amen was composed by Richard Ham to meet a need for a choral prayer response in the worship of First Baptist Church, Richmond, Kentucky, where he has been the minister of music since 1983. *The Baptist Hymnal* (1991) is the first collection in which this response has appeared. *H.T.M.*

America the Beautiful—See *O beautiful for spacious skies*

And God will raise you up 71

This is the refrain of a hymn written in 1978 by Michael Joncas. It draws its imagery from Exodus 19:4. The refrain originally began "And he will raise you up." The first line of the four-stanza text, which is an interpretation of Psalm 91, is "You who dwell in the shelter of our God." Joncas wrote the hymn after a visit with a friend who, during his visit, received a call that his father had suffered a heart attack. The author/composer sang it for the first time, with guitar accompaniment, at the visitation service before the funeral Eucharist. He arranged it in several forms and recorded it the following year in a collection entitled, "On Eagle's Wings." It was first published as a congregational piece in *Glory and Praise* (Phoenix, 1979). *The Baptist Hymnal* (1991) is the first collection in which Southern Baptists have included this.

On Eagle's Wings takes its name from the biblical image of the first line. The same name is used for the complete tune. *P.A.R.*

And can it be 147

According to John Julian, this text and "Where Shall My Wondering Soul Begin?" were written at Little Britain, London, in May, 1738, in a time when Charles Wesley underwent his great spiritual change. Charles wrote in his journal on May 23, 1738, "At nine I began a hymn on my conversion but was persuaded to break off for fear of pride…. I prayed Christ to stand by me and finished the hymn." It is not known to which of the two hymns Charles referred. One of them was written in the two days between Charles's conversion and John's conversion. After 10 o'clock the evening of John's conversion, they and several friends went to Charles's room and "sang the hymn with great joy, and parted with prayer." Both hymns are typical of the dynamic declarations of the Wesleyan conversion experience.

"And Can It Be" was first published in John Wesley's *Collection of Psalms and Hymns* (1738). In the *Collection of Hymns for the use of the People called Methodists* (1780), John dropped the fifth of the six six-line stanzas. The present version also drops the second stanza and is to be found for the first time in a Southern Baptist collection in *The Baptist Hymnal* (1991).

Sagina appeared in Thomas Campbell's 1825 collection called *The Bouquet,* where each of the 23 original tunes were named with botanical terms. The dictionary describes "Sagina" as a genus of small herbs with some supposed nutritive value and native to temperate and cool areas. *The Baptist Hymnal* (1991) is the first Southern Baptist hymnal to contain the tune.   *S.W.G.*

Angels we have heard on high 100

This carol of unknown authorship was originally in French with the first line, "Les anges dans nos campagnes." It is believed to date from the 18th century, but its first publication was in *Nouveau recueil de cantiques* (1855), where it was paired with the present tune. The translator of this version, one of several in English, is not known. This is a macaronic carol, combining Latin and English. The refrain is the Latin version of the angels' song, "Glory to God in the highest" (Luke 2:14).

GLORIA first appeared in the collection cited above. It is also called IRIS or identified by the first line of the French text. The present arrangement was made for *Baptist Hymnal* (1956) by Warren Angell. This text and tune first entered Southern Baptist hymnody in *Baptist Hymnal* (Nashville, 1956, No. 64).   *P.A.R.*

Angels, from the realms of glory 94

This hymn text by James Montgomery was first published in *The Sheffield Iris*, a Sheffield, England newspaper edited by Montgomery, on December 24, 1816, under the title "Nativity." It was included in the eighth and ninth editions of Cotterill's *Selection* (1819 and 1820). Montgomery included a slightly altered version in his *Christian Psalmist* (1825), and it has been that latter version which has been widely used. A fifth stanza, which is often omitted as it is in this hymnal, is as follows:

Sinners, wrung with true repentance
Doomed for guilt to endless pains,

Justice now revokes the sentence.
Mercy calls you—break your chains;
(Refrain)
The first use of this text in a Southern Baptist hymnal was in *The Sacred Lute* (Charleston, 1855, No. 130).

REGENT SQUARE was composed by Henry Smart as a setting for Horatius Bonar's "Glory Be to God the Father" in *Psalms and Hymns for Divine Worship* (London, 1867). Perhaps due to its origin in this English Presbyterian collection, it has continued to be associated with that text in the Church of Scotland. The tune was named for the Regent Square Presbyterian Church by Dr. James Hamilton, minister of the church and editor of the collection in which it first appeared.   *M.P.*

Are You Washed in the Blood—See *Have you been to Jesus*

Are you weary, are you heavyhearted 451

This text, known as "Tell It to Jesus Alone," was originally in German as "Sage es Jesu Allein," written by Edmund S. Lorenz and set to his tune. It was published in 1876 in the *Froelicher Botschafter* (*Joyful Messenger*—a German-American periodical of the United Brethren Church), and also in *Pilgerlieder* (*Pilgrim Songs*—a songbook edited by Lorenz for the United Brethren). Lorenz's text was translated into English by Jeremiah E. Rankin (author of "God Be with You Till We Meet Again") and published with the original tune in Lorenz's Sunday School songbook, *Songs of Grace* (1879). It is of interest that Lorenz's songbooks containing this hymn through as late as *Songs of Refreshing* (1894) list Rankin as the author. In the 1975 *Baptist Hymnal*, the tune was named DAYTON for the city in which it was composed and first published.

(This information is taken from Edmund

S. Lorenz's unpublished autobiography, provided by his granddaughter, Ellen Jane Lorenz Porter, a distinguished church musician in Dayton, Ohio.) This song's first inclusion in a Southern Baptist collection was in *Songs of Redemption* (Atlanta, 1920, No. 34).   H.E.

Arise, your light is come! 83

Ruth C. Duck wrote this hymn in 1973 while she was serving as a coeditor of *Because We Are One People* (1974), a collection of hymns using inclusive language published by the Ecumenical Women's Center of Chicago. In a letter to David Music, the author stated that the text came to her while she was working on an adaptation of William P. Merrill's "Rise Up, O Men of God." In her words, it was "as if the new wine of the faith I wanted to express would not fit into the old wineskin of the earlier text." The present hymn received its initial printing in *Because We Are One People* and subsequently appeared in the Reformed Church in America collection *Rejoice in the Lord* (1985) and in the 1990 *Presbyterian Hymnal*. The first publication of Duck's text in a Southern Baptist hymnal is in *The Baptist Hymnal* (1991).   D.M.

FESTAL SONG appears in *The Baptist Hymnal* (1991) set to "Come, We That Love the Lord" and to "Arise, Your Light Is Come." However, it may be best known as a setting for "Rise Up, O Men of God." The tune was written by William H. Walter and first appeared in 1872 in John Ireland Tucker's *The Hymnal with Tunes Old and New*, a collection compiled for the Protestant Episcopal Church. However, *Companion to Baptist Hymnal*, the *Methodist Hymnal Companion*, and the *Companion to Hymnal 1940* all three state the tune first appeared in 1894 in John I. Tucker and W. W. Rousseau's *Hymnal Revised and Enlarged*.   D.B.

As He gathered at His table 369

Paul A. Richardson wrote this text in 1986 in response to a search for new hymns on the ordinances sponsored by the Church Music Department of the Sunday School Board. Its purpose is the relation of the events in the upper room and Gethsemane to the present experience of Christians at the Lord's table. The final stanza emphasizes the intimacy and immediacy of this relationship. Omitted from this hymnal is the original sixth stanza:

> As he went into the garden
> praying, "Father, use your Son,"
> Christ alone could know its meaning;
> Still we pray, "God's will be done."

This text was originally set to Richardson's own tune, STUART, with which it appeared in its first publication in *The Worshiping Church* (Carol Stream, 1990).

The Baptist Hymnal (1991) is the first Southern Baptist collection to include this text.

STUTTGART—See hymn 21, O my soul, bless God the Father.   P.A.R.

As men of old their first fruits brought 639

This was one of the winning entries in a search for new hymns on stewardship conducted in 1960 by The Hymn Society of America. The search was jointly sponsored by the Department of Stewardship and Benevolence of the National Council of Churches of Christ in the United States of America in celebration of its 40th anniversary. Author Frank von Christierson wrote the hymn out of his concern as a pastor that the challenge to give needs repeated emphasis.

The text was first printed in *Ten New Stewardship Hymns* (New York, 1961), a pamphlet containing the 10 winning entries from the search. *The Methodist Hymnal* (Nashville,

1964) was the first hymnal to include it.

The text's first appearance in a Southern Baptist collection was in *The Baptist Hymnal* (1991).

FOREST GREEN—See hymn 79, Blessed be the God of Israel. *P.A.R.*

As we gather around the table 367

Mark Blankenship wrote both the words and the music for an observance of the Lord's Supper at the North Phoenix Baptist Church, Phoenix, Arizona, on December 24, 1973. The entire piece was written on December 17, 1973, and was first sung *a cappella* in an SATB setting by the adult choir on Christmas Eve. *Baptist Hymnal* (Nashville, 1975, No. 251) was the first Southern Baptist collection to contain this hymn.

NORTH PHOENIX was the tune name given by the composer in honor of the church where he was serving at the time. *P.H.*

As with gladness men of old 117

According to the editor's manuscript, this hymn was "written about 1860 during an illness." K. L. Parry says, more specifically, "written one evening during Epiphany about 1858 during convalescence from a serious illness" (62). Percy Dearmer adds, "after reading the Gospel of the day" (58). It was first printed in *Hymns of Love and Joy*, a little collection for private circulation. In 1861 the five six-line stanzas appeared in *Hymns Ancient and Modern*. The present version retains the original though the author approved the change of "manger" to "cradle" because Matthew 2:11 says that the wise men came into the house, not to the stable.

This hymn first appeared in a Southern Baptist hymnal in *New Baptist Hymnal* (Nashville, 1926, No. 88).

DIX—See hymn 44, For the beauty of the earth. *S.W.G*

Ask ye what great thing I know 538

The famous German preacher, Johann Christoph Schwedler (1672-1730), wrote this text based on 1 Corinthians 2:2 and Galatians 6:14. The first of the six four-line stanzas begins in the original German, "Wollt ihr wissen, was mein Preis?" and the responding refrain is "Jesu, der Gekreuzigte." It was published for the first time in 1741 (11 years after Schwedler's death) in *Hirschberger Gesangbuch*. The English translation by Benjamin H. Kennedy first appeared in the 1863 *Hymnologia Christiana, or Psalms and Hymns Selected and Arranged in the Order of the Christian Seasons*. Its first appearance in America was in 1869 in the Dutch Reformed *Hymns of the Church* and in Philip Schaff's *Christ in Song* (New York). Its first appearance in a Southern Baptist hymnal was in the *New Baptist Hymnal* (Nashville, 1926, No. 129).

HENDON appeared first in 1827 (some say 1823) in France in one of Henri A. C. Malan's several collections of his own texts and tunes. Hendon is a village in Middlesex, England, which Malan may once have visited. Lowell Mason arranged and published the tune in his *Carmina Sacra* (1841), its first appearance in America. Its first inclusion in a Southern Baptist hymnal was in the *Baptist Hymn and Praise Book* (Nashville, 1904, Nos. 48, 342). *S.W.G.*

At Calvary—See *Years I spent in vanity and pride*

At the Cross—See *Alas, and did my Savior bleed*

At the name of Jesus 198

Caroline Noel wrote this processional hymn for Ascension Day, which occurs 40 days after Easter in the church year. The hymn is based on Philippians 2:5-11. The present version omits three of the original seven stanzas. Noel's hymn first appeared in the author's collection *The Name of Jesus, and Other Verses for the Sick and Lonely* (1870). The first inclusion of this text in a Southern Baptist hymnal was *Baptist Hymnal* (Nashville, 1975, No. 363).

WYE VALLEY—See hymn 58, Like a river glorious.   *P.H.*

Away in a manger 103

This carol is by an unidentified 19th-century American, though its history has been clouded by a story that appeared with an early printing. Fact and fiction were separated by Richard S. Hill in "Not So Far Away in a Manger" (*MLA Notes*, Dec. 1945).

Stanzas one and two appeared anonymously in *Little Children's Book: For Schools and Families*, published in Philadelphia in 1885 for the General Council of the Evangelical Lutheran Church in North America. The tune provided was ST. KILDA, by J. E. Clark. In 1887, James R. Murray of Cincinnati printed the same stanzas with the present tune in *Dainty Songs for Little Lads and Lasses*. The confusion began with this publication, for Murray supplied the erroneous heading, "Luther's Cradle Hymn," with the note: "Composed by Martin Luther for his children, and still sung by German mothers to their little ones."

The third stanza, which first appeared in Charles H. Gabriel's *Gabriel's Vineyard Songs* (Louisville, 1892), is the work of yet another unknown writer. It has often been credited incorrectly to John Thomas McFarland.

MUELLER, the tune in *Dainty Songs*, is probably Murray's composition. It appeared there with the initials "J. R. M." The name comes from a misattribution to a Carl Mueller in *Worship and Song* (Boston, 1920). No such person has been identified; it is not the work of the well-known anthem composer. The tune is also known as AWAY IN A MANGER.

New Baptist Hymnal (Nashville, 1926, No. 92) was the first Southern Baptist hymnal to include this carol.   *P.A.R.*

Baptized in water 362

Michael Saward wrote this text in 1981 for *Hymns for Today's Church* (1982) to fill the void of baptismal hymns related to God's initiative in this event. In a letter to the author Saward relates: "I wrote the hymn having spent the day recording interviews for the Church of England's National 'Partners in Mission' Consultation 1981." The first draft of stanza two (line five) originally read "freed from the judgement" but was altered before publication "as a result of a comment that baptism was *first* a symbol of forgiveness." *The Baptist Hymnal* (1991) is the first Southern Baptist collection to include this hymn.

BUNESSAN—See hymn 48, Morning has broken.   *P.H.*

Be not dismayed 64

Civilla Durfee Martin (1869-1948), a native of Nova Scotia, wrote this hymn in 1904. She has supplied the following information:

"I was confined to a sick bed in a Bible school in Lestershire, New York. My husband was spending several weeks at the school, making a songbook for the president of the school. 'God Will Take Care of You' was written one Sunday afternoon while my husband went to a preaching appointment. When he returned I gave the words to him. He immediately sat down to his little Bilhorn organ and wrote the music. That evening he and two of the teachers sang the completed song. It was then printed in the songbook he was compiling for the school" (Reynolds, 1976, 41).

GOD CARES was composed in 1904 by Walter Stillman Martin for his wife's text, "Be not dismayed." This hymn of God's providential care was first published in *Songs of Redemption and Praise* (1905), which was compiled by John A. Davis, who was an evangelist and founder of the Practical Bible Training School, Lestershire, New York. The first Southern Baptist hymnal to contain this hymn was Coleman and Reynolds' *Kingdom Songs* (Dallas, 1921, No. 53), though Coleman had published it earlier in *The New Evangel* (Dallas, 1911, No. 8). *S.W.G.*

Be strong in the Lord 476

Linda Lee Johnson's text abounds in biblical imagery (Deuteronomy 31:1, 6, 7, 23; Joshua 1:6, 9, 18; Isaiah 40:31; Ephesians 6:11), and yet there is a simplicity achieved through the familiar symbols and the repetition of words and phrases. This Christian expression of a buoyant affirmation was written on an airplane on the way to her grandfather's funeral. It was one of her first texts. Both text and tune make their first appearance in a Southern Baptist collection in *The Baptist Hymnal* (1991).

STRENGTH, composed by Tom Fettke, is a straightforward, singable tune that complements the text. Both text and tune are in the gospel song tradition, using repeated sections to achieve an appropriate immediacy. *S.W.G.*

Be Thou my vision 60

The hymn had its roots in an Irish poem probably written in the eighth century. An English prose translation by Mary Byrne appeared in 1905 in Volume II of the Irish periodical *Erin*. Eleanor Hull published a versification of the prose translation in *Poembook of the Gael* (1912). Its first appearance in a hymnal was in the revised *Church Hymnary* (Edinburgh, 1927). *Baptist Hymnal* (Nashville, 1956, No. 62) is the first inclusion of this hymn in a Southern Baptist collection.

"SLANE is a traditional Irish air from Patrick W. Joyce's *Old Irish Folk Music and Songs* (1909), set to the text 'With my love on the road.' It was harmonized by David Evans and set to this text for the revised *Church Hymnary* (Edinburgh, 1927). Slane is a hill some ten miles from Tara in County Meath where Ireland's patron saint, Patrick (*c.* 389-461), lit the paschal fire on Easter eve, challenging King Loegaire" (Reynolds, 1976, 41). *D.B.*

Because He Lives—See *God sent His Son*

Because I have been given much 605

This text by Grace Noll Crowell was first published under the title "Because of Thy Great Bounty" in *Light of the Years* (New York, 1936), a collection of her poetry. Its first hymnal use was in *The New Church Hymnal* (New York, 1937), edited by H. Augustine Smith. The 1975 *Baptist Hymnal* (Nashville, No. 414) was the first Southern Baptist collection to include it.

SEMINARY was written for this text by Phillip Landgrave at the request of the 1975 Hymnal Committee. It was written at a time when the Landgrave family was considering building a new house. The text and its new tune became an expression of their commitment to use their new home for ministry to others. The tune was named by the composer for The Southern Baptist Theological Seminary, Louisville, Kentucky, where he teaches. *M.P.*

Behold the Lamb 233

Joyce Reba (Dottie) Rambo's text, copyrighted in 1979, draws from John 1:36 and the book of Revelation (13:8; 4:11; 5:12). The irregular metered text is set to her own tune. The first Southern Baptist hymnal to include it was *The Baptist Hymnal* (1991).

BEHOLD THE LAMB is the solo-song-like

tune which carries smoothly the irregular meter of the text.   *S.W.G.*

Believers all, we bear the name 399

This text by Milburn Price was written for a festival held at The Southern Baptist Theological Seminary in October, 1986, honoring Dr. Findley Edge, retired member of the faculty of the School of Christian Education in that institution. When the hymn was first sung for a seminary chapel service on October 27, 1986, it was introduced by its author as follows:

"The hymn which we sing at this time was written specifically for this occasion in honor of Findley Edge. The text incorporates three themes which have been prominent in his writings: the importance of continuing pilgrimage toward mature faith; the diversity of tasks of ministry to which persons are called; and the inclusiveness of the call to ministry, embracing male and female, clergy and laity, and persons of varying theological perspectives. The inclusive theme provides a unifying element to the entire text through the recurring phrase, 'Believers all,' which begins each stanza."

EDGE was also written by Milburn Price as a setting for the text of this hymn. In recognition of the occasion for which both text and tune were written, the tune was named for Findley Edge. As the tune was introduced at its first singing, "the musical setting for the text is intended to be sturdy, vigorous, reflecting the quality not only of Findley Edge's writings, but also of his own life and ministry."   *M.P.*

Beneath the cross of Jesus 291

Elizabeth Clephane wrote this hymn in 1868, and it was published posthumously in the *Family Treasury* magazine in 1872. The hymn's original five stanzas have been consistently reduced to three, owing to the Calvinistic theology of the second and third stanzas. Eight of her hymns were printed in the *Family Treasury* between 1872 and 1874. "Beneath the Cross of Jesus" was the first of these; "There were ninety and nine that safely lay," made famous by Ira D. Sankey, was the last. *The Modern Hymnal* (Dallas, 1926, No. 200) was the first Southern Baptist hymnal to include Clephane's hymn, although it was also published in *The New Baptist Hymnal* (Nashville, 1926, No. 110).

ST. CHRISTOPHER, named for the early Christian martyr, was written for this hymn by Frederick C. Maker and first appeared in the supplement to the *Bristol Tune Book* (1881).   *P.H.*

Bless His Holy Name—See *Bless the Lord, O my soul*

Bless that wonderful name 236

In a letter to Harry Eskew dated May 12, 1991, William Farley Smith of the Drew Theological Seminary faculty, a specialist in African-American sacred music, classified "Bless That Wonderful Name" as "a twentieth-century folk hymn utilizing quoted melodic elements from various very old slave songs." Smith further states that this song "appears to be a corruption rearranged to facilitate words not originally wedded to the melody." A traditional spiritual related to "Bless That Wonderful Name" is "Woke Up This Morning" (*Songs of Zion: Supplemental Worship Resource 12*. Nashville, 1981, No. 146). Both songs share very similar "response" phrases beginning in the third measure. The melody of the final phrase of "Bless That Wonderful Name" (No other name I know) is taken from a number of slave songs which end with the declamation, "Hallelujah!" A one-stanza version of "Bless That Wonderful Name" was published earlier in *Yes, Lord! Church of God in*

Christ Hymnal (Memphis and Nashville, 1982, No. 44).

WONDERFUL NAME is the tune name assigned by the committee for *The Baptist Hymnal* (1991).   *H.E.*

Bless the Lord, O my soul 22
Andraé Crouch wrote this song, based on Psalm 103:1, in 1973. The first hymnal to include it was *Hymns for the Family of God* (Nashville, 1976). Stanzas two and three were added in 1990 and first appear in *The Baptist Hymnal* (1991).

The tune, BLESS HIS HOLY NAME, differs slightly from the solo original and is also known as BLESS THE LORD.   *P.A.R.*

Blessed assurance, Jesus is mine! 334
This song was copyrighted by the composer of the tune, Mrs. Phoebe Palmer Knapp, in 1873, the year it was written by Fanny Crosby. Many of Fanny Crosby's hymnic themes were suggested by ministers wishing to have new songs on particular subjects. At other times, musicians would first compose tunes to which Crosby was asked to supply words. Such was the case with "Blessed Assurance."

The story goes, as related by Crosby herself in *Memories of Eighty Years* (London, 1906), that Mrs. Knapp played the tune in Fanny's hearing once or twice asking, "What does that melody say to you?" Fanny Crosby replied with the precise words of stanza one of the hymn.

It first appeared in John R. Sweney's *Gems of Praise* (Philadelphia, 1873) and was included subsequently in Ira D. Sankey's collections. Thereby it achieved immense popularity in Great Britain as well as in the United States and Canada. It has been used with effectiveness in the Billy Graham Crusades. In 1904 it appeared for the first time in two Baptist collections, *The Baptist Hymn and*

Praise Book (Nashville, 1904, No. 350) and Doane and Kirkpatrick's *Glorious Praise* (Louisville, No. 16).

ASSURANCE is the name assigned to this tune by the hymnal committee for *Baptist Hymnal* (1956).   *H.T.M.*

Blessed Be the Name—See *O for a thousand tonges to sing*

Blessed Redeemer—See *Up Calvary's mountain*

Blessed Savior, we adore Thee 204
"Blessed Savior, we adore Thee" was written by B. B. McKinney in 1942. It first appeared in the Sunday School periodical *The Teacher* (July, 1942). Its inclusion in a song collection was in *Look and Live Songs* (Nashville, 1945, No. 124). It achieved wide use among Southern Baptists when it was included in *Baptist Hymnal* (Nashville, 1956, No. 138).

GLORIOUS NAME is the name given B. B. McKinney's tune for this hymn in *Baptist Hymnal* (1956). There are similarities in the form and style of this tune with those of the French carol GLORIA ("Angels We Have Heard on High").   *H.T.M.*

Blessed be the God of Israel 79
This hymn is a paraphrase of Luke 1:68-79, the canticle of Zacharias (*Benedictus Dominus Deus Israel*). It was written by James Quinn for *New Hymns for All Seasons* (1982), which contains scriptural paraphrases for the Roman Catholic Mass. Like other hymns in the collection, it was paraphrased without rhyme to allow for greater scriptural fidelity. *The Baptist Hymnal* (1991) is the first Southern Baptist hymnal in which this text has appeared.

FOREST GREEN was arranged by Ralph Vaughan Williams from an English folksong, "The Ploughboy's Dream." The composer recorded this song at Forest Green, Surrey, England, in 1903. It was originally used as a setting for Phillips Brooks' hymn "O Little Town of Bethlehem" in *The English Hymnal* (1906).   *P.H.*

Blest be the tie that binds 387

This hymn of Christian fellowship was written by John Fawcett (1739-1817), an English Baptist minister. A lovely story is associated with the writing of this hymn. Duffield's version is as follows:

"It was in 1772, after a few years spent in pastoral work, that he was called to London to succeed the Rev. Dr. Gill. His farewell sermon had been preached near Wainsgate, in Yorkshire; six or seven wagons stood loaded with his furniture and books...but his loving people were not ready. They gathered about him, and 'men, women, and children clung around him and his family in perfect agony of soul.' Finally, overwhelmed with the sorrow of those they were leaving, Dr. Fawcett and his wife sat down on one of the packing-cases and wept bitterly. Looking up, Mrs. Fawcett said: 'Oh, John, John, I cannot bear this! I know not how to go!'

"'Nor I either,' said the good man; 'nor will we go. Unload the wagons, and put everything in the place where it was before.'...this hymn is said to have been written to commemorate the event" (73).

Other resources record Fawcett's decision to reject the call of the London church (and give up the badly-needed salary increase) in order to remain in Yorkshire, but there appears to be no convincing evidence that connects the hymn to the decision to remain with his congregation. Reynolds lists Josiah Miller's *Singers and Songs of the Church* (1869, 273) as the first publication to claim the hymn was connected with Fawcett's decision to stay in Wainsgate (1964, 25). The

original version of the hymn contained six stanzas and was published in Fawcett's *Hymns Adapted to the Circumstances of Public Worship* (Leeds, 1782). Stanzas five and six have been omitted.

This glorious hope revives
    Our courage by the way;
When each in expectation lives,
    And longs to see the day.

From sorrow, toil, and pain,
    And sin, we shall be free;
And perfect love and friendship reign
    Throughout eternity.

This Baptist hymn in all its six stanzas was included in Southern Baptists' first hymn collection, Manly's *The Baptist Psalmist* (Charleston, 1850, No. 1148).

DENNIS is the name (after a village in the Cape Cod area of Massachusetts) given by Lowell Mason to this tune which he arranged from one set to "O selig, selig, wer vor dir" in J. G. Nägeli's *Christliches Gesangburch* (1828).

The tune first appeared in *The Psaltery* (1845) edited by Mason and George J. Webb where it is set to Philip Doddridge's "How Gentle God's Commands."

Routley claims that, though the original idea came from the Swiss composer's collection, it is really Mason's composition since Nägeli's tune is hardly recognizable in DENNIS (1981, 123).

It appeared set to "Blest Be the Tie That Binds" as early as 1883 in *The Baptist Hymnal* (Philadelphia, 1883, No. 463).

The first Southern Baptist collection to include DENNIS with "Blest Be the Tie That Binds" was *The Baptist Hymn & Praise Book* (Nashville, 1904, No. 428).   *D.B.*

Break forth, O beauteous heavenly light 114

The first stanza of this text is a translation

by John Troutbeck of a stanza from a hymn by Johann Rist. Rist's hymn, "Ermuntre dich, mein schwacher Geist" ("Rouse yourself, my feeble spirit"), was based on Isaiah 9:2-7 and published in the first edition of his *Himmlische Lieder* (Lüne-burg, 1641). There it had 12 stanzas and appeared under the heading, "A Hymn of Praise on the Joyful Birth and Incarnation of our Lord and Savior Jesus Christ." "Break forth" is a translation of the ninth stanza, which begins "Brich an du schönes Morgenlicht." J. S. Bach used this stanza in the second cantata of his *Christmas Oratorio* (1734). When Troutbeck prepared an Eng-lish translation of that work for Novello, Ewer, and Company (London, *c.* 1873), he included this stanza.

The second stanza was written by Arthur Tozer Russell and published in his *Psalms and Hymns* (Cambridge, 1851).

ERMUNTRE DICH was composed for Rist's text by Johann Schop and appeared with it in *Himmlische Lieder*. It takes its name from the first line of the German hymn. The tune was originally in triple meter, but it was altered to 4/4 by Johann Crüger in *Praxis Pietatis Melica* (Berlin, 1647). The harmonization is based on that by J. S. Bach at number 12 in the *Christmas Oratorio*. The tune is sometimes called SCHOP.

The first hymnal by Southern Baptists to include this hymn was *The Baptist Hymnal* (1991).   *P.A.R.*

Break out, O Church of God 401

Written by Wesley L. Forbis in 1989, this hymn, in a classic style, offers a challenge to the contemporary church to cast off those traditions and concepts that hamper our ministry to a lost and suffering world. *The Baptist Hymnal* (1991) is the first hymn collection to publish this hymn.

ST. THOMAS—See hymn 354, I love Thy kingdom, Lord.   *D.B.*

Break Thou the bread of life 263

Mary A. Lathbury wrote the first two stanzas of this hymn at the request of Dr. John H. Vincent in the summer of 1877 at Lake Chautauqua in New York. Stanzas 3 and 4 in the present version were by Alexander Groves and these two stanzas first appeared in the *Wesleyan Methodist Magazine* (London, September, 1913).

The hymn was designed to be sung in connection with the Chautauqua Bible Study hour. Its focus is on the Scriptures and (in the added stanzas) on Jesus Christ who said, "I am the bread of life" (John 6:35). Its use on the occasion of the Lord's Supper could therefore be misunderstood.

The first two stanzas of this text and its tune first appeared in an official Southern Baptist collection in *Songs of Redemption* (Atlanta, 1920, No. 261) compiled by W. Plunkett Martin and James W. Jelks. However, it is found with four stanzas two years earlier in Robert H. Coleman's *The Popular Hymnal* (Dallas, 1918, No. 71).

BREAD OF LIFE was composed by William F. Sherwin in 1877 for Miss Lathbury's stanzas. Words and music were first published in *The Chautauqua Carols* (Chautauqua Sunday School Assembly, 1877).   *W.J.R.*

Breathe on Me—See *Holy Spirit, breathe on me*

Breathe on me, Breath of God 241

Edwin Hatch based the four-stanza hymn on the scriptural account of Jesus with His disciples: "And when he had said this, he breathed on them and saith unto them, 'Receive ye the Holy Ghost' " (John 20:22). Hatch first published the hymn in a privately printed pamphlet titled *Between Doubt and Prayer* (1878). The first hymnal inclusion was in Allon's *Congregational Psalmist Hymnal* (London, 1886). It was included in *The New*

Baptist Hymnal (Nashville, 1926, No. 146).

TRENTHAM—See hymn 278, Make me a captive, Lord. *W.J.R.*

Brethren, we have met to worship 379

This is one of the few examples of an early 19th-century campmeeting text to be found in modern hymnals. The first known printing of the text was in the *Spiritual Songster* (Frederick-Town , 1819) where it was one of five hymns attributed to "the late Rev. George Atkins." In this source, the hymn contained five stanzas; the original third stanza read as follows:

> Brethren there are poor backsliders,
> Who were once near heaven's door,
> But they have betray'd the Saviour,
> And are worse than e'er before;
> Yet the Saviour offers pardon,
> If they will repent the wound;
> Brethren pray, and Holy Manna
> Will be shower'd all around.

HOLY MANNA received its initial printing in William Moore's *Columbian Harmony* (Cincinnati, 1825), one of the many oblong shape-note tunebooks published by southern compilers before the Civil War. Nineteen tunes—including this one—were credited to "Moore" in the collection. However, HOLY MANNA has several earmarks of a melody originating in oral tradition, including its use of a pentatonic scale and its similarity to other folk hymns and secular folk songs. William Moore's part in composing this tune was probably limited to bringing together several preexisting fragments from other tunes to form a new melody.

"Brethren, We Have Met to Worship" and HOLY MANNA have been used for over 100 years to open the *Southern Harmony* "Big Singing" held annually in Benton, Kentucky, on the fourth Sunday in May.

This hymn and tune first entered an "official" Southern Baptist hymnal in *The Broad-*

man Hymnal (Nashville, 1940, No. 198). However it is to be found as early as 1918 in Baptist Robert H. Coleman's *The Popular Hymnal* (Dallas, 1918, No. 107). *D.M.*

Bring ye all the tithes 616

Lida Shivers Leech wrote the words and music in 1923 and Charles H. Gabriel copyrighted them in that same year. The text is based on Malachi 3:10. In 1924 the text and tune appeared in Robert H. Coleman's *Harvest Hymns* and, in 1926, in Coleman's *The Modern Hymnal* with the indication that it was the property of Coleman. The text and tune first appeared in a Southern Baptist hymnal in *The Broadman Hymnal* (Nashville, 1940, No. 393).

GIVING is the name which the composer suggested for the tune. *S.W.G.*

Bring your sin to Him and confess 319

This hymn of four-line stanzas with refrain was written by Ralph Parks and makes its first appearance in *The Baptist Hymnal* (1991).

DESMOND (KUM BA YAH) is a folk melody that seems to have originated in the offshore islands of South Carolina. It was taken back to Africa by slaves returning to their homeland where missionaries heard it and brought it back to America as an African folk song. The version in *The Baptist Hymnal* (1991) was made by Ralph Parks. In *The United Methodist Hymnal* (1989), the tune was named DESMOND by William Farley Smith for Desmond Tutu, Anglican Archbishop of Capetown and anti-apartheid activist in South Africa. *The Baptist Hymnal* (1991) is the first Southern Baptist standard collection to include this song. *W.J.R.*

Built on the Rock 351

This is regarded as Grundtvig's greatest hymn, "Kirken den er et gammelt hus" (literally, "The church is an old house"), first published in the author's *Sang-Värk til den Danske Kirke* ("Song-Work for the Danish Church," Copenhagen, 1837). It was translated into English by the Norwegian-American hymnologist and Lutheran pastor, Carl Doving (1867-1937), in 1909, and published in *The Lutheran Hymnary* (1913). For the 1958 *Service Book and Hymnal* (compiled for Lutheran bodies in the United States) Fred C. M. Hansen, a Danish-American Lutheran pastor, revised Doving's seven stanzas into five stanzas with some alterations. Stanzas 1, 2, and 3 of Hansen's version are used in both *Baptist Hymnal* (1975) and *The Baptist Hymnal* (1991). The two omitted stanzas begin with the lines "Yet in this house, an earthly frame" and "Through all the passing year, O Lord." Grundvig's hymn is rich in scriptural allusions, including Matthew 16:18, 1 Corinthians 3:16, 1 Corinthians 10:4, and Matthew 18:20.

KIRKEN (also called KIRKEN DEN ER ET GAMMELT HUS), which was composed by Ludwig M. Lindeman for Grundtvig's text, was first published in W. A. Wexel's *Christelige Psalmer* (Oslo, 1840). This tune, Lindeman's first, is in the Dorian mode and the traditional German Barform (AAB). This majestic tune has the character of a chorale and has often been equated to Luther's EIN' FESTE BURG.   *H.E.*

Burn in me, Fire of God 496

The text was written by the Canadian, Margaret Clarkson, who comments in the collection of her hymns, *A Singing Heart* (Carol Stream, 1987, 26): "These verses were written in Kirkland Lake, Ontario in 1938. They were included in *Clear Shining After Rain* in 1962 and adapted as a hymn in 1986. While they can be sung to TRENTHAM, a new tune would enhance their usefulness."

The Bible verse given by Clarkson with this hymn is Hebrews 12:29: "Our God is a consuming fire." *The Baptist Hymnal* (1991) is the first Southern Baptist hymnal to include this text.

TRENTHAM—See hymn 278, Make me a captive, Lord.   *H.E.*

Carols sing 90

This new carol, and its tune, BETHLEHEM SONG, was created by the husband-wife team of Martha and Paul Puckett in the course of preparing for an annual Christmas concert at the First Baptist Church of Bartow, Florida, where they served as church musicians for 30 years.

Two days before the program scheduled for Christmas Eve, 1987, Martha was sitting at the keyboard recalling the story behind the composing of "Silent Night" and thinking how great it would be to have a new carol like that for Paul to sing at the Christmas concert. Certainly, Bartow, Florida had no frigid weather like that of Oberndorf, Austria in the winter of 1818, and the First Baptist Church organ was in good condition, but a similar inspiration prevailed and as Martha's fingers moved over the keys in improvisation, the simple tune was born together with its first stanza of text. Paul's poetic gifts were then used to add the other two stanzas. "Carols Sing" was first sung on that Christmas Eve in 1987 and subsequently printed in the Puckett's Christmas letter to friends.

The utter artlessness of its words and music qualifies "Carols Sing" to be a welcome addition to a venerable carol tradition. It was first made generally known by its inclusion in *The Baptist Hymnal* (1991).   *H.T.M.*

Child in the manger 105

This text is Lachlan Macbean's translation of Mary Macdonald's Gaelic poem "The Child of Agh" (which means child of happiness, good fortune, power, or wonder). It was first published in Macbean's *Songs and Hymns of the Gael* (Edinburgh, 1888). Its first appearance in a hymn collection published in the United States was in *Christian Praise* (Chicago, 1957). *Baptist Hymnal* (Nashville, 1975, No. 84) was the first Southern Baptist hymnal to include it.

BUNESSAN—See hymn 48, Morning has broken.   *M.P.*

Children of God 479

Anderson T. Dailey wrote both the text and tune (with the same name) for this hymn. As related in correspondence to Harry Eskew, CHILDREN OF GOD was written in the basement of his church while he waited for the Junior Choir to come for rehearsal. He needed a number that would appeal to them using solo voices.

This hymn was privately published in Indianapolis by Dailey in 1972 in *Gospel Songs for Children's Choirs*. Its first appearance in a hymnal was in *The New National Baptist Hymnal* (Nashville, 1977, No. 468). *The Baptist Hymnal* (1991) marks the first appearance of this hymn in a Southern Baptist collection.   *H.E.*

Children of the heavenly Father 55

This hymn text by Caroline V. Sandell-Berg was written while she was in her teens and was first published in her *Andeliga Daggdropper* (1855). Ernst William Olson translated it from Swedish to English for use in *The Hymnal* (Rock Island, 1925), published for the Evangelical Lutheran Augustana Synod. Stanzas 1, 2, 3, and 6 from that translation are included in this hymnal. This text first appeared in a Southern Baptist hymnal in *Christian Praise* (Nashville, 1964, No. 248).

TRYGGARE KAN INGEN VARA was first used with the original Swedish version of the Sandell-Berg text in Fredrik Engelke's *Lofs*

ångeroch andeliga wisor (1873). The origin of this tune, which became popular in Sweden during the last half of the 19th century, is uncertain. One theory suggests that it came to Sweden from England with the pietistic revivalism of the second half of the century. Another perspective considers it to be a Scandinavian folksong with German origins. Its first publication in America was in the *Hemlåndssanger* (1890), published by the Evangelical Lutheran Augustana Synod. When this tune appeared with the "Children of the Heavenly Father" text in the Southern Baptist hymnal *Christian Praise*, it was designated AHNFELT, after Oskar Ahnfelt, a prominent musician and arranger of Swedish songs.   *M.P.*

Christ is alive! 173

"Christ Is Alive" was first sung by the congregation of Hockley Congregational Church, Essex, England, on Easter Sunday, 1968, ten days after the assassination of Dr. Martin Luther King. Brian Wren, the author and minister of the church at the time, sought in the hymn to reflect on that tragic event in the light of the living Christ and to reinterpret the biblical imagery of Christ "reigning at the right hand of God." He wanted to balance the idea of Christ's reigning above and its implication of remoteness and lack of involvement with the truths of the third and fourth stanzas.

The hymn was first published in *New Church Praise* (Edinburgh, 1975, No. 9) with the original form of the last stanza, as follows:

Christ is alive! Ascendent Lord,
   He rules the world his Father made
Till, in the end, his love adored
   Shall be to every man displayed.

Wren rewrote this stanza in 1978. It appeared in *Mainly Hymns* (Leeds, 1980, No. 17) as follows:

Christ is alive! His Spirit burns
  Through this, and every future age,
Till all creation lives and learns
  His joy, his justice, love and praise.

The Baptist Hymnal (1991), the first Southern Baptist collection to include the hymn, has yet a third version of the last stanza as well as some alterations of Wren's original lines in stanzas one, two, and four.

TRURO—See hymn 128, Lift up your heads. *H.T.M.*

Christ is made the sure foundation 356

This anonymous hymn is one of two translated from the Latin hymn beginning "Urbs beata Hierusalem," which appears in the oldest extant manuscript of hymns, dating from the 9th century. It is thought to be several centuries older, possibly as early as the 6th century. John Mason Neale, who translated the Latin to English in his *Medieval Hymns and Sequences* (1851), regarded it as an eighth century hymn.

The first stanza, translated "Blessed city, heavenly Salem," appears as a picture of the heavenly Jerusalem in many hymnals. The present hymn consists of stanzas 5, 7, 8, and 9 of Neale's translation. Neale's "Consubstantial, co-eternal" in the doxological final stanza have been altered to "One in might and one in glory." In medieval manuscripts this hymn is the proper office hymn for the dedication of a church. The text evolved over several centuries in the Latin, and its original 15.15.15. meter was changed in translation by Neale to 8.7.8.7.8.7. Neale's translation in his *The Hymnal Noted* (1851) was freely altered for *Hymns Ancient and Modern* (1861). This hymn is appropriate not only for the dedication of a church building, but is also fitting for any sermon dealing with the church.

UNSER HERRSCHER (also NEANDER, MUNICH,

or EPHESUS) is believed to have been composed by Joachim Neander for his hymn, "Unser Herrscher, unser König" (Our Ruler, Our King), first published together in his *A und Ω, Glaub- und Liebesübung* (Bremen, Germany, 1680). In the original version of this tune, the last line shifted to 6/4 time. UNSER HERRSCHER was altered to its present form in Freylinghausen's 1704 *Gesangbuch*. The first Southern Baptist collection to include "Christ Is Made the Sure Foundation" is *The Baptist Hymnal* (1991). *H.E.*

Christ is risen 167

"Christ Is Risen" is Fred Kaan's translation of "Christo vive" written by Argentinian Nicolás Martiéz in 1960. It is one of several translations specially prepared by Kaan in 1972 for the international ecumenical hymnal, *Cantate Domino* (Kassel, 1973, No. 89). In all three stanzas Kaan has been careful to be true to Martiéz' original. "Christ Is Risen" was included in *The Hymn Texts of Fred Kaan* (Carol Stream, 1985, No. 13) where the final word of line four in the first stanza is "laid," thus rhyming with line two "unafraid." *The Baptist Hymnal* (1991) is the first Southern Baptist collection to include the hymn.

CENTRAL is the name given the tune to "Christ Is Risen" composed by Pablo D. Sosa in Buenos Aires, Argentina, in 1960. It was first published with its original Spanish text in *Cantico Nuevo* (Buenos Aires, 1962). The arrangement by Mark Blankenship in *The Baptist Hymnal* (1991) contains slight rhythmic alterations from Sosa's original. *H.T.M.*

Christ Receiveth Sinful Men—See *Sinners Jesus will receive*

Christ the Lord is risen today 159

Charles Wesley (1707-88) composed over

6,500 hymns representing the broad spectrum of Christian doctrines. His Easter hymn, "Christ the Lord Is Risen Today," consisted originally of 11 four-line stanzas and was entitled "Hymn for Easter Day." It first appeared in *Hymns and Sacred Poems* (1739). The present version consists of stanzas 1, 4, the first two lines of stanza 2, the last two lines of stanza 3, and stanza 5 of the original. According to Erik Routley, it is possible that Martin Madan, an Anglican vicar and follower of the Wesleys, added the "Alleluias" (1952, 158).

This hymn first appeared in a Southern Baptist hymnal in *Baptist Hymn and Praise Book* (Nashville, 1904, No. 139).

EASTER HYMN appeared anonymously in *Lyra Davidica* (London, 1708) and the present form is derived from John Arnold's *Compleat Psalmodist* (London, 1741). John Wesley called the tune SALISBURY TUNE and included it in his *Foundery Collection* (London, 1742). *New Baptist Hymnal* (Nashville, 1926, No. 120) was the first Southern Baptist hymnal to contain this tune, although there it is called ANGLIA.   *S.W.G.*

Christ was born in a distant land 566

Gene Bartlett wrote both the words and music in 1968 on a commission from the Foreign Mission Board of the Southern Baptist Convention to be sung at the convention's annual meeting in Houston, Texas. Bartlett related to William J. Reynolds that he wrote the text during a "very boring meeting" (1976, 48).

The tune name RHEA was given in honor of Claude H. Rhea, Jr., who as a member of the Foreign Mission Board, communicated the request to Bartlett. The hymn was first published in the Foreign Mission Board's annual report to the convention in 1968 and was later included in the *Baptist Hymnal* (Nashville, 1975, No. 48).   *P.H.*

Christ, we do all adore Thee 647

This work is the final selection in *The Seven Last Words of Christ*, a cantata by the French composer, Theodore Dubois. The translation of the Latin text, "Adoramus te, Christe," was made by Theodore Baker. His translation has been popularized in this country by its use with the G. Schirmer edition of the cantata.

ADORE THEE is the name that has been given to the tune by the committee for *The Baptist Hymnal* (1991), the first Southern Baptist collection to include it.   *D.B.*

Christian hearts, in love united 378

This hymn was written in 1725 by Nicolaus Ludwig von Zinzendorf, and it is said to have been the result of the healing of strife in the Brethren's unity by common love to the Savior. It was published that same year in *Die letzten Reden unsers Herrn und Heylandes Jesu Christi vor seinem Creutzes-Tode* in Frankfurt and Leipzig.

This work contains a poetic version of John 14-17, Jesus' farewell discourse. Each of the four chapters is presented in a series of eight-line stanzas—chapter 14 in 43 stanzas, chapter 15 in 83 stanzas, chapter 16 in 81 stanzas, and chapter 17 in 113 stanzas! Stanzas 53-59 of chapter 15 were included in the hymnal, *Sammlung geist-und lieblicher Lieder* (1725). In the next few years several hymnals included various forms of the text. The English translation by Frederick W. Foster appeared in the *Moravian Hymn Book* (London, 1789), with the first line being, "Flock of Jesus, be united." The 1886 edition of that hymnbook altered the first line to "Christian hearts, in love united." The *Baptist Hymnal* (Nashville, 1975, No. 253) was the first Southern Baptist hymnal to include the hymn.

CASSELL, though sometimes attributed to Johann Thommen, is probably an anonymous tune from a Moravian source in Her-rnhut around the year 1735. Ludwig Erk , a German editor of folk songs, suggests that it has its origin in a secular source, perhaps *Sollen nun die grünen Jahre*. It was first published in Johann Thommen's *Erbaulicher Musicalischer Christen-Schatz* (Basel, 1745). In its present form, it first appeared in Parr, *Church of England Psalmody* (1889). *Baptist Hymnal* (Nashville, 1975, No. 253) was the first Southern Baptist hymnal to include this tune. *S.W.G.*

Christmas has its cradle 152

In a letter to the writer, Rae Whitney reports she wrote this text about 1980 (copyrighted 1985) on a favorite theme, the tying together of Easter and Christmas. "Christmas," she writes, "would have little meaning if it weren't for Easter."

Whitney's use of repetition underscores the relationship of the two great seasons of the Christian year. Each stanza begins "Christmas has its cradle" and, although in slightly differing forms, the phrase returns in each seventh line. "Easter" appears in the eighth line of each stanza.

PETHEL is the name given to the tune Stan Pethel was asked to write for this text. It bears a 1986 copyright. In a letter to Don Brown (Oct. 4, 1990), Pethel wrote: "This text struck me with its linking the events of Christ's birth and crucifixion. I tried to reflect this in the music with the shifts from major to minor and the use of the universal interval of the fifth."

Rae Whitney wrote, "He has caught beautifully the mood of my text." *D.B.*

Close to Thee—See *Thou, my everlasting portion*

Come, all Christians, be committed 604

Eva B. Lloyd wrote the hymn in 1963 to fit John Zundel's tune BEECHER. Mrs. Lloyd submitted it for the 1966 Southern Baptist Hymn Writing Competition sponsored by the Church Music Department in Nashville, and it was judged the winning hymn. The hymn was published with the tune BEACH SPRING in a pamphlet, *Eight New Christian Service Hymns* (Nashville, 1966), and then in the periodical *The Church Musician* (August 1967). The first hymnal inclusion was in *Baptist Hymnal* (Nashville, 1975, No. 362). For a fuller discussion of the hymn, see "Come, All Christians, Be Committed," by David W. Music, *The Church Musician* (October 1986, pp. 14-16). The difficulty of the exclusive language using "man" and "brother" in stanza three has been resolved in *The Baptist Hymnal* (1991) with this alteration:

God's command to love each other
Is required of ev'ry one.
Showing mercy to each other
Mirrors His redeeming Son.

BEACH SPRING, in duple meter and set to "Come, Ye Sinners, Poor and Needy," appears in *The Sacred Harp* (1844, No. 81), credited to B. F. White. White named the tune for a Baptist church in Harris County, Georgia (constituted in 1832) located near two beech trees at a spring. The Beech Spring Baptist Church still exists near Pine Mountain, Georgia. White's misspelling of the name "Beach Spring" has been retained in all editions of *The Sacred Harp*. James H. Wood's harmonization is taken from his choral arrangement, published in 1958 by Broadman Press. Wood, then on the faculty of The Southern Baptist Theological Seminary, Louisville, Kentucky, made the choral arrangement during the Billy Graham Crusade in Louisville. He has commented:

"I had just acquired a copy of the *Sacred*

Harp and fell upon this lovely melody which, it seemed to me, was the most appropriate setting of "Come, ye sinners" I had seen. The spirit of Dr. Graham's meetings certainly had something to do with the attraction of both the text and melody."

Wood's SATB choral arrangement appeared in *The Church Musician* (May, 1958). Wood's hymn tune version first appeared in a Southern Baptist hymnal in *Christian Praise* (Nashville, 1964, No. 224).   *W.J.R.*

Come, Christians, join to sing 231

Christian H. Bateman wrote this hymn and published it in *The Sacred Song Book,* a children's hymnal which he edited in 1843. It was in five stanzas and had the first line, "Come, children, join to sing." In a revision of the book, *Melodies for Sabbath Schools and Families* (1854), he reduced it to the present three stanzas. According to Julian's *Dictionary of Hymnology,* Bateman's hymn is a rewriting of "Join now in praise, and sing," written in 1836 by W. E. Hickson. With the change by an unknown editor from "children" to "Christians," this text became widely used by all ages. Its first appearance in a Southern Baptist hymnal was in *Christian Praise* (Nashville, 1964, No. 55).

MADRID is a tune of unknown origin which has appeared in many versions. Benjamin Carr published a piano arrangement in two different collections in 1825. In the following year, he issued a choral arrangement. In these, he identified the tune as a "Spanish hymn" or "an ancient Spanish melody." Another form of this tune that omits the repeat of the first four measures and divides note values to accommodate a 7.7.7.7.7.7. text is called SPANISH HYMN. The present harmonization of MADRID was made by David Evans for the Revised Edition of *The Church Hymnary* (London, 1927). *P.A.R.*

Come, every soul by sin oppressed 317

John Stockton, who wrote both text and tune, included this item in *Salvation Melodies, No. 1* (Philadelphia, 1874). According to the *Dictionary of American Hymnology,* it had appeared as early as 1869 in Phoebe Palmer (Mrs. J. F.) Knapp's *Notes of Joy for the Sabbath School* (New York). This would account for Ira Sankey's use of it in meetings in London in 1873, before the publication of Stockton's book.

Sankey altered the refrain from the original "Come to Jesus" to "Only trust him." He often substituted various phrases according to the mood of the service. In *Crowning Glory, No. 2* (Chicago, 1891), the following all appear: (1) Only trust him; (2) Come to Jesus; (3) Don't reject him; (4) I will trust him. Stockton's fifth stanza is omitted:

O Jesus, blessed Jesus, dear,
    I'm coming now to thee;
Since thou hast made the way so clear
    And full salvation free.

STOCKTON, the name of the author-composer, was applied to the tune as early as *The Methodist Hymnal* of 1932. It is also known as MINERVA and ONLY TRUST HIM.

This gospel song entered Southern Baptist hymnody in *The Baptist Hymn and Praise Book* (Nashville, 1904, No. 231).   *P.A.R.*

Come, Holy Spirit 239

Marian Wood Chaplin (Pille) wrote these words and this tune following the death of her first husband, Robert M. Chaplin, in 1978. The second word in the first and last lines of stanza one was originally "gentle," but this was altered to "Holy" for *The Baptist Hymnal* (1991).

The hymn was first published in an SATB choral octavo arrangement by Jean Williams Culpepper (Broadman, 1982). *The Baptist Hymnal* (1991) marks its first hymnal appearance.

CHAPLIN was the tune name assigned in memory of the composer's husband. *D.M.*

Come, Holy Spirit, Dove divine 364

This hymn is composed of stanzas 7, 4, 5, and 6 from "Our Saviour Bowed Beneath the Wave," a seven-stanza text written in Burma about 1829 by Adoniram Judson. The first hymnal to include this was the second edition of Thomas B. Ripley's *A Selection of Hymns* (Bangor, Maine, 1831), under the heading "Hymn written by Mr. Judson, Missionary; and sung at the baptism of several soldiers, at Maulmein, British Pegu." Winchell's *Collection* (Boston, 1832) and Babcock's *Manual of Christian Psalmody* (Boston, 1832; a Baptist edition of Mason and Greene's *Church Psalmody*) included the present excerpt of the hymn as well as a three-stanza cento with the original first line.

The present version of the hymn contains many alterations. Judson's fifth (now third) stanza read:

We plunge beneath the mystic flood.

O plunge us in thy cleansing blood;

We die to sin, and seek a grave

With thee, beneath the yielding wave.

His original sixth (now fourth) stanza began "And as we rise with thee to live" and concluded "The breath of life, the fire of love!" Further, Ripley gave the second line of the seventh (now first) stanza as "On us with beams of mercy shine." The pronouns for God were modernized for *The Baptist Hymnal* (1991).

This hymn was included in *The Baptist Psalmody* (Charleston, 1850, No. 906), Southern Baptists' first hymnal, as was "Our Savior Bowed Beneath the Wave" (No. 892).

MARYTON was composed by H. Percy Smith for John Keble's "Sun of My Soul, Thou Savior Dear." It was first printed in Sullivan's *Church Hymns with Tunes* (London, 1874). *P.A.R.*

Come, let us reason 313

The words and music of this song, COME, LET US REASON, were written by Ken Medema and copyrighted in 1972. The text is based on Isaiah 1:18. The arrangement of the tune in *The Baptist Hymnal* (1991) was the work of David Allen and first appeared in *The Hymnal for Worship & Celebration* (Word Music, 1986, No. 591). *The Baptist Hymnal* (1991) is the first Southern Baptist collection to include this song. *D.M.*

Come, Thou Almighty King 247

As late as the mid-19th century, English hymnal compilers occasionally failed to credit the Wesleys for the hymns they wrote. Benson reports "there was a common ignorance concerning Charles Wesley and his work" (261). In the October 1849 issue of the *Christian Remembrancer*, John Mason Neale attributed the authorship of "Hark! The Herald Angels Sing" to Doddridge.

However, in the case of "Come, Thou Almighty King," the reverse is true, for Charles Wesley has often been cited as the author, despite the lack of proper evidence. The Methodist hymnals of 1878, 1889, and 1905 (the latter one with a question mark) indicated Charles Wesley as the author. Evidently this occurred because the hymn and six stanzas of Wesley's "Jesus, Let Thy Pitying Eye" were bound together in the British Museum's copies of the 1757, 1759, and 1760 editions of Whitefield's *Collection of Hymns for Social Worship* (London, 1753). There is no convincing proof Wesley wrote the hymn. English Methodists have not included the work in their collections.

Samuel Duffield reports the hymn first appeared around 19 years after the 1745 publication of the British national song, "God Save the King," in the *Gentleman's Magazine*. For many years "Come, Thou Almighty King" was sung to that tune which survives in our hymnals as AMERICA. Duffield also relates the story of British troops' interrupting a worship service on Long Island during the American Revolution and ordering the congregation to sing "God Save the King." They complied, but substituted the words for "Come, Thou Almighty King" (113-14).

This hymn in five stanzas is found in the first "official" Southern Baptist collection, *The Baptist Psalmody* (Charleston, 1850, No. 130).

ITALIAN HYMN was not the only tune Felice de Giardini contributed to Martin Madan's *The Collection of Psalm and Hymn Tunes Sung at the Chapel of the Lock Hospital* (London, 1769), but it is the only one that remains in use. It first appeared in three-part harmony with the melody in the middle voice. The original version may be found in R. G. McCutchan's *Our Hymnody: A Manual of the Methodist Hymnal* (New York, 1937). The tune has been given other names such as: TRINITY, MOSCOW, HERMON, FLORENCE, and GIARDINI'S. The composer died in Moscow, a fact explaining the use of one of the designations. Giardini was known in England as "the Italian," thus its present designation. There is no known explanation for the HERMON and FLORENCE names.

This tune first appeared in a Southern Baptist collection in *The Casket* (Charleston, 1855, p. 149) where the melody is in the tenor part after the manner of the tunebooks of the day.   *D.B.*

Come, Thou Fount of every blessing 15, 18

Robert Robinson wrote this hymn in 1758. The original, in four stanzas of eight lines, was printed the following year in *A Collection of Hymns, Used by the Church of Christ in Angel Alley, Bishopsgate*. In *Psalms and Hymns* (London, 1760), Martin Madan

omitted the fourth stanza which began, "Oh! that day when free from sinning," putting the hymn in its usual form. As early as 1790 the text appeared in two books published in the United States. One of these was *A Selection of Psalms and Hymns . . .*, compiled by Samuel Jones and Burgis Allison for the Philadelphia Baptist Association. It is this version of the text that is set to NETTLETON.

In the folk traditions that formed the background of the shaped-note tune books, standard English hymn texts were sung, often in fragmentary form, to a variety of tunes. "Come, Thou Fount" is one of the texts that were treated in this way. Another aspect of this pattern was the addition of simple refrains, which were probably borrowed from oral tradition. These refrains may have originated with a particular text, but then "traveled" to be associated with other, often unrelated, words. Such appears to be the case in the setting to WARRENTON. This uses only the first half of Robinson's three stanzas in juxtaposition to the refrain:

I am bound for the kingdom,
    Will you go to glory with me?
Hallelujah, praise the Lord.

This combination dates from *The Sacred Harp* (Philadelphia, 1844), which was compiled by Baptists B. F. White and E. J. King. William J. Reynolds, in *Companion to Baptist Hymnal* (Nashville, 1976), gives an account of the history of this material.

"Come, Thou Fount of Every Blessing" has appeared in Southern Baptist books since the denomination's first hymnal, *The Baptist Psalmody* (Charleston, 1850, No. 578).

NETTLETON was first printed in John Wyeth's *Repository of Sacred Music, Part Second* (Harrisburg, 1813), where it set "Come, thou Fount." There it was called HALLELUJAH and differed from the present version in rhythm and melody. Wyeth listed it as a new tune, but did not identify the composer. The tune's present name derives from an incorrect attribution to Asahel Nettleton, an evangelist who compiled *Village Hymns* in 1824. GOOD SHEPHERD is another name by which it is known.

WARRENTON is a folk tune which appeared with this text in *The Sacred Harp*, as noted above. This arrangement of the tune first appeared in *Songs of Salvation* (Nashville, 1956), where it was attributed to John Drakestone.   *P.A.R.*

Come, Thou long-expected Jesus 77

Charles Wesley's fine Advent hymn appeared in the little book, *Hymns for the Nativity of Our Lord* (1744). Because it was not included in the 1780 *Collection of Hymns for the Use of the People Called Methodists*, it disappeared from English Wesleyan use until the revised edition of 1875. It first appeared in a Southern Baptist hymnal in *Baptist Hymnal* (Nashville, 1956, No. 70) where the first word is "Hail," rather than "Come." It was also set to the HARWELL tune. In *Baptist Hymnal* (Nashville, 1975, No. 79) and *The Baptist Hymnal* (1991), the first word is "Come," and the HYFRYDOL tune is used.

HYFRYDOL—See hymn 36, Praise the Lord! Ye heavens, adore Him.   *H.T.M., S.W.G.*

Come, we that love the Lord 524, 525

Isaac Watts' short meter hymn "Come, we that love the Lord" first appeared in his *Hymns and Sacred Songs* (1707) in 10 four-line stanzas entitled "Heavenly Joy on Earth." The text of the refrain was added by Robert Lowry when he composed the tune MARCHING TO ZION (hymn 524) in 1867. It first appeared in *Silver Spray* (1868), a collection of Sunday School songs.   *W.J.R.*

George Sampson in *The Century of Divine Songs* referred to this hymn as "that lively quickstep for happy Christians!"

Watts' text in six stanzas appeared in Southern Baptists' first "official" collection, *The Baptist Psalmody* (Charleston, 1850, No. 622). The two stanzas not currently included are:

> The sorrows of the mind
> Be banished from the place;
> Religion never was designed
> To make our pleasures less.

> There we shall see his face,
> And never, never sin;
> There, from the rivers of his grace,
> Drink endless pleasures in.

The four present stanzas with Robert Lowry's tune first appeared together in a Southern Baptist hymnal in *The Baptist Hymn and Praise Book* (Nashville, 1904, No. 17).

FESTAL SONG (hymn 525)—See hymn 83, Arise, your light is come.   *D.B.*

Come, ye disconsolate 67

The first two stanzas of this hymn, in their original form, were published in *Sacred Songs* (1816) by the author (Thomas Moore) under the title "Relief in Prayer." Thomas Hastings made several revisions when the hymn was included in Hastings' and Lowell Mason's *Spiritual Songs for Social Worship* (Boston, 1831). Changes were made in the second line of the first stanza and the second and third lines of stanza two. A new third stanza was added. This revised text appeared in the first Southern Baptist hymnal, *The Baptist Psalmody* (Charleston, 1850, No. 348).

CONSOLATOR was first published in an arrangement for solo voice in Samuel Webbe's *Collection of Motetts or Antiphons* (London, 1792). Thomas Moore attributed to this tune the inspiration for his writing the text to "Come, ye disconsolate." Text and tune were published together in *Spiritual Songs for Social Worship* (1831).   *M.P.*

Come, ye sinners, poor and needy 323

This text by Joseph Hart was first published in his *Hymns Composed on Various Subjects* (London, 1759), as "Come, and Welcome to Jesus Christ." Hart's original first line was "Come, ye, sinners, poor and wretched," and his hymn (according to Julian) received more than 20 alterations, most of them made in collections of Con-yers (1774) and Toplady (1776). This hymn consisted of seven stanzas of six lines each with no refrain. The present cento comprises the first four lines of stanzas 1, 2, 4, and 3, with only stanza 3 (present stanza 4) being an unaltered selection from Hart's original.

Hart's hymn was published in the American colonies as early as 1774 in Samuel Occum's *A Choice Collection of Hymns and Spiritual Songs* (New London, CT). A refrain was added to this hymn as early as *Hymns and Spiritual Songs for the Use of Christians* (2nd ed., Baltimore, 1802):

Turn to the Lord and seek salvation,
 Sound the praise of his dear name;
Glory, honor and salvation,
 Christ the Lord's come to reign.

The present refrain modified to, "I will arise and go to meet him," appeared in Methodist compiler Steth Mead's *A General Selection of the Newest and Most Admired Hymns and Spiritual Songs Now in Use* (Richmond, 1807), there associated with "Come, thou fount of every blessing."

The tune RESTORATION is a pentatonic early American folk melody in the Aeolian mode. It seems to have first appeared in print in 1835 in the first edition of William Walker's *Southern Harmony* (Spartanburg, p. 5) where it is set to the text "Mercy, O thou son of David." George Pullen Jackson, in his *Spiritual Folk-Songs of Early America* (pp. 232-33) cites several early American folk hymn melodies and secular folk melodies that are closely related to this tune.   *H.E.*

Come, ye thankful people, come 637

This hymn was written in 1844 by Henry Alford for the English Harvest Festival, a celebration similar in some ways to the American Thanksgiving. First published in the author's *Psalms and Hymns* (London, 1844), it was revised by him in *Poetical Works* (4th ed., London, 1865) and again in *The Year of Praise* (London, 1867). Another revision, of which Alford disapproved, was made for *Hymns Ancient and Modern* (London, 1861). The present version draws from each of these, but most closely resembles the poet's 1865 revision. Though based on the imagery of the agricultural harvest, the subject of this hymn is the final judgment. It alludes to Matthew 13:24-30, 36-43, and Mark 4:26-29.

ST. GEORGE'S WINDSOR was composed by George J. Elvey to set James Montgomery's "Hark, the Song of Jubilee" in Edward H. Thorne's *Selection of Psalm and Hymn Tunes* (London, 1858). It is named for St. George's Chapel at Windsor castle, where Elvey served the English royal family for 47 years. The tune was first matched with Alford's text in the original edition of *Hymns Ancient and Modern* (1861).

The first appearance of this hymn in a Southern Baptist collection was in *New Baptist Hymnal* (Nashville, 1926, No. 307). *P.A.R.*

Coming now to Thee 466

B. B. McKinney wrote this revival song in 1925. It was first printed in a collection by the Baptist independent publisher, Robert H. Coleman in *The Little Evangel* (Dallas, 1925, No. 4). It also appeared in Coleman's *The Modern Hymnal* (Dallas, 1926, No. 287), a book that was later published by Broadman Press. Its first inclusion in an "official" Southern Baptist denominational collection was in *Baptist Hymnal* (Nashville, 1956, No. 342).

TRAVIS AVENUE is the name given B. B. McKinney's tune for "Send a Great Revival" in *Baptist Hymnal* (1956). It refers to Travis Avenue Baptist Church, Ft. Worth, Texas, where McKinney served as music director and assistant to the pastor (1931-35). *H.T.M.*

Count Your Blessings—See *When upon life's billows*

Creator God, creating still 51
Jane Parker Huber wrote this text in 1977 as a fresh expression of the Trinitarian revelation of God. It draws from the first two chapters of Genesis and from John 1:10-18 and 15:26 in identifying the Persons of the Trinity by function (Creator, Redeemer, Sustainer). It was first published in the August 1977 issue of *Concern*, a Presbyterian periodical, under the title, "A Hymn to the Trinity." It subsequently appeared in *A Singing Faith* (Philadelphia, 1987), a collection of 73 of the author's hymns. The third line of the first stanza was changed by the editors of *The Baptist Hymnal* (1991). It originally read: "Create a new humanity."

This hymn entered Southern Baptist hymnody in *The Baptist Hymnal* (1991), the first major hymnal to include it.

ST. ANNE—See hymn 73, God moves in a mysterious way. *P.A.R.*

Creator of the universe 549
Wesley L. Forbis wrote this hymn in 1988. Forbis has indicated a primary reason for writing the hymn was to help Christians avoid delimiting our view of creation. God is, indeed, the creator of the universe. He is also responsible for the Christ-child, the call to witness, and the triumphant Christ.

Its first inclusion in a Southern Baptist collection is in *The Baptist Hymnal* (1991).

PORTALES was composed by Barry Braman for this text on June 24, 1989. At that time he was minister of music of the First Baptist Church of Portales, New Mexico. *D.B.*

Crown Him with many crowns 161
This hymn originated as six eight-line stanzas by Matthew Bridges published in the second edition of his *Hymns of the Heart* (1851). Based upon Revelation 19:12 ("and on His head were many crowns"), each stanza begins with a "crown Him" motif ("Crown Him with many crowns," "Crown Him the Virgin's Son," "Crown Him the Lord of love," "Crown Him the Lord of peace," "Crown Him the Lord of years," and "Crown Him the Lord of heaven"). The second line of the first stanza also carries an allusion to Revelation 5:11-14.

At the request of a minister who did not approve of Bridges' text, Godfrey Thring wrote a six-stanza hymn based upon Bridges' model and published it in his *Hymns and Sacred Lyrics* (1874). Though Thring wrote with the intention of his text's becoming a substitute for Bridges', hymnal editors have often used a combination of stanzas from both versions. In the present version, stanzas 1, 3, and 4 are from Bridges, and stanza 2 is from Thring (the fourth stanza of his text). The first Southern Baptist hymnal to include this text, along with the DIADEMATA tune, was *The Chapel Book* (Nashville, 1923, No. 30).

DIADEMATA was written for this hymn by George J. Elvey. The tune, whose name is taken from the Greek word for "crown" in Revelation 19:12, was first published in the Appendix to *Hymns Ancient and Modern* (London, 1868, No. 318). *M.P.*

Day by day 66
The original version of this text was written in Swedish by Caroline V. Sandell-Berg as "Blott en dag, ett ögonblick i sänder." For 37 years, Sandell-Berg published an annual

"Bible Calendar" (*Korsblomman*) which contained poetry and other devotional materials. This text was first published in her *Korsblomman* for 1866. The English translation by A. L. Skoog first appeared in *Mission Hymns* (1921). Its first inclusion in a Southern Baptist hymnal was in the *Baptist Hymnal* (Nashville, 1975, No. 222).

BLOTT EN DAG was composed for this text by Oscar Ahnfelt in 1872 and was published in *Andeliga Sånger* ("Spiritual Songs") in the same year. The tune name comes from the first three words of the original Swedish text. *M.P.*

Dear Lord and Father of mankind 267

This hymn is taken from the last six stanzas of John Greenleaf Whittier's 17-stanza poem, "The Brewing of Soma." The poem was first published in the April, 1872, issue of *Atlantic Monthly*. Soma was an intoxicating concoction of milk and honey which was used to induce a religious frenzy in the priests of the Hindu God Indra. Whittier compared this type of worship to the hysteria of the revivals and camp meetings of his day. His own Quaker practice was the antithesis of this emotion-filled worship. The concluding stanzas to the poem express the poet's concept of true worship. An English Baptist editor, W. Garrett Horder, first extracted stanzas 12 and 14-17 for his *Worship Song* (1884). The present version uses Horder's stanzas 1, 4, 5, and 2. The *New Baptist Hymnal* (Nashville, 1926, No. 63) was the first Southern Baptist hymnal to include Whittier's hymn.

REST (also called ELTON) was composed for this text by Frederick Maker for inclusion in G. S. Barrett's *Congregational Church Hymnary* (1887). The tune name refers to the serenity portrayed in the text. *P.H.*

Dear Lord, lead me day by day 459

Francisca Asuncion adapted this hymn around 1980 from a Filipino folk song, "Planting rice is never fun." The hymn first appeared in *Hymns from the Four Winds* (Nashville, 1983). She modified the original phrase in the refrain, "bent from morn till the set of sun" into "praise from morn till the set of sun." *The Baptist Hymnal* (1991) is the first Southern Baptist collection to include this song.

COTTAGE GROVE is the name given to the Philippine folk melody adapted by the author for this text. *P.H.*

Deep in my heart there's a gladness 541

The words and music of this hymn were written by Albert A. Ketchum in the early 1920s while he was a student at Moody Bible Institute in Chicago. Ketchum sold the song to a fellow student named Harry D. Clarke, who published it in his *Gospel Truth in Song, No. 2* (1922). The song was not copyrighted until 1931.

Ketchum's composition became familiar as a special number for soloists and small ensembles in revival and worship services. It has become increasingly popular as a congregational hymn since its inclusion in Donald P. Hustad's *Crusader Hymns* (1967). Its first inclusion in a Southern Baptist hymnal was in *Baptist Hymnal* (Nashville, 1975, No. 429).

KETCHUM is the tune name given for the composer. *D.M.*

Depth of mercy! 306

This hymn was first published in John and Charles Wesley's *Hymns and Sacred Poems* (1740). It was under the heading "After a Relapse into Sin" and was written in 13 four-line stanzas. It was included in almost all Methodist hymnals. In 1849 it was reduced to five stanzas and in 1935 to four stanzas. It appeared in the first Southern Baptist collection, *The Baptist Psalmody* (Charleston, 1850, No. 423).

SEYMOUR is the tune name taken from the opening chorus of Carl Maria von Weber's last opera, *Oberon*, composed in 1825 and 1826 and first performed in Covent Garden, London, on April 12, 1826, less than two months before the composer's death. The tune was arranged by Henry W. Greatorex, organist of the Center Church, Hartford, Connecticut, and named for Mr. Seymour, a bass singer in the church choir. The tune is also known as CHATHAM, HOLSTEIN, SHORE, WEBER, AND VESPERS. *S.W.G.*

Down at the cross 140

This text by Elisha A. Hoffman appeared with a tune by John R. Sweeney in *Joy to the World* (Cincinnati, 1878), a collection compiled by Sweeney, T. C. O'Kane, and C. C. McCabe. There each stanza ended "Glory, glory, glory to his name," and the refrain was:

Down at the cross, Down at the cross,
Down at the cross where the Saviour died,
Down at the cross was the blood applied,
Glory, glory, glory to his name.

GLORY TO HIS NAME was composed for this text by John H. Stockton and takes its name from the refrain.

Songs of Redemption (Atlanta, 1920, No. 196) was the first Southern Baptist book to include this. *P.A.R.*

Doxology—See *Praise God, from Whom All Blessings Flow*

Dying with Jesus, by death reckoned mine 415

A chance remark by a friend inspired Daniel W. Whittle to write this hymn. During the World's Columbian Exposition in Chicago in 1893, Henry Varley, an English lay preacher, said to Whittle, "I do not like the hymn 'I Need Thee Every Hour' very well, because I need the Lord every moment of the day." Varley's comment lingered in Whittle's mind, and he wrote these words with the opening line of the refrain, "Moment by moment I'm kept in His love."

Its first inclusion in a Southern Baptist "official" collection was in *Songs of Faith* (Nashville, 1933, No. 9). However, it appeared in Baptist Robert Coleman's publications from as early as 1926 in *The Modern Hymnal* (Dallas, 1926, No. 274).

WHITTLE was composed for the words by May Whittle Moody in 1893. Words and music first appeared in Ira D. Sankey's *Christian Endeavor Hymns* (Boston, 1894). Southern Baptists found the hymn in Robert H. Coleman's *The Modern Hymnal* (Dallas, 1926, No. 274) and in *Songs of Faith* (Nashville, 1933, No. 9). The tune was named WHITTLE in *Baptist Hymnal* (1975). *W.J.R.*

Easter people, raise your voices 360

This text by William M. James was written in 1976 for services at the Metropolitan Community United Methodist Church in New York City, where the author served as pastor at that time. It was first published in *Songs of Zion* (1979) and was later included in *The United Methodist Hymnal* (1989). This hymn was sung for the opening of the 1980 General Conference of the United Methodist Church. Two of the original five stanzas have been omitted in the published versions of the hymn. *Baptist Hymnal* (1991) marks its first inclusion in a Southern Baptist hymnal. Lines 3, 4, and 6 of stanza three differ in *The Baptist Hymnal* (1991) from earlier published versions. These lines from the original version read:

When in trouble move the faster
to our God who rights the wrong.
......

See the power of heavenly throngs.
REGENT SQUARE—See hymn 94, Angels, from the realms of glory. *M.P.*

Emmanuel 82
The words and music of this song were written by Bob McGee about 1975. The author/composer has stated that he was preparing for an interchurch family camp. While he was in prayer, the words and music began forming in his mind. The first publication of the song in a Southern Baptist hymnal is in *The Baptist Hymnal* (1991).

MCGEE is named for the composer. *D.M.*

Emptied of His glory 178
The words and music of the chorus, "He Is Lord," were written first and are of unknown origin. The earliest appearance of the chorus in a major hymnal was in *Hymns for the Family of God* (Nashville, 1976, No. 234). In *The Hymnal for Worship and Celebration* (Waco, 1986, No. 105), the chorus was used as the refrain for a three-stanza hymn with words by Linda Lee Johnson, Claire Cloninger, and Tom Fettke. A new tune (HE IS LORD) was supplied by Fettke for the stanzas. This three-stanza version is the one found in *The Baptist Hymnal* (1991). The present hymnal is the first Southern Baptist collection to contain the song. *D.M.*

Encamped along the hills of light 413
This is one of the texts which John H. Yates sent to Ira D. Sankey, for which Sankey composed the music. It first appeared in print, according to the best research, in 1891 in *The Christian Endeavor Handbook* and in *Gospel Hymns No. 6*. Its first appearance in a Baptist collection was in *Kingdom Songs*, compiled by I. E. Reynolds and Robert H. Coleman (Dallas, 1921, No. 158).

SANKEY is named for the composer. *W.J.R.*

Eternal Father, strong to save 69
William Whiting wrote the hymn in 1860 for a student at Winchester College who was about to sail for America. The school is located only 12 miles from Southampton, a port second only in size to London, and the boys of the school were familiar with the lore of the sea. The hymn was first published, in a somewhat revised version, in *Hymns Ancient and Modern* (London, 1861, No. 222) under the heading "For those at sea. 'These see the works of the Lord, and his wonders in the deep' " (Psalm 107:24). Other biblical allusions are to Job 28:10-11 and Mark 4:35-41. In the United States, the hymn first appeared in Nehemiah Adams' *Church Pastorals: Hymns and Psalms for Public and Social Worship* (Boston, 1864). Albert Bailey, in his *The Gospel in Hymns* (1950), writes, "I have crossed the Atlantic forty-nine times, and to the best of my recollection this hymn was sung at Morning Prayer every Sunday we were at sea under the British flag." The hymn and tune of English origin is known in the United States as the "Navy Hymn." Its opening lines are inscribed over the chancel of the chapel at the Naval Academy at Annapolis. A favorite of Franklin Delano Roosevelt, it was sung at his funeral at Hyde Park, New York, April 14, 1945. On November 24, 1963, as the body of John Fitzgerald Kennedy was borne up the steps of the Capitol Building in Washington, to the rotunda, where it would lie in state, the hymn was played by the Navy Band. The following day, at Arlington National Cemetery, it was played by the Marine Band at the conclusion of his burial service. It first appeared in a Southern Baptist collection in *New Baptist Hymnal* (Nashville, 1926, No. 69).

MELITA was composed by John B. Dykes for this hymn, and it was first published in the musical edition to *Hymns Ancient and Modern* (London, 1861, No. 222). Dykes named the tune MELITA, the Roman name for the Mediterranean island of Malta, where Paul the apostle was shipwrecked while traveling as a prisoner to Rome. "When they were escaped, they knew that the island was called Melita" (Acts 28:1). Erik Routley in *Companion to Congregational Praise* (London, 1953, p. 288), comments, "Although efforts have been made to displace it, experience has shown that no other tune in this meter sets the present words with half the felicity that Dykes shows here. No other hymn should be sung to this tune, but it is useless to attempt any other tune for these words." *W.J.R.*

Eternal God, may we be free 299

This text by Michael G. Dell was written in October 1981 as a class assignment for a course in hymnology taught by William J. Reynolds at Southwestern Baptist Theological Seminary. Upon Reynolds' encouragement, the text (set to a tune also written by Dell) was sent to the Church Music Department of the Baptist Sunday School Board. Text and tune were published together in the April/May/June 1986 issue of *Choral Praise*. The tune CANONBURY, however, was chosen to accompany Dell's text in *The Baptist Hymnal* (1991), the first hymnal in which this text has appeared.

CANONBURY—See hymn 568, Lord, speak to me, that I may speak. *M.P.*

Everything was made by God 45

This text and tune by Tina English was commissioned by Word for the collection, *Sing 'n Celebrate for Kids* (1977). This marks its first appearance in a Southern Baptist hymnal.

CANDICE CHRISTOPHER is named by the composer for her daughter, Candice, and son, Christoper. *H.E.*

Face to face with Christ, my Savior 519

Grant Colfax Tullar was assiting in an evangelistic meeting in the Methodist Episcopal Church, in Rutherford, New Jersey, in 1898, when he composed this tune just before an evening service. The tune was composed for Tullar's own words which began, "All for me the Savior suffered." The next day, Tullar received several poems from Carrie E. Breck. One of these, "Face to Face with Christ, My Savior," just fitted the tune Tullar had written the previous evening. He was so delighted with this coincidence that he discarded his own poem and replaced it with Mrs. Breck's poem. It appeared in Tullar's *Sermons in Song* (1899). Its first inclusion in a Baptist collection was in Coleman's *Kingdom Songs,* compiled by I. E. Reynolds and Robert H. Coleman (Dallas, 1921, No. 38).

FACE TO FACE is the name given this tune by the hymnal committee for *Baptist Hymnal* (1956). *W.J.R.*

Fairest Lord Jesus 176

One of hymnody's great ironies is that a hymn so rich in gentle images of nature came to be erroneously associated with the Crusades. The first English printing in Richard S. Willis' *Church Chorals and Choir Studies* (New York, 1850) perpetuated the myth that this hymn was "wont to be sung by the German knights on their way to Jerusalem."

The text appears to have had Jesuit origins and was first published in the Catholic collection *Muensterisch Gesangbuch* (1677), although it was probably written at least 15 years earlier. A German version with the present tune, "Schoenster Herr Jesu," was transcribed from the singing of haymakers in Silesia and printed in altered form in a collection of folk songs entitled *Schlesische Volkslieder* (Leipzig, 1842).

An anonymous English translation of the first three stanzas appeared in Willis' *Church Chorals and Choir Studies* in 1850. The popularity of the hymn was verified by its inclusion in every important collection for the two decades following. The fourth stanza is a translation by Joseph A. Seiss and first appeared in *The Sunday School Book* (Philadelphia, 1873) for Evangelical Lutherans. "Beautiful Savior" is the Lutheran version of the hymn. *The Modern Hymnal* (1926, No. 68) was the first Southern Baptist hymnal to contain this hymn.

The tune CRUSADERS' HYMN (also known as SCHÖNSTER HERR JESU or ST. ELIZABETH), and its text, were first notated from the singing of Silesian haymakers in 1839 by Heinrich Hoffmann von Fallersleben (1798-1874) and Ernst Friedrich Richter (1808-79). Both text and tune first appeared in *Schlesische Volkslieder* (Leipzig, 1842). Richard S. Willis' *Church Chorals and Choir Studies* (New York, 1850) contained the first American printing of this tune. A tune composed by Christian Ernst Graaf in the Hague in 1766 and used in a set of piano variations by Mozart (K. 24) contains a strikingly similar first phrase.

The name derives from Willis' acceptance of the Crusade myth mentioned above. ST. ELIZABETH comes from Franz Liszt's incorporation of the tune in his oratorio *The Legend of St. Elizabeth* (1862). The tune first appeared in a Southern Baptist hymn collection in *Kingdom Songs* (Nashville, 1921, No. 248). *P.H.*

Faith Is the Victory—See *Encamped along the hills of light*

Faith of our fathers! 352

Frederick W. Faber wrote this hymn as a reflection on the persecution that Catholics had suffered at the hands of the established church in England. It appeared in his collection *Jesus and Mary; or Catholic Hymns for Singing and Reading* (London, 1849), in two versions: one for England with four stanzas; and one for Ireland with seven. That the faith of which Faber wrote was Catholicism may be seen in stanzas two and three of the text for England, on which ours is based:

Our fathers, chained in prisons dark,
Were still in heart and conscience free:
How sweet would be their children's fate,
If they, like them, could die for thee.
Faith of our fathers, holy faith!
We would be true to thee till death.

Faith of our fathers! Mary's prayers
Shall win our country back to thee;
And through the truth that comes from God,
England shall then indeed be free.
Faith of our fathers....

Several persons have altered Faber's hymn to make it more generally acceptable. These changes have distorted the author's intent, but have enabled a wider range of Christians to aspire toward the faith of persecuted forebears. *The Baptist Hymnal* (1991) basically follows *Hymns for the Church of Christ* (Boston, 1853), a book compiled for Unitarians.

The first inclusion of this hymn in a collection for Southern Baptists was in *Songs of Redemption* (Atlanta, 1920, No. 264).

ST. CATHERINE is named for a fourth century Christian martyr of Alexandria. It was composed by Henri F. Hemy to set a text about her and included in Part Two of *Crown of Jesus Music* (London, 1864) which he edited. James G. Walton put the tune in its present form by adding the last eight measures for his *Plainsong Music for the Holy Communion Office* (London, 1874). This tune goes by several other names, including TYNEMOUTH, ST. FINBAR, and PRINCE. *P.A.R.*

Father, Father, You are Jehovah! 250

This chorus by Mark Blankenship appeared in the trilogy "Praise to the Trinity." The composer conducted the premiere at the dedication of the worship center at North Phoenix Baptist Church, Phoenix, Arizona, on May 25, 1980. *The Baptist Hymnal* (1991) marks the first inclusion of this work in a Southern Baptist hymnal.

JACKSON is named for Richard Jackson, pastor at North Phoenix Baptist Church. *P.H.*

Father, I adore You 256

This song was improvised in the summer of 1972 by Terrye Coelho Strom as she was driving near her home in Southern California. The simple Trinitarian praise chorus was copyrighted later that year by Maranatha! Music and spread quickly by publication in various chorus collections and by oral transmission. The first hymnal to include it was *Hymns of the Christian Life* (Harrisonburg, 1978).

MARANATHA, a Greek liturgical salutation meaning "our Lord, come," is also the name of the first publisher of this song. The tune is also known as COELHO, the author and composer's maiden name.

The Baptist Hymnal (1991) is the first Southern Baptist hymnal to include this song. *P.A.R.*

Father, Son, Holy Spirit—See *Father, Father, You are Jehovah!*

Father, we love You 249

The words and music of this song were written by Donna W. Adkins in 1975. In the October/November 1988 issue of the *Psalmist Magazine* (p. 16), the author provided the following information about the writing of the song.

"One morning while reading the 17th chapter of John, I began to meditate on the prayer of Jesus. I saw in a new way that Jesus was not only praying for His disciples,

but for all who would follow Him in years to come. He was actually praying for me! I was impressed that Jesus was placing such great emphasis on the unity of believers with the Lord. I also saw that it was very important to Jesus that the Father's name be glorified, and that there seemed to be a correlation between glorifying the Father's name and achieving unity. In that same moment I was inspired to sit at the piano and write GLORIFY THY NAME."

The first publication of the song was in a small booklet used at a pastor's conference. Subsequently, it appeared in *The Hymnal for Worship and Celebration* (Waco, 1986, No. 29). *The Baptist Hymnal* (1991) is the first printing of the words and music in a Southern Baptist collection. *D.M.*

Fill the earth with music 614

"Fill the Earth with Music" was judged the winner in the first hymn search sponsored by the Southern Baptist Church Music Conference in 1989. The hymn search committee had specified that hymns submitted should make strong missionary statements concerning the sharing of the Good News through the ministry of music. After undergoing some alteration and rearrangement, R. G. Huff's original text was first sung congregationally on June 12, 1989, at the Las Vegas meeting of the conference using the tune KING'S WESTON. At the author's suggestion, WYE VALLEY was substituted for the inclusion of the hymn in *The Baptist Hymnal* (1991) and, accordingly, a refrain was added using, again, the opening four lines of the first stanza.

The author states that Colossians 3:16 and Ephesians 5:19 were the scriptural bases for the hymn and that this represents his very first attempt at hymn writing. An original third stanza has been omitted in *The Baptist Hymnal* (1991):

In the voice of children, with the trumpet's blast,
All of God's creation, turn to Him at
last.
This will be our calling, this our mission
true;
Take the world this message: "Christ
makes all things new!"
WYE VALLEY—See hymn 58, Like a river
glorious.   *H.T.M.*

Footsteps of Jesus—See *Sweetly, Lord, have
we heard Thee calling*

For all the saints 355
William Walsham How wrote this majestic hymn for All Saints Day (Nov. 1). It was
first published in 11 stanzas in Earl Nelson's
Hymns for Saints' Days, and Other Hymns
(1864), and was accompanied by the text "a
cloud of witnesses" (Heb. 12:1). The original version, later altered with the author's
permission, read "For all *thy* saints." The
hymn comments on the idea of the "communion of saints" on earth as well as in
heaven. *Baptist Hymnal* (Nashville, 1975,
No. 144) was the first Southern Baptist hymnal to contain this hymn.
SINE NOMINE was written for this text by
Ralph Vaughan Williams and included in
The English Hymnal (1906). It was, however,
ascribed to an anonymous composer. SINE
NOMINE means "without a name," and is a
spoof on hymn tune names.   *P.H.*

For God so loved the world 548
In a September 1990 letter to the writer,
Rae Whitney reports she wrote this text
about 1978 (copyright 1985) because she was
"overwhelmed by contemplating the wonder and the glory of God's love." Galatians
1:5, "To whom be glory for ever and ever,"
was one of several Scriptures that inspired
her. Acts 3:10, "and they were filled with

wonder," was another. John 3:16 is the basis for stanza one. Stanza two reminds us that
being a Christian does not exempt one from
temptation and sin. Fortunately, Jesus continues to call us back to Him. Stanza three
begins with a reminder that we must live in
God's Word. Whitney says stanza four
"moves from contemplation to action" as we
are reminded "It is a wondrous thing God's
glory to proclaim." The hymn with its tune
LEDOUX was used as the theme song for the
1986 music leadership weeks at Ridgecrest
and Glorieta Baptist Conference Centers.
LEDOUX was composed by Joanne Brown-
LeDoux and was copyrighted in 1986. It was
written at the invitation of Mark Blankenship of the Church Music Department, Baptist Sunday School Board. A gifted pianist,
LeDoux read the text and developed the
tune during a time of keyboard improvisation.   *D.B.*

For He alone is worthy 427
No information is available concerning
the origin of this chorus, which has been circulated in the oral tradition repertory of
those churches which use praise choruses extensively. The hymnal committee for *The
Baptist Hymnal* (1991) found it in print in *Yes
Lord: Church of God in Christ Hymnal* (1982).
ADESTE FIDELIS (refrain)—See hymn 89, O
come, all ye faithful.   *M.P.*

For the beauty of the earth 44
Folliott S. Pierpoint (1835-1917) wrote this
as an eight-stanza communion hymn. Six of
the stanzas appear here and a number of minor alterations have developed through the
years. The hymn enumerates some 23 items
for which the Christian can be grateful and
culminates with gratitude for Christ, the
"best Gift Divine." The hymn was first published in the second edition of Orby Shipley's
Lyra Eucharistica (1864), and its first appear-

ance in a Southern Baptist hymnal was in *New Baptist Hymnal* (Nashville, 1926, No. 309).

DIX is the tune adapted from the chorale "Treuer Heiland wir sind hier" and included in Conrad Kocher's *Stimmen aus dem Reiche Gottes* (Stuttgart, 1838). The tune was given its present form by William Henry Monk in the original edition of *Hymns Ancient and Modern* (1861), where it was used for the text "As With Gladness Men of Old," by William Chatterton Dix, from whom the tune gets its name. The first appearance of the tune in a Southern Baptist hymnal was in *New Baptist Hymnal* (Nashville, 1926, Nos. 88, 309). *S.W.G.*

For the fruit of all creation 643

This text by Fred Pratt Green appeared as "Harvest Hymn" in the *Methodist Recorder* of August, 1970. It was written as a new text for EAST ACKLAM, the tune Francis Jackson wrote in 1957 as an alternate tune to AR HYD Y NOS, the Welsh folksong used for "God That Madest Earth and Heaven." Ironically, *The Baptist Hymnal* (1991) joins the folksong tune with the text written for the replacement tune. The original first line read "For the fruits of his creation." *The Baptist Hymnal* (1991) is the first Southern Baptist collection to include this hymn.

AR HYD Y NOS—See hymn 218, 'Tis the church triumphant singing. *D.B.*

For Thine is the kingdom 659

This excerpt of the Lord's Prayer (Matthew 6:13) appears in *Celebrate Life!*, a Christian musical by Buryl Red and Ragan Courtney (Nashville, 1972, p. 102). The first Southern Baptist hymnal to include it is *The Baptist Hymnal* (1991).

THE LORD'S PRAYER is the tune name given by the hymnal committee (1991), and is the original song title in *Celebrate Life!* *P.H.*

"Forever with the Lord!" 529

This text by James Montgomery was first published in the 1835 edition of *The Amethyst* and appeared in the same year in Montgomery's *Poet's Portfolio*. In its original form, it consisted of 22 stanzas of four lines each, divided unequally between two parts (nine stanzas in Part i and 13 stanzas in Part ii). It was initially published under the heading, "At Home in Heaven, 1 Thess. iv. 17."

The earliest *Dictionary of American Hymnology* listing of this text in this country is 1843, when it was published in *Select Melodies* (Cincinnati). The first appearance of portions of this text in a Southern Baptist hymnal was in *The Baptist Psalmody* (Charleston, 1850, No. 1292), in which six four-line stanzas were included. Only two of those stanzas are present in the version which appears in *The Baptist Hymnal* (1991), wherein six of the original four-line stanzas are combined to form three stanzas of eight lines each. The text used in this hymnal combines stanzas 1 and 3 of the original Part i and stanzas 5, 6, 7, and 13 from Part ii.

TERRA PATRIS—See hymn 43, This is my Father's world. *M.P.*

Forgiven 341

This hymn and tune were cowritten by Buryl Red and Mark Blankenship during a retreat for those involved in the Southern Baptist Convention's television program "At Home with the Bible." It was later used on one of the telecasts and subsequently published as a choral octavo. *The Baptist Hymnal* (1991) is the first Southern Baptist hymnal to contain this work.

The tune name RIDGECREST refers to the Southern Baptist Convention Conference Center located at Ridgecrest, North Carolina. *P.H.*

Free from the law, O happy condition 332

Philip P. Bliss wrote both words and music. Major Daniel W. Whittle gave the following account of this song's origin:

"Just before Christmas, 1871, Mrs. Bliss asked a friend, 'What shall I get for my husband as a Christmas present?' and, at the suggestion of this friend, purchased and presented him with the bound volume of a monthly English periodical called *Things New and Old.* Many things in these books of interpretation of Scripture and illustrations of Gospel truth were blessed to him, and from the reading of something in one of these books, in connection with Romans 8 and Hebrews 10:10, suggested this glorious gospel song" (132).

This hymn was first published in 1873 in Bliss' *Sunshine for Sunday Schools* (Cincinnati, No. 82), and then in his *Gospel Songs* (Cincinnati, 1874, No. 13). The original title, ONCE FOR ALL, is now used as the hymn tune name. The tune name was assigned by the hymnal committee for *Baptist Hymnal* (1956). The first Baptist hymnal to include this hymn is S. L. Caldwell's and A. J. Gordon's *The Service of Song for Baptist Churches* (New York, 1876, No. 283).

George C. Stebbins, a musical associate of evangelist D. L. Moody, as was Bliss, stated that this hymn "is conceded to be the clearest statement of the doctrine of grace in distinction from the law to be found in hymnology. Indeed, it was said at the time of Moody and Sankey's first visit to Scotland in 1873 that the singing of that hymn had more to do in breaking down the prejudice that existed against Gospel hymns up to that time than anything else, as its teaching was so scriptural and in such perfect accord with the teaching of the Scottish divines. The music setting of it, too, could not have been improved upon" (194).   *H.E.*

Freely, Freely—See *God forgave my sin in Jesus' name*

From all that dwell below the skies 13

Isaac Watts based this hymn on Psalm 117. It first appeared in Watts' *Psalms of David, Imitated in the Language of the New Testament* (1719). Its first printing in a hymnal for Southern Baptists was in *The Baptist Psalmody* (Charleston, 1850, No. 1016) where the word "who" rather than "that" is used in the first line.

DUKE STREET—See hymn 587, Jesus shall reign.   *D.B.*

Gentle Mary laid her Child 101

Joseph Simpson Cook wrote this text and entered it in a Christmas carol competition sponsored by *The Christian Guardian*, Christmas, 1919. The poem won first place and was published that year in *The Christian Guardian* by the Methodist Publishing House, Toronto. The first hymnal inclusion of the text was in *The Hymnary of the United Church of Canada* (Toronto, 1930). The first Southern Baptist hymnal to include this Christmas carol was *Baptist Hymnal* (Nashville, 1956, No. 73).

TEMPUS ADEST FLORIDUM is a melody that appeared in *Piae Cantiones*, compiled by Theodoricus Petrus of Nyland, Finland, 1582, where it is set to a Latin carol of spring, the first line of which is "Tempus adest floridum." In 1853, John Mason Neale made a metrical version of the legend of Good King Wenceslas for this tune, which has resulted in the association of this music with the Christmas season. The present harmonization was made by Sir Ernest MacMillan for *The Hymnary of the United Church of Canada* (Toronto, 1930, No. 57), where this text and tune appeared together for the first time. The first Southern Baptist usage of the tune was in *Baptist Hymnal* (Nashville, 1956, No. 73).   *W.J.R.*

Glorify Thy Name—See *Father, we love You*

Glorious Is Thy Name—See *Blessed Savior, we adore Thee*

Glorious things of thee are spoken 398

John Newton's hymn appeared in five eight-line stanzas in the *Olney Hymns*, Book I (1779, No. 60). The scriptural basis is Psalm 87:3, "Glorious things are spoken of thee, O city of God." The first appearance in the United States was in the unauthorized edition of John Rippon's *A Selection of Hymns from the Best Authors, Intended as an Appendix to Dr. Watts's Psalms and Hymns* (New York, 1792). Rippon's first edition had been published in London in 1787. The hymn appeared in Jesse Mercer's *The Cluster of Spiritual Songs, Divine Hymns, and Sacred Poems* (Augusta, 1810, 3rd ed., No. 287). The present version alters line six of the second stanza which originally read "Ever flows their thirst t'assuage." Southern Baptists' first hymnal, *The Baptist Psalmody* (Charleston, 1850, No. 969), contained selected stanzas of Newton's great hymn.

AUSTRIAN HYMN—See hymn 262, Word of God, across the ages.   *W.J.R.*

Glory be to the Father 252

"Glory Be to the Father" is a translation of the *Gloria Patri* which was used in its present form in Christian worship by the end of the 4th century. It is called the "Lesser Doxology" in contrast to the "Greater Doxology" which is the "Gloria in Excelsis." The "Lesser Doxology" was used in praise to the Trinity and as a means of combating the Arian heresy which denied the divinity of Christ. Three settings of the "Gloria Patri"

are to be found in *The Baptist Hymn and Praise Book* (Nashville, 1904, Nos. 578, 579, 580).

GLORIA PATRI (Greatorex) was written by Henry W. Greatorex and published in his *Collection of Psalm and Hymn Tunes* (Boston, 1851). It appears under the title "Gloria Patri No. 1."   *D.B.*

Go forth and tell! O Church of God 596

The words of this hymn were written by James Edward Seddon about 1960. The text was first printed in leaflets for use at meetings of the English Bible Churchmen's Missionary Society, of which the author was Home Secretary. In his travels representing the Society, the author began to feel the need for more relevant missionary hymns and sought to improve the situation by writing some himself, of which the present one is probably the best known. The first hymnal appearance of the text was in *Youth Praise* (1966). *The Baptist Hymnal* (1991) marks its first printing in a Southern Baptist collection.

NATIONAL HYMN—See hymn 629, God of our fathers.   *D.M.*

Go now in peace 660

This benediction is a canon composed by Natalie Sleeth in 1976 after attending a workshop in Dallas on church music for children using Orff instruments. The workshop had been led by Betty Bedsole, professor in the School of Church Music at The Southern Baptist Theological Seminary.

GO NOW IN PEACE is a repetitive pentatonic melody accompanied by ostinatos that may be played by keyboard, handbells, and/or Orff instruments. This work was first published in the composer's choral collection, *Sunday Songbook* (Hinshaw Music, 1976). The first hymnal to include this benediction was *The United Methodist Hymnal*

(Nashville, 1989, No. 665). Its first inclusion in a Southern Baptist collection is *The Baptist Hymnal* (1991, No. 660).   *H.E.*

Go Out and Tell—See *Go out in peace*

Go out in peace 657
This benediction chorus was written for the First Baptist Church of Plano, Texas, before its author became a member of the staff there. The church was experiencing disappointment in a prospective pastor's declining the call to their church. Christopher shared with his friend, the minister of music, this affirmation of "peace," of "joy," and of "trusting in His Word" and the chorus became particularly meaningful to the choir and congregation during this period. A short time later the minister felt that God was indeed calling him to the church and did accept the call as pastor. The text has reference to Isaiah 55:12.

"Go Out and Tell," with words and music by Keith Christopher, appeared in the July 1988 issue of *Choral Praise,* a choral periodical published by the Church Music Department of The Sunday School Board of the Southern Baptist Convention. It was used as a theme song for music weeks at the Southern Baptist Convention conference centers in Glorieta, New Mexico, and Ridgecrest, North Carolina, in that same year. *The Baptist Hymnal* (1991) is the first denomination-wide collection to include it.

PLANO was the name given the tune by the author and composer, Keith Christopher, in reference to the First Baptist Church of Plano, Texas, for which this work was written.   *S.W.G.*

Go, tell it on the mountain 95
The melody of this spiritual appears in the 1909 edition of Thomas P. Fenner's *Religious Folk Songs of the Negro as Sung on the Plantations* (Hampton, 1909, p. 174). Labeled a "Christmas Plantation Song," it is given there with its usual refrain and the following traditional stanzas:

> When I was a seeker,
>   I sought both night an' day,
> I ask' de Lord to help me,
>   An' He show' me de way.
> He made me a watchman,
>   Upon a city wall,
> An' if I am a Christian,
>   I am de least of all.

The present two stanzas were written by John W. Work, Jr., a faculty member of Fisk University. As recalled by his son, John W. Work, III, at Fisk it was customary before sunrise on Christmas morning in the early years of this century for students to go caroling from building to building singing, "Go, tell it on the mountain, Jesus Christ is born." These stanzas were published in John W. Work, III's *American Negro Songs and Spirituals* (New York, 1940, p. 215).

George Pullen Jackson pointed to the similarity of the stanza melody to the tune "We'll March Around Jerusalem" (358). William Arms Fisher noted the similarity of the refrain to George F. Root's Civil War song "Tramp, tramp, tramp, the boys are marching," suggesting the possibility that this spiritual took shape after the song by Root had become widely known (xxvi). As in many spirituals, the melody is pentatonic (with no fourth or seventh steps).

The present harmonization by John W. Work, III, was published in his *American Negro Songs and Spirituals* (New York, 1940). The first inclusion in a Southern Baptist hymnal was in *Baptist Hymnal* (Nashville, 1975, No. 82).

GO TELL IT is the tune name is taken from the common title of the hymn.   *H.E.*

Go to dark Gethsemane 150

James Montgomery wrote two versions of this hymn text. The first version was included in the ninth edition of Thomas Cotterill's *A Selection of Psalms and Hymns for Public and Private Use* (London, 1820). The second version, which was published in Montgomery's *A Selection of Hymns for the Use of the Protestant Dissenting Congregations of the Dissenting Order in Leeds* (Leeds, 1822), had changes from the original in 13 lines in stanzas two through four. The latter version also appeared in the author's *Christian Psalmist* (Glasgow, 1825). It is the revised version which is used in *The Baptist Hymnal* (1991). This text was included in the first hymnal published by Southern Baptists, *The Baptist Psalmody* (Charleston, 1850, No. 157).

REDHEAD 76 (also called GETHSEMANE, PETRA, OR AJALON) was composed by Richard Redhead and was first published in his *Church Hymn Tunes, Ancient and Modern, for the Several Seasons of the Church Year* (London, 1853), a collection of old and new tunes which Redhead compiled and edited. In this collection, each tune was given a Roman numeral instead of a name. Tune LXXVI was paired with the text "Rock of Ages, Cleft for Me," and continues to be used with that text in England.   *M.P.*

Go with God—See *May God's grace go before you*

God forgave my sin in Jesus' name 273

Carol Owens wrote this text and tune, FREELY, FREELY, for inclusion in *Come Together*, a 1972 musical she and her husband, Jimmy, jointly composed. It was placed in the worship segment of the musical and centers on the theme of freely giving oneself to whatever God asks. In a telephone conversation with the writer, Owens reported the text and tune came to her early one morn-

ing as she was reading from the Gospels. *The Baptist Hymnal* (1991) is the first Southern Baptist collection to include this song. *D.B.*

God is so good 23

No information is currently available concerning the origin of this anonymous song or its tune, GOD IS SO GOOD. *The Baptist Hymnal* (1991) marks its first appearance in a Southern Baptist hymnal.   *M.P.*

God Moves in a mysterious way 73

William Cowper wrote this hymn in 1773. It was published anonymously in John Newton's *Twenty-six Letters on Religious Subjects: to which are added Hymns* (London, 1774) under the subtitle "Light Shining Out of Darkness." In Book III of *Olney Hymns* (1779), in which Newton acknowledged Cowper's authorship, the hymn speaks of the greatness of God's providence and the mystery of God's being. It appeared in the first official Southern Baptist collection, *The Baptist Psalmody* (Charleston, 1850, No. 50) in five stanzas. Cowper's original consisted of six stanzas, the fifth being:

> His purposes will ripen fast,
> Unfolding every hour;
> The bud may have a bitter taste,
> But sweet will be the flower.

ST. ANNE first appeared anonymously in *A Supplement to the New Version of the Psalms by Dr. Brady and Mr. Tate,* sixth edition (London, 1708), as a setting for Psalm 42 and named ST. ANNE. In Philip Hart's *Melodies Proper to be sung to any of ye versions of the Psalms of David* (*c.* 1720), and John Church's *Introduction to Psalmody* (1723), William Croft is named as composer. The tune is named for St. Anne's Church, Soho, London, where Croft was organist. Croft is generally assumed to be the composer, although in the seventh edition of Abraham Barber's *Book of Psalm Tunes* (1715) the tune is titled

LEEDS and is attributed to Mr. Denby. Handel used the melody in his sixth Chandos anthem, "O Praise the Lord," and the opening phrase of the melody appears in J. S. Bach's "Fugue in E flat," more popularly known now as "St. Anne's Fugue."   D.B., S.W.G.

God of grace and God of glory 395

This hymn was written in the summer of 1930 while Harry Emerson Fosdick was vacationing at his summer home in Boothbay Harbor, Maine. It was written for the opening of Riverside Church on October 5, 1930. It was also sung for the dedication service on February 8, 1931. The hymn was first published in H. Augustine Smith's *Praise and Service* (New York, 1932). Its first appearance in a Southern Baptist hymnal was *Baptist Hymnal* (Nashville, 1956, No. 465). The present version includes the original third stanza as the fourth stanza.

CWM RHONDDA, a sturdy and singable Welsh tune, was composed by John Hughes and printed in leaflet form for the annual Baptist Cymanfa Ganu (Singing Festival) at Capel Rhondda, Pontypridd. Some sources give 1905 as the date of composition while others give 1907. It is said that by 1930, the tune had been heard at 5000 such festivals, and it has continued to be an extremely popular hymn tune. The tune name means "the low valley of the Rhondda." Rhondda, now called East Glamorgan, Wales, was a booming coal-mining area in the first decades of the 20th century. In 1933 the tune appeared in *Fellowship Hymn Book* (London), *Methodist Hymn Book* (London), and the Presbyterian (U.S.A.) *The Hymnal* (Philadelphia). The first Southern Baptist hymnal to include CWM RHONDDA was *Baptist Hymnal* (Nashville, 1956, Nos. 55, 465). S.W.G.

God of our fathers 629

This patriotic text was written for the centennial Fourth of July in 1876 by Daniel Crane Roberts when he was rector of St. Thomas' Church (Episcopal), Brandon, Vermont. It is interesting that this American centennial hymn was initially sung to "Russian Hymn," the tune of the Russian national anthem. Roberts sent his text anonymously to the commission revising the Episcopal hymnal and it was accepted, appearing in *The Hymnal 1892*. Although American in its origin, Roberts' hymn of praise and of prayer for peace can be sung by people of any freedom-loving nation.

Roberts' text was selected in 1892 for use as the hymn for the centennial of the United States Constitution. For this centennial George W. Warren composed NATIONAL HYMN, used in the Columbia celebration on October 8, 1892, at New York City's St. Thomas' Church (Episcopal) where Warren was organist. Warren's tune was published in 1893 in Arthur H. Messiter's musical edition of *The Hymnal 1892*, where it is named AMERICA. This early publication of NATIONAL HYMN appears to be conceived for choral rather than congregational use, for it is in the key of F and above the first line of the hymn is the indication, "Voices alone."

NATIONAL HYMN is the tune name was given in J. Ireland Tucker and William W. Rousseau's musical edition of *The Hymnal 1892*, published in 1894. Yet a third name given to Warren's tune is COLUMBIA, found in James H. Darlington's musical edition of *The Hymnal 1892*, published in 1897. This is the only hymn of ecumenical acceptance with a musical setting that features trumpet fanfares for the organ.

"God of Our Fathers" seems to have made its first appearance in a Baptist hymnal in *The New Baptist Praise Book: or Hymns of the Centuries* by Benjamin Shepherd and

William N. Lawrence (Philadelphia, 1914). Its first publication in a Southern Baptist hymnal was in *The New Baptist Hymnal* (Nashville, 1926, No. 26).   *H.E.*

God sent His Son 407
Bill and Gloria Gaither wrote words and music in 1971, shortly after the birth of their son, Benjy. The condition of the world politically, economically, and spiritually gave them great concern. Yet, they both felt the assurance and affirmation that we all can face the unknown future with confidence because Jesus Christ, our Savior, lives. *Baptist Hymnal* (1975) was the first hymnal to include the hymn, and at Bill Gaither's request, named the tune RESURRECTION. *W.J.R.*

God Will Take Care of You—See *Be not dismayed*

God's Son has made me free 649
The words of this song originally formed part of a hymn by Hans Adolph Brorson, *"Guds Son har gjort mig fri"* (God's Son has made me free). In 1906, Edvard Grieg set Brorson's text as the second of his *Fire Salmer frit efter aeldre norske Kirkemelodier* (Four Psalms freely arranged from old Norwegian church melodies) for baritone solo and mixed chorus, Opus 74. The present version of the tune, FREE, is an adaptation by Oscar R. Overby of the last 12 measures of Grieg's composition. *The Baptist Hymnal* (1991) marks the first appearance of the song in a Southern Baptist collection. That hymnal committee assigned the tune name.   *D.M.*

God, give us Christian homes! 504
Written in 1949 by B. B. McKinney, "God, Give Us Christian Homes" first appeared as a theme song for Christian Home Week in 1950. It was first printed for this purpose in

the Southern Baptist periodical for family living, *Home Life* (May, 1950). In that year (1950) it was also introduced at the annual meeting of the Southern Baptist Convention in Chicago by the Oklahoma Baptist University Bison Glee Club. Before its inclusion in *Baptist Hymnal* (Nashville, 1956, No. 377), it had widespread use in single sheet form.

CHRISTIAN HOME was the name chosen for the tune to the hymn by the committee for *Baptist Hymnal* (1956).   *H.T.M.*

God, our Author and Creator 590
Carl Daw wrote this text in 1985, submitting it to a hymn writing competition sponsored by the Southern Baptist Women's Missionary Union. It was selected as the WMU Centennial Hymn. The three stanzas are based on a Trinitarian structure. The guidelines for the WMU competition pointed to the need for attention to carrying out mission in daily life. The word "lives" consequently appears in all three stanzas of Daw's hymn. The author also sought to avoid the attitude of Western superiority found in many 19th-century mission hymns.

NALL AVENUE, composed by A. L. (Pete) Butler for this text in 1986, was chosen in a competition for a tune for the WMU text. Butler's tune is named for the Nall Avenue Baptist Church, Prairie Village, Kansas, the congregation Butler was serving as part-time minister of music when it was composed. Both the text and tune were published and widely sung during the 1987-88 centennial celebration of the Woman's Missionary Union. An additional tune suggested by Daw for his hymn is PLEADING SAVIOR, an early American folk hymn tune found in *The Hymnal 1982* (No. 596). *The Baptist Hymnal* (1991) is the first inclusion of this hymn for general public worship.   *H.E.*

God, our Father, we adore Thee! 248

George W. Frazer, an Irishman of Scottish descent, wrote this hymn of praise. Its first inclusion in an American hymnal was in a Loizeaux Brothers publication titled *Hymns of Grace and Truth* (New York, 1904). In this version, the hymn lacked a stanza addressed to the Holy Spirit. Gordon Shorney of the Hope Publishing Company wished to correct this and include the revision in his *Tabernacle Hymns No. 5*. Alfred Loizeaux informed Shorney there was no such stanza, but then submitted several for his consideration. Shorney chose the one that appears as stanza three in *The Baptist Hymnal* (1991). According to William Reynolds (*Companion to Baptist Hymnal*, p. 78), Loizeaux explained in a letter of November 23, 1954:

"I believe that the reason no stanza on the Holy Spirit appeared in the Grace and Truth Book is that the Brethren, so called "Plymouth Brethren" have felt quite strongly that we have no precedent in Scripture for directing worship personally to the Holy Spirit, even though we believe definitely that He is the third person of the Trinity. Personally, I do not hold invariably to this rule and thought that the hymn would be more complete with a stanza addressed to the Holy Spirit."

Baptist Hymnal (Nashville, 1956, No. 5) was the first Southern Baptist collection to include this hymn.

BEECHER—See hymn 208, Love divine, all loves excelling.   *D.B.*

God, our Father, You have led us 454

In 1984, Dr. Russell R. Tuck was elected president of California Baptist College, Riverside, California. In preparation for the inauguration of the president, the committee charged with planning the program invited Terry W. York, a 1973 graduate of the college, to write a new hymn for the event.

"God, Our Father, You Have Led Us" was first sung (to the tune CWM RHONDDA) at the inauguration of Dr. Tuck on November 2, 1984, in the sanctuary of Magnolia Avenue Baptist Church, Riverside. The text was subsequently adopted as the official hymn of the college.

CLAY was composed by Crystal Davis Clay in June of 1986. According to the composer, "The text came to mean a great deal to me as I studied and meditated upon its truth. As a believer, it is encouraging to know that, as Proverbs 3:5-6 says, 'Trust in the Lord with all all thine heart, and lean not unto thine own understanding. In all thy ways acknowledge Him, and He will direct thy paths.' "

The text and tune were first published together in the July 1987 issue of *Opus One*, a Baptist Sunday School Board magazine for youth choirs. The first hymnal publication of the words and music is in *The Baptist Hymnal* (1991).   *D.M.*

God, the Father of Your people 382

The stanzas of this hymn were the work of three different people. The first stanza was written in 1978 by Alfred E. Mulder and published in the *Psalter Hymnal* (Grand Rapids, 1987, No. 322). Stanza two was written by Ralph Parks for the present hymnal. The third stanza, a paraphrase of 2 Corinthians 13:14, is an altered version of a single-line hymn by John Newton which was first published in *Olney Hymns* (1779). The third stanza appeared in *Baptist Hymnal* (1956) in truncated form. The other two stanzas mark their first Southern Baptist publication in *The Baptist Hymnal* (1991).

HOLY MANNA—See hymn 379, Brethren, we have met to worship.   *D.M.*

God, who made the earth 50

This text by Sarah Betts Rhodes was written in 1870 for the Sheffield (England) Sunday School Union Whitsuntide (Pentecost) Festival. The earliest known publication of the hymn was in the *Methodist Sunday School Hymn Book* (1879).

Mrs. Rhodes wrote a tune to accompany her text, but her melody appears to have fallen out of favor, and several other composers have tried their hand at setting this text.

The tune SPRING was composed by Robert G. McCutchan and first published in the *American Junior Church School Hymnal* (1929), of which he was music editor. The first Southern Baptist collection to include this text and tune was *Songs for Juniors* (Nashville, 1953, No. 119).   *D.M.*

God, who stretched the spangled heavens 47

Catherine Cameron wrote this hymn about 1965; it was first published in 1971 in *The Hymn Book* of the Anglican and United Churches of Canada. According to the author, "This hymn was inspired by the magnificent union of Harry Emerson Fosdick's 'God of Grace and God of Glory' linked to the tune CWM RHONDDA by John Hughes. I wanted to express our unity with God in the gift of creativity, and to make it especially relevant to modern life. After examining many hymn tunes, I chose Haydn's AUSTRIAN HYMN, and began to wed words and ideas to the music. Over the weeks that followed, as I searched for just the right words to convey my thoughts into poetry, that wonderful music flooded my being. My hymn has been used with other tunes but it is far more meaningful to me when Haydn's triumphant music accompanies it. Probably my happiest moment came in 1966 when I first heard my hymn sung—by a chorus of young ministerial students. In 1988, it was sung at a hymn service in Westminster Abbey, London." Dr. Cameron has modern-ized the wording of this hymn slightly, changing words like "thou" to "you," and neutralizing male terminology. She has expressed regret that our hymnals omit her second stanza, which speaks to the condition of the homeless and dispossessed in today's society:

Proudly rise our modern cities,
    Stately buildings, row on row;
Yet their windows, blank, unfeeling,
    Stare on canyoned streets below,
Where the lonely drift unnoticed
    In the city's ebb and flow,
Lost to purpose and to meaning,
    Scarcely caring where they go.

HYMN TO JOY—See hymn 7, Joyful, joyful, we adore Thee.   *H.E.*

God, who touches earth with beauty 500

Canadian Mary Susannah Edgar wrote this hymn text in 1925, and the following year it was awarded first prize in a contest sponsored by the American Camper's Association. Written for campers, Stanley L. Osborne stated that "No hymn has been used more frequently by campers in Canada than this one... Recent translations into Spanish, French, Portuguese, and Japanese will extend its influence further" (243). This hymn appeared in *Baptist Hymnal* (1956, No. 45) with the tune GENEVA by C. Harold Lowen, but was omitted from the *Baptist Hymnal (1975)*.

The present tune, composed by A. L. (Pete) Butler, was given the composer's name for *The Baptist Hymnal* (1991). In a letter to this writer, the composer describes the circumstances concerning the origin of his setting in 1966:

"I began working on it during a revival at First Baptist Church, Anadarko, Oklahoma. The following summer it was introduced at an area (five associations) Children's Music Camp which met annually at Falls Creek

Baptist Assembly. My wife, Jo Ann, served as choral director for this camp for several years and almost every summer I wrote a new song for the occasion."

Butler's setting was first published in the January-February-March 1972 issue of *Young Musicians*. BUTLER has been arranged for congregational unison singing in this hymnal by Anna Laura Page.   *H.E.*

God, whose purpose is to kindle 618

This hymn by Elton Trueblood, originally titled "Baptism by Fire" and beginning "Thou, whose purpose is to kindle," first appeared in his book *The Incendiary Fellowship* (New York, 1967, p. 11). In the preface, the author observed that the hymn was written to present the message of the book in a succinct form; gave the scriptural references for the hymn as Luke 12:49, Acts 2:3, John 10:10, and Matthew 10:34; and noted that the text was written to be sung to the tune HYFRYDOL. The hymn was printed in three stanzas of eight lines each.

The first hymnal appearance of Trueblood's text was in *The Worshipbook* (Philadelphia, 1972). Its initial Southern Baptist publication was in *Baptist Hymnal* (1975) where it was printed in six stanzas of four lines each and set to the tune LIBERTY. *The Baptist Hymnal* (1991) uses stanzas 1, 2, 4, 5, and 6 of the *Baptist Hymnal* (1975) version and incorporates a number of textual changes to eliminate archaic language. It is also set to yet a different tune.

HOLY MANNA—See hymn 379, Brethren, we have met to worship.   *D.M.*

Good Christian men, rejoice 96

The earliest mention of this text and tune is by a 14th-century writer who stated that these words were first sung by angels to the Dominican mystic Heinrich Susa (d. 1366), who was drawn into a dance with his heav-enly visitors. The carol is "macaronic" (a combination of Latin with a vernacular language, which in this case is German). The earliest existing version is at the Leipzig University Library, Codex 1305, dating from around 1400.

After publication in an early German Lutheran Hymnal, Joseph Klug's *Geistliche Lieder* (Wittenberg, 1533), "In dulci jubilo" entered numerous Protestant and Catholic collections. In 1646 an entirely German version beginning "Nun singet und seid froh" was published in the Hanover *New Ordenlich Gesang-Buch*. Leonard Ellinwood records (in *The Hymnal Companion* 1940, p.26) that the "macaronic character of the text was fully tested on September 14, 1745, at the Moravian Mission in Bethlehem, Pennsylvania, where the mission diary records that it was sung simultaneously in 13 languages, European and Indian."

John Mason Neale's free translation of this carol first appeared in his *Carols for Christmastide* (London, 1853), a collection of 12 carols he edited, along with Thomas Helmore, as an inexpensive publication available to Anglican church choirs.

IN DULCI JUBILO (meaning "in sweet shouting") appeared in the 14th century manuscript mentioned above. This lilting melody reflects the dance-like character of the medieval carol. *Baptist Hymnal* (Nashville, 1975, No. 90) was the first Southern Baptist collection to include this ancient carol. *H.E.*

Grace Greater than Our Sin—See *Marvelous grace of our loving Lord*

Grace to you 663

This fellowship song was the finale of the musical *Stearns and Company* (1975) which commemorated both the Separate Baptists and the bicentennial of the United States. It was premiered at Freedom '76 in San Antonio, Texas. John Hendrix and Norman Bowman wrote the words; Mark Blankenship wrote the music, which has been given the tune name STEARNS in honor of Separate Baptist leader Jubal Stearns. *The Baptist Hymnal* (1991) marks the initial appearance of this song in a Southern Baptist hymn collection.   *P.H.*

Grace to you and peace 664

This scriptural benediction based on 2 John 3 was set to music by Alice Parker in 1962 for a Mennonite Summer Music Conference. It was first published in *The Mennonite Hymnal* (1969) without a tune name. The name PARKER was first given in *The Baptist Hymnal* (1991). In a letter to this writer, the composer suggested how it may be learned by a congregation:

"It is best taught by lining out, without accompaniment, and having the entire congregation sing it in unison until it is familiar. Then add the canon—I like Soprano, Alto, Men. I always sing it once through in unison before starting the canon."   *H.E.*

Grace, Love, and Fellowship—See *May the grace of Christ, our Savior*

Grace, love, and peace abide 655

The words of this response were written by Ann Brown Sims and the music by her husband, W. Hines Sims. The response was first published in the March 1951 issue of *The Church Musician* (p. 23). The first hymnal publication of the response was in *Baptist Hymnal* (1956).

The tune was named MERIDIAN by the composer for Mrs. Sims' birthplace, Meridian, Mississippi.   *D.M.*

Great is the Lord 12

The words and tune of this song were written by Michael W. and Deborah D. Smith on June 25, 1982, and recorded by Michael W. Smith in 1983. The song became an instant success and appeared in numerous arrangements for choir and other media. The arrangement in *The Baptist Hymnal* (1991) first appeared in *The Hymnal for Worship and Celebration* (1986). *The Baptist Hymnal* (1991) marks the first publication of the song in a Southern Baptist collection.

GREAT IS THE LORD is the tune name taken from the song title.   *D.M.*

Great is Thy faithfulness 54

Thomas O. Chisholm wrote this hymn in 1923 while living in Vineland, New Jersey. Its use was not widespread for several years, until it became a favorite of Dr. Will H. Houghton, president of Moody Bible Institute. Its frequent use in that institution gave it exposure which contributed to its subsequent popularity. Both words and music were published first in *Songs of Salvation*, compiled by William M. Runyan (Chicago, 1923, No. 70). Their first appearance in a Southern Baptist hymnal was in the 1956 *Baptist Hymnal* (Nashville, No. 47).

FAITHFULNESS was composed for this text by William M. Runyan after he had received the text, along with several others, from Chisholm. It was written in Baldwin, Kansas, in 1923. About this tune, Runyan wrote: "This particular poem held such an appeal that I prayed most earnestly that my tune might carry over its message in a worthy way" (Reynolds, 1976, 80-81). The tune was named by the composer for inclusion in *Baptist Hymnal* (1956).   *M.P.*

Great Redeemer, we adore Thee 209

John Roy Harris wrote the hymn and composed original music for it in December, 1934, while he was on the faculty of Oklahoma Baptist University. Based on Isaiah

47:4, "As for our redeemer, the Lord of hosts is his name." Harris' words and music, entitled "Great Redeemer," first appeared in *Echoes of Heaven* (Fort Worth, 1937, No. 25).

REDENTORE (Italian for "redeemer") was composed by Paolo Conte for the text in 1936, replacing Harris' tune. It first appeared in *The Broadman Hymnal* (Nashville, 1940, No. 362). Conte suggested the tune name for its inclusion in *Baptist Hymnal* (1956). *W.J.R.*

Greater is He that is in me 437

The words and music to this chorus were written by Lanny Wolfe in 1973. The Gospel Music Association voted this chorus one of the Top Ten Songs for 1973. It was first published in sheet music folio by the Benson Publishing Company (Dimension Music, SESAC, 1973). In correspondence with Dr. Harry Eskew, the composer noted that "There was no special occasion for writing this song. It came from Scripture at what I call a 'moment of truth.' " *The Baptist Hymnal* (1991) is the first Southern Baptist collection to include this song.

GREATER IS HE is the name assigned to this tune and is taken from the common title and first line of the hymn. *H.E.*

Guide me, O Thou great Jehovah 56

This hymn, rich in biblical symbolism of the Exodus experience, was written by William Williams in Welsh and published in his *Alleluia* (Bristol, 1745). The original was in five six-line stanzas. The present version uses the English translation of stanza 1 made by Peter Williams and included in his *Hymns on Various Subjects* (1771). The other two stanzas are from a version made either by William Williams himself or by his son John in 1772. That version was first published as a leaflet and then in Lady Huntingdon's *Collection of Hymns*, fifth edition

(1772 or 1773). The earliest use of the hymn in Southern Baptist hymnals was in *The Baptist Psalmody* (Charleston, 1850, No. 537).

CWM RHONDDA—See hymn 395, God of grace and God of glory. *S.W.G.*

Hail the day that sees Him rise 165

Charles Wesley's hymn was first published in *Hymns and Sacred Poems* (1739) in 10 four-line stanzas titled "Hymn for Ascension Day." The hymn has been greatly altered many times, but the most popular form of the hymn has been Thomas Cotterill's as it appeared in his ninth edition of *Selections* (1820). Alleluias were added first in G. C. White's *Introits and Hymns* (1852). The present version is basically Wesley's with the extensive alterations of Cotterill and minor alterations by others. John Julian noted that "when all its various forms are taken into account, this hymn ranks as one of the three hymns by C. Wesley which of all his compositions have attained to the greatest popularity. The other two are 'Hark! The Herald Angels Sing' and 'Jesu, Lover of My Soul' " (Julian, 479).

This text first appeared in a Southern Baptist hymnal in *The Baptist Hymn and Praise Book* (Nashville, 1904, No. 125).

ASCENSION is the tune composed by W. H. Monk for the 1861 *Hymns Ancient and Modern* to replace "the old Wesleyan tune . . . of enormous compass, ranging from low B flat to the upper G" (245). The first Southern Baptist hymnal to include it is *The Baptist Hymnal* (1991). *S.W.G.*

Happy the home when God is there 505

Written by Henry Ware, Jr., and titled "The Happy Home," this hymn first appeared in Elizabeth Mayo's *Selection of Hymns and Poetry for the Use of Infant and Juvenile Schools and Families* (3rd ed., 1846). An alteration of Ware's text by Bryan Jeffery Leech was published in *Hymns for the Family of God* (1976, No. 540), of which Leech was assistant editor. The version in *The Baptist Hymnal* (1991) follows this revision of the text. In its unaltered version, the hymn had previously appeared in *Baptist Hymnal* (1956, No. 374).

ST. AGNES—See hymn 116, Our Savior's infant cries were heard.   *D.M.*

Hark to the story angels are telling 97

Alta C. Faircloth is the author of the words and is the arranger of this Polish carol. It was first published as an arrangement for four-part women's voices in the monthly periodical *The Church Musician* (December, 1959). The hymn tune version was made for the hymnal *Christian Praise* (Nashville, 1964, No. 70) and subsequently was included in *Baptist Hymnal* (Nashville, 1975, No. 92).

MCCRAY was the name of Alta Faircloth's son-in-law, and she named the tune for him. *W.J.R.*

Hark! the herald angels sing 88

Charles Wesley's original version of this hymn was published in *Hymns and Sacred Poems* (1739) as "Hark, how all the welkin rings,/Glory to the King of kings." George Whitefield's *Collection of Hymns for Social Worship* (1753) contained the present form of the first two lines.

According to Julian, the hymn was one of 10 four-line stanzas, the present version being substantially taken from its first appearance in the Supplement to the *New Version of the Psalms of David* (1782) by Tate and Brady. There the hymn is cast in three eight-line stanzas with the refrain taken from the first two verses of stanza one. The first Southern Baptist hymnal to include Wesley's hymn was Manly's *Baptist Psalmody* (Charleston, 1850, No. 141).

MENDELSSOHN was adapted from Felix Mendelssohn's *Festgesang an die Kunstler* (Op. 68, No. 7, 1840), a work scored for male voices and brass in commemoration of the art of printing. This tune is taken from the second movement, which praises Gutenberg, the inventor of movable type. The movement titled "Vaterland in deinen Gauen" was adapted by William Cummings in 1855 and first published in Richard Chope's *Congregational Hymn and Tune Book* (London, 1857). Chope's book calls the tune ST. VINCENT. *Hymns for the Use of the Methodist Episcopal Church with Tunes for Congregational Worship* (1857), the first American Methodist hymn- and tune-book coupled the text with the tune HENDON. The tune is found with an altered version of the hymn in *The Baptist Hymn and Praise Book* (Nashville, 1904, No. 91).   *P.H.*

Hark, the voice of Jesus calling 591

Daniel March, a Congregational minister, was invited to deliver a sermon to the Philadelphia Christian Association meeting in his church, the Clinton Avenue Congregational Church, Philadelphia, on October 18, 1868. His text was "Also I heard the voice of the Lord, saying, Whom shall I send, and who will go for us? Then said I, Here am I; send me" (Isa. 6:8). He was unable to find a suitable hymn for the occasion. Shortly before the service, he wrote this hymn in four stanzas, and it was used in the service. It was first published the following year in Robert Lowry's *Bright Jewels for the Sunday School* (New York, 1869, No. 51). The text first appeared in a Southern Baptist collection in *The Baptist Hymn and Praise Book* (Nashville, 1904, No. 457) with the tune ELLESDIE (but designated there DISCIPLE, fr. Mozart, by H. P. Main). Originally, the first stanza began, "Hark, the voice of Jesus crying." To make it more acceptable in contemporary contexts, other minor alterations have been made in the text for *The Baptist Hymnal* (1991).

ELLESDIE—See hymn 471, Jesus, I my cross have taken.   *W.J.R.*

Have faith in God 405

This strong hymn of assurance was written in 1934 by B. B. McKinney during a revival meeting in which he was leading music at the First Baptist Church, Muskogee, Oklahoma. In a time of economic depression and uncertainty, he keenly felt the need of expressing a secure faith in God. During the sermon one evening, he began writing "Have faith in God." Later that evening, upon returning to his hotel room, he completed the song, both words and music.

The manuscript was sent to music publisher Robert H. Coleman who copyrighted it in 1934 and published it in *Glad Tidings* (Dallas, 1935, No. 28). Upon becoming music editor of the Southern Baptist Sunday School Board, McKinney included the song in his first collection, *Songs of Victory* (Nashville, 1937, No. 29). It has since enjoyed wide usage among Southern Baptists and is generally considered one of McKinney's finest inspirations.

MUSKOGEE, after the town in Oklahoma where the song was inspired, was the name given B. B. McKinney's tune to his "Have Faith in God" by the committee for *Baptist Hymnal* (Nashville, 1956, No. 253).   *H.T.M.*

Have Thine own way, Lord! 294

According to Ernest K. Emurian, this hymn by Adelaide A. Pollard was written in 1902 (39). He also suggests that it is autobiographical. The first stanza is based on Jeremiah 18:1-6. The following stanzas recall Psalm 51:7; Matthew 28:18; and Galatians 2:20, respectively.

ADELAIDE was composed for this text in 1907 by George C. Stebbins. It appeared that

year in several collections, including his *Northfield Hymnal with Alexander's Supplement* (Chicago). The tune is also known as POLLARD.

Kingdom Songs (Nashville, 1921, No. 175) was the first Southern Baptist collection to include this hymn.   *P.A.R.*

Have You Been to Calvary—See *Have you been to the cross*

Have you been to Jesus 136

Elisha A. Hoffman wrote both words and music (WASHED IN THE BLOOD) for this gospel hymn, which was first published in *Spiritual Songs for Gospel Meetings and the Sunday School*, edited by Hoffman and J. H. Tenney (Cleveland, 1878, p. 15). Three years later it was published in England in Sankey's *Sacred Songs and Solos*. However, this song is not found in the four editions of the American counterpart of Sankey's songbook that appeared after Hoffman's song was written.

By the turn of the century, this hymn had become associated with the Salvation Army, founded by General William Booth. In 1912, the American poet Vachel Lindsay used Hoffman's hymn as a basis for his poem, "General Booth Enters into Heaven." In 1915, Charles Ives discovered Lindsay's poem in *The Independent* and composed a setting that has become one of Ives' best known songs. This hymn's first appearance in a Baptist collection was in *The Baptist Hymn and Praise Book* edited by Lansing Burrows (Nashville, 1904, No. 209).   *H.E.*

Have you been to the cross 324

Richard D. Baker wrote both words and music in 1978, during an evangelistic emphasis in Denton, Texas. It was published in a musical, *This Is Living*, by Crescendo Music Publications, 1978, and was also released as a single octavo. *The Baptist Hymnal* (1991) marks it's first appearance in a Southern Baptist collection.

McKINNEY is the name given Richard D. Baker's tune in *The Baptist Hymnal* (1991). *W.J.R.*

Have you failed in your plan 318

B. B. McKinney, in both writing and conversation with friends, recalled the circumstances surrounding the writing of this hymn. In 1924 while he was teaching at Southwestern Baptist Theological Seminary, he went to Allen, Texas, for a Sunday School Conference. The preacher for the conference had made a passionate plea for the lost to accept Christ, closing with the words "Place your hand in the nail-scarred hand." This statement so gripped McKinney's heart and imagination that he jotted it down on an envelope.

As the meeting closed, a threatening storm cloud came up, requiring McKinney to rush to the home of Mr. and Mrs. Elzir Leach where he spent the night. During the terrific storm which struck immediately upon his arrival at the home, McKinney composed the first stanza of "The Nail-Scarred Hand." Before retiring he had completed the other stanzas and the music.

It was first published in Coleman's *Harvest Hymns* (Dallas, 1924, No. 46). Coleman later included it in his larger hymn collection, *The Modern Hymnal* (Dallas, 1926, No. 291), which later was published by the Baptist Sunday School Board, Nashville, Tennessee. Then, as editor of *The Broadman Hymnal* (Nashville, 1940, No. 397), McKinney included his song written 15 years earlier.

LUBBOCK is a city in west Texas where the hymnal committee for *Baptist Hymnal* (Nashville, 1956) mistakenly thought "The Nail-Scarred Hand" had been written by B. B. McKinney and thus gave his tune that name.   *H.T.M.*

He Hideth My Soul—See *A wonderful Savior is Jesus my Lord*

He Included Me—See *I am so happy in Christ today*

He Is Able to Deliver Thee—See *'Tis the grandest theme*

He is born 112

This is a translation by George K. Evans of an anonymous French carol, "Il est ne', le divin enfant." The French words and the tune of the carol—also of French origin—probably date from the 18th century. According to William E. Studwell, *Christmas Carols: A Reference Guide* (New York, 1985, p. 105), the carol may have received its first publication in 1867 and the tune is that of the air *La tete bizarde*. The text has appeared in a number of English translations in addition to the present one. The first Southern Baptist collection to include this carol is *The Baptist Hymnal* (1991).

IL EST NE' is taken from the French title of the carol.   *D.M.*

He Is Lord—See *Emptied of His glory*

He is risen! He is risen 166

This text by Cecil Frances Alexander was first published in 1846 in her *Verses for Holy Seasons*. The preface to this collection indicated that its purpose was to provide hymns which would help children to understand the Christian year. In its original form, the text consisted of five stanzas of six lines each. The version which appears in *The Baptist Hymnal* (1991) uses stanzas 1, 3, and 5 from the original, with several textual alterations. Its appearance in that hymnal is its first in a Southern Baptist hymn collection.

HE IS RISEN is a hymn tune adaptation by Bob Burroughs of his anthem setting of this text which was originally published in 1984 as the last of four *a cappella* anthems in an Easter choral cycle. The hymn tune arrangement was prepared for *The Baptist Hymnal* (1991). *M.P.*

He Is So Precious to Me—See *So precious is Jesus, my Savior*

He Keeps Me Singing—See *There's within my heart a melody*

He leadeth me! O blessed thought 52
This hymn text was written by Joseph H. Gilmore on March 26, 1862, following a midweek service at the First Baptist Church of Philadelphia, Pennsylvania, in which he had delivered an exposition on the first part of Psalm 23, with emphasis upon the phrase "He leadeth me." During a subsequent discussion that same evening in the home of one of the church deacons, he wrote the hymn in pencil and handed it to his wife. Several months later she sent it to the *Watchman and Reflector,* a Boston paper which published the hymn on December 4, 1862. The hymn appeared under the title, "He Leadeth Me Beside Still Waters," and was signed CONTOOCOOK, a pseudonym presumably supplied by Mrs. Gilmore. When William B. Bradbury set the text to music for publication in *The Golden Censer* (1864), he expanded Gilmore's refrain from two to four lines, retaining the four verses as originally written.

For a more complete version of the origin of this hymn in Gilmore's own words, see William J. Reynolds, *Companion to Baptist Hymnal* (Nashville, 1976, pp.84-85). The first Southern Baptist hymnal to include this text, along with Bradbury's tune, was *The Baptist Hymn and Praise Book* (Nashville, 1904, No. 406).

HE LEADETH ME (also known as AUGHTON)

was written for this text by William B. Bradbury and was first published in *The Golden Censer* (1864). *M.P.*

He Lives—See *I serve a risen Savior*

He's got the whole world in His hands 346
An anonymous African-American spiritual, "He's Got the Whole World in His Hands" has appeared in youth and gospel collections since the 1950s, often including indications for guitar chords. A number of Southern Baptists became acquainted with this spiritual from the 1952 choral arrangement by William J. Reynolds (Oklahoma City, Century Press). The first denominational hymnals to include the hymn were *The Johannine Hymnal* (Oak Park, 1971) and *The Hymn Book* (n.p., the Anglican Church of Canada and the United Church of Canada, 1971). A significant factor in the popularity of this spiritual has been its frequent inclusion in recitals by such renowned singers as Marian Anderson and Leontyne Price. This song's textual repetition and its rhythmic syncopation is typical of the spiritual. Among the additional stanzas not included in *The Baptist Hymnal* (1991) are:

> He's got the gambling man right in His hands
> He's got the lying man right in His hands,
> He's got the crap-shooting man in His hands,
> He's got you and me brother in His hands,
> He's got you and me sister in His hands.

Richard Starr is a pseudonym for the arranger of WHOLE WORLD. The tune name was given by the hymnal committee for *The Baptist Hymnal* (1991). *The Baptist Hymnal* (1991) is the first Southern Baptist hymnal to include this spiritual. *H.E.*

Hear our prayer, O Lord 658

This prayer response was probably written in the 1890s and was first published in 1924 in leaflet form in H. Augustine Smith's *Hymns for American Youth* (New York, 1924). It is apparently based on such passages as Psalm 17:6 and Psalm 102:1-2. Its first appearance in a Southern Baptist collection was in *Voice of Praise* (Nashville, 1947, No. 307).

WHELPTON is named for the composer George Whelpton.   *S.W.G.*

Heaven Came Down—See *O what a wonderful, wonderful day*

Heavenly hosts in ceaseless worship 40

This hymn was written in 1972 by Timothy Dudley-Smith and was first published in *Psalm Praise* in 1973. The author based the text on Revelation 4 and 5, in which the apostle John views the transcendant worship of heaven. The hymn particularly reflects verses 4:1, 8, 9, 11 and 5:9, 11, and 12-14 of John's Revelation. No Southern Baptist hymnal contained this hymn prior to *The Baptist Hymnal* (1991).

HARWELL was composed by Lowell Mason in 1840 for Thomas Kelly's "Hark, Ten Thousand Harps and Voices." The tune first appeared in Mason's *Carmina Sacra* (1841). Its first appearance in a Southern Baptist collection was in *The Baptist Hymn and Praise Book* (Nashville, 1904, No. 130).   *P.H.*

Heavenly Sunlight—See *Walking in sunlight*

Here am I, send me 597

The text and music of this song were written by John Purifoy in 1975 while he was serving as an editor for Word Music. In a letter dated November 28, 1990, the writer of the song observed that it "was composed as a direct response to my first year of service in the Christian music publishing field. As a 23-year-old freshman out of college, I was overwhelmed with gratitude to God as well as [with] the responsibility in serving as music editor for Word, Inc. The musical and spiritual influences of people like Kurt Kaiser and Charles F. Brown had a great effect upon me, and my prayer was that I could dedicate my talents and personhood to the tasks that lay ahead." The words and music were first published in the form of a choral anthem in 1976 (Word Music, Inc.). The first hymnal to include it is *The Baptist Hymnal* (1991).

The tune was named SALLY TOWNSEND by the composer in memory of a friend and fellow church member who died at the age of 15 after a long struggle with cancer. During her illness, Sally had served as a source of inspiration to her youth group and the church as a whole.   *D.M.*

Here at Your table, Lord 368

The hymn, written by May P. Hoyt, first appeared in *The Church Hymnary* (New York, 1891), compiled by Edward A. Bedell. The text has been altered by the substitution of "you" and "your" for "thee" and "thy" in both stanzas for *The Baptist Hymnal* (1991). Its first appearance in a Southern Baptist collection was in *Baptist Hymnal* (Nashville, 1956, No. 392).

BREAD OF LIFE—See hymn 263, Break Thou the bread of life.   *W.J.R.*

Here, O Lord, your servants gather 179

This text was written by Tokuo Yamaguchi for the Fourteenth World Christian Education Convention, held in 1958 in Tokyo, Japan. It is based on the conference theme, "Jesus Christ, the Way, the Truth, and the Life" (John 14:6), and celebrates

Christ as the source of unity and peace amid cultural pluralism and international confrontation. This last aspect reflects the widespread concern stemming from the launching of the first Sputnik by the USSR shortly before the meeting. The Japanese text, "Sekai no tomo to te o tsunagi," and this English translation by Everett M. Stowe (originally "Here, O Lord, Thy Servants Gather") were sung at the conference.

This hymn was first published in *Christian Shimpo* on January 25, 1958. Its first inclusion in a hymnal was in *Hymns of the Church* (Tokyo, 1963). The first American hymnal to include it was *The Mennonite Hymnal* (Kansas, 1969).

TOKYO was commissioned to set this text for the meeting cited above. It is the work of Isao Koizumi, who used the *gagaku* mode in its composition. *Gagaku* is the traditional style of Japanese court music, which dates as early as the 8th century and has even older roots in Chinese music. The tune is pentatonic.

The first appearance of this hymn in a Southern Baptist hymnal is in *The Baptist Hymnal* (1991).   *P.A.R.*

Higher Ground—See *I'm pressing on the upward way*

His name is Wonderful 203

Audrey Mieir, who wrote both words and music, has provided the following information:

"We were working in the Bethel Union Church, Duarte, California (a suburb of Los Angeles), where my husband's brother, Dr. Luther Mieir was pastor. Christmas was on Sunday and we had made all the usual preparations that small churches make to present the Christmas story in its simplicity and beauty. The church was decorated with pine boughs. The choirloft had been converted into a manger scene, and we had chosen to use the young people to present the story. As the morning service began, I was almost overwhelmed with the fragrance, the sound, and most of all, with the gentle moving of the Spirit in that church. The pastor stood to his feet, opened the Bible, and said, 'His name shall be called Wonderful.' I tell you the truth, that's all it took. I wrote words and music on the flyleaf of my Bible.

"In the Sunday evening service I taught the chorus to a group of young people, and it was sung for the first time. The song was first published in 1959 by Manna Music, and has been recorded many times" (Reynolds, 1976, 88).

This gospel song recalls seven different names or descriptions of Jesus. Its first appearance in a Southern Baptist hymnal was in *Baptist Hymnal* (Nashville, 1975, No. 71).

MIEIR is the name given the tune in *Baptist Hymnal* (1975) for Audrey Mieir, the composer.   *S.W.G.*

Holy Bible, Book divine 260

This text was written by John Burton, Sr., an English Baptist Sunday School teacher, and was first published in his *Youth's Monitor in Verse, a Series of Little Tales, Emblems, Poems and songs* (1803). It subsequently appeared in the *Evangelical Magazine* (June, 1805) under the signature "Nottingham—J. B." The hymn was included in Burton's *Hymns for Sunday Schools, or Incentives for Early Piety* (1806), which contained 96 of his hymns. Its first publication in the United States was in *Hymns for the Nursery* (New Haven, 1813). The first Southern Baptist collection to include it was C. J. Elford's *The Confederate Sunday School Hymn Book* (Greenville, 1864, No. 52).

ALETTA, by William B. Bradbury, was first published in his *Jubilee* (New York, 1858) as a setting for "Weary Sinner, Keep Thine

Eyes." Here it was identified as a new tune. It first appeared with "Holy Bible, Book Divine" in a Southern Baptist collection, *The Baptist Hymn and Praise Book* (Nashville, 1904, No. 162).   *M.P.*

Holy Bible, Book of love 264

The words, written by Evone Wood Capell in 1954, were included in lesson material which she wrote for *The Primary Leader* (April, May, June, 1955, p. 55). In its first publication, the text was set to William B. Bradbury's hymn tune ALETTA. Its first appearance in a Southern Baptist song collection was in *Songs for Children* (Nashville, 1964, No. 109).

Saxe Adams and Nettie Lou Jones, compilers of *Songs for Children* (Nashville, 1964), asked Irving Wolfe to compose a new tune for Mrs. Capell's text for their publication. In *The Baptist Hymnal* (1991), the tune was named WOLFE for the composer.   *W.J.R.*

Holy Ground—See *We are standing on holy ground*

Holy Is His Name—See hymn 343, *Holy, God is holy*

Holy Is the Lord—See hymn 9, *Holy, holy, holy is the Lord*

Holy Is the Lord—See hymn 666, *Holy, holy, holy, Holy is the Lord*

Holy, holy, holy is the Lord 9

The author of the three-stanza hymn, based on Revelation 4:8, is unknown.

JUBILATE is a melody of unknown origin arranged by Bill Newton for *The Baptist Hymnal* (1991).   *W.J.R.*

Holy Lord 622

This text was adapted from Isaiah 6:3 to fit the tune DONA NOBIS PACEM , a canon of unknown origin, possibly from the 16th century. Both the words and the tune were adapted by a musician whose pseudonym is Gerald S. Henderson.   *P.H.*

Holy Spirit, breathe on me 238

"Holy Spirit, breathe on me" was written in 1937 by B.B. McKinney who based it on the 19th-century hymn "Breathe on Me, Breath of God" by the British clergyman, Edwin Hatch. McKinney's song with its appealing chorus is a considerable alteration and extension of the original hymn. (See *The Baptist Hymnal*, 1991, No. 241). It was first published in a Southern Baptist collection in *Songs of Victory* (Nashville, 1973, No. 5) which was edited by McKinney.

TRUETT is the name chosen for B. B. McKinney's tune to his "Breathe on Me" by the committee for *Baptist Hymnal* (Nashville, 1956). It was named for George W. Truett (1867-1944), outstanding Southern Baptist preacher who for 47 years was the pastor of First Baptist Church, Dallas, Texas.   *H.T.M.*

Holy, God is holy 343

This text and tune were composed by David Danner in 1985 as a part of his musical *Praise*. This musical was composed for the Youth Choir of the Buncombe County Baptist Association at Asheville, North Carolina, the group that gave the work its premier performance at the Ridgecrest Baptist Conference Center in 1985. During *Praise*, this hymn is to be sung by a four-part choir and the congregation. "Holy Is His Name" was also published as a three-part round for children's choir in the January-February-March 1988 issue of *Young Musicians* (31-34). Its first publication in a hymnal is in *The Baptist Hymnal* (1991).

HICKS, the tune name, is named for John E. Hicks (1917-85), Director of Missions for the Buncombe County Baptist Association when this musical was commissioned. *H.E.*

Holy, holy 254

In a telephone conversation with Donald Brown, Jimmy Owens told of writing this text and tune (also named HOLY, HOLY) as part of the musical *Come Together* which was published in 1972. Owens wrote the musical as a way of expressing his belief that every Christian should be a minister and that the three primary ministries of the church are (1) to the Lord in worship, prayer, praise, and obedience; (2) to one another; and (3) to the world in evangelism. This piece was the final song of a segment dealing with reverential praise. *The Baptist Hymnal* (1991) is the first Southern Baptist collection to include this song. *D.B.*

Holy, holy, holy! 2

Written by Reginald Heber for Trinity Sunday while he was vicar of Hodnet, Shropshire (1807-23), this hymn text was first published in *A Selection of Psalms and Hymns of the Parish Church of Banbury,* third edition (1826). It was included in Heber's *Hymns Written and Adapted to the Weekly Church Service of the Year,* published posthumously in 1827.

The hymn is based upon Revelation 4: 8-11, and the opening half-line of each stanza also calls to mind Isaiah 6:3, the *Kedusha* of Jewish synagogue worship, and the *Sanctus* of the early Christian church. This text is illustrative of the early 19th-century movement in England which emphasized higher literary standards for the hymn. Its first appearance in a Southern Baptist hymnal was in *The Baptist Hymn and Praise Book* (Nashville, 1904, No. 83), where it was paired with the NICAEA tune.

NICAEA (also called SANCTUS) was written for this text by John B. Dykes. Often cited as the finest of Dykes's hymn tunes, it was first published, along with six other of his tunes, in *Hymns Ancient and Modern* (London, 1861). Dykes named the tune for the Council of Nicaea, A.D. 325, which formulated the Nicene Creed, a statement of faith which included an affirmation of the doctrine of the Trinity in response to the Arian heresy. *M.P.*

Holy, holy, holy, Holy is the Lord 666

This traditional text is based on the ancient Sanctus. The tune HOLY IS THE LORD was composed by Franz Shubert. In Volume 6 of the Dover reprint of the Breitkopf & Härtel edition of Schubert's complete works, the piece is printed as "For the Sanctus" under the general heading, "Songs for the Celebration of the Holy Offering of the Mass." Except for a change or two in the harmonization, the piece appears in our hymnal exactly as Schubert published it. The editor's comments in the critical edition suggest the song was first published in 1827 in Vienna. *D.B.*

Hosanna, loud hosanna1 30

Jennette Threlfall's text related to Jesus' triumphal entry into Jerusalem (see Matthew 21:9, Mark 11:9-10, and John 12:13) was first published in *Sunshine and Shadow,* a collection of 70 of her poems published in 1873. John Julian considered it to be the most widely used of her hymn texts. It appeared in this country in *Worship in Song* (New York and Chicago, *c.* 1880). It is included for the first time in a Southern Baptist hymnal in *The Baptist Hymnal* (1991).

ELLACOMBE's origins can seemingly be traced to a melody used as a setting of the text, "Ave Maria, klarer und lichter Morgenstern," in the *Gesangbuch der Herzoglichen Wirtembergischen Katholischen Hofkapelelle* (1784). In this collection used in the private chapel of the Duke of Würtemberg, it was listed as "Melodie No. 16." A German variant more closely resembling the present form of ELLACOMBE appeared in *Vollständige Sammlung der gewöhnlichen Melodien zum Mainzer Gesangbuche* (1833) by Xavier L. Hartig. (For a comparison of these two predecessors of ELLACOMBE, see Marilyn Stulken's *Hymnal Companion to the Lutheran Book of Worship*, pp. 325-26.) The tune as it is currently used was included as a setting for "Come, sing with holy gladness" in the 1868 Appendix to *Hymns Ancient and Modern*. The tune name currently used was apparently ascribed by an editor of a hymnal published in England, since Ellacombe is the name of a village in Devonshire.   *M.P.*

How can I say thanks 153

Both words and music of this gospel song were written in 1971 by Andraé Crouch. It made its first appearance in a hymnal in *Hymns for the Family of God* (Nashville, 1976). The first inclusion of this item in a collection for Southern Baptists is in *The Baptist Hymnal* (1991).

MY TRIBUTE, the tune name and common title of the song is also known by the first words of the chorus, TO GOD BE THE GLORY. *P.A.R.*

How firm a foundation 338

This hymn first appeared in John Rippon's *A Selection of Hymns from the Best Authors* (1787), with only the ascription "K-." The immediate and lasting popularity of the hymn has evoked considerable speculation about its authorship. Most attempts to identify the author have focused upon Robert Keene (or Keen), who was precentor at Rippon's Carter Lane Baptist Church (1776-93). Keene's name appears, however, only in conjunction with six hymn tunes published

in Rippon's *Selection of Psalm and Hymn Tunes* (1791), including the one to which the present hymn is set. William J. Reynolds cites W. T. Whitley, as documented from internal evidence, that Keene actually compiled this tune source (1976, 90-91). The question remains why Keene's name would be omitted from the hymn text and not the tune if he were the creator of both. Other names cited in later books include Kirkham and George Keith. Barring further substantiation, the authorship must remain the anonymous "K—."

Originally, the hymn was published in seven stanzas. Previous Southern Baptist hymnals contained stanzas 1, 3, 5, and 7. The present version restores the original fourth stanza. The stanzas omitted are:

In every condition, in sickness, in health,
    In poverty's vale, or abounding in wealth;
    At home and abroad, on the land, on the sea,
    As thy days may demand, shall thy strength ever be!

Even down to old age, all my people shall prove
    My sovereign, eternal, unchangeable love;
    And when hoary hairs shall their temples adorn,
    Like lambs they shall in my bosom be borne.

In Rippon's *Selection*, the hymn was titled "Exceeding Great and Precious Promises." The first Southern Baptist hymnal, Basil Manly's *The Baptist Psalmody* (Charleston, 1850, No. 828), contained this text with seven stanzas.

FOUNDATION is an anonymous American folk tune which appears in Joseph Funk's *Genuine Church Music* (1832) as PROTECTION.

With slight variations, the tune was used in other shape-note books such as *The Sacred Harp* (1844), where it is called BELLVUE, and the *Southern Harmony* (3rd. ed., 1854), where it is associated with a different text and entitled THE CHRISTIAN'S FAREWELL. The present version of this pentatonic tune and its harmonization are derived from R. M. McIntosh's *Tabor: or, the Richmond Collection of Sacred Music* (1866). Called CONVENTION, the tune appears in *The Baptist Hymn and Praise Book* (Nashville, 1904, No. 236). As early as Robert Coleman's *The Popular Hymnal* (Dallas, 1918, No. 108), the tune is called FOUNDATION. *P.H.*

How great our God's majestic Name! 70

Timothy Dudley-Smith wrote this hymn in August, 1989, at his family's summer home in Cornwall, England. It is based on the Revised Standard Version's rendering of Psalm 8. In a letter to this author dated November 20, 1990, Dudley-Smith related: "I had before me F. D. Kidner's *Tyndale Commentary* on Psalm 8 (Inter-Varsity Press, 1973). Verse 3 is an attempt to meet his point that the right inference to draw from God's ordered heavens is not his remoteness but his eye for detail. 'He planned no meaningless and empty universe but a home for his family.' Hence the reply to 'What is man?' is not 'a few random atoms' but 'Creation's crown.' "

The Baptist Hymnal (1991) is the first Southern Baptist hymnal to include this text.

DUKE STREET—See hymn 587, Jesus shall reign. *P.H.*

How Great Our Joy—See *While by the sheep we watched*

How Great Thou Art—See *O Lord my God! When I in awesome wonder*

How I Love You—See *Jesus, how I love You!*

How lovely is Thy dwelling place 523

This version of Psalm 84 came into use through the Scottish Psalter, *The Psalms of David in Meter* (1650), having 14 four-line stanzas but reduced to 12 four-line stanzas and much altered by the 1929 edition. The present version is that of *The Hymnal 1982* of the Episcopal Church. This version has been changed from the four-line common meter to the six-line 8 6. 8 6. 8 6 meter. At the request of the text committee for *The Hymnal 1982*, Carl Daw edited the first two stanzas from the Scottish psalter and then wrote the remaining stanzas to provide a paraphrase of the entire psalm in the same style. Its first inclusion in a Southern Baptist collection was in *The Baptist Hymnal* (1991).

The tune BROTHER JAMES' AIR (also MAROSA) is a traditional melody recorded by James Leith Bain (pen name: James Macbeth). It has become widely known as BROTHER JAMES' AIR through a choral version arranged for mixed voices by Gordon Percival Septimus Jacob (Oxford University Press, 1934) and set to "The Lord's my Shepherd, I'll not want" from the Scottish Psalter of 1650. BROTHER JAMES' AIR was apparently first published in Bain's tract, *The Great Peace* (1915). Bain, a Christian Scientist, was popularly known as Brother James and wrote numerous books on mysticism and related topics. *H.E.*

How Majestic Is Your Name—See *O Lord, our Lord, how majestic*

How sweet the name of Jesus sounds 453

Written by John Newton, the hymn of seven stanzas first appeared in the *Olney Hymns* (London, 1779, p. 72), titled "The

Name of Jesus," based on Song of Solomon 1:3, "Thy name is as ointment poured forth." The present version is made up of stanzas 1,2,3, and 5. In stanza four, line one, "brother" was originally "husband."

There were two additional stanzas in Newton's original text. The hymn first appeared in the United States in *The Christian Duty, Exhibited in a Series of Hymns,* a hymnal for the Dunkers (Church of the Brethren) compiled by a Fraternity of Baptists (Germantown, 1791). It was included in Southern Baptists' first "official" hymn collection, *The Baptist Psalmody* (Charleston, 1850, No. 583).

ORTONVILLE was composed by Thomas Hastings for Samuel Stennett's hymn "Majestic Sweetness Sits Enthroned." The tune first appeared in Hastings' *The Manhattan Collection* (New York, 1837), where it was in the key of C. It is first found in a Southern Baptist collection in *The Baptist Hymn and Praise Book* (Nashville, 1904, No. 309). *W.J.R.*

I am happy today 421

Both the text and the tune for this hymn were written by J. Edwin McConnell in 1910. Charlie D. Tillman purchased the manuscript of the song and secured a copyright in 1914. In an April 25, 1955, letter to William Reynolds, Mrs. Jean McConnell Larkin, the sister of the hymn writer, wrote:

"One very cold, below zero, day in a hotel in Spirit Lake, Iowa, an 18-year-old youth was at the piano and humming to himself. His father, who had been opening his mail nearby, asked what he was playing. 'Oh, just another song aborning, Dad,' answered the boy.... That night they introduced 'Whosoever Surely Meaneth Me' to the audience of their evangelistic meeting, where it soon became their 'theme song' of the campaign" (1976, 93).

The hymnal committee of the *Baptist*

Hymnal (1956) named the tune MCCONNELL. The first Southern Baptist collection to include this song was *Kingdom Songs* (Nashville, 1921, No. 11). *D.B.*

I Am His, and He Is Mine—See *Loved with everlasting love*

I am resolved 301

The origin of this hymn was related to William J. Reynolds in a letter dated January 28, 1955, from Mrs. J. L. Toll, daughter of the composer, James H. Fillmore.

"[This tune] was written in 1896 as a delegation song for Ohio—fourteen train loads—for the World Christian Endeavor Convention in San Francisco, honoring Frances E. Clarke, founder of Christian Endeavor. The song became so popular Mr. Hartsough wrote new words for it for our hymnals" (1976, 195).

Palmer Hartsough's new text first appeared with Fillmore's tune in *The Praise Hymnal,* compiled by Gilbert G. Ellis and Fillmore (Cincinnati, 1896, No. 228). (This was also the first hymnal to include "I Know That My Redeemer Liveth.") Except for minor changes in the tenor part in the last two phrases, the hymn tune appears unaltered from that of *The Praise Hymnal.* In 1915, this hymn appeared in Southern Baptist compiler-editor Robert H. Coleman's *The Herald* (Dallas, No. 26) and continued to be published in Coleman's numerous edited songbooks and hymnals, including *The Modern Hymnal* (Dallas, 1926, No. 235).

The tune name RESOLUTION was used first in the 1956 *Baptist Hymnal.* *H.E.*

I am satisfied with Jesus 472

B. B. McKinney wrote "Satisfied with Jesus" on a Saturday afternoon while on the faculty at Southwestern Baptist Theological Seminary, Ft. Worth, Texas. He had been pondering what God as Savior, Comforter, and Friend had done for him and how little he had done for God. He was altogether satisfied with Jesus but altogether dissatisfied with his own life. Therefore he wrote "Satisfied with Jesus" out of a deep sense of his own need to live a life more dedicated to God's service. With some emotion and even tears, he completed the song that afternoon. The details of that experience in McKinney's own words are recorded in Reynolds' *Companion to Baptist Hymnal* (Nashville, 1976, p. 94). The hymn was first published in Robert H. Coleman's *The Modern Hymnal* (Dallas, 1926, No. 427). Sixteen years later McKinney included it in the widely popular Southern Baptist collection *The Broadman Hymnal* (Nashville, 1940, No. 375).

ROUTH was the name given B. B. McKinney's tune for "Satisfied with Jesus" by the hymnal committee for *Baptist Hymnal* (Nashville, 1956, No. 436). This was the maiden name of McKinney's wife, Leila, whose brother Dr. E. C. Routh, preacher, journalist, and author, was for many years editor of the Oklahoma Baptist weekly, *Baptist Messenger*. Dr. Porter Routh, son of E. C. Routh and nephew of Mrs. McKinney, served as executive secretary of the Executive Committee of the Southern Baptist Convention (1951-79).   *H.T.M.*

I am so happy in Christ today 436

The text of this gospel song was written by Johnson Oatman, Jr. It first appeared with the present tune in *Hymns of Glory, No. 2* (Atlanta, 1914), compiled by Hampton H. Sewell.

SEWELL is named for its composer, an evangelistic singer. He wrote it in 1909 during a series of services which he was leading with preacher Charles Dunway. In *Companion to Baptist Hymnal*, William J. Reynolds quoted a letter from Sewell's widow:

"In April, 1909, they had a wonderful revival in Waycross, Georgia, and many souls were saved. ...It was also in this meeting that my husband was inspired to write the hymn 'He Included Me'" (95).

The first Southern Baptist hymnal to include this gospel song was *Kingdom Songs* (Nashville, 1921, No. 110).   *P.A.R.*

I am Thine, O Lord 290

The popular lyric "I Am Thine, O Lord" was written by Fanny Crosby in Cincinnati, Ohio, in the home of her friend, William H. Doane. One evening during her visit, they had been discussing the nearness of God. Upon retiring, the author formulated the entire four stanzas of the song that very night. She gave it to her host who later supplied the tune. Since its first publication in 1875, the hymn has remained unaltered in all subsequent Baptist hymn and gospel song books. Its first inclusion in an official Southern Baptist collection was in *The Baptist Hymn and Praise Book* (Nashville, 1904, No. 333), where the original title "Draw Me Nearer" was kept.

I AM THINE was composed by William H. Doane to the Crosby text. It was first published in *Brightest and Best*, an oblong Sunday School collection by Doane and Robert Lowry (New York and Chicago, 1875). There the title of the gospel song appears as "Draw Me Nearer," and beneath is the Scripture quotation, "Let us draw near with a true heart" (Hebrews 10:22). The tune name was first used in a Baptist collection in *Baptist Hymnal* (Nashville, 1956).   *H.T.M.*

I am weak but Thou art strong 448

The origin of this song is not known. Its earliest publications seem to have been in the evangelistic songbooks of the Stamps-Baxter Music and Printing Company in the late 1940s.

CLOSER WALK takes its name from the first line of the refrain.

Its first appearance in a hymnal for Southern Baptists was in *Baptist Hymnal* (Nashville, 1975, No. 481). *P.A.R.*

I can hear my Savior calling 288

Little is known about the origin of this hymn, except that it was copyrighted in 1890 by the composer of the tune, J.S. Norris, and that the words were attributed to E.W. Blandy. The earliest known printing of the hymn was in W.G. Cooper's *Pearls of Paradise* (Chicago, 1891).

The tune was named NORRIS in *Baptist Hymnal* (1956). This hymn and tune first entered into Southern Baptist use in Robert H. Coleman's *The Evangel* (Philadelphia, 1909, No. 155). *D.M.*

I come to the garden alone 187

One day in March, 1912, C. Austin Miles was sitting in his home, in a combination study and photographic darkroom, reading the 20th chapter of John's gospel which describes the arrival of Mary, Peter, and John at the tomb where Christ had been buried. As he read this account, in his imagination he saw all of this happening, heard the voices, and watched as a silent observer. From the inspiration of this experience, he remained at his desk and completed the words of the hymn. Later that evening he composed the music. The tune name GARDEN is taken from the first line of the hymn.

The first appearance of the hymn corrected was in *The Gospel Message No. 2*, compiled by J. H. Hall, C. Austin Miles, and Adam Geibel (Philadelphia, 1912). Its first appearance in a Southern Baptist collection was in *Songs of Redemption* compiled by W. Plunket Martin and James W. Jelks (Atlanta, 1920, No. 9). *W.J.R.*

I come with joy to meet my Lord 371

"I Come with Joy to Meet my Lord" was written in July, 1968, for the author's congregation at Hockley, England, to sum up a series of sermons on the meaning of communion. Brian Wren saw his hymn first published in *The Hymn Book of the Anglican Church of Canada and the United Church of Canada* (Canada, 1971, No. 328). A revised form of the text was later printed in Wren's *Mainly Hymns* (Leeds, 1980, No. 22). The revised text is the one found in *The Baptist Hymnal* (1991) but omitted there is the author's original stanza two:

I come with Christians far and near
    To find, as all are fed,
The new community of love
    In Christ's communion bread.

The Baptist Hymnal (1991) is the first Southern Baptist collection to include this hymn.

LAND OF REST—See hymn 510, O Lord, may church and home combine. *H.T.M.*

I gave My life for thee 606

Frances R. Havergal's collected poems cite a motto found under a picture of Jesus in the study of an eminent German pastor as the basis of this hymn: "I did this for thee; what hast thou done for Me?" In addition to this motto, each of the six stanzas of this hymn, given in *The Poetical Works of Frances Ridley Havergal* (1884), lists a Scripture reference to the right of each line. For the four stanzas in our hymnal (stanzas 1, 3, 4, and 5 of the original), the six scripture references corresponding to six lines of each stanza are:

1. (1) Galatians 2:20, (2) 1 Peter 1:19, (3) Ephesians 1:7, (4) Ephesians 2:1, (5) Titus 2:14, (6) John 21:15-17.

2. (1) John 17:5, (2) Revelation 4:3, (3) Philippians 2:7, (4) Matthew 7:20, (5) 2 Corinthians 28:9, (6) Luke 10:29.

3. (1) Isaiah 53:5, (2) Matthew 26:39, (3)

Luke 22:44, (4) Romans 5:9, (5) 1 Peter 2:21-24, (6) Romans 8:17,18.

4. (1) John 4:10,14, (2) John 3:13, (3) Revelation 21:6, (4) Acts 5:31, (5) Psalm 68:18, (6) Romans 7:1.

The author's sister, Maria V. G. Havergal, provided the following account:

"On January 10, 1858, she (the writer) had come in weary, and sitting down she read the motto, and the lines of her hymn flashed upon her. She wrote them in pencil on a scrap of paper. Reading them over she thought them so poor that she tossed them on the fire, but they fell out untouched. Showing them some months after to her father [the Rev. William Henry Havergal], he encouraged her to preserve them, and wrote the tune BACA specially for them. The hymn was printed on a leaflet, 1859, and in *Good Words*, February, 1860" (Reynolds, 1976, 97).

The first American publication of this text was in Philip Phillips' *New Standard Singer* (New York, 1868).

The tune KENOSIS, composed for this hymn by Philip P. Bliss and dedicated to the "Railroad Chapel Sunday School, Chicago," was first published in *Sunshine for Sunday Schools* by P. P. Bliss (Cincinnati, 1873, p. 56). It was included in *The Baptist Hymnal* by W. H. Doane and E. H. Johnson (Philadelphia, 1883, No. 459). The name "Kenosis" is from the Greek New Testament, referring to Christ's self-emptying (Phil. 2:7). The original key is C, and the following dynamic markings are given to the corresponding repeated lines at the close of each stanza:

Forte: I gave, I gave my life for thee,
Piano: What hast thou given for me?

The hymn became widely known among Southern Baptists by its publication in *The Baptist Hymn and Praise Book* (Nashville, 1904, No. 451).   *H.E.*

I have a song I love to sing 543

Both text and tune of this gospel song were written by E. O. Excell, who first published it in *Echoes of Eden for the Sunday School* (Chicago, 1884). The original contained another stanza between the present third and fourth. Its first and third lines were:

I have a joy I can't express,
All through His blood and righteousness.

OTHELLO was Excell's middle name. It was first affixed to the tune by the editors of *Baptist Hymnal* (Nashville, 1956).

The Broadman Hymnal (Nashville, 1940, No. 108) was the first Southern Baptist collection to include this hymn.   *P.A.R.*

I have come from the darkness 532

The words and music of this hymn were written by Marian Wood Chaplin (Pille) in 1964. In a letter dated May 8, 1990, the author noted that the hymn was inspired by "a young Jewish singer who was converted to Christianity when he lay very ill in a Baptist hospital in Cincinnati, Ohio. Upon returning to his home in Lexington, he called me to say, 'I have come from the darkness'—hence, the title to the song."

At the time the song was written, Mrs. Chaplin (as she was then) was living in Lexington, Kentucky. She drove to Nashville to present it to the Baptist Sunday School Board for possible publication. According to her own account, she was "ushered into the office of Dr. William Reynolds, who, upon hearing me play and sing it, decided almost immediately that this was the song they were looking for to use at the Baptist World Convention [sic] in the Orange Bowl in Miami, Florida. Since then it has been sung in the Billy Graham Crusade chorus, on radio, and has been recorded by George Beverly Shea and Frank Boggs, among others."

TO THE LIGHT is the tune name assigned to this hymn. The first hymnal appearance of the song is in *The Baptist Hymnal* (1991). *D.M.*

I have decided to follow Jesus 305

Here is a folk song that originated among one of the hill tribes in India. The Garo tribe lives in an area which is now the state of Meghalaya, but was, until 1970, the state of Assam, in northeastern India. The northern part of Meghalaya borders on the Himalayan Mountain range and the Brahmaputra and Barak, principal rivers. About two-thirds of the people are Hindus, and about a fourth of the population are Muslims. Many of the hill tribes, such as the Garos, have been converted to Christianity by missionaries, but the majority of the people still observe the customs and rituals of their traditional region. In this culture, to become a Christian could be a costly decision with "no turning back."

The first appearance in the United States seems to have been in *Choice Light and Life Songs*, compiled by LeRoy M. Lowell & Others (Winona Lake, 1950), a publication of the Free Methodist Church. The present version consists of two original stanzas, a third stanza by John Clark, with a fourth stanza which is considered traditional. The harmonization was made by William J. Reynolds. In this form it was published in *Assembly Songbook* (Nashville, 1959, No. 17). The tune was named ASSAM by the arranger for inclusion in *Christian Praise* (Nashville, 1964, No. 153).   *W.J.R.*

I have found a friend in Jesus 189

The late Lieutenant Colonel Gordon Avery, Salvation Army hymnologist, supplied William J. Reynolds the following information on this hymn and its author, Charles W. Fry:

"Soon after Fry's death on August 24, 1882, the manuscript of these words, writ-ten to a secular melody, was found among his personal effects by his widow. Attached to the song was a note stating it had been written at a Mr. Wilkinson's home in Lincoln, England, in June 1881, where Fry was a guest during his service with the Salvation Army in that city. The words were first published in *The War Cry* for December 29, 1881. Words and music first appeared in *Salvation Music, Vol. 2* (1883)" (1976, 97-98).

The original publication of Fry's hymn begins, "I've found a friend in Jesus" and used the contractions "I've" (st. 2, 1.3) and "He'll" (st. 3, 1.1). As early as 1890 these three contractions were altered to the present version in W. F. Strong's *Chapel Chimes* (Valparaiso) and in John McPhail's *Songs of Saving Power* (Chicago).

The earliest American publication of this hymn found by Reynolds is in J. S. Inskip's supplement to *Songs of Triumph* (Philadelphia, 1885; 1st ed. 1882). As pointed out by Avery in his *Companion to the Song Book of the Salvation Army* (London, 1961, p. 92), this hymn was adopted by Ira D. Sankey in his evangelistic campaigns with D. L. Moody in Britain, and he included it in his *Sacred Songs and Solos*. In 1887, Fry's hymn was included in the fifth volume of this collection's American counterpart entitled *Gospel Hymns No. 5* by Sankey, James McGranahan, and George C. Stebbins (New York; Chicago; Cincinnati, No. 102).

As pointed out to the present writer in a letter dated August 22, 1989, from Colonel Brindley Boon, English Salvation Army composer and music historian, the tune SALVATIONIST has on the authority of Fry himself been associated with the music of the American minstrel song by Will S. Hays, "The Little Old Log Cabin in the Lane" (Boston, 1871). The initial publication of Fry's hymn is the December 29 issue of *The War Cry* and bears the designation: "Tune—

'The Little, Old Log Cabin.' " The poetry of Fry's hymn and Hays' song vary in length, for the former has six-line stanzas and a two-line chorus, and the latter, eight-line stanzas and a four-line chorus. The meters of both are irregular, and Fry's hymn can only be sung to Hays' tune by adding or subtracting notes and omitting four phrases:

	Stanza	Chorus
SALVATIONIST	14.11.14.11.13.10	14.11
Hays' tune	14.10.14.10.14.10.14.11	13.9.15.11

Although one may hear the melody of Hays' song without associating it with that of "The Lily of the Valley," there are similar motives, and the closing pitches of their phrases are often the same. Early publications of SALVATIONIST demonstrate much uncertainty concerning its origin as well as variations in melody, harmony, rhythm, and meter. No composer attribution is given in *Salvation Music, Vol. 2* (1883), where the melody varies slightly from the present version and contains chromatic alterations. In *Gospel Hymns No. 5*, SALVATIONIST is given in 6/8 meter with the indication, "Arr. by Ira D. Sankey." In *Gospel Hymns No. 1 to 6 Complete* (1894, No. 367), the attribution is changed to "Arr. from J. R. Murray by I. D. Sankey." A search of available collections by James R. Murray has not located this tune. Later, Sankey even attributed this tune to Fry: "Mr. Fry is one of the leaders of the Salvation Army in London. In addition to writing the words, he also set the hymn to music, and later arranged it to slower time and published it in Gospel Hymns" (387).

In the Baptist collection *Select Gems* by Robert Lowry and W. H. Doane (Philadelphia, 1889, No. 154), this tune bears the designation, "English Melody." The version of SALVATIONIST in this Baptist collection is practically identical to that in our hymnal. Although there are uncertainties concerning the origin of SALVATIONIST, the conclusion of Colonel Brindley Boon may well be correct: "My opinion is that Charles Fry's words, 'I've found a friend in Jesus,' were set to 'The Little Old Log Cabin in the Lane' as he remembered the tune. In those days people heard the tune and sought to commit it to memory without ever having seen the music, and took the liberty of writing down the melody as they thought they had heard it. Or it could have been wrongly passed on. Today's stringent copyright laws would prohibit such a practice, but I guess there was no such worry in 1881" (Boon).

The first Southern Baptist collection to contain this song was *Songs of Faith* (Nashville, 1933, No. 95).   *H.E.*

I have heard the voice of Jesus 482

Both words and music were written by Richard D. Baker in 1966 for a month-long evangelistic crusade in First Baptist Church, Dallas, Texas. Prior to this meeting, he was inspired to write the hymn; it became the theme song for the revival. He named the tune LORIANN after his daughter, for inclusion in *Baptist Hymnal* (Nashville, 1975), its first appearance in a Southern Baptist collection. For a full discussion of the hymn, see "All to Thee," by David W. Music in *The Church Musician* (July, 1987, p. 14).   *W.J.R.*

I hear the Savior say 134

Elvina M. Hall was a member of the choir at Monument Street Methodist Church in Baltimore, Maryland, when she wrote this hymn. The words were composed one Sunday morning in 1865 during a long prayer by the pastor and were written on the flyleaf of a hymnal, the *New Lute of Zion*. Mrs. Hall subsequently gave a copy of her poem to the pastor.

Meanwhile, Mrs. Hall's choir director, John T. Grape, wrote a tune for another text—also called "Jesus Paid It All"—which had appeared in William B. Bradbury's *Golden Censer* (1864). Grape later observed that the choir and his friends thought the new tune (ALL TO CHRIST) was "very poor," but that his wife thought it was "a good piece of music." The composer showed his tune to the pastor, who noted that the tune would fit Mrs. Hall's new text. This pairing of text and tune first appeared in Theodore Perkins' *Sabbath Chords* (New York, 1868, No. 93).

Mrs. Hall's original text contained five stanzas and has undergone considerable revision (Reynolds, 1976, 99-100).

The first inclusion in a Southern Baptist hymnal of this text (five stanzas) and tune was in *The Baptist Hymn and Praise Book* (Nashville, 1904, No. 221). *D.M.*

I hear Thy welcome voice 302

Both the words and music (WELCOME VOICE) of this hymn were written by Lewis Hartsough in 1872. The text originally contained six stanzas, of which the present hymnal uses stanzas one, two, three, and six. The first publication of the hymn was in Joseph Hillman's *The Revivalist* (Troy, 1872), of which Hartsough was music editor.

Ira D. Sankey discovered Hartsough's hymn in 1873 in a monthly magazine, *Guide to Holiness,* a copy of which had been sent to him while he was conducting revival meetings in England with Dwight L. Moody. Sankey published the song in the first edition of his *Sacred Songs and Solos* (1873) and subsequently in *Gospel Hymns and Sacred Songs* (1875). There are a number of similarities between the words and music of this hymn and those of "Jesus Paid It All."

The first publication of "I Hear Thy Welcome Voice" in a Southern Baptist collection was in *The Baptist Hymn and Praise Book* (Nashville, 1904, No. 235). *D.M.*

I heard an old, old story 426

E. M. Bartlett, Sr. wrote the words and music to this, his last song, in 1939. The words expressed a strong Christian hope in spite of a stroke which had left him partially paralyzed. The first printing of the hymn was in James D. Vaughn's *Gospel Choruses* (Lawrenceburg, 1939). Bartlett was for many years a representative for the Vaughn Music Company. He subsequently sold the copyright to the Stamps-Baxter Music Company, Dallas, Texas. The second term of copyright renewal rights were assigned to Albert E. Brumley and Sons, Powell, Missouri. The tune name HARTFORD was given by his son Gene to commemorate the Arkansas town where E. M. Bartlett, Sr.'s music publishing firm was located. *Baptist Hymnal* (Nashville, 1975, No. 475) was the first Southern Baptist hymnal to contain Bartlett's work and where the tune name HARTFORD was first used. *P.H.*

I heard the bells on Christmas day 98

Henry Wadsworth Longfellow wrote the hymn on Christmas Day in 1863 for the children of the Sunday School of the Unitarian Church of the Disciples, Boston. The Civil War was at its worst. Six months earlier the Battle of Gettysburg had resulted in 40,000 men having been killed, wounded, or reported missing on both sides. Following a long siege, Vicksburg had been taken by the Union forces and 30,000 Confederate soldiers taken prisoner. In fact, Longfellow's own son Charley, 19 years of age, had been wounded in the war about a month before. Longfellow, a recent widower, was caring for his son in their own home. It is not difficult to understand how Longfellow bowed his head in despair and thought "there is no peace on earth." The poet pours out his soul for peace and good will in a very troubled day. References to the war are found in the omitted two stanzas that follow stanza four.

Then from each black, accursed mouth
The cannon thundered in the South,
And with the sound the carols drowned
Of peace on earth, good will to men.

It was as if an earthquake rent
The hearth-stones of a continent,
And made forlorn, the households born
Of peace on earth, good will to men.

The hymn first appeared in James R. Murray's *Pure Diamonds* (Cleveland, 1872). Southern Baptists first sang it from *The Modern Hymnal* (Dallas, 1926, No. 407).

WALTHAM was composed by John Baptiste Calkin for George W. Doane's "Fling out the banner, let it float." It was published in Sir Arthur Sullivan's *The Hymnary* (London, 1872).   *W.J.R.*

I heard the voice of Jesus say 551

Horatius Bonar wrote the hymn while he was pastor at Kelso, Scotland (1837-43). It first appeared in three eight-line stanzas in his *Hymns, Original and Selected* (1846), and later in his *Hymns of Faith and Hope* (1862), where it was entitled "The Voice from Galilee." The scriptural basis is "of his fulness have all we received, and grace for grace" (John 1:16). The hymn first appeared in the United States in *Spiritual Songs for the Month*, compiled by John C. Ryles (New York, 1855), and in *The Baptist Praise Book* (New York, 1871, No. 870). It first appeared in a Southern Baptist collection in *The Baptist Hymn and Praise Book* (Nashville, 1904, No. 307).

VOX DILECTI is a tune composed by John B. Dykes for this text for *Hymns Ancient and Modern* (London, 1868 ed., No. 317), and Dykes named it VOX DILECTI (which is Latin for "voice of the Beloved"). For Baptists it was used first in *Sursum Corda* (Philadelphia, 1898, No. 421). Leonard Ellinwood in *The*

Hymnal 1940 Companion comments that the "combination of minor and major for the contrasting quotation and narrative has made it a popular bit of Victorian romanticism" (p. 267). VOX DILECTI was not found to "I Heard the Voice of Jesus Say" in a Southern Baptist publication until its appearance in *New Baptist Hymnal* (Nashville, 1926, No. 175).   *W.J.R.*

I know a fount 155

This is the refrain of a text and tune by Oliver M. Cooke beginning "Say, are you weary? Are you heavy laden?" Gordon Taylor, in his *Companion to the Song Book of The Salvation Army* (London, 1988, No. 161) has given Cooke's account of the origin of this hymn:

"Describing how this song came to be written, the author said that, one day, as he was closing his accounts, he found a mistake which he could not correct. To clear his thoughts, he went for a short bus ride, and had not gone far when the chorus 'I know a fount' started to form in his mind. Before his journey ended, the first two stanzas and the chorus were almost finished. When he arrived home, he wrote the music and two other stanzas and immediately sent the song to the Music Editorial Department. It appeared shortly afterwards in *The Musical Salvationist*, April 1923, entitled 'I Know a Fount.' " This four-stanza hymn appears at No. 257 in *The Song Book of The Salvation Army* (Verona, 1987). Its first appearance in a Southern Baptist collection is in *The Baptist Hymnal* (1991), with the tune name I KNOW A FOUNT.   *H.E.*

I know not why God's wondrous grace 337

This text was written by renowned 19th century evangelist Major D. W. Whittle, who often wrote under the pseudonym "El

Nathan." The refrain quotes 2 Timothy 1:12 (KJV) verbatim.

EL NATHAN was composed by Whittle's musical director, James McGranahan, and first published with the text in *Gospel Hymns No. 4* (1883). The tune was named in *Baptist Hymnal* (1956) for Whittle's pen name. *The Baptist Hymn and Praise Book* (Nashville, 1904, No. 237) was the first Southern Baptist collection to contain this hymn and tune.   *P.H.*

I know that my Redeemer liveth 191

Jessie Brown Pounds wrote this text, based on a Christological interpretation of Job 19:25, for an Easter cantata composed by James H. Fillmore entitled *Hope's Messenger* (Cincinnati, 1893). Its first hymnal inclusion was *The Praise Hymnal: A Collection of Hymns and Tunes* (Cincinnati and New York, 1896, No. 112), compiled by Gilbert J. Ellis and Fillmore.

This hymn was published first in a Baptist collection in 1904 in the Baptist Book Concern's *Glorious Praise*, by William H. Doane and William J. Kirkpatrick (Louisville, No. 41). The tune was named HANNAH for the composer's mother, Hannah Lockwood Fillmore, in *Baptist Hymnal* (1956).   *H.E.*

I Know Whom I Have Believed—See *I Know not why God's wondrous grace*

I lay my sins on Jesus 272

This hymn was written by Horatius Bonar, who is considered the greatest of the Scottish hymn writers. It was written about 1834 in four eight-line stanzas and is thought to be Bonar's initial effort at hymn writing. The text was revised and published in Bonar's *Songs for the Wilderness* (1st series, 1843), with the heading "The Fulness of Jesus." The scriptural basis for the hymn is

"Behold the Lamb of God, which taketh away the sin of the world" (John 1:29). The first appearance of the text in the United States is found in *New Union Hymns* (Philadelphia, 1850); it was included in *The Baptist Praise Book* (New York, 1871, No. 855). The text, indicated to be sung to the tune SELBORNE, is first found in a Southern Baptist collection in *The Baptist Hymn and Praise Book* (Nashville, 1904, No. 214). The present version is made up of Bonar's stanzas 1, 2, and 4.

AURELIA—See hymn 350, The church's one foundation.   *W.J.R.*

I love Thee 211

The text of this anonymous folk hymn first appeared in Richard Allen's *Collection of Hymns & Spiritual Songs* (Philadelphia, 1801, p. 4). The title page of this book listed Allen as a "Minister of the African Methodist Episcopal Church." The hymn contained seven stanzas, the first of which began "O Jesus my Saviour, to Thee I submit." The present version uses the original stanzas 2, 4, 5, and 7, with alterations. In later hymnals the text was sometimes attributed to Mrs. Sarah Jones or to John Adam Granade.

The tune I LOVE THEE, which is also of folk origin, received its initial publication in Jeremiah Ingalls' *Christian Harmony* (Exeter, 1805, p. 44), where it was titled CHARITY and set to five stanzas of the text noted above. The tune was printed in 3/8 meter and given a three-part setting with the melody in the middle voice.

The hymn and tune first appeared in a Southern Baptist collection in *Baptist Hymnal* (Nashville, 1956, No. 150).   *D.M.*

I love Thy kingdom, Lord 354

This Psalm paraphrase is the oldest American hymn in continuous use. Timothy Dwight, president of Yale College, included

33 original hymns in his edition of the *Psalms of David by Isaac Watts* (1801). This is the only one of Dwight's hymns to have survived. Verses five and six of Psalm 137 were the basis for the paraphrase. Originally in eight stanzas, this commonly used version incorporates stanzas 1, 2, 5, 6, and 8. The "kingdom" of God and "Zion" are used synonymously with the church. Basil Manly's *The Baptist Psalmody* (Charleston, 1850, No. 982) was the first Southern Baptist hymnal, and Dwight's hymn was included in that collection.

St. Thomas was originally one-fourth of the extended English tune Holborn, published in Aaron Williams' *Universal Psalmodist* (2nd ed., 1763). There it was the setting for four stanzas of Charles Wesley's hymn "Soldiers of Christ, Arise." This tune first appeared with the name St. Thomas in the fifth edition of the *Universal Psalmodist* (1770) and in Isaac Smith's *Collection of Psalm Tunes* in the same year.

Set to two other hymns and attributed to G. F. Handel, St. Thomas first appeared in a Southern Baptist collection in *The Baptist Hymn and Praise Book* (Nashville, 1904, Nos. 438, 478).   *P.H.*

I love to tell the story 572

In 1866, Katherine Hankey was recovering from a serious illness when she wrote a two-part poem of 50 stanzas based on the life of Christ. Part one, "The Story Wanted," was dated January 29, 1866, and is the source for the hymn "Tell Me the Old, Old Story" (*Baptist Hymnal*, 1956, No. 222). The second part, "The Story Told," was completed on November 18, 1866. "I Love to Tell the Story" was drawn from this section of the poem.

The text of the refrain and the tune, Hankey, were written by William G. Fischer. The hymn was first published in *Joyful Songs Nos.*

1 to 3, a pamphlet issued in 1869 by the Methodist Episcopal Book Room, Philadelphia.

It is first found in Southern Baptist collections in 1904 in both *The Baptist Hymn and Praise Book* (Nashville, 1904, No. 280) and W. H. Doane and W. J. Kirkpatrick's *Glorious Praise* (Louisville, 1904, No. 138). *D.M.*

I love You, Lord 212

Both text and tune of "I love You, Lord" came as a gift to Laurie Klein after a morning devotion time when she had prayed for God to give her a song she could sing from her heart. She reports, "I picked up my guitar and the words and music seemed to flow effortlessly." The song which was copyrighted in 1978 has been widely used. It became a theme song at the National Foursquare Convention in California and quickly spread to many churches. It was first recorded on "Follow the Leader" by Sparrow Records. *The Baptist Hymnal* (1991) is the first Southern Baptist collection to include "I Love You, Lord."

I Love You, Lord is the tune name assigned to this hymn.   *D.B.*

I must needs go home 151

Jessie P. Pounds wrote the words, and Charles H. Gabriel the music, of this gospel song which was first published in Gabriel and W. W. Dowling's *Living Praises No. 2* (St. Louis, 1906, No. 52). E. O. Excell, one of the most successful compilers, publishers, and distributors of gospel song books once observed that: "It is to Gabriel's songs—"Hail Emmanuel," "He Is So Precious to Me," "The Way of the Cross," and many others—I owe so much for any success I have gained" (325).

It first came to Southern Baptists in Robert H. Coleman and W. W. Hamilton's *The Evangel* (Philadelphia, 1909, No. 27).

WAY OF THE CROSS, for obvious reasons, is the tune name assigned to this hymn. *D.M.*

I must tell Jesus 455

Both words and music were written by Elisha A. Hoffman, and it was copyrighted in 1894 by the Hoffman Music Company. In the same year it was first published in *Pentecostal Hymns* (Chicago, No. 4). Hoffman served as a music editor for this hymnal along with W. A. Ogden and J. H. Tenny, the hymns being selected by Henry Date, founder of the Hope Publishing Company. Hoffman's hymn also appeared in 1894 in his *Christian Endeavor Hymnal*. He related that this hymn was inspired by the response of one of his church members he had counseled: "Yes," she exclaimed, "I must tell Jesus!"

The tune ORWIGSBURG is named for Hoffman's hometown, Orwigsburg, Pennsylvania. The first publication of this hymn contains a fermata on the word "me" near the end of the refrain, followed by a ritard marking for the closing words, "Jesus alone."

"I Must Tell Jesus" was first published for Southern Baptist usage in Robert H. Coleman's *The World Evangel* (Dallas, 1913, No. 78). It later appeared in *New Baptist Hymnal* (Nashville, 1926, No. 347).   *H.E.*

I need Thee every hour 450

This hymn is the result of a collaboration between Annie S. Hawks and Dr. Robert Lowry, her pastor. Mrs. Hawks, in explaining the circumstances that inspired her poem, stated: "I was so filled with the sense of nearness to the Master that, wondering how one could live without Him, either in joy or pain, these words, 'I Need Thee Every Hour,' were ushered into my mind, the thought at once taking full possession of me" (Reynolds, 1964, 86). Pastor Lowry wrote

the tune NEED and the text of the refrain.

Its first appearance was in a small song book used during the National Baptist Sunday School Convention at Cincinnati in November, 1872. Its first appearance in a publication designed for widespread use was in Lowry's and William H. Doane's *Royal Diadem for the Sunday School* (New York, 1873). The Scripture heading was John 15:5, "Without me you can do nothing."

Ira Sankey introduced the hymn to England during the Moody-Sankey evangelistic meetings in London in 1874.

The first Southern Baptist collection to include this text and tune was *The Baptist Hymn and Praise Book* (Nashville, 1904, No. 391).   *D.B.*

I saw the cross of Jesus 286

This hymn by Frederick Whitfield was one of 26 poems included in his *Sacred Poems and Prose* (1861). Its first appearance in an American hymnal seems to have been in Alexander Campbell's *The Christian Hymn Book* (rev. enl. ed., Cincinnati, 1865). The earliest Baptist publication of this hymn in America was in Adoniram J. Gordon's and Arthur T. Pierson's *The Coronation Hymnal* (Philadelphia, 1894, No. 130), and includes two of Whitfield's stanzas to William G. Fisher's tune HANKEY, each followed by the refrain of Katherine Hankey, "I love to tell the story."

The tune name WHITFIELD was given by the committee for the 1956 *Baptist Hymnal*. Also known as CALCUTTA and PATNA, the following background information for WHITFIELD was given by the distinguished English hymnologist, Maurice Frost, in *The Choir* (LI, No. 5, 91):

"It is generally attributed to Bishop Heber, but it was certainly not written by him. An article in the *Oxford Diocesan Magazine* for August, 1932, by the late Rev. C.C. Inge, gave its source, and also related its history. It appeared in a manuscript book of tunes belonging to his family set to his grandfather's version of Psalm 61 (*The Cleveland Psalter*, by Archdeacon Churton), 8.8.8.3.8.7. Mr. W. W. Inge of Rugby kindly looked up the manuscript for me and sent me a copy of the tune.

"It goes back to a benefit concert arranged by Thomas Moore at the Theatre Royal, Dublin, in 1811, where it appears in a 'Melologue upon National Music' as a 'Greek Air resumed,' with a note, 'For this pretty Greek melody I am indebted to Mr. Gell who brought it with him from Athens.' A copy is in the British Museum, G. 806c. (66).

"The harmonization suggests that the first version in the manuscript book was taken directly from the concert programme."

The versions of this tune cited by Frost are given in William J. Reynolds' companion to the 1956 *Baptist Hymnal, Hymns of Our Faith* (p. 87). No one knows who altered this melody and recast it as a hymn tune. The earliest appearance Reynolds found of WHITFIELD as a hymn is in *The Sunday-Scholar's Tune Book* (London, 1869, No. 132), where it is named PATNA. It is interesting that the tune WHITFIELD has several melodic motives in common with another hymn tune said to be of Greek origin—William B. Bradbury's arrangement named SWEET STORY (*Baptist Hymnal*, 1956, No. 506), set to Jemima T. Luke's children's hymn, "I Think When I Read That Sweet Story of Old." H.E.

I serve a risen Savior 533

The stimulus for this text and tune by Alfred H. Ackley are reported in George Sanville's *Forty Gospel Hymn Stories* (1945). In 1933, Ackley was witnessing to a young Jew and was asked, "Why should I worship a dead Jew?"

Ackley replied, "He lives! I tell you, He is not dead, but lives here and now! Jesus Christ is more alive today than ever before." After this encounter, Ackley produced the words and music as well as a sermon on the subject of Jesus' resurrection. The hymn first appeared among Southern Baptists in *Triumphant Service Songs* (1933). Its first inclusion in a Southern Baptist collection was in *Voice of Praise* (Nashville, 1947, No. 48).

ACKLEY is the name given this tune by the hymnal committee for *Baptist Hymnal* (1956). P.H.

I sing the mighty power of God 42

In his "Preface to All That Are Concerned in the Education of Children" in *Divine Songs Attempted in Easy Language, for the Use of Children* (1715), Isaac Watts spoke of the urgent need to train properly the minds of children. To that end he offered his *Divine Songs* to which were added some Sonnets on Moral Subjects. That explains the occasional reference to this work as *Divine and Moral Songs for Children*. The hymn is drawn from Song No. 2, which consists of eight four-line stanzas under the heading "Praise for Creation and Providence." *The Baptist Hymnal* (1991) version uses three eight-line stanzas consisting of the first five from the original version plus an altered version (source unknown) of the sixth. The original sixth stanza (which is still used in English Baptist hymnals) reads:

Creatures (as num'rous as they be)
    Are subject to thy care;
There's not a place where we can flee,
    But God is present there.

Divine Songs ... is contained in Volume IV of a six-volume work which is part of the Spurgeon Collection of William Jewell College, Liberty, Missouri.

The first Southern Baptist collection to include this hymn was *Baptist Hymnal* (Nashville, 1975, No. 154).

FOREST GREEN—See hymn 79, Blessed be the God of Israel.   *D.B.*

I stand amazed in the presence 547

The text and music of this hymn were written by Charles H. Gabriel and first published in E. O. Excell's *Praises* (Chicago, 1905, No. 3).

Its first appearance in a Southern Baptist collection was in Robert H. Coleman's *The Popular Hymnal* (Dallas, 1918, No. 191).

MY SAVIOR'S LOVE is the name assigned to the tune.   *D.M.*

I Surrender All—See *All to Jesus I surrender*

I wandered in the shades of night 444

The text of this hymn was written by Judson W. Van DeVenter and the tune (SUNLIGHT IN MY SOUL) was composed by Winfield S. Weeden. Copyrighted in 1897, it was published in two collections of the following year: Henry Date's *Pentecostal Hymns No. 2* (Chicago, 1898, No. 365) and Harold E. Sayles' *Best Hymns No. 2 for Services of Song* (Chicago, 1898). This hymn gained wide use among Southern Baptists through its publication in *The Broadman Hymnal* compiled by B. B. McKinney (Nashville, 1940, No. 376). It was not included in the Baptist hymnals of 1956 and 1975.   *H.E.*

I want Jesus to walk with me 465

The overall difficulties of life depicted in the text of this African-American spiritual fit the context of slavery. "In my trials," "when I'm troubled," "when my heart is almost breaking," and "when my head is bowed in sorrow" reflect the heartfelt need of all persons, whether slave or free, for divine companionship on life's journey, especially during hardships. In *The Hymns of the United Methodist Hymnal* (Nashville, 1989, p. 178), William Farley Smith comments on this spiritual as follows: "The tune SOJOURNER is named for Sojourner Truth, the courageous freed slave woman who took to the dangerous byways of antebellum America preaching the abolition of slavery and equality of 'all o' Gawd's chillun's.' Sojourner Truth is identified with the singing of this spiritual, and it is quite possible that the stanzas refer to the dangers she encountered on her many treks." The basic structure of this spiritual follows the call and response pattern, the response being a repeated "walk with me" at the end of phrases 1, 2, and 4. However, the call and response pattern is not retained within the text of this arrangement of SOJOURNER, although Mark Blankenship reinstates it in the repeated notes of his accompaniment. Most recent hymnals, for instance *The United Methodist Hymnal* (1989) and *The Presbyterian Hymnal* (1990), have preserved the original call and response patterns within the text itself. The first Southern Baptist collection to include this spiritual is *The Baptist Hymnal* (1991).   *H.E.*

I was sinking deep in sin 546

In a letter to William J. Reynolds dated May 23, 1955, Mrs. Louise Rowe Mayhew, daughter of James Rowe, the author of the text, writes:

"Howard E. Smith was a little man whose hands were so knotted with arthritis that you would wonder how he could use them at all, much less play the piano, but he could and did. I can see them now, my father striding up and down humming a bar or two and Howard E. playing it and jotting it down. Thus was 'Love Lifted Me' composed. That was in Saugatuck, Connecticut, a good many years ago.

"This occurred in 1912, and the hymn was purchased and copyrighted June 1, 1912, by Charlie D. Tillman. On May 25, 1915, Tillman sold the copyright to Robert

H. Coleman for $100, and Coleman's first publication of the song was in his songbook *The Herald* (Dallas, 1915, No. 61). Of unusual interest is the fact that at the end of the first term of the copyright (28 years), Tillman negotiated the renewal rights from the composer's heirs in the interest of John T. Benson, Jr., who filed the renewal application on June 5, 1939, without Coleman's knowledge" (Reynolds, 1976, 107).

This gospel hymn's first appearance in an official Southern Baptist collection was in W. Plunkett Martin and James W. Jelks' *Songs of Redemption* (Atlanta, 1920, No. 50).

SAFETY is the name given this tune in *Baptist Hymnal* (1956).   W.J.R.

I will not be afraid 72

These words were written by Ellis Govan for use with a folklike tune of unknown origin. The first printing of the hymn occurred in *Songs of Victory*, a publication of the Faith Mission, an evangelistic organization founded in Scotland and Ireland in 1886 by Govan's father. *Baptist Hymnal* (1975) represented its first publication among Southern Baptists.

UNAFRAID is an anonymous tune.   D.M.

I will sing of my Redeemer 575

This text was found in an undamaged trunk in the train wreck which killed Philip P. Bliss and his wife near Ashtabula, Ohio, in 1876. Neither the date when it was written nor whether Bliss composed a tune for the text is known. The text and the present tune were first published in *Welcome Tidings, A New Collection for Sunday School* (1877), compiled by Robert Lowry, William H. Doane, and Ira D. Sankey. *The Baptist Hymn and Praise Book* (Nashville, 1904, No. 107) was the first Southern Baptist printing of this gospel song.

MY REDEEMER was composed by James Mc-Granahan while visiting Major D. W. Whittle in Chicago following Bliss' death. George C. Stebbins relates that the song was sung by four men's voices in a tabernacle service in Chicago with "two of the most prominent baritone soloists of the city . . . singing the lower parts, Mr. McGranahan taking the alto, an octave higher, and I the melody" (224-25). Stebbins later recorded the song at an exhibition of the Edison phonograph, thus making this hymn one of the earliest recorded songs.   P.H.

I will sing the wondrous story
535, 537

Francis H. Rowley wrote this text in 1886 during revival services at the First Baptist Church of North Adams, Massachusetts, where he was pastor. Peter P. Bilhorn was leading the music for the revival and asked Rowley to write a text which he might set. The original first line, "Can't you sing the wondrous story," was altered by the author. He did not approve, however, several other changes made by Ira Sankey, who registered the copyright and included it in *Gospel Hymns, No. 5* and *Sacred Songs and Solos*, both published in New York and Cincinnati in 1887. The original version of stanzas two through four may be seen in Reynolds' *Companion to Baptist Hymnal* (Nashville, 1976).

HYFRYDOL (hymn 535)—See hymn 36, "Praise the Lord! Ye Heavens, Adore Him."

WONDROUS STORY (hymn 537) was written by Bilhorn, as noted above. In *Modern Gospel Song Stories* (Kansas City, 1952), Haldor Lillenas retold George C. Stebbins' account of its publication. Bilhorn had gone to Brooklyn to meet Stebbins:

"During the winter Bilhorn wrote his first song, so far as I know, and I harmonized it for him, as he had not studied harmony up to that time. The song was entitled, "I Will Sing the Wondrous Story." I took Peter with me to call on Ira D. Sankey, and showed him the song. It impressed him as being serviceable and he accepted it as a gift. It was published in his next book and became one of the most popular numbers in the collection" (Reynolds, 1976, 110).

British hymnologist Frank Colquhoun called this "an example of the American gospel song at its best" (173).

The Baptist Hymn and Praise Book (Nashville, 1904, No. 320) was the first Southern Baptist collection to include this text and tune.   *P.A.R.*

I will trust in the Lord 420

The melody of this traditional African-American spiritual resembles the shape-note tune PISGAH, which appeared in print as early as 1817 in the second edition of Ananias Davisson's *Kentucky Harmony* (Harrisonburg, p. 44), where it is credited to J. Lowry and set to Watts' hymn "When I Can Read My Title Clear." William Farley Smith says that I WILL TRUST "was likely adapted from it [PISGAH], since the camp meetings of frontier U.S.A. allowed interracial attendance, resulting in many shared, borrowed, and adapted tunes and texts (*The Hymns of the United Methodist Hymnal*, Nashville, 1989, p. 161). In the widely used African-American Baptist hymnal, *The Baptist Hymnal* (Nashville, 1924, No. 300), "I Will Trust in the Lord" serves as an opening refrain to Charles Wesley's "Father, I Stretch My Hands to Thee." In the *A.M.E. Hymnal* (1954, No. 249), "I Will Trust in the Lord" appears as the refrain after Watts' "When I Can Read My Title Clear" beginning with the line "I'm goin' to trust in the Lord."

The tune for Watts' stanzas in this hymnal is a version of PISGAH, making the refrain [I WILL TRUST] an interesting variation of PISGAH. According to Gwen Williams, Southern Baptist home missionary serving among inner-city Blacks in New Orleans, "I Will Trust in the Lord" is traditionally sung unaccompanied in Black Baptist churches at the "Speaking Meeting," which occurs before Communion Sunday, a time of spiritual preparation for the observance of the Lord's Supper. Smith (*The Hymns of the United Methodist Hymnal*, p. 161) indicates that "This spiritual of conviction traditionally is sung moderately slow with heavy rhythmic accents, producing a dignified swaying body motion."   *H.E.*

I'd rather have Jesus 550

Mrs. Rhea F. Miller wrote this text and also composed a musical setting, both copyrighted in 1922. At the age of 20, George Beverly Shea composed his musical setting, according to his autobiography, *Then Sings My Soul*:

"One Sunday morning [Mother] placed on the piano a little poem by Mrs. Rhea F. Miller. Mother thought its message beautiful. I did, too.

"Instead of practicing the hymn I had intended to play that Sunday morning in church, I turned to this poem. Melody just seemed to form around the words. When I had played and sung it through for the first time, Mother came from the kitchen where she had overheard. She wrapped both arms around my shoulders and placed her wet cheek next to mine.

"In church that morning, I sang for the first time, 'I'd Rather Have Jesus.' " (31).

This became Beverly Shea's theme song, sung around the world in the Billy Graham evangelistic crusades. As of 1968, over a million copies of this song had been distributed in sheet music form.

I'D RATHER HAVE JESUS, appropriately enough, is the name of the tune as well as the text.   *H.E.*

I'll Live for Him—See *My life, my love I give to Thee*

I'll praise my Maker 35

Isaac Watts wrote two versions of Psalm 146 for his *Psalms of David, Imitated in the Language of the New Testament* (1719). Each carried the title "Praise to God for His Goodness and Truth." John Wesley altered the second version and published it in his 1727 *Charlestown Collection*, his 1741 *Collection of Psalms and Hymns*, and his 1780 *Collection of Hymns for the Use of the People Called Methodists*. *The Baptist Hymnal* (1991) uses Wesley's alteration of the second version. Southern Baptists' first hymnal, *The Baptist Psalmody* (Charleston, 1850, No. 568), included "I'll Praise My Maker" where the following stanza appears, instead of the one which appears as stanza three in *The Baptist Hymnal* (1991):

> Why should I make a man my trust?
> Princes must die and return to dust;
> Vain is the help of flesh and blood:
> Their breath departs, their pomp and
> power
> And thoughts all vanish in an hour,
> Nor can they make their promise
> good.

OLD 113TH comes from the *Strassburger Kirchenamt* of 1525. It is attributed to Matthias Greiter and was set to Psalm 36 in John Calvin's *Aulcuns Pseaumes et cantiques mys en chant* (Strassburg, 1539). The tune was altered in the *Anglo-Genevan Psalter* of 1561 and set to Psalm 113. It has also been known as LUCERNE. *The Baptist Hymnal* (1991) is the first appearance of this tune in a Southern Baptist collection. *D.B.*

I'll tell the world that I'm a Christian 553

"I'll tell the world..." was written and composed by Baynard L. Fox while he was living in Louisville, Kentucky, in 1955. Both text and tune came to him in a few moments of sudden inspiration. He sold it along with some of his other compositions in 1958 but when the owner failed to promote their sales, he bought them back in 1963. The hymn was then published by his own company, Fox Music Publications, in both solo and choral versions and subsequently was popularly used in revivals, conventions, and special events by several music evangelists including Martha Branham and Cliff Barrows. It became widely known when Martha Branham recorded it and sang it at the annual meeting of the Southern Baptist Convention in Atlantic City, New Jersey, in 1964.

The Baptist Hymnal (1991) is the first Southern Baptist collection to include this popular song of testimony.

TUCKER is the name of the Georgia city where Fox lived and served as a minister of music for several years prior to his death. *H.T.M.*

I'm just a child 488

The song is from *Musical Stories for Puppets and People* (Nashville, 1977), a collection of short musicals for children, words by Ed Seabough and music by Terry Kirkland. One of the musical stories was based on Matthew 14:13-23, the feeding of the 5000. To teach the concept of sharing, Seabough explained that when confronted with the question "Whacha Gonna Do for the Hungry People?" he felt even small children could understand the concept of sharing. He thought that maybe they could also understand the way you commit your life to Christ is by what you do in serving persons. So, he had the lad say, "Whatever I *have* I give it all to you, Lord." And then, make the commitment, "Whatever I *am* I give it all to you, Lord." Seabough wrote "Lord, I'm Just a

Child" as a commitment song for children, committing *self* and *possessions* to God.

KIRKLAND was composed for Seabough's words "I'm just a child" by Terry Kirkland and first appeared in *Musical Stories for Puppets and People* (1977). The tune was named for the composer when it appeared in *The Baptist Hymnal* (1991).   *W.J.R.*

I'm pressing on the upward way 484

This text was written by Johnson Oatman, Jr. It has been a favorite in holiness camp meetings.

HIGHER GROUND was written in 1892 by Charles H. Gabriel, who then sold it to J. Howard Entwisle, a compiler of gospel song books. Entwisle published it in *Songs of Love and Praise, No. 5* (Philadelphia, 1898), which he edited with John R. Sweney and Frank M. Davis.

Its first appearance in a Southern Baptist collection was in *Songs of Redemption* (Atlanta, 1920, No. 204).   *P.A.R.*

I'm so glad I'm a part of the family of God 386

In the church in Alexandria, Indiana, where William J. Gaither and his wife Gloria were active members, a young father was severely burned in an explosion in 1970. The church family prayed earnestly for his recovery. The next day was Easter morning and those who had prayed all night learned that their friend was still alive and the possibility of his survival was good. Prayers had been answered and the celebration of the resurrection of Christ had new meaning that morning. On their way home, Bill and Gloria Gaither talked about the family of believers and the love and concern they had shown. At home they began to piece together the words and music of the song as their noon meal was forgotten. By the time they sat down to eat, the song was completed.

The original version of the Gaithers' song consisted of the refrain and two stanzas. These stanzas are:

You will notice we say "brother and
    sister" 'round here—
    It's because we're a family and these
        folks are so near;
When one has a heartache, we all share
        the tears
    And rejoice in each victory in this
        family so dear.

From the door of an orphanage to the
        house of the King—
    No longer an outcast, a new song
        I sing;
From rags unto riches, from the weak
        to the strong,
    I'm not worthy to be here, but, praise
        God, I belong!

After being widely used by the Gaithers in their concerts and recordings, the hymn appeared in *Hymns for the Family of God* (Nashville, 1976, No. 543). The first inclusion in a Southern Baptist collection is *The Baptist Hymnal* (1991).

FAMILY OF GOD is the tune name taken from the common title of the hymn. *W.J.R.*

I've come to tell 222

"I've come to tell" is Frank Sawyer's translation of a three-stanza hymn by Juan M. Isáis. "Te vengo a decir" was given to the author while he was leading the music in an evangelistic campaign. He felt the need for a worship song with Spanish flavor. In a letter to Dr. Hugh T. McElrath, Isáis indicated that in this song he wanted to share with the people the truth that worship and adoration must be closely related to witnessing for Christ. This message is more fully communicated in the following two stanzas:

I've come to tell, I've come to tell,
    Oh my Savior,

And give you my being, and give
you my being,
my Friend, my God,
I've come to serve, I've come to serve,
my King, my Lord;
I've come to place before you all
that I am,
Receive it, God.

Wherever, Lord, wherever, Lord, I
will follow you,
And to the end, and to the end,
your servant I will be.
Send me, Lord, send me, Lord,
I will go anywhere;
I know I am nothing, I know I am
nothing,
but faithful I will be.

TE VENGO are the first two words in the
original Spanish version of "I've come to
tell" and therefore has been given as the
name of Isáis' tune composed for it.   *H.T.M.*

I've found a friend who is all to me 540

According to a letter of August 6, 1954 to
William J. Reynolds, Jack P. Scholfield (1882-
1972) wrote both the words and music in
1911 while he was assisting Dr. Mordecai F.
Hamm in evangelistic meetings. Scholfield
explained:

"The melody just came to me, almost as
a gift. Then I tried to make the words fit the
tune. It was popular from the start and
Robert H. Coleman told me some years ago
that it had been published in several foreign
languages" (1976, 119).

This hymn was first published in Robert
H. Coleman's *New Evangel* (Dallas, 1911, No.
89). The first Southern Baptist hymnal to
contain the hymn was *Kingdom Songs*, compiled by I. E. Reynolds and Coleman (Dallas, 1921, No. 311).

Scholfield named the tune RAPTURE for the
Baptist Hymnal (1956). The tune first appeared in a Southern Baptist hymnal in *Kingdom Songs* (Dallas, 1921, No. 311).   *S.W.G.*

I've found a friend, O such a friend! 183

James G. Small, a Scottish Free Church
minister, wrote the text, which was first published in *The Revival Hymn Book*, second series (1863), and later in his own collection
Psalms and Sacred Songs (1866). The hymn's
original title was "Jesus, the Friend."

FRIEND was composed by George C. Stebbins in January, 1878, and published in
Gospel Hymns No. 3 (1878). Stebbins was assisting George F. Pentecost in a revival in
Providence, Rhode Island, at the time. *The
Baptist Hymn and Praise Book* (Nashville,
1904, No. 275) was the first Southern Baptist hymnal to contain this hymn.   *P.H.*

I've got peace like a river 418

The origin of this spiritual is unknown.
The present arrangement was made by
William J. Reynolds for *Baptist Hymnal*
(Nashville, 1975, No. 458). This was the first
Southern Baptist collection and the first ma-
jor hymnal of any denomination to include
it.

PEACE LIKE A RIVER is the tune name tak-
en from the common title of the hymn.
P.A.R.

I've wandered far away from God 309

William J. Kirkpatrick wrote both words
and music of this well-known hymn of invitation, which was first published in *Winning Songs, for Use in Meetings for Christian
Worship or Work*, compiled by John R.
Sweney, H. L. Gilmour, and Kirkpatrick
(Philadelphia, 1892, No. 141). Its first appearance in a Southern Baptist hymnal was
in *Songs of Redemption* (Atlanta, 1920, No.
190).

COMING HOME was the name assigned to this tune in *Baptist Hymnal* (1956). *M.P.*

If you are tired of the load of your sin 311

This hymn was written by Mrs. C. H. Morris during a camp meeting at Mountain Lake Park, Maryland, in 1898. In the course of a Sunday morning invitation, Mrs. Morris was praying with a woman who had come forward. She sought to encourage the woman's decision by saying "Just now your doubtings give o'er." H.L. Gilmour, the song leader, evidently overheard her and added his own exhortation, "Just now reject Him no more." The preacher, L. H. Baker, made an additional entreaty, "Just now throw open the door," and Mrs. Morris concluded the appeal with the words "Let Jesus come into your heart." Mrs. Morris quickly formed this improvised verse into a refrain, complete with tune. The stanzas and the remainder of the tune were written before the end of the camp meeting, and the song was published in William J. Kirkpatrick and H.L. Gilmour's *Pentecostal Praises* (Philadelphia, 1898, No. 72). The hymn originally contained five stanzas; the omitted fourth stanza read:

If friends, once trusted, have proven
    untrue,
Let Jesus come into your heart;
Find what a Friend He will be unto you,
Let Jesus come into your heart.

The refrain was given in two forms, the current one and an alternate version:

Just now, my doubtings are o'er;
Just now, rejecting no more;
Just now, I open the door
And Jesus comes into my heart.

The tune was named MCCONNELSVILLE for its appearance in *Baptist Hymnal* (1956). McConnelsville is the Ohio town in which Mrs. Morris made her home. However the words (in five stanzas) and music first appeared in a Southern Baptist Collection in Doane and Kirkpatrick's *Glorious Praise* (Louisville, 1904, No. 136). *D.M.*

If you will only let God guide you 57

Georg Neumark wrote this hymn in gratitude for God's assistance in very trying times. On a journey he hoped would take him to Königsberg, the location of the only German university not disrupted by the Thirty Years War, Neumark was robbed of all his possessions save his prayer book and a few coins he had sewn in the lining of his clothing. After much travel and disappointment in search of work, he, with the help of Nicolaus Becker, the chief pastor in Kiel, secured the position of tutor in the home of a wealthy judge in that city. In a spirit of thanksgiving he wrote this hymn (based on Psalm 55:22) and gave it the title "A Song of Comfort: God Wll Care for and Help Everyone in His Own Time." Although the hymn was written in the early 1640s, it was first published in Neumark's *Musikalisch-poetischer Lustwald* (Jena, 1657).

Catherine Winkworth made two English translations of this text. Her second appeared in her *Chorale Book for England* (London, 1863), and is the one used by most hymnal compilers. Her version begins, "If thou but suffer God to guide thee." The Presbyterian *Worshipbook* of 1972 made minor changes including the substitution of "you" and "your" for "thou" and "thy." That is the version used in *The Baptist Hymnal* (1991). The first Southern Baptist collection to include the hymn was *Baptist Hymnal* (Nashville, 1975, No. 203).

NEUMARK was written by Georg Neumark for "If You Will Only Let God Guide You." It first appeared in 1657 in *Musikalisch-poetischer Lustwald*. J.S. Bach made several organ settings of the tune and used it in Cantatas 21, 27, 84, 88, 93, 166, 179, and 197.

Mendolssohn used the tune in *St. Paul* with the text "To Thee, O Lord, I yield my spirit." *D.B.*

Immortal Love, forever full 480

John Greenleaf Whittier's hymns are excerpts from his longer poems. In this case, the source was the poem "Our Master" from his collection *Tent on the Beach and Other Poems* (1867). Stanzas 1, 5, 14, and 16 of the original comprise the present version. The hymn's earliest appearance in a Southern Baptist hymnal was *The New Baptist Hymnal* (Nashville, 1926, No. 178) but without the first stanza.

SERENITY was adapted from William V. Wallace's love song, "Ye Winds That Waft My Sighs to Thee" (1856). The earliest appearance may have been in Charles S. Robinson's and Robert S. MacArthur's *Calvary Selection of Spiritual Songs* (1878), where the tune is named INVITATION and is cast in duple meter. By 1883, however, *Baptist Hymnal* (Philadelphia, 1883, Nos. 170, 340) listed the tune name as SERENITY and set the tune in triple meter. *P.H.*

Immortal, invisible, God only wise 6

Walter Chalmers Smith's hymn is based on 1 Timothy 1:17, "Now unto the King eternal, immortal, invisible, the only wise God, be honor and glory for ever and ever. Amen." After the hymn was first published in six four-line stanzas in the author's *Hymns of Christ and Christian Life*, Garrett Horder persuaded Smith to make a few alterations and included the hymn in his *Congregational Hymns* (London, 1884) and *Worship Song* (1905). The first appearance of the hymn in the United States was in *Hymnal, Amore Dei* (Boston, 1890). The present version uses the first three original stanzas; the fourth stanza is made up of the opening couplets of Smith's fourth and fifth stanzas.

ST. DENIO, sometimes called JOANNA, first appeared as a hymn tune in Wales in John Roberts' *Caniadau y Cyssegr* (Sacred Songs, 1839), where it is called PALESTRINA. The tune is based on a Welsh folk song, "Can Mlynedd i 'nawr" ("A hundred years from now"), well known in the early 19th century. The first English hymnal to include the tune was *The English Hymnal* (Oxford, 1906), where it was used with this text. Southern Baptists began singing the hymn and tune in *Baptist Hymnal* (Nashville, 1956, No. 43). *W.J.R.*

In Christ there is no East or West 385

John Oxenham [William Arthur Dunkerly] wrote this hymn in 1908 as part of a pageant for the London Missionary Society's exhibition, "The Orient in London." This poem, entitled "No East or West," appeared in the concluding section, which focused on India. Its first publication as a separate poem was in Oxenham's *Bees in Amber* (London, 1913). It has obvious links to Luke 13:29, John 13:35, and Galatians 3:28. In recent years several different revisions have been produced to make it as inclusive of gender as of geography. Accordingly, stanza three has changed "brothers" to "children" and "son" to "child."

This text first appeared in a Southern Baptist collection in *Baptist Hymnal* (Nashville, 1956, No. 443).

ST. PETER was composed by Alexander R. Reinagle and included in his *Psalm Tunes, for the Voice and Pianoforte* (London, 1836). In *A Collection of Psalm and Hymn Tunes* (London, 1840), also edited by Reinagle, he named it for St. Peter's-in-the-East, Oxford, the church for which he was organist. *P.A.R.*

In Christ, Our Liberty—See *We bind ourselves in freedom's chains*

In heavenly love abiding 348

Anna L. Waring's hymn was one of 19 she published in *Hymns and Meditations by A.L.W.* (1850) when she was 27 years old. The hymn was titled "Safety with God," with the heading "I will fear no evil: for thou art with me" (Psa. 23:4). The hymn reflects the confidence of Psalm 23. The first inclusion of the hymn in the United States was in the Baptist edition of *The Sabbath Hymn Book* (New York, 1858). Waring's hymn, set to the Finnish hymn melody NYLAND, was first used by Southern Baptists in *Baptist Hymnal* (Nashville, 1956, No. 303).

WHITFIELD—See hymn 286, I saw the cross of Jesus.   *W.J.R.*

In His time 53

Diane Ball was inspired by Ecclesiastes 3:1, 11 to write the words and music of this chorus in 1975. She was traveling with her family on the way to a speaking engagement for which she was late. After reading the Scripture text, she "heard a heavenly choir singing a melody. The words ...swept through my troubled heart; and... the Lord established His peace in my spirit" (Bauman, 26-27). A stanza was added in 1979:

> God would have us know, time makes
>   all things grow;
> He will make it so in His time.
> And by His great hand, all our life is
>   planned;
> Someday we will understand in
>   His time.

The tune name IN HIS TIME is the same as the hymn title. *The Baptist Hymnal* (1991) marks the first Southern Baptist use of the hymn.   *P.H.*

In loving-kindness Jesus came 542

On September 1, 1904, Charles H. Gabriel entered into an agreement with the evangelistic music publisher Charles M. Alexan-der whereby Gabriel would compose 200 pages of gospel songs during the course of a year. One of the pieces written under this contract was "In Loving-Kindness Jesus Came," both the words and music of which were by Gabriel. The first printing of the hymn occurred in Daniel B. Towner and Charles M. Alexander's *Revival Hymns* (Chicago, 1905, No. 28). In this collection, the words were attributed to "Charlotte G. Homer," one of many pseudonyms used by Gabriel.

The tune name, HE LIFTED ME, was the original title of the song, and was first used as the tune name in *Baptist Hymnal* (1956). It first appeared with this text for Southern Baptists in Baptist Robert H. Coleman's *The Popular Hymnal* (Dallas, 1918, No. 349). *D.M*

In my life, Lord, be glorified 457

The words and music of this song were written by Bob Kilpatrick in 1978. According to the author/composer, the song was written while he was sitting in his mother-in-law's living room. He had been searching for a song that he and his wife, Cindy, could sing together before beginning a concert or as a dedication of themselves to the ministry. In his own words:

"I didn't want to share it with anyone else—it was going to be our own "private" worship song—so I didn't write it with public scrutiny in mind."

However, the composer reports that "within a year, it had gone to every continent of the world." He has pointed out that "the melody is comprised of only 5 notes ... and the lyric is the simplest of prayers. This has led me to the firm belief that God is not waiting for us to do big things for Him.... He is waiting for us to offer Him what we have, even if it is only 5 notes and a simple prayer."

BE GLORIFIED is the tune name assigned by the hymnal committee.

The Baptist Hymnal (1991) represents the first appearance of the song in a Southern Baptist hymnal. *D.M.*

In remembrance 365

This hymn and its tune RED are excerpted from the musical *Celebrate Life!*, written by Ragan Courtney and Buryl Red in 1972. Ragan Courtney related in a letter to this writer:

"I wrote 'In Remembrance' as a song to sing during the acting out of the last supper. ...I was a relatively new Christian, and all of my writings were erupting out of my newfound relationship to the Lord. I remember being concerned that the lyric was just a trifle and not at all up to the occasion. Then I heard Buryl's setting, and I wept. His composition ennobled the words."

Celebrate Life! continues to be an outstanding example of the Christian message. As evidence of its staying power, a new edition was published in 1990. "In Remembrance" did not appear in a Southern Baptist hymnal until *The Baptist Hymnal* (1991). *P.H.*

In the cross of Christ I glory 554

John Bowring wrote this text and included it in his *Hymns* (1825) under the title "Glorying in the Cross." Galatians 6:14 was the scriptural inspiration. Many find it interesting that this hymn was written by a Unitarian, but it has brought comfort to countless numbers. There exists a legend that Bowring, while governor of Hong Kong, traveled to nearby Macao where his view of the impressive facade of the ruined church of St. Paul's inspired the writing of the hymn. However, "In the Cross of Christ I Glory" was written some 30 years before the hymnist ever saw Macao. The striking imagery came from his poetic imagination and wide grasp of world history. The hymn was first printed in a Southern Baptist collection in *The Baptist Hymn and Praise Book* (Nashville, 1904, No. 138).

RATHBUN was first published set to Mühlenberg's "Saviour, Who Thy Flock Art Feeding" in Greatorex's *Collection of Psalm and Hymn Tunes*. RATHBUN was composed in 1849 by Ithamar Conkey for Bowring's hymn. Conkey was organist of the Central Baptist Church in Norwich, Connecticut. Guy McCutchan, in *Our Hymnody*, gives portions of an article in a 1907 edition of the *Norwich Bulletin* which describes the writing of the tune:

"Doctor Hiscox was ...pastor of the church. He had prepared a series of seven sermons from 'The Words on the Cross.'

"One Sunday during the series it was a very rainy day. Mr. Conkey was sorely disappointed that the members of the choir did not appear, as only one soprano came. Mr. Conkey was so discouraged and disheartened that after the prelude he closed the organ and locked it and went to his home on Washington Street. The pastor and choir gallery were at opposite ends of the church, and he could leave without attracting the attention of the congregation.

"That afternoon he sat down at the piano for practice, the thoughts suggested in the series of sermons Doctor Hiscox had prepared and the words of the hymn suggested to be sung, 'In the cross of Christ I glory,' passing and repassing through his mind. He then and there composed the music which is now so universally familiar in churches of every denomination, known as RATHBUN. He admitted afterward the inspiration was a vivid contradiction of his feelings at the morning service (Reynolds, 1976, 115)."

The tune was named for the church's leading soprano, Mrs. Beriah S. Rathbun. *D.B.*

In the Family of God—See *The family of God is born from above*

In the Garden—See *I come to the garden alone*

In the lightning flash across the sky 59

Barbara Fowler Gaultney wrote both words and music, which were first published in the April 1960 issue of *The Church Musician* (pp. 36-39) as an SATB anthem, arranged by Julian Wilson, her minister of music at the First Baptist Church, Forest Park, Georgia. The next year it was included in *Songs of Salvation No. 2* (Nashville, 1961, No. 15).

When this hymn was first published in *Baptist Hymnal* (Nashville, 1975, No. 209), its tune was named FOREST PARK for the Atlanta suburb where Mrs. Gaultney lived. H.E., W.J.R.

In the little village of Bethlehem 102

The text and music of this hymn were written by William H. Neidlinger and published in 1890 as a solo song with piano accompaniment. In this form it became a perennial favorite for soloists during the Christmas season. In his 1976 dissertation, "The Sacred Art Song in the United States, 1869-1975" (Southwestern Baptist Theological Seminary, Fort Worth, Texas, p. 72), James W. Glass observed that most solo songs from this period have fallen out of common use, but that this one has survived because of the "appealingly simple nature" of the text and the "inventiveness of the melodic line."

The first known arrangement of the song for congregational singing was made by Robert F. Douglas and published in *The Hymnal for Worship and Celebration* (Waco, 1986, No. 162). *The Baptist Hymnal* (1991) is the first appearance of the song in a Southern Baptist compilation.

NEIDLINGER is named for the composer. D.M.

In the Name of the Lord—See *There is strength in the name*

In the Presence of the Lord—See *There is joy, there is joy*

Infant holy, Infant lowly 106

The original text was an anonymous Polish carol beginning "W zlobie lezy." The English version was made by Edith M. G. Reed and published in the December 1925 issues of *Panpipes* and *Music and Youth*, periodicals which she edited. It first appeared in a hymnal in *School Worship* (London, 1926).

Reed's original phrases, "Swift are winging, angels singing," were altered to "Angels winging, praises singing" for the present hymnal.

W ZLOBIE LEZY is a Polish carol tune in the dance rhythm of the mazurka. It takes its name from the first words of the Polish text. This harmonization, one of many, is attributed to Wilbur Lee. It first appeared in *Songs for Christmas* (Nashville, 1958). The harmonization made by Reed ended with the melodic pattern 4-3-1, rather than 3-2-1; it also had a two-bar coda after each strophe. *Baptist Hymnal* (Nashville, 1975, No. 94) was the first Southern Baptist book to include this carol. P.A.R.

Is your life a channel of blessing? 564

Harper G. Smyth wrote both the words and music in 1903. The hymn was published in James McGranahan's *Hymns, Psalms, and Gospel Songs* (Pittsburgh, 1904).

EUCLID is the name given this tune in *Baptist Hymnal* (1956) commemorating the Euclid Avenue Baptist Church, Cleveland,

Ohio, which Smyth served as music director for many years. *The Evangel* (Philadelphia, 1909, No. 83), published by Robert H. Coleman and W. W. Hamilton, was Southern Baptists' first inclusion of this text and tune.   *P.H.*

It came upon the midnight clear 93

This carol-hymn of social concern was written by a Unitarian minister, Edmund H. Sears, and first printed in the December 29, 1849 issue of the *Christian Register*. Fifteen years earlier, Sears had written a similar Christmas hymn, beginning "Calm on the listening ear of night come heaven's melodious strains," but this text did not carry the strong social implications of "It Came upon the Midnight Clear," which Erik Routley called "the first Christmas hymn in English with a social message" (42). In his collection of *Sermons and Songs of the Christian Life* (1875), Sears placed these two hymns, one at the beginning and the other at the end, in a sermon for Christmas Eve based on 1 Timothy 2:6.

"It Came upon the Midnight Clear" originally contained five stanzas, the second of which is omitted in the present hymnal:

> Still through the cloven skies they come
> With peaceful wings unfurled,
> And still their heavenly music floats
> O'er all the weary world;
> Above its sad and lowly plains
> They bend on heavenly wing,
> And ever o'er its Babel sounds,
> The blessed angels sing.

CAROL was first published in Richard S. Willis' *Church Chorals and Choir Studies* (New York, 1850), as a setting of Philip Doddridge's "See Israel's Gentle Shepherd Stand" and titled STUDY NUMBER 23. In 1860, Willis published an adaptation of the tune with the text "While shepherds watched their flocks by night." This arrangement subsequently became associated with Sears' text and the two have become indelibly linked together.

This hymn and its tune first appeared in a Southern Baptist collection in Robert H. Coleman's *The Popular Hymnal* (Dallas, 1918, No. 133).   *D.M.*

It Is Well with My Soul—See *When peace, like a river*

It's So Wonderful—See *To me, it's so wonderful*

Jerusalem, my happy home 517

These four stanzas are from a poem of 26 four-line, common meter stanzas found in a manuscript book in the British Museum (*Add.* 15.225). There it is headed "A Song Made by F: B: P. To the tune of Diana." There is no date on the manuscript, but it is thought to be from the late 16th or early 17th century. Nothing is known of the writer, nor has the "tune of Diana" been identified with certainty. Leonard Ellinwood, in *The Hymnal 1940 Companion* (p. 342), comments, "Here is sacred folk-literature at its very finest, coming at a time when the singing of English congregations was limited to the metrical paraphrases of the Psalms."

John Julian's careful treatment of this hymn in his *Dictionary of Hymnology* (pp. 580-83) reveals the complexity of its various forms. He gives another version of 44 stanzas, dating from 1585, suggesting that both versions may have had an earlier common source. New versions appeared retaining certain stanzas of earlier versions and adding new stanzas by unknown writers. One stanza, now a part of John Newton's "Amazing Grace! How Sweet the Sound," has been found in *A Collection of Sacred Ballads* (1790), compiled by two Baptists, Andrew Broaddus and Richard Broaddus, of Caroline County, Virginia. In a ten-stanza version, this is the final stanza:

> When we've been there ten thousand years
> Bright shining as the sun,
> We've no less days to sing God's praise,
> Than when we first begun.

The first Southern Baptist collection to publish "Jerusalem, My Happy Home" was *Christian Praise* (Nashville, 1964, No. 431).

LAND OF REST—See hymn 510, O Lord, may church and home combine.   *W.J.R.*

Jerusalem, the golden 527

This is one of several hymns in English translated from *De Contemptu Mundi* (On the Contemptibleness of the World), a poem of almost 3000 lines written about 1145 by Bernard of Cluny. Written in the difficult meter of dactylic hexameter, each line was composed of three parts, with rhyme between the first two parts as well as end rhyme between successive lines, as follows:

Hora novis*sima* Tempora pes*sima*sunt: vigil*emus!*

Ecce mina*citer*imminet ar*biter*ille supre-*mus....*

John Mason Neale translated this difficult pattern of poetry into simple ballad meter (7.6.7.6.D.), his version of 218 lines becoming the leading translation of what has been called "a bitter satire on the fearful corruption of the age." Other hymns from Neale's translation of Bernard's poem include "The world is very evil," "Brief life is here our portion," and "For thee, O dear, dear country."

"Jerusalem, the Golden" was introduced to Baptists in America through several hymnals published in 1871: *The Baptist Praise Book* (New York), *The Baptist Hymn Book, The Baptist Hymn and Tune Book* (Philadelphia), and *The Service of Song for Baptist Churches* (Boston). Beginning with A. B. Cates' *Bap-*

tist Songs with Music (Louisville, 1873), this hymn has appeared frequently in hymnals compiled for Southern Baptist churches. The first appearance of both text and tune in an "official" Southern Baptist collection was in *The Baptist Hymn and Praise Book* (Nashville, 1904, No. 550)

EWING was first composed by Alexander Ewing for "For Thee, O Dear, Dear Country" in 1853, being printed first in broadside form and then in John Grey's *Manual of Psalms and Hymn-tunes* (London, 1857) with the name ST. BEDE. Its original rhythm in 3/2 meter was altered by William Henry Monk for publication in *Hymns Ancient and Modern* (1861).   *H.E.*

Jesu, Jesu, fill us with Your love 501

This hymn was adapted from a folk song collected in 1963 at Chereponi in northern Ghana by Tom Colvin. Fifteen new African Christians were engaged in a three-week leadership course at Chereponi led by Presbyterian missionaries Al Drass and Bob Thelin. The melody of this hymn was one that was shared with Colvin by the nationals. At a later time he wrote the words which are based on John 13:3-5 and also reflect Luke 10:25-28. It was published with an original text in his collection of African hymns, *Free to Serve* (1968). Colvin's arrangement appears in several contemporary hymnals, and its first appearance in a Southern Baptist hymnal is in *The Baptist Hymnal* (1991).

CHEREPONI was obviously named for the place where the tune was first heard by Colvin.   *P.H.*

Jesus, at Your holy table 377

This hymn was written by Tom Allen as part of a research paper assignment on the Lord's Supper while he was a student at Furman University. The inspiration for the text came from childhood remembrances of the

Supper as well as from a service of holy communion in Westminster Abbey, attended by the author in the summer of 1986. The third stanza was rewritten while Allen was at seminary and the revised hymn was first used for a communion service at the Audubon Baptist Church, Louisville, Kentucky, where he served as organist. *The Baptist Hymnal* (1991) is the first hymnal to include the hymn, slightly altered from the author's original.

BEACH SPRING—See hymn 604, Come, all Christians, be committed.   *H.T.M.*

Jesus calls us o'er the tumult 293

This hymn by Cecil Frances Alexander was written for St. Andrew's Day and is based on Matthew 4:18-20. It was first published by the Society for the Propagation of Christian Knowledge in Tract No. 15, "Hymns for Public Worship" (1852, No. 116). The original hymn had five stanzas. The omitted second stanza is:

As, of old, Saint Andrew heard it
  By the Galilean lake,
Turned from home and toil and kindred,
  Leaving all for His dear sake.

GALILEE was composed by William Herbert Jude for the text "Jesus Calls Us O'er the Tumult," and first appeared in *The Congregational Church Hymnal* (London, 1887), edited by George S. Barrett and E. J. Hopkins. *Kingdom Songs* (Dallas, 1921, No. 196) was the first Southern Baptist hymnal to contain this hymn, although it appeared in the very first compilation of Baptist Robert H. Coleman (with W. W. Hamilton) in *The Evangel* (Philadelphia, 1909, No. 195). *S.W.G.*

Jesus Calls You Now—See *Bring your sin to Him and confess*

Jesus, how I love you! 230

In a simple, straightforward way, this three-stanza chorus offers love, thanks, and praise for Christ's goodness, grace, and presence. Aaron Tomes wrote this text in 1979 as a senior in high school at a Colorado youth camp.

TOMES is named for its composer, Aaron Tomes. He composed this tune to his own text, "How I Love You." Like its text, it is a simple, straightforward tune in a comfortable singing range and with repeated melodic figures. Text and tune were copyrighted in 1981, and first appeared in *Singing Is Fun, Vol. II*, Broadman Press, 1981. It later appeared in *DiscipleYouth Songs* (1984, No. 26), compiled by Mark Blankenship. *The Baptist Hymnal* (1991) marks its first appearance in a Southern Baptist hymnal.   *S.W.G.*

Jesus, I my cross have taken 471

The hymn first appeared signed by the initial "G" in Henry F. Lyte's *Sacred Poetry* (3rd. ed., Edinburgh, 1824). The heading for the six eight-line stanzas was "Lo, we have left all, and followed thee" (Mark 10:28). Nine years later, in his *Poems, Chiefly Religious*, Lyte claimed authorship of the hymn. The first appearance of the hymn in the United States occurred in Archibald Alexander's *A Selection of Hymns* (New York, 1831). Two stanzas of this hymn were published in the first Southern Baptist hymnal, *The Baptist Psalmody* (Charleston, 1850, No. 516), but the text was attributed to "Grant," perhaps a derivation from the letter "G" used as a signature in its earliest publications. The first Baptist usage was in *The Baptist Praise Book*, compiled by Richard Fuller, E. M. Levy, S. D. Phelps, H. C. Fish, Thomas Armitage, E. T. Winkler, W. W. Everts, George C. Lorimer, and Basil Manly, Jr. (New York, 1871, No. 705). The first "official" Southern Baptist collection to include the three stanzas as found in *The Baptist Hymnal* (1991) was *The Baptist Hymn and Praise Book*

(Nashville, 1904, No. 340).

ELLESDIE appeared in Joshua Leavitt's *The Christian Lyre, Vol. II* (New York, 1833), where it is called DISCIPLE. It is set to this text and no composer is indicated. In *The Baptist Praise Book* (New York, 1871, p. 278), it appears with this text bearing the notation "Arr. by J. P. Holbrook," who was the music editor. In *Winnowed Hymns* (New York, 1873), the source is given as "Air, Mozart, Arr. by H. P. M." These are the initials of Hubert P. Main, whose harmonization of the melody attributed to Mozart appears in many late 19th-century hymnals. There seems to be no evidence to support crediting the tune to Mozart. Robert G. McCutchan, in *Hymn Tune Names*, suggests that ELLESDIE "is said to be a 'made name'—from the initial letters 'L. S. D.' of some person unknown." *The Baptist Hymn and Praise Book* (Nashville, 1904, No. 457) calls the tune DISCIPLE and attributes it to Mozart.   *W.J.R.*

Jesus is all the world to me 184

Both words and music of this gospel song were written by Will L. Thompson. It first appeared in *The New Century Hymnal* (East Liverpool, OH, 1904), which he edited and published.

ELIZABETH was the name of Thompson's wife. This name was first applied to the tune in *Baptist Hymnal* (Nashville, 1956).

Songs of Redemption (Atlanta, 1920, No. 17) was the first Southern Baptist book to include this hymn.   *P.A.R.*

Jesus is coming to earth again 195

Written and composed by Mrs. C. H. (Lelia N.) Morris, this text and tune were first published in H. L. Gilmour, George W. Sanville, William J. Kirkpatrick, and Melvin J. Hill's *The King's Praises No. 3* (Philadelphia, 1912). Eight years after its initial publication, the song appeared in W. Plunkett Mar-

tin and J. W. Jelks' *Songs of Redemption* (Atlanta, 1920, No. 108).

SECOND COMING is the name assigned to this tune by the hymnal committee for *Baptist Hymnal* (1956).   *D.M.*

Jesus Is Lord of All—See *Jesus is Savior and Lord of my life*

Jesus is Savior and Lord of my life 296

LeRoy McClard wrote both words and music for this hymn. He recalls that the teaching of the lordship of Christ first became a reality to him in a New Testament class taught by Dr. Jack MacGorman at Southwestern Baptist Theological Seminary in 1948. This experience made a deep impression on his life. In the summer of 1966 he led the music for the Southern Baptist Youth Conference at Glorieta, New Mexico, and "Jesus Is Lord" was the conference theme. All during the week he was concerned because there was no appropriate hymn to support this theme. At the close of the week he returned to Illinois, where he was then working as state music director for the Illinois Baptist State Association. The first day after his return, in his home in Carterville, he wrote the words and music. It was first published in *Songs of Salvation No. 3* (Nashville, 1966, No. 19), and then in *Baptist Hymnal* (Nashville, 1975, No. 353).

The tune is named LORDSHIP OF CHRIST by the author/composer.   *W.J.R.*

Jesus is tenderly calling 316

Fanny J. Crosby wrote this text in 1883. It was later given its tune by George C. Stebbins. In the first appearance in *Gospel Hymns No. 4* compiled by Ira D. Sankey, James McGranahan and George C. Stebbins (Chicago, 1883), it is headed with the Scripture reference, "Arise, he calleth thee" (John 11:28). In an earlier 1881 edition of *Gospel Hymns No. 4*,

"Jesus Is Tenderly Calling Thee Home" is not to be found. It first appeared in a Southern Baptist collection in *The Baptist Hymn and Praise Book* (Nashville, 1904, No. 186).

CALLING TODAY is the name ascribed in *Baptist Hymnal* (1956) to the tune composed by George C. Stebbins for "Jesus Is Tenderly Calling" by Fanny Crosby. In his *Reminiscences and Gospel Hymn Stories* (New York, 1924), Stebbins states that Fanny Crosby's words did not impress him as being of more than ordinary merit, even for evangelistic work, and that it never entered his mind that the song would meet with the instant favor it enjoyed for many years   .H.T.M.

Jesus Is the Song—See *My Savior is the Lord and King*

Jesus is the sweetest name I know 205

This chorus is the refrain of the hymn, "There Have Been Names That I Have Loved to Hear," of which words and music were written by Lela B. Long. The earliest listing of the hymn in the *Dictionary of American Hymnology* is in *The Christian Witness Songs* (Chicago, 1930). No information is available concerning its origin or its author/composer. *The Baptist Hymnal* (1991) is the first Southern Baptist hymnal to include it.

LOVELY NAME, the tune name, is taken from the second line of the refrain.   *M.P.*

Jesus, Jesus, Jesus 177

This hymn with one stanza, words by William J. and Gloria Gaither, and music by William J. Gaither, was written in 1970. Many experiences of joy and sorrow—the birth of their first child, the death of Bill's grandmother, and others—inspired a song that is a statement of what Bill and Gloria Gaither had found to be true: there *is* something about that name—JESUS! The first hymnal inclusion was *Hymns for the Family*

of God (Nashville, 1976, No. 227). *The Baptist Hymnal* (1991) is the first Southern Baptist collection to include it.

THAT NAME is the name given the tune by the composer for its first hymnal inclusion. *W.J.R.*

Jesus, keep me near the cross 280

This gospel hymn text was written by Fanny Crosby to fit its tune which was composed by W. H. Doane. It appears in *The Baptist Hymnal* (1991) as originally written with the exception of one word ("his" substituted for "its" in the fourth phrase of the second stanza)—a change first made in *Baptist Hymnal* (Nashville, 1956, No. 97). Its first inclusion in an "official" Southern Baptist collection was in *The Baptist Hymn and Praise Book* (Nashville, 1904, No. 117).

NEAR THE CROSS was written first by W. H. Doane and given to Fanny Crosby who provided the text. The text and tune first appeared in *Bright Jewels* edited by Robert Lowry and assisted by W. F. Sherwin and Chester G. Allen (New York, 1869). Its first appearance in a Doane collection was in *Songs of Devotion* (New York; Chicago, 1870). The tune name was used first for Baptists in *Baptist Hymnal* (Nashville, 1956).   H.T.M.

Jesus, lover of my soul 180

This hymn was written shortly after Charles Wesley's conversion experience in 1738 and was published within a few months of the official date (1739) of the founding of Methodism. It was first published in the Wesleyan *Hymns and Sacred Poems* (1740) and headed "In Temptation." It has been one of the best-loved hymns in the English language. Though rich in imagery, it is a simple and clear hymn with a remarkably high number of monosyllabic words. The first word was originally "Jesu," Wesley's favorite form. A number of liberties have been taken with the hymn in various hymnals. The third stanza has been omitted in the present version. Its first appearance in a Southern Baptist hymnal was in *The Baptist Psalmody* (Charleston, 1850, No. 543).

MARTYN was written by Simeon B. Marsh in the fall of 1834 while he was on his way from Amsterdam, New York, to Johnstown, New York, to conduct a singing school. It is said that he stopped his horse, dismounted, and sketched the tune. The tune was first published in Volume I of Thomas Hastings' *Musical Miscellany* (1836), with John Newton's text "Mary, At Her Saviour's Tomb." Its first appearance with "Jesus, Lover of My Soul" was in 1842 in *Sacred Songs for Family and Social Worship* edited by Thomas Hastings. The *Baptist Hymn and Praise Book* (Nashville, 1904, No. 282) was the first Southern Baptist hymnal to include the tune.   *S.W.G.*

Jesus loves me! 344

The words of this hymn first appeared in a book entitled *Say and Seal*, written by Anna B. Warner, in collaboration with her sister, Susan, and published in 1860. In the novel is a scene in which Johnny Fax, a young boy who is ill, is comforted by his Sunday School teacher, John Linden. When Linden is asked by the child to sing, he begins a new song—the four stanzas of the hymn written by Anna B. Warner. *Kingdom Songs* (Dallas, 1921, No. 262) was the first Southern Baptist hymnal to include this text and its familiar tune.

CHINA was composed in 1861 by William B. Bradbury for this text. To the four stanzas of Warner's hymn, Bradbury added the words of the refrain. Text and tune were published in his *Golden Shower* (1862, No. 68), a Sunday School songbook. The tune name was assigned because of the popularity of the tune among children in China as the result of missionary work there. Such popularity might be attributed to the pentatonic structure of the melody.   *M.P.*

Jesus loves the little children 592

This is the refrain of a hymn text written by Clarence Herbert Woolston beginning "Jesus loves the children dear." The tune CHILDREN is that of George Frederick Root's popular Civil War song, "Tramp! Tramp! Tramp!" (Chicago, 1864), with the refrain:

Tramp, tramp, tramp, the boys are
   marching,
   Cheer up, comrades. They will come,
And beneath the starry flag
   We shall breathe the air again,
Of the free land in our own beloved
   home.

Woolston's three-stanza hymn was first published in *The Gospel Message No. 3* (Philadelphia, 1913, No. 355).

It was an obvious outgrowth of Woolston's ministry to children through his church and through children's meetings at summer conference centers. The chorus "Jesus Loves the Little Children" appeared as anonymous in Robert H. Coleman's *The American Hymnal* (Dallas, 1933, No. 441) and in B. B. McKinney's *The Broadman Hymnal* (Nashville, 1940, No. 311), where it became widely known among Southern Baptists. Woolston's complete hymn with refrain set to Root's tune became available to children in Southern Baptist Sunbeam bands through the publication in *Missionary Melodies*, compiled by Louanah Riggs Holcomb (Nashville, 1950, p. 18). Published under the auspices of the Woman's Missionary Union, this collection included additional second and third stanzas to Woolston's text, apparently submitted anonymously by Sunbeam leaders.

Woolston's original lines: "Red and yellow, black and white, They are precious in his sight" have been altered for *The Baptist Hymnal* (1991) to "Every color, every race, All are covered by His grace."   *H.E.*

Jesus, my friend, is great 190

The original Japanese words and the music of this song were written by Yuji Abe and Katsuhiko Shimada during a Kanto Gakuin (Yokohama) High School YMCA summer retreat in 1963. In a letter to the author of this article, the translator, Nobuaki Hanaoka, who was present at the retreat, made the following observations about the song:

"Though this was almost extemporaneously written, we all liked it. We added a few words here and there. The song remained popular among the members of the High-Y and we sang it almost every year at retreat during our school days. Years later, I wrote it down from my memories and translated it into English for our church youth. Before this was published in *Hymns from the Four Winds,* a United Methodist hymnal supplement, it had never been published anywhere to my knowledge."

Translated by Mr. Hanaoka in 1981, the song appeared in *Hymns From the Four Winds* (Nashville, 1983, No. 101) as a single-line melody. The first appearance of the song in a Southern Baptist hymnal is *The Baptist Hymnal* (1991).

KANTO, the tune name, is taken from the name of the high school.   *D.M.*

Jesus, my Lord and Savior 186

"Walking Along with Jesus" was written in 1977 while Nelson A. Sosa, the author and composer, was living in Cuba. Sosa gives testimony of the assurance of God's companionship which gave him this song at a very difficult period of his life. For 10 years he had been longing to leave Cuba, yet there were those who sought to discourage him

in his desire to come to the United States. In great doubt and anguish of spirit after the pleas of a particular individual that he withdraw his request to leave the country, he turned to the Scriptures for help. Psalm 48:14, "For this God is our God forever and ever; he will be our guide even to the end," provided the assurance he needed that, whether in Cuba or elsewhere, he would continue to walk with Jesus by his side. In the joy and peace that came with this realization, Sosa found himself singing the stanzas of "Walking Along with Jesus."

Hymnal committee member, Paul Bobbitt, Director of the Church Music Department of the Florida Baptist Convention, was instrumental in getting this song to the committee for consideration, and *The Baptist Hymnal* (1991) is the first Southern Baptist collection to include it.

SOSA is the name given by *The Baptist Hymnal* (1991) editorial staff committee to Nelson Sosa's tune for "Walking Along with Jesus."   *H.T.M.*

Jesus, my Lord, will love me forever 345

Norman J. Clayton wrote the tune now called ELLSWORTH about 1942, while he was living in Malverne, Long Island, New York. A year later, while compiling a new collection of songs, he remembered the tune and wrote the present stanza and refrain text. Words and music first appeared in Clayton's *Word of Life Melodies No. 1* (1943). Text and tune were first included in a Southern Baptist collection in *Baptist Hymnal* (Nashville, 1975, No. 477).   *W.J.R.*

Jesus, our Lord and King 363

No information is known about the hymn or the author.

TRENTHAM—See hymn 278, Make me a captive, Lord.   *W.J.R.*

Jesus Paid It All—See *I hear the Savior say*

Jesus shall reign 587

This is another of the great hymns taken from Isaac Watts' *Psalms of David, Imitated in the Language of the New Testament* (1719). Stanzas 1, 3, and 4 in *The Baptist Hymnal* (1991) are the original stanzas 1, 4, and 5 of Watts' setting of part 2 of Psalm 72. In order to divest the hymn of its British colonial flavor, stanza 2 in *Baptist Hymnal* (1975) has been omitted. It read:

> From north to south the princes meet
> To pay their homage at his feet;
> While western empires own their Lord,
> And savage tribes attend his word.

Its replacement is stanza 6 of the original. One of the earliest hymns on missions, it seldom appeared in 18th-century hymnals. Perhaps this was caused by the century's strong Calvinist emphasis on predestination. The great missionary movements did not begin until the 19th century. However Southern Baptists' first published hymnal, *The Baptist Psalmody* (Charleston, 1850, No. 1002) included the hymn without the stanza quoted above.

DUKE STREET was first published as ADDISON'S 19TH PSALM in *Select Collection of Psalm and Hymn Tunes* (Glasgow, 1793) by Henry Boyd. No composer was given. It appeared as DUKE STREET in William Dixon's *Euphonia* (Liverpool, 1805) and was attributed to John Hatton who lived on Duke Street in St. Helen's, England. It has also appeared as NEWRY, WINDLE, and ST. HELEN'S.   *D.B.*

Jesus, the very thought of Thee 225

This text is a translation into English of a segment of the extended Latin hymn "*Jesu dulcis memoria.*" The hymn was once attributed to Bernard of Clairvaux, but this claim is now generally considered to be inaccurate. Though differing opinions continue to exist among scholars concerning its origin, general consensus supports an English origin around the 12th century, with the text later gaining wider circulation on the continent. The version appearing in *The Baptist Hymnal* (1991) uses the first four stanzas of Edward Caswall's translation which was published in his *Lyra Catholica* (London, 1849), with minor alterations in stanza 2, lines 1 and 3, and in stanza 4, lines 2 and 4. Caswall's translation was first published in the United States in three collections issued in 1851 by Edward Dunigan & Brothers: *The Catholic Hymn Book*, *The Little Catholic Hymn Book*, and *Lyra Catholica*. Its first publication in a Southern Baptist hymnal was in *The Baptist Hymn and Praise Book* (Nashville, 1904, No. 273).

ST. AGNES—See hymn 116, Our Savior's infant cries were heard.   *M.P.*

Jesus, Thy boundless love to me 123

Paul Gerhardt's original hymn, "O Jesu Christ, mein schoenstes Licht," was based on a prayer of thanks, No. 5 in Class II of Johann Arndt's *Paradissgaertlein* ("Little Paradise Garden," 1612). Gerhardt's hymn of 16 stanzas was first published in the fifth edition of his friend Johann Crüger's famous hymnal, *Praxis Pietatis Melica* ("Practice of Piety in Song," Berlin, 1653). At least five translations have been made into English, the most popular of which is John Wesley's version, described by Haeussler as an inspired paraphrase almost like an original creation. This is one of 33 hymns that Wesley translated from the Moravian *Herrnhut Gesangbuch* (1735) while he was in the colony of Georgia (1735-38). Following Wesley's return to England, this version of 16 stanzas was first published in his *Hymns and Sacred Poems* (1739) under the title "Living by Christ." In his comprehensive hymnal of 1780, *A Collection of Hymns for the Use of the*

People Called Methodists, Wesley reduced this hymn to nine stanzas. The earliest Baptist hymnal in America to include this hymn was Stow and Smith's *The Psalmist* (Boston, 1843), followed by Manly's *The Baptist Psalmody* (Charleston, 1850), where number 667 is reduced to four stanzas.

ST. CATHERINE—See hymn 352, Faith of our fathers.   *H.E.*

Jesus was a loving teacher 602

No information is available about the author or the circumstances under which this children's hymn was written. The words were copyrighted in 1946 by Westminster Press, and the hymn seems to have first appeared in *Songs and Hymns for Primary Children* (Philadelphia, 1963). The first printing in a Southern Baptist collection is in *The Baptist Hymnal* (1991).

The tune BARNARD was named for its composer, Charlotte A. Barnard. However the tune is named BROCKLESBURY in *Songs and Hymns for Primary Children* (No. 114), and BARNARD is previously found with another Barnard tune set to Howard B. Grose's "Give of Your Best to the Master" (*Baptist Hymnal*, 1956, No. 353).   *H.T.M.*

Jesus! what a friend for sinners! 185

The *Dictionary of American Hymnology* cites the earliest publication of this text by J. Wilbur Chapman in *Conference Hymnal* (Philadelphia, 1907), compiled by Charles M. Alexander. When the text appeared in *Alexander's Gospel Songs No. 2* (New York, 1910) under the heading "Our Great Saviour," a copyright date of 1910 was listed for it. For this latter collection, a foreword was written by J. Wilbur Chapman, and the text was set to a harmonization of the HYFRYDOL tune (with which the text continues to be paired) by Robert Harkness, who was the pianist for several of Chapman's evangelis-

tic campaigns. The text contains both quotations from and allusions to Charles Wesley's "Jesus, Lover of My Soul." The first Southern Baptist collection to include this hymn was *Baptist Hymnal* (Nashville, 1975, No. 64).

HYFRYDOL—See hymn 36, Praise the Lord! Ye heavens, adore Him.   *M.P.*

Jesus' hands were kind hands 477

The words of this song were written by Margaret Cropper. Set to an anonymous French folk melody, AU CLAIR DE LA LUNE appeared in Gordon John Freer's *Bless the Lord: Songs and Hymns for Young Children* (Toronto, 1967) and subsequently in *The Hymnal* of the Baptist Federation of Canada (1973, No. 448). The present arrangement of the tune is the work of Bill Newton. *The Baptist Hymnal* (1991) represents the first publication of the words and music in a Southern Baptist collection.   *D.M.*

Joy to the world! the Lord is come 87

Perhaps the most significant attempt "to make David sing like a Christian" was Isaac Watts' *Psalms of David Imitated in the Language of the New Testament* (London, 1719). "Joy to the World! The Lord Is Come" is taken from the second part (vv. 4-9) of Watts' rendering of Psalm 98. The wording in our hymnal is the same as in the original. This is not the case with some other collections. Reynolds, in *Hymns of Our Faith*, describes two interesting alterations: (1) A Seventh-Day Adventist version which focuses on the second coming by altering the verb to read "Joy to the world, the Lord *will* come," and (2) a disfigurement which appeared in *Social Hymns for Use of Friends of the Rational System of Society* (1838):

Joy to the world! the light has come,
   The only lawful King:
Let every heart prepare it room

And moral nature sing
(Reynolds, 1976, 128).

Several Methodist collections substitute "world" for "earth" in the opening line of the second stanza. The text unaltered first appeared in a Southern Baptist collection in *The Baptist Psalmody* (Charleston, 1850, No. 146).

ANTIOCH (also called COMFORT, HOLY TRIUMPH, and MESSIAH) was said to be arranged or adapted "from Handel." McCutchan notes: "Some authorities state it is a sort of medley, the opening phrase being taken from the chorus, 'Lift up your heads,' and the part set to the words 'and heaven and nature sing' (four measures), from the introduction to the tenor recitative, 'Comfort ye, my people' " (McCutchan, 123). ANTIOCH, which probably was "written" in 1836, was included in Lowell Mason's *Modern Psalmist* (Boston, 1839). A notation in the index indicated the tune had "either been arranged, adapted, or composed for this work, or taken from other recent works of the Editor" (Reynolds, 1964, 107). While there is disagreement as to Handel's contribution to the tune, there is no denying it has served as a useful setting for Watts' text.

The tune first appeared in a Southern Baptist collection, *The Casket*, an oblong tune-book (Charleston, 1855, p. 87) which places the melody in the tenor of a four-part setting. *D.B.*

Joyful, joyful, we adore Thee 7

According to Tertius Van Dyke, this hymn was written in 1907 by his father, Henry Van Dyke, when he was a guest preacher at Williams College, Williamstown, Massachusetts, nestled in the Berkshires. Coming to breakfast, he placed a manuscript on the table before college president Garfield, saying, "Here is a hymn for you. Your mountains were my inspiration. It must be sung to the music of Beethoven's 'Hymn to Joy'." It is included in the third edition of Van Dyke's *Poems*, there dated 1908. The first hymnal publication was in the *Presbyterian Hymnal* (Philadelphia, 1911, No. 115).

HYMN TO JOY is drawn from Beethoven's *Ninth Symphony*, composed 1817-23, and published in 1826. Beethoven's tune, a setting to Schiller's "Ode to Joy," was the inspiration for Van Dyke's hymn. Three arrangements of this tune, all called BONN, were published in Elam Ives, Jr.'s *The Mozart Collection* (New York, 1846). An adaptation of the Ives' version was used with Van Dyke's hymn in the *Presbyterian Hymnal* in 1911. The present adaptation of this tune, made by Edward Hodges, was first published in S. P. Tuckerman, *Trinity Collection of Church Music* (New York, 1864). *H.E.*

Just a Closer Walk with Thee—See *I am weak but Thou art strong*

Just as I am 303, 307

This hymn was written by Charlotte Elliott in 1834, while she was living at Westfield Lodge, Brighton, England. Because of a weakened physical condition, she was unable to go with her brother, an Anglican minister, and other members of the family to a bazaar to raise funds for St. Mary's Hall, a college for daughters of poorer clergy in Brighton. In the midst of a restless night during which she found sleep difficult, due to her preoccupation with her own physical weakness, she began writing the verses of this hymn as an expression of trust and personal faith. The hymn was first published in a leaflet in 1835, without her knowledge, and was included the following year in her *Invalid's Hymn Book* in six four-line stanzas with the Scripture text, "him that cometh to me I will in no wise cast out" (John 6:37). A seventh stanza was added when the hymn appeared later in that same year in *Hours of Sorrow Cheered and Comforted*. This text appeared in the first Southern Baptist hymnal, *The Baptist Psalmody* (Charleston, 1850, No. 472).

WOODWORTH (hymn 307) by William B. Bradbury was first published in the *Mendelssohn Collection, or Third Book of Psalmody* (1849, p. 60), compiled by Bradbury and Thomas Hastings. In this collection it was set in the key of C and used with "The God of Love Will Sure Indulge." It became closely associated with Charlotte Elliott's text through its use by Moody and Sankey and its inclusion in the collection of *Gospel Hymns and Sacred Songs* published from 1875-91.

TABERNACLE (hymn 303) was written by Phillip Landgrave as the result of a suggestion from Dr. Kenneth Chafin, then professor of evangelism at The Southern Baptist Theological Seminary, that he compose a new tune for "Just As I Am." It was subsequently included in a youth musical, *Purpose* (1968), which Landgrave wrote for the youth choir at Tabernacle Baptist Church, Louisville, Kentucky, where he served as minister of music. The tune was named for that church.   *M.P.*

Just when I need Him, Jesus is near 65

This was one of William C. Poole's first attempts at hymn writing. In 1907, Poole submitted this and several other texts to composer Charles H. Gabriel. Gabriel wrote the tune and published the hymn in his *The Victory: A Collection of Popular Sunday School Songs New and Old* (Cincinnati, 1908). In this source the first stanza read:

Just when I need Him, Jesus is near,
  Willing to help me, anxious to cheer;
In all my trials answering prayer,
  Just when I need him most.

E. O. Excell bought the hymn from Gabriel and printed it in his *Service in Song*

(Chicago, 1909). In the same year, the hymn also appeared in Southern Baptist Robert H. Coleman's first collection, *The Evangel* (Philadelphia, 1909, No. 37), which was co-compiled by W. W. Hamilton and edited by Excell.

The tune GABRIEL was named for its composer in *Baptist Hymnal* (1956).   *D.M.*

Just When I Need Him Most—See *Just when I need Him, Jesus is near*

King of kings 234

This chorus was written around 1974 by Naomi Batya and Sophie Conty when they were both 13 years old. It spread through many congregations and was first published by Maranatha! Music as an anonymous or traditional work. The girls' pastor recognized the song and contacted Maranatha! Music. Since then, authorship has been correctly ascribed. *The Baptist Hymnal* (1991) marks its first publication among Southern Baptists.

KING OF KINGS is a Hebrew folk tune that may be sung as a two-part canon.   *P.H.*

King of my life, I crown Thee now 490

This text was written by Jennie E. Hussey and first published in *New Songs of Praise and Power No. 3* (1921), where it was set to William J. Kirkpatrick's tune DUNCANNON.

The tune was assigned the name DUNCANNON in *Baptist Hymnal* (1975) because that was the town in which Kirkpatrick was born. The first Southern Baptist hymnal to include this text and tune was *Christian Praise* (Nashville, 1964, No. 305).   *M.P.*

Lead Me to Calvary—See *King of my life, I crown Thee now*

Lead me to some soul today 560

This chorus was written in 1936. The

words were written by Will H. Houghton, President of Moody Bible Institute, and the music composed by Wendell P. Loveless, Director of Moody's Department of Religious Broadcasting. It was written "In memory of D. L. Moody, who said: 'I must speak to one soul each day about Christ.' " This chorus, composed in 1936, was the theme song for the annual Founder's Week at Moody Bible Institute in 1937, the year of the centenary of D. L. Moody's birth, when it became popular. It was published in Loveless' and William M. Runyan's *Radio Songs and Choruses of the Gospel Number Two* (Chicago, 1937, No. 25). This chorus soon became widely known among Southern Baptists through its inclusion in Robert H. Coleman's *World Revival Hymns* (Dallas, 1939, No. 77). The following year it appeared in *The Broadman Hymnal* (Nashville, 1940, No. 323).

LEAD ME is the name assigned to the tune by the hymnal committee for *The Baptist Hymnal* (1991).   *H.E., D.M.*

Lead on, O King Eternal 621

Ernest W. Shurtleff wrote this hymn in 1887 for the graduation ceremony of his class at Andover Theological Seminary in Massachusetts. The occasion for which the hymn was written is reflected in the references to "days of preparation" and "fields of conquest." The text was first published in Shurtleff's *Hymns of the Faith* (1887).

Henry Smart composed the tune LANCASHIRE as a setting of Reginald Heber's "From Greenland's icy mountains." The tune was first sung on October 4, 1835, at a festival in Blackburn, Lancashire, celebrating the 300th anniversary of the English Reformation. Thirty-two years later, the tune made its first hymnal appearance in Smart's *Psalms and Hymns for Divine Worship* (London, 1867). The earliest known association between LANCASHIRE and "Lead On, O King

eternal" occurred in the 1905 *Methodist Hymnal* (New York, No. 408).

The hymn and its tune does not appear in a Southern Baptist hymn collection until *The New Baptist Hymnal* (Nashville, 1926, No. 210). The same year it appeared in Baptist Robert H. Coleman's *The Modern Hymnal* (Dallas, 1926, No. 203).   *D.M.*

Leaning on the Everlasting Arms—See *What a fellowship, what a joy divine*

Let all mortal flesh keep silence 80

Here is the Cherubic Hymn from the Liturgy of St. James of Jerusalem that was used in Eastern Orthodox churches, probably as early as the fifth century. It is still sung as the sacred elements are brought to the sanctuary. A literal prose translation was made for Neale and Littledale's *Translations of the Primitive Liturgies* (1868-69), and from this Gerard Moultrie made the metrical translation for Orby Shipley's *Lyra Eucharistica*, (2nd ed., 1864). This hymn made its first appearance in the United States in Bernhard Pick's *Hymns and Poetry of the Eastern Church* (New York, 1908). Southern Baptists' singing of this hymn developed when it appeared in *Baptist Hymnal* (Nashville, 1956, No. 80).

PICARDY is a French tune, probably from the 17th century. It is found in *Chansons populaires des provinces de France*, (Vol. IV, Paris, 1860, p. 6), in which it is identified as having been sung by Mme. Pierre Dupont to the words "Jesus Christ s' habille en pauvre," a folk song she remembered from her childhood in Picardy. The tune was adapted for the present text in *The English Hymnal* (London, 1906, No. 318) by Ralph Vaughan Williams.   *W.J.R.*

Let all the world in every corner sing 28

George Herbert wrote this two-stanza poem as part of his *The Temple* (Cambridge, p. 45), a collection of verse which was published posthumously in 1633. This is one of two lyrics in the book which were originally titled "Antiphon." In the medieval Latin church, an antiphon was a short refrain which was sung before and after the chanting of a psalm. Herbert's poem preserved this form by beginning, ending, and separating the two stanzas with the words "Let all the world in ev'ry corner sing, *My God and King.*" The title and format of "Antiphon" suggest that, unlike most of the poems in *The Temple*, Herbert intended for these stanzas to be sung. The poem was adapted for hymnic use as early as 1697, when it was included (in altered form) in *Select Hymns taken out of Mr. Herbert's Temple and turn'd into the common Meeter to be Sung in the Tunes ordinarily us'd in Churches* (London, 1697, p. 12).

ALL THE WORLD was composed by Robert G. McCutchan for use with this text in *The Methodist Hymnal* (1935, No. 8), of which he was editor. Not wishing his identity as composer to be known, McCutchan credited this and three other tunes in the book to "John Porter." The tune originally contained a first and second ending, with the last two melody notes of the second ending rising to E and F-sharp.

This text and tune made their first Southern Baptist hymnal appearance in *Christian Praise* (Nashville, 1964, No. 5).   *D.M.*

Let all things now living 640

This text was written and first published with the Welsh folk tune, ASH GROVE, by Katherine K. Davis in 1939. The text was attributed to John Cowley, which was one of Davis' pseudonyms. *The Baptist Hymnal* (1991) is the first Southern Baptist hymnal to include this hymn.

ASH GROVE—See hymn 497, The Master hath come.   *P.H.*

Let Jesus Come into Your Heart—See *If you are tired of the load of your sin*

Let Others See Jesus in You—See *While passing through this world*

Let us break bread together 366

The origin of this text representing the African-American spiritual tradition is unknown. It has been surmised that this spiritual was a "gathering song"—a type of song intended to announce a secret meeting of African-Americans at a time when such meetings had been declared illegal. It has become associated with the Lord's Supper because of the first two stanzas. In his *English-Speaking Hymnal Guide*, Erik Routley suggested that the text was first published in James Weldon Johnson's *Negro Spirituals*, Book II (1927). Its first appearance in a Southern Baptist hymnal was in the *Baptist Hymnal* (Nashville, 1975, No. 252).

BREAK BREAD is the tune traditionally associated with this text. It is usually identified as LET US BREAK BREAD.   *M.P.*

Let your heart be broken 611

This text was written by Bryan Jeffery Leech and copyrighted in 1975. Its first hymnal inclusion was in *Hymns for the Family of God* (1976), where it was set to Leech's own tune, BJORKLUND MAJOR, in an arrangement by Fred Bock. *The Baptist Hymnal* (1991) marks its first appearance in a Southern Baptist collection.

WYE VALLEY—See hymn 58, Like a river glorious.   *D.M.*

Lift every voice and sing 627

Poet James Weldon Johnson and composer John Rosamond Johnson pooled their efforts to produce this song first sung by a chorus of Black schoolchildren in Jacksonville, Florida, in celebration of the birthday of Abraham Lincoln. It is a song of hope, which recognizes, even in the darkest of days, the ultimate triumph of God.

In his autobiography, *Along This Way* (1933), James Weldon Johnson related how he started with his first line: "Lift ev'ry voice and sing." He then worked along grinding out the next five, when there came to him the lines:

"Sing a song full of the faith
    that the dark past has taught us,
Sing a song full of the hope
    that the present has brought us."

The spirit of the poem had taken hold of him. He composed two other stanzas without pen and paper while his brother worked at his musical setting of them. After the feverish ecstasy of creation, he sensed the serene joy that makes complete the poet's experience.

Although the brothers had no idea of the wide reception it would receive, in only 20 years after its introduction, their song had spread throughout the South and beyond. Typed or printed copies were frequently found pasted in the backs of hymnals and songbooks. It was subsequently adopted by the National Association for the Advancement of Colored People, and considered by many as the "Black National Hymn."

Although almost a century had to pass after the Civil War before most American hymnals would reflect the rich African-American heritage of song, the second half of the 20th century has seen a significant shift in the cultural diversity of major hymnals. Following its inclusion in *The Lutheran Book of Worship* (1978), "Lift Every Voice and Sing" has appeared in such major American hymnals as *The Hymnal 1982* (Episcopal), *The United Methodist Hymnal* (1989), and *The Presbyterian Hymnal* (1990). *The Baptist Hymnal* (1991) is the first Southern Baptist collection to include it.

LIFT EVERY VOICE is the name assigned to this tune, and is taken from the first line of stanza one.   *H.E.*

Lift high the cross 594

This wonderful hymn by George W. Kitchin and Michael R. Newbolt appeared in the 1916 *Supplement of Hymns Ancient & Modern*. Many are reminded of John 12:32: "And I, if I be lifted up from the earth, will draw all men unto me." Sydney H. Nicholson wrote CRUCIFER for this text. *The Baptist Hymnal* (1991) is the first Southern Baptist collection to include this vibrant song.   *D.B.*

Lift Him up 220

Phillip Landgrave wrote this chorus as a recurring theme in an anthem composed in 1986 for the Adult Choir at Lyndon Baptist Church, Louisville, Kentucky. The anthem, based upon John 12:32, was published by Van Ness Press in 1988. The chorus appears in a hymnal for the first time in *The Baptist Hymnal* (1991).

LIFT HIM UP is named for the hymn title. *M.P.*

Lift up your heads 128

Georg Weissel's hymn, "Macht hoch die Thür, das Thor macht weit," in five eight-line stanzas, first appeared in the *Preussische Fest-Lieder*, Part I (1642). Based on Psalm 24, it is a triumphal hymn written for the First Sunday of Advent. Catherine Winkworth's English translation first appeared in her *Lyra Germanica* (1855). The present version is made up of the first half of her stanzas one, four, and five. The hymn first appeared in the United States in an American edition of Winkworth's *Lyra Germanica* (New York, 1856). Its first appearance in a Southern Baptist collection was in *Baptist Hymnal* (Nashville, 1956, No. 247).

TRURO first appeared anonymously in Thomas Williams' *Psalmodia Evangelica: A Collection of Psalms and Hymns in Three Parts for Public Worship*, Part II (London, 1789), where it was set to Isaac Watts's "Now to the Lord a Noble Song." The tune bears the name of an ancient town in southwestern Cornwall, England, a cathedral city and an English Channel port.   *W.J.R.*

Like a river glorious 58

These words were completed by Frances Ridley Havergal on November 3, 1874, at Leamington, England, and published in her *Loyal Responses* (1878).

James Mountain's tune WYE VALLEY was written for Havergal's text and first appeared in the composer's *Hymns of Consecration and Faith* (London, 1876, No. 272).

Baptist Hymnal (Nashville, 1956, No. 294) was apparently the first Southern Baptist collection to include this hymn.   *D.M.*

Living for Jesus 282

This text was written by Thomas O. Chisholm in 1917, at the request of C. Harold Lowden. Lowden had composed the tune in 1915 under the title "Sunshine Song" for use in a Children's Day service. Later, while preparing a collection of hymns for publication, he decided that the tune needed a stronger text and sent it to Chisholm under the title "Living for Jesus." After initially declining because he had not previously written a hymn on request, Chisholm was persuaded by Lowden, who insisted that he had been led by God to make the request. Soon thereafter, Chisholm completed the text of four stanzas and refrain.

Text and tune were published by the composer in single sheets in the spring of 1917, and it was first used in summer youth conferences in this form. Later in 1917 it appeared in *Uplifting Songs*, compiled by Lowden and Rufus W. Miller and published by Heidelberg Press.

LIVING is the tune name given by the composer. Both text and tune first appeared in a Southern Baptist collection in *Songs of Faith* (Nashville, 1933, No. 254).   *M.P.*

Living Stones—See *Our God has built with living stones*

Lo, He comes with clouds descending 199

Charles Wesley wrote more than 6000 hymns covering a broad range of Christian doctrines. The best of Wesley's hymns are among the finest in the English language and the present text portrays in vivid imagery the eschatology which is so much a part of the Christian faith.

The hymn is an example of how texts are often altered in the course of time. Wesley was moved, obviously inspired by John Cennick's hymn for the second advent, "Lo! He Cometh, Countless Trumpets," and wrote a finer hymn in the same meter on the same theme. Martin Madan made a combination (with alterations) of both Cennick's and Wesley's texts and such combinations and alterations have appeared until today. The present version uses stanzas 1, 2, and 4 of Wesley (except in stanza 2 "dreadful" is replaced with "splendor's"; in stanza 4, "Jah, Jehovah" has been replaced with "Oh, come quickly!" and repeats have been made in the fifth line of each stanza to make the hymn 8.7.8.7.8.7 rather than Wesley's 8.7.8.7.4.7). Cennick's fifth stanza is used here in place of Wesley's third, and even here Cennick's word "redemption" has been replaced with "the Savior."

Wesley's hymn was designated for the second Sunday of Advent and appeared in *Hymns of Intercession for all Mankind* (1758) entitled there, "Thy Kingdom Come." The first two stanzas of Wesley (altered) with the fifth stanza of Cennick (altered) first appeared in a Southern Baptist hymnal in *New Baptist Hymnal* (Nashville, 1926, No. 122).

REGENT SQUARE—See hymn 94, Angels, from the realms of glory.   *S.W.G.*

Lo, how a Rose e'er blooming 78

The source from which this text was translated is an anonymous German carol, "Es ist ein' Ros' entsprungen," based on Isaiah 11:1, Luke 1 and 2, and Matthew 2. The earliest known source of the German text is a manuscript from St. Alban's Carthusian monastery in Trier which was compiled between 1582-88, although the text is thought to have originated much earlier. It was first published in the *Alte Catholische Geistliche Kirchengeseng* (Cologne, 1599). The first two stanzas as they appear in this hymnal were translated by Theodore Baker. The earliest inclusion of Baker's translation in a hymn cited by the *Dictionary of American Hymnology* was the *Wartburg Hymnal for Church, School, and Home* (Chicago, 1918). Harriet Krauth Spaeth's translation of the third stanza is taken from her translation of the German text in 1875 under the title, "Behold, a Branch Is Growing." *The Baptist Hymnal* (1991) is the first Southern Baptist collection to include this text and tune. Two changes have been made from Baker's translation. In line five of the first stanza, "flow'ret" has been replaced by "flower," and in the seventh line of the first two stanzas, "half-gone" has replaced the original "half spent."

ES IST EIN' ROS' is an arrangement of a traditional German melody which is thought to have originated as early as the 15th century, but which was first published in the *Alte Catholische Geistliche Kirchengeseng* with the "Es ist ein' Ros' entsprungen" text. Michael Praetorius' setting of the tune used

in *The Baptist Hymnal* (1991) first appeared in Volume VI of his *Musae Sionae* (1609). The irregularity of the rhythm links this melody with the style of numerous other chorale melodies and Genevan metrical psalm tunes in their original form.   *M.P.*

Look ye saints! the sight is glorious 169

Revelation 11:15 provided the inspiration for this hymn by Thomas Kelly. It was first published in the third edition of Kelly's *Hymns on Various Passages of Scripture* (1809). Southern Baptists' first "official" hymn collection, *The Baptist Psalmody* (Charleston, 1850, No. 238) included this hymn.

BRYN CALFARIA, one of the tunes used with this hymn, was written by the Welsh composer, William Owen. The translation of the Welsh tune name is "Mount Calvary." It was first published in 1886 in Volume II of Owen's *Y Perl Cerddorol* (The Pearl of Music), a collection of the composer's anthems and hymn tunes.   *D.B.*

Lord Jesus, I long to be perfectly whole 325

James L. Nicholson wrote the text, and William G. Fischer the tune, of this hymn based on Psalm 51:7. The hymn first appeared in a pamphlet, *Joyful Songs No. 4* (Philadelphia, 1872), where it contained six stanzas, of which stanzas 1, 3, 5, and 4 are found in the present hymnal. The first line of each stanza originally began "Dear Jesus."

The tune was given the name FISCHER for its appearance in *Baptist Hymnal* (1956). The hymn and tune first appeared in a Southern Baptist collection in *Songs of Redemption*, compiled by W. Plunkett Martin and James W. Jelks (Atlanta, 1920, No. 165).   *D.M.*

Lord, as of old at Pentecost 242

Both the words and music of this hymn

were written by Charles H. Gabriel. The hymn was first published in Homer Rodeheaver and B.D. Ackley's *Great Revival Hymns, No. 2* (Chicago, *c.* 1913, No. 65), of which Gabriel was musical editor. The words were attributed to "Charlotte G. Homer," one of several pseudonyms adopted by Gabriel, and the copyright date for the hymn was given as 1912. The first Southern Baptist collection to include the hymn was I. E. Reynolds' *Jehovah's Praise* (Fort Worth, 1925, No. 107).

OLD-TIME POWER is the name given this tune by the hymnal committee for *Baptist Hymnal* (1956). *D.M.*

Lord, Be Glorified—See *In my life, Lord, be glorified*

Lord, for the gift of children 508
Duane Blakely's "Lord, for the Gift of Children" was written for parent/child dedication services at the author's church, First Baptist Church of Garland, Texas. Through the hymn, parents and church members express to God their gratitude for the gift of children, acknowledge God's ownership of the children, commit themselves to be faithful in teaching and living before the children, and pray that the children will always follow the teachings of God. *The Baptist Hymnal* (1991) is the first Southern Baptist collection to contain this hymn.

NYLAND is a Finnish folk melody from the parish of Kuortane (the tune is also called KUORTANE in some hymnals) in Etalapohjanmaa (South Ostrobothnia). It appeared in the Appendix of the 1909 edition of Finland's Evangelical Lutheran Church Chorale Book (*Suomen Evankelis Luterilaisen Kirken Koraalikirja*). The tune first appeared in English hymnody in 1927 in *The Church Hymnary*, harmonized by David Evans and set to Anna Waring's text, "In Heavenly Love

Abiding." The first appearance of NYLAND in a Southern Baptist hymnal was in *Baptist Hymnal* (Nashville, 1956, No. 303) for the text "In Heavenly Love Abiding." *S.W.G.*

Lord, Here Am I—See *Master, Thou callest*

Lord, I want to be a Christian 489
As with most African-American spirituals, the origin of "Lord, I Want to Be a Christian" is unknown. This version is based on that in *Folk Songs of the American Negro* (Nashville, 1907), edited by Frederick J. Work. There are several differences from the Work version, however. It sets the first line as a solo, places a fermata over the second syllable of "Christian" in the second line (and at the parallel place in the last line), and moves the melody to the octave, rather than the sixth, in the middle of the third line. Also, the word "in" is presented as "in a," the last line of every stanza is "Lord, I want to be a Christian," and there is another stanza before our last: "I don't want to be like Judas."

The tune, I WANT TO BE A CHRISTIAN, is titled from the text.

This spiritual first appeared in a Southern Baptist hymnal in *Christian Praise* (Nashville, 1964, No. 306). *P.A.R.*

Lord, I'm Coming Home—See *I've wandered far away from God*

Lord, lay some soul upon my heart 570
This is a simple soul winner's prayer song, created or adapted by B. B. McKinney in collaboration with Mack Weaver in 1939. Its first publication in a Baptist collection was in *The Broadman Hymnal* (Nashville, 1940, No. 451). The first stanza is anonymous, but the second and third stanzas are the work of Weaver and McKinney.

LEILA is the name given B. B. McKinney's tune for "Lord, Lay Some Soul upon My Heart" by the committee for *Baptist Hymnal* (1956). It is named for the composer's wife, Leila Routh McKinney.   *H.T.M.*

Lord, make our homes 511

This text by Esther Burroughs was the first-prize winner in the 1981 Broadman Press Hymn Contest which encouraged the writing of new hymns on the Christian home in support of the Southern Baptist Convention's denominational emphasis on "Strengthening Families" in 1982. Another hymn text by the author, "Father, In This World," was one of four texts selected for Honorable Mention designation in the same hymn search. The emphasis of the text reflects the author's concern that the home should both minister to the family and serve as a witness to the surrounding community.

BURROUGHS was written by Bob Burroughs in 1981 as a setting for "Lord, Make Our Homes," written by his wife, Esther. This tune was selected as the setting for its companion text in the 1981 Broadman Hymn Contest.   *M.P.*

Lord, Send a Revival—See *Send a revival, O Christ, my Lord*

Lord, speak to me, that I may speak 568

Frances Ridley Havergal wrote this hymn on April 28, 1872, at Winterdyne, England. In a letter to a friend, dated May 25, 1872, Miss Havergal noted that she had written a poem titled "A Worker's Prayer" for *Woman's Work*, probably a magazine or newspaper. Under the title, and with a reference to Romans 14:7, "Lord, Speak to Me That I May Speak" was published the same year in a leaflet. Subsequently, the text appeared in Havergal's *Under the Surface* (1874). The present hymnal uses stanzas 1, 4, 6, and 7 of the seven-stanza original.

CANONBURY is an adaptation of the fourth piano piece in Robert Schumann's Opus 23, *Nachtstuecke* (1839). The earliest known use of Schumann's melody as a hymn tune was in J. Ireland Tucker's *Hymnal with Tunes, Old and New* (1872).

Both text and tune entered Southern Baptist hymnody in the *New Baptist Hymnal* (Nashville, 1926, No. 211).   *D.M.*

Lord, the light of Your love is shining 579

This hymn was written by Graham Kendrick in 1987 out of a longing for spiritual awakening across the world. The song was first used at Kendrick's home church, The Ichthus Christian Fellowship in London, England. Its first major use was at a "Spring Harvest" convention in the United Kingdom. First published in *Spring Harvest Songbook*, it was sung with great enthusiasm at the 11th Baptist Youth World Conference meeting in Glasgow, Scotland, July 27-31, 1988. It has since gained worldwide popularity. *The Baptist Hymnal* (1991) is its first appearance in a Southern Baptist collection.

SHINE is the name given Graham Kendrick's tune to his popular song beginning "Lord, the light of Your love is shining" in *The Baptist Hymnal* (1991), where it is arranged by Tom Fettke.   *H.T.M., D.B.*

Lord, Thy church on earth is seeking 391

This text by Hugh Sherlock was written as the "theme hymn" for the Methodist Church in Jamaica in 1960, which was designated as the "Year of Renewal." The author was Chairman of the Jamaica District at the time. His experiences working in the depressed area of West Kingston, Jamaica, influenced his emphasis upon social concerns in stanzas two and three. *The Baptist Hymnal* (1991) is the first Southern Baptist hymnal in which this text has been included.

HARRIS—See hymn 429, Who can cheer the heart like Jesus.   *M.P.*

Lord, who across the ages 624

The text and tune for this hymn were written for the celebration of the 180th anniversary of the First Baptist Church, Alexandria, Virginia, by the church's pastor, M. Vernon Davis. The hymn was first sung on April 24, 1983. Dr. Davis relates the following interpretation of his hymn:

"The three stanzas of the anniversary hymn reflect the spirit of three distinct eras in the life of First Baptist Church, Alexandria, Virginia. The closing lines of each stanza attempt to relate the meaning of those historical moments to the lives of the present members of the church. Each stanza expresses gratitude to God for what he accomplished through his people in the past and also a petition that the Lord of history will work through his people today.

"Stanza one was inspired by the founding pastor and members. Jeremiah Moore was a staunch defender of religious liberty and was imprisoned for his convictions. The second stanza recalls the difficult years of the Civil War, during which the First Baptist Church was the only Alexandria congregation to continue regular worship services under the leadership of pastor C. C. Bitting. Stanza three remembers the visionary leadership of Ernest Campbell in the building of a new church facility."

This hymn appears in a Southern Baptist collection for the first time in *The Baptist Hymnal* (1991).

ALEXANDRIA, the tune, is named for the city where First Baptist Church is located.   *P.H.*

Love came down at Christmas 109

The date of composition of this poem by Christina Rossetti is unknown, but it was first published in her *Time Flies; a Reading Diary* of 1885. Several minor alterations have been made. The most significant was the author's change of the original last line "Love, the universal sign" to "Love for plea and gift and sign." *The Baptist Hymnal* (1991) is the first Southern Baptist collection to include this Christmas song.

GARTAN is a traditional Irish tune said to be especially popular in County Donegal. The tune is named for Lough Gartan, a small lake in Donegal, Ireland. The harmonization in *The Baptist Hymnal* (1991) collection was made by David Evans and bears a copyright date of 1927.   *D.B.*

Love divine, all loves excelling 208

This hymn, written in four eight-line stanzas, was first published under the title "Jesus, Show Us Thy Salvation" in Charles Wesley's pamphlet, *Hymns for Those That Seek and Those That have Redemption in the Blood of Jesus Christ* (Bristol, 1747). With its emphasis on God's love, the hymn was a significant addition to Wesleyan church song.

Several textual alterations have been made with, perhaps, the most famous being the change in stanza 2, line 5, "Take away the power of sinning." John Fletcher wrote, "Would it not be better to soften it by saying, 'Take away the love of [or the bent to] sinning? Can God take away from us our *power of sinning,* without taking away our power of free obedience?' " (Creamer, 337).

Other changes were also made. In the original poem, stanza 2, line 4 read "Let us find that second rest"; stanza 3, line 2, "let us all Thy life receive"; and stanza 4, line 2, "pure and sinless let us be." By 1761 there was enough concern with the second stanza that it was omitted entirely from Wesleyan collections. John Wesley did not include the stanza in *A Collection of Hymns for the Use of the People Called Methodists* (London, 1780). Other English collections continued to use the second stanza, often changing "power" to "love."

The hymn is found in the earliest Southern Baptist collection, *The Baptist Psalmody* (Charleston, 1850, No. 664) with the second half of the second stanza as follows:

Take away the love of sinning;
Take our load of guilt away;
End the work of thy beginning;
Bring us to eternal day.

The third stanza is completely omitted and the fourth stanza considerably altered in this early Baptist hymnal.

BEECHER (sometimes designated ZUNDEL or LOVE DIVINE) was the tune John Zundel composed in 1870 for "Love Divine, All Loves Excelling." For many years Zundel served as organist for the Pilgrim Congregational Church in Brooklyn. His pastor was Henry Ward Beecher, one of the most influential clergymen of the 19th century. The tune's first appearance was in *Christian Heart Songs, A Collection of Solos, Quartettes and Choruses of All Meters* (New York, 1870, No. 91). Zundel gave tempo suggestions by giving the length of time required to sing one stanza. A stanza of BEECHER was supposed to take 65 seconds (Reynolds, 1976, 138).

The tune made its first appearance in a Southern Baptist collection in *The Baptist Hymn and Praise Book* (Nashville, 1904, No. 393).   *D.B.*

Love Is the Theme—See *Of the themes that men have known*

Love Lifted Me—See *I was sinking deep in sin*

Loved with everlasting love 336
This hymn, with text by George W. Robin-son and tune EVERLASTING LOVE by James Mountain, was first published in Mountain's *Hymns of Consecration and Faith* (1876). *Baptist Hymnal* (Nashville, 1975, No. 342) was the first Southern Baptist collection to include these words and music.   *D.M.*

Low in the grave He lay 160
"Low in the Grave He Lay" and its tune CHRIST AROSE were written in 1874. Robert Lowry, the author/composer, was serving as pastor of the First Baptist Church of Lewisburg, Pennsylvania, and teacher at the University of Lewisburg (later Bucknell). Luke 24:6, "He is not here, but is risen," served as the inspiration for the text. Its first appearance was in a compilation edited by Lowry and W. H. Doane and published as *Brightest and Best* (New York; Chicago, 1875, No. 113).

Its first appearance in a Southern Baptist hymnal was in *Songs of Redemption* (Atlanta, 1920, No. 243).   *D.B.*

Majestic sweetness sits enthroned 219
The original version of this hymn text by Samuel Stennett, a Baptist pastor in England, had nine stanzas. The version appearing in *The Baptist Hymnal* (1991) includes stanzas 3, 4, 5, and 7 from the original hymn. The text was influenced by images from Song of Solomon 5:10-16. It was first published in John Rippon's *Selection of Hymns from the Best Authors* (London, 1787), under the heading "Chief Among Ten Thousand; or, the Excellence of Christ." Its first publication in the United States was in Asahel Nettleton's *Village Hymns for Social Worship* (1824). The hymn was included in the first hymnal published by Southern Baptists, *The Baptist Psalmody* (Charleston, 1850, No. 215).

ORTONVILLE—See hymn 453, How sweet the name of Jesus sounds.   *M.P.*

Majesty 215

The words and music of this song were written by Jack W. Hayford in 1977. Hayford and his wife Anna were vacationing in Britain at the time. The author later wrote that the experience of visiting many of the castles of the land led him to: "sense the influence one might feel if raised as a child in such regal settings…. [It] became quite credible how a person used to such an environment might more likely conceive of themselves as being bred to influence their world.

"One day, as Anna and I drove along together, at once the opening lyrics and melody of 'Majesty' simply came to my heart. I continued driving, asking her to jot the words and the melody line in the notebook she had beside her."

The remainder of the song was written after the Hayfords returned to their home in California.

The first publication of the song in a major hymnal was in *The Hymnal for Worship & Celebration* (Waco, 1986, No. 74). *The Baptist Hymnal* (1991) is its first publication in a Southern Baptist collection.

MAJESTY is the tune name taken from the hymn title.   *D.M.*

Make Me a Blessing—See *Out in the highways and byways of life*

Make me a captive, Lord 278

George Matheson wrote this hymn in 1890 at Row, Dumbartonshire, Scotland, and published it in his *Sacred Songs*. Ephesians 3:1 inspired the writing of the poem. Matheson gave it the title "Christian Freedom." *The Baptist Hymnal* (1991) is the first Southern Baptist collection to include it.

TRENTHAM was composed by Robert Jackson for Henry W. Baker's poem, "O Perfect Life of Love." The tune was first published in 1888 in *Fifty Sacred Leaflets*. It was named

after a village in Staffordshire, England. *D.B.*

Make Me a Channel of Blessing—See *Is your life a channel of blessing?*

Make room within my heart, O God 491

Bryan Jeffery Leech wrote these words while serving on the hymnal commission for the Evangelical Covenant Church. The hymn received its first publication in *The Covenant Hymnal* (Chicago, 1973, No. 448).

FOREST GREEN—See hymn 79, Blessed be the God of Israel.   *D.M.*

"Man of sorrows!" what a name 175

This text and tune by Philip P. Bliss was first published in the *International Lessons Monthly* (1875), entitled "Redemption." Its first hymnal inclusion was in Bliss and Ira D. Sankey's *Gospel Hymns No. 2* (New York; Chicago; Cincinnati, 1876, No. 7), titled "Hallelujah, What a Savior!" The Scripture verse excerpt given above this hymn is Isaiah 53:3: "A man of sorrows, and acquainted with grief." Stanza 3 of its original 5 stanzas is omitted:

Guilty, vile and helpless we;
  Spotless Lamb of God was he;
"Full atonement!" can it be?
  Hallelujah, what a Savior!

" 'Man of Sorrows,' What a Name" was introduced to Southern Baptists in Plunkett Martin and James W. Jelks' *Songs of Redemption* (Atlanta, 1920, No. 244).

The tune name HALLELUJAH, WHAT A SAVIOR is taken from the common title of the hymn. As given in *Gospel Hymns No. 2*, each of the four phrases of Bliss' hymn are to be sung progressively louder, for they bear the dynamic markings: *p, m, f,* and *ff.* The original key is C major. Although this hymn tune has the characteristic dotted eighth and sixteenth note pattern of the gospel hymn style in its brief refrain, its even-note rhythms and varied harmonies overall are more typical of the churchly hymn tunes of an earlier era.   *H.E.*

Many and great, O God 49

Joseph Renville wrote the original version of this hymn in the Dakota language for use at the *Lac-qui-Parle* (French for "lake which speaks") mission in what is now western Minnesota. In its original form, consisting of seven stanzas based upon Jeremiah 10:12-13, the hymn was published in the 1842 edition of *Dakota Odowan* ("Dakota Hymnal") with words only. It appeared with the LACQUIPAR-LE tune in the 1879 edition of that hymnal, published by The Dakota Mission of the American Missionary Association and the Presbyterian Board of Foreign Missions. Because of the growing popularity of the hymn with YWCA groups in the early 20th century, Philip Frazier was asked by the chairman of the music committee of the national YW-CA in 1929 to provide an English version. Frazier's paraphrase of the first and last stanzas of Renville's hymn was introduced at the YWCA national convention 1930 and was subsequently published in *Young Camp* songbooks and in *Hymns of the Rural Spirit* (Protestant Episcopal Church, 1947). It is included in a Southern Baptist hymnal for the first time in *The Baptist Hymnal* (1991), in which the last word of the first line has been changed from "things" to "works."

LACQUIPARLE was first published in the 1879 *Dakota Odowan* with a harmonization by James R. Murray. That hymnal carried a notation that the tune was a "Dakota native air" harmonized by Murray in 1877. The harmonization used in *The Baptist Hymnal* (1991) was written by Bill Newton for this hymnal.

(Some of the information in this article is drawn from the unpublished research of Lois C. Willand, a copy of which was provided the author by Carlton Young.)   *M.P.*

Marvelous grace of our loving Lord 329

Julia Harriette Johnston (1849-1919) wrote this text and Daniel Brink Towner composed the tune in 1910. The earliest appearance of the text and tune seems to have been in *Hymns Tried and True,* compiled by Towner (Chicago, 1911, No. 2). *Baptist Hymnal* (Nashville, 1956, No. 200) was the first Southern Baptist hymnal in which this hymn appeared.

The tune MOODY was composed in 1910 by Daniel B. Towner (1850-1919), who was head of the Music Department of Moody Bible Institute in Chicago. The tune was given this name in *Baptist Hymnal* (Nashville, 1956, No. 200), which was the first Southern Baptist hymnal to contain it.   *S.W.G.*

Master, Thou callest 486

"Lord, Here Am I" was dictated by Fanny Crosby and indicated to have been written down by an anonymous scribe on August 15, 1877. Exactly 100 years later it was one of 120 unpublished poems that were compiled by Donald P. Hustad and published by Hope Publishing Company under the title *Fanny Crosby Speaks Again* (Carol Stream, 1977). The composer John Ness Beck supplied the tune in 1984.

The Baptist Hymnal (1991) includes stanzas 1, 2, and 4 of Crosby's four-stanza original. The omitted stanza reads:

Ready to labor while life shall remain;
Ready for trials, affliction or pain;
Ready to witness, my Savior, for Thee;
Ready to publish Thy mercy to me.

Only one alteration has been made from the author's text. In stanza one, line two, the original is:

Only direct me, and I will away.

The Baptist Hymnal (1991) is the first Southern Baptist collection to include this hymn.

BECK is named for its composer, John Ness Beck. It was originally published by Beckenhorst Press of which Beck was co-founder. A relatively simple tune with chorus, it is written in a traditional but continually popular gospel song style. *H.T.M.*

May God's grace go before you 648

Wesley Forbis wrote this text and the tune GO WITH GOD in May of 1990. The intent was to write a dismissal song that would combine a meaningful text with an easily-learned tune. *D.B.*

May the grace of Christ, our Savior 661

Tom Fettke's benediction chorus is based on 2 Corinthians 13:14. Text and tune were written by Fettke and copyrighted in 1986. The song's first appearance in a Southern Baptist collection was *The Baptist Hymnal* (1991).

CANE PEAK is the name given this tune by the composer in honor of his wife's parents whose home in southern California is located on a street with this name. *S.W.G.*

Mine eyes have seen the glory 633

In the fall of 1861 Julia Ward Howe, with her husband, Dr. Howe, their pastor, Dr. James Freeman Clarke, and Governor Andrews of Massachusetts, were visiting Washington, D.C., and were invited to watch a military review of federal troops some distance from the city. On their return to Washington, on a road congested with troops, they heard some soldiers singing "John Brown's body lies a-mouldering in the grave." Dr. Clarke commented on the stirring character of the tune and suggested that

Mrs. Howe write a better text for it. During that night the words came to her and the stanzas were completed before daybreak. On her return to Boston, she showed the poem to James T. Fields, editor of the *Atlantic Monthly*, who suggested the title "Battle Hymn of the Republic," and published it in the February, 1862 issue. Its first appearance in a tune book was in J. W. Dadmun's *The Aeolian Harp* (Boston, 1862). Its first appearance in a collection intended for Southern Baptist use was in Robert H. Coleman's *The Popular Hymnal* (Dallas, 1918, No. 366).

BATTLE HYMN is of obscure origin, apparently a variant of a camp meeting tune that originated in South Carolina. It was well known many years prior to the Civil War. The John Brown text really involves two people by the same name. The first was an obscure private in the northern troops. By the time of John Brown's raid on Harper's Ferry, October 16, 1859, and his execution on December 2, of the same year, this text, made up for Pvt. John Brown was used for John Brown, the ardent abolitionist, and it was in this form that it came to Mrs. Howe's attention.

The fascinating story behind the Battle Hymn of the Republic is told by Charles Eugene Cleghorn in Paper XXIX of the Hymn Society of America (Ft. Worth, 1974). *W.J.R.*

Moment by Moment—See *Dying with Jesus, by death reckoned mine*

More about Jesus 600

Eliza Edmunds Hewitt suffered from a spinal disease for many years. When her health improved and she was sufficiently recovered to resume her work, she became interested in writing poetry. Some of her poems for children came to the attention of John R. Sweney who set many of them to music. SWENEY was composed by John R. Sweney for the text, "More about Jesus would I know," and first appeared with that text in W. J. Kirkpatrick and J. R. Sweney's *Glad Hallelujahs* (1887). After this initial contact, they collaborated on many hymns. Her interest in teaching young people can be seen in this hymn which, with its 16 uses of the word "more," stresses the desire to grow in Christlikeness.

The first Southern Baptist hymnal in which this hymn appeared was *Kingdom Songs* (Dallas, 1921, No. 1), although one of its compilers, Robert H. Coleman had published it earlier for the first time in *The World Evangel* (Dallas, 1913, No. 81).   *S.W.G.*

More love to Thee, O Christ 473

The husband of the author of "More Love to Thee," George L. Prentiss, wrote in the posthumously published *The Life and Letters of Elizabeth Prentiss* (New York, 1882) concerning its origin that it belonged probably to a time as far back as the year 1856. Like most of the hymns of Elizabeth Payson Prentiss, it is simply a prayer put into verse form. It was written so hastily that the last stanza was left incomplete, one line having been added in pencil when it was printed. The author did not show it, even to her husband, until many years after it was written; and she wondered why, when published, it met with such favor.

For Mrs. Prentiss the 1850s were years of both physical and emotional suffering, which included her own feeble health and the death of two of her children. The years are reflected in the lines of the now omitted stanza:

Let sorrow do its work,
  Come grief and pain;
Sweet are the messengers,
  Sweet their refrain,
When they can sing with me,

More love, O Christ, to Thee,
  More love to Thee!

The hymn was printed on a leaflet in 1869 for distribution to friends. In 1870 William Howard Doane published it in his *Songs of Devotion* (New York; Chicago, No. 379), set to his tune MORE LOVE TO THEE. The hymn was sung at the graveside of the author by her friends when she was buried in 1878. It first appeared in a Southern Baptist collection in *The Baptist Hymn and Praise Book* (Nashville, 1904, No. 283).   *H.E.*

Morning has broken 48

Eleanor Farjeon was asked by the editors of *Songs of Praise* to write a hymn of thanksgiving for each new day to fit the unusual meter of the Gaelic tune to which it is set. Her three stanzas first appeared in the revised and enlarged edition of *Songs of Praise* in 1931. Southern Baptists first included this hymn in *Baptist Hymnal* (Nashville, 1975, No. 151).

BUNESSAN was notated by Alexander Fraser from the singing of a wandering Highlander. It was first published in Lachlan Macbean's *Songs and Hymns of the Gael* (1888) with the text "Child in the Manger." The hymn and text subsequently were contained in the *Irish Church Hymnal* (1917). Mark Hayes harmonized the tune for *The Baptist Hymnal* (1991).   *P.H.*

Must Jesus bear the cross alone 475

This hymn was derived from several sources, and its origins therefore remain shrouded in obscurity. The first stanza was altered from Thomas Shepherd's *Penetential Cries* (1693), a hymnal for English Independents. The hymn's original form read:

Shall Simon bear the Cross alone,
  And other Saints be free?
Each Saint of thine shall find his own,
  And there is one for me.

The person responsible for changing "Simon" to "Jesus" is unknown. John Julian dates stanza two from a missionary collection published at Norwich, England, around 1810. Stanza three appeared with the other two in the *Oberlin Social and Sabbath School Hymn Book* (1844), compiled by George N. Allen. The first two lines of stanza two read:

'll bear the consecrated cross,
Till from the cross I'm free.

In his *Plymouth Collection* (1855), Henry Ward Beecher attributed these three stanzas to Allen along with three others ascribed to his brother Charles Beecher. Stanza five is altered slightly from this first printing, in which the final couplet read:

Ye angels! from the stars flash down,
And bear my soul away.

Manly's Choice (Louisville, 1892) was the first Southern Baptist collection to print the text.

MAITLAND was composed by George N. Allen for this text in his *Oberlin Social and Sabbath School Hymn Book* (1844). In Beecher's *Plymouth Collection* it is called CROSS AND CROWN with the misnomer "Western Melody." The success of the *Plymouth Collection* helped to disseminate this hymn tune, particularly among Baptists, Presbyterians, and Congregationalists.

The tune to the hymn "Precious Lord, Take My Hand" (PRECIOUS LORD), by Thomas A. Dorsey, is based on an imitation of MAITLAND.

This text and tune are first found in an "official" Southern Baptist collection in *The Baptist Hymn and Praise Book* (Nashville, 1904, No. 441).   *P.H.*

My country, 'tis of thee 634

Samuel F. Smith wrote this hymn in 1831, while preparing for the Baptist ministry at Andover Theological Seminary. Smith was a friend of the prominent musician and edu-

cator, Lowell Mason. Another friend, William C. Woodbridge, had traveled in Europe and had brought to Mason several German hymnals and tunebooks. Mason, who couldn't read German, asked Smith, a proficient linguist, to look through the books to see if anything could be translated for American use. Smith was intrigued by a German patriotic text, "Gott segne Sachsenland" (God bless Saxony), written in 1815 by Siegfried A. Mahlmann. He decided to write a patriotic hymn in the same poetic meter and quickly produced the present text. This was sung by a children's choir under Mason's direction in a service sponsored by the Boston Sabbath School Union at Park Street Church on July 4, 1831. The third of the original five stanzas was dropped after its initial use. It read:

No more shall tyrants here
With haughty steps appear,
And soldier bands;
No more shall tyrants tread
Above the patriot dead—
No more our blood be shed
By alien hands.

AMERICA was the tune accompanying the German text and the one used at the first singing of Smith's hymn. Of course, it is only called AMERICA in the United States. It is known as NATIONAL ANTHEM throughout the British empire, where sets to their national hymn, "God Save the Queen." Other names are CREATION, STAMFORD, and WHITEFIELD'S TUNE. The last, reflecting its use in the services of George Whitefield, appeared in James Lyon's *Urania*, a 1790 American tunebook. Thus the tune was known in this country before its association with Smith's text.

The Baptist Psalmody (Charleston, 1850, No. 1104), Southern Baptists' first hymnal, included this hymn. One of its editors, Basil Manly, Jr., was a personal friend of Smith.   *P.A.R.*

My faith has found a resting place 412

This text was written by Eliza E. Hewitt under the pseudonym Lidies H. Edmunds. It was first published in *Songs of Joy and Gladness, No. 2* (Boston and Chicago, c. 1890), under the title "No Other Plea." It apparently did not appear in another collection until 1944, when it was included in *Choice Hymns of the Faith*, a Plymouth Brethren hymnal. Its first publication in a Southern Baptist collection was in *Assembly Songs* (Nashville, 1959, No. 74).

LANDÅS is a Norwegian folk melody arranged by William J. Kirkpatrick, one of the compilers of *Songs of Joy and Gladness, No. 2*, in which it first appeared with Eliza E. Hewitt's text. The name LANDÅS was given to the tune in *Christian Praise* (Nashville, 1964, No. 236) by William J. Reynolds, who named it after a Norwegian village that he discovered in an atlas. The tune is called NORSE AIR in the 1964 *Methodist Hymnal*, and the *Companion* to that hymnal says that it was originally set to "The Hardy Norseman's House of Yore."   *M.P.*

My faith looks up to Thee 416

In 1888, hymnologist Samuel Duffield considered "My faith looks up to Thee" one of the three most popular hymns in America. The author, Dr. Ray Palmer, gave the circumstances related to the writing of the hymn in his collected *Poems* of 1875. Combining his information with that given by Rev. J. E. Rankin and "with the best accounts given by others," Duffield presented this summary:

"The hymn was written in 1830, but not published (as a hymn) until 1832. The author was in New York City, 'between his college and theological studies,' and was in poor health and a teacher in a ladies' school. Dr. Palmer says: 'I gave form to what I felt, by writing, with little effort, the stanzas. I recollect I wrote them with very tender emotion and ended the last line with tears.' The manuscript was then placed in a pocketbook, where it remained for some time. Its true discoverer was Lowell Mason, the musician, who asked young Palmer if he had not some hymn or hymns to contribute to his new book. The pocket-book was produced, and the little hymn (then between two and three years old and never previously utilized, though it had been in print as a poem) was brought to light. Dr. Mason was attracted by it, and desired a copy. They stepped together into a store (it was in Boston), and the copy was made and taken away without any further comment. On carefully re-reading the hymn at home, Dr. Mason was so much interested that he wrote for it the tune of OLIVET, to which it is usually sung.

"Two or three days later he again met the author on the street, and, scarcely waiting to salute him, he said in substance: 'Mr. Palmer, you may live many years and do many good things, but I think you will be best known to posterity as the author of 'My faith looks up to thee.'

"The first publication of this hymn really occurred in 1832, but it received no particular notice in America. It had, however, obtained a reprint in some religious newspapers, from one of which the Rev. Andrew Reed of Scotland secured it while he was in this country. Dr. Reed took it, a waif, for his prospective hymn-book, and published it anonymously. 'It had,' says Dr. J. E. Rankin, 'several years of transatlantic life before it was much known in America; and possibly was indebted to its foreign and uncertain origin for its first recognition here, as many another native production has been' " (361-62).

This hymn was published in the first Southern Baptist collection, *The Baptist Psalmody* (Charleston, 1850, No. 541)

OLIVET by Lowell Mason was first published in *Spiritual Songs for Social Worship* (1832), edited by Lowell Mason and Thomas Hastings.

It did not appear in a Southern Baptist collection until *The Baptist Hymn and Praise Book* (Nashville, 1904, No. 256).   *D.B.*

My Father is rich in houses and lands 555

The inspiration for the hymn came to Harriet E. Buell during a Sunday morning service at the Methodist Episcopal Church in Thousand Island Park, New York. She submitted the poem of six four-line stanzas to the *Northern Christian Advocate*, a periodical published in Syracuse, New York, to which she was a frequent contributor. It was published in the February 1, 1877 issue.

Many Baptists were first exposed to this song in *The Evangel* (Philadelphia, 1909, No. 78), compiled by Southern Baptists Robert H. Coleman and W. W. Hamilton. Its first entry in an "official" Southern Baptist collection was in *New Baptist Hymnal* (Nashville, 1926, No. 342).

BINGHAMTON was composed for "A Child of the King" by John B. Sumner, who found the poem in the *Northern Christian Advocate*. He added the text of the refrain and composed the music while he was pastor of the Methodist Church in Binghamton, New York, which accounts for the name of the tune. A few months after the hymn was completed, Buell was surprised to hear the hymn sung as a solo in the Methodist church in Manlius, New York. Words and music were first published in *Beulah Songs*, by William McDonald and Lewis Hartsough (Philadelphia, 1879, No. 88). In some later publication, Buell's original line "I'm *the* child of *a* King" was changed to "I'm *a* child of *the* King."   *W.J.R.*

My God, how wonderful You are 11

Frederick W. Faber wrote this hymn under the heading, "Our Heavenly Father," and included it in his *Jesus and Mary; or Catholic Hymns for Singing and Reading* (London, 1849). *The Baptist Hymnal* (1991) includes stanzas 1, 3, 4, and 5 of the original nine and restates Faber's language in a more contemporary idiom (as in "You are" for "thou art" in stanza 1). Other changes have been made by various editors over the years: "wonderful" for "beautiful" and "glorious" for "awful" (st. 2); "deep and tender" for "deepest, tenderest" (st. 3); and "too, O Lord" for "Living God" (st. 4).

The first Southern Baptist hymnal to include this hymn was *The Baptist Hymn and Praise Book* (Nashville, 1904, No. 59).

AZMON—See hymn 216, O for a thousand tongues to sing.   *P.A.R.*

My hope is built on nothing less 406

This text as it is currently sung is an adaptation of a six-stanza hymn written by Edward Mote in 1834. According to Mote's account of its origin, the words of the refrain came to him as he was walking up Holborn Hill, London, on his way to work. The first four stanzas were written during that same day. The final two stanzas were written on the following Sunday after a visit to see the ailing wife of a fellow churchman.

A copy was sent to *Spiritual Magazine*, in which it was published without attribution to Mote. Subsequently it was included in a hymn collection issued by Rees in 1836 and was attributed to Rees in some later collections. The hymn was published in Mote's *Hymns of Praise* (1836) under the title "The immutable Basis of a Sinner's hope," along with approximately 100 of Mote's hymns. The first line of Mote's original version of the hymn is "Nor earth, nor hell my soul can move." (For a more detailed account of the origin of this hymn, in Mote's own words, see William J. Reynolds' *Companion to Baptist Hymnal*, pp. 147-49.) The first appearance of this text and its companion tune in a Southern Baptist hymnal was in *The Baptist Hymn and Praise Book* (Nashville, 1904, No. 248).

SOLID ROCK was composed by William B. Bradbury for this text in 1863. It appeared first in Bradbury's *The Golden Censer,* a small collection for use with children which was published in June, 1864. Three months later it was included in Bradbury's *Devotional Hymn and Tune Book* (Philadelphia, 1864, No. 52), which was the only new Baptist hymnal to be published in this country during the Civil War.   *M.P.*

My Jesus, I love Thee 210

Paul told Timothy to "let no man despise thy youth" (1 Tim. 4:12). This hymn is proof young Christians have much to offer, for the author, William Ralph Featherston (some sources indicate the name ends with an 'e'), was probably only 16 years old when he wrote the hymn. Traditionally, the year 1858 has been given as the date of its writing along with a notation that the author was 16. William Reynolds has pointed out that one of these pieces of information is incorrect. If the hymn were written in 1858, then the author was only twelve. If he were 16, then the year of composition would be 1862. Some confusion exists concerning the dates of the author's birth and death. McCutchan lists 1842-78 (276). This would substantiate the claim the hymn was written in 1858 when its author was 16. However, Reynolds gives 1846-73 as the life span of Featherston (308). His information appears to be more reliable since it came from the records of the Methodist church in Montreal where the author and his parents were members.

According to McCutchan, Featherston sent his poem to an aunt who, at that time, lived in Los Angeles. She encouraged him to publish it. Evidently the hymn first appeared in England in *The London Hymn Book* (1864). Reynolds indicates the earliest inclusion he has found in an American collection is D. L. Moody's *The Northwestern Hymn Book* (Chicago, 1868).

This text is first found for Southern Baptists in *The Baptist Hymn and Praise Book* (Nashville, 1904, No. 281).

GORDON was composed by Adoniram Judson Gordon who had found the text in *The London Hymn Book* of 1864. Although the text had appeared in U.S. hymnals as early as 1868, the hymn did not become popular until it was joined with Gordon's tune in *The Service of Song for Baptist Churches,* published by Gordon and S. L. Caldwell (New York, 1876, No. 1105).   *D.B.*

My life, my love I give to Thee 298

This text by Ralph E. Hudson, with this tune by C. R. Dunbar, first appeared in *Salvation Echoes,* compiled and published by R. E. Hudson (Alliance, 1882, No. 62).

DUNBAR is named for the composer C. R. Dunbar. *Kingdom Songs* (Dallas, 1921, No. 226) was the first Southern Baptist hymnal to contain the tune, although as early as 1913 it is found in the hymn collections of Robert H. Coleman (*The World Evangel,* 1913, No. 156).   *S.W.G.*

My Lord Is Near Me All the Time—See
In the lightning flash across the sky

My Lord, I did not choose You 289

This text is an adaptation into more contemporary language of Josiah Conder's " 'Tis Not That I Did Choose Thee," which was first published in Leifchild's *Original Hymns* (1843). The earliest appearance of Conder's original version in a hymn in this country, according to the *Dictionary of American Hymnology*, was in the Baptist edition of *The Sabbath Hymn Book* (New York, 1858). *The Baptist Hymnal* (1991) is the first Southern Baptist hymnal to include either version of this Conder text.

WHITFIELD—See hymn 286, I Saw the cross of Jesus.   *M.P.*

My Savior First of All—See *When my life-work is ended*

My Savior is the Lord and King 552
This text was written by David Danner for his anthem published under the title "Jesus Is the Song" in *He Is Lord* (1979), his first major collection of choral compositions and arrangements. According to the author, this is the only instance in which he has written a text for a tune already in mind.

SIMPSON is the name given by Danner to the hymn-tune adaptation of his original anthem. This adaptation was made for inclusion in *The Baptist Hymnal* (1991). The tune was named for Mrs. Lorene Simpson, who served for many years as church pianist in Danner's home church, Crown Heights Baptist Church in Oklahoma City, Oklahoma, as a way of recognizing and expressing appreciation for her encouragement of the author-composer's early musical development.   *M.P.*

My Shepherd will supply my need 68
Isaac Watts made this paraphrase of Psalm 23. It was first published in his *The Psalms of David Imitated in the Language of the New Testament* of 1719. Its first appearance in a Southern Baptist collection is in *The Baptist Hymnal* (1991).   *D.B.*

According to recent research by Marion Hatchett of the University of the South, the tune now called RESIGNATION apparently was first printed in the 1828 enlarged edition of Lewistown, Pennsylvania, surveyor Freeman Lewis' *Beauties of Harmony* (1st ed., Pittsburg, 1814) where it was titled HOPEWELL and associated with the hymn "Come Humble Sinner in whose Breast." The Methodist clergyman Samuel Wakefield then published RESIGNATION with this same text in his *American Repository of Sacred Music* (Pittsburg, 1830).Other earlier printings of RESIGNATION include Joseph Funk's *Genuine Church Music* (1832, p. 144), set to "And let this feeble body fail." Its first appearance with Watts' text was in John Steffy's *The Valley Harmonist* (1836, p.29). It also appeared in the 1854 edition of *The Southern Harmony* (p.38). An anthem setting by Virgil Thomson brought the tune to the notice of many choral musicians.   *H.E.*

My singing is a prayer 603
Novella Dillard Preston Jordan, the author of the text, gave it to Bill F. Leach, then editor of the quarterly periodical *The Junior Musician*. Leach sent the text to David H. Williams, requesting that he compose a unison anthem setting of the text for children's voices. The completed anthem was published in *The Junior Musician* (Oct. 1964, p. 20), and the hymn tune version appeared in *Junior Hymnal* (Nashville, 1964, No. 155).

VERMONT is the name given the tune by the composer for inclusion in *Junior Hymnal*.

Its first appearance in an official standard Southern Baptist collection was in *Baptist Hymnal* (Nashville, 1975, No. 412).   *W.J.R.*

My Tribute—See *How can I say thanks*

Name of all majesty 207
Timothy Dudley-Smith wrote this hymn in August, 1979, at Ruan Minor, Cornwall, where most of his recent hymns have been written. This hymn reflects the inspiration

of Walter de la Mare's poetry. In *Lift Every Heart* (Carol Stream, 1984), he states, "the final affirmation of each verse is 'Jesus is Lord' ...the primitive creed of Christianity."

MAJESTAS resulted from the frequent partnership of Michael Baughen and Timothy Dudley-Smith. Baughen wrote in a letter to this writer:

"MAJESTAS was possibly the 'finale' of the partnership [with Timothy Dudley-Smith] and I am delighted that it has been a widely appreciated climax. The words demanded a tune of majesty but had to get a climactic sequence in the second half of each verse. The slight alteration of pattern in the seventh line is deliberate, of course, to help the climax. I love to hear it sung and to join in singing, when adequate emphasis is put upon line 8—'Jesus is Lord.' To him be the glory—forever."

The text and tune first appeared together in *Hymns for Today's Church* (1982). *The Baptist Hymnal* (1991) is the first inclusion of either in a Southern Baptist hymnal.   *P.H.*

Near to the Heart of God—See *There is a place of quiet rest*

Nearer, my God, to Thee 458
Inspired by the Genesis 28:10-22 account of Jacob at Bethel, Sarah Fuller Adams wrote this hymn in 1840. It was first published in William Johnson Fox's *Hymns and Anthems* (1841), compiled for his Unitarian congregation in Finsbury, England. The first American appearance was in James Freeman Clarke's *Disciples' Hymn Book* (Boston, 1844). It is found first in a collection used by Baptists in the South in A. B. Cates' *Baptist Songs with Music* (Louisville, 1879, No. 131).

Robert Guy McCutchan (*Our Hymnody*, Nashville, 1937, p. 381) suggests Lowell Mason had the air "Oft in the stilly night" in mind when he wrote this tune. It first ap-

peared in the Andover *Sabbath Hymn and Tune Book* (1859). In 1868 Mason stated: "When we were compiling the collection known as the *Sabbath Hymn and Tune Book*, they [that is, Edward A. Park and Austin Phelps] applied to me for a musical setting for the hymn, 'Nearer, My God, to Thee.' The metre was irregular. But one night some time after, lying awake in the dark, eyes wide open, through the stillness of the house the melody came to me, and the next morning I wrote down the notes of BETHANY."

It is widely known that the text was sung as the *Titanic* sank on April 14, 1912. The use of BETHANY in the movie based on the tragedy gave credence to the notion this tune was sung and played on the ship. However, many Englishmen were quick to let it be known that BETHANY is not used with this text in their country. A different tune was sung and played as the ship sank.   *D.B.*

No prison wall can hold 628
This text by L. W. Terley was written to support the doctrine of the priesthood of the believer and to emphasize the servant role of Christian ministry. *The Baptist Hymnal* (1991) is the first hymnal to include this hymn.

DIADEMATA—See hymn 161, Crown Him with many crowns."   *M.P.*

No, not despairingly 270
This hymn of five seven-line stanzas, written by Horatius Bonar, first appeared in his *Hymns of Faith and Hope* (3rd series, 1866, p. 83), with the heading "Confession and Peace." The hymn describes vividly the conversion experience—trusting in Jesus, confessing sin, finding peace and light, with "nothing between." The first appearance of the hymn in the United States was in Philip Phillips' *Song Life for Sunday Schools* (New York, 1872). Its first appearance in a South-

ern Baptist collection was in *Baptist Hymnal* (Nashville, 1956, No. 206).

KEDRON, attributed to Ann B. Spratt, is of unknown origin. James Edmund Jones states that this is one of two tunes by Spratt which appeared in the *Book of Common Praise* (1866). In J. Ireland Tucker's *Parish Hymnal* (New York, 1870), the tune is set to "Nearer, My God, to Thee" and is called "Hymn 51 First Tune." In Tucker's *Tunes Old and New* (New York, 1872, No. 507), it is called KE-DRON and is set to the same hymn. The first association of the tune to the present hymn seems to have been in the *Westminster Sabbath School Hymnal* (1883, p. 62).   *W.J.R.*

No, Not One—See *There's not a friend like the lowly Jesus*

Not what my hands have done 339

Horatius Bonar, the Scottish preacher, is the author of the hymn, which appeared in his *Hymns of Faith and Hope* (2nd series, 1861). Originally in twelve four-line stanzas, the first line read, "Not what these hands have done." The present version includes three eight-line stanzas made up of Bonar's stanzas 1, 2, 5, 6, 7, and 11, with some alteration. Who made this altered eight-line version is not known. The first appearance of the hymn in the United States was in *Hymns and Offices of Public Worship* (Bethlehem, 1865), and it then appeared in *Sursum Corda* (Philadelphia, 1898, No. 330).

The Baptist Hymnal (1991) marks its first inclusion in a Southern Baptist collection in this form. However, Bonar's stanzas 7 and 11 with alterations are used with the hymn "I Bless the Christ of God" in *Baptist Hymnal* (Nashville, 1975, No. 286).

LEOMINSTER is a hymn tune adapted from an anthem entitled "The Pilgrim Song" by George Walter Martin, published in his *The Journal of Part Music* (Vol. II, 1862). The

adaptation was made by Sir Arthur Sullivan, and it appeared in *Church Hymns with Tunes* (London, 1874). Robert G. McCutchan, in *Hymn Tune Names* (New York, 1957, p. 92), states that the tune name comes from the town Leominster in Herefordshire, England. The name is thought to have been derived from Leofminster, "the church of Leofic." Leofic, the Earl of Mercia (d. 1057), is best remembered as the husband of the celebrated Lady Godiva. *The Baptist Hymnal* (1991) is the first Southern Baptist collection to include the tune.   *W.J.R.*

Nothing but the Blood—See *What can wash away my sin?*

Now I Belong to Jesus—See *Jesus, my Lord, will love me forever*

Now thank we all our God 638

This hymn of gratitude was written in the midst of one of history's most devastating wars, the Thirty Years' War (1618-48). Martin Rinkart was pastor at Eilenburg, Saxony, Germany, and was for a time the only pastor in the city. In the year 1637 alone, he was responsible for nearly 4500 burials. This hymn, however, was originally a table grace and reflects little of this calamitous time. The first printing is believed to have occurred in his *Jesu Heartz-Büchlein* (1636), although the earliest edition extant is from 1663. Rinkart's text was based on Ecclesiasticus 50:22-24 and is cast in a three-part structure by stanzas: thanksgiving, petition, and a paraphrase of the Gloria Patri. The present translation was by Catherine Winkworth in *Lyra Germanica* (2nd series, 1858), and was reprinted in her *Chorale Book for England* (1863). Southern Baptists first included the chorale in the *New Baptist Hymnal* (Nashville, 1926, No. 44).

NUN DANKET has been inextricably associated with Rinkart's text since their first publication together in Johann Crüger's *Praxis Pietatis Melica (The Practice of Piety in Song;* 1647 ed.). In *The Music of Christian Hymns,* Erik Routley calls Crüger's tune "one of the greatest melodies in the world" (1981, 61). The melody has often been incorporated into other compositions, notably by J. S. Bach and Felix Mendelssohn. The harmonization employed in this version is from Mendelssohn's *Lobgesang (Song of Praise,* Op. 52, 1840), where it was set in six parts. Mendelssohn altered the original melody. *P.H.*

O beautiful for spacious skies 630

This text was written by Katherine Lee Bates on a summer evening in Colorado Springs, Colorado, in 1893, after she had visited the summit of Pike's Peak with a group of friends. The view from that point provided inspiration for the opening lines. The imagery of the "alabaster cities" used in the last stanza was prompted by a visit to the Columbian Exposition in Chicago during that same year. The poem was first published in *The Congregationalist* on July 4, 1895. In 1904 Bates made extensive revisions in the four stanzas, simplifying the flow of language, and this version was published in the *Boston Evening Transcript* (November 19, 1904). Slight additional alterations were later made in the third stanza.

MATERNA (also known as CIVITAS DEI) was composed by Samuel A. Ward for the hymn "O Mother Dear, Jerusalem." There are two versions of the origin of this tune. According to an employee in Ward's music store, it was written by Ward in 1882 while he was crossing New York harbor, following an outing at Coney Island and was first performed at Grace Episcopal Church, Newark, New Jersey, where Ward was organist, by a choir of 200 men and boys. The other version, by Ward's son-in-law, the Rev. Henry W. Armstrong, holds that it was composed in 1885 in memory of Ward's oldest daughter, Clara, upon her death. The tune first appeared in print in *The Parish Choir* (July 12, 1888). Its first hymnal use was in *Church Hymnal,* compiled by Charles L. Hutchins (1894). The uniting of this tune with Katherine Lee Bates's text occurred in 1912, when the president of Massachusetts Agricultural College requested permission of Ward's widow to do so. This pairing of text and tune became popular during World War I. The first Southern Baptist hymnal to include this text and tune was *Kingdom Songs* (Dallas, 1921, No. 326), in which the MATERNA tune was designated as WARD. *M.P.*

O Christ, our hope, our heart's desire 414

This is a translation of the Latin hymn, "Jesu, nostra redemptio," which was written as early as the seventh or eighth century. A translation was prepared by John Chandler and included in his *Hymns of the Primitive Church* (London, 1837). The current text is essentially the same as one "based on" Chandler's work in *Hymns Ancient and Modern* (London, 1861), though the fourth of Chandler's five stanzas is omitted.

MANOAH first appeared in *A Collection of Psalm and Hymn Tunes* (Hartford, 1851) by Henry W. Greatorex. It is probably Greatorex' arrangement of a pre-existent tune, though he did not indicate its source. The name is that of Samson's father (Judges 13).

The Baptist Hymnal (1991) is the first Southern Baptist collection to include this text. *P.A.R.*

O come, all ye faithful 89

The Latin hymn from which this text was translated exists in seven manuscripts which have been found, the most recent by British hymnologist Maurice Frost in 1946. Each of these manuscripts was signed by John Francis Wade. There has been uncertainty as to whether the hymn text and its tune should be credited to Wade or to an unknown source from which Wade, who earned his living by copying and selling music, might have copied them. In *Adeste Fideles: A Study on Its Origin and Development* (1947), Dom John Stéphan suggests that the hymn and tune should be credited to Wade and attributes its origin to *c.* 1743. The first known printing of the text in its original Latin was in Wade's *Cantus Diversi pro Dominicis et Festis per Annum* ("Various Songs for Worship Services and Festivals of the Year") published in 1751.

Four stanzas appear in each of the seven manuscript sources. In the early 19th century, the original four stanzas were partially rewritten by Abbé Etienne Jean Francois Borderies, who added three stanzas. The version used in this hymnal is based upon "Ye faithful, approach ye," a translation made by Frederick Oakeley in 1841 for use by his congregation at Margaret Street Chapel, London. The first line was changed to "O come, all ye faithful" in F. H. Murray's *A Hymnal for Use in the English Church* (London, 1852). *The New Baptist Hymnal* (Nashville, 1926, No. 90) was the first Southern Baptist hymnal to include this text, along with the ADESTE FIDELES tune.

ADESTE FIDELES (also known as PORTUGUESE HYMN) appears in the original manuscripts and in *Cantus Diversi* in triple meter. Its first publication in duple meter was in Samuel Webbe's *An Essay on the Church Plain Chant* (London, 1782). The first publication in America was in Benjamin Carr's *Musical Journal* (Philadelphia, Dec. 29, 1800). The tune name is derived from the opening words of the original Latin text.   *M.P.*

O come, O come, Emmanuel 76

This hymn is drawn from a group of seven medieval Latin texts known as the "Great" or "O" Antiphons, from the fact that each opens with the word "O." The original prose versions of the antiphons date from the ninth century or earlier. One antiphon was to be sung before and after the Magnificat at Vespers on each of the seven days from December 17 to 23. The antiphons were turned into Latin verse, probably during the 12th century, and these versifications were published in *Psalteriolum Cantionum Catholicarum* (1710). John Mason Neale's translation of antiphons two through five and seven appeared in his *Mediaeval Hymns* (1851) under the first line "Draw nigh, draw nigh, Emmanuel." Neale's translation, which is the source of stanzas one and two of the present version, was altered to its current form in *Hymns Ancient and Modern* (London, 1861). The translation of stanzas three and four was the work of Henry Sloane Coffin and first appeared in his *Hymns of the Kingdom of God* (New York, 1916).

The earliest known source for the tune VENI EMMANUEL is a 15th-century Processional in the Bibliotheque Nationale, Paris. Here, the tune is used as a setting for extra verses to the *Libera me* Responsory of the Requiem Mass, beginning "Bone Jesu dulcis cunctis." The manuscript featured an immediate repeat of the first two musical phrases. This repeat was omitted in the earliest publication of the tune, J.M. Neale and Thomas Helmore's *The Hymnal Noted* (Part II, 1854). This book was the first to pair the tune with Neale's translation of *Veni Emmanuel* and is the source for the version of the tune found in most modern hymnals. The text and tune first entered Southern Baptist hymnody in *Baptist Hymnal* (Nashville, 1975, No. 78).   *D.M.*

O day of God, draw nigh 623

This hymn on peace and judgment was written in 1937 by Robert B. Y. Scott for the Fellowship for a Christian Social Order. Scott was concerned that Christian practice be brought in line with prophetic ideals. It was first included in *Hymns for Worship* (1939). *The Baptist Hymnal* (1991) marks the first Southern Baptist collection to include Scott's hymn.

OLD 134TH—See hymn 30, Stand up and bless the Lord.   *P.H.*

O for a thousand tongues to sing 206

Charles Wesley wrote the stanzas in 1739, as he approached the first anniversary of his conversion of May 21, 1738. The adaptation used here, made by Ralph E. Hudson, substitutes "blessed be the name of the Lord," for the second and fourth lines of each stanza. The adapted text and the tune, BLESSED NAME, first appeared in Hudson's *Songs for the Ransomed*, published in Alliance, Ohio, 1887.   *W.J.R.*

A variation of BLESSED NAME arranged by W. J. Kirkpatrick appeared in *Glorious Praises* (Louisville, 1904, No. 271) by Baptist tune writer, W. H. Doane, but it is set to a text by W. H. Clark, "All Praise to Him Who Reigns Above."

The tune harmonized by J. M. Hunt set to the Wesley text appeared in *The Evangel* (Philadelphia, 1909, No. 226), the first collection by Baptist Robert H. Coleman with co-compiler W. W. Hamilton. The text and tune have been included in all subsequent Southern Baptist collections.   *H.T.M.*

O for a thousand tongues to sing 216

On Pentecost Sunday, May 21, 1738, Charles Wesley experienced his spiritual conversion and in 1739, approaching the anniversary of his conversion, he wrote the 18-stanza hymn entitled "For the Anniversary Day of One's Conversion."

In *Hymns and Human Life*, the English hymnologist Erik Routley remarks that "the hymnody of the Wesleys . . . is always intellectually disciplined, always anchored down to Christian doctrine, and always leads the believer away from himself in the end to the communion of saints and the eternal life" (1952, 71).

The original version began with the words, "Glory to God, and praise, and love." The present version is made up of stanzas 7, 8, 9, and 10 of the original. The original stanza 7 is based on the words of the Moravian missionary, Peter Boehler, "Had I a thousand tongues, I would praise him with them all." R. Conyer's *Psalms and Hymns* of 1767 was the first to use the seventh stanza as the initial stanza and John Wesley did the same in his *Collection of Hymns* of 1780 where "O for a thousand tongues" is the first hymn. *Baptist Hymn and Praise Book* (Nashville, 1904, No. 310) was the first Southern Baptist hymnal to contain this hymn, though doubtless it was intended to be sung to the ORTONVILLE tune.

The tune AZMON first appeared anonymously in Lowell Mason's (1792-1872) *Modern Psalmist* (Boston, 1839). Mason states in the preface that his recent European tour was made primarily "to obtain materials for a work like this. In the prosecution of this design he [Mason] visited many of the most important cities, and obtained from distinguished composers of different nations much manuscript music; and also a great variety of recent musical publications, English, German, and French, which had not before reached this country" (3).

In his "List of European Authors," Mason included "Glaser, J. M., German, 1780" and in *The Sabbath Hymn and Tune Book* (1859) he named this tune DENFIELD and attributed it to "C. G." The tune is apparently a Mason arrangement of a tune by Carl Gotthelf Glaser. AZMON first appeared in a Southern Baptist hymnal in *New Baptist Hymnal* (Nashville, 1926, No. 128), although it appeared in Baptist Robert H. Coleman's collections from 1911 onward.   *S.W.G.*

O God of love, enable me 580

David B. Duncan wrote this hymn in October 1988 for a service on "Worship Through the Arts" at First Southern Baptist Church, Salt Lake City, Utah. It reflects his awareness of the many unsaved persons in that urban setting and of his responsibility to be God's agent for the love, grace, and hope enumerated in the first three stanzas. The fourth stanza is an acknowledgment of God as the Power who supplies these things through Jesus Christ. The text was originally set to VERMONT, by David H. Williams. The author changed the tune to ST. PETER because it is more widely known and is in the public domain.

The Baptist Hymnal (1991) contains the first publication of this hymn.

ST. PETER—See hymn 385, In Christ there is no East or West.   *P.A.R.*

O God of love, O King of peace 619

This text by Sir Henry W. Baker was written for and first published in the original edition of *Hymns Ancient and Modern* (1861), where it appeared under the caption, "The Lord shall give his people the blessing of peace" (Psalm 29:11). It was published in this country in *Church Pastorale* (Boston, 1864), edited by Nehemiah Adams. *The Baptist Hymnal* (1991) is the first Southern Baptist hymnal to include it. In this hymnal the original fourth stanza is omitted.

GERMANY—See hymn 402, The church of Christ in every age.   *M.P.*

O God of might, O Son of light 582

"Send Me, O Lord, Send Me" was written by Southern Baptist missionary Ross Coggins in 1955 in the city of Surabaja on the island of Java (Indonesia). At that time he and his family were new to that country which seemed to them strange, forbidding, and unsympathetic. Upon going to the Immanuel Baptist Church of Surabaja for an early Sunday morning service in October, 1955, Coggins was comforted by the warmth and friendliness of the Indonesian Christians in general and by their singing of a beautiful hymn about the Lord's return in particular.

The appealing melody of that hymn kept recurring in the new missionary's mind for days thereafter until he found himself fitting English words to it. The three stanzas of the text soon evolved as a reaffirmation of the author's commitment to the will of God. The story of this experience in Coggins' own words can be found in Reynolds' *Companion to Baptist Hymnal* (Nashville, 1976, pp. 157-58).

Coggins decided to share the song in the hope that others in singing it would catch a new vision of the common task of taking the gospel to all the world. He sent his text and the tune to his close friend, Dr. Wesley Forbis, then on the music faculty at the University of Corpus Christi. Forbis hurriedly made a harmonized arrangement of the tune in hymnic form to be sung by the Texas All-State BSU Choir, of which he was conductor. It was first sung by the choir and student congregation at the 1956 Texas State BSU Retreat in Latham Springs.

It thus came to the attention of G. Kearnie Keegan, secretary of the Student Department of the Baptist Sunday School Board, who used it as the theme song for the World Mission Conference for students in Nashville, Tennessee, in December, 1956. It was also the theme song for Student Night at Christmas that year.

In Toronto, Canada, for the Fifth Baptist Youth World Conference (June 27-July 2, 1958), it was sung with great enthusiasm by thousands of youth as the final song of each session. It first appeared in a Southern Baptist collection in *Christian Praise* (Nashville, 1964, No. 417).

SURABAJA is the name of the city in Indonesia where the tune was first heard by the author of the words. This tune name was given to what was thought to be an "Indonesian Folk tune" when it was first published in a Southern Baptist collection in *Christian Praise* (Nashville, 1964, No. 417). It also appeared as an "Indonesian Melody" in *Baptist Hymnal* (Nashville, 1975, No. 293).

Subsequently, music missionary Bill H. Ichter in Rio de Janeiro, Brazil, made known his discovery that the tune heard by Ross Coggins was derived from the gospel song "The Lord Is Coming" by Elisha A. Hoffman. Hoffman's better known texts are "Down at the cross where my Savior died" and "What a fellowship, what a joy divine." He also wrote both words and music to the gospel song "Are You Washed in the Blood." The first appearance of "The Lord Is Coming" was in Ira Sankey's *Gospel Hymns No. 6* (New York/Chicago, 1891, No. 36). The original song printed there has an added chorus which is not used as part of the SURABAJA tune. The tune is arranged by James Bigelow, a pseudonymn for a writer who wishes to remain anonymous.   *H.T.M.*

O God of prophets, known of old 646

Written in 1984, Wesley Forbis penned this hymn to be used for ordination services. While it fits this need admirably, it also could be effectively used in any service that recognizes or commissions those called out for service. Its first inclusion in a Southern Bap-

tist collection is in *The Baptist Hymnal* (1991) of which Forbis was the executive editor.

The tune COTHEN was written by David Danner, while Design Editor for GENEVOX Music Group. The tune was named in honor of Grady C. Cothen, president of the Baptist Sunday School Board (1975-84).   *D.B.*

O God, our help in ages past 74

Isaac Watts' *Psalms of David Imitated in the Language of the New Testament* (1719) is the source of this hymn. Included in *Baptist Hymnal* (1991) are stanzas 1, 2, 3, 5, 7, and 9 of the original nine which were a paraphrase of the first five verses of Psalm 90. Stanza five did not appear in *Baptist Hymnal* (1956). Its addition restores the so-called "Hebrew" pattern in which the first four stanzas describe God's power, perfection, and never-ending life (the thesis) and are contrasted with the fifth stanza which depicts man's weakness and mortality (the antithesis). In the sixth stanza (the synthesis) man's weakness is caught up in God's power and care. Watts began the hymn with "Our God." John Wesley made the change to "O God."

The Baptist Psalmody (Charleston, 1850, No. 2), the first Southern Baptist hymnal, contained Watts' great paraphrase.

ST. ANNE—See hymn 73, God moves in a mysterious way.   *D.B.*

O God, to those who here profess 506

The first and third stanzas of this trinitarian-form wedding hymn are by Charles Philip Price. The second stanza is by Charles Wesley. Price states that he made a conscious effort to heap up words in a Wesley-like way. The hymn's first appearance in a Southern Baptist hymnal is in *The Baptist Hymnal* (1991).

ST. AGNES—See hymn 116, Our Savior's infant cries were heard.   *S.W.G.*

O God, Almighty Father 258

This is a translation by Irvin Udulutsch of an anonymous German hymn, "Gott Vater! sei gepriesen," which was taken from the *Maintzesch Gesangbuch* of 1661. Udulutsch prepared his translation in 1955 for use in worship at St. Lawrence Seminary in Mt. Calvary, Wisconsin. *Our Parish Prays and Sings* (Collegeville, 1959) was the first hymnal to publish this text.

GOTT VATER SEI GEPRIESEN, which first appeared in the *Limburg Collection* (1838), is a chorale tune by an unknown composer. Its name is the German incipit of the text with which it is associated. The present harmonization was prepared by Geoffrey Price for *The Baptist Hymnal* (1991), the first Southern Baptist collection to include this hymn. *P.A.R.*

O God, we ask for strength 498

This hymn was written in 1988 while its author was a student in the hymnology class of Dr. Hugh T. McElrath. His motivation was not only to receive extra credit in course work but to make a contribution to Southern Baptist hymnody. Disturbed by the unkind words and actions of some Southern Baptists during times of controversy and believing that Christians can cooperate while holding differing viewpoints, he wrote the hymn as a prayer for Southern Baptists. Though Larry Schultz has composed words and music in other genres, some of which have been published, this is his first hymn and *The Baptist Hymnal* (1991) is its first appearance in print.

ST. AGNES—See hymn 116, Our Savior's infant cries were heard. *H.T.M.*

O happy day that fixed my choice 439

This hymn by Philip Doddridge first appeared in Job Orton's edition of Doddridge's *Hymns Founded on Various Texts in the Holy Scriptures* (London, 1755). Based on 2 Chronicles 15:15, the title given was "Rejoicing in Our Covenant Engagements to God." The refrain was added much later when the text was set to HAPPY DAY. *The Baptist Psalmody* (Charleston, 1850, No. 530), the first "official" Southern Baptist collection, included this hymn.

Although it may have been known earlier, the first documented appearance of the tune HAPPY DAY was in William McDonald's *Wesleyan Sacred Harp* (Boston, 1854). It was set to the hymn "Jesus, My All, to Heaven Is Gone" with the refrain "Happy day, happy day, when Jesus washed my sins away!" The hymn by Doddridge was listed as an alternate text. The source of the tune is not clear. Some sources report the tune to have been derived from a well-known tune by E. F. Rimbault entitled "Happy Day." This is at least true of the refrain, for the opening notes appear to be almost an exact copy. Researchers speculate that the remainder of the tune may have been the work of one or more unknown composers. *The Baptist Hymn and Praise Book* (Nashville, 1904, No. 323) was the first Southern Baptist collection to print the tune. *D.B.*

O holy Dove of God descending 240

Both the words and the tune (LOIS) of this song were written by Bryan Jeffery Leech. The hymn first appeared in *Hymns for the Family of God* (Nashville, 1976). This is the initial publication of the text and tune in a Southern Baptist collection. *D.M.*

O how He loves you and me 146

Kurt Kaiser jots down new ideas for music or words when they come to him spontaneously. Frequently he refers to these bits and pieces for a spark to ignite further creative writing. One day in 1975 he ran across the phrase "O how He loves you and me," which he had written down earlier, and decided to write a melody for it. In ten minutes he had completed words and music. *The Baptist Hymnal* (1991) is the first Southern Baptist collection to include this song.

PATRICIA is the name given the tune by the composer for his wife.   *W.J.R.*

O Jesus, I have promised 276

John Ernest Bode's hymn was written in 1866 for the confirmation of his daughter and his two sons. The hymn was first published in the 1869 *Appendix to Psalms and Hymns* by the Society for the Promotion of Christian Knowledge under the text of Luke 9:57, "Lord, I will follow thee whithersoever thou goest." *New Baptist Hymnal* (Nashville, 1926, No. 193) was the first Southern Baptist hymnal to include the hymn. The present version uses stanzas 1, 5, 2, and 3 of the original and minor changes have been made in the wording.

ANGEL'S STORY was composed by Arthur H. Mann for Emily Miller's text, "I love to hear the story which angel voices tell," and the tune name has been taken from that text. The tune first appeared in *The Methodist Sunday School Hymnbook* (London, 1881). The first Southern Baptist hymnal to contain the tune was *New Baptist Hymnal* (Nashville, 1926, No. 193).   *S.W.G.*

O land of rest, for thee I sigh! 608

The earliest appearance of this text recorded in the *Dictionary of American Hymnology* (*DAH*) is on page 56 of the Appendix to Samuel Wakefield's *The Christian Harp* (Pittsburgh, 1836). Lazarus B. McLain, then of Greensburgh, Pennsylvania, compiled this Appendix, and published and revised this edition of the *Harp*. The six stanzas in the *Harp* begin with the following lines:

1. O, land of rest, for thee I sigh!
2. No tranquil joys on earth I know

3. To Jesus Christ I sought for rest
4. I would at once have quit this field
5. When by affliction sharply tried
6. Weary of wand'ring round and round.

A footnote directs the singer to create a refrain by repeating the tune to the last two lines of each stanza, for example:

And dwell in peace at home,
And dwell in peace at home,
When shall I lay my armor by,
And dwell in peace at home[?]

Within six years this text appeared with an altered first line, "Sweet land of rest for thee I sigh," in David Benedict's *Conference Hymns for Social Worship* (Providence, 1842). The *DAH* records a number of publications of this altered version until 1879. This text also appears as "O home of rest," "O land of tranquil rest," and "O sweet land of rest." The *DAH* also records this text in other tongues, as in the German, "Wir zieh'n nach dem verheiss'nen Land." Both versions of this text appear with and without a refrain. The refrain beginning "We'll wait till Jesus comes" appeared as early as 1858 in Benjamin Lloyd's *The Primitive Hymns* (Greenville, No. 689). This refrain was altered to "We'll work till Jesus comes" as part of the late 19th-century revival movement, possibly as late as *Gospel Hymns No. 3* (Chicago, 1878, No. 83), reflecting a change of theological emphasis and corresponding less well with the contemplative sentiment of the original hymn. Other refrains with this text include "I'm goin' home and it won't take long," "O Eden is a land of rest," "Home, home, sweet, sweet home," and "O this is not my home."

Although this text is attributed to the English hymnist Elizabeth Mills (1805-29), its first known publication was seven years after her death. The hymn was well known in the early American shape-note tradition.

George Pullen Jackson published it with five different tunes (See his *Another Sheaf of White Spirituals*, Gainesville, 1952, p. 226).

The tune O LAND OF REST was published with this text without composer or author indications as early as 1859 in A. S. Jenks' *Devotional Melodies* (2nd ed., Philadelphia). This text and tune appeared in a Southern Baptist publication as early as *The Baptist Hymn and Praise Book* (Nashville, 1904, No. 456), but was apparently shortened to its present three-stanza version in the hymnals of Robert H. Coleman, such as *The Modern Hymnal* (Dallas, 1926, No. 126), continuing in B. B. McKinney's *The Broadman Hymnal* (Nashville, 1940, No. 167) and in *Baptist Hymnal* (Nashville, 1956, No. 284). This popular hymn was omitted from the 1975 *Baptist Hymnal* but was reinstated in *The Baptist Hymnal* (1991). No primary source evidence has been found supporting William Miller as the composer of LAND OF REST. This pentatonic tune is probably an American folk hymn.   *H.E.*

O little town of Bethlehem 86

On Christmas Eve 1865, the outstanding American preacher, Phillips Brooks (1835-93), rode on horseback from Jerusalem to Bethlehem and visited the Field of the Shepherds. In 1868, for the children of the Sunday School of Holy Trinity Episcopal Church in Philadelphia, he wrote this hymn which conveys something of what he saw and felt on his trip to the little town. The hymn was printed in leaflets and used locally. It was first published in William R. Huntington's *Church Porch* (1874) and has become one of the best-loved Christmas hymns in the English language. The fourth stanza of the original five is usually omitted today.

The tune ST. LOUIS was composed in 1868 by Lewis H. Redner, organist at Holy Trinity Church in Philadelphia, at the request of the pastor, Phillips Brooks, for Brooks's text "O little town of Bethlehem." It is said that the melody came to Redner during the night before Christmas and that he got out of bed to jot down the melody. He filled out the harmony before going to church the next morning. The tune and text were first published in William R. Huntington's *Church Porch* (1874). The first Southern Baptist hymnal to contain the tune was *New Baptist Hymnal* (Nashville, 1926, No. 82), although it also appeared in the same year in Coleman's *The Modern Hymnal* (Dallas, 1926, No. 406).   *S.W.G.*

O Lord my God! When I in awesome wonder 10

This Swedish hymn written by Carl Boberg, had its beginning in 1886, as he wrote the words to fit a Swedish folk melody. After appearing in several religious periodicals, Boberg published it in a Christian weekly paper, *Sanningsvittnet* (Witness of the Truth), of which he was editor. A German translation appeared in 1907, and the singing of the German text spread throughout Germany. Twenty years later a Russian translation was made from the German text, and was published in 1927 in a collection of 1,233 hymns, *Kimvali* (Cymbals), published by the Baptist Kompas Press, Lodz, Poland. The Russian translation was discovered by Stuart K. Hine, a Methodist missionary serving in the Ukraine, who was unaware that it was originally a Swedish hymn. Some years later, while serving in a Carpathian mountain village in Czechoslovakia, Hine translated the first stanza during a thunderstorm. Later Hine added the second and third stanzas that were largely his own creation. In 1939, at the outbreak of World War II, Hine returned to England, and there, in 1948, he added stanza four. Subsequently the hymn was printed in leaflet form, and one of the leaflets was given to George Beverly Shea during the Billy Graham London Crusade in 1954. Later Shea and Cliff Barrows felt impressed to introduce the song for the first time in the Billy Graham Crusade in Toronto in 1955.

O STORE GUD is a Swedish melody of unknown origin. Its earliest publication seems to have been *Sanningsvittnet* (Apr. 16, 1891), where it was notated in triple time for piano and guitar by Ad. Edgren. The hymnbook of the Swedish Missionary Alliance of 1894, notated the tune in quadruple time.

This text and tune first appeared in a Southern Baptist collection in *Baptist Hymnal* (Nashville, 1975, No. 35). *W.J.R.*

O Lord, may church and home combine 510

This text by Carlton Buck was first published in *Thirteen New Marriage and Family Life Hymns*, a collection issued in 1961 by the Hymn Society of America, in cooperation with the Department of Family Life of the National Council of Churches of Christ in the U.S.A. and the Canadian Council of Churches, for the North American Conference on Church and Family held from April 30 - May 5 of that year. The original version of the hymn consisted of three eight-line stanzas under the title "Bless Thou Our Christian Homes, O Lord." The current version omits the entire first stanza and the first half of the last stanza of the original. The remaining material is set as three four-line stanzas. Additionally, the first line of the version used in this hymnal is a revision of the original "May church and Christian home combine."

The Baptist Hymnal 1991 is the first Southern Baptist collection to include this hymn. *M.P.*

LAND OF REST is a folk melody which appears in *The Baptist Hymnal* (1991) with a harmonization by Annabel Morris Buchanan, first published in her *Folk Hymns of America* (New York, 1938), where it carries the notation, "Heard as a child from my grandmother, Mrs. S. J. (Sarah Ann Love) Foster." Mrs. Buchanan attributed the tune to Scottish or Northern English origins and speculated that the version she heard from her grandmother had been brought to Texas by way of South Carolina and Tennessee. A version of this tune bearing the tune name NEW PROSPECT and attributed to W. S. Turner appeared in *The Sacred Harp* (1844) with the text "O land of rest! for thee I sigh." In J. R. Graves' *Little Seraph* (Memphis, 1873, p.24), this tune is given as SWEET LAND OF REST with no composer indicated. *W.J.R.*

O Lord, our Lord, how majestic 29

Michael W. Smith wrote the words and music of this song on November 1, 1981. It was published a few days after its composition and was recorded by Sandi Patti in 1982. The arrangement in *The Baptist Hymnal* (1991) received its first printing in *The Hymnal for Worship and Celebration* (1986). *The Baptist Hymnal* (1991) is the first Southern Baptist book to include the song.

HOW MAJESTIC takes its name from the first line and title. *D.M.*

O Love that wilt not let me go 292

On June 6, 1882, during a time of "the most severe mental suffering," George Matheson wrote this hymn. He claimed to have written it in five minutes. At the suggestion of the hymnal committee of the Church of Scotland, he changed one word. The original version read "I climb the rainbow in the rain." Matheson removed "climb" and substituted "trace." It first appeared in a Southern Baptist collection in Martin and Jelk's *Songs of Redemption* (Atlanta, 1920, No. 236).

ST. MARGARET was composed in 1804 for "O Love That Wilt Not Let Me Go" by Albert Peace and was included in the music edition of the *Scottish Hymnal* (Edinburgh, 1885). Peace, the music editor of the *Scottish Hymnal*, had been requested by the hymnal committee to write the tune because none was available for the metric structure (8.8.8.8.6.) Matheson had used for his hymn.   D.B.

O Master, let me walk with Thee 279

Washington Gladden wrote this poem in 1879 and published it in *Sunday Afternoon*, a magazine which he edited. There it appeared in a devotional column, "The Still Hour," under the title, "Walking with God." It originally consisted of three eight-line stanzas, but Charles H. Richards made it an effective hymn by omitting the second stanza when he published it in *Christian Praise* (New York, 1880). (The omitted lines are found in Reynolds' *Companion to Baptist Hymnal*, Nashville, 1976.) The original poetic structure may be seen by noting that the present stanzas three and four are part of the same sentence. An early editor substituted "tell" for "teach" in the third line of the first stanza. *Kingdom Songs* (Nashville, 1921, No. 195) was the first Southern Baptist collection to include this hymn.

Though he had not intended this text as a hymn, Gladden observed that many persons set it to tunes he considered unsuitable. Thereafter, he would permit its use only with MARYTON.

MARYTON—See hymn 364, Come, Holy Spirit, Dove divine.   P.A.R.

O my soul, bless God the Father 21

This is a metrical version of the first eight verses of Psalm 103, published in eight stanzas in the *Sabbath-School Psalmodist, Prepared Expressly for Use in the Families, Sabbath Schools and Congregations of the United Pres-*

byterian Church (Philadelphia, 1866, p. 112), where it is set to the tune NETTLETON (with two stanzas for each singing of the tune). The original first line is "O my soul, bless thou Jehovah;" this was one of what was referred to as "the twenty-five new versions complete, as adopted by the General Assembly." The first line was altered to its present form in *The Methodist Hymnal* of 1935.

STUTTGART is an adaptation of a tune first published in *Psalmodia Sacra* (Gotha, Germany, 1715), edited by A. C. Ludwig and C. F. Witt. Its original form is given in *Companion to the Hymnal: A Handbook to the 1964 Methodist Hymnal* (p. 166). Apparently composed or arranged by Witt, STUTTGART was adapted by Henry J. Gauntlett for *Hymns Ancient and Modern* (1861) for use with "Earth Has Many a Noble City." Rather than the usual German custom of taking its name from its original text (*Sollt es gleich besweilen scheinen*), McCutchan (*Hymn Tune Names*, p. 159) has related how this tune was known as STUTTGART in German use from the early 19th century.

This text and tune were first included in a Southern Baptist collection in *Baptist Hymnal* (Nashville, 1956, No. 51).   H.T.M.

O perfect Love 512

This wedding hymn was written by Dorothy Frances Gurney in 1883 at Pull Wyke, Windermere, England, for the marriage of her sister. The author has given the following account concerning the origin of this hymn:

"We were all singing hymns one Sunday evening, and had just finished "O Strength and Stay," the tune which was an especial favourite of my sister's, when someone remarked what a pity it was that the words should be unsuitable for a wedding. My sister, turning suddenly to me, said, "What is the use of a sister who composes poetry if she cannot write me new words for this tune?" I picked up my hymn-book, and said, "Well, if no one will disturb me, I will go into the library and see what I can do." After about 15 minutes I came back with a hymn, "O Perfect Love," and there and then we all sang it to the tune of STRENGTH AND STAY. It went perfectly, and my sister was delighted, saying that it must be sung at her wedding. For two or three years it was sung privately at many London weddings, and then it found its way into the hymnals. The writing of it was no effort whatever after the initial idea had come to me of the two-fold aspect of perfect union, love and life, and I have always felt that God had helped me to write it."

O PERFECT LOVE (also known as SANDRINGHAM) was originally in an anthem composed by Joseph Barnby for the marriage of the Duke of Fife to Princess Louise of Wales, July 27, 1889. It was published as a hymn tune in *The Hymnal* (Episcopal) edited by Charles Hutchens in 1892. The first appearance of this hymn in a Baptist hymnal in America was in *Sursum Corda: A Book of Praise* (Philadelphia, 1898, No. 834), edited by E. H. Johnson and E. E. Ayres.   *H.E.*

O praise the gracious power 226

This text by Thomas H. Troeger is based on Ephesians 2:11-22 and evolved from an object lesson used by the author to relate that passage to third- and fourth-graders in Sunday School. These thoughts were developed into a sermon and, finally, into this hymn. It was written in the early 1980s and was first published in *New Hymns for the Lectionary: To Glorify the Maker's Name* (with Carol Doran; New York, 1986). There it was set to CHRISTPRAISE RAY, a tune composed for it by Carol Doran. *The Presbyterian Hymnal* (Louisville, 1990) was the first hymnal to include this text.

Several changes have been made for this hymnal. An omitted final stanza reads:
O praise the living Christ
    with faith's bright songful voice!
Announce the gospel to the world
    and with these words rejoice:
Troeger's original refrain is: "We praise you, Christ! Your cross has made us one!" *The Baptist Hymnal* (1991) is the first Southern Baptist hymnal to include this text.

MARION—See hymn 39, Rejoice, ye pure in heart.   *P.A.R.*

O sacred Head, now wounded 137

This hymn was based on a medieval Latin poem, captioned as a "rhythmical prayer to the various members of Christ's body suffering and hanging on the Cross." It is in seven parts:
1. "Salve mundi salutare" (to the feet)
2. "Salve Jesu, Rex sanctorum"
   (to the knees)
3. "Salve Jesu, Pastor bone"
   (to the hands)
4. "Salve Jesu, summe bonus"
   (to the sides)
5. "Salve salus mea, Deus" (to the breast)
6. "Summi Regis cor aveto" (to the heart)
7. "Salve caput crentatum" (to the face)
"Salve mundi salutari" has been attributed to Bernard of Clairvaux (1091-1153) or to Arnulf of Louvain (1200-51). Its appearance in manuscripts is no earlier than the 14th century, so its authorship remains uncertain. The poem's seven parts may not be a unity, for the last sections may not have been a part of the original poem. The hymn is of a type known as "crucifix hymns," one part being used for each of the seven days of the week to address the limbs of Christ hanging on the cross.

Paul Gerhardt translated part seven, "Salve caput crentatum," into the German beginning "O Haupt voll Blut und Wunden." Gerhardt's version was first published in 10 eight-line stanzas in Crüger's *Praxis Pietatis Melica* (1656 ed.). Armin Haeussler has agreed with Percy Dearmer's assessment that Gerhardt's version was "more fervent and more scriptural than the original."

James Waddell Alexander rendered Gerhardt's translation into English, and it was first published in Joshua Leavitt's *The Christian Lyre* (New York, 1830, No. 136). Hymnologist Philip Schaff published Alexander's translation in his *Christ in Song* (1868), where he commented:

"This classical hymn has shown an imperishable vitality in passing from the Latin into the German, and from the German into the English, and proclaiming in three tongues, and in the name of three confessions—the Catholic, the Lutheran, and the Reformed—with equal effect, the dying love of our Savior, and our boundless indebtedness to Him" (Schaff, 178).

The text is first found in a Southern Baptist collection in *The Baptist Hymn and Praise Book* (Nashville, 1964, No. 123).

PASSION CHORALE was originally the melody of a German love song, "Mein G'müth ist mir verwirret, Das macht ein Jungfrau zart" (My heart is distracted by a gentle maid), composed by Hans Leo Hassler and published in his *Lustgarten neuer teutscher Gesäng* (Nuremberg, 1601). It was first used as a hymn tune to "Herzlich tut mich verlangen" in *Harmoniael Sacrae* (3rd ed., Gorlitz, 1613). Crüger first published this tune to Gerhardt's text, as noted above. This melody was a favorite of J.S. Bach, who used it five times in his *St. Matthew Passion*. The original vigorous rhythmic style of Hassler's melody had been smoothed out to mostly quarter note values by the time of Bach. The original and altered rhythms of PASSION CHORALE are given side by side in the *Lutheran Book of Worship* (Minneapolis;

Philadelphia, 1978, Nos. 116 and 117). The text in Alexander's translation first entered a Southern Baptist collection in *The Baptist Hymn* and *Praise Book* (Nashville, 1904, No. 123). However the Hassler tune PASSION CHORALE is not found in a Southern Baptist hymn book until *Baptist Hymnal* (Nashville, 1956, No. 92).   *H.E.*

O say, can you see 635

Francis Scott Key wrote this patriotic song on September 14, 1814, in Baltimore, Maryland, near the end of the War of 1812. Key had been on assignment as an agent of the United States to negotiate the release of a prisoner held by the British fleet. Though the British agreed to free the prisoner, they kept Key with the fleet to keep secret the plans of an attack on Fort McHenry. The author and his party could only watch helplessly as the bombardment continued all day on September 13 and into the night. Seeing by the first light of day that the U.S. flag still flew over the garrison, Key began to write this poem, finishing it that evening upon arrival in the city. It was printed the next day as a handbill and soon appeared in newspapers. Joseph Carr published a sheet music version about a month later.

Key's original had four stanzas. The second and third, omitted here, may be seen in Reynolds' *Companion to Baptist Hymnal* (167). Congress made "The Star-Spangled Banner" the national anthem on March 3, 1931.

NATIONAL ANTHEM is the work of an unknown composer. Its first extant publication was in *Vocal Magazine* (London, 1778), where it set the text "To Anacreon in Heaven," by Ralph Tomlinson. The tune was apparently not new at that time. John Stafford Smith, to whom it is often credited mistakenly, was the arranger of a three-voice version published in 1799. The tune was known in the United States as early as 1793, when the first of more than 100 patriotic parodies appeared with it. Key himself wrote a set of words for an 1805 Washington dinner honoring Stephen Decatur. It was perhaps because of his familiarity with this tune that his patriotic poem was written in this form and so quickly.

Kingdom Songs (Nashville, 1921, No. 327) was the first Southern Baptist book to include this song. Its absence from earlier collections is probably because it was not considered a hymn. *P.A.R.*

O sing a song of Bethlehem 120

Louis F. Benson, a Presbyterian minister, teacher, and hymnologist, wrote this hymn which focuses on four locations significant in the life of Christ—Bethlehem, Nazareth, Galilee, and Calvary. *Baptist Hymnal* (Nashville, 1975, No. 99) was the first Southern Baptist hymnal to include this hymn.

KINGSFOLD was one of the most widely sung English folk tunes of its day and has been included in numerous hymnals following its introduction in *The English Hymnal* (1906) in an arrangement by Ralph Vaughan Williams. The tune is associated with ballads about Job and about Dives and Lazarus in the *Oxford Book of Carols*. It was first published in *English Country Songs* (1893), edited by Lucy Broadwood and J.A. Fuller Maitland. This Aeolian mode tune is named for the village in Surrey, England, where Vaughan Williams heard a version of the tune sung. *P.H.*

O sing a song to God 38

This translation is from the Spanish hymn, "Cantemos al Senor," by Carlos Rosas. In a letter to the author, Rosas states that his inspiration for writing "Aleluya!" (Cantemos al Senor) was "the fruit of biblical reflection and liturgical experiences."

Hugh Warner, the hymn's translator, is the pseudonym of an author who wishes to remain anonymous. *The Baptist Hymnal* (1991) is the first Southern Baptist hymn collection to include this song.

The tune is named ROSAS for the composer. *P.H.*

O soul, are you weary and troubled? 320

In a pamphlet written by missionary Lillias Trotter, Helen Howarth Lemmel read the lines "So then, turn your eyes upon Him. Look full into His face, and you will find that the things of earth will acquire a strange, new dimness." In a moment of sheer inspiration, she shaped the stanzas and the refrain and added the musical setting. Four years later, in 1922, the hymn was published in *Glad Songs,* a publication of the British National Sunday School Union. The book consisted of 67 poems by Lemmel. The song's popularity in England caught the attention of Harry D. Clarke, an American song writer and publisher. Clarke included it in his *Gospel Truth in Song, No. 3* (Chicago, 1925). The first Southern Baptist collection to include this song was *Baptist Hymnal* (Nashville, 1975, No. 198).

LEMMEL is the tune name given for the composer. *W.J.R.*

O That Will Be Glory—See *When all my labors and trials are o'er*

O the deep, deep love of Jesus 409

This text by S. Trevor Francis appeared as an eight-stanza poem titled "Love of Jesus" in the author's *Whence-Whither, and Other Poems* (1898). The present three-stanza version is from *The Song Companion to the Scriptures* (1911), compiled by G. Campbell Morgan. Although its first publication has not been located, the Irish *Church Hymnal*

(1919) dates this hymn 1873. So well known was this hymn of Francis that his posthumously published collected works are titled *O the Deep, Deep Love of Jesus, and Other Sacred Poems* (London, 1926).

The first Southern Baptist collection to include this hymn was *Baptist Hymnal* (Nashville, 1975, No. 340).

HARRIS—See hymn 429, Who can cheer the heart like Jesus.   *H.E.*

O the King is coming 194

The inspiration for the song came from a sermon on the second coming of Christ by evangelist James Crabtree. At the end of the sermon, Crabtree walked through the congregation shouting "The King is coming! The King is coming!"

With that cry ringing in her heart, Gloria Gaither wrote the words in collaboration with her husband Bill Gaither and a close family friend, Charles Millhuff. When finished, the song shouted out the news of the reality of Christ's return. The year was 1970. The version that appears in *The Baptist Hymnal* (1991) is the refrain of the original song, which appeared in *Hymns for the Family of God* (Nashville, 1976, No. 313).

KING IS COMING is the name given the tune in the first hymnal publication. *W.J.R.*

O What a Wonder It is—See *For God so loved the world*

O what a wonderful, wonderful day 438

John W. Peterson, who wrote both text and tune, has provided the following account of this hymn's origin: "This was written in the summer of 1961, when I was directing the singing one week at the Montrose Bible Conference in Montrose, Pennsylvania. During one of the sessions, an opportunity for personal testimony was given to the audience. An old gentleman rose to his feet and told of his conversion experience. In describing that night when he met Christ, he used the phrase, 'It seemed like heaven came down and glory filled my soul.' Right away I knew that it would be a fine title for a song, so I wrote it down and later in the week completed the song." It was first published in *Miracle Melodies No. 4* (Grand Rapids, 1961), and became a favorite almost immediately.

The first Southern Baptist collection to include this hymn was *Baptist Hymnal* (Nashville, 1975, No. 425).

HEAVEN CAME DOWN is the same as the title.   *H.E.*

O worship the King 16

"O Worship the King" is based on the Old Testament hymn of praise, Psalm 104, or more precisely, on William Kethe's version of Psalm 104 which appeared in the *Anglo-Genevan Psalter* in 1561. It was written in 1833 by Robert Grant (1779-1838) near the end of his career in the English parliament and about a year before he became Governor of Bombay. The hymnologist Erik Routley describes the hymn as England's "earliest genuine hymn from a distinguished public servant" and says that the hymn "with its fine lofty phrases, is immortal" (1952, 190). The hymn, with its first two stanzas about God and the last two directed to God, is rich in biblical imagery and lofty descriptions of both the transcendence and immanence of God.

It was first published in Henry Bickersteth's *Christian Psalmody* (1833). Its first appearance in a Southern Baptist hymnal was in *Baptist Hymn and Praise Book* (Nashville, 1904, No. 18).

The tune LYONS appeared in the second volume of William Gardiner's *Sacred*

Melodies (London, 1815) and is there attributed to "Haydn," though it cannot be traced precisely to the works of either Franz Joseph Haydn (1732-1809) or Johann Michael Haydn (1737-1806). This tune first appeared in a Southern Baptist hymnal in *Baptist Hymn and Praise Book* (Nashville, 1904, No. 18). *S.W.G.*

O Zion, haste 583

Mary Ann Thomson wrote this text one night in 1868 while watching over one of her children who was ill. She wished to write a missions text to the tune which she knew with Faber's "Hark, Hark, My Soul." (It is not known if the tune she had in mind was that by Henry Smart or another by John Dykes.) She had difficulty completing the refrain to her own satisfaction and did not finish the text for another three years.

The hymn originally had six stanzas, of which the third and sixth were:

'Tis thine to save from peril of perdition
    The souls for whom the Lord his life laid down;
Beware lest, slothful to fulfill thy mission,
    Thou lose one jewel that should deck his crown.

He comes again, O Sion, ere thou meet him,
    Make known to every heart his saving grace;
Let none whom he hath ransomed fail to greet him,
    Through thy neglect, unfit to see his face.

The hymn first appeared in the 1892 Episcopal *Hymnal.*

TIDINGS takes its name from the refrain of Thomson's text, with which it has been associated since *The Church Hymnal*, a tunebook for the Episcopal hymnal, was published in 1894. James Walch had written this tune in 1875 as a setting for "Hark, Hark, My Soul," because he felt tunes by Smart and Dykes were not adequate. It is also called ANGELIC SONGS and PROCLAMATION.

Kingdom Songs (Nashville, 1921, No. 209) was the first Southern Baptist collection to include this hymn. *P.A.R.*

Of all the Spirit's gifts to me 442

Fred Pratt Green wrote this hymn for a United Women's Rally in Croydon near London. It was sung during a session planned around the theme "The Fruits of the Spirit." The influence of Galatians 5:22 is evident. The hymn bears a 1979 copyright date.

THREEFOLD GIFTS was written by Austin C. Lovelace for this text. It bears a copyright date of 1987. In a conversation with the writer, Lovelace indicated he offered the tune to felllow members of the editorial board of *Hymn Supplement II.* The inclusion of the tune in *Baptist Hymnal* (1991) is the first time it has been used in a Southern Baptist hymn collection. *D.B.*

Of the Father's love begotten 251

Early in the fifth century, Aurelius Clemens Prudentius, a Spanish lawyer and poet, published a volume with the title, *Cathemerinon.* It included a long poem, "Da plectrum puer, choreis," which stated orthodox Christian theology in the manner of the secular epics. Later manuscripts contain a version of this poem beginning with its fourth stanza, "Corde natus ex Parentis," and adding a refrain, "saeculorum saecula." On this Latin model, John Mason Neale wrote a five-stanza English text, which began "Of the Father, sole begotten" and ended with a doxology (not in the Latin). This was published in the 1854 edition of *The Hymnal Noted* (London). Neale later altered the opening phrase to its present form. Henry W. Baker revised and added to Neale's hymn in the draft version of *Hymns Ancient and Modern* (London, 1859), creating a nine-stanza text. *The Baptist Hymnal* (1991) uses stanzas 1 (Neale, alt.), 4 (Neale, alt.), and 9 (Baker) of this composite.

DIVINUM MYSTERIUM takes its title from the first words of a Latin Sanctus trope, sometimes attributed to Thomas Aquinas, with which it was associated from the 13th century. Though originally an unmeasured plainsong, it gained currency in a triple-meter version included in the Swedish Lutheran anthology, *Pies Cantiones Ecclesiasticae et Scholasticae* (Greifswald, 1582). It came into use with Neale's text in *The Hymnal Noted*, compiled by Neale and Thomas Helmore. The present form of the melody is an approximation of plainsong style developed by C. Winfred Douglas for *The Hymnal* of the Episcopal Church (New York, 1916). The harmonization was made by Mark Blankenship for *The Baptist Hymnal* (1991).

Baptist Hymnal (Nashville, 1975, No. 62) was the first Southern Baptist collection to include this hymn.   *P.A.R.*

Of the themes that men have known 545

Both this text and the music were written by the Texas Methodist pastor and evangelist, Albert C. Fisher (1886-1946). The name FISHER was given to the tune in *Baptist Hymnal* (1956). The text and tune first appeared in Robert H. Coleman's *World Evangel* (Dallas, 1913, No. 7). *Kingdom Songs* (Dallas, 1921, No. 57) was the first Southern Baptist hymnal to include the hymn.   *S.W.G.*

Oh, come, little children 107

Johann Abraham Peter Schulz, an early German Classical composer, wrote this text and tune in 1794. The text is a translation

of the original tune, IHR KINDELEIN KOMMET.

SCHULZ takes its tune name from the composer. Erik Routley says this nursery rhyme tune became very popular during the Romantic era (64-66). Its appearance in *The Baptist Hymnal* (1991) is the first in a Southern Baptist hymnal, although both text and tune appeared in *Songs for Children* (Nashville, 1964).   *P.H.*

Oh, how good is Christ the Lord! 228

There is no information on the text or tune, OH QUE BUENO, of this Puerto Rican Folk Hymn. It was arranged by Richard Starr.

Oh, How I Love Jesus—See *There is a name I love to hear*

On a hill far away 141

The Michigan Historical Commission has erected a historical marker in front of the Delta Tau Delta fraternity house on the campus of Albion College, a United Methodist school in Albion, Michigan. The marker reads: "The Old Rugged Cross, one of the world's best loved hymns, was composed here in 1912 by Rev. George Bennard (1873-1958)." This claim is disputed by the members of the Friends' Church of Sturgeon Bay, Wisconsin, since they celebrate "The Old Rugged Cross Day" on the second Sunday in January each year, for they believe the song was written in Sturgeon Bay. Another congregation, the Methodist church of Pokagon, Michigan, celebrates a similar day each year on June 7, for they claim the song was written in Pokagon. At any rate, we know that Bennard wrote both the words and the tune of this beloved hymn. The tune is named OLD RUGGED CROSS for obvious reasons.

Late in the fall of 1912, Bennard began writing the hymn and continued working on it over several weeks. In revival meetings in

Michigan and New York State, he carried the words with him. He may have made some revisions or additions at Sturgeon Bay, thus the claim of the Friends' Church states that Bennard completed the hymn during a revival meeting, December 29, 1912, through January 12, 1913. The first publication of the hymn occurred in *Heart and Life Songs, for the Church, Sunday School, Home and Campmeeting* (Chicago, 1915). It appeared for Southern Baptists in Robert H. Coleman's *Hosannas* (Dallas, 1923, No. 13).   *W.J.R.*

On Eagle's Wings—See *And God will raise you up*

On Jordan's stormy banks 521

This hymn was written by the English Baptist minister Samuel Stennett, and it was first published in Baptist pastor John Rippon's famous hymn compilation, *A Selection of Hymns* (London, 1787; reprinted, New York, 1792). With the title "Heaven Anticipated," Stennett's hymn consisted of eight four-line stanzas with no refrain. The refrain, an American addition, probably originated in the frontier camp meeting revivals of the early 19th century.

PROMISED LAND was first published in William Walker's *Southern Harmony* (Spartanburg, 1835), where it is attributed to "Miss M. Durham." As is usual in Southern shape-note tunebooks before the Civil War, PROMISED LAND appears in three voice parts—treble, tenor, and bass—with the melody in the tenor part.

The tune exists in two modes, major and minor. In *Southern Harmony* and in subsequent tunebooks such as *The Sacred Harp* (1844), it was published in F-sharp minor. The tune is still sung in this mode in shape-note tunebook singings. In the late 19th century, PROMISED LAND was changed to F major to accomodate it to the newer gospel

hymn style. This change to F major was made by Rigdon M. McIntosh, and seems to have been first published in *A Collection of Hymns and Tunes for Public Social, and Domestic Worship* (Nashville, No. 807). In addition to the change to major, the rhythms beginning and ending most of the phrases have been altered. Reynolds has rightly observed that "Although a great deal of the folk character of the original tune was lost in this alteration, the tune has enjoyed immense popularity and has far surpassed other tunes for the hymn" (1976, 175). The text can be found in Southern Baptist's first collection, *The Baptist Psalmody* (Charleston, 1850, No. 1276). The major mode version of PROMISED LAND first appeared in a Southern Baptist collection in *Songs of Redemption* (Atlanta, 1920, No. 37).   *H.E.*

Once to every man and nation 470

In his 90-line poem of December, 1845, "The Present Crisis," the distinguished New England poet, James Russell Lowell, made a strong protest against the war with Mexico. Lowell felt that the war was unjust and that it would expand slavery. The poem was first published in the *Boston Courier* (Dec. 11, 1845). The English Congregational minister and hymnologist, W. Garrett Horder, selected, rearranged, substituted, and edited the lines which now make up this hymn. Horder published the hymn in his *Hymns, Supplemental to existing collections* of 1896 and again in his 1905 *Worship Song. Baptist Hymnal* (Nashville, 1956, No. 418) was the first Southern Baptist collection to include the hymn.

BEECHER—See hymn 208, Love divine, all loves excelling.   *S.W.G.*

One by one 561

In 1989 the California Southern Baptist Church Music Conference commissioned

David Justice to write a new missions hymn. Justice wrote the text and tune for a hymn of three stanzas and a refrain; this received its premier at the annual meeting of the Church Music Conference in Redding, California, November, 1989. *The Baptist Hymnal* (1991) uses only the refrain, which, according to the author/composer, was the first part of the hymn to be written. The author has observed that the text was written to reemphasize the fundamental truth that, in spite of all our mass-evangelism efforts, the people of the world must come to Christ "one by one." The song makes its first hymnal appearance in *The Baptist Hymnal* (1991).

ONE BY ONE is the tune name taken from the refrain text.   *D.M.*

One day 193

Charles H. Marsh had just completed high school when J. Wilbur Chapman invited him to be the organist and accompanist at the Winona Lake Chautauqua and Bible Conference (IN). Later, in 1908 or 1909, Marsh joined Chapman at Stony Brook, Long Island, for a Bible conference. It was there that Chapman gave Marsh the poem "One Day" to set to music. Marsh later sold the copyright to Chapman's assistant, Parley E. Zartmann. A full account of the subsequent copyright dispute involving Charles M. Alexander, Hope Publishing Company, and Rodeheaver Publishing Company is contained in a letter from Marsh reprinted in Reynolds' *Companion to Baptist Hymnal* (175-76). The first three stanzas were first included in a Southern Baptist collection in *Kingdom Songs* (Nashville, 1921, No. 248).

CHAPMAN is named for the author of the hymn, J. Wilbur Chapman.   *P.H.*

Only believe 534

In 1921, Paul Rader and his four-year-old daughter, Harriet, were walking across one of Chicago's busiest boulevards. Tightly holding Harriet's hand, he asked her if she were afraid to cross the street.

"No," she replied, "not when you're with me. Why should I be afraid?"

Her words provided the inspiration to Rader that Christians should have the same childlike faith in God. When he returned home, he completed words and music, based on Luke 12:32: "Fear not, little flock; for it is your Father's good pleasure to give you the kingdom." The three stanzas are:

Fear not, little flock, from the cross to
    the throne,
    From death into life He went for His
    own;
All power in earth, all power above,
    Is given to Him for the flock of His
    love.

Fear not, little flock, He goeth ahead,
    Your Shepherd selected the path you
    must tread;
The waters of Marah He'll sweeten for
    thee—
    He drank all the bitter in Gethsemane.

Fear not, little flock, whatever your lot;
    He enters all rooms, "the doors being
    shut."
He never forsakes, He never is gone—
    So count on His presence in darkness
    and dawn.

The refrain following each stanza is:
    Only believe, only believe,
    All things are possible, only believe.

The hymn's first appearance was in Harry D. Clarke's *Gospel Truth in Song* (Chicago, 1923). Rader's stanzas have been largely forgotten, but the refrain has been widely used. Its first appearance in a Southern Baptist collection was in *Songs of Faith* (Nashville, 1933, No. 260).

ONLY BELIEVE is named for the hymn title and refrain text.   *W.J.R.*

Only Trust Him—See *Come, every soul by sin oppressed*

Onward, Christian soldiers 493
This text was written in 1864 by Sabine Baring-Gould for a children's festival at Horbury Bridge, Yorkshire, England, for a processional with cross and banners. Such an event was a traditional practice in 19th-century England, as children marched from one village to another. The hymn was first published in *The Church Times* on October 15, 1864, in its original version of six stanzas. The first Southern Baptist hymnal to include the text, as well as the ST. GERTRUDE tune, was *The Baptist Hymn and Praise Book* (Nashville, 1904, No. 436).

ST. GERTRUDE, written in 1871 by Arthur S. Sullivan for use with this text in his *The Hymnary* (London, 1872), was first published in the December 1871 issue of the *Musical Times.* The tune was named for Mrs. Gertrude Clay-Ker-Seymer, in whose home in Hanford, Dorsetshire, Sullivan was visiting when he wrote it. Sullivan honored ("canonized") friends in this manner on occasion. The first known printing of the tune in America is believed to be in John R. Sweney's *Gems of Praise* (Philadelphia, 1873).   *M.P.*

Open my eyes, that I may see 502
The text and tune are the work of Clara H. Scott. It was first published in 1895 in *Best Hymns No. 2* (Chicago) compiled by E. A. Hoffman and Harold F. Sayles. The 1956 *Baptist Hymnal* committee named the tune SCOTT. This text, with tune appeared in Baptist publisher Robert Coleman's *The American Hymnal* (Dallas, 1933, No. 457) and in B. B. McKinney's *Broadman Hymnal* (Nashville, 1940, No. 351).   *D.B.*

Open our eyes, Lord 499
This worship chorus was written by Robert M. Cull and copyrighted in 1976 by Maranatha! Music. He was a composer and arranger with Maranatha! Music at the time of its composition. *The Baptist Hymnal* (1991) is the first Southern Baptist compilation to contain this chorus.

OPEN OUR EYES is the name of the tune, and is taken from the first line of the text.   *P.H.*

Our Father, which art in heaven 462
This setting of Matthew 6:9-13 is taken from Albert Hay Malotte's solo song "The Lord's Prayer" written in 1935. *The Baptist Hymnal* (1991) is the first Southern Baptist collection to include it.

MALOTTE is taken from the solo song "The Lord's Prayer" and is named for the composer, Albert Hay Malotte.   *S.W.G.*

Our God has built with living stones 353
The words of this hymn by Terry W. York originally formed part of a cycle of five texts commissioned by Judson Baptist Church, Nashville, Tennessee, in celebration of the church's 75th anniversary (1985). The author is a member of this church, where he sings in the choir. The first hymnal publication of this text is in *The Baptist Hymnal* (1991).

ARLINGTON—See hymn 358, This is the day the Lord has made.   *D.M.*

Our God has made us one 388
In 1984 Niles Borop and Jim Weber, both of whom were staff writers for Word Music and Meadowgreen Music at the time, collaborated in writing a new hymn on the theme of Christian unity. Borop wrote the text, and Weber provided the tune (WEBER) first used with these words. Borop has de-

scribed the concerns which prompted him and Weber to write the hymn:

"We believe that the Body of Christ is united. We have one Lord Jesus, one faith in his intervening love, one hope in his saving grace, one Spirit poured out for our comfort and equipping, and one God who is Father of all. The church may be fractured in many ways, but as we obey the will of our Lord, cling to the faith, rest in the hope, listen to the Spirit, and enjoy the mercies of the Father, we are drawn together as well."

The text, along with the WEBER tune, was published in *The Hymnal for Worship & Celebration* (Word Music, 1986). The appearance of the text in *The Baptist Hymnal* (1991) is its first in a Southern Baptist collection. However, the tune used here is OLD 134TH.

OLD 134TH—See hymn 30, Stand up and bless the Lord. *M.P.*

Our life and its sustaining breath 642

Terry W. York wrote this hymn in 1974 while he was an M.C.M. student at New Orleans Baptist Theological Seminary. The text was printed that year in an informal student newsletter and was later sung at a special Thanksgiving service held by church music students at the seminary. Encouragement from a seminary professor, who had discovered the hymn at the student-led Thanksgiving service and subsequently had used it with his own family as a table grace, led the author to enter the text into the selection process for Southern Baptists' *The Baptist Hymnal* (1991).

The tune MARIANNA was composed for this text in 1989 by Dennis Allen, and named for the town of Marianna, Florida, where he served as minister of music at the First Baptist Church from 1979 to 1986.

The Baptist Hymnal (1991) marks the first hymnal appearance of this text and tune. *D.M.*

Our Savior's infant cries were heard 116

Thomas H. Troeger wrote this hymn in 1986 for the Barium Springs Home for Children, a Presbyterian institution in North Carolina. It was commissioned in anticipation of the 1991 centennial of that ministry, with the objective that it celebrate the care and nurture of children and "be useful as a gift to the church." It appeared in *New Hymns for the Life of the Church: To Make Our Prayer and Music One* (New York, 1992), a collection of Troeger's hymns.

Omitted from *The Baptist Hymnal* (1991) is the second stanza, which the author considers the crux of the hymn:

In Joseph's arms, at Mary's breast,
while Herod's violence spread,
God's love by human love was blessed,
protected, nurtured, fed.

The first hymnal to publish this text was *The Worshiping Church* (Carol Stream, 1990). The first Southern Baptist collection to include it is *The Baptist Hymnal* (1991).

ST. AGNES was composed for the hymn "Jesus, the Very Thought of Thee" and first appeared in the *Hymnal for Use in the English Church* (London, 1866) edited by John Grey. The tune was named by Dykes for the 13-year-old Christian girl who, according to legend, was martyred in Rome on January 21, 304 A.D. She was sentenced to death for refusing to marry a young nobleman and reportedly said, "I am already engaged to one—to him alone I keep my troth." St. Agnes is the patron saint of young girls in the Roman Catholic Church. In England, the tune is known as ST. AGNES, DURHAM, to differentiate it from another tune, ST. AGNES composed by James Langran. The tune first appeared in a Southern Baptist collection in *The Baptist Hymn and Praise Book* (Nashville, 1904, No. 249), where it is set, not to "Jesus, the Very Thought of Thee," but to

William Bathurst's "Oh, for a Faith That Will Not Shrink." *S.W.G., P.A.R., M.P.*

Out in the highways and byways of life 569

According to the composer, George S. Schuler, the words for this hymn were written by Ira B. Wilson about 1909, but he did not compose the tune until 1924. As related by Schuler, "oddly enough, neither of us can recall how we came to write the song. To this day he [Wilson] claims to have no part in authorizing the work, but I do know he wrote it. When the song was in manuscript it was submitted to a publisher. It was rejected as 'being unsuited for our need.' I had plates made and one thousand copies printed, costing me a sum I could ill afford at the time. George Dibble, well known as an evangelist in those days, introduced the number at an International Sunday School Convention at Cleveland, Ohio. Here it became a great favorite, and it is needless to say that within a short time I received many offers for the song" (Reynolds, 1976, 177).

This song was published in *Songs of Evangelism* (No. 16) edited and compiled by Schuler, Edwin O. Excell, and W. E. Biederwolf (Fort Wayne, 1925). Originally composed as a choir selection, this hymn was dedicated to the Moody Memorial Church Choir, Chicago. The choral version of this hymn with pianistic accompaniment in the chorus appeared in B. B. McKinney's *The Broadman Hymnal* (Nashville, 1940, No. 130), but was changed to four-part harmony on the chorus in *Baptist Hymnal* (1956, No. 431), where it was given its tune name, SCHULER. *H.E.*

Out of my bondage, sorrow, and night 310

This hymn, along with "Ye Must Be Born Again," was a product of the collaboration of Congregational minister William T. Sleeper and George C. Stebbins, who composed the tune JESUS, I COME. The text and tune were first printed in *Gospel Hymns No. 5* (1887) with the scriptural subtitle "Deliver me, O my God" (Ps. 71:4). The first printing in a Southern Baptist hymnal occurred in *The Baptist Hymn and Praise Book* (Nashville, 1904, No. 191). *P.H.*

Pass me not, O gentle Savior 308

Written by Fanny J. Crosby in 1868, this song first appeared in William H. Doane's *Songs of Devotion* (New York; Chicago, 1870). The current text differs from the original in two respects: At the end of line three in stanza one, "smiling" in Crosby's original has been changed to "calling." In line one of stanza three "merits" has been made singular thus aiding its rhyming with "spirit."

Despite some theological objections to the song's apparent concern for self above the needs of others and the hint of God's capriciousness or unwillingness to look in mercy on all who call for it, this song has continued in popular use. It first appeared with its tune in a Southern Baptist collection in *The Baptist Hymn and Praise Book* (Nashville, 1904, No. 218), though it had earlier appeared in collections such as *The Baptist Hymnal* (Philadelphia, 1883, No. 361).

The tune PASS ME NOT was composed to Fanny Crosby's "Pass Me Not, O Gentle Savior" by William H. Doane. The tune was first given this name in *Baptist Hymnal* (1956). It is unaltered from its original publication in *Songs of Devotion* (1870) and has remained wedded to the Crosby text. *H.T.M.*

Pentecostal Power—See *Lord, as of old at Pentecost*

People need the Lord 557

The words and music to this chorus were written in 1983 by Greg Nelson and Phill McHugh as the refrain of the song "People Need the Lord." The idea for the song emerged from a luncheon meeting in a Nashville, Tennessee, restaurant. According to the composers, as McHugh became aware of the pain in the eyes of their waitress, he said to Nelson, "People need the Lord, don't they?"

Nelson responded, "Yes, people do need the Lord." From that brief exchange came the idea for the song, which was sketched in outline during the remainder of the meal. It was subsequently recorded and became a popular song with soloists and choirs.

PEOPLE NEED THE LORD is the tune name taken from the first line of the chorus.   *M.P.*

Praise and thanksgiving 645

This anonymous round comes from the Alsace region of France, near the German border. The English translation from the German was made by Edith Lowell Thomas and published by her in *The Whole World Singing* (New York, 1950). Stanzas two and three were written by Marie Post and added to Thomas' text in the *Psalter Hymnal Supplement* (Grand Rapids, 1974).

LOBET UND PREISET takes its name from the incipit of the original German text for this canon. The harmonization was prepared by Geoffrey Price for *The Baptist Hymnal* (1991).

The Baptist Hymnal (1991) is the first Southern Baptist collection to include this hymn.   *P.A.R.*

Praise God, from whom all blessings flow (Doxology) 253

Protestant churches in the English-speaking world refer to this hymn as "The Doxology." In reality, a doxology is any expression of praise to God. Two of the better known doxologies are the "Greater Doxology" (the *Gloria in excelsis*) and the "Lesser Doxology" (the *Gloria Patri*). This doxology was written by Thomas Ken and served as the final stanza of his "Morning," "Evening," and "Midnight," hymns which were published around 1692 and included in the Appendix to the second edition (1695) of Ken's *A Manual of Prayers for Use of the Scholars of Winchester College*. Ken made several alterations. The version used in *The Baptist Hymnal* (1991) was done in 1709. Ken's "Doxology" is the first of 16 Trinitarian Doxologies included at the end of Southern Baptists' first "official" hymnal, *The Baptist Psalmody* (Charleston, 1850, No. 1296).

OLD 100TH—See hymn 5, All people that on earth do dwell.   *D.B.*

Praise Him! praise Him! 227

This praise song by Fanny Crosby was first published in *Bright Jewels* (Chicago, 1869). An oblong Sunday School collection, it was edited by Robert Lowry, William F. Sherwin, and Chester G. Allen, the composer of the tune. The title was given as "Praise! Give Praise."

JOYFUL SONG is the tune given to Crosby's "Praise Him! Praise Him!" in *Baptist Hymnal* (Nashville, 1956). Like most gospel songs, the tune had no name in most hymnals but when first referred to, it was called ALLEN. Robert H. Coleman's *The Popular Hymnal* (Dallas, 1918, No. 258) was the first collection used by Southern Baptists to include the text and tune.   *H.T.M.*

Praise Him, All Ye Little Children—See *Praise Him, praise Him, all ye little children*

Praise Him, praise Him, all ye little children 31

The text of this children's hymn is by an unknown author. Its simple words are much like those of many other songs written in the 19th century for use in Sunday School. Similar texts are found in British and American collections published in the 1880s and 1890s.

BONNER appeared with this text for the first time in the 1908 edition of *Child Songs* (London), edited by Carey Bonner. There it was attributed to "E. Rawdon Bailey," a pseudonym used by Bonner for his arrangements or harmonizations of melodies from other sources. It is therefore unclear to what extent this is an original work. The tune is simple and is similar to that of other children's songs of the time, both sacred and secular. It is also called PRAISE HIM, GOD IS LOVE, and HE IS LOVE.

The first appearance of this song in a collection for Southern Baptists (other than in those intended exclusively for children) was in Robert Coleman's *The Modern Hymnal* (Dallas, 1926, No. 393).   *P.A.R.*

Praise the Father 257

Michael A. Perry wrote this hymn in 1978, while working with the team preparing *Hymns for Today's Church* (London, 1982), in which it was first published. It was written to meet a perceived need for new hymns expounding the doctrine of the Trinity. *The Baptist Hymnal* (1991) is the first hymnal for Southern Baptists to include this text.

STUTTGART—See hymn 21, O my soul, bless God the father.   *P.A.R.*

Praise the Lord who reigns above 33

This hymn by Charles Wesley is based on Psalm 150 and first appeared in the Wesleyan *Collection of Psalms and Hymns* (London, 1743). It appeared in America in Manning's *Boston Collection of Sacred and Devotional Hymns* (Boston, 1808) and in 1975 it appeared in the Southern Baptist hymnal *Baptist Hymnal* (Nashville, 1975, No. 23). It

was written in four stanzas of eight lines. This present version omits stanza 2.

AMSTERDAM was one of six tunes which John Wesley adapted from Freylinghausen's *Geistreiches Gesangbuch* (Halle, 1704, revised in 1714, completed and augmented in 1741) for his first compilation of tunes, the *Foundery Collection*, published in London in 1742. For some reason, Wesley credited the tune to the English organist and composer, James Nares (1715-83). AMSTERDAM's first appearance in a Southern Baptist hymnal was in *New Baptist Hymnal* (Nashville, 1926, No. 240).   *S.W.G.*

Praise the Lord! ye heavens, adore Him 36

The first two stanzas of this hymn are an anonymous paraphrase of Psalm 148. They first appeared as four four-line stanzas under the heading "Hymn from Psalm CXLVIII, Haydn" in an undated leaflet titled *Hymns for Foundling Apprentices Attending Divine Service to Return Thanks*. The reference to Haydn indicates the intent that these lines be sung to AUSTRIAN HYMN. The leaflet was pasted in the back of the 1797 and 1801 editions of *Psalms, Hymns, and Anthems of the Foundling Hospital,* a charitable institution in London. The first printing of this text which can be dated with certainty is that in *Psalms and Hymns* for Magdalen College (London, 1804).

The last stanza, which has no direct link to the first two, was written by Edward Osler and first published in the *Mitre Hymn Book* (London, 1836). The texts were joined in Cooke and Denton's *The Church Hymnal* (London, 1853).

The anonymous text appeared in *The Baptist Psalmody* (Charleston, 1850, No. 124), the first hymnal published for Southern Baptists. *Baptist Hymnal* (Nashville, 1975, No. 11) was the first Southern Baptist collection to add Osler's stanza.

HYFRYDOL was composed about 1830 by Rowland H. Prichard and was first published in his collection, *Cyfaill y Cantorion* (1844). Hyfrydol is Welsh for "good cheer." *P.A.R.*

Praise the Lord, the King of glory 232

Delma B. Reno wrote the hymn in 1964, and it was submitted in the 1964 Hymn Writing Competition sponsored by the Church Music Department of the Baptist Sunday School Board, Nashville. The hymn was judged the winner in the competition. Paired with the tune CHARLES, its first appearance in a Southern Baptist collection was in *Christian Praise* (Nashville, 1964, No. 16).

CHARLES was composed by W. Hines Sims for this winning text. The first public use of the text and tune was at the Nationwide Conference of Southern Baptist Church Musicians in Louisville, Kentucky, February 11-13, 1964. *W.J.R.*

Praise to the Lord, the Almighty 14

This is generally regarded as one of the great hymns of praise of the Christian church and appears in most major hymnals. It was written by Joachim Neander (1650-80) and is based on Psalm 103:1-6 and Psalm 150. The original "Lobe den Herren, den mächtigen König der Ehren!" was published in the author's *A und Ω, Glaub-und Liebesübung*, in Bremen in 1680. This translation is by Catherine Winkworth who selected four of the original five stanzas and included it in her *Chorale Book for England*, 1863. "If with His love He befriend thee" is not the best translation of the original German in stanza 3 and some prefer "He who with love does befriend thee." The hymn first appeared in America in the *Hymnbook for the Use of Evangelical Lutheran Schools and Congregations* (Decorah, 1879) and first appeared in a Southern Baptist hymnal in *Bap-*

tist Hymnal (Nashville, 1956, No. 6).

LOBE DEN HERREN is taken from the first line of Neander's text which is the same as Luther's translation of Psalm 103:1 and the basis of the text. The tune first appeared in 1665 in the *Ander Theil des Erneuerten Gesangbuchs* of Stralsund but is given there with the text, "Hast du denn, Liebster dein Angesicht gäntzlich verborgen." It appeared in 1680 in Neander's A *und* Ω with his text and since that time the tune and Neander's text have usually appeared together. There is the possibility that before it was associated with a sacred text the tune was used with the secular text, "Seh ich nicht blinkende, flinkende Sterne aufgehen."

Bach used the melody in Cantatas 57 and 137, in an unfinished cantata, "Herr Gott, Beherrscher aller Dinge," and in an organ setting, "Kommst du nun, Jesu," in the *Schübler Chorales*.

Baptist Hymnal (Nashville, 1956, No. 6) was the first appearance of this tune in a Southern Baptist hymnal. The present version uses the Sterndale Bennett harmonization which appeared in the *Chorale Book for England* (1863). *S.W.G.*

Praise ye the name of the Lord 665

Gordon Young's organ and choral music is well known to American church musicians. This piece is excerpted from an anthem by the same name published in 1967. The anthem was written as a successor to "Now Let Us All Praise God and Sing." No previous Southern Baptist hymnal has contained this piece.

PRAISE YE is the tune name taken from the first line of the text. *P.H.*

Praise, my soul, the King of heaven 32

This paraphrase of Psalm 103 by Henry F. Lyte was first published in Lyte's *Spirit of the Psalms* (1834), which contained over 280 new paraphrases of the psalms. This collection was written for use by his congregation in the small fishing village in Lower Brixham, Devonshire, England, which Lyte served from 1823 until his death in 1847. There were five stanzas in the original version. In that version the fifth line of each stanza was "Praise him, praise him," but that was later changed to the present "Alleluia! Alleluia!"

The first publication of this hymn in the United States was in Nehemiah Adams' *Church Pastorale* (Boston, 1864). Its first appearance in a Southern Baptist hymnal was in the *New Baptist Hymnal* (Nashville, 1926, No. 31), where it was paired with the REGENT SQUARE tune.

This hymn was used as the processional hymn for the wedding of Queen Elizabeth II at Westminster Abbey, November 20, 1947, which happened to be the 100th anniversary of the death of its author.

In 1931 Mark Andrews composed LAUDA ANIMA (Andrews) for this text. That same year G. Schirmer published it as an anthem with the title "Lauda Anima." The composer's name was added to the tune name to distinguish it from the LAUDA ANIMA (Goss) tune by John Goss.   *M.P.*

Precious Lord, take my hand 456

Thomas A. Dorsey wrote this hymn in 1932 a few days after the death of his first wife, Nettie, and their infant son. She died in childbirth, and the child died within 24 hours of the mother. Dorsey had been away in St. Louis on a gospel music tour with Theodore Fry when he received the telegram from Chicago about his wife. For several days he was lost in grief.

"I felt that God had done me an injustice. I didn't want to serve Him anymore or write gospel songs. I just wanted to go back to that jazz world I once knew so well," he

said. A friend helped him through this period and encouraged him to sit down at the piano. There he began to play a melody, and as he did, he once again felt close to God and the words to "Precious Lord, Take My Hand" came to him. It was not copyrighted until 1938. An additional stanza begins with the line, "When the darkness appears and the night draws near." This personal song of consolation has become Dorsey's most popular composition, having been translated into more than 50 languages.

The tune PRECIOUS LORD is Dorsey's arrangement of the mid-19th century hymn tune MAITLAND, commonly sung to the text "Must Jesus Bear the Cross Alone." *The Baptist Hymnal* (1991) is the first Southern Baptist collection to include this song.   *H.E.*

Purer in heart, O God 492

Fannie Estelle Davison is the author of the text, and the tune PURER IN HEART was composed by James H. Fillmore for the text. The hymn first appeared in Fillmore's *Songs of Gratitude* (Cincinnati, 1877, No. 67). It has appeared in every Southern Baptist hymnal since *The Broadman Hymnal* (1940).   *W.J.R.*

Redeemed, how I love to proclaim it! 544, 531

"Redeemed, How I Love to Proclaim It" was written by Fanny Crosby and first published, appropriately enough, in *Songs of Redeeming Love,* edited by John R. Sweney, C. C. McCabe, T. C. O'Kane, and the composer of its original tune, W. J. Kirkpatrick (Philadelphia, Chicago and St. Louis, 1882, No. 7). On the title page of this volume appeared the quotation of the final lines of William Cowper's "There Is a Fountain": "Redeeming love has been my theme, And shall be till I die."

The popular gospel song did not appear in a Southern Baptist collection until *The*

Broadman Hymnal (Nashville, 1940, No. 92).

REDEEMED is the name given W. J. Kirkpatrick's tune for Fanny Crosby's "Redeemed, How I Love to Proclaim It" by the committee for *Baptist Hymnal* (1956).

ADA was composed by A. L. "Pete" Butler in 1966 for Fanny Crosby's "Redeemed, How I Love to Proclaim It." It was first sung as a choral number for male voices and was later published for mixed choir in *The Church Musician* (July 1967). Widely circulated in anthem form, it was frequently used by Cliff Barrows with the Billy Graham Crusade choirs. As a hymn tune, it first appeared in *Crusade Hymns* (Nashville, 1968, No. 31). The tune name, first found in *Baptist Hymnal* (1975), comes from the town in Oklahoma where Butler was minister of music at the time of its composition.   *H.T.M.*

Rejoice in the Lord always 433

These words are those of Philippians 4:4 (KJV), and the music is traditional. This simple Scripture setting is the sort of song that has often been sung around campfires at summer camps, unaccompanied, or perhaps accompanied by guitar. It may be sung in unison or as a round.

REJOICE is the tune name taken from the chorus title.   *H.E.*

Rejoice, the Lord is King 197

"Rejoice, the Lord is King" is based on Philippians 4:4 and was first published in John Wesley's *Moral and Sacred Poems* (1744), and two years later in Charles Wesley's collection of 16 hymns entitled *Hymns for our Lord's Resurrection* (1746). The present version uses four of the original six stanzas. This hymn is one of the three Wesley hymns for which the famous composer George F. Handel wrote tunes. *Baptist Hymnal* (Nashville, 1956, No. 108) was the first appearance of the text in a Southern Baptist hymnal.

DARWALL, or DARWALL'S 148TH was composed by John Darwall for the new version of Psalm 148, "Ye Boundless Realms of Joy," which was included in Aaron Williams's *New Universal Psalmist* and published in London in 1770. This is the only tune to survive of the two-part tunes which Darwall provided for all of the 150 psalms. The first appearance of the tune in a Southern Baptist hymnal was in *Baptist Hymnal* (Nashville, 1956, No. 108).   *S.W.G.*

Rejoice, ye pure in heart 39

Using Psalm 20:4 and Philippians 4:4 as a source of inspiration, Edward Plumptre wrote this poem for the annual choir festival at Peterborough Cathedral (England) in May of 1865. Some sources indicate its next appearance was in the second edition (1865) of Plumptre's *Lazarus and Other Poems*. Others indicate it was in the third edition (1868). Its first inclusion in a hymnal was in the Appendix to the 1868 edition of *Hymns Ancient and Modern*. There were 11 stanzas in the original version. The first Southern Baptist collection to include it was *New Baptist Hymnal* (Nashville, 1926, No. 47).

MARION, composed in 1883 with "Rejoice, Ye Pure in Heart" in mind, was the product of Arthur H. Messiter, the organist-choirmaster at New York's Trinity Episcopal Church. The tune, named for his mother, was published in the *Hymnal with Music As Used in Trinity Church* (New York, 1893).   *D.B.*

Rescue the perishing 559

Fanny Crosby gave a vivid account of the writing of "Rescue the Perishing" in 1869 after she had been addressing a gathering of working men on a hot summer evening. She was concerned that some mother's son in that meeting would have to be rescued from sin that night or not at all. After her pressing pleas to the men, a young man of 18 came forward to inquire if Fanny had him in mind. After extended prayer, he arose with a new light in his eye for he had "found God."

Mr. William H. Doane, Fanny's musical collaborator, a few days before this incident had suggested the subject, "Rescue the Perishing." After that meeting on that hot summer evening, Fanny went home thinking of nothing else than producing a hymn on that theme. Before retiring she already had in her mind the entire four stanzas and refrain which were written down the next day and sent to Mr. Doane.

RESCUE, the name given this tune in *Baptist Hymnal* (1956), was composed by W. H. Doane to the Fanny Crosby text "Rescue the Perishing" and first published in his *Songs of Devotion* (New York, 1870). The words and music are unaltered from their appearance in print.

Though "Rescue the Perishing" to RESCUE first appeared in a Southern Baptist collection in *The Baptist Hymn and Tune Book* (Nashville, 1904, No. 448), it was sung earlier by many Baptists who used W. H. Doane's collections, including *The Baptist Hymnal* (Philadelphia, 1883, No. 361). H.T.M.

Revive Us Again—See *We praise Thee, O God!*

Ring the bells of heaven! 428

"Ring the Bells of Heaven" was originally a secular song ("Glory! Glory! or the Little Octoroon") by George F. Root (1820-95). William Orcutt Cushing (1823-1902), the author of the text and a successful pastor in Christian churches in New York for more than 30 years, heard the song and remarked later in his *Story of a Musical Life*:

"The melody ran in my head all day long, chiming and flowing in its sweet musical ca-

dence. I wished greatly that I might secure the tune for use in Sunday School and for other Christian purposes. When I heard the bells of heaven ringing of some sinner that had returned, it seemed like a glad day. Then the word "Ring the Bells of Heaven" at once flowed down into the waiting melody" (Reynolds, 1976, 185).

The earliest appearance which William J. Reynolds found is in one of Root's popular collections, *Chapel Gems for Sunday School,* compiled by Root and B. R. Hanby (Chicago: Root & Cady, 1866). The first Southern Baptist hymnal to include the hymn was *Broadman Hymnal* (Nashville, 1940, No. 124), though Baptist Robert H. Coleman had included it in his hymnals as early as 1911.

RING THE BELLS was originally a secular song by George F. Root, and listed among his published sheet music as "Glory! Glory! or the Little Octoroon." The earliest appearance of the tune seems to be in a compilation by Root and B. R. Hanby, *Chapel Gems for Sunday School* (Chicago, 1866). The first Southern Baptist hymnal in which the tune appeared was *Broadman Hymnal* (Nashville, 1940, No. 124), but it is found in Coleman's *The New Evangel* (with J. F. Scholfield, Louisville, 1911, No. 86).   S.W.G.

Rise up, O men of God! 400

William Pierson Merrill wrote this hymn for the Brotherhood Movement within the Presbyterian Church and therefore is not intended to be inclusive of both sexes. The initial suggestion for the text came from Nolan R. Best, editor of the *Continent*, and was reinforced by Merrill's reading an article by Gerald Stanley Lee entitled "The Church of the Strong Men" (1911). The words were written aboard a steamer on Lake Michigan as the author was returning to his pastorate in Chicago. The text was first published in the *Continent* (Feb. 16, 1911), and with music in *The Pilgrim Hymnal* (1912). Southern Baptists first included this hymn in *The Broadman Hymnal* (Nashville, 1940, No. 186). ST. THOMAS—See hymn 354, I love Thy kingdom, Lord.   *P.H.*

Rock of Ages, cleft for me 342
A single four-line stanza of this hymn by Augustus Toplady first appeared in the October, 1775, issue of *The Gospel Magazine* in an article entitled "Life—A Journey," signed "Minimus," a pseudonym used by Toplady. The complete four stanzas of the hymn were published in the March, 1776, issue of the same magazine, under the title "A Living and Dying Prayer for the Holiest Believer in the World," following an article by Toplady in which he discussed the impossibility of persons paying their indebtedness to God. The full text also appeared, with minor modifications, in Toplady's *Psalms and Hymns for Public and Private Worship* published in the same year.

Toplady's original four-stanza version has undergone several alterations, of which the most significant include the one which appeared in Cotterill's *Selection of Psalms and Hymns* (1815) and the version published in the 1830 *Supplement* to the *Wesleyan Hymn Book* (which was strongly influenced by Cotterill's changes). The version used in this hymnal combines Cotterill's 1815 version of the first stanza, a second stanza which juxtaposes the first two lines from Toplady's original second stanza with the last four lines from the second stanza appearing in the 1830 *Supplement*, and the final stanza from the latter collection.

This text was among those included in the first Southern Baptist hymnal, *The Baptist Psalmody* (Charleston, 1850, No. 208).

TOPLADY (also known as ROCK OF AGES) was written in 1830 by Thomas Hastings and was first published, under the tune name ROCK OF AGES, in *Spiritual Songs for Social Worship* (1832). The name was changed and the rhythm altered in Lowell Mason's *Sabbath Hymn and Tune Book* (1859).   *M.P.*

Room at the Cross—See *The cross upon which Jesus died*

Satisfied—See *All my life I had a longing*

Satisfied with Jesus—See *I am satisfied with Jesus*

Saved, Saved—See *I've found a friend who is all to me*

Savior, like a shepherd lead us 61
The authorship of this hymn is uncertain, but it is usually attributed to Dorothy A. Thrupp. It was first published, without indication of authorship, in the fourth edition of *Hymns for the Young* (1836), compiled by Thrupp. In Carus Wilson's *Children's Friend* (1838) it was ascribed to "Lyte," but in the same year it appeared in Mrs. Herbert Mayo's *Selection of Hymns and Poetry for the use of Infant and Juvenile Schools*, again without an author being listed. Miss Thrupp contributed to this collection other hymns and poems which were signed "D. A. T." Because these initials do not appear with this hymn, its attribution to Thrupp is generally regarded as questionable. The first Southern Baptist hymnal to include this text and its tune (designated as SHEPHERD) was *Kingdom Songs* (Dallas, 1921, no. 271).

BRADBURY (also known as SHEPHERD) was composed by William B. Bradbury for use with this hymn. It was first published in the 1859 edition of his *Oriola*, a Sunday School collection.   *M.P.*

Savior, teach me day by day 461
This text was written by Jane E. Leeson

and was first published in her *Hymns and Scenes of Childhood, or A Sponsor's Gift* (London, 1842) under the title "Obedience." The recurring line "Loving Him who first loved me" is based upon 1 John 4:19. The original poem consisted of four stanzas of eight lines each. The four four-line stanzas used in this hymnal include the first half of stanzas 1 and 2 and the last half of stanzas 3 and 4 from the original version. The first Southern Baptist hymnals to include this text and the POSEN tune were the *New Baptist Hymnal* (Nashville, 1926, No. 196) and the *Modern Hymnal* (Dallas, 1926, No. 65). In the *New Baptist Hymnal*, two stanzas of this text also appeared with the EMMELAR tune (No. 404).

POSEN was written by George C. Strattner. It was first published in the fifth edition of Joachim Neander's *Bundesleider* (Frankfurt, 1691), which Strattner edited.   *M.P.*

Savior, Thy dying love 607

This is the one hymn by which Baptist pastor Sylvanus Dryden Phelps wished to be remembered. In fact, he requested that "Author of the hymn 'Saviour, Thy Dying Love'" be placed on his gravestone where he is buried in New Haven, Connecticut.

The hymn was written in 1862 and sent to the editors of the *Watchman and Reflector* where it appeared unsigned in March, 1864. As first published, it appears in Reynolds' *Companion to Baptist Hymnal*, but the author recast it in its present form when fellow Baptist pastor Robert Lowry solicited it and others from him for inclusion in his and William H. Doane's collection, *Pure Gold*, published by Biglow and Main in 1871 (1976, 189).

Its heading there was: "Lord, What Wilt Thou Have Me Do?" (Acts 9:6).

The hymn is a prayerful meditation on the supreme sacrifice made by Christ for every individual, requiring a response of love

and fidelity. It has continued to be useful because the spiritual aspirations expressed are universally valid.

Its first appearance in a Southern Baptist collection was *The Baptist Hymn and Praise Book* (Nashville, 1904, No. 344).

SOMETHING FOR JESUS is the tune composed by Robert Lowry for "Savior, Thy dying love."   *H.T.M.*

Search me, O God 297

This hymn was written during an Easter Conference in Ngaruawahia, New Zealand, in 1936. It was a time of evangelistic fervor, and it inspired J. Edwin Orr to write the text and set it to the tune of a Maori native song that began "Now is the hour when we must say goodbye." The text was first published in *All Your Need* (London, 1936). For *The Baptist Hymnal* (1991), several alterations were made. Some are minor in that they exchange "you" for "thee" and "your" for "thy." More extensive changes occur in the first two lines of stanza three which originally read:

Lord, take my life and make it wholly
    thine;
Fill my poor heart with thy great love
    divine.

Another change was made in the second line of stanza four which read:

Send a revival, start the work in me.

Baptist Hymnal (Nashville, 1975, No. 266) was the first Southern Baptist collection to include this hymn.

ELLERS was composed by Edward J. Hopkins and first used for "Savior, Again to Thy Dear Name." It appeared in the third edition (1869) of Brown-Borthwick's *Supplemental Hymn and Tune Book* as a unison setting with a different accompaniment for each stanza. Hopkins made the harmonization in *The Baptist Hymnal* (1991) from the *Appendix to the Bradford Tune Book* (1872).

Some hymnals use a slightly different harmonization which Arthur S. Sullivan prepared for *Church Hymns* (1874). *D.B.*

See, to us a Child is born 104

This Christmas hymn, based on Isaiah 9:6, 7, was written in 1982 by Timothy Dudley-Smith. It was first published in 1983 with the tune INNOCENTS as suggested by the author. He relates in his book (*Lift Every Heart*, Carol Stream, 1984, p. 253) that the hymn is antiphonal in form and suggests alternating verses within each stanza between choir (or solo) and congregation. *The Baptist Hymnal* (1991) is the first Southern Baptist hymnal that has included this hymn.

INNOCENTS first appeared in *The Parish Choir* (November, 1850), an Anglican periodical of the Society for Promoting Church Music, which was for a time edited by William H. Monk. Speculations as to the source of this tune have ranged from Handel's opera *Siroe* to "Venetian Air" arranged in 1838 by Samuel Webbe, Jr., and finally to an unpublished song by Joseph Smith entitled "The Sun." None of these are defensible, thus William H. Monk is generally given credit for arranging the tune. *P.H.*

Seek ye first 478

This chorus by Karen Lafferty was born of a decision she made in 1971 to "seek first the Kingdom of God" rather than her personal career goals. She had been an entertainer in restaurants and hotel lounges, where she had a platform to be a witness. The call in 1971, however, was one to channel her efforts into ministry. She quit her job and began to teach guitar lessons. The lack of income led her to doubt the wisdom of her action. When she attended a Bible study at her home church, Calvary Chapel, Costa Mesa, California, the words of Matthew 6:33 became real to her. That night she composed the chorus that has become known world-wide. She has developed a missionary outreach through music in The Netherlands. This chorus makes its first appearance in a Southern Baptist collection in *The Baptist Hymnal* (1991).

LAFFERTY is the tune named for the composer of "Seek Ye First." *P.H.*

Send a Great Revival—See *Coming now to Thee*

Send a revival, O Christ, my Lord 468

"Lord, Send a Revival" was written by B. B. McKinney in 1927 and first published in Robert H. Coleman's *Evangel Bells* (Dallas, 1927, No. 1). It did not appear in a Southern Baptist publication until *Baptist Hymnal* (Nashville, 1956, No. 333).

MATTHEWS, the name given "Lord, Send a Revival" by the committee for *Baptist Hymnal* (1956), is in reference to Dr. Charles E. Matthews. Dr. Matthews was secretary of the Department of Evangelism of the Southern Baptist Home Mission Board (1947-56) and pastor of the Travis Avenue Baptist Church, Ft. Worth, Texas (1923-47). During part of that time, B. B. McKinney served the church as music director. *H.T.M.*

Send forth Your Word, O God 588

The first three stanzas of this text were written by Milburn Price for the Commissioning Service held by the Foreign Mission Board of the Southern Baptist Convention in Lexington, Kentucky, in April 1987. The text was written at the invitation of William B. Williams, minister of music at Immanuel Baptist Church in Lexington, who coordinated the music for that service. The fourth stanza was added in 1989 when the text was being considered for inclusion in *The Baptist Hymnal* (1991).

PROCLAMATION was composed by Price as

a setting for this text for its use in the Foreign Mission Board Commissioning Service. *M.P.*

Send Me, O Lord, Send Me—See *O God of might, O Son of light*

Send the Light—See *There's a call comes ringing*

"Serve the Lord with gladness" 495

B. B. McKinney, the author and composer of "Serve the Lord with Gladness," told how he came to write the song in the summer of 1930. He had been asked by the Convention-wide leader of preadolescent training among Southern Baptists to write a song based on Psalm 100 to go with their theme for the year. After McKinney read the psalm while on a train journeying to New Orleans, the text and tune came to him in moments of quick inspiration, and upon reaching his destination, he completed the song. The account of the experience in McKinney's own words may be found in Reynolds' *Companion to Baptist Hymnal* (Nashville, 1976, pp. 190-91).

"Serve the Lord with Gladness" was first published by Robert H. Coleman in *Service Songs* (Dallas, 1931, No. 2). Its first appearance in a Southern Baptist collection was *The Broadman Hymnal* (Nashville, 1940, No. 347).

LEE is the name given B. B. McKinney's tune for "Serve the Lord with Gladness" by the committee for *Baptist Hymnal* (1956). It is named for Miss Mary Virginia Lee, Southern Baptist Convention-wide leader of work with intermediate-age young people. She had requested the song from McKinney. *H.T.M.*

Set my soul afire 573

Gene Bartlett wrote the text of this hymn in 1964 during a sermon preached by Robert

S. Scales at the Trinity Baptist Church, Oklahoma City, Oklahoma. The sermon was titled "The Fire That Cannot Be Quenched." In 1965, the Capital Baptist Association in Oklahoma City requested a theme song for a series of revivals. Bartlett then wrote the tune and named it SCALES for his pastor (Reynolds, 1976, 191). This text has been translated into Spanish and Portuguese. *Baptist Hymnal* (Nashville, 1975, No. 302) was the first Southern Baptist collection to contain this hymn and tune. *P.H.*

Shall we gather at the river 518

Robert Lowry, a prominent Baptist minister, wrote the text and tune of this hymn. It was first published in *Happy Voices* (New York, 1865), a Sunday School collection compiled by Lowry and William H. Doane. Not many years afterward, Samuel Duffield claimed the hymn "is now familiar to all Sunday School children throughout the world" (113).

Reynolds relates Lowry's account of the writing of the hymn:

"One afternoon in July, 1864, when I was pastor at Hanson Place Baptist Church, Brooklyn, the weather was oppressively hot, and I was lying on a lounge in a state of physical exhaustion. I was almost incapable of bodily exertion, and my imagination began to take to itself wings. Visions of the future passed before me with startling vividness. The imagery of the apocalypse took the form of a tableau. Brightest of all were the throne, the heavenly river, and the gathering of the saints. My soul seemed to take new life from that celestial outlook. I began to wonder why the hymn writers had said so much about the 'river of death' and so little about the 'pure water of life, clear as crystal, proceeding out of the throne of God and of the Lamb.' As I mused the words began to construct themselves. They came first as a question of Christian inquiry, 'Shall we gather?' Then they broke out in a chorus, as an answer of Christian faith, 'Yes, we'll gather.' On this question and answer the hymn developed itself. The music came with the hymn" (1964, 176).

Aaron Copland's arrangement for solo voice (*Old American Songs*, Second Set, 1954) has brought the hymn to the attention of serious vocal students and recital and concert audiences.

"Shall We Gather at the River" first appeared in a Southern Baptist collection in *The Baptist Hymn and Praise Book* (Nashville, 1904), No. 549.

HANSON PLACE was the name given this tune by the 1956 *Baptist Hymnal* committee in recognition of the church Lowry was serving when he wrote text and tune. *D.B.*

Share His Love—See *The love of God is broader*

Shine, Jesus, Shine—See *Lord, the light of Your love is shining*

Silent night, holy night 91

The story of this familiar Christmas carol began on Christmas Eve in 1818, in the village of Oberndorf in Upper Austria. Sometime during the day Father Joseph Mohr, at St. Nicholas Church, discovered that the organ would not play. This was a major crisis, because the music of the Christmas service depended so much on the instrument. As a partial solution to this situation, he decided to compose a new song and substitute it for the music previously planned. Father Mohr wrote out some lines which began "Stille nacht, heilige nacht," and asked his organist friend Franz Gruber to write the music. The completed song was sung for the first time at the Christmas Eve service as the two men sang the song accompanied by Gruber playing the guitar.

Later, Karl Mauracher came to Oberndorf to repair the organ. Father Mohr sang the song for him and told him of the Christmas Eve service. In the months that followed, Mauracher told others of the song as he traveled around servicing organs. A family of glovemakers, the Strassers, discovered "Stille nacht, heilige nacht," as they worked various fairs displaying their beautiful gloves. The Strasser family was a singing group, and they sang the song at the Leipzig fair in 1831. From Leipzig the song traveled in every direction. In a Catholic hymnal published in Leipzig in 1838, the song appeared in print for the first time—20 years after that "organless" Christmas Eve service at Oberndorf.

German-speaking immigrants brought the song to America, and the first English version appeared in an 1849 hymnal published for Methodists in America. Nine years later an English translation was published in England. The most popular translation in America is that made by John Freeman Young, and in the present version stanzas 1 and 3 are by Young, and stanzas 2 and 4 are anonymous.

Robert H. Coleman's *The Popular Hymnal* (Dallas, 1918, No. 318) was the first unofficial Southern Baptist collection to contain "Silent Night" (though having considerable variation in text from the present version).

STILLE NACHT is the German tune name for "silent night." *W.J.R.*

Simply trusting every day 417

This text was written about 1876 by Edgar Page Stites.

TRUSTING JESUS was composed for these words in 1876 by Ira D. Sankey. Dwight L. Moody had been given a newspaper clipping containing the text and asked Sankey to set it. The tune name is the common title of the song, which was first published in

Gospel Hymns, No. 2 (New York and Cincinnati, 1876). There the text was attributed to Edgar Page.

The first Southern Baptist hymnal to include this gospel song was *The Baptist Hymn and Praise Book* (Nashville, 1904, No. 257). P.A.R.

Since I Have Been Redeemed—See *I have a song I love to sing*

Since Jesus Came into My Heart—See *What a wonderful change*

Sing hallelujah to the Lord 214
This praise song was composed by Linda Stassen Benjamin in July 1974. It was written as an assignment in a class for artists and musicians held at Calvary Chapel in Costa Mesa, California, and taught to a congregation the following week. Soon thereafter it was recorded by the composer for Maranatha! Music. Its first publication was in *Praise* (Laguna Hills, 1975). It has since been printed in many other countries.

STASSEN is the composer's maiden name, which was her surname at the time this piece was written. The tune is also known as SING ALLELUIA.

The first appearance of this song in a hymnal compiled for Southern Baptists is in *The Baptist Hymnal* (1991). P.A.R.

Sing Hosannas—See *Hark to the story the angels are telling*

Sing praise to God who reigns above 20
This German hymn of Johann Jakob Schütz, "Sei Lob und Ehr dem höchsten Gut," was first published in his *Christliches Gedenkbüchlein* (Frankfurt-am-Main, 1675). Originally in nine stanzas, it is based on Deuteronomy 32:3. Frances E. Cox's trans-

lation in eight stanzas was published in *Lyra Eucharistica* (2nd ed., 1864) and in her collection, *Hymns from the German* (London, 1864). The earliest publication of this translation in America was in *Hymnbook for the Use of Evangelical Lutheran Schools and Congregations* (Decorah, 1879). *Baptist Hymnal* (Nashville, 1956, No. 22) was the first Southern Baptist collection to include the hymn.

The tune MIT FREUDEN ZART is from the Bohemian Brethren *Kirchengeseng* (1566). A version prior to that of the Bohemian Brethren hymnal is found in the French metrical Psalm 138, "Il faut que de tous mes esprits," in the edition of the *Genevan Psalter, Trente quatre pseaumes de David* (Geneva, 1551). Walter Blankenburg, in *Protestant Church Music: A History* (London, 1975, p. 598), regarded this tune as having originated in the late Middle Ages. H.E.

Sing the wondrous love of Jesus 514
The author, Eliza E. Hewitt, and the composer, Emily D. Wilson, regularly attended the Methodist camp meetings at Ocean Grove, New Jersey, and, apparently, their collaboration in writing this hymn resulted from this mutual interest. The hymn first appeared in *Pentecostal Praises*, compiled by William J. Kirkpatrick and Henry L. Gilmour (Philadelphia, 1898, No. 148).

HEAVEN is the name given the tune in *Baptist Hymnal* (1956). The first appearance for Southern Baptists was in Robert H. Coleman's *Hosannas* (Dallas, 1923, No. 70). W.J.R.

Sing them over again to me 261
Philip P. Bliss wrote both words and music for this song, first published in *Words of Life* (1874), the first issue of a Sunday School paper published in New York by Fleming H. Revell. It was later published in *Gospel Hymns No. 3* (1878). Its first inclusion in a Baptist compilation was not until 1904,

when it appeared in two hymnals: *Glorious Praise* by W. H. Doane and W. J. Kirkpatrick (Louisville) and *The Baptist Hymn and Praise Book* by Lansing Burrows (Nashville). George C. Stebbins, in his *Memoirs and Reminiscences* (New York, 1924, pp.91-92), tells of using Bliss' hymn in an evangelistic meeting with Dr. George F. Pentecost in New Haven, Connecticut, in 1878. Two years earlier Mr. Revell had given Stebbins a copy of the Sunday School paper that contained this hymn.

Stebbins had kept it through two seasons of evangelistic work, not thinking it possessed merit, particularly for solo use. During a campaign in New Haven, he decided to sing it as a duet with his wife. It was received with great enthusiasm and from then on became a great favorite with the people.

The song first appeared in a Southern Baptist collection in *The Baptist Hymn and Praise Book* (Nashville, 1904, No. 202).

WORDS OF LIFE is the name assigned to this tune based on the recurring theme.   *H.T.M.*

Sing to the Lord of harvest 641

John S. B. Monsell published this hymn in the second edition of his *Hymns of Love and Praise* (London, 1866). The present version uses the first and third of the original four eight-line stanzas, dividing each and adding the word "O" in the middle of the second stanza. It also has "Bring to" for "Heap on" at the beginning of stanza three and "you" for "ye" in the second phrase of the final stanza.

JEWELL was written by Paul Yeary to set this text for *The Baptist Hymnal* (1991).

Baptist Hymnal (Nashville, 1975, No. 232) was the first Southern Baptist Hymnal for general congregational use to include Monsell's text. It had appeared earlier in *The Junior Hymnal* (Nashville, 1964, No. 215). In both collections, it was set to NORTHAVEN, a tune derived by Jane Marshall from her uni-

son anthem, which was published in the September 1960 issue of *The Church Musician*.   *P.A.R.*

Sing we now of Christmas 111

This translation/adaptation of the French Christmas carol "Noel nouvelet" first appeared in *Christmas Carols from Many Countries* (New York, 1934), which contained carols arranged for unchanged voices by Satis N. Coleman and Elin K. Jorgensen. Both the title page and foreword to that collection indicated that many of the carols had been "newly translated," and "Sing We Now of Christmas" was listed in the index under the heading, "New Translations of Old French Carols." However, it was not specified whether the translations had been made by the compiler/arrangers or by someone else. The structure of the text in its English translation differs from that of the original French text, which consisted of six three-line stanzas, each followed by a one-line refrain. The final stanza of the French carol was not translated.

The United Methodist Hymnal (1989) was the first hymnal to include this English translation, with a few alterations to accommodate the text to a more regular metrical structure for hymnal usage. For example, the first line of stanza five was revised from "Then they offered gold and myrrh" to "Gold and myrrh they took there." The English text appears for the first time in a Southern Baptist hymnal in *The Baptist Hymnal* (1991).

FRENCH CAROL is the name given to the tune which has been associated with the traditional French carol "Noel nouvelet." The melody was used by Marcel Dupré as the principal theme for *Variations on a Noel* (Opus 20, 1922). The harmonization for *The Baptist Hymnal* (1991) was provided by Mark Blankenship.   *M.P.*

(A substantial portion of this article is

based upon information provided to the author by Carlton R. Young.)

Sing, Congregation, Sing—See *With boldness in your speech*

Sinners Jesus will receive 563

"Jesus nimmt die Sünder an!/Saget doch dies Troswort allen" is the original German text by Lutheran pastor Erdmann Neumeister. This hymn was written as the conclusion to his sermon on Luke 15:1-7 and was first published in Neumeister's *Evangelischer Nachklang* (1718). Originally a text of eight six-line stanzas, the present version employs only the first four lines of each stanza. The chorus was excerpted from stanza six. The English translation was made by Emma F. Bevan in her *Songs of Eternal Life* (1858). Tune composer James McGranahan adapted the stanzas in their present form from Bevan's translation.

The first stanza appears in the *Lutheran Book of Worship* (1978) in this version:

Jesus sinners will receive;
  May they all this saying ponder
Who in sin's delusions live
  And from God and heaven wander!
Here is hope for all who grieve:
Jesus sinners will receive.

The first appearance of this text with its NEUMEISTER tune in a Southern Baptist collection was in *Songs of Redemption* (Atlanta, 1920, No. 106), although it had appeared over a decade earlier in Robert Coleman's first collection, with W. W. Hamilton, *The Evangel* (Philadelphia, 1909, No. 81).

NEUMEISTER was composed by James McGranahan for male voices, a medium which he pioneered in 19th-century evangelism. The male voicing was first published in *The Gospel Male Choir, No. 2* (1883) and in the same year for mixed voices in *The Gospel Choir*, edited by Ira D. Sankey and McGranahan. The tune name was first used in the *Mennonite Hymnary* (1940).   *P.H.*

So precious is Jesus, my Savior 452

This hymn by Charles H. Gabriel was first published in his *Joyful Praise* (Chicago, 1902, No. 2). The first stanza originally read:

I'm happy in Jesus, my Saviour, my King,
  And all the day long of His goodness
  I sing,
To Him in my weakness I lovingly cling,
  For He is so precious to me.

E. O. Excell, who purchased the hymn from Gabriel in 1907, was probably responsible for the alteration of this stanza to its present form.

The tune was named PRECIOUS TO ME in *Baptist Hymnal* (1956).

The hymn and tune made their first appearance in a Southern Baptist collection in I. E. Reynolds and Robert H. Coleman's compilation, *Kingdom Songs* (Nashville, 1921, No. 114).   *D.M.*

So send I you 565

Under the title "So send I you," E. Margaret Clarkson wrote a five-stanza hymn in the winter months of 1938 which was published in 1939 in a Canadian magazine, *The Evangelical Christian*. Its first stanza reads:

So send I you to labor unrewarded,
  To serve unpaid, unloved, unsought, unknown,
To bear rebuke, to suffer scorn and scoffing—
So send I you to toil for me alone.

Miss Clarkson has given the following account of this hymn and its successor:

"I was reading in John's Gospel one cold night in February, 1938, in the mining town of Kirkland Lake where I was teaching, when suddenly the words of John 20:21 leaped from the page—'As the Father has sent me, even so send I you.' As I pondered on their significance, God seemed to speak to me. I had long known that because of a physical disability I could never go to the mission field, but that night God seemed to say to me that this lonely spot was where he had put me—my mission field. I had written verse all my life so it was natural for me to respond in the words of a poem; I wrote the first version of "So Send I You" that evening....

"As I grew in knowledge of the Scriptures, I came to realize that this text, written when I was only 22, was really very one-sided: it told only of the difficulties and privations of the missionary call, and none of its triumph and glory.... In 1962, while on vacation at the Severn River, I wrote a second text. This set forth the true teaching of the Word of God on our Lord's missionary call, showing its sorrows but also showing its triumph and joy. I used the same rhythm so that the stanzas of the two texts can be used interchangeably. It was published by Singspiration Music in 1963 to a second tune by John Peterson.

"While the original song is still widely sung, I am happy to see that many of the newer hymnals are dropping that text in favor of the newer one, which undoubtedly is the more biblical hymn. I wish above all to be a biblical writer" (Clarkson, 153).

John W. Peterson has related how he came to compose the tune TORONTO:

"In the summer of 1954, I was on the staff of Moody Bible Institute radio station, WM-BI, in Chicago. One of the girls in the office handed me a poem one day that had impressed her. She thought I could possibly read it on one of the programs I conducted called, 'The Shut-In Hour.' The poem was 'So Send I You.'

"I did use it and was deeply moved by the verses, so much so, that I tucked them away in my briefcase that I would be carrying to Kansas a few weeks later for a summer vacation. One morning during my vacation in Wichita, Kansas, while improvising at the piano at the home of my mother, with the lines of this poem before me, the melody came.... Somehow I sensed in my heart that God was going to use this song. It was first published in *Low Voice*, one of a group of books called 'Melody-Aire Series' that I produced for Moody Press in 1954" (Reynolds, 1975, 197).

The tune name TORONTO was given to Peterson's tune in *Baptist Hymnal* (1975), which was its first appearance in a Southern Baptist collection (No. 280).

Miss Clarkson's second hymn has been used by the InterVarsity Christian Fellowship in its Urbana conferences. The committee for *Baptist Hymnal* (1975) compared the latter stanzas with the original ones and chose the 1963 version.   *H.E.*

Softly and tenderly 312

The words and music of this gospel song were written by Will L. Thompson. According to George Swetnam (*The Pittsburgh Press*, Jan. 31, 1943), it is based on a prayer which the author heard. Its first publication was in *Sparkling Gems, Nos. 1 and 2 Combined* (Chicago, 1880), edited by J. Calvin Bushey (believed to be a pseudonym of Thompson's) and published by Thompson. Its popularity and usefulness in the revivals of the late 19th century is attested by a story connected with Dwight L. Moody. During his last illness, Moody is said to have told Thompson, "Will, I would rather have written 'Softly and tenderly Jesus is calling' than anything I have been able to do in my whole life."

THOMPSON was the name given to this tune in *Baptist Hymnal* (Nashville, 1956, No. 236). It was also known earlier as SOFTLY AND TENDERLY.

The first Southern Baptist book to include

this was *The Baptist Hymn and Praise Book* (Nashville, 1904, No. 184).   *P.A.R.*

Soldiers of Christ, in truth arrayed 574

This hymn by Basil Manly, Jr., was written at the request of James P. Boyce, chairman of the faculty, for the first commencement of The Southern Baptist Theological Seminary in 1860. Appearing in *The Baptist Hymnal* (1991) are stanzas 1, 4, 5, and 6 of Manly's original six-stanza hymn. The second and third stanzas, which have been omitted from all commencement programs since 1871, are:

> Forth to realms of darkness go,
> Where, like a river's ceaseless flow,
> A tide of souls is drifting down,
> Blasted beneath th' Almighty's frown.

> No human skill nor power can stay
> That flood upon its gloomy way;
> But God's own love devised the plan
> To save the ruined creature, man.

This "seminary hymn" entered an "official" Southern Baptist collection in *Baptist Hymnal* (Nashville, 1975, No. 315), although it had been published earlier in other books used by Baptists.

MENDON is the name of a village in Worcester County, Massachusetts. The name was applied early in the 19th century to the anonymous tune which in the hymn collections is variously designated as from the German, an old German melody and traditional German melody. The tune has had many arrangers, including Lowell Mason and Samuel Dyer. The arrangement in *The Baptist Hymnal* (1991) was made by Donald Winters who served on the first faculty of Southern Seminary's School of Church Music. (1945-51).   *H.T.M.*

Something for Thee—See *Savior, Thy dying love*

Songs of praise the angels sang 235

The first publication of this text by James Montgomery was in the eighth edition of Thomas Cotterill's *Selection* (1819), where it appeared in six stanzas of four lines each under the heading "God Worthy of All Praise." When it was published in Montgomery's *Christian Psalmist* in 1825, the heading was changed to "Glory to God in the Highest."

The earliest publication of this text in America, according to the *Dictionary of American Hymnology*, was in *Hymns Suited to the Feasts and Fasts of the Church* (1826). Its first appearance in a Southern Baptist collection was in *The Sacred Lute* (Charleston, 1855, No. 43). In *The Baptist Hymnal* (1991) stanza six of the original version is deleted, and the first two lines of stanza four differ from the original version, which read:

> And shall men alone be dumb
> Till that glorious kingdom come?

MONKLAND is an arrangement made by John Bernard Wilkes of a tune known as FAHRE FORT which came from J. A. Freylinghausen's *Geistreiches Gesangbuch* (1704). It passed into English popular use through the Moravian communities. However, the real origin of the tune is to be found in the Scandinavian song collection, *Piae Cantiones* (1582). The Moravian collection, *Hymn Tunes of the United Brethren* (Manchester, 1824) was the source from which Wilkes organist at Monkland, arranged the tune for the original music edition of *Hymns Ancient and Modern* (1861).   *M.P., H.T.M.*

Soon and very soon 192

This gospel song was written in 1976 by Andraé Crouch. The first stanza draws from the repeated "I am coming soon" phrases of the twenty-second chapter of Revelation, while the second and third stanzas echo the promises of Revelation 21:4. The first stanza is often repeated after the third.

The tune, SOON AND VERY SOON, is also known as VERY SOON. The present arrangement was made in 1987 by William Farley Smith (see separate entry) for *The United Methodist Hymnal* (Nashville, 1989). It omits one section of the original solo.

The Baptist Hymnal (1991) is the first Southern Baptist collection to include this. *P.A.R.*

Sound aloud the trumpet! 171

This hymn was written in 1979 by Janie Alford. It was the Easter text in a set of *Nine Hymns for the Church Year* prepared for her congregation, Westminster Presbyterian Church in Nashville, Tennessee, and added as a supplement to their hymnal. In the original, the "Alleluias" in stanzas one and four and the "anthems" in stanza one were plural.

MARTHA'S SONG was composed for this text by Hal H. Hopson, who was, at that time, director of music at Westminster Presbyterian Church and Alford's collaborator and encourager. The tune originally was named MILLER, but it was renamed for the composer's wife because it was a favorite of hers.

The first major hymnal to include this is *The Baptist Hymnal* (1991). *P.A.R.*

Speak to my heart 281

"Speak to My Heart" was written by B. B. McKinney in 1927 and first published in Robert H. Coleman's *Evangel Bells* (Dallas, 1927, No. 12). Its first appearance in a Southern Baptist collection was in *The Broadman Hymnal* (Nashville, 1940, No. 415). A simple prayer hymn, it has achieved wide usage.

HOLCOMB is the name given by the committee for *Baptist Hymnal* (1956) to B. B. McKinney's tune for "Speak to My Heart." It honors Dr. T. L. Holcomb who was Executive Secretary-Treasurer of the Baptist Sunday School Board (1935-53) and the one responsible for McKinney's coming to the Board as its first music editor. *H.T.M.*

Spirit of God, descend upon my heart 245

This hymn, which was inspired by Galatians 5:25, was first published in Charles Rogers' *Lyra Brittanica* (London, 1869). The hymn was attributed to George Croly. Of the original five stanzas, *The Baptist Hymnal* (1991) omits stanza four:

> Hast Thou not bid me love Thee, God
> and King?
> All, all Thine own, soul, heart and
> strength and mind
> I see Thy cross; there teach my heart
> to cling:
> O let me seek Thee, and O let me find!

The first inclusion in an American hymnal appears to have been in Prime's *Songs of the Soul, Gathered Out of Many Lands* (New York, 1880). *New Baptist Hymnal* (Nashville, 1926, No. 150) is the first Southern Baptist collection to include the hymn.

MORECAMBE, originally designated HELLESPONT, was published in 1870 in leaflet form as a tune for "Abide with Me." Frederick Cook Atkinson wrote the tune for use at St. Luke's Church in Bradford, England, where he served as organist. Its first appearance in a collection was in *Congregational Church Hymnal* (London, 1887), compiled by G. S. Barrett and E. J. Hopkins. *D.B.*

Spirit of the living God 244

Daniel Iverson wrote both words and music. During January and February of 1926, the George T. Stephens Evangelistic Party conducted a citywide revival in a tabernacle in Orlando, Florida. Iverson, a Presbyterian minister from Lumberton, North Carolina, spent several days in Orlando visiting with the Stephens team. The day he arrived, he was greatly impressed by a message on the Holy Spirit given by Dr. William Barron, a physician from Columbia, South Carolina.

Later that day Iverson went to the First Presbyterian Church in Orlando, sat down at a piano, and wrote the song. Miss Birdie Loes, the pianist for the Stephens team, wrote out a manuscript copy. E. Powell Lee, the team song leader, taught the song to the people in the tabernacle that evening and used it throughout the campaign. Printed in single sheets, the song was distributed privately in revivals and church services.

Without Iverson's knowledge and without his name, the song appeared in Robert H. Coleman's *Revival Songs* (Dallas, 1929, No. 92) with the notation "Arr. E. L. Wolslagel." In this version, the original melody had been changed by repeating measures 1-2 in measures 5-6. In B. B. McKinney's *Songs of Victory* (Nashville, 1937, No. 79), the song was titled "Fall Fresh on Me," without Iverson's or Wolslagel's name, and with the notation "Arr. B. B. McKinney." Here the melody is the same as Wolslagel's version, with slight changes in part writing and harmonic structure. McKinney's version was included in his *Broadman Hymnal* (Nashville, 1940, No. 329), and in the first printings of *Baptist Hymnal* (Nashville, 1956, No. 523).

In the early 1960s, E. Powell Lee brought this entire matter to the attention of the Church Music Department's music editor, W. J. Reynolds, and contact was made with Iverson. In subsequent printings of the 1956 hymnal, Iverson was credited with both words and music. However, since by this time the melody was so well known in the present version, it did not seem wise to restore Iverson's original melody, even though

it has a stronger melodic line.

IVERSON is the name given the tune in *Baptist Hymnal* (1975). *W.J.R.*

Spirit, Now Live in Me—See *O holy Dove of God descending*

Stand up and bless the Lord 30

This hymn text was written by James Montgomery for the Red Hill Wesleyan Sunday School anniversary, Sheffield, England, on March 15, 1824. The first two stanzas are based upon Nehemiah 9:5. The second line of the original version read "Ye children of His choice," but Montgomery changed "children" to "people" for the hymn's publication in the *Christian Psalmist* (1825). It was first published in the United States in 1831, when it appeared in two collections, *A Selection of Hymns, adapted to the Devotions of the Closet, the Family, and the Social Circle* (New York), compiled by Alexander Archibald, and *Church Psalmody* (Boston). Its first appearance in a Southern Baptist hymnal was in *New Baptist Hymnal* (Nashville, 1926, No. 28).

OLD 134TH (also called ST. MICHAEL) originated as a tune used to set Psalm 101 in the 1551 *Genevan Psalter*. It was adapted to short meter as a setting for Psalm 134 in the 1561 *Anglo-Genevan Psalter*, which accounts for its currently used tune name. It disappeared from common usage for an extended period of time, but was published in its present form in William Crotch's *Psalm Tunes* (London, 1836), where it was given the name ST. MICHAEL. The tune made its first appearance in a Southern Baptist collection in *Baptist Hymnal* (Nashville, 1956, No. 16). *M.P.*

Stand up, stand up for Jesus 485, 487

Written by George Duffield, Jr., in 1858, the text of this hymn was inspired in part by a sermon preached by Reverend Dudley

A. Tyng and by Tyng's untimely death a short time later. Tyng's sermon, delivered before an audience of 5,000 men in Jayne's Hall, Philadelphia, on March 30, 1858, was based on Exodus 10:11, "Go now ye that are men, and serve the Lord."

Several days later, Tyng was fatally injured when the sleeve of his study gown caught in the cogs of a machine; death came in a matter of hours. Tyng's dying words were an exhortation for the members of the Young Men's Christian Association before whom he had preached on that day earlier to "stand up for Jesus!"

On the following Sunday, Duffield preached a sermon from Ephesians 6:14, at the conclusion of which he read the text of his new hymn, "Stand Up, Stand Up for Jesus." The hymn originally consisted of six stanzas and contained allusions not only to Tyng's dying exhortation and to the scriptural bases for the sermons of both Tyng and Duffield, but also—in an omitted stanza—to the void caused by the death of his friend:

Stand up, stand up for Jesus,
    Each soldier to his post;
Close up the broken column,
    And shout through all the host;
Make good the loss so heavy,
    In those that still remain,
And prove to all around you,
    That death itself is gain.

The text was first printed in a *Supplement to The Church Psalmist* (Philadelphia, 1843. The Supplement was apparently issued in 1858).

The tune WEBB was initially a setting of a secular text, " 'Tis Dawn, the Lark Is Singing," composed by George J. Webb during a voyage from England to America. The song was first published in Webb and Lowell Mason's *The Odeon* (1837). Five years later the melody made its first known appearance as a hymn tune in Moses L. Scudder's

The Wesleyan Psalmist (1842) as a setting for Samuel F. Smith's "The Morning Light Is Breaking." Until 1850 it was known as GOODWIN. The association of WEBB with Duffield's text seems to date from William B. Bradbury's *Golden Chain* (New York, 1861).

The four stanzas of this hymn without the tune is first found in an official Southern Baptist collection in *Kind Words* (Memphis, 1871, p. 81) compiled by G. W. Linton and Howard M. Teasdale. In this earliest appearance there are two instances of variation from the present version:

Stanza 2e "Ye are the men, now serve
    him," and
Stanza 3f "And, watching unto prayer."

The first three stanzas first appeared with the WEBB tune in a Southern Baptist book in *The Baptist Hymn and Praise Book* edited by Lansing Burroughs (Nashville, 1904, No. 445).

GEIBEL, by Adam Geibel, was composed for Duffield's text and published in his *Uplift Voices* (New York, 1901, No. 18). The first known Southern Baptist hymnal inclusion of GEIBEL was in *New Baptist Hymnal* (Nashville, 1926, No. 365). *D.M.*

Standing on the promises 335

R. Kelso Carter wrote both the words and music of this gospel song which first appeared in Carter and John L. Sweney's *Songs of Perfect Love* (Philadelphia, 1886, No. 120). The text originally contained five stanzas (Reynolds, 1976, 202). The tune was given the name PROMISES in *Baptist Hymnal* 1956.

The first appearance of this text and tune in a Southern Baptist collection was in Robert Coleman's *The Popular Hymnal* (Dallas, 1918, No. 203). *D.M.*

Stir Your church, O God, our Father 392

The original version of this hymn was

written in July, 1970, by Milburn Price and submitted to the Church Music Department of the Sunday School Board in response to a search for new hymn texts. It was subsequently published in a pamphlet entitled "New Hymns for This Day" (Nashville, 1971) and included in the 1975 *Baptist Hymnal*. The version which appears in *The Baptist Hymnal* (1991) was revised by the author to provide inclusive language for persons and to substitute "you-your" pronouns for "thee-thou" language. The latter issue necessitated rewriting portions of the following lines: line 6 of stanza 1; lines 6 and 8 of stanza 2; and line 4 of stanza 3.

Church Music Department personnel of the Baptist Sunday School Board selected a tune by A. L. Butler as their choice to fit the text. Butler named the tune MADILL for the Oklahoma town where he had served as minister of music at the First Baptist Church (Reynolds, 1976, 202).   *M.P.*

Sunlight—See *I wandered in the shades of night*

Sunshine in My Soul—See *There is sunshine in my soul*

Surely Goodness and Mercy—See *A pilgrim was I*

Sweet hour of prayer 445

When the four stanzas of this hymn were first published in *The New York Observer* on September 13, 1845, there was an accompanying account of its origin in which Rev. Thomas Salmon (1800-54) attributed its authorship to a blind preacher named W. W. Walford. Salmon had come to the United States in 1842 following a four-year pastorate at Coleshill, Warwickshire, England, where he supposedly had known Walford and became acquainted with the poem. Re-

search by William J. Reynolds found no record of anyone by the name of Walford living in Coleshill at that time. Joseph F. Green, Jr., has suggested that the author could have been William Walford on the basis of similarities in content between Walford's book, *The Manner of Prayer* (1836), and the hymn. The earliest appearance of this text in a hymnal, according to the *Dictionary of American Hymnology* index, was in 1849, in the Baptist collection *Conference Hymns, A New Collection of Hymns, designed especially for use in Conference and Prayer Meetings and Family Worship* (New York), compiled by Dowling. (For more detailed information concerning attempts to discern authorship of this hymn, see William J. Reynolds, *Companion to Baptist Hymnal*, 1976, pp. 203-05.)

SWEET HOUR (also known as WALFORD) was composed for this text by William B. Bradbury. Concerning this tune, William J. Reynolds has written: "The earliest book to contain this tune that the writer has found is Bradbury's *Golden Chain* (New York, 1861, No. 10). Bradbury's *Cottage Melodies* (1859) is usually given as the source of this tune. While this tune does appear in later editions of this collection, it does not appear in the first edition in 1859. It seems to have been the common custom of such compilers as Bradbury, Mason, and Hastings to insert a particular tune that had been published in a new collection and begun to be popular into subsequent editions and printings of earlier collections with which the compilers were associated. Such practice has resulted in considerable confusion in accurately designating sources for many of these tunes" (1976, 205).

The first Southern Baptist hymnal to include this text and tune was *The Baptist Hymn and Praise Book* (Nashville, 1904, No. 28).   *M.P.*

Sweet, Sweet Spirit—See *There's a sweet, sweet spirit*

Sweetly, Lord, have we heard Thee calling 483

Mary Bridges Canedy Slade (1826-82), a native of Fall River, Massachusetts, the wife of a clergyman and for some time assistant editor of *The New England Journal of Education,* wrote this text in seven stanzas. The present version of her text consists of stanzas 1, 2, 3, and 7.

The hymn and tune seem to have first appeared in a Sunday School collection for the Methodist Episcopal Church, South, *The Amaranth,* compiled by Atticus G. Haygood and R. M. McIntosh (Nashville, 1871, No. 124). The hymn first appeared in a Southern Baptist hymnal in *The Broadman Hymnal* (Nashville, 1940, No. 228), although it is to be found in Baptist Robert H. Coleman's widely used hymn collection, *The Modern Hymnal* (Dallas, 1926, No. 397).

FOOTSTEPS was composed by Asa B. Everett, and it seems to have first appeared with the text "Sweetly, Lord, have we heard thee calling" in a Sunday School collection for the Methodist Episcopal Church, South, *The Amaranth,* compiled by Atticus G. Haygood and R. M. McIntosh (Nashville, 1871, No. 124). *The Broadman Hymnal* (Nashville, 1940, No. 228) was the first "official" Southern Baptist hymnal in which this tune appeared, although it appeared earlier in Robert Coleman's *The Modern Hymnal* (Dallas, 1926, No. 397).   *S.W.G.*

Take my life, and let it be 277, 283

Frances R. Havergal wrote this hymn on February 4, 1874. About the occasion she wrote: "There were ten persons in the house, some unconverted and long prayed for, some converted but not rejoicing Christians. He gave me the prayer, 'Lord, give me all in this house.'And He just did. Before I left the house everyone had got a blessing. The last night of my visit I was too happy to sleep, and passed most of the night in praise and renewal of my own consecration, and these little couplets formed themselves and chimed in my heart, one after another till they finished with 'Ever, only, all for thee'" (Reynolds, 1976, 206).

The poem appeared in Havergal's *Loyal Responses* (London, 1878) in twelve couplets headed, "Self-consecration to Christ." Ten aspects of self-commitment were listed between the introductory verse and the conclusion. The present version pairs the couplets in this way: 1 and 3, 4 and 5, 7 and 2, 9 and 10. Omitted are 6 (lips), 8 (intellect), 11 (love), and the climactic "ever, only, all for thee." The words of the refrain for the tune YARBROUGH are not by Havergal.

This text became popular within the year, being published in Charles B. Snepp's *Songs of Grace and Glory* (London) and Philip Phillips' *The Gospel Singer* (Philadelphia).

YARBROUGH has been attributed to William B. Bradbury, but there is no evidence for this. Its earliest publication seems to have been in *New Life* (Nashville, 1880) with the arrangement credited to Rigdon M. McIntosh, one of the book's compilers. The poet wrote a tune for her text called CONSECRATION, but it is said that the family preferred PATMOS, a tune composed by her father, William H. Havergal.

The first Southern Baptist collection to include this text was *The Baptist Hymn and Praise Book* (Nashville, 1904, No. 342). *P.A.R.*

HENDON was composed by Henri A. C. Malan. This tune is usually dated 1827 and probably received its first printing in one of Malan's collections of hymns, for which he generally wrote both the words and music. The first American publication of the tune was in Lowell Mason's *Carmina Sacra* (1841).

The harmonization that appears in *the Baptist Hymnal* (1991) was Mason's work. The first publication of the tune in a Southern Baptist collection was apparently in *New Baptist Hymnal* (Nashville, 1926, Nos. 129, 327). *D.M.*

Take my life, lead me, Lord 287

Maines Rawls wrote both words and music in 1968. During a plane flight from Nashville to Dallas for an engagement he wrote this song, which was first published in *Songs for Fun and Fellowship No. 3* (Nashville, 1969). The tune is named LANGLEY after the writer's father, Langley A. Rawls (1882-1979), a Baptist pastor in Florida and Georgia for 65 years. This hymn was included in *Baptist Hymnal* (1975, No. 366). *H.E.*

Take the name of Jesus with you 576

This is another enduring gospel song whose first appearance was in William H. Doane's and Robert Lowry's *Pure Gold* (New York, 1871). Lydia Baxter wrote the text in 1870. Doane supplied the tune PRECIOUS NAME (Reynolds, 1976, 207ff). This hymn first appeared in a Southern Baptist collection in *The Baptist Hymn and Praise Book* (Nashville, 1904, No. 422). *D.B.*

Take time to be holy 446

A wealthy English ship owner, William D. Longstaff, wrote the hymn about 1882, after hearing a sermon preached from the text "Be ye holy; for I am holy" (1 Peter 1:16). The speaker told of Griffith John, a missionary to China, and quoted a statement the missionary had made at a conference in China, "Take time and be holy." Longstaff gave the hymn text to Ira D. Sankey, and Sankey passed it on to George C. Stebbins to provide a musical setting. The hymn first appeared in William H. Doane's *Sunny Side Songs for the Sunday School* (New York, 1883).

The Baptist Hymn and Praise Book (Nashville, 1904, No. 396) was the first Southern Baptist collection to include the hymn.

HOLINESS was composed by George C. Stebbins while he was assisting in meetings and conferences in India. During the days there he discovered Longstaff's poem which he had forgotten among his papers. He composed the tune and mailed it to Ira D. Sankey in New York. The text and tune were first published in Sankey's *Winnowed Songs for Sunday School* (1891, No. 40), and the following year appeared in *Gospel Hymns No. 6* (New York, 1890, No. 35), which guaranteed its wide circulation. According to the *Dictionary of American Hymnology*, the text first appeared in *The Baptist Hymn and Praise Book* (Nashville, 1904, No. 396). *W.J.R.*

Take up thy cross and follow Me 285

"Wherever He Leads I'll Go" was written by B. B. McKinney in January 1936 in Clanton, Alabama. The occasion was a sectional meeting of the Alabama Baptist Sunday School Convention in which McKinney was leading the music and the featured speaker was long-time missionary to Brazil, Robert S. Jones. For reasons of health, Jones had come back to the States and a few days prior to the convention, had learned he would not be able to return to Brazil. Expressing heart-felt concern, McKinney inquired as to Jones' future plans. Jones' reply was that he did not know but "wherever He leads, I'll go."

With those poignant words lingering in his mind, McKinney went to his hotel room and wrote out both words and music of "Wherever He Leads I'll Go." At the evening session of the convention, after Jones had spoken, McKinney handed a manuscript copy of the song to the organist and sang it as a solo.

(Jones later became associated with the Southern Baptist Annuity Board, Dallas, where he served effectively until his retirement in 1957. He died at his birthplace, Murray, Kentucky, May 19, 1960.)

"Wherever He Leads I'll Go" first appeared in print in *Songs of Victory* (Nashville, 1937, No. 4), the first collection prepared by McKinney in his position as music editor of the Baptist Sunday School Board. It has been in every Southern Baptist hymnal published since—a testimony to its influence as an expression of consecration.

FALLS CREEK, the name given the tune for "Wherever He Leads I'll Go" by the committee for *Baptist Hymnal* (1956), refers to Falls Creek Baptist Assembly in the Arbuckle Mountains of Oklahoma. For 20 years (1925-45), McKinney was the music director of this annual summer assembly of Oklahoma Baptists. A dynamic leader of church song, McKinney wielded great influence on the church music of that area and, because of his inspiration, great congregational singing has become a noble tradition at Falls Creek. "Wherever He Leads I'll Go" was first introduced at this assembly by its author and composer in 1936, prior to his publication of it the following year. *H.T.M.*

"Take up your cross," 494

Charles W. Everest wrote this text based on Mark 8:34, in 1833, and published it that year in his *Visions of Death, and Other Poems*. Its first inclusion in a hymnal was in *Union Hymns* (Philadelphia, 1835). This was one of only two American hymns (the other being G. W. Doane's "Thou Art the Way: to Thee Alone") to appear in the first edition of *Hymns Ancient and Modern* (London, 1861). Everest's original text of five stanzas, which may be seen in Routley's *A Panorama of Christian Hymnody* (Chicago, 1979), has been much altered through the years. The language was updated for this hymnal.

The Baptist Hymn and Praise Book (Nashville, 1904, No. 454) was the first Southern Baptist hymnal to include this hymn.

QUEBEC was composed by Henry Baker in 1854, while he was a student at Exeter College, Oxford. In 1862 it was submitted, unsigned, by "S.C.C.," perhaps a friend of Baker's, to the *Penny Post*, a London newspaper, as a new tune for John Keble's "Sun of My Soul, Thou Savior Dear." John B. Dykes named it WHITBURN and credited it to Baker when it was published with Keble's text in John Grey's *Hymns for Use in the English Church* (London, 1866). When it appeared in the music edition of Bickersteth's *The Hymnal Companion* (London, 1871) with the name HESPERUS and without attribution, Baker asserted his claim to its composition. It is known by other names as well, including ELIM and VENN. The tune's first inclusion in a Southern Baptist collection is in *New Baptist Hymnal* (Nashville, 1926, No. 134). *P.A.R.*

Teach me, O Lord, I pray 601

This text by G. Kearnie Keegan was written, at the request of W. Hines Sims and W. L. Howse, to support the 1959 Southern Baptist Convention emphasis, "Teaching and Training." It was written at night when Keegan was on a flight to California for a speaking engagement. The metrical form was shaped so that the text could be sung to the tune DIADEMATA. The hymn was originally printed in single sheets and distributed widely. The first Southern Baptist collection to include it was *Assembly Songbook* (Nashville, 1959, No 21). For *The Baptist Hymnal* (1991), the original use of "thee-thou" language has been revised to "you" and "your" pronouns.

DIADEMATA—See hymn 161, Crown Him with many crowns. *M.P.*

Tell it! Tell it out with gladness 585

This hymn appears in *Fifteen New Bible Hymns* published in a pamphlet by the Hymn Society of America in 1966 for the celebration of the 150th anniversary of the American Bible Society. These hymns were selected from 365 submitted to the Hymn Society. The search was not for new hymns about the Bible but, rather, for hymns about the putting of the written Word of God into the hands of men and women for their salvation.

This three-stanza hymn was published with the tunes HYMN TO JOY and HYFRYDOL suggested. Its first hymnal inclusion was in the 1971 *Hymnal for the Church of God* (Anderson, IN). The first Baptist publication of this hymn was in *Baptist Hymnal* (1975, No. 275).

HYMN TO JOY—See hymn 7, Joyful, joyful, we adore Thee.   *H.E.*

Tell It to Jesus—See *Are you weary, are you heavyhearted*

Tell me the stories of Jesus 129

William H. Parker, an English Baptist layman, was greatly interested in Sunday School work. One Sunday afternoon in 1885, after he had returned from Sunday School, he sat alone thinking over his experiences of the day. Recalling the oft-repeated request of the children, "Teacher, tell us another story," he composed the lines of this hymn. The hymn was first printed in sheets used for Sunday School anniversaries of the Chelsea Street Baptist Church, New Basford, Nottingham, England. It was published in the *Sunday School Hymnary* (London, 1905). The first appearance of the text in the United States was in *Junior Carols* (Boston, 1906). For Southern Baptists it was first included in *New Baptist Hymnal* (Nashville, 1926, No. 405).

STORIES OF JESUS was the prize-winning tune submitted by Frederic A. Challinor in a competition sponsored by the National Sunday School Union of England in 1903, its centennial year. The competition was for new hymn tunes for several texts that were to be printed in a leaflet. Parker's hymn was one of those included. Sir Frederick Bridge, organist at Westminster Abbey, was the judge. When he had examined the manuscripts that had been submitted, he handed Challinor's manuscript to Carey Bonner, secretary of the National Sunday School Union, and remarked, "This is the best. A fine hymn, too. In a few years both will be sung all over the kingdom." Its first hymnal inclusion was the *Sunday School Hymnary* (London, 1905). *The New Baptist Hymnal* (Nashville, 1926, No. 405) was the first Southern Baptist hymnal to include it. *W.J.R.*

Tell me the story of Jesus 122

This gospel song by Fanny Crosby tells of the birth, temptation, ministry, rejection, crucifixion, burial, and resurrection of Jesus. "Tell Me the Story of Jesus," with the STORY OF JESUS tune by John R. Sweney (1837-99), first appeared in *The Quiver of Sacred Song*, compiled by William J. Kirkpatrick and John R. Sweney (Philadelphia, 1880, No. 52). The first Southern Baptist hymnal to include the hymn was *Broadman Hymnal* (Nashville, 1940, No. 367).   *S.W.G.*

Tell out, my soul, the greatness of the Lord 81

This is Timothy Dudley-Smith's most widely circulated hymn. The basis for its text is the New English Bible translation of the Magnificat (The Song of Mary) in Luke 1:46-55. It was written as a devotional poem in May, 1961 in Blackheath, while he was associated with a home missionary society of the Anglican Church. The text is equally useful at Christmas, as a majestic hymn of praise, and as a missions hymn. *The Baptist Hymnal* (1991) is the first Southern Baptist collection to contain this work.

WOODLANDS was first linked to this text by the editors of *100 Hymns for Today* (1969). The author credits the expanded use of his hymn to this partnership. The tune was written by Walter Greatorex, the music master at Gresham's School, Holt, England, in 1919. The tune's name comes from one of the houses at Gresham's School.   *P.H.*

Tell the Good News—See *Christ was born in a distant land*

Thanksgiving/Thanks-living—See *Our life and its sustaining breath*

That boy-child of Mary 110
Tom Colvin served in Malawi for much of his missionary career. His efforts as a hymnist were directed toward providing English texts for African hymns and folk melodies. This text on the name(s) for Mary's child relates to a common African practice of naming a child in such a way as to express the parents' aspirations for their offspring or of relating the events associated with the birth. *The Baptist Hymnal* (1991) is the first Southern Baptist collection to include this song.

BLANTYRE is a traditional dance tune from Malawi which Colvin adapted for singing. *P.H.*

The Birthday of a King—See *In the little village of Bethlehem*

The blood that Jesus shed for me 133
Andraé Crouch wrote both words and music for this gospel song in 1962. *Hymns for the Family of God* (Nashville, 1976) was the first hymnal to include it. The first line is

shared with a text by Fanny Crosby that continues "when groaning, dying on the tree."

THE BLOOD takes its name from the first two words that are common both to the text and the common title, "The Blood Will Never Lose Its Power." The congregational version has minor rhythmic and melodic changes from the original solo.

The Baptist Hymnal (1991) is the first Southern Baptist collection to include this. *P.A.R.*

The Blood Will Never Lose Its Power—
See *The blood that Jesus shed for me*

The Bond of Love—See *We are one in the bond of love*

The church of Christ, in every age 402
This hymn was written by Fred Pratt Green in 1969. In 1975 it appeared in the Supplement (*New Church Praise*) compiled for the United Reformed Church. The five-stanza version we use omits one of the original stanzas and moves the second one to the last. This change was made at the request of Lutherans in the United States. The hymn in *The Baptist Hymnal* (1991) was first published in *The Lutheran Book of Worship* (1978). Green felt the changes asked for by that committee resulted in an improved hymn. *The Baptist Hymnal* (1991) is the first Southern Baptist collection to include this hymn.

GERMANY was published in 1815 in William Gardiner's *Sacred Melodies from Haydn, Mozart, and Beethoven, adapted to the best English Poets, and appropriated to the use of the British Church.* Gardiner indicated the tune was from the music of Beethoven, although in a later work (*Music and Friends*, 1838) he seemed less certain when he reported the tune "is somewhere in the works of Beethoven, but I cannot point it out."

Some feel the tune is based on a German folk melody, while others support the Beethoven theory. The introduction to the aria "O Isis und Osiris" in Mozart's opera *The Magic Flute* is the most likely source of the first phrase of GERMANY. The remainder may be Gardiner's creation.   *D.B.*

The church's one foundation 350

In 1866, Samuel J. Stone (1839-1900), then curate at Windsor, wrote 12 hymns based on the Apostles' Creed and in defense of Bishop Gray who was embroiled in a controversy which shook the Church of England. Bishop John William Colenso of Natal, South Africa, had employed higher criticism to challenge the historicity of the Pentateuch and as a result was deposed by Bishop Gray of Capetown. "The Church's One Foundation" was based on the ninth article of the Creed and appeared in his *Lyra Fidelium; Twelve Hymns on the Twelve Articles of the Apostles' Creed,"* published in 1866. The present version is made up of stanzas 1, 2, and 5 of the original seven eight-line stanzas. The hymn, set to the present tune, appeared in the appendix to *Hymns Ancient and Modern* (London, 1868). It first appeared in a Southern Baptist hymnal in *New Baptist Hymnal* (Nashville, 1926, No. 244).

The tune AURELIA was composed by Samuel Sebastian Wesley (1810-76), grandson of Charles Wesley and one of the most significant musicians in 19th-century England, for the text, "Jerusalem the Golden." The name of the tune comes from "aurum," the Latin word for "gold," and was suggested by the composer's wife. It first appeared with that text in *A Selection of Psalms and Hymns* (London, 1864), which was edited by Wesley and Charles Kemble. It seems to have appeared with the text, "The Church's One Foundation," for the first time in the *Appendix to Hymns Ancient and Modern* (1868).

Baptist Hymn and Praise Book (Nashville, 1904, Nos. 24, 380) was the first Southern Baptist hymnal to contain the tune, though in neither case is it set to Stone's hymn.   *S.W.G.*

The cross upon which Jesus Died 315

The words and music of this song were written by Ira F. Stanphill in 1945 while he was holding a revival meeting in Kansas City. During a Sunday morning service, the evangelist asked the congregation to suggest titles for new songs. One member recommended the title "Room at the Cross." Using this suggestion as a basis, the song was written that afternoon. According to Stanphill's autobiography, *This Side of Heaven* (1983), the song was cowritten with his wife Zelma, who sometimes collaborated with him in such efforts. However, published versions listed only Ira's name as author and composer. The song's first appearance in a published collection was in Stanphill's *Hymntime Harmonies* (1946).

The first publication of the words and music in a Southern Baptist hymnal was in *Baptist Hymnal* (1975).

STANPHILL is the tune named for the composer.   *D.M.*

The day of resurrection 164

The hymn comes from the first of the eight odes by John of Damascus making up "The Golden Canon." The canon is a form of hymn that developed in the Greek church near the close of the seventh century. It consists of nine odes on the nine canticles from Scripture and is sung at midnight on Easter morn, just as the congregation kindles their candles producing a sudden glow of light. A cannon is fired, drums and trumpets sound, and the cry goes up, "Christ is risen!" John Mason Neale's free translation of this Greek ode appeared in his *Hymns of the Eastern Church* (London, 1862). For congregational singing it was published in *The Parish Hymn Book* (London, 1863). The hymn first appeared in the United States in *Hymns for the Use of the Evangelical Lutheran Church* (Philadelphia, 1865) and was included in *The Baptist Hymnal* (Philadelphia, 1883, No. 649). *Baptist Hymnal* (Nashville, 1956, No. 111) was the first Southern Baptist collection to include the hymn.

LANCASHIRE—See hymn 621, Lead on, O King Eternal.   *W.J.R.*

The Family of God—See *I'm so glad I'm a part of the family of God*

The family of God is born from above 380

Mark Blankenship wrote the words and music of this chorus as part of a larger work titled *Children of God*. The occasion for the composition was the 50th anniversary in 1980 of Broadmoor Baptist Church, Shreveport, Louisiana. The entire work was based on 1 John. *The Baptist Hymnal* (1991) is the first Southern Baptist collection in which this work appears.

The tune name FAMILY is taken from the text theme.   *P.H.*

The first day of the week 357

This text by Fred Pratt Green was the result of a request by the *Hymns and Songs* committee for a hymn that would relate the Lord's Day with the Sabbath. Stanzas three and four were altered at the suggestion of Lutherans in this country and the hymn appeared in *The Lutheran Book of Worship* (1978). Those same alterations have been included in *The Baptist Hymnal* (1991). The original stanzas read:

And each day of the week,
And on the Lord's own day,
They walked in Christian liberty
His new and living way.

So on the Lord's own day,
From needless burdens freed,
We keep a Sabbath made for us
To fit our inmost need.

HILL was written for this text by Mark Blankenship at the request of Wesley L. Forbis, general editor of the hymnal. The tune is named for the street on which the composer lives.   *D.B.*

The First Lord's Day—See *They rolled a stone before the door*

The first Nowell 85

A "Nowell" (*Noël* in French) was a joyous expression, shouted or sung, commemorating the birth of Christ. This English carol is thought to be around 300 years old. It first appeared with nine stanzas in the second edition of Davis Gilbert's *Some Ancient Christmas Carols* (1823). An altered version was printed in *Chrismas Carols, Ancient and Modern* (1833) by W. Sandys. The hymnal version incorporates stanzas 1, 2, 3, and 8 of the original. An alteration of the original second stanza, "They looked up and saw a star," brings the text into agreement with Scripture. The star was seen by the wise men, not the shepherds (Matt. 2:2). *The Broadman Hymnal* (Nashville, 1940, No. 140) was the first Southern Baptist collection to contain this carol.

THE FIRST NOWELL accompanied the text of the carol in W. Sandys' *Christmas Carols, Ancient and Modern* (1833). Although the source is unknown, Millar Patrick, in *Handbook to the Church Hymnary Supplement* (1935), theorized that the melody was originally a descant to Jeremiah Clark's "A Hymn for Christmas Day." This tune was an elaborated form of Clark's ST. MAGNUS. The harmonization by John Stainer was taken from Bramley and Stainer's *Christmas Carols New and Old* (1871).   *P.H.*

The God of Abraham praise 34

This hymn is a metrical version of the *Yigdal*, a doxology of the 13 articles of the Hebrew faith, drawn up by the 12th-century Hebrew scholar Moses Maimonides. The metrical form of the *Yigdal*, usually attributed to Daniel ben Judah, 14th-century Hebrew poet, was sung antiphonally by the precentor and congregation at the close of divine service on the eve of the Sabbath and other festivals. A literal translation of the *Yigdal* may be found in Julian's *Dictionary of Hymnology* (pp. 1149-50). Thomas Olivers heard the *Yigdal* sung at the Great Synagogue, Duke's Place, London, in 1770. While staying at the home of John Blakewell in Westminster, London, Olivers, an evangelical English preacher, made the poetic version in 12 eight-line stanzas. He published these in an undated leaflet entitled *A Hymn to the God of Abraham*. Olivers' hymn first appeared in the United States in 1790 in *A Selection of Psalms and Hymns*, compiled by Samuel Jones and Burgis Allison for the churches of the Philadelphia Baptist Association. In the same year it was included in *The Pocket Hymn Book of the Methodist Episcopal Church* (Philadelphia, 1790), compiled by Thomas Coke and Francis Asbury.

In the mid-1880s, Rabbi Max Landsberg of Temple B'rith Kodesh, Rochester, New York, asked his friend, the Rev. Newton Mann, minister of the First Unitarian Church, Rochester, New York, to make a metrical translation of the *Yigdal* that was more faithful to the original Hebrew. While it was a more accurate translation, it did not fit the meter of the tune LEONI. In 1889, William Channing Gannett, who had succeeded Mann as minister in Rochester, was asked by Landsberg to recast Mann's stanzas to fit LEONI. Gannett's version, in five stanzas, beginning "Praise to the living God" (*c.* 1900), appeared in Jewish *Union Hymnal* (1910). The version in *The Baptist Hymnal* (1991) uses stanzas 1, 3, and 5.

An unknown hymnal editor, sometime around 1914, replaced Gannett's opening line with Olivers' first line, "The God of Abraham praise." This substitution has resulted in much confusion and erroneous information in hymnals and hymnal companions. This version appeared in *The Hymnal* (Philadelphia, 1933), compiled by Clarence Dickinson, all attributed to Olivers. The first use of this version by Southern Baptists was in *Baptist Hymnal* (1975).

LEONI is an adapted version of the tune which cantor Meyer Lyon transcribed for Thomas Olivers after Olivers had heard it in the Great Synagogue, in London, in 1770. Olivers named the tune LEONI for Meyer Lyon (Meier Leoni). While the source of the tune is unknown, it seems to be no older than the 17th century.　　*W.J.R.*

The great Physician 188

William Hunter wrote these words and published them in his *Songs of Devotion* (Pittsburgh, 1859). The original text, titled "Christ, the Physician," had seven stanzas, of which 4, 5, and 7 are omitted here. They may be seen in William J. Reynolds' *Companion to Baptist Hymnal* (Nashville, 1976).

The refrain bears a striking resemblance to these lines from the hymn, "Burst, ye emerald gates, and bring":

Sweetest sound in seraphs' song,
　　Sweetest notes on mortal tongue,
Sweetest carol ever sung,
　　Jesus! Jesus! flows [rolls] along.

This text by Richard Kempenfelt first appeared in his *Original Hymns and Poems* (Exeter [England], 1777) and was widely reprinted in 19th-century American collections.

GREAT PHYSICIAN was composed for these words by John H. Stockton. It appeared in *Joyful Songs, Nos. 1, 2, and 3 Combined*

(Philadelphia, 1869).

The first Southern Baptist collection to include this gospel song was *Songs of Faith* (Nashville, 1933, No. 116).   *P.A.R.*

The King Is Coming—See *O the King is coming*

The King of glory comes 127
This text by Fr. Willard F. Jabusch was written in 1965 for a Sunday youth mass at St. Celestine's Church (Roman Catholic) in Elmwood Park, Illinois. It was first published the following year in *Hymnal for Young Christians*, one of the first Roman Catholic hymnals to be published in English in this country after Vatican II. *The Baptist Hymnal* (1991) is the first Southern Baptist collection in which it has appeared.

The text was written to be sung to an Israeli folk tune which the author had heard during a visit to Israel. The refrain and the first stanza draw upon Psalm 24: 7-8. The original third stanza does not appear in this hymnal.

PROMISED ONE is a setting of the Israeli folk tune for which Jabusch wrote the text. This setting was written by John Ferguson for Advent services at the United Church of Christ in Kent, Ohio, in 1973 and was first published in *The Hymnal of the United Church of Christ* (1974), of which Ferguson was music editor.   *M.P.*

The Lily of the Valley—See *I have found a friend in Jesus*

The Lord bless you and keep you 662
Peter C. Lutkin published this in 1900 as a "Farewell Anthem with Sevenfold Amen." It was dedicated to William Smedley. Beginning with the 1905 *Methodist Hymnal*, it has appeared in several hymnals. Lutkin did not feel the sevenfold Amen was suitable for the congregational use. The text is taken from Numbers 6:24-26. Lutkin's tune is named BENEDICTION. The first appearance of this benedictory song in a Southern Baptist collection was in *New Baptist Hymnal* (Nashville, 1926, No. 426).   *D.B.*

The Lord's Prayer—See *Our Father, which art in heaven*

The love of Christ who died for me 268
Timothy Dudley-Smith wrote this hymn a few days before "How Great Our God's Majestic Name" in August, 1989, during his family's summer holiday in Cornwall, England. In a letter to this writer he said, "I wanted to write a hymn about the cross and response to the gospel of Christ's love." Galatians 2:20 is one example of the many New Testament verses that underlie the text. It was first published in *Mission Praise* (1990). *The Baptist Hymnal* (1991) is the first Southern Baptist hymnal to include this hymn.

AZMON—See hymn 216, O for a thousand tongues to sing.   *P.H.*

The love of God is broader 567
Both words and music were written by William J. Reynolds as part of a "musical service," entitled *Reaching People* (Nashville, 1972), a work supporting an outreach emphasis of the Sunday School program among Southern Baptists.

SULLIVAN is the name given the tune by the composer in the *Baptist Hymnal* (Nashville, 1975, No. 285). The tune was named for James L. Sullivan, then president of the Baptist Sunday School Board, Nashville, Tennessee, and one of the outstanding denominational statesmen of his generation.   *W.J.R.*

The Majesty and Glory of Your Name—See *Alleluia, Alleluia! The majesty and glory*

The Master hath come 497

Sarah Doudney is the author of the hymn which first appeared in the Sunday School Union's *Songs of Gladness* (London, 1871), with the heading "Jesus and Mary of Bethany." It is based on Martha's words "The Master is come, and calleth for thee" (John 11:28). The author was a prolific contributor to religious magazines and periodicals of her day, and it is quite possible that this hymn appeared in such a publication prior to its inclusion in the above named collection. The first appearance of the hymn in the United States was in the *Sunday School Service Book and Hymnal* (Boston, 1885). Southern Baptists first sang this hymn with this tune in *Baptist Hymnal* (Nashville, 1956, No. 427).

ASH GROVE is a traditional Welsh melody of unknown origin. It was originally associated with a secular text about lovers strolling in a grove of ash trees. *W.J.R.*

The Nail-Scarred Hand—See *Have you failed in your plan*

The Old Rugged Cross—See *On a hill far away*

The Old Ship of Zion—See *'Tis the old ship of Zion*

The Savior is waiting 321

Ralph Carmichael wrote both words and music in 1958 while he was minister of music at the Temple Baptist Church, Los Angeles. It was tended as an invitation hymn for use by the pastor, Dr. J. Lester Harnish. The first hymnal inclusion was *Hymns of Glorious Praise* (Springfield, 1969). The tune was named CARMICHAEL by the Hymnal Committee of *Baptist Hymnal* (1975), the first Southern Baptist collection to include it. *W.J.R.*

The Servant Song—See *We are travelers on a journey*

The sky shall unfold 196

Joyce Reba (Dottie) Rambo's hymn links phrase to phrase, referring to the sky, the stars, the light, the angel, the sleeping, and those who remain, and climaxes with WE SHALL BEHOLD HIM, which is the tune name. There are reminiscences of Mrs. Frank A. Breck's hymn "Face to face," and allusions to John 17:24, 1 Corinthians 13:12, and 2 Corinthians 4:6. *The Baptist Hymnal* (1991) is the first Southern Baptist collection to include this song. *S.W.G.*

The Solid Rock—See *My hope is built on nothing less*

The Star-Spangled Banner—See *O say, can you see*

The strife is o'er 172

This is Francis Pott's translation of an anonymous Latin hymn, "Finita iam sunt praelia," which has been traced to *Symphonia Sirenum Selectarum* (Cologne, 1695). Pott's translation first appeared in his *Hymns Fitted to the Order of Common Prayer* (London, 1861) and was extensively altered for inclusion in *Hymns Ancient and Modern* (London) later the same year. Many other changes have been made in this text over the years.

VICTORY is an adaptation by William H. Monk of the opening phrases of the "Gloria Patri" from G. P. da Palestrina's "Magnificat tertii toni" (1691). Monk took the first two phrases from Palestrina's piece, altered them slightly, restated the first with a different harmonization, and added music for a single alleluia to set Pott's text for *Hymns Ancient and Modern*. He also wrote music, omitted in this hymnal, for three alleluias to begin the hymn. Monk had prepared an unsuccessful adaptation of Palestrina's theme to set John Cosin's "Come, Holy Ghost, Our Souls Inspire" in *The Parish Choir* (London, 1851). The tune is also known as PALESTRINA or CONQUEROR.

The first Southern Baptist collection to include this hymn was *Baptist Hymnal* (Nashville, 1956, No. 107), which retained the opening alleluias but altered the rhythmic structure.   *P.A.R.*

The Way of the Cross Leads Home—
See *I must needs go home*

The whole world is singing 593
The words and music of this song were written in 1962 by Margaret Baker as part of a study unit on missions written for Primary choirs and published by the Church Music Department of the Sunday School Board of the Southern Baptist Convention. At the time, she was directing children's choirs at the First Baptist Church of Pine Bluff, Arkansas. The song was later included in *Songs for Primaries* (Nashville, 1964).

BAKER is the tune named for the composer.   *M.P.*

The Word of God is alive 265
This text about Holy Scripture was written in 1990 by L. W. Terley. It is based on the *New International Version* of Hebrews 4:12.

PARKS was composed by Paul Yeary to set this text for *The Baptist Hymnal* (1991).

The Baptist Hymnal (1991) is the first hymnal to include this text and tune.   *P.A.R.*

There is a balm in Gilead 269
This African-American spiritual is of unknown origin. In *White and Negro Spirituals*, however, George Pullen Jackson points to hymnist John Newton's use of the phrase "sin-sick soul" in 1779 in a hymn that became popular with Southern singers:

How lost was my condition
Till Jesus made me whole,
There is but one Physician
Can cure a sin-sick soul (198).

The spiritual text refers to the ointment mentioned in Jeremiah 8:22 and 46:11 and provides a positive response to the prophet's question, "Is there no balm in Gilead?" The present version of the hymn is taken from the source in which it first appeared, *Folk Songs of the American Negro* (Nashville, 1907), edited by Frederick J. Work and John W. Work, Jr. *Baptist Hymnal* (Nashville, 1975, No. 205) was the first Southern Baptist collection to include this spiritual.

BALM IN GILEAD is the tune name taken from the common title of the hymn.   *P.H.*

There is a fountain 142
William Cowper wrote this hymn based on Zechariah 13:1: "In that day there shall be a fountain opened to the house of David and to the inhabitants of Jerusalem for sin and for uncleanness." Probably written in 1771, it first appeared in Conyer's *Collection of Psalms and Hymns* (1772) in seven four-line stanzas and was included in *Olney Hymns* (1779). The first appearance in the United States seems to have been in John Rippon's *Selection of Hymns* (New York, 1792), and John Stanford's *A Collection of Evangelical Hymns* (New York, 1793)—both collections for Baptists. It is found in five stanzas in Southern Baptist's first collection, *The Baptist Psalmody* (Charleston, 1850, 409).

CLEANSING FOUNTAIN is called "Western Melody" or "unknown" in most of the 19th-century American tunebooks. It is a pentatonic (five tone) melody, characteristic of the camp meeting songs and folk songs of the early part of the century.   *W.J.R.*

There is a name I love to hear 217

This text (without the refrain) by Frederick Whitfield was first published in hymn sheets and leaflets in 1855. He then published it in a group of 26 poems in his *Sacred Poems and Prose* (Dublin, 1859; 2nd ed. enl., 1861; 4th ed. enl., 1864). This text apparently was first published in America in Goodman's *Village Hymn Book* (Taunton, 1864) and in Bradbury's *Devotional Hymn and Tune Book* (Philadelphia, 1864, No. 584).

The refrain, "Oh, how I love Jesus," is a chorus of American folk origin, being attached to various other hymns, including "Amazing Grace! How Sweet the Sound" and "Alas! and Did My Savior Bleed." Ellen Jane Lorenz, in her study, *Glory, Hallelujah! The Story of the Campmeeting Spiritual* (Nashville, 1978, p. 120), found this chorus 42 times, the earliest in 1868. Concerning OH, HOW I LOVE JESUS, she comments that the tune was popular with African-Americans and is part of a tune family of four campmeeting songs, all in 6/8 and with similar melodic outlines and dancelike movement. The earliest publication of OH, HOW I LOVE JESUS is possibly in Joseph Hillman and Lewis Hartsough's *The Revivalist* (Troy, 1869, No. 456), where it is associated with "Jesus, the Name High Over All" by Charles Wesley. The tune bears the indication, "Arr. by Mrs. Helen M. Bradley."

Whitfield's hymn with its refrain to OH, HOW I LOVE JESUS was published for Southern Baptists as early as Robert H. Coleman's *The New Evangel* (Dallas, 1911, No. 257). *H.E.*

There is a place of quiet rest 295

Soon after he completed theological training at Union Theological Seminary, Cleland B. McAfee returned to his alma mater, Park College, Parkville, Missouri, to serve as pastor of the college church and director of the choir. Frequently, for his communion services, McAfee would write a response for the choir to sing that was appropriate to the theme of the service. Shortly before a Communion Sunday, his brother Howard's two little girls died of diphtheria. The college, the church, and the town were in shock. McAfee, as he contemplated this sorrow, recalled that he had not written the song for Communion. He quickly finished it and taught it to the choir on Saturday evening. After rehearsal, the choir went to Howard McAfee's darkened, quarantined house, and sang it standing in the yard. It was sung again on Sunday morning at the Communion service.

McAfee submitted the manuscript to the Lorenz Publishing Company of Dayton, Ohio, and it first appeared in the monthly choir magazine, *The Choir Leader* (October, 1903).

MCAFEE is the name given the tune in *Baptist Hymnal* 1956. Its first appearance in a Southern Baptist collection was in B. B. McKinney's *The Broadman Hymnal* (Nashville, 1940, No. 273).   *W.J.R.*

There is a Savior 536

The words of this song were written by Sandi Patti Helvering and Phill McHugh, and the music by Greg Nelson and Bob Farrell in 1985. The song was recorded in the same year on Sandi Patti's album, *Morning Like This. The Baptist Hymnal* (1991) marks its first publication in a major hymnal.

SAVIOR is the tune name taken from the common title of the hymn.   *D.M.*

There is joy, there is joy 440

This hymn appears in *Kneel at the Cross*,

a large work written by Mark Blankenship for Easter, 1974, at North Phoenix Baptist Church, Phoenix, Arizona. *The Baptist Hymnal* (1991) is the first Southern Baptist collection to include this text and tune.

KNEEL was obviously chosen for the tune name, since it is the first word in the title of the cantata *Kneel at the Cross* (Nashville, 1975) in which this selection appeared. *P.H.*

There is never a day so dreary 434

A number of years after he set this hymn to music, the composer E. O. Sellers wrote the author, Anna B. Russell, requesting the story concerning the writing of this hymn. Miss Russell replied that there was no information she could give.

NEW ORLEANS was composed in 1921, two years after Sellers joined the faculty of Baptist Bible Institute (now New Orleans Baptist Theological Seminary), New Orleans, Louisiana. Under the title "A Song in the Heart," it first appeared in *Hosanna in the Highest*, compiled by Gypsy Smith and William McEwan with music edited by McEwan and Ensign Edwin Young (Brooklyn, n.d., No. 7). A favorite hymn of evangelist Gypsy Smith, it was used as the theme song for his evangelistic meetings. This hymn appeared in two Southern Baptist collections of 1929: *Revival Songs* by Robert H. Coleman (Nashville, No. 38) and *Select Sacred Songs* Souvenir Edition 74th Session (Nashville, No. 8). Sellers' music, originally in the key of B-flat, is a sensitive setting of the contrasting moods of Russell's text, utilizing word painting and chromatic harmonies often found in compositions for male quartets. *H.E.*

There Is Power in the Blood—See *Would you be free from the burden of sin?*

There is strength in the name 174

Sandi Patti Helvering was inspired with the idea behind this song after reading the book *Lord, I Want to Know You* by Kay Arthur. She was assisted in the writing of the lyrics by Gloria Gaither and Phill McHugh. Mrs. Helvering wrote the tune. The song was recorded on her album, *Morning Like This*, which was released in 1986. *Morning Like This* was honored with a Grammy Award from the National Academy of Recording Arts and Sciences and a Dove Award from the Gospel Music Association. It was also certified a Gold Album.

The congregational arrangement of the song was the work of Robert F. Douglas and first appeared in *The Hymnal for Worship & Celebration* (1986, No. 90). *The Baptist Hymnal* (1991) marks its first printing in a Southern Baptist collection.

NAME OF THE LORD is the tune name taken from the common title of the hymn. *D.M.*

There is sunshine in my soul 430

According to William J. Reynolds, Eliza E. Hewitt (1851-1920) wrote this tune "while she was teaching school in Philadelphia. One day she was attempting to correct an incorrigible; he struck her across the back with a heavy slate, causing severe injury. She was placed in a heavy cast for six months. After the long confinement, her doctor permitted her to go for a short walk in nearby Fairmount Park on a warm spring day. With her heart overflowing with joy for recovery, she returned home and wrote these lines" (1976, 221).

The third stanza originally began "There's springtime in my soul today." "Springtime" was later changed to "gladness" and the beginning of each stanza was changed from "there's" to "there is."

The text with the tune SUNSHINE, by John

R. Sweney (1837-99), first appeared in *Glad Hallelujahs*, edited by William J. Kirkpatrick and Sweney (Philadelphia, 1887, No. 84). The first Southern Baptist Hymnal to include the hymn was *Baptist Hymn and Praise Book* (Nashville, 1904, No. 356).   *S.W.G.*

There shall be showers of blessing 467

This gospel song was one of many collaborative efforts by noted 19th-century evangelist Major D. W. Whittle and his musical associate James McGranahan. The tune SHOWERS OF BLESSING by McGranahan first appeared with the text in *Gospel Hymns No. 4* (1883). The text and tune first appeared in a Southern Baptist collection in *The Baptist Hymn and Praise Book* (Nashville, 1904, No. 444).   *P.H.*

There's a call comes ringing 595

This gospel song was written by Charles H. Gabriel in 1890 while he was serving as chorister of the Sunday School at Grace Methodist Episcopal Church in San Francisco, California. On Easter Sunday, March 6, 1890, the Sunday School took up a "Golden Missionary Offering." The superintendent had asked Gabriel to provide a new song for the occasion, and the composer had responded by writing the words and music of this hymn, the second stanza of which contains a reference to the "golden offering."

Gabriel later recalled that a visiting field missions secretary who was present at the special service carried the song to the eastern part of the country, where it quickly became popular through the singing of Methodist Chaplain C. C. McCabe. The song was first printed in George D. Elderkin's *The Finest of the Wheat* (Chicago, 1890, No. 60), under the title "Send the Light." In this source, an eight-measure bass solo was inserted between the stanzas and

the present refrain, with the notation that the solo "may be omitted." The text for the last two lines of the refrain originally read:

Send the light! and let its radiant beams
Light the world forevermore.

The immediate and widespread acceptance of this song represented a significant turning point in Gabriel's life. He had previously written and published a number of other hymns and gospel songs, but—as the composer subsequently observed—with the popularity of "Send the Light," "ambition again awoke within me, and marked the beginning of my second entry into song writing," a career he pursued with great success until his death in 1932.

Robert H. Coleman's *The Popular Hymnal* was the first Southern Baptist hymn collection to include this gospel song (Dallas, 1918, No. 215).

McCABE is the name given this tune by the hymnal committee for *Baptist Hymnal* (1956).   *D.M.*

There's a glad new song 431

Both words and tune were written by Albert Christopher Fisher in 1940. He sold them and four other songs to Robert H. Coleman. William J. Reynolds, in his *Companion to Baptist Hymnal*, tells that this text and tune remained in Coleman's files of unpublished materials, which were purchased in 1945 by the Baptist Sunday School Board. W. Hines Sims, the editor of *Baptist Hymnal* (Nashville, 1956), discovered the song and included it in that hymnal (No. 311). The tune name, REDEEMING LOVE, was taken by Sims from Fisher's title for the song. *S.W.G.*

There's a land that is fairer than day 515

Sanford Fillmore Bennett, a druggist, moved to Elkhorn, Wisconsin, in 1859 and joined forces with a local musician, Joseph P. Webster, to produce a collection of songs titled *The Signet Ring* (1868), which contained this hymn. Sankey's *My Life and the Story of the Gospel Hymns*, quoting Bennett, contains the following account of the hymn's origin:

"Mr. Webster, like many musicians, was of an exceedingly nervous and sensitive nature, and subject to periods of depression, in which he looked upon the dark side of all things in life. I had learned his peculiarities so well that on meeting him I could tell at a glance if he was in one of his melancholy moods, and I found that I could rouse him from them by giving him a new song or hymn to work on. On such an occasion he came into my place of business, walked down to the stove, and turned his back to me without speaking. I was at my desk writing. Presently I said: 'Webster, what is the matter now?'

"'It is no matter,' he replied. 'It will be all right by and by!'

"The idea of the hymn came to me like a flash of sunlight, and I replied: 'The sweet by and by! Would that not make a good hymn?'

"'Maybe it would,' said he indifferently.

"Turning to the desk I penned the three verses and the chorus as fast as I could write. In the meantime two friends, Mr. N. H. Carswell and Mr. S. E. Bright, had come in. I handed the hymn to Mr. Webster. As he read it his eye kindled, and his whole demeanor changed. Stepping to the desk, he began writing the notes in a moment. Presently he requested Mr. Bright to hand him his violin, and then he played the melody. In a few moments more he had the notes for the four parts of the chorus jotted down. I think it was not over thirty minutes ...before [we] were singing the hymn" (285-286).

The text and tune first came into a South-ern Baptist collection in *The Baptist Hymn and Praise Book* (Nashville, 1904, No. 555).

SWEET BY AND BY is the tune name taken from the text of the refrain.   *P.H.*

There's a Spirit in the air 393

This hymn was written by Brian Wren in June, 1969, for the Pentecost season at his church in Hockley, England. His purpose was to try to celebrate the idea of the Holy Spirit "working in our world." Originally written in seven stanzas with alternating refrains, the version in *The Baptist Hymnal* (1991) omits two of the stanzas having the refrain "We can see his power today." The hymn was first published in *Praise for Today* (London, 1974, No. 84) which was the supplement to the British *Baptist Hymn Book* (London, 1962). The first Southern Baptist hymn collection to include this text and its tune is *The Baptist Hymnal* (1991).

LAUDS was composed by John Wilson in 1969 for the James Montgomery hymn "Songs of Praise the Angels Sang" and published in *Hymns and Songs* (London, 1969, No. 64). The descant was written at the same time and has been included in subsequent printings of the tune. Both tune and descant were first used with Brian Wren's "There's a Spirit in the Air" in December, 1972, when the composer introduced it in a program of new hymns at an annual celebration of the Royal School of Church Music. The association has since been widely adopted.   *H.T.M.*

There's a sweet, sweet spirit 243

Both words and music were written by Doris Akers. The inspiration for the song came during a prayer service as she and her choir felt the presence of the Holy Spirit. First published in solo music by Manna Music in 1965, it appeared the same year in a choral version arranged by Kurt Kaiser, and this has become, for many, the accepted version. The present hymn tune version was made for *Baptist Hymnal* (1975), its first hymnal inclusion, where it was named MANNA.

The hymnal committee for *The Baptist Hymnal* (1991) requested and received permission from the copyright holder to change the word "stay" to "You're" in the refrain. That change is noted by an asterisk on the hymn page. *W.J.R.*

There's a wideness in God's mercy 25

These five stanzas are excerpted from a hymn by Frederick W. Faber with the first line, "Souls of men, why will ye scatter." An eight-stanza version of this poem appeared in his *Oratory Hymns* (London, 1854). The selection here uses stanzas 4, 6, 9, 8, and 13 from a thirteen-stanza version, published with the title, "Come to Jesus," in Faber's *Hymns* (London, 1862). The entire text may be seen in Routley's *A Panorama of Christian Hymnody* (Chicago, 1979).

The final stanza is extensively revised in the present hymnal. The original read:
If our love were but more simple
    We should take him at his word;
And our lives would be all sunshine
    In the sweetness of our Lord.

WELLESLEY was composed by Lizzie S. Tourjée as the setting for a text to be used at her high school graduation in Newton, Massachusetts. It is named for Wellesley College, which she subsequently attended. Its first appearance in a hymnal was as the setting for three texts, including Faber's, in the *Hymnal of the Methodist Episcopal Church with Tunes* (New York, 1878). The composer's father, Eben Tourjée, was a "special musical editor" of this collection.

The first Southern Baptist hymnal to include this hymn was *The Baptist Hymn and Praise Book* (Nashville, 1904, No. 294). *P.A.R.*

There's not a friend like the lowly Jesus 181

The text of this gospel song was written by Johnson Oatman, Jr., about 1895. It was first printed in a collection in *Heaven's Echo* (Philadelphia, 1895), edited and published by George C. Hugg.

HARPER MEMORIAL was composed for this text in 1895 by Hugg. It is named for the Presbyterian church in Philadelphia where he was a member. It is sometimes called NO, NOT ONE, the popular title of the song, or EVANGELINE.

The Baptist Hymn and Praise Book (Nashville, 1904, No. 317) was the first Southern Baptist hymnal to include this hymn. *P.A.R.*

There's Something About That Name—
See *Jesus, Jesus, Jesus*

There's within my heart a melody 425

The words and music of this hymn were written by Luther B. Bridgers in 1910, apparently in the aftermath of a house fire which claimed the lives of his wife and three sons. Stanzas one and four may be a reflection of this tragic event. The hymn was first published in Charlie D. Tillman's *The Revival No. 6* (Atlanta, 1910, No. 21). The hymn was subsequently purchased by Robert H. Coleman and printed in his *Popular Hymnal* (Dallas, 1918, No. 181), through which it became familiar to Southern Baptists.

The tune was first called SWEETEST NAME in *Baptist Hymnal* (1956). *D.M.*

They rolled a stone before the door 162

"The First Lord's Day" was written by William N. McElrath in the summer of 1959, as one of several hymns for preadolescents. As editor of children's materials at the Baptist Sunday School Board, he felt the need for hymns simple enough for older children, yet not as easy and repetitive as those sung by younger boys and girls. When he shared these hymns with editorial colleagues, they were met with limited enthusiasm, and he laid them aside. In 1964 when Bill F. Leach was preparing the contents of a children's hymnal along with Paul Bobbitt, he selected this hymn because of the need for more selections on the resurrection. *Junior Hymnal* (Nashville, 1964, No. 94) was the first Southern Baptist collection in which the hymn appeared but it has found wide acceptance and thus been included in all standard hymnals of the denomination published since.

SPRINGBROOK is the name selected by William N. McElrath for his tune to "The First Lord's Day." The name comes from the street where he and his family lived in Nashville, Tennessee, from 1959 to 1964. *H.T.M.*

Thine is the glory 163

Edmond L. Budry, a pastor in Vevey, Switzerland, wrote "Thine Is the Glory" in 1884. It was first published in *Chants Evangeliques* (Lausanne, 1885). It appeared in the *Y.M.C.A. Hymn Book* published in Lausanne in 1904 and in *Cantate Domino* (Geneva, 1925), the hymnal of the World Student Christian Federation. In 1923 it was translated into English by Richard Birch Hoyle. *The Baptist Hymnal* (1991) is the first Southern Baptist collection to include this hymn and its tune.

MACCABEUS is taken from "See, the Conquering Hero Comes," a chorus from Handel's oratorio, *Judas Maccabaeus*. The chorus was not a part of the original (1747) performance of the oratorio. In fact, it originally appeared in *Joshua* written a year later in 1748. The chorus was added to *Judas Maccabaeus* in 1751. Around 1760 it was used as

a hymn tune for Charles Wesley's "Christ the Lord Is Risen Today" in Thomas Butts' *Harmonia Sacra.* *D.B.*

This is a day of new beginnings 370

The original version of this hymn was written by Brian Wren for a New Year's Day Service (1978) at Holy Family Church, Blackbird Leys, Oxford, England, and was set to DRONFIELD, a tune by the author himself, arranged by Peter Cutts. In its first version, the first stanza was written in the form of a question: "Is this a day of new beginnings?" For the second stanza the author was thinking of 2 Corinthians 5:16-17.

The hymn was given its present form when it was included in *Hymnal Supplement II* (Carol Stream, 1987), where it was set to Carlton R. Young's BEGINNINGS. *The Baptist Hymnal* (1991) is the first Southern Baptist publication to include the hymn and tune.

BEGINNINGS was composed in 1983 by Carlton R. Young to Wren's original version of "This Is the Day of New Beginnings" which included two stanzas ending in questions. To quote the composer from a letter to the writer of this article: "Since the poet's first two stanzas are questions and the third (the second in the later version) is a gesture towards the future, all stanzas except the last end on a V chord—incomplete, unfinished and to become. The melody and the parallel/altered harmonies are in the style of a 1930s Broadway ballad."

Hymnal Supplement II (Carol Stream, 1987), of which Young was the executive editor, was the first collection to print the tune. *H.T.M.*

This is my Father's world 43

The three eight-line stanzas of this hymn as it currently appears contain six of the 16 stanzas of a poem by Maltbie D. Babcock which first appeared in *Thoughts for Every-*

day *Living* (New York), published posthumously in 1901. The first line of each of the 16 stanzas begins "This is my Father's world." The hymn suggests some of the implications of Psalm 24:1 regarding God's ownership of the world and his continuing care of it. This text, along with its familiar tune (designated TERRA BEATA), first appeared in a Southern Baptist hymnal in *New Baptist Hymnal* (Nashville, 1926, No. 406).

TERRA PATRIS (also called TERRA BEATA) was composed for this text by Franklin L. Sheppard and first published in his *Alleluia* (1915), a Presbyterian Sunday School songbook. Because Sheppard thought this tune to be an English melody which he heard from his mother during childhood, he cited it as a "Traditional English Melody arranged by F.L.S." in *Alleluia*. The tune was originally named TERRA BEATA ("Blessed Earth"), but was changed to TERRA PATRIS ("Father's Earth") by the editors of *The Hymnal* (1933) to refer more precisely to the recurring theme of the text.   *M.P.*

This is the day 359

The author and composer of this Scripture song, Leslie Garrett, recounts that "the song was given to us in Brisbane, Australia, in 1967 at the time we were having a very hard time really going through a valley. Then one morning, the Lord gave this song to us from Psalm 118:24."

The psalm itself is a litany of thanksgiving and is the last of the Hallel group (Psalms 113-118) which has long been a part of the liturgy of the great festivals of Judaism. Like many of the psalms, this Scripture song lends itself to antiphonal or responsorial singing. *The Baptist Hymnal* (1991) is the first Southern Baptist hymnal in which the hymn has appeared.

THIS IS THE DAY is the tune name taken from the common title of the hymn. *S.W.G.*

This is the day the Lord has made 358

Isaac Watts included this hymn as the final of four sections of Psalm 118 in his *Psalms of David Imitated in the Language of the New Testament* (1719). The heading was "Hosanna: or, the Lord's Day." *New Baptist Hymnal* (Nashville, 1926, No. 7) was the first Southern Baptist collection to include this hymn.

ARLINGTON is based on the minuet of the overture to *Artaxerxes*, an opera by Thomas A. Arne produced in London in 1762. The hymn tune version was the work of Ralph Harrison who included it in his *Sacred Harmony—A Collection of Psalmtunes, Ancient and Modern* (London, 1784).   *D.B.*

This is the threefold truth 408

The Baptist Hymnal (1991) uses stanzas 1, 3, and 4 of Fred Pratt Green's original five-stanza hymn. The hymn bears a 1980 copyright. Each stanza ends with "Christ has died! Christ is risen! Christ will come again!" one of the oldest expressions of Christian worship. The first Southern Baptist collection to include the hymn is *The Baptist Hymnal* (1991).

ACCLAMATIONS was adapted by Jack Schrader from an anthem setting which he made of the text. According to Schrader, he was drawn to the text for what it has to say about the content of worship.   *D.B.*

This joy that I have 443

This is an anonymous contemporary African-American spiritual. According to the arranger, Houston Simmons, the tune has origins in the pre-Civil War jubilee. The jubilee, a type of Black spiritual, was a rhythmic musical religious expression of life, love, hope, and freedom. The text of the song probably dates from the 1930s or 1940s and apparently grew out of the services of the Black Pentecostal Church of God in Christ under Bishop Charles Mason. The words probably originated in improvised performance. The first known publication of the song is in *The Baptist Hymnal* (1991).

THIS JOY is the tune name taken from the common title of the hymn.   *D.M.*

Thou didst leave Thy throne 121

The hymn, written by Emily E. S. Elliott, was privately printed by the author for the choir and children of the parish school of St. Mark's Church, Brighton, England, in 1864. The hymn is based on Luke 2:7, "Because there was no room for them in the inn." It was published in the *Church Missionary Juvenile Instructor* (1870), which Miss Elliott edited, and in her *Chimes for Daily Service* (1880). The refrain in the final stanza was not in the original version, and its source is unknown. The first appearance of the text in the United States was in *The Sunday School Hymnal* (Boston, 1871). It appeared in *Sursum Corda* (Philadelphia, 1898, No. 174), and in *New Baptist Hymnal* (Nashville, 1926, No. 123).

MARGARET was composed by Timothy R. Matthews for Miss Elliott's words. Text and tune appeared in *Children's Hymns and Tunes* (London, 1876).   *W.J.R.*

Thou, my everlasting portion 464

"Thou, my everlasting portion" was written in 1874 when the gospel song composer, Silas J. Vail, brought the tune now named CLOSE TO THEE to Fanny Crosby asking her to provide for it a text. The story goes that as he played the tune for her, Mrs. Crosby said the melody of the refrain suggested to her the words "Close to Thee." As was her custom often, she immediately wrote out the words of all three stanzas of the song. First appearing in *Songs of Grace and Glory for Sunday Schools* (New York, 1874, No. 17), compiled by W. F. Sherwin and Vail, it later became the property of Biglow and Main

publishing firm and appeared in *Gospel Hymns No. 2* (1876). Its first appearance in a Southern Baptist collection was in *The Baptist Hymn and Praise Book* (Nashville, 1904, No. 274).

CLOSE TO THEE takes its name from the refrain of the hymn beginning with the words "Thou, my everlasting portion" and was first so designated in *Baptist Hymnal* (Nashville, 1956).   *H.T.M.*

Though I may speak with bravest fire 423

This paraphrase of 1 Corinthians 13:1-3 was written in 1971 by Hal H. Hopson and was published the following year as a two-part anthem by Hope Publishing Company. The hymnic form of the piece was prepared for inclusion in that publisher's *Hymnal Supplement* (Carol Stream, 1974).

GIFT OF LOVE is Hopson's arrangement of the English folk melody, "O Waly Waly." It has been paired with his text from its inception. A traditional American variant of this same tune is known as "The water is wide."

The Baptist Hymnal (1991) is the first collection for Southern Baptists to include this text and tune.   *P.A.R.*

'Tis finished! The Messiah dies 148

Charles Wesley's Good Friday hymn based on John 19:30 appeared in 1762 in his *Short Hymns* in two eight-line stanzas. The hymn was published in A.M. Toplady's *Psalms and Hymns* (1776), and in this way came into use in the Church of England. However, Charles Wesley was not satisfied with those stanzas and, at his death in 1788, left in manuscript another hymn in eight four-line stanzas on the same Scripture. Stanzas 1 and 8 are, respectively, stanza 1, lines 1-4 and stanza 2, lines 5-8 slightly altered from the text of 1762. Stanzas 2-7 were new. In the present version, stanza 1 is the first four lines of stanza 1 of the 1762 version and stanza 3 is the first four lines of stanza 2 (slightly altered) of that earlier version. Stanzas 2 and 4 come from the version left in manuscript at his death on March 29, 1788.

The Baptist Hymnal (1991) is the first Southern Baptist hymnal to include the hymn. In the second stanza of this version, Wesley interweaves Matthew 27:51 (Mark 15:38 and Luke 23:45) "the veil of the temple was rent in twain," with Ephesians 2:14, "[Christ] hath broken down the middle wall of partition." The present version ends with 1 Corinthians 15:54, "Death is swallowed up in victory."

Olive's Brow was written by William B. Bradbury for William B. Tappan's hymn, " 'Tis Midnight, and on Olive's Brow," which appeared in Tappan's *Poems* (Philadelphia, 1822). The tune was first published in *The Shawm* (New York, 1853), compiled by Bradbury and George F. Root. That collection was called a "Library of Church Music, embracing about one thousand pieces, consisting of psalm and hymn tunes adapted to every meter in use." The work had a special index for "all the Peculiar Metres of the Methodist hymnbooks as used in the North, these hymns being differently marked from those of the other religious denominations." The tune first appeared in a Southern Baptist hymnal in *New Baptist Hymnal* (Nashville, 1926, No. 105).   *S.W.G.*

'Tis so sweet to trust in Jesus 411

This hymn text was written by Louisa M. R. Stead. There is no definitive information available concerning the circumstances surrounding the hymn's origin. It was first published, along with William J. Kirkpatrick's tune written for it, in *Songs of Triumph*, compiled by Rev. J. S. Inskip (Philadelphia, 1882, No. 46).

Trust in Jesus was composed by Kirkpatrick specifically for this text. The first use of both text and tune in a Southern Baptist collection was in *Songs of Redemption* (Atlanta, 1920, No. 103).   *M.P.*

'Tis the church triumphant singing 218

John Kent, an English shipwright with limited formal education, wrote this hymn in 1803. Its obvious emphasis on praise made the hymn acceptable to some who rejected others of his hymns because of their Calvinistic leanings. The repeated phrase "Worthy the Lamb" is drawn from Revelation 5:12. *The Baptist Hymnal* (1991) is he first Southern Baptist collection to include this hymn.   *D.B.*

Ar Hyd y Nos is the name of a traditional Welsh tune, which translated means "On length of night." It has long been associated with the text "All Through the Night." Lowell Mason used this air in some of his collections and one of his followers, Luther O. Mason, harmonized it. The arrangement by Mark Blankenship was made for *The Baptist Hymnal* (1991).   *H.T.M.*

'Tis the grandest theme 24

William A. Ogden wrote both the words and music of this gospel song which was first published in Edwin O. Excell's *Triumphant Songs for Sunday School and Gospel Meetings* (Chicago; New York, 1887, No. 64). The first known appearance of the song in a Baptist collection was in Robert H. Coleman's and W. W. Hamilton's *The Evangel* (Philadelphia, 1909, No. 38).

Deliverance is the tune name derived from the theme of the refrain.   *D.M.*

'Tis the old ship of Zion 577

This African-American spiritual appears to be a combination of a commonly used metaphor of the gospel ship and "The Old Time Religion." Versions of a distantly related spiritual, "Old ship of Zion," are recorded by George Pullen Jackson in *White and Negro Spirituals* (New York, 1944, pp. 148-49); Dena Epstein in *Sinful Tunes and Spirituals* (Urbana, 1977, p. 223); and Newman I. White in *American Negro Folk-Songs* (Cambridge, 1928, pp. 93 ff.). Spirituals often traded such musical and textual ideas in the process of oral transmission. "The Old Time Religion" was a camp-meeting song sung by both blacks and whites in the 19th century. It appears for the first time in a Southern Baptist hymnal in *The Baptist Hymnal* (1991).

YARMOUTH, also known as "The Old Time Religion," is a camp-meeting song sung by both blacks and whites during the 19th century. The present version is the first to be included in a Southern Baptist hymnal. *P.H.*

To God be the glory 4

"To God Be the Glory" is one of the finest hymns to come from the combined work of Fanny J. Crosby and William M. Doane. It was written by the blind poet in 1875 and was submitted to Doane who first published it in his and Robert Lowry's collection, *Brightest and Best* (New York & Chicago, 1875). Besides numerous other selections by both Crosby and Doane, the two collaborated on 28 other songs in that collection, including "I Am Thine, O Lord," "Jesus, Keep Me Near the Cross," and "Rescue the Perishing."

Many of these songs found their way into the famous *Gospel Hymn* series published by Ira D. Sankey and thereby became well known in both Great Britain and the United States. But "To God Be the Glory" was not included in Sankey's American editions. Consequently, it was little known in this country until it was used by Cliff Barrows in the Nashville Billy Graham Crusade in 1954.

Since then it has become immensely popular. Its noble mood of praise inspired by numerous references to the Psalms (29:2; 67:3, 5; 126:3; 150:1) lifts it beyond the subjective themes more usual in gospel songs. Nearly 80 years after its first publication by Baptists Lowry and Doane, it was reintroduced into a Baptist collection in *Baptist Hymnal* (Nashville, 1956, No. 41), the first Southern Baptist hymnal to include the hymn.

TO GOD BE THE GLORY was composed by W. H. Doane who was profoundly moved by Fanny Crosby's text of objective praise. It has enjoyed wide acceptance in hymnals of great theological and cultural diversity. Much of its usefulness can be attributed to Doane's tune which aptly fits the text in both meaning and mood. *H.T.M.*

To me, it's so wonderful 432

Ralph H. Good Pasteur wrote both words and music in 1955, and they were first sung by the choir of the First Church of Deliverance, Chicago, Illinois, where Good Pasteur was music director. The song was later published and distributed in pamphlet form. In the early 1970s it became widely known when Ethel Waters sang it in Billy Graham Crusade meetings. The first hymnal inclusion was in *Baptist Hymnal* (Nashville, 1975, No. 467), using an arrangement made by William J. Reynolds.

COBBS is the tune name given by Good Pasteur to honor Clarence H. Cobbs, founder and pastor of Chicago's First Church of Deliverance. *W.J.R.*

To the work! 615

Fanny Crosby wrote this song in 1869. Two years later William H. Doane, who set many of her texts to music, composed the tune and published it in *Pure Gold for the Sunday School* (New York; Chicago, 1871, No. 74). The title given in the original publication was "Toiling On," and the Scripture text subsumed was Hebrews 4:11: "Let us labour therefore to enter into that rest." The text with its tune was introduced to many Southern Baptists in Robert Coleman's *The Popular Hymnal* (Dallas, 1918, No. 327), although it was sung earlier by some Southern Baptists from Doane's own *Glorious Praise* (Louisville, 1904, No. 54).

TOILING ON is from the refrain of "To the Work" and was first used as a tune title in *Baptist Hymnal* (Nashville, 1956).   *H.T.M.*

To worship, work, and witness 389

Written by Henry Lyle Lambdin, this was one of over 800 texts submitted to the Hymn Society of America (now the Hymn Society in the United States and Canada) in response to an appeal for new hymns on "the mission of the church." Nine hymns, including Lambdin's were selected for publication in a pamphlet, *Nine New Hymns on the Mission of the Church* (1969). "To Worship, Work, and Witness" also appeared on the cover of *The Hymn* (July, 1969). The first appearance of the text in a Southern Baptist collection was in *Baptist Hymnal* (Nashville, 1975, No. 238).

WIE LIEBLICH IST DER MAIEN was composed by Johann Steuerlein. Originally published in 1575 with secular words, the tune first appeared with a sacred text in Gregor Gunderreiller's *Dauids Himlische Harpffen* (Nuernberg, 1581). This is the first publication of the tune in a Southern Baptist hymnal. *D.M.*

Trials dark on every hand 522

The words and music of this hymn were written by Charles Albert Tindley and first published in four stanzas beginning with the first line "We are tossed about and driven" in L. B. Goodall's *Living Hymns* (1905). This same first line appears in *New Songs of*

Pentecost No. 3 by C. Austin Miles, Adam Geibel, and J. Lincoln Hall (Philadelphia, 1918, No. 66), copyrighted in 1905 and credited to Tindley with the designation "arr. by F. A. Clark." This same designation was given in the first Southern Baptist publication of Tindley's hymn, *Songs of Redemption* by W. Plunkett Martin and James W. Jelks (Atlanta, 1920, No. 150). The *Dictionary of American Hymnology: First Line Index* (New York, 1984) lists eight more publications of Tindley's hymn beginning with "We are tossed about and driven" through the year 1968.

The arrangement of Tindley's hymn beginning "Trials dark on every hand" has been more widely published, appearing in more than 30 hymnals through 1975. Perhaps B. B. McKinney was familiar with the unattributed publication of "Trials dark on every hand" in *Victory Songs*, for he arranged and published it in three stanzas in E♭ in *Songs of Victory* (Nashville, 1937, No. 30) with the designation "Southern Melody, arr. by B. B. McKinney" and "Words Adapted." He gave no credit to Tindley. Minor changes were made in the music, and new words were provided for the first half of stanza two. In place of:

> We are often destitute
>   of the things that life demands,
> Want of shelter and of food,
>   thirsty hills and barren land;

McKinney substituted what was apparently his own wording:

> Oft our cherished plans have failed,
>   Disappointments have prevailed,
> And we've wondered in the darkness,
>   heavy-hearted and alone.

This was the arrangement that appeared in *The Broadman Hymnal* (1940, No. 134) that introduced this hymn anonymously to thousands of Southern Baptist congregations. It is interesting that *The Broadman Hymnal* gives Tindley credit for two of his other hymns: "Stand by Me" (No. 30) and "Nothing Between" (No. 66). In the 1956 *Baptist Hymnal* Tindley was given recognition as the author and composer of "Trials dark on every hand" as arranged by McKinney.

BY AND BY is the tune name taken from the refrain text.   *H.E.*

Trust and Obey—See *When we walk with the Lord*

Trust, Try, and Prove Me—See *Bring ye all the tithes*

Trusting Jesus—See *Simply trusting every day*

Tune your hearts that all may hear 578

In the spring of 1988, Hugh T. McElrath, then President of the Southern Baptist Church Music Conference, sent a letter to John McKay, then music director of the annual meetings of the Southern Baptist Convention, inviting him to become a member of the conference. McElrath included in the letter a brochure of the 1988 conference program which was to take place in San Antonio, Texas, with its announced theme: "Tune Your Hearts That All May Hear."

Upon receiving the letter, McKay was immediately struck by the musical sound of that phrase. While driving to a singing engagement, he found himself singing those words over and over. Suddenly the music and lyrics came and within an hour, he had the song as it now appears in *The Baptist Hymnal* (1991). McKay's accompanist, Reba Jones, took his original words and tune and made the four-part arrangement. It was mailed to McElrath along with McKay's registration for membership in the Church Music Conference. It was fittingly sung for the

first time at the Castle Hills Baptist Church, San Antonio, immediately following the conference president's address. Its first appearance in a Baptist collection is *The Baptist Hymnal* (1991).

McKay is the tune named for the composer.   *H.T.M.*

Turn Your Eyes upon Jesus—See *O soul, are you weary and troubled?*

Up Calvary's mountain 149

The composer of the tune REDEEMER, Harry Dixon Loes, once observed that many of his songs were written after hearing sermons. Such was the case with this tune, which was inspired by a sermon on "Our Blessed Redeemer." After completing the tune, Loes sent it and the subject matter to his friend and collaborator, Avis B. Christiansen, who supplied the words. The hymn was first published in W. Plunkett Martin and James W. Jelks' *Songs of Redemption* (Atlanta, 1920, No. 117), a collection designed for use by the music evangelists employed by the Home Mission Board. The tune was given its present name by Loes when it was included in *Baptist Hymnal* (1956).   *D.M.*

Victory in Jesus—See *I heard an old, old story*

Walking Along with Jesus—See *Jesus, my Lord and Savior*

Walking in sunlight 424

In this hymn, the usual process of composing text, then music, was reversed. The composer of SUNLIGHT, George H. Cook, brought his tune to Rev. Henry J. Zelley, a Methodist pastor, who supplied the text. Evidently the song was sold to H. L. Gilmour who had it copyrighted in 1899. Reynolds indicated the earliest collection he had found that contained the hymn was *Songs of Praise and Victory* (Philadelphia, 1900) compiled by William Kirkpatrick (1976, 231).

The text and its tune made their first appearance in a Southern Baptist collection in *The Broadman Hymnal* (Nashville, 1940, No. 119). *D.B.*

We are called to be God's people 390

This text was written in 1973 by Thomas A. Jackson for McLean Baptist Church, McLean, Virginia, of which he was pastor. He had expressed frustration over not finding a text to express the concept that God calls persons to be His people in the church. The writing of the hymn was his response to a friend who suggested that he meet this need. He subsequently wrote two other stanzas, but these have not come into common use. (These may be seen in *The Church Musician*, October 1987.) With permission of the author, minor revisions were made for this hymnal by Hugh T. McElrath.

Baptist Hymnal (Nashville, 1975, No. 405) was the first Southern Baptist collection to include this hymn. It was selected as the WMU hymn-of-the-year in 1982-83 and as the hymn-of-the-year by the Church Music Department of the Sunday School Board in 1987-88.

AUSTRIAN HYMN—See hymn 262, Word of God, across the ages. *P.A.R.*

We are climbing Jacob's ladder 474

This anonymous spiritual is based on the story of Jacob's dream as recorded in Genesis 28:11-22. It also incorporates New Testament references to Jesus and "soldiers of the cross." Belden and Hudson (*The Frank C. Brown Collection of North Carolina Folklore*, v. 3, p. 504) state that this Scripture "passage provided the theme of one or more of the early spirituals, sung by whites and blacks."

Lomax (*The Folk Songs of North America*, p. 453) even views this song as "One of the spirituals which emerged from white tradition, but was early remade by Negroes." However, he does not give a clear basis for his opinion. In the earliest collection of Negro spirituals, *Slave Songs of the United States* (1867, p.vi, note), the compilers rejected as inauthentic several songs they heard (as being slave songs) but had seen in (white) Methodist hymn books, including "Climb Jacob's Ladder." This spiritual appears in harmonized form in R. Nathaniel Dett's *Religious Folk-Songs of the Negro as Sung at Hampton Institute* (1927, p. 118). Its first appearance in a hymnal seems to have been in H. Augustine Smith's *American Student Hymnal* (New York, 1928, No. 318). Two additional stanzas begin "I'm gonna ride the golden chariot" and "I'm gonna sit at the welcome table." A remarkable feature of JACOB'S LADDER is its constant syncopation, which occurs in every measure but the last. The tune name is taken from the hymn title.

Its first appearance in a Southern Baptist collection was in *Baptist Hymnal* (Nashville, 1975, No. 147). *H.E.*

We are God's people 383

The words of this hymn were written by Bryan Jeffery Leech and first published in *Hymns for the Family of God* (1976, No. 546). The text is based upon a number of significant New Testament passages, including 1 Peter 2:9; Ephesians 1:22-23, 5:25; and 1 Corinthians 3:16.

The tune SYMPHONY is an arrangement of the opening theme from the fourth movement of Johannes Brahms' Symphony No. 1 in C minor. The composer made the first sketches for this symphony in 1855. However, it was not until 1862 that the first movement was more or less completed (it still lacked the opening slow section).

Brahms then abandoned work on the symphony, returned to it in the summer of 1874, and finished it in September of 1876, though he continued to make minor revisions before its first performance in Karlsruhe, Germany, on November 4, 1876.

The symphony was an instant success and was nicknamed "Beethoven's Tenth Symphony," because it seemed a logical continuation of the work of Brahms' famous predecessor. The first publication of the symphony occurred in 1877.

The adaptation of Brahms' theme as a hymn tune was suggested by Bryan Jeffery Leech because of the strength and singability of the melody. The actual arrangement was the work of Fred Bock. It received its initial publication in *Hymns for the Family of God* (1976, No. 546), where it was set to the present text. The use of classical melodies as hymn tunes was common in the 19th century. The present arrangement is one of the relatively few examples of such adaptations in the late 20th century.

The Baptist Hymnal (1991) is the first publication of both text and tune in a Southern Baptist collection.   *D.M.*

We are one in the bond of love 384

Otis Skillings wrote both words and music and included this song in his musical for youth choirs entitled *Love* (Kansas City, 1971). Because of its popular acceptance, it was also published in song sheets in the present version. Its first inclusion in a hymnal was *Baptist Hymnal* (1975).

The tune SKILLINGS is named for the composer.   *W.J.R.*

We are standing on holy ground 224

This chorus by Geron Davis was originally written as the refrain of a song composed for the dedication of a new sanctuary for the New Life Church in Savannah, Tennessee,

in 1979. Davis had been asked by his father, who was pastor of the church, to write a new song for the first Sunday service in the new building. According to the composer, he went into the sanctuary around 1:30 a.m. on Sunday morning, sat down at the piano in the empty sanctuary, and began to create the new song.

In Davis' words, "When I walked through the door I sensed His presence." Both words and music were completed within 15 minutes. "Holy Ground" has been recorded by several gospel artists and was nominated in 1988 by the Gospel Music Association for the Song of the Year.

For its inclusion in *The Baptist Hymnal* (1991), the first Southern Baptist collection in which has appeared, the tune has been assigned the name HOLY GROUND.   *M.P.*

We are travelers on a journey 613

The text of the hymn was written by Richard Gillard in 1974 and first published in *Songs of the Kingdom* (Auckland, New Zealand, 1977). It was originally written in six four-line stanzas, but has been rearranged into three four-line stanzas for *The Baptist Hymnal* (1991). The author has related in correspondence with the present writer details of this hymn's formation: "Early in 1974 I wrote verse 3 (beginning "I will hold the Christ-light for you") and had no further inspiration. After 5-1/2 months backpacking around England and Europe and visiting Israel, my wife and I returned to New Zealand just prior to Christmas '74. It was then that I was able to write the other 4 verses. The melody was basically written along with the third verse but was 'polished up through that Christmas holiday.' " The original six stanzas of this hymn begin as follows:

1. Sister, let me be your servant
2. We are pilgrims on a journey

3. I will hold the Christ-light for you
4. I will weep when you are weeping
5. Brother, let me be your servant
6. When we sing to God in heaven.

With the recasting of this hymn into three eight-line stanzas, the eight-line tune BEACH SPRING was selected for its musical setting.

BEACH SPRING—See hymn 604, Come, all Christians, be committed.   *H.E.*

We bind ourselves in freedom's chains 626

This hymn grows out of a basic New Testament concept seen in such passages as John 8, Romans 6 and 8, and Galatians 5. The hymn begins with the paradox of being bound by freedom's chains which are forged with love by God in Christ. The imagery of the hymn is rich and vivid and rooted in the New Testament. There is a strong contrast of the false liberty which men seek in creeds and laws and power, in priest and king, with the true liberty which is found in dying to self and in servanthood to Christ. The final stanza is a challenge to stand fast in that freedom and to cry the message of what that freedom means. *The Baptist Hymnal* (1991) is the first Southern Baptist collection to include this hymn.

ST. ANNE—See hymn 73, God moves in a mysterious way.   *S.W.G.*

We gather together 636

"Wilt heden nu treden voor God den Heere" was an anonymous Dutch hymn written in the late 16th century to celebrate Holland's freedom from Spain. It was first included in Adrianus Valerius' *Nederlandtsch Gedenckclanck* (1626 edition). The collection was revived in 1877 when Viennese musician Edward Kremser included a German translation of the text in his *Sechs Altniederlandische Volkslieder* for male chorus and or-

chestra. The English translation by Theodore Baker in 1894 was published in Coenraad V. Bos' *Dutch Folk Songs* (1917).

KREMSER was a folk song also found in Valerius' collection mentioned above. Edward Kremser included it in his 1877 collection of Netherlands folk songs. The tune name commemorates Kremser's rediscovery of this hymn of protection. The hymn and tune appeared in *Baptist Hymnal* (Nashville, 1956, No. 492) for the first time in any Southern Baptist hymnal.   *P.H.*

We give Thee but Thine own 609

The text in six stanzas was written in 1858 and first published in the enlarged edition (1864) of *Psalms and Hymns*, edited by Thomas Baker Morrell and William W. How. Above How's hymn was printed Proverbs 19:17: "He that hath pity upon the poor lendeth unto the Lord." The omitted third and fourth stanzas of the original are:

Oh, hearts are bruised and dead,
    And homes are bare and cold,
And lambs, for whom the Shepherd bled,
    Are straying from the fold.
To comfort and to bless,
    To find a balm for woe,
To tend the lone and fatherless,
    Is Angels' work below.

The first Baptist hymnal in America to include How's text was *The Baptist Praise Book* (New York, 1871). Among Southern Baptists it was introduced in *Baptist Hymnal* (Nashville, 1956, No. 402).

ST. ANDREW was composed in 1866 by Joseph Barnby for the hymn, "Sweet Is Thy Mercy, Lord," by John S. B. Monsell. This tune is named for St. Andrew's Church, Wells Street, London, where Barnby was organist from 1863 to 1871. ST. ANDREW was first published unnamed in Barnby's *Hymn Tunes* (London, 1869), and under its name in his posthumous *Hymn Tunes* (1897). This tune has also been known as AILEEN and MONSELL. *H.E.*

We have come into His house 361

This praise chorus was composed in 1975 by Bruce Ballinger while he was minister of music at Kennedy Road Tabernacle in Brampton, Ontario, Canada. It was written to remind the congregation why they had come together and to focus their attention on God. An omitted third stanza encouraged the raising of hands as an act of worship. Following inclusion in several chorus collections, it made its first hymnal appearance in *The Hymnal for Worship and Celebration* (Waco, 1986).

WORSHIP HIM takes its name from the phrase that occurs six times in the two stanzas.

The Baptist Hymnal (1991) is the first Southern Baptist collection to include this hymn. *P.A.R.*

We have heard the joyful sound 581, 584

This text was written by Priscilla J. Owens for a Sunday School mission anniversary in Baltimore and was adapted to the chorus of "Vive le Roi," from the opera *Les Huguenots* by Giacomo Meyerbeer. The first line originally read, "We have heard *a* joyful sound." The first appearance of the first line as it now is used was in *Gospel Hymns No. 5* (1887). The first Southern Baptist hymnal use of this text was in *The Baptist Hymn and Praise Book* (Nashville, 1904, No. 210), where it was paired with the JESUS SAVES tune.

JESUS SAVES was written for this text by William J. Kirkpatrick and was first published in *Songs of Redeeming Love*, edited by John R. Sweney, C. C. McCabe, T. C. O'Kane, and Kirkpatrick (Philadelphia, 1882). The text and tune appeared in the same year in *The Royal Fountain No. 3*, edited by Sweney

and Kirkpatrick (Philadelphia).

LIMPSFIELD was composed by Josiah Booth as a setting for "We Have Heard the Joyful Sound" in John Stainer's *Church Hymnary* (Edinburgh and Oxford, 1898). *M.P.*

We meet within this holy place 376

Beth Rice Luttrell's Lord's Supper hymn begins in general worship and moves increasingly into the Last Supper experience. This hymn placed second in the 1987 "B. B. McKinney Memorial Hymn Writing Competition" sponsored by the Church Music Department of the Sunday School Board of the Southern Baptist Convention. *S.W.G.*

NICHOLS is the tune is the was written for these words by Ted Nichols in 1988 while he was serving on a church staff in Phoenix, Arizona. This was one of a number of texts that had been sent to the composer by the Church Music Department of the Baptist Sunday School Board with the challenge to write music to any one he chose. The tune was named for the composer by personnel in the Church Music Department.

The Baptist Hymnal (1991) marks the first appearance of both text and tune in any hymnal. *D.M.*

We praise Thee, O God! 469

This hymn was written by William P. Mackay in 1863 and revised in 1867. Originally a hymn of five stanzas, the present version omits stanza four:

All glory and praise to the God of all grace,
Who has brought us, and sought us, and guided our ways.

The scriptural bases are found in Habakkuk 3:2 ("O Lord, revive thy work") and in Psalm 85:6 ("Wilt thou not revive us again").

REVIVE US AGAIN was composed by John J. Husband around 1815 and may have been used with a secular text. Its first pairing with this text seems to have been in Biglow and Main's *New Praises of Jesus* (1867). In *Gospel Hymns and Sacred Songs* (1875), this tune is set to Horatius Bonar's "Rejoice and Be Glad!" with Mackay's text listed as an alternate. Subsequently, Mackay's hymn and Husband's tune became inextricably linked, and they first appeared in a Southern Baptist hymnal in *The Baptist Hymn and Praise Book* (Nashville, 1904, No. 19). The tune name REVIVE US AGAIN appears first in *New Baptist Hymnal* (Nashville, 1926, No. 328). *P.H.*

We praise You with our minds, O Lord 599

"We Praise You with Our Minds, O Lord" was written by Hugh T. McElrath in the summer of 1962. Turning at his desk from a thorny research problem for which interest was lagging, he tried his hand at formulating some verses for the appealing Gaelic melody CLONMEL. Being a teacher charged with the task of challenging the minds of students as well as all other facets of their being, he took Mark 12:30 for his organizing guide and inspiration. During the course of a hot afternoon all three stanzas of the hymn slowly came. The experience in McElrath's own words is recorded in Reynolds' *Companion to Baptist Hymnal* (Nashville, 1975, No. 235). After later making some revisions, McElrath entered the hymn in the Southern Baptist Hymn Writing Competition of 1962 where it received honorable mention.

In addition to Mark 12:30, it has been pointed out that the hymn presents a veritable mosaic of scriptural allusion:

Stanza 1: 1 Corinthians 14:15; John 14:26; John 15:26; Psalm 111:10; Proverbs 1:7; John 14:13; John 16:23-24; James 1:5.

Stanza 2: Romans 6:12-13; Romans 12:1; 1 Corinthians 6:13-20; 1 Corinthians 3:16-17.

Stanza 3: Psalm 24:34; Psalm 73:1; 2 Timothy 2:22; Mark 12:30; Philippians 2:5-11.

The hymn's first appearance in a Southern Baptist collection was in *Christian Praise* (Nashville, 1964, No. 17). In the version found in *The Baptist Hymnal* (1991), minor alterations in language have been made by the author.

CLONMEL is a very old Gaelic tune which may be found in Petrie's *Ancient Music of Ireland* (London, 1902) without words or a name. It is quite possible that it dates back to the ancient Irish church of St. Columba (6th century). The tune was published in 1892 with pensive words of longing for Ireland by the poet Alfred P. Graves and arranged by Sir Charles Villiers Stanford. Known as "The Flight of the Earls," it was first used as a modern hymn tune in the *Church and School Hymnal* (London, 1926). Dr. Eric H. Thiman, chair of the Musical Advisory Committee for the hymnal *Congregational Praise* (London, 1951), gave it the name CLONMEL from a small town in Ireland.

Dr. William J. Reynolds discovered the tune in the *Christian Science Hymnal* (Boston, 1932, No. 136, there called HEAVENWARD and arranged by Sir H. Walford Davies) and arranged it as a unison anthem for children. This was published in *The Church Musician* (March, 1952, pp. 18-19). He later arranged it as a hymn tune for *Baptist Hymnal* (1956) where it was set to Edwin Hodder's text "Thy Word Is Like a Garden, Lord." The tune was first mated with "We Praise You with Our Minds, O Lord" in *Christian Praise* (1964). Obviously the tune has good wearing qualities to have survived so long and such varied experience. *H.T.M.*

We praise You, O God, our Redeemer 19

This text was written by Julia Cady Cory in 1902 as a substitute text for the tune

KREMSER, which is most often sung to "We gather together to ask the Lord's blessing." The organist at Brick Presbyterian Church in New York City, J. Archer Gibson, asked the 19-year-old author for a new text. In a letter to William J. Reynolds (Oct. 21, 1954), Mrs. Cory said she "struggled for two weeks and finally produced what we have today" (1976, 288). The hymn was first sung on Thanksgiving Day, 1902, at Brick Presbyterian Church and at the Church of the Covenant in New York City. One month later, a Christmas stanza was added which is not generally known. The hymn's first publication came in *Hymns of the Living Church* (1910). Slight modernizations of language were made in the present version. The first inclusion of this hymn in a Southern Baptist hymnal was *Baptist Hymnal* (Nashville, 1956, No. 11).

KREMSER—See hymn 636, We gather together.   *P.H.*

We Shall Behold Him—See *The sky shall unfold*

We stand united in the truth 625

Philip M. Young, a minister of music, wrote this hymn for the Southern Baptist Historical Society meeting in 1986. *The Baptist Hymnal* (1991) marks the first inclusion in a Southern Baptist hymnal.

TALLIS' ORDINAL first appeared in Matthew Parker's Psalter (1557) set to the common meter version of "Veni Creator Spiritus." This was the last of Thomas Tallis' tunes in the appendix to the Archbishop of Canterbury's psalter. The term "ordinal" refers to the use of "Veni Creator" for the ordination of priests. The chords at the beginning of the first and third phrases, as well as the final chord, lacked thirds in the original.   *P.H.*

We three kings of Orient are 113

Both words and music were written in 1857 by John Henry Hopkins, Jr., and first appeared in his *Carols, Hymns, and Songs* (1863). The story of the wise men occurs only in the second chapter of Matthew's Gospel: "There came wise men from the east to Jerusalem." Other than the vague reference that they were "from the east," there is no specific information as to their origin. Matthew gives no hint as to exactly how many there were, nor does he name them. Slowly over the years, the wise men have taken on distinct personalities and individual characteristics. The legend now generally accepted has settled on three wise men, and, furthermore, has given each a name, a background, and a life story. *The Baptist Hymnal* (1991) is the first Southern Baptist hymnal to include this Christmas song.

KINGS OF ORIENT is the name given Hopkins' tune in recent hymnals.   *W.J.R.*

We utter our cry 631

Fred Kaan wrote this text in February 1983 while on vacation in Cuba. It was written at the request of Olle Dahlen, Swedish ambassador to the United Nations, for the opening service of the Christian World Conference on Life and Peace. Kaan was a delegate to the conference and was present at the service, held in the Uppsala Cathedral on April 20, at which the hymn was first sung to the tune HANOVER. The delegates, from 62 countries, sang the hymn several times and included it in the conference's official message. The present version employs stanzas 1, 2, 4, and 6 of the original six. *The Hymn Texts of Fred Kaan* (Carol Stream, 1985) includes the complete text under the heading, "A hymn on life and peace." Its first publication in a book for congregational use was in Nancy Rosenberger Faus' *Singing for Peace* (Carol Stream, 1986), which substituted "leaders" for "statesmen."

The Baptist Hymnal (1991) is the first Southern Baptist collection to include this hymn.

LYONS—See hymn 16, O worship the King.   *P.A.R.*

We welcome glad Easter 168

This anonymous hymn first appeared in *Junior Hymnal* (1964), published by Broadman Press for older children. Nothing is known of the origins of the text. Alterations were made for the present hymnal to begin each stanza with "we" and to replace "ye" with "all" and "sweet" with "glad" in the refrain.

ST. DENIO—See hymn 6, Immortal, invisible, God only wise.   *P.H.*

We will glorify 213

Both the words and music of this song were written by Twila Paris. Copyrighted in 1982, the song was recorded by the author/composer and published in a sheet music version. The first hymnal publication of the song—in an arrangement by David Allen—was in *The Hymnal for Worship & Celebration* (Waco, 1986), edited by Tom Fettke. *The Baptist Hymnal* (1991) follows the version from this collection and is the first Southern Baptist hymnal to include the song.

WE WILL GLORIFY is the tune named for the common title.   *D.M.*

We worship round this table 373

Helen Sims Smaw wrote the words of this hymn about 1976 while she was serving as an Editorial Assistant in the Sunday School Division of the Baptist Sunday School Board, Nashville, Tennessee. The author has stated that the inspiration for the writing of the hymn came primarily from two sources: her editorial work with Ralph L. Murray on Page Kelley's January Bible Study textbook on Ex-

odus, and the influence of a series of noonday prayer services led by Dr. Hogan L. Yancey, pastor of Downtown Presbyterian Church, Nashville. The use of the term "mercy seat" in stanza one was probably derived from Exodus (see Ex. 25:17-22). Other scriptural passages, most notably Psalm 18:1, also serve as part of the background to the hymn (see stanza five). *The Baptist Hymnal* (1991) is the first publication of the text.

QUEBEC–See hymn 494, Take up your cross.   *D.M.*

We'll Work Till Jesus Comes—See *O land of rest, for thee I sigh*

We're Marching to Zion—See *Come, we that love the Lord*

We've a story to tell 586

Henry Ernest Nichol wrote both the text and the tune in 1896. It was published that same year in *The Sunday School Hymnary* (London). It came into American use in *Hymns and Tunes for Schools* (New York, 1907).

MESSAGE was the name given by the author/composer to summarize the content of the hymn.

New Baptist Hymnal (Nashville, 1926, No. 261) was the first Southern Baptist book to include this hymn. It was adopted as the hymn of the Girls Auxiliary (predecessor of Girls in Action and Acteens) in 1924.   *P.A.R.*

Were you there 156

As is typical of folk hymnody, the origin of this spiritual is unknown. It was one of the first songs of African-American Christians to be included in hymnals of predominantly White denominations. The present version is based on that in *Folk Songs of the American Negro* (Nashville, 1907), edited by John J. Work, Jr. and Frederick J. Work.

In that collection there were two additional stanzas before the last: "Were you there when they pierced him in the side?" and "Were you there when the sun refused to shine?" *Baptist Hymnal* (Nashville, 1975, No. 108) was the first Southern Baptist collection to include "Were You There."

WERE YOU THERE is named from the repeated question of the text.   *P.A.R.*

What a fellowship, what a joy divine 333

Showalter's account, quoted in Lester Hostetler's *Handbook to the Mennonite Hymnary* (1949), related that while he was teaching a singing school at Hartsells, Alabama, he received correspondence from two former pupils in South Carolina, both of whom had lost their wives. In his expression of sympathy to them he quoted from Deuteronomy 33:27: "The eternal God is thy refuge, and underneath are the everlasting arms." As Showalter pondered these words, he felt they ought to be expressed in a song. He then wrote the words and music of the refrain, and requested his friend Elisha A. Hoffman to write appropriate stanzas.

Hoffman's three stanzas with Showalter's refrain and music first appeared as the opening hymn of two 1887 songbooks which are identical in all aspects except for the words "Glad" and "Song" in their titles: *The Glad (Song) Evangel for Revival, Camp, and Evangelistic Meetings*, compiled by Showalter, L.M. Erlsinger, and A. J. Perry (Dalton, 1887, No. 1). *The Glad Evangel* is in the personal library of William J. Reynolds, and *The Song Evangel* is in the Library of Congress. The tune's original key is A major. The earliest Baptist inclusion of this hymn is in *Glorious Praise* by William H. Doane and William J. Kirkpatrick (Louisville, 1904, No. 90). This hymn, arising from the seven-shape gospel tradition of the South, has also become popular among Black Baptist congregations, where it is sung in a compound meter at a slow tempo.

SHOWALTER is the tune named for the composer.   *H.E.*

What a friend we have in Jesus 182

This hymn was written in 1855 by Joseph Scriven (1819-86) in Canada and sent to his mother in Ireland to comfort her in a time of sorrow. Scriven once explained to a friend, "The Lord and I did it between us." The first appearance of the hymn in a hymnal seems to have been in J. B. Packard's *Spirit Minstrel: a Collection of Hymns and Music* (Boston, 1857). It was included in Horace Hasting's *Social Hymns, Original and Selected* (Boston, 1865). *Baptist Hymn and Praise Book* (Nashville, 1904, No. 355) was the first Southern Baptist hymnal to contain this hymn.

CONVERSE is the tune composed by Charles C. Converse in 1868. It appeared first in *Silver Wings* (Boston, 1870, No. 98) edited by "Karl Reden," the German form of Converse's name and a pseudonym used by him. The tune is there attributed to "Karl Reden."

Ira D. Sankey recounts in his autobiography how the hymn came to his attention: "Returning from England in 1875, I soon became associated with P. P. Bliss in the publication of what later became known as *Gospel Hymns No. 1*. After we had given the completed compilation to our publishers I chanced to pick up a small paper-covered pamphlet of Sunday-School hymns, published at Richmond, Virginia. I discovered this and sang it through, and determined to have it appear in *Gospel Hymns*. As the composer of the music was my friend C. C. Converse, I withdrew from the collection one of his compositions and substituted for it, 'What a Friend We Have in Jesus.' Thus the last hymn that went into the book became one of the first in favor" (334-35).

The tune is also called ERIE for the city in Pennsylvania where Converse lived for many years and has also been called FRIENDSHIP. The tune's first appearance in a Southern Baptist hymnal was in *Baptist Hymn and Praise Book* (Nashville, 1904, No. 355). Although found in hymnals published earlier, CONVERSE as a tune name is first used in a Southern Baptist Hymnal in the *Chapel Book* (Nashville, 1923, No. 44).   *S.W.G.*

What a wonderful change 441

The words of this hymn were written by Rufus H. McDaniel in 1914 as a response of faith to the death of his son, Herschel, in 1913. Charles H. Gabriel composed the tune for McDaniel's text in 1914 and the completed hymn was published in *The Message in Song Numbers 1 and 2*, compiled by Arthur S. Magann, Charles F. Allen, and John P. Hillis (Philadelphia, 1914, No. 155).

McDaniel's text originally consisted of five stanzas. The omitted second stanza read:

I have ceased from my wand'ring and going astray,
Since Jesus came into my heart!
And my sins which were many are all washed away
Since Jesus came into my heart!

The tune was given the name MCDANIEL in *Baptist Hymnal* (1956).

Its first appearance in a Southern Baptist collection was in *Songs of Redemption* compiled by W. Plunkett Martin and James W. Jelks (Atlanta, 1920, No. 35).   *D.M.*

What can I give Him 610

This text is stanza five of Christina Rossetti's beautiful poem, "In the Bleak Midwinter." The date of composition is unknown, but it was first published in January of 1872 in *Scribner's Monthly* with the title "A Christmas Carol." *The English Hymnal* of 1906 was the first hymnal to use the po-

em. *The Baptist Hymnal* (1991) is the first Southern Baptist collection to include both text and tune.

CASTLE was written by Don Cason for *The Hymnal for Worship and Celebration*. The copyright date for the tune is 1986.   *D.B.*

What can wash away my sin? 135

This hymn first appeared in *Gospel Music* (New York, 1876, No. 7) compiled by William H. Doane and Robert Lowry. Lowry, was pastor of the Park Avenue Baptist Church in Plainfield, New Jersey, from 1875 to 1885 when he resigned because of poor health. He remained in Plainfield until his death in 1899. Hebrews 9:22, "Without the shedding of blood there is no remission," was the Scripture reference given. The refrain and frequent repetition of "Nothing but the blood of Jesus" (it is sung 12 times when all four stanzas are used) is reminiscent of camp-meeting style. The first stanza in particular is an example of the "Question and Answer" hymn pattern described by Carl Price (431-42). We do not use Lowry's final two stanzas:

Now by this I'll overcome-
Nothing but the blood of Jesus,
Now by this I'll reach my home-
Nothing but the blood of Jesus.

Glory! Glory! this I sing-
Nothing but the blood of Jesus,
All my praise for this I bring-
Nothing but the blood of Jesus.

This text with its tune first appeared as early as 1909 in the American Baptist publication compiled by Southern Baptists, Robert H. Coleman and W. W. Hamilton, *The Evangel* (Philadelphia, 1909, No. 117).

PLAINFIELD was chosen by the 1956 Baptist Hymnal committee as the name of the tune for "Nothing But the Blood."   *D.B.*

What Child is this 118

This text is from William Chatterton Dix's poem, "The Manger Throne" written around 1865. This and his "As with Gladness Men of Old" are among the most widely known of his many Christmas and Easter carols. Although this hymn was included in William J. Reynolds' compilation for Broadman Press (Nashville, 1958), *Songs for Christmas*, this is its first appearance in a Southern Baptist hymnal.

While the tune GREENSLEEVES may have been popular even earlier, it is referred to in the registers of the Stationers' Company, September 1580, where Richard Jones was licensed to print "A new Northern Dittye of the *Lady Greene Sleeves*." At the same time a license was granted to Edward White to print "A ballad, being the Ladie Green Sleeves *Answere* to Donkyn his frende." Within a few days, it appeared with a sacred text, "*Greene Sleves* moralised to the Scripture, declaring the manifold benefites and blessings of God bestowed on sinful man." In *The Merry Wives of Windsor*, Shakespeare has Mrs. Ford speak of Falstaff's inconsistency of speech and life in saying, "I would have sworn his disposition would have gone to the truth of his words; but they do no more adhere and keep pace together, than the Hundredth Psalm to the tune of 'Green Sleeves.'"   *S.W.G.*

What If It Were Today—See *Jesus is coming to earth again*

What wondrous love is this 143

The text of "Wondrous Love," a well-known folk hymn in the South, appeared anonymously in Methodist compiler Stith Mead's *A General Selection of the Newest and Most Admired Hymns and Spiritual Songs Now in Use* (2nd ed., Lynchburg, 1811, No. 121) in six stanzas. This text was also published anonymously in the same year in Baptist compiler Starke Dupuy's *A Selection of Hymns and Spiritual Songs from the Best Authors* (Frankfort, 1811, No. 198) in seven stanzas. The present stanzas are 1, 2, 5, and 6 of those in Mead's collection and 1, 2, 4, and 6 in Dupuy's. The two omitted stanzas in both books begin "Ye winged seraphs fly, Bear the news" and "Ye friends (sons) of Zion's King, Join his praise." Dupuy also included a third stanza missing from the present version, beginning "And when to that bright world, We arrive." The present four stanzas from Dupuy are identical except for 4, which begins, "And when from death we're free, we'll sing on." In Mead there are variants in two stanzas of the present version. Stanza 1 ends "To send this precious peace, To my soul." The final stanza begins, "And while from death I'm free, I'll sing on."

The earliest publication of the tune WONDROUS LOVE was in the appendix of the 1840 [2nd] edition of William Walker's *The Southern Harmony, and Musical Companion* (Spartanburg; Flat Rock, NC; Philadelphia; [1st ed.] 1835,p.220) Only the first stanza of the anonymous text is given, while the tune is attributed to "Christopher." Walker gives all six stanzas as found in Mead in his *The Christian Harmony* (Philadelphia, 1867, p. 359), where he comments further on the tune: "Arranged by James Christopher, of Spartanburg, S.C. A very popular old southern tune." Thus WONDROUS LOVE, whose hexatonic melody is in the Dorian mode, existed in oral tradition for some time before it was arranged by Christopher, whose identity is uncertain. Christopher's arrangement of WONDROUS LOVE was republished anonymously four years later in the first edition of *The Sacred Harp* (Hamilton; Philadelphia, 1844, p. 159). Although WONDROUS LOVE is in the same stanzaic form as the ballad of Captain Kidd, it is not in the same melodic family, as Ellen

Jane Porter has demonstrated in her study, *Two Early American Tunes: Fraternal Twins?* (New York, 1975). (The tune CAPTAIN KIDD also appears in Walker's *Southern Harmony,* 1835, p. 50.) In addition to its acceptance in the *Southern Harmony* and *Sacred Harp* singing traditions, "What Wondrous Love Is This" has gained a firm place in recent American hymnals and is also widely known in various choral arrangements.

This folk hymn did not enter a Southern Baptist hymnbook until *Baptist Hymnal* (Nashville, 1975, No. 106).   *H.E.*

When all my labors and trials are o'er 520

The words and music of this hymn were written by Charles H. Gabriel. On February 28, 1900, Gabriel sold the song to E. O. Excell, who published it in *Make His Praise Glorious* (Chicago, 1900, No. 54) under the title "Oh, That Will Be Glory." In the early years of the 20th century, Gabriel's song was nicknamed the "Glory Song," which accounts for the name of the tune, GLORY SONG. The song was inspired by Gabriel's acquaintance with Ed Card, superintendent of the Sunshine Rescue Mission in St. Louis, Missouri. Card was nicknamed "Old Glory Face" because of his exuberant personality and frequent use of the word "glory." Card's manner of ending his prayers with the expression "and that will be glory for me" served as the basis for the refrain of Gabriel's hymn.

This song appeared in the very first collection compiled by Robert H. Coleman in collaboration with W. W. Hamilton, later to be president of Baptist Bible Institute in New Orleans, Louisiana (now New Orleans Baptist Theological Seminary). The hymnal was titled *The Evangel* (Philadelphia, 1909, No. 14).   *D.M.*

When Christ was lifted from the earth 562

This hymn was written by Brian Wren in October, 1970, in response to some now-forgotten controversy and tension in the congregation at Hockley, England, where he ministered at the time. Delaying for some time the use of the hymn which originally had six stanzas, Wren later reduced it for publication to the four he considered the more lasting. The hymn is based on two New Testament references: John 12:32-33 and Romans 15:7. *The Baptist Hymnal* (1991) is the first Southern Baptist collection to include the hymn.

HAYES, a bold common meter tune, named for its composer (*The Baptist Hymnal* [1991] music subcommittee member Mark Hayes), was accepted as the musical setting for Brian Wren's text "When Christ was lifted from the Earth." *The Baptist Hymnal* (1991) is the first Southern Baptist collection to include both text and tune.   *H.T.M.*

When I pray 460

This children's song (words and music by Marie Ingham) was first published in the August 1959 issue of *The Church Musician* magazine. The composer prefers to remain anonymous. *The Baptist Hymnal* (1991) is the first Southern Baptist hymnal to contain this song.

WHEN I PRAY is the tune named for the common hymn title.   *P.H.*

When I survey the wondrous cross 144

Galatians 6:14 inspired Isaac Watts to write a five-stanza poem entitled "Crucifixion to the World by the Cross of Christ." Its first appearance was in Book II of *Hymns and Spiritual Songs* (London, 1707) where it began:

When I survey the wondrous cross
Where the young Prince of Glory died.

Beginning with *The Hymnal 1940* and continuing in *The Hymnal 1982*, the Episcopalians use this original version. The altered version used in *The Baptist Hymnal* (1991) was made by Watts himself in an enlarged edition of *Hymns and Spiritual Songs* (London, 1709). Watts' fourth stanza was marked by brackets indicating it could be omitted. It reads:

His dying crimson, like a robe,
Spreads o'er his body on the tree;
Then I am dead to all the globe,
And all the globe is dead to me.

A supplement to George Whitefield's *Collection of Hymns* (London, 1757) contained the first appearance of the four-stanza version in common use today. The hymn is found in the first Southern Baptist Collection, *The Baptist Psalmody* (Charleston, 1850, No. 933).

HAMBURG was written by Lowell Mason in 1824 while he was living in Savannah, Georgia, where it was first sung in the First Presbyterian Church. "It first appeared in print in *The Boston Handel and Haydn Society Collection of Church Music* (3rd. ed., 1825) with the information that it was arranged from a Gregorian chant" (Reynolds, 1976, 241). *D.B.*

When in our music God is glorified 435

This hymn was written by Fred Pratt Green in 1972 at the request of John Wilson who wanted a praise or choir anniversary text for Charles V. Stanford's tune EN-GLEBERG. Several musical settings have been made. The original first line read "When in man's music, God is glorified." The change to "our" was done to meet sexist-language objections. However, Green feels the loss of the juxtaposition of "man" and "God" weakens the line. *The Baptist Hymnal* (1991) marks the first Southern Baptist collection to include this hymn.

ENGELBERG was written by Charles V. Stanford for William Walsham How's "For All the Saints." It was set to that text in the 1904 edition of *Hymns Ancient and Modern*. After the text was set to Ralph Vaughan Williams' tune SINE NOMINE in the *English Hymnal* of 1906, ENGELBERG declined in popularity. It offers a fine setting for Green's text and deserves wide use. *D.B.*

When morning gilds the skies 221

The German hymn, "Bein frühen Morgenlicht" ("By early morning light"), appeared in the *Katholisches Gesangbuch* for the diocese of Würzburg (1828), being found in several forms to 1858 such as "Wach ich früh Morgens auf" and "Wach' ich am Morgen auf," so it may have appeared before 1828. Edward Caswall took one of these German versions and translated it into English, publishing six stanzas in Fromby's *Catholic Hymns* (London, 1854) and eight more in his own *Masque of Mary* (London, 1858). A second widely used translation of this German hymn with the same first line in English was made by Robert Bridges for his *Yattendon Hymnal* (Oxford, 1899), consisting of 20 three-line stanzas. In *The Baptist Hymnal* (1991) there are four six-line stanzas, 1, 2, and 4 of which are from Caswall, with stanza 3 from Bridges.

LAUDES DOMINI was composed by Joseph Barnby for Caswall's translation and published as an alternate tune in the Appendix to the original edition of *Hymns Ancient and Modern* (London, 1868, No. 314). Robert Coleman introduced this hymn to Southern Baptists in *The Popular Hymnal* (Dallas, 1918, No. 1). *H.E.*

When my life-work is ended 528

This song expressing delight in the anticipation of meeting the Savior in the heavenly realm was written by Fanny Crosby in

1891. As in the case of many of her creations, she had been asked to set words to a preexistent melody. In this instance it was a peppy tune by the well-known bandmaster and song leader, John R. Sweney. The music, reminiscent of popular song, helped "My Savior First of All" gain wide use in both England and America, although one critic has wondered if almost any other kind of tune could have more appropriately expressed the thought of the words.

The song with Sweney's tune first appeared in *Songs of Love and Praise* (Philadelphia, 1894, No. 128), edited by Sweney along with William J. Kirkpatrick and H. L. Gilmour. The first Southern Baptist collection to contain it was *The Baptist Hymn and Praise Book* (Nashville, 1904, No. 561).

I SHALL KNOW HIM is a brass band sort of tune typical of many of the gospel songs of its era. Written by a former Civil War bandmaster, John R. Sweney, it achieved enormous popularity in the late 19th and early 20th centuries. The tune was first given its name in *Baptist Hymnal* (1956).   H.T.M.

When peace, like a river 410

An event of great tragedy is associated with the writing of this hymn. Its author, Horatio G. Spafford, was a Chicago lawyer and the respected friend of prominent evangelists such as Moody, Sankey, and Bliss. In 1873, Spafford, his wife, and their four daughters were advised by their family doctor to take a European holiday, primarily to improve the state of Mrs. Spafford's health. Unexpected business matters forced Spafford to postpone his departure, but his wife and daughters sailed as scheduled on the S. S. *Ville du Havre* in November, 1873. An English sailing vessel, the *Lochearn*, collided with the ship on November 22. The *Ville du Havre* sank in a matter of minutes. The daughters were lost, but Mrs. Spafford was

rescued. On December 1, when the survivors had been brought to Cardiff in Wales, Mrs. Spafford sent the message "Saved alone." Spafford wrote the words of this hymn as the ship taking him to meet his wife neared the spot of the tragedy.

This hymn and its tune was first included in a Southern Baptist collection in *The Baptist Hymn and Tune Book* (Nashville, 1904, No. 253).

VILLE DU HAVRE, named for the fatal ship whose sinking took the lives of four of the author's daughters, was composed by Philip B. Bliss for the "It Is Well with My Soul" text. It appeared in *Gospel Hymns No. 2* (Chicago, 1876) compiled by Ira D. Sankey and Bliss. *D.B.*

When the church of Jesus 396

Fred Pratt Green wrote this hymn in 1968 for a Stewardship Renewal Campaign for the Trinity Methodist Church in Sutton, a borough of London. While the stewardship emphasis is evident (particularly in stanza three), there is also a strong challenge to the church to minister to the world around us. *D.B*

KING'S WESTON was composed by Ralph Vaughan Williams for Caroline M. Noel's "At the Name of Jesus," and first appeared in *Songs of Praise* (1925). The tune name comes from that of a country house on the Avon River near Bristol, England. *P.H.*

When the Morning Comes—See *Trials dark on every hand*

When the Roll Is Called Up Yonder— See *When the trumpet of the Lord shall sound*

When the trumpet of the Lord shall sound 516

James M. Black, the writer of both the words and music, relates the following account of the inspiration for this hymn in *My Life and the Story of the Gospel Hymns* (1906) by Ira D. Sankey:

"While a teacher in a Sunday-school and president of a young people's society, ...I one day met a girl, fourteen years old, poorly clad and the child of a drunkard. She accepted my invitation to attend the Sunday-school, and joined the young people's society. One evening at a consecration-meeting, when members answered the roll-call by repeating Scripture texts, she failed to respond. I spoke of what a sad thing it would be, when our names are called from the Lamb's Book of Life, if one of us should be absent; and I said, 'O God, when my own name is called up yonder, may I be there to respond!' I longed for something suitable to sing just then, but I could find nothing in the books. We closed the meeting, and on my way home I was still wishing that there might be a song that could be sung on such occasions. The thought came to me, 'Why don't you make it?' I dismissed the idea, thinking that I could never write such a hymn. When I reached my house my wife saw that I was deeply troubled, and questioned me, but I made no reply. Then the words of the first stanza came to me in full. In fifteen minutes more I had composed the other two verses. Going to the piano, I played the music just as it is found to-day in the hymn-books, note for note, and I have never dared to change a single word or a note of the piece since" (302-03). *H.T.M.*

William J. Reynolds notes that the earliest known appearance of the song is in J. H. Alleman's *Songs of the Savior's Love* (1892). The words and music are first found in a collection for Baptists in Robert Coleman and W. W. Hamilton's *The Evangel* (Philadelphia, 1909, No. 126).

ROLL CALL is the tune named for the central theme of the hymn. *P.H.*

When upon life's billows 644

This text was written by Johnson Oatman, Jr., and first published with this tune in *Songs for Young People* (Cincinnati, 1897) which E. O. Excell compiled for the Methodist Book Concern.

BLESSINGS was composed by Excell. This name was given to the tune in *Baptist Hymnal* (Nashville, 1956).

Kingdom Songs (Nashville, 1921, No. 164) was the first Southern Baptist collection to include this gospel song. *P.A.R.*

When We All Get to Heaven—See *Sing the wondrous love of Jesus*

When we walk with the Lord 447

John H. Sammis wrote this text. Daniel Brink Towner, the composer of the tune TRUST AND OBEY, recalls the writing of the hymn and tune:

"Mr. Moody was conducting a series of meetings in Brockton, Massachusetts, and I had the pleasure of singing for him there. One night a young man rose in a testimony meeting and said, 'I am not quite sure—but I am going to trust, and I am going to obey.' I just jotted that sentence down, and sent it with the little story to the Rev. J. H. Sammis, a Presbyterian minister. He wrote the hymn, and the tune was born. The chorus 'Trust and obey, for there's no other way to be happy in Jesus, But to trust and obey' was written before the hymn was" (Sankey, 326).

The text and tune first appeared in *Hymns Old and New* (Chicago, 1887, No. 59). *Songs of Redemption*, a volume compiled by W. Plunkett Martin and James W. Jelks and published by the Home Mission Board (Atlanta, 1920, No. 226), was the first Southern Baptist hymnal collection to contain this text and tune. Robert Coleman published it earlier in *The Popular Hymnal* (Dallas, 1918, No. 226). *S.W.G.*

Where He Leads Me—See *I can hear my Savior calling*

Wherever He Leads I'll Go—See *"Take up thy cross and follow Me"*

While by the sheep we watched 108

This anonymous German carol comes from a 16th-century Nativity play. Theodore Baker translated the first three and last of the original nine stanzas for an octavo published in New York in 1895 by G. Schirmer. The opening line and the last two stanzas have been recast by unknown writers. Baker's first line, "While by my sheep I watched at night," was closer to the German original, "Als ich bei meinen Schlafen wacht."

JÜNGST is named for Hugo Jüngst, who arranged the music for the octavo cited above. It is also known as the "Echo Carol" because of its repeated phrases. *Songs of Hope* (Chicago, 1948) was the first hymnal to include this text and tune.

The first appearance of this carol in a collection for Southern Baptists is in *The Baptist Hymnal* (1991). *P.A.R.*

While passing through this world 571

"Let Others See Jesus in You" was written by B. B. McKinney and first published by Robert H. Coleman in *Harvest Hymns* (Dallas, 1924, No. 7). The chorus, however, was written earlier and appeared in Coleman's *Pilot* (Dallas, 1922, No. 248). It was then included in *The Modern Hymnal* (Dallas, 1926, No. 244) and subsequently in most of the Southern Baptist collections published since. Typical of many McKinney songs, it challenges Christians to be faithful in their living and witnessing.

COLEMAN is the name assigned to B. B. McKinney's tune for "Let Others See Jesus in You" by the committee for *Baptist Hymnal* (1956). It is in recognition of Robert H. Coleman, Baptist publisher, with whom McKinney worked for many years. *H.T.M.*

Whiter than Snow—See *Lord Jesus, I long to be perfectly whole*

Who can cheer the heart like Jesus 429

Thoro Harris wrote both words and music, sometimes referred to as "All That Thrills My Soul Is Jesus," in 1931 when he lived in Chicago, Illinois. The song was published in Harris' *Revival Echoes* (1931). In 1942 he assigned the copyright of the song to the Nazarene Publishing House, Kansas City, Missouri. Southern Baptists first sang Harris' song from *Baptist Hymnal* (Nashville, 1975, No. 434).

HARRIS was named for the composer by the Hymnal Committee for *Baptist Hymnal* (Nashville, 1975, No. 434). *W.J.R.*

Who is He in yonder stall 124

This hymn by Benjamin R. Hanby first appeared in *The Dove: A Collection of Music for Day and Sunday Schools, Juvenile Singing Classes, and the Social Circle* (Chicago, 1966), one of a series of quarterly songbooks, *Our Song Birds*, that Hanby edited with George F. Root. Hanby's original text has eight two-phrase stanzas, to which unknown writers have made additions and alterations. These may have emerged from oral tradition. The stanzas in *The Baptist Hymnal* (1991) consist of: Hanby's 1 and 4; two anonymous lines; Hanby's 3 and an anonymous line; Hanby's 5 and an anonymous line; and Hanby's 7 and 8. The only major change from Hanby's own words is in the last line of the final stanza, which read "Rules the world of light alone?"

WHO IS HE, by Hanby, appeared with the text at its first publication. It is also called LOWLINESS. Donald P. Hustad made the present arrangement, which pairs the stanzas and slightly alters the harmonization, for *Worship and Service Hymnal* (Chicago, 1957).

The Baptist Hymnal (1991) is the first Southern Baptist collection to include this hymn.   *P.A.R.*

"Whosoever heareth" 314

Both words and music of this hymn were written by Philip P. Bliss. It grew out of a series of meetings conducted by the English evangelist Henry Morehouse in the winter of 1869-70. For seven consecutive services, Morehouse preached sermons based on John 3:16. Bliss attended these services and inspired to write this hymn. It was first published in George F. Root's *The Prize, a Collection of Songs, Hymns, Chants, Anthems and Concert Pieces, for the Sunday School* (Chicago, 1870; reprint, Cincinnati, n.d., p.7). In 1874 Bliss included this hymn in his *Gospel Songs*. It was published in a Southern Baptist collection in *Jehovah's Praise* by Isham E. Reynolds and B. B. McKinney (Fort Worth, 1925, No. 82).

WHOSOEVER is the tune name taken from the opening statement of each stanza.   *H.E.*

"Whosoever" Meaneth Me—See *I am happy today*

"Whosoever Will"—See *"Whosoever heareth"*

Why Do I Sing About Jesus—See *Deep in my heart there's a gladness*

With boldness in your speech 397

Terry W. York wrote these words on June 13, 1980, while he was serving as minister of music and youth at the First Southern Baptist Church of Sacramento, California. The author has stated that there was no particular occasion for the writing of the hymn. In its original form, the text did not contain the tag line, "sing, congregation, sing." This was added in 1984 when the hymn was selected by the Church Music Department of the Baptist Sunday School Board as the theme song for that summer's Ridgecrest and Glorieta Church Music Leadership Weeks. The words were sent out to several composers for a setting. David Schwoebel's tune MICHELLE, named for his wife, was selected for publication with the text.

The composer of the tune has stated that it was written in about 20 minutes' time on January 17, 1984, while he was serving as minister of music at St. Matthew United Methodist Church, Belleville, Illinois.

This hymn was first published in the program booklets for the Church Music Leadership Weeks at Ridgecrest, North Carolina, and Glorieta, New Mexico, in the summer of 1984. *The Baptist Hymnal* (1991) marks the first hymnal appearance of both text and tune.   *D.M.*

Without Him 300

Mylon R. LeFevre wrote both words and music when he was 18 years of age. More than 125 artists have recorded the song since it was first written in 1963. Its first hymnal inclusion was in *Baptist Hymnal* (1975).

The hymnal committee for *The Baptist Hymnal* (1991) requested and received permission from the copyright holder to change the words "You can't" to "Do not" in the refrain. That change is noted by an asterisk on the hymn page.

WITHOUT HIM is the tune name taken from the opening words of the two stanzas.   *W.J.R.*

Wonderful grace of Jesus 328

Haldor Lillenas, who was then pastor of the Church of the Nazarene in Auburn, Illinois (1916-19), wrote this text and tune for music evangelist Charles H. Alexander. It was introduced in 1918 by Homer Hammontree at the Bible Conference at Northfield, Massachusetts, and first published in *Tabernacle Choir* (1922), edited by R. J. Oliver and Lance Latham. *Great Gospel Songs* (1929) was the first Nazarene hymnal to contain Lillenas' hymn.

In Lillenas' autobiography he cautions against distorting the words of the hymn by singing WONDERFUL GRACE at too fast a tempo.

The Baptist Hymnal (1991) is the first Southern Baptist collection to include this hymn, although it was known to many Southern Baptists through its appearance in Robert Coleman's *The Modern Hymnal* (Dallas, 1926, No. 466). *P.H.*

Wonderful Words of Life—See *Sing them over again to me*

Wonderful, Wonderful Jesus—See *There is never a day so dreary*

Word of God, across the ages 262

In 1951 the Hymn Society of America invited the writing of hymns on the Bible in connection with the publication of the Revised Standard Version of the Bible which was to appear in 1952. Ferdinand Q. Blanchard's hymn was one of the winning hymns and was first published in a Hymn Society of America pamphlet entitled "Ten New Hymns on the Bible" which appeared in 1953. Some minor alterations of language have been made in *The Baptist Hymnal* (1991). *Baptist Hymnal* (Nashville, 1956, No. 176) was the first Southern Baptist hymnal to contain this hymn.

AUSTRIAN HYMN is the tune written in January 1797, by the famous Austrian composer Franz Joseph Haydn (1732-1809) for the Austrian national anthem, "Gott erhalte Franz den Kaiser," by Lorenz Leopold Hauschka. It was first performed for the birthday of Emperor Franz II on February 12, 1797. The hymn served as the Austrian national anthem for many years. The tune is based on a Croatian folk song, "Vjatvo rano se ja vstanem." The melody was used later by the composer as the theme for variations in the slow movement of his String Quartet in C, Opus 76, No. 3, which is known as the "Emperor" Quartet. The tune first appeared in English collections in Edward Miller's *Sacred Music* (London, 1802). The tune appears for the first time in a Southern Baptist hymnal in the *New Baptist Hymnal* (Nashville, 1926, No. 127). *S.W.G.*

Worship the Lord 115

John S. B. Monsell's original hymn was entitled "O Worship the Lord in the Beauty of Holiness" and was published in his *Hymns of Love and Praise* (1863) as five four-line stanzas. There is another version by Monsell and a number of versions altered by other writers. The second stanza of the present version was written by David Steele. The hymn is intended for Epiphany (January 6) in which the church celebrates the wise men's adoration of Christ and His first manifestation to the Gentiles. The hymn is based on Psalm 96:9 and is rich in biblical imagery.

JANICE is the tune, named for the composer's (Tom Fettke) wife. It is a simple, singable melody in a standard hymn-like style. It especially complements David Steele's second stanza. *The Baptist Hymnal* (1991) is the first Southern Baptist hymnal to contain this tune. *S.W.G.*

Worthy is the Lamb 157

Both text and tune of this hymn were written by Stephen Leddy in 1963 while he was a student at Baylor University. One day as he was studying in his dormitory room, his eyes rested on the title of a book, *Worthy Is the*

Lamb, by Ray Summers. Feeling an inspiration to write a song based upon the words of that title, he set to work immediately and completed the hymn in about an hour.

WORTHY LAMB is the tune name given to Leddy's setting of his text. Both text and tune name are based upon Revelation 5:12: "Worthy is the Lamb that was slain to receive power, and riches, and wisdom, and strength, and honour, and glory, and blessing." Words and music were first published in *A Time to Sing* (Carol Stream, 1967). The appearance of this hymn in *The Baptist Hymnal* (1991) is its first in a Southern Baptist collection.   *M.P.*

Worthy of worship 3

Terry W. York wrote the words, and Mark Blankenship the music, of this hymn in 1988 as part of an Easter musical, *Praise the Risen Savior*, which was published by GENEVOX in 1989. The author has noted that this hymn was written partly as an attempt to blend the style of the praise chorus with that of the traditional hymn.

The tune JUDSON is named for Judson Baptist Church, Nashville, Tennessee, of which both the author and composer are members. *The Baptist Hymnal* (1991) is the first hymnal to include this text and tune.   *D.M.*

Would you be free from the burden of sin? 132

Lewis E. Jones wrote both words and music of this hymn while attending a camp meeting at Mountain Lake Park, Maryland. The manuscript was purchased by Dr. H. L. Gilmour, and the hymn was first published in *Songs of Praise and Victory*, compiled by William J. Kirkpatrick and Gilmour (Philadelphia, 1899, No. 58). It also appeared in the same year in *Gospel Praises*, compiled by Kirkpatrick, Gilmour, and J. L. Hall (Philadelphia, No. 69).

POWER IN THE BLOOD was the name assigned to this tune in *Baptist Hymnal* 1956. *Songs of Redemption* (Atlanta, 1920, No. 121) was the first Southern Baptist hymnal to include this text and tune.   *M.P.*

Would you bless our homes and families 507

This text was written in 1974 by Walter Farquharson. In a letter to Harry Eskew, the author has described his purpose in writing this hymn:

"It attempts to celebrate real families, not some ideal family, for pressures are great on the family, whatever its configuration. The hymn therefore recognizes that the way for families is often that of 'anxious walking.' At the same time, it celebrates family as a school of grace and place of preparation and enabling for service of the whole human family."

This hymn was first published in a collection of songs for worship, *Worship the Lord* (Oakville, Ontario, Canada: 1977), where it is set to a tune by Canadian Ron Klusmeier. The first inclusion of this hymn in a Southern Baptist collection is *The Baptist Hymnal* (1991).

NETTLETON—See hymn 15, Come, Thou Fount of every blessing.   *H.E.*

Ye Must Be Born Again—See *A ruler once came to Jesus*

Ye servants of God 589

This hymn was published in the Wesleys' *Hymns for Times of Trouble and Persecution* (1744) in six four-line stanzas. It was the first hymn in the section "Hymns to be sung in Tumult." The "tumult" has reference to the dynastic quarrels of the 1740s in England and the ridiculous claims that the Wesleys were involved in an attempt to overthrow the Crown. The text first appeared in a

Southern Baptist hymnal in *The Baptist Psalmody* (Charleston, 1850, No. 127).

LYONS—See hymn 16, O worship the King. *S.W.G.*

Years I spent in vanity and pride 138

This hymn was written by William R. Newell (1868-1956) and the tune, CALVARY, by Daniel B. Towner (1850-1919), both of whom were associated with Moody Bible Institute in Chicago. William J. Reynolds recounts the writing of the text and tune:

"The words had been vaguely in his mind for a few weeks and then, one day, on his way to lecture, they suddenly began crystallizing in his mind. He stepped into an unoccupied classroom and wrote them down quickly on the back of an envelope as they now appear. Proceeding to his class, he met Daniel B. Towner, then director of music at the Institute, handed him the verses and suggested that he compose suitable music for them. When the author returned from his class, Dr. Towner had completed the tune, and they sang it together. It first appeared in *Famous Hymnal* (1895, No. 79)" (1976, 249).

This hymn first appeared in a Southern Baptist hymnal in *Kingdom Songs* (Dallas, 1921, No. 52) although it is found three years earlier in Coleman's *The Popular Hymnal* (Dallas, 1918, No. 177).   *S.W.G.*

Your love, O God, has called us here 509

This wedding hymn was written in 1981 by Russell Schulz-Widmar for *The Hymnal 1982* (New York, 1985). In that hymnal it was set to the tune WAREHAM. It was the author's intent to provide an accessible hymn that acknowledged God as the source of all good, including love; that recognized the revelation of God's love in Jesus; and that sought blessing on the couple being married, as well as on others present, especially other married couples.

This text entered Southern Baptist hymnody in *The Baptist Hymnal* (1991).

CANONBURY—See hymn 568, Lord, speak to me, that I may speak.   *P.A.R.*

Your supper, Lord, before us spread 374

Joseph F. Green wrote this text at the request of Bill F. Leach of the Church Music Department of the Baptist Sunday School Board for a children's choir curriculum unit on the Lord's Supper. Leach then asked Irving Wolfe to make a unison and two-part anthem setting of this text, which was published in *The Church Musician* (December, 1961, p. 44). The hymn tune version was made for *The Junior Hymnal* (Nashville, 1964, No. 169), in which the composer named the tune REYNOLDS for William J. Reynolds, who had been his doctoral student at George Peabody College for Teachers (now a part of Vanderbilt University). This text and tune appeared in the *Baptist Hymnal* (1975) with its original first line, "Thy supper, Lord, before us spread." The present version of this text is a revision made by the author and the hymnal editing staff. In place of the tune REYNOLDS, the familiar tune HAMBURG was preferred for use in the current hymnal.

HAMBURG—See hymn 144, When I survey the wondrous cross.   *H.E.*

AUTHORS, COMPOSERS, AND SOURCES

Abe, Yuji–Little information is available about this Japanese Christian. He is known to have attended Kanto Gakuin High School in Yokohama, Japan, in the late 1950s or early 1960s. According to Nobuaki Hanaoka, a friend from Abe's high school days, and the translator of his song, Mr. Abe had no musical training except for singing in the school choir.   *D.M.*

KANTO–Jesus, My Friend, Is Great–190

Ackley, Alfred Henry (b. Spring Hill, PA, Jan. 21, 1887; d. Whittier, CA, Jul. 3, 1960) received his early music instruction from his father, and later studied harmony and composition in New York with Hans Kronald and in London at the Royal Academy of Music. He was an accomplished cellist. A graduate of Westminster Theological Seminary, he was ordained to the Presbyterian ministry in 1914 and served churches in Wilkes-Barre, Pennsylvania; Pittsburgh, Pennsylvania (as assistant to Dr. Hugh Thompson Kerr, editor of the Presbyterian *Hymnal*, 1933); and Escondido, California. With his elder brother Bentley, who was pianist and private secretary for Billy Sunday, he helped compile hymnals and gospel songbooks for the Rodeheaver Publishing Company. He claimed to have written around 1500 hymns, gospel songs, children's songs, secular songs, and college glee club songs. "He Lives" was his most popular. He was awarded an honorary Doctor of Sacred Music degree by John Brown University, Siloam Springs, Arkansas.   *P.H.*

ACKLEY–He Lives–533

Adams, Sarah Fuller Flower (b. Harlow, Essex, England, Feb. 22, 1805; d. London, England, Aug. 14, 1848) was the second daughter of Benjamin Flower, editor of *The Cambridge Intelligencer* and *The Political Review*. In 1834 she married William Bridges Adams, an inventor and civil engineer. An actress, her 1837 portrayal of Lady Macbeth in London's Richmond Theater was favorably received. Concern for her health caused her to abandon a stage career. She began to write poetry and prose for *The Repository*, a periodical edited by her minister, William Johnson Fox, of the South Place Unitarian Church, Finsbury, London. Mrs. Adams contributed 13 hymns to Fox's *Hymns and Anthems* (1841) including "Nearer, My God, to Thee." Her sister, Eliza, was the music editor.

Other literary works include a religious dramatic poem, *Vivia Perpetua* (1841), and a child's catechism. She worked with Vincent Novello on the music edition of *Songs for the Months*.   *D.B.*

Nearer, My God, to Thee–458

Adkins, Donna (b. Louisville, KY, Jun. 18, 1940) was born to a mother and father who were both church musicians and traveled as gospel singers. Donna began singing publicly when she was two years old and at age twelve began playing for the family quartet. She attended Asbury College, Wilmore, Kentucky, and the University of Louisville. Donna has served on the music staff at several churches. In addition to her current position as secretary to the Senior Pastor at Covenant Church of Pittsburgh, where her husband, Jim, is Administrative Pastor, she is actively involved in the music ministry of the church. She and her husband are the parents of two grown children.   *D.M.*

GLORIFY THY NAME–Glorify Thy Name–249

Ahnfelt, Oscar (b. Gullarp, Skåne Province, Sweden, May 21, 1813; d. Karlshamn, Sweden, Oct. 22, 1882), the son of a Swedish Lutheran pastor, became a popular singer of sacred songs through his association with Carl Olof Rosenius, an outstanding Swedish lay preacher in the mid-19th century. Ahnfelt received his early education from his older brothers and began studying for the ministry at Lund University in 1929. He withdrew from school, however, and worked as a tutor for several years before beginning music study at Stockholm in 1840. It was there that he met Rosenius (with whom he traveled in Denmark and Norway) and Caroline V. Sandell-Berg. The first collection of Ahnfelt's songs was published in 1850 under the sponsorship of the famous singer Jenny Lind. Twelve editions of his *Andeliga Sånger* were published between 1850-1877, containing approximately 200 songs.   *M.P.*

BLOTT EN DAG–66

Akers, Doris (b. Brookfield, MO, May 21, 1922) wrote her first gospel song when she was 10 years old. Although lacking in any formal music training, she has ably conducted choirs throughout the nation. She organized the Los Angeles Sky Pilot Choir in 1957. On one occasion, when told she possessed something "magic" that captured the attention of the congregation, she replied, "Magic, nothing–it's just letting go and releasing the Spirit of God." She now makes her home in Columbus, Ohio.   *W.J.R.*

MANNA–Sweet, Sweet Spirit–243

Alexander, Cecil Frances Humphreys (b. Tyrone Co., Ireland, 1818 [some older sources give 1823]; d. Londonderry, Ireland, Oct. 12, 1895) was the daughter of Major John Humphreys. Around 1835 the family moved to Miltown House in Tyrone County where she wrote several hymns and published *Verses from the Holy Scripture* (1846) and, perhaps her most important volume, *Hymns for Little Children* (1848) which went through more than 100 editions. Being interested in the poor and needy, she and her sister established a school for the deaf. In 1850 she married the Reverend William Alexander, rector of the county of Tyrone, who later became bishop of Derry and Raphoe, and finally, archbishop of Armagh and primate of all Ireland. For a time she walked miles daily ministering to the sick and taking food to the poor regardless of their creed. She founded a Girl's Friendly Society in Londonderry when she and her husband were there. Her collections of poetry also include *Narrative Hymns for Village Schools* (1853), *Poems on Subjects in the Old Testament* (in two parts, 1854 and 1857), and *Hymns Descriptive and Devotional* (1858).   *S.W.G.*

All Things Bright and Beautiful–46
He Is Risen! He Is Risen!–166
Jesus Call Us O'er the Tumult–293

Alexander, James Waddell (b. Hopewell, VA, Mar. 13, 1804; d. Sweetsprings, VA, Jul. 31, 1859) was born on the estate named Hopewell, the home of his maternal grandfather, James Waddell, in Louisa County, Virginia. He was a son of Archibald Alexander (1772-1851), a prominent Princeton theologian. At the age of only 13 he entered the College of New Jersey (now Princeton University), being graduated near the top of his class in 1820. In 1821 he entered Princeton Theological Seminary, leaving in 1824 to become a teacher of mathematics at the College of New Jersey. In 1825 Alexander was given a license to the ministry by the Presbytery of New Brunswick, thereafter he moved to Virginia, where he was ordained to the ministry in 1827. After serving as pastor in Charlotte County, Virginia, he became pastor of the First Presbyterian Church of Trenton, New Jersey, 1829-32. For the following 12 years (1833-44) he was professor of belles lettres and rhetoric at the College of New Jersey. From 1844 to 1849 he was pastor of Duane Street Presbyterian Church, New York City. Returning once more to Princeton, he was professor of church history and church government at Princeton Theological Seminary, 1849-1851. After spending the summer of 1851 in Europe, he became pastor of the Fifth Avenue Presbyterian Church, a congregation consisting largely of persons from his previous pastorate in New York. He served as pastor there until his death eight years later. A recognized scholar, Alexander contributed often to the *Princeton Quarterly Review* and wrote more than 30 volumes for the American Sunday School Union. He demonstrated much interest in Latin and German hymnody, his writings and translations appearing in the *New York Observer*, the *Princeton Review*, and *Kirchenfreund*. In addition to his widely used translation, "O sacred Head, now wounded," he translated "Stabat Mater" (Near the cross was Mary weeping) and "Jesu dulcis memoria" (Jesus, how sweet Thy memory is). His translations were published in *The Breaking Crucible: And Other Translations of German Hymns* (New York, 1861).   *H.E.*

O Sacred Head, Now Wounded (tr.)–137

Alford, Henry (b. London, England, Oct. 7, 1810; d. Canterbury, England, Jan. 12, 1871) was an Anglican minister. The son of a rector, he was ordained in the Church of England in 1833, a year after graduation from Trinity College, Cambridge. After service with his father, he was vicar of Wymeswold, Leicestershire (1835-53), and minister at Quebec Chapel, London (1853-57). He became dean of Canterbury in 1857, serving there until his death. He was a distinguished lecturer and author, producing 50 books, including 18 of hymns and poetry. His four-volume commentary on the Greek New Testament established him as one of the leading biblical scholars of his day.   *P.A.R.*

Come, Ye Thankful People, Come–637

Alford, Janie (b. Nashville, TN, Oct. 8, 1887; d. Nashville, TN, Jun. 10, 1986) was a Presbyterian layperson and poet. She attended Watkins Institute Night School and the University of Tennessee at Nashville, but was prevented by family obligations from completing her college education. After 40 years as a medical secretary, she opened her own letter shop, which she ran until she was 87. She was president of the Tennessee Federation of Women's Clubs and editor of its magazine. A lifelong Presbyterian, she was a charter member of Westminster Presbyterian Church in Nashville, where she served as librarian and church school teacher. That congregation published a booklet of her poetry, *Poems by Janie*, in 1981. She was encouraged in her hymnwriting by composer and arranger Hal Hopson, who was director of music at the church. They collaborated on *Nine Hymns for the Church Year* (1979), a supplement to the hymnal used at the Westminster church.   *P.A.R.*

Sound Aloud the Trumpet–171

Allen, Chester G. (b. 1838; d. 1878) was an American gospel tune writer and editor who shared in the publication of a number of collections of evangelistic songs such as *Bright Jewels* (Chicago, 1869). To this collection, in which he collaborated with W. F. Sherwin and W. H. Doane, he contributed 10 other musical settings besides JOYFUL SONG, his tune for Fanny Crosby's "Praise Him! Praise Him!." His wife also was a tune writer. Other than this, little is known of him. *H.T.M.*

JOYFUL SONG–227

Allen, David Jonathan is the pseudonym of an arranger who prefers to remain anonymous. *D.M.*

WE WILL GLORIFY (arr.)–213
COME, LET US REASON (arr.)–313
OPEN OUR EYES (arr.)–499

Allen, Dennis Clyde (b. Anniston, AL, Nov. 27, 1952) is the son of Rev. L. C. and Virginia (Dixon) Allen. Dennis was educated at the University of Georgia (B.A., 1974) and The Southern Baptist Theological Seminary (M.C.M., 1976). While in seminary, he served as minister of music at Mill Creek Baptist Church, Radcliff, Kentucky. Following his graduation, he held similar positions at the First Baptist Church of Summerville, Georgia (1977-79), and the First Baptist Church of Marianna, Florida (1979-86). In 1987 he became a music design editor in the Youth/Adult/General Materials Development section of the Baptist Sunday School Board's Church Music Department (1987-1991). Currently a freelance composer, his choral compositions are found in the catalogs of many publishers. He is also heavily involved in electronic music technology and in concertizing

with his wife, Nan. The Allens are the parents of two sons, Mark and Drew. *D.M.*

MARIANNA–642

Allen, George Nelson (b. Mansfield, MA, Sep. 7, 1812; d. Cincinnati, OH, Dec. 9, 1877) was Professor of Sacred Music and Geology at Oberlin College from 1837 until his retirement in 1864. A pupil of Lowell Mason, he founded the Oberlin Musical Association, known today as the Musical Union. Allen established the piano department at Oberlin, raised funds for the first Music Hall, and invited nationally known conductors to lead the Musical Association in "Grand Concerts" at commencements. The renowned Oberlin Conservatory of Music, founded in 1865, evolved from the foundations laid by Allen. He compiled *The Social and Sabbath Hymn Book* (1844) and *Hymns for Social Worship* (1844?), neither of which contained tunes. His MAITLAND tune, however, was set to "Must Jesus Bear the Cross Alone" in the former collection. *P.H.*

PRECIOUS LORD–456
MAITLAND–475

Andraé, Reba Jones (b. San Antonio, TX, Nov. 30, 1939) was born in the Salvation Army Hospital, San Antonio, and was adopted by George (now deceased) and Ada Vanderslice. She graduated from Baylor University (B.A. in piano performance, 1962). Since 1961, she has served as pianist for music evangelist John McKay, who wrote both text and tune to MCKAY. Reba took the original words and tune and made the four-part arrangement. (See "Tune your hearts that all my hear.") She is the mother of four children, one of whom is Melody Tunney. Reba is married to Andy Andraé. Both Reba and Andy are volunteers for the

Home Mission Board, serving at First Baptist Church, South Lake, Fort Worth, Texas. Reba has a cassette tape entitled "Piano Praise" (Rainbow Recording, 1986). *J.V.A./H.T.M.*

McKay (arr.)–578

Allen, Richard (b. Philadelphia, PA, Feb. 14, 1760; d. Philadelphia, PA Mar. 26, 1831), was born a slave and at an early age was sold to a farmer near Dover, Delaware. After his conversion Allen began to preach and conduct services in his master's house, ultimately converting the slave-owner himself, who allowed him to purchase his freedom in 1777. In 1787 he and Absalom Jones were ejected from white St. George Methodist Episcopal Church, Philadelphia. Allen and a number of other blacks then formed Bethel Church, the first black Methodist church in the country. He was instrumental in the formation of the African Methodist Episcopal Church in 1794. When the African Methodist Episcopal Church was incorporated in 1816 Allen was chosen as its first bishop, an office he held until his death. Allen's *Collection of Hymns & Spiritual Songs* (Philadelphia, 1801) contained a number of folk-hymn texts, including the first known printing of the hymn "I love thee." *D.M.*

I Love Thee–211

Allen, Tom (b. Fayetteville, NC, Nov. 14, 1958) is a graduate of Furman University (BA, 1985) and the Southern Baptist Theological Seminary (M.Div., 1989). He has served as organist in churches in North Carolina, Indiana, and Kentucky. At the present writing he is a bivocational pastor at Weston Baptist Church, North Vernon, Indiana. *H.T.M.*

Jesus, at Your Holy Table–377

Andrews, Mark (b. Gainsborough, Lincolnshire, England, Mar. 21, 1875; d. Montclair, NJ, Dec. 10, 1939) had training from John Thomas Ruck at Westminster Abbey before emigrating to the United States in 1902. He lived and worked as a church musician in several churches in Montclair and became quite active in the affairs of the American Guild of Organists. A versatile composer, he had string quartets, cantatas, anthems, organ pieces, and songs to his credit. *H.T.M.*

Lauda Anima (Andrews)–32

Angell, Warren Mathewson (b. Brooklyn, NY, May 13, 1907) is a Southern Baptist best known for his many years as Dean of the School of Fine Arts at Oklahoma Baptist University. Trained as both a singer and a pianist at Syracuse University (B.M., 1929; M.M., 1933) and Teachers College, Columbia University (Ed.D., 1944), he taught at Murray State Teachers College from 1934 until 1936, when he moved to OBU. Between that time and his retirement as dean in 1973, he developed a reputation as an outstanding teacher, administrator, and choral conductor. He has also made important contributions as a composer, arranger, and author. He lives in active retirement in Black Mountain, North Carolina. *P.A.R.*

Gloria (harm.)–100

Antes, John (b. Frederick, PA, 1740; d. Bristol, England, 1811) is credited with the original version of Monkland, which was included in a manuscript *Collection of Hymn Tunes Chiefly Composed for Private Amusement* lodged in the archives of the

Moravian Church, London, England. Antes was born in America into a large family of early German settlers. In 1752 he was a student in a boys' school in Bethlehem, Pennsylvania. In 1764 he was called to Herrnhut, Saxony, the international center of the Moravians. After being ordained as a Moravian minister, he spent 11 years (1770-81) in Cairo as the first American-born missionary to Egypt. Returning to Herrnhut for a while, he then went in 1783 to Fulneck, England where he remained with the Moravian Brethren for a period of 25 years. In 1808 he moved to Bristol, remaining there until his death.

In addition to his work as a clergyman, Antes was known as a watchmaker, a violin maker, an inventor, and a composer of concerted vocal compositions, string trios, and chorales. These musical works establish him as one of the finest early American composers of sacred music.   *H.T.M.*

MONKLAND–235

Arne, Thomas Augustine (b. London, England, Mar. 12, 1710; d. London, England, Mar. 5, 1778), although overshadowed by Handel, is considered England's finest native-born composer of the 18th century. Following study at Eton, his career in music was delayed by law studies at his father's request. Eventually music prevailed, and he won fame as a composer of oratorios, masques, and operas. He is best known today for the patriotic song, "Rule Britannia."   *D.B.*

ARLINGTON–353, 358, 481

Asuncion, Francisca (b. Philippines, 1927) graduated from Westminster Choir College. She served as a choir director and pianist in Manila before immigrating to the United States. She adapted Philippine folk songs for use with Christian texts for the hymnal *Hymns from the Four Winds* (Nashville, 1983). According to I-to Loh, Director/Editor for *Hymns from the Four Winds*, in a letter to this writer, she has been the choir director of Rosewood United Methodist Church in Los Angeles, California.   *P.H.*

COTTAGE GROVE (arr.)–Dear Lord, Lead Me Day by Day–459

Atkins, George. The identity of this author is not known. Earlier attempts to identify him with a Methodist circuit-riding preacher of East Tennessee, George Atkins (d. 1827), have been apparently in error, since the author of "Brethren, we have met to worship" was referred to in 1819 as "the late Rev. George Atkins" (see *The Hymn*, October 1980, p. 247 and April 1985, p. 18).   *D.M.*

Brethren, We Have Met to Worship–379

Atkinson, Frederick Cook (b. Norwich, England, Aug. 20, 1841; d. East Dereham, England, Nov. 30, 1896) was chorister and assistant organist at Norwich Cathedral for 11 years. After receiving his Bachelor of Music degree from Cambridge in 1867, he served as organist and choirmaster in Bradford, returned to Norwich Cathedral from 1881 to 1885, and then moved to St. Mary's Parish Church in Lewisham. He composed services, anthems, hymn tunes, songs, and piano music.   *D.B.*

MORECAMBE–245

Babcock, Maltbie Davenport (b. Syracuse, NY, Aug. 3, 1858; d. Naples, Italy, May 18, 1901) was educated at Syracuse

University and Auburn Theological Seminary. As a student, he excelled in academics, athletics, and music, including the development of skills on the organ, piano, and violin. Following his ordination to the Presbyterian ministry, he became pastor of the First Presbyterian Church, Lockport, New York. For 14 years he was pastor of the Brown Memorial Church in Baltimore and in 1899 was called to succeed Henry van Dyke as pastor of the Brick Presbyterian Church of New York City. He had served this church for only 18 months when he died while on a Mediterranean cruise during a trip to the Holy Land. A collection of his sermons and poems, *Thoughts for Everyday Living,* was published in 1901, a few months after his death. *M.P.*

This Is My Father's World–43

Bach, Johann Sebastian (b. Eisenach, Germany, Mar. 21, 1685; d. Leipzig, Germany, Jul. 28, 1750) is regarded as the most distinguished musician of the most distinguished family in the history of music. After musical training at Ohrdruf and Lüneburg, he served briefly at Arnstadt and Mühlhausen. His three main posts for which he composed music were as organist-cappellmeister at Weimar (1708-17), director of the court orchestra at Cöthen (1717-23), and cantor, organist, and teacher at Leipzig (1723-50). Bach was little known during his day outside of Germany, and there primarily as a fine organist and teacher. His music came to be recognized for its greatness in the past century, due to the efforts of distinguished musicians, such as Felix Mendelssohn in Germany and England and Samuel S. Wesley in England. The details of Bach's life and music are readily available in standard reference works.

Bach was primarily a church musician and composer. His faith commitment is reflected in the words which he wrote at the close of nearly all of his works: *Soli Deo Gloria* (To God alone be praise). In his choral works, especially his cantatas (over 200 survive), Bach harmonized with unsurpassed genius the older chorale melodies to be sung by choirs. His chorale harmonizations, known as the "Bach chorales," are used as models for harmony classes today. Although he composed few if any chorale melodies, he edited the tunes for Schmelli's *Musicalisches Gesangbuch* (1736), to which he contributed 16 original tunes. A collected edition of Bach's chorale harmonizations was brought out by his son Carl Philipp Emanuel (1765-69) titled *371 Vierstimmige Choral Gesänge.* These congregational song melodies were a significant influence on Bach's surviving organ works, 173 of them which are based on chorales. *H.E.*

ERMUNTRE DICH MEIN SCHWACHER (harm.)–114
PASSION CHORALE (harm.)–137

Bain, James Leith (b. Scotland, *c.* 1860; d. Wallasey, Cheshire, England, Sep. 19, 1925) was a poet, a composer of tunes, a mystical writer, and a spiritual healer known as "Brother James." After abandoning his early Christian beliefs for agnosticism, his lost faith was restored in part through the help of the Christo Theosophic Society. His revival of religious faith resulted in his writing numerous melodies and poems. A Christian Scientist, he organized a Brotherhood of Healers to treat both spiritual and physical infirmities. He reportedly would often sing to his patients during healing sessions as part of their treatment. His latter years were spent in Liverpool working among children in the slums of that city. He lived with his sister in retirement for about 20 years in West Kirby, a coastal town about 10 miles from Liverpool. He was buried at the West Kirby Parish Church.

One of his books dealing with healing is *The Brotherhood of Healers. Being a Message to all Practical Mystics... and an Introduction to the Study of the Essential Principles of Spiritual, Psychic and Mental Healing* (1906). A collection of Bain's hymns and prayers is titled *In the Heart of the Holy Grail, Being the Hymns and Prayers of the Christ-Child to the Christ-Mother...* . (Bradford and London, 1911). His tune BROTHER JAMES'S AIR was published at the end of his book addressed to the nations involved in World War I: *The Great Peace: Being a New Year's Greeting to our Motherland and the Nations at Present in Conflict and a Welcome to Them All to the Feast of the Great Peace...* (London, 1915). Bain's works were published under the pen name, James Macbeth.   *H.E.*

BROTHER JAMES' AIR–523

Baker, Henry (b. Nuneham Courtenay, Oxfordshire, England, Jun. 16, 1835; d. Wimbledon, Surrey, England, Feb. 1, 1910), the son of an Anglican minister, was both an engineer and a musician. He was educated at Winchester and studied civil engineering at Cooper's Hill. For many years he constructed railroads in India. John Bacchus Dykes encouraged Baker to study music and, in 1867, he earned a music degree at Exeter College, Oxford. Several of his hymn tunes appeared in W. Garrett Horder's *Worship Song* (1905).   *S.W.G.*

QUEBEC–373, 494

Baker, Henry Williams (b. Belmont House, Vauxhall, England, Jun. 21, 1821; d. Monkland, England, Feb. 12, 1877) was

educated at Trinity College, Cambridge. In 1844 he was ordained to the Anglican clergy, becoming Vicar of Monkland in 1851 and serving in that capacity until his death. His work as chairman of the committee that prepared *Hymns Ancient and Modern* (1861) had a significant impact on English hymnody. He contributed original hymns as well as translations. The last words he reportedly uttered were the third stanza of his "The King of Love My Shepherd Is:"

Perverse and foolish oft I stray'd,
But yet in love He sought me,
And on His shoulder gently laid,
And home, rejoicing, brought me.
D.B.

Of the Father's Love Begotten (tr.)–251
O God of Love, O King of Peace–619

Baker, Margaret Reaves (b. Honey Grove, TX, Oct. 3, 1922), earned degrees in music at Stetson University (B.A., 1944) and Southwestern Baptist Theological Seminary (M.S.M., 1957). She married Frank J. Baker in 1947. Her ministry through music has included serving as Minister of Music at Dauphin Way Baptist Church, Mobile, AL (1951-54) and Miami Shores Baptist Church, Miami, FL (1957-59). In 1964 she and her husband were appointed by the Foreign Mission Board of the Southern Baptist Convention to serve as missionaries in Taejon, South Korea, where they remained until 1970. Subsequent assignments with the Foreign Mission Board took them to Zambia, Africa (1970-80) and Johannesburg, South Africa (1980-87). In each missionary assignment, Margaret Baker worked actively in using music as an expression of faith. In South Africa she served as chairman of the national music committee of the Baptist Union of South Africa.   *M.P.*

BAKER–The Whole World Is Singing–593

Baker, Richard D. (b. Farmersville, TX, May 12, 1927) was educated at Baylor University, Southwestern Baptist Theological Seminary, University of California, and San Diego State University. He served as minister of music, Birchman Avenue Baptist Church, Fort Worth, Texas (1950-56). For more than 20 years he was involved in an international ministry of concerts and crusades, singing on "The Baptist Hour," in Billy Graham Crusades, and in evangelistic work with his preacher brother, Bo Baker. Since 1980 he has served as minister of music at Prestonwood Baptist Church, Dallas, Texas. In addition to being an evangelistic singer and recording artist, he has written more than 200 songs. *W.J.R.*

MCKINNEY–Have You Been to Calvary–324
LORIANN–All to Thee–482

Baker, Theodore (b. NY, Jun. 3, 1851; d. Dresden, Germany, Oct. 13, 1934) was preparing for a business career, but decided upon music. He received his doctorate from the University of Leipzig (1882), where his dissertation on the music of the Seneca tribe became the first serious study of native American music. Edward MacDowell used it as a source for themes in his Second (Indian) Suite for orchestra. From 1892-1926, he was literary editor and translator of books, librettos, and articles for G. Schirmer. Upon retirement, he returned to Germany. In 1900, he published *Baker's Biographical Dictionary of Musicians* (now in its 7th edition, 1984; ed. Nicolas Slonimsky). *P.H.*

Lo, How a Rose E'er Blooming
  (tr. st. 1,2) –78
We Gather Together (tr.)–636

Christ, We Do All Adore Thee
  (English version)–647

Ball, (Linda) Diane (b. TN, Apr. 29, 1941) is youth and outreach director for Koloa Assembly of God Church, Koloa, Kauai, Hawaii. She is married to Jay Ball, and they have five children. She is also area manager for the Kauai 700 Club, Director of Koamalu Shelter for the Homeless, and Director of Springs of Living Water Camps in northern California. Her father, Cecil Cooper, sang with the San Francisco Opera. "In His Time" was her first published song. She has also been published in *Virtuous Woman*, a Christian magazine. *P.H.*

IN HIS TIME–In His time–53

Ballinger, Bruce Thomas (b. Montreal, Quebec, Canada, Apr. 19, 1945) is a church musician and composer. Before shifting his professional attention to music, he was trained as a mathematician at McMaster University (B. Sc., 1967) and McGill University (M. Sc., 1969, and doctoral study). He served three Pentecostal Assemblies of Canada/Assemblies of God congregations as minister of music: Kennedy Road Tabernacle, Brampton, Ontario (1972-80); Evangelistic Temple, Houston (1980-85); and Calvary Temple, Denver (1985-86). Since 1986 he has devoted himself to leading workshops and composing. His publications include more than 40 original songs and choruses as well as anthems and musicals. *P.A.R.*

WORSHIP HIM–We Have Come into
  His House–361

Baring-Gould, Sabine (b. Exeter, Devonshire, England, Jan. 28, 1834; d. Lew-Trenchard, North Devonshire, England,

Jan. 2, 1924), the son of an English squire, traveled extensively in Germany and France during his early years. He earned B.A. and M.A. degrees at Clare College, Cambridge, and taught in the choir school of St. Barnabas, Pimlico, London, and at Hurstpierpoint College, Sussex. After being ordained in 1864, he became curate of Horbury, near Wakefield, where he ministered until 1867. Some of his best-known hymns were written for the children of the mission at Horbury Bridge. He served at Dalton, Yorkshire, and as rector at East Mersea, Essex, before becoming rector of Lew-Trenchard, in 1881, after inheriting the family estate there upon his father's death.

Baring-Gould was a prolific writer, whose publications included books of history, biography, travel, theology, fiction, and poetry. It was said that he had more works listed in the British Museum catalog than any other writer of that day. His collaboration with H. Fleetwood Shephard in publishing *Songs and Ballads of the West* (1889-91) reflected his interest in collecting folk songs. He collaborated with Cecil J. Sharp, England's noted authority on folk song, in the publication of *English Folk-songs for Schools.*   *M.P.*

Onward, Christian Soldiers–493

Barnard, Charlotte Alington (b. Louth, Lincolnshire, England, Dec. 23, 1830; d. Dover, Kent, England, Jan. 1, 1869) studied music theory under William Henry Holmes, professor of piano at the Royal Academy of Music. She was married to Charles Cary Barnard in 1854. Publishing over 100 ballads under the pseudonym "Claribel," she is best known for "Come Back to Erin." She is the composer of another tune also named BARNARD sung to the once popular song for youth, "Give of your best to the Master."   *H.T.M.*

BARNARD–602

Barnby, Joseph (b. York, England, Aug. 12, 1838; d. London, England, Jan. 28, 1896) was a prolific composer of hymn tunes in the Victorian period. In 1897, the year after his death, 246 of his settings were published. The son of Thomas Barnby, an organist, Joseph was a highly gifted musician. He was a chorister at York Minster at the age of seven, a teacher at ten, an organist at twelve, and a choirmaster at fourteen. At the age of 16 he went to London to study music at the Royal Academy of Music. In London his two most important organist-choirmaster positions were at St. Andrew's Wells Street, 1863-71, where he developed a choir recognized as the finest in the city; and at St. Anne's, Soho, 1871-86 (the church where William Croft, composer of the hymn tune ST. ANNE, served 1700-11), where he established an annual performance of Bach's passion music. From 1875 to 1892 he was precentor of Eton College, resigning to become the second principal of the Guildhall School of Music. From 1861 to 1876 he was musical advisor to the firm Novello, Ewer & Co., where, beginning in 1867, he directed a choral group that became known as "Barnby's Choir." A widely recognized musician in his country, he became a Fellow of the Royal Academy of Musicians and in 1892 was knighted by Queen Victoria. Barnby's compositions include 46 anthems, numerous services, the oratorio *Rebekah*, and partsongs. For High Anglican churches he edited *The Hymnary* (1872). He also edited *The Congregational Mission Hymnal* (1890), *The Congregational Sunday School Hymnal* (1891), and *The Home and School Hymnal* (1893), the last-named for the (Presbyterian) Free Church of Scotland. Among his most popular hymn tunes in addition to those in this hymnal are MERRIAL (Now the day is over), LONGWOOD (Spirit of God, descend upon my heart), JUST AS I AM (Just as I am, thine own to be), and SARUM (For all the saints, who from their labors rest).   H.E.

LAUDES DOMINI–221
O PERFECT LOVE–512
ST. ANDREW–609

Bartlett, Eugene Monroe (b. Waynesville, MO, Dec. 24, 1885; d. Siloam Springs, AR, Jan. 25, 1941), the son of Hiram Bartlett, was educated at Hall-Moody Institute, Martin, Tennessee, and at the William Jewell Academy (1913-14), Liberty, Missouri. As president of the Hartford Music Company, Hartford, Arkansas (1918-1935), he published many song books and edited a music magazine, *Herald of Song.* Later he was affiliated with the Stamps-Baxter Music Company, Dallas, Texas, and the James D. Vaughan Music Company, Lawrenceburg, Tennessee. He was widely known as a gospel singer, composer, singing school teacher, editor, and publisher. His best known song is "Victory in Jesus." The Gospel Music Hall of Fame inducted him as a member in 1979. His "Victory in Jesus" is included in *The United Methodist Hymnal* (1989).   P.H.

HARTFORD–Victory in Jesus–426

Bartlett, Eugene (Gene) Monroe, Jr. (b. Greenwood, AR, May 4, 1918; d. Oklahoma City, OK, Jul. 10, 1988) began his career in the gospel music field. Under the auspices of his father's Hartford (Ark.) Music Company, Gene attended singing schools led by teachers such as Will H. and

J. H. Ruebush and Homer Rodeheaver. He studied for two years at Ruebush's Shenandoah (VA) Conservatory of Music (1935-37). When his father was employed by the Stamps-Baxter Publishing Company in Dallas, Texas, Gene joined the Stamps-Baxter Quartet and simultaneously attended Southern Methodist University as an English literature major. His father suffered a stroke, and Gene was forced to withdraw from school.

He was invited to become student choir director at the First Baptist Church, Batesville, Arkansas, and to attend Arkansas College in the same city. It was here he met his future wife Emma-Jeanne who was also a student. His last year of college was spent at John Brown University, Siloam Springs, Arkansas, where he received the B.A. degree in 1940. The Bartletts were married on August 25, 1940.

Gene traveled with a gospel quartet in Arkansas, Missouri, and Oklahoma until he was called to the Ohio Street Baptist Church, Pine Bluff, Arkansas in 1941. He served a series of churches including First Baptist Church, North Little Rock, Arkansas; First Baptist Church, Blytheville, Arkansas; Springdale Baptist Church, Tulsa, Oklahoma; Central Baptist Church, Muskogee, Oklahoma; and Trinity Baptist Church, Oklahoma City. From 1948-1951, Gene pursued a second bachelor's degree at Oklahoma City University and completed the Bachelor of Music in 1954 at Oklahoma Baptist University, Shawnee, Oklahoma.

In 1954 he became the director of church music for the Baptist General Convention of Oklahoma. His accomplishments included leading music for the Falls Creek Baptist Assembly (where he was affectionately called "Uncle Gene"), founding the Singing Churchmen of Oklahoma in 1961, and serving as president of the Southern Baptist

Church Music Conference, 1963-65. He received the honorary Doctor of Music degree from Oklahoma Baptist University in 1954 and the W. Hines Sims Award from the Southern Baptist Church Music Conference in 1985. He died three years later as the result of Parkinson's disease. *P.H.*

RHEA–Tell the Good News–566
SCALES–Set My Soul Afire–573

Bateman, Christian Henry (b. Wyke, Yorkshire, England, Aug. 9, 1813; d. Carlisle, Cumberland, England, Jul. 27, 1889) was a pastor and hymnal editor. His ministry was wide ranging as he served Moravian, Congregational, and Anglican churches in England, Scotland, Wales, and the Channel Islands. In 1843 he compiled *The Sacred Song Book*, a children's hymnal which went through many editions and at least two name changes. These books, with sales exceeding six million, greatly influenced Sunday School hymnody in Scotland. He also edited *The Congregational Psalmist* (London, 1846) and *The Children's Hymnal and Christian Year* (1872). *P.A.R.*

Come, Christians, Join to Sing–231

Bates, Katherine Lee (b. Falmouth, MA, Aug. 12, 1859; d. Wellesley, MA, Mar. 28, 1929) was the daughter and granddaughter of Congregational ministers. Her grandfather, Joshua Bates, was president of Middlebury College from 1818-38. Her secondary education was pursued at Wellesley and Newton high schools, and she was graduated from Wellesley College in 1880. Following graduation she taught at the high school level for six years before accepting a position on the faculty at Wellesley College, where she later became head of the English Department. She was the au-

thor or editor of more than 20 books, including *History of American Literature* (1908), *America, the Beautiful* (1911), *Fairy Gold* (1916), and *The Pilgrim Ship* (1926). She was awarded a Litt.D. by Middlebury College in 1914, by Oberlin College in 1916, and received the LL.D. from Wellesley College in 1925. *M.P.*

America the Beautiful–630

Batya, Naomi (b. Bronx, NY, Apr. 21, 1961), also known as Nomi Yah-Wanag, lives in Berkeley, California, and is self-employed. She attended the University of California-Santa Barbara and San Francisco City College. Her only published song is "King of Kings," written with Sophia Conty. *P.H.*

King of Kings–234

Baughen, Michael Alfred (b. Borehamwood, Hertfordshire, England, Jun. 7, 1930) has served as Bishop of Chester since 1982. His father was the London manager of an American steel company. He received the Bachelor of Divinity from London University and was rector of All Souls, Langham Place, London, from 1970-1982 before assuming his present position. His association with Timothy Dudley-Smith began in 1959 when both joined the Church Pastoral-Aid Society. Baughen began collecting music for youth from his visits throughout England. The two men jointly edited *Youth Praise 1* (1966) and *2* (1969), which sold over one million copies. Baughen has written about 35 hymns, Psalm versions, and spiritual songs. In a letter to the author, Baughen spoke of "an affinity of the Spirit between Timothy Dudley-Smith [and myself] in that his words of hymns would frequently 'speak music' to me as soon as I read them for the first time." Their last partnership as of this printing was Dudley-Smith's hymn "Name of All Majesty" and Baughen's tune MAJESTAS. *P.H.*

MAJESTAS–207

Baxter, Lydia (b. Petersburg, NY, Sep. 8, 1809; d. New York, NY, Jun 22, 1874) was an enthusiastic Christian. She and her sister were converted under the preaching of Rev. Eben Tucker, a Baptist missionary, and played a major role in the founding of a Baptist church in Petersburg. Her active interest in the church continued after her marriage and move to New York City. Even though she became an invalid, her home continued to serve as a gathering place and source of encouragement to those involved in Christian work. In addition to numerous gospel songs, she published in 1855 a book of religious poems titled, *Gems by the Wayside.* "Take the Name of Jesus with You" is the only one of her hymns used today. *D.B.*

Take the Name of Jesus with You–576

Beck, John Ness (b. Warren, OH, Feb. 16, 1930; d. Columbus, OH, Jun. 25, 1987) was a graduate of Ohio State University with degrees in science and music and took graduate work at the same school. Later he taught music theory at Ohio State and directed musicals at the Stadium theater there. For several years Beck was music director at University Baptist Church and also operated the University Music House.

Well known as a composer of sacred choral music, he was the president and co-founder of Beckenhorst Press. In the latter part of his career, he was a frequent conductor and clinician at workshop events in which he promoted the publications of Breckenhorst Press. He was also chairman of the board of the John Ness Beck Foundation (in memory of well-known choral composers Randall Thompson and Joseph Clokey) for composers and arrangers of traditional American choral music. As a composer he is remembered for many popular anthems ("Upon This Rock" and "Every Valley") and for his hymns and vocal solos. *H.T.M.*

BECK–486

Beethoven, Ludwig van (b. Bonn, Germany, Dec. 16, 1770; d. Vienna, Austria, Mar. 26, 1827), primarily a composer of instrumental music, brought to full maturity the sonata, concerto, string quartet, and symphony. His sacred choral compositions include *Mass in C* (1807), *Mass in D* (*Missa Solemnis,* 1819-23), and the oratorio *Christ on the Mount of Olives* (1803). Hymn tunes attributed to Beethoven are adaptations from his larger works made by others. Biographies and complete lists of Beethoven's works are found in *Baker's Biographical Dictionary of Musicians* and in *The New Grove Dictionary of Music and Musicians.* *H.E.*

HYMN TO JOY–7, 47, 585

Benjamin, Linda Lee Stassen (b. La Porte, IN, Sep. 19, 1951) is a singer and songwriter. She attended Ball State University and El Camino Junior College (California). Among her compositions are concert pieces and sing-along songs for congregations. *P.A.R.*

STASSEN–Sing Hallelujah to the Lord–214

Bennard, George (b. Youngstown, OH, Feb. 4, 1873; d. Reed City, MI, Oct. 10, 1958) moved with his family to Iowa when he was a small child. At a Salvation Army revival in Lucas, Iowa, he was converted and felt the call to the gospel ministry. His father died when he was 16, and he became the sole support of his mother and four sisters. Further education was impossible, but he gained his theological knowledge through his association with other ministers and by his own disciplined study. He and his wife became Salvation Army workers, and he became a brigade leader of the corps. After several years he resigned this work, joined the Methodist Episcopal Church, and spent a number of years in evangelistic work in the United States and Canada. Although he wrote more than 300 gospel songs, he is remembered for the one song he wrote in 1913. *W.J.R.*

Old Rugged Cross–The Old Rugged Cross–141

Bennett, Sanford Fillmore (b. Eden, Erie County, NY, Jun. 21, 1836; d. Richmond, IN, Jun. 12, 1898) was educated at Waukegan Academy and the University of Michigan. Converted in a Methodist revival, he later declared himself a Universalist, although he never formally joined that fellowship. After two years as superintendant of schools in Richmond, Illinois, he became the associate editor of *The Independent*, a weekly newspaper at Elkhorn, Wisconsin. During the Civil War he served with the Union Army. After the war he returned to Elkhorn, where he became the proprietor of a drugstore and began the study of medicine. Graduating from Rush Medical College in 1874, he practiced medicine for the remainder of his active life. As a youth, his first poems appeared in the Waukegan *Gazette* in the early 1850s. He wrote a considerable amount of both prose and verse but is solely remembered

for "There's a Land that Is Fairer Than Day." *P.H.*

There's a Land that Is Fairer Than Day–515

Bennett, William Sterndale (b. Sheffield, England, Apr. 13, 1816; d. London, England, Feb. 1, 1875) entered the choir of King's College Chapel in Cambridge at the age of eight, the Royal Academy of Music at the age of ten, and later studied in Leipzig. Among his close friends were Robert Schumann and Felix Mendelssohn. Together with Otto Goldschmidt, the German-born pianist-composer and husband of Jenny Lind, he was musical editor of Catherine Winkworth's *Choral Book for England* (1863). Bennett was a composer as well as conductor, and in 1866 became Principal of the Royal Academy of Music. Nicholas Temperley, in the *New Grove Dictionary of Music and Musicians* (Washington, D.C., 1980), refers to Bennett as "the most distinguished English composer of the Romantic School" (Sadie, "Sir William Sterndale Bennett"). He was knighted in 1871 and is buried at Westminster Abbey. *S.W.G.*

Lobe Den Herren (harm.)–14

Benson, Louis Fitzgerald (b. Philadelphia, PA, Jul. 22, 1855; d. Philadelphia, PA, Oct. 10, 1930) received a law degree from the University of Pennsylvania and practiced for seven years before being led to the ministry. He entered Princeton Theological Seminary and was ordained a Presbyterian minister in 1886. After serving as pastor of the Church of the Redeemer, Germantown, Pennsylvania until 1892, the remainder of his life was spent as a hymnbook editor, lecturer, and hymnologist. Benson lectured on liturgics at Auburn

Theological Seminary and on hymnology at Princeton. His most noteworthy achievement was *The English Hymn: Its Development and Use in Worship* (1915), still a standard resource for hymnologists. The hymnals which he compiled were *The Hymnal* (Presbyterian; 1895 and revised 1911), *The Hymnal for Congregational Churches* (1896), *The Chapel Hymnal* (1898), *The School Hymnal* (1899), and *The Book of Common Worship of the Presbyterian Church in the United States of America* (with Henry Van Dyke, 1905). His own hymns were collected in *Hymns, Original and Translated* (1925). *P.H.*

O Sing a Song of Bethlehem–120

Bernard of Cluny (*c.* 1145) Almost nothing is known of him, except that he wrote *De Contemptu Mundi* about 1145 at the abbey of Cluny, France, which was under the leadership of Peter the Venerable, who served as its abbot from 1122 to 1156. Bernard of Cluny, possibly an Englishman, has often been confused with his more famous contemporary, Bernard of Clairvaux. *H.E.*

Jerusalem, the Golden–527

Bevan, Emma Frances (b. Oxford, England, Sep. 25, 1827; d. Cannes, France, Feb. 13, 1909) was the daughter of Rev. Philip Nicholas Shuttleworth, Warden of New College, Oxford, and subsequently Bishop of Chichester. She married London banker R. C. L. Bevan in 1856. Her translations of German verse appeared in *Songs of Eternal Life* (1858) and *Songs of Praise for Christian Pilgrims* (1859). *P.H.*

Christ Receiveth Sinful Men (tr.)–563

Bigelow, James–This is a pen name. The writer wishes to remain anonymous. *H.T.M.*

Surabaja (arr.)–582

Bilhorn, Peter Philip (b. Mendota, IL, Jul. 22, 1865; d. Los Angeles, CA, Dec. 13, 1936) was an evangelistic singer, writer of gospel songs, and music compiler and publisher. Though his first trade was carriage building in Chicago, his avocation was as a popular singer. Converted in 1883 during a revival led by George F. Pentecost and George C. Stebbins, he decided to enter evangelistic work. He studied music with Stebbins, Frederick W. Root, and Jean de Reske. He travelled extensively with such preachers as Pentecost, D. D. O'Dell, and John Currie, and preceded Homer Rodeheaver as Billy Sunday's coworker. To meet the needs of traveling musicians, he invented and manufactured a portable organ, donating the profits to religious work in Chicago. For much of his time in Chicago he was associated with Baptist congregations, belonging from 1916 to 1920 to the North Shore Baptist Church, where he served as choir director. He wrote more than 2000 songs, held copyright to hundreds of others through Bilhorn Publishing Company, and produced numerous collections. *P.A.R.*

Wondrous Story–537

Black, James Milton (b. South Hill, NY, Aug. 19, 1856; d. Williamsport, PA, Dec. 21, 1938) was a singing school teacher and the editor of more than a dozen gospel songbooks published by the Methodist Book Concern (New York and Cincinnati), McCabe Publishing Company (Chicago), and the Hall-Mack Company (Philadelphia). His most popular collection was *Songs of the Soul* (1894) which sold over 400,000 copies in its first two years. An active Methodist, Black was appointed to serve on the Joint Commission for the *Methodist Hymnal* (1905). None of his gospel songs were included in the hymnal, however. He was a member of the Pine Street Methodist Church, Williamsport, from 1904 until his death.   *P.H.*

Roll Call–When the Roll Is Called up Yonder–516

Blakley, Duane (b. Portales, NM, Jul. 24, 1937) received the Bachelor of Music Education from Eastern New Mexico University in 1959 and, in 1962, the Master of Church Music degree from Southwestern Baptist Theological Seminary in Fort Worth, Texas. He served a number of churches as minister of music–First Baptist Church of Forest Hill, Fort Worth, Texas; First Baptist Church of Leonard, Texas; and First Baptist Church of Cleburne, Texas. In 1963 he became minister of music at Calder Avenue Baptist Church of Beaumont, Texas, and in 1968 at Manor Baptist Church of San Antonio, Texas. From November 1969 until May 1971, he was Instructor and Director of the A Cappella Choir at East Texas Baptist College, Marshall, Texas. In May 1971, he became minister of music at the First Baptist Church of Brownwood, Texas. Following his service there, he became the minister of music at the First Baptist Church of Garland, Texas, in April, 1977. He was one of the writers of *The Music Ministry Resource Manual*. His anthems, cantatas, and musicals have been used extensively. Perhaps his best known work is the anthem, "Ask Ye What Great Thing I Know."   *S.W.G.*

Lord, for the Gift of Children–508

Blanchard, Ferdinand Quincy (b. Jersey City, NJ, Jul. 23, 1876; d. Cleveland, OH, Jul. 2, 1966) received the A.B. degree from Amherst College in 1898, the B.D. degree from Yale Divinity School in 1901, and received honorary D.D. degrees from Amherst College in 1918 and from Oberlin University in 1919. He was ordained to the Congregational ministry and served as pastor in Southington, Connecticut (1901-04), in East Orange, New Jersey (1904-15), and at Euclid Avenue Congregational Church, Cleveland, Ohio for 40 years, from 1915 until his retirement in 1955. He was a respected leader in his denomination and was elected moderator of the Congregational Christian Churches of the U.S.A. (1942-44).   *S.W.G.*

Word of God, Across the Ages–262

Blandy, E. W. Nothing is known of this author.   *D.M.*

Where He Leads Me–288

Blankenship, Lyle Mark (b. Chicago, IL, May 11, 1943), the son of a Southern Baptist pastor, was educated at Oklahoma Baptist University (B.M., 1965) and at The University of Texas (M.M., 1967). After serving churches in Luling and Midland, Texas, and Phoenix, Arizona, he joined the Church Music Department of the Baptist Sunday School Board in 1974. Since 1986, he has served as manager over all the editorial work done by the Youth/Adult/General section. Mark is an active choral composer; his compositions number around 250. He was an important member of the Editorial Committee (Design/Organization) for *The Baptist Hymnal* (1991).   *P.H.*

JUDSON–3
FRENCH CAROL (arr.)–111
IL EST NÉ (arr.)–112
CENTRAL (arr.)–167
AR HYD Y NOS (arr.)–218
JACKSON–Father, Son, Holy Spirit–250
DIVINUM MYSTERIUM (arr.)–251
Forgiven–341
HILL–357
NORTH PHOENIX–As We Gather Around the
  Table–367
FAMILY–In the Family of God–380
KNEEL–In the Presence of the Lord–440
SOJOURNER (arr.)–465
BROTHER JAMES' AIR (arr.)–523
TO THE LIGHT (adapted)–532
YARMOUTH (arr.)–577
STEARNS–663

Bliss, Philip Paul (b. Huston Township
area, Clearfield County, PA, Jul. 9, 1838; d.
near Ashtabula, OH, Dec. 29, 1876) was
born in a log house on his parents' farm in
central Pennsylvania, west of the Allegheny Mountains. At the age of 11 he left
home to work on farms and in lumber
camps. He was converted at the age of 12
and joined a Baptist church near the
school he attended at Elk Run, Pennsylvania. He was married June 1, 1859, to Lucy
J. Young, and began teaching singing
schools. After their marriage, Mr. and Mrs.
Bliss united with the Presbyterian Church
of Rome, Pennsylvania. In the summers of
1860, 1861, and 1863 he attended the Normal Academy of Music at Genesco, New
York, conducted by such teachers as T.E.
Perkins, T.J. Cook, Bassini, and Pychowski.
Bliss is thought to have been taught to play
the reed organ by his wife, who both accompanied and sang duets with him. With
income saved from teaching singing
schools, Bliss purchased a house in Rome
in 1863, which since the mid-1960s, has

been the home of the P.P. Bliss Gospel
Songwriters Museum.

At the invitation of George F. Root, Bliss
went to Chicago in 1865, working four
years for the Root and Cady Company,
holding musical conventions, giving concerts, and writing articles for that firm's
monthly, *The Song Messenger of the North-
West*. From 1870 Bliss spent four more
years in similar musical activities on his
own, including leading the choir at the
First Congregational Church in Chicago.
After repeated urgings of the evangelist
Dwight L. Moody, Bliss gave up his music
teaching to become an evangelistic singer.
From March 1874 he was associated with
Major D.W. Whittle, holding meetings in
Illinois, Michigan, Pennsylvania, Kentucky,
Tennessee, Minnesota, Missouri, Alabama,
and Georgia.

After spending Christmas with their family in Rome in 1876, Mr. and Mrs. Bliss left
their children there and took a train to
Chicago for a meeting with Whittle at
Moody's Tabernacle, scheduled for Sunday,
December 31. As the train crossed a ravine
approaching Ashtabula, Ohio, the bridge
collapsed and the train fell 70 feet, bursting
into flames. Bliss reportedly survived the
fall, but then died in a desperate attempt to
rescue his wife.

In addition to secular songs, Bliss composed words and/or music to over 300 sacred selections, including almost 200 gospel
hymns. His collection, *Gospel Songs* (1874)
and Ira D. Sankey's *Gospel Hymns and Sacred
Songs* (1875), helped to establish the widely
accepted term for this genre of sacred music. The latter collection and *Gospel Hymns
No. 2* (1876), also jointly compiled with
Sankey, were expanded after Bliss' death by
Sankey, McGranahan, and Stebbins to six
volumes and then published as *Gospel
Hymns Nos. 1-6 Complete* (1894). This col-

lected edition contained 24 selections by Bliss. Its British counterpart, *Sankey's Sacred Songs and Solos* (*1200 Pieces*, 1903), included 34 Bliss selections. Bliss' other collections are *The Charm: A Collection of Sunday School Music* (1871), *The Song Tree: A Collection of New Songs, Duets, Trios and Quartets* (1872), *Sunshine for Sunday Schools* (1873), and *The Joy: A Collection of New and Carefully Selected Music, for Classes, Choirs, and Conventions* (1873). In addition to his selections listed below, his most popular Sunday School songs and gospel hymns include: "Almost Persuaded," "Let the Lower Lights Be Burning," "Dare to Be a Daniel," "Hallelujah, 'Tis Done," "Hold the Fort," "Jesus Loves Even Me," "More Holiness Give Me," and "The Light of the World Is Jesus."   *H.E.*

HALLELUJAH, WHAT A SAVIOR!–"Man of Sorrows," What a Name–175
WORDS OF LIFE–Wonderful Words of Life–261
WHOSOEVER–"Whosoever Will"–314
ONCE FOR ALL–Free from the Law, O Happy Condition–332
VILLE DU HAVRE–410
I Will Sing of My Redeemer–575
KENOSIS–606

Boberg, Carl (b. Monsteras, Sweden, Aug. 16, 1859; d. Kasimar, Sweden, Jan. 7, 1940) was reared in Monsteras on the southeast coast of Sweden. He was converted at the age of 19, attended a Bible school in Kristinehamn, and began preaching in his hometown. For 26 years he edited a Christian weekly paper. Representing his hometown, he served in the Upper House of the Swedish Parliament (1911-1924). (See entry under "O Lord, my God! When I in awesome wonder" for more information.)   *W.J.R.*

How Great Thou Art (st. 1)–10

Bock, Fred (b. New York, NY, Mar. 30, 1939) received his B.S. in Music Education from Ithaca College, Ithaca, New York, and an M.M. in Church Music from the University of Southern California (1962). In 1986 he was awarded an honorary D. Mus. from Taylor University, Upland, Indiana. A well-known composer of music for choir, keyboard, and other media, he is also President of the Fred Bock Music Company and Director of Music at the First Presbyterian Church, Hollywood, California. He served as General Editor of *Hymns for the Family of God* (Paragon, 1976).   *D.M.*

SYMPHONY (arr.)–383

Bode, John Ernest (b. St. Pancras, Middlesex, England, Feb. 23, 1816; d. Castle Camps, Cambridgeshire, England, Oct. 6, 1874) was educated at Eton, the Charter House, and at Christ Church, Oxford (B.A., 1837; M.A., 1840). From 1837 to 1843 he was a tutor at Christ Church and in 1841 he was ordained. He became rector at Westwell, Oxfordshire in 1847. In 1855 he delivered the Bampton Lectures at Oxford. In 1857 Bode lost to Matthew Arnold, by one vote, the election as professor of poetry at Oxford. He became rector at Castle Camps, Cambridgeshire in 1860. He published two collections of poems, *Ballads from Herodotus* (1853), and *Short Occasional Poems* (1858), as well as *Hymns from the Gospel of the Day, for Each Sunday and the Festivals of Our Lord* (1860).   *S.W.G.*

O Jesus, I Have Promised–276

Bohemian Brethren *Kirchengesänge*
See *Kirchengesänge.*

MIT FREUDEN ZART–20

Bonar, Horatius (b. Edinburgh, Scotland, Dec. 19, 1808; d. Edinburgh, Scotland, Jul. 31, 1889) was educated at the University of Edinburgh. Ordained to the ministry of the Church of Scotland in 1837, he settled at Kelso and was given charge of the North Parish. Amid controversy in the Church of Scotland, he was very active in the movement that led to the founding of the Free Church of Scotland in 1843. He remained in Kelso as minister of a Free Church congregation. He was one of the editors of *The Border Watch*, the official paper of the Free Church, and for many years, because of his keen interest in the second coming of Christ, edited *The Journal of Prophecy*. In 1866 he became minister of the Chalmers Memorial Free Church, Grange, Edinburgh, named for Thomas Chalmers, the leader and first moderator of the Free Church Movement. In 1883 Bonar was elected Moderator of the General Assembly of his church. He wrote about 600 hymns and 60 paraphrases of psalms. Among his collections of hymns are: *Songs of the Wilderness* (1843); *The Bible Hymn Book* (1845); *Hymns, Original and Selected* (1846); *Hymns of Faith and Hope* (1857); second series (1861); third series (1866); *The Song of the New Creation* (1872); and *Hymns of the Nativity* (1879). *W.J.R.*

No, Not Despairingly–270
I Lay My Sins on Jesus–272
Not What My Hands Have Done–339
I Heard the Voice of Jesus Say–551

Bonner, Carey (b. Southwark, Surrey, England, May 1, 1859; d. Muswell Hill, Hornsey, Middlesex, England, Jun. 16, 1938) was a Baptist minister and hymnologist. He was the son of a Baptist pastor and was named for William Carey, the pioneer Baptist missionary. A sermon by C. H. Spurgeon convinced him to study for the ministry, which led him to Rawdon College. He was ordained in 1884 and served as pastor of two congregations, Oakfield Union Church, Sale, Chester (1884-95) and Portland Chapel, Southampton (1895-1900), before becoming Secretary of the National Sunday School Union in 1900. He remained in that role until his retirement in 1929. He was also President of that organization in 1922-23 and President of the Baptist Union of Great Britain in 1931-32.

Bonner's other principal interest besides Sunday School work was music. He was music editor for *The Christian Endeavor Hymnal* (London, 1896), a widely distributed collection. He edited *The Sunday School Hymnary* (London, 1905), which sold more than four million copies, and three volumes of *Child Songs* (London, 1908, 1923, 1936). He was also chair of the committee that prepared *The Baptist Church Hymnal (Revised)* (London, 1933) and, with W. T. Whitley, he compiled its handbook (London, 1935). *Some Baptist Hymnists* (London, 1937) was his overview of the denomination's contributions to hymnody. He was an authority on authorship and copyright and a founding member of The Hymn Society of Great Britain and Ireland.

Bonner composed cantatas, anthems, sacred songs, and part-songs, and contributed to the body of hymnody as author, composer, and arranger. He hid the extent to which he included his own works in the books that he edited through the use of pseudonyms. Among those listed by Bernard S. Massey (*The Hymn Society of Great Britain and Ireland Bulletin*, Vol. 12, No. 3 [July, 1988]) are A. Bryce and Nora C.E. Byrne (both anagrams), R.Y. Harding, Ernest B. Leslie, Hermann von Mueller, Frank Ernest Newton, Edwyn Vincent, and E. Rawdon Bailey.   *P.A.R.*

Book of Psalms, The was a prominent compilation of metrical psalms made for The United Presbyterian Church in the United States in 1871. Two metrical versions surviving in current use from this collection are the one for Psalm 84, "Lord God of Hosts, How Lovely," and the one for Psalm 103, "O My Soul, Bless God the Father." So far as is known, the names of the writers of these metrical psalms have never been published. *H.T.M.*

O My Soul, Bless God the Father (para.)–21

Booth, Josiah (b. Coventry, Warwickshire, England, Mar. 27, 1852; d. Hornsey, Middlesex, England, Dec. 29, 1929 or 1930) studied at the Royal Academy of Music. His first organ position was at the Wesleyan Chapel, Banbury. In 1877 he became organist-choirmaster at Park Chapel (Congregational), Crouch End, London, where he served for 41 years. He served as music editor for Parts II and III of the *Congregational Hymnal* (London, 1888) and was musical consultant for the *Congregational Hymnary* (London, 1916). In addition to chants and hymn tunes, his compositions include an oratorio (*Nehemiah*, 1885), a cantata for women's voices, anthems, and service music. *M.P.*

LIMPSFIELD–584

Bork, Lester–This is a pen name. The writer wishes to remain anonymous. *S.W.G.*

In Christ, Our Liberty–626

Borop, Niles A., III (b. Aiken, SC, Oct. 13, 1956) has earned degrees from Mercer University (B.A., 1978) and Vanderbilt University (M.Div., 1981). He has served as youth minister and pastor for Baptist, Methodist, and Disciple of Christ churches in Georgia, Kentucky, and Tennessee. He was staff writer for Word Music Group from 1982-87 and since 1987 has been owner of N. B. Music Group. His songs have been recorded by contemporary Christian artists such as Denise Williams, Sandi Patti, Steve Green, Larnelle Harris, Michael Card, and The Imperials. He has received two Dove Awards and seven Gospel Music Association Awards Nominations. Recordings of several of his songs have reached the "Top Ten" in the Gospel Charts. *M.P.*

Our God Has Made Us One–388

Bourgeois, Louis (b. Paris, France, *c.* 1510; d. *c.* 1561) was a French courtier and composer who became a follower of John Calvin. In Geneva he was appointed cantor (1540) and then master of the choristers (1545) at St. Peter's Church. Under Calvin's patronage, he became musical editor of successive editions of the *Genevan Psalter* (1542 to 1557). In 1550 he published a textbook for singers. He is revealed in the psalters as a skillful composer and adapter of existing melodies. He harmonized and published two sets of psalms in four to six parts for nonliturgical use. However, it has been difficult to determine just how many of the psalter tunes are his original compositions. On the basis of the singable psalm tunes attributed to him, such as OLD HUNDREDTH, he has been considered the architect of the modern hymn tune. *H.T.M.*

OLD 100TH (attr.)–5, 253

Bowman, Norman (b. St. Louis, MO, Dec. 15, 1939) holds degrees in English and journalism from William Jewell College (1962); B.D. in theology, New Orleans Baptist Theological Seminary (1965); and art, M.A., Peabody College of Vanderbilt University (1975). He has been an editor at the Baptist Sunday School Board (1965-1976), a free-lance writer, artist, and photographer, and a publications coordinator for Dallas County Community College District (1979-1981). He is currently Director of Corporate Communications for Software of the Future, Inc. His writings include *College Is a Question Mark* (1970) and *New Beginnings* (1977), lyrics for anthems and musical dramas, and poems. In 1977, Bowman provided photographs for a special edition of the New Testament (American Bible Society).   *P.H.*

Grace to You–663

Bowring, John (b. Exeter, England, Oct. 17, 1792; d. Exeter, England, Nov. 23, 1872) was born into a Puritan family, but he eventually became a Unitarian. He left school at age 14 to work with his father in the family woolen business. Stimulated by his experience in world trade, his great gifts as a linguist grew until he claimed to have a reading knowledge of 200 languages and a speaking knowledge of 100. In 1825 he was appointed editor of the *Westminster Review*. He published many works, including a number dealing with the poetry of countries such as Russia, Poland, Holland, Spain, and Bohemia. He was twice elected to Parliament and served the British government in several capacities including Governor of Hong Kong. Queen Victoria knighted him in 1854. Most of his hymns were limited in their use to Unitarian congregations, but a few such as "God Is Love, His Mercy Brightens," "Watchman, Tell Us of the Night," and "In the Cross of Christ I Glory" have enjoyed widespread popularity.   *D.B.*

In the Cross of Christ I Glory–554

Bradbury, William Batchelder (b. York, ME, Oct. 6, 1816; d. Montclair, NJ, Jan. 7, 1868) moved in 1830 with his family to Boston, where he began taking organ lessons. In 1833 he entered the Boston Academy of Music, where he studied with Lowell Mason and George James Webb. His first organ position was at the Bowdoin Street Church, which he served for three months under Mason's direction. From 1836-40 he moved frequently as a singing school teacher and organist.

In 1840 Bradbury became organist and choir director at the First Baptist Church of Brooklyn. The following year he accepted a similar position at the Baptist Tabernacle, New York City, where he organized and conducted singing classes for young people similar to Mason's work in Boston. In 1847 he took his family to Europe, where his itinerary included visiting John Hullah's singing school classes in England and observing music classes in the Leipzig schools. During an extended stay in Leipzig, he studied theory and composition with Moritz Hauptmann, piano with Ernst Ferdinand Wenzel and Ignaz Moscheles, and voice with Franz Magnus Boehm. Returning to New York in 1849, he devoted his time to teaching, conducting singing classes, composing, and editing collections of vocal music.

Bradbury and his brother E. G. joined with Ferdinand Lighte and Henry Newton in forming the Lighte, Newton, and Bradbury Piano Company in 1854. William retired from this enterprise in 1867. Between 1841 and 1867 he was associated with the publication of over seventy collections of sacred and secular music. Four collections were collaborations with Thomas Hastings, beginning with *The Psalmodist* (1844). In

1861 he formed the William B. Bradbury Company to publish his own collections. The company was sold in 1867 to Biglow and Main of New York. Among the more important Bradbury collections, in addition to *The Psalmodist*, are *The Mendelssohn Collection* (1849), *The Shawm* (1853), *The Golden Chain* (1861), *Devotional Hymn and Tune Book* (1864), and *The Golden Censer* (1864).   *M.P.*

He Leadeth Me–52
Bradbury–61
Olive's Brow–148
Aletta–260
Woodworth–307
China–344
Solid Rock–406
Sweet Hour–445

Brahms, Johannes (b. Hamburg, Germany, May 7, 1833; d. Vienna, Austria, Apr. 3, 1897), one of the great German composers of the 19th century, was the son of a Hamburg street and dance musician who also served as a double bass player in the Hamburg orchestra. Johannes studied piano with Otto Cossell and composition with Eduard Marxsen, and gave his first solo piano recital on September 21, 1848, in Hamburg. He met Robert Schumann in 1853. Schumann immediately became a close friend and an ardent champion of Brahms' music.

Following a period of travel and residence in various German cities, Brahms returned to Hamburg in 1859 where he founded and directed a women's chorus. He moved to Vienna in 1862. From 1863-64 he was director of the Vienna Singakademie. After his resignation from this position, he lived a rather unsettled existence in various cities, returning to Vienna in 1869. From 1871 to 1874 he conducted concerts of the

Gesellschaft der Musikfreunde. In 1875 Brahms again left Vienna, living for three years in Heidelberg. He returned to Vienna in 1878 where he remained until his death.

Brahms is often labeled a "classic romanticist" since his works are in the romantic style of the nineteenth century, but often rely upon forms and techniques from earlier periods. Brahms' works included four symphonies, several orchestral overtures, the *Variations on a Theme by Haydn*, chamber music, 11 chorale preludes for organ, *A German Requiem*, the *Liebeslieder Waltzes*, other sacred and secular choral works, music for piano, and many solo songs. *D.M.*

Symphony–383

Braman, Barry (b. Paragould, AK, Jun. 18, 1947) grew up in Waterford, California. He was educated at Modesto (California) Junior College (A.A., 1967), California State University in San Jose (B.A., 1969), and the School of Church Music, Southwestern Baptist Theological Seminary (M.C.M., 1976). His church service includes an internship at the First Baptist Church of Modesto; Bethel Baptist Church in Roswell, New Mexico; First Baptist Church of Portales, New Mexico; and Shady Oaks Baptist Church in Hurst, Texas. In 1978 he began to publish his work. To date (1990), he has published over 300 keyboard, choral, and handbell compositions.   *D.B.*

Portales–549

Breck, Carrie E. (b. Walden, VT, Jan. 22, 1855; d. Portland, OR, Mar. 27, 1934) moved to Portland, Oregon, after her childhood in Vermont and a short residence in New Jersey. She, her husband Frank A. Breck, and their five daughters were devout

Christians, members of the Presbyterian church. She gave lyric expression to her Christian devotion as she carried out her routine duties of the day about the home. *W.J.R.*

Face to Face with Christ, My Savior–519

Bridgers, Luther Burgess (b. Margaretsville, NC, Feb. 14, 1884; d. Atlanta, GA, May 27, 1948) was 17 years of age when he began to preach. He attended Asbury College in Wilmore, Kentucky, and became a Methodist pastor, serving in this capacity for more than 12 years. In 1910, while he was conducting a revival meeting, his wife and children were killed in a tragic fire at his father-in-law's house in Harrodsburg, Kentucky. In 1914 he married Aline Winburn, a music teacher at Shorter College, Rome, Georgia, and became a general evangelist for the Methodist Episcopal Church, South. For a brief time after World War I, he did mission work in Belgium, Czechoslovakia, and Russia, before returning to evangelistic work in the United States. He re-entered the pastorate after 1932, served churches in Georgia and North Carolina for 13 years, then retired to Gainesville, Georgia. *D.M.*

SWEETEST NAME–He Keeps Me Singing–425

Bridges, Matthew (b. Malden, Essex, England, Jul. 14, 1800; d. Sidmouth, Devon, England, Oct. 6, 1894) was educated in the Church of England. However, he later came under the influence of John Henry Newman and followed Newman and others into the Roman Catholic Church in 1848 during the Oxford Movement. His published works include political works, several volumes of history, and poetry, in addition to his hymns, which appeared in his *Hymns of the Heart* (1847; enlarged in 1851) and *The Passion of Jesus* (1852). His hymns were introduced first in America by Henry Ward Beecher in his *Plymouth Collection* (1855). Bridges spent several years living in the Canadian province of Quebec, but returned to England, where he died at the Convent of the Assumption, Devon. *M.P.*

Crown Him with Many Crowns
   (st. 1,3,4)–161

Bridges, Robert (b. Walmer, Kent, England, Oct. 23, 1844; d. Boar's Hill, Abingdon, Berkshire, England, Apr. 21, 1930) was educated at Eton and at Corpus Christi College, Oxford. After a period of travel in Europe and the East, he studied medicine at St. Bartholomew's Hospital, London. Upon qualifying, he practiced casualty medicine at the Great Northern Hospital and also engaged in general practice.

In 1882, he retired from medicine and settled in the Berkshire village of Yattendon to devote himself to literature and hymnody. Taking over the training of the choir boys in the local parish church, he prepared for them his own selection of 100 hymns, published (1895-99) as *The Yattendon Hymnal*. This collection has been hailed as one of the most distinguished of individual contributions to English hymnody. His own views on hymns were published in an essay "A Practical Discourse on Some Principles of Hymn-Singing" in *The Journal of Theological Studies* (1899).

In hymnic circles he is remembered for several original hymns and particularly for his translations from the Latin and German. He was named English Poet Laureate in 1913 in recognition of his great contribution to English letters. *H.T.M.*

When Morning Gilds the Skies (trans. st. 3)–221

Broadwood, Lucy (b. Melrose, Scotland, Aug. 8, 1858; d. London, England, Aug. 22, 1929) was a pioneering British folk song collector. The daughter of Henry Fowler Broadwood, of the famous London piano manufacturing firm, she was joint editor (with J.A. Fuller Maitland) of *English County Songs* (1893). This collection is now a classic and was then a forerunner of the folk song revival which began in earnest with the formation of The Folk Song Society (1898) of which Lucy Broadwood was a founder-member. In 1908 she published *English Traditional Songs and Carols* with her own piano accompaniments. For many years she was editor of the *Journal of the Folk Song Society* which contained many songs that she herself collected and carefully annotated, thus revealing her wide knowledge of folklore and religious history as well as of music in general. *H.T.M.*

Kingsfold–120

Bromehead, Joseph (b. London, England, Nov. 29, 1747; d. Eckington, Derbyshire, England, Jan. 30, 1826), after schooling at Queen's College, Oxford, was ordained a priest of the Church of England. He served as curate of Eckington, Derbyshire, where he compiled *Psalms and Hymns for Public or Private Devotion* (Sheffield, 1795). Known as the "Eckington Collection," this volume contained 47 psalm versions and 37 hymns. Among the hymns which were signed as being by Bromehead himself was one of the many known versions of "Jerusalem, My Happy Home." The entire collection was reprinted by James Montgomery in 1802, and thus "Jerusalem, My Happy Home" was con-nected with Bromehead's name for several years. However, there is no hard evidence that Bromehead had any connection with the hymn other than to include it in a compilation. *H.T.M.*

Jerusalem, My Happy Home (attr.)–517

Brooks, Phillips (b. Boston, MA, Dec. 13, 1835; d. Boston, MA, Jan. 23, 1893) has been considered one of America's outstanding preachers. He attended Harvard University and after he was unsuccessful at teaching at the Boston Latin School, he studied for the ministry at the Episcopal Theological Seminary in Alexandria, Virginia. He was ordained in 1859 and began his ministry at the Church of the Advent in Philadelphia. In 1861 he was called to the Holy Trinity Church in Philadelphia and it was here that his best-known hymn, "O Little Town of Bethlehem," was written. But in his day, it was for his powerful preaching and personality that he was known. In 1869 he became rector of Holy Trinity in Boston where he served for 22 years. People came in large numbers to his Sunday sermons and his Wednesday evening lectures. He preached regularly at the Episcopal Theological School and at Harvard University. His famous *Lectures on Preaching* at Yale Divinity School were delivered in 1877 and circulated in America and in England. In 1878 the first volume of his sermons was published, and it sold over 200,000 copies. In 1891 he was elected bishop of Massachusetts and served in that position until his untimely death on January 23, 1893. *S.W.G.*

O Little Town of Bethlehem–86

Brorson, Hans Adolph (b. Randerup, Denmark, Jun. 20, 1694; d. Ribe, Denmark,

Jun. 3, 1764) was the son of a Danish pastor, who died when Hans was ten. Hans studied at the cathedral school of Ribe and the University of Copenhagen. While in school he came under the influence of Pietism, a movement in the Lutheran faith that stressed devotional life over confessional orthodoxy.

After his graduation, Brorson was called to minister to a congregation in Randerup. In 1729 he became one of the pastors at a church in Toender. In 1747 he was appointed bishop of the Ribe diocese.

Brorson began writing hymns during his first pastorate and continued this practice throughout the remainder of his life. Approximately three-fourths of his texts were translations or paraphrases of German hymns. As a result of the excellence and number of his Christmas hymns, he has been given the nickname "poet of Christmas." Among his collections of hymns were *Troens rare Klenodie* (Faith's Rare Jewel, 1739) and *Den ny Salmebog* (The New Hymnbook, 1740). In 1765, his son published *Hans Adolph Brorson's Swan-Song*, a collection of 70 hymns Brorson had written during the last year of his life. The most famous of these posthumously-published hymns, "Behold a Host Arrayed in White," is still found in many hymnals.   *D.M.*

God's Son Has Made Me Free–649

Brown, Ann (See Ann Brown Sims).

Brown-LeDoux, Joanne (b. DeRidder, LA, Jul. 1, 1956) was educated at McNeese (Louisiana) State University (B.M.E., 1978) and East Texas University (M.M., 1981). She is the pianist at First Baptist Church, Charlotte, North Carolina, where her husband, Milton LeDoux, serves as minister of music. She has worked as a music librarian, public

school music teacher, and as a private music instructor. An accomplished pianist, she has published piano solos and anthems for children, youth, and adults. She has produced two instructional cassettes that teach language arts and music skills.   *D.B.*

LeDoux–548

Buchanan, Annabel Morris (b. Groesbeck, TX, Oct. 22, 1888; d. Paducah, KY, Jan. 6, 1983) pursued music studies at the Landon Conservatory of Music (Dallas) and the Guilmant Organ School (New York City) and taught piano, organ, theory, and composition in colleges in Texas, Oklahoma, and Virginia. She married John Preston Buchanan, a lawyer and writer, in 1912. She was president of the Virginia Federation of Music Clubs from 1927-30 and held office in the National Federation of Music Clubs. She was one of the founders of the Virginia State Choral Festival and the White Top Folk Festival, and was associated with the latter festival from 1931-40. Widely recognized for her work with American folk music, her publications include *Adventures in Virginia Folkways, American Folk Music, Folk Hymns of America*, and numerous articles in periodicals. Her valuable collection of folk music materials, which included books, photographs, recordings, and manuscripts, was donated to the University of North Carolina at Chapel Hill in 1978.   *M.P.*

LAND OF REST (arr.)–371, 510, 517

Buck, Carlton C. (b. Salina, KS, Aug. 31, 1907) was educated at Biola Institute (now Biola University), California Christian College (now Chapman College, Certificate of Church Music), Whittier College, Los Angeles Bible Seminary (now Talbot Seminary,

Bachelor of Sacred Music, 1946), and San Gabriel College (M.A., 1950). He was awarded an honorary D.D. from San Gabriel College in 1955. After serving as Director of Music at the First Christian Church of Bell, California, from 1929-34, he was ordained into the ministry in the Christian Church (Disciples of Christ) on Nov. 20, 1934. He subsequently served as pastor in Christian Churches in southern California for over 25 years. In 1960 he became pastor of the First Christian Church in Eugene, Oregon, and remained there until 1974. Since his retirement from that position, he has served in an interim capacity in churches in Oregon, Idaho, Utah, Tennessee, and Montana. He has served on numerous state and national commissions and committees in the Christian Church, and was president of the Oregon Christian Convention. His publications include *At the Lord's Table* (1956), *At the Lord's Treasury* (1959), *Communion Thoughts and Prayers* (1976), *Quiet Time Verse* (1965), and *Special Time Verse* (1970). The first three are worship manuals published by Bethany Press, and the latter two are collections of poetry. His writings also have appeared in several anthologies of sermons and poetry. *M.P.*

O Lord, May Church and Home
  Combine–510

Budry, Edmond Louis (b. Vevey, Switzerland, Aug. 30, 1854; d. Vevey, Switzerland, Nov. 12, 1932) studied theology in Lausanne. After serving from 1881 to 1889 as pastor at Cully, he moved to Vevey, Switzerland to begin a 35-year ministry as pastor of the Free Church. He is responsible for the texts of over 60 hymns, several of which were versions of German, English, or Latin works. *D.B.*

Thine Is the Glory–163

Buell, Harriet Eugenia Pack (b. Cazenovia, NY, Nov. 2, 1834; d. Washington, D.C., Feb. 6, 1910) was a regular contributor to the *Northern Christian Advocate*, Syracuse, New York, for half a century. A resident of Manluis, New York, she was a member of the Methodist church there. After 1898 she made her home in Washington, D.C., but spent her summers in Thousand Island Park, New York. *W.J.R.*

A Child of the King–555

Burroughs, Bob Lloyd (b. Tazewell, VA, Mar. 10, 1937) pursued his undergraduate musical studies at Mars Hill College (1955-57) and Oklahoma Baptist University (1957-59) and earned a seminary degree in music from Southwestern Baptist Theological Seminary (1961) with a double major in music theory and composition. He served as minister of music at the First Baptist Church in Muskogee, Oklahoma (1962-65) and the First Baptist Church of Abilene, Texas (1965-70). From 1970-80 he was Assistant Professor of theory and Composition and Composer-in-Residence at Samford University. In 1990 he accepted an appointment as Associate Professor of Theory and Composition at Palm Beach Atlantic College. A prolific composer, Burroughs has had over one thousand compositions and arrangements published by a variety of music publishers. He served as President of the Southern Baptist Church Music Conference from 1969-71. In 1975 he organized the Baptist Festival Singers and has conducted their annual overseas concert tours since that time. In 1987 he received the "Profile in Excellence" award from the Oklahoma Baptist University Alumni Association. He was a member of the Hymnal Committee for *The Baptist Hymnal* (1991).   *M.P.*

He Is Risen–166
Lord, Make Our Homes–511

Burroughs, Esther Milligan (b. Calgary, Alberta, Canada, Feb. 6, 1937) attended Mars Hill College (1955-57) and Oklahoma Baptist University (1957-59), receiving the B.S. degree with a major in Physical Education/Recreation from the latter institution in 1959. She served as minister of youth activities at the First Baptist Church, Abilene, Texas (1969-71) and as Director of Campus Ministries at Samford University (1971-80). Since 1980 she has been with the Home Mission Board of the Southern Baptist Convention, serving as Assistant Director of the Special Mission Ministries Department from 1980-86 and as National Evangelism Consultant with Women in the Evangelism Section from 1986-90. As a lyricist she has collaborated with her composer husband, Bob Burroughs, in the writing of eight musicals. Articles that she has written have appeared in several denominational periodicals. She received the Alumni Achievement Award from Oklahoma Baptist University in 1988.   *M.P.*

Lord, Make Our Homes–511

Burton, John, Sr. (b. Nottingham, England, Feb. 26, 1773; d. Leicester, England, Jun. 24, 1822) was a Baptist layman who devoted much of his attention to Sunday School work. His first hymns were written for the children in his Sunday School. His publications include *Youth's Monitor in Verse, a Series of Little Tales, Emblems, Poems and Songs* (1803), *Hymns for Sunday Schools, or Incentives for Early Piety* (1806), and other collections of verse for children. He was one of the compilers of the *Nottingham Sun-*

day School Union Hymn Book (1812), which went through 20 editions by 1861.   *M.P.*

Holy Bible, Book Divine–260

Butler, A. L. (b. Noble, OK, Jun. 29, 1933) was educated at Oklahoma Baptist University (B.M.) and The Southern Baptist Theological Seminary (M.S.M.). He served as the Minister of Music at First Baptist Church, Madill, Oklahoma (1957-60); First Baptist Church, Ada, Oklahoma (1960-83) and Nall Avenue Baptist Church, Prairie Village, Kansas (1983-86). In 1983 he joined the faculty of Midwestern Baptist Theological Seminary, Kansas City, Missouri, and led in the establishment of its church music degree program of which he has been the chairperson. In 1991, he was named Professor of Church Music. A member of the American Society of Composers, Authors and Publishers (ASCAP) since 1971, he is the composer of the hymn tunes listed below and of several anthems and a cantata. He was a member of the committee for *The Baptist Hymnal* (1991) and served on its music subcommittee.   *H.T.M.*

Madill–392
Butler–500
Ada–531
Nall Avenue–590

Byrne, Mary Elizabeth (b. Dublin, Ireland, 1880; d. Dublin, Ireland, 1931) was educated at the Dominican Convent in Dublin and at the University of Ireland. A researcher for the Board of Intermediate Education, she received scholarly recognition for her contribution to the *Old and Mid-Irish Dictionary* and to the *Dictionary of the Irish Language*. For her treatise on *England in the Age of Chaucer*, she received the Chancellor's gold medal in the Royal University.   *D.B.*

Be Thou My Vision (trans.)–60

Calkin, John Baptiste (b. London, England, Mar. 16, 1827; d. Islington, London, England, Apr. 15, 1905) received his first musical instruction from his father, a well-known music teacher. At the age of 20 the son succeeded Edwin G. Monk as organist at St. Columba's College, Rathfarnham, near Dublin. Returning to London six years later, he held various organ positions, including Woburn Chapel. In 1883 he was appointed to the faculty of the Guildhall School of Music. He was a member of the Council of Trinity College, London, and a Fellow of the Royal College of Organists. *W.J.R.*

Waltham–98

Cameron, Catherine (b. Catherine Cameron Bonnell at St. John, New Brunswick, Canada, Mar. 27, 1927) moved to the United States at the age of eight, returning to Canada to study at McMaster University (B.A. in English, 1949). Her father, John Sutherland Bonnell, served for many years as pastor of the Fifth Avenue Presbyterian Church, New York City. She studied sociology at the University of Southern California, receiving the Ph. D. in 1971. She is Professor of Sociology at the University of La Verne and is married to another professor, Stuart Oskamp. They share four adult children and three grandchildren from previous marriages.

Concerning her interest in writing hymns, Dr. Cameron writes: "As a child and teenager with a gift for writing poetry, I was troubled by the mismatch between words and music in some of the hymns sung in our church. The beauty of words and meanings were sometimes lost. I thought that one day I might write a hymn that was a harmony of poetry and music. Many years later, I remembered my childhood goal and wrote two hymns."

In addition to the present hymn, her other hymn, written in 1964, is "O Christ, Who Came to Share Our Human Life," first published in *The Hymn Book* (1971) of the Anglican and United Church of Canada. *H.E.*

God, Who Stretched the Spangled Heavens–47

Campbell, Thomas (b. 1777; d. 1844) Little is known of Thomas Campbell. It is believed that he was a native of Sheffield, England, and that he was, in some way, related to the Methodist movement. *S.W.G.*

Sagina–147

Capell, Evone Wood (b. Dodge County, GA, Aug. 16, 1918), the daughter of Edgar Lee Wood and Leila (Pierce) Wood, was educated at the high school in Eau Gallie, Florida, Massey Business College, Jacksonville, Florida, and Stetson University (B.A.). She has done postgraduate work in Jacksonville University, the University of South Florida, and the University of Florida. In 1946 she married Frank Warren Capell, a Baptist minister in Florida, who served as an associate in the Training Union Departments in Alabama and Florida until his retirement in 1973. For 23 years Mrs. Capell was an elementary school teacher, retiring in 1984. She wrote curriculum material for children and leaders in Church Training for the Baptist Sunday School Board, 1954-79, and has contributed articles to *Home Life* and *The Church*

Training Magazine. The Capells make their home in Lake City, Florida.   *W.J.R.*

Holy Bible, Book of Love–264

Carmichael, Ralph (b. Quincy, IL, May 27, 1927) attended Southern California College, Costa Mesa. As a college student he became music director at the Calvary Assembly, Inglewood, California, and, in 1949, had his first experience in television, "The Campus Christian Hour," which ran for 76 consecutive weeks on a Pasadena television station and won a TV "Emmy" award. His first sacred recording was produced in 1950, and a year later he wrote the musical score for the first of several Billy Graham films. He established Lexicon Music, his publishing firm, in 1963, and Light Records, his record label, in 1967. He was an early contributor to the area of Christian musicals for youth choirs with such works as *Tell It Like It Is, Natural High,* and others. His music catalog and his copyrights are now controlled by Spectra Music of Nashville, Tennessee.   *W.J.R.*

CARMICHAEL–The Savior Is Waiting–321

Carr, Benjamin (b. London, England, Sep. 12, 1768; d. Philadelphia, PA, May 24, 1831) was a composer, performer, editor, and publisher. He came to the United States in 1793, after studying in England with Samuel Arnold, the younger Charles Wesley, and Samuel Wesley. He, his brother Thomas, and their father, Joseph, became quite successful as music publishers, with operations in New York, Philadelphia, and Baltimore. As publisher, promoter, and editor of *Musical Journal for the Piano Forte,* he was a positive influence on the development of music in America. He was also a church musician, serving Roman Catholic

and Episcopal congregations in Philadelphia and preparing several collections of hymns and choral music. His compositions and arrangements in many genres include many works for the church.   *P.A.R.*

MADRID (arr.)–231

Carter, Russell Kelso (b. Baltimore, MD, Nov. 18, 1849; d. Catonsville, MD, Aug. 23, 1926) attended the Pennsylvania Military Academy, where he was an outstanding athlete and a member of its first graduating class (1867). He returned to this school in 1869 to become successively instructor, then professor of chemistry and natural sciences (1872). In 1873 he moved to California, where he raised sheep until 1876. In 1881 he returned again to his alma mater, this time as professor of civil engineering and mathematics. He resigned this position in 1887, was ordained to the Methodist ministry, and became active in Holiness campmeetings. Subsequently, he studied medicine and became a practicing physician in Baltimore.

Carter wrote widely in the areas of mathematics, science, and religion, published several novels, and a number of hymnals, including *Songs of Perfect Love* (with John L. Sweney, 1886) and *Hymns of the Christian Life* (with A. B. Simpson, 1891).   *D.M.*

PROMISES–Standing on the Promises–335

Cason, Don (b. Plano, TX, Jun. 11, 1954) was influenced by the ministry of the First Baptist Church of Plano. In 1976 he received a Bachelor of Music Education degree from Baylor University. An experienced songwriter and arranger, he has been associated with Word Music since 1978 and currently serves that organization as Vice President.   *D.B.*

Caswall, Edward (b. Yately, Hampshire, England, Jul. 15, 1814; d. Edgbaston, Birmingham, England, Jan. 2, 1878) was a son of the vicar of Yately. Following preparatory schools at Chidwell and Malborough, he studied at Brasenose College, Oxford, where he graduated with honors (B.A. 1836; M.A. 1838). Following ordination in the Church of England as deacon in 1838 and as priest in 1839, he served as curate of Stratford-sub-Castle near Salisbury from 1840 to 1847. In 1841 he married Louisa Walker, a scholar who shared her husband's interest in the Roman Catholic ritual. This interest grew as they took journeys to Ireland and the Continent. In January 1847 he and his wife became Roman Catholics. Following her death in 1849, Caswall in 1850 entered the Oratory of St. Philip Neri at Edgbaston joining John Henry Newman. Julian says that his life from this point, "although void of stirring incidents, was marked by earnest devotion to his clerical duties and a loving interest in the poor, the sick, and in little children" (Julian, 215). Most of his original poems and hymns were written during his years at the Oratory. Although, for doctrinal reasons, his original hymns have had little use outside the Roman Church, his translations from the Latin are second only to those of Neale. *H.E.*

When Morning Gilds the Skies
 (tr. st. 1,2,4)–221
Jesus, the Very Thought of Thee (tr.)–225

Cennick, John (b. Reading, Berkshire, England, Dec. 12, 1718; d. London, England, Jul. 4, 1755), although of Quaker background, was reared in the Church of England. His family was probably of Bohemian extraction. Under the influence of John Wesley, he forsook his work as a land surveyor at Reading to teach coal miners' children at Kingswood. Subsequently he became the first lay preacher among the Methodists. Doctrinal differences with the Wesleys led him to follow George Whitfield for a time, but in 1745 he joined the Moravian Brethren and was ordained by them in 1749. Thereafter he ministered among the Moravians in both Germany and Northern Ireland. Having published no less than four collections of hymns, Cennick was widely known and respected as a hymnist during his lifetime although few of his works have survived in current use. *H.T.M.*

Lo, He Comes with Clouds Descending
 (st. 3)–199

Challinor, Frederic Arthur (b. Longton, Staffordshire, England, Nov. 12, 1866; d. Paignton, Devonshire, England, Jun. 10, 1952) worked in a brickyard when he was 10, then in a coal mine, and at age 15 was employed in a china factory. His musical interest greatly increased when a piano was received by his family as part of a legacy. He was educated at the Royal College of Music and the University of London, where he received the Mus.D. degree in 1903. He had over a thousand musical compositions published. *W.J.R.*

STORIES OF JESUS–129

Chandler, John (b. Witley, Surrey, England, Jun. 16, 1806; d. Putney, Wandsworth, Surrey, England, Jul. 1, 1876) was an Anglican clergyman and hymn translator. He was educated at Corpus Christi College, Oxford (B.A., 1827; M.A., 1830) and was ordained deacon in 1831 and priest in 1832. In 1837, the year in which he succeeded his father as vicar of Witley, he published *Hymns of the Primitive Chuch* (London). He was a skilled translator of hymns from the Latin, as well as an able author of sermons and other prose works. *P.A.R.*

O Christ, Our Hope, Our Heart's
  Desire (tr.)–414

Chaplin (Pille), Marian Wood (b. Defiance, OH, Jul. 5, 1914) attended Defiance High School and Defiance College, where she majored in music. She married Robert M. Chaplin in 1934, rearing two children, a son and a daughter. After the death of her first husband in 1978, she married Richard Pille (1980). She is a member of the American Society of Composers, Authors, and Publishers and of the National League of American Pen Women. Her compositions–including sacred and secular songs and music for church choir–are in the catalogs of several publishers. She has also appeared as a performer in concerts and on radio and television. Mrs. Pille makes her residence in Fort Myers, Florida. *D.M.*

CHAPLIN–Come, Holy Spirit–239
To The Light–I Have Come from the
  Darkness–532

Chapman, J. Wilbur (b. Richmond, IN, Jun. 17, 1859; d. Jamaica, Long Island, NY, Dec. 25, 1918) was a noted evangelist and Bible conference leader in the early twentieth century. After receiving his education at Lake Forest (Illinois) University and Lane Theological Seminary (Cincinnati, Ohio), he entered the pastorate, serving churches in Albany, New York; Philadelphia, Pennsylvania; and New York City between 1884 and 1905. In that year, Chapman became an itinerant evangelist traveling throughout the world. Charles M. Alexander, the

man who later claimed to own the copyright for Chapman's hymn "One Day," was his evangelistic singer and choir director. In 1917, Chapman was elected moderator of the General Assembly of the Presbyterian Church, U.S.A. A popular Bible conference leader, he became the first director of the Winona Lake (Indiana) Bible and Chautauqua Conference. He helped initiate similar conferences at Montreat, North Carolina, and Stony Brook, New York. Chapman wrote eight books and several hymn texts. *P.H.*

Jesus! What a Friend for Sinners–185
One Day–193

Chisholm, Thomas Obediah (b. near Franklin, Simpson County, KY, Jul. 29, 1866; d. Ocean Grove, NJ, Feb. 29, 1960) received his early education in a small country school, but had no formal education beyond the elementary level. He began teaching school at the age of 16 in the country schoolhouse where he had received his own early education. At the age of 21, he became the associate editor of *The Franklin Advocate*, a weekly newspaper in his hometown. He made a profession of faith at the age of 27 during a revival meeting conducted by Dr. H. C. Morrison, founder of Asbury College and Theological Seminary. Dr. Morrison invited Chisholm to become office editor and business manager of the *Pentecostal Herald*, which had its offices in Louisville, Kentucky.

Chisholm was ordained to the Methodist ministry in 1903. Following a one-year pastorate in Scottsville, Kentucky, it became necessary for him to leave the pastorate because of failing health. After spending five years with his family on a farm near Winona Lake, Indiana, he became a life insurance agent in that city and continued in this same line of work when he moved to Vineland, New Jersey, in 1916. He retired in 1953 and spent the last years of his life at the Methodist Home for the Aged in Ocean Grove, New Jersey. Chisholm wrote over 1200 poems, a large number of which appeared in religious periodicals. Of these, two have become widely known–"Great Is Thy faithfulness" and "Living for Jesus." *M.P.*

Great Is Thy Faithfulness–54
Living for Jesus–282

Christian Harmony was one of the earliest oblong tunebooks (though not using shape-notes) that contained songs set to formerly secular or folk melodies. It was compiled by Jeremiah Ingalls, a prominent singing master, and published at Exeter, New Hampshire in 1805, bearing the title: *The Christian Harmony, or Songster's Companion.*

Over half of its 137 tunes were composed in the indigenous New England style, but the other settings are spiritual folk songs–a genre that came into vogue in the Southern shape-note tunebooks that were to appear throughout the nineteenth century. Since Ingalls' book thus belongs to both the New England and the Southern traditions, it occupies a unique position in American tunebook literature. *H.T.M.*

I Love Thee–I Love Thee–211

Christian Lyre, The (1831, Leavitt) is the title of a collection of lively hymns and "choruses" intended for use in revivals. It was compiled in 1831 by the Reverend Joshua Leavitt, a prominent American Congregational minister, and is historically important as one of the first to have tunes printed alongside hymn texts rather than

in separate tunebooks. Despite its generally lower standard of song, it was the first book in America to publish Dr. J. W. Alexander's well-known "O Sacred Head, Now Wounded"–a translation of Paul Gerhardt's "O Haupt voll Blut und Wunden." Leavitt's collection is also the first-known source of several popular hymn tunes, including ELLESDIE, which is attributed to Mozart without substantiation. *H.T.M.*

ELLESDIE–471, 591

Christiansen, Avis Marguerite Burgeson (b. Chicago, IL, Oct. 11, 1895), wrote her first poems as a child. Her earliest published hymns appeared in *Tabernacle Praises* (1916) with musical settings by D. B. Towner. She has lived her entire life in Chicago, where she is a member of Moody Memorial Church (at the time of this writing). Her late husband, Ernest C. Christiansen, was a vice president of Moody Bible Institute. Mrs. Christiansen has published two books of poetry, as well as numerous gospel song texts. *H.E.*

Blessed Redeemer–149

Christierson, Frank von (b. Lovisa, Finland, Dec. 25, 1900) is a Presbyterian pastor and hymnist. He and his family came to the United States in 1904 and settled in California. He became a naturalized citizen in 1921 and received his education at Stanford University (B.A., 1923) and San Francisco Theological Seminary (B.D., 1929; M.A., 1930). While a student, he was Director of Youth at First Presbyterian Church in San Luis Obispo for three years. Following his ordination in 1929, he served as pastor of three Presbyterian churches in California: Calvary, in Berkeley (1930-44); Trinity, in North Hollywood (1944-61);

and Celtic Cross, in Citrus Heights (1961-62), founding the latter two. He was moderator of both the San Francisco and Los Angeles presbyteries. Since his retirement in 1962, he has remained active in interim and volunteer ministries. In his seventies he served First Presbyterian Church of Roseville, California, as assistant minister and was named pastor emeritus when he concluded that work.

Christierson is the author of more than 100 hymns, many first published by The Hymn Society of America, which named him a Fellow in 1982. His texts have been printed in hymnals in Great Britain, Canada, and the United States and have been translated into Norwegian and Portuguese. *P.A.R.*

As Men of Old Their First
  Fruits Brought–639

Christopher, Keith (b. Rockwall, TX, Dec. 8, 1958) attended North Texas State University and Southwestern Baptist Theological Seminary. He served as minister of instrumental music at Prestonwood Baptist Church in Dallas and is, at the time of this writing, the Creative Director for Anthem and Instrumental Music with Word Music in Plano, Texas. *S.W.G.*

Plano–Go Out and Tell–657

Clark, John is the pseudonym of an author who prefers to remain anonymous. *H.T.M.*

I Have Decided to Follow Jesus (st. 3)–305

Clarkson, E. Margaret (b. Saskatchewan, Canada, Jun .8, 1915) was four when her family moved to Toronto. There her family attended St. John's Presbyterian Church,

where she gained a great love for hymns. After being educated at Toronto Teachers' College, she taught elementary school in Ontario, for two years in a lumber camp, for five years in a gold-mining camp, and then in Toronto schools until her retirement in 1973. She is a member of the Knox Presbyterian Church, Toronto. Her first hymn, "We Come, O Christ, to Thee," was written for the Inter-Varsity Christian Fellowship and published in 1947. She has published hundreds of poems, articles, songs, and sketches, as well as 17 books in seven languages. Her hymns include "Praise the Lord, Sing Hallelujah," the official hymn of the Lausanne Congress. Her collected hymns, entitled *A Singing Heart* (Carol Stream: Hope Publishing Co.), were published in 1987. *H.E.*

Burn in Me, Fire of God–496
So Send I You–565

Clay, Crystal Davis (b. Petersburg, VA, Jun. 4, 1957) was graduated with a Bachelor of Music in Piano Performance from Wheaton College Conservatory of Music (1979) and a Master of Church Music (Piano Performance) from The Southern Baptist Theological Seminary (1981). She served as pianist and music associate at the First Baptist Church of Lake City, South Carolina (1981-86), and is currently employed as pianist, music associate, and children's choir coordinator at Spring Valley Baptist Church, Columbia, South Carolina, where her husband Mark is minister of music. Mrs. Clay is also active as a private piano instructor. Her published compositions and arrangements include music for solo piano, anthems for children, youth, and adult choirs, as well as hymns and Scripture choruses. Mrs. Clay is a member of ASCAP and was named to "Outstanding Young

Women of America" in 1987. The Clays are the parents of two children.   *D.M.*

Clay–454

Clayton, Norman J. (b. Brooklyn, NY, Jan. 22, 1903), as a lad, played the pump organ and later a trumpet in the South Brooklyn Gospel Church. Music became the major interest of his life and he began to compose. In 1942 he joined the staff of Jack Wyrtzen's "Word of Life" radio program and worked for 12 years as organist, vibraharpist, and director of the inquiry room. In 1945 he began his music publishing business and released 30 gospel song books during the years 1945-59. In 1959 he transferred his music publishing and all his copyrights to the Rodeheaver Company and joined that firm as writer, editor, and arranger. Since 1960 he spends his summers in New York and winters in Florida and is engaged in meetings, personal appearances, and other opportunities to share his testimony for Christ.   *W.J.R.*

Ellsworth–Now I Belong to Jesus–345

Clephane, Elizabeth Cecilia (b. Edinburgh, Scotland; Jun. 18, 1830; d. Melrose Roxburghshire, Scotland, Feb. 19, 1869) was in delicate health from her youth, but earned the nickname "Sunbeam" for her service to the poor and sick in Melrose. Her family moved from Edinburgh following the death of her father, Andrew Clephane, and their new home in Melrose was near Abbotsford, the home of Sir Walter Scott. Eight of her poems were published posthumously between 1872 and 1874 in a Free Church magazine, *The Family Treasury*, edited by William Arnot. The editor noted: "These lines express the experiences, the hopes, and the longings of a young Chris-

tian lately released" (Julian, V.I, 238). Her hymn, "The Ninety and Nine," was set to music by Ira D. Sankey when he visited Edinburgh with Dwight L. Moody in 1873.   *P.H.*

Beneath the Cross of Jesus–291

Cloninger, Claire (b. Lafayette, LA, Aug. 12, 1942) received her B.A. (1966) and M.A. (1967) degrees in education from the University of Southwestern Louisiana in Lafayette. She has been a professional freelance writer since 1979. In 1986 she became a staff writer for Word Music, Inc. Her books include *The Kaleidoscope* (1988), *Faithfully Fit* (1991, with Laura Barr), and *Postcards From Heaven* (1992). She has written the book and lyrics for 12 musicals. Two of these, *Come Celebrate Jesus* and *A Son! A Savior!*, received Dove Awards, as did her song "Friend of a Wounded Heart." Claire and her husband, Robert, now reside in Alabama. They are the parents of two sons.   *D.M.*

He Is Lord–178

Coelho, Terrye–(See Strom, Terrye Coelho)

Coffin, Henry Sloane (b. New York, NY, Jan. 5, 1877; d. Lakeville, CT, Nov. 25, 1954) received his B.A. (1897) and M.A. (1900) degrees from Yale University, and a B.D. from Union Theological Seminary (1900). Ordained to the Presbyterian ministry in 1900, he served as pastor of the Bedford Park (1900-05) and Madison Avenue (1905-26) Presbyterian churches and as associate professor of practical theology at Union Seminary. His duties at the seminary included the teaching of hymnology. In 1926 he became president of the seminary, holding this post until 1945. In 1943 he was elected moderator of the General Assembly of the Presbyterian Church in the U.S.A. In addition to writing a number of books on issues facing the church of his day, Coffin served as coeditor of *Hymns of the Kingdom of God* (1910 and later eds.). *D.M.*

O Come, O Come, Emmanuel
(trans. st. 3, 4)–76

Coggins, Ross Calvin (b. Wichita Falls, TX, Nov. 23, 1927) is a graduate of Baylor University (B.A., 1948) and Southwestern Baptist Theological Seminary (B.D., 1951). After serving for a time (1951-53) as an associate in the Baptist Student Department of the Baptist General Convention of Texas, he became, for two years, Baptist Student Union Director at North Texas State University, in Denton, Texas. In 1955 he went as a missionary under appointment of the Southern Baptist Foreign Mission Board to Indonesia, serving in various capacities there until 1961. At that time he resigned from foreign mission service and joined the staff of the Southern Baptist Christian Life Commission. He remained in that position until 1967 when he became head of the southeast region of Vista, located in Atlanta, Georgia.

In 1972 he began service as a regional director with the Inter-American Foundation in Washington, D.C., with responsibilities for the Caribbean area, Mexico, and Central America. In 1980 he went back to Indonesia as director of the State Department's AID's office of Voluntary and Humanitarian Programs. After five years in that capacity, he went to Rome, Italy, as U. S. representative to the United Nations Food and Agricultural Agencies. He has more recently been director of the Africa Emergency Coordination Office which coodinates relief funds for famine-stricken areas in Africa. *H.T.M.*

Send Me, O Lord, Send Me–582

Collection of Psalm and Hymn Tunes or ***Collection*** (1851) is a short title designation for *Collection of Psalm and Hymn Tunes, Chants, Anthems and Sentences for the Use of the Protestant Episcopal Church in America*, compiled in 1851 and published in Boston by Henry Wellington Greatorex (1813-1858), British organist and composer. The collection is the original source of several hymn tunes used in many American churches in the late 19th and early 20th centuries. Among the better known of these tunes are SEYMOUR, MANOAH, and Greatorex's setting of the GLORIA PATRI. *H.T.M.*

GLORIA PATRI (Greatorex)–252
MANOAH–414

Colvin, Thomas Stevenson (b. Glasgow, Scotland, Apr. 16, 1925) was for several years a Lieutenant with the Royal Indian Engineers in Burma and Singapore. He left military service to answer the call to ministry, becoming a divinity student at Trinity College, Glasgow University. Shortly thereafter, he became a member of the Iona Community, where Scottish Christianity began in 563, and was ordained a minister in the Church of Scotland in 1954. Colvin was appointed a missionary to serve the Church of Central Africa Presbyterian in Malawi. From 1959-64 he served in Ghana and was appointed District Pastor at Tamale, Northern Ghana. He was recalled to Malawi in 1964 to help form the first joint Protestant-Roman Catholic development Christian Service

Committee in Africa, a program which he headed until 1974. His work in Africa included community development projects for wells, dams, roads, latrines, and water supplies as well as famine and flood relief, refugee rehabilitation, and long-term settlement programs. Colvin then served as Warden and Leader of Ministry of the Grove Centre Church of Sydenham United Free Church in South East London, involved in urban community development. He has served as a consultant to the World Council of Churches in Geneva and Zambia. As a result of his work in Africa, he published two books of African hymns, *Free to Serve* (1968) and *Leap My Soul* (1976), many of which had never before appeared in print. Rev. Colvin currently resides in Edinburgh, Scotland.   *P.H.*

BLANTYRE (adapt.)–That Boy-Child
of Mary–110
CHEREPONI (arr.)–Jesu, Jesu, Fill Us
with Your Love–501

Conder, Josiah (b. Aldersgate, London, England, Sep. 17, 1789; d. St. John's Wood, London, England, Dec. 27, 1855) was the son of a bookseller and engraver. While in his early teens, he began working in his father's bookshop and became its proprietor in 1811. He acquired the *Eclectic Review* in 1814 and edited that publication for more than 20 years. He began writing at an early age and published an extended list of works in both prose and verse. His books of prose include writings on geography, travel, biography, and biblical stories. His collections of verse included *The Withered Oak* (1805); *The Reverie* (1811); *The Star in the East* (1824); *Sacred Poems, Domestic Poems, and Miscellaneous Poems* (1824); *The Choir and the Oratory, or Praise and Prayer* (1837). One year after his death, *Hymns of Praise,*

Prayer, and Devout Meditation (1856), a collection of his poems and hymns personally revised, was published by his son, Rev. E. R. Conder. Josiah Conder edited *The Congregational Hymn Book: a Supplement to Dr. Watts's Psalms and Hymns* (1836), the first official hymnbook of the Congregational Union, in which 56 of his own hymn texts were included. His wife, Joan Elizabeth Conder, a granddaughter of the sculptor L. F. Roubiliac, was also a hymn writer whose texts appear in several of her husband's collections, including four in *The Congregational Hymn Book.*   *M.P.*

My Lord, I Did Not Choose You–289

Conkey, Ithamar (b. Shutesburg, MA, May 5, 1815; d. Elisabeth, NJ, Apr. 30, 1867) was an outstanding church musician often serving in Baptist churches. After having been organist for a time at the Central Baptist Church in Norwich, Connecticut, he moved in 1850 to New York City where he had a distinguished career as a church soloist and in oratorio. After singing as bass solist in the choirs of Calvary Episcopal Church and Grace Church for many years, in 1861 he became the bass soloist and conductor of the quartet choir at the Madison Avenue Baptist Church where he served until his death.   *H.T.M.*

RATHBUN–554

Conte, Paolo (b. Palermo, Italy, Feb. 24, 1891; d. Colorado Springs, CO, Sep. 11, 1966) was educated at Liceo Benedetto, Marcello, Venice, Italy, and received his master's degree in 1913. He emigrated to the United States and taught music at the University of North Dakota (1914-23). He was dean of fine arts, Oklahoma Baptist University (1923-36), and taught at the

University of Wichita (1936-52). He moved to Colorado Springs and served as music director for the First Baptist Church there for several years. He was well known as a distinguished organist; his music compositions include piano, organ, vocal, and orchestral works. *W.J.R.*

Conty, Sophie (b. 1961) is coauthor, along with Naomi Batya, of the chorus "King of Kings," which they wrote when they were 13 years old. No other information is available about her. *P.H.*

Converse, Charles Crozat (b. Warren, MA, Oct. 7, 1832; d. Highwood, NJ, Oct. 18, 1918) attended the academy at Elmira, New York, and in 1855 went to Germany where he studied law and philosophy. He also studied music theory and composition under Louis Plaidy, E. Friedrich Richter, and Moritz Hauptmann at the Leipzig Conservatory. While in Europe, he developed friendships with Franz Liszt and Louis Spohr. He returned to America in 1859. In 1861 he earned a degree in law from the Law School in Albany, New York and practiced law in Erie, Pennsylvania from 1875. He was also in charge of the Burdetta Organ Company. In 1895 Rutherford College conferred on him the degree of LL.D. He declined an offer by Sterndale Bennett of a Doctor of Music degree from Cambridge University in England for the five-voice double fugue concluding his Psalm-Cantata on Psalm 126. He composed two symphonies, string quartets, oratorios, some overtures, and a large number of hymn tunes. Together with William B. Bradbury and others, he edited various collections of songs and Sunday School songbooks and was a friend of Ira D. Sankey, the gospel hymn tune writer and associate of Dwight L. Moody. He used the German form of his name, Karl Reden, as a pseudonym for most of his composing, editing, and compiling. *S.W.G.*

Cook, George Harrison (b. Manahawkin, NJ, Apr. 16, 1864; d. Marlboro, NJ, Jun. 8, 1946) "was converted at the age of 14 and had a fruitful ministry, preaching, singing, composing tunes, directing choirs, and leading bands and orchestras. He spent his last years at Ocean Grove, New Jersey" (Reynolds, 1976, 287). *D.B.*

Cook, Joseph Simpson (b. Durham Co., England, Dec. 4, 1859; d. Toronto, Canada, May 27, 1933) had his early education in England, then studied at Wesleyan Theological College, McGill University, Montreal. He earned doctoral degrees in sacred theology and philosophy. Ordained in 1885 to the Methodist ministry, he served churches in Ontario. Later he served churches in the United Church of Canada. In the fellowship of both churches he was held in high regard as a scholarly minister. *W.J.R.*

Cooke, Oliver Mark (b. Little London, Dennington, Berkshire, England, Jul. 13, 1873; d. West Ashford, Kent, England, Mar. 5, 1945) was the son of Mark Cooke, a professional singer who had been a chorister in Oxford Cathedral. After his family moved to London, Oliver studied music, including organ with John Stainer, and earned a London College of Music certificate for organ playing. Although his music teacher wanted him to become an organist-choirmaster, Cooke's father, then an enthusiastic member of the Salvation Army, influenced him to give his talents to this ministry. He served as a bandmaster at Peckham, then as a song leader, first at Nunhead, and then at Lewisham where he remained for 35 years. His first song appeared in *The War Cry* (Oct. 1888), and he wrote regularly for *The Musical Salvationist* for the next 50 years. *H.E.*

I KNOW A FOUNT–I Know a Fount–155

Cory, Julia Bulkley Cady (b. New York, NY, Nov. 9, 1882; d. Englewood, NJ, May 1, 1963) was the daughter of noted architect J. Cleveland Cady. She attended Brearley School and Reynolds School in New York. Although a hymn writer from the age of eight, she is known only for "We Praise You, O God, Our Redeemer." Her family attended Brick Presbyterian Church in New York City. In 1911, she married Robert Haskell Cory, and they had three sons. She attended First Presbyterian Church in Englewood, New Jersey, where she lived for several years before her death. *P.H.*

We Praise You, O God, Our Redeemer–19

Cotterill, Thomas (b. Cannock, Staffordshire, England, Dec. 4, 1779; d. Sheffield, Yorkshire, England, Dec. 29, 1823) was the son of a woolstapler. He was educated at the Free School, Birmingham, and received the B.A. and M.A. degrees from St. John's College, Cambridge. He was ordained in 1803 and became curate of Tutbury in June of that year. His other charges were incumbent of Lane End, Staffordshire, and per-

petual curate of St. Paul's, Sheffield. His *Selection of Psalms and Hymns* had a significant impact on later collections, and to it he contributed 25 original hymns and versions of individual psalms. Julian notes that Cotterill was more happy in the alterations he made to some hymns and in his compilation of centos.

Reynolds notes that "it was at the church in Sheffield, in 1819, that a legal controversy occurred, regarding Cotterill's efforts to introduce for congregational singing, the use of the eighth and enlarged edition of his *Selection of Psalms and Hymns* (first edition, 1810). Those in the congregation who opposed hymn singing sought to have this hymnal prohibited. The Archbishop of York persuaded him to withdraw the hymnal and prepare another collection (ninth edition, 1820), which was officially accepted, and thus became the first hymnal so recognized for use in the Anglican church" (Reynolds, 1976, 288-89).

John Julian wrote that Cotterill's suppressed book of 1819, *A Selection of Psalms and Hymns for Public & Private Use*, "did more than any other collection in the Church of England to mould the hymnbooks of the next period; and nearly nine-tenths of the hymns therein, and usually in the altered form given them by Cotterill, or James Montgomery who assisted him, are still in common use in Great Britain and America" (Julian, 334). *S.W.G.*

Hail the Day That Sees Him Rise–165

Courtney, Ragan (b. Ruston, LA, Nov. 3, 1941) is a free-lance playwright, actor, and poet who lives in Houston, Texas. He was educated at Louisiana College (B.A., 1964) and the Neighborhood Playhouse School of the Theatre. He served as Associate Professor of Church Drama at The Southern Baptist Theological Seminary, Louisville, Kentucky (1984-89). His published works include *Hello, World!*, *Celebrate Life, Beginnings, Acts, Suddenly Single, Lottie D., Bright New Wings,* and a collection of poems simply titled *Poems* (Broadman Press, 1973). *P.H.*

In Remembrance–365

Cowper, William (b. Berkhampstead, Hertfordshire, England, Nov. 26, 1731; d. East Dereham, Norfolk, England, Apr. 25, 1800). His father served as chaplain to King George II. His mother, a descendant of John Donne, the poet, died when he was six years old. After attending a boarding school, he was a student at Westminster School. He was called to the Bar in 1754, but never practiced law. His dread of appearing before the House to stand examination resulted in mental illness and deep melancholia. Later he made his home with the family of Reverend Morley Unwin, whose wife became his devoted friend and guardian. After Unwin's death in 1767, John Newton persuaded Mrs. Unwin and her family to move to Olney. Cowper joined them and remained in Olney for 19 years, working with Newton both in literary and church activities. Together they produced the *Olney Hymns* (1779), one of the significant collections of English hymnody. Cowper's poetry was widely acclaimed. He became recognized as the greatest English poet of his day. *W.J.R.*

God Moves in a Mysterious Way–73
There Is a Fountain–142

Cox, Frances E. (b. Oxford, England, May 10, 1812; d. Headington, England, Sep. 23, 1897) contributed 49 translations from the German in *Sacred Hymns from the German*

(1841) which contained the original texts and notes on the authors. In the second edition of this work (1864), the translations were increased to 56 with revisions of the earlier translations and additional notes. Her friend Baron Bunsen was instrumental in suggesting for her consideration German texts he thought worthy of translation. Miss Cox was also the author of a few original hymns that were contributed for periodical publication. *H.T.M.*

Sing Praise to God Who Reigns
  Above (tr.)–20

Croft, William (b. Nether Eatington, Warwickshire, England, Dec. 30, 1678; d. Bath, Somerset, England, Aug. 14, 1727) served as a chorister under John Blow at St. James's Chapel Royal. He became organist at St. Anne's, Soho, in 1700 and remained in this position for 11 years. He and Jeremiah Clark were appointed joint organists at the Chapel Royal in 1704, and in 1707, on the death of Clark, he became sole organist. In 1708 he succeeded John Blow as organist at Westminster Abbey and composer to the Chapel Royal. His epitaph in Westminster Abbey concludes (as translated from Latin):
"Having resided among mortals for fifty years, behaving with the utmost candor (not more conspicuous for any other office of humanity than the friendship and love truly paternal to all whom he had instructed) he departed to the heavenly choir on the fourteenth day of August, 1727, that, being near, he might add his own Hallelujah to the Concert of Angels."
  In his earlier life he composed music for the theater, as well as other secular music. However, in later life he devoted himself entirely to sacred music and became one of the great names in English sacred music

history. Of particular significance are his psalm tunes, which are the earliest examples of English psalm tunes as distinguished from the Genevan or French psalm tunes. *W.J.R.*

St. Anne–51, 73, 74, 626

Croly, George (b. Dublin, Ireland, Aug. 17, 1780; d. Holborn, England, Nov. 24, 1860) received his M.A. from the University of Dublin in 1804 and was ordained a clergyman in the Church of Ireland. Around 1810 he moved to London and spent the remaining 50 years of his life engaged in various literary activities. His many publications reflected his staunch conservatism. In 1835 he was made a rector of St. Bene't Sherehog and St. Stephen's, Walbrook. In this poorer section of London, his effective preaching drew large crowds. *D.B.*

Spirit of God, Descend upon My Heart–245

Cropper, Margaret Beatrice (b. Kendal, Westmoreland, England, Aug. 29, 1886; d. Woodlands, Kendal, Westmoreland, England, Sep. 27, 1980) was the daughter of Charles James Cropper. She was a prolific writer of poetry, drama, biography, and literary criticism. Among her books were *Flame Touches Flame* (1949), *Sparks Among the Stubble* (1955), and *Life of Evelyn Underhill* (1959); her dramatic works included *Christ Crucified* (1932) and *Country Cottage* (1939). *D.M.*

Jesus' Hands Were Kind Hands–477

Crosby, Fanny Jane (b. Putnam County, NY, Mar. 24, 1820; d. Bridgeport, CT, Feb. 12, 1915) is considered the most significant writer of gospel songs America has produced. Blinded by an unfortunate instance of medical malpractice at six weeks of age, she was educated at the New York City School for the Blind. Upon graduation she taught there for several years and was married to Alexander van Alstyne, a blind musician who was also an instructor there.

Possessing from childhood a natural gift for poetry, she had considerable experience in writing secular verse and supplying texts for minstrel songs and cantatas before she turned her talents to the writing of sacred poetry at age 44. During a long life of over 90 years, she produced between 8500 and 9000 texts, many of which were set to music by the leading gospel song composers of the day, including William B. Bradbury, Robert Lowry, George Root, William Howard Doane, and Ira D. Sankey. Most of her lyrics were published by Biglow and Main Company of Chicago. This company was acquired in 1922 by the Hope Publishing Company which presently holds many of Crosby's copyrights and possesses many of her devotional texts which have yet to be set to music. Fanny Crosby used more than 200 pseudonyms in signing her hymns.

Much of Fanny Crosby's life was spent in New York City and, as a life-long Methodist, she frequently attended the John Street Methodist Episcopal Church of that city. In 1924 the Fanny Crosby Memorial Home for the Aged was established in Bridgeport, Connecticut, where the poet spent her final years. *H.T.M.*

To God Be the Glory–4
All the Way My Savior Leads Me–62
Tell Me the Story of Jesus–122
Praise Him! Praise Him!–227
Jesus, Keep Me Near the Cross–280
I Am Thine, O Lord–290
Pass Me Not, O Gentle Savior–308

Jesus Is Tenderly Calling–316
Blessed Assurance, Jesus Is Mine–334
He Hideth My Soul–340
Close to Thee–464
Lord, Here Am I–486
My Savior First of All–528
Redeemed–531
Redeemed, How I Love to Proclaim It–544
Rescue the Perishing–559
To the Work–615

Crotch, William (b. Norwich, England, Jul. 5, 1775; d. Taunton, Somerset, England, Dec. 29, 1847) was a child prodigy who, at age two, could play a small organ constructed by his father, a master carpenter. Before age four, he was touring with his mother, giving recitals in London and other places. After studies in Cambridge, he went to Christ Church, Oxford, in order to study theology. Soon changing to music study, he became organist there at age 15 and completed his doctorate in music in 1799. After serving as Professor of Music for Oxford University, he moved in 1807 to London to become the first principal of the newly established Royal Academy of Music.

Though as a composer he did not quite fulfill his early promise, he was highly respected as a man of musical learning. He wrote piano and organ music, hymn tunes, Anglican chants, oratorios, and the variations on a Handel theme that is now known as the "Westminster Chimes" sounded every quarter hour from the large bells of the tower clock ("Big Ben") on the Houses of Parliament, Westminster, London, England.   *H.T.M.*

OLD 134TH (adapt.)–30, 388, 623

Crouch, Andraé (b. Los Angeles, CA, Jul. 1, 1945) is a writer and singer of gospel songs and a member of the Church of God in Christ. He attended Valley Junior College in California. As a child, he began playing the piano for services in the church where his father was pastor. While in high school, he organized a singing group, the COGICS (an acronym of Church of God in Christ Singers). After this group was dissolved, he formed the Disciples, with whom he has made several national and international tours in the past 25 years. His accomplishments as composer and recording artist have brought him several Grammy and Dove awards. He has written more than 300 songs and published an autobiography, *Through It All* (with Nina Bell, Waco, 1974).   *P.A.R.*

BLESS HIS HOLY NAME–Bless His
  Holy Name–22
THE BLOOD–The Blood Will Never Lose
  Its Power–133
MY TRIBUTE–My Tribute–153
SOON AND VERY SOON–Soon and
  Very Soon–192

Crowell, Grace Noll (b. Inland, IA, Oct. 31, 1877; d. Dallas, TX, Mar. 31, 1969) published her poetry for the first time in 1906 and continued writing and publishing for the remainder of her life. She was Poet Laureate of Texas from 1935-37. In 1938 she was named Honor Poet of the Year by the New York Poetry Center and was selected by American Publishers as one of the 10 outstanding American women of the year. The following year she was awarded a D. Litt. from Baylor University. Her literary contributions, both poetry and prose, were published in 41 books, and she also contributed poetry to numerous periodicals. She was a Methodist, and among her published collections are *Light of the Years* (1936), *Songs of Hope* (1938), *Songs for Com-*

fort (1947), *A Child Kneels to Pray* (1950), *Proofs of His Presence* (1958), and *God's Masterpieces* (1963). *M.P.*

Because I Have Been Given Much–605

Crüger, Johann (b. Gross-Breesen, Prussia, Apr. 9, 1598; d. Berlin, Germany, Feb. 23, 1662) attended schools at Guben, Sorau, and Breslau, before entering the Jesuit College at Olmütz. He also studied under Paul Homberger, a pupil of Giovanni Gabrieli, at Regensburg in a "poet's school." He settled in Berlin in 1615 and was a private tutor. In 1620, he began theological studies at the University of Wittenburg. He became the cantor of St. Nicholas' Church, Berlin, in 1620, and a master at the gymnasium of the Grey Cloister. Crüger held both posts until his death. He is remembered for composing fine chorale tunes for texts by his pastor Paul Gerhardt, as well as Franck, Herrmann, Rinkart, Rist, *et al.* Crüger's *Praxis Pietatis Melica* (1644; 44 subsequent editions) was the primary hymnal of the Pietistic movement and the source of many excellent tunes. Its later editions contained 1316 hymns. *P.H.*

Nun Danket—638

Cull, Robert M. (b. Los Angeles, CA, May 24, 1949) is a worship leader, former pastor, composer, and arranger. He attended Southern California College (1967-70), Costa Mesa, and worked in California as a freelance composer and arranger. For six years, he was associated with Maranatha! Music. He later served as producer and arranger for Challace Music Company. His catalog contains over 55 songs, the first published work being "Someone to Follow" (1969, Lillenas). His other songs include "Sail Away," "Welcome to the Family," and "Remember." *P.H.*

Open Our Eyes–Open Our Eyes, Lord–499

Cummings, William Hayman (b. Sidbury, Devonshire, England, Aug. 22, 1831; d. Dulwich, Camberwell, London, England, Jun. 6, 1915) was a chorister at St. Paul's Cathedral and then at The Temple Church, London. In 1847 he became organist of Waltham Abbey and soon afterward joined the choirs of The Temple Church, Westminster Abbey, and the Chapel Royal where he was highly acclaimed as a tenor soloist, especially in his role as the Evangelist in the Bach *Passions*. In 1847 he sang under Mendelssohn in the oratorio, *Elijah*.

From 1879-1896 he was professor of singing at the Royal Academy of Music, and for a time he was conductor of the Sacred Harmonic Society and precentor at St. Anne's, Soho (London). In 1896 he succeeded Joseph Barnby as principal of the Guildhall School of Music where he remained until his retirement in 1911.

Also renowned as a musicologist and antiquarian, Cummings was an authority on Henry Purcell and became one of the founders of the Purcell Society. In 1882 he prepared a biography of Purcell and contributed articles to *Grove's Dictionary of Music and Musicians*. His compositions include church music, orchestral music, and songs. In 1900 he received an honorary Doctor of Music degree from the University of Dublin, Ireland. *H.T.M.*

Mendelssohn (arr.)–88

Cushing, William Orcutt (b. Hingham Center, MA, Dec. 31, 1823; d. Lisbon, NY, Oct. 19, 1902) was, for over 20 years, a successful pastor of Christian churches in Searsburg, Auburn, Brookley, Buffalo, and Sparta, New York. His wife died in 1870 and Cushing's ill health forced him to retire from the active ministry. In his last years he joined the Wesleyan Methodist Church. He became intensely interested in hymn writing, and his more than 300 hymns have been set to music by George F. Root, Robert Lowry, Ira D. Sankey, and others.   *S.W.G.*

Ring the Bells of Heaven–428

Dailey, Anderson T. (b. Louisville, KY, Aug. 9, 1927) was educated at Butler University (B.M., M.M.) and also attended Ball State University, Marion College, and the University of Pittsburgh. He and his wife, Anna L. Dailey, have a son and a daughter. He resides in Indianapolis, Indiana, where he is the minister of music of the St. Paul Baptist Church and is the administrator of the St. Paul Home for the Aged. He is also owner of Dailey's Nursing Home. For 24 years he was a high school music teacher. He is director of the Sounds of Music, a community chorus. In 1987 he was one of five Indianians receiving the National Black Music Caucus Award for service to music education. He composed and published *Gospel Songs for Children's Choirs* (Indianapolis, 1972) and several anthems. His anthem, "Bless the Lord, Oh My Soul," (1971) was published in *The New National Baptist Hymnal* (Nashville, 1977, No. 519).   *H.E.*

CHILDREN OF GOD–Children of God–479

Danner, David (b. Tulsa, OK, Aug. 8, 1951; d. Nashville, Feb. 6, 1993) was educated at Central State University, Edmond, Oklahoma (B.M.Ed., 1973) and George Peabody College for Teachers (now part of Vanderbilt University, (M.M.Ed., 1978). From 1973-91 he was employed by the Baptist Sunday School Board, serving in music editing positions and, from 1987, as

production manager and then as design editor for the GENEVOX Music Group. Danner now works as a free-lance composer/arranger/conductor and has his own production company, David Danner Productions. As of 1991, he had over 120 compositions and arrangements for choirs and various instrumental groups with such publishers as GENEVOX, Hinshaw, Cantus, Laurel, and Theodore Presser. His major works include *Joy Comes in the Morning* (1981) and *And We Beheld His Glory* (1984). He served as a member of the Hymnal Committee for *The Baptist Hymnal* (1991). *H.E.*

HICKS–Holy is His name–343
SIMPSON–Jesus is the song–552
COTHEN–646

Darwall, John (b. Haughton, Staffordshire, England, 1731; d. Walshall, Staffordshire, England, Dec. 18, 1789) received a Bachelor of Arts degree from Brasenose College, Oxford (1756). In 1761 he was appointed curate of St. Matthew's Church in Walshall, Staffordshire, and in 1769, vicar of that church where he remained until his death. He was an enthusiastic amateur musician and though a pastor, he composed two volumes of piano sonatas and settings for all 150 psalms of Tate and Brady's *New Version*.   *S.W.G.*

DARWALL–197

Davis, Geron LaRay (b. Bogalusa, LA, Dec. 1, 1960) became acquainted with church music at an early age as the son of a pastor. He served as minister of music at Christ Temple in Irving, Texas from 1982-84, and since 1984 has held a similar position at the Pentecostals of Alexandria (Louisiana) Church. He has gained recognition as a composer of contemporary gospel songs. *M.P.*

Davis, Katherine Kennicott (b. St. Joseph, MO, Jun. 25, 1892; d. Concord, MA, Apr. 20, 1980) earned her Bachelor of Arts degree in 1914 from Wellesley College. After two years of graduate study at the New England Conservatory of Music, she taught at her alma mater from 1916-18. She credited her interest in music for treble choir and her concern for practicality in composition to the English-born Concord musician Thomas Whitney Surette. She was also a pupil of the renowned French musician Nadia Boulanger, who taught many important American composers. From 1921-29 she taught music in private schools in Concord and Philadelphia. From that time on, she devoted her energies to composing and arranging until 1977, when her eyesight failed. She did, however, complete one final composition in May, 1980–a setting of Watts' text "Come, we that love the Lord." Of her nearly 800 compositions and arrangements, the best known is "The Little Drummer Boy," which she composed under the pseudonym John Cowley. *P.H.*

Davis, M. Vernon (b. Houston, TX, Aug. 22, 1934) is currently Vice President for Academic Affairs and Dean of the Faculty at the Midwestern Baptist Theological Seminary, Kansas City, Missouri, a position he has held since 1987. After graduating from Baylor University (B.A., 1955) and Southwestern Baptist Theological Seminary (M.Div., 1958; Th.D., 1964), he served in campus ministries in Texas (1960-65). He was associate pastor of the South Main Baptist Church, Houston, Texas (1965-67) and pastor of Grace Temple Baptist Church, Denton, Texas (1967-71). Before joining the faculty of Midwestern Theological Seminary in 1983, he was pastor of the First Baptist Church of Alexandria, Virginia (1971-83). Davis is the author of numerous articles for periodicals and theological journals. His interest in music includes singing, playing the piano, and composition. He is married to the former Bennie Ruth Smith, and they have a son and a daughter. *P.H.*

Davison, Fannie Estelle (b. Cuyahoga Falls, OH, 1851; d. Chicago, IL, Mar. 10, 1887) was the daughter of Philo and Sarah Ann (Linsted) Church. Her father was killed when she was 10 years old and her mother later married Henry Christian Warner. The family moved to Carthage, Missouri, where Mr. Warner owned a hotel. Fannie Estelle Church was married to Asa Lee Davison, a court reporter, and they settled in Chicago, later living in Madison, Wisconsin. Mrs. Davison was in poor health during her last years and was cared for by her mother. Upon her death, in 1887, she was buried in Carthage, Missouri. She is the author of a number of hymns, most of which appeared in collections published by Fillmore Bros., a music publishing firm in Cincinnati, Ohio. She wrote the libretto for the cantata *Faith, Hope and Love* (1886), for which J. H. Rosecrans composed the music. *W.J.R.*

Daw, Carl Pickens, Jr. (b. Louisville, KY, Mar. 18, 1944) grew up in a Baptist pastor's home, becoming an Episcopalian as an adult. While growing up in Tennessee (Nashville and Murfreesboro), he studied cello and then piano. He was educated at Rice University (B.A., English) and at the University of Virginia (M.A., Ph.D., English). During his graduate years he met and married May Joan Bates, also a trained musician. After teaching English for eight years at the college of William and Mary, he enrolled in the School of Theology at The University of the South, Sewanee, Tennessee, to prepare for the Episcopal ministry, and studied there from 1978 to 1981. During his years at Sewanee he became a member of the text committee for the new Episcopal hymnal, an experience which led to his becoming a hymn writer. Several of his original hymns, translations, and paraphrases appeared in *The Hymnal 1982* of the Episcopal Church, including his best-known "Like the Murmur of the Dove's Song" (1981). Following his theological studies, he served for three years as assistant rector at Christ and Grace Episcopal Church, Petersburg, Virginia. Since 1984 he has been Vicar-Chaplain of St. Mark's Chapel, Storrs, at the University of Connecticut. In 1990 Hope Publishing Company released *The Collected Hymns of Carl P. Daw, Jr.: A Year of Grace: Hymns for the Church Year.*   H.E.

How Lovely Is Thy Dwelling Place
  (st. 3,4)–523
God, Our Author and Creator–590

Dayyan, Daniel ben Judah (*c.* 14th century) was the medieval rabbi who is credited with being the author or arranger of the metrical version of the Thirteen Articles of Faith or Jewish "Doxology" known as The Yigdal. It was first Christianized and paraphrased in English by the 18th century

Wesleyan preacher Thomas Olivers in the hymn beginning "The God of Abraham praise." The Yigdal is traditionally sung antiphonally by precentor and congregation at the close of Sabbath eve services and other festivals.   H.T.M.

The God of Abraham Praise–34

Dell, Michael Glenn (b. Jacksonville, FL, Feb. 17, 1959) earned degrees in church music from Stetson University (B.M., 1981) and Southwestern Baptist Theological Seminary (M.C.M., 1983). Since January 1984 he has served as organist/music associate at the First Baptist Church of Huntsville, Alabama. Previously he was organist/music assistant at Sagamore Hill Baptist Church, Fort Worth, Texas, from March 1982 to January 1984. Several of his organ compositions and arrangements have been published by GENEVOX Music Group.   M.P.

Eternal God, May We Be Free–299

DeVenter, Judson W. Van (see Van Deventer, Judson W.)

Dix, William Chatterton (b. Bristol, England, Jun. 14, 1837; d. Cheddar, Axbridge, Somerset, England, Sep. 9, 1898) was the son of a surgeon in Bristol who wrote a biography of the Bristol poet, Chatterton, for whom his son was named. William attended the Bristol Grammar School and developed a love for poetry and language. He later became manager of a marine insurance company in Glasgow. He composed a number of hymns that appeared in his *Hymns of Love and Joy* (1861), *Altar Songs, Verses on the Holy Eucharist* (1867), *A Vision of All the Saints* (1871), and *Seekers of a City* (1878). He also put into metrical form the translations of a number of Greek and Abyssinian hymns. He wrote two devotional books, *Light* and *The Risen Life* (1883), and one book of instruction for children, *The Pattern of Life*. Following his retirement, he lived in Clifton with a married daughter. He is buried in the Parish Church at Cheddar, Somerset.   *S.W.G.*

As with Gladness Men of Old–117
What Child Is This–118

Doane, William Howard (b. Preston, CT, Feb. 3, 1832; d. South Orange, NJ, Dec. 24, 1915) was the chief musical collaborator with Fanny Crosby in the production of gospel songs. Having a devoutly religious background, he was educated at Woodstock Academy and early on showed musical promise as a performer (flute and organ) as well as a choral conductor. Converted in 1847, he was baptized in 1851 and became a life-long active member of Baptist churches.

After being associated with his father in cotton manufacturing during his younger years, Doane moved into woodworking machinery manufacturing, working for the J. A. Fay and Company in Norwich, Connecticut; Chicago, Illinois; and finally (1860) in Cincinnati, Ohio, where he was promoted to the position of president. In Cincinnati, Doane was a highly respected civic leader as well as a man of outstanding achievement in business. However, after a bout of severe illness in early life, he had purposed to devote the greater portion of his time and talent to his avocation of writing gospel song tunes and editing gospel song collections. Of his over 2000 tunes, well over 30 are still in common use. He was the compiler and editor, often in collaboration with Robert Lowry and others, of some 40 song collections. He was also the musical editor of *The Baptist Hymnal*

(Philadelphia, 1883). For over 25 years the superintendent of the Sunday School at the Mount Auburn Baptist Church in Cincinnati, he also served as president of the Ohio Baptist Convention (1899-1902) and of the American Baptist Publication Society (1911-12). Doane was an active supporter of the YMCA and a generous contributor to charitable endeavors. He donated large sums of money to Denison University, Granville, Ohio, where a number of buildings are named in his memory. In 1875 that Baptist institution conferred on him the Mus. D. degree. The Doane Memorial Music Building at the Moody Bible Institute is further evidence of his benefactions. He is best remembered, however, for his singable gospel song tunes.   *H.T.M.*

To God Be the Glory–4
Near the Cross–280
I Am Thine–290
Pass Me Not–308
More Love to Thee–473
Rescue–559
Precious Name–576
Toiling On–615

Doddridge, Philip (b. London, England, Jun. 26, 1702; d. Lisbon, Portugal, Oct. 25, 1751) was the youngest of 20 children and only one of two who survived infancy. His father was a London merchant. His paternal grandfather was one of many nonconformist clergymen who lost their pastorates as a result of the Act of Uniformity (1672). His mother's father, a Lutheran pastor named John Bauman, left Prague, Bohemia, to escape religious persecution. When his parents died in 1715, he was offered a university education and an opportunity for a life of ministry in the Church of England. Instead, he chose to enter a dissenting academy at Kibworth in Leicestershire. In

1729 he became minister at Northampton where he became the head of his own academy. The University of Aberdeen recognized his work by awarding him the D.D. degree in 1736. In 1751 he journeyed to Portugal in an unsuccessful attempt to cure his consumption. He died in Lisbon at the age of 49. In addition to many theological works, Doddridge wrote approximately 370 hymns. These were published in 1755 by his friend, Job Orton. While most observers feel he did not possess the poetic gifts of Isaac Watts, the hymns of Doddridge indicate a missionary zeal and a social consciousness to a greater degree than his older contemporary.   *D.B.*

O Happy Day That Fixed My Choice–439

Dorsey, Thomas Andrew (b. Villa Rica, GA, Jul. 1, 1899; d. Chicago, IL, Jan. 23, 1993) traveled as a boy with his father, an itinerant Baptist preacher, playing the reed pump organ for his services. In 1910 he moved to Atlanta, where in the following year he attended a "Colored Night" service at a Billy Sunday revival and was impressed by Homer Rodeheaver's musical leadership. In Atlanta he also came under the influence of blues pianists and began to play for dances. About 1916 he moved to Chicago where he studied at the Chicago College of Composition and Arranging, continuing to support himself as a pianist, plus working with record companies and music publishers. His composition *Riverside Blues* was recorded by King Oliver's Creole Jazz Band in 1923, and from 1923 to 1926 he toured with the famed blues singer Gertrude (Ma) Rainey, accompanying her with his Wildcats Jazz Band as well as composing and arranging music for her performances.

Dorsey was also composing sacred music and, after hearing the Rev. A. W. Nix sing at the 1921 National Baptist Convention, was inspired to write his first gospel song, "If I Don't Get There," published in *Gospel Pearls* (Nashville, 1921, No. 117). After several years of involvement in both blues and gospel, he turned in the early 1930s to gospel music exclusively. In 1931 he and Theodore Fry organized the first Black gospel chorus at the Ebenezer Baptist Church, Chicago. He and singer Sallie Martin founded the National Convention of Gospel Choirs and Choruses in 1932, the year in which the Dorsey House of Music was established. Between 1932 and 1944, he toured America with "Evenings of Dorsey." Fry and Martin sang with him during the thirties, and from 1939 to 1944 he toured with Mahalia Jackson.

Dorsey reportedly composed nearly 1,000 songs, publishing more than half of them. He was influenced by the gospel hymns of Charles A. Tindley but sought to incorporate in his sacred songs "the feelings and the pathos and the moans of the blues" (Southern, *Biographical Dictionary of Afro-American and African Musicians*). Three of his best known songs published in *The New National Baptist Hymnal* (1977) are "Precious Lord, Take My Hand" (1932, copyrighted in 1938), "Peace in the Valley" (1939), and "When I've Done My Best" (1939). Among African-Americans, Dorsey is known as "The Father of Gospel Music." *H.E.*

Precious Lord (adapt.)–Precious Lord, Take My Hand–456

Doudney, Sarah (b. Portsea, Hampshire, England, Jan. 15, 1841; d. Oxford, England, Dec. 15, 1926) at an early age revealed unusual literary ability and wrote "The Lessons of the Water-Mill" when she was 15. One of the oft-quoted lines from this poem is, "The mill cannot grind with the water that is past." A prolific writer, she published a number of novels and contributed numerous articles to the *Sunday Magazine*. She spent most of her life in quiet seclusion in the remote village of Cobham in Hampshire.   *W.J.R.*

The Master Hath Come–497

Douglas, Robert F. This is the pseudonym of a composer/arranger who wishes to remain anonymous.   *H.T.M.*

NAME OF THE LORD (arr.)–174

Doving, Carl (b. Norddalen, Norway, Mar. 21, 1867; d. Chicago, IL, Oct. 2, 1937) immigrated to the United States in 1890 and attended Luther Seminary (C.T., 1896) and Luther College (B.A., 1903). After serving as pastor of Lutheran churches in Red Wing and Montevideo, Minnesota and Brooklyn, New York, he became city missionary to Chicago. He was a respected hymnologist and translator of German and Scandinavian hymns. His extensive hymnological library is located at Luther College, Decorah, Iowa.   *W.J.R.*

Built on the Rock (tr.)–351

Drakestone, John. This is the pen name of a hymnist who wishes to remain anonymous.   *D.B.*

WARRENTON (arr.)–18

Draper, William Henry (b. Kenilworth, Warwickshire, England, Dec. 19, 1855; d. Clifton, Bristol, England, Aug. 9, 1933) attended Chiltenham College and graduated from Oxford University (Keble College, 1877; M.A., 1880). He was ordained in the

Church of England in 1880 and served in various positions throughout his life including: assistant curate, St. Mary's, Shrewsbury; vicar of Alfreton (1883-89); vicar of the Abbey Church, Shrewsbury (1889-99); rector of Adel, Leeds (1899-1919); Master of the Temple, London (1919-30); and vicar of Axbridge, Somerset (1930-33). He wrote over 60 hymns, among the finest being his translations from Greek and Latin. His publications include *Hymns for Holy Week* (1899; translations from the Greek), *The Victoria Book of Hymns* (1897), *Hymns for the Tunes of Orlando Gibbons* (1925), and *Seven Spiritual Songs by Thomas Campion* (ed.; 1919).   *P.H.*

All Creatures of Our God and King (parap.)–27

Dubois, Francois Clement Theodore (b. Rosnay, France, Aug. 24, 1837; d. Paris, France, Jun. 11, 1924) was known as a composer, organist, and music educator. He studied at the Paris Conservatoire where in 1861 he received the *Prix de Rome*. From 1896 to 1905 he was Director of the Paris Conservatoire. His departure from that position was hastened by public protests over the refusal of the Conservatoire to award the *Prix de Rome* to Ravel. Dubois published operas, church music, chamber music, and orchestral works.   *D.B.*

ADORE THEE–647

Duck, Ruth C. (b. Washington, D.C., November 21, 1947), studied at Southwestern University, Memphis, Tennessee (B.A., 1969), Chicago Theological Seminary (M. Div., 1973), the University of Notre Dame (M.A., 1987), and the Boston University School of Theology (Ph.D., 1989). She also received an honorary D.D. from Chicago

Theological Seminary. Duck is currently Assistant Professor of Worship at Garrett-Evangelical Theological Seminary, Evanston, Illinois. An ordained minister in the United Church of Christ, she served as pastor of St. John's United Church of Christ, Hartford, Wisconsin (1975-79) and Bethel-Bethany United Church of Christ, Milwaukee, Wisconsin (1979-84), as well as in various staff positions in other churches.

Ruth Duck was a coeditor of one of the earliest inclusive language hymn collections, *Because We Are One People* (1974). She has also edited or coedited other collections of hymns and worship resources, including *Everflowing Streams: Songs for Worship* (1981), *Becoming One* (1986), and *Touch Holiness: Resources for Worship* (1990). Duck is in wide demand as a speaker and conference leader on worship, theology, and hymnody. Her hymns have appeared in a number of recent hymnals, including *The United Methodist Hymnal* (1989) and *The Presbyterian Hymnal: Hymns, Psalms, and Spiritual Songs* (1990).   *D.M.*

Arise, Your Light Is Come–83

Dudley-Smith, Timothy (b. Manchester, England, Dec. 26, 1926) was the Bishop of Thetford, Norfolk (1981-91). The call to ministry came at age 11 or 12, following his father's death. He was educated at Pembroke College, Cambridge, and Ridley Hall, Cambridge, and was ordained in 1950 to the Anglican ministry. He has served in numerous positions: Assistant Curate, St. Paul's Church, Northumberland Heath, 1950-53; Head, Cambridge University Mission in Bermondsey, 1953-55; Honourary Chaplain to the Bishop of Rochester, 1953-60; Editorial Secretary of the Evangelical Alliance and first editor of *Crusade*, 1955-60, founded in the wake of the Billy

Graham Crusade in 1955; Assistant Secretary of the Church Pastor-Aid Society, 1959-65; Secretary of the Church Pastoral-Aid Society, 1965-73; Archdeacon of Norwich, 1973-81. He is married to Arlette (née MacDonald), and they have three children. Along with Michael Baughen, he was responsible for *Youth Praise 1 & 2* (1966, 1969), which sold over one million copies by May 1973. Among his other books are *A Collection of Hymns, 1961-1981* (1981), *Lift Every Heart* (1983), *A Flame of Love* (1987), *Songs of Deliverance* (1988) and *Praying with the English Hymn Writers* (1989). In *Lift Every Heart*, he relates that his purpose in writing hymns is to fulfill the commission given him upon the receipt of a Bible at his consecration as Bishop of Thetford: "Receive this Book; here are the words of eternal life. Take them for your guide and declare them to the world" (Dudley-Smith, 10).   *P.H.*

Heavenly Hosts in Ceaseless Worship–40
How Great Our God's Majestic Name–70
Tell Out, My Soul, the Greatness–81
See, to Us a Child Is Born–104
A Purple Robe–154
Name of All Majesty–207
The Love of Christ Who Died for Me–268

Duffield, George, Jr. (b. Carlisle, PA, Sep. 12, 1818; d. Bloomfield, NJ, Jul. 6, 1888) was a third-generation Presbyterian minister whose grandfather had been a chaplain to the Continental Congress during the Revolutionary War. He graduated from Yale University (1837) and Union Theological Seminary (1840) and received his ordination to the Presbyterian ministry in 1840. He pastored churches in Brooklyn, New York (1840-47), Bloomfield, New Jersey (1847-52), Philadelphia (1852-61), Adrian, Michigan (1861-65), Galesburg,

Illinois (1865-69), Saginaw, Michigan (1869), and Ann Arbor and Lansing, Michigan (1869-84). He also served for seven years as a regent of the University of Michigan. His literary work included the editing of a Presbyterian newspaper, the *Christian Observer*. Upon his retirement, he returned to Bloomfield, New Jersey, where he lived for a time with his son, Rev. Samuel W. Duffield, the author of two important books on hymnology, *English Hymns, Their Authors and History* (1886) and *Latin Hymn Writers and Their Hymns* (1889).   *D.M.*

Stand Up, Stand Up for Jesus–485, 487

Dunbar, C. R. No information has been found on C. R. Dunbar.   *S.W.G.*

DUNBAR–298

Duncan, David Brian (b. Cape Girardeau, MO., Oct. 5, 1958) is a Southern Baptist musician-minister. He was educated at Southeast Missouri State University (B.M.E., 1981) and The Southern Baptist Theological Seminary (M.C.M., 1983). While a student, he served First Baptist Church, Chaffee, Missouri, and Sardinia Baptist Church, Sardinia, Indiana. Upon graduation from seminary, he was called to Miner Baptist Church, Sikeston, Missouri, as Minister of Music and Youth. In 1987, he moved to Salt Lake City, Utah, as Minister of Music and Education at First Southern Baptist Church. He has published choral arrangements of hymns and has written several pieces for the use of the churches he has served.   *P.A.R.*

O God of Love, Enable Me–580

Dwight, Timothy (b. Northampton, MA, May 14, 1752; d. Philadelphia, PA, Jan. 11, 1817) was the grandson of the renowned New England theologian Jonathan Edwards. His mother, Mary (Edwards) Dwight, was responsible for his early education, which enabled him to read the Bible at age four. He entered Yale at 13 with a significant portion of the first two years completed. After graduating with highest honors in 1769, he remained at Yale as a tutor. During the Revolutionary War, Dwight served as a chaplain in the Continental Army, became friends with George Washington, and wrote patriotic songs. He became pastor of the Congregational Church at Greenfield, Connecticut, in 1783, supplementing his income by conducting an academy there. In 1795 he became president of Yale and professor of theology. His chapel preaching helped ignite the revival on the campus which was part of the Second Great Awakening. At the request of the General Association of Connecticut, Dwight revised Isaac Watts' *Psalms of David* (1801), adding 33 of his own hymns. As the result of extended reading by candlelight and a smallpox innoculation, he was continually plagued by poor eyesight and pain.   *P.H.*

I Love Thy Kingdom, Lord–354

Dyke, Henry van (see Van Dyke, Henry)

Dykes, John Bacchus (b. Kingston-upon-Hull, England, Mar. 10, 1823; d. Ticehurst, Sussex, England, Jan. 22, 1876) displayed musical abilities at an early age. He began playing the organ in the church in Hull, where his grandfather was a minister, at the age of 10. Following his graduation from St. Catherine's College, Cambridge, in 1847, he received ordination as deacon, and later as priest, at Walton, Yorkshire. Two years later he was appointed to Durham, where he became precentor at the Durham Cathedral. Dykes was awarded a doctorate from Durham University in 1861, and the following year he became vicar of St. Oswald's, Durham, where he served for the remainder of his life. He was a prolific composer of hymn tunes and is credited with having written approximately 300. Most of these were first published in one of the editions of *Hymns Ancient and Modern* or Chope's *Congregational Hymn and Tune Book.* *M.P.*

NICAEA–2
MELITA–69
ST. AGNES–116, 225, 498, 505, 506
VOX DILECTI–551

Edgar, Mary Susanne (b. Sundridge, Ontario, Canada, May 23, 1889; d. Toronto, Ontario, Canada, Sep. 17, 1973) attended primary school in Sundridge, followed by her secondary education at Havergal College, Toronto. During high school she won prizes for her literary efforts. She then enrolled in extension courses at the University of Chicago and the University of Toronto, majoring in English. In 1912 she became Girl's Work secretary in Montreal, and in 1914-15 attended the National Training School of the Young Women's Christian Association in New York. She worked for the YMCA in Japan in 1920-21, and then traveled in India and Ireland. In 1922 she founded Camp Glen Bernard, a private camp for girls on Lake Bernard at Sundridge in northern Ontario. She was known to her campers as "Ogimaqua" (friend of children). Her publications include *Five One-Act Plays* (1916-18), *Woodfire and Candlelight* (1945), *Under Open Skies* (1956), *The Christmas Wreath* (1966), and *Once There Was a Camper* (1970). Most of her hymns and poems were written for campers. *H.E.*

God, Who Touches Earth with Beauty–500

Edmunds, Lidie H. is a pseudonym used by Eliza Edmunds Hewitt for "My Faith Has Found a Resting Place." Information on Hewitt can be found in this book. *M.P.*

My Faith Has Found a Resting Place–412

Elliott, Charlotte (b. Clapham, England, Mar. 18, 1789; d. Brighton, England, Sep. 22, 1871) lived most of the first 32 years of her life in Clapham. After a serious illness in 1821 left her an invalid, she moved to Brighton in 1823, where she lived for the remainder of her life. A friendship with the Genevan evangelist, H.A. César Malan, with whom she corresponded for 40 years, contributed to the development of her spirituality, which was expressed in her hymn texts and other poetry. In spite of pain and suffering, she pursued her literary interests. She assisted in the compilation of the six editions of *The Invalid's Hymn Book* from 1834-1854, and the 1854 edition contained 112 of her hymns. Her hymns also appear in *Psalms and Hymns for Public, Private and Social Worship* (1835-48, edited by her brother, Rev. Henry V. Elliott) and in her *Hours of Sorrow* (1836); *Morning and Evening Hymns for a Week* (1839); and *Thoughts in Verse on Sacred Subjects* (1869). *M.P.*

Just As I Am–303, 307

Elliott, Emily Elizabeth Steele (b. Brighton, Sussex, England, Jul. 22, 1836; d. Islington, London, England, Aug. 3, 1897) was the daughter of Edward B. Elliott, rector of St. Mark's Church, Brighton, a brother of Charlotte Elliott. A prolific poet and quite active in mission work, Elizabeth Elliott published 70 hymns and poems in her

Chimes of Consecration (1873), and 71 more in her *Chimes for Daily Service* (1880). Some of her poems appeared in the *Church Missionary Juvenile Instructor* of which she was editor.   *W.J.R.*

Thou Didst Leave Thy Throne–121

Ellor, James (b. Droylsden, Lancashire, England, 1819; d. Newburgh, NY, Sep. 27, 1899) was a hatter by trade but gave evidence of musical prowess at an early age. By age 18 Ellor was leading the choir at the Wesleyan Chapel in Droylsden. He later secured employment with a railroad being constructed in the north of England. In 1843 he emigrated to the United States and returned to his hatmaking trade. In the last years before his death, he became blind. He died at his son's home in Newburgh, New York, and was buried in Bloomfield, New Jersey.   *P.H.*

Diadem–200

Elvey, George Job (b. Canterbury, Kent, England, Mar. 27, 1816; d. Windlesham, Surrey, England, Dec. 9, 1893) was educated as a chorister at Canterbury Cathedral. While in his teens, he developed notable skills as an organist and, at the age of 19, became organist and master of the choristers at St. George's Chapel, Windsor, the home church of the royal family. For that position he was appointed by King William IV and was selected over Samuel Sebastian Wesley, among others. Elvey attended the Royal Academy of Music and in 1838 received his Bachelor of Music degree at New College, Oxford. In 1840 he was awarded the Doctor of Music degree. He served for 47 continuous years at St. George's Chapel, during which he played for many services involving the royal family. He was knight-

ed by Queen Victoria after writing the *Festival March* for the wedding of Princess Louise. In addition to hymn tunes, Elvey composed anthems, service music, and two oratorios–*The Resurrection and Ascension* (1840) and *Mount Carmel* (1886).   *M.P.*

Diademata–161, 601, 628
St. George's Windsor–637

Emerson, Luther O. (b. Parsonfield, ME, Aug. 3, 1820; d. Hyde Park, MA, Sep. 29, 1915), after studying in local schools, attended Dracut Academy in Massachusetts. He forsook the study of medicine early on to pursue a career in music. After study with I. B. Woodbury, then prominent as a music teacher, he served six years as music teacher and choir director in Salem, Massachusetts. Then moving to Boston, he became organist of the Bulfinch Street Church and was associated with the Oliver Ditson Company. Much of his time was devoted to conducting musical conventions and compiling collections for singing schools, Sunday Schools, and churches. Findlay College in Ohio honored him with the Mus. D. degree.   *H.T.M.*

Ar Hyd Y Nos (harm.)–218, 643

English, Tina (b. Dallas, TX, May 21, 1952) is the pseudonym of Christine English Wilkerson. She is a graduate of Baylor University (B.S., 1974), where professor Frank Leavell was an influence in her style of writing lyrics. Kurt Kaiser and Charles F. Brown were instrumental in providing her first opportunities in music composition. Her first published work was "Cast Your Cares" (Word, 1972). She is a concert artist who sings her own compositions, playing piano and guitar. A conductor of choral clinics, she has served as a youth choir director and an educator-music specialist. Tina English is married to Chris Wilkerson, and they are the parents of a son and a daughter. Presently she is Artist-in-Education at the Second Baptist Church, Lubbock, Texas. In 1990 she also became an Artist-in-Education with the Texas Commission on the Arts. As of 1990, her list of published works included over 100 compositions released by Benson, Broadman, Jenson, Lorenz, Purifoy, and Word.   *H.E.*

CANDICE CHRISTOPHER–Everything Was
   Made by God–45

Evans, David (b. Resolven, Glamorganshire, Wales, Feb. 6, 1874; d. Rhosllanerchrugog, Wrexham, Denbighshire, Wales, May 17, 1948) was the outstanding Welsh musician of his generation. He was educated at Arnold College (Swansea), University College (Cardiff), and Oxford University, where he received the Mus. Bac. degree in 1895. He was organist at Jewin Street Presbyterian Chapel in London from 1899 to 1903 when he returned to University College, Cardiff, as head of its music department, serving there until his retirement in 1939. He was also associated with the University College of South Wales and Monmouthshire and the University of Wales. As editor of the journal, *Y Cerddor* (1916-21), adjudicator of the National Eisteddfod, and conductor of many *cymnafa ganu* (the great traditional singing festivals), he was a leader in his nation's music. He composed many pieces for the church and compiled an influential collection of standard hymn tunes, *Moliant Cenedl* (1920). He was music editor of the 1927 Revised Edition of *The Church Hymnary*, a book used around the world by English-speaking Presbyterians, and *Llyfr Tonau ac Emynau* (1929), a Welsh Methodist hymnal.   *P.A.R.*

SLANE (harm.)–60
GARTAN (harm.)–109
MADRID (harm.)–231
NYLAND (arr.)–508

Everest, Charles William (b. East Windsor, CT, May 27, 1814; d. Waterbury, CT, Jan. 11, 1877) was an Episcopalian minister. He was graduated from Trinity College, Hartford. In 1842, he was ordained and served as rector in Hampden, Connecticut, from that time until 1873.   *P.A.R.*

Take Up Your Cross–494

Everett, Asa Brooks (b. VA, 1828; d. near Nashville, TN, Sep., 1875) completed his medical training, but abandoned the practice of medicine to pursue a career in music. He spent some time in Boston studying music and then for a brief time was a teacher in Virginia. He studied music in Leipzig, Germany, for four years. He was associated with the L. C. Everett Company in Richmond, Virginia. The firm later moved to Pennsylvania. Before the Civil War, the firm employed more than 50 teachers in the Southern and mid-Atlantic states. Everett composed numerous gospel songs, and edited a number of collections. His best known collection was *The Sceptre* (New York).   *S.W.G.*

FOOTSTEPS–483

Ewing, Alexander C. (b. Old Machar, Aberdeenshire, Scotland, Jan. 3, 1830; d. Taunton, Somerset, England, Jul. 11, 1895) was a son of Alexander Ewing, M.D., lecturer on surgery at Marichal College, Aberdeen, Scotland. The younger Ewing first studied law at that school, but did not enter law practice, his major interest being music. He then studied music at Heidelberg

University. Although never a professional musician, he became an excellent performer on the piano, violin, cello, and cornet. He was devoted to the study of old English music, becoming a member of both the Haydn Society and the Harmonic Choir of Aberdeen. At the beginning of the Crimean War in 1855, Ewing enlisted in the Army Commissariat Department, and was stationed at Constantinople. He rose to the rank of Lieutenant-Colonel. He served later in South Australia and China, remaining in foreign service until 1867. In that year at the age of 37, he married Julianna Horatia Scott-Gatty, a distinguished author of children's literature. It is curious that this hymn tune is the only music that Ewing is known to have composed.   *H.E.*

Ewing–527

Excell, Edwin Othello (b. Stark Co., OH, Dec. 13, 1851; d. Chicago, IL, Jun. 10, 1921) was a leader in the composition and publication of gospel songs. His father was a minister in the German Reformed Church. While employed as a construction laborer, he began to conduct singing schools. He was converted in the mid-1870s during a Methodist revival for which he was leading the music. He then obtained his musical training in sessions known as "normal schools" under such prominent leaders as George W. Root and his son, Frederick. He settled in Chicago in 1883 and became a leader in Sunday School work, not only composing tunes and compiling songbooks, but helping to found the International Sunday School Lessons. He began his own publishing company and was at one time the largest agent in the country. He also worked with other publishers, including Hope, Benson, and Robert H. Coleman, a Southern Baptist. In addition to composing more than 2000 tunes and editing nearly 90 collections, he was active as a song leader in revivals, working principally with Sam P. Jones. He became ill while assisting Gypsy Smith in a meeting in Louisville, Kentucky, returned to Chicago, and died there some weeks later.   *P.A.R.*

New Britain (arr.)–330
Othello–Since I Have Been Redeemed–543
Blessings–644

Faber, Frederick William (b. Calverley, Yorkshire, England, Jun. 28, 1814; d. Brompton, Kensington, Middlesex, England, Sep. 26, 1863) was a Roman Catholic priest and hymnist. He was reared in a Calvinistic Anglican home and educated at Balliol and University Colleges, Oxford (B.A., 1836; M.A., 1839). He was ordained an Anglican deacon in 1837, made a priest in 1839, and appointed rector in 1842. He became an ardent follower of the Oxford Movement and, like many in that movement, shifted his allegiance to the Roman Catholic Church. The Wilfridians, a religious order which he founded in Birmingham, merged with the order of St. Philip Neri, headed by Faber's mentor, John Henry Newman (also a hymnist). From 1849 until his death, Faber headed the Brompton Oratory (London) of that order. It was his desire as a writer to produce a body of popular devotional hymnody for English Catholics, such as John Newton and William Cowper had done for Anglicans in their *Olney Hymns*. His 150 texts appeared in four volumes.   *P.A.R.*

My God, How Wonderful You Are–11
There's a Wideness in God's Mercy–25
Faith of Our Fathers–352

Faircloth, Alta Cook (b. Valley Mills, TX, Nov. 8, 1911; d. Franklin, TN, May 8, 1983) taught in the public schools in Memphis, Tennessee, and then was assistant to the superintendent and supervisor of music, Louisiana Baptist Children's Home, Monroe, Louisiana (1942-51). In 1951 she joined the Church Music Department of the Baptist Sunday School Board and contributed significantly to the editing of music publications until her retirement in 1976. She wrote numerous anthems and songs and compiled and arranged three collections of music for women's voices. She served on the editorial staff for *Baptist Hymnal* (1956), *Christian Praise* (1964), and *Baptist Hymnal* (1975).   *W.J.R.*

McCray (arr.)–Sing Hosannas–97

Farjeon, Eleanor (b. Westminster, London, England, Feb. 13, 1881; d. Hampstead, London, England, Jun. 5, 1965) was the daughter of novelist B.L. Farjeon and the granddaughter of actor Joseph Jefferson. She was educated privately and wrote novels, plays, poetry, music, and books for children. The first of her approximately 80 works was *Nursery Rhymes of London Town* (1916). Subsequent volumes won her the Carnegie Medal, the Hans Anderson International Medal, and the Regina Medal. Among her works were *A Nursery in the Nineties* (1935), *Martin Pippin in the Daisyfield* (1937), *The Glass Slipper* (1944), *Silversand and Snow* (1951), and *The Last Four Years* (1958). She became Roman Catholic at age 70.   *P.H.*

Morning Has Broken–48

Farquharson, Walter (b. near Rosetown, Saskatchewan, Canada, May 30, 1936) was reared on his family's seed grain farm, where he was imbued with a concern for matters of justice and ecology. He was educated at the University of Saskatchewan (B.A., 1957) and St. Andrew's College, Saskatchewan (B.D., 1961). Following his ordination in 1960 he went to Edinburgh, Scotland for a year of post-graduate studies. In July of 1961 he became pastor of the Saltcoats-Bredenbury pastoral charge of the United Churches of Canada in Saskatchewan. For 13 years he served in what he called a tent-making ministry. In addition to fulfilling his ministry as pastor, he taught English and other subjects in the local school. In 1990 Farquharson was elected Moderator of the United Church of Canada. In recognition of his contribution to rural and pastoral ministry and hymn writing, he was awarded the honorary D.D. by St. Andrew's College in 1975. Stanley Osborne, in *If Such Holy Song* (Whitby, Ontario, 1976, No. 88) has described Farquharson's developing interest in writing hymn texts:

"In his youth the author had a deep interest in horticulture as well as writing. Both were very important to him, but gradually the latter became dominant. He grew up in an atmosphere where precision was the rule in the written and spoken word. He remembers the frustration he experienced whenever he encountered mediocrity in hymns. 'How realistic is it to stand and sing "all is safely gathered in,"' he said to himself, 'when you know that only one farmer in twelve has his work done!' The time came when he could not resist the inner compulsion to write hymns himself. When he did, his congregation responded enthusiastically."   *H.E.*

Would You Bless Our Homes and
  Families–507

Farrell, Bob (b. Corpus Christi, TX, Oct. 23, 1948) received his B. S. in Economics from the University of Houston in 1972. Since his graduation, he and his wife Jayne have been in full-time music ministry, most recently (from 1977 to present) as the contemporary Christian duo Farrell & Farrell. The Farrells have recorded ten albums since 1977. Bob has also functioned as a songwriter/publisher for his own companies, Summerdawn Music and Mint To Be Music, and, since his move to Nashville, Tennessee in 1984, as a staff writer for Warner Chappell Music.

Bob's songs have been recorded by Amy Grant, Tennessee Ernie Ford, Sandi Patti, The Imperials, and many other artists. In 1984 his song "Because of Who You Are" was nominated for Song of the Year by the Gospel Music Association. Bob's songwriting credits also include "Shine Down," "People All Over the World," "Heirlooms," and "Who Will Call Him King of Kings?" *D.M.*

There Is a Savior–536

Fawcett, John (b. Lidget Green, near Bradford, Yorkshire, England, Jan. 6, 1739 or 1740; d. Hebden Bridge, Yorkshire, England, Jul. 25, 1817) was greatly moved, as a 16-year-old, by the preaching of George Whitefield and joined the Methodists for a time. In 1758 he united with the Baptists at Bradford and began preaching in 1763. He served churches in Wainsgate, Yorkshire, and at Hebden Bridge, refusing invitations to prestigious appointments elsewhere.

At Hebden Bridge he converted a portion of his home into a school for neighborhood children. There he trained many students who later became prominent, including Ward of Serampore and John Foster, the essayist. He declined an invitation to

become principal of Bristol Baptist College, but founded the Northern Education Society (later known as Rawdon College). Fawcett was one of the earliest supporters of the new Baptist Missionary Society and the author of many works of both prose and poetry. Of the several hymns written as expressions or expositions of his sermons, two are still in common use: "Blest Be the Tie That Binds" and "Lord, Dismiss Us with Thy Blessing." *H.T.M.*

Blest Be the Tie–387

Featherston, William Ralph (b. Montreal, Quebec, Canada, Jul. 23, 1846; d. Montreal, Quebec, Canada, May 20, 1873) was the son of John and Mary (Stephenson) Featherston and seems to have spent his life in Montreal. No other information has been found about this author except that he and his parents were members of the Wesleyan Methodist Church of Montreal, which was later named the St. James Methodist Church, and now is the St. James United Church, from whose records the above information was secured. *W.J.R.*

My Jesus, I Love Thee–210

Ferguson, John (b. Cleveland, OH, Jan. 27, 1941) earned degrees from Oberlin College (B.M., 1963), Kent State University (M.A., 1965), and the Eastman School of Music (D.M.A., 1976). His doctoral study in organ was taken with Russell Saunders. Following 15 years on the music faculty at Kent State University, during which he was also Organist-Choirmaster of the United Church of Christ, Kent, Ohio, he served as Music Director and Organist at the Central Lutheran Church in Minneapolis from 1978-83. In 1983 he joined the music faculty at St. Olaf college, where he is Elliot and Klara Stockdal Johnson Professor of Organ and Church Music and Minister of Music to the student congregation. He has served as visiting professor at the University of Notre Dame and the Yale Institute of Sacred Music. Ferguson is author of *Worship Blueprints: Guide to Planning for Music* and *Walter Holtkamp: American Organ Builder* and co-author of *A Musician's Guide to Church Music*. He served as music editor of *The Hymnal of the United Church of Christ* (1975).   *M.P.*

PROMISED ONE (arr.)–127

Fettke, Thomas Eugene (b. Bronx, New York, NY, Feb. 24, 1941) is a composer, arranger, producer, and editor. He received his education at Oakland City College and California State University (Hayward). For 33 years he served as a minister of music and as a private and public school teacher. His last minister of music position was at the Oak Creek Church in Danville, California. He was also a staff member at Redwood Chapel Community Church and Redwood Christian School system. In 1986 he was the senior editor of *The Hymnal for Worship & Celebration* (Word). He continues to serve as guest conductor, clinician, and workshop leader. His first published work was "My God, How Wonderful Thou Art" in 1972. Among the best known of his numerous works is the anthem, "The Majesty and Glory of Your Name."   *S.W.G.*

SOLI DEO GLORIA–37
JANICE–115
HE IS LORD–He Is Lord–178
WE SHALL BEHOLD HIM (arr.)–196
THIS IS THE DAY (arr.)–359
STRENGTH–476
SHINE (arr.)–579
CANE PEAK–Grace, Love, and Fellowship–661

Fillmore, James Henry (b. Cincinnati, OH, Jun. 1, 1849; d. Cincinnati, OH, Feb. 8, 1936) was a member of a family of musicians, composers, and music publishers active in Ohio in the latter 19th and earlier 20th centuries. He was the eldest of seven children born to Augustus Dameron and Hannah (Lockwood) Fillmore. His father (1823-69), a frontier preacher in Illinois before settling his family in Cincinnati in the 1840s, was an ordained Baptist minister and later a minister among the Disciples of Christ. He was also a professional musician, composing hymn tunes and revival songs and compiling tunebooks using both shape-notes and a numeral notation invented by his brother, Comfort Lavius Fillmore. After his father's death in 1869, twenty-one-year-old son James took over his singing schools to support the family. Having learned the printing trade and music typesetting, he joined two of his brothers, Frederick A. Fillmore (b. 1856) and Charles M. Fillmore (b. 1860) in founding Fillmore Brothers in 1874. Specializing in educational and band music, as well as church music, Fillmore Brothers became known as Fillmore Music House at the turn of the century and was sold to Carl Fischer in 1951. Fillmore also published a monthly periodical, *The Musical Messenger*, from 1891 to 1897.

J.H. Fillmore's music collections included *The New Harp of Zion* (1872), *Songs of Glory* (1874), *Songs of Gratitude* (1878), *New Christian Hymn and Tune-Book* (1882), *The Praise Hymnal* (with Palmer Hartsough, orchestration by Henry Fillmore, 1912). Fillmore's gospel songs include the music to "I Am Resolved No Longer to Linger" and "Purer in Heart, O God."   *H.E.*

HANNAH–191
RESOLUTION–301

Fischer, William Gustavus (b. Baltimore, MD, Oct. 14, 1835; d. Philadelphia, PA, Aug. 12, 1912) learned to read music in a singing class held at a German-speaking church in Philadelphia. Later, while learning the bookbinding trade at J. B. Lippincott's, he devoted his evenings to the study of music. From 1858 to 1868 he taught music at Girard College, Philadelphia. In the latter year he became a partner with John E. Gould in a piano business. He was a member of Christ Methodist Episcopal Church during his residence in Philadelphia.

Fischer was well known as a choral conductor and as a song leader for revival meetings. He led a choir of 1000 voices for the Moody-Sankey campaign in Philadelphia (1875) and a large choir of Welsh singers at the bicentennial celebration of the landing of William Penn. He composed over 200 Sunday School and gospel hymn tunes, many of which were first published in pamphlet form. *D.M.*

FISCHER–325
HANKEY–572

Fishel, Donald (b. Hart, MI, Nov. 1, 1950) received a Bachelor of Music from the University of Michigan, Ann Arbor, (1972) and a Bachelor of Science in Computer Science from Eastern Michigan University, Ypsilanti (1983). He was reared in the Methodist church, though he never became a member. During his college years (1968-69) he became interested in the Roman Catholic church. In 1969 he became a member of The Word of God, a charismatic Catholic community in Washtenaw County, Michigan, and was baptized in 1970. Donald was active in the music ministry of The Word of God from 1971 to 1981, directing the orchestra from about 1975 to 1981. He also served from 1980 to 1982 as music director at a Roman Catholic church in Ann Arbor, for which he wrote a large amount of liturgical music, most of which remains unpublished.

From 1973 to 1981 Donald was publications editor for The Word of God Music and Servant Music, typesetting music and helping produce record albums. Since 1983 he has worked as a systems programmer, helping to design and build computer systems. *D.M.*

ALLELUIA NO.1–Alleluia, Alleluia! Give Thanks–170

Fisher, Albert C. (b. New Bern, NC, Mar. 10, 1886; d. Dallas, TX, Feb. 6, 1946) received his education at Polytechnic College (Fort Worth, Texas), Vanderbilt University, and Southern Methodist University. In 1908 he moved back to Fort Worth and served for 10 years as general evangelist for the Methodist Episcopal Church, South. During World War I, he served as a chaplain. For 12 years he ministered in the East Oklahoma Conference, but, in 1944, he was transferred to the North Texas Conference. He wrote both text and tune for a number of gospel songs and edited *Best Revival Hymns* (Cokesbury Press, 1923). *S.W.G.*

REDEEMING LOVE–There's a Glad New Song–431
FISHER–Love Is the Theme–545

Forbis, Wesley L. (b. Chickasha, OK, Oct. 31, 1930) was educated in the public schools of Chickasha, the University of Tulsa (B.M.E., 1952; M.A., Religion, 1955), Baylor University (M.M., 1957), and George

Peabody College (Ph.D., 1968). While at Baylor he directed the Baylor Religious Hour Choir.

During the years 1955-59 he served in a variety of positions including Instructor of Church Music and Assistant Football Coach at the University of Corpus Christi, and Baptist Student Union director and Bible Teacher at Del Mar Junior College. In 1957 he married the former Ginger Parks. During his years at George Peabody, he was active as a church and school musician in Nashville.

In 1962 he moved to Liberty, Missouri, as music department chairman of William Jewell College where he served for 19 years. He became widely known as an adjudicator, clinician, choral director, music worship leader, and music educator. He served as president of the Missouri American Choral Directors Association and the Southwest Division ACDA. He is a recipient of the Hines Sims Award of the Southern Baptist Church Music Conference and was named by William Jewell College a Walter Pope Binns Scholar. In 1990 he was selected for membership in the William Jewell Teachers Hall of Fame. Since 1981 he has been responsible for the program of church music for the Southern Baptist Sunday School Board.   *D.B.*

Break Out, O Church of God–401
Creator of the Universe–549
O God of Prophets, Known of Old–646
Go with God–Go with God–648

Fosdick, Harry Emerson (b. Buffalo, NY, May 24, 1878; d. Bronxville, NY, Oct. 5, 1969) was educated at Colgate University (A.B., 1900), Union Theological Seminary (B.D, 1904), and Columbia University (M.A., 1908). He received 12 honorary degrees from universities in America and Scotland. He was ordained a Baptist minister in 1903 and from 1904 to 1915 was minister of First Baptist Church in Montclair, New Jersey. From 1908 to 1915 he was also a teacher of homiletics at Union Theological Seminary and from 1915 to 1946 he was professor of practical theology. During World War I, he served as a chaplain to the American troops. From 1919-26 he was pastor of First Presbyterian Church of New York City.

In 1926 he was called to Park Avenue Baptist Church in New York City. From 1926 to 1946, he was preacher on the National Vespers nationwide radio broadcasts. Using funds from John D. Rockefeller, Jr., the congregation of the Park Avenue Baptist Church constructed the large interdenominational Riverside Church overlooking the Hudson River in Manhattan, New York City, near Columbia University. He was the author of 32 books. The title of his autobiography, *The Living of These Days*, is taken from the hymn which he wrote for the opening of the Riverside Church.   *S.W.G.*

God of Grace and God of Glory–395

Foster, Frederick William (b. Bradford, England, Aug. 1, 1760; d. Ockbrook, near Derby, England, Apr. 12, 1835) was educated at the Moravian Brethren educational center in Fulneck, Yorkshire, and later on the continent at the Moravian College in Saxony, at Barby near Magdeburg. Upon his return to England he became a minister of the Moravian Church, later a provincial superintendent, and finally consecrated a bishop in the Moravian Church in 1818. He was a translator of German hymns, composer of original English hymns, and editor of the 1801 *Moravian Hymn Book*, the 1808 supplement, and the revised edition of 1826.   *S.W.G.*

Christian Hearts, in Love United (tr.)–378

Foundery Collection–The "Foundery" was for a number of years an English government site for the casting of cannon. In 1716 an explosion killed several workmen and almost demolished the facilities. John Wesley purchased the site and rebuilt it for use as the first Methodist meetinghouse in London. Today a chapel stands on the location which is near the building where John Wesley lived and near where he is buried. The *Foundery Collection* [*A Collection of Tunes as they are Sung at the Foundery* (London, 1742)] contained 42 tunes, which John Wesley selected from several sources, and was the first Wesleyan collection to provide tunes for the Wesleyan hymns.   *S.W.G.*

AMSTERDAM–33

Fox, Baynard Layne (b. Louisville, KY, Sep. 21, 1932; d. Tucker, GA, Sep. 30, 1982) attended Georgetown College, Georgetown, Kentucky, and the School of Church Music of The Southern Baptist Theological Seminary, Louisville, Kentucky, and was a graduate of the University of Louisville (B.M.E., 1959). Following graduation, he taught public school music in Bullitt County, Kentucky, for two years.

A gifted composer of gospel music, Fox achieved popularity with his best-known composition, "I'll Tell the World That I'm a Christian." He also wrote and published other vocal solos and choral works including *A New Creation* (an evangelistic cantata), *All God's Children, Sing unto the Lord a New Song, Like a Thief in the Night, He Is Risen,* and *Amazing Grace, How Can It Be?* He was a talented instrumentalist, playing the piano "by ear" and frequently entertaining with his accordion and giving private instruction in the instrument.

He served as minister of music at Fourth Avenue Baptist Church (1954-57) and Rockford Lane Baptist Church (1959-61) in Louisville and at Ridgecrest Baptist Church, Dothan (1961-63), and Second Baptist Church, Huntsville, Alabama (1964). His last position of service was as minister of music at Rehoboth Baptist Church, Tucker, Georgia (1964-73). For reasons of health, he took early retirement from full-time church work in 1973. However in retirement, he founded the Atlanta Christian Chorus, a non-denominational choir of 150 voices, and its children's wing, a chorus of approximately 100 boys and girls, which he directed in concerts and recordings until 1980. In his last years, Fox suffered blindness, owing to complications from long-term diabetes.   *H.T.M.*

TUCKER–I'll Tell the World That I'm a Christian–553

Francis of Assisi (b. Assisi, Italy, 1182; d. Assisi, Italy, Oct. 3, 1226) was born Giovanni Bernadone. His father was a wealthy textile merchant; his mother came from a distinguished French family. Reared in comfortable circumstances, Francis spent his youth in the pursuit of pleasure. He was imprisoned in 1202-03 as a leader in the war between Assisi and Perugia. A serious illness caused him to reexamine his style of living. While on his way to another war in 1205, he saw a vision at Spoleto which caused him to return to Assisi. He was converted following an encounter with a leper and after hearing a voice from the cross in the ruined church at San Damiano. The voice instructed Francis to rebuild churches. During the years 1206-08 he followed this command, broke off relations with his father, and took vows of poverty and ministered to the poor and ill. The Franciscan order was founded in 1209 on the principles espoused by Jesus in Matthew 10:5-14. This first order was followed by an order of nuns and a third order of laypersons. Francis was obsessed with a desire to preach to Mohammedans. His first missionary endeavor to Syria was thwarted by a shipwreck, the second by illness. A journey to France had to be postponed so that Francis could quell dissension brought on when some followers attempted to mitigate the order's rule of simplicity.

At Christmas in 1223 he reportedly built the first creche, from which we derive our modern custom. He gradually retired from administering the order in favor of a life of prayer and singing. The last two years of his life were marked by constant pain and blindness. The most typical trait associated with Francis was his love of nature. His "Canticle to the Sun" was the first poetic work in modern Italian.   *P.H.*

All Creatures of Our God and King–27

Francis, Samuel Trevor (b. Chesthunt, Hertsfordshire, England, Nov. 19, 1834; d. Worthing, Sussex, England, Dec. 28, 1925) spent his early life in Hull, where he was a member of the surpliced choir in the parish church. He began to write poetry at an early age. He later moved to London, where he became a merchant and was affiliated with the Plymouth Brethren assembly at Kennington. His biography appears in H. Pickering's *Chief Men Among the Brethren* (1931). He was an evangelist and an open air preacher. He accompanied R.C. Morgan, editor of *The Christian*, on a visit to North Africa. From 1873-75 he was an assistant to Ira D. Sankey during the Moody-Sankey meetings in Great Britain. His works include *Gems from the Revised Version, with Poems* (1891), *Whence-Whither, and Other Poems* (1898), and his collected works, *O the Deep, Deep Love of Jesus, and Other Sacred Poems* (London, 1926). He died at Groomsbridge Nursing Home in Worthing, Sussex. *H.E.*

O the Deep, Deep Love of Jesus–409

Frazer, George West (b. Bally, near Sliso, Ireland, 1830; d. Cheltenham, Gloucestershire, England, Jan. 24, 1896) was descended from the Lovat-Frazer of Inverness, Scotland. His conversion, at the age of 20, was the result of a revival meeting conducted in Dublin by Grattan Guiness. He earned his living as a bank employee but devoted much of his time to evangelistic work. He spent much time in England and eventually moved to Cheltenham. He wrote many hymns which were published in *Midnight Praises*, *Day-Dawn Praises*, and *The Day Spring.*   *D.B.*

God, Our Father, We Adore Thee
   (st. 1,2,4)–248

Frazier, Francis Philip (b. Santee, NE, Jun. 2, 1892; d. Yankton, SD, Sep. 28, 1964) was the son and grandson of Sioux Native Americans who were Congregational ministers. He received his early education at the Santee Indian School, Yankton Academy, and Mt. Herman School (MA), and attended Dartmouth College for one year. Following military service in France and Germany from 1917-19, he earned degrees from Oberlin College (B.A., 1922) and Chicago Theological Seminary (B.D., 1925). He was ordained in 1926 and invested his life in ministry among Native Americans, including assignments in Oklahoma, North Dakota, South Dakota, and California. From 1956 until his death in 1964 he was supervisor for the churches of the Sioux Indian Mission of the Standing Rock Reservation. He was awarded the D.H.L. degree by Oberlin in 1960 and honored by Dartmouth College with the Doctor of Divinity degree in 1964.   *M.P.*

Many and Great, O God (parap.)–49

Fry, Charles William (b. Alderbury, Wiltshire, England, May 30, 1838; d. Park Hall, Polmont, England, Aug. 23, 1882) was the first bandmaster of the Salvation Army. At an early age he and his brothers learned to play one or more musical instruments. As a youth he was appointed conductor in the small ensemble that accompanied the singing in the Wesleyan Chapel where his family worshiped and where at the age of 17 he was converted. Like his father and grandfather, Fry became a builder, bringing his three sons into business with him. When the Salvation Army began its work in 1878, Fry, in spite of opposition, offered himself and his three sons to play for their outdoor meetings. This was the beginning of brass band music in the missions of the Salvation Army. The Fry Family Band toured with the Army's founder General William Booth, and were so much in demand that their business began to suffer. After conferring with General Booth and much prayer, they closed their business to work full-time for the Salvation Army in 1880. After two years, Fry's service was cut short by illness. He was cared for in the home of Mr. Livingston Learmouth, Park Hall, Polmouth, where he died. He was buried in the Necropolis Cemetery, Glasgow, Scotland. Arch R. Wiggins has described the work of the Fry Family Band:

"The Frys made up their parts as they went along; they required no printed music. Fred (the eldest son) and his brothers all knew shorthand, so whenever they heard a fresh song they would take down the words and Fred would write the music in tonic sol-fa. Once, when the Founder's (General Booth) Sunday night meeting was unusually stiff, he dropped on Fred Fry for a vocal solo, and as suddenly Fry had the inspiration to sing "Depth of Mercy" to the then popular secular air, "It is years since we last met," which resulted in completely changing the atmosphere of the gathering and a number of people deciding for Christ" (Wiggins, 24).

The Salvation Army's pioneer musician Lt. Col. Richard Slater wrote concerning Fry's songs:

"His power of expression made his singing arrestive. It was the power of religion, the outcome of a personal fellowship with God, which gave him his emotional force as a vocalist. He was a song-writer and often set words to simple melodies.... He drew from personal experience the matter for his verses" (Avery, 14).   *H.E.*

SALVATIONIST (adapt.)–The Lily of the Valley–189

Funk, Joseph (b. PA, Apr. 6, 1778; d. Singers Glen, VA, Dec. 24, 1862). See *Genuine Church Music.*

Foundation–338

Gabriel, Charles Hutchinson (b. Wilton, IA, Aug. 18, 1856; d. Los Angeles, CA, Sep. 15, 1932) was one of the more prominent and prolific figures in the development of the gospel song. He was reared by Methodist parents and encouraged to develop his interest in music. He followed his father as a singing school teacher. After a failed marriage, perhaps because of his frantic schedule as a musician and music teacher, he moved to California in 1887.

While there he remarried and became music director of the Sunday School at Grace Methodist Episcopal Church in San Francisco. In 1892 he settled in Chicago to be nearer the publishing houses. From that time until his retirement, he was active as poet, composer, and editor. He was associated principally with the Rodeheaver Company, but worked also with Hope and E.O. Excell. His output has been estimated at 7,000 songs, in addition to anthems, cantatas, and other works. He was also a prolific writer of prose, producing two volumes of memoirs, two volumes of biographical sketches of gospel song writers, and one on philosophy of church music. Terry W. York, in his doctoral dissertation on Gabriel, sees him as a pivotal figure, being one of the last to write for the urban revivals and one of the first to provide music for the local church.   *P.A.R.*

GABRIEL–65
WAY OF THE CROSS–151
OLD-TIME POWER–Pentecostal Power–242
MCDANIEL–441
PRECIOUS TO ME–He Is So Precious to Me–452
HIGHER GROUND–484
GLORY SONG–O That Will Be Glory–520
HE LIFTED ME–In Loving-Kindness
  Jesus Came–542
MY SAVIOR'S LOVE–I Stand Amazed in
  the Presence–547
MCCABE–Send the Light–595

Gaither, Gloria (b. Battle Creek, MI, Mar. 4, 1942) was educated at Anderson College (B.A., M.A.), majoring in English, French, and Sociology. She married William J. Gaither, whom she met during college. She taught three years in Alexandria High School, Alexandria, Indiana. She shares in song writing and public appearances with her husband, and her unusual singing abil-

ity adds warmth and beauty to the sound of the Gaither concerts and recordings. *W.J.R.*

NAME OF THE LORD–In the Name of
  the Lord–174
There's Something About That Name–177
The King Is Coming–194
The Family of God–386
Because He Lives–407

Gaither, William J. (b. Alexandria, IN, Mar. 28, 1936) was educated at Anderson College (B.A., M.A.), majoring in English. He taught English at Alexandria High School. After six years his music activities and the Gaither Music Company, which he had established, demanded his full time. A prolific composer with musical sensitivity, he has composed more than 300 songs. Among these are "Because He Lives," "There's Just Something About That Name," "The Family of God," "He Touched Me," "Something Beautiful," and "Let's Just Praise the Lord." His song writing is usually done in collaboration with his wife Gloria. The Gaithers' success as writers of songs, recording artists, and concert artists has made them exceedingly popular. In spite of the recognition they have received, they have maintained their family lifestyle and have remained committed to their local church fellowship.   *W.J.R.*

THAT NAME–There's Something About That
  Name–177
KING IS COMING–The King Is Coming–194
FAMILY OF GOD–The Family of God–386
RESURRECTION–Because He Lives–407

Gannett, William Channing (b. Boston, MA, Mar. 13, 1840; d. Rochester, NY, Dec. 15, 1923) was educated at Harvard University, Harvard Divinity School, and Cambridge Theological School. For three and a half years during the Civil War, he worked among the freed slaves. Ordained to the Unitarian ministry in 1868, following several pastorates, he became pastor of the First Unitarian Church, Rochester, New York, where he served from 1889 to 1908. Among his published works are *A Year of Miracle* (1882), *The Thought of God in Hymns and Poems* (in collaboration with Frederick L. Hosmer, 1885), *The Childhood of Jesus* (1890), and *Frances David* (1914). *W.J.R.*

The God of Abraham Praise
  (versification)–34

Garo Christians are people of Mongolian extraction living in the hills of Assam on the northeastern frontier of India who were evangelized in the 19th century by Christian missionaries. Through the years they developed their own modes of worship and styles of singing. Certain stanzas of the song "I Have Decided to Follow Jesus" are derived from the musical worship of these Garo Christian converts. *H.T.M.*

I Have Decided to Follow Jesus (st. 1,2)–305

Gardiner, William (b. Leicester, England, Mar. 15, 1770; d. Leicester, England, Nov. 16, 1853) successfully ran the hosiery manufacturing business he inherited from his father. He was devoted to music and through his travels, met such musicians as Haydn and Beethoven. In 1794 he provided the music for (and played viola in) a performance of Beethoven's string trio, Opus 3. For this he is recognized by many as the first to introduce Beethoven's music into England. In addition, he fostered the introduction of the works of Haydn and Mozart to English audiences. The three volumes of his *Music and Friends* (1838-53) de-

scribed his travels and contacts with famous musicians. The first two volumes of Gardiner's *Sacred Melodies from Haydn, Mozart, and Beethoven adapted to the best English Poets and Appropriated to the use of the British Church* (6 vols., London, 1812 and 1815) contained many hymn tune adaptations of themes from 18th-century masterpieces. His pattern of excerpting and adapting tunes from the classics became fashionable and influenced others in England and the United States, including Lowell Mason, who borrowed from Gardiner's collections. Nineteenth-century hymnal compilers frequently turned to this work as a source of tunes. *D.B., P.A.R.*

GERMANY–402

Garrett, Leslie Norman (b. Mamatmata, New Zealand, Jul. 15, 1943) received his education at the Word of Faith Bible School. He is pastor of the Christian Family Centre in Maddington, Western Australia. His first published work was the text and tune of "This Is the Day." His musical works include *Scripture in Song* and *Song of Praise*. His books are *Which Bible Can We Trust* and *Best of All God Is with Us.* *S.W.G.*

THIS IS THE DAY–This Is the Day–359

Gaultney, Barbara Fowler (b. Atlanta, GA, Jul. 14, 1935; d. Riverdale, GA, Jan. 21, 1974) was educated in the Atlanta public schools and attended the Georgia State University in Atlanta. In 1957 she moved her membership from the Columbia Drive Baptist Church, Decatur, Georgia, to the First Baptist Church, Forest Park, both suburbs of Atlanta. For a period of time she was poet laureate of Clayton County, Georgia, writing for local newspapers. A privately published volume of her poems and essays is *"...Of Such Is the Kingdom!...: Devotional Thoughts* (1965). A sensitive person and in poor health, she was home-bound during much of her later life. Both blind and crippled, she frequently turned to writing as an expression of her faith.   *H.E., W.J.R.*

Forest Park–My Lord Is Near Me All the Time–59

Gauntlett, Henry John (b. Wellington, Hampshire, England, Jul. 9, 1805; d. Kensington, Middlesex, England, Feb. 21, 1876) in early life was organist and choirmaster of Olney Church, Buckinghamshire, where his father was vicar. After a short career as a lawyer, he turned his full-time energies to music in 1846. He was chosen by Mendelssohn to be the organist for the premier performance of *Elijah* in Birmingham (1846) and was associated with Dr. Henry Allon in the well-known psalmody classes conducted at Union Chapel, Islington (London). An enthusiast for plainsong, he wrote much on church music and composed anthems, songs, and some 10,000 hymn tunes! This was in addition to his organ compositions. Preeminently interested in hymnody, he helped edit several hymnals. Gauntlett served as organist of All Saints, Notting Hill (1861-63) and St. Bartholomew-the-Less (1872-76) and for years exerted considerable influence as an organ designer.   *H.T.M.*

Stuttgart (adapt.)–21, 257, 369

Geibel, Adam (b. Baden, Germany, Sep. 15, 1885; d. Philadelphia, PA, Aug. 3, 1933) was brought to America at an early age. At eight or nine, he was given improper treatment for an eyelid infection, which caused him to become totally blind. In later years,

Geibel remarked that his blindness caused him to develop his musical abilities and was not a source of regret on his part. He became widely known as an organist, conductor, and composer, and founded the Adam Geibel Music Company. This later became the Hall-Mack Company and eventually the Rodeheaver Hall-Mack Company. Geibel composed a number of popular secular songs, including "Kentucky Babe," "Little Cotton Dolly," and "Sleep, Sleep, Sleep," and was known particularly as a composer of pieces for four-part men's voices. Geibel served for many years as organist at Philadelphia's Stetson Mission.   *D.M.*

Geibel–487

Geistliche Kirchengesäng (1599) is the short title for *Alte Katholische Geistliche Kirchengesäng* which was published in 1599 in Cologne, Germany. This collection is the earliest known source of several old Rhineland carols, including the original of "Lo, How a Rose E'er Blooming."   *H.T.M.*

Es Ist Ein Ros'–78

Geistliche Kirchengesäng (1623) is the short title for *Ausserlesene Catholische Geistliche Kirchengesäng* which was printed by Peter von Brachel in Cologne, Germany in 1623. This collection is the earliest source known for a number of German hymn tunes, including Lasst uns Erfreuen to which "All Creatures of Our God and King" is sung.   *H.T.M.*

Lasst uns Erfreuen–27

Genevan Psalter (1551) was one of several incomplete collections of metrical versions of the psalms published under the direction of John Calvin in Geneva, Switzerland. Calvin's collaborators were the poet Clement Marot and the theologian Theodore de Beza who provided most of the metrical texts (in French) and Louis Bourgeois, who provided most of the 85 psalm tunes in this 1551 collection. The *Genevan Psalter* was completed in 1562 with a total of 125 tunes. It continues to be the original source of several metrical psalm tunes in current use. *H.T.M.*

Old 100th–5, 253
Old 134th–30, 388, 623

Genuine Church Music (compiled by Joseph Funk) is a singing-school tunebook in shape notation first printed in Winchester, Virginia, in the Shenandoah Valley in 1832. A significant source of American folk hymns, this tunebook is one of only five that continue to be used in singings. Its full title, *A Compilation of Genuine Church Music*, was changed in its fifth edition (1851) to *Harmonia Sacra, being a Compilation of Genuine Church Music*, and its notation was changed from four- to seven-shape. Beginning with the fourth edition (1847), this tunebook was printed by Joseph Funk and his sons at Mountain Valley, Virginia. A 24th edition, *The New Harmonia Sacra: a Compilation of Genuine Church Music* (1980), is still in use among the Mennonites of the Shenandoah Valley. In the early 1980's about ten *New Harmonia sacra* singings were being held annually. *Genuine Church Music* was compiled by Joseph Funk, a Mennonite singing-school teacher, composer, and printer. Funk lived in Mountain Valley, near Harrisonburg, Virginia, a village whose name was changed to Singers Glen in 1860 to reflect its musical significance. Alice Parker's opera *Singers Glen* (Hinshaw, 1978) is based on the life of Joseph Funk and his *Genuine Church Music*. *H.E.*

Foundation–338

Gerhardt, Paul (b. Gräfenhayniches, near Wittenberg, Germany, Mar. 12, 1607; d. Lübben, Germany, May 27, 1676) was the son of the mayor of Gräfenhayniches. He was educated at the Elector's school at Grimma (1622-27), and at the University of Wittenberg (1628-42). From the age of twelve he experienced the trials and tribulations of the Thirty Years' War during which Swedish soldiers burned his home town. Possibly due to these conditions, he was not ordained to the Lutheran ministry until 1651, when he was 44. About 1643 he moved to Berlin and became a tutor in the home of Andreas Barthold, whose daughter Anna Maria became Gerhardt's wife in 1655. Gerhardt served Lutheran parishes at Mittenwalde (1651-57); the great St. Nicholas' Church in Berlin (1657-68); and at Lübben (1669-76).

In addition to the tragedies of the Thirty Years' War, Gerhardt experienced much personal suffering. Four of his five children died in infancy, and his wife died in 1668. From 1666-68 he was involved in political and theological controversy because he refused to sign the edict of Elector Frederick William I, which limited free discussion of Lutheran and Reformed issues. Following his refusal Gerhardt was dismissed from his position at St. Nicholas' Church.

Gerhardt and Luther are regarded as the greatest German hymn writers. While Luther's hymns are objective and sometimes militant (as in "A mighty fortress"), Gerhardt's are subjective, emphasizing devotion and trust in God. Gerhardt's 132 hymns mark a transition from the confessional to the pietistic in German hymnody.

Much of the initial popularity of his hymns can be attributed to their relevance to a people suffering amid war and controversy.

At St. Nicholas' Church Gerhardt served along with the cantor and hymn tune composer Johann Crüger, who published many of his hymns in the 1648 edition of his *Praxis Pietatis Melica* ("Practice of Piety in Song"). Crüger's successor, Johann G. Ebeling, also published a number of settings of Gerhardt's hymns in *Das andere Dutzend geistlicher Andachtslieder Herrn Paul Gerhardts mit neuen Melodien* ("The Other Dozen Sacred Devotional Songs of Paul Gerhardt, with New Melodies," 1666-67). The first English translations of Gerhardt's hymns appear to be those of John Wesley (1739-40).   *H.E.*

Jesus, Thy Boundless Love to Me–123
O Sacred Head, Now Wounded–137

Gesangbuch der Herzogl (Wittenberg, 1784) is the short designation for a well-known 18th-century German songbook entitled *Gesangbuch der Herzoglichen Wirtembergischen Katolischen Hofkapelelle* (1784). Possibly its significant place in the worship of the ducal chapel in Wittenberg lent popularity to certain of its hymn tunes, including the one subsequently named ELLACOMBE.   *H.T.M.*

ELLACOMBE–130

Giardini, Felice de (b. Turin, Italy, Apr. 12, 1716; d. Moscow, Russia, Dec. 17, 1796) was a chorister in Milan Cathedral and later a violin pupil of G. B. Somis. He became a well-known violinist and played in various orchestras in the opera houses of Rome and Naples. From 1752 to 1784 he lived in England as a leader at the Italian opera and later as an impressario. His growing reputation opened the doors of the aristocracy to him, and among those who befriended him, as she did many others, was the outstanding leader in the Evangelical Revival, Lady Huntingdon. Through her influence he wrote four tunes for Martin Madan's *A Collection of Psalms and Tunes* (London, 1769), generally known as the "Lock Hospital Collection." Of these four, only the ITALIAN HYMN tune has remained in usage. Giardini left England in 1784 but returned in 1790. After unsuccessful opera ventures in London, he took his troupe to Moscow where he died, apparently in great poverty.   *H.T.M.*

ITALIAN HYMN–247

Gillard, Richard Arthur Moss (b. Malmsbury, Wiltshire, England, May 22, 1953) is a graduate of Primary Teachers Training College, Auckland, New Zealand, 1974. He and his wife Suzanne Rae Gillard have three children. In 1956 he moved from his native England to New Zealand, where he lives at Birkenhead, Auckland. He has served as warehouse or dispatch manager of several firms. A member of Willow Avenue Chapel (Brethren), Birkenhead, he grew up in the Assemblies of God, returning to Anglicanism as a young adult.

A particularly important influence, as described in a letter to this writer, "was St. Paul's Anglican Church, an inner city Anglo-Catholic/charismatic parish, home of the St. Paul's Singers (I was a part of this group) and the St. Paul's Outreach Trust. I also spent some time as a member of a folk music club. I have very little formal music training and rely heavily on my two ears and on guitar chord symbols, and my instrumental abilities are confined to fretted, plucked stringed instruments. The biggest outlet for my (and my wife's) talents was with the St. Paul's Singers. We travelled throughout New Zealand leading worship at a number of conferences and introducing new music to other congregations (particularly Anglican ones) as well as leading our own congregation in worship three times as week. We also were involved in making six record albums and in the publishing of several songbooks and in writing original songs and liturgical music." His songs include "Lift High the Banners of Love" (1975), "Worthy the Lamb" (1975), and "Between the Singing Mountains" (1976), published by St. Paul's Outreach Trust.   *H.E.*

The Servant Song–613

Gilmore, Joseph Henry (b. Boston, MA, Apr. 29, 1834; d. Rochester, NY, Jul. 23, 1918) was educated at Phillips Academy, Andover, Massachusetts, Brown University, and Newton Theological Institution. Following his graduation from Newton in 1861, he taught Hebrew there for one year. After being ordained to the Baptist ministry in 1862, he became pastor of the Baptist church in Fisherville, New Hampshire. From 1863-64 he was editor of the Concord *Daily Monitor* and private secretary for his father, who at that time was Governor of New Hampshire. After serving for a time as pastor of the Second Baptist Church in Rochester, New York, in 1868 he was appointed professor of logic, rhetoric, and English literature at the University of Rochester, where he remained until his retirement in 1911. An author and poet, his publications included *The Art of Expression* (1876), *He Leadeth Me, and other Religious Poems* (1877), and *Outlines of English and American Literature* (1905).   *M.P.*

He Leadeth Me! O Blessed Thought–52

Gladden, Washington (b. Pottsgrove, PA, Feb. 11, 1836; d. Columbus, OH, Jul. 2, 1918) was a writer, editor, and pastor. He graduated from Williams College in 1859 and in 1860 was ordained a Congregationalist minister. He served churches in Brooklyn (1860-61) and Morrisania, New York (1861-66), and in North Adams, Massachusetts (1866-71), before joining the editorial staff of the *Independent* (New York). In 1874, he became pastor of the North Congregational Church of Springfield, Massachusetts. He spent the longest portion of his ministry at First Congregational Church in Columbus, Ohio, where he was pastor from 1882 until his retirement in 1914.

Through his writing and preaching, Gladden became one of the best-known American ministers of his day. His speaking, more than 30 books, and numerous journal articles helped to increase public understanding of biblical scholarship and of the social aspects of the Christian witness. He served from 1904 to 1907 as moderator of the National Council of Congregational Churches and was recognized with honorary doctorates from the University of Wisconsin, Roanoke College, and the University of Notre Dame. He was among the editors of *The Pilgrim Hymnal* (1904).   *P.A.R.*

O Master, Let Me Walk with Thee–279

Gläser, Carl Gotthelf (b. Weissenfels, Germany, May 4, 1784; d. Barmen, Germany, Apr. 16, 1829) was a chorister at St. Thomas' Church in Leipzig where J. S. Bach had served earlier. Gläser later studied law at the University of Leipzig, but finally turned to music and studied violin with the Italian master, Bartholomeo Campagnoli, who taught in Leipzig. Gläser moved to Barmen and became a teacher of piano, violin, and voice and owned a music shop.

He composed motets, school songs, and instrumental works and directed choral groups. *S.W.G.*

AZMON–11, 216, 268

Good Pasteur, Ralph H. (b. Columbus, IN, Dec. 12, 1923) was named from two ancestors–brothers who were named Goode and Pasteur. His family was originally from Haiti. Following his childhood spent in Richmond, Indiana, he attended the University of Southern California, Los Angeles, where he majored in English and minored in music. On April 4, 1948, he became music director for the First Church of Deliverance, Chicago, Illinois; he has served on the church staff since then. He was chief administrator for the First Church of Deliverance Convalescent Home (1969-80). The music of this church is well known in Chicago, largely because of the late Sunday evening radio broadcasts that began in 1935 and are still heard each week on radio station WLUP. Musicians trained under his leadership have become effective leaders in other churches. *W.J.R.*

COBBS–It's So Wonderful–432

Gordon, Adoniram Judson (b. New Hampton, NH, Apr. 19, 1836; d. Boston, MA, Feb. 2, 1895), named for the pioneer Baptist missionary to Burma, was educated at Brown University and Newton Theological Seminary. Ordained to the Baptist ministry in 1863, he was called as pastor of the Baptist church at Jamaica Plain, Massachusetts, and six years later succeeded Dr. Baron Stow as pastor of the Clarendon Street Baptist Church, Boston. He was one of the editors of *The Service of Song for Baptist Churches* (1871) and editor of *The Vestry Hymn and Tune Book* (1872). For a time, in addition to his pastoral work, he served as editor of the monthly publication *The Watchword*. In 1878 he received the D.D. degree from Brown University. He was a close friend of Dwight L. Moody and was of great assistance in Moody's evangelistic efforts in Boston . *W.J.R.*

GORDON–210

Govan, Ellis (b. Biggar, Scotland, 1897) served in World War I, then spent several years in business in Kenya. He returned to the British Isles to work in the Faith Mission, an evangelistic agency that had been founded by his father in 1886. Govan retired from the Faith Mission after 34 years of service. *D.M.*

I Will Not Be Afraid–72

Grant, Sir Robert (b. Bengal, India, 1779; d. Dalpoorie, India, Jul. 9, 1838) was educated at Magdalen College, Cambridge and later became a Fellow there. In 1808 he entered Parliament. In 1831 he was made a member of the Privy Council and in 1832 Judge Advocate General. A year later he introduced in Commons a Bill for the emancipation of the Jews. In 1834 he was made Governor of Bombay and was knighted on that occasion. After his death at Dalpoorie, Western India, a medical college bearing his name was erected as a memorial to him. *S.W.G.*

O Worship the King–16

Grape, John Thomas (b. Baltimore, MD, May 6, 1835; d. Baltimore, MD, Nov. 2, 1915) was the son of George and Charlotte Grape. He was a coal merchant by trade, pursuing music as an avocation. He directed the choir of Baltimore's Monument

Street Methodist Church and later that of the Hartford Avenue Methodist Church in the same city. *D.M.*

ALL TO CHRIST–134

Gray, Marie is the pseudonym of a composer who wishes to remain anonymous. *H.E.*

I WILL TRUST (arr.)–420
ALL DAY LONG (arr.)–463

Greatorex, Henry Wellington (b. Burton-upon-Trent, Derbyshire, England, Dec. 24, 1813; d. Charleston, SC, Sep. 10, 1858) was an Anglican church musician. He received his early training from his father, Thomas, organist at Westminster Abbey. He came to Center Congregational Church in Hartford, Conneticut, in 1836, and subsequently served at St. Paul's Episcopal and Calvary Protestant Episcopal churches in New York City. In 1853 he moved to Charleston, where he was a church organist until his death from yellow fever. In 1851, his *Collection of Psalm and Hymn Tunes, Chants, Anthems and Sentences for the Use of the Protestant Episcopal Church in America* (Boston, 1851) was published in Hartford and in New York. It had several later editions under other titles. *P.A.R.*

GLORIA PATRI (GREATOREX)–252
MANOAH–414

Greatorex, Walter (b. Mansfield, Nottinghamshire, England, Mar. 30, 1877; d. Bournemouth, Hampshire, England, Dec. 29, 1949) was music master at Gresham's School, Holt, Norfolk, from 1911 until his death in 1949. He received his education at Derby School and St. John's College, Cambridge. He was a chorister at King's College, Cambridge (1888-93). From 1900-10 he was the assistant music master at Uppingham School. His most famous pupils included organist Henry G. Ley and Benjamin Britten. *P.H.*

WOODLANDS–81

Green, Fred Pratt (b. Roby [Liverpool] England, Sep. 2, 1903) grew up with Methodist and Anglican influences in his life. His father, at one time a Wesleyan Methodist, occasionally served as a local preacher. His mother was an Anglican. While at Roby, the Green family worshiped at Childwell Parish Church. When the family moved to Wallasey, just prior to World War I, they worshiped at Claremont Road Wesleyan Church. Following a decision to enter the ministry, Green entered Didsbury Theological College in 1924. In 1928 he began his work as chaplain to Hunmanby Hall, a Methodist girls boarding school. Here he wrote his first hymn. He also fell in love and married the teacher of French, Marjorie Dowsett. His ministry took him to several areas, but his service at Grange Park was particularly important with regard to his hymn writing. While visiting one of his Sunday School pupils, Green met Fallon Webb. Webb, a competent poet himself, encouraged Green to write poetry on a regular basis. For nearly 20 years the two men evaluated each other's work.

His retirement in 1969 resulted in greater involvement as a member of the group preparing *Hymns and Songs,* a supplement to the *Methodist Hymn-Book.* At the urging of fellow committee members, he wrote hymns to meet specific needs of the collection. Erik Routley played a major role in making Green's work known in the United States and considered him the most important hymnist in Methodism since Charles

Wesley. Green's hymns have found their way into all standard hymn collections. *D.B.*

The First Day of the Week–357
When the Church of Jesus–396
The Church of Christ, in Every Age–402
This Is the Threefold Truth–408
When in Our Music God Is Glorified–435
Of All the Spirit's Gifts to Me–442
For the Fruit of All Creation–643

Green, Joseph Franklin (b. Waco, TX, Jun. 6, 1924), the son of a Baptist minister, graduated from Texas Wesleyan College (B.S.), Baylor University (M.A.), and Southwestern Baptist Theological Seminary (Th.D.). From 1943 to 1946 he served in the United States Army. An ordained Baptist minister, he was a pastor in Texas and Colorado until he began editorial work with Broadman Press, Nashville, in 1954. He wrote several books, including *The Heart of the Gospel* (1968) and *Biblical Foundations for Church Music* (1967). In addition to texts for hymns and anthems, numerous articles, and curriculum pieces, he wrote brief hymn interpretations for *The Church Musician* and other publications of the Baptist Sunday School Board. Along with the present hymn, his revision of "Come, Come Ye Saints" appeared in the *Baptist Hymnal* (1975). Since retirement in 1979, he has worked as an editor, writer, and pastor. He presently resides in Grandin, North Dakota. *H.E.*

Your Supper, Lord, Before Us Spread–374

Greiter, Matthias (b. Aichach, Bavaria, *c.* 1490; d. Strasbourg, France, Dec. 20, 1550) was trained at Strasbourg Minster to be a singer and monk, but in 1524 he became a Lutheran minister there. He served as assis-

tant pastor, pastor, and director of a choir school. Before he died, he returned to the Roman Catholic Church. Seven of Greiter's melodies appeared in his *Strassburger Kirchenamt* of 1525. He also served as music editor of Calvin's first psalter (Strassburg, 1539). *D.B.*

Old 113th–35

Grieg, Edvard Hagerup (b. Bergen, Norway, Jun. 15, 1843; d. Bergen, Norway, Sep. 4, 1907) received early musical instruction from his mother, an amateur pianist, and subsequently attended the Leipzig Conservatory of Music (1858-1862). From 1863 to 1867 he lived in Copenhagen, Denmark. In 1867 he married his cousin, Nina Hagerup, and returned to Norway, where the Griegs settled in Christiania (now Oslo). In 1877 the Griegs moved to the Norwegian mountain region of Hardanger. Eight years later they built a home in Troldhaugen, near Bergen, where they lived during the remainder of Edvard's life.

By the age of 25, Grieg was internationally recognized as the most significant composer of his country and one of the major composers in all of Europe. He was in frequent demand as a pianist and conductor of his own works, not only in his own country, but throughout Europe as well. At Grieg's request, upon his death his remains were cremated and placed in the side of a cliff at the Troldhaugen fjord.

Grieg was best known for writing music that reflected the romantic spirit and beauty of his native land. The lyrical, national character of his music caused critics to dub him the "Chopin of the North." Grieg excelled particularly in music in the smaller forms, such as piano miniatures, folk song arrangements, and solo songs, of which "I

Love Thee" is the best known. His Piano Concerto in A Minor and two suites arranged from the incidental music to Henrik Ibsen's play *Peer Gynt* continue to form part of the standard orchestral repertory.   *D.M.*

FREE–649

Grotenhuis, Dale (b. Cedar Rapids, WI, Dec. 1, 1931) was educated at Calvin College, Grand Rapids, Michigan (B.A., 1949), Michigan State University (M.M., 1961), and Ohio State University (doctoral studies). Since 1960 he has been professor of music and choral conductor at Dordt College, Sioux City, Iowa. The composer of numerous band and choral works, he was a member of the revision committee for the *Psalter Hymnal* (1987) published by the Christian Reform Church.   *H.T.M.*

TE VENGO (harm.)–222

Groves, Alexander (b. Newport, Isle of Wight, England, 1842; d. Henley-on-Thames, Oxfordshire, England, Aug. 30, 1909), at the age of 18, settled in Henley, where he worked as a grocer and accountant. In 1887 he began work for the Henley Savings Bank, as a trustee for 10 years, then auditor, and later became bank actuary. A highly respected churchman, he served for some years as organist at the Henley Wesleyan Chapel but later was associated with the Anglican parish church.   *W.J.R.*

Break Thou the Bread of Life (st. 3,4)–263

Gruber, Franz Xaver (b. Unterweizberg, near Hochburg, Austria, Nov. 25, 1787; d. Hallein, near Salzburg, Austria, Jun. 7, 1863) was discouraged from pursuing his musical ambitions by his father, a linen weaver, who urged him to follow a more remunerative profession. Nevertheless, Franz learned to play the violin and later studied organ with Georg Hardobler. He taught school at Arnsdorf (1807-29), and to supplement his income he accepted the position of organist at St. Nicholas Church at nearby Oberndorf. He was headmaster at Berndorf (1828-32), and from 1833 until his death he was organist and choirmaster at Hallein near Salzburg. More than 90 musical compositions are credited to him, but his fame is based on the Christmas song he wrote in 1818.   *W.J.R.*

STILLE NACHT–91

Grundtvig, Nicholai Frederik Severin (b. Udby, near Vordlingbor, Denmark, Sep. 8, 1783; d. Vartou, Denmark, Sep. 2, 1872) is regarded as the last and greatest of Denmark's triumvirate of hymn writers: Kingo (17th century), the "Poet of Easter;" Brorson (18th century), the "Poet of Christmas;" and Grundtvig (19th century), the "Poet of Whitsuntide." Grundtvig's father was a Lutheran pastor who remained faithful to evangelical Christianity at a time when rationalism was strong. The young Grundtvig's contact with rationalism at the University of Copenhagen caused him to lose interest in Christianity, and he graduated "without spirit and without faith." Before long his eyes were opened, and he became violently opposed to the new teaching. After several years of teaching, Grundtvig was asked by his father to become the assistant pastor of the parish at Udby. In his trial sermon for ordination, Grundtvig spoke so boldly against the rationalism of the clergy that the bishop vetoed his assignment to Udby, and he was for many years a pastor without a parish, being in constant controversy.

Nevertheless, his preaching attracted large

audiences and his poetry and hymns attracted much attention. His hymnal, *Sang-Värk til den Danske Kirke* (1837), was well received by the people. His leadership in education spread to other Scandinavian countries, bringing him recognition as "the father of the public school in Scandinavia." In contrast to his stormy earlier career, Grundtvig's latter years were relatively serene, his greatness being widely recognized. In addition to being elected to posts in the Danish government, he was given the title of Bishop when he celebrated his golden jubilee as a pastor in 1861. In addition to "Built on the Rock, the Church Doth Stand," his most popular hymn, Grundtvig is represented by seven other hymns in the *Lutheran Book of Worship* (1978).   *H.E.*

Built on the Rock–351

Gurney, Dorothy Frances, née Blomfield (b. London, England, Oct. 4, 1858; d. Notting Hill, Kensington, London, England, Jun. 15, 1932) was a daughter of the Rev. Frederick George Blomfield, rector of St. Andrew's Undershaft, London, and a granddaughter of Bishop Blomfield of Chester and London. In 1897 she married Gerald Gurney, an actor who was ordained in the Church of England and was also the son of an Anglican clergyman and hymn writer, the Rev. Archer Gurney. In 1919 Dorothy Frances and Gerald Gurney were received into the Roman Catholic communion at Farnborough Abbey. From *A Little Book of Quiet*, one of her two volumes of poems, are the lines:

"The kiss of the sun for pardon,
　The song of the birds for mirth;
One is nearer God's heart in a garden
　　Than anywhere else on earth."
H.E.

O Perfect Love–512

Hall, Elvina Mabel (b. Alexandria, VA, Jun. 4, 1820; d. Ocean Grove, NJ, Jul. 18, 1889), the daughter of Captain David Reynolds, was a member of the Monument Street Methodist Church, Baltimore, for over 40 years. Following the death of her first husband, Richard Hall, she married Rev. Thomas Myers of the Baltimore Conference of the Methodist Church (1885). *D.M.*

Jesus Paid It All–134

Ham, Richard Wendell (b. Louisville, KY, Jun. 5, 1935) attended public schools in Louisville and graduated from Georgetown College and the School of Church Music of The Southern Baptist Theological Seminary, Louisville. He has served as Minister of Music at Walnut Street Baptist Church, Owensboro, Kentucky (1958-59); Immanuel Baptist Church, Lexington, Kentucky, (1961-66); First Baptist Church, Pine Bluff, Arkansas (1966-68), and since 1983 at the First Baptist Church, Richmond, Kentucky. He has also served in part-time and interim positions in churches while a Consultant in the Church Music Department of the Sunday School Board of the Southern Baptist Convention (1968-83). He is married and the father of two daughters. From some 20 choral prayer responses that he has composed for his choir in Richmond, two were selected for inclusion in *The Baptist Hymnal* (1991), where they were first published.   *H.T.M.*

THREEFOLD 2–Amens–653
THREEFOLD 3–Amens–654

Hanaoka, Nobuaki (b. Saga, Japan, Dec. 25, 1944) is a graduate of Kanto Gakuin

University School of Theology, Yokohama, Japan, and Colgate Rochester Center for Theology, Rochester, New York. Currently pastor of Pine United Methodist Church in San Francisco, California, he previously pastored Buena Vista United Methodist Church, Alameda, California, and Japanese Baptist Church of Seattle, Washington. *D.M.*

Jesus, My Friend, Is Great (tr.)–190

Hanby, Benjamin Russel (b. Rushville, OH, Jul. 22, 1833; d. Chicago, IL, Mar. 16, 1867) was a United Brethren minister and musician. He was educated at Otterbein University (now College, A.B., 1858), an institution that his father, a United Brethren bishop and hymnal editor, had helped to found. Following his graduation, he served as a fund-raising agent for the college, as principal of Seven Mile Academy (Ohio), and as pastor of three congregations in Ohio: Lewisburg, New Paris, and Otterbein Chapel. He encountered resistance in his pastorates because of his progressive views on theology, politics, and the use of music in the church.

In 1864 he turned to music, his long-standing avocation, as a profession. He subsequently worked as a composer, arranger, editor, and singing school leader with the firms of John Church (Cincinnati) and Root and Cady (Chicago). At the latter firm, he worked with George M. Root on such books as *Chapel Gems for Sunday Schools* (Chicago, 1866). Hanby composed patriotic, day school, and Sunday School songs, three of which, "Darling Nelly Gray," "Santa Claus [Up on the House-top]," and "Who Is He in Yonder Stall," achieved lasting popularity. He died in Chicago following a long struggle with tuberculosis. *P.A.R.*

Who Is He–Who Is He in Yonder Stall–124

Handel, George Frederick (b. Halle, Germany, Feb. 23, 1685; d. London, England, Apr. 14, 1759) is best remembered as a composer of oratorios, including *Messiah*. However, his early fame came as a result of opera composition. For a time, a career in music was in doubt, for his father encouraged him to pursue a career in law. Handel was a skilled performer on the organ, harpsichord, and violin. As a young man he studied counterpoint and fugue with F. W. Zachow, cathedral organist in Handel's native city of Halle. Before he was 20 he went to Hamburg, the principal center of German opera. His first opera, *Almira*, was performed at the Hamburg opera house in 1705. Handel spent most of the next four years in Italy with travels to Rome, Florence, Naples, and Venice. He met and was influenced by Corelli, the Scarlattis, and Steffani.

Soon after accepting an appointment as music director at the Electoral Court of Hanover, Handel took a leave of absence and visited London during the season of 1710-11. The production of his opera *Rinaldo* there was a triumph. In the fall of 1712 he was granted a second leave to visit London with the understanding he would return after a resonable time. He was still in London two years later when his employer, the Elector of Hanover, was crowned King George I of England. Handel eventually made the best of this awkward situation and became England's most famous composer.

After almost 30 years of writing and producing operas, his chief interest shifted to oratorio composition. His impressive list of works may be found in sources such as *The New Grove Dictionary of Music and Musicians*. Handel knew the Wesleys and wrote three hymn tunes (GOPSAL, CANNONS, and FITZWILLIAM) for texts by Charles Wesley. These were discovered in 1826 by Samuel Wesley, the son of Charles. Other Handel hymn tunes have been adapted from his oratorios and operas.   *D.B.*

ANTIOCH–87
MACCABEUS–163

Hankey, Katherine (b. Clapham, England, 1834; d. London, England, 1911) was christened Arabella Catherine, but nicknamed "Kate." Her father, Thomas Hankey, was a banker and member of William Wilberforce's "Clapham Sect," a group of evangelicals who sought to abolish slavery in the British Empire. Katherine devoted her life to religious work, particularly to teaching Bible classes for girls and to hospital visitation. She was also interested in foreign missions and, in later life, devoted the proceeds from her writings to this cause. She published a book *The Old, Old Story and Other Verses*, in 1879.   *D.M.*

I Love to Tell the Story–572

Hansen, Fred C. M. (b. Vejle, Denmark, Jun. 25, 1888; d. Blair, NE, Apr. 4, 1965) came to the United States at an early age when his parents immigrated. Educated at Dana College, the University of Nebraska, and Trinity Seminary, he was ordained in 1914 to the ministry of the United Evangelical Lutheran Church. He served as pastor of churches in Iowa, Wisconsin, and Illinois, and was considered one of the most important translators of hymns from the Danish language. Hansen was a member of the hymnal commission for *Service Book and Hymnal* (1958).   *H.T.M.*

Built on the Rock (revised tr.)–351

Harkness, Georgia (b. Harkness, NY, Apr. 21, 1891; d. Claremont, CA, Aug. 30, 1974) was a pioneering Methodist woman theologian and educator who earned degrees from Cornell University (B.A., 1912) and Boston University (M.A., 1920; M.R.E., 1920; Ph.D., 1923). She did additional study at Harvard, Yale, and Union Theological Seminary. Her teaching career, which spanned nearly 50 years, began in New York high schools, and during the 1920s and '30s moved to the college level and into applied theology. She taught at Elmira College (1923-37), Mount Holyoke College (1937-39), Garrett Biblical Institute (1939-50), and Pacific School of Religion (1950-61). After retiring in 1961, she resided in Claremont, California. When she moved to Garrett in 1939, she became the first woman to hold a full professorship in a theological seminary. Ordained to the Methodist ministry, she was an active leader in her denomination and in the World Council of Churches. After nearly three decades of work on behalf of full clergy rights for women, she saw her dream fulfilled by a vote of the Methodist General Conference in 1956. A prolific author, she wrote 37 books and several hundred published articles, speeches, and sermons. A pacifist, she envisioned and worked for a world united through Christ. She wrote a large number of poems and published three volumes of verse which include the hymns: *Holy Flame* (1935), *The Glory of God* (1943), and *Be Still and Know* (1953). Five of her 18 hymns were published from 1945-66 in pamphlets of the Hymn Society of America.   *H.E.*

Tell It Out with Gladness–585

Harris, John Roy (b. Fayetteville, AR, Dec. 5, 1891; d. Lawton, OK, Mar. 5, 1987), while still a child, moved with his family to the Indian Territory, where his father was a United States marshal and a farmer in what is now Sequoyah County, Oklahoma. After meager schooling in this frontier community, he finished high school in Muskogee, Oklahoma, attended Oklahoma Baptist University, and later the University of Oklahoma. A pioneer music and education director in Oklahoma Baptist churches, he began his work at Bristow in 1922. After serving at Ardmore and Shawnee, he taught music for seven years at Oklahoma Baptist University and was also principal of the academy (high school). At various times he was an evangelistic singer, traveling with several evangelists throughout Oklahoma, Texas, and Arkansas. He was music director and assistant to the pastor, First Baptist Church, Ada, Oklahoma (1939-55). In 1955 he became director of city mission work, First Baptist Church, Lawton, Oklahoma, and continued this work until his retirement in 1980.   *W.J.R.*

Great Redeemer, We Adore Thee–209

Harris, Thoro (b. Washington, DC, Mar. 31, 1873; d. Eureka Springs, AR, Mar. 27, 1955) attended college in Battle Creek, Michigan, and published his first hymnal in Boston in 1902. The following year he was invited by Peter Bilhorn to move to Chicago to assist him in music publishing. There Harris wrote and edited publications for a number of music publishers and prepared Bible school services and hymnbooks. He moved to Eureka Springs, Arkansas, a beautiful spot in the Ozark Mountains, in 1932. There he continued composing songs and making compilations, and he also served as organist for local churches. A fellow townsman in Eureka Springs recalled to R. W. Stringfield that

Harris was "a very energetic person, walking about the city almost constantly carrying a little canvas handbag in which he carried copies of his songbooks for sale." *W.J.R.*

HARRIS–391, 409, 429

Harrison, Ralph (b. Chinley, Derbyshire, England, Sep. 10, 1748; d. Manchester, Lancashire, England, Nov. 4, 1810) was the son of a Dissenting minister. He was educated at a Unitarian school–Warrington Academy. After leaving school in 1769, he served an independent chapel at Shrewsbury and then in 1771 became organist of Cross Street Chapel (Independent), Manchester, a position he held until his death.

Beginning in 1774 he conducted a school in Manchester and was professor of classics and belles lettres at the Manchester Academy. He published *The Rudiments of English Grammar* (1777) but is best known for his tunebooks, *Sacred Harmony*, Volume I in 1784 and Volume II in 1791. As an amateur musician, he exerted considerable influence on the shaping of Independent collections of psalm and hymn tunes. *H.T.M.*

ARLINGTON (arr.)–353, 358, 481

Hart, Joseph (b. London, England, 1712; d. London, England, May 24, 1768), although brought up by devout parents and given a good education, strayed from their teaching and spent many years in an intense struggle between good and evil, as he related in his "Experience," published as a preface to his hymns. He was able to read the Bible in its original Greek and Hebrew, and became a teacher of languages in London. Not until Whitsunday 1757, at the age of 47, was he converted following a sermon on Revelation 3:10 in the Moravian Chapel in Fetter Lane, London. Many of his most passionate hymns were written in the following two years and published in his *Hymns Composed on Various Subjects, with the Author's Experience* (London, 1759; *Supplement*, 1762; *Appendix*, 1765). From 1759 until his death he was the greatly esteemed pastor of Jewin Street Independent Chapel, London. A strong Calvinist, he was often critical of John Wesley's theology, at one time writing a tract on "The Unreasonableness of Religion, Being Remarks and Animadversions on the Rev. John Wesley's Sermon on Romans 8:22." Next to Isaac Watts, Hart was the most popular of the Independent hymnists of 18th-century England. Some 20 thousand people are reported to have attended his funeral in London's Bunhill Fields Cemetery, where in 1875, over a century later, a monument was placed in his memory.   *H.E.*

Come, Ye Sinners, Poor and Needy–323

Hartsough, Lewis (b. Ithaca, NY, Aug. 31, 1828; d. Mount Vernon, IA, Jan. 1, 1919) entered the ministry of the Methodist Episcopal Church in 1851 and held several pastorates in the Oneida Conference of New York. Poor health led him to request a transfer to the western states, where he organized and became the first superintendent of the Utah (Methodist) Mission. Hartsough subsequently held denominational positions and pastorates in the Wyoming District, in Epworth, Iowa, and in the Northwest Iowa Conference. He retired in 1895 and made his home in Mount Vernon, Iowa, until his death.

Hartsough was coeditor of *The Sacred Harmonist* (Boston, 1864) and *Beulah Songs* (Philadelphia, 1879). He also served as music editor of Joseph Hillman's *The Revivalist*

(Troy, 1868), an important revival songbook that preceded the famous *Gospel Hymns* series of Sankey, Bliss, and their collaborators. *The Revivalist* is said to have sold over 150,000 copies and gone through at least 11 printings, one of which included 12 texts, 14 tunes, and 30 arrangements credited to Hartsough.   *D.M.*

Welcome Voice–I Hear Thy Welcome Voice–302

Hartsough, Palmer (b. Redford, MI, May 7, 1844; d. Plymouth, MI, Oct. 24, 1932) was the son of Wells and Thankful (Palmer) Hartsough. His father, an active layman, had helped organize the Michigan Baptist Convention in 1836. When Palmer was 12 years old, the family moved to Plymouth, Michigan.

Later, he attended Kalamazoo College, a Baptist school, and also Michigan State Normal. There he became interested in music and, while still a student, began teaching singing schools in rural areas. Beginning in 1867, he was an itinerant singing school teacher traveling throughout Michigan, Illinois, Iowa, Ohio, Kentucky, and Tennessee. When the interest in singing schools waned, about 1877, he settled in Rock Island, Illinois, opened a music studio, taught vocal and instrumental music, and served as music director at the Baptist church of which he was a member. In 1893 he became associated with the Fillmore publishing firm in Cincinnati where he worked for 10 years. He also served as music director for the Ninth Street Baptist Church. A prolific writer of texts for hymns, gospel songs, Sunday School songs, cantatas, and programs, he produced more than a thousand texts for publications. In 1906 he was ordained to the Baptist ministry and, following several brief pastorates, he became pastor of the Baptist church at Ontario, Michigan (1914-27). He retired in 1927, returned to Plymouth, Michigan, where he remained until his death at the age of 88. *W.J.R.*

I Am Resolved–301

Hassler, Hans Leo (b. Nuremberg, Germany, baptized Aug. 17, 1562; d. Frankfurt-am-Main, Germany, Jun. 8, 1612) was the most famous of three musical sons of the Nuremberg organist Isaak Hassler. He first studied music with his father and then went to Venice in 1584 and became a composition student of Andrea Gabrieli and a friend of fellow student Giovanni Gabrieli. The following year Hassler returned to Germany, becoming organist to Octavian II of the house of Fuggers in Augsburg. After Octavian's death in 1600, Hassler went to Prague as court organist to Emperor Rudolph II. In Prague he also manufactured and installed musical clocks. From 1601 Hassler was once more in Nuremberg, serving as organist of the Frauenkirche and director of town music. During these four years in Nuremberg he was quite active and his reputation as a gifted organist and composer grew. In 1604 he moved to Ulm where he married. In 1608 he moved to Dresden to become chamber organist to the Elector Christian II of Saxony. Soon thereafter he developed tuberculosis, an illness which led to his death four years later while accompanying the Elector to the election and coronation of the Emperor Matthias at Frankfurt-am-Main. Hassler was succeeded as music director of the Saxon court chapel by Michael Praetorius and Heinrich Schütz.

Regarded as the greatest German composer of the late 16th century, Hassler wrote a large number of secular and sacred choral works and some works for organ and clavier. Publications of his compositions are listed in *The New Grove Dictionary of Music and Musicians*. A collected edition of Hassler's works is being published in Wiesbaden, Germany by Breitkopf and Härtel under the auspices of the Society for Bavarian Music History. *H.E.*

PASSION CHORALE–137

Hastings, Thomas (b. Washington, CT, Oct. 15, 1784; d. New York, NY, May 15, 1872), at the age of 12, moved with his family to Clinton, Oneida County, New York. An albino and afflicted with extreme nearsightedness, he taught himself the fundamentals of music. With his country school education, he was leading the village choir at the age of 18. An active member of the Oneida County Musical Society, he published for this group his first collection. Called *The Utica Collection*, it was combined with Warriner's *Springfield Collection* in 1816 and became known as *Musica Sacra*. He edited *The Western Recorder* (1823-32), a religious periodical published in Utica, and used the columns of this paper to promote his ideas regarding the improvement of church song. He moved to New York City in 1832, at the invitation of 12 churches who sought his services as choir director. He was dedicated to the cause of good church music and, together with Lowell Mason, did much to shape the development of church music in America in the nineteenth century. He wrote more than 600 hymns and 1000 hymn tunes, and compiled more than 50 collections. He was awarded the Mus.D. degree by the University of the City of New York in 1858. *W.J.R.*

Come, Ye Disconsolate (alt.)–67

ORTONVILLE–219, 453
TOPLADY–342

Hatch, Edwin (b. Derby, England, Sep. 4, 1835; d. Headington, Oxford, England, Nov. 19, 1889) was born of Nonconformist parents, but he joined the Church of England when he was 18. Educated at Pembroke College, Oxford, he received the Bachelor of Arts degree with honors in 1857. Ordained in the Church of England in 1859, he held teaching positions in Toronto and Quebec, Canada for eight years. He returned to Oxford in 1867 as vice-principal of St. Mary Hall and became the first editor of the Oxford University *Gazette* in 1870. In 1884 he became university reader in ecclesiastical history at Oxford. He was widely acclaimed for his Bampton Lectures (1880), and Hibbert lectures (1888). A man of deep piety and humility, Hatch earned an international reputation for his scholarship and historical research. His last public speech was made at a breakfast, part of the opening celebration of Mansfield College, Oxford.   *W.J.R.*

Breathe on Me–238
Breathe on Me, Breath of God–241

Hatton, John (b. Warrington, England, *c.*1710; d. St. Helen's, England, 1793), sometimes known as John of Warrington, lived on Duke Street in St. Helen's in the township of Windle. Other than the fact that his funeral service was held in the Presbyterian Chapel in St. Helen's, on December 13, 1793, almost nothing is known about him.   *D.B.*

DUKE STREET–13, 70, 587

Havergal, Frances Ridley (b. Astley, Worcestershire, England, Dec. 14, 1836; d.

Oystermouth, Glamorganshire, Wales, Jun. 3, 1879) began writing verses at the age of seven, and they soon appeared in *Good Words* and other religious periodicals. Her father, William H. Havergal, was the rector of St. Nicholas, Worcester, where Frances grew up as a girl. At the age of 14 she had a deep religious experience and later wrote, "There and then I committed my soul to the Savior–and earth and heaven seemed bright from that moment." All of her hymns reflect the joy of this experience of commitment and consecration. She was confirmed a member of the Church of England in 1853. Early in life she memorized large portions of the Scriptures and became proficient in French, Italian, German, Latin, Greek, and Hebrew. She was a frequent visitor to Switzerland and loved climbing in the Swiss Alps. Her contributions to Christian song number more than 100.   *W.J.R.*

Like a River Glorious–58
Take My Life, and Let It Be
   Consecrated–277, 283
Lord, Speak to Me, That I May
   Speak–568
I Gave My Life for Thee–606

Hawks, Annie Sherwood (b. Hoosick, NY, May 28, 1836; d. Bennington, VT, Jan. 3, 1918), a Baptist, was the author of some 400 Sunday school hymns. Only "I Need Thee Every Hour" is still used today, however. A resident of Brooklyn for many years, where she was a member of the Hanson Place Baptist Church, Mrs. Hawks was encouraged by her pastor, Dr. Robert Lowry, to develop her considerable talent as a writer of verse, especially for children.
   During the eight years in which Dr. Lowry had charge of the church, Mrs. Hawks probably wrote most of her poems, many of

them being provided with tunes by Dr. Lowry. In 1857 she was married to Charles H. Hawks and became the mother of three children. After Mr. Hawks' death in 1888, she lived with a daughter and her husband, Dr. and Mrs. W. E. Putnam in Bennington, Vermont, until her death in 1918.   *H.T.M.*

I Need Thee Every Hour–450

Haydn, Franz Joseph (b. Rohrau, Austria, Mar. 31, 1732; d. Vienna, Austria, May 31, 1809) was the son of Matthias, a master wheelwright, and his mother, Maria Koller, was a cook in Count Harrach's household. At the age of eight he became a boy chorister at the Vienna Cathedral, St. Stephen's. On May 1, 1761, Haydn was appointed vice *Kapellmeister* to Paul Anton Esterhazy. In 1766, he became *Kapellmeister*. When the court chapel dissolved in 1790, Haydn remained titular *Kapellmeister* but moved to Vienna. On New Year's Day 1791 he crossed the Channel from Calais to Dover in nine hours for an extended and successful visit to England. In July of that year he was awarded an honorary Doctor of Music degree by Oxford. Another visit to England was made in 1794-95. In 1792, Beethoven took lessons from Haydn.

Haydn was a prolific composer. His works include 104 symphonies, sinfonia concertante for various instruments, 83 string quartets, 52 piano sonatas, 18 operas, cantatas, songs, vocal ensembles, sacred music including 14 Masses, and four oratorios including *The Creation* and *The Seasons*. He was a devout Christian and regarded his musical abilities as God-given. He began his works with "In nomine Domini" (In the name of the Lord) and ended them with "Laus Deo" (Praise God).

He called his servants around him for a final time on May 26, 1809. He was carried to the piano and solemnly played the Emperor's Hymn (AUSTRIAN HYMN) three times. Five days later, at one o'clock in the morning, he died.   *S.W.G.*

AUSTRIAN HYMN–262, 390, 398

Haydn, Johann Michael (b. Rohrau, Austria, Sep. 14, 1737; d. Salzburg, Austria, Aug. 10, 1806) was the younger brother of the more famous Franz Joseph Haydn. When the latter's voice broke as a boy soprano at St. Stephen's Cathedral in Vienna, Michael succeeded him. Like his brother, a self-taught musician, Michael went in 1762 as musical director to Archbishop Sigismund of Salzburg, where he remained until his death. He was the teacher of famous musicians, including Carl Maria von Weber. Franz Joseph held his brother's sacred compositions in high esteem, claiming them as superior to his own. Michael wrote some 360 works for church use, a number of which have been sources for hymn tunes. He was a devout Christian, initialing his works with "O. a. M. D. Gl" (*Omnia ad Majorem Dei Gloriam*–"All to the major glory of God").   *H.T.M.*

LYONS (attr.)–16, 589, 631

Hayes, Mark (b. Ladysmith, WI, Mar. 28, 1953) is a free-lance composer, arranger, and record producer. He received the Bachelor of Music degree in piano performance from Baylor University (1975). He has served as a free-lance arranger and recording session singer for Word Records (1975-77) and as music editor for Tempo Records (1977-80). Hayes' catalog includes over 300 original compositions and arrangements and more than 20 recordings. His album, "I've Just Seen Jesus," won the Dove award from the Gospel Music Association. Mark lives in Kansas City, Missouri and is a member of Broadway Baptist Church.   *P.H.*

BUNESSAN (arr.)–48, 105, 362
HAYES–562

Hayford, Jack W. (b. Los Angeles, CA, Jun. 25, 1934) is a graduate of LIFE Bible college, Los Angeles, California (1956), Azusa Pacific University, Azusa, California (1970), and is the recipient of honorary doctorates from LIFE Bible College, Oral Roberts University, and the California Graduate School of Theology. From 1956 to 1960 he and his wife Anna served a pastorate in Fort Wayne, Indiana, returning to Los Angeles in the latter year to become National Youth Directors for the International Church of the Foursquare Gospel. From 1965 to 1973, Jack was a member of the faculty at LIFE Bible College, serving as Dean of Students from 1965 to 1970. In 1977 he became president of this institution, a position he held until 1982, while simultaneously serving as pastor of The Church On The Way.

In 1969, Hayford began what was supposed to be a temporary assignment to pastor a small church of 18 people. However, he has remained pastor of this church, The Church On The Way, for over 21 years, and in that time the church has grown to more than 7000 members.

Hayford is widely known as an author of 16 books, a conference leader and speaker, and a media personality. He has written over 400 songs, hymns, and other musical works.   *D.M.*

MAJESTY–Majesty–215

Hays, William Shakespeare (b. Louisville, KY, Jul. 19, 1837; d. Louisville, KY, Jul. 23, 1907) attended colleges at Hanover, Indiana; Clarksville, Tennessee; and Georgetown, Kentucky. While a student at Georgetown College in 1856 he published his first song, "Little Ones at Home." The following year he left Georgetown College to work as a riverfront reporter for the Louisville *Democrat.* He wrote verse for popular songs and often set them to music, although he had no formal musical training. Hays' most famous Civil War song was "The Drummer Boy of Shiloh" (1862). His songs reflected Confederate sentiments, leading to his imprisonment by the Union army in New Orleans. As a result of spending his early adult years working on the riverboats of the Ohio and Mississippi, he acquired knowledge that he drew upon for his 30 years of writing a "River" column for the Louisville *Courier-Journal.* His songs include sentimental ballads, call-and-response spirituals, and dialect minstrel songs, the last category including "The Little Old Log Cabin in the Lane" (1871). According to Cockrell, Hays' work includes at least 546 poems, three published books of poetry, nine piano pieces, and 322 songs. It has been estimated that over 20 million copies of his songs have been sold. Hays' papers and music are housed in the Kentucky Library at Western Kentucky University, Bowling Green, Kentucky.   *H.E.*

SALVATIONIST–189

Heber, Reginald (b. Malpas, Cheshire, England, Apr. 21, 1783; d. Trichinopoly, India, Apr. 3, 1826) attended Brasenose College, Oxford, where he won a literary prize for his poetry, and later became a fellow at All Souls' College. Ordained in 1807, he became vicar of his family's parish, Hodnet, Shropshire, and served there for 16 years (1807-23). During this time he developed an interest in hymn writing, and his first published hymns appeared in the *Christian Observer* in 1811. Around 1819 he began compiling a collection of hymns to meet the worship needs of the Christian year, but he was unsuccessful in securing the approval of the Bishop of London for the publication of his collection. In 1823 he became Bishop of Calcutta and served in India for less than three years before his death. Heber's *Hymns Written and Adapted to the Weekly Church Service of the Year*, published posthumously in 1827, was the first English hymnal to be arranged according to the church year. Each Sunday and most Holy Days of the Anglican Church were provided with appropriate hymns, which were usually based upon the Epistle or Gospel lesson for the day. The collection was also influential through its contributions to the early 19th-century literary movement in English hymnody. Hymns by Milman and other distinguished poets were included, in addition to the 57 hymns by Heber.   *M.P.*

Holy, Holy, Holy–2

Hedge, Frederic Henry (b. Cambridge, MA, Dec. 12, 1805; d. Cambridge, MA, Aug. 21, 1890) was a precocious child who at the age of 10 was able to give long passages from Homer in Greek. After four years of study in Germany, he graduated from Harvard in 1825. In 1829 he was ordained to the ministry, serving Unitarian churches at West Cambridge, Massachusetts; Bangor, Maine; Providence, Rhode Island; and Brookline, Massachusetts. A leader in the Unitarian movement, he served as president of the American Unitarian Association (1859-62). While pastor at the Brookline Unitarian Church from 1857-72, he also served Harvard as professor of ecclesiastical history (1857-76), and professor of German

from 1872 until his retirement in 1884. Hedge was an important figure in the Transcendental movement, pioneering in introducing German poetry and metaphysics to the United States. A recognized scholar in German literature, his monumental work in this field was *Prose Writers of Germany* (1848). His contribution to hymnody, compiled with F. Dan Huntington, was *Hymns for the Church of Christ* (Boston, 1853), which include Hedge's translations and original hymns.   *H.E.*

A Mighty Fortress Is Our God (tr.)–8

Helmore, Thomas (b. Kidderminster, Worcester, England, May 7, 1811; d. Westminster, London, England, Jul. 6, 1890) received his B.A. (1840) and M.A. (1845) degrees from Magdalen Hall, Oxford. He was ordained to the Anglican ministry and served two years as curate of St. Michael's Church, Lichfield. In 1840 he became vicar of Lichfield Cathedral and, in 1842, vice-principal and precentor of St. Mark's College in Chelsea. He retained the latter position for 35 years, retiring in 1877. For much of this time (beginning in 1846), he also served as master of the choristers in the English Chapel Royal.

Helmore played an important part in the introduction of plainsong into the Church of England. Among the many musical publications for which he was at least partly responsible were the *Psalter Noted* (1849), *Canticles Noted* (1849), *A Manual of Plainsong* (1850), *The Hymnal Noted* (1854), *Carols for Christmas* (1853), *Carols for Easter* (1855), *St. Mark's Chant Book* (1863), *A Catechism of Music* (1878), *Plain Song* (1878), and *A Fuller Directory of the Plain Song of the Holy Communion Service* (1881).   *D.M.*

Veni Emmanuel (adapt.)–76

Helvering, Sandi Patti (b. Anderson, IN, Jul. 12, 1956) received her Bachelor of Arts degree from Anderson College, Anderson, Indiana, in 1979. A well-known artist in the field of contemporary Christian/gospel music, her first album, *Sandi's Song*, was recorded in 1979. Currently, she performs in approximately 100 concerts annually throughout the United States and other countries and has appeared as guest on a variety of secular and religious television shows. At the time of this writing, she has recorded 11 albums, one of which has been certified platinum and five certified gold. Her recordings have been the recipients of a number of Grammy and Dove Awards. Her husband, John L. Helvering, also serves as her manager. The Helverings are the parents of four children.   *D.M.*

NAME OF THE LORD–In the Name of
  the Lord–174
There Is a Savior–536

Hemy, Henri Frederick (b. Newcastle-on-Tyne, England, Nov. 12, 1818; d. Hartlepool, England, Jun. 10, 1888) was the son of German parents. A Roman Catholic, he was organist at St. Andrew's Church in his native city. The collection of church music which he compiled, *Crown of Jesus Music* (London, 1864) was widely used in his communion. He also taught music at Tynemouth and at St. Cuthbert's College, Ushaw, Durham, and wrote a popular piano method book, *Royal Modern Tutor for the Pianoforte* (1858).   *P.A.R.*

ST. CATHERINE–123, 352

Henderson, Gerald S. is the pseudonym of an author who prefers to remain anonymous.   *P.H.*

Holy Lord (st. 1)–622

Hendrix, John D. (b. Kansas City, MO, Jul. 26, 1935) is Basil Manly, Jr. Professor of Christian Education at The Southern Baptist Theological Seminary, Louisville, Kentucky. He received his degrees from William Jewell College (B.A.), Midwestern Baptist Theological Seminary (M. Div.), and New Orleans Baptist Theological Seminary (M.R.E. and Ed.D.). Before joining the faculty of Southern Seminary, he served in various positions at the Baptist Sunday School Board and as a minister in the areas of music, youth, and education in Louisiana and Missouri churches. Dr. Hendrix and his wife Lela have two children. Among his publications are *Experiential Education: X-Ed* (1975), *The Equipping of Disciples* (1976), *We Have These Treasures: A Profile of Youth Leadership Gifts* (1979), *To Thessalonians with Love* (1982), and *Finding Your Place in Ministry* (1988).   *P.H.*

Grace to You–663

Herbert, George (b. Montgomery, England, Apr. 3, 1593; d. Bemerton, Wilts, England, Mar. 1, 1633) attended Westminster school and received his B.A. (1613) and M.A. (1616) from Trinity College, Cambridge. Upon his graduation he became a major fellow of the College, which involved him in teaching responsibilities, and in 1620 he began service as its Public Orator, a post he retained until 1628. The favor of King James I seemed to promise a governmental career, but the death of this monarch in 1625 and the subsequent dissolution of Parliament (to which Herbert had been elected in 1624) by Charles I in August of the same year put an end to these aspirations. Herbert then took orders in the Church of England and became rector of the Anglican church in Bemerton (1630), where he served until his death.

Herbert's best-known literary work was *The Temple*, a collection of poems which he gave to his friend Nicholas Ferrar shortly before his death, with the request that Ferrar either publish or destroy them as he saw fit. Fortunately, Ferrar chose to print the book, and *The Temple* subsequently became recognized as a masterpiece of religious literature. The hymnic potential of Herbert's poems was recognized as early as 1697 when 32 of them were included in the anonymously-compiled *Select Hymns, taken out of Mr. Herbert's Temple, and turn'd into the Common Metre. To be Sung in the Tunes ordinarily us'd in Churches* (Cambridge, 1697). John Wesley printed six Herbert poems in his *Collection of Psalms and Hymns* (1737) and over 40 in *Hymns and Sacred Songs* (1739).   *D.M.*

Let All the World in Every Corner Sing–28

Herrington, Leland Howard (Lee) (b. 1941) composed six arrangements for *The Hymnal for Worship & Celebration* published in 1986 by Word Music.   *S.W.G.*

Behold the Lamb (arr.)–233

Hewitt, Eliza Edmunds (b. Philadelphia, PA, Jun. 28, 1851; d. Philadelphia, PA, Apr. 24, 1920) was educated in the public schools and the Girls' Normal School, where she was the valedictorian of her class and later spent several years there as a teacher. She was interested in the Sunday School Movement and devoted much of her life to it in Philadelphia's Northern Home for Friendless Children. She was also active in the Olivet Presbyterian Church. After moving to another part of the city, she became active in the Calvin Presbyteri-

an Church where she served as superintendent of the Primary department until her death. For many years she suffered from a spinal disease, but recovered sufficiently to resume her work. Following her illness, she developed an interest in writing poetry and some of her poems came to the attention of John R. Sweney who set a number of them to music. They later collaborated on several hymns. Her hymns were published by John R. Sweney and William J. Kirkpatrick. She also wrote texts for B. D. Ackley, Charles H. Gabriel, E. S. Lorenz, and Homer Rodeheaver.   *S.W.G.*

Sunshine in My Soul–430
When We All Get to Heaven–514
More About Jesus–600

Hine, Stuart Wesley Keene (b. London, England, Jul. 25, 1899) was educated at the Cooper's Company School, London. During World War I, he served in the British Army in Belgium and France (1917-19). Ordained to the Methodist ministry, he and his wife served as missionaries in Poland (1923-32), then in Russia, Czechoslovakia (1932-39). When World War II began, Hine returned to England and did evangelistic work among families of Russian and Ukranian refugees, and Polish prisoners of war. He conducted weekly meetings of Slavs in Earls Court (1950-59). In his latter years he continues his ministry in his writings and publications. Among his publications are *Not You, But God: A Testimony to God's Faithfulness* (1982).   *W.J.R.*

O Store Gud (arr.)–How Great Thou Art (tr.)–10

Hoffman, Elisha Albright (b. Orwigsburg, PA, May 7, 1839; d. Chicago, IL, Nov. 25, 1929) was the son of the Reverend Francis A. and Rebecca Ann (Waggoner) Hoffman. His father was a minister of the Evangelical Association, and his middle name represented the Hoffmans' esteem for Jacob Albright, the founder of this denomination. (Through several mergers, the Evangelical Association is now absorbed into the United Methodist Church.) He was educated in the public schools of Philadelphia and at Union Bible Seminary at New Berlin, Pennsylvania. During the Civil War he served with the 47th Pennsylvania Infantry Division. About 1866 Hoffman married Susan Orwig, daughter of Bishop William H. Orwig of the Evangelical Association. One of their sons, Ira Orwig, was also a hymn writer who harmonized many of his father's hymn tunes. From 1868 the Hoffmans lived in Cleveland, Ohio, where for 11 years he was a publishing agent for Board of Publications of the Evangelical Association. An ordained Evangelical minister, he served as pastor of Evangelical, Congregational, and Presbyterian churches in Ohio, Illinois, and Michigan. In 1894 Hoffman became the first music editor of Hope Publishing Company of Chicago, serving until 1912. He was music editor of about 50 songbooks and hymnals, writing the words and/or music to at least 1,000 gospel hymns for Sunday School and revival use. *H.E.*

WASHED IN THE BLOOD–Are You Washed in the Blood–136
Down at the Cross–140
Leaning on the Everlasting Arms–333
ORWIGSBURG–I Must Tell Jesus–455
SURABAJA–582

Holden, Oliver (b. Shirley, MA, Sep. 18, 1765; d. Charlestown, MA, Sep. 4, 1844) was an important early American composer and tune book compiler. He was trained as a carpenter, but his diverse activities included teaching singing schools, acquiring substantial real estate holdings, operating both a general store and a music store, serving six terms in the Massachusetts House of Representatives (1818-33), pastoring a Puritan church, and teaching and publishing music. Holden gave the land upon which a Baptist church was built in Charlestown.

His publications included: *The American Harmony* (1792); *Union Harmony* (1793); *The Massachusetts Compiler* (with H. Gram and S. Holyoke, 1795); *The Worcester Collection* (6th ed., 1797); *Modern Collection of Sacred Music* (attr. to Holden, 1800); *Plain Psalmody* (attr. to Holden, 1800); *Charlestown Collection of Sacred Songs* (1803). *P.H.*

CORONATION–202

Hopkins, Edward John (b. Westminster, London, England, Jun. 30, 1818; d. St. Pancras, London, England, Feb. 4, 1901) began his musical career as a chorister at the Chapel Royal in 1826. While there he studied theory with T.F. Walmsley. After serving as organist at the parish church of Mitcham, Surrey, St. Peter's in Islington, and St. Luke's in Berwick Street, he began, in 1843, a 55-year tenure as organist at Temple Church in London. Upon his retirement in 1898 he was succeeded by H. Walford Davies. In 1882 he received the honorary Mus.D. from the Archbishop of Canterbury. In 1886 Trinity College, Toronto, recognized him in the same manner. He composed service music, anthems, hymns, and chants. In conjunction with Edward Rimbault he published *The Organ: Its History and Construction* (1855). Other publications included the *Wesleyan Tune Book* (1876), which he completed after the deaths of H.J. Gauntlett and George Cooper, the original compilers, and *Congregational Church Hymnal* (1887) for which work he served as music editor.   *D.B.*

ELLERS–297

Hopkins, John Henry, Jr. (b. Pittsburgh, PA, Oct. 28, 1820; d. Troy, NY, Aug. 14, 1891) was educated at the University of Vermont (B.S., 1839; M.A., 1845) and at General Theological Seminary in New York City, 1850. He founded the *Church Journal* of the Episcopal Church and served as its editor (1853-68). He was the first instructor in church music at General Seminary (1855-57). In 1872 he was ordained in the Episcopal Church and served as rector of Trinity Church, Plattsburg, New York (1872-76), and Christ Church, Williamsport, Pennsylvania (1876-87). Leonard Ellinwood in *The Hymnal 1940 Companion* states that Hopkins was "one of the great leaders in the development of hymnody in the Episcopal church during the mid-19th century."   *W.J.R.*

KINGS OF ORIENT–We Three Kings of Orient Are–113

Hopson, Hal Harold (b. Mound, TX, Jun. 12, 1933) is a composer, teacher, and church musician. He earned the Bachelor of Music degree from Baylor University in 1954 and the Master of Sacred Music degree from The Southern Baptist Theological Seminary in 1956. He did additional study in conducting with Lloyd Pfautsch and in organ with Dora Barclay and Helmut Schuller. In addition to serving several congregations, principally in Nashville, Tennessee, he has taught church music at Westminster Choir College (1983-84) and at Scarritt Graduate School (1984-88). Active in several professional oganizations, he

is a popular conductor, clinician, and workshop leader. His published compositions and arrangements number more than 800.   *P.A.R.*

MARTHA'S SONG–171
GIFT OF LOVE–Though I May Speak with Bravest Fire–423

Houghton, William Henry (Will H.) (b. South Boston, MA, Jun. 28, 1887; d. Hollywood, CA, Jun. 14, 1947), as a young man, was an actor with extensive experience as a professional entertainer in vaudeville. In 1909 he responded to a call to the ministry, gave up the stage, and entered Eastern Nazarene College, North Scutuate, Rhode Island. He left college to become an evangelistic song leader for Reuben A. Torry. In 1915 he was ordained by the First Baptist Church, Canton, Pennsylvania. After two years he became pastor at New Bethlehem and, a little later, at Norristown, Pennsylvania. In 1925 he conducted evangelistic meetings in Ireland. He was pastor of the Baptist Tabernacle in Atlanta (1925-30), and of Calvary Baptist Church, New York City (1930-34). In 1931 he received an honorary D.D. degree from Wheaton College, and in 1942, an honorary LL.D. from Bob Jones College. In 1934 he became president of Moody Bible Institute, serving there until his death in 1947. In the Institute hymnal, *The Voice of Thanksgiving No. 5* (1946), six hymns and choruses bear his name as author of texts and the chorus "Trust Him" was entirely composed by him. His books include *Let's Go Back to the Bible* (1940), *The Living Christ* (1936), and *Rhymes from a City Tower* (1940).   *H.E.*

LEAD ME–560

How, William Walsham (b. Shrewsbury, Shropshire, England, Dec. 13, 1823; d. Leenane, County Mayo, Ireland, Aug. 10, 1897) earned the accolade, "the poor man's bishop," for his unselfish service among the destitute in London's East End. Throughout his life he was characterized as a plain, unassuming man who was interested in living among and serving his people. How received a B.A. in 1845 and a M.A. in 1847 from Wadham College, Oxford, and was ordained an Anglican priest in 1847. He served as curate of St. George's, Kidderminster, and of Holy Cross, Shrewsbury; rector of Whittington; rural dean of Oswestry; and honorary canon of the English Church at Rome. His service in East London began in 1879 when he became suffragan bishop, with the title Bishop of Bedford. He was appointed the first Bishop of Wakefield in 1888. He was honored with two D.D. degrees, the first from the Archbishop of Canterbury in 1879 and the second from Oxford University in 1886. How died while on a vacation in Ireland. His work as a hymn writer included 54 hymns. He edited *Psalms and Hymns* with Thomas B. Morrell (1854) and chaired the committee of *Church Hymns* (1871) for which Arthur Sullivan was musical editor. *P.H.*

For All the Saints–355
We Give Thee But Thine Own–609

Howe, Julia Ward (b. New York, NY, May 27, 1819; d. Newport RI, Oct. 17, 1910) married Samuel Gridley Howe, who became director of the Perkins Institute for the Blind, Boston. Mrs. Howe was greatly devoted to her husband's work, and became, in her own right, a distinguished and influential public speaker. She was an ardent abolitionist, and, in 1870, she pro-

posed that the women of the world organize to end war for all time. An active writer, she published three volumes of verse. A member of the Unitarian church, she frequently spoke in churches of her own faith, as well as others. *W.J.R.*

Mine Eyes Have Seen the Glory–633

Hoyle, Richard Birch (b. Cloughfold, Lancashire, England, Mar. 8, 1875; d. London, England, Dec. 14, 1939) was trained at Regent's Park College for the Baptist ministry. For over 25 years he pastored English Baptist churches. His pastoral work was hindered by deafness. For a time he worked for the YMCA and edited their journal, *The Red Triangle*. He made English translations of around 30 French hymns. In 1934 he moved to the United States and taught at Western Theological Seminary in Philadelphia for two years before returning to England to become pastor of the Baptist church in Kingston-upon-Thames. *D.B.*

Thine Is the Glory (tr.)–163

Hoyt, May Pierpont (late 19th century) No information has been found to identify this author. Because her Lord's Supper hymn has appeared quite generally in hymn collections of the Christian Church (Disciples of Christ), it has been assumed that she was a member of that fellowship. Hymnologist Arthur N. Wake says that this is one of the favorite communion hymns of the Disciples of Christ (268). *W.J.R.*

Here, at Your Table, Lord–368

Huber, Jane McAfee Parker (b. Jinan, China, Oct. 24, 1926) is a Presbyterian elder and poet. She was born in China of American missionary parents and grew up in

Hanover, Indiana, where her father served as president of Hanover College. She received her education at Wellesley College and Hanover College (B.A., 1948). In 1947 she married William A. Huber, a Presbyterian pastor, and with him reared five daughters and one son. She presently makes her home in Hanover. She began writing hymns in 1976, with particular concern for peacemaking, justice, and inclusiveness–areas of ministry in which she has been actively involved within and beyond her denomination. Her hymns have been widely published, and 73 of them were collected in *A Singing Faith* (Philadelphia, 1987). *P.A.R.*

Creator God, Creating Still–51

Hudson, Ralph E. (b. Napoleon, OH, Jul. 9, 1843; d. Cleveland, OH, Jun. 14, 1901) moved to Pennsylvania during his childhood. He enlisted as a private on June 20, 1861 at the beginning of the Civil War and served in Company K, 10th Pennsylvania Reserves (later renamed the 39th Pennsylvania Volunteers). From June 1862 to February 1863 he served as a nurse at the General Hospital, Annapolis, Maryland. On March 4, 1863 he married Mary Smith of Annapolis. He was honorably discharged on June 11, 1864 at Pittsburgh. For five years he taught music at Mount Vernon College, Alliance, Ohio, and later became active as a singer, song composer, and music publisher at Alliance. He also devoted much of his time to evangelistic work and was a licensed preacher in the Methodist Episcopal Church. His published works include *Salvation Echoes* (1882); *Gems of Gospel Songs* (1884); *Songs of Peace, Love and Joy* (1885) and *Songs of the Ransomed* (1887). He was a Prohibitionist, wrote a number of temperance songs, and published *The Temperance Songster* (1886). *S.W.G.*

HUDSON–At the Cross (refrain)–139
BLESSED NAME (arr.)–Blessed Be the Name (refrain)–206
I'll Live for Him–298
SATISFIED–539

Huff, R. G. (b. Pigeon Forge, TN, Oct. 21, 1949) was educated at Carson Newman College (B.A., Bible) and Southwestern Baptist Theological Seminary (M.C.M.). After serving churches in Tennessee, Texas, and Colorado, he went in 1988 to be minister of music at University Hills Baptist Church, Denver, Colorado. He has been active as clinician for children's and youth/adult choirs as well as workshop leader in worship planning conferences. A frequent contributor of articles to *The Church Musician*, *Worship*, and other periodicals as well as guest lecturer in Baptist colleges and seminaries. Huff has conducted his Young Musicians Choir as the featured children's choir during Music Week at the Baptist Conference Center, Glorieta, New Mexico. *H.T.M.*

Fill the Earth with Music–614

Hugg, George C. (b. Haddonfield, NJ, May 23, 1848; d. Philadelphia, PA, Oct. 13, 1907) was a church musician, composer, and publisher. At the age of 12 he became choirmaster of the Presbyterian church in Berlin, New Jersey. After moving to Philadelphia, he led choirs at Tabernacle Presbyterian Church and Broad Street Methodist Episcopal Church. Later he served Harper Memorial Presbyterian Church as deacon, elder, and trustee, and assistant Sunday School superintendent. Active in Sunday School work and in annual campmeetings in the mid-Atlantic states, he wrote many tunes and published numerous collections of music for Sunday Schools. *P.A.R.*

Hughes, John (b. Dowlais, Wales, 1873; Llantwit Fardre, Pontypridd, Wales, May 14, 1932) moved with his family in 1874 to Llantwit Fardre, where he lived the rest of his life. At the age of 12 he went to work as a doorboy at a local mine, Glyn Colliery. He was later employed as a clerk, and then an official in the traffic department of the Great Western Railway and remained in that employment for the rest of his life. He succeeded his father in the offices of deacon and precentor of Salem Baptist Church in Llantwit Fardre and was a lifelong member there until his death. *S.W.G.*

CWM RHONDDA–56, 395

Hull, Eleanor H. (b. Manchester, England, Jan. 15, 1860; d. London, England, Jan. 13, 1935) supported the revival of Gaelic culture and literature by founding and serving as secretary of the Irish Text Society. The author of several books on Irish history and literature, she also served as president of the Irish Literary Society of London. *D.B.*

Be Thou My Vision (versified)–60

Hunter, William (b. Ballymena, County Antrim, Ireland, May 26, 1811; d. Cleveland, OH, Oct. 18, 1877) was a Methodist minister, professor, and editor. He and his family immigrated to York, Pennsylvania, when he was six years old. After graduating in 1833 from Madison College (Pennsylvania), he was ordained by the Pittsburgh Conference. He edited their *Journal* from 1836 to 1840 and its successor, the *Christian Advocate*, from 1844 to 1852 and again from 1872 to 1876. From 1855 until 1870 he was professor of Hebrew and Biblical Literature at Allegheny College. Then he became pastor of the Methodist Episcopal Church in Alliance, Ohio. He was a presiding elder in the Virginia and East Ohio Conferences. More than 125 of his hymns appear in collections he edited: *Select Melodies* (1st ed., Cincinnati, 1838), *The Minstrel of Zion* (with Samuel Wakefield, 1845), and *Songs of Devotion* (Pittsburgh, 1859). He was appointed to the committee which revised the Methodist hymnal of 1878, but died before the book's publication. *P.A.R.*

The Great Physician–188

Husband, John Jenkins (b. Plymouth, England, 1760; d. Philadelphia, PA, Mar. 19, 1825) was clerk at Surrey Chapel, Plymouth, England, before coming to the United States in 1809. He was a singing school teacher in Philadelphia and clerk at St. Paul's Protestant Episcopal Church until his death. He is buried in St. Paul's churchyard. He composed a number of tunes and anthems and contributed "an improved mode of teaching music to facilitate the progress of the learner" to a subsequent edition of Andrew Adgate's *Philadelphia Harmony* (1st ed., 1790). *P.H.*

REVIVE US AGAIN–469

Hussey, Jennie Evelyn (b. Henniker, NH, Feb. 8, 1874; d. Concord, NH, 1958) lived most of her life in a small rural New Hampshire community in the same farmhouse where four generations of her Quaker ancestors had lived. She began writing poetry early in life. Some of her devotional texts were set to music by gospel song composers. Her last years were spent in the Home for the Aged in Concord, New Hampshire. *M.P.*

Lead Me to Calvary–490

Hustad, Donald Paul (b. Sioux Agency, Yellow Medicine County, MN, Oct. 2, 1918) is a Baptist teacher, conductor, organist, author, composer, and arranger. He earned degrees from John Fletcher College (B.A., 1940) and Northwestern University (M.Mus., 1945; D.Mus., 1963), and has done post-graduate study at Indiana University and with Jean Langlais in Paris, France. He is an Associate of the American Guild of Organists. His contributions to church music have been recognized by the W. Hines Sims Award from the Southern Baptist Church Music Conference in 1984, and the Fellowship of The Hymn Society in the United States and Canada in 1989. His academic appointments include service at Olivet College (1946-50); Moody Bible Institute, where he was director of the Sacred Music Department (1950-63); New Orleans Baptist Theological Seminary (visiting professor 1964-65); and The Southern Baptist Theological Seminary (1966-86), where, from 1975 until 1986 he held the V. V. Cooke Professorship. He continues as senior professor at Southern Seminary. From 1961 to 1967 he was team organist with the Billy Graham Evangelistic Association.

Hustad is a prolific writer, composer, and arranger, and is widely sought after as a speaker and recitalist. He is the editor of *Fanny Crosby Speaks Again* (1977), and the author of *Jubilate! Church Music in the Evangelical Tradition* (1981) and *Choral Musicianship and Voice Training* (with Kerchal Armstrong; 1986), all published by Hope Publishing Company of Carol Stream, Illinois. In his role as hymnal editor with Hope, he has edited eight collections, including *Hymns for the Living Church* (1974) and its *Dictionary-Handbook* (1978) and *The Worshiping Church* (1990), together with its *Worship Leaders' Edition* (1991). He was a member of the committee that edited *Baptist Hymnal* (1975). His numerous hymn tunes, harmonization, and arrangements appear in a variety of hymnals.   *P.A.R.*

WHO IS HE (arr.)–124

Hymns Ancient and Modern (1875) is very likely the most popular hymnal ever published for English-speaking Christians. A legacy of the Oxford Movement in British church life, it was printed in its first complete form in 1861. It underwent a thorough revision (the first of several) in 1875 at which time many new hymns and tunes were added. The book is the work of many hymnists and tune writers but principally that of Henry W. Baker (texts) and William H. Monk (tunes).

Its long and continued use can be accounted for by its broad inclusion of congregational songs from the evangelical as well as the high church traditions. Although it was never the official hymnal of the Church of England, in actuality it has virtually fulfilled that role through the years.   *H.T.M.*

CANONBURY–509

Hymns for the Young (1836) was the fourth edition of a collection of songs for children edited by Miss Dorothy Ann Thrupp. She was the author of several hymns which appeared in other collections. Because "Savior, Like a Shepherd Lead Us" first appeared in this collection, it is generally attributed to her authorship.   *H.T.M.*

Savior, Like a Shepherd Lead Us–61

Ingalls, Jeremiah (b. Andover, MA, Mar. 1, 1764; d. Hancock, VT, Apr. 6, 1838) settled in Newbury, Vermont, about 1791, where he was occupied variously as a farmer, cooper (barrel-maker), and tavern-keeper. He also served as choir director, bass viol player, and deacon in the New-bury Congregational Church and taught singing schools in the area. In 1810 he moved to a farm between Rochester and Hancock, Vermont, where he remained until his death. His first published tunes appeared in books by other compilers in the 1790s and, in 1805, he put forth *The Christian Harmony*, one of the earliest American collections to contain a significant number of folk hymn tunes. In addition to the tune listed below, Ingalls is remembered as the composer of two popular fuging tunes, NEW JERUSALEM and NORTHFIELD.   *D.M.*

I LOVE THEE–I Love Thee–211

Ingham, Marie is the pseudonym of a composer who prefers to remain anonymous.   *P.H.*

WHEN I PRAY–When I Pray–460

Isáis, Juan Martínez (b. Zacatecas, Mexico, 1926) graduated from the Central American Bible Institute of Guatemala City, Guatemala (1952), studying also in various schools in the United States. He is a member of the National Presbyterian Church of Mexico and serves as director of Latin America Mission in Mexico. He has been active in evangelistic work and in Christ for the Cities, an urban mission outreach program of Latin America Mission. The author of several books published in both English and Spanish, he also is the composer of numerous hymns and choruses.   *H.T.M.*

TE VENGO–I've Come to Tell–222

Iverson, Daniel (b. Brunswick, GA, Sep. 26, 1890; d. Asheville, NC, Jan. 3, 1977) was educated at the University of Georgia, Moody Bible Institute, Columbia Theological Seminary, and the University of South Carolina. Ordained to the Presbyterian ministry in 1914, he began his pastoral work at the First Presbyterian Church, Tifton, Georgia, and later served churches in South Carolina and North Carolina. In 1927 he organized the Shenandoah Presbyterian Church, Miami, Florida, and served as pastor of this congregation until his retirement in 1951. During these 24 years he led in the organization of seven Presbyterian churches in the Miami area. Throughout his ministry he was involved in evangelistic endeavors and was in demand as speaker, preacher, and evangelist. From 1962 until his death in 1977, he lived in Asheville, North Carolina, and was active in supplying pulpits in various churches thoughout that region.   *W.J.R.*

IVERSON–Spirit of the Living God–244

Jabusch, Willard Francis (b. Chicago, IL, Mar. 12, 1930) was educated at St. Mary of the Lake Seminary (S.T.B., M.A., 1956), Loyola University of Chicago (M.A., 1961), and Northwestern University (Ph.D., 1968). He served St. James Catholic church in Chicago as assistant pastor (1956-61), taught at Niles College (1963-66), and was on the faculty of Mundelein Seminary (1968-90). In 1990 he became Director of Calvert House, the Roman Catholic student center at the University of Chicago. His published books include *The Person in the Pulpit* (1980), *Walk Where Jesus Walked* (1986), *The Spoken Christ* (1990), and *City on the Tiber* (1990).   *M.P.*

The King of Glory Comes–127

Jackson, Robert (b. Oldham, Lancashire, England, 1840; d. Royton, Oldham, Lancashire, England, Jul. 12, 1914) was a student at the Royal Academy of Music and began his organ career at St. Mark's, Grosvenor Square, London. For some time he was a member of the Halle Symphony Orchestra at Birmingham. In 1868, he succeeded his father as organist at St. Peter's Church, Oldham, a position his father had held for 48 years. He served there for 46 years. The tenure of service of father and son at St. Peter's Church, Oldham, covering almost a century, seems to be an unequaled record in the annals of church music. Jackson published several collections of hymn tunes.   *W.J.R.*

TRENTHAM–241, 278, 363, 496

Jackson, Thomas Albert (b. Baltimore, MD, May 1, 1931) is a Baptist pastor. He is a graduate of Towson State University (A.A., 1951), the University of Richmond (B.A., 1953), Southeastern Baptist Theological Seminary (B.D., 1957), and Johns Hopkins University (Ph.D., 1970). He has been pastor of Wake Forest Baptist Church, Wake Forest, North Carolina, since 1988. Prior to that time he was pastor of Wilderness Road Baptist Church, Fredericksburg, Virginia (1951-57); associate pastor of First Baptist Church, Baltimore, Maryland (1957-63); pastor of Reistertown Baptist Church, Reistertown, Maryland (1963-65), and pastor of McLean Baptist Church, McLean, Virginia (1965-88). He has served on the governing boards of Golden Gate Baptist Theological Seminary, the Baptist General Association of Virginia, and the University of Richmond and has taught in an adjunctive capacity for several institutions. He has been president of the Southeastern Seminary Alumni Association and

the Virginia Baptist Pastor's Conference and has served on the Ethics Commission of the Baptist World Alliance.   *P.A.R.*

We Are Called to Be God's People–390

James, William Marceus (b. Meadville, MS, Jun. 4, 1915) earned degrees from Mt. Beulah College (A.A.), Butler University (Bachelor of Sacred Literature, 1938), and Drew University (B.D., 1942, and M.A., 1945). His pastorates include East Calvary Methodist Church, New York City (1940-44), Trinity Methodist Church of the Bronx, New York City (1944-52), and Metropolitan Community United Methodist Church, New York City (1952-85). During his pastorates in New York City, he helped to organize the East Harlem Triangle Housing Program and was founder and first president of the Ministerial Interfaith Association of Harlem. A major focus of his pastoral leadership was ministry to street people and street gangs. In 1985 James became Executive Director of the Multi-Ethnic Center for Ministry of the Northeastern Jurisdiction of the United Methodist Church located at Drew University. In recognition of his effective ministry in an urban setting, he was awarded a Doctor of Humane Letters degree from Drew University in 1985.   *M.P.*

Easter People, Raise Your Voices–360

John of Damascus (b. Damascus, Syria, *c.* 700; d. Jerusalem, *c.* 780) was educated by Cosmas, a learned Sicilian monk. After a political career as chief councillor to the caliph of Damascus, he retired to the cloister of Mar Saba in the desert near Jerusalem. There he devoted himself to a life of writing, compiling huge works in the areas of science, philosophy, and theology. His most lasting work, however, was in the realm of Greek music and hymnody. What Gregory the Great achieved in the collection and codification of Christian chant in the West, John achieved in the East, thus making a great contribution to the music and hymnody of the Greek Church.

John was the perfector of the characteristic Greek worship form known as the canon (kanon). This extended poetic form consists of eight (sometimes nine) odes, each of which in turn is made up of several stanzas. The most famous of these canons composed by John is known as the "Golden Canon" for Easter, generally recognized as the grandest piece of Greek sacred poetry in existence. The first ode of this canon is the source for John's well-known Easter hymn translated as "The Day of Resurrection." *H.T.M.*

The Day of Resurrection–164

Johnson, J. (John) Rosamond (b. Jacksonville, FL, Aug. 11, 1873; d. New York, NY, Nov. 11, 1954) was an African-American composer, lyricist, and performer. He was educated at the New England Conservatory of Music and also studied privately in London with Samuel Coleridge-Taylor. After teaching school for several years in Jacksonville, he moved to New York City to enter show business. In 1899 he was joined by his older brother, James Weldon Johnson, and they collaborated with Bob Cole to become a successful songwriting team, producing some 200 songs. Although James Weldon Johnson's contribution was limited to writing lyrics, J. Rosamond Johnson and Bob Cole provided both lyrics and music. They performed in vaudeville and Broadway shows and also produced their own musical comedies, such as *The Shoo-fly Regiment* (1907). In 1913 Rosamond Johnson became music director of Hammerstein's Grand Opera House in London, and from 1914 to 1919 he was director of the Music School Settlement for Colored People in Harlem. His compositions range in style from the popular idioms of the time, as found in his songs, to longer works which reflect his classical training. He performed in such musical dramas as *Porgy and Bess* (1935). He edited four significant collections of black music: *The Book of Negro Spirituals* (1925); *The Second Book of Negro Spirituals* (1926), both in collaboration with his brother; *Shout Songs* (1936); and *Rolling Along in Song* (1937). *H.E.*

Lift Every Voice–627

Johnson, James Weldon (William) (b. Jacksonville, FL, Jun. 17, 1871; d. Wiscasset, ME, Jun. 26, 1938) was a leading public figure among African-Americans and one of the greater lights of the Harlem Renaissance in the '20s, a "coming of age" in African-American art, literature, and music. He was distinguished as an author, educator, lyricist, and writer of music, interpreter of black culture, and champion of black rights. After graduating from Atlanta University in 1894, he was a school principal and lawyer in Jacksonville, Florida–the first black attorney in that state. In the summer of 1899 he and his brother, the composer J. Rosamond Johnson, went to New York, and in collaboration with Bob Cole, became a successful song writing team. Many of their songs were included in musical comedies. In 1906 Johnson began a career with the United States diplomatic service, being appointed to a post in Venezuela. He was married to Grace Nail of New York City in 1910. In 1912 Johnson published a short novel, *The Autobiography of an Ex-colored Man*, a work recognized as a valuable document concerning African-American culture and its music during this era. His other works include two volumes of Negro spirituals, published in 1925 and 1926, and *God's Trombones–Seven Negro Sermons in Verse* (1927). *God's Trombones* has become well known through choral settings such as that of Roy Ringwald (1950). In 1914 Johnson became editorial writer for the *New York Age*, the oldest black newspaper in that state. In 1916 he became field secretary and later executive secretary for the NAACP, speaking throughout the nation on behalf of black rights for a share in democracy. In 1930 he resigned this position to return to writing, and in the following year became professor of creative literature at Fisk University, Nashville, Tennessee. His autobiography, *Along This Way*, was published in 1933.   *H.E.*

Lift Every Voice and Sing–627

Johnson, Linda Lee (b. Seattle, WA, Nov. 9, 1947) describes herself as the full-time wife of the superintendent of Redwood Christian Schools and the mother of two children. She is a member of the Redwood Chapel Community Church in Castro Valley, California. She considers Tom Fettke to be the greatest influence on her as a lyricist. Her first published text was "Lord, Let Me Serve," written in 1978. Her other texts include "The Majesty and Glory of Your Name," "Changed," "Be Strong in the Lord" and over 20 others.   *S.W.G.*

The Majesty and Glory of Your Name–37
He Is Lord–178
Be Strong in the Lord–476

Johnston, Julia Harriette (b. Salineville, OH, Jan. 21, 1849; d. Peoria, IL, Mar. 6, 1919) moved with her family in 1855 to Peoria, Illinois, where she spent the rest of her life. Her father was pastor of the First Presbyterian Church of Peoria from 1856 until he died in 1864. Julia was superintendent of the younger children's department of the Sunday School for 41 years and teacher of the infant class. Her mother founded the Presbyterian Missionary Society of Peoria, and Julia was president of the organization for 20 years. She published *School of the Master* (1880), *Bright Threads* (1897), *Indian and Spanish Neighbors* (1905), and *Fifty Missionary Heroes* (1913). She wrote Primary Sunday School lesson material and about 500 hymns.   *S.W.G.*

Grace Greater than Our Sin–329

Joncas, Jan Michael (b. Minneapolis, MN, Dec. 20, 1951) is a Roman Catholic priest, scholar, and musician. He earned a B.A. from the College of St. Thomas, a M.A. from the University of Notre Dame, and the License in Sacred Liturgy from the Pontificio Istituto Liturgico, Collegio Sant'Anselmo (Rome, Italy), where, in 1991, he was working toward a Doctorate in Sacred Liturgy. Following his ordination in 1980, he served as associate pastor at Presentation Parish in Maplewood, Minnesota, and as chaplain at the Newman Center at the Twin Cities campus of the University of Minnesota before being sent to Rome for doctoral study. He has published a number of articles on church music and several collections of compositions for worship, which total more than 100. He has recorded many of his own compositions.   *P.A.R.*

On Eagle's Wings–On Eagle's Wings–71

Jones, Lewis Edgar (b. Yates City, IL, Feb. 8, 1865; d. Santa Barbara, CA, Sep. 1, 1936) attended Moody Bible Institute, from which he graduated in the same class with Billy Sunday. His vocational life was given to YMCA work, serving as physical director at Davenport, Iowa, general secretary in Fort Worth, Texas, and general secretary in Santa Barbara, California. He served in the latter position from 1915 until his retirement in 1925. For Jones hymn writing was a hobby, and he typically wrote both words and music for his hymns, some of which were published under one of the pseudonyms he used, such as Lewis Edgar, Edgar Lewis, and Mary Slater.   *M.P.*

POWER IN THE BLOOD–There Is Power in the Blood–132

Jones, Reba (See Andrae, Reba Jones)

Jordan, Novella Dillard Preston (b. Putnam County, TN, May 25, 1901, d. Nashville, TN, Dec. 21, 1991) was the daughter of Calvin C. and Margaret Dillard and the granddaughter of John L. Dillard, D.D., one of the founders of the Cumberland Presbyterian Church. She attended business college in Nashville, Tennessee, then joined the editorial department of the Baptist Sunday School Board in 1922, and with the exception of one year, 1947-48, she worked in various positions there until her retirement in 1966. She was assistant literary editor of *The Church Musician*, a monthly periodical, from 1951 to 1966. Related to her special interest in journalism, she attended George Peabody College for Teachers, the University of Tennessee, and Belmont College. She wrote two biographical books for children, *Makers of Music* (Convention Press, 1960) and *Makers of Hymns* (Convention Press, 1962). Later these two books were revised, added to, and combined into one published by Broadman Press in 1982, *Makers of Music*. She also

wrote "We Shall All Be Changed," a text set to music by Stan Pethel and published in the Simply Gospel Choral Series published by GENEVOX Music Group.   *W.J.R.*

My Singing Is a Prayer–603

Jude, William Herbert (b. Westleton, Suffolk, England, Sep. 18, 1851; d. London, England, Aug. 8, 1922) was organist at the Blue Coat Hospital in Liverpool and, beginning in 1889, at the Stretford Town Hall near Manchester. He traveled extensively in Great Britain and Australia as a popular lecturer and recitalist. Among the works he edited on hymnody and sacred music are *Music and the Higher Life* (1904); *Mission Hymns* (1911); *Festival Hymns* (1916); and the *Monthly Hymnal* and *Minister of Music*. He also composed an operetta *(Innocents Abroad)*, songs, and anthems.   *S.W.G.*

GALILEE–293

Judson, Adoniram (b. Malden, MA, Aug. 9, 1788; d. Bay of Bengal, Apr. 12, 1850) was the first Baptist missionary from the United States. The son of a Congregationalist minister, he was educated at Rhode Island College (now Brown University; A.B., 1807) and Andover Theological Seminary. In 1812, while enroute to India for service as a Congregationalist missionary, he and his wife, Ann Hasseltine, became convinced, through the study of Scripture, of the Baptist view of baptism. Upon his arrival in Calcutta, he was immersed by English Baptist missionary William Ward. When forced to leave India in 1813, Judson began work in Burma. Despite imprisonment and resistance to the gospel, his labor over many years produced a Bible in Burmese, a Burmese-English dictionary, and a Burmese grammar. His letters and his

1845 visit to the United States stimulated interest in missions among Baptists in America. He wrote many poems, among which were a few hymns. His versification of the Lord's Prayer, "Our Father God, who art in heaven," appeared in several nineteenth-century Baptist collections.

Judson remarried after the deaths of his first two wives. The second and third Mrs. Judsons, Sarah Hall Boardman and Emily Chubbock, were also hymnists. One of his sons, the noted Baptist pastor, Edward Judson, coedited a hymnal, *The New Laudes Domine* (New York, 1892).   *P.A.R.*

Come, Holy Spirit, Dove Divine–364

Jüngst, Hugo (b. Dresden, Germany, Feb. 26, 1853; d. Dresden, Germany, Mar. 3, 1923) was a conductor, composer, and arranger. He was educated at the Dresden Conservatory (1871-76) and founded the Dresden Male Choral Society in the year of his graduation. He arranged and composed for that group and became well known as a leader of festivals. In 1898, the King of Saxony awarded him the title Professor. *P.A.R.*

Jüngst (arr.)–108

Justice, David Michael (b. Long Beach, CA, Jul. 26, 1948), the son of Ralph and Nadean Justice, received his B.A. degree in economics from California State University, Long Beach, in 1972. From 1978 to 1983 he served as minister of music at Truett Memorial Baptist Church in Long Beach. Since 1984 he has been minister of music at Mid-Cities Baptist Church, Westminster, California. In addition to writing hymn tunes and texts, he is a composer of choral anthems and music for handbells.   *D.M.*

One by One–One by One–561

Kaan, Frederik Herman (b. Haarlem, The Netherlands, Jul. 27, 1929), a minister in the United Reformed Church, spent most of his childhood in Ziest and began his higher education at the University of Utrecht. He then entered Western College, in Bristol, England, and subsequently earned the B.A. at the University of Bristol in 1954. After a year of post-graduate study, Kaan was called to Windsor Road Congregational Church in Barry, South Wales. He served there for eight years (1955-63), then became minister of the Pilgrim Church in Plymouth. In 1968, he became minister-secretary of the International Congregational Council in Geneva, Switzerland; and, upon its merger into the World Alliance of Reformed Churches, became executive secretary of the new body. In 1978 he returned to England as moderator of the Western Midlands Province of the United Reformed Church. From 1985-1989, he was a member of the ministerial team at Central Church in Swindon and minister of Penhill United Reformed Church. The Reformed Theological Seminary in Debrecen, Hungary, awarded him an honorary Th.D. in 1978. A dissertation on "Emerging Language in Hymnody" earned him a Ph.D. from Geneva Theological College in 1984. His varied places of service, linguistic abilities, and ardent ecumenical service in the cause of the poor, hungry, and dispossessed have made him a Christian citizen of the world.

Kaan has written more than 200 hymns, which have been translated into more than 15 languages. They are collected in two volumes, *The Hymn Texts of Fred Kaan* (Carol Stream, 1985) and *Planting Trees and Sowing Seeds* (Carol Stream, 1989). He has also contributed to hymnody as a consultant, editor, and translator.   *P.A.R.*

Christ Is Risen (tr.)–167
We Utter Our Cry–631

Kaiser, Kurt Frederick (b. Chicago, IL, Dec. 17, 1934) was educated at the American Conservatory of Music and Northwestern University (B.M., 1958; M.M., 1959). For more than 30 years he was associated with Word, Incorporated, and had a significant role in developing the international image of this firm in the fields of sacred recordings. He makes his home in Waco, Texas, and devotes his time to free-lance composing, arranging, and producing. He is a deacon in the Seventh and James Baptist Church, Waco, Texas. He and his wife Patricia, parents of four children and grandparents of two, are active in the fellowship of this church family. His compositions and choral arrangements are widely sung. Recordings of his own piano artistry and orchestral scorings have been exceedingly popular. *W.J.R.*

PATRICIA–O How He Loves You and Me–146
MANNA (arr.)–Sweet, Sweet Spirit (arr.)–243

Katholiches Gesangbuch (Würzburg, 1828) was one of several German Catholic hymn collections containing texts that were later translated into English by the followers of the 19th-century Oxford Movement in England. Included in this particular hymnal published at Würzburg in 1828 was the German hymn "Beim frühen Morgenlicht" which came into English through the translation of Edward Caswall as "When Morning Gilds the Skies." *H.T.M.*

When Morning Gilds the Skies (st. 1, 2,4)–221

Keegan, Gilbert Kearnie (b. Bunkie, LA, Jan. 31, 1907; d. St. Louis, MO, Sep. 13, 1960) was educated at Northwestern Louisiana State College (B.A., 1927) and Southwestern Baptist Theological Seminary (Th.M., 1933). He was ordained to the Baptist ministry and served as pastor at First Baptist Church, Natchitoches, Louisiana (1932-35); Emmanuel Baptist Church, Alexandria, Louisiana (1937-41); First Baptist Church, Longview, Texas (1941-45); and Temple Baptist Church, Los Angeles, California (1945-50). In 1950 he became secretary of the Student Department of the Baptist Sunday School Board, Nashville, Tennessee, and directed Southern Baptist student work on college campuses. He was exceedingly popular as a speaker, a soloist, and a writer. His own inimitable singing of "The Lily of the Valley" became his trademark. While president of the Southwestern Baptist Theological Seminary Alumni, he led in the campaign to raise $750,000 toward the erection of the Truett-Fleming, Scarborough Building on that campus. *W.J.R.*

Teach Me, O Lord, I Pray–601

Kelly, Thomas (b. Kellyville, Stradbally, County Queens, Ireland, Jul. 13, 1769; d. Dublin, Ireland, May 14, 1855) was educated at Trinity College, Dublin. Forsaking his early plans to pursue a legal career, Kelly was ordained in the Church of England. His fervent evangelical preaching brought opposition. The archbishop of Dublin forbade him to preach in any of the churches of his diocese. He eventually left the Church of England and built churches at Athy, Portarlington, and Wexford. Kelly wrote 765 hymns which were published in *A Collection of Psalms and Hymns* (1800), *Hymns of Various Passages of Scripture* (1804), and *Hymns not before Published* (1815). *D.B.*

Look, Ye Saints! The Sight Is Glorious–169

Ken, Thomas (b. Little Berkhampsted, Hertfordshire, England, Jul. 1637; d. Longbridge Deverill, Wiltshire, England, Mar. 19, 1711) was an Anglican bishop and writer. His parents died when he was a child, and Izaak Walton, who had married Ken's half-sister, Anne, became his guardian. He was educated at Winchester and at Hart Hall and New College, Oxford (B.A., 1661; M.A., 1664). Following his ordination in 1662, he served in a number of parishes and, from 1679 to 1680, as chaplain to Princess Mary at the Hague before being consecrated Bishop of Bath and Wells in 1685. His firm principles and forthrightness both earned him respect and brought him into frequent conflict with the crown. He was imprisoned in the Tower of London in 1688 for refusing to subscribe to the Declaration of Indulgences of James II (though he was subsequently acquitted). When he declined to take the Convocation Oath upon the accession of William IV in 1691, he was deprived of his see. From that time until his death, he lived at the home of Lord Weymouth in Longleat, Wiltshire.

Ken's most fruitful relationship was with Winchester College. He was a student there in the early 1650s, was elected a fellow in 1666, and became prebendary in 1669, with simultaneous responsibilities at the college, at the cathedral, and as chaplain to the bishop. It was out of his devotion to the students at Winchester that he wrote his most famous work, *A Manual of Prayers for the Use of the Scholars at Winchester College* (1st ed., London, 1674). The 1695 edition of this book included his morning, evening, and midnight hymns, with their shared doxology, "Praise God, from whom all blessings flow." Four volumes of his poetic works were published posthumously in 1721.   *P.A.R.*

All People That on Earth Do Dwell–5
All Creatures of Our God and King–27
Praise God, from Whom All
  Blessings Flow–253
All Praise to You, My God, This Night–449

Kendrick, Graham (b. Blisworth, Northamptonshire, England, Aug. 2, 1950) is the son of a Baptist pastor. His full-time ministry began in 1972 after leaving Teacher Training College. After a year singing his songs in evangelistic meetings, he toured for three years with "In the Name of Jesus," a team working in evangelism and church renewal. In 1976 he became music director of British Youth for Christ. He spent five years based in York at St. Michael le Belfrey church. Since 1984 he and his family have lived in London where they belong to the Ichthus Christian Fellowship. He travels extensively as a part of their ministry team. He is widely known as a writer of popular praise and worship songs. Each year he serves as a worship leader for "Spring Harvest," an interdenominational convention that draws as many as 60,000 people. *D.B.*

SHINE–Shine, Jesus, Shine–579

Kennedy, Benjamin Hall (b. Summerhill, Warwickshire, England, Nov. 6, 1804; d. Apr. 6, 1889) was educated at King Edward's School, Birmingham, Shrewsbury School, and St. John's College, Cambridge. He became the Regius Professor of Greek in the University of Cambridge. He was an important educator, author of a Latin grammar, editor of some of the classics, hymn writer, compiler, and translator. His hymns and translations appeared in his *Psalter, or the Psalms of David, in English Verse* (1860) and *Hymnologia Christiana, or Psalms and Hymns Selected and Arranged in* the *Order of the Christian Seasons* (1863), the last of which became a significant storehouse for subsequent hymnal compilers and editors.   *S.W.G.*

Ask Ye What Great Thing I Know (tr.)–538

Kent, John (b. Bideford, Devonshire, England, Dec., 1766; d. Nov. 15, 1843) worked as a shipwright. His opportunities for formal education were limited. A few of his hymns were published in Samuel Reece's *Collection* of 1799. The first edition of Kent's *Collection of Original Gospel Hymns* was published in 1803. A 10th edition published in 1861 contained some longer works and a *Life* written by his son (Julian, I, 623). Calvinistic theology was prominent in his hymns and, as a result, some compilers avoided them. Charles H. Spurgeon used several in his *Our Own Hymnbook* of 1866.   *D.B.*

'Tis the Church Triumphant Singing–218

Ketchum, Albert A. (b. Feb. 12, 1894) was a student at Moody Bible Institute, Chicago, in the early 1920s when he wrote a number of songs which were sold to Harry D. Clark. In the 1940s Ketchum was living in Long Beach, California, and working for Delco Products Company, Los Angeles. No other information is available.   *D.M.*

KETCHUM–Why Do I Sing About Jesus–541

Kethe, William (b. *c.* 1530, Scotland [?]; d. Dorsetshire, England, before Jun. 2, 1594) is generally considered to have been a native of Scotland though little is known of the place or exact date of his birth. During 1555-58 he lived in exile in Frankfurt and Geneva and afterwards was employed as an envoy from Geneva to other English-

speaking congregations on the Continent.

He doubtless was one of the scholars among the English refugees who remained in Geneva after 1558 to complete the English translation of the Bible and the *Anglo-Genevan Psalter*. Twenty-five of his metrical psalm versions appeared in that psalter published in 1561, the most famous of which is the one for Psalm 100, "All People That on Earth Do Dwell."   *H.T.M.*

All People That on Earth Do Dwell–5

Key, Francis Scott (Pipe's Creek, MD, Aug., 1779; d. Baltimore, MD., Jan. 11, 1843) was an Episcopalian layman, a lawyer, and a poet. After attending St. John's College in Annapolis, he studied law and served three terms as United States District Attorney for the District of Columbia. Among his roles in the church were vestryman, lay reader, Bible teacher, delegate to the General Convention, organizer of the Domestic and Foreign Missionary Society, and member of a committee to prepare a new hymnal for the denomination. His collected poetic works, published in 1857, include several hymns in addition to his famous patriotic song.   *P.A.R.*

The Star-Spangled Banner–635

Kilpatrick, Bob (b. Louisville, KY., Oct. 25, 1952), the son of an Air Force chaplain, was born while his father was attending The Southern Baptist Theological Seminary, Louisville, Kentucky. By the time he was 15, Bob had lived on three continents. He was converted during the Christmas holidays of 1968. Bob is widely known as a performer of contemporary Christian music in concert and on evangelistic crusades, a recording artist and producer, and a composer of worship choruses. He and his wife,

Cindy, were married on November 13, 1971, and are the parents of five children. They presently reside in Redding, California, where they are members of Bethel Church.   *D.M.*

BE GLORIFIED–Lord, Be Glorified–457

Kingsway Carol Book, one of several such (probably 19th-century) carol collections, was edited by Leslie Russell and published in London. It contained the particular translation and paraphrase of the Polish carol, W ZLOBIE LEZY which subsequently entered most hymnals and carol collections as "Infant Holy, Infant Lowly." This was the work of the British scholar and editor, Edith M.G. Reed.   *H.T.M.*

Infant Holy, Infant Lowly–106

Kirchengesänge (1566) (Bohemian Brethren) is the short title for *Kirchengesänge darinnen die Heubtartikel des christliche Glaubens Kurtz gefasset und ausgeleget sind* which was published in Berlin by the Bohemian Brethren in 1566. It contained over 500 hymns reflecting the strong singing tradition of the Brethren and is one in the long line of fine Bohemian Brethren hymnals that were published in 16th and 17th century Germany. This particular 1566 collection was the original source of the tune MIT FREUDEN ZART.   *H.T.M.*

MIT FREUDEN ZART–20

Kirkland, Terry (b. West Plains, MO, Aug. 17, 1940) was educated at Samford University (B.M., 1962), and University of Alabama (M.M., 1964). He served as minister of music, Forest Lake Baptist Church, Tuscaloosa, Alabama (1963-66), Morningview Baptist Church, Montgomery, Al-

abama (1967-71), and Belmont Heights Baptist Church, Nashville, Tennessee (1980-84). He was children's music editor and recording specialist in the Church Music Department, Baptist Sunday School Board, Nashville (1972-81). For several years he worked as a free-lance writer and composer, and, since 1987, has been president of Kirkland House, a Lorenz Corporation publishing company specializing in music and music educational materials for children.   *W.J.R.*

KIRKLAND–488

Kirkpatrick, William James (b. Duncannon, PA, Feb. 27, 1838; d. Germantown, PA, Sep. 20, 1921) was the son of Irish immigrants. His early musical studies were taken with his father. Through these and subsequent studies, he became proficient on flute, violin, and cello. In 1855 he moved to Philadelphia and became a member of the Wharton Street Methodist Episcopal Church. In 1859, at the age of 21, he edited his first collection, *Devotional Melodies,* a collection of camp meeting songs. He married Miss S. T. Doak in 1861. During the Civil War he served in the 91st Regiment of the Pennsylvania Volunteers as a fife-major. From 1862-78 he worked in the furniture business in Philadelphia. During these years he was also active in Sunday School work and camp meeting singing. Following the death of his wife in 1878, Kirkpatrick pursued his musical interests full-time. He served as music director at Grace Methodist Episcopal Church in Philadelphia from 1886-97. He married Mrs. Sara Kellogg Bourne in 1893. The second Mrs. Kirkpatrick died around 1910, and in 1917 he married Mrs. John R. Sweney, the widow of his long-time business associate and collaborator in music publishing.

From 1880 until his death, Kirkpatrick was involved in the publication of approximately 100 collections of gospel songs. His principal business partner and collaborator was John R. Sweney. Sweney and Kirkpatrick edited and published nearly 1,000 of Fanny Crosby's hymns. In addition to Sweney, Kirkpatrick collaborated with H. L. Gilmour, John H. Stockton, and J. Howard Entwhistle. He served as president of Praise Publishing Company in Philadelphia, which published many of his collections. *M.P.*

Kitchin, George William (b. Naughton, Suffolk, England, Dec. 7, 1827; d. Durham, England, Oct. 13, 1912) was educated at Ipswich Grammar School, King's College School and College, and Christ Church, Oxford. His distinguished career included service as Dean of Winchester and Durham Cathedrals and as Chancellor of Durham University. *D.B.*

Klein, Laurie (b. Watertown, WI, Nov. 29, 1950) holds a degree in Art from St. Olaf College. In 1972 she married Bill Klein. They have recorded three albums and have traveled in ministry throughout most of the western states. In recent years she has been a student of theater arts. She has worked as a professional storyteller, an actress for Books in Motion, Artistic Director of Programming at Calvary Chapel of Spokane, and is currently teaching theater arts at Whitworth College in Spokane, Washington. *D.B.*

Knapp, Phoebe Palmer (b. New York City, NY, Mar. 9, 1839; d. Poland Springs, MA, Jul. 10, 1908) was a close friend and fellow church member with Fanny Crosby. The daughter of a Methodist evangelist, she demonstrated an unusual gift for music at an early age. When 16 she married John Fairfield Knapp who became the founder of the Metropolitan Life Insurance Company. Upon the death of her husband, she shared her considerable inherited wealth in numerous charitable causes. Her son, Joseph Palmer Knapp (d. 1951) was the president of Crowell-Collier Publishing Company. Mrs. Knapp published more than 500 gospel song tunes, many of which found acceptance in both England and America. Today, aside from ASSURANCE, she is remembered only for the music of "Open the Gates of the Temple," the words of which were also written by Fanny Crosby. *H.T.M.*

Kocher, Conrad (b. Ditzingen, Würtemberg, Germany, Dec. 16, 1786; d. Stuttgart, Germany, Mar. 12, 1872) went to St. Petersburg, Russia at the age of 17 where he studied composition. He returned to Germany and in 1811 went to Stuttgart. In 1819 he spent a year in Rome studying music. He became concerned with the improvement of choral music in the churches. Therefore, in 1821 in Stuttgart, he founded a School of Sacred Song, the Gesangvereins Liederkranz, which popularized four-part singing in the churches. In 1823 he published *Die Tonkun-*

st in der Kirche, a treatise on church music. He edited several chorale books for which he supplied a number of tunes. He wrote an oratorio, *Der Tod Abels*, two operas, and several sonatas. He received an honorary Doctor of Philosophy degree from the University of Tübingen in 1852. In 1855, he compiled his set of chorales, *Zions Harfe*. He was organist and choirmaster of the Stiftskirche in Stuttgart from 1827 until his retirement in 1865.   *S.W.G.*

Dix–44, 117

Koizumi, Isao (b. Osaka, Japan, Nov. 3, 1907) is an economist and church musician. He studied organ and composition privately and earned the Bachelor of Economics degree from Osaka University of Commerce in 1932. He served that institution until 1942, when he moved to Tokyo. In 1951, he was appointed General Music Director at the U.S. Far East Air Force Chapel Center in Tokyo. For many years, he was conductor of the Tokyo Choral Society.

Koizumi has been an important figure in church music, both in his congregation, Higashi-Nakano United Church of Christ, and in the preparation of hymnals. He was music editor of two collections published by the United Church of Christ in Japan–*The Hymnal* (Tokyo, 1954) and *The Sunday School Hymnal* (Tokyo, 1954) and wrote the notes on the music for the companion to the former book. He also served on the committee that edited the 1967 revision of *The Hymnal*. Among his publications are hymn tunes, works for organ, and books and articles about church music.   *P.A.R.*

Tokyo–179

Kremser, Edward (b. Vienna, Austria, Apr. 10, 1838; d. Vienna, Austria, Nov. 27, 1914) was an outstanding chorus master of the Vienna Männergesangverein and conductor of other choral groups in that city. He was the composer of many operettas, cantatas, and part-songs as well as piano music. His *Sechs Altniederländische Volkslieder* (1877) consisted of arrangements from an earlier collection of old Dutch folksongs by Valerius (1616). This popular collection arranged for men's chorus and orchestra is the source for the hymn tune that bears the compiler's name.   *H.T.M.*

Kremser (arr.)–19, 636

Lafferty, Karen Louise (b. Alamogordo, NM, Feb. 29, 1948) is currently serving as a missionary in The Netherlands for Youth with a Mission and is director of that organization's Musicians for Missions, which she founded in 1980. She was reared in a Southern Baptist church in New Mexico and received the Bachelor of Music Education degree from Eastern New Mexico State University. She points to the musical influences of Peter, Paul, and Mary, Joni Mitchell, the Kingston Trio, and Brasil '66 in her music missionary endeavors. She first worked with Maranatha! Music, an outreach of her home church, Calvary Chapel, Costa Mesa, California. She has recorded five solo albums, a music video, and regularly makes radio and television appearances.   *P.H.*

Lafferty–Seek Ye First (based on Scripture)–478

Lambdin, Henry Lyle (b. Rutledge, TN, Nov. 18, 1892) was a native of Tennessee who spent all his ministerial career in New Jersey. Ordained a Methodist minister, he served pastorates at Morristown and Summit and for six years was a District Superintendent in the Northern New Jersey

Methodist Conference. He spent the latter part of his career as Professor of Homiletics in the Theological School of Drew University. He was the author of several hymns including the Newark Conference Centennial Hymn and "To Worship, Work, and Witness," published in 1969 by the Hymn Society in the United States and Canada in "Nine New Hymns on the Mission of the Church." He now lives in Florham Park, New Jersey. *H.T.M.*

To Worship, Work, and Witness–389

Landgrave, Phillip (b. Marion, IN, May 9, 1935) earned degrees from Eastern Kentucky State College (B.A., 1957) , The Southern Baptist Theological Seminary (B.C.M., 1961; M.C.M., 1963; D.M.A., 1966), and has pursued postdoctoral studies at the University of Southern California (1971-72), Indiana University (1978), and in London, England (1980). He has served as minister of music in churches in Kentucky, Alabama, California, Georgia, and England. While serving in the military he was composer/arranger for the Third Army Band and Chorus (1959-60). He became a member of the faculty of the School of Church Music, The Southern Baptist Theological Seminary, in 1965 and has taught in the areas of voice, composition, and music ministry since that time. A prolific composer, his published works include one oratorio, two church music dramas, three Christian musicals, five cantatas, and more than one hundred anthems. His most frequently performed larger works include *Purpose* (1968), *The Church* (1968), *Christ in You the Hope* (1969), *When Jesus Comes* (1973), *The Upper Room* (1982), and *Redemption's Hour* (1982). He maintains an active schedule as conductor, singer, and clinician for workshops and conferences. *M.P.*

LIFT HIM UP–Lift Him Up–220
TABERNACLE–303
SEMINARY–605

Landsberg, Max (b. Berlin, Germany, Feb. 26, 1845; d. Rochester, NY, Dec. 8, 1928) was taught privately by his father, Meyer Landsberg, rabbi of Hildescheim. He studied further at the universities of Göttingen, Breslau (now Wroclaw), Berlin, Halle, and at the Breslau Jewish seminary. He was on the faculty at the seminary for Jewish teachers at Hanover (1866-71) and became a rabbi in 1870. He was called to the Temple B'rith Kodesh, Rochester, New York, in 1870. He served there for 34 years and became known for his scholarship and service to both Jewish and Gentile communities. He was active in the Jewish reform movement in the United States. *W.J.R.*

The God of Abraham Praise–34

Lathbury, Mary Artemisia (b. Manchester, Ontario County, NY, Aug. 10, 1841; d. East Orange, NJ, Oct. 20, 1913) was the daughter of a Methodist preacher and became a well-known professional artist. Associated with the Rev. John H. Vincent while he was secretary of the Methodist Sunday School Union, she served as general editor of publications for children and young people. Much of her poetic writing first appeared in these publications. She was actively involved in the summer assemblies in Lake Chautauqua in New York, and her poetic ability earned her recognition as the "Poet Laureate of Chautauqua." *W.J.R.*

Break Thou the Bread of Life (st. 1,2)–263

Leddy, Stephen Dale (b. San Angelo, TX, Sep. 15, 1944) began writing music while a junior at San Angelo Central High School, from which he graduated in 1962. He attended Baylor University and graduated from the University of Texas in 1970 with a B.S. degree, majoring in physical education. After teaching physical education in an elementary school for one year, he began traveling extensively as a music evangelist in 1971. Leddy later enrolled for studies at Southwestern Baptist Theological Seminary and completed the Master of Divinity degree there in 1977. Following graduation he resumed his full-time ministry in music evangelism, which he continued until his travel was curtailed due to open-heart surgery in February of 1987. He has written a number of songs, several of which have been published by Hope Publishing Company. He has appeared as a sacred concert artist and has recorded two albums of his own music.   *M.P.*

WORTHY LAMB–Worthy Is the Lamb–157

Lee, Wilbur is the pseudonym of a composer-arranger who wishes to remain unidentified.   *H.T.M.*

W ZLOBIE LEZY (harm.)–106

Leech, Bryan Jeffery (b. Buckhurst Hill, Essex, England, May 14, 1931) attended London Bible College and held a pastorate in Surrey, England, before emigrating to the United States in 1955. Further education was received at Barrington College (M.A., B.A.), North Park Seminary, Illinois, and Westmont College, California. His pastorates in the United States have included churches in Boston, Massachusetts; Montclair, New Jersey; San Francisco, and Santa Barbara, California. In addition to cowriting a novel, *It Must Have Been McNutt*, and making a musical adaptation of Charles Dickens' *A Christmas Carol*, he has written sever-

al hymn texts and tunes which are found in a number of recent hymnals. He was a member of the Hymnal Commission that prepared *The Covenant Hymnal* for the Evangelical Covenant Church (1973) and served as assistant editor of *Hymns for the Family of God* (Nashville, 1976). His "Let God Be God" won first place in a competition to select a theme hymn for the ecumenical evangelistic movement "Key 73."   *D.M.*

LOIS–Spirit, Now Live in Me–240
We Are God's People–383
Make Room Within My Heart, O God–491
Happy the Home When God Is
    There (alt.)–505
Let Your Heart Be Broken–611

Leech, Lida Shivers (b. Mayville, NJ, May 12, 1873; d. Long Beach, CA, Mar. 4, 1962) lived at Cape May Court House in New Jersey during her childhood. She was educated at Columbia and Temple Universities. She wrote some 500 gospel songs, was organist at Bethany Methodist Church in Camden, New Jersey, and traveled extensively as a pianist in evangelistic services.   *S.W.G.*

GIVING–Trust, Try, and Prove Me–616

Leeson, Jane Eliza (b. London, England, 1809; d. Leamington, Warwickshire, England, Nov. 18, 1881) was active for many years in the Catholic Apostolic Church, Gordon Square, London. Some of her hymns were improvised as "prophetic utterances" for meetings at that church, to whose hymnal she contributed nine hymns and translations. She published several collections of religious verse, much of which was written for children.   *M.P.*

Savior, Teach Me Day by Day–461

LeFevre, Mylon R. (b. Atlanta, GA, Oct. 6, 1944), the youngest son of Urias and Eva Mae LeFevre, well-known gospel singers, was educated at Bob Jones University and the West Coast Bible College. His professional background includes singing with the LeFevres, the Stamps Quartet, and his own group, Broken Heart. He is the composer of many gospel songs, including "Happiness," "I Want to Live for Him," and "He's the Only One." His 1970 album *Mylon,* released on Cotillion Records, was one of the first Christian rock albums. He hoped to reach unbelievers in the street by fusing rock music with the message of the gospel. In his own life, as well as in his music, it was only a matter of time before the gospel message was taken over by the rock 'n' roll. His lifestyle changed drastically as did the message of his songs. His return to his family, his faith and his music was a gradual process spreading over several years. In 1974 he successfully broke his addiction to heroin. He recommitted his life to Christ in April 1980, and in November 1981, was ordained as a minister and elder at Atlanta's Mount Paran Church of God.   *W.J.R.*

WITHOUT HIM–Without Him–300

Lemmel, Helen Howarth (b. Wardle, Manchester, England, Nov. 14, 1863; d. Seattle, WA, Nov. 1, 1961) was brought to the United States by her family when she was nine years of age. She lived several years in Milwaukee and Madison, Wisconsin. A gifted singer, she organized a women's quartet that traveled with the Chautauqua Circuit. From 1904 until her death she made her home in Seattle, where she was a member of the Ballard Baptist Church. For many years she traveled as a concert singer; she also conducted religious services for children, for whom she wrote and published stories and songs. She is credited with more than 400 hymns.   *W.J.R.*

LEMMEL–Turn Your Eyes upon Jesus–320

Lillenas, Haldor (b. Stord, near Bergen, Norway, Nov. 19, 1885; d. Aspen, CO, Aug. 18, 1959) was the dominant personality in the early development of music within the Nazarene church. His family immigrated to America, settling first in South Dakota and then in Astoria, Oregon, in 1889. Confirmed in the Lutheran church at age 15, he soon joined the newly founded Nazarene church. The call to the ministry led him to Deets Pacific Bible College (now Pasadena College), Los Angeles. He married Bertha Mae Wilson, also a song writer and elder in the church of the Nazarene. While a pastor, he received his musical education by correspondence courses and self-study. His first published song book was *Special Sacred Songs* (1919), which he published privately. On October 26, 1925, he organized the Lillenas Publishing Company while pastoring the First Church of the Nazarene, Indianapolis, Indiana. The company was purchased by the Nazarene Publishing House and became its music division. Lillenas moved to Kansas City to become manager of the music department and remained in that position until his retirement in 1950. He edited the first official Nazarene hymnal, *Glorious Gospel Hymns* (1931), which contained 81 of his pieces. *Worship in Song* (1972), the current Nazarene hymnal, included 19 of Lillenas' songs. During his lifetime Lillenas wrote over 4,000 texts and tunes. He was awarded the honorary D.Mus. degree by Olivet Nazarene College, Kankakee, Illinois.   *P.H.*

WONDERFUL GRACE–Wonderful Grace of Jesus–328

Limburg Gesangbuch is a hymnal published in 1838 by the Roman Catholic diocese of Limbur- an-der-Lahn in Germany. It is the source of the tune GOTT VATER SEI GEPRIESEN. *P.A.R.*

GOTT VATER SEI GEPRIESEN–258

Lindeman, Ludwig Mathias (b. Trondhjem, Norway, Nov. 28, 1812; d. Christiana [Oslo], Norway, May 23, 1887) was the most famous member of a family of musicians. He received his early musical instruction from his father, substituting for him at the organ at the age of 12. He started theological studies at Oslo, but his love of music led him to choose music as a profession. In 1839 he succeeded his brother as organist at Our Savior's Church, Oslo, where he formed a friendship with its pastor Wilhelm Andreas Wexels, a noted hymn writer. He served this church as organist for 47 years. Lindeman composed tunes for the new hymns in Magnus Landstad's *Salmebog* (1869), which he completed in 1872 and published with church approval in 1877 as a *Koralbog*. The contemporary Norwegian Bishop Skaar wrote, "Landstad's hymns and Lindeman's tunes have given to church song new life in our country." In addition to KIRKEN, five other tunes by Lindman are found in the *Lutheran Book of Worship* (1878). Lindeman collected more than 2,500 Norwegian folk songs, many of them published in his collection of 1853. He was highly regarded as a teacher, and his influence was felt on subsequent generations of Norwegian organists. At the age of 71, Lindeman and his son Peter established what is now Oslo Conservatory, the first music conservatory in Norway. *H.E.*

KIRKEN–351

Liturgy of St. James (5th century) is one of the earliest forms of Christian liturgical worship. It was developed in the church at Jerusalem. The bishop at Jerusalem was James, the half brother of our Lord, for whom the liturgy is named. It was used in the Eastern Orthodox Church as early as the fifth century and is the source of the prayer that is translated and revised as the hymn "Let All Mortal Flesh Keep Silence." *H.T.M.*

Let All Mortal Flesh Keep Silence–80

Lloyd, Eva Brown (b. Jameson, MO, Mar. 9, 1912) was educated at Northwest Missouri State University (B.A.), the University of Missouri at Kansas City (M.A.), and the University of Colorado. She has had extensive teaching experience at the elementary, secondary, and college levels. Her secondary and college teaching have been in the fields of English and English literature. More recently she has served as an English tutor for internationals. She lives in Maryville, Missouri, where she and her husband, Clarence Lloyd, are members of the First Baptist Church. *W.J.R.*

Come, All Christians, Be Committed–604

Loes, Harry Dixon (b. Kalamazoo, MI, Oct. 20, 1892; d. Chicago, IL, Feb. 9, 1965) was born Harold Loes, but called "Harry" throughout his life. He selected his own middle name, calling himself after the pastor of Moody Church in Chicago, Dr. A. C. Dixon. Loes attended Moody Bible Institute, where he studied under D. B. Towner, who inspired him to begin writing gospel songs. He received further education at the American Conservatory of Music, the Metropolitan School of Music, and Chicago Musical College. He was engaged in full-time evangelistic work for 12 years. In 1927 he became music and educational director for the First Baptist Church in Okmulgee, Oklahoma, following this with a similar position in the First Baptist Church, Muskogee, Oklahoma. In 1939 he returned to Moody Bible Institute as a member of the music faculty, where he remained until his retirement. Loes wrote about 1500 hymn texts and 3000 hymn tunes.   *D.M.*

REDEEMER–149

Loizeaux, Alfred Samuel (b. Vinton, IA, Feb. 12, 1877; d. Towson, MD, May 7, 1962) was active in Christian work while employed for many years as an executive with the Baltimore Consolidated Light, Heat, and Power Company. In addition to his work with the Baltimore School of the Bible, he also edited a monthly magazine for Christians entitled *Help and Food*, published by Loizeaux Brothers, Incorporated, New York City.   *D.B.*

God, Our Father, We Adore Thee (st. 3)–248

Long, Lela B. No biographical information is available concerning this author/composer of the chorus "Jesus is the sweetest name I know."   *M.P.*

LOVELY NAME–Jesus Is the Sweetest
  Name I Know–205

Longfellow, Henry Wadsworth (b. Portland, ME, Feb. 27, 1807; d. Cambridge, MA, Mar. 24, 1882) was the son of Stephen and Zilpah (Wadsworth) Longfellow. His mother was a descendant of John Alden and Priscilla Mullins. After his graduation from Bowdoin College in 1825, he studied in Europe. He was professor of modern languages and literature at Bowdoin College

(1829-34), then became professor of literature at Harvard University, where he taught for 17 years. In addition to being an outstanding scholar and teacher, he was the most influential American poet of his day. Among his poetic works that became extremely popular are *Evangeline* (1847), *The Song of Hiawatha* (1855), *The Courtship of Miles Standish* (1858), and *Tales of a Wayside Inn* (1863, 1872, and 1874).   *W.J.R.*

I Heard the Bells on Christmas Day–98

Longstaff, William Dunn (b. Sunderland, Durham, England, Nov. 6, 1822; d. Sunderland, Durham, England, Apr. 2, 1894) was the son of a wealthy ship owner. Being a man of independent means, he was generous in gifts to charitable and philanthropic interests. A close friend of the Reverend Arthur A. Rees, who left the Church of England and established Bethesda Free Chapel, Longstaff served as treasurer for the chapel and looked after the maintenance and improvements of the building. He became a close friend of Moody and Sankey during the 1870s and was active in their work in England. It is not known that he wrote any hymns other than "Take Time to Be Holy."   *W.J.R.*

Take Time to Be Holy–446

Lorenz, Edmund Simon (b. near Canal Fulton, OH, Jul. 13, 1854; d. Dayton, OH, Jul. 11, 1942) was the eldest son of the Rev. Edward and Barbara (Gueth) Lorenz, his father serving as a missionary to German-speaking immigrants in northern Ohio. Following graduation from high school in Toledo, Ohio, he taught school, then studied at Otterbein University; Union Biblical Seminary, Dayton, Ohio; and Yale Theological Seminary. In 1883 and 1884 he studied at the University of Leipzig, concentrating on philosophy and church history. Having had training in music and having composed tunes since his youth, Lorenz, at the age of 20, served as music editor for the first United Brethren hymnal with tunes, *Hymns of the Sanctuary, and Social Worship* (Dayton, 1874).

After returning from Europe he was pastor of High Street United Brethren Church in Dayton from 1884-86. He then served for two years as president of Lebanon Valley College, Annville, Pennsylvania. Lorenz's health broke in 1888. While recuperating he turned his attention to music once again, and in 1890 he began publishing music in Dayton as Lorenz and Company, later changed to Lorenz Publishing Company. He began publishing monthly music periodicals: *The Choir Leader* (1894), *The Choir Herald* (1897), *Kirchenchor* (Church Choir, 1897), and numerous magazines for choirs and organists. He composed hymn tunes and gospel hymns, and wrote books on revival work and on church music, the latter including *Practical Church Music* (1909), *Church Music* (1923), *Music in Work and Worship* (1925), and *The Singing Church* (1937), and *Practical Hymn Studies* (1937).

From 1876 to 1935 Lorenz was editor or co-editor of about 40 collections of sacred music, including songbooks, choral collections, cantatas, and hymnals. Several of these collections were in German. Representative titles are *Gates of Praise* (with Isaiah Baltzell, 1880), *Songs of Refreshing* (1886), *The Otterbein Hymnal* (1890), *Manly Praise* (1896), *Heils-Lieder* (1904), and *United Praise* (with Ira Wilson, 1908).

He lived to see the Lorenz Publishing Company become one of America's largest and most influential publishers of church music. He remained active in its operation until shortly before his death at the age of 88. The Lorenz Corporation with four divisions, celebrated its centennial in 1990. *H.E.*

DAYTON–451

Lovelace, Austin C. (b. Rutherfordton, NC, Mar. 26, 1919) was trained at High Point College (A.B., 1939) and Union Theological Seminary (M.S.M., 1941; D.S.M., 1950). He has served churches in Lincoln, Nebraska and in Charlotte and Greensboro, North Carolina. From 1952 to 1962 he was minister of music at First Methodist Church, Evanston, Illinois. After serving (1962-64) at Christ Church Methodist Church, New York City, he moved to Denver, Colorado to become Minister of Music at the Montview Boulevard Presbyterian Church. He also served the Lovers Lane Methodist Church in Dallas, Texas, for a time. In 1986 he retired from the church music position at the Wellshire Presbyterian Church in Denver.

His career as an educator in church music is impressive. He has taught at the University of Nebraska, Queens College in Charlotte, Garrett Theological Seminary of Chicago, and Union Theological Seminary, New York, as well as at Temple Buell College and Iliff School of Theology in Denver. He was a leading founder of the National Fellowship of Methodist Musicians and served as its first president (1955-57). He is a past president of the Hymn Society in the United States and Canada and has served as a vice-president of the Choristers Guild. A respected author of books and journal articles, he has published over 600 compositions, including choral pieces, vocal solos, organ works, and hymn tunes.

Of particular significance are his *Music and Worship in the Church* (co-written with

William Rice, 1960; rev. and en., 1976) and *The Anatomy of Hymnody* (New York, 1965; Chicago, 1985).   *D.B., H.T.M.*

THREEFOLD GIFTS–442

Loveless, Wendell Phillips (b. Wheaton, IL, Feb. 2, 1892; d. Honolulu, HI, Oct. 3, 1987) was reared in Wheaton, a suburb of Chicago, where he attended the College Church (Congregational) but was disinterested in spiritual matters until his thirties. After being in business in Chicago, in 1914 he was selected as a member of a group of entertainers that toured the United States for six seasons providing training and experience as a vocalist, pianist, and master of ceremonies–all of which he later put to good use in Christian ministry. During World War I he was an officer in the Marine Corps. He became a Christian after he began to read the Bible seriously at home, seeking to become a better example for his family. He was employed by Moody Bible Institute in 1926, serving initially in the Extension Department. When MBI decided to begin radio broadcasting, he was selected to head station WMBI, serving in this capacity from 1926 to 1947, thus having opportunity to grow up with this new medium. Later he was pastor of several churches, including the Wheaton Free Church, the Boca Raton (Florida) Conference Church, and associate pastor of the First Chinese Church, Honolulu, Hawaii. He and his wife, Velma S. Loveless, have three sons: Robert C., David S., and Wendell P., Jr. The oldest son, Robert C. Loveless, collaborated with him on some of his songs such as the chorus "Every Day with Jesus" (1936). Loveless' publications include several Bible study books, a manual on Christian radio broadcasting, and five volumes of *Radio Songs and Choruses*.   *H.E.*

Lead Me to Some Soul Today–560

Lowden, Carl Harold (b. Burlington, NJ, Oct. 12, 1883; d. Collingswood, NJ, Feb. 27, 1963) was musically precocious as a child. He learned to play the violin as a child and played in the church orchestra. He began writing songs at the age of 12 and sold his first song to the Hall-Mack Company, where he was later employed. Lowden served for 12 years as musical editor for the Evangelical and Reformed Church, but resigned this position to enter private business in Camden, New Jersey. He taught music for 8 years at the Bible Institute of Pennsylvania and served as minister for 28 years at the Linden Baptist Church of Camden. He retired in 1861 and lived in Collingswood, New Jersey, until his death two years later.   *M.P.*

LIVING–282

Lowell, James Russell (b. Cambridge, MA, Feb. 22, 1819; d. Cambridge, MA, Aug. 12, 1891) came from a distinguished New England Lowell family which included lawyers, clergymen, and outstanding poets. After James Russell Lowell, there came Amy Lowell and Robert Lowell, all poets of the first rank. He attended Harvard but was suspended for neglecting his duties. After reinstatement, he graduated in 1838 and continued studies in law. He opened a law office in Boston, but because of so few clients, gave himself to reading and writing. In 1855, he succeeded Longfellow as professor of modern languages and literature at Harvard. Lowell was strongly anti-slavery and contributed many articles on the subject to periodicals. He edited *The Atlantic Monthly* (1857-62) and *The North American Review* (1863-72). He had a distinguished literary career and was Minister to Spain (1877-80).

From 1880-85, he served as Ambassador to Great Britain.   *S.W.G.*

Once to Every Man and Nation–470

Lowry, Robert (b. Philadelphia, PA, Mar. 12, 1826; d. Plainfield, NJ, Nov. 25, 1899) was educated at Bucknell University, graduating with honor in 1854. Following pastorates at West Chester, Pennsylvania, 1854-58, and New York City, 1859-61, he became pastor of the Hanson Place Baptist Church, Brooklyn, 1861-69. During his pastorate at Lewisburg, Pennsylvania, 1869-75, he was also professor of belles-lettres at Bucknell University and received the D.D. degree in 1875. He then became pastor of the Park Avenue Baptist Church, Plainfield, New Jersey, where he remained until his death. During his pastorate in Brooklyn he became intensely interested in writing hymns and tunes. He succeeded William B. Bradbury as editor of Sunday School song collections for Biglow and Main, New York, in 1868, and collaborated with William H. Doane in most of these publications. Among them are: *Happy Voices* (1865), *Gospel Melodies* (1868), *Bright Jewels* (1869), *Pure Gold* (1871), *Royal Diadem* (1873), *Temple Anthems* (1873), *Hymn Service* (1871, 1872, 1873), *Tidal Wave* (1874), *Brightest and Best* (1875), *Welcome Tidings* (1877), *Fountain of Song* (1877), *Chautauqua Carols* (1878), *Gospel Hymn and Tune Book* (1879), *Good as Gold* (1880), *Our Glad Hosanna* (1882), *Joyful Lays* (1884), and *Glad Refrain* (1886).   *W.J.R.*

ALL THE WAY–62
PLAINFIELD–What Can Wash Away
 My Sin–135
CHRIST AROSE–Low in the Grave He Lay–160
NEED–450
HANSON PLACE–Shall We Gather at the

River–518
MARCHING TO ZION–524
SOMETHING FOR JESUS–607

Luther, Martin (b. Eisleben, Saxony, Germany, Nov. 10, 1483; d. Eisleben, Saxony, Germany, Feb. 18, 1546) was the son of a copper miner. He studied at Magdeburg, Eisenach, and Erfurt (M.A. 1505). In 1505 he entered the Augustinian monastery at Erfurt, being ordained a priest in 1507. The following year he became a lecturer at the University of Wittenberg and began to preach. In 1512 he received the Doctor of Divinity degree from Wittenberg University. While on a trip to Rome (1509-10) Luther was shocked by the corruption of the clergy. His feelings came to a climax in 1517 when the Dominican monk Tetzel came through Saxony selling indulgences, which led to Luther's famous 95 theses or articles which he nailed to the door of the Wittenberg Castle Church. This marked the beginning of a long, open struggle with Rome, climaxing in his defense of his writings before the imperial Diet of Worms in 1521 during which he refused to recant. Luther translated the Bible into German, (1521-34). He prepared the way for the first German hymn book, the so-called "Achtliederbuch" (Nüremberg, 1524) of eight hymns, four of which were written by Luther. Luther's 37 hymns and paraphrases drew from several sources: Latin hymns, versification of the Psalms and other parts of Scripture, and revisions of pre-Reformation German hymns, plus his own originals. There is considerable uncertainty concerning which tunes Luther, a trained musician with a great love for music, actually composed. Riedel has shown how the tunes attributed to Luther were strongly influenced by the work of his contemporary Hans Sachs and the Meistersinger tradition. The vigorous rhythmic chorale melodies of Luther's century lost much of their vitality by the time they were harmonized in the eighteenth century by J.S. Bach. Thus much of the excitement of the early chorales of Luther and others is largely unknown to English-speaking congregations. Luther's greatest contribution to hymnody lay in the restoration of singing by the congregation. His thoughts on music and congregational song have been summarized by W.E. Buszin, *Musical Quarterly* (v. 32, 80-97), and his collected hymns are in volume 53 of *Luther's Works* (St. Louis and Philadelphia, 1955-).   *H.E.*

EIN' FESTE BURG–A Mighty Fortress Is
  Our God–8

Lutkin, Peter Christian (b. Thompsonville, WI, Mar. 27, 1858; d. Evanston, IL, Dec. 27, 1931) was a noted church musician and music educator. He received his first training in the Chicago Public Schools and at St. James' Cathedral Choir School. He studied in Europe from 1881-84. Upon his return to Chicago he served as organist-choirmaster at St. Clements (1884-91) and at St. James (1891-96) while also serving as a teacher of music theory at the American Conservatory of Music. In 1896 he became the first dean of Northwestern University's School of Music. He was a champion of church music, one of the founders of the American Guild of Organists, and a driving force in the Music Teacher's National Association, an organization he served as president in 1911 and again in 1920. He was a member of the editorial boards of the 1905 Methodist hymnal and the 1918 Episcopal hymnal. He composed hymn tunes, anthems, and instrumental works.   *D.B.*

BENEDICTION–662

Luttrell, Jo Beth Rice (b. Decatur, TX, Mar. 7, 1934) received a B.A. in English literature from Central State University, Edmond, Oklahoma. She was a member of the faculty at Central State University and associate editor of the *Home Mission* magazine. She serves as administrative assistant to her husband. She is a member of First Baptist Church of Griffin, Georgia, and is co-director of Children Four in Sunday School. She has written other hymn texts including "In the age of noise and turmoil" and numerous articles and books for children.   *S.W.G.*

We Meet Within This Holy Place–376

Lyall, Max (b. Tonkawa, OK, Feb. 14, 1939) has been a member of the faculty of Golden Gate Baptist Theological Seminary since 1974. There he is professor of church music. He had previously served on staff at Belmont College (now Belmont University, Nashville). Lyall was educated at Oklahoma Baptist University (B.M.), University of Oklahoma (M.M.), and Peabody Conservatory of Music (D.M.A.). He has done additional study at Teachers College of Columbia University and at the Juilliard School of Music.

From 1963 to 1966 he was assistant music director for the church music department of the Baptist Sunday School Board in Nashville. *Authentic Original* (1977), a collection of hymn-tune improvisations for piano, was his first record album. His second album, *Max, Rhythm, and Song*, was released in 1980.

Lyall has been pianist for meetings of the Southern Baptist Convention, Baptist World Alliance, and is a frequent performer as pianist, organist, and singer for

Broadman Press and Buryl Red Productions. He has toured Europe as accompanist for the Baptist Festival Singers (1982, 1985, 1988) and also for the Baptist Youth World Alliance in Argentina (1984). In addition, he has been piano and harpsichord soloist with the Nashville Symphony and Chamber Orchestras. He was honored by Oklahoma Baptist University with a "Profiles in Excellence" award in 1987. He is a member of ASCAP and is the accompanist for the Centurymen of the Southern Baptist Radio and Television Commission.

He has written and arranged a number of works appearing in Southern Baptist publications including *Favorite Hymns for the Piano, Music From Way Back When,* and *Klassics for Kids.* His hymn arrangements are also included in *A Heritage of Hymns....J.V.A.*

To The Light (arr.)–532

Lyon, Meyer (b. London (?), 1751; d. Kingston, Jamaica, 1797) was cantor in various London synagogues including the Great Synagogue in Dukes Place (1768-72). Because his powerful singing voice attracted Gentiles as well as Jews wherever he sang, Lyon had ambitions to sing in opera. However because of his unwillingness to sing on Friday nights or during religious high holy days, and because of his general lack of acting ability, he did not succeed in that field. In 1787 when the Ashkenazic (German and English) congregation in Kingston, Jamaica, needed a cantor for their new synagogue, Lyon took the position and remained there until his death. *H.T.M.*

Leoni (trans.)–34

Lyra Davidica, or a Collection of Divine Songs and Hymns, Partly New Composed, Partly Translated from the High German and Latin Hymns; and Set to Easy and Pleasant Tunes, was published in 1708 in London by J. Walsh. The compiler is unknown and it seems to have been a private venture with only a few copies being printed. The only surviving copy is in the British Museum. There were only 31 hymns and 25 tunes in its approximate 80 pages. Most of the tunes are probably English, nine of which may have been written for this work. Two were Latin melodies and there are nine German chorales. The compiler states his purpose in the Preface saying that the work was intended to introduce "a little freer air than the grave movement of the Psalmtunes, as being both seasonable and acceptable.... In Germany, where they have abundance of divine songs and hymns, set to short and pleasant tunes, the peasant at his plow, the servants at their labour, the children in the street... make use of these for the expression of their mirth; and have no such custom as we unhappily labour under, of ballads and profane songs" (Reynolds, 1976, 364). *S.W.G.*

Easter Hymn–159

Lyte, Henry Francis (b. Ednam, Roxburghshire, Scotland, Jun. 1, 1793; d. Nice, France, Nov. 20, 1847) studied at Portora Royal School, Enniskillen, Ireland, and received a B.A. degree from Trinity College, Dublin, in 1814. While at Trinity he received a prize for an English poem three times. After first considering a medical career, he was ordained in 1815. Following periods of service in the parishes of Wexford, Marazion, and Lymington, he was appointed curate at Lower Brixham, Devonshire, a fishing village where he served for 23 years. His physical condition was weakened in his later years because of asthma and tuberculosis. He died in Nice, France, after going to the continent for health reasons. Lyte's publications include *Tales on the Lord's Prayer* (1826); *Poems, Chiefly Religious* (1844), and *The Spirit of the Psalms* (1834).   M.P.

Praise, My Soul, the King of Heaven–32
Abide with Me–63
Jesus, I My Cross Have Taken–471

Macbean, Lachlan (b. Kiltarlity, Inverness-shire, Scotland, 1853; d. Kirkcaldy, Fifeshire, Scotland, Jan. 24, 1931) moved to Inverness at the age of 15 to pursue a business career. Owing to his interest in journalism, he joined the staff of *The Fifeshire Advertiser*, the newspaper at Kirkcaldy. He later became editor of that paper and also edited the *Kirkcaldy Burgh Records*. He published several books concerning the Scottish Highlands and was an advocate for the renewal of interest in the older Gaelic songs. His publications include *Lessons on Gaelic* and *Songs and Hymns of the Gael* (1888).   M.P.

Child in the Manger (tr.)–105

MacDonald, Mary McDougall (b. Ardtun, Isle of Mull, Argyllshire, Scotland, 1789; d. Isle of Mull, Argyllshire, Scotland, May 21, 1872) was a devout Baptist who wrote over 80 hymns and psalm paraphrases in Gaelic. Her brother, a Baptist preacher on the island of Mull, and her nephew also wrote Gaelic poetry. She was known by her neighbors for her joyful singing as she worked at her spinning wheel. Following her marriage to Neill MacDonald, a tenant farmer, she lived in the village of Cnocan on Mull.   M.P.

Child in the Manger–105

Mackay, William Paton (b. Montrose, Scotland, May 13, 1839; d. Portree, Scotland, Aug. 22, 1885) was educated at the University of Edinburgh and practiced medicine for a number of years. Feeling called to the ministry, he was ordained and became pastor of the Prospect Street Presbyterian Church, Hull, Scotland, in 1868. He wrote several hymns, 17 of which appeared in W. Reid's *Praise Book* (1872).   P.H.

Revive Us Again–469

MacMillan, Ernest (b. Mimico, Ontario, Canada, Aug. 18, 1893; d. Toronto, Canada, May 6, 1973) was the son of Dr. Alexander MacMillan, a Presbyterian minister and editor of the *Hymnary of The United Church of Canada* (1930) and author of its companion *Hymns of the Church* (1935). He was educated at the University of Toronto, University of Edinburgh, and Oxford University. Visiting in Germany at the outbreak of World War I, he was imprisoned and remained there for four years. After the war he returned to Canada and became conductor of the Toronto Symphony Orchestra and the Mendelssohn Choir. MacMillan served as dean of the music faculty, Toronto University, (1927-52), and he was also principal of the Music Conservatory. In 1935 he was knighted by King George V in recognition of his work as composer, teacher, conductor, and organist.   W.J.R.

Tempus Adest Floridum (arr.)–101

Main, Hubert Platt (b. Ridgefield, CT, Aug. 17, 1839; d. Newark, NJ, Oct. 7, 1925) was the son of Sylvester Main, a singing school teacher associated with I. B. Woodbury and William B. Bradbury in their publishing endeavors. He gained valuable experience through his association with Philip Phillips in Cincinnati and with the music firm of F. J. Huntington & Company, New York. In 1866 he assisted Phillips in the compilation of the *Methodist Episcopal Hymn and Tune Book*. In 1867 he accepted a position with the William B. Bradbury Company, New York. Following Bradbury's death the following year, the new firm of Biglow and Main was formed, with Sylvester Main as junior partner; this firm became Bradbury's successor. Young Main stayed with the new firm throughout his lifetime and, with few exceptions, was involved in some way–in the making, compiling, editing, proofreading, etc.–with every publication of the firm. Because of his intimate knowledge of music copyrights, his counsel was frequently sought by other publishers.

While he is credited with having written more than 1000 compositions, his greatest contribution to American hymnody was through his role as a publisher and hymnologist. His personal collection of old music books now is a part of the Newberry Library, Chicago, and is known as the Main Library. The publishing interests of Biglow and Main were purchased by the Hope Publishing Company in 1920.   *W.J.R.*

ELLESDIE (arr.)–471, 591

Maker, Frederick Charles (b. Bristol, England, 1844; d. Bristol, England, Jan. 1, 1927) was trained as a chorister in the cathedral at Bristol. He studied organ with Alfred Stone and later contributed seven hymn tunes to *The Bristol Tune Book* (1881 supplement), compiled by his former teacher. He was organist at the Milk Street Methodist Free Church, the Clifton Downs Congregational Church, and the Redland Park Congregational Church (1882-1910). For 27 years, he was visiting professor of music at Clifton College. He accompanied the Bristol Festival Choirs, directed by Alfred Stone, conducted the Bristol Free Church Choir Association, and composed hymn tunes, anthems, cantatas, and piano works.   *P.H.*

REST(ELTON)–267
ST. CHRISTOPHER–291

Malan, Henri Abraham César (b. Geneva, Switzerland, Jul. 7, 1787; d. Vandoeuvres, Switzerland, May 18, 1864) was the son of Jacques Imbert Malan, a professor at the College of Geneva, where César received his education. In 1810 he was ordained a minister in the Reformed Church and became pastor of the Chapelle du Temoignage in Geneva, where his preaching attracted large crowds. However, his outspoken criticism of the spiritually impoverished state of the national church led to his resignation from this position. He then built a chapel on his own property, where he preached for 43 years. He also made evangelistic preaching tours to France, Belgium, and the British Isles. Malan was the most important writer of hymns in the French language during the nineteenth century with over 1000 texts and tunes to his credit. His first collection, *Cantiques cretiens,* containing 35 hymns for domestic use, was published in 1823. In subsequent editions, most of which appeared under the title *Chants de Sion,* the number of hymns was increased to 300 (1836); the last edition was issued in 1855. He also published a book of hymns for children, *Soixante chants et chansons pieuses* (1837), which went through four editions, the last in 1853.   *D.M.*

HENDON–277, 538

Malotte, Albert Hay (b. Philadelphia, PA, May 19, 1895; d. Los Angeles, CA, Nov. 16, 1964), an American organist and song composer, became a member of the choir of St. James Episcopal Church and later studied with W.S. Stansfield and, in Paris, with Georges Jacob. He served as organist in Chicago and in London. He later moved to Hollywood and became a member of the music staff of the Walt Disney Studios where he composed the scores for some of Disney's "Silly Symphonies" and "Ferdinand, the Bull." He composed settings of the 23rd Psalm and other religious texts. His 1935 setting of "The Lord's Prayer" became enormously popular. *S.W.G.*

Malotte–462

Manly, Basil, Jr. (b. Edgefield County, SC, Dec. 19, 1825; d. Louisville, KY, Jan. 31, 1892), the son of Basil Manly, Sr. (who became pastor of the First Baptist Church, Charleston, South Carolina, and later the president of the University of Alabama), was educated at the University of Alabama (B.A. 1843), Newton Theological Center, Massachusetts, and Princeton Theological Seminary. Manly was licensed to preach in 1844 and in 1848 was ordained by the First Baptist Church, Tuscaloosa, Alabama.

After serving part-time at three churches in Alabama and Mississippi, he was called in 1850 to the pastorate of the First Baptist Church, Richmond, Virginia. After four years in that capacity, he resigned to become the founding president of the Richmond Female Institute. When The Southern Baptist Theological Seminary was founded in Greenville, South Carolina in 1859, he joined its first faculty. During the Civil War while the Seminary was inactive, Manly turned his attention to the establishment of the Sunday School Board

(1863) of which he was president.

In 1871 he became president of Georgetown College, Georgetown, Kentucky, but later rejoined the seminary faculty after the school had been moved to Louisville, Kentucky (1877). He had a distinguished career there as professor of Old Testament until his death.

Throughout his life Manly was deeply interested in hymnody. In a day when hymnology was a fledgling discipline in America, he was regarded as something of an authority in the field. He was dedicated to the goal of lifting the standard of musical worship among Baptists and served as critic and arbiter of the content of their hymnody through several compilations and contributions to various hymn collections.

Together with his father, he compiled the first "official" hymnal for Southern Baptists, *The Baptist Psalmody* (Charleston, 1850). He also compiled and published *Baptist Chorals* (Richmond, 1859), and *Manly's Choice* (Louisville, 1891). To these and other hymnals he contributed both texts and tunes in a variety of styles. His most widely published text was "Work for the Day Is Coming," which appeared in a hymnal as recently as 1950, but never in a Southern Baptist collection. His one hymn that endures among Southern Baptists is "Soldiers of Christ, in Truth Arrayed." *H.T.M.*

Soldiers of Christ, in Truth Arrayed–574

Mann, Arthur Henry (b. Norwich, England, May 16, 1850; d. Cambridge, England, Nov. 19, 1929) became a chorister at the cathedral in Norwich. He was educated at New College, Oxford (B.M., 1874; D.Mus., 1882). He was organist at St. Peter's, Wolverhampton in 1870, at Tettenhall Parish Church in 1871, and at Beverly Minster in

1875. For 53 years he was organist at King's College, Cambridge; a member of the Royal College of Organists; and a fellow of King's College. He was a composer, a collector of early hymn books, and was the musical editor of Charles D. Bell's *The Church of England Hymnal* (1895). He spent much time working with the manuscripts of George F. Handel. *S.W.G.*

ANGEL'S STORY–276

Mann, Newton (b. Cazenovia, NY, Jan. 16, 1836; d. Chicago, IL, Jul. 25, 1926) was a Unitarian minister. While he was a student at Cazenovia Seminary, the death of his father made it necessary for Mann to assume the family farming responsibilities. By his own efforts he learned five languages and was knowledgeable of the finest in literature. He became a Unitarian, but discovered that his liberal thinking was quite extreme, even for this fellowship. For a while he was principal of a school in Alton, Illinois, and later was superintendent of the Western Sanitary Commission's soldiers' home in Vicksburg, Mississippi. He returned north in 1865, was ordained to the ministry, and pastored Unitarian churches in Kenosha, Wisconsin; Troy and Rochester, New York; and Omaha, Nebraska. He was the author of *Natural History of the Jewish and Christian Scriptures* (1905) and *The Evolution of a Great Literature* (1906-09), and poems on religious and philosophical subjects. *W.J.R.*

The God of Abraham Praise (tr.)–34

March, Daniel (b. Millbury, MA, Jul. 21, 1816; d. Woburn, MA, Mar. 2, 1909), the son of Samuel and Zoa (Park) March, spent his childhood on his father's farm. He was educated at Millbury Academy, later

Amherst College (1834-36). He graduated from Yale University (1840), and became principal of Fairfield Academy in Connecticut (1840-43). He completed his theological studies at Yale, was ordained to the Congregational ministry in 1845, and became pastor in Cheshire, Connecticut. In addition to pastorates in Nashua and Brooklyn, New York, and Philadelphia, Pennsylvania, he was twice pastor at Woburn, Massachusetts (1856-64 and 1877-95). He traveled extensively and was greatly interested in missionary endeavors around the world. He was awarded the D.D. degree by Western University of Pennsylvania. "Hark, the Voice of Jesus Calling" seems to be the only hymn he ever wrote. *W.J.R.*

Hark, the Voice of Jesus Calling–591

Marsh, Charles Howard (b. Magnolia, IA, Apr. 8, 1886; d. La Jolla, CA, Apr. 12, 1956) was an accomplished organist and composer who served the last 20 years of his life as organist-choirmaster at St. James-by-the-Sea Episcopal Church, La Jolla, California. His parents immigrated from England a few months before Charles was born. His father pastored the Congregational Church in Magnolia, Iowa. Upon graduating from high school, J. Wilbur Chapman invited him to be pianist at Winona Lake (Indiana) Bible and Chautauqua Conference, where, in his early twenties, he wrote the tune CHAPMAN. After serving as both a private and conservatory teacher, he joined the faculties of the Bible Institute of Loas Angeles (1915-19) and the University of Redlands (1919-26). In the summer of 1924, he studied at the Fontainbleu Conservatory in France with organists Charles-Marie Widor and Henri Libert. During the years 1926 and 1928, Marsh returned to Paris to study with Isidor Philipp, Camille Decreaus, Marcel Dupre, and Nadia Boulanger. Upon his return to America, he became president of the European School of Music and Art, Fort Wayne, Indiana. He was appointed professor of organ in 1932 at Orlando (Florida) College of Music and later the University of Florida, Gainesville, where he also served as organist-choirmaster at First Baptist Church. From 1935-39 he was district supervisor of the Federal Music Project, San Diego, California, and organist-choirmaster in La Jolla from 1936 until his death. In addition to his accomplishments as an organist, (for which he earned a F.A.G.O. certificate) he was noted as a poet, painter, and composer of songs, anthems, and instrumental works.   *P.H.*

CHAPMAN–193

Marsh, Simeon Butler (b. Sherburne, NY, Jun. 1, 1798; d. Albany, NY, Jul. 14, 1875) grew up on a farm and had little musical training until he was 16, but at 19 began teaching in singing schools. In 1818 he attended a singing school conducted by Thomas Hastings who encouraged Marsh in his work. He conducted singing schools in the churches of Albany Presbytery for the next 30 years. He also taught voice, violin, and piano and was choir director and Sunday School superintendent in the Presbyterian church in Sherburne. He was also knowledgeable about editing, printing, and publishing. In 1837 he founded the *Intelligencer* in Amsterdam, New York, and edited it for seven years. Later he published the Sherburne *News* and set the type and layout for the three children's songbooks he published.   *S.W.G.*

MARTYN–180

Martin, Civilla Durfee (b. Jordan, Nova Scotia, Aug. 21, 1866; d. Atlanta, GA, Mar. 9, 1948) taught in village schools for several years and then studied music for a short time. Her husband, Walter Stillman Martin, was an evangelist, teacher, and pastor, and Mrs. Martin used her musical talents to help him. They collaborated on the writing of a number of gospel songs.   *S.W.G.*

God Will Take Care of You–64

Martin, George W. (b. London, England, Mar. 8, 1828; d. Wandsworth, Surrey, England, Apr. 16, 1881) was a chorister at St. Paul's Cathedral, London. He became professor of music in the Normal College for Army Schoolmasters, music-master in St. John's Training College, Battersea, and organist of Christ Church, Battersea. Composer of many glees, madrigals, and part-songs, he edited *The Journal of Part Music* (1861-62). The concerts of the Metropolitan Schools Choral Society under his direction had a high reputation.   *W.J.R.*

LEOMINSTER–339

Martin, Walter Stillman (b. Rowley, Essex County, MA, 1862; d. Atlanta, GA, Dec. 16, 1935) attended Harvard University. He was an ordained Baptist minister, but later joined the Christian Church (Disciples of Christ). He became professor of Bible at the Atlantic Christian College, North Carolina in 1916. He conducted Bible conferences and evangelistic meetings across the nation. His wife, Civilla Durfee Holde, a native of Nova Scotia, collaborated with him in the writing of a number of gospel songs. He moved to Atlanta, Georgia, in 1919 and lived there until his death.   *S.W.G.*

GOD CARES–64

Martinéz, Nicolás (b. Buenos Aires, Argentina, Oct. 7, 1917; d. Aug. 19, 1972) was born into a Roman Catholic family. While yet a youth, he embraced evangelical Christianity, studied in the Evangelical Faculty of Theology in Buenos Aires and did postgraduate study in Puerto Rico. In 1948 he was ordained in the Disciples of Christ Church and served as pastor in both Argentina (el Chaco) and Paraguay. An active promoter of ecumenical cultural activity in his community, he was one of the editors of *Cantico Nuevo* (Buenos Aires, 1962). Martinéz was the author and translator (into Spanish) of several hymn texts to be found both in *Cantico Nuevo* and *Himnario Bautista* (El Paso, 1978). *H.T.M.*

Christ Is Risen–167

Mason, Lowell (b. Medfield, MA, Jul. 8, 1792; d. Orange, NJ, Aug. 11, 1872) was directing a church choir and teaching singing schools at the age of 16. In 1812 he moved to Savannah, Georgia, and served there as a bank clerk until 1827. While there he studied harmony and composition with the German musician F. L. Abel and collaborated with him in compiling what was to become in 1822 the first edition of *The Boston Handel and Haydn Society Collection of Church Music*. The work was based on William Gardiner's *Sacred Melodies* and was sponsored by the Handel and Haydn Society. While in Savannah, he became a charter member of the First Independent Presbyterian Church and served there as organist for seven years and was active in Sunday School and mission society work. In 1827, he returned to Boston and served as choir director of Bowdoin Street Church where Lyman Beecher, father of Harriet Beecher Stowe, was minister. From 1827 until 1832 he was president and conductor of the

Boston Academy of Music. He set up the teacher training session in his academy and was successful in establishing music education in the public schools of Boston. He published numerous collections for church and school and contributed many original hymn tunes as well as adaptations and arrangements of tunes from other sources. In 1855, New York University conferred on him an honorary doctorate. *S.W.G.*

AZMON (arr.)–11, 216, 268
HARWELL–40
ANTIOCH (arr.)–87
HAMBURG–144, 374
HENDON (harm.)–277, 538
DENNIS (arr.)–375, 387
OLIVET–416
BETHANY–458

Matheson, George (b. Glasgow, Scotland, Mar. 27, 1842; d. North Berwick, Scotland, Aug. 28, 1906) was the son of a wealthy Glasgow merchant. Almost blind by the age of 18, he nevertheless was a brilliant student. His sisters learned Hebrew, Greek, and Latin in order to assist him. He was licensed to preach in 1866 and served churches in Glasgow and Innellan in Argyllshire. From 1886 to 1899 he was minister of St. Bernard's Church, Edinburgh. He was widely known as a preacher, lecturer, and author. Included in his works was one book of poems, *Sacred Songs* (1890). Because he was greatly respected and loved, the University of Edinburgh awarded him the D.D. degree in 1879. He received the LL.D. from the University of Aberdeen in 1902. *D.B.*

Make Me a Captive, Lord–278
O Love That Wilt Not Let Me Go–292

Matthews, Timothy Richard (b. Colmworth, Bedfordshire, England, Nov. 4, 1826; d. Tetney, Louth, Lincolnshire, England, Jan. 5, 1910) was educated at Caius College, Cambridge (B.A., 1853). He became a private tutor at Windsor and while there studied organ under George Elvey, with whom he enjoyed a lifelong friendship. Ordained in 1853, after a curacy at Nottingham, he became curate at North Cotes in 1859–ten years later becoming rector–where he remained until his retirement in 1907. He composed more than 100 hymn tunes and edited several collections of hymn tunes and organ music. *W.J.R.*

MARGARET–121

McAfee, Cleland Boyd (b. Ashley, MO, Sep. 25, 1866; d. Jaffrey, NH, Feb. 4, 1944) graduated from Park College, Parkville, Missouri, in 1884, and studied at Union Theological Seminary. He returned to Park College to teach, served as pastor of the college church, and directed the church choir. He entered pastoral work, serving the Forty-first Street (now First) Presbyterian Church, Chicago (1901-04), and the Lafayette Avenue Presbyterian Church, Brooklyn (1904-12), where a memorial plaque was placed in the sanctuary. At McCormick Theological Seminary, Chicago, he served as professor of systematic theology (1912-30), and was then elected secretary of the Presbyterian Board of Foreign Missions (1930-36). After retirement he made his home at Jaffrey, New Hampshire, but continued writing, preaching, and teaching. *W.J.R.*

MCAFEE–Near to the Heart of God–295

McClard, LeRoy (b. Cape Girardeau, MO, Mar. 18, 1926) was educated at Southeast Missouri State University, Oklahoma Baptist University (B.M.), and Southwestern Baptist Theological Seminary (B.C.M.). He served as minister of music at East Henderson Baptist Church, Cleburne, Texas (1948-50), Immanuel Baptist Church, Shawnee, Oklahoma (1950-52), and Immanuel Baptist Church, Little Rock, Arkansas (1952-55). He served two states as state music director–Arkansas Baptist State Convention (1955-63), and Illinois Baptist State Association (1964-66). He served in responsible leadership positions in the Church Music Department of the Baptist Sunday School Board, Nashville, Tennessee (1963-64; 1966-91). In retirement he makes his home in Franklin, Tennessee. *W.J.R.*

LORDSHIP OF CHRIST–Jesus Is Lord of All–296

McConnell, James Edwin (b. Atlanta, GA, Jan. 12, 1892; d. Newport Beach, CA, Jul. 24, 1954) was the son of J. Lincoln and Mary (White) McConnell. He attended Webb Preparatory School in Bell Buckle, Tennessee, and in September 1907, enrolled in the Academy Division of William Jewell College, Liberty, Missouri. He listed "Methodist" as his denominational preference. In the 1920s his father served as pastor of the First Baptist Church of Oklahoma City. McConnell had a successful career in radio as "Smilin' Ed." He hosted a popular children's program and "Hymn Time" carried by NBC. He also appeared on television. *D.B.*

MCCONNELL–"Whosoever" Meaneth Me–421

McCutchan, Robert Guy (b. Mt. Ayr, IA, Sep. 13, 1877; d. Claremont, CA, May 15, 1958) attended Park College, Parkville, Missouri (1893-94), and Simpson College, Indianola, Iowa (B. M., 1904). After graduation he accepted a position as voice instructor at Baker University in Baldwin, Kansas, eventually becoming chair of the music department. He remained at Baker until 1910, when he resigned to do additional study in Germany. He returned to the United States late in 1910 to take up duties as Dean of the School of Music at DePauw University, Greencastle, Indiana. He remained at DePauw until his retirement to Claremont, California, in 1937. In addition to his administrative and teaching responsibilities, McCutchan served on the Commission on Church Music of the Methodist Episcopal Church (1924-28), the Joint Commission for the Revision of the Methodist Hymnal (1928-35), and, after his retirement, the General Conference Committee on Music of the Methodist Episcopal Church. He was music editor of the *American Junior Church and School Hymnal* (1928), *Standard Hymns and Gospel Songs* (1929), and editor of *The Methodist Hymnal* (1935). His writings on church music and hymnology included *Better Music in Our Churches* (1925), *Music in Worship* (1927), *Our Hymnody: A Manual of The Methodist Hymnal* (1937), *Hymns in the Lives of Men* (1945), *Hymn Tune Names* (1957), and numerous articles in magazines, journals, dictionaries, and encyclopedias. He collected a valuable personal library of over 3,000 volumes on church music and hymnody, which was donated to the Claremont College Graduate School, where it is housed in the Honnold Library.   *D.M.*

ALL THE WORLD–28
SPRING–50

McDaniel, Rufus Henry (b. near Ripley, Brown County, OH, Jan. 29, 1850; d. Dayton, OH, Feb. 13, 1940) attended school at Bentonville, Ohio, and at Parker's Academy,

Claremont County, Ohio. At the age of 19 he was licensed to preach and, in 1873, was ordained to the ministry of the Christian Church. He served in the Southern Ohio Conference of the Christian Church as a pastor of churches in Hamersville, Higginsport, Centerburg, and Sugar Creek. McDaniel wrote over 100 hymns.   *D.M.*

Since Jesus Came into My Heart–441

McDonald, William (b. Belmont, ME, Mar. 1, 1820; d. Monrovia, CA, Sep. 11, 1901) was of Scottish descent. He was a member of the Maine Conference of the Methodist Episcopal Church (1843), transferring later to the Wisconsin Conference (1855) and then to the New England Conference (1859). (See *Wesleyan Sacred Harp*).   *D.B.*

HAPPY DAY–439

McElrath, Hugh Thomas (b. Murray, KY, Nov. 13, 1921) was educated at Murray State University (B.A.), The Southern Baptist Theological Seminary (B.S.M., M.S.M.) and the Eastman School of Music, the University of Rochester (Ph.D.). He also pursued sabbatical studies in Bologna, Italy; Oxford, England; and Zürich, Switzerland. In the first class to be graduated from the School of Church Music of The Southern Baptist Seminary, he joined its faculty in 1948, becoming the V. V. Cooke Professor of Church Music in 1986. His teaching areas have included music history, hymnology, worship, voice, vocal and choral literature, and ministry formation.

A member of The Music Teachers National Association, the National Association of Teachers of Singing, the Sonneck Society (American Music), and the American Musicological Society, McElrath is also a world traveler, having spent sabbatic leaves throughout the world, lecturing, holding workshops, singing recitals, and leading in musical worship. He has been active in the work of the Southern Baptist Church Music Conference, having served intermittently through the years as executive council member, vice-president, and editor of its journal. In 1987-89 he was President of the conference, and in 1992 was the recipient of the Hines Sims Award, the highest honor granted by the Conference to those who are judged to have made significant contributions in the field of church music. In 1988 McElrath was recognized by the Southern Baptist Church Music Department, the State Baptist Music Secretaries, and the music deans of the Baptist seminaries for outstanding service as a music educator and "Musician on Mission."

Since the 1940's, McElrath has been a practicing church musician, having served churches in North Carolina and Kentucky. For 22 years (1955-77) he and his wife, Ruth, were co-ministers of music at the Beechwood Baptist Church in Louisville.

A frequent contributor to denominational and scholarly periodical literature, Dr. McElrath is the author of several books on hymnody and related areas. The co-author, with Dr. Harry Eskew, of *Sing with Understanding* (Nashville, 1980), a widely used textbook in hymnology, he was also the coordinating editor for this volume, *Handbook to The Baptist Hymnal* (Nashville, 1992). He was member of the hymnal committees for both *Baptist Hymnal* (1975) and *The Baptist Hymnal* (1991), serving on theological and doctrinal evaluation subcommittees. Also active in the affairs of The Hymn Society in the United States and Canada, McElrath has worked on its executive and research committees and in 1991 was made a Fellow of the Society.   *H.T.M.*

We Praise You with Our Minds, O Lord–599

McElrath, William Nold (b. Murray, KY, Mar. 1, 1932) was educated at Murray State University (B.A.) and The Southern Baptist Theological Seminary (M. Div., Th. M.). He was editor of older children's Bible study materials, Baptist Sunday School Board, Nashville, Tennessee (1959-64). Since 1965, he has been a missionary under appointment of the Southern Baptist Foreign Mission Board, helping produce literature and train writers and editors in developing countries–especially in Indonesia, where he and his wife live in Bandung, West Java. He has written more than 60 books in two languages, besides other hymns, songs, librettos for music dramas, and hundreds of articles, stories, and church curriculum materials. Some of his better-known published works include *A Bible Dictionary for Young Readers*; *Bible Guidebook*; *Music in Bible Times*; *Judges and Kings: God's Chosen Leaders*; *Sing His Song Around the Earth*; *Oz and Mark Quick: Taiwan Team-mates*; *Bold Bearers of His Name: Forty World Mission Stories*; and the practical learning exercises in *Survival Kit for New Christians*.   *H.T.M.*

SPRINGBROOK–The First Lord's Day–162

McFarland, John Thomas (1851-1913) is the name of an individual who has been erroneously connected with the text of the Christmas song "Away in a Manger." See the article on "Away in a Manger." *H.T.M.*

Away in a Manger (st. 3)–103

McGee, Bob (b. Vancouver, British Columbia, Canada, Jun. 18, 1949) graduated from Glad Tidings Bible College, Vancouver, in 1971. He has served as a pastor for the Vineyard Churches for many years. *D.M.*

McGee–Emmanuel–82

McGranahan, James (b. near Adamsville, PA, Jul. 4, 1840; d. Kinsman, OH, Jul. 7, 1907) was an evangelistic song leader and composer of gospel songs. He received musical training through singing schools and, by age 19, was conducting his own classes. While attending Bradbury's Normal Music School at Genesco, New York (1861-62), he became friends with P.P. Bliss. He became the musical associate of professor J.G. Towner in 1862. In 1875 he studied under Frederick W. Root and became a teacher and director of George F. Root's National Normal Institute for three summers. P.P. Bliss urged him to take up mass evangelism. After Bliss' death, McGranahan joined D.W. Whittle in 1877, and the pair spent 11 years together. They toured Great Britain twice in 1880 and in 1883. He wrote tunes for Whittle's texts and pioneered the use of men's choruses in his meetings. He became an editor with Ira D. Sankey and George Stebbins of *Gospel Hymns and Sacred Songs* (1878-1891; Nos. 3-6). When his health declined in 1887, he gave up active evangelistic work and settled in Kinsman, Ohio. In addition to the *Gospel Hymns* series, his compilations include *The Gospel Male Choir* (1878, 1883), *The Choice, Harvest of Song* (with C.C. Case), and *Gospel Choir* (with Ira D. Sankey). *P.H.*

El Nathan–337
Showers of Blessing–467
Neumeister–563
My Redeemer–575

McHugh, Phillip (Phill) James (b. Aberdeen, SD, Apr. 25, 1951) is a writer of contemporary Christian songs whose works have been recorded by Steve Green, Larnelle Harris, Sandi Patti, Scott Wesley Brown, and others. His songs "Lamb of Glory" and "People Need the Lord" were nominated for Dove Awards in 1985 and 1986 respectively, and he has received numerous other award nominations. Phill became associated with the River Oaks Music company in 1983 and entered a long-term exclusive songwriting agreement with River Oaks in 1987. *D.M.*

Name of the Lord–In the Name of the Lord–174
People Need the Lord–People Need the Lord–557

McIntosh, Rigdon McCoy (b. Maury County, TN, Apr. 3, 1836; d. Atlanta, GA, Jul. 4, 1899) was the son of Hector and Nancy (Biggs) McIntosh. He was educated at Jackson College, Columbia, Tennessee. He received his musical training under L. C. and Asa B. Everett, with whom he was associated for several years in composing and editing music books, and in teaching both singing schools and normal music schools throughout the South. He was married to Sarah (Sallie) McGlasson of Farmville, Virginia, through whose influence he was converted and joined the Methodist Episcopal Church, South.

In 1875 he was appointed to the faculty of Vanderbilt University, Nashville. Two years later he joined the faculty of Emory College, Oxford, Georgia. Owing mainly to poor health, he resigned his teaching position in 1895. He then devoted his time exclusively to his previously established firm, the R. M. McIntosh Company. In the 1870s and 1880s, he edited a number of

Sunday School songbooks and hymnals for the Methodist Episcopal Church, South. McIntosh was one of the most prominent musicians in the southern states during his time, excelling as a choral director, teacher, composer, and editor. His collections for church and Sunday School include *Tabor* (1866), *Glad Tidings* (1867), *Amaranth* (1871), *Emerald* (1872), *The Gem* (1873), *Hermon* (1873), *A Collection of Hymns and Tunes for Public, Social, and Domestic Worship* (1874), *Good News* (1876), *New Life* (1879), *Life and Light* (1881), *Prayer and Praise* (1883), *New Life No. 2* (1886), *Christian Hymns* (1889), *Pure Songs* (1890), *Living Songs* (1892), *Words of Truth* (1892), *McIntosh's Anthems* (1894) *Gospel Grace* (1895), and *Songs of Service* (1897). Several of these collections were co-edited with Atticus Haygood or W.G.E. Cunnyngham, Sunday School secretaries for the Methodist Episcopal Church, South. Two pseudonyms used by McIntosh were Emilius Laroche and Franz Volk. Three texts of Mrs. M.B.C. Slade with music by McIntosh were published in *The Broadman Hymnal* (1940): "The Kingdom Is Coming," "Gathering Home," and "Tell It Again."   *H.E.*

PROMISED LAND (arr.)–521

McKay, John (b. Turkey, TX, Feb. 27, 1934) is the son of David Lee and Fannie Collins McKay. His father died the day after his first birthday, and John was sent to live with his maternal grandparents. At age nine, they moved to Ft. Worth, Texas, where he continues to reside. He became a Christian at age 13 and made a decision for full-time Christian ministry at age 15. Winning an athletic scholarship to Texas Christian University, Ft. Worth, he received All-Southwest Conference honors during his freshman year. The next year he transferred

to North Texas State University School of Music to prepare for a vocal ministry. He was baritone soloist with the A Cappella Choir and won a full scholarship to Julliard School of Music but declined so he could pursue a ministry in church music. Upon graduation, he served for five years in local church music ministries. In 1961 McKay entered into a full-time evangelistic singing ministry, teaming with James Robison in 1965. They conducted over 450 crusades together, which included a televised program, "James Robison Presents." John has more than 15 albums to his credit.

In May 1985 McKay received an honorary doctor of letters degree from Dallas Baptist University, Dallas, Texas. Since 1984, he has served as the music director for the annual meetings of the Southern Baptist Convention. In addition, he serves as a trustee of Southwestern Baptist Theological Seminary and as director of Spiritual Awakening Conferences based in Ft. Worth.

McKay is married to Julia Leslie McKay, and they have five children–one daughter and four sons. *J.V.A.*

McKAY–Tune Your Hearts That All May Hear–578

McKinney, Baylus Benjamin (b. Heflin, LA, Jul. 22, 1886; d. Bryson City, NC, Sep. 7, 1952) was educated at Southwestern Baptist Theological Seminary, Siegel-Myers Correspondence School of Music (B.M., 1922), and Bush Conservatory, Chicago. In 1942 he was awarded the Mus. D. degree by Oklahoma Baptist University, Shawnee, Oklahoma.

For more than a decade, McKinney taught voice, conducting, and theory as a member of the music faculty of Southwestern Baptist Theological Seminary, Ft. Worth, Texas. In addition to teaching responsibilities, he served as music editor for the Dallas firm of Robert H. Coleman (1918-35) as well as director of music in various churches. From 1915 onward he pursued an active career of composing hymns and songs for church and evangelistic use.

During the economic depression of the early 1930's, he resigned his position at the seminary to become assistant pastor and director of music at the Travis Avenue Baptist Church, Ft. Worth (1931-35). In 1935 he became the first music editor of the Baptist Sunday School Board and in 1941 the first secretary of the newly established Church Music Department. In this position McKinney continued to write songs and to compile hymnals, notably *The Broadman Hymnal* (1940). He organized and promoted the Church Music Emphasis Weeks at Ridgecrest Baptist Assembly (from 1941), fostered the establishment of Church Music Departments with secretaries in the state Baptist conventions (from 1944), inaugurated and developed the Church Music Training Course (from 1946) and served as the first music editor of *The Church Musician* periodical (from 1950).

Throughout his career McKinney published over 500 works, including both words and music for nearly 180 compositions and the tunes for 185 in addition to the texts for 16 others. The greater parts of his output were original hymns and gospel songs, but he was also arranger, adapter, and editor of numerous items for solo, duet, quartet, and choir. The great popularity of his songs reflects his sensitivity to the musical tastes and spiritual needs of a broad spectrum of Southern Baptists. For years McKinney was widely known for his inspiring leadership of congregational singing, being in constant demand as a director of music for revivals. Before his untimely death by automobile accident while returning from the 1952 Church Music Leadership Week at Ridgecrest Baptist Assembly, he was generally considered as the archtypical "Mr. Southern Baptist Church Music." Two years after his death, the B. B. McKinney Research Foundation was established at Oklahoma Baptist University to be a repository for his papers and a center for studies in Southern Baptist church music. *H.T.M.*

GLORIOUS NAME–Glorious Is Thy Name–204
TRUETT–Breathe on Me (adapt.)–238
IVERSON (arr.)–244
HOLCOMB–Speak to My Heart–281
FALLS CREEK–Wherever He Leads I'll Go–285
LUBBOCK–The Nail-Scarred Hand–318
ALTAR–All on the Altar–326
MUSKOGEE–Have Faith in God–405
TRAVIS AVENUE–Send a Great Revival–466
MATTHEWS–Lord, Send a Revival–468
ROUTH–Satisfied with Jesus–472
LEE–Serve the Lord with Gladness–495
CHRISTIAN HOME–God, Give Us
    Christian Homes–504
BY AND BY (alt. and arr.)–When the
    Morning Comes (alt. and arr.)–522
LEILA–Lord, Lay Some Soul upon My
    Heart (st. 2,3)–570
COLEMAN–Let Others See Jesus in You–571

Medema, Ken (b. Grand Rapids, MI, Dec. 7, 1943) received his bachelor's degree in music from Michigan State University (1965). Following his marriage, he and his wife Jane Smith moved to Indiana where they both worked in a state hospital as music therapists. Further study at Michigan State University led to a master's degree in music therapy (1969), after which the Medemas moved to New Jersey, where Ken continued his career as a music therapist and first began seriously composing Christian songs. Since January 1, 1973, Ken has dedicated himself to full-time composition and performing of contemporary Christian music. Though blind from birth, Medema has toured extensively in the United States and many other countries as a vocalist and performer on piano and synthesizer. His compositions include numerous popular Christian songs, including "Lord, Listen to Your Children Praying," "And This Is Love," and "Come, Let Us Reason." Reared in the Christian Reformed tradition, Medema is currently a member of the Dolores Street Baptist Church, San Francisco, California. Ken and his wife are the parents of two children. *D.M.*

Come, Let Us Reason–Come, Let Us Reason–313

Mendelssohn-Bartholdy, Jacob Ludwig Felix (b. Hamburg, Germany, Feb. 3, 1809; d. Leipzig, Germany, Nov. 4, 1847) was born into the banking family of Abraham and Lea Mendelssohn. His grandfather was the renowned philosopher Moses Mendelssohn. In 1811 the family was forced to flee to Berlin to escape persecution by French occupation forces. The cultural life of Berlin and the influence of Felix's mother nurtured the prodigious talents of the boy. The family was baptized into the Christian faith in 1816 (the father in 1822) and adopted the name Bartholdy from the name of family property. He debuted as a pianist at age nine and had composed several works by age 12. Mendelssohn's most popular work, *A Midsummer Night's Dream*, was first performed in 1827. At age 20 he conducted a revival of Bach's *St. Matthew Passion*, which stimulated interest once again in the works of the Baroque master.

Mendelssohn traveled widely as a performer and conductor and became ac-

quainted with notable musicians and literary figures, especially Goethe. In 1835 he was named conductor of the Leipzig Gewandhaus orchestra. He married in 1837, and from a happy relationship were born three sons and two daughters. He was instrumental in founding the Leipzig Conservatory in 1840. In addition to his symphonies, overtures, chamber music, concertos, organ and piano works, Mendelssohn is known for two oratorios, *St. Paul* (1840) and *Elijah* (1846). *P.H.*

Mendelssohn–88
Nun Danket (harm.)–638
Almighty Father–656

Merrill, William Pierson (b. Orange, NJ, Jan. 10, 1867; d. New York City, NY, Jun. 19, 1954) was converted at age 11. He received his A.B. (1887) and M.A. (1890) degrees from Rutgers College and his B.D. (1890) from Union Theological Seminary. Merrill was ordained to the Presbyterian ministry in 1890. He served churches in Philadelphia and Chicago before becoming pastor of the Brick Presbyterian Church, New York City (1911-38). He published several hymns and ten books, including *Footings for Faith* (1915), *Christian Internationalism* (1919), *The Common Creed of Christians* (1920), *The Freedom of the Preacher* (1922), *Liberal Christianity* (1925), *Prophets of the Dawn* (1927), *The Way* (1933), and *We See Jesus* (1934). From 1915, he was president of the trustees of the Church Peace Union. *P.H.*

Rise Up, O Men of God–400

Messiter, Arthur Henry (b. Frome, Somersetshire, England, Apr. 12, 1834; d. New York, NY, Jul. 2, 1916) came to this country in 1863 and for a while sang as a volunteer in the choir of Trinity Episcopal Church, New York City. His education, which had all been from private tutors, included four years of music study in Northampton. After a brief period of service as church organist in Vermont and then in Philadelphia, he returned to Trinity Church in 1866 and began a distinguished 31-year career as organist-choirmaster. His choir of men and boys was considered one of the finest in the country. He composed several anthems, edited a music edition of the *Hymnal, 1893*, edited a *Psalter* (1889), and in 1906 wrote *A History of the Choir and the Music of Trinity Church. D.B.*

Marion–39, 226

Mieir, Audrey Mae (b. Leechburg, PA, May 12, 1916) was educated at L.I.F.E. Bible College. In 1936 she married Charles B. Mieir and in 1937 was ordained to the gospel ministry in the International Church of Foursquare Gospel. From 1937 until 1945, she was an evangelistic pianist in radio and personal appearances. From 1946 until 1958 she organized various choirs and in 1959 was director of Mieir Choir Clinics in Hollywood, California. The following year she became vice-president of Mieir Music Foundation Incorporated in Hollywood. *S.W.G.*

Mieir–His Name Is Wonderful–203

Miles, C. Austin (b. Lakehurst, NJ, Jan. 7, 1868; d. Pitman, NJ, Mar. 10, 1946) was educated at the Philadelphia College of Pharmacy and the University of Pennsylvania, and was a pharmacist for several years. After writing his first gospel song and submitting it to the Hall-Mack Publishing Company of Philadelphia, he abandoned

pharmacy to work for the music publisher. For 37 years he was employed by the Hall-Mack Publishing Company as editor and manager, and when the firm merged with the Rodeheaver Company to become Rodeheaver-Hall-Mack, he continued in an editorial capacity. During these years he was a well-known music director in churches, camp meetings and conventions. *W.J.R.*

Garden–In the Garden–187

Miller, Rhea Florence (b. North Syracuse, NY, Mar. 5, 1894; d. Kankakee, IL, Mar. 2, 1966) was born Rhea Florence Ross. In 1912 she became a member of the Main Street Baptist Church in Binghampton, New York. She attended Binghampton Central High School, graduating in 1912. In 1917 she was married to Howard Vassar Miller (1894-1948), who had been ordained to the Baptist ministry a week before his wedding. In 1922 they became members of the Church of the Nazarene, in which denomination he served as pastor of churches in Connecticut, New York, and Illinois, and then became dean of the School of Religion at Northwest Nazarene College, Nampa, Idaho. From 1940 to 1948 he was general superintendent of the Church of the Nazarene, the highest office of his denomination, traveling extensively throughout the United States, Canada, and the British Isles. Mrs. Miller, a pianist, traveled with her husband and played during meetings in which he spoke. She attended the Ithaca College Conservatory in 1931 and 1932. Rhea Miller composed words and music to several hymns and choruses. She served for many years as a member of the General Missionary Council of the Church of the Nazarene. The Millers had two daughters, Lois Caroll, who died at birth, and Elizabeth, who married Robert Quanstrom, a Nazarene minister. Rhea Florence Miller is buried in Quick Cemetery, Brooktondale, New York.   *H.E.*

I'd Rather Have Jesus–550

Miller, William is an individual whose identity (even existence) is in doubt. See article on "O land of rest, for thee I sigh." *H.T.M.*

O LAND OF REST–608

Millhuff, Charles (Chuck) (b.Chicago, IL, Mar. 9, 1938) was educated at Olivet Nazarene University (A.B.) and Nazarene Theological Seminary (B.D.). He received the honorary D.D. from Mid-America Nazarene College, Olathe, Kansas. An ordained elder in the Church of the Nazarene, he has been involved in evangelistic endeavors throughout the nation, preaching in churches, on radio, and television. He has been blessed with the gift of evangelism and uses it effectively. The author of four books, and one evangelistic musical, *New World*, he makes his home in Olathe, Kansas.   *W.J.R.*

The King Is Coming (collaborator)–194

Mills, Elizabeth (1805-29) is a person whose identity is unknown and whose connection with the song "We'll Work Till Jesus Comes" is highly questionable. See the article on this song entitled "O land of rest, for thee I sigh!"   *H.E.*

We'll Work Till Jesus Comes–608

Mohr, Joseph (b. Salzburg, Austria, Dec. 11, 1792; d. Wagrein, Austria, Dec. 4, 1848), as a boy, was a chorister in the cathedral choir at Salzburg. Ordained a priest in the Roman Catholic Church in 1815, he served

as assistant priest at St. Nicholas Church, Oberndorf, 1817-19, where he wrote the carol that made him famous. Following several other appointments, he became vicar at Hintersee in 1828 and at Wagrein, near St. Johann, in 1837, where he remained until his death.   *W.J.R.*

Silent Night, Holy Night–91

Monk, William Henry (b. St. George Hanover Square, Middlesex, England, Mar. 16, 1823; d. Stoke Newington, London, England, Mar. 1, 1889) served as organist at three London area churches (Eaton Chapel, Pimlico; St. George's Chapel, Albemarle Street; Portman Chapel, Marylebone) before being appointed choir director at King's College, London, in 1847. From 1852 until his death he was organist at St. Matthias Church, Stoke Newington, where he promoted congregational singing and established a daily choral service. In addition to his church appointments, he also held positions as professor of vocal music at King's College, London, and professor of music at the School for the Indigent Blind, the National Training School for Music, and Bedford College, London. Monk is perhaps most significant for his work as music editor for several hymnals, including the 1861, 1875, and 1889 editions of *Hymns Ancient and Modern*. For those editions he composed 50 hymn tunes. He also edited the *Parish Choir* from 1840-51. Monk was awarded the Doctor of Music degree from Durham University in 1882.   *M.P.*

DIX (adapt.)–44, 117
EVENTIDE–63
INNOCENTS–104
ASCENSION–165
VICTORY (adapt.)–172

Monsell, John Samuel Bewley (b. St. Columb's, Londonderry, Ireland, Mar. 2, 1811; d. Guildford, Surrey, England, Apr. 9, 1875) received the B.A. degree from Trinity College, Dublin, in 1832 and was ordained in 1834. He had several appointments in Ireland and then went to England where, in 1853, he became vicar of Egham, Surrey. In 1870 he became rector at St. Nicholas, Guildford where he was accidentally killed when repairs were being made to the roof of the church. He was an ardent advocate of congregational singing, pleading that our hymns be "more fervent and joyous. We are too distant and reserved in our praises; we sing, not as we should sing to Him who is Chief among ten thousand, the Altogether Lovely." He wrote nearly 300 hymns which were published in his 11 volumes of poetry.   *S.W.G.*

Worship the Lord (st. 1)–115
Sing to the Lord of Harvest–641

Montgomery, James (b. Irvine, Ayrshire, Scotland, Nov. 4, 1771; d. Sheffield, Yorkshire, England, Apr. 30, 1854) was the son of a Moravian minister. At the age of seven he was left at the Brethren ministry at Fulneck when his parents went to Barbados as missionaries. He remained at Fulneck until 1787. For several years he tried a variety of jobs before settling in Sheffield in 1792, where he was employed by Joseph Gales, an auctioneer, bookseller, and printer of the *Sheffield Register* newspaper. In 1794 Gales left England to avoid political prosecution, following which Montgomery began to operate the *Register* and changed its name to *The Sheffield Iris*. During this 31 years editing the *Iris* he was imprisoned twice, once for reprinting a song in commemoration of the fall of the Bastille and once for writing about a riot in Sheffield.

Montgomery was a strong advocate for foreign missions and the British Bible Society. He also strongly supported the singing of hymns in Anglican worship, and became involved in the controversy over the hymnal compiled by Thomas Cotterill first published in 1810. The hymnal finally was approved for use in 1820, advancing the cause of hymn singing in the Church of England.

He lectured on poetry in Sheffield and at the Royal Institution, London. He wrote approximately 400 hymns (including Psalm versions), which were published in his *Songs of Zion* (1822), *The Christian Psalmist* (1825), and *Original Hymns for Public, Private, and Social Devotion* (1853).   *M.P.*

Stand Up and Bless the Lord–30
Angels, from the Realms of Glory–94
Go to Dark Gethsemane–150
Songs of Praise the Angels Sang–235
According to Thy Gracious Word–372
Forever with the Lord–529

Moody, May Whittle (b. Chicago, IL, Mar. 20, 1870; d. Northfield, MA, Aug. 20, 1963), the daughter of Daniel W. and Abbie Hanson Whittle, was educated in the Girls' School, Northfield, Massachusetts, Oberlin College (1888-89), and the Royal Academy of Music, London (1890-91). She was a gifted singer. In many of her father's meetings, she appeared as a soloist and sang duets with her mother. In 1894 she married Will R. Moody, eldest son of the evangelist. In Northfield, she lived a long and fruitful life, dying there in 1963 at the age of 93.   *W.J.R.*

WHITTLE–415

Moore, Thomas (b. Dublin, Ireland, May 28, 1779; d. Chittoe, Wiltshire, England,

Feb. 25, 1852) had a dual career in government service and as a writer. Following his education at Trinity College, Dublin, and Middle Temple, London (where he studied law), he went to Bermuda in 1804 as registrar to the Admiralty Court. Because he found the position to be monotonous, he appointed a deputy and returned to England. When the deputy embezzled funds, Moore went into temporary exile and did not return to England until the indebtedness was repaid in 1822. He was a prolific writer whose publications included *A Selection of Irish Melodies* (1807-34) and *Sacred Songs* (1816). Thirty-two of his hymns appeared in the latter collection.   *M.P.*

Come, Ye Disconsolate–67

Moore, William. Little information has come to light regarding this composer. In 1825 he published a four-shape-note tune-book, *The Columbian Harmony*, the preface of which placed him in Wilson County, Tennessee. In the 1820's Wilson County was home to at least four men bearing the name William Moore, any one of whom could have been the tunebook compiler.

While *The Columbian Harmony* apparently did not achieve enough popularity to merit a second edition, several of the tunes which were credited to "Moore" and received their first printing in this book became widely used in later shape-note tunebooks.   *D.M.*

Holy Manna–379, 382, 618

Morris, Lelia Naylor (b. Pennsville, OH, Apr. 15, 1862; d. Auburn, OH, Jul. 23, 1929) moved with her family to Malta, Ohio, following her father's return from the Civil War in 1866. After her father's death, she, her mother, and a sister opened a millinery shop in McConnelsville. She married Charles H. Morris in 1881, changing her membership from the Methodist Protestant Church to the Methodist Episcopal Church to be with her husband. Both she and Mr. Morris were active in their church and in camp meetings.

Encouraged by Henry L. Gilmour, Mrs. Morris began writing gospel songs in the 1890's. Her eyesight began to fail in 1913 and she became totally blind within a year. Nevertheless, she continued to write, ultimately producing over 1,000 hymn texts, for many of which she also wrote the music.   *D.M.*

Second Coming–What If It Were Today–195
McConnelsville–Let Jesus Come into Your Heart–311

Mote, Edward (b. London, England, Jan. 21, 1797; d. Horsham, Sussex, England, Nov. 13, 1874) was neglected by his parents, who managed a London pub, so he grew up in the streets of London. As a youth, he was apprenticed to a cabinet-maker. He came under the influence of the preaching of Rev. John Hyatt at the Tottenham Court Road Chapel in 1813 and was baptized in 1815 at another church, pastored by Rev. John Bayley. Mote settled at Southwark, a suburb of London, where he became a successful cabinetmaker and also earned money writing for the press. In 1852 he became pastor of the Baptist Church in Horsham, Sussex, which he served for 21 years. It is said that he did not miss a worship service during his lengthy pastorate there. He resigned in 1873, due to ill health, and died the following year.

Mote wrote approximately 100 hymns and included them in his *Hymns of Praise, A New Selection of Gospel Hymns, Combining*

All the Excellencies of Our Spiritual Poets, with many Originals (London, 1836). This collection, which contained 606 hymns from various sources, may have been the first to use the term "gospel hymn." *M.P.*

The Solid Rock–406

Moultrie, Gerard (b. Rugby, Warwickshire, England, Sep. 16, 1829; d. Southleigh, Oxfordshire, England, Apr. 25, 1885) was the son of an Anglican minister, the Reverend John Moultrie. According to Armin Haeussler, his great-grandfather Moultrie, a native of South Carolina, went back to England from South Carolina after the outbreak of the Revolutionary War. Fort Moultrie at Charleston, South Carolina, was named for General William Moultrie, a great-granduncle, who served two terms as governor of South Carolina in 1785-87 and 1792-94. Gerard Moultrie was educated at Rugby and Exeter College, Oxford (B.A., 1851; M.A., 1856) and became assistant master and chaplain of Shrewsbury School, 1852-55. After various chaplaincies, he became vicar of Southleigh in 1869 and warden of St. James' College, 1873, where he remained until his death. He is the author of much religious verse and numerous hymns, including translations from Greek, Latin, and German. Among his publications are *Hymns and Lyrics for the Seasons and Saints' Days of the Church* (1867) and *Cantica Sanctorum* (1880). *W.J.R.*

Let All Mortal Flesh Keep Silence (tr.)–80

Mountain, James (b. New Wortley, Yorkshire, England, Jul. 16, 1844; d. Tunbridge Wells, Kent, England, Jun. 27, 1933) was educated at Gainford Academy, Rotherham College, Nottingham Institute, and Cheshunt College. Following his ordination, he became pastor of a church in Great Marlow, Buckinghamshire, but ill health forced him to resign this position and travel on the Continent, where he engaged in further study at the universities of Heidelberg and Tuebingen. Back in England, he came under the influence of Dwight L. Moody and Ira Sankey and conducted evangelistic meetings in Britain (1874-82) and in a world-wide tour (1882-89). From 1889 to 1897 he served as pastor of the Countess of Huntingdon's Chapel at Tunbridge Wells. In the latter year he changed his views on baptism, resigned his pastorate, became a Baptist, and founded St. John's Free Church in Tunbridge Wells. Though he wrote a number of religious books, articles, and hymn texts, Mountain is best known today as a composer of hymn tunes. Assisted by Frances Ridley Havergal, he compiled *Hymns of Consecration and Faith* (1876), a book which is said to show the influence of Sankey's music on Mountain. *D.M.*

Wye Valley–58, 198, 611, 614
Everlasting Love–336

Mozart, Wolfgang Amadeus (b. Salzburg, Austria, Jan. 27, 1756; d. Vienna, Austria, Dec. 5, 1791) was one of the master composers of all time, combining German depth of emotion with Italian frankness in instrumental and dramatic works of classic freshness. Mozart and his sister (the children of Leopold Mozart, official musician to the Archbishop of Salzburg) were both prodigies and were taken on extensive performing tours at an early age. From age four young Wolfgang was composing works of amazing quality and performing them with dazzling virtuosity.

When, after many worrisome years, he

was finally released from the service of the Salzburg archbishop, he settled in Vienna, married Constanze Weber, and sought to pursue an independent career as a composer and performer. Poor management of financial matters led to poverty and hardship. Prolonged overwork and overindulgence undermined his health, and he died at age 35. He left over 600 compositions in every area of musical performance, many considered to be timeless masterpieces. In his last years, Mozart was attracted to Freemasonry but remained faithful to the Roman Catholic Church. His church music reflects influences from both institutions. Although he composed a considerable amount of music for church use, insofar as is known, he wrote no hymn tunes as such. Several melodies have been adapted, however, from his works by hymn book editors. Sometimes anonymous tunes have been spuriously attributed to him, possibly to enhance the attractiveness and marketability of the collections in which they are found. Such is the case with the tune ELLESDIE. *H.T.M.*

ELLESDIE (attr.)–471, 591

Mulder, Alfred E. (b. near Ireton, IA, Apr. 4, 1936) is a graduate of Calvin College (A.B., 1957) and Calvin Theological Seminary (B.D., 1960; M.Div., 1975). From 1960 to 1964 he served as pastor of the Luctor Christian Reformed Church in Prairie View, Kansas, and from 1964 to 1968 as pastor of the Christian Reformed Church in Brigham City, Utah. In 1968 he accepted the pastorate of Bethany Christian Reformed Church in Gallup, New Mexico, where he ministered until 1983. Since January, 1984, he has served as Director of Ministries for Christian Reformed Home Missions in Grand Rapids, Michigan. *D.M.*

God, the Father of Your People–382

Münster Gesangbuch (1677) is the title of the collection which contained the first printing of the German hymn which is translated in English, beginning with the words "Fairest Lord Jesus." The German text can be traced back as far as 1662 in a manuscript of that date found in Münster, Westphalia (Germany), where the *Gesangbuch* was later printed. *H.T.M.*

Fairest Lord Jesus–176

Murray, James Ramsey (b. Andover, MA, Mar. 17, 1841; d. Cincinnati, OH, Mar. 10, 1905) was the son of Scottish parents who had immigrated the year before his birth. He received his musical education from Lowell Mason, George W. Root, George J. Webb, and William B. Bradbury at the Musical Institute in North Reading, Massachusetts. After service in the Union army during the Civil War, he returned home to teach music before moving to Chicago in 1868 to become an editor for the firm of Root and Cady. When the 1871 fire destroyed their facilities, he returned to Andover and taught music in the public schools. In 1881 he joined the John Church Company of Cincinnati, a major publisher of Sunday School and gospel music. He remained with that company until his death, composing many pieces and editing a periodical and several collections. *P.A.R.*

MUELLER–103

Nägeli, Johann (Hans) Georg (b. Wetzikon, Zürich, Switzerland, May 26, 1773; d. Wetzikon, Zürich, Switzerland, Dec. 26, 1836) was a Swiss music educator, composer, author, lecturer, and music publisher, whose editions of the music of Bach, Handel, Frescobaldi, and other masters were outstanding. He was the founder and president of the Swiss Association for the Cultivation of Music. A musical periodical started by him in 1803 published new piano works by then contemporary composers, including sonatas by Beethoven. He lectured in Switzerland and Southern Germany on what would now be called music appreciation. He was a pioneer in applying the principles of the Pestalozzian system to music instruction. The American Lowell Mason was greatly influenced by Nägeli's writings on music education, and after the latter's death visited schools where his methods were being used. As a composer Nägeli is best known for his collections of songs, many of which remain popular in Switzerland. Some of his melodies intended for other purposes have been adapted as hymn tunes, principally by Lowell Mason. *H.T.M.*

DENNIS–375, 387

Neale, John Mason (b. London, England, Jan. 24, 1818; d. East Grinstead, Sussex, England, Aug. 6, 1866) was the only son of the Reverend Cornelius and Susanna Neale, both of whom were evangelical Anglicans. He studied at Trinity College, Cambridge, on a scholarship. He earned a number of prizes as a student, including (eleven times!) the Seatonian Prize for sacred poetry. Graduating in 1840, he was elected fellow of Downing College. While at Cambridge he was also closely associated with the local expression of the Oxford Movement, being one of the founders of the Ecclesiological or Cambridge Camden Society. In 1841 he was ordained deacon in the Anglican Church, and in the following year, priest. His Anglo-Catholic leanings and chronic ill health kept Neale from the parish ministry.

In 1846 he was appointed warden of Sackville College, East Grinstead, a home for old men. For the remainder of his life he occupied this position, a position that enabled him to devote himself to research and writing. He also became a champion for social ministry, founding a nursing sisterhood (St. Margaret's) and extending the ministry of Sackville College to include orphans and fallen women. His research resulted in volumes on medieval church history and liturgy that won him world-wide recognition. His bishop forbade Neale from administrating in the religious services, a restriction that was in effect from 1847 until 1863, three years before his death.

Neale's greatest literary achievements are his translations and paraphrases from the Greek and Latin. He introduced the hymnic traditions of Eastern Christianity, unknown up to that time. The publication in 1862 of his *Hymns of the Eastern Church* was the culmination of 12 years of research. The chief collections of his translations from the Latin are *Medieval Hymns and Sequences* (1851 and 1853), *Hymns, Chiefly Medieval, on the Joys and Glories of Paradise* (1865). *The Hymnal Noted* (with Thomas Helmore, 1851 and 1854) brought into English the hymns of the *Sarum Breviary*, a collection of Medieval office hymns. In the original "trial" edition of *Hymns Ancient and Modern* which was published in 1859, he contributed nearly one-eighth of the texts. No translator of hymns from the Latin and Greek is more widely represented in current English-language hymnals than Neale. Julian lists his numerous prose writings, collections of original poetry, and his translations.

Paradoxically, Neale's work lacked official English recognition, his honors coming from elsewhere. In 1860 the Metropolitan of Russia presented him an inscribed copy of an ancient liturgy. In 1853 and in 1861 he received honorary degrees from Trinity College, Hartford, Conneticut.   *H.E.*

O Come, O Come, Emmanuel
   (tr. st.1, 2)–76
Good Christian Men, Rejoice (tr.)–96
All Glory, Laud, and Honor (tr.)–126
The Day of Resurrection (tr.)–164
Of the Father's Love Begotten (tr.)–251
Christ Is Made the Sure Foundation
   (tr.)–356
Jerusalem, the Golden (tr.)–527

Neander, Joachim (b. Bremen, Germany, 1650; d. Bremen, Germany, May 31, 1680) attended the Pädagogium and Gymnasium Illustre at Bremen. At the age of 20, as a wild and rebellious student, he attended a service at St. Martin's Church in Bremen to ridicule Pastor Theodore Under-Eyck. He later came under the influence of Pastor Under-Eyck and was led to an experience of Christian conversion. He became a tutor in Frankfurt-am-Main and in 1674 he became rector of the German Reformed (Calvinistic) Church's Latin School in Düsseldorf. In Heidelberg, Neander came under the powerful influence of two devout and godly Pietists–Jakob Spener and Johann J. Schütz. In 1679, at the age of 29, he returned to Bremen as an unordained assistant to Pastor Under-Eyck at St. Martin's Church.

Neander wrote about 60 hymns and provided tunes for many of them. Many of his hymns are subjective and typical of seventeenth-century Pietism. Others are hymns of objective praise. He is considered by many to be the first important German hymnist after the Reformation and is regarded as the outstanding hymn writer of the German Reformed Church. He has been called the "Paul Gerhardt of the Calvinists." He died of tuberculosis at the age of 30.   *S.W.G.*

Praise to the Lord, the Almighty–14
Unser Herrscher–356

Neidlinger, William Harold (b. Brooklyn, NY, Jul. 20, 1863; d. East Orange, NJ, Dec. 5, 1924) was a pupil of Dudley Buck in New York and Edward Dannreuther in London. An organist, choral director, and teacher of singing, he was also known as a composer of songs and compiler of music books for children. His most popular children's collection was *Small Songs for Small Singers* (1896), which gained wide acceptance in kindergartens. In addition to his musical pursuits, Neidlinger was a student of child psychology and founded a school for exceptional children in East Orange, New Jersey. His compositions included an opera, *In Corsica* (1896-1897), the cantata *Prayer, Promise, and Praise* (1906), and many songs. He was the author of *A Primer on Voice and Singing* (1903).   *D.M.*

Neidlinger–The Birthday of a King–102

Nelson, Gregory Allan (b. Bismarck, ND, Sep. 10, 1948) began piano study when he was in first grade and string study when he was in fourth grade. During high school he was student arranger and conductor of the school orchestra. He attended the University of North Dakota, Grand Forks, and Mary College, Bismarck, from which he received a Bachelor of Arts in Social Science and Music in 1972.

In the 1970s, Nelson built a 16-track recording studio in his home, producing many local and regional commercials, albums, theme songs for films, etc. He founded Spirit Records in 1977, and in 1978 moved to Los Angeles, California, where he became Director of Publishing at Sparrow Records. In 1979, he sold Spirit Records. Nelson continued at Sparrow until

1980, when he moved to Nashville, Tennessee, where he worked first for Paragon Music, then Meadowgreen Music. He now operates his own company, Greg Nelson Music, in Nashville, where he lives with his wife Pamela and their children Sarah and Benjamin.

Nelson has served as composer, arranger, orchestrator, and producer for albums recorded by Sandi Patti, Larnelle Harris, Steve Green, Scott Wesley Brown, and other contemporary Christian artists. Many of the albums he has produced have achieved the status of Gold LPs and have been nominated for or won Dove Awards.

In addition to his compositional and production work, Nelson has been a teacher in both grade school and high school, and has served various churches as choir or youth director. *D.M.*

SAVIOR–There Is a Savior–536
PEOPLE NEED THE LORD–People Need
  the Lord–557

Neumark, Georg (b. Langensalza, Thuringia, Mar. 16, 1621; d. Weimar, Germany, Jul. 18, 1681) was born into the family of a clothing merchant just three years after the beginning of the Thirty Years War. After a *Gymnasium* education, he eventually studied law and poetry at Königsberg University. A few years later he settled in Thuringia where he became court poet, librarian, and registrar to the Duke of Sachse-Weimar. His literary gifts were recognized in 1653 when he was admitted to the Fruitbearing Society, the most important German literary society of the time. *D.B.*

NEUMARK–If You Will Only Let God
  Guide You–57

Neumeister, Erdmann (b. Uchteritz, Germany, May 12, 1671; d. Hamburg, Germany, Aug. 18, 1756) is best known today as the originator of cantata texts which were used by J. S. Bach and other composers. He was highly regarded for his more than 650 hymn texts. Neumeister was educated at the University of Leipzig (M.A., 1695), where he later served as a lecturer. In 1697 he became assistant pastor at Bibra. The following year he became pastor and assistant superintendent of the Eckartsberg district. Duke Johann Georg called him to Weissenfels in 1704 as his daughter's tutor and assistant court preacher and, shortly thereafter, court preacher. The princess died in less than two years, and the Duke's sister invited Neumeister to Sorau where, in 1706, he became senior court preacher, member of the consistory, and superintendent. His final pastorate was of St. James' Church in Hamburg from 1715 until his death. He was renowned as an eloquent, sincere preacher and defender of High Lutheranism against the Pietists and Moravians. His hymns appeared in *Der Zugang zum Gnadenstuhle Jesu Christo* (1705) and *Evangelischer Nachklang* (1718). *Funffache Kirchen-Andachten* (1716) contains his cantata texts. *P.H.*

Christ Receiveth Sinful Men–563

Newbolt, Michael R. (b. Dymock, Gloucestershire, England, 1874; d. Bierton, Bucks, England, Feb. 7, 1956) was educated at St. John's College, Oxford, England (B.A. 1895, M.A. 1912). He was ordained a deacon in 1899 and a priest in 1900. After church positions in Wantage and Iffley, he served as Principal of the Missionary College in Dorchester from 1910 to 1916. From 1916 to 1927 he was Perpetual Curate of St. Michael and All Angels in

Brighton. From 1927 to 1946 he was Canon of Chester Cathedral.   *D.B.*

Lift High the Cross (alt.)–594

Newell, William Reed (b. Savannah, OH, May 22, 1868; d. Deland, FL, Apr. 1, 1956) received the A.B. degree from Wooster College in 1891 and attended seminary at Princeton and Oberlin. He was pastor of several churches before going to Chicago in 1895 where he became pastor of the Bethesda Congregational Church. Later that year he became assistant superintendent of the Moody Bible Institute. He conducted interdenominational Bible classes in Chicago, Detroit, Toronto, and St. Louis and did extensive writing. His expositions on the books of Romans, Hebrews, and Revelation, and his Old Testament studies were all published. He moved to Deland, Florida to retire.   *S.W.G.*

At Calvary–138

Newton, Bill is the pseudonym of an arranger who prefers to remain anonymous. *D.M., W.J.R.*

Jubilate (arr.)–9
Rosas (arr.)–38
Lacquiparle (harm.)–49
Ascension– (arr.)165
Au Clair De La Lune (arr.)–477

Newton, John (b. London, England, Jul. 24, 1725; d. London, England, Dec. 21, 1807) was the son of a devout Christian mother who died when he was seven. His father, a sea captain, did not share her religious interest. The lad went to sea with his father when he was 11, and later served in the Royal Navy on a British man-of-war. He joined the crew of a slave-trading ship and engaged in slave-trading for a number of years. His Christian experience came through his reading of Thomas a Kempis' *Imitation of Christ*, and his experience of a stormy night in 1748 on a waterlogged ship when he faced imminent death. The memory of his mother and his love for Mary Catlett, who later became his wife, served as restraining influences. In 1754 he left the sea and became tide surveyor in Liverpool, where he came under the influence of the preaching of Whitefield and Wesley. By 1758, sensing God's call to the ministry, he began to preach. He was ordained in the Church of England and was appointed curate of the parish church at Olney in 1764. William Cowper came to Olney in 1767, and together they published *Olney Hymns* (1779), to which Newton contributed 280 hymns. In 1780 he became vicar at St. Mary Woolnoth, London, where he continued to preach until after his eightieth year.

In his latter years a servant would stand by his side in the pulpit and help him find the headings in his manuscript. When he was no longer able to read and was advised to give up preaching, he replied, "What, shall the old African blasphemer stop while he can speak!" He was buried in the church crypt at St. Mary Woolnoth with the epitaph that he himself wrote:

John Newton, Clerk
Once an infidel and libertine,
A servant of slaves in Africa:
Was by the rich mercy of our
Lord and Savior, Jesus Christ,
Preserved, restored, pardoned,
And appointed to preach the Faith
He had labored long to destroy.
Near sixteen years at Olney in Bucks;
And twenty-seven years in this church.

In 1893 when the Bank Station of the London Underground (subway) was built under St. Mary Woolnoth, the remains of John and Mary Newton were removed from the church crypt to the churchyard at Olney.   *W.J.R.*

Amazing Grace! How Sweet the Sound
  (st. 1-4)–330
God, the Father of Your People (st. 3)–382
Glorious Things of Thee Are Spoken–398
How Sweet the Name of Jesus Sounds–453

Nichol, Henry Ernest (b. Hull, Yorkshire, England, Dec. 10, 1862; d. Skirlaugh, Yorkshire, England, Aug. 30, 1926) was a writer of hymns in support of the Sunday School movement. Though he began training to be a civil engineer, he shifted his focus to music and earned the B.M. degree from Oxford in 1888. Many of his works were signed with the pseudonym "Colin Sterne," a rough anagram of his middle and last names.   *P.A.R.*

MESSAGE–We've a Story to Tell–586

Nichols, Ted (b. Missoula, MT, Oct. 1, 1928) received degrees from Baylor University (B.M.) and the Texas University of Arts and Industry (M.S. in Music Composition), and has done additional study at Syracuse University in New York, the University of California at Los Angeles, the University of Southern California, and Claremont Graduate School, Claremont, California. His career has spanned a wide gamut of musical activities. These include over twenty-five years as a minister of music in local churches; a teacher of band and orchestra in junior high school, high school, junior college, and university settings; International Music Director of Campus Crusade For Christ; Director of Music and Creative Arts at Western Conservative Baptist Seminary (seven years); and nearly a decade as Musi-

cal Director for Hanna-Barbera TV Productions of Hollywood.

As a composer, Nichols has provided music for numerous films, television programs, commercials, and record albums. He has written two operas, three stage musicals, and two dramatic cantatas, as well as many anthems and hymn arrangements for both choir and instruments. In 1986 he received a commendation from the House of Representatives of the state of Kentucky for his work in composing biblical musical drama. He presently serves as Minister of Music and Worship at Sunset Presbyterian Church, Portland, Oregon.   *D.M.*

NICHOLS–376

Nicholson, James (b. Ireland, *c*. 1828; d. Washington, D.C., Nov. 6, 1876) emigrated to the United States in the early 1850s, settling in Philadelphia, where he participated in Sunday School and evangelistic work in the Wharton Street Methodist Episcopal church. He moved to Washington, D. C., about 1871. There he was employed as a clerk in the Post Office Department, but remained active in positions of Christian leadership–teaching Sunday School, leading singing, and taking part in evangelistic efforts. Though he died in Washington, his body was returned to Philadelphia for burial.   *D.M.*

Whiter than Snow–325

Nicholson, Sydney Hugo (b. London, England, Feb. 9, 1875; d. Ashford, Kent, England, May 30, 1947) was the son of Sir Charles Nicholson, one of the founders and the first Chancellor of the University of Sydney. He was educated at Rugby and at New College, Oxford. He also studied at the Royal College of Music. Perhaps his most prestigious service was as organist at Manchester Cathedral and at Westminster Abbey. In 1927 he retired to found the School of English Church Music and served as its director until his death in 1947. *D.M.*

CRUCIFER–594

Noel, Caroline Maria (b. London, England, Apr. 10, 1817; d. London, England, Dec. 7, 1877) was the daughter of Anglican clergyman and hymnwriter Gerard Thomas Noel. Her uncle, Baptist Noel, also a hymnist and Anglican clergyman, left the Church of England and later became a Baptist minister. Caroline wrote some hymns as a teenager, but did not return to writing until a prolonged illness caused her to do so later in life. The hymns written during her last 25 years as an invalid were meant to comfort other sufferers. She published *The Name of Jesus, and Other Verses for the Sick and Lonely* in 1870, while other poems of hers were published posthumously. *P.H.*

At the Name of Jesus–198

Norris, John Samuel (b. West Cowes, Isle of Wight, England, Dec. 4, 1844; d. Chicago, IL, Sep. 23, 1907) was the son of John and Harriet (Chalk) Norris. He received his education and ordination to the Methodist ministry (1868) in Canada and served Methodist churches in Canada, New York, and Wisconsin. In 1878 he became a Congregationalist and pastored churches of that denomination in Wisconsin and Iowa, also serving as a conference evangelist in the latter state. He retired in 1901, moving to Chicago, where he remained until his death. He published one collection of hymns, *Songs of the Soul. D.M.*

NORRIS–288

Oakeley, Frederick (b. Shrewsbury, England, Sep. 5, 1802; d. Islington, London, England, Jan. 29, 1880) received a B.A. degree from Christ Church, Oxford, in 1824 and was elected a Fellow of Balliol in 1827. He became a Prebendary at Lichfield Cathedral in 1832 and began serving at Margaret Chapel, London, in 1839, where he collaborated with the organist, Richard Redhead, to reform the worship services. Oakeley became involved in the Oxford Movement and was author of some of the Tractarian pamphlets supporting Roman Catholic doctrine. He left the Church of England in 1845 and entered the Roman Catholic Church. In 1852 he became a Canon of Westminister Pro-Cathedral, where he worked among the poor in the district. *M.P.*

O Come, All Ye Faithful (tr.)–89

Oatman, Johnson, Jr. (b. Medford, NJ, Apr. 21, 1856; d. Norman, OK, Sep. 25, 1922) was a Methodist minister and a writer of gospel song texts. Though ordained as a young man, he worked in business rather than serving in the pastorate. He joined his father in the mercantile business in Lumberton, New York, then, after his father's death, moved to Mount Holly, New Jersey, and sold insurance. His first hymn was written in 1892, set by John R. Sweney, and published the next year. Forced by ill health to retire in 1893, he devoted himself to writing and produced more than 7000 texts. Many of his poems were set by leading gospel song composers, such as Sweney, E. O. Excell, Charles H. Gabriel, and William J. Kirkpatrick. *P.A.R.*

No, Not One–181
He Included Me–436
Higher Ground–484
Count Your Blessings–644

Ogden, William Augustine (b. Franklin County, OH, Oct. 10, 1841; d. Toledo, OH, Oct. 14, 1897) began his musical education by attending local singing schools. Following a four-year stint with the 30th Indiana Volunteer Infantry during the Civil War, he continued his music study under Lowell Mason, Thomas Hastings, E. E. Bailey, and B. F. Baker. Ogden himself became a singing-school teacher and was well-known for his activities at musical conventions and music schools. In 1887 he became supervisor for public school music in Toledo, Ohio, a position he retained until his death. Among the many gospel songs he wrote were "Look and Live," the tune for "Bring Them In," and "He Is Able to Deliver Thee." Ogden was also active as a compiler of gospel song books.   *D.M.*

DELIVERANCE–He Is Able to Deliver Thee–24

Olivers, Thomas (b. Tregynon, Montgomeryshire, Wales, 1725; d. London, England, Mar. 1799) was orphaned at the age of four and reared on the farm of a distant relative. He was apprenticed to a shoemaker at the age of 18 but was fired because of bad conduct. Olivers was converted by a sermon preached by George Whitefield at Bristol and joined the Methodist Society at Bradford-on-Avon. For 22 years he served as an itinerant Methodist preacher, traveling throughout England and Ireland. Upon the separation of Whitefield and the Wesleys, Olivers remained with the Wesleys, and in 1775 became supervisor of all publications. However, he was discharged by John Wesley in 1789 and spent his retirement in London.   *W.J.R.*

The God of Abraham Praise (st. 1)–34

Olson, Ernst William (b. Skåne, Finja parish, Sweden, Mar. 16, 1870; d. Chicago, IL, Oct. 6, 1958) came to the United States with his parents in 1875. The family settled first near Wahoo, Nebraska, but later moved to Texas. Olson graduated from Augustana College, Rock Island, Illinois, in 1891. After working for several Swedish newspapers, he was office editor for the Engberg-Holmberg Publishing Company from 1906 until 1911, when he became editor for the Augustana Book Concern, a position he held until 1949. A writer and a poet who wrote in both English and Swedish, he wrote *A History of the Swedes in Illinois* (1908). Twenty-eight of his hymn translations and four original hymns were included in *The Hymnal* (Rock Island, IL, 1925) of the Evangelical Lutheran Augustana Synod. Olson served as a member of the hymnal committee for that collection and for the Lutheran *Service Book and Hymnal* (1958). He was awarded an honorary doctorate from Augustana College in 1926.   *M.P.*

Children of the Heavenly Father (tr.)–55

Orr, J. Edwin (b. Belfast, Ireland, Jan. 15, 1912; d. Asheville, NC, Apr. 22, 1987) left Ireland in 1933 to begin his work as an evangelist. In 1939 he became assistant pastor of The People's Church of Toronto, Canada. In 1940 he was ordained in New Jersey to the Baptist ministry. He received an M.A. from Northwestern University in 1941 and a Th.D. in 1943 from Northern Baptist Seminary. From 1942 to 1946 he served in the United States Air Force. Following that he enrolled in Oxford University receiving a Ph.D. in 1948. Throughout his life he was involved in evangelistic work throughout the world. In 1967 he joined the faculty of the School of World

Missions of Fuller Theological Seminary in Pasadena in an adjunct relationship that allowed him to continue to write and to conduct conferences. At Fuller he taught the History of Awakenings. He was a member of the Commission of Cooperative Christianity of the Baptist World Alliance. He was serving as a conference leader at Ridgecrest Baptist Conference Center in April of 1987 when he suffered what proved to be a fatal heart attack.   *D.B.*

Search Me, O God–297

Osler, Edward (b. Falmouth, Cornwall, England, Jan. 30, 1798; d. Truro, Cornwall, England, Mar. 7, 1863) was a physician and editor. He practiced medicine privately and in a naval hospital until 1836, when he devoted himself to religious and literary pursuits. For a while he was associated with the Society for Promoting Christian Knowledge. In 1841 he moved to Truro to edit the *Royal Cornwall Gazette.* He wrote books on several subjects and worked with W.J. Hall in compiling the *Mitre Hymn Book* (London, 1836). He contributed 15 psalm paraphrases and 50 hymns to that collection and published others in *Church and King,* a journal which he edited.   *P.A.R.*

Praise the Lord! Ye Heavens, Adore Him (st. 3)–36

Overby, Oscar R. (b. 1892; d. 1964) was educated at Concordia College, Moorhead, Minnesota; Northwestern Conservatory of Music, Minneapolis, Minnesota; the New England Conservatory of Music, Boston, Massachusetts; St. Olaf College, Northfield, Minnesota; and Columbia University, New York, New York. He served as professor of Music Theory and Choral Director at Concordia College, Moorhead, Minnesota; pro-

fessor of Music Theory, Chorus, Band, Piano, and Voice at Park Region College, Fergus Falls, Minnesota; and from 1921 to 1950 was on the music faculty of St. Olaf College, Northfield, Minnesota. Later, he became Director of the Choral Union of the Evangelical Lutheran Church, which subsequently merged with other Lutheran bodies in the United States. Overby's publications included arrangements and original compositions for mixed choir, women's choir, two volumes of songs for children's choirs, and an album of sacred solos.   *D.M.*

FREE (arr.)–649

Owen, William (b. Bangor, Caernarvonshire, Wales, Dec. 12, 1813; d. Caernarvonshire, Wales, Jul. 20, 1883) followed in his father's trade and worked as a slate miner in the Penrhyn quarries. He enjoyed a local reputation as a fine singer. At the age of 18 he wrote his first hymn tune. His anthems and hymn tunes were published in 1866 in his *Y Perl Cerddorol* (The Pearl of Music). *D.B.*

BRYN CALFARIA–169

Owens, Carol (b. El Reno, OK, Oct. 30, 1931) lived in various parts of California and went to college in San Jose. She met her husband, Jimmy, in the San Francisco area. They attended the Neighborhood Church in Oakland, a Christian Missionary Alliance fellowship. Later she and her husband moved to southern California where they were active in music writing and recording. In recent years she and her husband have been involved in mission enterprises under the sponsorship of the Church of the Way in Los Angeles.   *D.B.*

FREELY, FREELY–Freely, Freely–273

Owens, Jimmy (b. Clarksdale, MS, Dec. 9, 1930) graduated from Central High School in Jackson, Mississippi, and attended Millsaps College and Southwestern College. His early religious training was in Baptist churches. He recalls a godly grandmother who urged him to memorize Scripture. As a very young man, he played trumpet in a traveling jazz band, but after a few months, at age 19, he underwent a religious renewal and left the band. He knew he was called to ministry, but didn't know in what area. During part of a four-year stint in the Navy, he was stationed near San Francisco. There, under the influence of a Christian Missionary Alliance congregation, he became involved in the music ministry. He has had an extensive career in composing and recording. In recent years he and his wife have been involved in overseas missions under the auspices of the Church of the Way in Los Angeles.   *D.B.*

Holy, Holy–Holy, Holy–254

Owens, Priscilla Jane (b. Baltimore, MD, Jul. 21, 1829; d. Baltimore, MD, Dec. 5, 1907) spent her entire life in Baltimore, where she was a public school teacher for 49 years. She was a member of the Union Square Methodist Episcopal Church, where she was active in the work of the Sunday School. She wrote both prose and poetry, and her writings were published in religious periodicals such as the *Methodist Protestant* and the *Christian Standard.*   *M.P.*

We Have Heard the Joyful Sound–581, 584

Oxenham, John (b. Cheetham, Manchester, England, Nov. 12, 1852; d. High Salvington, Worthing, Sussex, England, Jan. 23, 1941) was the pen name of William Arthur Dunkerly. He took the name from a character in Charles Kingsley's novel, *Westward Ho!* Educated at Old Trafford School and Victoria University, Dunkerly joined his father's mercantile house upon graduation. While in this work he lived for five years in France and for two years in the United States. He became interested in journalism and literature and, upon his return to England, published *The Idler, Today,* and a London edition of the *Detroit Free Press*. He subsequently devoted himself fully to his writing, producing more than 60 volumes of poetry and prose under his pseudonym. Because he went to some pains to avoid discovery, many of his friends did not identify Oxenham as Dunkerly until after his death. He was an active churchman, serving as a deacon and Bible teacher in the Ealing Congregational Church in London. Much of his writing has a religious element.   *P.A.R.*

In Christ There Is No East or West–385

Page, Anna Laura (b. Louisville, KY, Jan. 11, 1943) is the daughter of Kenneth and Beulah Hood, who greatly encouraged her musical development. From the age of 11 she has played preludes and offertories in church. She is a graduate of the University of Kentucky (B.M. in music education/piano and M.M. in music theory with an organ emphasis). She has taught organ part-time at Mercer University (1976-78) and theory and organ part-time at Lander College (1978-87). Churches she has served as organist include Beech Haven Baptist, Athens, Georgia (1971-78), Vineville Baptist, Macon, Georgia (1972-78), and South Main Baptist, Greenwood, South Carolina (1978-89). She served also as minister of music in the latter church (1980-87). Her numerous sacred compositions include works for organ, piano, handbells, and choral works for children, youth, and adults released by such publishers as Alfred, Candela, Coronet, CPP/Belwin, Doxology, Flammer, GENEVOX, Hinshaw, Lorenz. She is married to Oscar Page, president of Austin Peay State University, Clarksville, Tennessee. They have a daughter, Kristen, and a son, Matt.   *H.E.*

BUTLER (arr.)–500

Palestrina, Giovanni Pierluigi da (b. Palestrina, Italy, 1525/26; d. Rome, Italy, Feb. 2, 1594) was a major composer of his time and the dominant figure in the music of the Roman church during that era. His name was taken from a small village near Rome where he served and where, probably, he was born. His life was spent as a musician in the Catholic church. As a child, he was a choirboy at Santa Maria Maggiore in Rome. In 1544 he became the organist at St. Agapito Cathedral in Palestrina. When his bishop was elected Pope Julius III in 1551, he appointed the young musician, then in his mid-twenties, as *maestro* of the Capella Giulia, the musical establishment of St. Peter's. Four years later, he was appointed to the Sistine Chapel, despite the fact that he was married and the chapel was supposedly restricted to those who had taken a vow of celibacy. When, later the same year, a new pope enforced the regulations, Palestrina became *maestro di cappella* of St. John, Lateran. He served there until 1650, when he returned to Santa Maria Maggiore. This responsibility was overlapped from 1564 to 1566 by service at the estate of Cardinal d'Este, a position which was his major employment from 1567 until 1571. From 1566 until 1571 he also taught music at the Seminario Romano. He returned to the Capella Giulia in 1571 and remained there until his death.

Palestrina composed an enormous amount of music for the services of the Roman church, as well as a smaller number of madrigals. The degree of perfection which he attained in transparent contrapuntal writing established him as the premier musical figure of the Counter Reformation and made his works the aesthetic standard for composers of Catholic church music into the present century.   *P.A.R.*

VICTORY–172

Palmer, Ray (b. Little Compton, RI, Nov. 12, 1808; d. Newark, NJ, Mar. 29, 1887) was the son of Judge Thomas Palmer. At the age of 13 he worked as a clerk in a Boston dry-goods store. He united with Boston's famous Park Street Congregational Church and soon felt a calling to the ministry. His formal education was at Phillips Academy and at Yale. Following a position with a ladies seminary in New Haven, he was licensed to preach and was ordained when called to the pastorate of the Central Congregational Church of Bath, Maine. Some of his finest hymns were written during that 15-year pastorate. In 1850 he became the pastor of the First Congregational Church of Albany, New York, and remained there until 1865 when he moved to New York City to become Corresponding Secretary of the American Congregational Union where he served until his retirement in 1878. Palmer contributed 15 original hymns and Latin translations to Park & Phelps's *Sabbath Hymn-Book* of 1858. He wrote several collections of religious poetry and essays. Samuel Duffield claimed Palmer "has written more and better hymns than any other American" (Duffield, 363).   *D.B.*

My Faith Looks Up to Thee–416

Paris, Twila (b. Springdale, AR, Dec. 28, 1958) is the daughter, granddaughter, and great-granddaughter of preachers. She is a contemporary Christian singer and song-writer whose first album, *Knowin' You're Around*, was recorded in 1981. Eight other albums have followed through 1990. Most of the songs on these recordings were written by Twila. She has produced nine number one single records and has received numerous Gospel Music Association Dove Award nominations. In addition to "We Will Glorify," her songs "Lamb of God" and "Faithful Men" have been included in recent hymnals.   *D.M.*

WE WILL GLORIFY–We Will Glorify–213

Parker, Alice (b. Boston, MA, Dec. 16, 1925) is a graduate of Smith College and the Juilliard School of Music, with honorary doctorates from Hamilton and Macalester Colleges. She makes her home in New York City. In 1984 she founded Melodious Accord, Inc., an organization involved in concerts and educational activities. In 1954 she married baritone Thomas Pyle (d. 1976), who collaborated with her on translations for the Robert Shaw Chorale and joined her in recitals and workshops. Her compositions include operas, cantatas, song cycles, chamber music, and many shorter works for voice and instruments. She has arranged hundreds of hymn tunes and has done much research into early American hymnody. She has taken a particular interest in the early American folk hymn tradition, having arranged a number of folk hymns herself or in collaboration with Robert Shaw. Her gift for inspiring improvisatory group singing has been demonstrated in workshops and neighborhood "Sings." She is the author of *Creative Hymn Singing* (Chapel Hill, NC, 1976).   *H.E.*

PARKER–664

Parker, William Henry (b. New Basford, Nottinghamshire, England, Mar. 4, 1845; d. New Basford, Nottinghamshire, England, Dec. 2, 1929) was apprenticed as a youth in the machine construction department of a large lace-making plant in New Basford and remained with the same company for a number of years. Later he became head of an insurance company. An active member of the Chelsea Street Baptist Church, Nottingham, he was greatly interested in Sunday School work. Most of his hymns were written for Sunday School anniversaries. The National Sunday School Union acquired his hymns and 15 appear in the *Sunday School Hymnary* (London, 1905).   *W.J.R.*

Tell Me the Stories of Jesus–129

Parks, Ralph is the pseudonym of an author/composer who wishes to remain anonymous.   *W.J.R.*

Jesus Calls You Now–319
God, the Father of Your People (st. 2)–382

Patti, Sandi (See Helvering, Sandi Patti).

Peace, Albert Lister (b. Huddersfield, England, Jan. 26, 1844; d. Liverpool, England, Mar. 14, 1912) was a true child prodigy. At the age of nine he was appointed organist at the parish church in Holmfirth, Yorkshire. He received the B. Mus. (1870) and Mus. D. (1875) degrees from Oxford University. He became organist at Glasgow Cathedral in 1879. In 1897 he succeeded W. T. Best as organist at St. George's Hall, Liverpool, a position he held until his death. He was a composer of cantatas, service music, organ pieces, and hymn tunes.

The Church of Scotland called on him to edit several collections including *The Scottish Hymnal* (1885), *Psalms and Paraphrases with Tunes* (1886), *The Psalter with Chants* (1888), and *The Scottish Anthem Book* (1891).   *D.B.*

ST. MARGARET–292

Perronet, Edward (b. Sundridge, Kent, England, 1726; d. Canterbury, England, Jan. 2, 1792) was born in a family of Huguenot emigrés who came from Switzerland to England in 1680. Edward's father, Vincent, was the vicar of Shoreham, Kent. Both Edward and his father were closely aligned with the Wesleyan movement within the Anglican church. Edward's satiric poem *The Mitre* (London, 1757), however, attacked abuses in the Church of England and provoked John Wesley's anger. A later controversy over the right of Methodist ministers to administer the ordinances led to Perronet's breaking with the Wesleys in 1771. He then became a minister in one of Lady Huntingdon's chapels in Canterbury. However, she also resented his attitude toward the Church of England. Perronet concluded his career as an independent minister in Canterbury. Though he was the author of several hymns and versified Scriptures, only the present hymn remains in common use, "All Hail the Power of Jesus' Name."   *P.H.*

All Hail the Power of Jesus' Name
(st. 1,2)–200, 201, 202

Perry, Michael Arnold (b. Beckenham, Kent, England, Mar. 8, 1942) is an Anglican minister and hymnwriter. He was educated at Dulwich College; University College, London; Oak Hill Theological College and Ridley College, Cambridge; and the University of Southampton and holds the B.D. and M.Phil. degrees. He has served as curate of St. Helens, Lancashire (1965-68); curate of Bitterne, Southampton (1968-72); vicar of Bitterne (1972-81); rector of Eversley, Hampshire (1981-89); and vicar of Tonbridge, Kent (since 1989). He has held several important posts within his church and was also, from 1981 until 1987, chaplain/lecturer at the national Police Staff College in Bramshill. He is a prolific hymnist and has been influential in the field of hymnody as Honorary Secretary of Jubilitate Hymns, Ltd., compilers of *Hymns for Today's Church* (1st ed., London: 1982), *Carols for Today* (London: 1986), and *Come Rejoice!* (Carol Stream, Ill.: 1989). He was also joint editor of *Carol Praise* (Basingstoke, 1987).   *P.A.R.*

Praise the Father–257

Peterson, John W. (b. Lindsborg, KS, Nov. 1, 1921) was the youngest child in a Swedish-American family and his father died when he was four. He was converted at the age of 12 and wrote his first song when in high school. During World War II, he was an Army Air Force pilot based in Burma flying the famed "China Hump" over the Himalaya mountains. After the war, he was educated at Moody Bible Institute and the American Conservatory of Music. In 1954, he became the editor of Singspiration, Inc. in Montrose, Pennsylvania. He became president and part owner when the firm was moved to Grand Rapids, Michigan, in 1963. He presently makes his home in Scottsdale, Arizona, where he oversees the activities of the John W. Peterson Music Company. For more than three decades, he has been writing gospel songs and choir music for church use. His cantatas have sold over eight million copies. Among these are *Night of Miracles, Born a King, No Greater Love, Carol of Christmas, Jesus Is Coming,* and *I Love America.* He has compiled two major hymnals, *Great Hymns of the Faith* and *Praise.* From John Brown University, he received the honorary Sac. Mus. D. degree (1967); from Western Conservative Baptist Seminary, the honorary D.D. degree (1971); and from Grand Canyon College the honorary Doctor of Fine Arts (1979).   *H.E.*

Goodness–Surely Goodness and Mercy–422
Heaven Came Down–Heaven Came
   Down–438
Toronto–565

Pethel, Stan (b. Gainesville, GA, Feb. 3, 1950) is a graduate of South Hall High School, Gainesville, Georgia; the University of Georgia (B.M., 1972 and M.F.A., 1973); and the University of Kentucky (D.M.A., 1981). In 1972-73 he was the band director for the Clarke County (Georgia) Middle Schools. In 1973 he joined the music faculty of Berry College in Rome, Georgia. Widely recognized as a composer and arranger, he has published over 375 works. In addition to his work at Berry, Pethel also serves the Garden Lakes Baptist Church in Rome as minister of music.   *D.B.*

Pethel–152

Phelps, Sylvanus Dryden (b. Suffield, CT, May 15, 1816; d. New Haven, CT, Nov. 23, 1895) received his formal education at the Connecticut Literary Institute, Brown University, and Yale Divinity School. In 1846 he became pastor of the First Baptist Church of New Haven. He served until 1874 when he left to assume the pastorate of the Jefferson Street Baptist Church of Providence, Rhode Island. He resigned that

position in 1876 to become editor of *The Christian Secretary.* His devotional publications include: *Eloquence of Nature, and Other Poems* (1842); *Sunlight and Hearthlight* (1856); and the *Poet's Song* (1867). His son, William Lyon Phelps, was well known as a professor of English at Yale University and an author of renown.   *D.B.*

Something for Thee–607

Pierpoint, Folliott Sandford (b. Spa Villa, Bath, England, Oct. 7, 1835; d. Newport, Monmouthshire, England, Mar. 10, 1917) was graduated in classical honors in 1871 from Queen's College, Cambridge, and later served as classical master at Somersetshire College. Following his resignation from Somersetshire College, he lived for a time at Babbicombe, Devonshire, and did occasional teaching. He published *The Chalice of Nature and Other Poems,* which was republished as *Songs of Love, The Chalice of Nature, and Lyra Jesu.* His hymns appeared in the *Churchman's Companion* and the *Lyra Eucharistica.*   *S.W.G.*

For the Beauty of the Earth–44

Plumptre, Edward Hayes (b. London, England, Aug. 6, 1821; d. Wells, England, Feb. 1, 1891) followed education at King's College, London, and University College, Oxford, with a distinguished career as a teacher, scholar, and preacher. His publications dealt with a variety of topics including the classics, biography, history, and poetry, as well as theological works. He held many important positions, including chaplain at King's College (1847-68); professor of pastoral theology (1853-63); professor of New Testament exegesis (1864-81); dean of Queen's College, Oxford; and prebendary of St. Paul's Cathdral. During the last 10 years of his life he served as Dean of Wells Cathedral.   *D.B.*

Rejoice, Ye Pure in Heart–39

Pollard, Adelaide Addison (b. Bloomfield, IA, Nov. 27, 1862; d. New York, NY, Dec. 20, 1934) was a teacher and missionary. Her parents named her Sarah Addison, but she adopted the name Adelaide. Though she was reared in a strong Presbyterian home, her own spiritual quest led her to many marginal expressions of Christianity. She was educated in Iowa and Indiana and at the Boston School of Oratory. Upon completing her training, she moved to Chicago and taught in several schools for young women. Suffering from diabetes, she was persuaded by a friend to attend the healing services of evangelist John Alexander Dowie, who called himself "Elijah III." Believing that she had been cured, she began to work with Dowie and his Christian Catholic Apostolic Church in Zion. Soon she fell under the spell of another faith healer, named Sanford, who led his group to set up a watch tower on the coast of Maine to await the return of Christ. Following recovery from a debilitating collapse in 1895, she joined other followers of Sanford in an attempt to raise funds to begin mission work in Africa. After this effort failed, she taught for some years at the Christian and Missionary Alliance Training School in Nyack, New York. She finally reached Africa just prior to World War I, but was forced to leave by its outbreak. She spent the war years in Scotland, then returned to the Northeastern United States to work with a variety of sectarian groups. She lived an isolated and itinerant life, resuming contact with her family only when illness forced periods of recuperation. She wrote many hymns, but only "Have thine own way, Lord" is in common use. *P.A.R.*

Have Thine Own Way, Lord–294

Poole, William Charles (b. Easton, MD, Apr. 14, 1875; d. Lewes, DE, Dec. 24, 1949) was reared on a farm and became a Christian at age 11. He attended Washington College, Chestertown, Maryland, was ordained to the Methodist ministry in 1900, and served as a pastor in the Wilmington Conference for 35 years. His first efforts at writing gospel song texts came about as a result of encouragement by Charles H. Gabriel.   *D.M.*

Just When I Need Him Most–65

Post, Marie J. Tuinstra (b. Jenison, MI, Feb. 8, 1919; d. Grand Rapids, MI, May 24, 1990) was a poet and a member of the Christian Reformed Church. She earned the B.A. degree from Calvin College in 1941. She was a prolific writer whose poems were published in newspapers, religious journals, and poetry collections, as well as in an anthology of her own works, *I Had Never Visited an Artist Before* (Grand Rapids: 1977). Her poems appeared almost daily in the *Grand Rapids Press* for 30 years. She served on the editorial committee for the *Psalter Hymnal* (Grand Rapids: 1977) and contributed more than 40 hymns and psalm paraphrases to that collection. *P.A.R.*

Praise and Thanksgiving (st. 2, 3)–645

Pott, Francis (b. Southwark, Surrey, England, Dec. 29, 1832; d. Speldhurst, Kent, England, Oct. 26, 1909) was an Anglican clergyman and hymnist. He was educated at Brasenose College, Oxford (B.A., 1854;

M.A., 1867), and was ordained in 1856. He was curate at Bishopsworth, Somerset (1856-58); Ardingly, Sussex (1858-61); and Ticehurst, Sussex (1861-66), before becoming rector at Norhill, Ely (1866-91). When deafness forced his retirement, he moved to Speldhurst, Kent, and devoted the remaining years of his life to the improvement of worship and hymnody in his communion. He was a member of the committee for *Hymns Ancient and Modern* (London, 1861) and editor of *The Free-Rhythm Psalter* (London, 1898). In addition to translations from Latin and Syriac sources, he wrote original hymns.   *P.A.R.*

The Strife Is O'er (tr.)–172

Pounds, Jessie Brown (b. Hiram, OH, Aug. 31, 1861; d. Hiram, OH, Mar. 3, 1921) was the daughter of Holland Brown, a pioneer preacher among the Disciples of Christ, and Jane Abell Brown, who greatly influenced her daughter's love for literature. From kindergarten age Jessie Brown created verse and, from the age of 15, wrote regularly for religious periodicals, including the *Christian Standard*. For more than 30 years she collaborated with James H. Fillmore, writing religious poetry which he set to music. Her published writings include nine books, 50 cantata librettos, and over 400 gospel hymn texts. Her most popular hymns include "Anywhere with Jesus," "The Touch of His Hand on Mine," and "Beautiful Isle of Somewhere." In 1897 she married the Rev. John E. Pounds, who was then pastor of the Central Christian Church, Indianapolis, Indiana. During the last two years of her life, she was on the editorial staff of *The Christian Century*.   *H.E.*

The Way of the Cross Leads Home–151
I Know That My Redeemer Liveth–191

Praetorius, Michael (b. Creuzburg an der Werra, Germany, Feb. 15, 1571; d. Wolfenbüttel, Germany, Feb. 15, 1621), the son of a Lutheran pastor, was a distinguished German composer, theorist, and organist. His first church position was as organist at St. Marien Church, Frankfurt, which he assumed in early 1587 and where he remained for three years. He became organist at the court of Duke Heinrich Julius at Wolfenbüttel in 1590 and was appointed court Kapellmeister there in 1604. He held this post until 1620, when failing health necessitated his retirement. His service at Wolfenbüttel was occasionally interrupted by temporary engagements elsewhere (Dresden, Magdeburg, and Kassel), and his travels brought him into contact with Heinrich Schütz, as well as the current Italian style of composition. Praetorius was a prolific composer whose work focused predominantly upon music for the Lutheran liturgy of the time. The nine-volume collection, *Musae Sioniae* (1605-19) contains a major portion of his vocal compositions for this purpose; volumes IV-VIII provide a rich resource of German Protestant hymn texts and tunes. The three volumes of his *Syntagma Musicum* (1614-19) are an important resource for studying the Protestant church music (the first volume), musical instruments (volume II), and music theory and composition (volume III) of his day.   *M.P.*

Es Ist Ein Ros'–78

Prentiss, Elizabeth Payson (b. Portland, ME, Oct. 26, 1818; d. Dorset, VT, Aug. 13, 1878) was the fifth of eight children born to the Rev. Edward and Ann (Shipman) Payson. She was educated at schools in New York (1830) and in Portland (1830-34). Her literary career began at the age of 16 in 1834 with a piece published in *Youth's Companion*, a magazine in Boston for children and youth with a wide reputation for high spiritual and literary standards. Many of her short didactic tales and sketches were published in this magazine under the signature "E." After several years of teaching in Portland and in Richmond, Virginia, she married the Rev. George Lewis Prentiss in 1845. They resided mainly in New York City, where her husband was pastor of the Mercer Street Presbyterian Church and then the Church of the Covenant. Later he became a professor at Union Theological Seminary. In 1858 she went to Europe with her family for reasons of her husband's health, remaining until 1860. In 1868 they built a summer home in Dorset, Vermont, which became their annual family retreat.

In addition to *Youth's Companion*, Mrs. Prentiss' shorter works appeared primarily in the *New York Observer* and the *Advance* (Chicago). Beginning with *Little Suzy's Six Birthdays* (1853), her series of "Little Suzy" books for young children were popular in America and in England. Two of her works, *Peterchen and Gretchen* (1860) and *Griselda* (1876), were translations from the German. Her most popular book was *Stepping Heavenward* (1869), which sold over one hundred thousand copies in America and also appeared in more than a dozen editions in Europe. For several decades *Stepping Heavenward* was regularly used in Sunday School libraries and was considered ideal for a prize to be awarded to school children. Her religious verse appeared in two editions, best known as *Golden Hours* (1872), some of them appearing in church hymnals. Ten of her texts are indexed in the *Dictionary of American Hymnology*, but the only one to survive beyond the 19th century is "More love to Thee, O Christ."   *H.E.*

More Love to Thee, O Christ–473

Price, Charles Philip (b. Pittsburgh, PA, Oct. 4, 1920) studied piano with Ferguson Webster in his youth and later sang in the Harvard Glee Club. He received an A.B. degree from Harvard, a B.D. degree from Virginia Theological Seminary, and a Th.D. from Union Theological Seminary in New York. He served as rector of St. Michael's of the Valley in Ligonier, Pennsylvania, as assistant at St. James Church in New York City, as professor of theology at the Virginia Theological Seminary, and as preacher to the University of Harvard. He wrote articles for the *Anglican Theological Review* as well as *Principles of Christian Faith and Practice* (1974), *Liturgy for Living* (with L. Weil, 1975), *A Matter of Faith* (1980), and *The Gifts of God* (with E. Goetchius, 1984). Price, an Episcopalian, considers himself a Tillichian theologian. He married Betty Farley and they have one daughter, Edith Arensburg (Price) Majors.   *S.W.G.*

O God, to Those Who Here Profess (st. 1, 3)–506

Price, Geoffrey is the pseudonym of a Southern Baptist composer who wishes to remain anonymous.   *P.A.R.*

Gott Vater Sei Gepriesen (arr. and harm.)–258
Lobet Und Preiset (harm.)–645

Price, Milburn (b. Electric Mills, MS, Apr. 9, 1938) earned degrees in music from the University of Mississippi (B.M., 1960), Baylor University (M.M., 1963), and the University of Southern California (D.M.A., 1967), and has been a Visiting Scholar at Princeton Theological Seminary (1987) and the Candler School of Theology at Emory

University (1991). He has taught at the University of Southern California (1966-67), at Furman University (1967-81), and served as chairman of the department of music at Furman from 1972-81. In 1981 he became Dean of the School of Church Music at The Southern Baptist Theological Seminary. He has been an active conductor, choral clinician, and lecturer on various aspects of church music. His choral compositions and arrangements have appeared in the catalogues of nine different publishing companies. He is co-author, along with William J. Reynolds, of *A Survey of Christian Hymnody* (3rd ed., 1987). He married Barbara Stevens in 1961, and they have one son, Steven, born in 1963. *M.P.*

Stir Your Church, O God, Our Father–392
EDGE–Believers All, We Bear the Name–399
PROCLAMATION–Send Forth Your Word,
   O God–588

Prichard, Rowland Huw (b. Graienyn, Merionethshire, Wales, Jan. 14, 1811; d. Holywell, Flintshire, Wales, Jan. 25, 1887) was a laborer and amateur musician. He spent most of his life in Bala, where he was known as a singing leader. In 1844 he published *Cyfaill y Cantorion* (The Singer's Friend), a children's songbook that contained many of his tunes. *P.A.R.*

HYFRYDOL–36, 77, 185, 535

Prudentius, Aurelius Clemens (b. Northern Spain, 348; d. *c.* 413) was a Catholic lawyer and poet. He came from a prominent family and was trained in the law. He served as a judge and was made chief of the Imperial Guard to Emperor Honorius. At the age of 57 he converted to Christianity, entered a monastery, and de-

voted himself to prayer and writing, becoming one of the principal Christian poets of his time. *P.A.R.*

Of the Father's Love Begotten–251

Psalmodia Evangelica (1789, Thomas Williams) is the title of a two-volume collection of psalm and hymn tunes compiled by Thomas Williams in 1789. The musical items were arranged by Williams in three parts and were intended for "Churches, Chapels and Dissenting Meetings in England, Scotland and Ireland." In the second volume may be found the original printing of the tune TRURO. *H.T.M.*

TRURO–128

Psalms of David in Meter, The (1650) is the short title for the Scottish metrical psalter of 1650 which was a revision of the first Scottish metricization of the psalms completed in 1564. This revision, the source of numerous familiar metrical psalm versions, remained intact until the 20th century. The full title of this 1650 revision was *The Psalms of David in Meeter* (sic): *Newly translated, and diligently compared with the original Text, and former translations: More plaine* (sic)*, smooth and agreeable to the Text, than any heretofore.* This psalter has often been cited as a classic of English Protestant literature, taking its place beside the King James Version of the Bible (with which it was often bound) and *The Book of Common Prayer. H.T.M.*

How Lovely Is Thy Dwelling Place–523

Puckett, Martha Roberts (b. Columbia, SC, Oct. 2, 1927) has served as a church musician (organist) with her music minister husband during most of their married career of over 40 years. She is a writer, composer, keyboard teacher, and mother of two children, both trained musicians. She served as organist at Baptist churches in Lancaster, South Carolina, and Bartow, Florida, and is presently (1990) interim pianist at Eastside Baptist Church in Plant City, Florida. Several of her compositions have been published.   *H.T.M.*

BETHLEHEM SONG–Carols Sing–90

Puckett, Paul Etheridge (b. Atlanta, GA, Jan. 5, 1923) is a graduate of the University of South Carolina (B.S. in economics). He received further training at Columbia (SC) Bible College Graduate School of Missions and The Southern Baptist Theological Seminary School of Church Music, Louisville, Kentucky.

After working as minister of music and education in churches in Pageland, Lancaster, and Camden, South Carolina, and Gastonia, North Carolina, he accepted the call of the First Baptist Church of Bartow, Florida, where he served in various positions as minister of music and education, minister of music and youth, and minister of music and administration over a period of 30 years. He was active as an officer in the Southeastern Religious Education Association. For his long career, Paul was honored by election to the presidency of the Florida Church Music Conference and subsequently with life membership in that organization. In 1987 he was honored by the Southern Baptist Convention state music directors and the Church Music Department of the Sunday School Board as "Musician on Mission."

He and his wife have collaborated in the publishing of several compositions. "Carols Sing" is their first piece to be included in a standard hymnal. In 1990 Paul was serving as interim director of music at the Eastside Baptist Church in Plant City, Florida. *H.T.M.*

Carols Sing–90

Purifoy, John (b. Camden, AR, Sep. 30, 1952) received his Bachelor of Music at the University of Arkansas in 1974 and has done graduate study in music theory at the University of Texas. From 1975 through 1982 he served as Music Editor (1975-78) and Director of Music Publishing (1978-82) at Word, Incorporated. In 1983 he became owner of his own company, Purifoy Publishing, which was bought by the Lorenz Corporation in 1991. John now serves as a composer/arranger for Lorenz.

Purifoy is the composer of over 100 choral anthems in the catalogues of various publishers. He has also written larger choral works, including a patriotic oratorio, *We Hold These Truths*, which was commissioned by the Knoxville Community Chorus and Orchestra. This received its premiere in 1985 with Alex Haley as narrator. *We Hold These Truths* was the recipient of the Freedoms Foundation at Valley Forge Award for 1985. The composer is also a five-time recipient of the ASCAP Standard Awards Panel.

John makes his home in Knoxville, Tennessee, with his wife Vicki and his sons Michael and Drew.   *D.M.*

SALLY TOWNSEND–Here Am I, Send Me–597

Quinn, James, S.J. (b. Glasgow, Scotland, Apr. 21, 1919) is a member of the British Province of the Society of Jesus. He received the M.A. from Glasgow University in 1939. His published works include *New Hymns for All Seasons* (1967), for which he served as editor, and *Theology of the Eu-*

charist (1973). He presently lives in Edinburgh, Scotland.   *P.H.*

Blessed Be the God of Israel–79

Rader, Paul (b. Denver, CO, Aug. 24, 1879; d. Hollywood, CA, Jul. 19, 1938) was the son of a Methodist minister. He was converted at the age of nine and was educated at the University of Denver and the University of Colorado. He served on the faculty of the athletic departments of the University of Puget Sound, Tacoma, Washington, and Hamline University, St. Paul, Minnesota. He became a gifted evangelistic preacher, was pastor of Chicago's Moody Church (1915-21), was elected international president of the Christian and Missionary Alliance (1921-23), then founded the Chicago Gospel Tabernacle, which he pastored for 11 years. He was a pioneer in gospel radio broadcasting and was associated in its beginning with the Tabernacle Publishing Company, Chicago. He wrote a number of hymns and hymn tunes.   *W.J.R.*

Only Believe–Only Believe–534

Rambo, Joyce Reba (Dottie) (b. Madisonville, KY, Mar. 2, 1934) is a well-known composer and singer. As a member of the Singing Rambos, she toured full-time for over 25 years. She composed the children's musical, *Down by the Creek Bank*, has written over 1000 songs and made over 50 recordings. Her compositions include "He Looked Beyond My Faults," "Remind Me," "If That Isn't Love," "Glory in the Cross," and "Tears Will Never Stain the Streets of That City."   *S.W.G.*

We Shall Behold Him–We Shall Behold Him–196
Behold the Lamb–Behold the Lamb–233

Rankin, Jeremiah Eames (b. Thornton, NH, Jan. 2, 1828; d. Cleveland, OH, Nov. 28, 1904), the son of the Rev. Andrew and Lois (Eames) Rankin, graduated from Middlebury College in 1848. After teaching in New London, Connecticut, and Warren County, Kentucky, and serving at Middlebury College as a tutor (1850-51), he studied at Andover Seminary, graduating in 1854. He married Mary Howell Birge Nov. 28, 1854 in Washington, D.C. Following his ordination to the Congregational ministry in 1855, he served as pastor of the Congregational Church, Potsdam, New York (1855-56) and then at St. Albans, Vermont (1857-62). He then served the Appleton Street Church, Lowell, Massachusetts (1862-64) and the Winthrop Church, Charleston, Massachusetts (1864-69). In 1869 he began a distinguished pastorate of almost 15 years at the First Congregational Church, Washington, DC. There large audiences attended, among them judges and members of Congress. During this period he served on the board of Howard University. After five years (1884-89) as pastor of the Valley Congregational Church, Orange, New Jersey, he served as president of Howard University until 1903. Rankin often closed his sermons with an original poem. Three volumes of his verses were printed privately: *Broken Cadences* (1889), *Hymns Pro Patria* (1889), and *German-English Lyrics* (translations; 2nd ed., 1898). He compiled and edited *Gospel Temperance Hymnal* (with E.S. Lorenz; New York, 1878) and *Gospel Bells* (with J.W. Bischoff and Otis F. Presbrey (Chicago, 1880).   *H.E.*

Tell It to Jesus–451

Rawls, Rooks Maines (b. Lake Butler, FL, Jul. 12, 1916) was educated at Mercer University (A.B.), and did graduate work at

George Peabody College for Teachers and Scarritt College. He served as an associate in the Church Training Department, Georgia Baptist Convention (1938-43), and as state secretary of Church Training and Baptist Student Work for the Alabama Baptist Convention (1943-44). From 1944 he served in various positions at the Baptist Sunday School Board, Nashville, Tennessee: director of young people's work (1944-52), manager of the Nashville Baptist Book Store (1952-55), and director of associational work (1955-64) in the Church Training Department; he then served in the Church Recreation Department as director of field services (1965-72), and as coordinator of special projects (1972-81). He retired in 1981 and now lives in Brentwood, Tennessee.   *H.E.*

LANGLEY–Take My Life, Lead Me, Lord–287

Red, Buryl (b. Little Rock, AR, Oct. 7, 1936) was educated at Baylor University (B.M., 1957) and at Yale University (M.M., 1961). He received honorary doctorates from William Jewell College, Independence, Missouri, and from William Carey College, Hattiesburg, Mississippi. Red is active as a composer, arranger, and orchestrator of music in diverse settings. Since 1961, he has served in various capacities–editor, producer, and consultant–to publishers of music education textbooks. His work as a project consultant with the Radio and Television Commission is ongoing. He continues to record preschool materials for the Baptist Sunday School Board. He has directed the Centurymen, a male chorus of 100 Southern Baptist ministers of music, since 1969. Their appearance on Chinese television in 1989 was the first telecast of religious music ever permitted in that country. An NBC documentary containing footage of that historic event won an Emmy Award. Red's work as orchestrator and arranger extends also to Broadway, Radio City Music Hall, and commercial television. He is currently preparing performing editions of early masterpieces–a practice begun with his edition of Pergolesi's *Magnificat*. Many of his activities are conducted under the auspices of his companies, BR Productions and Generic Music, in New York City. His larger works include *Celebrate Life, It's Cool in the Furnace, Beginnings, Acts,* and *Christmas Time.*   *P.H.*

RIDGECREST–341
RED–365
THE LORD'S PRAYER–659

Redhead, Richard (b. Harrow-on-the-Hill, Middlesex, England, Mar. 1, 1820; d. Hellingly, Hailsham Sussex, England, Apr. 27, 1901) received his early musical education as a chorister at Magdalen Chapel, Oxford, beginning in 1829. He accepted a position at Margaret Street Chapel, London, in 1839 and served that congregation until 1864. (In 1859, following an extended period of construction on a new church building during which the congregation worshiped at a temporary site, the Chapel became All Saints' Church and came to be known as the "Tractarian Cathedral.") From 1864 until 1894, Redhead was organist at St. Mary Magdalene, Paddington. The strong influence of the Tractarian Movement upon his work is seen in *Laudes Diurnae* (1843), on which he collaborated with Frederick Oakley. This collection was the first plainsong psalter used in the Anglican church. In 1849 he provided tunes for *Hymns and Introits*, edited by G. Cosby White. His other major publication was *Church Hymn Tunes, Ancient and Modern, for the Several Seasons of the Church Year* (London, 1853). An enlarged edition of *Church Hymn Tunes* which more than doubled the number of tunes included was issued in 1859. *M.P.*

REDHEAD–150

Redner, Lewis Henry (b. Philadelphia, PA, Dec. 14, 1831; d. Atlantic City, NJ, Aug. 29, 1908) was educated in the public schools of Philadelphia and at the age of 16 entered the real estate business and ultimately became a wealthy real estate broker in the city. He was organist in four other churches before serving at Holy Trinity Church from 1861 to 1864. For 19 years he served as superintendent of the Sunday School of the Chapel of Holy Trinity Church, beginning with 36 children and increasing to over 1,000. An endowment fund started by Redner still supports the work of the Holy Trinity Church in downtown Philadelphia. He died on August 29, 1908 at the Hotel Marlborough in Atlantic City where he had gone to recuperate from an illness. *S.W.G.*

ST. LOUIS–86

Reed, Edith Margaret Gellibrand (b. Islington, Middlesex, England, Mar. 31, 1885; d. Barnett, Hertfordshire, England, Jun. 4, 1933) was a musician and editor. She received her musical training at the Guildhall School of Music and became an Associate of the Royal College of Organists. Percy Scholes was her mentor in editorial work for several journals, including *Panpipes*, *The Music Student*, and *Music and Youth*. She was the author of *Story Lives of the Great Composers* (London, 1925). *P.A.R.*

Infant Holy, Infant Lowly
 (tr. and parap.)–106

Reinagle, Alexander Robert (b. Brighthelmstone, Sussex, England, Aug. 21, 1799; d. Kidlington, Oxfordshire, England, Apr. 6, 1877) was an Anglican organist and composer. He came from a family of professional musicians. His father was a well-known cellist; his grandfather was trumpeter to the king; and an uncle, also named Alexander Reinagle, was an influential musician in the United States after his immigration in 1786. He studied organ with his father at Oxford, where he later became a teacher. During his 31 years as organist at St. Peter's-in-the-East, Oxford, Reinagle published two collections, *Psalm Tunes, for the Voice and Pianoforte* (London, 1836) and *A Collection of Psalm and Hymn Tunes* (1840). *P.A.R.*

ST. PETER–385, 580

Reno, Delma B. (b. Long Leaf, LA, Sep. 27, 1916; d. Dallas, TX, Dec. 15, 1981), after public school in Glenmora, Louisiana, received the R.N. degree from the Grady Memorial Hospital School of Nursing, Atlanta, Georgia. She served in the Army Nurse Corps during World War II. A writer of hymns and poems, she published *The Meditations of My Heart* (1975), a collection of poetry. A member of the First Baptist Church, Dallas, Texas, she was superintendent of the Special Education Department, working with mentally and emotionally handicapped children. *W.J.R.*

Praise the Lord, the King of Glory–232

Renville, Joseph R. (b. St. Paul, MN, 1779; d. 1846) was a fur trader whose father was a French-Canadian trader and whose mother was a Dakota Native American. He received his education in Canada from a Roman Catholic priest. He established the Fort

Renville trading post on the Minnesota River (in what is now Chippewa County, Minnesota) and assisted the Dakotas in adapting to a changing environment. With his help, a mission was established at Lac-qui-Parle near his trading post, and he helped translate the Bible into the Dakota language. Renville wrote several hymns in the Dakota language which he set to Native American melodies. (The information for this article is drawn from the unpublished research of Lois C. Willand, a copy of which was provided the author by Carlton Young.)   *M.P.*

Many and Great, O God–49

Repository of Sacred Music, Part Second (1813) (Wyeth) is the earliest American singing school tunebook to contain a significant number of folk hymns that have survived to the present. It was published in Harrisburg, Pennsylvania, by the printer John Wyeth as a supplement to his earlier *Repository of Sacred Music* (1810). There were 149 tunes in *Repository of Sacred Music, Part Second*, 58 of which were new tunes, and most had folk hymn characteristics. According to Irving Lowens in his *Music and Musicians in Early America* (p. 150), it is highly probable that the person responsible for the organization and editorial supervision of the tunebook was the Reverend Elkanah Kelsay Dare (1782-1826), a Methodist clergyman and musician. In view of the important influence played by this collection on the content of later tunebooks such as *The Southern Harmony* (1835) and *The Sacred Harp* (1847), Wyeth's compilation is historically significant as a Northern precursor of Southern folk hymnody.   *H.T.M.*

NETTLETON–15
NETTLETON–507

Reyes, Gus (b. Corpus Christi, TX, Mar. 7, 1953) was trained at Delmar College, Corpus Christi, Texas (A.A.), the University of Texas, Austin (B.B.A.), Angelo State University, San Angelo (M.B.A.), and was graduated from Southwestern Baptist Theological Seminary (M.R.E.; Ed.D.). He has served as a bivocational minister of education in Texas churches and as instructor in the areas of business and marketing at Tarrant County Junior College, Ft. Worth, and Texas Christian University.

In 1987 he left the position of minister of education and youth at Mountain View Baptist Church, El Paso, to become a consultant in the Sunday School Division of the Baptist Sunday School Board. Currently, he is manager of the church and direct marketing planning section of the Board's marketing planning and promotion department. He and his wife Leticia have a daughter, Andrea. His translation of Nelson Sosa's "Caminando con Jesús" was made at the request of Terry W. York, project coordinator for *The Baptist Hymnal* (1991).   *H.T.M.*

Walking Along with Jesus (tr.)–186

Reynolds, William Jensen (b. Atlantic, IA, Apr. 2, 1920) moved with his parents, George Washington and Ethel (Horn) Reynolds to Oklahoma when he was only five months old. His father was a church music director and evangelistic singer. He was educated at Southwest Missouri State College (B.A., 1942), Southwestern Baptist Theological Seminary (M.S.M., 1945), North Texas State College (M.M., 1946), Westminster Choir College, and George Peabody College for Teachers (Ed.D., 1961). He served as minister of music at First Baptist Church, Ardmore, Oklahoma (1946-47), and First Baptist Church, Oklahoma City, Oklahoma (1947-55). From 1955 to 1980 he was employed in the Church Music Department of the Baptist Sunday School Board, Nashville, Tennessee. Since 1980 he has served as professor of church music, Southwestern Baptist Theological Seminary, Fort Worth, Texas. He has served as music director for meetings of the Southern Baptist Convention and the Baptist World Alliance. He served as chairman of the hymnal committee and general editor for *Baptist Hymnal* (1975), and *The New Broadman Hymnal* (1977). He is the author of *Hymns of Our Faith* (1964), *Companion to Baptist Hymnal* (1976), *Congregational Singing* (1975), *Songs of Glory* (1989), and co-author with Milburn Price of *A Survey of Christian Hymnody* (3rd ed., 1987). He served as president of the Hymn Society of America, 1978-80.   *W.J.R.*

WONDROUS LOVE (arr.)–143
ASSAM (arr.)–305
BREAK BREAD (arr.)–366
PEACE LIKE A RIVER (arr.)–418
COBBS (arr.)–432
SULLIVAN–Share His Love–567
CLONMEL (arr.)–599

Rhodes, Sarah Betts (b. Sheffield, Yorkshire, England, 1829; d. Wakefield, Yorkshire, Nov. 21, 1904) was born Sarah Betts Bradshaw and married a Sheffield silversmith, J. Alsop Rhodes. A sculptor and hymn writer, she was an active member of the Congregational church. No other information is available.   *D.M.*

God, Who Made the Earth–50

Richardson, Paul Akers (b. Stuart, VA., Aug. 4, 1951) is a Baptist church musician and teacher. He holds degrees from Mars Hill College (B.M., 1973) and The Southern

Baptist Theological Seminary (M.C.M., 1975; D.M.A., 1979), and has done postdoctoral study at the Eastman School of Music of the University of Rochester and at Colgate Rochester Divinity School/Bexley Hall/Crozer Theological Seminary. Since 1977, he has served in various positions on the administrative staff and faculty of Southern Seminary, where he is presently Associate Professor and Chair of Doctoral Studies in Church Music. He has served as minister of music on a part-time or interim basis in North Carolina, Indiana, and Kentucky. Among his hymnological activities have been two terms as Secretary-Treasurer of The Hymn Society in the United States and Canada, membership on the editorial committee for *The Worshiping Church* (Carol Stream, Ill.: 1990), the publication of numerous articles, and the contribution of annotations to this handbook.   *P.A.R.*

As He Gathered at His Table–369

Rinkart (also Rinckart), Martin (b. Eilenburg, Saxony, Germany, Apr. 23, 1586; d. Eilenburg, Saxony, Germany, Dec. 8, 1649) attended the Latin school at Eilenburg, St. Thomas' School, Leipzig, as a foundation scholar and chorister, and the University of Leipzig in 1601. He returned to his native Eilenburg in 1617 as archdeacon after appointments in Eisleben at the gymnasium and pastorates in Erdeborn and Lyttichendorf. In that same year, Rinkart wrote a cycle of seven dramas commemorating the centennial of the Reformation. Eilenburg was a walled city and thus became a refuge for fugitives. During the Thirty Years' War, overcrowding and poor sanitation brought on famine and pestilence. In 1637, Rinkart was left as the only pastor in the city and buried nearly 4500 people in that year alone. He was responsible for

40 to 50 burials a day. Rinkart twice convinced the victorious Swedish forces not to demand excessive tribute from the city. In spite of this outstanding service, he was harassed by the authorities over finances and other matters in his later years and died an exhausted man. Rinkart wrote 66 hymns which reflect his faith in and assurance of God's providence.   *P.H.*

Now Thank We All Our God–638

Rippon, John (b. Tiverton, Devonshire, England, Apr. 29, 1751; d. London, England, Dec. 17, 1836) was for 63 years pastor of the Carter Lane Baptist Church in London. He joined the Baptist church in his hometown when he was 16. The following year he began his education for the ministry at the Baptist College in Bristol. When John Fawcett declined the call from the Carter Lane church in 1722, John Rippon became the interim pastor. In 1723 he was named the permanent pastor, succeeding John Gill, who had served the church for 54 years.

Rippon was one of the most popular and influential Dissenting ministers of his day, both in England and America. He edited and revised John Gill's nine-volume *Exposition of the Old and New Testaments*. His periodical, the *Baptist Annual Register* (1790-1802), chronicled important events among Baptists on both sides of the Atlantic. He is most noted as the compiler of *A Selection of Hymns from the Best Authors, Intended As an Appendix to Dr. Watts' Psalms and Hymns* (1787). This hymnal became an important source of material for later compilers and introduced hymns by English Baptists Ann Steele, Samuel Stennett, John Fawcett, and Samuel Medley. *A Selection of Psalm and Hymn Tunes* (1791) was published under his name, but was probably compiled by

the precentor at his church, Robert Keene. Rippon was awarded the Doctor of Divinity degree, by what is now Brown University, in 1792.   *P.H.*

All Hail the Power of Jesus' Name
  (st. 3,4)–200, 201, 202
How Firm a Foundation (comp.)–338

Rist, Johann (b. Ottensen, Holstein, Germany, Mar. 8, 1607; d. Wedel, Holstein, Germany, Aug. 31, 1667) was a Lutheran pastor, teacher, and author. While a student at the University of Rinteln he began to write hymns under the influence of Josua Stegmann, a hymnist and professor of theology. He subsequently studied Hebrew, mathematics, and medicine at the University of Rostock and settled in Hamburg as a teacher. Most of his career was spent as a pastor in Wedel, a town near Hamburg, though he had many opportunities to move to more prominent positions as his fame grew.

Rist, a prolific writer in many genres, was named Poet Laureate by Emperor Ferdinand III. He wrote more than 680 hymns, intending to cover in them the whole of Christian theology. He published his texts in a series of small hymnals, the first being *Himmlische Lieder* (Lüneburg, 1641), which had settings by his friend, Johann Schop.
P.A.R.

Break Forth, O Beauteous Heavenly Light
  (st. 1)–114

Roberts, Daniel Crane (b. Bridgehampton, Long Island, NY, Nov. 5, 1841; d. Concord, NH, Oct. 31, 1907) was educated at Kenyon College, Gambier, Ohio. Following service as a private in the 84th Ohio Volunteers during the Civil War, he was ordained deacon in the Protestant Episcopal Church in 1865 and priest in 1866. He served as rector at Christ Church, Montpelier, Vermont; St. John's, Lowell, Massachusetts; St. Thomas', Brandon, Vermont; and vicar for the last 29 years of his life at St. Paul's, Concord, New Hampshire. He was for many years president of the New Hampshire State Historical Society. He also served as chaplain of the New Hampshire department of the Grand Army of the Republic, as commander of his state commandery of the Knights Templars (1894 and 1895), and as their national grand prelate (1901-1904). In 1885 Norwich University conferred on him the Doctor of Divinity degree. "God of Our Fathers, Whose Almighty Hand" is the only hymn for which he is remembered. *H.E.*

God of Our Fathers–629

Robinson, George Wade (b. Cork, Ireland, 1838; d. Southhampton, England, Jan. 28, 1877) attended Trinity College, Dublin, and New College, St. John's Wood, London. He was ordained to the ministry of the Congregational church and served with Dr. Urwick as co-pastor of York Street Chapel, Dublin. Later pastorates included St. John's Wood Chapel, London, and Union Street Chapel, Brighton. His poetic works included *Iona and Other Sonnets* (Dublin, 1868), *Loveland* (London, 1870), and *Songs in God's World* (London, 1872). *D.M.*

I Am His, and He Is Mine–336

Robinson, Robert (b. Swaffham, Norfolk, England, Sep. 27, 1735; d. Birmingham, England, Jun. 9, 1790) was a prominent Baptist preacher and historian. He early demonstrated a keen mind and skill in languages, and it was his mother's hope that he might become an Anglican priest. The family's impoverishment following the desertion and subsequent death of his father, however, put an end to his formal education, and at age 14 he was apprenticed to a barber in London. In 1752 he heard George Whitefield preach a sermon based on Matthew 3:7, with the repeated warning, "The wrath's to come!" This prompted a period of spiritual searching which culminated three years later in a profession of faith.

At age 22, he moved to East Anglia and there began to preach. In 1758 he became a minister of the Calvinistic Methodist Tabernacle in Mildenhall, Norwich. After a short time, he led a group from that congregation which formed an Independent (Congregational) church. During this period he rejected an invitation to return to the Anglican communion. In 1759, having adopted Baptist views on baptism as a result of Bible study, he was baptized by John Dunkham, a Baptist pastor and hymn writer in Ellingham. In that same year, he began to preach at the Stone Yard Baptist Church in Cambridge. In 1761 he accepted the call of the Stone Yard congregation to become its pastor. He continued in this role for nearly three decades, until the year of his death.

His oratorical skill, knowledge, wise counsel, and, above all, advocacy of personal, civil, and religious liberties made him a prominent figure, not only among Baptists, but in the wider Christian community. Because of his open-mindedness and toleration of views of others for the sake of liberty, he was accused by many, especially among the Calvinists, of departing from Baptist positions. Though largely self-educated, he wrote, translated, and published widely. Commissioned in 1781 to prepare a history of English Baptists, he undertook a monumental study. As a result, he produced *A History of Baptism* (1790) and left incomplete at his death the first of three projected volumes of *Ecclesiastical Researches* (published posthumously, 1792). He wrote 13 hymns and in 1768 prepared a new edition of William Barton's *Psalms*. *P.A.R.*

Come, Thou Fount of Every Blessing–15, 18

Root, George Frederick (b. Sheffield, MA, Aug. 30, 1820; d. Bailey Island, ME, Aug. 6, 1895), the eldest of eight children in a musical family, grew up on a farm at North Reading, near Boston. His first formal lessons in music took place when he, at the age of 18, went to Boston to study piano with A. N. Johnson and was his assistant organist at both Winter Street and Park Street churches. He also took singing lessons from George James Webb and joined the Handel and Haydn Society. After two years of study, he became an assistant in Lowell Mason's public school classes, and by 1841 he was directing sessions in vocal technique. In 1844 he introduced Mason's methods to New York, teaching music at Abbott's School for Young Ladies, Rutgers Female Institute, Union Theological Seminary, and the New York Institute for the Blind, where one of his students was Fanny Crosby. In 1845 he married Mary Olive Woodman, an accomplished singer. He directed the choir of Mercer Street Church, then went to Paris (1850) for vocal study, returning the following year to resume teaching. When Mason moved to New York in 1853, Root helped him establish there the first Normal Musical Institute for training teachers, its first session being led by Mason, Root, William B. Bradbury, Thomas Hastings, J. C. Woodman, and John Zundel. In the 1850s Root

began publishing parlor songs under the pseudonym G. Friedrich Wurzel (his name in German). His first song was "The Hazel Dell" (1852) with text by Fanny Crosby. He later became a leading composer of Civil War songs, including "The Battle Cry of Freedom" (1862) and "Just Before the Battle, Mother" (1862). In 1858 Root moved to Chicago, where he and his brother E. T. Root were partners in the firm of Root and Cady, a music store and publisher of popular songs. Following the great Chicago fire of 1871, Root withdrew from the firm but continued to write materials in music education, sacred music, and teacher training. In addition to some 200 songs, Root composed cantatas (sacred and secular) and compiled a number of collections of music and music method books. A selective list of Root's works is given in *The New Grove Dictionary of American Music*. A deeply religious man, in 1864 he and his wife signed the constitution of the Chicago Society of the New Jerusalem, remaining followers of Swedenborg for the remainder of their lives. Nineteen of Root's hymn tunes appeared in *Gospel Hymns Nos. 1 to 6 Complete* (1894).   *H.E.*

RING THE BELLS–428
CHILDREN–592

Rosas, Carlos (b. Linares, Nuevo Leon, Mexico, Nov. 4, 1939) serves as music director of the Mexican-American Cultural Center, San Antonio, Texas, a position he has held from 1976 to 1980 and again from 1990 to the present. Rosas attended a religious seminary between ages 12 and 19, during which time he had no contact with the outside world. He left the seminary in 1959 and took a series of jobs which included that of a bellboy in a Monterrey, Mexico, hotel. In this setting he met his future wife, Maria Teresa De Leon. After their marriage in 1965, the couple divided their time between Monterrey and her home city, San Antonio. He became a United States citizen in 1968. Rosas obtained employment as an insurance agent shortly thereafter and held that job until he began attending San Antonio College in 1976. He began the church choir at San Juan de los Lagos Catholic Church in 1970 with five members. The group now numbers 70 and includes a mariachi band. In 1991 his choir sang in St. Peter's Basilica in Rome. Rosas conducts workshops in music and liturgy throughout the United States. His most renowned hymn is "San Antonio y Roman Cantan," which was selected in a contest to be sung during the 1987 visit of Pope John Paul II to San Antonio. He relates, "Music should be used at the service of the Kingdom of God. It should awaken people to fight for the Kingdom instead of sleeping while injustices are being committed. The Christian value of the gospel is to share, to live in community and to serve" (Salazar).   *P.H.*

Rosas–O Sing a Song to God–38

Rossetti, Christina Georgina (b. London, England, Dec. 5, 1830; d. London, England, Dec. 29, 1894) was a member of a talented family. Her father, Gabriele Rossetti, was an Italian refugee who taught Italian at King's College, London. Her brother Dante Gabriel Rossetti, was the acknowledged leader of the Pre-Raphaelite Movement, made up of English artists and poets. He used Christina as a model for his painting of the madonna. Through religious devotion she sought relief from personal disappointments and poor health. She wrote many books of poetry and prose. Two of her best known poems which be-

came hymns are "In the Bleak Midwinter" and "Love Came Down at Christmas."   *D.B.*

Love Came Down at Christmas–109
What Can I Give Him–610

Rowe, James (b. Devonshire, England, Jan. 1, 1865; d. Wells, VT, Nov. 10, 1933), the son of John and Jane (Gillard) Rowe, came to the United States in 1890, settled at Albany, New York, and was married to Blanche Clapper. After working as an employee of a railroad and being superintendent of the Hudson River Humane Society, Albany, he devoted the rest of his life to literary pursuits. Writing song texts and editing music journals, he was successively associated with the Trio Music Company, Waco, Texas; A. J. Showalter Music Company, Chattanooga, Tennessee; and James D. Vaughn Music Company, Lawrenceburg, Tennessee. In his later years he made his home in Wells, Vermont, and devoted his time to writing serious and humorous verse for greeting card publishers. His daughter, Louise Rowe Mayhew, a gifted artist, was associated with him in his work. By his own record, he wrote more than 19,000 song texts, among the best known of which are 'I Walk with the King,' and 'I Would Be Like Jesus'."   *W.J.R.*

Love Lifted Me–546

Rowley, Francis Harold (b. Hilton, NY, Jul. 25, 1854; d. Boston, MA, Feb. 14, 1952) was a prominent Baptist pastor and humanitarian. He was educated at the University of Rochester (A.B., 1875) and Rochester Theological Seminary (B.D., 1878) and selected for membership in Phi Beta Kappa. He served churches in Titusville, Pennsylvania (1879-84); North

Adams, Massachusetts (1884-92); Oak Park, Illinois (1892-96); Fall River, Massachusetts (1896-1900); and Boston (1900-10). Upon retirement from the pastorate of First Baptist Church, Boston, he became president of the Massachusetts Society for Prevention of Cruelty to Animals, serving with this group until his death. He was also a leader in the Massachusetts Bible Society, the New England Baptist Hospital, and other humanitarian causes. The Rowley School of Humanities at Oglethorpe University (Georgia) memorializes his work. *P.A.R.*

I Will Sing the Wondrous Story–535, 537

Runyan, William Marion (b. Marion, NY, Jan. 21, 1870; d. Pittsburg, KS, Jul. 29, 1957) began serving as church organist at the age of 12. In 1884 he moved with his family to Marion, Kansas, where he continued his musical studies and became successful as a music teacher while still in his teens. The son of a Methodist preacher, he was ordained to the Methodist ministry in 1891 and held pastorates in Kansas for 12 years. In 1903, Runyan became evangelist for the Central Kansas Methodist Conference and served in this role for approximately 20 years, when increasing deafness necessitated his resignation. In 1924 he became associated with John Brown University, Sulphur Springs, Arkansas, where he served as pastor of the Federated Church and editor of the *Christian Workers Magazine*. From 1925 until his retirement in 1948 he lived in Chicago, where he was associated with Moody Bible Institute and also worked with the Hope Publishing Company. A songbook compiler and editor during these years, Runyan had written his first gospel song in 1915 and was encouraged in these pursuits by D.B. Towner. He received an honorary Doctor of Letters degree from Wheaton College in 1948. *M.P.*

Faithfulness–54

Russell, Anna Belle (b. Pine Valley, Chemung Co., N.Y., Apr. 21, 1862; d. Corning, N.Y., Oct. 29, 1954), the daughter of Chancey and Jane (Denson) Russell, spent most of her life in Corning, New York, where she was an active member of the First Methodist Church. She made her home with her sister, Cora C. Russell, and they both wrote a number of hymns. Russell composed at least eight hymn-tune settings of her poems between 1917 and 1942. William J. Reynolds reported to this writer that she "had three or four dozen texts published with hymn tunes composed by many composers of her day. The best known of these are D.B. Towner, George C. Stebbins, B.D. Ackley, J.H. Fillmore, I.H. Meredith, Grant Colfax Tullar, and Fred B. Holton." Mary Louise VanDyke, director of the Dictionary of American Hymnology Project of the Hymn Society of the United States and Canada, reported that their files list 32 hymn texts ascribed to Russell. *H.E.*

Wonderful, Wonderful Jesus–434

Russell, Arthur Tozer (b. Northampton, England, Mar. 20, 1806; d. Southwark, Sussex, England, Nov. 18, 1874) was an Anglican minister and hymnwriter. The son of a Congregationalist pastor, he was educated at Manchester College, York, and at St. John's College, Cambridge. Following his ordination in 1829, he served parishes in Huntingdonshire, Caxton, Cambridgeshire, Liverpool, Shropshire, and Southwick, Sussex. He was a critic of the Oxford movement and the author of several books. He compiled *Hymn Tunes, Original and Selected* (London, 1840) and published many of his approximately 140 hymns in *Psalms and Hymns* (Cambridge, 1851).   *P.A.R.*

Break Forth, O Beauteous Heavenly Light (st. 2)–114

Sacred Harp, The (1844) is an oblong, shape-note, "fasola" tunebook, compiled by Benjamin Franklin White and Elisha James King. The book of 262 pages was published in Philadelphia, Pennsylvania, by S. C. Collins, and has been the most durable of the 19th-century tunebooks by southern compilers. In the preface to the first edition, White states that he has "taught music for the last twenty years, and being necessarily thrown among churches of various denominations, and all the time observing wants in that of a variety of church music, has in this work endeavored to supply that deficiency which heretofore existed, by placing all the church music within his reach in one book."

This variety is reflected in White's choice of English psalm and hymn tunes, New England fuging tunes, hymn tunes, anthems, and odes, as well as Southern folk tunes and original tunes by southern composers. Many of these tunes, referred to by George Pullen Jackson as "Old Baptist Tunes," were those sung to the hymns in the "words only" Baptist collections of Andrew Broaddus, Jesse Mercer, Staunton S. Burdett, and William Dossey.   *W.J.R.*

WARRENTON–18
BEACH SPRING–377, 604, 613

Sacred Melodies from Haydn, Mozart, and Beethoven, Adapted to the Best English Poets and Appropriated to the Use of the British Church (London)

was published in 1812 by William Gardiner. A second volume was published in 1815. Gardiner was born in Leicester, England, on March 15, 1770. He had a hosiery mill in Leicester and once sent six pairs of stockings to Joseph Haydn with Haydn's melodies woven into the design (AUSTRIAN HYMN was one of the tunes included). He made frequent business trips to the Continent and collected the melodies of classic works which he adapted into hymn tunes for his two collections. Nineteenth-century English and American compilers followed his lead and adapted classic melodies as hymn tunes. Lowell Mason drew heavily on the collections of Gardiner.   *S.W.G.*

LYONS–16, 589, 631
GERMANY–402, 619

Sammis, John H. (b. Brooklyn, NY, Jul. 6, 1846; d. Los Angeles, CA, Jun. 12, 1919) moved to Logansport, Indiana in 1869 where he became a successful businessman. He felt the call to the ministry while serving as a YMCA worker. He attended McCormick Theological Seminary and graduated from Lane Theological Seminary in 1881. In 1880, he was ordained to the Presbyterian ministry and held pastorates in Glidden, Iowa; Indianapolis, Indiana; Grandhaven, Michigan; Red Wing, Minnesota; and Sullivan, Indiana. He joined the faculty of the Los Angeles Bible Institute following many years as a successful pastor.   *S.W.G.*

Trust and Obey–447

Sandell-Berg, Caroline V. (b. Fröderyd, Sweden, Oct. 3, 1832; d. Stockholm, Sweden, Jul. 26, 1903), also known as Lina Sandell, was the daughter of a Lutheran minister. She experienced both difficulty and tragedy early in her life. At the age of 12 she became paralyzed, but eventually recovered her health. She saw her father fall from a boat and drown when she was 26, and her mother died two years later. In 1861 she took a position on the editorial staff of the Evangelical National Foundation, where she met Carl Olof Rosenius, a leading lay-preacher. It was during this time that she devoted part of her time to writing religious poems, many of which were set to music by Oskar Ahnfelt, Rosenius' musical associate. One hundred and twenty-six of her original hymns and translations were published by the Evangelical National Foundation in *Sionstoner*. She is credited with having written 650 poems, and she has been called "the Fanny Crosby of Sweden." In 1867 she married Carl Oscar Berg, a wealthy Stockholm merchant.   *M.P.*

Children of the Heavenly Father–55
Day by Day–66

Sankey, Ira David (b. Edinburgh, PA, Aug. 28, 1840; d. Brooklyn, NY, Aug. 13, 1908) was perhaps the best-known and most influential of the song leaders of the 19th-century urban revivals. After moving with his family to Newcastle, Pennsylvania, in 1857, he joined the Methodist Episcopal Church and became its Sunday School superintendent and choir director. He returned to Newcastle after service in the Civil War and worked with his father, who was collector of internal revenue.

Sankey became a leader in the local Y.M.C.A. and met Dwight L. Moody at its 1870 convention in Indianapolis. After six months of persuasion, Moody convinced him to become the music leader for his meetings. He worked with Moody for nearly 30 years and established a new model of the evangelistic musician through his decorous song leading and his practice of accompanying his own solos on a reed organ.

After he was unable to get permission to add his own songs to an edition of Philip Phillips' *Hallowed Songs* (Cincinnati, 1865) for a London meeting in 1872, Sankey published *Sacred Songs and Solos* (London, 1873), which went through many editions and sold more than 80 million copies. Upon his return to the United States, Sankey discovered P. P. Bliss' *Gospel Songs* (Cincinnati, 1874) and proposed that they combine their efforts. The result was *Gospel Hymns and Sacred Songs* (New York and Cincinnati, 1875). The *Gospel Hymns* series continued through six volumes, as Sankey collaborated with Bliss and, after his death, with James McGranahan and George C. Stebbins. These books were so widely disseminated that they effectively established the core of the gospel hymn repertory. Sankey's work in publication continued as president of Biglow and Main from 1895 until his death. He spent his last years in Brooklyn, struggling with blindness, illness, and depression.

Sankey wrote more than 100 tunes, many of which were harmonized by others. *P.A.R.*

Sankey–413
Trusting Jesus–417

Saward, Michael John (b. Blackheath, Kent, England, May 14, 1932) is the vicar of Ealing, London. He was educated at Eltham College, London, and at Bristol University (B.A. Theology, 1955). From 1967-72 he served in the Radio and Television Office of the Church of England. He became Vicar of St. Matthew, Fulham, London, in 1972. He is a Church Commissioner, a member of the General synod, and a

Church Urban Fund Trustee. He is married and has four children. Since 1962 Saward has written 58 hymns which have been published worldwide. He was an editor of *Hymns for Today's Church* (1982) and is a director of Jubilate Hymns, Ltd. *P.H.*

Baptized in Water–362

Sawyer, Laurence Frank (Victoria, British Columbia, Canada, Aug. 4, 1946), since 1986, has served with Christian Reformed World Ministries as a seminary professor for Iglesia Cristiana Reformaca in Tegucigalpo, Honduras. Previously he held pastorates in Zoetermeer, The Netherlands (1977-80) and in Ponce, Puerto Rico (1983-85). Educated at Calvin College, Grand Rapids, Michigan (B.A., 1971), and at the Reformed Seminary in Kampen, The Netherlands, he is the author of occasional poems and meditations. *H.T.M.*

I've Come to Tell (trans.)–222

Schlesische Volkslieder (1842) is a collection of German folk songs published in Leipzig in 1842 which contained an altered text to "Schönster Herr Jesu" ("Fairest Lord Jesus") with a melody marked as having been taken down from the oral tradition in the region around Glaz, Silesia. This collection is therefore the original source of the anonymous tune named variously CRUSADER'S HYMN and ST. ELIZABETH to which "Fairest Lord Jesus" is sung. *H.T.M.*

CRUSADERS' HYMN (ST. ELIZABETH)–176

Scholfield, John (Jack) P. (b. Beulah, KS, Jul. 17, 1882; d. Poplar Bluff, MO, Jun. 2, 1972) received a B.A. degree from Baker University in 1906. Before joining the staff of the Home Mission Board (1912-1917,

1919), he was a school teacher and evangelistic singer, writing a number of songs which were purchased and published by Robert H. Coleman. In 1931, Scholfield moved to Fort Scott, Kansas, and entered the real estate business. He retired in 1950 and moved to Poplar Bluff, Missouri, where he died. *S.W.G.*

RAPTURE–Saved, Saved–540

Schop, Johann (b. Hamburg [?], Holstein, Germany, ca. 1595; d. Hamburg, Germany, 1667) was a Lutheran musician and composer. The first record of his employment was as a probationary musician in Wolfenbüttel in 1614. In the following year, he moved to the court of Christian IV in Copenhagen. By 1621 he had settled in Hamburg, where he lived for the remainder of his life, though he traveled widely and was sought after for other positions. He was skilled on many instruments, including the lute, cornet, trombone, and was an outstanding violinist. In various roles in Hamburg–court music director, church music director, and organist–he contributed to the flourishing of music in that city. He composed solo songs and sacred concertos and wrote numerous tunes to set the hymn texts of his friend, Johann Rist. Among his many chorales that figure prominently in the Lutheran repertory, perhaps the most famous is "Werde munter, mein Gemuthe," written for a text by Rist and known through J. S. Bach's cantata number 147 as "Jesu, Joy of Man's Desiring." *P.A.R.*

ERMUNTRE DICH MEIN SCHWACHER–114

Schrader, Jack (b. St. Louis, MO, Jul. 16, 1942) was educated at Brentwood High School (St. Louis), Moody Bible Institute (Dip. Church Music, 1964), and the University of Nebraska-Lincoln (B.M.E., 1966). After further studies in theology, he was ordained by the Evangelical Free Church in America in 1975. For 20 years he served as a minister of music in local churches including 15 years (1969-84) at the Evangelical Free Church in Wheaton, Illinois. After six years on a half-time basis, in 1984 he joined Hope Publishing Company as a full-time editor and church music specialist. In 1991 he assumed the position of music editor. *D.B.*

ACCLAMATIONS–408

Schubert, Franz (b. Lichtental, Austria, Jan. 31, 1797; d. Vienna, Austria, Nov. 19, 1828) was a prolific composer of art songs, operas, church music, chamber music, and orchestral music. His total output is all the more amazing when one realizes he was only 31 when he died. He is noted for his ability to write beautiful melodies and for the ability to compose with great speed. *D.B.*

HOLY IS THE LORD–666

Schuler, George Stark (b. New York, NY, Apr. 18, 1882; d. Sarosota, FL, Oct. 30, 1973) received his musical training in New York City and then in Chicago at the Chicago Musical College, the Cosmopolitan School of Music, and the American Conservatory of Music. He enrolled at Moody Bible Institute intending to prepare for the pastorate, but then turned to music. In 1909 he began teaching music at Moody, serving 42 years until his retirement on January 1, 1951. He taught organ, piano, harmony, and choral conducting, and wrote several texts for use in his classes, including *Choral Directing* (Chicago, 1922), *Evangelistic Piano Playing* (Bryn Mawr,

1922), and *Gospel Song and Hymn Tune Composition: Formerly Four-Part Harmony and Composition* (New York, 1927). He was a regular contributor to *The Etude* magazine. Twice he served as minister of music of the Moody Memorial Church, Chicago. His most popular songs include "I'm a Pilgrim" (1909), used by Charles Alexander in his evangelistic meetings, "Oh, What a Day!" (1933), and "Overshadowed" (1935). From 1946 to 1973, Schuler served on the editorial staff of The Rodeheaver Company. *H.E.*

SCHULER–569

Schultz, Lawrence Edmond (b. Tulsa, OK, Oct. 3, 1965) is a graduate of Oklahoma Baptist University (B.M.; Magna cum Laude, 1986) and The Southern Baptist Theological Seminary (MCM, 1989). He is married to Cynthia Smith who is also a seminary music school graduate. During student days Schultz served in music ministry positions in the Phoenix Avenue Baptist Church, Tulsa, Oklahoma, and the Yorktown Baptist Church, Louisville, Kentucky. While in high school, he won a composition competition sponsored by the Church Music Department of the Baptist General Convention of Oklahoma. This helped him discover his creative gifts. Several of his choral pieces and vocal solos have been published in *The Church Musician* and by GENEVOX Music Group. In 1990 he became the Minister of Music at the First Baptist Church, Walterboro, South Carolina. *H.T.M.*

O God, We Ask for Strength–498

Schulz, Johann Abraham Peter (b. Luneburg, Germany, Mar. 31, 1747; d. Schwedt-an-der-Oder, Germany, Jun. 10,

1800) became a musician against his father's desire that he pursue a ministerial career. At the age of 15, he ran away from home with the help of Joseph Kirnberger to Berlin to further his musical aspirations. Schulz was persuaded to return to school but did study with Kirnberger three years later. From 1768-73 he toured Europe with the Polish princess Sapieha Woiwodin von Smolensk. He returned to Berlin in 1773 and assisted Kirnberger in editing his *Treatise on Pure Composition* without receiving credit for his work. In 1776, he became musical director of the French theatre in Berlin. Schulz served as court composer to Prince Henry of Prussia at Rheinsburg from 1780-87. The pinnacle of his career came in 1787 when he obtained the post of Hofkapellmeister and director of the Royal Danish Theatre in Copenhagen. Through his leadership, the Danish court became a leading musical center. He was pensioned in 1795 and then divided his time between Berlin and Rheinsberg. He was an important early composer of lieder, opera, and oratorio.   *P.H.*

SCHULZ–Oh, Come, Little Children–107

Schulz-Widmar, Russell (b. Harvard, IL, Jul. 29, 1944) is a Lutheran church musician and teacher. He was educated at Valparaiso University (B.Mus., 1966), Union Theological Seminary (S.M.M., 1968), and The University of Texas (D.M.A., 1974). He is co-director of music at University United Methodist Church in Austin, Texas; adjunct professor of church music at The Episcopal Theological Seminary of the Southwest; and visiting lecturer in church music at Austin Presbyterian Seminary. From 1988 to 1990, he served as president of The Hymn Society in the United States and Canada. He was editor of *Songs of*

Thanks and Praise (Chapel Hill, 1980), chair of the music committee for *The Hymnal 1982* (New York, 1985), and coeditor, with Jeffrey Rowthorn, of *A New Hymnal for Colleges and Schools* (New Haven, 1992). *P.A.R.*

Your Love, O God, Has Called Us Here–509

Schumann, Robert Alexander (b. Zwickau, Saxony, Germany, Jun. 8, 1810; d. Endenich, near Bonn, Germany, Jul. 29, 1856) was one of the great Romantic composers of the 19th century. The son of a bookseller and publisher, Schumann manifested considerable musical talent at an early age. He was composing by the age of seven and writing for chorus and orchestra by 11. However, his father died when he was 15, and his mother insisted on his studying for the bar. Consequently, he was enrolled as a law student first at the University of Leipzig, then at the University of Heidelberg, but spent most of his time studying music, until his mother finally gave in to his musical aspirations. In 1840 Schumann married the daughter of his piano teacher, Clara Wieck, one of the great pianists of the 19th century and an excellent composer in her own right. Schumann wrote symphonies, concertos, and chamber music, but excelled especially as a composer of songs and short piano works. The literary background of his youth led him into the field of music criticism. He helped found the influential journal *Neue Zeitschrift fuer Musik* and served as its editor for 10 years. Through this journal and other writings, he championed the cause of musical Romanticism and brought the compositions of Frederic Chopin and Johannes Brahms to the attention of the public. Toward the end of his life, Schumann was afflicted with bouts of insanity and, after an attempt at suicide, was confined by his own request to an asylum, where he died at age 46.   *D.M.*

Canonbury–299, 509, 568

Schütz, Johann Jacob (b. Frankfurt-am-Main, Germany, Sep. 7, 1640; d. Frankfurt-am-Main, Germany, May 22, 1690) studied at Tübingen and was licensed to practice civil and canon law. He worked in Frankfurt, in later years earning the title of *Rath* (counselor). A close friend of Philipp Jacob Spener, Schütz suggested that Spener begin his later-to-be-famous *Collegia Pietatis* (prayer meetings), the establishment of which in 1670 is regarded as the beginning of the Pietist movement in German religious life. Schütz was the author of many hymns which were published in his *Christliches Gedenckbüchlein zu Beförderung lines anfangenden neuen Lebens* . . (Christian Devotional Booklet for the Development of a New Life, Frankfurt, 1675).   *H.E., H.T.M.*

Sing Praise to God Who Reigns Above–20

Schwedler, Johann Christoph (b. Krobsdorf, Silesia, Dec. 21, 1672; d. Niederwiese, Silesia, Jan. 12, 1730) was educated at the Gymnasium at Zittau and received a M.A. from the University of Leipzig in 1697. In 1701 he became pastor at Niederwiese where he was noted for the gift of prayer, and was popular for his powerful preaching. He would sometimes begin services at five or six in the morning and people would come in succession to fill the church until two or three in the afternoon. It is said that the principal theme of his some 500 hymns was the grace of God through Christ and the joyful confidence of the soul that experienced that grace. He died suddenly during the night of January 12, 1730.   *S.W.G.*

Ask Ye What Great Thing I Know–538

Schwoebel, David Gene (b. East St. Louis, IL, Dec. 2, 1957) studied at McKendree College, Lebanon, Illinois (B.A., 1979), and Southwestern Baptist Theological Seminary (M.C.M., 1980). He served as minister of music at St. Matthew United Methodist Church, Belleville, Illinois (1981-84), as assistant minister of music at First Baptist Church, Montgomery, Alabama (1984-87), and as minister of music at First Baptist Church, Chamblee, Georgia (1987-91). Since 1991 he has been minister of music at Briarlake Baptist Church, Decatur, Georgia. His publications include over 70 compositions for choir, handbells, organ, and piano, as well as "A Ministry in Handbells" in *Music Idea Kit* (Franklin House Publishing, 1984). He is active as a workshop leader, adjudicator, clinician, and pianist for church music festivals. David and his wife Michelle are the parents of three children.   *D.M.*

Michelle–397

Scott, Clara H. (b. Elk Grove, Cook Co. IL, Dec. 3, 1841; d. Dubuque, IA, Jun. 21, 1897) was the daughter of Abel Fiske and Sarah (Rockwell) Jones. In 1856 she attended the first musical institute in Chicago, conducted by C. M. Cady. Three years later she began teaching music in the Ladies' Seminary at Lyons, Iowa. In 1861 she was married to Henry Clay Scott. She became an acquaintance of Horatio R. Palmer, who greatly encouraged her in creative writing. She contributed a large number of songs to his collections, as well as numerous piano music in sheet music form. She published *The Royal Anthem Book* (1882), the first collection of anthems published by a woman, *Happy Songs, Truth in Song for Lovers of*

Truth (1896), and *Short Anthems* (1897). While visiting in Dubuque, Iowa, she was tragically killed when thrown from a buggy by a runaway horse.   *W.J.R.*

Scott–Open My Eyes That I May See–502

Scott, Robert Balgarnie Young (b.

Toronto, Canada, Jul. 16, 1899; d. Toronto, Canada, Nov. 1, 1987) was an Old Testament scholar and ordained minister of the United Church of Canada. He earned a B.B. degree from Knox College, Toronto (1926), and several degrees from the University of Toronto (B.A., M.A., and Ph.D). His studies also took him to Westminster Hall, Vancouver; New College, Edinburgh; and Westminster College, Cambridge. After two years as minister in a mission church in Long Branch, Ontario, Scott embarked upon his teaching career. He taught at Union College of British Columbia, Vancouver; United Theological College, Montreal (1931-48); and McGill University, Montreal (1948-55), before joining the religion department at Princeton University in 1955. Scott served as chairman of the department from 1963 until his retirement in 1965. He served as president of The Fellowship for a Christian Social Order, working closely with Gregory Vlastos. Together they edited *Toward the Christian Revolution* (1936), which was widely read in the United States and Canada. His best known book was *The Relevance of the Prophets* (1945; revised 1968). Other books include *The Way of Wisdom in the Old Testament* (1971) and *Treasures from the Judean Caves* (1955). His hymns are contained in nearly 30 hymnals.   *P.H.*

O Day of God, Draw Nigh–623

Scriven, Joseph Medicott (b. Seapatrick,

County Down, Ireland, Sep. 10, 1819; d. Bewdley, Rice Lake, Ontario, Canada, Oct. 10, 1886) was the son of a captain in the Royal Marines, and his mother was a sister to an English vicar. Scriven entered Trinity College in Dublin, but after two years decided on an Army career and entered Addiscombe Military College, Surrey in 1837. He returned to Trinity College after poor health caused him to abandon his military ambitions, receiving a B.A degree in 1842.

On the evening before his wedding, his bride-to-be was accidentally drowned. Possibly seeking to start life anew, he moved to Canada in 1844. He taught school for a time in Woodstock and Brantford. Then he moved to Bewdley near Rice Lake and became a tutor to the family of Lieutenant Pengelley, a retired naval officer. Again, shortly before he was to be married, his bride-to-be, Miss Eliza Roche, a relative of the Pengelley family, died suddenly after a brief illness.

Scriven attempted to follow literally Christ's teachings in the Sermon on the Mount and gave away his property. As a member of the Plymouth Brethren he spent his time in menial work for the physically handicapped and financially destitute. He himself suffered physical and financial problems in his later years. He became extremely depressed because of failing health, little income, and the fear of becoming physically helpless and a burden to others. He drowned on October 10, 1886 at Rice Lake in Ontario, Canada and it was never determined whether his death was suicidal or accidental. A monument to him was erected in 1910 at Rice Lake, 10 miles north of Port Hope, Ontario.   *S.W.G.*

What a Friend We Have in Jesus–182

Seabough, Edward Ellis (b. Aurora, MO, Oct. 27, 1932) was educated at Southwest Baptist College, Southwest Missouri State University, and Southwestern Baptist Theological Seminary. He served as student and music secretary for the Baptist General Convention of Oregon-Washington and as a consultant in the Student Department, Baptist Sunday School Board, Nashville, Tennessee. Following his work as associate to the executive director of the Southern Baptist Home Mission Board, he was minister of single adults and college students for the South Main Baptist Church, Houston, Texas. He is presently vice-president for Wilcox World Travel and Tours, Asheville, North Carolina. *W.J.R.*

I'm Just a Child–488

Sears, Edmund Hamilton (b. Sandisfield, MA, Apr. 6, 1810; d. Weston, MA, Jan. 16, 1876), after receiving his education at Union College, Schenectady, New York, and Harvard Divinity School, was ordained to the Unitarian ministry and held pastorates in Wayland and Lancaster, Massachusetts. Despite his Unitarian education and pastorates, Sears claimed to believe and preach the divinity of Jesus Christ. He served as coeditor of *Monthly Religious Magazine* and authored a number of books, including *Regeneration* (1854), *Pictures of the Olden Time* (1857), *Athanasia, or Foregleams of Immortality* (1858), *The Fourth Gospel, the Heart of Christ* (1872), and *Sermons and Songs of the Christian Life* (1875). *D.M.*

It Came upon the Midnight Clear–93

Seddon, James Edward (b. Ormskirk, Lancashire, England, Aug. 24, 1915; d. London, England, Sep. 19, 1983), the son of James and Ellen Seddon, attended King George V Grammar School, Southport. He received Associate degrees in music from the London College of Music and Trinity College, London, and trained for the ministry at the Bible Churchmen's Theological College (now Trinity College) in Bristol. From 1939 to 1945 he held three curacies in the Church of England. In 1945 he became a missionary to Morocco, returning to England in 1955 to become Home Secretary of the Bible Churchmen's Missionary Society, a post he held until 1967. From 1967 to 1980 he held two incumbencies in the Church of England. Seddon wrote about 30 hymns in English on missions and other topics, as well as several hymns in Arabic during his service in Morocco. *D.M.*

Go Forth and Tell! O Church of God–596

Seiss, Joseph Augustus (b. Graceham, MD, Mar. 18, 1823; d. Philadelphia, PA, Jun. 20, 1904) was born in a German Moravian settlement and confirmed as a Moravian at age 16. He ignored the advice of his father and his bishop by studying for the ministry at Pennsylvania College, Gettysburg, and by pursuing private theological study. The Evangelical Lutheran Synod of Virginia licensed him in 1842. He held pastorates in Virginia and Maryland before becoming pastor of St. John's Lutheran Church in Philadelphia in 1858. He later established the Church of the Holy Communion in that city. Among some 80 publications are *The Last Times* (1856), *The Evangelical Psalmist* (1859), *Lectures on the Gospels* (1868-72), works on Lutheran literature, and hymn collections. *P.H.*

Fairest Lord Jesus (st.4)–176

Selection of Hymns (1787, John Rippon) is the short title of *A Selection of Hymns* from the Best Authors intended to be An Appendix to Dr. Watts' Psalms and Hymns which was published in London in 1787 by John Rippon, prominent Baptist pastor, editor, publisher, historian, and first president of the Baptist Union of Great Britain. This book of hymns, which went through some 30 editions in Britain and America, served the cause of hymnody possibly better than any other Baptist collection not only because of its wide circulation, but by virtue of its use as a source book–indeed a sort of standard reference work–drawn upon by many compilers and editors of hymnals. It is best remembered as the original source of the anonymous "How Firm a Foundation." *H.T.M.*

How Firm a Foundation–338

Sellers, Ernest Orlando (b. Hastings, MI, Oct. 29, 1869; d. Eola, LA, Oct. 19, 1952) was the son of William A. and Kate (Armstrong) Sellers, who were both devout Methodists and brought Ernest up in that church. The family moved during his early years to Lansing, Michigan, where Ernest graduated from high school. He then was apprenticed to a surveyor and civil engineer and, after five years, was appointed city engineer and superintendent of public works. He met Edith Lavinia Simmons in the Methodist Church in Lansing, and in 1892 they were married in Hillsdale, Michigan.

Sellers reportedly possessed a beautiful tenor voice and had studied piano and voice privately for a short time. Notwithstanding his limited musical training, he had a strong desire to lead evangelistic music, and in 1896 he became associated with evangelist Fred B. Smith for several months. From April to July of 1897, he studied at the Moody Bible Institute. While a student he joined the Moody Memorial Church

and was baptized into its fellowship. In January 1899 Sellers began directing the music at the First Baptist Church, Macon, Georgia, during which time he became gradually more involved in the Macon YMCA, becoming its general secretary in January 1900. This was followed by YMCA positions in Washington, D.C. (1901-02) and Wilmington, Delaware (1902-03), and then the position of director of men's work at the Euclid Avenue Baptist Church, Cleveland, Ohio (1903-07). Sellers returned to Moody Bible Institute as assistant director of the music course (under D.B. Towner) and professor of Sunday School pedagogy, 1907-18. His hymn "Thy Word Have I Hid in My Heart" was copyrighted in 1908. During these years he led music for such well known evangelists as R.A. Torry, Gypsy Smith, A.C. Dixon, and J. Wilbur Chapman. In 1918 Sellers resigned his position at Moody to do YMCA work among men in the armed forces, including service in England and France. Upon his return, Sellers was ordained to the gospel ministry September 22, 1919, by the Belden Avenue Baptist Church, Chicago.

On October 1, 1919, Sellers became a member of the faculty of the one-year-old Baptist Bible Institute (now New Orleans Baptist Theological Seminary), beginning as Professor of Christian Music, Personal Work, and Director of Student Activities. Sellers, then 50 years of age, served on the faculty 25 years until his retirement in 1944. He was affectionately known as "Uncle Fuller," receiving the respect and esteem of colleagues and students. During the financial hardships of the Great Depression, Sellers was one of several faculty members who served the school for a period of time without salary. His later years were made financially secure by the discovery of oil on his property at Eola,

Louisiana, where he made his retirement home, "Bayou Grove." He is buried in the Pythian Cemetery, Bunkie, Louisiana.

Sellers wrote several books for use in his classes: *Personal Evangelism* (1923), *How to Improve Church Music* (1928), *Elements of Music Notation and Conducting* (1938), *Worship, Why and How* (1944), and *Evangelism in Sermon and Song* (1946). He was a member of the committee for *The New Baptist Hymnal* (1926). His compositions were published in three collections: *Songs by Sellers* (self-published, 1942), *Wonderful Songs* (Singspiration, 1948), and *Sacred Songs and Anthems* (Broadman, 1951). In addition to hymn texts and tunes, Sellers wrote more than 300 poems, which have been collected in the Martin Music Library of New Orleans Baptist Theological Seminary. Sellers also wrote numerous articles, including several in the 1951 and 1952 issues of *The Church Musician*.

The music building of New Orleans Baptist Theological Seminary, built shortly after his death, is named the Sellers Music Building. This building houses a Mason and Hamlin reed pump organ formerly in the Moody Memorial Church that Sellers used for many years and bequeathed to the seminary.   *H.E.*

New Orleans–434

Sewell, Hampton Haygood (b. Atlanta, GA, Jan. 7, 1874; d. Temple, GA, Mar. 11, 1937) was an evangelistic singer, and a composer and compiler of gospel songs. His formal education was limited, but he studied music with gospel songwriter and publisher A. J. Showalter at the Southern Normal Music Institute. He began his evangelistic work in 1909 with preacher Charles Dunaway, after having been a merchant and farmer. His three collections, *Hymns of*

Glory (Atlanta, 1909), *Hymns of Glory, No. 2* (Atlanta, 1914), and *World Revival Hymns* (Atlanta, 1918), include many of his 500 hymns.   *P.A.R.*

Sewell–436

Shea, George Beverly (b. Winchester, Ontario, Canada, Feb. 1, 1909) was the fourth of eight children of the Rev. Adam Joseph and Maude (Whitney) Shea. His mother was a church pianist, and he did his first singing in the choir of the Wesleyan Methodist church where his father served as pastor in Ottawa. He came to the United States in 1928, studying at Houghton (New York) College, 1928-29, where he sang in the Glee Club directed by Wilfred C. Bain, a friend since childhood. Houghton awarded Shea an honorary D.F.A. in 1956. He also received an honorary D.S.M. from Trinity College in 1969. He was married to Erma Letta Scharfe June 16, 1934, and they had two children, Ronald and Elaine. In 1941 Shea became an American citizen. While working for Mutual of New York Insurance Company in New York City, he studied with several voice teachers including Gino Monaco. During the thirties he had opportunities to sing on several radio programs in the New York area, and in 1938 he moved to Chicago to work at the Moody Bible Institute. He joined the staff of WMBI the following year. For several years he sang hymns on the ABC network program, "Club Time." In 1944 he joined the young preacher Billy Graham in singing on his radio program, "Songs in the Night." This was the beginning of an association in an evangelistic ministry that continues to the present. Shea has recorded 49 albums of hymns and spirituals for RCA Victor and for WORD Records. In 1966 he received a Grammy award. His publications include the collections *George Beverly Shea's Favorites* (1957), *The Crusade Soloist* (1963), *Songs That Lift the Heart* (1972), and his autobiography, *Then Sings My Soul* (1968). Much of the popularity of "I'd Rather Have Jesus" along with "How Great Thou Art" is due to his singing of these hymns in Billy Graham Crusades. In addition to the present hymns, he composed the words and music to "The Wonder of It All" (1956) and a few other lesser known songs. Several years after the death of his first wife, he married Karlene Johnson (1985) and moved from the Chicago area to Montreat, North Carolina. *H.E.*

I'D RATHER HAVE JESUS–550

Shepherd, Thomas (b. England, 1665; d. Bocking, Essex, England, Jan. 29, 1739) was ordained in the Church of England, but left it in 1694. He became pastor of the Castle Hill Meeting House at Nottingham, where Philip Doddridge was later to assume the pastorate. He moved to Bocking, near Braintree, Essex, in 1700 and preached in a barn for seven years before a small chapel was built. He remained as pastor of this church for 39 years. *P.H.*

Must Jesus Bear the Cross Alone –475

Sheppard, Franklin Lawrence (b. Philadelphia, PA, Aug. 7, 1852; d. Germantown, PA, Feb. 15, 1930) was educated at the University of Pennsylvania, where he was a charter member of the University's chapter of Phi Beta Kappa, and from which he graduated in 1872. In 1875 he assumed responsibility for the foundry of his father's firm, Isaac A. Sheppard & Company, manufacturers of stoves and heaters. He was a member of the Zion Episcopal Church, Baltimore, and served that church as organist and vestryman. He later joined the Second Presbyterian Church of Baltimore, where he was music director and an active Sunday School worker. Sheppard served as a lay delegate to the General Assembly and was a member of the Presbyterian Board of Publication, later serving as president. His musical interests are reflected in his editing *Alleluia* (1915), a Presbyterian Sunday School songbook. He also served on the editorial committee for *The Hymnal* (1911), used by Presbyterian churches. *M.P.*

TERRA PATRIS–43, 529

Sherlock, Hugh Braham (b. Portland, Jamaica, West Indies, Mar. 21, 1905), the son of a Methodist minister, was educated at Beckford and Smith's School, Calabar High School, and Caenwood Methodist Theological College in Jamaica. He served as a Methodist minister in Turks Islands from 1932-37 and in Jamaica, succeeding his late father in the Ocho Rios Circuit, from 1937-40. From 1940-56 he was Founder-Director of the Y.M.C.A.-sponsored Boys' Town in Western Kingston. Sherlock became the first National Chairman of the Jamaica Methodist District in 1956 and served in that position until 1966. He subsequently became the first President of the Autonomous Methodist Conference of the Caribbean and the Americas in 1967 and held that position until 1972. His honors include an honorary D.D. degree from Baldwin-Wallace College in 1962 and an honorary LL. D. from the University of the West Indies in 1977. He is the author of the words of the national anthem of Jamaica, written in 1972. In 1979 he was awarded the "Order of Jamaica," that country's highest national honor. *M.P.*

Lord, Thy Church on Earth Is Seeking–391

Sherwin, William Fiske (b. Buckland, MA, Mar. 14, 1826; d. Boston, MA, Apr. 14, 1888) received his music education under Lowell Mason and other teachers of his day and later taught at New England Conservatory of Music in Boston. He possessed extraordinary ability in the organizing and directing of amateur choruses, and, because of this, he was chosen to be the musical director of Chautauqua Assembly in New York. He was a Baptist layman. *W.J.R.*

BREAD OF LIFE–263, 368

Shimada, Katsuhiko–Little information is available about this Japanese Christian. He is known to have been a student at Kanto Gakuin High School in Yokohama, Japan, in the late 1950s or early 1960s. According to the translator of the text, Nobuaki Hanaoka, who knew Mr. Shimada in his youth, he had no musical training "except that we all sang in the school choir and loved to sing." *D.M.*

KANTO–Jesus, My Friend, Is Great–190

Showalter, Anthony Johnson (b. Cherry Grove, Rockingham County, VA, May 1, 1858; d. Chattanooga, TN, Sep. 16, 1924) was a direct descendant of Heinrich Funck (Henry Funk), America's first Mennonite bishop and the father of the musical Funk family of the Shenandoah Valley. Showalter received his early musical training from his father, a leading singing school teacher of the Shenandoah Valley. A.J. Showalter's teachers included Benjamin C. Unseld, George F. Root, H.R. Palmer, and F.W. Root. He began teaching singing schools at the age of 14 as his father's assistant, and in 1878 he taught his own singing schools as an employee of the Ruebush-Kieffer Company of Dayton, Virginia. His work

soon extended into other southern states.

In 1884 Showalter moved to Dalton, Georgia, where he founded his own firm, The A.J. Showalter Company. By Showalter's death in 1924, his collections of songs were reported to be selling about 100,000 copies a year. From 1884 to at least 1924, Showalter published a monthly, *The Music Teacher*. He trained a number of prominent southern gospel musicians through his normal music schools, including J.D. Patton, T.B. Mosley, and J.R. Baxter, Jr. In 1925, the year after Showalter's death, a memorial service was held for him in Dalton by the Seventh Congressional District Singing Association, which, with 5,000 in attendance, was considered the greatest event of its kind ever held in Georgia. The memorial service at his grave site in Hardwick Private Cemetery was begun with the singing of his most famous hymn, his setting of E.A. Hoffman's "Leaning on the Everlasting Arms." *H.E.*

SHOWALTER–333

Shrubsole, William (baptized Canterbury, England, Jan. 13, 1760; d. London, England, Jan. 18, 1806) was a close friend of Edward Perronet, for whose hymn "All Hail the Power of Jesus' Name" he wrote the tune MILES LANE. The son of a blacksmith, Shrubsole received musical training as a chorister at Canterbury Cathedral between 1770 and 1777. In 1782, he was appointed organist at Bangor cathedral, but he was dismissed in less than two years because of his association with Methodists and Dissenters. He became a private music teacher in London until his appointment in 1784 as organist at Spa Fields Chapel, where he remained until his death. A phrase from MILES LANE is carved on Shrubsole's tombstone in Bunhill Fields, London. *P.H.*

MILES LANE–201

Shurtleff, Ernest Warburton (b. Boston, MA, Apr. 4, 1862; d. Paris, France, Aug. 24, 1917) attended Harvard University, New Church Theological Seminary (Swedenborgian) in Cambridge, and was graduated from Andover Theological Seminary (1887). He was ordained to the Congregational ministry and pastored churches in Ventura, California (1883-91), Plymouth and Palmer, Massachusetts (1891-98), and Minneapolis, Minnesota (1898-1905) before moving to Frankfurt, Germany, where he founded the American Church. In 1906 he became student activities director at the Academy Vitti in Paris, and, during World War I, he and his wife Helen became involved in relief work. Shurtleff wrote a number of books, including *Poems* (1883), *New Year's Peace* (1885), *Song of Hope* (1886), *Shadow of the Angel* (1886), *Hymns of Faith* (1887), and *Song on the Waters* (1913).   *D.M.*

Lead On, O King Eternal–621

Simmons, Houston (b. New Orleans, LA, May 10, 1956) is a graduate of Loyola University of the South, New Orleans, Louisiana (B.M., 1978), and New Orleans Baptist Theological Seminary (M.C.M., 1980). He served as minister of music at Greater St. Stephen Baptist Church, New Orleans (1975-76), and First Baptist Church, Vacherie, Louisiana (1979-84, 1986-87). From 1982-87 he was also president/producer of Kingdom Enterprises, Incorporated. In this capacity he was responsible for all aspects of production, recording, marketing, publication, and distribution of recorded and printed Christian music, including arranging, orchestrating, and post production studio work. His production credits include seven full-length album recordings. In 1987 Houston became minister of music at Emmanuel Baptist Church, San Jose, California, a large, urban Southern Baptist church. He is the composer of numerous classical and sacred choral and orchestral works.   *D.M.*

THIS JOY (arr.)–443

Sims, Ann Brown (b. Meridian, MS, Feb. 20, 1908; d. Franklin, TN, Jul. 8, 1988) was the daughter of Wiley B. And Mary (Rives) Brown. She graduated from Centenary College *summa cum laude* in 1927 and became a public school teacher in Shreveport. In 1936 she married Walter Hines Sims, who was employed in 1945 by B. B. McKinney to work as editor in the Church Music Department of the Baptist Sunday School Board. Later he became Secretary of the Church Music Department upon McKinney's death and in 1956, was editor of *Baptist Hymnal*. After their move to Nashville, Tennessee, Ann Sims became head of the Latin Department of Montgomery Bell Academy, a preparatory school for boys where she taught for 25 years. Following 17 years of retirement in Florida, she and Dr. Sims returned to middle Tennessee in 1986 where she died in 1988.   *H.T.M, C.L.K..*

Grace, Love, and Peace Abide–655

Sims, Walter Hines (b. Urania, LA, Sep. 30, 1907), the son of Walter Heiman and Annie Elizabeth (Rogers) Sims, was reared in Louisiana and Texas, where his father held various pastorates of Baptist churches. He was educated at Hardin-Simmons University (A.B., 1928), Centenary College (B.Mus., 1937), and George Peabody College for Teachers (M.A., 1946). He has done graduate work at Southwestern Baptist Theological Seminary, the University of Nebraska, and Northwestern University. He was awarded the honorary Mus.D. degree by Hardin-Simmons University in 1948. He was director of instrumental music in the public schools of Shreveport, Louisiana, 1935-45, and during this same period was music director, Queensborough Baptist Church, Shreveport. In 1945-46 he was a member of the faculty of George Peabody College for Teachers, Nashville, and served as minister of music, First Baptist Church, Nashville. He came to the Church Music Department of the Baptist Sunday School Board, Nashville, as associate secretary in 1946, working with B. B. McKinney, head of the department. He became secretary of the department in 1952, following McKinney's death.

In this position he gave guidance to the program of church music for Southern Baptist churches, which included publication, curriculum and program development, and field promotion. He served as director of the annual Southern Baptist Church Music Leadership Conferences at Ridgecrest, North Carolina, and Glorieta, New Mexico. He was editor of *The Church Musician,* the monthly periodical for Southern Baptist musicians (1950-70). He served as editor and chairman of the Hymnal Committee for *Baptist Hymnal* (1956) and also compiled and edited other collections published by Broadman Press. He is the author of *Instrumental Music in the Church* (1947), *Song Leading* (1959), and *Church Music Manual* (1957). In his honor, the Southern Baptist Church Music Conference which he helped found in 1956, established the W. Hines Sims Award to recognize individuals who have significantly contributed to Southern Baptist church music. After 24 years in the Church Music Department, he retired in 1970. He makes his home near Nashville, Tennessee.   *W.J.R.*

CHARLES–232
MERIDIAN–655

Sinclair, Jerry (b. Calais, ME, Mar. 25, 1943) is a singer, publisher, and businessman. He began writing songs as a teenage preacher in Northern Maine. During the early days of the Jesus Movement, he traveled with The Chosen Ones, a singing group that worked with Arthur Blessitt and other evangelists. He presently divides his time between his music publishing company, Southern California Music, and work as an executive of a cellular telephone company.   *P.A.R.*

ALLELUIA–Alleluia–223

Skillings, Otis (b. Hamilton, OH, Jul. 27, 1935) is the son of a minister, and his unusual musical talents were evident at an early age. He studied music at St. Paul's College. His skills as composer, arranger, pianist, and orchestra conductor have been evident in his professional achievements in multi-media productions. His sacred compositions and arrangements are found in the catalogs of many publishers, and his music has been recorded on many labels. After 29 years in church music activities in San Diego, California, he moved to Rockford, Illinois, in 1984. There, as minister of music for the First Evangelical Free Church, he gives direction to a comprehensive music ministry that includes music activities involved in the church's SummerWood Amphitheater.   *W.J.R.*

SKILLINGS–The Bond of Love–384

Skoog, Andrew L. (b. Värmland, Sweden, Dec. 17, 1856; d. Minneapolis, MN, Oct. 30, 1934) came to the United States with his family in 1869 to live in St. Paul, Minnesota. His formal education extended only to the sixth grade. However, he developed broad interests and abilities in a variety of areas. He served on the Minneapolis City Council, was an organist-choirmaster in churches in Chicago and Minneapolis, edited a popular Swedish language journal published monthly, and became a leader in the music of the Evangelical Covenant Churches of America. His contributions included the writing of hymns and anthems and the editing of seven hymnals and several choral collections. *The Covenant Hymnal* (Chicago, 1973) contained two Swedish hymns, four English hymns, six translations, and four hymn tunes by Skoog.   *M.P.*

Day by Day (trans.)–66

Slade, Mary Bridges Canedy (b. Fall River, MA, 1826; d. Fall River, MA, 1882) was the wife of a clergyman and spent her entire life in Fall River. She was a schoolteacher and, for some time, assistant editor of *The New England Journal of Education.* She wrote the texts for a number of gospel songs.   *S.W.G.*

Footsteps of Jesus–483

Sleeper, William True (b. Danbury, NH, Feb. 9, 1819; d. Wellesley, MA, Sep. 24, 1904) was pastor of the Summer Street Congregational Church in Worcester, Massachusetts, for over 30 years. He was educated at Phillips-Exeter Academy, the University of Vermont, and Andover Theological Seminary. After his ordination to the Congregational ministry, he served as a home missionary in Worcester, Massachusetts, and later in Maine, helping to found three churches. He returned to Worcester in 1876 to pastor the Summer Street Congregational Church, which he

had served earlier as a missionary. His children were outstanding in their fields of service. His son, William W. Sleeper, was a Congregational pastor at Wellesley; Henry Dyke Sleeper was professor of music at Smith College and a respected organist and composer; May Sleeper Ruggles was a renowned contralto in Boston. Helen Joy Sleeper, daughter of William W. Sleeper, was music librarian at Wellesley College and was widely respected as a scholar. Sleeper published a book of poems in 1883 entitled *The Rejected King, and Hymns of Jesus.*   *P.H.*

Out of My Bondage, Sorrow, and Night–310
Ye Must Be Born Again–322

Sleeth, Natalie Allyn Wakeley (b. Evanston, IL, Oct. 29, 1930; d. Denver, CO, Mar. 21, 1992) was the only daughter of musical parents. She began piano lessons at the age of four. She majored in music theory at Wellesley College (B.A., 1952). Shortly after college she married the Reverend Ronald E. Sleeth, a Methodist clergyman and professor of homiletics, and for 33 years until his death in 1985 they resided in university communities in Nashville, Dallas, Evanston, and Denver. There are two children, Molly Sleeth French and David Thompson Sleeth. From 1969 to 1976 she was music secretary at Highland Park United Methodist Church, Dallas. She credited a course she audited under Dr. Lloyd Pfautsch at Southern Methodist University as the influence that led her into composition. In 1969 the Choristers Guild of Dallas released her first published work, *Canon of Praise.* Additional publishers of her many choral works are AMSI, Sacred Music Press, Carl Fischer, Broadman Press, Hope Publishing Company, Hinshaw Music, and Sonos Music Resources. She was author of a book, *Adventures for the Soul* (Hope, 1987) and the subject of a videotape, *Words and Music* (Hope, 1990). Until her death she resided in Denver, where she was a member of the Wellshire Presbyterian Church. Natalie Sleeth was awarded an honorary Doctor of Humane Letters by West Virginia Wesleyan College in 1989 and an honorary Doctor of Music by Nebraska Wesleyan College in 1990.   *H.E.*

Go Now in Peace–Go Now in Peace–660

Small, James Grindlay (b. Edinburgh, Scotland, 1817; d. Renfrew-on-the-Clyde, Scotland, Feb. 11, 1888) was educated at the University of Edinburgh. He joined the Free Church of Scotland and was ordained in 1847, pastoring a church at Bervie near Montrose. His publications included two hymn collections, *Hymns for Youthful Voices* (1859) and *Psalms and Sacred Songs* (1866), as well as two volumes of poems.   *P.H.*

I've Found a Friend, O Such a Friend!–183

Smart, Henry Thomas (b. London, England, Oct. 26, 1813; d. London, England, Jul. 6, 1879) was the son of Henry Smart, violinist, music publisher, and orchestra conductor. He was educated at Highgate, studied toward the legal profession, and later left the practice of law for music. He had received early music training from his father in fundamentals and was largely self-taught as an organist. He became highly proficient as an organist and served in that capacity at the parish church, Blackburn, Lancashire, 1831-36; St. Philip's Church, Regent Street, London, 1838-39; St. Luke's Church, Old Street, 1844-64; and St. Pancras Church, London, from 1865 until his death. He suffered failing eyesight for several years and became completely blind in 1865. However, he continued to play the organ after that time, and his daughter transcribed his compositions for him.

Smart became an authority on organ design and served as a consultant for new organ installations in England and Scotland. He designed the organs at St. Andrew's Hall, Glasgow, and Town Hall, Leeds. He composed an opera, an oratorio, choral music and organ music, in addition to his hymn tunes. His publications include *Chorale Book* (1865) and *Collection of Sacred Music* (1863), and he served as musical editor for *Psalms and Hymns for Divine Worship* (1867) and the *Presbyterian Hymnal* (1875), the hymnbook of the United Presbyterian Church of Scotland. His tunes also appeared in *Hymns Ancient and Modern* (1861). *M.P.*

Regent Square–94, 199, 360
Lancashire–164, 621

Smaw, Helen Sims (b. Chattanooga, TN, Jan. 19, 1935) received her Bachelor of Arts in English from Belmont College, Nashville, Tennessee (1957). On June 9, 1959 she married Owen Meredith Smaw in Nashville. From 1962 to 1970, Mrs. Smaw was a public school teacher in New Bern, North Carolina. In 1971 she received the Master of Religious Education degree from Southeastern Baptist Theological Seminary, Wake Forest, North Carolina. Two years later (1973) she joined the Sunday School Division of the Baptist Sunday School Board as an Editorial Assistant, working mainly on materials for January Bible Study and Vacation Bible School. In 1977 she became an Assistant Editor in the Sunday School Division, with primary responsibilities in the areas of Children's Bible Study and Vacation Bible School.

Mrs. Smaw has been listed in *Who's Who in Poetry* (1986, 1990, USA), *International*

Who's Who in Poetry (1991), and International Who's Who of Intellectuals (1991). Her hymn texts and poems have appeared in various denominational publications and in anthologies of poetry, including Our Western World's Greatest Poems (1983), American Poetry Anthology (1983), The Art of Poetry: A Treasury of Contemporary Verse (1985), and Our World's Most Cherished Poems (1986). She has also written a number of articles for The Sunday School Growth Journal, Children's Leadership Magazine, The Church Musician, and other periodicals. D.M.

We Worship Round This Table–373

Smith, Alfred Barnerd (b. Wortendyke, NJ, Nov. 8, 1916) studied at Juilliard School of Music, Moody Bible Institute, and Wheaton College (B.A. 1943). He was a boy prodigy violinist and a student of the renowned Leopold Auer; was concert master of New Jersey High School Symphony Orchestra, 1932; and in 1933 appeared as Youth Soloist with the New York Symphony (now the Philharmonic) Orchestra with Walter Damrosch conducting. In 1942-43, he was concert master of the Wheaton Symphony Orchestra. While a student at Wheaton College he was closely associated with fellow classmate Billy Graham and was Graham's first song leader in the early Youth for Christ movement. In 1941, while a student at Wheaton, he began his first publishing venture, a collection titled Singspiration. This book became an immediate success and paved the way for the founding of the Singspiration Music Company in which he edited, compiled, and published numerous chorus books and the hymnal Inspiring Hymns. He was also instrumental in launching the composing and arranging career of John W. Peterson. In 1962 he sold "Singspiration" to the Zondervan

Company of Grand Rapids, Michigan. Ten years later he again entered the publishing field, introducing the hymnal Living Hymns. His major contribution to the singing church in recent years has been his Hymn Histories, a presentation of hymns and gospel songs and their origins. Smith has been given several honorary degrees including a Mus.D. from John Brown University. He now lives in Greenville, South Carolina, and is still actively involved in publishing through his company, Better Music Publications. H.E.

Goodness–Surely Goodness and Mercy–422

Smith, Deborah D. (b. Nashville, TN, Mar. 3, 1958) received her Bachelor of Science degree from Wheaton College in 1980. She is married to Michael W. Smith with whom she occasionally collaborates on songs. The Smiths are the parents of five children and live in a rural area near Franklin, Tennessee. D.M.

Great Is the Lord–Great Is the Lord–12

Smith, Henry Percy (b. Malta, 1825; d. Bournemouth, Hampshire, England, Jan. 28, 1898) was an Anglican cleric. Subsequent to his education at Balliol College, Oxford, he was curate at Eversley (1849-51) and St. Michael's, Yorktown, Camberley, Surrey (1851-68); vicar of Great Barton, Suffolk (1868-82); chaplain at Christ Church, Cannes, France (1882-95); and canon of the cathedral at Gibraltar (1892-98). P.A.R.

Maryton–279, 364

Smith, Howard E. (b. Jul. 16, 1863; d. Norwalk CT, Aug. 13, 1918). Very little is known about Smith, except that he was an active musician throughout his life and served many years as a church organist in Connecticut. He composed a number of hymn tunes, but only the present one remains in common usage." *W.J.R.*

Smith, John Stafford (b. Gloucester, England, 1750; d. London, England, Sep. 3, 1836) was an organist, singer, composer, and antiquary who has often been mistakenly credited with the tune NATIONAL ANTHEM. See the article on "O Say Can You See." *H.T.M.*

Smith, Michael Whitaker (b. Kenova, WV, Oct. 7, 1957) is a songwriter, performer, and recording artist/producer of contemporary Christian music. He moved from his hometown to Nashville, Tennessee, in 1978. In 1980 he joined a gospel singing group, *Higher Ground*, and became a staff writer for Paragon Music. When his contract with Paragon expired, Michael joined the staff of Meadowgreen Music. He subsequently became associated with Edward Grant Publishing Company. His songs have been recorded by a number of prominent contemporary Christian artists, including Amy Grant, Sandi Patti, Pat Boone, Larnell Harris, David Meece, and the Bill Gaither Trio. Michael's credits also include songs written for television and recordings featuring his own performances. Michael is married to Deborah Smith, with whom he occasionally collaborates in writing music. They have five children and live in Franklin, Tennessee. *D.M.*

Smith, Samuel Francis (b. Boston, MA, Oct. 21, 1808; d. Newton Centre, MA, Nov. 16, 1895) was an important Baptist leader. Stimulated by the work of Adoniram Judson, he was strongly interested in foreign missions, but his health prevented him from entering that field. After graduation from Harvard University (A.B., 1829) and Andover Theological Seminary (B.D., 1832), he became editor of the *Baptist Missionary Magazine*. From 1834 until 1842 he was pastor of the Baptist church in Waterville, Maine, and professor of modern languages at Waterville (now Colby) College. For the next 12 years he was pastor of First Baptist Church in Newton Centre. He left that position in 1854 to become editorial secretary of the American Baptist Missionary Union, serving in that role until his retirement in 1869. He wrote several books, including *Rambles in Missionary Fields* (Boston, 1883), his impressions from an 1880 tour of mission stations in Europe and Asia. His zeal for missions was passed on to his son, A. W. Smith, who served as president of the Baptist seminary in Rangoon, Burma.

With Baron Stow, Smith compiled *The Psalmist* (Boston, 1843), the most influential Baptist hymnal of its time. It included 26 of the approximately 100 hymns which he wrote. *P.A.R.*

Smith, Walter Chalmers (b. Aberdeen, Scotland, Dec. 5, 1824; d. Kinbuck, Perthshire, Scotland, Sep. 20, 1908) was educated at the Grammar School, University of Aberdeen, and at New College, Edinburgh. He was ordained a minister in the Free Church of Scotland in 1850, and served Free churches in London, Milnathort, Glasgow, and Edinburgh. He became pastor of the Free High Church, Edinburgh (1876-94), and was elected moderator of the Free Church of Scotland in 1893. His hymns were published in *Hymns of Christ and the Christian Life* (1876), and his poems, other than his hymns, were published as *Poetical Works* (1902).   W.J.R.

Immortal, Invisible, God Only Wise–6

Smith, William Farley (b. Durham, NC, Apr. 23, 1941) is a United Methodist musician and teacher. He holds degrees from the Manhattan School of Music (B.M., 1962; M.M., 1963) and Columbia University (M.Ed., 1982; Ed.D., 1984). He taught for more than 20 years in the public school system of New York City and also served on the faculty at Montclair State College in New Jersey. In 1990 he accepted a dual appointment as Professor of Music at Drew University and Professor of Worship Music at Drew Theological Seminary. He serves St. Mark's United Methodist Church in Harlem as minister of music. Known for his research and "restorations" in the area of African-American music, he contributed to *Songs of Zion* (Nashville, 1981) and was a consultant/editor/arranger for *The United Methodist Hymnal* (Nashville, 1989). P.A.R.

Soon and Very Soon (arr.)–192

Smyth, Harper G. (b. New York, NY, Mar. 16, 1873; d. Cleveland, OH, Aug. 25, 1945) studied at the Institute of Music Art, New York, and was a member of the Metropolitan Opera Company for two years. He directed church choirs in Atlanta and Indianapolis and was the song leader for Maud Ballington Booth of the Salvation Army and evangelist J. Wilbur Chapman. He became music director of the Euclid Avenue Baptist Church in Cleveland, Ohio, in 1913 and maintained a private voice studio. During World War I, he became known for writing and directing pageants. He was the official song leader for the Republican National Convention in 1924 and served in the same capacity for Rotary International. He published *Let's Adventure in Personality* in 1941. In April, 1945, he suffered a stroke while leading the singing for a group of Army inductees and died four months later. Of his approximately 25 songs, only the present one is commonly sung.   P.H.

Euclid–Make Me a Channel of Blessing–564

Sosa, Nelson Arthur (b. Camagüey, Cuba, Feb. 1, 1935) is the grandson of a British emigré, who so revered the British admiral Horatio Nelson that Sosa's father was asked to name his son Nelson. Charles Sosa, the father, was a worker in a cigarette factory in Havana. By means of a scholarship and by dint of hard work, Sosa was graduated from Havana University with an M.D. degree. A specialist in the treatment of ear, nose, and throat, he also studied at Emory University, Atlanta, Georgia (1957-59), and practiced medicine at Camagüey General Hospital for 18 years.

In 1977, after a decade of frustration, he was allowed to leave Cuba for Jamaica where he hoped to use his British citizenship to obtain entry into the United States. Through the special efforts of Bonnie Anderson, a reporter for *The Miami Herald*, and Florida senator Claude Pepper, Sosa, his sister and parents finally were able to emigrate to Miami in February, 1978. He has worked there as a medical technician in the Human Resources Department of the federal government. For over a decade he has been Director of Spanish-speaking work for the Baptist Brotherhood in Miami Association. In 1986 the Southern Baptist Brotherhood Commission presented Sosa an award for outstanding service in this capacity. He has also served as a member of the Florida Baptist State Board of Missions.

Though not formally trained in music, Sosa has had a life-long interest in music. He plays the guitar by ear and sings solos with confidence. A creator of songs for years, he has written words and music for over 60 compositions (30 while in Cuba; the remainder since leaving Cuba). Many of his beginning songs were inspired during an illness. Often while working as a physician in the hospital, melodies have come to him, and the services of a friend, a pianist, were used to write them down. In recent years Sosa has shared his faith through his songs which have been sung around the world.   *H.T.M.*

Sosa–Walking Along with Jesus–186

Sosa, Pablo D. (B. Chivilcoy, Argentina, Dec. 16, 1933), the son and nephew of Methodist pastors in Argentina, has himself served as a pastor. He studied theology in his native country and specialized in music studies in both the United States and Germany. A coordinator in the Department of Communication of the Interconfessional Association of Theological Studies, he has also functioned as professor in the National Conservatory of Music in Buenos Aires. The writer, composer, and translator of several hymns, he has a special interest in promoting Latin-American religious folk song.   *H.T.M.*

Central–167

Southern Harmony (1835, William Walker) is one of several important oblong tune-books using the four-shape notation (fa, sol, la, mi) published in 1835 by William "Singing Billy" Walker. The extended title was *The Southern Harmony, and Musical Companion; containing a choice of Tunes, Hymns, Psalms, Odes, and Anthems Selected from the Most Eminent Authors in the United States,* etc. (New Haven, CT, 1835). Containing some 218 tunes, 25 of which were composed by Walker himself, *The Southern Harmony* became one of the most popular of tunebooks in the 19th century. Its 1854 edition has been reprinted four times, most recently in 1987 with Dr. Glenn C. Wilcox as editor (Lexington, KY, 1987).

Among the sources for Walker's texts in *The Southern Harmony* were Jesse Mercer's *The Cluster of Hymns* (1813) and Andrew Broaddus' *The Dover Selection* (1828), both Baptist collections. Walker published other tunebooks, including *Southern and Western Pocket Harmonist* and *Christian Harmony* (1866) which used seven-shape notation. Followers of Walker's music migrated from South Carolina to western Kentucky where an annual "Big Singing" using *The Southern Harmony* was inaugurated in 1844. That tradition has been steadfastly maintained to the present day in Benton, Kentucky, at the Marshall County Court House on the fourth Sunday of each May.   *H.T.M.*

Resignation–68
Wondrous Love–143
Restoration–323

Spaeth, Harriet Reynolds Krauth (b. Baltimore, MD, Sep. 21, 1845; d. Philadelphia, PA, May, 1925) was the daughter, granddaughter, and wife of distinguished Lutheran ministers. An active church musician, she was an organist, author, hymnal editor, and translator of hymns from German into English. The Lutheran *Church*

Book with Music (1872), which she edited, contains many of her translations. Others were included in The Sunday School Hymnal (1901), published by the American Lutheran Publication Board. Her books include A Life of Hans Sachs and a biography of her husband, Rev. Adolph Spaeth, who at one time served as president of the General Council of the Lutheran Church in America.   *M.P.*

Lo, How a Rose E'er Blooming (tr. st.3)–78

Spafford, Horatio Gates (b. North Troy, NY, Oct. 20, 1828; d. Jerusalem, Oct. 16, 1888),after early life in New York, moved to Chicago in 1856, where he established a successful legal practice and served as professor of medical jurisprudence of Lind University, later Chicago Medical College. A Presbyterian layman, he was a Sunday School teacher and active in YMCA work. He served as a director and trustee for the Presbyterian Theological Seminary of the Northwest, established in Chicago by Cyrus McCormick. In 1870 he spent four months in England and Scotland. In Edinburgh he met Dr. Piazza Smith, Astronomer Royal for Scotland, and became greatly interested in the archaeology of the Bible.

Some months prior to the Chicago fire in 1871, Spafford had invested heavily in real estate on the shore of Lake Michigan, and his holdings were wiped out by the fire. The tragic deaths of his four daughters (see discussion of the hymn) were compounded by the death of his son in 1880. The unsympathetic attitude of Christian friends in the midst of their sorrow caused the Spaffords to decide to leave Chicago, and the interest in the Holy Land, which had begun a decade before, turned their attention to Jerusalem. In 1881, with a group of friends, they settled in Jerusalem, where they established the American Colony. The unusual experiences of this extraordinary family and the significant work of the American Colony in Jerusalem are vividly told by his daughter, Bertha Spafford Vester, in her book Our Jerusalem. On July 24, 1963, the writer visited with Mrs. Vester in her apartment at the American Colony in Jerusalem, Jordan.   *W.J.R.*

It Is Well with My Soul–410

Spohr, Louis (b. Brunswick, Germany, Apr. 5, 1784; d. Kassel, Germany, Oct. 22, 1859) was a German violinist, conductor, and significant composer of instrumental music and opera in the early Romantic period. Born into a musical family, his early musical development was supported by Karl Wilhelm Ferdinand, Duke of Brunswick. Spohr studied violin with J. A. Riemenschneider, Dufour, C. L. Maucourt, and Franz Eck, and gained widespread acclaim for his virtuosic playing. In 1806 he married Dorette Scheidler, a virtuoso harpist, and together they concertized throughout Europe. He became Kapellmeister and director of opera at Kassel in 1822, was appointed Generalmusikdirector there in 1847, and retired in 1857. As a composer he wrote oratorios, operas, violin concertos, symphonies, and chamber music. He was a friend of both Beethoven and von Weber and an early champion of the operas of Wagner.   *M.P.*

Spohr–46

Spratt, Ann Baird (b. 1829). No information has been discovered as to the identity of this composer.   *W.J.R.*

Kedron–270

Stainer, Sir John (b. Southwark, Surrey, England, Jun. 13, 1840; d. Verna, Italy,

Mar. 31, 1901) was an organist, composer, and educator. From 1847 until 1856 he was a chorister at St. Paul's Cathedral in London. He served as organist and choirmaster of St. Benedict and St. Peter's, Paul's Wharf, and in 1856 became organist of St. Michael's College at Tenbury. In 1859 he entered Christ Church, Oxford, and earned the B.Mus. degree. He became organist at Magdalen College, Oxford, and in 1863 took a B.A. degree. He was appointed organist to the University of Oxford and received both a D.Mus. degree and a M.A. degree. In addition to his work at Oxford, he had close ties with Cambridge, the University of London, and The Royal Academy of Music. In 1872 he became the organist of St. Paul's Cathedral in London and, as a result of his high standards, the choir became a model throughout England. In 1888 failing sight caused him to resign his post at St. Paul's, and in that year he was knighted by Queen Victoria. From 1889 to 1899, he was Professor of Music in the University of Oxford. Following his death in Italy he was buried at Holywell Cemetery, Oxford on April 6, 1901. He composed more than 150 hymn tunes, anthems, services, cantatas, and oratorios (the most famous of which is *The Crucifixion*). He also composed the famous "Sevenfold Amen." He wrote books on harmony and organ playing, as well as *The Music of the Bible* and the scholarly *Dufay and his Contemporaries* (1898). He was musical editor for the *Church Hymnary* (1898) and co-edited *The Dictionary of Musical Terms* (1879). Stainer was well loved and respected, an excellent musician in many respects, especially as an organist. He was noted for his concern for excellence in church music. *S.W.G.*

GREENSLEEVES (harm.)–118
O PERFECT LOVE (arr.)–512

Stanford, Charles Villiers (b. Dublin, Ireland, Sep. 30, 1852; d. London, England, Mar. 29, 1924) was one of England's most successful early 20th-century musicians. A student from 1870 in Queen's College, Cambridge, he was appointed organist at Trinity College, Cambridge in 1873. He had a long and distinguished teaching career not only at Cambridge but at the Royal College of Music in London. A composer of operas, choral works, songs, and symphonies, he, along with his Edwardian contemporaries, C. H. H. Parry and H. Walford Davies, represented a mild revolt against the hegemony of the Victorian part-song–a reaction which came to full strength with the fresh original tunes and folk-song arrangements of Ralph Vaughan Williams in *The English Hymnal* (1906). *H.T.M.*

ENGELBERG–435

Stanphill, Ira Forest (b. Bellvue, NM, Feb. 14, 1914) spent his early years in various small towns in New Mexico, Oklahoma, and Kansas. When Ira was eight, he moved with his family to Coffeyville, Kansas, where at the age of 15 he became host of a radio program on station KGGF. After graduation from Coffeyville Junior College, he became Minister of Youth and Music at the First Assembly of God Church in Breckenridge, Texas. During this time he also began publishing his own gospel songs. In 1936 Stanphill was called to the pastorate of a church in Springfield, Missouri. After his ordination to the ministry in 1939, he became a full-time evangelist, also serving numerous short-term pastorates and ministry positions in various states. In 1966 he became pastor of the Rosen Heights (now Rockwood Park) Assembly of God Church, Fort Worth, Texas, retiring from this position in 1979. Since his retirement, he has kept an active schedule as a speaker and gospel singer.

Stanphill showed musical and compositional abilities at an early age. His first song, a chorus titled "Move Forward," was written while he was still in high school. His first published song, "Afterwhile," appeared in 1935. He later founded his own publishing company, Hymntime Publishers, which was sold to Zondervan Publishing House in 1968. In addition to "The cross upon which Jesus died" ("Room at the Cross"), Stanphill wrote "Happiness Is the Lord," "Mansion Over the Hilltop," "I Know Who Holds Tomorrow," and many other popular gospel songs. *D.M.*

STANPHILL–Room at the Cross–315

Starr, Richard. This is a pen name. The writer wishes to remain anonymous. *J.V.A.*

RESIGNATION (arr.)–68
OH QUE BUENO (harm. and arr.)–228
WHOLE WORLD (arr.)–346

Stassen-Benjamin, Linda. (b. 1951-)

Sing Hallelujah to the Lord-214

Stead, Louisa M. R. (b. Dover, England, *c.* 1850; d. Penkridge, near Umtali, Southern Rhodesia, Jan. 18, 1917) was born in England, but in 1871 moved to the United States where she lived with friends in Cincinnati, Ohio. At a camp meeting in Urbana, Ohio, she made a commitment to missionary service, but was unable to be appointed at the time because of health limitations. She married a Mr. Stead in 1875, and subsequently gave birth to a daughter, Lily. Four years after the birth of the daughter, Mr. Stead died in a drowning accident

while trying to rescue a child at Long Island, New York. Around 1880 Mrs. Stead and Lily went to South Africa, where she served as a missionary for 15 years. She married a Mr. Wodehouse, a native of South Africa, but poor health necessitated their return to the States in 1895. When her health was restored, she and her husband were appointed to the Methodist Mission at Umtali, Southern Rhodesia, where they arrived on April 4, 1901. She retired there in 1911. Her daughter, Lily, who had married and also served as a missionary in Southern Rhodesia, took care of her mother in her retirement. Mrs. Stead-Wodehouse died in 1917 after a prolonged illness and was buried near her African home in Penkridge, near Mutambara Mission. *M.P.*

'Tis So Sweet to Trust in Jesus–411

Stebbins, George Coles (b. East Carlton, NY, Feb. 26, 1846; d. Catskill, NY, Oct. 6, 1945) had his music interest whetted when a teenager by attending a rural singing school. Later he took voice lessons in Buffalo and Rochester, New York, and became tenor soloist in a Rochester church choir. In 1869 he went to Chicago to be associated with Lyon and Healy Music Company and to serve as director of music at the First Baptist Church. While engaged in evangelistic work, he arranged music for male quartets, sharing with James McGranahan an innovation that was used with great success in mass evangelism. In 1874 he moved to Boston, Massachusetts, to become song leader at the Clarendon Street Baptist Church whose pastor was A. J. Gordon (composer of the tune for "My Jesus, I Love Thee") and later he went to a similar capacity at the Tremont Temple Baptist Church of the same city.

From 1876 until 1899 he was associated with Dwight L. Moody and Ira D. Sankey in evangelistic campaigns in this country and abroad. He followed Sankey as the musical director of Moody's Northfield (Massachusetts) Bible Conference. Upon the death of P. P. Bliss, he became one of the editors of the series of the Moody and Sankey gospel hymn collections. His *Reminiscences and Gospel Hymn Stories* (New York, 1924) is a significant first person account of the music and musicians of the late 19th-century urban revivals.

Suffering from deafness, he retired from active evangelical work in 1908 but continued to write hymns and edit hymnals through a long and productive life. Many of his some 1500 songs were written under the pseudonym, George Coles. He composed his last song at age 98.   *H.T.M.*

FRIEND–183
ADELAIDE–294
JESUS, I COME–310
CALLING TODAY–316
BORN AGAIN–322
HOLINESS–446

Steele, David Horatio (b. Cincinnati, OH, Mar. 7, 1950) received a Bachelor of Music in composition from the University of Cincinnati College Conservatory of Music. He is a member of the Church of the Nazarene and has been active in the music publishing industry for many years.   *S.W.G.*

Worship the Lord (st. 2)–115

Stennett, Samuel (b. Exeter, Devonshire, England, 1727; d. Muswell Hill, Middlesex, England, Aug. 25, 1795) was born into a family that had held a prominent place for generations in Seventh Day Baptist churches of England. Samuel's grandfather Joseph Stennett (1663-1713) was a pastor and a pioneer Baptist hymn writer. Stennett was

educated under the Rev. John Hubbard of Stepney and Dr. John Walker of the Academy at Mile End. In 1747 he became assistant to his father, and following his father's death he became pastor in 1758. In 1767 he received a call to become pastor of the Seventh Day Baptist Church in London where his grandfather had served for 23 years. Although he did not accept the call to be pastor, he preached the sermon every Saturday morning for 20 years in addition to serving his own church. Stennett was recognized as one of the outstanding dissenting preachers of his day. At the age of only 36 his scholarship was recognized by King's College, Aberdeen, which conferred the D.D. degree upon him. King George III was a personal friend. John Howard, noted English philanthropist and prison reformer, was a member of his congregation. Stennett was much respected by some of the statesmen of his day, and he used his influence in support of the principles of religious freedom. As observed by Haeussler, "Had he chosen to renounce his non-conformist principles he could have held high position in the Church of England, but he chose to follow his grandfather's example" (Haeussler, 921). Stennett contributed 38 hymns to his friend Dr. John Rippon's *Selection* (London, 1787). Stennett's collected poems and hymns were published in volume II of his *Works* (4 vols., 1824).   *H.E.*

Majestic Sweetness Sits Enthroned–219
On Jordan's Stormy Banks–521

Stephens, Wilhelmina D'A. No information is available about this author.   *P.H.*

Jesus Was a Loving Teacher–602

Steuerlein [Steurlein], Johann (b. Schmolkulden, Germany, Jul. 5, 1546; d.

Meiningen, May 5, 1613) was the son of a Lutheran pastor. He became a student of law, and in 1589 was appointed Chancery secretary in Meiningen and in 1590, town-clerk of Wasungen. Later he became mayor of Meiningen. He followed music and literature as an avocation, and various compositions of his were published. His most important work was *Sieben und Zwantzigk newe geistliche Gesenge* (1588). Of these 27 hymns, three are marked as by Steuerlein [Steurlein], and several others with no authors named could well have been written by him. In 1581 he was given official recognition as both an excellent poet and musician by the Emperor Rudolph II. *H.T.M.*

Wie Lieblich Ist Der Maien–389

Stites, Edgar Page (b. Cape May, NJ, Mar. 22, 1836; d. Cape May, NJ, Jan. 7, 1921) was a Methodist lay preacher. He was a direct descendant of John Howland, a passenger on the *Mayflower*, and the cousin of hymnist Eliza E. Hewitt. During the Civil War, Stites was responsible for distributing rations to the troops passing through Philadelphia. For a time afterward, he piloted ships on the Delaware River. He was a member of First Methodist Church in Cape May, a local preacher, and, for a short time, a missionary in the Dakotas. He often signed his texts "Edward Page." *P.A.R.*

Trusting Jesus–417

Stockton, John Hart (b. New Hope, PA, Apr. 19, 1813; d. Philadelphia, PA, Mar. 25, 1877) was reared in a Presbyterian home, but converted in a Methodist camp meeting at Paulsboro, New Jersey, in 1832. He was ordained a Methodist minister and be-

came a member of the New Jersey Conference. After illness forced his retirement from the pastorate in 1874, he continued part-time work in evangelistic causes, including the Moody and Sankey meetings in Philadelphia. He wrote several gospel songs and compiled *Salvation Melodies* (Philadelphia, 1874) and *Precious Songs* (Philadelphia, 1875). *P.A.R.*

Down at the Cross–140
The Great Physician–188
Stockton–Only Trust Him–317

Stone, Samuel John (b. Whitmore, Staffordshire, England, Apr. 25, 1839; d. Charterhouse, London, England, Nov. 19, 1900) attended Charterhouse and received the Bachelor of Arts degree from Pembroke College, Oxford in 1862 and later the Master of Arts degree. He was ordained in 1862 and served as curate of Windsor from 1862 until 1870 and then at St. Paul's Haggerston where he succeeded his father as vicar in 1874. The St. Paul's, Haggerston parish had no church, school, or vicarage when his father became its vicar, but by the work of the two of them it became a fully-equipped parish. In 1809, Stone became rector of All Hallows-on-the-Wall in London and remained there until his death at the Charterhouse. Stone served as a member of the committee which prepared the 1909 edition of *Hymns Ancient and Modern*. He published several collections of poems and hymns including *The Knight of Intercession, and Other Poems* (1872); *Sonnets of the Christian Year* (1875); *Hymns* (1866); and *Order of the Consecutive Church Service for Children, with Original Hymns* (1883). His *Collected Poems and Hymns* was published by F. G. Ellerton after Stone's death. *S.W.G.*

The Church's One Foundation–350

Stowe, Everett M. Nothing has been discovered about this translator. *P.A.R.*

Here, O Lord, Your Servants Gather (tr.)–179
Stralsund Gesangbuch was a hymn collection in two parts published in 1665 for the region around Stralsund, a German town on the coast of the Baltic Sea. It bore the fuller title *Erneuerten Gesangbuch*, and its second part, entitled *Ander Theil des Erneuerten Gesangbuch*, included the first appearance of the hymn tune Lobe Den Herren.. *S.W.G, H.T.M..*

Lobe Den Herren–14

Strattner, Georg Christoph (b. Gols, Germany, *c.* 1644; d. Weimar, Germany, 1704) went to Pressburg as a chorister *c.* 1651 to live and study with Samuel Friedrich Capricornus. He served as Kapellmeister at the court of Baden-Durlach from 1666 until 1682, when he became Kapellmeister at the Barfusserkirche in Frankfurt am Main. He also taught music in the Gymnasium in Frankfurt. After leaving Frankfurt in the midst of a scandal in 1692, he eventually settled in Weimar, where he became vice-Kapellmeister in 1695 and director of the Weimar opera house in 1697. Strattner wrote primarily sacred music, including cantatas and hymn tunes, and was editor of the fifth edition of Joachim Neander's *Bundeslieder* (Frankfurt, 1691). *M.P.*

Posen–461

Strom, Terrye Coelho (b. Camp Roberts, CA, Aug. 6, 1952) is a nondenominational lyricist and homemaker. She attended Arizona State University and completed training as a medical assistant in Anaheim, California. She became a Christian in 1971 and has, since that time, written words for many songs, most of which are unpublished. In 1978 she married James Strom. They and their four children live in Walnut, California. *P.A.R.*

Maranatha–Father, I Adore You–256

Sullivan, Arthur Seymour (b. Bolwell Terrace, Lambeth, England, May 13, 1842; d. Westminster, London, England, Nov. 22, 1900) became a chorister at the Chapel Royal at the age of 12. He was educated at the Royal Academy of Music, where he studied with Sterndale Bennett and John Goss. He also studied with Moritz Hauptmann, Ferdinand David, and Ignaz Moscheles at the Leipzig Conservatory. Following his return to England, he held several organist positions and became professor of composition at the Royal Academy of Music in 1866. In the field of church music, Sullivan wrote anthems (he was 15 when his first anthem was published), hymn tunes, and oratorios. Most of his hymn tunes were written between 1867 and 1874 and were published in *The Hymnary* (1872) and *Church Hymns with Tunes* (1874), both of which he edited. Sullivan's greatest acclaim as a composer came from his association with Sir W. S. Gilbert in writing music for the Savoy Operas. The Gilbert and Sullivan operettas have gained international popularity which continues to this day. Sullivan strongly opposed adapting hymn tunes from popular melodies and consistently refused permission to make hymn tune adaptations from his operettas. He was knighted by Queen Victoria in 1883 and given honorary Doctor of Music degrees by both Cambridge and Oxford University. *M.P.*

St. Gertrude –493

Sumner, John B. (b. Lime Hill, PA, Mar. 25, 1838; d. Binghamton, NY, May 9, 1918) was educated at Wyoming Seminary, Pennsylvania. For a number of years he was a music teacher, conducting singing schools in the Susquehanna Valley. Ordained to the Methodist ministry, he entered the Wyoming Conference (Pennsylvania) in 1869 and held numerous pastorates until his retirement in 1908. He had a fine tenor voice and, with two other Methodist ministers, he organized the Wyoming Conference Trio, which became quite popular at Methodist conferences and Chautauqua meetings. Of the 11 hymn tunes he composed, only BINGHAMTON is known today. *W.J.R.*

BINGHAMTON–555

Sweney, John R. (West Chester, PA, Dec. 31, 1837; d. PA, Apr. 10, 1899) had an early interest in musical composition and by the time he was 22 he was teaching music in Dover, Delaware. He was a director of the Third Delaware Regiment Band during the Civil War. After the war, he became a professor of music at the Pennsylvania Military Academy and remained there for 25 years. Ten years of that time he was also song leader of the Bethany Presbyterian Church Sunday School, one of the largest Sunday Schools in Philadelphia. He was in great demand as a song leader in church assemblies in the northeastern section of the country. He composed over 1000 gospel hymn tunes and edited or coedited over 60 gospel hymnbooks, Sunday School music, and anthems. *S.W.G.*

STORY OF JESUS–122
SUNSHINE–430
I SHALL KNOW HIM–528
SWENEY–600

Tallis, Thomas (b. Kent [?], England, *c.* 1505; d. Greenwich, Kent, England, Nov. 23, 1585) was a prominent English composer and church musician. His first known service was as organist of the Benedictine Priory of Dover in 1532. He was then at St. Mary-on-the-Hill, London (1537-38); Waltham Abbey, London (1538-1540); and Canterbury Cathedral (1541-1542). In 1543 he was named a Gentleman of the Chapel Royal, with which he may have been associated earlier. His outstanding skills as organist and composer and his sagacity in religious and political matters enabled him to serve the royal court through the reigns of Henry VIII, Edward VI, Mary Tudor, and Elizabeth I.

Tallis composed for both Roman and Anglican services. He accommodated the shifts in language, liturgical function, performing resources, and musical style which accompanied the changes of monarchs and religious allegiances. Though he composed a small number of secular works, his fame rests upon his compositions for the church, which range from the 40-voice motet, "Spem in alium," to simple anthems in keeping with the new Anglican liturgy. Because of his achievements as one of the first to write for the Church of England, he has been called both the "Father of English Cathedral Music" and the "Father of English Church Music." He wrote nine tunes for John Day's publication of *The whole Psalter, translated into English Metre* (London, *c.* 1567) to texts by Matthew Parker, Archbishop of Canterbury. *P.A.R.*

TALLIS' CANON–449
TALLIS' ORDINAL–625

Terley, L. W. is a pseudonym of one who wishes to remain anonymous. *H.T.M.*

The Word of God Is Alive–265
A Servant of the Least–628

Teschner, Melchior (b. Fraustadt, Silesia, Apr. 29, 1584; d. Oberpritschen, Posen, Dec. 1, 1635) attended school at the Gymnasium in Zittau and the University of Frankfurt-an-der-Oder. From 1605 to 1608 he served as cantor and teacher in the village of Schmiegel. In 1609 he returned to his hometown of Fraustadt to become cantor and teacher at the Kripplein Christi church. He accepted a call to the pastorate of a church in nearby Oberpritschen in 1614. Two years later he married Elizabeth Klee, with whom he had seven children. Teschner died during an attack by the Cossacks. He was succeeded in his pastorate by one of his sons and later by a grandson.   *D.M.*

St. Theodulph–126

The Sacred Harp (1844) is an oblong, shape-note, "fasola" tunebook compiled by Benjamin Franklin White and Elisha James King. The book of 262 pages was published in Philadelphia, Pennsylvania, by S. C. Collins and has been the most durable of the 19th-century tunebooks by Southern compilers. In the preface to the first edition, White states that he has "taught music for the last twenty years, and being necessarily thrown among churches of various denominations, and all the time observing wants in that of a variety of church music, has in this work endeavored to supply that deficiency which heretofore existed, by placing all the church music within his reach in one book." This variety is reflected in White's choice of English psalm and hymn tunes, New England fuging tunes, hymn tunes, anthems, and odes, as well as Southern folk tunes and original tunes by Southern composers. Many of these tunes,

referred to by George Pullen Jackson as "Old Baptist Tunes," were those sung to the hymns in the "words only" Baptist collections of Andrew Broaddus, Jesse Mercer, Staunton S. Burdett, and William Dossey.   *W.J.R.*

Warrenton–18
Beach Spring–377, 604,613

Theodulph of Orleans (b. *c.* 750; d. Angers, Sep. 18, 821) was born of a noble Gothic family, probably in Italy. He became abbot of a monastery in Florence, but in 781 was brought to France by Charlemagne to become abbot of Fleury and subsequently Bishop of Orleans. Upon the death of Alcuin (804), Theodulph became Charlemagne's chief theologian and played a large part in setting up a system of education for the Empire. After the death of the Emperor in 814, Theodulph was accused of conspiring against Charlemagne's son and successor, Louis the Pious. He was stripped of his ecclesiastical offices and imprisoned at Angers in 818. It is thought that, despite a legend to the contrary, he died in prison, perhaps as a result of poisoning.   *D.M.*

All Glory, Laud, and Honor–126

Thesaurus Musicus (1744) was long thought to be the source of the tune America (or National Hymn, as it is known in Great Britain). Recent research by Malcolm Boyd, as reported in *The New Grove Dictionary of Music and Musicians* (London, 1980), asserts that the source cited is actually a copy of *Harmonia anglicana* (London, 1744), with its title altered to read *Thesaurus Musicus*. Thus *Harmonia anglicana* seems to be the earliest extant source of this tune in a version similar to that known today, though other forms of the tune were known prior to that time, both in England and on the continent.   *P.A.R.*

AMERICA–634

Thomas, Edith Lowell (b. Eastford, CT, Sep. 11, 1878; d. Claremont, CA, Mar. 17, 1970) was a Methodist musician and educator. She was educated at Boston University (B.R.E., 1922; M.Ed., 1927), and Union Theological Seminary, New York (M.S.M., 1932), and taught at Boston University from 1920 until 1932. She served churches and church schools in New York, New Jersey, Connecticut, and Massachusetts and was cofounder and coprincipal of The Misses Thomas (Preparatory) School in Collingswood, New Jersey. A well-known writer, speaker, and conference leader, she published several resources for the use of music in the religious education of children, including *Sing, Children, Sing* (New York, 1939), *The Whole World Singing* (New York, 1950), and *Music in Christian Education* (New York, 1953).   *P.A.R.*

Praise and Thanksgiving (tr. st. 1)–645

Thomas, Eugene. This is a pen name. The writer wishes to remain anonymous. *H.T.M.*

I LOVE YOU, LORD (arr.)–212
MAJESTY (arr.)–215

Thompson, Will Lamartine (b. Smith's Ferry, PA, Nov. 7, 1847; d. New York, NY, Sep. 20, 1909) was a leading writer and publisher of gospel songs. He was educated at Mount Union College (Ohio) and the New England Conservatory of Music. His early fame as a composer was earned through popular songs. From this he learned a style which made his gospel songs accessible and which made him quite wealthy through his own publishing company. He served for a time as music director in a Methodist congregation, but became a Presbyterian when he married in 1891.   *P.A.R.*

ELIZABETH–Jesus Is All the World to Me–184
THOMPSON–Softly and Tenderly–312

Thomson, Mary Ann Faulkner (b. London, England, Dec. 5, 1834; d. Philadelphia, PA, Mar. 11, 1923) was an Episcopalian layperson and hymnist who came to the United States as a child. She and her husband, John, the first librarian of the Free Library of Philadelphia, were active members of the Church of the Annunciation. She wrote more than 40 hymns, most of which were published in *The Churchman* (New York) or *The Living Church* (Chicago). *P.A.R.*

O Zion, Haste–583

Threlfall, Jeannette (b. Blackburn, Lancashire, England, Mar. 24, 1821; d. Westminster, Middlesex, England, Nov. 30, 1880) was left an orphan at an early age and spent her life with relatives–first with an uncle and an aunt at Blackburn and Leyland successively, and later with their daughter and her husband at Westminster. A series of two accidents caused her to become an invalid, but she maintained a gentle, pleasant spirit through her adversity and became known for her generosity to charitable causes. She spent much of her time reading and, in her "idle moments," began to write sacred poems and hymns, which at first were sent anonymously to various periodicals. Thirty-five of her poems were collected and published in *Woodsorrel, or Leaves from a Retired Home* (1856). In 1873, 15 poems selected from *Woodsorrel* were added to 35 others and published under the title *Sunshine and Shadow*. In his introduction to *Sunshine and Shadow*, Bishop Christopher Wordsworth wrote: "... considerable mental powers and graces of composition are blended with pure religious feelings, and hallowed by sound doctrine and fervent devotion." *M.P.*

Hosanna, Loud Hosanna–130

Thring, Godfrey (b. Alford, Somerset, England, Mar. 25, 1823; d. Shamley Green, Guildford Surrey, England, Sep. 13, 1903) was educated at Shrewsbury School and Balliol College, Oxford, from which he received a B. A. degree in 1845. Following ordination in the Church of England in 1846, he served as curate at Strathfield-Turgis (1846-50) and subsequently other parishes before succeeding his father as rector of Alford-with-Hornblotton, Somerset, in 1858. In 1876 he was appointed prebend of East Harptree in Wells Cathedral, in which position he remained until his retirement in 1893. His hymns were published in his *Hymns Congregational and Others* (1866); *Hymns and Verse* (1866); *Hymns and Sacred Lyrics* (1874); and *A Church of England Hymn Book Adapted to the Daily Services of the Church throughout the Year* (1880). A revised edition of the latter collection appeared in 1882 under the title *The Church of England Hymn Book.*   *M.P.*

Crown Him with Many Crowns (st. 2)–161

Thrupp, Dorothy Ann (b. London, England, Jun. 20, 1779; d. London, England, Dec. 14, 1847) wrote hymns intended primarily for use by children. Several of her hymns were included under the pseudonym of "Iota" in Rev. W. Carus Wilson's *Friendly Visitor* and *Children's Friend*. Others appeared with the attribution "D.

A. T." in Mrs. Herbert Mayo's *Selection of Hymns and Poetry for the use of Infant Schools and Nurseries* (1838). Thrupp edited *Hymns for the Young*, which appeared in four editions from 1830-36 and in which all of the hymns were unsigned.   *M.P.*

Savior, Like a Shepherd Lead Us–61

Tindley, Charles Albert (b. Berlin, MD, Jul. 7, 1851 or 1856; d. Philadelphia, PA, Jul. 26, 1933) was an African-American Methodist preacher of widespread fame and a pioneer author-composer in the Black gospel hymn tradition. His year of birth is uncertain. Born of slave parents, his mother died when he was a young child, and soon thereafter he was separated from his father. Charles, determined to gain an education, plowed all day in the field and walked or ran 14 miles at night to learn from a school teacher.

After his marriage to Daisy Henry, the Tindleys moved from Maryland's Eastern Shore area to Philadelphia. There he worked as a hod carrier and became a janitor at John Wesley (later Bainbridge Street) Methodist Episcopal Church, attending school at night. In 1885, Tindley passed the examination for the Methodist ministry and joined the Delaware Annual Conference, serving in Cape May, New Jersey; South Wilmington, Delaware; Odessa, Delaware; Pocomoke, Maryland; Pocomoke Circuit (four churches), Maryland; Fairmount, Maryland; and Wilmington, Delaware, where he served the historic Ezion Methodist Church, 1897-1900. From 1900 to 1902 he was presiding elder of the Wilmington District. In 1902, Tindley became pastor of the Philadelphia church he was to serve the rest of his life–Bainbridge Street Methodist (later Calvary and East Calvary). The church's growth to more than 7,000 members under his leadership led to a new building in 1924 seating 3,000. The building was named, over his protests, the Tindley Temple Methodist Church.

Tindley wrote more than 45 gospel hymns, the earliest copyrighted in 1901. Often he would emphasize a point in a sermon with a familiar hymn or one he had written. Tindley's more popular gospel hymns include "Nothing Between," "Leave It There," "Stand by Me," and the present hymn, "When the Morning Comes." Two of these four hymns were introduced to Southern Baptists in Robert Coleman's *The Modern Hymnal* (1926). Three of these hymns appeared in B.B. McKinney's *The Broadman Hymnal* (1940). William J. Reynolds has observed that Tindley's song of 1901, "I'll Overcome Some Day," "served as a basis, more in spirit and thought than in actual words or melody, for 'We Shall Overcome,' a theme song of the Civil Rights Movement" that began in the 1960s.   *H.E.*

By And By–When the Morning Comes–522

Tomes, Aaron (b. Amarillo, TX, Sep. 10, 1960) received a B.C.M. degree from Oklahoma Baptist University in 1983 and a M.M. from Southwestern Baptist Theological Seminary in 1987. In 1984 he became associate minister of music at Travis Avenue Baptist Church, Fort Worth, Texas. In 1989 he became minister of music at the North Fort Worth Baptist Church, Fort Worth, Texas.   *S.W.G.*

Tomes–How I Love You–230

Toplady, Augustus Montague (b. Farnham, Surrey, England, Nov. 4, 1740; d. London, England, Jul. 26, 1778) was educated at Westminster School, London, and at Trinity College, Dublin. While in Ireland he was converted during a sermon given by a Wesleyan Methodist lay preacher, James Morris, at a service in a barn. Following ordination in the Church of England in 1762, he served as curate at Blagdon and Farleigh, and later as vicar at Broadhembury, Devonshire. He moved to London in 1776 to serve at the Chapel of the French Calvinists in Leicester Fields. An outspoken Calvinist, he was a strong critic of John Wesley because of the latter's Arminian beliefs. Toplady's hymns and poetry were published in his *Poems on Sacred Subjects* (1759); *The Gospel Magazine* (1771-1776); and *Psalms and Hymns for Public and Private Worship* (1776).   *M.P.*

Rock of Ages, Cleft for Me–342

Tourjée, Lizzie Shove (b. Newport, RI, Sep. 9, 1858; d. Auburndale, MA, Dec. 28, 1913) was the daughter of Eben Tourjée, founder of the New England Conservatory of Music. She was a student at the Conservatory in 1876 and attended Wellesley College for one year, 1877-78. In 1883 she married Franklin Estabrook, a Boston industrialist, with whom she reared two sons. She spent her adult life in Auburndale, Massachusetts, as a music teacher and as organist at the Centenary Methodist Church.   *P.A.R.*

Wellesley–25

Towner, Daniel Brink (b. Rome, PA, Mar. 5, 1850; d. Longwood, MO, Oct. 3, 1919) was taught music early by his father, who had a considerable reputation as a singer and music teacher. John Howard, George F. Root, and George J. Webb provided his more formal training. From 1870 to 1882 he was music director of the Centenary Methodist Episcopal Church in

Binghamton, New York; from 1882 to 1884 he served the York Street Methodist Episcopal Church in Cincinnati, Ohio; and from 1884 to 1885 the Union Methodist Episcopal Church of Covington, Kentucky. In the fall of 1885, Dwight L. Moody invited him to use his fine baritone voice and his skill as a choral conductor in the Moody evangelical work. In 1893, he became head of the Music Department of Moody Bible Institute where he trained evangelical church musicians. In 1900 he was awarded a Mus.D. by the University of Tennessee. He was involved in the publication of 14 collections and is credited with more than 2000 songs. He died while leading the music in an evangelistic meeting in Longwood, Missouri.   *S.W.G.*

CALVARY–138
MOODY–329
TRUST AND OBEY–447

Tredinnick, Noël (b. London, England, Mar. 9, 1949) was educated at St. Olaves Grammar School, The Guildhall School of Music, and The Institute of Education in London. Having won organ prizes while a student at the Guildhall School, he became a professor there in 1975. Simultaneously he worked as a freelance conductor and arranger with the British Broadcasting Company.

During and after a period as music director at the Langley Park School, he took the position of organist/music director of All Souls Church, Langham Place, London, in 1972. In this important center of evangelical worship music, he has exerted wide influence as a performer, composer, and arranger of congregational and choral songs as well as of organ music. As an editor and member of the Jubilate Group he has contributed numerous original songs and ar-

rangements to *Hymns for Today's Church* (London, 1982; 1987), and *Carols for Today* (London, 1987).

Tredinnick was also one of the music editors of *Carol Praise* (London, 1987) and has served as an editor for Oxford University Press. He is also a council member of The Music Worship Trust and an advisor at The Royal School of Church Music.   *H.T.M.*

MAJESTAS (arr.)–207

Troeger, Thomas Henry (b. Suffern, NY, Jan. 30, 1945) is a Presbyterian minister, teacher, and writer. He earned a B.A. degree from Yale University in 1967 and a B.D. degree from Colgate-Rochester Divinity School in 1970. From 1970 until 1977 he was Associate Pastor of New Hartford Presbyterian Church in New York. In 1977 he joined the faculty of Colgate Rochester Divinity School/Bexley Hall/Crozer Theological Seminary in Rochester, New York, teaching preaching and parish ministry. In 1991 he was named Peck Professor of Preaching and Communication at the Iliff School of Theology, Denver, Colorado. Since 1991 he has taught at Iliff School of Theology in Denver. He is in great demand as a preacher and lecturer and is a prolific writer. In addition to devotional volumes and works on preaching and worship, he has written more than 80 hymns, many in collaboration with tune writer Carol Doran, a teaching colleague at Colgate Rochester. The major collections of his hymns are *New Hymns for the Lectionary: To Glorify the Maker's Name* (New York, 1986) and *New Hymns for the Life of the Church: To Make Our Prayer and Music One* (New York, 1992).   *P.A.R.*

Our Savior's Infant Cries Were Heard–116
O Praise the Gracious Power–226

Troutbeck, John (b. Blencowe, Cumberland, England, Nov. 12, 1832; d. London, England, Oct. 11, 1899) was an Anglican minister, church musician, and translator. He earned degrees from University College, Oxford (B.A., 1856; M.A., 1858), and was ordained deacon in 1855 and priest in 1856. From 1865 to 1869 he was precentor at Manchester Cathedral. In 1869 he became minor canon and precentor at Westminster Abbey. He also served as Chaplain and Priest in Ordinary to the Queen and as secretary to the New Testament Revision Company (1870-81). The Archbishop of Canterbury named him Doctor of Divinity in 1883. Troutbeck edited the *Manchester Psalter* (London, 1867), *Manchester Chant Book* (London, 1871), *Westminster Abbey Hymn-Book* (London, 1883), *Westminster Abbey Chant Book* (with J. Frederick Bridge; London, c. 1885), and *Cathedral Paragraph Psalter* (London, 1894). He also wrote *Music Primer for Schools* (with R. F. Dale; London 1873) and *Church Choir Training* (London, 1879). He was a prolific translator, rendering the texts of operas, oratorios, anthems, and solo songs from German, French, and Italian for the publishing house of Novello and Ewer.   *P.A.R.*

Break Forth, O Beauteous Heavenly Light
   (trans. st. 1)–114

Trueblood, David Elton (b. Pleasantville, IA, Dec. 12, 1900) received degrees from Hartford Theological Seminary (S.T.B., 1924) and Harvard University (Ph. D., 1926). He taught at Guilford College (1927-30), Haverford College (1933-36), Stanford University (1936-45), and Earlham College (1946-66). A member of the Society of Friends (Quakers), he has been widely recognized as a popular speaker and author. His numerous books include *The*

Yoke of Christ (1958), *The Company of the Committed* (1961), *The People Called Quakers* (1966), *The Incendiary Fellowship* (1967), *The New Man for our Time* (1970), *The Validity of the Christian Mission* (1972), and *Abraham Lincoln, Theologian of American Anguish* (1973).   *D.M.*

God, Whose Purpose Is to Kindle–618

Tucker, Francis Bland (b. Norfolk, VA, Jan. 6, 1895; d. Savannah, GA, Jan. 1, 1984) was an Episcopalian minister and hymnist. He was the youngest of 13 children of an Episcopalian bishop and his wife. Tucker was educated at the University of Virginia (B.A., 1914) and at Virginia Episcopal Seminary (B.D., 1920), his education having been interrupted by service as a medical corpsman in France during World War I. He served parishes in Brunswick County, Virginia (1920-25); Georgetown, District of Columbia (1925-45); and Savannah, Georgia (1945-67). Among his predecessors at Christ Church in Savannah had been John Wesley. As Russell Schulz-Widmar noted in an obituary in *The Hymn* (April, 1984, pp. 117-18), "Like Wesley, he came to realize that the whole world was his parish and that hymn writing was a part of his ministry." He died in Savannah only a few days short of his 89th birthday.

Tucker began to write hymns while serving on the committee that prepared *The Hymnal 1940* (New York, 1943). To that influential book he contributed six hymns, all of which were reprinted in other collections. He was the only person to work on that hymnal and its successor, *The Hymnal 1982* (New York, 1985). The latter book displayed his diverse contributions to hymnody by including 26 items written, revised, translated, or versified by Tucker.   *P.A.R.*

All Praise to Thee–229

Tullar, Grant Colfax (b. Bolton, CT, Aug. 5, 1869; d. Ocean Grove, NJ, May 20, 1950) was born when Ulysses S. Grant and Schuyler Colfax were president and vice-president of the United States, thus his name. When he was two years old, his mother died and he was reared by unsympathetic relatives. He worked in a woolen mill when he was 10. In Hartford, he clerked in a shoe store until he was 15. At the age of 19, he was converted at a Methodist camp meeting near Waterbury, Connecticut.

His time at Hackettstown Academy, New Jersey, 1889-91, was his only formal education. He was ordained to the Methodist ministry and served as pastor for one year at Dover, Delaware. He resigned the pastorate to enter evangelistic work and, for 10 years, was a song leader for the evangelist, Major George A. Hilton.

In 1893, with Isaac H. Meredith, he founded the Tullar-Meredith Publishing Company, New York, which became a successful publisher of church and Sunday School music.   *S.W.G.*

Face to Face–519

Udulutsch, Irvin Matthew (b. Norwich, WI, Feb. 19, 1920) is a Roman Catholic priest and musician. He entered the Capuchin-Franciscan Order in 1938 and was ordained a priest in 1946. He was educated at the University of Montreal (B.A., 1950) and at Notre Dame University (M.A., 1967). He taught liturgical music at St. Lawrence Seminary from 1947 to 1960 and at St. Anthony Seminary from 1960 to 1970, before becoming Director of Education for the midwest province of his order. Since 1975 he has served in pastoral roles

in parishes in Wisconsin and Minnesota. In addition to a variety of musical and liturgical items which have been published, he has written much unpublished material for worship.   *P.A.R.*

O God, Almighty Father (tr.)–258

Vail, Silas Jones (b. Brooklyn, NY, Oct. 6, 1818; d. Brooklyn, NY, May 20, 1884) worked for some time as a hatter and clerk in Danbury, Connecticut. Later he settled in New York City where he became a successful businessman. Having an interest in music as a hobby, he compiled *The Athenaeum Collection* which included 10 previously unpublished songs of Stephen Foster. He composed several hymn tunes and was engaged by the prohibitionist Horace Waters to compile the collection *Songs of Grace and Glory* (1874) with W. F. Sherwin.   *H.T.M.*

Close to Thee–464

Van DeVenter, Judson W. (b. near Dundee, MI, Dec. 5, 1855; d. Tampa, FL, Jul. 17, 1939), the son of John W. and Eliza (Wheeler) Van DeVenter, was educated in the public schools of Dundee and at Hillsdale College in Michigan. He received his musical training in singing schools. He studied art by touring Europe in 1885, visiting famous art galleries and studying painting. For a number of years, he taught art and penmanship in public schools, including five years as Supervisor of Drawing at Sharon, Pennsylvania, and five years at Bradford, Pennsylvania. An active member of the Methodist Episcopal church and singer in the choir, he experienced a call to the ministry and was licensed as a local preacher. He began evangelistic work, preaching in the United States, England, and Scotland, and being assisted for many years by the evangelistic singer, W. S. Weeden. He spent the last years of his life in Tampa, Florida, where he was an important influence upon the young evangelist, Billy Graham. His "My Mother's Prayer" (I never can forget the day) to a Weeden tune was included in *The Broadman Hymnal* (Nashville, 1940, No. 95).   *H.E.*

I Surrender All–275
Sunlight–444

Van Dyke, Henry (b. Germantown, PA, Nov. 10, 1852, d. Princeton, NJ, Apr. 10, 1933) was educated at Brooklyn Polytechnic Institute, Princeton University (B.A., 1873), and Princeton Theological Seminary (1877, with a year of study abroad.) He was ordained to the Presbyterian ministry and served as pastor of the United Congregational Church, Newport, Rhode Island (1879-83), and of Brick Presbyterian Church, New York City (1883-99). In 1899 he became Murray Professor of English Literature at Princeton for 23 years. His friend, President Woodrow Wilson, whom he had known when Wilson was president of Princeton University, appointed him United States minister to the Netherlands and Luxemburg, where he served from 1914-16. In 1917 he served as a lieutenant commander in the United States Navy Chaplain Corps. He retired from Princeton in 1923. He was a leader in his denomination, being elected moderator of the General Assembly, and chairman of the committee which prepared the *Book of Common Worship* (1905) and its revision in 1932. His hymn on the dignity of labor, "Jesus, Thou Divine Companion" (1909), was published in a number of earlier 20th century American hymnals. A biography by his son Tertius Van Dyke, published in 1935, lists his numerous publications. *H.E.*

Joyful, Joyful, We Adore Thee–7

Vaughan Williams, Ralph (b. Down Ampney, Gloucestershire, England, Oct. 12, 1872; d. St. Marylebone, London, England, Aug. 26, 1958) was the most significant figure in English church music during the first half of the 20th century and the most important English composer of his generation. He distinguished himself as a composer who found inspiration in earlier English music, particularly the country's folksongs. He was the son of the vicar of Christ Church, Down Ampney, but the family moved to Surrey (near London) in 1875 upon his father's death. He studied piano, violin, organ, and theory as a child, and switched to the viola upon entering Charterhouse School. He studied with Parratt, Parry, Stanford, and Wood at the Royal College of Music before entering Cambridge University. He received the Bachelor of Music in 1894 from Trinity College, Cambridge, and a Bachelor of Arts in history in 1895. That year he returned to the Royal College of Music, where he became lifelong friends with Gustav Holst. Vaughan Williams was awarded the Doctor of Music in 1901 from Trinity College. His studies outside England took him to Berlin in 1897 to study with Max Bruch and to Paris in 1908 to study with Maurice Ravel.
Vaughan Williams edited three important collections of church music: *The English Hymnal* (1906); *Songs of Praise* (1925 and 1931, with Percy Dearmer and Martin Shaw); and the *Oxford Book of Carols* (1928, with Percy Dearmer and Martin Shaw). Among his compositions are 14 original hymn tunes. He is remembered by the larger musical world for his symphonies, operas, ballets, orchestral music, chamber music, songs, and film music.   *P.H.*

LASST UNS ERFREUEN (harm.)–27
FOREST GREEN (arr.)–42, 79, 491, 639
KINGSFOLD–(arr.)120
SINE NOMINE–229, 355
KING'S WESTON–396

Virginia Harmony (1831) was an oblong tunebook of four-shape vintage, whose full title was *The Virginia Harmony: a New and Choice Selection of Psalm and Hymn Tunes, Anthems and Set Pieces, in Three and Four Parts, Some of Which Have Never Before Been Published* (Winchester, VA, 1831). Its compilers were David L. Clayton and James P. Carrell. The latter was a Methodist minister (b. Lebanon, VA, Feb. 13, 1787; d. Lebanon, VA, Oct. 28, 1854) who was a prosperous and prominent leader in the Methodist church. He gave the land for the Lebanon Methodist Church and made generous bequests to the Methodist Missionary Society and the Methodist Publishing House, Nashville, Tennessee. *H.T.M.*

NEW BRITAIN–330

Wade, John Francis (b. *c.* 1710; d. Aug. 16, 1786) was a music teacher who copied and sold plain chant and other music for use in the chapels and homes of Douay, France, which served as a refuge for English religious and political refugees from the Jacobite rebellion of 1745. Wade himself was an Englishman who lived in this city, which was a haven particularly for Roman Catholics from England. *M.P.*

ADESTE FIDELES–89, 427

Walch, James (b. Egerton, Lancashire, England, Jun. 21, 1837; d. Llandudno, Caernarvonshire, Wales, Aug. 30, 1901) was a church musician, conductor, and businessman. His musical training came from his father and from Henry Smart. He served as organist at Duke's Alley Congregational Church, Bolton (1851-57); Walmsley Church (1857-58); Bridge Street Wesleyan Chapel (1858-63); and St. George's, Bolton (1863-77). From 1870 until 1877, he was conductor of the Bolton Philharmonic Society. In 1877 he moved to Barrow-in-Furness, where he had a music business. He composed many works for the church, but only the tune TIDINGS remains in use. *P.A.R.*

TIDINGS–583

Walford, William (b. Bath, Somerset, England, 1772; d. Uxbridge, England, Jun. 22, 1850) is sometimes cited as the possible author of the text, "Sweet Hour of Prayer." Following his education at Homerton Academy, he was ordained to the Congregational ministry. Pastorates included Stowmarket, Suffolk (1798-1800), Great Yarmouth, Norfolk (1800-13), and Uxbridge, Middlesex (1824-31 and 1833-48). He taught classics at Homerton Academy from 1814-31. His publications include *The Manner of Prayer* (1836), *The Book of Psalms: A New Translation*; *A Catechism on Christian Evidences*; and an *Autobiography*, edited by John Stoughton and published posthumously in 1851. *M.P.*

Sweet Hour of Prayer–445

Walker, William (b. near Martin's Mills, near Cross Keys, Union County, SC, May 6, 1809; d. Spartanburg, SC, Sep. 24, 1875) was perhaps the most famous Southern Baptist composer of the singing school tradition in the pre-Civil War South. Having learned the folk hymn tradition as a child, Walker began composing, notating and harmonizing melodies from oral tradition as early as the age of 18. In the First Baptist Church of Spartanburg he served as a deacon, as a frequent messenger to the Tyger River Association, and as a leader of congregational singing. In 1835 he compiled his first and most famous singing school tunebook, *The Southern Harmony and Musical Companion* (New Haven, CT; later eds. at Philadelphia in 1840, 1847 [2 eds.], and 1854). In 1866 Walker reported that about 600,000 copies of *Southern Harmony* had been sold.

In the first edition of *Southern Harmony*, Walker first published the hymn text "Amazing grace, how sweet the sound" to the tune NEW BRITAIN and the hymn "On Jordan's stormy banks I stand" to the tune PROMISED LAND. In the 1840 [second] edition he published the text "What wondrous love is this, O my soul" for the first time with its tune, WONDROUS LOVE.

Three additional tunebooks published by Walker were *Southern and Western Pocket Harmonist* (Philadelphia, 1846), *Christian Harmony* (Philadelphia, 1867, 2nd ed. 1872), and *Fruits and Flowers* (Philadelphia, 1873). *Southern Harmony* is still in use at an annual singing in Benton, Kentucky, while *Christian Harmony* is still used at annual singings in North Carolina, Georgia, Mississippi, and especially in Alabama. *H.E.*

See *Southern Harmony*–68, 143, 323

Wallace, William Vincent (b. Waterford, Ireland, Jun. 1, 1812; d. Chateau de Bages, France, Oct. 12, 1865), of Scottish ancestry, received his early musical training from his father. Inspired by hearing Paganini, he began studying the violin and made his concert debut at age 15 in Dublin. He traveled extensively in Australia, New Zealand, India, South America, the United States, and Mexico. Two of his seven operas were staged at Drury Lane in London: *Maritana* (1845) and *Matilda of Hungary* (1847). He wrote tunes for four hymns by John Keble in addition to a cantata and several compositions. Failing eyesight caused him to spend his last years in the Pyrenees. *P.H.*

SERENITY–154, 480

Walter, William Henry (b. Newark, NJ, Jul. 1, 1825; d. New York City, NY, 1893) showed promise as an organist even as a young man. In his early teens he served as organist at a Presbyterian Church and at Grace Episcopal Church in Newark. At the age of 17 he became organist at the Church of the Epiphany in New York City. Following his work there, he was organist at St. John's Chapel, St. Paul's Chapel, and Trinity Chapel until 1869.

Columbia University awarded him a Doctor of Music Degree in 1864. He was named organist at Columbia the following year. In addition to various pieces of sacred music, his publications include a *Manual of Church Music* (1860), *Chorals and Hymns* (1857), and *The Common Prayer, with Ritual Song* (1868). *D.B.*

FESTAL SONG–83, 525

Walton, James George (b. Clitheroe, Lancashire, England, Feb. 19, 1821; d. Bradford, Yorkshire, England, Sep. 1, 1905) was the editor of *Plainsong Music for the Holy Communion Office* (London, 1874). No other details of his life are available. *P.A.R.*

ST. CATHERINE (last 8 measures)–123, 352

Ward, Samuel Augustus (b. Newark, NJ, Dec. 28, 1847; d. Newark, NJ, Sep. 28,

1903) received his musical training in New York City. He established a successful retail music store in Newark, New Jersey, and was active in the musical life of that city. He became organist at Grace Episcopal Church in 1880 and remained in that position for several years. In 1889 he founded the Orpheus Club of Newark and served as its director until 1900. In 1934 a plaque in his memory was placed on the exterior wall of the Parish House of Grace Church.   *M.P.*

Materna–630

Ware, Henry, Jr. (b. Hingham, MA, Apr. 21, 1794; d. Framingham, MA, Sep. 25, 1843) graduated from Harvard University–where his father was a renowned professor–in 1812 and became a teacher at Exeter Academy in New Hampshire. He was ordained to the Unitarian ministry in 1817 and installed as pastor of the Second Unitarian Church in Boston, where for a time his assistant pastor was Ralph Waldo Emerson. From 1830 to 1842 he was a professor of pulpit eloquence and pastoral care at Cambridge Theological School. Ware served as editor of *The Christian Disciple*, which subsequently became *The Christian Examiner*. Four volumes of his writings were published posthumously in 1846.   *D.M.*

Happy the Home When God Is There–505

Waring, Anna Laetitia (b. Plas-y-Velin, Neath, Glamorganshire, South Wales, Apr. 19, 1823; d. Clifton, near Bristol, England, May 10, 1910), the daughter of Elijah Waring, was brought up in the Society of Friends. However, she abandoned her Quaker background, joined the Church of England, and was baptized in 1842. Her *Hymns and Meditations by A.L.W.* (1850) contained 19 hymns; it was enlarged to 39

hymns in the tenth edition (1863). During her later years she lived at Clifton and spent much of her time visiting prisoners in the jails.   *W.J.R.*

In Heavenly Love Abiding–348

Warner, Anna Bartlett (b. Long Island, NY, 1820; d. Constitution Island, near West Point, NY, 1915) was a daughter of Henry W. Warner, a New York lawyer. After 1837 she, along with her father and older sister, Susan, lived on Constitution Island, near the United States Military Academy at West Point. She wrote novels in collaboration with her sister under the pen names of Amy Lothrop (Anna) and Elizabeth Wetherell (Susan). The two sisters conducted Sunday School classes for the cadets at West Point for many years. Their home, "Wood Crag," was willed to the Academy and has been made a national shrine. At her death, Anna was buried with military honors. In addition to her novels, she published two collections of hymns, *Hymns of the Church Militant* (1858) and *Wayfaring Hymns, Original and Translated* (1869).   *M.P.*

Jesus Loves Me–344

Warner, Hugh is the pseudonym of an author who wishes to remain anonymous.   *H.E.*

O Sing a Song to God (tr.)–38
Walking Along with Jesus (adapt.)–186

Warren, George William (b. Albany, NY, Aug. 17, 1828; d. New York, NY, Mar. 17, 1902) was educated at Racine College, Wisconsin. Largely self taught in music, he became organist at the age of 18 at St. Peter's Episcopal Church, Albany, serving until 1858 when he began two years service at St. Paul's, Albany. His later positions as organist were Holy Trinity, Brooklyn, 1860-1870, and St. Thomas', New York City, 1870-1900. He also was organist of Columbia University for several years before his death. He was considered an excellent trainer of voices at St. Thomas where he worked for 30 years. From 1895, he gave popular lectures on music to large and appreciative audiences. Racine College conferred on him the D.Mus. degree. His compositions include several salon pieces, anthems, and services; he edited *Warren's Hymns and Tunes as Sung at St. Thomas' Church* (1888).   *H.E.*

NATIONAL HYMN–596, 629

Watts, Isaac (b. Southampton, England, Jul. 17, 1674; d. Stoke Newington, London, England, Nov. 25, 1748) was the son of Enoch Watts, a cobbler, clothier, and Dissenting schoolmaster who kept a boarding house at Southampton and who suffered imprisonment for his convictions. His mother was of French Huguenot extraction. Isaac, a precocious young man, was offered an education at either Oxford or Cambridge University with a view to ordination in the Church of England, but he refused it to enter an Independent Academy at Stoke Newington. After graduation he returned home to Southampton where he wrote many of the hymns for which he has become famous and which were later published in 1707 and 1709.

For six years thereafter he was tutor in the family of Sir John Hartopp. Then in 1702 he was called to be the pastor of the distinguished Independent Congregation in Mark Lane, London. During his time in this capacity, he engaged in such intense theological and philosophical study that

his health was undermined. In 1712, after he had suffered a serious illness, an assistant was called to help carry his pastoral responsibilities. From this time until his death, he lived in semiretirement in the home of Sir Thomas Abney, serving as chaplain to the family and preaching occasionally in his church.

In spite of poor health, he remained a faithful pastor to his flock, took a leading part in the life of Dissenting churches in London, carried on a voluminous correspondence with the religious leaders of New England, and published some 60 books covering many scholarly fields. His volume, *Logic,* was used as a textbook at Oxford University well into the 19th century. In 1728 he was honored with a D.D. degree from Edinburgh. When he died, he was buried in Bunhill Fields (the London cemetery for those outside the Established Church), and a monument was erected to him in Westminster Abbey in 1779.

Generally considered to be the "Father of English Hymnody," Watts was the author of nearly 700 hymns and psalm paraphrases, many of which are considered among the greatest in the English language. Most of his sacred poems were published in four major collections: *Horae Lyricae* (1706); *Hymns and Spiritual Songs* (1707); *Divine Songs* (1715); and *The Psalms of David Imitated in the Language of the New Testament and Applied to the Christian State and Worship* (1719). These volumes contained the two types of congregational song for which he is remembered–paraphrases of Scripture and devotional poetry. The influence of his twofold theory of congregational praise–that truly Christian praise must go beyond the mere words of Scripture to become original expressions of devotion and that the Hebrew psalms had to be Christianized to be appropriate for authentically

Christian worship–dominated hymn content and practice in the 19th century and continues to the present. His hymns are models of true piety and simplicity. Using only a few basic meters and the plain language of common folk, almost single-handedly he was able to break the stranglehold of strict metrical psalmody and to establish a foundation for the English hymnody of a "Golden Age," dating roughly from Charles Wesley, through William Cowper and John Newton to James Montgomery. He was thus the true shaper of the pattern of the congregational hymn as we know it.

Therefore Isaac Watts was to English hymnody what Ambrose was to the medieval Latin office hymn, what Clement Marot was to the French metrical psalm, and what Martin Luther was to the German chorale. At least two dozen of his hymns and psalm paraphrases in current use testify to a legacy that is monumental.   *H.T.M.*

From All That Dwell Below the Skies–13
I'll Praise My Maker–35
I Sing the Mighty Power of God–42
My Shepherd Will Supply My Need (parap.)–68
O God, Our Help in Ages Past–74
Joy to the World! The Lord Is Come–87
At the Cross–139
When I Survey the Wondrous Cross–144
Alas, and Did My Savior Bleed–145
This Is the Day the Lord Has Made–358
Am I a Soldier of the Cross–481
We're Marching to Zion–524
Come, We That Love the Lord–525
Jesus Shall Reign–587

Weaver, Mack. The identity of this writer is unknown.
Lord, Lay Some Soul upon My Heart (st.2, 3)–570

Webb, George James (b. Rushmore Lodge, Wiltshire, near Salisbury, England, Jun. 24, 1803; d. Orange, NJ, Oct. 7, 1887) was the son of a prosperous farmer who wished him to enter the ministry. However, George wanted to become a musician, and to that end studied organ with Alexander Lucas at Salisbury Cathedral. He became organist at a church in Falmouth, but immigrated to America in 1830, where he settled in Boston. There he became organist of the Old South Church, a position he retained for 40 years. In 1833 he became a teacher in Lowell Mason's Boston Academy of Music, and in 1840 was elected president of the famous Handel and Haydn Society. He was widely known and highly respected as a conductor of choral and orchestral music. In 1870 he moved to Orange, New Jersey, then to New York City (1876), where he taught singing. He returned to Orange in 1885, where he remained until his death.

Webb's publications–some of which were co-compiled with Lowell Mason–included *The Massachusetts Collection of Psalmody* (1840), *The American Glee Book* (1841), *The Psaltery* (1845), *The National Psalmist* (1848), *Cantica Laudis* (1850), *The Melodist* (1850), and *Cantica Ecclesiastica* (1859). *D.M.*

WEBB–485

Webbe, Samuel (b. London, England, 1740; d. London, England, May 25, 1816) was apprenticed to a cabinetmaker at the age of 11. At the age of 20 he decided to become a musician and began to work as a music copyist for a London publisher, using his earnings to take music lessons. He studied organ with Carl Barbandt of the Bavarian Embassy Chapel in London. A Roman Catholic, Webbe became organist for the chapels of the Sardinian and Portuguese embassies in London and occasionally played at the Bavarian and Spanish chapels. He composed masses, motets, anthems, and glees. For the latter genre, he is considered to be England's most outstanding composer, having won several prizes during his lifetime for his glees. Webbe published *A Collection of Sacred Music As Used in the Chapel of the King of Sardinia in London* (*c.* 1785), *A Collection of Masses* (1792), *A Collection of Motetts and Antiphons* (1792), and nine collections of glees and catches. He also wrote *An Essay on the Church Plain Chant* (1782). *M.P.*

CONSOLATOR–67

Weber, Carl Maria von (b. Eutin, Germany, Nov. 18, 1786; d. London, England, Jun. 5, 1826) received his muscial training under Michael Haydn, the brother of Franz Joseph Haydn, and under Abt Bogler, who was influential in getting Weber appointed Kapellmeister of the Breslau Municipal Theatre. Weber grew up in theater life under the aegis of his father and became one of the outstanding opera composers in Germany. He is considered by some to be the "father" of German Romantic opera, paving the way for Richard Wagner. He died of tuberculosis. *S.W.G.*

SEYMOUR–306

Webster, Joseph Philbrick (b. Manchester, NH, Mar. 22, 1819; d. Elkhorn, WI, Jan. 18, 1875) graduated from Pembroke Academy, New Hampshire (1840), and studied music under Lowell Mason in Boston (1840-43). He spent a number of years in New York, New Jersey, and Connecticut teaching music and giving concerts. He was a versatile musician, playing the flute, violin, and piano. In Connecticut he managed a singing troupe, The Euphonians, and composed for them their most successful songs. After short periods in Madison, Indiana; Chicago, Illinois; and Racine, Wisconsin, he settled in Elkhorn, Wisconsin (from 1859). He is said to have composed over 400 songs, including sentimental ballads, patriotic songs, and hymn tunes. His most popular works were "Lorena," a ballad, and the hymn tune SWEET BY AND BY. *H.T.M.*

SWEET BY AND BY–515

Weeden, Winfield Scott (b. Middleport, OH, Mar. 29, 1847; d. Bisby Lake, NY, Jul. 31, 1908), the son of Isaac and Sarah (Faar) Weeden, was educated in the Middleport public schools. Converted in early manhood, he taught singing schools for several years before entering evangelistic work. Gifted with a fine voice and ability as a song leader, he was frequently invited to lead music for YMCA, Christian Endeavor, and Epworth League conventions. He was associated with Judson W. Van DeVenter in evangelistic meetings for many years, composing music for van DeVenter's gospel hymns. Weeden compiled several collections, including *The Peacemaker* (1894), *Songs of Sovereign Grace* (1897), and *Songs of the Peacemaker* (1895). During his last years he lived in New York City, where he owned The Winona Hotel. On his tombstone in New York City's Woodlawn Cemetery is engraved the title of his best-known hymn, "I Surrender All." *H.E.*

SURRENDER–275
SUNLIGHT IN MY SOUL–444

Weissel, Georg (b. Domnau, Germany, 1590; d. Königsberg, Germany, Aug. 1,

1635) was the son of Johann Weissel, mayor of Domnau. He was educated at the University of Königsberg, and later at Wittenberg and several other universities. After serving for a period as rector of the school at Frieland, he returned to Königsberg to resume theological studies (1617). He became pastor of the newly-erected Altrossgart Church at Königsberg (1623) and remained there until his death. His some 20 hymns appeared in the hymn collections of the Pietists. *H.T.M.*

Lift Up Your Heads–128

Wesley, Charles (b. Epworth, Lincolnshire, England, Dec. 18, 1707; d. London, England, Mar. 28, 1788) was educated at Westminster School and Christ Church College, Oxford. He became a tutor at Christ Church and founded there the "Holy Club," a group of young Oxford students who pledged themselves "to observe with strict formality the method of study and practice laid down in the statutes of the University" and therefore were dubbed "Methodists" by their detractors.

In 1735 he was ordained in the Church of England and then accompanied his brother John on a journey to the English colony in Georgia. They arrived in February, 1736, and Charles served as private secretary and chaplain to Governor James E. Oglethorpe. Within a few months they returned to London and became associated with a group of Moravians. Wesley was converted on Whitsunday, May 20, 1738, and his older brother, John, had a similar experience a short time later.

Shortly after his conversion, he accepted a curacy at Islington, London, but in a few months he was forbidden to preach in the parish church, and from then on he was closely associated with his brother John. He devoted his energies and talents to their evangelistic work, traveling throughout England and Wales on horseback, preaching to throngs in the out-of-doors, and founding societies for disciplined prayer and Bible study.

Charles remained loyal to the Established Church and was never in sympathy with those of the "Methodists" who wanted to leave the Anglican Church. After his marriage in 1749, he confined his work largely to Bristol and London. More than 6500 hymns covering a broad spectrum of Christian experience and many new evangelical emphases flowed from his passionate pen. He expanded the limited hymnic forms of his day by employing 30 different meters. Always a faithful communicant of the Church of England, when he died at the age of 70, his body was buried in the Marylebone parish churchyard in London. *S.W.G., H.T.M.*

Praise the Lord Who Reigns Above–33
Come, Thou Long-Expected Jesus–77
Hark! The Herald Angels Sing–88
And Can It Be–147
'Tis Finished! The Messiah Dies–148
Christ the Lord Is Risen Today–159
Hail the Day That Sees Him Rise–165
Jesus, Lover of My Soul–180
Rejoice, the Lord Is King–197
Lo, He Comes with Clouds Descending
  (st. 1,2,4)–199
Blessed Be the Name–206
Love Divine, All Loves Excelling–208
O for a Thousand Tongues to Sing–216
Depth of Mercy–306
O God, to Those Who Here Profess
  (st. 2)–506
Ye Servants of God–589

Wesley, John (b. Epworth, Lincolnshire, England, Jun. 17, 1703; d. London, England, Mar. 2, 1791) was the son of the Anglican clergyman Samuel and his wife Susannah, a remarkable woman. As a small child, John was rescued from the Epworth rectory in 1709 as it burned, an experience which his mother regarded as a sign of his being saved for God's purposes. John was educated at Charterhouse School and Christ Church, Oxford (B.A. 1724, M.A., 1726-27). He was ordained priest in 1728, and from 1727 to 1729 served as curate to his father. In 1729 he returned to Oxford to serve for six years as tutor at Lincoln College, during which time he joined his brother Charles in the disciplined activities of the Holy Club, for which they were called "Methodists." In 1735 he and his brother Charles sailed to Savannah, Georgia under the sponsorship of the Society for the Propagation of the Gospel. Aboard ship he became acquainted with a group of Moravians, learned German, and began translating their hymns into English. While in Savannah John patterned his ministry after that of the Moravians, establishing a Sunday School for youth at the parish church he served (now Christ Church). John became embroiled in controversy and was brought to court, but left for England before the case was closed. In spite of his personal disappointments in Georgia, Wesley compiled the first hymnal to be published in the colonies, *A Collection of Psalms and Hymns* (1737), known as the "Charlestown Collection" after the city where it was printed. Shortly after returning to England in 1737, Wesley underwent a spiritual conversion in a Moravian meeting on Aldersgate Street. From this time he gave himself to preaching and teaching the Gospel with great fervor and zeal. For over 50 years he was an itinerant evangelist, often preaching outdoors, for many of the Anglican clergy would not permit him to occupy their pulpits. His *Journal* is a record of his remarkable ministry. He traveled over 250,000 miles on horseback, delivered about 40,000 sermons, and on occasions spoke to as many as 30,000 people. Over a period of 53 years the Wesleys published 64 collections of hymns. Since the hymns were not always identified as the work of John or Charles, there has been continuing speculation among hymnologists concerning their authorship. Henry Bett concluded that nine-tenths of the hymns in the Wesley's comprehensive *Collection of Hymns for the Use of the People Called Methodists* were written by Charles. Concerning John's hymnic contribution, W. Garrett Horder considered him, "as great a translator as Charles is an original hymnist. For congregational use they are probably the finest translations in the English language, whilst they have the honor of having opened to us the rich treasure of sacred song which Germany possesses" (Horder, 114).

By far the greatest contribution of John Wesley to hymnody was his editing and publishing the hymns of his brother, Charles.

Wesley was also concerned with the practice of congregational singing, as evidenced from his often-quoted "Directions for Singing" (preface to *Sacred Melody*, 1761) which can be found in *The United Methodist Hymnal* (Nashville, 1989, p.vii).   H.E.

I'll Praise My Maker (alt.)–35
Jesus, Thy Boundless Love to Me (tr.)–123

Wesley, Samuel Sebastian (b. London, England, Aug. 14, 1810; d. Gloucester, England, Apr. 19, 1876) was the grandson of Charles Wesley and one of the most significant musicians in 19th-century England. His father supplied his early music training and Samuel became a chorister of the Chapel Royal in 1820. In 1826, he held his first organ position and served several churches before becoming organist at Hereford Cathedral in 1832. He received the Doctor of Music degree from Oxford in 1839. He served as organist at Exeter Cathedral (1835-42), Leeds Parish Church (1842-49), Winchester Cathedral (1849-65), and Gloucester Cathedral (1865-76). He became professor of organ at the Royal Academy of Music in 1850. He was an ardent angler, and it is said that his choice of communities where he would serve as organist was sometimes influenced by the fishing possibilities. He was an advocate for improving English cathedral music and concerned for a reform among 19th-century church musicians. He published a large amount of church music (services, anthems, and hymn tunes) including *The European Psalmist* (1872), a compilation of 733 hymn tunes (130 of them his own). He died at Gloucester, but was buried at Exeter according to his wishes.   *S.W.G.*

AURELIA–272, 350

Wesleyan Sacred Harp (1854) was compiled by the Rev. William McDonald of the Maine Conference of the Methodist Church, together with "S.Hubbard, esq." in Boston in 1854. It is the earliest known source of the tune HAPPY DAY. Though the compilers in their Preface indicate "many of the tunes--not all together new--have never appeared in a work of this kind before," it is altogether likely that HAPPY DAY, as well as other tunes contained in this collection, were current at an earlier time. *H.T.M.*

HAPPY DAY–439

Whelpton, George (b. Redbourne, England, May 17, 1847; d. Oxford, OH, Nov. 25, 1930) came with his family to the United States in 1851. During the Civil War, at the age of 16, he enlisted in the Union Army.

He studied music with Horatio R. Palmer and for some 20 years was a recognized choral director in Buffalo, New York. In 1903 he joined the editorial staff of the Century Publishing Company in New York, publishing several collections including *Hymns of Worship and Service* and *The Church Hymnal*. He joined the editorial staff of A.S. Barnes Company in 1916 and remained there until his retirement in 1925.   *S.W.G.*

WHELPTON–658

White, Benjamin Franklin (b. near Cross Keys, Union County, SC, Sep. 20, 1800; d. Atlanta, GA, Dec. 5, 1879), 12th child of Robert and Mildred White, had little formal education and was self-taught in music. In 1825 he married Thurza Golightly of Spartanburg. To this marriage nine children were born. In 1842, he moved his family to Harris County, Georgia, and, in 1844, with E. J. King as co-editor, he published *The Sacred Harp*. He was the first editor of the Harris County weekly newspaper, *The Organ*, which began publication January 1, 1852. In 1858 he became clerk of the Inferior Court and was elected mayor of Hamilton in 1865. In the 1850s he was active in the Harris County militia and rose to the rank of major. From that time on he was always referred to as Major White. He was an active member of a missionary Baptist church. *W.J.R.*

See *Sacred Harp, The*–18, 377, 604, 613

Whitefield, George (b. Gloucester, England, Dec. 16, 1714; d. Newburyport, MA, Sep. 30, 1770), after a meager schooling, became a bartender in his mother's inn at Gloucester. Managing to prepare for Oxford University, he entered Pembroke College and became a disciplined member of the "Holy Club," made famous by the Wesley brothers, John and Charles. Ordained in the Anglican Church at age 22, he set about his evangelizing tours throughout England and Wales.

At first closely connected with the Wesleys, he parted company with them in 1741 over doctrinal differences. He came to America seven times where his powerful preaching was instrumental in inaugurating the spiritual revival known as "The Great Awakening." His contributions to hymnody consisted of his editing the widely-used *Collection of Hymns for Social worship* (1753), which contained his alteration of several hymns, including the beginning lines of Charles Wesley's Christmas hymn "Hark! The Herald Angels Sing." While in Massachusetts during the seventh tour, he died and was buried at Newburyport under the pulpit of the Old South Presbyterian Church.   *H.T.M.*

Hark! The Herald Angels Sing (alt.)–88

Whitfield, Frederick (b. Threapwood, Shropshire, England, Jan. 7, 1829; d. Lower Norwood [S.E. London], England, Sep. 13, 1904) graduated (B.A., 1859) at Trinity College, Dublin, Ireland. Ordained deacon in the Church of England in 1859, he was curate at Otley, Yorkshire, (1859-61). Following ordination as priest, he was vicar of Kirkby-Ravensworth, Yorkshire, (1861-65). He then served as senior curate at St. Giles-in-the-Fields, London, (1866-68); and Greenwich, (1868-70); and as vicar of St.

John's, Crayford, Bexley, Kent, (1871-73); and of Emmanuel, Wimbledon, (1873-75). His major appointment was as vicar of St. Mary-in-the-Castle, Hastings, where he served 24 years, from 1875 to 1899. In 1899 he resigned because of failing health, moving to Norfolk House, Lancaster Road, South Norwood. He had four sons who were clergymen. A prolific writer, the *British Library Catalog* lists 30 original works of his, including *Voices from the Valley Testifying of Jesus* (1861), *Earthly Shadows of the Heavenly Kingdom* (1872), and *Wellsprings of Life* (2nd ed., 1893). His poems and hymns were published in his *Sacred Poems and Prose* (Dublin, 1859) and *The Christian Casket; or Sacred Poems and Prose* (2nd series, 1864).   *H.E.*

Oh, How I Love Jesus–217
I Saw the Cross of Jesus–286

Whiting, William (b. Kensington, Middlesex, England, Nov. 1, 1825; d. Winchester, Hampshire, England, May 3, 1878) was educated at Clapham and Winchester Colleges. For 36 years Whiting was master of the Winchester College Choristers' School, an institution with a tradition dating from 1382. He taught and directed the 16 boys who sang regularly in the Anglican services in the school chapel. He published *Rural Thoughts and Other Poems*, 1851, and "Eternal Father, Strong to Save" is the only hymn he ever wrote.   *W.J.R.*

Eternal Father, Strong to Save–69

Whitney, Rae E. (b. Chippenham, Wilts, England, May 21, 1927) is the daughter of Arthur James Phillips and Alice Davis Phillips. She was educated at Chippenham Grammar School and at the University of Bristol where she received a B.A. (English Honors) in 1948 and a Certificate in Education in 1949. During her teenage years, she became a committed Christian and was baptized at the Station Hill Baptist Church in Chippenham. Her Christian growth during this same period was influenced by Ray and Nellie Montacute, prominent English Baptists. From 1949-60 she taught English and Religion in secondary schools. She also served as a Sunday School teacher and was active as a lay preacher in rural Baptist, Methodist, and Congregational Churches. In 1956 she was confirmed in the Church of England. From 1958 to 1960, she lived in London and worked as a resident secretary of the Fellowship of St. Alban and St. Sergius, a group devoted to better understanding between eastern and western churches. In 1960, on a trip to Italy, she met Rev. Clyde E. Whitney, Rector of St. Andrew's Episcopal Church in Scottsbluff, Nebraska. They were married December 31, 1960. Except for one year of service to the Church in Guatemala, she and her husband have lived in western Nebraska all their married lives. In 1991 they were residing in Gering, Nebraska. Rae Whitney began writing hymns as a teenager, but most (around 200) have been written since 1978. In addition to the two hymns in *The Baptist Hymnal* (1991), her text "Lord God, you now have set your servant free" was published in *The Hymnal, 1982*, the *Presbyterian Hymnal* (1990), and was one of seven of her hymns in *Songs of Rejoicing* (1989).   *D.B.*

Christmas Has Its Cradle–152
O What a Wonder It Is–548

Whittier, John Greenleaf (b. Haverhill, MA, Dec. 17, 1807; d. Hampton Falls, NH, Sep. 7, 1892), born of Quaker parents, spent his first 20 years on the family farm. He was largely self-educated and found his poetic talent, around age 14, stimulated by a book of Robert Burns' poetry. His first poem was published by abolitionist William Lloyd Garrison in his *Newburyport Free Press* in 1826. Under the influences of his Quaker background and Garrison, Whittier became a staunch abolitionist. Throughout his career, he edited several publications, including the *National Era* (1847-60). Whittier considered himself to be one of the founders of the Republican Party. His greatest work is generally believed to be "Snow-Bound" (1866). About 50 hymns have been excerpted from his poetry, even though Whittier disavowed any exceptional ability as a hymn writer.   *P.H.*

Dear Lord and Father of Mankind–267
Immortal Love, Forever Full–480

Whittle, Daniel Webster (b. Chicopee Falls, MA, Nov. 22, 1840; d. Northfield, MA, Mar. 4, 1901) moved to Chicago during his teenage years and became a cashier at the Wells Fargo Bank. He enlisted in the 72nd Illinois Infantry, Company B, in 1861. On the eve of his regiment's departure, August 22, 1862, he married Abbie Hanson. He eventually became provost marshall on O. O. Howard's staff and participated in Sherman's march to the sea. He was wounded in the battle of Vicksburg and was taken prisoner. At the end of the war, he received a brevet promotion to major, hence the title that remained a part of his identity for life. Upon returning to Chicago, he became treasurer of the Elgin Watch Company. Dwight L. Moody's influence, however, caused him to resign and enter evangelistic work in 1873. His music associates were among the notables of their day: P. P. Bliss, James McGranahan, and George C. Stebbins. Whittle wrote around 200 hymn texts, many under the pseudonym "El Nathan."   *P.H.*

I Know Whom I Have Believed–337
Moment by Moment–415
There Shall Be Showers of Blessing–467

Wilkes, John B. (b. London, England, 1785; d. London, England, 1869), after studying at the Royal Academy of Music in London, became organist of St. David's, Merthyr Tydfil, and later of Llandaff Cathedral. In 1860 he was organist ot the Monkland church near Leominster where Henry W. Baker, the chief promoter of *Hymns Ancient and Modern*, was the vicar. It was therefore natural that Wilkes should be one of the contributors to the origianl music edition of that epoch-making hymnal. In 1865, he retired to live in London. *H.T.M.*

Monkland (arr.)–235

Williams, Aaron (b. London, England, 1731; d. London, England, 1776) was a singing teacher, music engraver, and publisher. He served as clerk for the Scots Church, London Wall. His publications included: *The Universal Psalmodist* (1763), *The Royal Harmony* (1766), *The New Universal Psalmodist* (1770), *Harmonia Coelestis* (6th ed., 1775), and *Psalmody in Miniature* (1778). *The Royal Harmony* was reprinted many times, including an American edition titled *The American Harmonist* (1769), published by Daniel Bailey. *P.H.*

St. Thomas–354, 400, 401

Williams, Clara Tear (b. Painesville, OH, Sep. 22, 1858; d. Caneadea, NY, Jul. 1, 1937) lived in Houghton, New York, where she was a member of the Wesleyan Methodist Church. George Beverly Shea, himself a Wesleyan Methodist, was introduced by his father to Mrs. Williams short-

ly after his family moved to Houghton in 1917. He described the encounter in *Crusade Hymn Stories* (Carol Stream, 1967, p. 75): "Walking together in Houghton one day, Dad pointed out a tall, elderly lady moving slowly on the sidewalk. He told me that she was Mrs. Clara Tear Williams, a much loved and respected hymn writer–author of one of his favorite Christian songs, 'Satisfied.' ....She had a regal and dignified bearing and yet she had the kindness and gentleness of Christ in her face.... Hers was a beautiful life exhibited not only to the whole community, but expressed also in the pages of hymnody." *D.B.*

Satisfied–539

Williams, David H. (b. Caerphilly, Wales, Nov. 21, 1919) emigrated to the United States, was educated at the Juilliard School of Music, and studied privately with Roy Harris, A. Madely Richardson, and Walter Wild. He served as organist and choirmaster at churches in New York, Connecticut, Vermont, and Arizona. For a number of years he served as director of the ministry of music of the Catalina United Methodist Church, Tucson, Arizona. He has written numerous compositions for children, youth, and adult choirs. *W.J.R.*

Vermont–603

Williams, Peter (b. Llansadurnin, Carmarthenshire, Wales, Jan. 7, 1722; d. Llandyfeilog, Wales, Aug. 8, 1796) was educated in Llansadurnin in grammar school and there converted under the preaching of George Whitefield. In 1744 he was ordained and became curate at Eglwys Cummyn. His fervent preaching brought much opposition, and he was forced out of the Established Church. In 1746 he joined the

Calvinistic Methodist Church and became an itinerant preacher. He became one of the outstanding leaders of the Methodist Revival in Wales. He was later expelled by the Methodists on the grounds of heresy and built his own chapel in Water Street, Carmarthen. In 1759 he published a volume of Welsh hymns and in 1771 he published *Hymns on Various Subjects*. He also published a family edition of the Welsh Bible with a commentary (1767-70) and, in 1773, a Welsh concordance.   *S.W.G.*

Guide Me, O Thou Great Jehovah
  (tr. st. 1)–56

Williams, Ralph Vaughan (See Vaughan Williams, Ralph).

Williams, Thomas. Nothing is known of the compiler of the 1789 *Psalmodia Evangelica.*   *W.J.R.*

See Psalmodia Evangelica–128, 173

Williams, William (b. Cefn-y-Coed, Llanfair-y-bryn, Carmarthenshire, Wales, Feb. 11, 1717; d. near Llandovery, Wales, Jan. 11, 1791), the son of a prosperous farmer, received a good education and began the study of medicine at Llwynllwyd Academy at Carmarthen. He determined to enter the ministry after being deeply stirred by the preaching of Howell Harris. In 1740, he was ordained a deacon of the Established Church and served as a curate for a while, but was denied ordination as a priest because of his evangelistic views. He became associated with the Calvinistic Methodist Church and for more than half a century traveled throughout Wales doing evangelistic work. His wife was a singer and often traveled with him. He was a very popular preacher and John Julian refers to

him as "the Sweet Singer of Wales." Williams wrote more than 800 Welsh hymns and more than 100 English hymns. It has been said that he was to Wales what Paul Gerhardt was to Germany and what Isaac Watts was to England. He died at Pantycelyn, a farm three miles east of Llandovery and is buried in the churchyard of Llanfair church.   *S.W.G.*

Guide Me, O Thou Great Jehovah–56

Willis, Richard Storrs (b. Boston, MA, Feb. 10, 1819; d. Detroit, MI, May 7, 1900) received his bachelor's degree from Yale University in 1841. During his college days, he was president of the Beethoven Society (1837), for which he also composed choral and instrumental pieces. After graduation he went to Germany, where he studied music with Schnyder von Wartensee in Frankfurt and with Moritz Hauptmann in Leipzig. While in Leipzig he formed a close friendship with Felix Mendelssohn. Willis returned to the United States in 1848, becoming music critic for several magazines–*New York Tribune*, *The Albion*, and *The Musical Times*. From 1852-64 he edited the periodicals *Musical Times*, *Musical World*, and *Once a Month*. He authored a book (*Our Church Music*, 1856), and brought out several vocal collections, including *Church Chorals and Choir Studies* (1850), *Waif of Song* (1876)–a compilation of student and patriotic songs, and *Pen and Lute* (1883).   *D.M.*

CAROL–93
CRUSADERS' HYMN (ST. ELIZABETH) (arr.)–176

Wilson, Emily Divine (b. Philadelphia, PA, May 24, 1865; d. Philadelphia, PA, Jun. 23, 1942) was the daughter of John and Sarah (Lees) Divine, her father a native of

Ireland, and her mother a native of England. In 1887 she was married to Rev. John G. Wilson, a Methodist minister, who served as district superintendent of the Philadelphia Conference, and who was, at the time of his death in 1933, pastor of the Wharton Memorial Methodist Church, Philadelphia. She and her husband were well-known personalities at the Ocean Grove Assembly in New Jersey.   *W.J.R.*

HEAVEN–514

Wilson, Hugh (b. Fenwick, Ayrshire, Scotland, 1766; d. Duntocher, Dunbartonshire, Scotland, Aug. 14, 1824) was educated in the village school. Through self-study he broadened his knowledge of music and mathematics and learned to design sundials. From his father he learned shoemaking. He earned extra income by teaching classes in a variety of subjects including music. After 1800 he worked as a calculator and draftsman. An active churchman, he helped found a Sunday School in the village of Duntocher. Of the several tunes he composed or arranged, AVON is the only one in current use.   *D.B.*

AVON–145, 372

Wilson, Ira Bishop (b. Bedford, Taylor County, IA, Sep. 6, 1880; d. Los Angeles, CA, Apr. 3, 1950) was taught violin and organ by an older sister and began studying harmony while still a youth. In 1902 he entered Moody Bible Institute for training in musical evangelism. In 1905, however, he accepted a position as composer and editor with the Lorenz Publishing Company, Dayton, Ohio. He was a contributing editor to Lorenz's music periodicals, *The Choir Leader* and *The Choir Herald*, and editor-in-chief of *The Volunteer Choir*. For his com-

positions he used a number of pseudonymns, especially "Fred B. Holton." In addition to numerous hymn arrangements and anthems, he was particularly successful in composing seasonal choir cantatas, reportedly with sales of more than one and a half million copies. Ninety-three of his cantatas, both sacred and secular, are listed in Thurston J. Dox's *American Oratorios and Cantatas* (1986). He and E.S. Lorenz and D.B. Towner edited the Sunday School songbook, *His Worthy Praise* (1915). In 1930 he moved to Los Angeles, but continued his work with Lorenz. His son, Roger C. Wilson, was also a composer on the Lorenz editorial staff. In 1985, 35 years after his death, 21 of Ira B. Wilson's works were listed in *Sacred Choral Music in Print* (2nd ed.).   *H.E.*

Make Me a Blessing–569

Wilson, John Whitridge (b. Bournville, suburb of Birmingham, Warwickshire, England, Jan. 21, 1905) was educated at Cambridge University in physics and mathematics. In 1928, he decided upon music as a profession and studied at the Royal College of Music while living with and learning from his uncle, Sir Walford Davies, noted choirmaster and popular music educator. He also studied with England's premier composer, Ralph Vaughan Williams.

After a brief teaching appointment at Tonbridge School he went in 1932 to Charterhouse where, after a war-time break to teach science, he was director of music until 1965. He then taught at the Royal College of Music until his retirement in 1980. Reared in the Congregationalist tradition, he became a communicant of the Church of England and was for some time organist of Guildford Methodist Church, Surrey. For a quarter of a century, he served as the treasurer of the Hymn Society of Great Britain and Ireland (1965-90) and is widely recognized as a scholar-apostle of all musical aspects of hymnody in England. He is best known as the organizer, promoter, and director of the annual hymn singing events in Westminster Abbey known as *Come and Sing.*

He served on the editorial committees of numerous hymn collections including *The Clarendon Hymn Book* (1936); *Hymns for Church and School* (1964); *Hymns and Songs* (1969); *Broadcast Praise* (1981); and *Hymns and Psalms, A Methodist and Ecumenical Hymn Book* (1983). He was coeditor with Erik Routley of *Hymns for Celebration* (1974) and the compiler of *Sixteen Hymns of Today for Use as Simple Anthems* (1978) and *Twenty-one Hymns Old and New for Use as Simple Anthems* (1985). He presently is living in retirement in Guildford, Surrey, England. *H.T.M.*

LAUDS–393

Winkworth, Catherine (b. London, England, Sep. 13, 1827; d. Monnetier, Savoy, France, Jul. 1, 1878), because of her fidelity to both the word and the spirit of the original, is regarded as the foremost English translator of German hymns. Her mother died in 1841, and when her father remarried in 1845 she went to Dresden to live briefly with an aunt. Her stay in Germany aroused a lifelong interest in the study of the German language.

In 1855 she published *Lyra Germanica,* her first series of translations of German hymns then in common use. The book went through 30 editions and was followed by a second series published in 1858 which went through 12 editions. She also published her *Chorale Book for England* (1863) and *Christian Singers of Germany* (1869).

She lived in Manchester for most of her life, but in 1862 she moved to Clifton, near Bristol, to live with her father and sisters. She was a devout and well-informed woman who was interested in educational and social issues, especially in higher education for women. She died suddenly of a heart problem at the age of 51 at Monnetier in Savoy and was buried there.   *S.W.G.*

Praise to the Lord, the Almighty (tr.)–14
If You Will Only Let God Guide You (tr.)–57
Lift Up Your Heads (tr.)–128
Now Thank We All Our God (tr.)–638

Witt [Witte], Christian Friedrich (b. Altenburg, Germany, *c.* 1660; d. Altenburg or Gotha, Germany, Apr. 13, 1716) was first taught music by his father, Johann Ernst Witt, an Altenburg court organist. The younger Witt studied counterpoint and composition with C.C. Wecker in Nuremberg. In 1686 he became chamber organist at the Gotha court. In 1713 he took the position of Kapellmeister there. He composed vocal and instrumental music, including a cycle of 65 church cantatas. His keyboard works include several harpsichord suites and a *Passacaglia* in D minor once wrongly attributed to Bach. His *Psalmodia sacra* (Gotha, 1716), regarded as one of the most important German hymnals of the early eighteenth century, included 774 chorales with 356 melodies, including over 100 new tunes, most of which are regarded as being by Witt himself.   *H.E.*

STUTTGART–21, 257, 369

Wolfe, Aaron Robarts (b. Mendham, NJ, Sep. 6, 1821; d. Montclair, NJ, Oct. 6, 1902) graduated from Williams College (A.B., 1844) and Union Theological Seminary (1851). He was licensed to the ministry by the Third Presbytery of New York on April 9, 1851, but most of his career was spent in educational work. He was principal of a school for young women in Tallahassee, Florida, from 1852-55. In 1859 he established the Hillside Seminary for Young Ladies in Montclair, New Jersey, and served as its principal until 1872, when he retired due to failing health. Eight of his hymns, appearing under the signature "A.R.W.," were published in 1858 in Thomas Hastings' *Church Melodies.*   *M.P.*

A Parting Hymn We Sing–375

Wolfe, Irving Willis (b. Cedar Rapids, IA, May 4, 1903; d. Nashville, TN, Jul. 31, 1977) was educated at the University of Northern Iowa (B.A., 1925) and Northwestern University (M.S., 1931; Ph.D., 1936). He taught at Eastern Illinois University (1937-40) and George Peabody College for Teachers, where he was head of the division of music (1940-55) and professor of music (1955-71). A nationally known figure in the field of music education, he was active in all levels of the Music Educators National Conference. He was the author of *State Certification of Music Teachers* (Washington, 1972), and coauthor of the public school music series *Together We Sing* and *Discovering Music Together.* For many years he was an active member of Nashville's Vine Street Christian Church and sang in the choir. He directed music in various churches in Nashville and always maintained a keen interest in the field of church music. His own dedication to music education, desire to help children discover the joy of music experiences, and his genuine interest in the musical development of his students made him an inspiration to those whose lives he touched.   *W.J.R.*

Wolfe–264

Wolfe, Lanny Lavon (b. Columbus, OH, Feb. 2, 1942) was educated at Ohio State University, San Jose State College, and Southern Illinois University at Edwardsville. He has served as Dean of Music, Gateway College of Evangelism, St. Louis (1968-74) and Dean of Music, Christian Life College, Stockton, California (1975-76). Since 1974 he has been Dean of Music, Jackson [Mississippi] College of Ministries. He directs the Lanny Wolfe Singers and Band, ten students at the Jackson College of Ministries who present concerts nationwide. They are recording artists on the SpiritSong label, Cleveland, Tennessee. He also serves as Minister of Music, First Pentecostal Church, Jackson. In 1971 he published his first song, "Only Jesus Can Satisfy Your Soul." As of 1991, he had composed over 300 songs and 10 musicals. His songs have been voted among the Top Ten Songs of the Gospel Music Association for many years. The GMA has also nominated Lanny Wolfe for eight years as Best Gospel Composer and he has received SESAC's Gospel Composer of the Year Award for two consecutive years. For 16 years he was a composer and artist with the Benson Company, Nashville. He received a Dove Award for Gospel Songwriter of the Year for 1984 with "More than Wonderful" which was judged "Song of the Year." Since 1988 he has published with Pathway Press, Cleveland, Tennessee.   *H.E.*

Greater Is He–Greater Is He That Is in Me–437

Wood, James H. (b. Rochester, MN, Apr. 14, 1921) was educated at Macalester College (A.B.), Iowa University (M.A.), and Union Theological Seminary (S.M.D.), and was a member of the Robert Shaw Chorale

(1951-52). His earlier teaching career took him to Colorado A. and M. College, Bethany College, Duke University, and The Southern Baptist Theological Seminary. In 1958 he went to the music faculty of Morningside College, Sioux City, Iowa, where he served for 21 years as teacher of voice and choral work and head of the music department. In 1979 he moved to Frostburg State College, Frostburg, Maryland, as chairman of the music department. A versatile musician, Wood has made many solo appearances (bass-baritone) and has pursued a professional career that has included choral conducting and composition of vocal and choral works and arrangements. In 1986 he and his wife, Joyce, a piano teacher, retired to Owatonna, Minnesota, where they continue to reside.   *H.T.M.*

BEACH SPRING (harm.)–377, 604, 613

Woolston, Clarence Herbert (b. Camden, NJ, Apr. 7, 1856; d. Philadelphia, PA, May 20, 1927), son of Isaiah S. and Sarah B. Woolston of Camden, New Jersey, attended public schools at Camden, and studied at the South Jersey Institute at Bridgeton. Following his call to the ministry, he studied at Crozier Theological Seminary. After his ordination in 1880, he was pastor of Baptist churches at South River, New Jersey (1880-85) and Lambertville, New Jersey (1885-87). In 1887 he began a 40-year pastorate at the East Baptist Church, Philaelphia, serving until his death in 1927. Possessing dramatic gifts, he would sometimes illustrate his sermons with sleight-of-hand tricks. He was widely known for his work with children, serving on the program for children's work in the Billy Sunday meetings and in summer conferences at Ocean Grove, New Jersey and at Winona Lake, Indiana. He was founder of the Penny Concert movement for children. His books include *Seeing Truth: A Book of Object Lessons with Magical and Mechanical Effects* (Philadelphia and Chicago, 1910), *Penny Object Lessons* (with Homer A. Rodeheaver and Frank B. Lane; Chicago and Philadelphia, 1916), and *The Bible Object Book: A Book of Object Lessons Which Are Different, Written in Plain English and in Common Words* (Philadelphia, 1926).   *H.E.*

Jesus Loves the Little Children–592

Work, Frederick Jerome (b. Nashville, TN, Aug. 11, 1879; d. Bordentown, NJ, Jan. 17, 1942) was a teacher, composer, arranger, and collector of folk songs. His early training was with his father, John Wesley Work, Sr., who was associated with the Fisk Jubilee Singers and was the choir director at Nelson Merry's Church (later First Colored Baptist Church, now First Baptist Church, Capitol Hill) in Nashville. He earned a B.A. degree in music from Fisk University in 1903 and did further study at both Columbia University and Temple University. He taught in the public schools of Kansas City, Missouri; at Prairie View State College; and, from 1922 until his death, at the Bordentown Manual Training School in Bordentown, New Jersey.

Though he composed for several media, his enduring contribution was as a collector and arranger. He collaborated with his brother, John Wesley Work, Jr., in gathering, arranging, and publishing the spirituals and other folk songs of African-Americans. It was as a result of this work that many of these pieces were assembled from fragments and established in forms which are considered standard.

Among his publications are *New Jubilee Songs* (Nashville, 1902), *Folk Songs of the American Negro* (with introduction by John W. Work, Jr.; Nashville, 1907), and *Some*

American Negro Folksongs (Boston, 1909). *P.A.R.*

WERE YOU THERE (adapt.)–156
I WANT TO BE A CHRISTIAN (adapt.)–Lord, I Want to Be a Christian (adapt.)–489

Work, John Wesley, Jr. (b. Nashville, TN, Aug. 6, 1872; d. Nashville, TN, Sep. 7, 1925) studied music at Fisk University, Nashville (A.B., 1895; M.A., 1898), and classics at Harvard University in 1896-97. He taught Latin, Greek and history at Fisk from 1898 to 1923, then became president of Roger Williams University, Nashville, two years before his death. He gave himself to the preservation, development, and performance of African-American spirituals, assuming an important role which resulted in widespread renewed pride in these traditional melodies. In 1899 he led a reestablished company of Fisk Jubilee Singers in their first tour in more than 20 years. Through the efforts of Work and his brother Frederick J. Work, in folk song collecting and arranging, there were published such collections as *New Jubilee Songs as Sung by the Fisk Jubilee Singers* (Nashville, 1901) and *Folk Songs of the American Negro* (Nashville, 1969). In 1909 Work organized the Fisk University Jubilee Quartette which he directed and in which he sang first tenor. This quartet toured the country and was one of the earliest Black groups to be recorded commercially, becoming known through Victor and Columbia recordings. *H.E.*

Go, Tell It on the Mountain–95
WERE YOU THERE (adapt.)–156
Lord, I Want to Be a Christian (adapt.)–489

Work, John Wesley, III (b. Tullahoma, TN, Jun. 15, 1901; d. Nashville, TN, May 18, 1967) was the eldest son of John Wes-ley Work, Jr. and Agnes Haynes Work. After elementary and high school education in Nashville, where his father served as director of the Fisk Jubilee Singers and later as president of Roger Williams University, he earned the M.M.Ed. degree at Columbia University (1930) and went on to study at Yale University (B.M., 1933).

Returning to Nashville, he directed the Fisk University Men's Glee Club (which attained national fame) and the world-famous Fisk Jubilee Singers (1948-57). He was a composer and arranger of music throughout his career. His compositions include a choral cycle, *Isaac Watts Contemplates the Cross*, many orchestral works, and arrangements of African-American spirituals. A recognized authority on African-American music, Work was the author of *American Negro Songs and Spirituals* (1940) and the writer of numerous periodical and reference work articles on African-American music. *H.T.M.*

GO TELL IT (harm.)–95

Wren, Brian Arthur (b. Romford, Essex, England, Jun. 3, 1936) was educated at the Royal Liberty School, Romford. He enlisted in national service before entering New College, Oxford, in 1957. Upon receiving his Bachelor of Arts degree in 1960, he entered Mansfield College from which he was graduated in 1965 and was ordained a minister in the Congregational (now United Reform) Church. He served the Congregational Church at Hockley, Essex, from 1965 to 1970.

In 1970, Wren became secretary to Churches' Action for World Development, an ecumenical organization sponsored by the British Council of Churches, the Conference of British Missionary Societies and other entities. He also worked for Third World First and was Chairperson of the

Council of War on Want.

With the encouragement of Erik Routley, whom he first knew at Mansfield College, Wren began writing hymns in 1962. The author of well over 100 hymns and the composer of tunes for several of them, he is among the most prolific of hymnists in the mainline tradition. Many of his earliest texts were set to music by his friend Peter Cutts. In more recent times, as his hymns have achieved wide acceptance, other composers have written tunes for them. Wren's hymns may be found in three collections: *Faith Looking Forward* (1983), *Praising a Mystery* (1986), and *Bring Many Names* (1989), all published by Hope Publishing Company.

Besides his work on hymns, Wren has been an education consultant and writer on worship and social issues. His published works include *Contemporary Prayers for Public Worship* (1967), *Education for Justice* (1977), *Patriotism and Peace* (1983), and *What Language Shall I Borrow?* (1989). Since 1985 he has worked as a freelance writer and lecturer on worship and hymn writing and has taught courses and held workshops in universities, seminaries, and churches throughout the United States and Canada, as well as in his native country. *H.T.M.*

Christ Is Alive–173
This Is a Day of New Beginnings–370
I Come with Joy to Meet My Lord–371
There's a Spirit in the Air–393
When Christ Was Lifted from the Earth–562

Wyeth, John (b. Cambridge, MA, Mar. 31, 1770; d. Philadelphia, PA, Jan. 23, 1858) was a Unitarian editor and publisher. He spent most of his life in Harrisburg, Pennsylvania, where he published a weekly newspaper and several books. Among these books were hymnals, the best known of which are *Repository of Sacred Music* (Harris-

burg, 1810) and *Repository of Sacred Music, Part Second* (Harrisburg, 1813; 2d ed., 1820). Both of these collections were in shape notes, and the latter had a major influence on the tune repertory of subsequent books in the South, such as *The Southern Harmony*. Wyeth was neither a composer nor a musician. His interest seems to have been commercial. Irving Lowens, in his introduction to the reprint edition of *Repository, Part Second* (Rpt. New York, 1964), concludes that Elkanah Kelsay Dare (1782-1826), a Methodist minister and musician, was the principal editor of this collection. Its contents were designed to appeal to the Methodists and Baptists whose camp meetings and revivals were providing a ready market for publications of folk hymnody. *Repository, Part Second* included many anonymous tunes in a folk idiom which have endured.   *P.A.R.*

See **Repository of Sacred Music, Part Second**–15, 507

Yamaguchi, Tokuo (b. Fukue Island, Japan, 1900) is a minister of the United Church of Christ in Japan. He received his theological education at Aoyama Gakuin University, completing his work in 1924. Upon graduation he began service as a Methodist pastor. In 1937 he became pastor of the United Church of Christ in Toyohashi, where he served for many years. Efforts to find more recent information about him have been unsuccessful.   *P.A.R.*

Here, O Lord, Your Servants Gather–179

Yates, John H. (b. Batavia, NY, Nov. 21, 1837; d. Batavia, NY, Sep. 5, 1900) had parents who emigrated from England and settled in Batavia, New York. As a young man, he had a successful career in the retail business. In 1866 he became editor of a local newspaper and served there for 10 years. He was licensed to preach in the Methodist church in 1858. Later in life, he was ordained in the Baptist ministry, and served seven years as pastor of the West Bethany Free Will Baptist Church. *Poems and Ballads*, a collection of his works, was published in 1897.   *W.J.R.*

Faith Is the Victory–413

Yeary, Paul is the pseudonym of a contemporary Southern Baptist composer who wishes to remain unidentified.   *P.A.R.*

PARKS–265
Holy Lord (st. 2)–622
JEWELL–641

York, Terry Wayne (b. Atchison, KS, Mar. 29, 1949), following his graduation from high school, spent two years in the United States Marine Corps (1967-68). He received his B.A. (1973) from California Baptist College, Riverside, California, and his M.C.M. (1975) and D.M.A. (1985) degrees from New Orleans Baptist Theological Seminary, New Orleans, Louisiana. From 1976 to 1977 he served as minister of music and youth at Southside Baptist Church, Tempe, Arizona, and from 1977-80 held a similar position at First Southern (now Capitol City) Baptist Church, Sacramento, California. He joined the Church Music Department of the Baptist Sunday School Board in 1984, where he has served successively as a Youth/Adult Music Consultant, Literary Design Editor in the Youth/Adult/General Development Section, and Hymnal Project Coordinator for *The Baptist Hymnal* (1991). He now serves as manager of the Field Services Section in the same department. A member of ASCAP,

York's publications include a monograph, *Great Hymns of Missions* (1979), articles in scholarly and denominational periodicals, hymn texts, and anthem lyrics. In addition to interests in hymnology, church music philosophy and administration, and reading and writing poetry, Terry enjoys American history. He and his wife, Janna, have two children, Matthew and Melody.   *D.M.*

Worthy of Worship–3
Living Stones–353
Sing, Congregation, Sing–397
God, Our Father, You Have Led Us–454
Thanksgiving/Thanks-living–642

Young, Carlton Raymond (b. Hamilton, OH, Apr. 25, 1926) was educated at the College of Music, the University of Cincinnati (B.S., 1950) and Boston University School of Theology (S.T.B., 1953). He was ordained an elder in The Methodist Church (1953) and is a member of the East Ohio Annual Conference. He served as minister of music in Church of the Savior, Cleveland Heights, Ohio (1953-56), and Trinity United Methodist Church, Youngstown, Ohio (1956-59). As director of music for Abingdon Press, Nashville, Tennessee (1959-64), he began their program of music publishing and distribution. He taught church music at Perkins School of Theology and the School of the Arts, Southern Methodist University, Dallas, Texas (1965-75); at Scarritt College, Nashville, Tennessee (1975-78); and at Candler School of Theology, Emory University, Atlanta, Georgia.

He has directed the music for each General Conference of The United Methodist Church since 1966. A teacher, editor, composer, and conductor, he has had the unique distinction of having served as editor of two revisions of hymnals for

Methodists: *The Methodist Hymnal* (1964), the first to be authorized by a united Methodism since 1821, and *The United Methodist Hymnal* (1989). For the *Companion to the Hymnal: a handbook to the 1964 Methodist Hymnal* (1970), he prepared the biographies of authors, composers, and sources, and he is the author of the companion volume for the 1989 hymnal. A past president of the Hymn Society of America, he is now director of programs in music and other arts, Scarritt-Bennett Center, Nashville. He is professor of church music emeritus, Candler School of Theory, Emory University, Atlanta, Georgia. The author of numerous articles in the field of church music and hymnody, he has lectured in England and Europe. *W.J.R.*

BEGINNINGS–370

Young, Gordon (b. McPherson, KS, Oct. 15, 1919) is an organist-composer who is retired and living in Detroit, Michigan. He received his education at Southwestern College (B.M. 1940; Mus. D., 1960) and Curtis Institute of Music (1944-46). He served as organist at First Methodist Church, Tulsa, Oklahoma (1940-44), First Presbyterian Church, Lancaster, Pennsylvania (1944-48), and First Presbyterian Church, Detroit, Michigan (1952-72). He also taught at Texas Christian University (1950-52). He has received several ASCAP awards for his catalog of over 500 organ, choral, and solo voice and instrumental works. *P.H.*

PRAISE YE–Praise Ye the Name of the Lord–665

Young, John Freeman (b. Pittston, Kennebec County, ME, Oct. 30, 1820; d. New York, NY, Nov. 15, 1885) was educated at Wesleyan University, Middletown, Con-

necticut. He joined the Episcopal Church and took his theological training at the Virginia Theological Seminary at Alexandria. Ordained in 1845, he was assigned to the Diocese of Florida, serving at Jacksonville and Tallahassee. He then served in Texas, Mississippi, and Louisiana during the years 1848-55. For 12 years he served in New York City, and was then elected second bishop of Florida in 1867. For 18 years he served diligently the cause of Christ in Florida. Because of his interest and understanding of architecture, many church buildings of excellent appearance were built. His interest in educational opportunities led him to establish a boys' school in Jacksonville and girls' school at Fernandina. Following the Civil War he was instrumental in reopening the University of the South, Sewanee, Tennessee. He published *Hymns and Music for the Young* (1860-61) and his *Great Hymns of the Church* was published posthumously by John Henry Hopkins, Jr., in 1887. *W.J.R.*

Silent Night, Holy Night (tr., st.1,3)–91

Young, Philip M. (b. Greenville, SC, Jul. 3, 1937) has been minister of music at First Baptist Church, Henderson, North Carolina, since 1959. He received his baccalaureate education at North Greenville College (A.A.) and Furman University (B.A., 1958) and did graduate study at Florida State University. Campbell University honored him with the Doctor of Letters degree in 1987. He is actively involved in the pipe organ industry as a builder representative and designer. His hobby is building and restoring harpsichords and other keyboard instruments. Among his compositions are over 70 anthems and cantatas, numerous handbell compositions, and hymns and/or tunes. His anthem, "Fanfare with Alleluias"

(1967), was the first anthem commissioned by the Southern Baptist Church Music Conference. *P.H.*

We Stand United in the Truth–625

Zelley, Henry J. (b. Mount Holly, NJ, Mar. 15, 1859; d. Trenton, NJ, Mar. 16, 1942) was educated at Mount Holly public schools, Pennington Seminary, and Taylor University (A.M., Ph.D., and D.D.). He was ordained to the Methodist ministry and admitted to the New Jersey Conference in 1882. He served 19 charges in the conference before his retirement in 1929. He was active in Conference work, having served as statistical secretary, treasurer, and trustee. He was a member of the Home Mission and Church Extension Board and a trustee of Pennington Seminary. A successful gospel preacher and pastor, his ministry was marked with evangelistic fervor. He is the author of more than 1,500 poems, hymns, and gospel songs. *W.J.R.*

Heavenly Sunlight–424

Zinzendorf, Nicolaus Ludwig von (b. Dresden, Saxony, Germany, May 26, 1700; d. Herrnhut, Saxony, Germany, May 9, 1760) was educated at the Pädagogium at Halle and at the University of Wittenberg. Born to a noble and independently wealthy family, in 1722 he purchased Herrnhut, an estate which he made into a refuge for persecuted Moravian Brethren. The Moravian Brethren, largely under his leadership, developed extensive missionary endeavors. In 1734, he received from the Theological Faculty of the University of Tübingen a license to preach and was consecrated Bishop of the Moravian Brethren's Unity at Berlin on May 10, 1737. Zinzendorf traveled widely and on his visits to the American colonies, he was influential in establishing settlements in Pennsylvania at Bethlehem, Nazareth, Lancaster, Hebron, and York. The keynote of Zinzendorf's more than 2000 hymns was his deep personal devotion to and fellowship with Christ. *S.W.G.*

Christian Hearts, in Love United–378

Zundel, John (b. Hochdorf, Germany, Dec. 10, 1815; d. Cannstadt, Germany, Jul., 1882) began his musical career in Russia at St. Petersburg, where he was organist at St. Anne's Lutheran Church and bandmaster of the Imperial House Guards. In 1847 he arrived in America, and after brief service at the First Unitarian Church, Brooklyn, and St. George's Episcopal Church, New York, he became organist at Henry Ward Beecher's Plymouth Congregational Church, Brooklyn, on January 1, 1850. His organ playing became almost as popular as Beecher's preaching, and "We will go hear Beecher and Zundel" became a common expression as the services became celebrated for great preaching, skillful organ playing, and thrilling congregational singing. He published *The Choral Friend* (1852), *Psalmody* (1855), and *Christian Heart Songs* (1870). He assisted Beecher in the editing of *Temple Melodies* (1851), and the *Plymouth Collection* (1855). To this latter collection he contributed 28 tunes. In 1863 he founded the *Monthly Choir and Organ Journal*, but ceased publication after a year. In 1873 he became editor of *Zundel and Brandt's Quarterly*, which contained 12 pages of music in each issue.

Later he served for a few months as organist at Detroit's Central Methodist Episcopal Church. In 1880 he retired to Germany where he died two years later. *W.J.R.*

Beecher–208, 248, 470

SCRIPTURE INDEXES

Scriptural Bases for Hymns Index

Genesis

1	42	
1:1	549	st. 1.
1:1	549	
1:1	43	
1:1	49	
1:1-10	50	st. 1.
1:1-25	50	
1:2	69	st. 3.
1:3-5	48	st. 1.
1:3-5	623	st. 4.
1:6-18	42	st. 1.
1:9-10	49	st. 1.
1:11,16	48	st. 2.
1:11-12	50	st. 2.
1:14-18	44	st. 1.
1:14-18	44	
1:14-19	48	st. 3.
1:20-25	42	st. 2.
1:21	549	st. 2.
1:26-27	590	
1:29	643	
5:22,24	448	ref.
5:22,24	448	
5:24	444	st. 3.
5:24	445	
8:22	54	st. 2.
8:22	641	st. 2.
12:2	565	
12:2	565	st. 1.
17:1-8	34	
28:10-22	458	
28:10-22	474	
28:12	432	st. 2.
28:12	458	st. 2.
28:12	474	st. 1.
28:12-13	474	st. 2.
28:12-13a	80	st. 2.
28:12-17	224	st. 1.
28:13-17	458	st. 1.
28:15	432	st. 1.
28:18	458	st. 3.
32:10	323	st. 4.
32:24-26	242	st. 4.
32:30	519	ref.
42:36	522	st. 2.

Exodus

3:5	224	
3:7-8a	627	st. 3.
13:21	56	st. 3.
15:1-2, 11	435	
15:1-2,11	435	st. 1.
15:2	434	ref.
15:2	627	st. 1.
15:8	204	st. 4.
15:11	254	st. 1.
15:11,13	12	ref.
19:3-6	624	st. 1.
19:4	72	ref.
19:4	83	st. 4.
19:18-21	11	st. 3.
19:18-22	11	st. 2.
23:19	639	
23:19a	639	st. 1.
25:22	67	st. 1.
30:6	67	
33:22	340	ref.
33:22	340	st. 1.
33:22	340	
34:6-7	306	

Leviticus

26:4	467	st. 4.
26:12	465	
26:12	465	st. 2.

Numbers

6:24-26	662	st. 1.
6:24-26	662	
10:29	521	ref.
10:29b	301	st. 5.
14:21	622	
17:4	607	st. 2.

Deuteronomy

3:27	447	st. 3.
3:6	65	st. 1.
4:31	25	st. 1.
4:31	62	st. 3.
4:31	189	st. 3.
4:31	338	st. 2.
6:1-9	508	st. 2.

6:5	256	st. 1.
6:5	505	st. 1.
6:5	607	st. 1.
6:7-8	508	st. 4.
6:7-9	507	st. 4.
7:13	643	st. 1.
10:14-15	44	st. 1.
10:17	11	st. 1.
11:19	504	st. 1.
26:1-4	641	st. 3.
28:1-2,15	470	st. 1.
28:12	59	st. 3.
28:9-12	470	st. 2.
31:6	62	st. 1.
31:6	103	st. 2.
32:12	62	
33:26	10	
33:27	71	st. 3.
33:27	74	st. 2.
33:27	333	
33:27	333	ref.
33:27a	333	st. 1.

Joshua

1:5	185	st. 1.
1:6-7	476	ref.
1:6-7	476	st. 3.
1:7-9	629	st. 2.
1:9	64	st. 2.
3:17	56	st. 4.
4:20-22	353	st. 5.
22:19	633	st. 2.
24:15	470	

1 Samuel

3:8-10	116	st. 4.
7:12	15	st. 2.
7:12	18	st. 2.
12:22	181	st. 4.
16:23	517	st. 3.
30:3-6	522	st. 3.

2 Samuel

12:23	322	st. 4.
12:23	528	st. 3.
22:4	223	st. 4.

22:50 ....544 .....st. 3.

1 Kings
8:30 658
8:35-36 ....467 .....st. 3.
8:57 ....65 ....st. 2.
8:57 ....103 ...st. 3.
8:57 ....344 .....st. 4.
18:27-29 ....98 ....st. 4.
18:41 ....467 .....st. 2.
19:3-8 ....269 .....st. 1.
19:11-12 ....270 .....st. 3.

2 Kings
4:25-26 ....410 .....st. 1.
6:16 ....437 .....st. 1.

1 Chronicles
16:8-10 ....70 ....st. 4.
16:8-12 ....33 ....st. 1.
16:10 ....538 .....st. 1.
16:23 640
16:23-25 ....640 .....st. 1.
16:23-29 13
16:23-30 ....28 ....st. 1.
16:25 ....3 ....st. 1.
16:25a ....12 ....st. 1.
16:28-29 ....216 .....st. 1.
16:28-29 ....227 .....ref.
16:28-31 ....33 ....st. 3.
16:30-34 ....640 .....st. 2.
16:31 33
16:31-33 ....43 ....st. 1.
16:34 ....13 ....st. 2.
16:34 ....23 ....st. 1.
16:34 23
21:16 ....633 .....st. 1.
29:11 ....589 .....st. 4.
29:14 609
29:14-16 ....609 .....st. 1.

2 Chronicles
6:18 ....351 .....st. 2.
6:21,40 656
6:40 ....656 .....st. 1.
15:14-15 439
15:15 ....439 .....st. 1.
29:3-6 ....468 .....st. 2.

Nehemiah
1:6a ....658 .....st. 1.
9:5 30

Job
1:21 ....55 ....st. 4.
5:7 ....455 .....st. 1.
11:7 ....73 ....st. 1.
12:10 341
12:10 ....341 .....st. 1.
19:25 191
19:25 ....191 .....st. 1.
19:25 ....543 .....st. 1.
19:26-27 ....196 .....ref.
28:26 ....59 ....ref.
30:25 ....613 .....st. 4.
38:4-7 ....235 .....st. 1.
38:7 ....7 ....st. 4.
38:7 ....94 ....st. 1.

Psalms
3:5 ....453 .....st. 3.
4:1 ....182 .....st. 1.
4:3 ....509 .....st. 2.
5:11 434
5:3 ....221 .....st. 1.
5:3 221
5:8 ....287 .....st. 1.
5:8 287
5:8 ....621 .....st. 2.
6:2 ....309 .....st. 3.
6:6-9 ....451 .....st. 3.
8 70
8:1 29
8:1 ....70 ....st. 1.
8:1 ....174 .....st. 4.
8:1 ....204 .....ref.
8:1 ....232 .....st. 3.
8:1 ....29 ....st. 1.
8:1 ....213 .....st. 2.
8:1,9 ....37 ....st. 1.
8:1-4 ....629 .....st. 1.
8:2 ....31 ....st. 1.
8:3 ....70 ....st. 2.
8:3-5 ....50 ....st. 3.
8:3-8 ....50 ....st. 4.
8:4-6 ....70 ....st. 3.
8:5-6 ....44 ....st. 2.
8:9 37
8:9 ....373 .....st. 5.
8:9 ....449 .....st. 1.

9:14 ....524 .....st. 4.
12:5 ....540 .....st. 3.
16:8 ....529 .....st. 3.
16:8 ....648 .....st. 1.
16:11 ....211 .....st. 4.
16:11 440
16:11 ....529 .....st. 4.
17:5 ....483 .....ref.
17:6-7 ....450 .....ref.
17:8 ....64 ....st. 1.
17:15 ....535 .....st. 4.
18:2, 31 ....291 .....st. 1.
18:28 ....532 .....st. 1.
18:28 532
18:35 ....415 .....st. 3.
19:1 36
19:1-2 ....2 ....st. 4.
19:1-6 ....10 ....st. 1.
19:1-6 ....27 ....st. 1.
19:1-11 ....36 ....st. 1.
19:7-11 ....264 .....st. 2.
19:12-14 ....492 .....st. 3.
19:13-14 ....498 .....st. 5.
19:14 ....128 .....st. 2.
20:4-5 ....39 ....st. 4.
20:5 ....4 ....ref.
20:7-8 ....635 .....st. 1.
20:7-8 635
22:1,11 ....406 .....st. 2.
22:4 629
22:28 ....589 .....st. 2.
23 68
23:1-3 ....68 ....st. 1.
23:1-3 ....348 .....st. 2.
23:2 ....52 ....ref.
23:2 52
23:2-3 ....52 ....st. 1.
23:2-3 ....422 .....st. 2.
23:2-3 ....459 .....st. 2.
23:2-4 ....348 .....st. 3.
23:3 ....56 ....st. 1.
23:3 ....56 ....st. 2.
23:3 459
23:3 ....459 .....st. 1.
23:3a ....552 .....st. 4.
23:4 ....52 ....st. 2.
23:4 ....52 ....st. 4.
23:4 ....406 .....st. 3.
23:4 ....416 .....st. 4.
23:4 ....422 .....st. 3.
23:4 ....537 .....st. 4.

12:1	497	st. 3.
12:13-14	30	st. 2.

Song of Solomon
2:1	189	
2:1	189	st. 1.
2:1	550	st. 3.

Isaiah
1:12-17	396	st. 1.
1:18	134	st. 3.
1:18	313	st. 2.
1:18	313	
1:18a	313	st. 1.
2:2-4	93	st. 4.
2:4	631	st. 3.
5:14-16	398	st. 4.
6:1,5	633	
6:1-8	2	
6:2-3	80	st. 3.
6:3	2	st. 1.
6:3	343	
6:3	666	st. 1.
6:3	666	
6:5-7	2	st. 3.
6:8	275	st. 3.
6:8	287	st. 3.
6:8	486	ref.
6:8	486	
6:8	583	
6:8	591	st. 1.
6:8	591	
6:8	597	st. 1.
6:8	597	
6:8-13	486	st. 1.
7:14	76	ref.
7:14	76	st. 1.
7:14	78	st. 2.
7:14	82	st. 1.
7:14	112	st. 1.
7:14	127	st. 1.
8:10	621	st. 3.
8:20	322	st. 2.
9:2	78	st. 3.
9:2-3	468	st. 4.
9:3	641	st. 1.
9:6	3	st. 3.
9:6	104	st. 2.
9:6	203	st. 1.
9:6	203	
9:6-7	90	st. 3.

9:6-7	111	st. 1.
9:7	197	st. 3.
9:7	203	st. 2.
9:7	600	st. 4.
11:1	78	
11:1-5	78	st. 1.
11:9	221	st. 4.
12:2	71	st. 1.
12:2-3	411	
12:3	110	
12:5	425	ref.
12:6	314	st. 1.
16:10-12	525	st. 2.
24:15	236	st. 4.
25:4a	425	st. 3.
25:8	416	st. 3.
25:8a	192	st. 3.
25:8-9	161	st. 2.
25:9	317	ref.
25:9	317	st. 1.
25:9	317	
25:9	439	ref.
26:3	295	st. 3.
26:3	295	
26:3	302	st. 3
26:3-4	58	st. 2.
26:19	441	st. 3.
28:16	338	
28:16	338	st. 1.
29:13	299	st. 2.
30:18	316	st. 3.
30:18	334	st. 3.
30:18	546	st. 3.
30:21	333	st. 2.
30:27-29	633	st. 3.
33:5-6	524	st. 3.
35:1,10	87	st. 3.
35:10	322	st. 3.
35:10	524	
35:10	524	ref.
38:1-3	451	st. 4.
38:2-3,17	451	st. 2.
38:17	416	st. 2.
38:19	504	st. 2.
40:3-4	519	st. 3.
40:9	584	
40:10	414	st. 4.
40:11	61	st. 1.
40:11	61	
40:11	203	st. 3.
40:11	456	st. 1.

40:11	465	st. 1.
40:28-31	73	st. 2.
40:28-31	456	st. 2.
40:31	451	st. 1.
40:31	498	st. 1.
40:31	498	
41:13	456	
42:5,10a	38	st. 2.
42:16	424	st. 1.
43:2	338	st. 3.
43:2	464	st. 2.
43:18-19	370	st. 1.
44:8	392	st. 2.
44:22	239	st. 1.
44:23	457	st. 3.
44:24-28	43	st. 3.
45:5-8	213	st. 3.
45:12,18	631	st. 1.
45:22	320	
45:22	416	
45:22-23	179	st. 2.
47:4	209	
48:17	432	ref.
48:17	621	
48:18	58	st. 1.
49:5-6	30	st. 4.
51:11	477	st. 1.
51:11	541	st. 1.
53:3	175	
53:3-5	175	st. 1.
53:3-6	606	st. 3.
53:4-5	303	st. 1.
53:4-5	307	st. 1.
53:4-5	429	st. 2.
53:4-6	576	ref.
53:5	172	st. 5.
53:5	268	st. 2.
53:5-6	127	st. 3.
53:11-12	587	st. 4.
55:1	303	st. 2.
55:1	307	st. 2.
55:1	436	st. 2.
55:1	551	st. 2.
55:1	615	st. 2.
55:1,6	323	st. 2.
55:1-2	324	st. 2.
55:7	135	st. 2.
55:7	307	st. 5.
55:7	312	st. 4.
55:7	439	st. 2.
55:12	7	st. 2.

15:38	628	st. 2.
16:1-4	168	st. 2.
16:1-6	173	st. 3.
16:1-7	490	st. 3.
16:4-7	166	st. 1.
16:5-7	168	st. 3.
16:6	166	
16:15	98	st. 5.
16:15	236	st. 5.
16:15	595	ref.

Luke

1:17	587	st. 2.
1:29-33	105	st. 2.
1:31-32a	108	st. 1.
1:35	112	st. 2.
1:46-48	81	st. 1.
1:46-55	81	
1:49-50	81	st. 2.
1:51-53	81	st. 3.
1:54-55	81	st. 4.
1:68-69	79	st. 1.
1:68-79	79	
1:70-75	79	st. 2.
1:76-77	79	st. 3.
1:78-79	76	st. 2.
2:4-9	102	st. 1.
2:6-7	91	st. 1.
2:6-7	91	
2:6-7	97	st. 1.
2:6-7	101	
2:6-7	108	
2:6-7	112	
2:6-7	116	
2:6-7,16	101	st. 1.
2:7	96	st. 1.
2:7	102	st. 2.
2:7	103	
2:7	106	
2:7	107	st. 2.
2:7	112	st. 3.
2:7	152	st. 4.
2:7	152	
2:7, 16	103	st. 1.
2:7,12,16	118	st. 2.
2:7,16	95	st. 3.
2:7,34-35	152	st. 1.
2:7.16	106	st. 1.
2:8	94	st. 2.
2:8	95	st. 1.
2:8-9	97	st. 2.

2:8-10	110	st. 1.
2:8-11	85	st. 1.
2:8-11	120	
2:8-11	120	st. 1.
2:8-12,17	118	st. 1.
2:8-14	91	st. 2.
2:8-14	101	st. 2.
2:8-14	106	st. 2.
2:8-14	114	
2:8-14	114	st. 1.
2:8-15	111	st. 2.
2:9-11	95	st. 2.
2:9-12	90	st. 1.
2:9-14	121	st. 2.
2:10-11	85	
2:10-11	94	
2:10-11	108	st. 3.
2:10-12	97	
2:10-14	76	st. 4.
2:10-14	88	
2:10-14	88	st. 1.
2:11	104	
2:11	104	st. 1.
2:11	110	st. 2.
2:12-15	110	st. 3.
2:13-14	86	st. 2.
2:13-14	88	ref.
2:13-14	89	st. 2.
2:13-14	90	
2:13-14	93	
2:13-14	93	st. 1.
2:13-14	100	
2:13-14	100	st. 1.
2:13-14	102	ref.
2:13-14	235	st. 2.
2:13-15	97	ref.
2:13-20	118	ref.
2:14	100	ref.
2:15	89	st. 1.
2:15	107	st. 1.
2:15-16	124	st. 1.
2:15-17,23	152	st. 2.
2:16	107	st. 3.
2:16,34-35	90	st. 2.
2:16-19	100	st. 4.
2:16-19	111	st. 3.
2:16-20	110	st. 4.
2:17-18	95	
2:17-18	95	ref.
2:17-18	118	
2:20	85	st. 4.

2:20	100	st. 2.
2:25-28	94	st. 4.
2:28-32	407	st. 2.
2:29-32	77	st. 1.
2:30-35	116	st. 3.
2:39-40	120	st. 2.
4:18	216	st. 3.
4:18	310	st. 1.
4:18	536	st. 2.
4:18	537	st. 3.
4:18-19	391	st. 2.
4:18-19	392	st. 4.
4:18; 19:10	389	st. 2.
4:22	219	
5:11	471	st. 1.
5:11	483	
5:24	132	st. 2.
5:24-25	412	st. 4.
6:21-23a	445	st. 2.
6:38	605	st. 1.
7:47-50	540	ref.
9:1-2,6	466	st. 4.
9:2	589	st. 1.
9:22	463	st. 1.
9:23	137	st. 2.
9:23	151	ref.
9:23	471	
9:23	475	st. 1.
9:23	475	
9:23	490	st. 4.
9:23	494	st. 4.
9:23	497	st. 2.
9:23,62	305	st. 3.
9:24-25	454	st. 2.
9:41-43	602	st. 2.
9:57-58	279	st. 1.
9:58	121	st. 3.
10:1-3	445	st. 4.
10:2	641	
10:18	358	st. 2.
10:20	452	st. 4.
10:27	311	st. 1.
10:30-37	501	st. 3.
10:33-37	501	st. 4.
11:1-4	602	st. 1.
11:9-10	451	
11:13	254	st. 4.
11:28	262	st. 1.
12:28	385	st. 4.
12:32	127	st. 4.
12:35-38	400	st. 2.

13:2-4 646	5:5,8 ....663 .....st. 3.	8:3 ....353 .....st. 3.
13:32-33 77	5:6 ....145 .....st. 2.	8:9,14-16 ....256 .....st. 3.
16:9 595	5:6-8 ....175 .....st. 3.	8:9-11 ....115 .....st. 4.
16:9 ....595 .....st. 2.	5:6-8 ....219 .....st. 3.	8:11,14 ....446 .....st. 4.
16:9-10 ....595 .....st. 1.	5:6-8 ....548 .....st. 2.	8:14 ....454 .....st. 3.
16:23-25 ....181 .....st. 3.	5:6-11 ....140 .....st. 3.	8:14,17 ....450 .....st. 5.
16:23-25 ....552 .....st. 2.	5:6-11 ....141 .....st. 2.	8:14-17 ....258 .....st. 3.
16:25 ....579 .....st. 2.	5:6-11 ....286 .....st. 1.	8:15-17 ....7 ....st. 3.
17:11 ....599 .....st. 1.	5:8 ....135 .....st. 4.	8:15-17 ....96 ....st. 2.
17:11,32 ....600 .....ref.	5:8 139	8:16-17 ....332 .....st. 3.
17:24 45	5:8 ....139 .....st. 1.	8:17 555
17:28a ....584 .....st. 3.	5:8 143	8:17 ....555 .....ref.
20:20-21 562	5:8 ....143 .....st. 1.	8:23 ....310 .....st. 4.
20:20-21 ....562 .....st. 1.	5:8 ....319 .....st. 4.	8:24-25 ....279 .....st. 4.
20:20-24 ....483 .....st. 3.	5:8 ....535 .....st. 1.	8:27,34 ....165 .....st. 5.
20:21-22 ....402 .....st. 2.	5:8 ....545 .....st. 1.	8:32 ....429 .....st. 4.
20:22-24 ....569 .....st. 4.	5:8 ....546 .....ref.	8:32 ....442 .....st. 2.
20:24 ....330 .....st. 3.	5:8 ....584 .....st. 2.	8:32,37-39 ....142 .....st. 3.
20:28 ....378 .....st. 2.	5:8-11 ....606 .....st. 4.	8:34 ....24 ....st. 2.
20:36-38 ....387 .....st. 4.	5:10-11 ....554 .....st. 4.	8:35 ....336 .....st. 4.
22:10 ....296 .....st. 3.	5:11 ....162 .....ref.	8:35-39 ....286 .....st. 3.
22:28 ....630 .....st. 2.	5:14-17 ....167 .....st. 3.	8:37-39 334
26:26-29 ....571 .....st. 1.	5:15 ....218 .....st. 2.	8:38 ....55 ....st. 3.
	5:15 ....329 .....st. 3.	8:38-39 ....409 .....st. 2.
Romans	5:20 ....329 .....ref.	8:39 605
1:11-13 ....565 .....ref.	5:20-21 ....180 .....st. 4.	8:39 ....605 .....st. 3.
1:14-16 ....561 .....st. 1.	5:20-21 329	9:2-3 ....574 .....st. 2.
1:14-16 561	6:3-4 ....51 ....st. 4.	10:1 ....565 .....st. 2.
1:16 553	6:3-4 ....362 .....st. 2.	10:8-10 582
1:16-17 ....553 .....st. 1.	6:3-4 ....363 .....st. 4.	10:8-10 585
3:22 ....147 .....st. 5.	6:3-5,22 ....415 .....st. 1.	10:8-9 489
3:22-24 ....254 .....st. 3.	6:4 362	10:8-9 ....489 .....st. 1.
3:22-25 ....411 .....st. 2.	6:5 ....364 .....st. 4.	10:9-13 436
3:23 ....267 .....st. 2.	6:5-8 ....362 .....st. 3.	10:11-13 ....436 .....st. 1.
3:23-25 ....132 .....st. 1.	6:9 ....320 .....st. 2.	10:13 421
3:23-25 ....147 .....st. 4.	6:9,8:2 ....143 .....st. 4.	10:13 ....421 .....ref.
3:23-25a ....319 .....st. 2.	6:12-24 ....363 .....st. 3.	10:13-14 ....596 .....st. 2.
3:23-26 286	6:14 ....332 .....st. 1.	10:14-15 ....646 .....st. 3.
3:23-26 ....345 .....st. 2.	6:14 ....564 .....st. 3.	10:15 ....277 .....st. 2.
3:23-26 ....531 .....st. 2.	6:17-18 ....275 .....st. 1.	10:15 ....278 .....st. 2.
3:23-26 ....544 .....st. 2.	6:22-23 ....328 .....st. 1.	12:1 277
3:24 ....302 .....st. 4.	7:21-24 ....307 .....st. 3.	12:1 ....277 .....st. 1.
5:1 ....363 .....st. 2.	7:21-25 ....455 .....st. 4.	12:1 278
5:1-2 ....286 .....st. 4.	7:21-25 ....486 .....st. 3.	12:1 ....278 .....st. 1.
5:1-2 ....337 .....st. 2.	7:21-25a ....470 .....st. 4.	12:1 326
5:1-2,8-9 ....148 .....st. 3.	7:24-25a ....286 .....st. 2.	12:1 ....326 .....st. 1.
5:5 ....238 .....st. 3.	7:25a ....23 ....st. 4.	12:1 ....363 .....st. 1.
5:5 ....243 .....ref.	8:1-3 ....332 .....st. 2.	12:1 ....641 .....st. 4.
5:5 ....409 .....st. 1.	8:2 ....143 .....st. 4	12:1-2 ....445 .....st. 3.
5:5,8 ....209 .....st. 3.	8:2 ....148 .....st. 4.	12:1-2 604
5:5,8 ....480 .....st. 1.	8:2 ....298 .....st. 3.	12:1-2 ....604 .....st. 1.

4:6 .... 469 ..... st. 2.	12:9-10 .... 597 ..... st. 3.	6:8-10 .... 643 ..... st. 3.
4:6 .... 554 ..... st. 3.	13:11 581	6:9 .... 595 ..... st. 4.
4:6-8 .... 444 ..... st. 2.	13:14 250	6:9 .... 615 ..... ref.
4:7-11 .... 461 ..... st. 4.	13:14 .... 250 ..... ref.	6:10 .... 605 ..... st. 2.
4:8-10 .... 594 ..... st. 4.	13:14 .... 257 ..... st. 4.	6:14 .... 141 ..... ref.
4:8-11 .... 470 ..... st. 3.	13:14 .... 356 ..... st. 4.	6:14 144
4:15 .... 330 ..... st. 1.	13:14 .... 382 ..... st. 4.	6:14 .... 144 ..... st. 2.
4:15 .... 330 ..... st. 4.	13:14 661	6:14 .... 151 ..... st. 3.
4:16-18 .... 514 ..... st. 2.	13:14 .... 661 ..... st. 1.	6:14 280
4:16-18 .... 533 ..... st. 2.		6:14 .... 280 ..... ref.
5:1-6 .... 529 ..... st. 1.	**Galatians**	6:14 554
5:4 .... 292 ..... st. 1.	1:3-5 4	6:14 .... 554 ..... st. 1.
5:6-9 .... 410 ..... st. 4.	2:20 .... 140 ..... st. 4.	
5:11 .... 560 ..... st. 4.	2:20 .... 170 ..... st. 3.	**Ephesians**
5:14 292	2:20 180	1:3 .... 542 ..... st. 4.
5:14-15 .... 298 ..... st. 2.	2:20 .... 180 ..... st. 1.	1:3-8 .... 153 ..... ref.
5:14-15 .... 326 ..... ref.	2:20 .... 241 ..... st. 3.	1:4-6 226
5:14-17 .... 157 ..... st. 2.	2:20 .... 257 ..... st. 2.	1:4-8 .... 426 ..... ref.
5:15 .... 139 ..... st. 4.	2:20 268	1:4-9,11-12 ...... 542 ..... st. 2.
5:15 298	2:20 .... 282 ..... ref.	1:5 .... 221 ..... st. 2.
5:15 .... 626 ..... st. 3.	2:20 .... 353 ..... st. 4.	1:5-8 .... 329 ..... st. 1.
5:15-16 .... 336 ..... st. 2.	2:20 441	1:7 .... 226 ..... st. 6
5:15-17 .... 319 ..... st. 3.	2:20 .... 441 ..... ref.	1:7 575
5:17 .... 436 ..... ref.	2:20 .... 538 ..... st. 3.	1:7-8 330
5:18-19 .... 109 ..... st. 2.	2:20-21 .... 541 ..... ref.	1:13-14 .... 248 ..... st. 3.
5:18-20 .... 569 ..... st. 1.	3:1-3 .... 357 ..... st. 3.	1:13-14 .... 370 ..... st. 2.
5:21 .... 535 ..... st. 3.	3:8-9 570	1:18-23 .... 226 ..... st. 6.
6:2 311	3:13 149	1:19-21 .... 8 .... st. 4.
6:4-10 .... 415 ..... st. 2.	3:13 332	1:22-23 .... 480 ..... st. 4.
6:18 258	3:19 .... 496 ..... st. 3.	2:1-5 .... 441 ..... st. 1.
7:9-10 .... 306 ..... st. 5.	3:26 477	2:4 .... 25 .... st. 2.
8:2,5 .... 434 ..... st. 3.	3:26-28 .... 226 ..... st. 3.	2:4 .... 328 ..... st. 2.
8:5 .... 145 ..... st. 5.	3:26-28 .... 563 ..... st. 2.	2:4 .... 559 ..... st. 3.
8:5 610	3:28 385	2:4-5 .... 560 ..... st. 1.
8:9 328	4:4-5 .... 112 ..... ref.	2:4-5, 8-10 ...... 346 ..... ref.
8:9 .... 328 ..... st. 4.	4:4-7 .... 77 .... st. 2.	2:4-7 .... 25 .... st. 4.
8:9 .... 555 ..... st. 2.	4:6-7 .... 241 ..... st. 2.	2:4-7 .... 147 ..... st. 1.
8:11-12 .... 117 ..... st. 2.	4:19 571	2:4-7 .... 377 ..... st. 3.
9:15 .... 44 .... st. 6.	5:1 .... 421 ..... st. 3.	2:4-8 .... 582 ..... st. 2.
9:15 .... 145 ..... st. 4.	5:1 626	2:4-10 .... 546 ..... st. 2.
10:3-5 .... 355 ..... st. 3.	5:1 .... 634 ..... st. 1.	2:6-7 .... 291 ..... st. 3.
10:5 .... 491 ..... st. 2.	5:13 649	2:7 147
12:2-4 .... 484 ..... st. 4.	5:16,25 .... 477 ..... st. 2.	2:8 540
12:7-10 .... 434 ..... st. 2.	5:22 442	2:8-9 .... 336 ..... st. 1.
12:7-8 .... 405 ..... st. 2.	5:22 .... 442 ..... st. 1.	2:10 .... 290 ..... st. 2.
12:9 .... 62 .... st. 2.	5:22-23 .... 508 ..... st. 3.	2:12-13,19 ...... 555 ..... st. 3.
12:9 .... 315 ..... st. 1.	5:22-23 .... 511 ..... st. 1.	2:13-14 .... 226 ..... ref.
12:9 .... 318 ..... st. 1.	5:22-23 .... 512 ..... st. 3.	2:13-18 .... 226 ..... st. 1.
12:9 .... 663 ..... st. 1.	5:22-25 .... 294 ..... st. 4.	2:14-18 382
12:9-10 .... 339 ..... st. 2.	5:22-25 .... 370 ..... st. 3.	2:20 356
12:9-10 .... 566 ..... st. 3.	6:2 .... 613 ..... st. 2.	2:20 .... 356 ..... st. 1.

2:16 ....293 .....st. 3.	1:7 ....199 .....st. 2.	5:12 ....104 .....st. 4.
3:1 55	1:8 ....34 ....st. 1.	5:12 157
3:2 196	1:8 ....34 ....st. 3.	5:12 200
3:2 ....209 .....st. 4.	1:8 ....40 ....st. 1.	5:12 ....280 .....st. 3.
3:2 ....519 .....st. 4.	1:8 ....251 ....st. 1.	5:12 647
3:2-3 ....444 .....st. 5.	1:8 ....252 ....st. 1.	5:12-13 ....124 .....ref.
3:8 ....195 .....st. 2.	1:8 252	5:12-13 229
3:16-18 ....604 .....st. 3.	1:13-16 174	5:12-13 ....515 .....st. 2.
3:17-18 ....109 .....st. 3.	1:14 ....15 ....st. 3.	5:13 201
3:17-18 ....393 .....st. 3.	1:14 ....18 ....st. 3.	5:13 202
3:23-24 ....247 .....st. 4.	1:14-15 ....219 .....st. 1.	5:13 ....231 .....st. 3.
4:4 437	2:10 ....514 .....st. 3.	5:13 ....251 .....st. 2.
4:7-11 ....461 .....st. 3.	3:17-18 ....307 .....st. 4.	5:13 ....252 .....st. 1.
4:9 545	3:20 321	5:13 252
4:9-10 ....210 .....st. 1.	3:20 ....321 ....ref.	6:9 ....527 .....st. 3.
4:9-10 ....211 .....st. 3.	3:20 ....452 .....st. 2.	7:4 ....200 .....st. 2.
4:9-10 548	4:6 ....537 ....ref.	7:4 ....201 .....st. 2.
4:9-11 ....282 .....st. 2.	4:8 9	7:4 ....202 .....st. 2.
4:9-12 ....568 .....st. 2.	4:8 254	7:9,14 ....137 .....ref.
4:10 546	4:8b ....9 ....st. 1.	7:9-10 ....134 .....st. 4.
4:16 208	4:10-11 ....2 ....st. 2.	7:9-10 ....143 .....st. 3.
4:16 ....208 .....st. 1.	4:10-11 ....161 .....st. 1.	7:9-10 ....213 .....st. 5.
4:16 619	4:10-11 ....475 .....st. 4.	7:11-12 ....428 .....ref.
4:16,18 ....509 .....st. 1.	4:11 3	7:12 ....251 .....st. 3.
4:16-19 ....264 .....st. 1.	4:11 ....3 ....ref.	7:14 ....132 .....ref.
4:18 ....123 .....st. 3.	4:11 ....9 ....st. 2.	7:14-15 ....517 .....st. 2.
4:18 ....442 .....st. 3.	4:11 ....9 ....st. 3.	7:14-17 ....475 .....st. 2.
4:19 211	5:6,9-12 ....233 .....ref.	7:14-17 ....528 .....st. 4.
4:19 ....217 .....ref.	5:6-10 ....136 .....st. 3.	7:15 ....518 .....st. 2.
5:4-5 413	5:8-13 ....229 .....st. 1.	7:15-17 ....405 .....ref.
5:4-5 ....413 .....ref.	5:9 ....343 .....st. 2.	7:16-17 ....521 .....st. 3.
	5:9 ....544 .....st. 4.	7:17 ....192 .....st. 2.
2 John	5:9,12 427	11:15 ....169 .....st. 1.
3 664	5:9,12 ....427 .....st. 1.	11:15 169
3 ....664 .....st. 1.	5:9-10 ....200 .....st. 3.	11:15 173
	5:9-10 ....201 .....st. 3.	11:15 ....173 .....st. 4.
3 John	5:9-10 ....202 .....st. 3.	11:15-17 40
2 410	5:9-10 ....229 .....st. 2.	11:17 ....638 .....st. 3.
2 ....410 .....ref.	5:9-13 ....166 .....st. 3.	12:10-11 ....522 .....ref.
	5:9-13 ....431 .....ref.	15:2-4 ....229 .....st. 3.
Jude	5:9-13 ....431 .....st. 3.	15:3-4 ....213 .....st. 1.
14 194	5:9-13 ....527 .....st. 2.	15:3-4 213
22-23 560	5:9-13 ....613 .....st. 6.	15:3-4 ....311 .....st. 4.
23 ....392 .....ref.	5:11-12 ....536 .....st. 3.	15:3-4 ....594 .....st. 5.
24-25 ....472 .....st. 4.	5:11-12 ....537 .....st. 5.	17:14 124
	5:11-14 ....200 .....st. 1.	19:1 170
Revelation	5:11-14 ....200 .....st. 4.	19:1 214
1:5a ....344 .....st. 2.	5:11-14 ....201 .....st. 1.	19:1 223
1:5b ....410 .....st. 2.	5:11-14 ....201 .....st. 4.	19:1 ....478 .....ref.
1:5-6 ....206 .....st. 4.	5:11-14 ....202 .....st. 1.	19:1,3-4,6 ....214 .....st. 1.
1:5-6 ....398 .....st. 3.	5:11-14 ....202 .....st. 4.	19:1,3-4,6 ....355 .....ref.

Promises Index

Topical Index of Responsive Readings

Bold numbers indicate primary readings

The Glory of God

God the Father 1, 671, 703
Majesty and Power **669, 670,**
677, 700
Love, Mercy, and Grace **671,**
672, 1, 694
Praise and Adoration **673, 674,**
671, 672
God's Work 41, 670
Creation **675,** 41, 670
Providence **676, 677**

The Love of God

God the Son 75, 327, 349, 690
Advent **678,** 718
Birth **679,** 75
The Coming of the Wise Men
680
Life and Ministry **119, 681,** 617,
697
Triumphal Entry **682**
Cross, Suffering, and Death
131, 683, 684, 266, 404, 693
Resurrection **158, 685,** 513
Savior and Lord **686, 687,** 274,
404
Friend **688**
Return **689,** 702, 710
Praise and Adoration **690,** 404
God the Holy Spirit 237, 691, 706
God the Trinity 246, 697
God's Word 259, 692, 711, 714

The People of God

Our Sin 266, 688
Salvation 274, 693, 75, 686
Confession and Repentance **694,**
266, 700
Grace and Assurance 327, 695,
1, 676, 711

The Church 349, 707, 714, 717
The Lord's Day **696,** 695
Baptism **697,** 556
The Lord's Supper **698**
Family of God **699,** 503, 695
Mission **700,** 556, 712

The Christian Life 404, 598, 687
Faith, Hope, and Love **701,** 695
Joy and Triumph **702,** 676, 690,
710
Prayer and Fellowship with God
703, 704, 670, 687
Discipleship **705, 706,** 119, 617,
681, 688
Dedication **707,** 530, 717
Commitment **708,** 716
Home and Family 503, 709, 675
Life Eternal 513, 710, 1, 686

The Witness of the People of God

Testimony 530, 711, 274
Evangelism and Missions 556,
712, 700
Nurture, Education,
Stewardship, and Service 598
Nurture **713**
Education **714,** 692
Stewardship **715,** 705
The Christian and the
Social Order 617, 716
Cooperation **717,** 699, 713
Peace and War **718**
Religious Liberty **719**
Priesthood of the Believer **720,**
690, 695
God and Country **721**

Scriptural Index of Responsive Readings

TEXT INDEXES

Concordance of Key Words and Phrases

battle...............476......st. 3	bless.................030......st. 1	blood.................319......st. 2
bear....................071......ref.	bless.................103......st. 3	blood.................325......st. 2
beautiful.............515......ref.	bless.................450......ref.	blood.................334......st. 1
Beautiful Savior ..176......st. 4	bless.................523......st. 4	blood.................339......st. 2
beauty................044......st. 1	bless.................656......st. 1	blood.................342......st. 1
beauty................209......st. 4	blessed................206......ref.	blood.................365......ref.
beauty................500......st. 1	blessing.............007......st. 3	blood.................375......st. 3
beauty................623......st. 1	blessing.............087......st. 3	blood.................406......st. 1
bed.....................160......st. 2	blessing.............129......st. 2	blood.................411......st. 2
before.................072......st. 2	blessing.............242......st. 4	blood.................412......st. 3
beginning............252......st. 1	blessing.............275......st. 3	blood.................421......st. 1
beginning............370......st. 1	blessing.............452......st. 3	blood.................426......ref.
behold................196......st. 1	blessing.............467......ref.	blood.................531......ref.
belief..................004......st. 2	blessing.............564......ref.	blood.................544......ref.
believe................168......st. 4	blessing.............569......ref.	blood.................575......ref.
believe................273......ref.	blessing.............636......st. 1	blood.................606......st. 1
believe................298......st. 2	blessings.............081......st. 1	blood of the Lamb136......ref.
believe................306......st. 4	blessings.............184......st. 2	blood of the Lamb329......st. 1
believe................307......st. 5	blessings.............243......st. 2	blossoms.............292......st. 4
believe................320......st. 3	blessings.............253......st. 1	blot.....................303......st. 2
believe................329......st. 3	blessings.............340......st. 3	blot.....................307......st. 2
believe................337......ref.	blessings.............351......st. 3	boast...................144......st. 2
believe................534......st. 1	blessings.............449......st. 1	bodies.................599......st. 2
believe................548......st. 1	blessings.............644......st. 1	body...................372......st. 2
believed...............330......st. 2	blind..................073......st. 4	bond...................384......st. 1
bells...................098......st. 1	blind..................330......st. 1	bond...................439......st. 4
bells...................351......st. 1	bliss...................096......st. 2	bondage..............310......st. 1
bells...................428......st. 1	bliss...................221......st. 4	Book...................260......st. 4
bells...................545......st. 2	bliss...................336......st. 4	Book...................263......st. 4
bells...................614......st. 2	blissful................439......st. 3	book...................571......st. 2
beside.................072......st. 2	blood..................025......st. 2	born...................085......ref.
Bethlehem............086......st. 1	blood..................040......st. 2	born...................088......st. 3
Bethlehem............102......st. 1	blood..................085......st. 4	born...................095......ref.
Bethlehem............107......st. 1	blood..................132......st. 4	born...................428......st. 3
Bethlehem............108......st. 2	blood..................133......st. 1	born...................566......st. 1
Bethlehem............110......st. 1	blood..................134......st. 3	born again............273......st. 1
Bethlehem............120......st. 1	blood..................135......st. 1	born again............322......ref.
Bethlehem............367......st. 1	blood..................140......st. 1	bound..................371......st. 4
bias....................631......st. 3	blood..................141......st. 3	bound..................521......ref.
Bible...................260......st. 1	blood..................142......st. 1	bounties..............609......st. 2
Bible...................301......st. 5	blood..................147......st. 1	bounty.................605......st. 1
Bible...................344......st. 1	blood..................151......st. 2	bow....................178......ref.
Bible...................504......st. 1	blood..................155......st. 1	bow....................198......st. 1
billows................444......st. 2	blood..................175......st. 2	bow....................316......st. 3
bind....................385......st. 2	blood..................206......st. 3	Boy-Child.............110......ref.
bird....................046......st. 1	blood..................216......st. 4	branches..............378......st. 3
birds...................336......st. 2	blood..................217......st. 2	brass...................423......st. 1
birth...................086......st. 2	blood..................218......st. 3	brave..................571......st. 4
birth...................549......st. 1	blood..................270......st. 4	brave..................633......st. 5
bleeding..............149......ref.	blood..................302......st. 1	Bread..................067......st. 3
bless...................021......st. 1	blood..................303......st. 1	bread..................365......st. 1
bless...................021......st. 6	blood..................307......st. 1	bread..................366......st. 1
bless...................022......st. 1	blood..................317......st. 2	bread..................369......st. 3

death....................148 ......st. 4	died ....519 ......st. 1	duty.......................261 ......st. 1
death....................160 ......st. 3	dim ....320 ......ref.	duty.......................559 ......st. 4
death....................163 ......ref.	dimness................245 ......st. 2	dwell ....441 ......st. 4
death....................165 ......st. 2	disappointment....370 ......st. 3	dwelling................523 ......st. 1
death....................171 ......ref.	disappointments ..522 ......st. 2	dying....................192 ......st. 2
death....................172 ......st. 2	disciples ....646 ......st. 3	dying....................451 ......st. 4
death....................172 ......st. 4	disconsolate..........067 ......st. 1	eagle......................071 ......ref.
death....................191 ......st. 2	discord ....425 ......st. 2	eagles ....083 ......st. 4
death....................198 ......st. 2	discouraged ....269 ......st. 1	ears.......................499 ......st. 2
death....................268 ......st. 2	discouraged ....432 ......st. 2	ears.......................502 ......st. 2
death....................342 ......st. 3	discouraged ....644 ......st. 1	earth......................042 ......st. 2
death....................352 ......st. 2	diseases ....181 ......st. 1	earth......................050 ......st. 1
death....................415 ......st. 1	diseases ....272 ......st. 2	earth......................221 ......st. 4
death....................416 ......st. 4	distress ....035 ......st. 3	earth......................235 ......st. 3
death....................494 ......st. 4	distress ....219 ......st. 3	earth......................385 ......st. 4
death....................538 ......st. 3	distress ....442 ......st. 3	earth......................417 ......st. 4
deathbeds ....312 ......st. 3	distress ....455 ......st. 1	ease ....293 ......st. 3
deathless ....163 ......st. 3	diverse.................399 ......st. 3	ease ....481 ......st. 2
debt......................139 ......st. 5	divide....................562 ......st. 3	east.......................085 ......st. 2
debt......................145 ......st. 4	divine...................241 ......st. 3	Easter ....353 ......st. 4
debt......................268 ......st. 1	division.................371 ......st. 3	ecstasies ....245 ......st. 2
debtor ....015 ......st. 3	domain ....550 ......ref.	Eden......................048 ......st. 3
debtor ....018 ......st. 3	door ....096 ......st. 2	elect......................350 ......st. 2
decided ....305 ......st. 1	door ....151 ......st. 3	Emmanuel.............076 ......st. 1
dedicate ....390 ......st. 2	door ....314 ......st. 2	Emmanuel.............082 ......st. 1
deed ....399 ......st. 2	door ....321 ......ref.	empower...............051 ......st. 3
deeds....................611 ......st. 3	door ....452 ......st. 2	endless ....074 ......st. 3
defeated ....207 ......st. 3	door ....557 ......st. 1	endure...................624 ......st. 2
defender...............183 ......st. 4	doors ....596 ......st. 4	enlighten ....580 ......st. 2
Defender..............476 ......st. 1	doubt ....307 ......st. 3	enrich....................580 ......st. 3
defense.................074 ......st. 2	doubt ....335 ......st. 2	enslaved...............300 ......st. 2
defense.................476 ......st. 2	doubt ....412 ......st. 2	enthrone...............118 ......st. 3
defense.................629 ......st. 3	doubt ....441 ......st. 2	enthrone...............169 ......st. 2
defiled..................328 ......st. 3	doubt ....532 ......st. 2	enthrone...............198 ......st. 3
delay ....324 ......ref.	doubt ....644 ......st. 2	equality................626 ......st. 2
deliver..................455 ......st. 3	doubtings..............311 ......ref.	eternal...................034 ......st. 1
Deliverer ....056 ......st. 2	doubts...................133 ......st. 2	eternal...................074 ......st. 6
deny.....................184 ......st. 3	doubts...................209 ......st. 2	eternal...................104 ......st. 3
deny.....................494 ......st. 1	doubts...................484 ......st. 2	eternal...................191 ......st. 1
desert ....523 ......st. 3	Dove ....240 ......st. 1	eternal...................197 ......st. 4
desire....................051 ......st. 1	Dove ....243 ......ref.	eternal...................512 ......st. 3
Desire of nations 076 ......st. 4	Dove ....364 ......st. 1	eternal...................545 ......ref.
despair ....098 ......st. 3	dream....................639 ......st. 2	eternal...................638 ......st. 3
despair ....146 ......st. 2	dreams ....240 ......st. 1	eternally................543 ......st. 4
despair ....533 ......st. 2	dreams ....454 ......st. 1	eternal life ....034 ......st. 3
despair ....631 ......st. 1	dreams ....500 ......st. 4	eternity ....143 ......st. 4
despise ....471 ......st. 2	dreams ....557 ......st. 1	eternity ....180 ......st. 4
destiny ....207 ......st. 2	drear....................456 ......st. 2	eternity ....241 ......st. 4
devotion ....003 ......st. 2	dreary...................434 ......st. 1	eternity ....345 ......ref.
dew ....497 ......st. 3	drink ....366 ......st. 2	eternity ....431 ......ref.
die ....147 ......ref.	drink ....436 ......st. 4	eternity ....444 ......st. 5
die ....150 ......st. 3	dross.....................496 ......st. 2	everlasting ....074 ......st. 3
died ....319 ......st. 2	duties ....470 ......st. 3	everlasting ....333 ......ref.

follow	461	st. 3	free	121	st. 4	friends	562	st. 2
follow	471	st. 1	free	147	st. 2	friendship	371	st. 3
follow	483	st. 1	free	166	st. 1	friendship	511	st. 3
follow	486	st. 2	free	216	st. 4	fright	631	st. 2
follow	497	st. 1	free	278	st. 1	fruit	050	st. 2
follow	548	st. 3	free	299	st. 1	fruit	442	st. 2
follow	594	st. 1	free	301	ref.	fruitful	641	st. 2
followers	382	st. 2	free	332	st. 2	fullness	600	st. 1
footprints	483	st. 1	free	363	st. 3	future	407	ref.
footprints	497	st. 1	free	395	st. 2	future	508	st. 2
footsteps	532	st. 1	free	414	st. 2	Galilee	120	st. 3
footsteps	544	st. 4	free	421	st. 3	Galilee	121	st. 3
footsteps	611	st. 3	free	475	st. 3	Galilee	127	st. 2
forest	010	st. 2	free	480	st. 1	gall	157	st. 3
forever	008	st. 4	free	541	st. 2	garden	048	st. 2
forever	529	st. 3	free	562	st. 4	garden	171	st. 3
forgave	273	st. 1	free	579	st. 1	garden	187	st. 1
forget	361	st. 2	free	580	st. 1	garden	288	st. 2
forgive	021	st. 2	free	615	st. 3	garden	382	st. 2
forgive	149	st. 2	free	624	st. 1	garden	547	st. 2
forgive	188	st. 2	free	626	st. 1	gate	464	st. 3
forgive	267	st. 1	free	635	st. 2	gates	514	st. 4
forgive	407	st. 1	free	638	st. 2	gates of light	151	st. 1
forgive	449	st. 2	free	649	st. 1	gender	226	st. 3
forgive	559	st. 2	freed	362	st. 2	gentle	477	st. 2
forgive	569	st. 2	freedom	310	st. 1	gentle	498	st. 1
forgive	618	st. 2	freedom	357	st. 5	Gethsemane	124	st. 4
forgiven	341	st. 1	freedom	391	st. 2	Gethsemane	150	st. 1
forgiven	362	st. 2	freedom	625	st. 2	Gethsemane	372	st. 3
forgiven	371	st. 1	freedom	626	st. 1	Gethsemane	490	ref.
forgiven	542	st. 2	freedom	628	st. 1	gift	086	st. 3
forgiven	585	st. 1	freedom	634	st. 1	gift	108	st. 4
forgiveness	185	st. 5	freely	273	ref.	gift	109	st. 3
forgiveness	397	st. 1	friend	116	st. 4	gift	112	st. 2
forgiving	027	st. 3	friend	149	st. 3	gift	181	st. 5
forgiving	270	st. 4	friend	181	st. 1	gift	183	st. 2
forsake	055	st. 4	friend	182	st. 1	gift	302	st. 4
forsake	189	st. 3	friend	183	st. 1	gift	490	st. 3
forsake	338	st. 4	friend	184	st. 1	gift	515	st. 3
fortress	008	st. 1	friend	185	st. 1	gift	520	st. 2
foundation	338	st. 1	friend	189	st. 1	gift	549	st. 1
foundation	353	st. 2	friend	231	st. 2	gift	609	st. 1
foundation	356	st. 1	friend	268	st. 5	Gift divine	044	st. 6
foundation	538	st. 2	friend	290	st. 3	gifts	111	st. 5
foundation	623	st. 2	friend	315	st. 2	gifts	113	st. 1
fount	155	st. 1	friend	318	ref.	gifts	115	st. 2
fountain	136	st. 4	Friend	411	st. 4	gifts	117	st. 3
fountain	140	st. 3	friend	438	st. 1	gifts	396	st. 3
fountain	142	st. 1	friend	451	ref.	gifts	580	st. 2
fountain	280	st. 1	friend	492	st. 2	gifts	605	st. 1
fountain	436	st. 2	friend	540	st. 1	gifts	606	st. 4
frail	032	st. 3	friends	472	st. 2	gifts	607	st. 4
free	077	st. 1	friends	520	st. 3	gifts	638	st. 1

Jesus	103	st. 1	joy	187	ref.
Jesus	110	st. 1	joy	219	st. 4
Jesus	134	ref.	joy	260	st. 4
Jesus	136	st. 1	joy	290	st. 4
Jesus	138	st. 3	Joy	292	st. 3
Jesus	177	st. 1	joy	295	st. 3
Jesus	180	st. 1	joy	310	st. 4
Jesus	185	st. 1	joy	317	st. 4
Jesus	188	ref.	joy	345	st. 3
Jesus	191	ref.	joy	357	st. 1
Jesus	208	st. 1	joy	364	st. 4
Jesus	210	st. 1	joy	371	st. 1
Jesus	217	ref.	joy	373	st. 2
Jesus	229	st. 5	joy	388	st. 1
Jesus	250	st. 2	joy	414	st. 4
Jesus	256	st. 2	joy	418	st. 3
Jesus	270	st. 1	joy	428	st. 1
Jesus	300	ref.	joy	430	st. 4
Jesus	301	ref.	joy	436	st. 4
Jesus	311	st. 1	joy	440	st. 1
Jesus	316	ref.	joy	441	ref.
Jesus	323	ref.	joy	442	st. 1
Jesus	344	ref.	joy	443	st. 1
Jesus	463	st. 1	joy	447	st. 3
Jesus	474	st. 3	joy	450	st. 3
Jesus	483	ref.	joy	468	st. 4
Jesus	489	st. 4	joy	473	st. 2
Jesus	608	ref.	joy	475	st. 2
Jesus Christ	221	st. 1	joy	512	st. 3
Jesus Christ	538	st. 1	joy	517	st. 4
Jesus the Nazarene	547	st. 1	joy	525	st. 1
join	317	st. 4	joy	527	st. 1
Jordan	521	st. 1	joy	540	ref.
journey	056	st. 2	joy	547	st. 4
journey	424	st. 1	joy	554	st. 4
journey	464	st. 1	joy	571	st. 3
journey	497	st. 2	joy	574	st. 4
journey	576	st. 4	joy	576	ref.
journey	613	st. 3	joy	580	st. 3
journey	621	st. 3	joy	657	st. 1
joy	005	st. 3	joyful	020	st. 4
joy	007	st. 2	joyful	166	st. 1
joy	007	st. 3	joyful	484	st. 3
joy	044	st. 3	joyous	221	st. 3
joy	062	st. 2	joys	063	st. 2
joy	067	st. 2	joys	524	st. 1
joy	087	st. 1	joys	524	st. 2
joy	108	ref.	jubilee	581	st. 2
joy	120	st. 2	Judge	257	st. 4
joy	162	st. 2	judgment	288	st. 3
joy	164	st. 3	judgment	633	st. 3
joy	172	st. 2	justice	006	st. 2
joy	184	st. 4	justice	025	st. 1

justice	390	st. 3
justice	401	st. 1
justice	623	st. 2
justified	148	st. 3
justified	193	ref.
justified	363	st. 2
keep	337	ref.
keys	197	st. 3
kind	025	st. 4
kind	066	st. 1
kind	190	st. 2
kind	225	st. 3
kind	477	st. 2
kindle	618	st. 1
kindness	559	st. 3
kindness	607	st. 3
King	016	st. 1
King	028	st. 1
King	060	st. 4
King	077	st. 2
king	085	st. 3
King	091	st. 2
King	100	st. 3
King	104	st. 4
King	128	st. 1
King	138	st. 3
King	159	st. 2
King	162	st. 2
King	170	st. 1
King	175	st. 5
King	192	st. 1
King	195	ref.
King	203	st. 2
King	232	st. 1
King	234	st. 1
King	358	st. 3
King	525	st. 2
King of creation	014	st. 1
King of glory	127	st. 1
King of heaven	032	st. 1
King of Israel	085	ref.
King of Israel	126	st. 1
King of kindness	209	st. 3
King of kings	169	st. 2
King of kings	213	st. 4
King of kings	400	st. 1
King of kings	576	st. 4
kingdom	018	ref.
kingdom	127	st. 4
kingdom	197	st. 3
kingdom	199	st. 4
kingdom	268	st. 5
kingdom	301	st. 4

sinner	434	st. 4	song	100	st. 2
sinner	474	st. 3	song	130	st. 3
sinners	139	st. 1	song	164	st. 3
sinners	149	ref.	song	188	ref.
sinners	175	st. 1	song	200	st. 4
sinners	204	st. 3	song	201	st. 4
sinners	207	st. 2	song	202	st. 4
sinners	323	st. 1	song	221	st. 2
sinners	379	st. 2	song	227	ref.
sinners	545	st. 4	song	355	st. 4
sinners	563	st. 1	song	431	ref.
sinners	581	st. 2	song	434	ref.

First Lines and Title Index

Titles are in caps and small caps; first lines in lower case type.

A Child of the King, 555 (E♭)
A mighty fortress is our God, 8 (C)
A parting hymn we sing, 375 (E♭)
A pilgrim was I, 422 (E♭)
A purple robe, 154 (D)
A ruler once came to Jesus, 322 (E♭)
A Servant of the Least, 628 (D)
A wonderful Savior is Jesus my Lord,   340 (D)
Abide with me, 63 (E♭)
According to Thy gracious Word, 372 (G)
Alas, and did my Savior bleed (AVON), 145 (A♭)
Alas, and did my Savior bleed (HUDSON), 139 (E♭)
All creatures of our God and King, 27 (E♭)
All day long, 463 (F)
All glory, laud, and honor, 126 (B♭)
All hail the power of Jesus' name (CORONATION), 202 (G)
All hail the power of Jesus' name (DIADEM), 200 (B♭)
All hail the power of Jesus' name (MILES LANE), 201 (B♭)
All my life I had a longing, 539 (E♭)
All on the altar, 326 (F)
All people that on earth do dwell, 5 (G)
All praise to Thee, 229 (F)
All praise to You, my God, this night, 449 (G)
All That Thrills My Soul, 429 (B♭)
All the way my Savior leads me, 62 (G)
All things bright and beautiful, 46 (D)
All to Jesus I surrender, 275 (D)
All to Thee, 482 (F)
Alleluia, 223 (G)
Alleluia, Alleluia! The majesty and glory of Your name, 37 (C)
Alleluia, alleluia! Give thanks, 170 (F)

Almighty Father, hear our prayer, 656 (G)
Am I a soldier of the cross, 481 (D)
Amazing grace! How sweet the sound, 330 (G)
Amen (DANISH), 650 (A♭)
Amen (DRESDEN), 651 (C)
Amen (THREEFOLD 1), 652 (F)
Amen (THREEFOLD 2), 653 (C)
Amen (THREEFOLD 3), 654 (C)
America the Beautiful, 630 (B♭)
And can it be, 147 (G)
And God will raise you up, 71 (D)
Angels, from the realms of glory, 94 (B♭)
Angels we have heard on high, 100 (F)
Are You Washed in the Blood, 136 (A♭)
Are you weary, are you heavyhearted, 451 (G)
Arise, your light is come, 83 (A♭)
As He gathered at His table, 369 (F)
As men of old their first fruits brought, 639 (F)
As we gather around the table, 367 (D)
As with gladness men of old, 117 (A♭)
Ask ye what great thing I know, 538 (G)
At Calvary, 138 (C)
At the Cross, 139 (E♭)
At the name of Jesus, 198 (F)
Away in a manger, 103 (F)

Baptized in water, 362 (B♭)
Be not dismayed, 64 (B♭)
Be strong in the Lord, 476 (A)
Be Thou my vision, 60 (E♭)
Because He Lives, 407 (A♭)
Because I have been given much, 605 (A♭)
Behold the Lamb, 233 (E♭)
Believers all, we bear the name, 399 (D)
Beneath the cross of Jesus, 291 (D♭)
Bless His Holy Name, 22 (E♭)
Bless that wonderful Name, 236 (G)

Bless the Lord, O my soul, 22 (E♭)
Blessed assurance, Jesus is mine, 334 (D)
Blessed be the God of Israel, 79 (G)
Blessed Be the Name, 206 (A♭)
Blessed Redeemer, 149 (E♭)
Blessed Savior, we adore Thee, 204 (F)
Blest be the tie, 387 (F)
Break forth, O beauteous heavenly light, 114 (E♭)
Break out, O Church of God, 401 (E♭)
Break Thou the bread of life, 263 (D)
Breathe on Me, 238 (E♭)
Breathe on me, Breath of God, 241 (F)
Brethren, we have met to worship, 379 (A♭)
Bring ye all the tithes, 616 (E♭)
Bring your sin to Him and confess, 319 (D)
Built on the Rock, 351 (C minor)
Burn in me, Fire of God, 496 (F)

Carols sing, 90 (F)
Child in the manger, 105 (C)
Children of God, 479 (D)
Children of the heavenly Father, 55 (D)
Christ is alive, 173 (C)
Christ is made the sure foundation, 356 (C)
Christ is risen, 167 (E minor)
Christ Receiveth Sinful Men, 563 (D)
Christ the Lord is risen today, 159 (C)
Christ was born in a distant land, 566 (F)
Christ, we do all adore Thee, 647 (C)
Christian hearts, in love united, 378 (G)
Christmas has its cradle, 152 (D minor)
Close to Thee, 464 (G)
Come, all Christians, be committed, 604 (G)
Come, Christians, join to sing, 231 (A♭)

Come, every soul by sin oppressed, 317 (G)

Come, Holy Spirit, 239 (E♭)

Come, Holy Spirit, Dove divine, 364 (D)

Come, let us reason, 313 (D)

Come, Thou Almighty King, 247 (F)

Come, Thou Fount of every blessing (NETTLETON), 15 (E♭)

Come, Thou Fount of every blessing (WARRENTON), 18 (D)

Come, Thou long-expected Jesus, 77 (F)

Come, we that love the Lord (FESTAL SONG), 525 (B♭)

Come, we that love the Lord (MARCHING TO ZION), 524 (G)

Come, ye disconsolate, 67 (C)

Come, ye sinners, poor and needy, 323 (G minor)

Come, ye thankful people, come, 637 (F)

Coming now to Thee, 466 (C)

Count Your Blessings, 644 (E♭)

Creator God, creating still, 51 (C)

Creator of the universe, 549 (F)

Crown Him with many crowns, 161 (E♭)

Day by day, 66 (E♭)

Dear Lord and Father of mankind, 267 (D)

Dear Lord, lead me day by day, 459 (C)

Deep in my heart there's a gladness, 541 (A♭)

Depth of mercy, 306 (D)

Down at the cross, 140 (A♭)

Doxology, 253, 5, 449 (G); 27 (E♭)

Dying with Jesus, by death reckoned
    mine, 415 (F)

Easter people, raise your voices, 360 (C)

Emmanuel, 82 (C)

Emptied of His glory, 178 (G)

Encamped along the hills of light, 413 (E♭)

Eternal Father, strong to save, 69 (C)

Eternal God, may we be free, 299 (G)

Everything was made by God, 45 (D)

Face to face with Christ, my Savior, 519 (B♭)

Fairest Lord Jesus, 176 (E♭)

Faith Is the Victory, 413 (E♭)

Faith of our fathers, 352 (G)

Father, Father, You are Jehovah, 250 (C)

Father, I adore You, 256 (F)

Father, Son, Holy Spirit, 250 (C)

Father, we love You, 249 (B♭)

Fill the earth with music, 614 (E♭)

Footsteps of Jesus, 483 (E♭)

For all the saints, 355 (G)

For God so loved the world, 548 (C)

For He alone is worthy, 427 (G)

For the beauty of the earth, 44 (G)

For the fruit of all creation, 643 (F)

For Thine is the kingdom, 659 (F)

"Forever with the Lord", 529 (D)

Forgiven, 341 (C)

Free from the law, O happy
    condition, 332 (E♭)

Freely, Freely, 273 (E♭)

From all that dwell below the skies, 13 (D♭)

Gentle Mary laid her Child, 101 (G)

Gloria Patri, 252 (E♭)

Glorify Thy Name, 249 (B♭)

Glorious Is Thy Name, 204 (F)

Glorious things of thee are spoken, 398 (E♭)

Glory be to the Father, 252 (E♭)

Go forth and tell, 596 (E♭)

Go now in peace, 660 (C)

Go out and tell, 657 (C)

Go out in peace, 657 (C)

Go, tell it on the mountain, 95 (G)

Go to dark Gethsemane, 150 (E♭)

Go with God, 648 (E♭)

God forgave my sin in Jesus' name, 273 (E♭)

God, give us Christian homes, 504 (E♭)

God is so good, 23 (E♭)

God moves in a mysterious way, 73 (D♭)

God of grace and God of glory, 395 (G)

God of our fathers, 629 (E♭)

God, our Author and Creator, 590 (A)

God, our Father, we adore Thee, 248 (B♭)

God, our Father, You have led us, 454 (E♭)

God sent His Son, 407 (A♭)

God, the Father of Your people, 382 (A)

God, who made the earth, 50 (B♭)

God, who stretched the spangled heavens, 47 (F)

God, who touches earth with beauty, 500 (C)

God, whose purpose is to kindle, 618 (G)

God Will Take Care of You, 64 (B♭)

God's Son has made me free, 649 (B♭)

Good Christian men, rejoice, 96 (F)

Grace Greater than Our Sin, 329 (G)

Grace, Love, and Fellowship, 661 (D)

Grace, love, and peace abide, 655 (F)

Grace to you, 663 (G)

Grace to you and peace, 664 (D minor)

Great is the Lord, 12 (C)

Great is Thy faithfulness, 54 (E♭)

Great Redeemer, we adore Thee, 209 (E♭)

Greater is He that is in me, 437 (F)

Guide me, O Thou great Jehovah, 56 (F)

Hail the day that sees Him rise, 165 (A♭)

Happy the home when God is there, 505 (A♭)

Hark! the herald angels sing, 88 (F)

Hark, the voice of Jesus calling, 591 (A♭)

Hark to the story angels are telling, 97 (F)

Have faith in God, 405 (C)

Have Thine own way, Lord, 294 (E♭)

Have You Been to Calvary, 324 (E♭)

Have you been to Jesus, 136 (A♭)

Have you been to the cross, 324 (E♭)

Have you failed in your plan, 318 (F)

He Hideth My Soul, 340 (D)

He Included Me, 436 (B♭)

He Is Able to Deliver Thee, 24 (B♭)

He Is Born, 112 (F)

He is Lord, 178 (G)

He is risen! He is risen, 166 (C)
He Is So Precious to Me, 452 (G)
He Keeps Me Singing, 425 (A♭)
He leadeth me! O blessed thought, 52 (C)
He Lives, 533 (B♭)
Hear our prayer, O Lord, 658 (D)
Heaven Came Down, 438 (F)
Heavenly hosts in ceaseless worship, 40 (G)
Heavenly Sunlight, 424 (F)
Here am I, send me, 597 (D)
Here, at Your table, Lord, 368 (E♭)
Here, O Lord, Your servants gather, 179 (C dorian)
He's got the whole world in His hands, 346 (D)
Higher Ground, 484 (G)
His name is Wonderful, 203 (F)
Holy Bible, Book divine, 260 (F)
Holy Bible, Book of love, 264 (E♭)
Holy, God is holy, 343 (F)
Holy Ground, 224 (E♭)
Holy, holy, 254 (C)
Holy, holy, holy, 2 (D)
Holy, holy, holy is the Lord, 9 (G)
Holy Is His Name, 343 (F)
Holy Is the Lord, 9 (G)
Holy is the Lord (Schubert), 666 (E♭)
Holy Lord (DONA NOBIS PACEM), 622 (F)
Holy Spirit, breathe on me, 238 (E♭)
Hosanna, loud hosanna, 130 (A♭)
How can I say thanks, 153 (B♭)
How firm a foundation, 338 (A♭)
How great our God's majestic Name! 70 (D)
How Great Our Joy, 108 (C)
How Great Thou Art, 10 (B♭)
How I Love You, 230 (C)
How lovely is Thy dwelling place, 523 (D)
How Majestic Is Your Name, 29 (C)
How sweet the name of Jesus sounds, 453 (G)

I am happy today, 421 (A♭)
I Am His and He Is Mine, 336 (D)
I am resolved, 301 (B♭)
I am satisfied with Jesus, 472 (E♭)
I am so happy in Christ today, 436 (B♭)

I am Thine, O Lord, 290 (A♭)
I am weak, but Thou art strong, 448 (B♭)
I can hear my Savior calling, 288 (F)
I come to the garden alone, 187 (A♭)
I come with joy to meet my Lord, 371 (G)
I gave My life for thee, 606 (B♭)
I have a song I love to sing, 543 (G)
I have come from the darkness, 532 (C)
I have decided to follow Jesus, 305 (D♭)
I have found a friend in Jesus, 189 (F)
I have heard the voice of Jesus, 482 (F)
I hear the Savior say, 134 (E♭)
I hear Thy welcome voice, 302 (E♭)
I heard an old, old story, 426 (G)
I heard the bells on Christmas day, 98 (E♭)
I heard the voice of Jesus say, 551 (G minor)
I know a fount, 155 (D)
I know not why God's wondrous grace, 337 (D)
I know that my Redeemer liveth, 191 (C)
I Know Whom I Have Believed, 337 (D)
I lay my sins on Jesus, 272 (D)
I love Thee, 211 (E♭)
I love Thy kingdom, Lord, 354 (F)
I love to tell the story, 572 (A♭)
I love You, Lord, 212 (E♭)
I must needs go home, 151 (G)
I must tell Jesus, 455 (E♭)
I need Thee every hour, 450 (A♭)
I saw the cross of Jesus, 286 (E♭)
I serve a risen Savior, 533 (B♭)
I sing the mighty power of God, 42 (F)
I stand amazed in the presence, 547 (A♭)
I Surrender All, 275 (D)
I wandered in the shades of night, 444 (E♭)
I want Jesus to walk with me, 465 (C minor)
I was sinking deep in sin, 546 (B♭)
I will not be afraid, 72 (A♭)
I will sing of my Redeemer, 575 (A♭)

I will sing the wondrous story (HYFRODOL), 535 (G)
I will sing the wondrous story (WONDROUS STORY), 537 (E♭)
I will trust in the Lord, 420 (G)
I'd rather have Jesus, 550 (D♭)
If you are tired of the load of your sin, 311 (A♭)
If you will only let God guide you, 57 (G minor)
I'll Live for Him, 298 (F)
I'll praise my Maker, 35 (D)
I'll tell the world that I'm a Christian, 553 (D)
I'm just a child, 488 (C)
I'm pressing on the upward way, 484 (G)
I'm so glad I'm a part of the family of God, 386 (F)
Immortal, invisible, God only wise, 6 (A♭)
Immortal Love, forever full, 480 (E♭)
In Christ, Our Liberty, 626 (C)
In Christ there is no East or West, 385 (D)
In heavenly love abiding, 348 (D)
In His time, 53 (D)
In loving-kindness Jesus came, 542 (G)
In my life, Lord, be glorified, 457 (D)
In remembrance, 365 (A♭)
In the cross of Christ I glory, 554 (B♭)
In The Family of God, 380 (G)
In the Garden, 187 (A♭)
In the lightning flash across the sky, 59 (E♭)
In the little village of Bethlehem, 102 (G)
In the Name of the Lord, 174 (G)
In the Presence of the Lord, 440 (F)
Infant holy, Infant lowly, 106 (G)
Is your life a channel of blessing, 564 (A♭)
It came upon the midnight clear, 93 (B♭)
It Is Well with My Soul, 410 (D♭)
It's So Wonderful, 432 (G)
I've come to tell, 222 (G)
I've found a friend, O such a friend, 183 (A♭)

I've found a friend who is all to me, 540 (B♭)

I've got peace like a river, 418 (G)

I've wandered far away from God, 309 (A♭)

Jerusalem, my happy home, 517 (F)

Jerusalem, the golden, 527 (D♭)

Jesu, Jesu, fill us with Your love, 501 (D)

Jesus, at Your holy table, 377 (F)

Jesus calls us o'er the tumult, 293 (A♭)

Jesus Calls You Now, 319 (D)

Jesus, how I love You, 230 (C)

Jesus, I my cross have taken, 471 (G)

Jesus is all the world to me, 184 (A♭)

Jesus is coming to earth again, 195 (C)

Jesus Is Lord of All, 296 (D♭)

Jesus is Lord of all the earth, 170 (F)

Jesus is Savior and Lord of my life, 296 (D♭)

Jesus is tenderly calling, 316 (C)

Jesus Is the Song, 552 (A♭)

Jesus is the sweetest name I know, 205 (C)

Jesus, Jesus, Jesus, 177 (E♭)

Jesus, keep me near the cross, 280 (F)

Jesus, lover of my soul, 180 (F)

Jesus loves me, 344 (D)

Jesus loves the little children, 592 (A♭)

Jesus, my friend, is great, 190 (F)

Jesus, my Lord and Savior, 186 (C)

Jesus, my Lord, will love me forever, 345 (G)

Jesus, our Lord and King, 363 (E♭)

Jesus Paid It All, 134 (E♭)

Jesus shall reign, 587 (E♭)

Jesus, the very thought of Thee, 225 (G)

Jesus, Thy boundless love to me, 123 (F)

Jesus was a loving teacher, 602 (G)

Jesus! what a friend for sinners, 185 (G)

Jesus' hands were kind hands, 477 (F)

Joy to the world! the Lord is come, 87 (D)

Joyful, joyful, we adore Thee, 7 (G)

Just a Closer Walk with Thee, 448 (B♭)

Just as I am (TABERNACLE), 303 (E♭)

Just as I am (WOODWORTH), 307 (E♭)

Just when I need Him, Jesus is near, 65 (D♭)

Just When I Need Him Most, 65 (D♭)

King of kings, 234 (G minor)

King of my life, I crown Thee now, 490 (E♭)

Lead Me to Calvary, 490 (E♭)

Lead me to some soul today, 560 (G)

Lead on, O King Eternal, 621 (D)

Leaning on the Everlasting Arms, 333 (A♭)

Let all mortal flesh keep silence, 80 (D minor)

Let all the world in every corner sing, 28 (D)

Let all things now living, 640 (F)

Let Jesus Come into Your Heart, 311 (A♭)

Let Others See Jesus in You, 571 (A♭)

Let us break bread together, 366 (E♭)

Let your heart be broken, 611 (E♭)

Lift every voice and sing, 627 (A♭)

Lift high the cross, 594 (C)

Lift Him up, 220 (G)

Lift up your heads, 128 (D)

Like a river glorious, 58 (F)

Living for Jesus, 282 (F)

Living Stones, 353 (E♭)

Lo, He comes with clouds descending, 199 (A)

Lo, how a Rose e'er blooming, 78 (F)

Look, ye saints! The sight is glorious, 169 (G minor)

Lord, as of old at Pentecost, 242 (A♭)

Lord, Be Glorified, 457 (D)

Lord, for the gift of children, 508 (E♭)

Lord, Here Am I, 486 (C)

Lord, I want to be a Christian, 489 (E♭)

Lord, I'm Coming Home, 309 (A♭)

Lord Jesus, I long to be perfectly whole, 325 (A♭)

Lord, lay some soul upon my heart, 570 (F)

Lord, make our homes so loving, 511 (F)

Lord, Send a Revival, 468 (A♭)

Lord, speak to me, that I may speak, 568 (F)

Lord, the light of Your love, 579 (A♭)

Lord, Thy church on earth is seeking, 391 (A)

Lord, who across the ages, 624 (A♭)

Love came down at Christmas, 109 (F)

Love divine, all loves excelling, 208 (B♭)

Love Is the Theme, 545 (B♭)

Love Lifted Me, 546 (B♭)

Loved with everlasting love, 336 (D)

Low in the grave He lay, 160 (C)

Majestic sweetness sits enthroned, 219 (A♭)

Majesty, 215 (B♭)

Make Me a Blessing, 569 (C)

Make me a captive, Lord, 278 (D)

Make Me a Channel of Blessing, 564 (A♭)

Make room within my heart, O God, 491 (G)

"Man of Sorrows," what a name, 175 (B♭)

Many and great, O God, 49 (C minor)

Marvelous grace of our loving Lord, 329 (G)

Master, Thou callest, 486 (C)

May God's grace go before you, 648 (E♭)

May the grace of Christ, our Savior, 661 (D)

Mine eyes have seen the glory, 633 (B♭)

Moment by Moment, 415 (F)

More about Jesus, 600 (A♭)

More love to Thee, O Christ, 473 (G)

Morning has broken, 48 (C)

Must Jesus bear the cross alone, 475 (A♭)

My country, 'tis of thee, 634 (F)

My faith has found a resting place, 412 (A♭)

My faith looks up to Thee, 416 (E♭)

My Father is rich in houses and lands, 555 (E♭)

My God, how wonderful You are, 11 (G)

My hope is built on nothing less, 406 (F)

My Jesus, I love Thee, 210 (F)

My life, my love I give to Thee, 298 (F)

My Lord, I did not choose You, 289 (D♭)

My Lord Is Near Me All the Time, 59 (E♭)

My Savior First of All, 528 (A♭)

My Savior is the Lord and King, 552 (A♭)

My Shepherd will supply my need, 68 (C)

My singing is a prayer, 603 (D♭)

My Tribute, 153 (B♭)

Name of all majesty, 207 (B♭)

Near to The Heart of God, 295 (D♭)

Nearer, my God, to Thee, 458 (G)

No, not despairingly, 270 (E♭)

No, Not One, 181 (F)

No prison wall can hold, 628 (D)

Not what my hands have done, 339 (D)

Nothing but the Blood, 135 (G)

Now I Belong to Jesus, 345 (G)

Now thank we all our God, 638 (F)

O beautiful for spacious skies, 630 (B♭)

O Christ, our hope, our heart's desire, 414 (F)

O come, all ye faithful, 89 (G)

O come, O come, Emmanuel, 76 (E minor)

O day of God, draw nigh, 623 (A♭)

O for a thousand tongues to sing (AZMON,) 216 (A♭)

O for a thousand tongues to sing (BLESSED NAME), 206 (A♭)

O God, Almighty Father, 258 (F)

O God of love, enable me, 580 (E♭)

O God of love, O King of peace, 619 (B♭)

O God of might, O Son of light, 582 (G)

O God of prophets, known of old, 646 (B♭)

O God, our help in ages past, 74 (C)

O God, to those who here profess, 506 (G)

O God, we ask for strength, 498 (A♭)

O happy day that fixed my choice, 439 (F)

O holy Dove of God descending, 240 (C)

O how He loves you and me, 146 (A♭)

O Jesus, I have promised, 276 (G)

O land of rest, for thee I sigh, 608 (F)

O little town of Bethlehem, 86 (F)

O Lord, may church and home combine, 510 (E♭)

O Lord my God! when I in awesome wonder, 10 (B♭)

O Lord, our Lord, how majestic, 29 (C)

O Love that wilt not let me go, 292 (A♭)

O Master, let me walk with Thee, 279 (E♭)

O my soul, bless God the Father, 21 (G)

O perfect Love, 512 (E♭)

O praise the gracious power, 226 (G)

O sacred Head, now wounded, 137 (A minor)

O say, can you see, 635 (A♭)

O sing a song of Bethlehem, 120 (E minor)

O sing a song to God, 38 (D minor)

O soul, are you weary and troubled, 320 (F)

O That Will Be Glory, 520 (A♭)

O the deep, deep love of Jesus, 409 (A♭)

O the King is coming, 194 (A)

O What a Wonder It Is, 548 (C)

O what a wonderful, wonderful day, 438 (F)

O worship the King, 16 (A♭)

O Zion, haste, 583 (B♭)

Of all the Spirit's gifts to me, 442 (D)

Of the Father's love begotten, 251 (E♭)

Of the themes that men have known, 545 (B♭)

Oh, come, little children, 107 (D)

Oh, how good is Christ the Lord, 228 (D)

Oh, How I Love Jesus, 217 (A♭)

On a hill far away, 141 (B♭)

On Eagle's Wings, 71 (D)

On Jordan's stormy banks, 521 (F)

Once to every man and nation, 470 (A)

One by one, 561 (F)

One day, 193 (D♭)

Only believe, 534 (D♭)

Only Trust Him, 317 (G)

Onward, Christian soldiers, 493 (E♭)

Open my eyes, that I may see, 502 (A♭)

Open our eyes, Lord, 499 (D)

Our Father, which art in heaven, 462 (B♭)

Our God has built with living stones, 353 (E♭)

Our God has made us one, 388 (G)

Our life and its sustaining breath, 642 (G)

Our Savior's infant cries were heard, 116 (F)

Out in the highways and byways of life, 569 (C)

Out of my bondage, sorrow, and night, 310 (A♭)

Pass me not, O gentle Savior, 308 (A♭)

Pentecostal Power, 242 (A♭)

People need the Lord, 557 (C)

Praise and thanksgiving, 645 (F)

Praise God, from whom all blessings flow, 253 ,5 449, (G); 27, (E♭)

Praise Him, All Ye Little Children, 31 (E♭)

Praise Him! praise Him, 227 (G)

Praise Him, praise Him, all ye little children, 31 (E♭)

Praise, my soul, the King of heaven, 32 (D)

Praise the Father, 257 (G)

Praise the Lord, the King of glory, 232 (F)

Praise the Lord who reigns above, 33 (F)

Praise the Lord! ye heavens, adore Him, 36 (F)

Praise to the Lord, the Almighty, 14 (F)

Praise ye the name of the Lord, 665 (D)

Precious Lord, take my hand, 456 (A♭)

Purer in heart, O God, 492 (G)

Redeemed, (ADA), 531 (E♭)
Redeemed, how I love to proclaim it (REDEEMED), 544 (A♭)
Rejoice in the Lord always, 433 (F)
Rejoice, the Lord is King, 197 (C)
Rejoice, ye pure in heart, 39 (F)
Rescue the perishing, 559 (B♭)
Revive Us Again, 469 (G)
Ring the bells of heaven, 428 (B♭)
Rise up, O men of God, 400 (G)
Rock of Ages, cleft for me, 342 (B♭)
Room at the Cross, 315 (G)

Satisfied, 539 (E♭)
Satisfied with Jesus, 472 (E♭)
Saved, Saved, 540 (B♭)
Savior, like a shepherd lead us, 61 (D)
Savior, teach me day by day, 461 (E♭)
Savior, Thy dying love, 607 (G)
Search me, O God, 297 (G)
See, to us a Child is born, 104 (D)
Seek ye first, 478 (E♭)
Send a Great Revival, 466 (C)
Send a revival, O Christ, my Lord, 468 (A♭)
Send forth your Word, O God, 588 (C)
Send Me, O Lord, Send Me, 582 (G)
Send the Light, 595 (G)
"Serve the Lord with gladness," 495 (C)
Set my soul afire, 573 (F)
Shall we gather at the river, 518 (D)
Share His Love, 567 (G)
Shine, Jesus, Shine, 579 (A♭)
Silent night, holy night, 91 (B♭)
Simply trusting every day, 417 (G)
Since I Have Been Redeemed, 543 (G)
Since Jesus Came into My Heart, 441 (A♭)
Sing, Congregation, Sing, 397 (C)
Sing hallelujah to the Lord, 214 (C minor)
Sing Hosannas, 97 (F)
Sing praise to God who reigns above, 20 (E♭)
Sing the wondrous love of Jesus, 514 (C)
Sing them over again to me, 261 (F)
Sing to the Lord of harvest, 641 (D)

Sing we now of Christmas, 111 (E minor)
Sinners Jesus will receive, 563 (D)
So precious is Jesus, my Savior, 452 (G)
So send I you, 565 (F)
Softly and tenderly, 312 (G)
Soldiers of Christ, in truth arrayed, 574 (A♭)
Something for Thee, 607 (G)
Songs of praise the angels sang, 235 (B♭)
Soon and very soon, 192 (G)
Sound aloud the trumpet, 171 (G)
Speak to my heart, 281 (F)
Spirit, Now Live in Me, 240 (C)
Spirit of God, descend upon my heart, 245 (C)
Spirit of the living God, 244 (F)
Stand up and bless the Lord, 30 (G)
Stand up, stand up for Jesus (GEIBEL), 487 (F)
Stand up, stand up for Jesus (WEBB), 485 (B♭)
Standing on the promises, 335 (B♭)
Stir Your church, O God our Father, 392 (G)
Sunlight, 444 (E♭)
Sunshine in My Soul, 430 (A♭)
Surely Goodness and Mercy, 422 (E♭)
Sweet hour of prayer, 445 (C)
Sweet, Sweet Spirit, 243 (G)
Sweetly, Lord, have we heard Thee calling, 483 (E♭)

Take my life, and let it be consecrated (HENDON), 277 (F)
Take my life, and let it be consecrated (YARBROUGH), 283 (G)
Take my life, lead me, Lord, 287 (D♭)
Take the name of Jesus with you, 576 (A♭)
Take time to be holy, 446 (F)
"Take up thy cross and follow Me," 285 (F)
"Take up your cross," 494 (E♭)
Teach me, O Lord, I pray, 601 (D♭)
Tell It Out with Gladness, 585 (G)
Tell It to Jesus, 451 (G)
Tell me the stories of Jesus, 129 (C)
Tell me the story of Jesus, 122 (E♭)

Tell out, my soul, the greatness of the Lord, 81 (D)
Tell the Good News, 566 (F)
Thanksgiving/Thanks-living, 642 (G)
That boy-child of Mary, 110 (F)
The Birthday of a King, 102 (G)
The blood that Jesus shed for me, 133 (A♭)
The Blood Will Never Lose Its Power, 133 (A♭)
The Bond of Love, 384 (B♭)
The church of Christ, in every age, 402 (A♭)
The church's one foundation, 350 (E♭)
The cross upon which Jesus died, 315 (G)
The day of resurrection, 164 (C)
The Family of God, 386 (F)
The family of God is born from above, 380 (G)
The first day of the week, 357 (C)
The First Lord's Day, 162 (F)
The first Nowell, 85 (D)
The God of Abraham praise, 34 (E minor)
The great Physician, 188 (Eb)
The King Is Coming, 194 (A)
The King of glory comes, 127 (E minor)
The Lily of the Valley, 189 (F)
The Lord bless you and keep you, 662 (C)
The Lord's Prayer, 462 (B♭)
The love of Christ who died for me, 268 (F)
The love of God is broader, 567 (G)
The Majesty and Glory of Your Name, 37 (C)
The Master hath come, 497 (G)
The Nail-Scarred Hand, 318 (F)
The Old Rugged Cross, 141 (B♭)
The Old Ship of Zion, 577 (A♭)
The Savior is waiting, 321 (F)
The Servant Song, 613 (F)
The sky shall unfold, 196 (C)
The Solid Rock, 406 (F)
The Star-Spangled Banner, 635 (A♭)
The strife is o'er, 172 (E♭)
The Way of the Cross Leads Home, 151 (G)
The whole world is singing, 593 (D)

Topical Index of Hymns

ASSURANCE
(see also: FAITH AND TRUST;
SECURITY OF THE BELIEVER)
A Child of the King, 555
A Mighty Fortress Is Our God, 8
All People That on Earth Do
Dwell, 5
Amazing Grace! How Sweet the
Sound, 330
Ask Ye What Great Thing I Know,
538
Blessed Assurance, Jesus Is Mine,
334
God Will Take Care of You, 64
Grace Greater than Our Sin, 329
He Hideth My Soul, 340
He Leadeth Me! O Blessed
Thought, 52
He's Got the Whole World in His
Hands, 346
I Know Whom I Have Believed,
337
I Will Trust in the Lord, 420
In the Garden, 187
It Is Well with My Soul, 410
Jesus! What a Friend for Sinners,
185
Just a Closer Walk with Thee, 448
On Eagle's Wings, 71
Rock of Ages, Cleft for Me, 342
Standing on the Promises, 335
The Old Ship of Zion, 577
There Shall Be Showers of
Blessing, 467
This Joy That I Have, 443

ATONEMENT
(see: GRACE, JESUS CHRIST-
BLOOD, JESUS CHRIST-CROSS,
JESUS CHRIST-LOVE FOR US)

BAPTISM
Baptized in Water, 362
Come, Holy Spirit, Dove Divine,
364
Jesus, Our Lord and King, 363
When We Walk with the Lord, 447

BENEDICTIONS
(see: SERVICE MUSIC)

BIBLE
Break Thou the Bread of Life, 263
God, Give Us Christian Homes,
504

God of Our Fathers, 629
Holy Bible, Book Divine, 260
Holy Bible, Book of Love, 264
How Firm a Foundation, 338
Morning Has Broken, 48
Send Forth Your Word, O God,
588
Tell It Out with Gladness, 585
The Word of God Is Alive, 265
Wonderful Words of Life, 261
Word of God, Across the Ages,
262

BIRTH OF JESUS
(see: JESUS CHRIST-BIRTH)

BLOOD OF CHRIST
(see: GRACE; JESUS CHRIST-
BLOOD; JESUS CHRIST-CROSS;
JESUS CHRIST-LOVE FOR US)

CALLS TO WORSHIP
(see: SERVICE MUSIC)

CHILDREN'S HYMNS
(see also: HOME AND FAMILY)
All Creatures of Our God and
King, 27
All Glory, Laud, and Honor, 126
All Things Bright and Beautiful, 46
Away in a Manger, 103
Carols Sing, 90
Everything Was Made by God, 45
Fairest Lord Jesus, 176
For the Beauty of the Earth, 44
God, Who Made the Earth, 50
God, Who Touches Earth with
Beauty, 500
Holy Bible, Book of Love, 264
Hosanna, Loud Hosanna, 130
I'm Just a Child, 488
Infant Holy, Infant Lowly, 106
Jesus Loves Me, 344
Jesus Loves the Little Children,
592
Jesus Was a Loving Teacher, 602
Jesus' Hands Were Kind Hands,
477
My Singing Is a Prayer, 603
Oh, Come, Little Children, 107
Praise and Thanksgiving, 645
Praise Him, All Ye Little Children,
31
Purer in Heart, O God, 492
Rejoice in the Lord Always, 433

Savior, Teach Me Day by Day, 461
Sing to the Lord of Harvest, 641
Sing We Now of Christmas, 111
Tell Me the Stories of Jesus, 129
That Boy-Child of Mary, 110
The First Lord's Day, 162
The Whole World Is Singing, 593
This Is My Father's World, 43
We Praise You with Our Minds, O
Lord, 599
We Welcome Glad Easter, 168
What Can I Give Him, 610
When I Pray, 460
Your Supper, Lord, Before Us
Spread, 374

CHRISTIAN LIFE
(see: ASSURANCE; DISCIPLE-
SHIP; FAITH AND TRUST;
HOPE; JOY; PRAYER; FELLOW-
SHIP WITH GOD; SECURITY
OF THE BELIEVER; MINISTRY,
CHRISTIAN; CITIZENSHIP,
CHRISTIAN)

CHRISTMAS
(see: JESUS CHRIST-ADVENT;
JESUS CHRIST-BIRTH)

CHURCH
(see also: FAMILY OF GOD;
FELLOWSHIP OF BELIEVERS;
GROWTH; MISSION)
Blest Be the Tie, 387
Break Out, O Church of God, 401
Built on the Rock, 351
Christ Is Made the Sure
Foundation, 356
Christian Hearts, in Love United,
378
Glorious Things of Thee Are
Spoken, 398
Go Forth and Tell, 596
God, the Father of Your People,
382
How Lovely Is Thy Dwelling
Place, 523
I Love Thy Kingdom, Lord, 354
Lord, Be Glorified, 457
Lord, Thy Church on Earth Is
Seeking, 391
Lord, Who Across the Ages, 624
O Lord, May Church and Home
Combine, 510
Our God Has Made Us One, 388

Rise Up, O Men of God, 400
Stir Your Church, O God, Our
  Father, 392
The Church of Christ, in Every
  Age, 402
The Church's One Foundation,
  350
'Tis the Church Triumphant
  Singing, 218
To Worship, Work, and Witness,
  389
We Are God's People, 383
We Stand United in the Truth,
  625

CITIZENSHIP, CHRISTIAN
  (see also: SOCIAL CONCERNS)
America the Beautiful, 630
God of our Fathers, 629
Lift Every Voice and Sing, 627
Mine Eyes Have Seen the Glory,
  633
My Country, 'Tis of Thee, 634
The Star-Spangled Banner, 635
We Utter Our Cry, 631

COMFORT
  (see also: GUIDANCE AND
  CARE; SECURITY OF THE
  BELIEVER; GOD THE
  FATHER-PROVIDENCE; GOD
  THE FATHER-LOVE FOR US)
Abide with Me, 63
All Praise to You, My God, This
  Night, 449
All the Way My Savior Leads Me,
  62
Amazing Grace! How Sweet the
  Sound, 330
Arise, Your Light Is Come, 83
Be Strong in the Lord, 476
Because He Lives, 407
Beneath the Cross of Jesus, 291
Blessed Assurance, Jesus Is Mine,
  334
Children of the Heavenly Father,
  55
Come, Ye Disconsolate, 67
Come, Ye Sinners, Poor and
  Needy, 323
Count Your Blessings, 644
Day by Day, 66
Eternal Father, Strong to Save, 69
God Will Take Care of You, 64
Have Faith in God, 405
He Hideth My Soul, 340
He Leadeth Me! O Blessed
  Thought, 52
Here, O Lord, Your Servants
  Gather, 179

Holy Bible, Book Divine, 260
How Firm a Foundation, 338
How Lovely Is Thy Dwelling
  Place, 523
How Sweet the Name of Jesus
  Sounds, 453
I Am His, and He Is Mine, 336
I Heard the Voice of Jesus Say,
  551
I Lay My Sins on Jesus, 272
I Must Tell Jesus, 455
I Need Thee Every Hour, 450
I Saw the Cross of Jesus, 286
I Want Jesus to Walk with Me,
  465
I Will Not Be Afraid, 72
In Heavenly Love Abiding, 348
In Loving-Kindness Jesus Came,
  542
In the Cross of Christ I Glory, 554
In the Garden, 187
It Is Well with My Soul, 410
It's So Wonderful, 432
I've Found a Friend, O Such a
  Friend, 183
Jesus Is All the World to Me, 184
Jesus, Lover of My Soul, 180
Jesus! What a Friend for Sinners,
  185
Just a Closer Walk with Thee, 448
Just When I Need Him Most, 65
Like a River Glorious, 58
Love Lifted Me, 546
Moment by Moment, 415
My Faith Has Found a Resting
  Place, 412
My Faith Looks Up to Thee, 416
My Shepherd Will Supply My
  Need, 68
Near to the Heart of God, 295
No, Not One, 181
On Jordan's Stormy Banks, 521
Out of My Bondage, Sorrow, and
  Night, 310
Precious Lord, Take My Hand, 456
Surely Goodness and Mercy, 422
Sweet Hour of Prayer, 445
Take the Name of Jesus with You,
  576
Tell It to Jesus, 451
The Great Physician, 188
The Lily of the Valley, 189
There Is a Balm in Gilead, 269
There Is a Name I Love to Hear,
  217
Trust and Obey, 447
What a Friend We Have in Jesus,
  182
When the Morning Comes, 522
Wonderful, Wonderful Jesus, 434

**COMMITMENT AND
CONSECRATION**
  (see also: COURAGE; DISCIPLE-
  SHIP; GROWTH; HOLINESS
  AND PURITY; SERVANTHOOD)
All on the Altar, 326
All to Thee, 482
Am I a Soldier of the Cross, 481
Be Thou My Vision, 60
Beneath the Cross of Jesus, 291
Breathe on Me, 238
Burn in Me, Fire of God, 496
Close to Thee, 464
Come, All Christians, Be
  Committed, 604
Footsteps of Jesus, 483
God, Our Father, You Have Led
  Us, 454
God, Whose Purpose Is to Kindle,
  618
Hark, the Voice of Jesus Calling,
  591
Have Thine Own Way, Lord, 294
Here Am I, Send Me, 597
Higher Ground, 484
Holy, Holy, 254
I Am Thine, O Lord, 290
I Gave My Life for Thee, 606
I Have Decided to Follow Jesus,
  305
I Surrender All, 275
I'll Live for Him, 298
I'm Just a Child, 488
Jesus, I My Cross Have Taken, 471
Jesus Is Lord of All, 296
Jesus, Keep Me Near the Cross,
  280
Jesus, Our Lord and King, 363
Jesus, Thy Boundless Love to Me,
  123
Jesus! What a Friend for Sinners,
  185
Jesus' Hands Were Kind Hands,
  477
Lead Me to Calvary, 490
Lead On, O King Eternal, 621
Lift Up Your Heads, 128
Living for Jesus, 282
Lord, Here Am I, 486
Lord, I Want to Be a Christian,
  489
Lord, Lay Some Soul Upon My
  Heart, 570
Lord, Send a Revival, 468
Make Me a Captive, Lord, 278
Make Me a Channel of Blessing,
  564
Make Room Within My Heart, O
  God, 491
More Love to Thee, O Christ, 473

My Singing Is a Prayer, 603
Nearer, My God to Thee, 458
O Jesus, I Have Promised, 276
O Love That Wilt Not Let Me Go, 292
O Master, Let Me Walk with Thee, 279
Once to Every Man and Nation, 470
Open My Eyes, That I May See, 502
Open Our Eyes, Lord, 499
Purer in Heart, O God, 492
Satisfied with Jesus, 472
Savior, Like a Shepherd Lead Us, 61
Send a Great Revival, 466
Set My Soul Afire, 573
Speak to My Heart, 281
Spirit of God, Descend upon My Heart, 245
Spirit of the Living God, 244
Stand Up, Stand Up for Jesus (Geibel), 487
Stand Up, Stand Up for Jesus (Webb), 485
Take My Life, and Let It Be Consecrated (Hendon), 277
Take My Life, and Let It Be Consecrated (Yarbrough), 283
Take My Life, Lead Me, Lord, 287
Take Up Your Cross, the Savior Said, 494
The Love of Christ Who Died for Me, 268
The Nail-Scarred Hand, 318
This Is a Day of New Beginnings, 370
Thou Didst Leave Thy Throne, 121
Thou, My Everlasting Portion, 464
'Tis So Sweet to Trust in Jesus, 411
To Worship, Work, and Witness, 389
Turn Your Eyes upon Jesus, 320
We Are Called to Be God's People, 390
We Are Climbing Jacob's Ladder, 474
We Praise You with Our Minds, O Lord, 599
We'll Work Till Jesus Comes, 608
What Can I Give Him, 610
Where He Leads Me, 288
Wherever He Leads I'll Go, 285

CONFESSION AND REPENTANCE
(see also: INVITATION-CONSE-CRATION; INVITATION-SALVA-TION; FORGIVENESS)

At Calvary, 138
Beneath the Cross of Jesus, 291
Breathe on Me, 238
Depth of Mercy 306
Jesus Calls You Now, 319
Jesus Is Tenderly Calling, 316
Just As I Am (Tabernacle), 303
Just As I Am (Woodworth), 307
Lord, I'm Coming Home, 309
Lord, Send a Revival, 468
No, Not Despairingly, 270
Out of My Bondage, Sorrow, and Night, 310
Pass Me Not, O Gentle Savior, 308
Search Me, O God, 297
Send a Great Revival, 466
There's a Wideness in God's Mercy, 25

COURAGE
(see also: COMMITMENT AND CONSECRATION)

Am I a Soldier of the Cross, 481
Be Strong in the Lord, 476
Faith of Our Fathers, 352
God Moves in a Mysterious Way, 73
God of Grace and God of Glory, 395
God, Our Author and Creator, 590
God, Whose Purpose Is to Kindle, 618
Here, O Lord, Your Servants Gather, 179
Lead On, O King Eternal, 621
Lift Every Voice and Sing, 627
Lord, Thy Church on Earth is Seeking, 391
Lord, Who Across the Ages, 624
On Eagle's Wings, 71
Once to Every Man and Nation, 470
Onward, Christian Soldiers, 493
Stand Up, Stand Up for Jesus (Geibel), 487
Stand Up, Stand Up for Jesus (Webb), 485
We Are Called to Be God's People, 390

CREATION
(see also: GOD THE FATHER-MAJESTY AND POWER)

All Creatures of Our God and King, 27
All Things Bright and Beautiful, 46
Creator God, Creating Still, 51
Everything Was Made by God, 45
Fairest Lord Jesus, 176
God, Who Made the Earth, 50

God, Who Stretched the Spangled Heavens, 47
God Who Touches Earth with Beauty, 500
How Great Our God's Majestic Name, 70
How Great Thou Art, 10
I Sing the Mighty Power of God, 42
Let All Things Now Living, 640
Many and Great, O God, 49
Morning Has Broken, 48
O Sing a Song to God, 38
Praise the Lord! Ye Heavens, Adore Him, 36
Praise to the Lord, the Almighty, 14
Songs of Praise the Angels Sang, 235
This Is My Father's World, 43

CROSS OF CHRIST
(see: JESUS CHRIST-CROSS)

DEDICATION-CHILDREN AND PARENTS
(see: CHURCH)

DEDICATION-CHRISTIAN WORKERS
(see: MINISTRY, CHRISTIAN; SERVANTHOOD; SERVICE; STEWARDSHIP)

DEDICATION-CHURCH
(see: CHURCH)

DISCIPLESHIP
(see also: COMMITMENT AND CONSECRATION; FELLOWSHIP WITH GOD; SERVANTHOOD)

All Day Long, 463
Be Strong in the Lord, 476
Because I Have Been Given Much, 605
Believers All, We Bear the Name, 399
Break Out, O Church of God, 401
Children of God, 479
Christian Hearts, in Love United, 378
Come, All Christians, Be Committed, 604
Dear Lord and Father of Mankind, 267
Dear Lord, Lead Me Day by Day, 459
Eternal God, May We Be Free, 299
Footsteps of Jesus, 483
God, Our Author and Creator, 590

God, Our Father, You Have Led Us, 454
Hark, the Voice of Jesus Calling, 591
Have Thine Own Way, Lord, 294
Higher Ground, 484
I Am Resolved, 301
I Am Thine, O Lord, 290
I Have Decided to Follow Jesus, 305
I'll Tell the World That I'm a Christian, 553
In the Presence of the Lord, 440
I've Found a Friend, O Such a Friend, 183
Jesu, Jesu, Fill Us with Your Love, 501
Jesus Calls Us O'er the Tumult, 293
Jesus, I My Cross Have Taken, 471
Lead Me to Calvary, 490
Lead On, O King Eternal, 621
Living for Jesus, 282
Lord, Here Am I, 486
Lord, I Want to Be a Christian, 489
Lord, Send a Revival, 468
Lord, Speak to Me, That I May Speak, 568
Make Me a Blessing, 569
Make Me a Captive, Lord, 278
More Love to Thee, O Christ, 473
Must Jesus Bear the Cross Alone, 475
O God, We Ask for Strength, 498
O Jesus, I Have Promised, 276
O Master, Let Me Walk with Thee, 279
Open My Eyes, That I May See, 502
Praise and Thanksgiving, 645
Purer in Heart, O God, 492
Savior, Teach Me Day by Day, 461
Seek Ye First, 478
Send Me, O Lord, Send Me, 582
Sing, Congregation, Sing, 397
Soldiers of Christ, in Truth Arrayed, 574
Take My Life, Lead Me, Lord, 287
Take Up Your Cross, the Savior Said, 494
Teach Me, O Lord, I Pray, 601
The Master Hath Come, 497
This Is a Day of New Beginnings, 370
Though I May Speak with Bravest Fire, 423
Trust and Obey, 447
Walking Along with Jesus, 186
We Are Called to Be God's People, 390

We Are God's People, 383
We Give Thee But Thine Own, 609
Where He Leads Me, 288
Wherever He Leads I'll Go, 285

EASTER
(see: JESUS CHRIST-RESURRECTION)

EDUCATION
(see also: GROWTH; GUIDANCE AND CARE; NURTURE)
God, Our Father, You Have Led Us, 454
God, Who Stretched the Spangled Heavens, 47
Jesus Was a Loving Teacher, 602
Lord, for the Gift of Children, 508
Lord, Speak to Me, That I May Speak, 568
More About Jesus, 600
Savior, Teach Me Day by Day, 461
Teach Me, O Lord, I Pray, 601
Tell It Out with Gladness, 585
We Praise You with Our Minds, O Lord, 599

ENCOURAGEMENT
(see: COMFORT; COURAGE)

ETERNAL LIFE
(see also: FELLOWSHIP WITH GOD; HEAVEN; JESUS CHRIST-RETURN; SECURITY OF THE BELIEVER)
All That Thrills My Soul, 429
All the Way My Savior Leads Me, 62
Amazing Grace! How Sweet the Sound, 330
As with Gladness Men of Old, 117
Breathe on Me, Breath of God, 241
Christ Is Made the Sure Foundation, 356
Christ Is Risen, 167
Christ the Lord Is Risen Today, 159
Come, Christians, Join to Sing, 231
Come, Thou Almighty King, 247
Come, Thou Long-Expected Jesus, 77
Footsteps of Jesus, 483
Forever with the Lord, 529
Glorious Things of Thee Are Spoken, 398
Great Redeemer, We Adore Thee, 209

He Hideth My Soul, 340
How Great Thou Art, 10
I Am Thine, O Lord, 290
I Know That My Redeemer Liveth, 191
I Saw the Cross of Jesus, 286
I Stand Amazed in the Presence, 547
Jesus, Keep Me Near the Cross, 280
Jesus Paid It All, 134
Lo, He Comes with Clouds Descending, 199
My Faith Looks Up to Thee, 416
Nearer, My God to Thee, 458
O Love That Wilt Not Let Me Go, 292
O That Will Be Glory, 520
On Jordan's Stormy Banks, 521
Saved, Saved, 540
Since I Have Been Redeemed, 543
Sunlight, 444
Sweet Hour of Prayer, 445
The Day of Resurrection, 164
The Solid Rock, 406
There's a Land That Is Fairer than Day, 515
We Welcome Glad Easter, 168
When the Morning Comes, 522
When the Roll Is Called Up Yonder, 516

EVANGELISM
(see also: MISSION; TESTIMONY)
All on the Altar, 326
Bless That Wonderful Name, 236
Brethren, We Have Met to Worship, 379
Christ Receiveth Sinful Men, 563
Down at the Cross, 140
Faith of Our Fathers, 352
Fill the Earth with Music, 614
Go, Tell It on the Mountain, 95
Go Forth and Tell, 596
Go Out and Tell, 657
God, Our Author and Creator, 590
Hark, the Voice of Jesus Calling, 591
He Is Able to Deliver Thee, 24
Here Am I, Send Me, 597
I Love to Tell the Story, 572
I Will Sing of My Redeemer, 575
I'll Tell the World That I'm a Christian, 553
Lead Me to Some Soul Today, 560
Let Others See Jesus in You, 571
Lift High the Cross, 594
Living for Jesus, 282

Lord, Lay Some Soul upon My Heart, 570
Lord, Send a Revival, 468
Lord, Speak to Me, That I May Speak, 568
Make Me a Blessing, 569
Make Me a Channel of Blessing, 564
O God of Prophets, Known of Old, 646
O Zion, Haste, 583
One by One, 561
Pentecostal Power, 242
People Need the Lord, 557
Redeemed (Ada), 531
Redeemed, How I Love to Proclaim It (Redeemed), 544
Rescue the Perishing, 559
Ring the Bells of Heaven, 428
Room at the Cross, 315
Send Forth Your Word, O God, 588
Send Me, O Lord, Send Me, 582
Send the Light, 595
Set My Soul Afire, 573
Share His Love, 567
Sing, Congregation, Sing, 397
So Send I You, 565
Soldiers of Christ, in Truth Arrayed, 574
Take the Name of Jesus with You, 576
Tell It Out with Gladness, 585
Tell the Good News, 566
The Old Ship of Zion, 577
To Worship, Work, and Witness, 389
Tune Your Hearts That All May Hear, 578
Turn Your Eyes upon Jesus, 320
We Have Heard the Joyful Sound (Jesus Saves), 581
We Have Heard the Joyful Sound (Limpsfield), 584
We've a Story to Tell, 586
Word of God, Across the Ages, 262
Ye Servants of God, 589

FAITH AND TRUST
(see also: ASSURANCE; GOD THE FATHER-PROVIDENCE; GUIDANCE AND CARE; HOPE)
Ask Ye What Great Thing I Know, 538
At the Cross, 139
Be Strong in the Lord, 476
Believers All, We Bear the Name, 399
Christ Receiveth Sinful Men, 563

Day by Day, 66
Dear Lord and Father of Mankind, 267
Face to Face with Christ, My Savior, 519
Faith Is the Victory, 413
Faith of Our Fathers, 352
God Moves in a Mysterious Way, 73
Great Is the Lord, 12
Guide Me, O Thou Great Jehovah, 56
Have Faith in God, 405
He Hideth My Soul, 340
Higher Ground, 484
How Firm a Foundation, 338
I Know Whom I Have Believed, 337
I Will Not Be Afraid, 72
I Will Trust in the Lord, 420
If You Will Only Let God Guide You, 57
Leaning on the Everlasting Arms, 333
Like a River Glorious, 58
Lord, Who Across the Ages, 624
Moment by Moment, 415
My Faith Has Found a Resting Place, 412
My Faith Looks Up to Thee, 416
O God of Love, O King of Peace, 619
O God, Our Help in Ages Past, 74
Once to Every Man and Nation, 470
Only Believe, 534
Onward, Christian Soldiers, 493
Stand Up, Stand Up for Jesus (Geibel), 487
Stand Up, Stand Up for Jesus (Webb), 485
'Tis So Sweet to Trust in Jesus, 411
Trusting Jesus, 417
We Give Thee But Thine Own, 609
When the Morning Comes, 522
Wonderful Words of Life, 261

FAMILY OF GOD
(see also: CHURCH)
Blest Be the Tie, 387
Glorious Things of Thee Are Spoken, 398
God, the Father of Your People, 382
How Lovely Is Thy Dwelling Place, 523
In Christ There Is No East or West, 385
In the Family of God, 380

Living Stones, 353
Our God Has Made Us One, 388
The Family of God, 386
The Master Hath Come, 497
When Christ Was Lifted from the Earth, 562

FATHER'S DAY
(see: HOME AND FAMILY)

FELLOWSHIP OF BELIEVERS
(see also: CHURCH)
A Parting Hymn We Sing, 375
Believers All, We Bear the Name, 399
Blest Be the Tie, 387
Christian Hearts, in Love United, 378
Come, We That Love the Lord (Festal Song), 525
God, the Father of Your People, 382
Here, O Lord, Your Servants Gather, 179
I Come with Joy to Meet My Lord, 371
In Christ, Our Liberty, 626
In Christ There Is No East or West, 385
In the Family of God, 380
Living Stones, 353
Our God Has Made Us One, 388
Sing, Congregation, Sing, 397
Sweet, Sweet Spirit, 243
The Bond of Love, 384
The Family of God, 386
The Servant Song, 613
We Are God's People, 383
We Meet Within This Holy Place, 376
We Stand United in the Truth, 625
We're Marching to Zion, 524

FELLOWSHIP WITH GOD
(see also: DISCIPLESHIP; JESUS CHRIST-FRIEND; PRAYER; ETERNAL LIFE)
Abide with Me, 63
All Day Long, 463
Be Thou My Vision, 60
Blessed Assurance, Jesus Is Mine, 334
Children of the Heavenly Father, 55
Christ Is Alive, 173
Close to Thee, 464
Come, We That Love the Lord (Festal Song), 525
Face to Face with Christ, My

GROWTH

(see also: CHURCH; EDUCA-
TION; COMMITMENT AND
CONSECRATION; NURTURE)

All Day Long, 463
Be Thou My Vision, 60
Believers All, We Bear the Name,
399
Breathe on Me, 238
Burn in Me, Fire of God, 496
Eternal God, May We Be Free, 299
Footsteps of Jesus, 483
God, Our Father, You Have Led
Us, 454
God, Who Stretched the Spangled
Heavens, 47
God, Who Touches Earth with
Beauty, 500
Higher Ground, 484
How Lovely Is Thy Dwelling
Place, 523
I Am Thine, O Lord, 290
I Have Come from the Darkness,
532
In His Time, 53
Lord, for the Gift of Children, 508
Lord, I Want to Be a Christian,
489
Lord, Speak to Me, That I May
Speak, 568
Make Me a Captive, Lord, 278
More About Jesus, 600
Open My Eyes, That I May See,
502
Purer in Heart, O God, 492
Savior, Teach Me Day by Day, 461
Soldiers of Christ, in Truth
Arrayed, 574
Spirit, Now Live in Me, 240
Take My Life, Lead Me, Lord, 287
Take Time to Be Holy, 446
This Is a Day of New Beginnings,
370
We Give Thee But Thine Own,
609

GUIDANCE AND CARE

(see also: COMFORT; EDUCA-
TION; FAITH AND TRUST)

All the Way My Savior Leads Me,
62
Amazing Grace! How Sweet the
Sound, 330
Because He Lives, 407
Children of the Heavenly Father,
55
Count Your Blessings, 644
Day by Day, 66
Eternal Father, Strong to Save, 69

God, Our Father, You Have Led
Us, 454
God, Who Made the Earth, 50
God, Who Stretched the Spangled
Heavens, 47
God Will Take Care of You, 64
Great Is Thy Faithfulness, 54
Guide Me, O Thou Great Jehovah,
56
He Leadeth Me! O Blessed
Thought, 52
He Lives, 533
Holy Bible, Book Divine, 260
How Firm a Foundation, 338
I Have Come from the Darkness,
532
I Heard the Voice of Jesus Say, 551
I Must Tell Jesus, 455
I Need Thee Every Hour, 450
I Saw the Cross of Jesus, 286
I Will Not Be Afraid, 72
If You Will Only Let God Guide
You, 57
In Heavenly Love Abiding, 348
Jesus Is the Song, 552
Jesus, Lover of My Soul, 180
Jesus! What a Friend for Sinners,
185
Just a Closer Walk with Thee, 448
Just When I Need Him Most, 65
Like a River Glorious, 58
Moment by Moment, 415
My Faith Has Found a Resting
Place, 412
My Faith Looks Up to Thee, 416
My Lord Is Near Me All the Time,
59
My Shepherd Will Supply My
Need, 68
No, Not One, 181
Now Thank We All Our God, 638
O God, Our Help in Ages Past, 74
O Jesus, I Have Promised, 276
O What a Wonder It Is, 548
On Eagle's Wings, 71
Savior, Like a Shepherd Lead Us,
61
Sunlight, 444
Surely Goodness and Mercy, 422
Tell It to Jesus, 451
The Master Hath Come, 497
The Solid Rock, 406
There Is a Savior, 536
Trust, Try, and Prove Me, 616
Trusting Jesus, 417
What a Friend We Have in Jesus,
182
When the Morning Comes, 522
Without Him, 300

HEAVEN

(see also: ETERNAL LIFE)

Amazing Grace! How Sweet the
Sound, 330
Come, Thou Fount of Every
Blessing (Nettleton), 15
Come, Thou Fount of Every
Blessing (Warrenton), 18
Come, We That Love the Lord
(Festal Song), 525
Come, Ye Disconsolate, 67
Face to Face with Christ, My
Savior, 519
Forever with the Lord, 529
Glorious Things of Thee Are
Spoken, 398
Heaven Came Down, 438
I Know That My Redeemer Liveth,
191
Jerusalem, My Happy Home, 517
Jerusalem, the Golden, 527
My Jesus, I Love Thee, 210
My Savior First of All, 528
On Jordan's Stormy Banks, 521
Ring the Bells of Heaven, 428
Shall We Gather at the River, 518
Since Jesus Came into My Heart,
441
Soon and Very Soon, 192
The Old Rugged Cross, 141
The Way of the Cross Leads
Home, 151
There's a Land That Is Fairer than
Day, 515
We're Marching to Zion, 524
When the Roll Is Called Up
Yonder, 516
When We All Get to Heaven, 514

HOLINESS AND PURITY

(see also: COMMITMENT AND
CONSECRATION)

Breathe on Me, 238
Breathe on Me, Breath of God,
241
Burn in Me, Fire of God, 496
Come, Holy Spirit, 239
God, Who Touches Earth with
Beauty, 500
Jesus, Thy Boundless Love to Me,
123
Let Others See Jesus in You, 571
Lord, Be Glorified, 457
Lord, I Want to Be a Christian,
489
Make Me a Channel of Blessing,
564
Make Room Within My Heart,
O God, 491
Purer in Heart, O God, 492

Search Me, O God, 297
Speak to My Heart, 281
Spirit, Now Live in Me, 240
Take Time to Be Holy, 446
We Are Climbing Jacob's Ladder, 474
We Praise You with Our Minds, O Lord, 599

HOLY SPIRIT
(see also: PRAYER; TRINITY)
Break Thou the Bread of Life, 263
Breathe on Me, 238
Breathe on Me, Breath of God, 241
Burn in Me, Fire of God, 496
Come, Holy Spirit, 239
Come, Holy Spirit, Dove Divine, 364
Come, Thou Almighty King, 247
God, Our Father, We Adore Thee, 248
Greater Is He That Is in Me, 437
Of All the Spirit's Gifts to Me, 442
Pentecostal Power, 242
Revive Us Again, 469
Spirit, Now Live in Me, 240
Spirit of God, Descend upon My Heart, 245
Spirit of the Living God, 244
Sweet, Sweet Spirit, 243
This Joy That I Have, 443
We Praise You with Our Minds, O Lord, 599

HOME AND FAMILY
(see also: CHILDREN'S HYMNS)
God, Give Us Christian Homes, 504
Happy the Home When God Is There, 505
Lord, for the Gift of Children, 508
Lord, Make Our Homes, 511
O God, to Those Who Here Profess, 506
O Lord, May Church and Home Combine, 510
O Perfect Love, 512
Our Savior's Infant Cries Were Heard, 116
Would You Bless Our Homes and Families, 507
Your Love, O God, Has Called Us Here, 509

HOPE
(see also: FAITH AND TRUST)
And Can It Be, 147
Blessed Assurance, Jesus Is Mine, 334
Christ Is Risen, 167

Come, Thou Long-Expected Jesus, 77
Come, Ye Disconsolate, 67
God, Our Father, You Have Led Us, 454
Heaven Came Down, 438
If You Will Only Let God Guide You, 57
I'll Praise My Maker, 35
In the Name of the Lord, 174
Jesus, I My Cross Have Taken, 471
O Christ, Our Hope, Our Heart's Desire, 414
O God, Our Help in Ages Past, 74
Only Believe, 534
Out of My Bondage, Sorrow, and Night, 310
Rejoice, the Lord Is King, 197
Satisfied, 539
The Church's One Foundation, 350
The Solid Rock, 406
Wonderful, Wonderful Jesus, 434
Word of God, Across the Ages, 262

INVITATION-CONSECRATION
(see also: FORGIVENESS; CONFESSION AND REPENTANCE)
Footsteps of Jesus, 483
God, Whose Purpose Is to Kindle, 618
Have Thine Own Way, Lord, 294
Here Am I, Send Me, 597
Higher Ground, 484
I Have Decided to Follow Jesus, 305
I Surrender All, 275
I'll Live for Him, 298
Jesus Is Lord of All, 296
Jesus, Keep Me Near the Cross, 280
Jesus, Thy Boundless Love to Me, 123
Living for Jesus, 282
Lord, Here Am I, 486
Make Room Within My Heart, O God, 491
More Love to Thee, O Christ, 473
O Jesus, I Have Promised, 276
Open My Eyes, That I May See, 502
Purer in Heart, O God, 492
Satisfied with Jesus, 472
Savior, Like a Shepherd Lead Us, 61
Speak to My Heart, 281
Take My Life, and Let It Be Consecrated (Hendon), 277

Take My Life, and Let It Be Consecrated (Yarbrough), 283
Take My Life, Lead Me, Lord, 287
Take Time to Be Holy, 446
Take Up Your Cross, the Savior Said, 494
Thou Didst Leave Thy Throne, 121
'Tis So Sweet to Trust in Jesus, 411
Turn Your Eyes upon Jesus, 320
Where He Leads Me, 288
Wherever He Leads I'll Go, 285

INVITATION-SALVATION
(see also: FORGIVENESS; CONFESSION AND REPENTANCE)
All to Thee, 482
Are You Washed in the Blood, 136
Come, Let Us Reason, 313
Come, Ye Sinners, Poor and Needy, 323
Down at the Cross, 140
Grace Greater than Our Sin, 329
I Have Decided to Follow Jesus, 305
I Hear Thy Welcome Voice, 302
I Surrender All, 275
I'll Live for Him, 298
In Loving-Kindness Jesus Came, 542
Jesus Calls You Now, 319
Jesus Is Tenderly Calling, 316
Just As I Am (Tabernacle), 303
Just As I Am (Woodworth), 307
Let Jesus Come into Your Heart, 311
Lord, I'm Coming Home, 309
Only Trust Him, 317
Out of My Bondage, Sorrow, and Night, 310
Pass Me Not, O Gentle Savior, 308
Room at the Cross, 315
Softly and Tenderly, 312
The Nail-Scarred Hand, 318
The Savior Is Waiting, 321
There Is a Fountain, 142
Turn Your Eyes upon Jesus, 320
Whiter than Snow, 325
"Whosoever Will," 314
Without Him, 300
Ye Must Be Born Again, 322

JESUS CHRIST-ADVENT
Blessed Be the God of Israel, 79
Come, Thou Long-Expected Jesus, 77
Emmanuel, 82
Let All Mortal Flesh Keep Silence, 80
Lo, How a Rose E'er Blooming, 78
O Come, All Ye Faithful, 89

O Come, O Come, Emmanuel, 76
The King of Glory Comes, 127

JESUS CHRIST-ASCENSION
Christ the Lord Is Risen Today, 159
Hail the Day That Sees Him Rise, 165
One Day, 193
Tell the Good News, 566

JESUS CHRIST-BIRTH
Angels, from the Realms of Glory, 94
Angels We Have Heard on High, 100
As with Gladness Men of Old, 117
Away in a Manger, 103
Break Forth, O Beauteous Heavenly Light, 114
Carols Sing, 90
Child in the Manger, 105
Christmas Has Its Cradle, 152
Come, Thou Long-Expected Jesus, 77
Emmanuel, 82
Gentle Mary Laid Her Child, 101
Go, Tell It on the Mountain, 95
Good Christian Men, Rejoice, 96
Hark! The Herald Angels Sing, 88
He Is Born, 112
How Great Our Joy, 108
I Heard the Bells on Christmas Day, 98
Infant Holy, Infant Lowly, 106
It Came upon the Midnight Clear, 93
Joy to the World! The Lord Is Come, 87
Lo, How a Rose E'er Blooming, 78
Love Came Down at Christmas, 109
O Come, All Ye Faithful, 89
O Little Town of Bethlehem, 86
O Sing a Song of Bethlehem, 120
Oh, Come, Little Children, 107
See, to Us a Child Is Born, 104
Silent Night, Holy Night, 91
Sing Hosannas, 97
Sing We Now of Christmas, 111
That Boy-Child of Mary, 110
The Birthday of a King, 102
The First Nowell, 85
Thou Didst Leave Thy Throne, 121
We Three Kings of Orient Are, 113
What Can I Give Him, 610
What Child Is This, 118
Who Is He in Yonder Stall, 124

JESUS CHRIST-BLOOD
Alas, and Did My Savior Bleed (Avon), 145
And Can It Be, 147
Are You Washed in the Blood, 136
At the Cross, 139
Blessed Assurance, Jesus Is Mine, 334
Blessed Be the Name, 206
Blessed Redeemer, 149
Down at the Cross, 140
Free from the Law, O Happy Condition, 332
Grace Greater than Our Sin, 329
I Gave My Life for Thee, 606
I Hear Thy Welcome Voice, 302
I Know a Fount, 155
I Lay My Sins on Jesus, 272
I Will Sing of My Redeemer, 575
Jesus Paid It All, 134
Just As I Am (Tabernacle), 303
Just As I Am (Woodworth), 307
"Man of Sorrows," What a Name, 175
Nothing but the Blood, 135
O for a Thousand Tongues to Sing (Azmon), 216
O Happy Day That Fixed My Choice, 439
Redeemed (Ada), 531
Redeemed, How I Love to Proclaim It (Redeemed), 544
Rock of Ages, Cleft for Me, 342
The Blood Will Never Lose Its Power, 133
The Old Rugged Cross, 141
The Way of the Cross Leads Home, 151
There Is a Fountain, 142
There Is Power in the Blood, 132
'Tis the Church Triumphant Singing, 218
To God Be the Glory, 4
Victory in Jesus, 426
When I Survey the Wondrous Cross, 144
Whiter than Snow, 325
"Whosoever" Meaneth Me, 421

JESUS CHRIST-CROSS
(see also: REDEMPTION; SALVATION)
A Purple Robe, 154
According to Thy Gracious Word, 372
Alas, and Did My Savior Bleed (Avon), 145
All to Thee, 482
And Can It Be, 147

Ask Ye What Great Thing I Know, 538
At Calvary, 138
At the Cross, 139
Behold the Lamb, 233
Beneath the Cross of Jesus, 291
Blessed Redeemer, 149
Christmas Has Its Cradle, 152
Creator of the Universe, 549
Crown Him with Many Crowns, 161
Down at the Cross, 140
Glorious Is Thy Name, 204
Go to Dark Gethsemane, 150
Grace Greater than Our Sin, 329
Have You Been to Calvary, 324
How Great Thou Art, 10
I Am Thine, O Lord, 290
I Gave My Life for Thee, 606
I Hear Thy Welcome Voice, 302
I Know a Fount, 155
I Saw the Cross of Jesus, 286
I Stand Amazed in the Presence, 547
I Will Sing the Wondrous Story (Hyfrydol), 535
I Will Sing the Wondrous Story (Wondrous Story), 537
In the Cross of Christ I Glory, 554
Jesus, Keep Me Near the Cross, 280
Jesus Paid It All, 134
Lead Me to Calvary, 490
Lift High the Cross, 594
Low in the Grave He Lay, 160
"Man of Sorrows," What a Name, 175
Must Jesus Bear the Cross Alone, 475
Name of All Majesty, 207
Not What My Hands Have Done, 339
O Sacred Head, Now Wounded, 137
Oh, How Good Is Christ the Lord, 228
One Day, 193
Rejoice, Ye Pure in Heart, 39
Rock of Ages, Cleft for Me, 342
Room at the Cross, 315
Tell Me the Story of Jesus, 122
The Blood Will Never Lose Its Power, 133
The Nail-Scarred Hand, 318
The Old Rugged Cross, 141
The Strife Is O'er, 172
The Way of the Cross Leads Home, 151
There Is a Fountain, 142
There Is Power in the Blood, 132

This Is the Threefold Truth, 408
'Tis Finished! The Messiah Dies, 148
Victory in Jesus, 426
We Have Heard the Joyful Sound (Jesus Saves), 581
We Have Heard the Joyful Sound (Limpsfield), 584
Were You There, 156
When I Survey the Wondrous Cross, 144
Who Is He in Yonder Stall, 124
Worthy Is the Lamb, 157

JESUS CHRIST-FRIEND
(see also: FELLOWSHIP WITH GOD)
Come, Christians, Join to Sing, 231
Come, Holy Spirit, 239
Heaven Came Down, 438
How Sweet the Name of Jesus Sounds, 453
I Must Tell Jesus, 455
I Want Jesus to Walk with Me, 465
It's So Wonderful, 432
I've Found a Friend, O Such a Friend, 183
Jesus Is All the World to Me, 184
Jesus, My Friend, Is Great, 190
Jesus! What a Friend for Sinners, 185
Just a Closer Walk with Thee, 448
Just When I Need Him Most, 65
Leaning on the Everlasting Arms, 333
No, Not One, 181
Our Savior's Infant Cries Were Heard, 116
People Need the Lord, 557
Satisfied, 539
Satisfied with Jesus, 472
Saved, Saved, 540
Savior, Like a Shepherd Lead Us, 61
Tell It to Jesus, 451
The Lily of the Valley, 189
Walking Along with Jesus, 186
What a Friend We Have in Jesus, 182

JESUS CHRIST-KING
All Glory, Laud, and Honor, 126
Angels, from the Realms of Glory, 94
Angels We Have Heard on High, 100
Child in the Manger, 105

Christ the Lord Is Risen Today, 159
Come, Thou Long-Expected Jesus, 77
Glorious Is Thy Name, 204
His Name Is Wonderful, 203
I Love Thee, 211
Joy to the World! The Lord Is Come, 87
Of the Father's Love Begotten, 251
Rejoice, the Lord Is King, 197
Silent Night, Holy Night, 91
Soon and Very Soon, 192
The First Lord's Day, 162
The First Nowell, 85
This Is the Day the Lord Has Made, 358
We Will Glorify, 213
What If It Were Today, 195

JESUS CHRIST-LIFE AND MINISTRY
I Heard the Voice of Jesus Say, 551
Jesus, Lover of My Soul, 180
Jesus Was a Loving Teacher, 602
Jesus' Hands Were Kind Hands, 477
O Sing a Song of Bethlehem, 120
One Day, 193
Our Savior's Infant Cries Were Heard, 116
Savior, Teach Me Day by Day, 461
Tell Me the Stories of Jesus, 129
Tell Me the Story of Jesus, 122
Tell the Good News, 566
That Boy-Child of Mary, 110
The King of Glory Comes, 127
Thou Didst Leave Thy Throne, 121
Who Is He in Yonder Stall, 124
Wonderful Words of Life, 261

JESUS CHRIST-LORDSHIP
All Hail the Power of Jesus' Name (Coronation), 202
All Hail the Power of Jesus' Name (Diadem), 200
All Hail the Power of Jesus' Name (Miles Lane), 201
All Praise to Thee, 229
At the Name of Jesus, 198
Crown Him with Many Crowns, 161
Have Thine Own Way, Lord, 294
He Is Lord, 178
His Name Is Wonderful, 203
I'd Rather Have Jesus, 550
Jesus Is Lord of All, 296
Living for Jesus, 282
Name of All Majesty, 207

Praise the Lord, the King of Glory, 232
The Church's One Foundation, 350
To Worship, Work, and Witness, 389
Worthy of Worship, 3

JESUS CHRIST-LOVE FOR US
(see also: FORGIVENESS)
Alas, and Did My Savior Bleed (Azmon), 145
And Can It Be, 147
At the Cross, 139
For the Beauty of the Earth, 44
He Lives, 533
I Am His, and He Is Mine, 336
I Hear Thy Welcome Voice, 302
I Love to Tell the Story, 572
I Will Sing of My Redeemer, 575
Immortal Love, Forever Full, 480
In Loving-Kindness Jesus Came, 542
Jesus Is Tenderly Calling, 316
Jesus, Lover of My Soul, 180
Jesus Loves Me, 344
Jesus, the Very Thought of Thee, 225
Jesus, Thy Boundless Love to Me, 123
Jesus Was a Loving Teacher, 602
Just As I Am (Tabernacle), 303
Just As I Am (Woodworth), 307
Love Divine, All Loves Excelling, 208
Love Is the Theme, 545
Love Lifted Me, 546
More About Jesus, 600
No, Not One, 181
Now I Belong to Jesus, 345
O How He Loves You and Me, 146
O Love That Wilt Not Let Me Go, 292
O Sacred Head, Now Wounded, 137
O the Deep, Deep Love of Jesus, 409
Praise Him! Praise Him, 227
Savior, Like a Shepherd Lead Us, 61
Softly and Tenderly, 312
Something for Thee, 607
The Love of Christ Who Died for Me, 268
There Is a Fountain, 142
There Is a Name I Love to Hear, 217
There's a Glad New Song, 431
What Wondrous Love Is This, 143

When Christ Was Lifted from the Earth, 562
When I Survey the Wondrous Cross, 144
Why Do I Sing About Jesus, 541

JESUS CHRIST-NAME
All Hail the Power of Jesus' Name (Coronation), 202
All Hail the Power of Jesus' Name (Diadem), 200
All Hail the Power of Jesus' Name (Miles Lane), 201
All Praise to Thee, 229
Ask Ye What Great Thing I Know, 538
At the Name of Jesus, 198
Bless That Wonderful Name, 236
Blessed Be the Name, 206
Down at the Cross, 140
Emmanuel, 82
Freely, Freely, 273
For All the Saints, 355
Glorious Is Thy Name, 204
He Keeps Me Singing, 425
His Name Is Wonderful, 203
Holy Is His Name, 343
How Majestic Is Your Name, 29
How Sweet the Name of Jesus Sounds, 453
I'll Tell the World That I'm a Christian, 553
In the Name of the Lord, 174
Jesus Is the Sweetest Name I Know, 205
Jesus, Lover of My Soul, 180
"Man of Sorrows," What a Name, 175
Name of All Majesty, 207
O for a Thousand Tongues to Sing, 216
O Sing a Song of Bethlehem, 120
Oh, How I Love Jesus, 217
Praise Him! Praise Him, 227
Take the Name of Jesus with You, 576
The Great Physician, 188
The Solid Rock, 406
There's Something About That Name, 177
We Will Glorify, 213
Wonderful Grace of Jesus, 328

JESUS CHRIST-OUR LOVE FOR HIM
(see also: THANKFULNESS AND THANKSGIVING)
Blessed Redeemer, 149
Majestic Sweetness Sits Enthroned, 219

My Jesus, I Love Thee, 210
Open Our Eyes, Lord, 499
The Old Rugged Cross, 141
We Are Climbing Jacob's Ladder, 474

JESUS CHRIST-RESURRECTION
Alleluia, Alleluia! Give Thanks, 170
Because He Lives, 407
Christ Is Alive, 173
Christ Is Risen, 167
Christ the Lord Is Risen Today, 159
Christmas Has Its Cradle, 152
Crown Him with Many Crowns, 161
Easter People, Raise Your Voices, 360
Go to Dark Gethsemane, 150
Hail the Day That Sees Him Rise, 165
He Is Lord, 178
He Is Risen! He Is Risen, 166
He Lives, 533
I Know That My Redeemer Liveth, 191
Lead Me to Calvary, 490
Look, Ye Saints! The Sight Is Glorious, 169
Low in the Grave He Lay, 160
Oh, How Good Is Christ the Lord, 228
One Day, 193
Rejoice, the Lord Is King, 197
Sound Aloud the Trumpet, 171
The Day of Resurrection, 164
The First Day of the Week, 357
The First Lord's Day, 162
The Strife Is O'er, 172
Thine Is the Glory, 163
This Is the Day the Lord Has Made, 358
This Is the Threefold Truth, 408
Tune Your Hearts That All May Hear, 578
We Welcome Glad Easter, 168
Were You There, 156

JESUS CHRIST-RETURN
(see also: ETERNAL LIFE)
At the Name of Jesus, 198
How Great Thou Art, 10
I Know That My Redeemer Liveth, 191
I'll Tell the World That I'm a Christian, 553
It Is Well with My Soul, 410

Let All Mortal Flesh Keep Silence, 80
Lo, He Comes with Clouds Descending, 199
Look, Ye Saints! The Sight Is Glorious, 169
"Man of Sorrows," What a Name, 175
One Day, 193
Praise Him! Praise Him, 227
Songs of Praise, 235
Soon and Very Soon, 192
The King Is Coming, 194
This Is the Threefold Truth, 408
We Shall Behold Him, 196
We'll Work Till Jesus Comes, 608
What If It Were Today, 195

JESUS CHRIST-SAVIOR
A Purple Robe, 154
According to Thy Gracious Word, 372
Alas, and Did My Savior Bleed (Avon), 145
All That Thrills My Soul, 429
All the Way My Savior Leads Me, 62
Are You Washed in the Blood, 136
Ask Ye What Great Thing I Know, 538
At the Cross, 139
Blessed Be the God of Israel, 79
Blessed Be the Name, 206
Blessed Redeemer, 149
Child in the Manger, 105
Christ Receiveth Sinful Men, 563
Come, Ye Sinners, Poor and Needy, 323
Down at the Cross, 140
Face to Face with Christ, My Savior, 519
Free from the Law, O Happy Condition, 332
Glorious Is Thy Name, 204
Go, Tell It on the Mountain, 95
Good Christian Men, Rejoice, 96
Have You Been to Calvary, 324
He Hideth My Soul, 340
How Great Thou Art, 10
I Am Resolved, 301
I Have Come from the Darkness, 532
I Hear Thy Welcome Voice, 302
I Love Thee, 211
I Saw the Cross of Jesus, 286
I Stand Amazed in the Presence, 547
I Will Sing the Wondrous Story (Hyfrydol), 535

I Will Sing the Wondrous Story
(Wondrous Story), 537
I'll Live for Him, 298
Jesus, Keep Me Near the Cross,
280
Jesus, Lover of My Soul, 180
Jesus, the Very Thought of Thee,
225
Jesus! What a Friend for Sinners,
185
Just As I Am (Tabernacle), 303
Just As I Am (Woodworth), 307
Let Jesus Come into Your Heart,
311
Love Divine, All Loves Excelling,
208
Love Lifted Me, 546
Low in the Grave He Lay, 160
"Man of Sorrows," What a Name,
175
My Jesus, I Love Thee, 210
My Savior First of All, 528
Name of All Majesty, 207
No, Not Despairingly, 270
Not What My Hands Have Done,
339
Nothing but the Blood, 135
O Christ, Our Hope, Our Heart's
Desire, 414
O for a Thousand Tongues to Sing
(Azmon), 216
O How He Loves You and Me, 146
O Sacred Head, Now Wounded,
137
Oh, How I Love Jesus, 217
Only Trust Him, 317
Out of My Bondage, Sorrow, and
Night, 310
Pass Me Not, O Gentle Savior, 308
Praise Him! Praise Him, 227
Praise the Lord, the King of Glory,
232
Redeemed (Ada), 531
Redeemed, How I Love to
Proclaim It (Redeemed), 544
Rejoice, the Lord Is King, 197
Rejoice, Ye Pure in Heart, 39
Rescue the Perishing, 559
Rock of Ages, Cleft for Me, 342
Room at the Cross, 315
Satisfied with Jesus, 472
Saved, Saved, 540
Savior, Like a Shepherd Lead Us,
61
Shine, Jesus, Shine, 579
Since I Have Been Redeemed, 543
Since Jesus Came into My Heart,
441
Softly and Tenderly, 312
The Great Physician, 188

The Nail-Scarred Hand, 318
The Old Rugged Cross, 141
The Savior Is Waiting, 321
The Way of the Cross Leads
Home, 151
There Is a Fountain, 142
There Is a Savior, 536
There Is Power in the Blood, 132
'Tis Finished! The Messiah Dies,
148
To God Be the Glory, 4
Turn Your Eyes upon Jesus, 320
What Wondrous Love Is This, 143
"Whosoever Will," 314
Why Do I Sing About Jesus, 541
Without Him, 300
Your Supper, Lord, Before Us
Spread, 374

**JESUS CHRIST-
TRIUMPHAL ENTRY**
All Glory, Laud, and Honor, 126
Hosanna, Loud Hosanna, 130
In the Name of the Lord, 174
Lift Up Your Heads, 128
Tell Me the Stories of Jesus, 129
The King of Glory Comes, 127

JOY
(see also: PRAISE AND
ADORATION-GOD THE
FATHER; PRAISE AND
ADORATION-JESUS CHRIST;
THANKFULNESS AND
THANKSGIVING; VICTORY)
All the Way My Savior Leads Me,
62
Come, We That Love the Lord
(Festal Song), 525
For the Beauty of the Earth, 44
Good Christian Men, Rejoice, 96
He Included Me, 436
Heavenly Sunlight, 424
How Great Our Joy, 108
I Have Come from the Darkness,
532
In the Presence of the Lord, 440
I've Come to Tell, 222
I've Got Peace Like a River, 418
Jerusalem, My Happy Home, 517
Joy to the World! The Lord Is
Come, 87
Joyful, Joyful, We Adore Thee, 7
Let All the World in Every Corner
Sing, 28
Must Jesus Bear the Cross Alone,
475
My Savior First of All, 528
Now I Belong to Jesus, 345

O Happy Day That Fixed My
Choice, 439
Of All the Spirit's Gifts to Me, 442
Rejoice in the Lord Always, 433
Rejoice, Ye Pure in Heart, 39
Ring the Bells of Heaven, 428
Since Jesus Came into My Heart,
441
Sing, Congregation, Sing, 397
Sunshine in My Soul, 430
Take the Name of Jesus with You,
576
The Day of Resurrection, 164
This Is the Day, 359
This Joy That I Have, 443
We're Marching to Zion, 524

JUDGEMENT
(see: ETERNAL LIFE; JESUS
CHRIST-RETURN)

KINGDOM
(see: CHURCH; JESUS CHRIST-
RETURN)

THE LORD'S DAY
The First Day of the Week, 357
The First Lord's Day, 162
This Is the Day, 359
This Is the Day the Lord Has
Made, 358
We Have Come into His House,
361

LORD'S SUPPER
A Parting Hymn We Sing, 375
According to Thy Gracious Word,
372
As He Gathered at His Table, 369
As We Gather Around the Table,
367
Here, at Your Table, Lord, 368
I Come with Joy to Meet My
Lord, 371
In Remembrance, 365
Jesus, at Your Holy Table, 377
Let Us Break Bread Together, 366
The First Day of the Week, 357
This Is a Day of New Beginnings,
370
This Is the Threefold Truth, 408
We Meet Within This Holy Place,
376
We Worship Round This Table,
373
Your Supper, Lord, Before Us
Spread, 374

LOVE
(see: GOD THE FATHER-LOVE,
MERCY, AND GRACE; GOD
THE FATHER-LOVE FOR US;
JESUS CHRIST-LOVE FOR US)

MAJESTY OF GOD
(see: GOD THE FATHER-
MAJESTY AND POWER)

MARRIAGE
(see: HOME AND FAMILY)

MERCY
(see: GOD THE FATHER-LOVE,
MERCY, AND GRACE)

MINISTRY, CHRISTIAN
(see also: SERVANTHOOD)
A Servant of the Least, 628
Arise, Your Light Is Come, 83
As He Gathered at His Table, 369
As Men of Old Their First Fruits
Brought, 639
Because I Have Been Given Much,
605
Believers All, We Bear the Name,
399
Break Out, O Church of God, 401
Creator God, Creating Still, 51
Footsteps of Jesus, 483
For the Fruit of All Creation, 643
God, Our Father, You Have Led
Us, 454
God of Grace and God of Glory,
395
Hark, the Voice of Jesus Calling,
591
I Come with Joy to Meet My
Lord, 371
In Christ, Our Liberty, 626
Jesu, Jesu, Fill Us with Your Love,
501
Jesus' Hands Were Kind Hands,
477
Let Your Heart Be Broken, 611
Lord, Thy Church on Earth Is
Seeking, 391
Make Me a Blessing, 569
O Day of God, Draw Nigh, 623
O God, We Ask for Strength, 498
O Master, Let Me Walk with Thee,
279
O Praise the Gracious Power, 226
Of All the Spirit's Gifts to Me, 442
Our Savior's Infant Cries Were
Heard, 116
Rise Up, O Men of God, 400

Soldiers of Christ, in Truth
Arrayed, 574
Stir Your Church, O God, Our
Father, 392
The Church of Christ, in Every
Age, 402
The Family of God, 386
The Servant Song, 613
There's a Spirit in the Air, 393
To Worship, Work, and Witness,
389
We Give Thee But Thine Own,
609
When the Church of Jesus, 396

MISSION
(see also: CHURCH; EVANGE-
LISM; TESTIMONY)
Alleluia, Alleluia! Give Thanks,
170
Brethren, We Have Met to
Worship, 379
From All That Dwell Below the
Skies, 13
Go, Tell It on the Mountain, 95
Go Forth and Tell, 596
God, Our Author and Creator, 590
Hark, the Voice of Jesus Calling,
591
Here Am I, Send Me, 597
I Love to Tell the Story, 572
I Will Sing of My Redeemer, 575
Jesus Shall Reign, 587
Lead Me to Some Soul Today, 560
Lord, Thy Church on Earth Is
Seeking, 391
Make Me a Blessing, 569
O God of Love, Enable Me, 580
O Zion, Haste, 583
One by One, 561
People Need the Lord, 557
Rescue the Perishing, 559
Ring the Bells of Heaven, 428
Send Forth Your Word, O God,
588
Send Me, O Lord, Send Me, 582
Send the Light, 595
Set My Soul Afire, 573
Share His Love, 567
Shine, Jesus, Shine, 579
Sing to the Lord of Harvest, 641
So Send I You, 565
Soldiers of Christ, in Truth
Arrayed, 574
Take the Name of Jesus with You,
576
Tell It Out with Gladness, 585
Tell the Good News, 566
The Church of Christ, in Every
Age, 402

There's a Spirit in the Air, 393
Turn Your Eyes upon Jesus, 320
We Have Heard the Joyful Sound
(Jesus Saves), 581
We Have Heard the Joyful Sound
(Limpsfield), 584
We've a Story to Tell, 586
Ye Servants of God, 589

MOTHER'S DAY
(see: HOME AND FAMILY)

NATURE
(see: CREATION)

NURTURE
(see also: EDUCATION;
GROWTH)
Abide with Me, 63
Breathe on Me, Breath of God,
241
Day by Day, 66
God, Who Stretched the Spangled
Heavens, 47
God, Who Touches Earth with
Beauty, 500
God Will Take Care of You, 64
I Will Not Be Afraid, 72
Immortal, Invisible, God Only
Wise, 6
In His Time, 53
Jesus Was a Loving Teacher, 602
Lord, for the Gift of Children, 508
O Lord, May Church and Home
Combine, 510
Open My Eyes, That I May See,
502
Our Savior's Infant Cries Were
Heard, 116
Precious Lord, Take My Hand, 456
Would You Bless Our Homes and
Families, 507

OBEDIENCE
(see: DISCIPLESHIP; COMMIT-
MENT AND CONSECRATION)

ORDINATION
(see: COMMITMENT AND
CONSECRATION; SERVANT-
HOOD)

PALM SUNDAY
(see: JESUS CHRIST-TRIUMPHAL
ENTRY)

PATRIOTISM
(see: CITIZENSHIP, CHRISTIAN)

Blessed Assurance, Jesus Is Mine, 334

Blessed Be the God of Israel, 79

Blessed Be the Name, 206

Break Forth, O Beauteous Heavenly Light, 114

Christ Is Alive, 173

Christ Is Made the Sure Foundation, 356

Christ Is Risen, 167

Christ, We Do All Adore Thee, 647

Come, Christians, Join to Sing, 231

Crown Him with Many Crowns, 161

Fairest Lord Jesus, 176

Father, Son, Holy Spirit, 250

Fill the Earth with Music, 614

For All the Saints, 355

For He Alone Is Worthy, 427

For the Beauty of the Earth, 44

Glorify Thy Name, 249

Glorious Is Thy Name, 204

Great Is the Lord, 12

Great Redeemer, We Adore Thee, 209

Greater Is He That Is in Me, 437

Hail the Day That Sees Him Rise, 165

He Is So Precious to Me, 452

He Keeps Me Singing, 425

Heavenly Hosts in Ceaseless Worship, 40

Heavenly Sunlight, 424

His Name Is Wonderful, 203

Holy Ground, 224

Holy, Holy, 254

Holy Is His Name, 343

Hosanna, Loud Hosanna, 130

How Great Thou Art, 10

How I Love You, 230

How Majestic Is Your Name, 29

How Sweet the Name of Jesus Sounds, 453

I Am His, and He Is Mine, 336

I Love Thee, 211

I Love You, Lord, 212

I Will Sing the Wondrous Story (Hyfrydol), 535

I Will Sing the Wondrous Story (Wondrous Story), 537

I'd Rather Have Jesus, 550

Immortal Love, Forever Full, 480

In the Name of the Lord, 174

Jesus, the Very Thought of Thee, 225

Jesus, Thy Boundless Love to Me, 123

Jesus Is All the World to Me, 184

Jesus Is Lord of All, 296

Jesus Shall Reign, 587

King of Kings, 234

Let All Mortal Flesh Keep Silence, 80

Let Us Break Bread Together, 366

Lift Him Up, 220

Lift Up Your Heads, 128

Look, Ye Saints! The Sight Is Glorious, 169

Love Divine, All Loves Excelling, 208

Majestic Sweetness Sits Enthroned, 219

Majesty, 215

More Love to Thee, O Christ, 473

My Jesus, I Love Thee, 210

My Tribute, 153

Name of All Majesty, 207

O for a Thousand Tongues to Sing (Azmon), 216

O Praise the Gracious Power, 226

O the Deep, Deep Love of Jesus, 409

Oh, How Good Is Christ the Lord, 228

Praise Him! Praise Him, 227

Praise the Lord, the King of Glory, 232

Rejoice in the Lord Always, 433

Rejoice, the Lord Is King, 197

Revive Us Again, 469

Sing Hallelujah to the Lord, 214

Sing Hosannas, 97

The First Lord's Day, 162

The King of Glory Comes, 127

The Strife Is O'er, 172

The Whole World Is Singing, 593

There's a Spirit in the Air, 393

There's Something About That Name, 177

This Is the Day the Lord Has Made, 358

'Tis the Church Triumphant Singing, 218

Tune Your Hearts That All May Hear, 578

We Have Come into His House, 361

We Praise You with Our Minds, O Lord, 599

We Shall Behold Him, 196

We Will Glorify, 213

When in Our Music, God is Glorified, 435

When Morning Gilds the Skies, 221

When We All Get to Heaven, 514

Why Do I Sing About Jesus, 541

Wonderful Grace of Jesus, 328

Wonderful, Wonderful Jesus, 434

Worship the Lord, 115

Worthy Is the Lamb, 157

Worthy of Worship, 3

Ye Servants of God, 589

PRAYER

(see also: FELLOWSHIP WITH GOD; HOLY SPIRIT)

All Praise to You, My God, This Night, 449

Blest Be the Tie, 387

Brethren, We Have Met to Worship, 379

Dear Lord, Lead Me Day by Day, 459

Dear Lord and Father of Mankind, 267

Eternal Father, Strong to Save, 69

Have Faith in God, 405

I Must Tell Jesus, 455

Lord, Speak to Me, That I May Speak, 568

Make Room Within My Heart, O God, 491

My Singing Is a Prayer, 603

Near to the Heart of God, 295

Speak to My Heart, 281

Spirit of God, Descend upon My Heart, 245

Sweet Hour of Prayer, 445

Take Time to Be Holy, 446

Tell It to Jesus, 451

The Lord's Prayer, 462

What a Friend We Have in Jesus, 182

When I Pray, 460

When the Church of Jesus, 396

PRIESTHOOD OF THE BELIEVER

A Servant of the Least, 628

Glorious Things of Thee Are Spoken, 398

In Christ, Our Liberty, 626

We Stand United in the Truth, 625

PROVIDENCE

(see : GOD THE FATHER-PROVIDENCE)

RACE RELATIONS

(see: CITIZENSHIP, CHRISTIAN; FAMILY OF GOD; FELLOWSHIP OF BELIEVERS; SOCIAL CONCERNS)

REDEMPTION

(see also: GOD THE FATHER-
LOVE, MERCY, AND GRACE;
JESUS CHRIST-CROSS;
SALVATION)
Blessed Be the God of Israel, 79
Creator God, Creating Still, 51
He Is Able to Deliver Thee, 24
How Great Thou Art, 10
I Will Sing of My Redeemer, 575
Not What My Hands Have Done,
339
O My Soul, Bless God the Father,
21
Redeemed (Ada), 531
Redeemed, How I Love to
Proclaim It! (Redeemed), 544
Since I Have Been Redeemed, 543
Victory in Jesus, 426
We Praise You, O God, Our
Redeemer, 19

REPENTANCE

(see: CONFESSION AND
REPENTANCE)

RESURRECTION

(see: JESUS CHRIST-
RESURRECTION)

SALVATION

(see also: GOD THE FATHER-
LOVE, MERCY, AND GRACE;
JESUS CHRIST-CROSS;
FORGIVENESS, REDEMPTION)
A Purple Robe, 154
All to Thee, 482
Amazing Grace! How Sweet the
Sound, 330
Are You Washed in the Blood, 136
At Calvary, 138
Free from the Law, O Happy
Condition, 332
Grace Greater than Our Sin, 329
He Included Me, 436
He Is Able to Deliver Thee, 24
I Know Whom I Have Believed,
337
I Will Sing of My Redeemer, 575
Let Jesus Come into Your Heart,
311
Lord, I'm Coming Home, 309
Love Lifted Me, 546
Majestic Sweetness Sits Enthroned,
219
My Lord, I Did Not Choose You,
289
No, Not Despairingly, 270
Nothing but the Blood, 135
Now I Belong to Jesus, 345

O Christ, Our Hope, Our Heart's
Desire, 414
O What a Wonder It Is, 548
Only Trust Him, 317
Rock of Ages, Cleft for Me, 342
Saved, Saved, 540
The Old Ship of Zion, 577
The Savior Is Waiting, 321
The Way of the Cross Leads
Home, 151
There Is Power in the Blood, 132
There's a Glad New Song, 431
This Is the Day the Lord Has
Made, 358
'Tis Finished! The Messiah Dies,
148
When Christ Was Lifted from the
Earth, 562
"Whosoever" Meaneth Me, 421
Ye Must Be Born Again, 322

SCRIPTURES

(see: BIBLE)

SECOND COMING

(see: JESUS CHRIST-RETURN)

SECURITY OF THE BELIEVER

(see also: ASSURANCE; GOD
THE FATHER-PROVIDENCE;
COMFORT; ETERNAL LIFE)
Children of the Heavenly Father,
55
Free from the Law, O Happy
Condition, 332
I Am His, and He Is Mine, 336
I've Found a Friend, O Such a
Friend, 183
Love Lifted Me, 546
"Man of Sorrows," What a Name,
175
Not What My Hands Have Done,
339
Now I Belong to Jesus, 345
O the Deep, Deep Love of Jesus,
409
Redeemed (Ada), 531
Redeemed, How I Love to
Proclaim It (Redeemed), 544
Standing on the Promises, 335
The Old Ship of Zion, 577
Trust, Try, and Prove Me, 616

SERVANTHOOD

(see also: COMMITMENT AND
CONSECRATION; DISCIPLE-
SHIP; MINISTRY, CHRISTIAN;
SERVICE; STEWARDSHIP;
TESTIMONY)
A Servant of the Least, 628

Believers All, We Bear the Name,
399
Let Your Heart Be Broken, 611
Lord, Who Across the Ages, 624
O Day of God, Draw Nigh, 623
O God of Love, Enable Me, 580
O Jesus, I Have Promised, 276
O Master, Let Me Walk with Thee,
279
Teach Me, O Lord, I Pray, 601
The Servant Song, 613
To the Work, 615
We Are Called to Be God's People,
390
We Stand United in the Truth, 625

SERVICE

(see also: SERVANTHOOD;
TESTIMONY)
Arise, Your Light Is Come, 83
Believers All, We Bear the Name,
399
Come, All Christians, Be
Committed, 604
Creator God, Creating Still, 51
For the Fruit of All Creation, 643
God, Our Author and Creator, 590
God, Who Stretched the Spangled
Heavens, 47
Hark, the Voice of Jesus Calling,
591
I Gave My Life for Thee, 606
In Remembrance, 365
Jesu, Jesu, Fill Us with Your Love,
501
Jesus Calls Us O'er the Tumult,
293
Let Your Heart Be Broken, 611
Lord, Speak to Me, That I May
Speak, 568
O Jesus, I Have Promised, 276
O Master, Let Me Walk with Thee,
279
Savior, Teach Me Day by Day, 461
Serve the Lord with Gladness, 495
Stir Your Church, O God, Our
Father, 392
Teach Me, O Lord, I Pray, 601
Thanksgiving/Thanks-living, 642
The Church of Christ, in Every
Age, 402
The Servant Song, 613
There's a Spirit in the Air, 393
To the Work, 615
To Worship, Work, and Witness,
389
We Are Climbing Jacob's Ladder,
474
We Are God's People, 383

We Stand United in the Truth,
625
We'll Work Till Jesus Comes, 608
When the Church of Jesus, 396
Ye Servants of God, 589

SERVICE MUSIC
A Parting Hymn We Sing, 375
Almighty Father, Hear Our Prayer,
656
Amen (Danish), 650
Amen (Dresden), 651
Amen (Threefold 1), 652
Amen (Threefold 2), 653
Amen (Threefold 3), 654
Bless His Holy Name, 22
Christ, We Do All Adore Thee,
647
Doxology, 253 (5, 27, 449)
For Thine Is the Kingdom, 659
Glory Be to the Father, 252
Go Now in Peace, 660
Go Out and Tell, 657
Go with God, 648
God's Son Has Made Me Free, 649
Grace, Love, and Fellowship, 661
Grace, Love, and Peace Abide, 655
Grace to You, 663
Grace to You and Peace, 664
Hear Our Prayer, O Lord, 658
Holy Is the Lord (Schubert), 666
Holy Lord (Dona Nobis Pacem),
622
Let All Mortal Flesh Keep Silence,
80
Praise Ye the Name of the Lord,
665
The Lord Bless You and Keep You,
662
Worship the Lord, 115

SIN
Are You Washed in the Blood, 136
At the Cross, 139
Blessed Be the God of Israel, 79
Christ Receiveth Sinful Men, 563
Come, Let Us Reason, 313
Depth of Mercy, 306
Free from the Law, O Happy
Condition, 332
God Forgave My Sin in Jesus'
Name, 273
Grace Greater than Our Sin, 329
I Am Resolved, 301
I Lay My Sins on Jesus, 272
It Is Well with My Soul, 410
Jesus, Lover of My Soul, 180
Let Jesus Come into Your Heart,
311
No, Not Despairingly, 270

Nothing but the Blood, 135
Out of My Bondage, Sorrow, and
Night, 310
Saved, Saved, 540
Search Me, O God, 297
Send a Great Revival, 466
Softly and Tenderly, 312
The Love of Christ Who Died for
Me, 268
Turn Your Eyes upon Jesus, 320

SOCIAL CONCERNS
(see also: CITIZENSHIP,
CHRISTIAN; PEACE ON EARTH)
Arise, Your Light Is Come, 83
As He Gathered at His table, 369
Because I Have Been Given Much,
605
Believers All, We Bear the Name,
399
Break Out, O Church of God, 401
Christ Is Alive, 173
Come, All Christians, Be
Committed, 604
Eternal God, May We Be Free,
299
For the Fruit of All Creation, 643
God of Grace and God of Glory,
395
God, Our Author and Creator,
590
God, Who Stretched the Spangled
Heavens, 47
God, Whose Purpose Is to Kindle,
618
Hark, the Voice of Jesus Calling,
591
Jesu, Jesu, Fill Us with Your Love,
501
Let Your Heart Be Broken, 611
Lord, Thy Church on Earth Is
Seeking, 391
O Day of God, Draw Nigh, 623
O Praise the Gracious Power, 226
Once to Every Man and Nation,
470
Rise Up, O Men of God, 400
Soldiers of Christ, in Truth
Arrayed, 574
Stir Your Church, O God, Our
Father, 392
Teach Me, O Lord, I Pray, 601
The Church of Christ, in Every
Age, 402
The Servant Song, 613
There's a Spirit in the Air, 393
There's a Wideness in God's
Mercy, 25
To the Work, 615

To Worship, Work, and Witness,
389
We Are Called to Be God's People,
390
We Stand United in the Truth,
625
We Utter Our Cry, 631
When Christ Was Lifted from the
Earth, 562
When the Church of Jesus, 396

STEWARDSHIP
(see also: SERVANTHOOD)
All to Thee, 482
As Men of Old Their First Fruits
Brought, 639
As with Gladness Men of Old, 117
Because I Have Been Given Much,
605
Come, All Christians, Be
Committed, 604
For the Fruit of All Creation, 643
I'm Just a Child, 488
Living for Jesus, 282
Sing to the Lord of Harvest, 641
Something for Thee, 607
Trust, Try, and Prove Me, 616
We Give Thee But Thine Own,
609
What Can I Give Him, 610
When the Church of Jesus, 396
Worship the Lord, 115

SUBMISSION
(see: COMMITMENT AND
CONSECRATION; CONFESSION
AND REPENTANCE; FAITH
AND TRUST)

SURRENDER
(see: COMMITMENT AND
CONSECRATION; CONFESSION
AND REPENTANCE; FAITH
AND TRUST)

TEMPTATION
(see: SIN)

TESTIMONY
(see also: EVANGELISM;
MISSION; SERVANTHOOD;
SERVICE)
A Child of the King, 555
All on the Altar, 326
All That Thrills My Soul, 429
All Things Bright and Beautiful,
46
All to Thee, 482
At Calvary, 138
At the Cross, 139

Because He Lives, 407
Blessed Assurance, Jesus Is Mine, 334
Blessed Be the Name, 206
Christ Receiveth Sinful Men, 563
Close to Thee, 464
Down at the Cross, 140
Forever with the Lord, 529
Forgiven, 341
Go, Tell It on the Mountain, 95
He Included Me, 436
He Is Lord, 178
He Is So Precious to Me, 452
He Lives, 533
Heavenly Sunlight, 424
I Am His, and He Is Mine, 336
I Am Resolved, 301
I Have Come from the Darkness, 532
I Have Decided to Follow Jesus, 305
I Know That My Redeemer Liveth, 191
I Know Whom I Have Believed, 337
I Love Thee, 211
I Love to Tell the Story, 572
I Love You, Lord, 212
I Saw the Cross of Jesus, 286
I Stand Amazed in the Presence, 547
I Will Not Be Afraid, 72
I Will Sing the Wondrous Story (Hyfrydol), 535
I Will Sing the Wondrous Story (Wondrous Story), 537
I Will Trust in the Lord, 420
I'd Rather Have Jesus, 550
I'll Live for Him, 298
I'll Tell the World That I'm a Christian, 553
In Loving-Kindness Jesus Came, 542
It Is Well with My Soul, 410
It's So Wonderful, 432
I've Come to Tell, 222
I've Found a Friend, O Such a Friend, 183
I've Got Peace Like a River, 418
Jesus, I My Cross Have Taken, 471
Jesus Is All the World to Me, 184
Jesus Is Lord of All, 296
Jesus, My Friend, Is Great, 190
Jesus Paid It All, 134
Let Others See Jesus in You, 571
Living for Jesus, 282
Lord, Be Glorified, 457
Love Lifted Me, 546

My Savior First of All, 528
My Singing Is a Prayer, 603
My Tribute, 153
Now I Belong to Jesus, 345
O for a Thousand Tongues to Sing (Azmon), 216
O Happy Day That Fixed My Choice, 439
Oh, How I Love Jesus, 217
Redeemed (Ada), 531
Redeemed, How I Love to Proclaim It (Redeemed), 544
Satisfied with Jesus, 472
Saved, Saved, 540
Share His Love, 567
Since I Have Been Redeemed, 543
Since Jesus Came into My Heart, 441
Sunlight, 444
Sunshine in My Soul, 430
Surely Goodness and Mercy, 422
Tell Out, My Soul, the Greatness of the Lord, 81
The Blood Will Never Lose Its Power, 133
The Lily of the Valley, 189
The Solid Rock, 406
There Is a Savior, 536
There's a Glad New Song, 431
Though I May Speak with Bravest Fire, 423
"Whosoever" Meaneth Me, 421
Why Do I Sing About Jesus, 541
Without Him, 300

THANKFULNESS AND THANKSGIVING
(see also: PRAISE AND ADORA-
TION-GOD THE FATHER;
JESUS CHRIST-OUR LOVE FOR
HIM; PRAISE AND ADORA-
TION-JESUS CHRIST; JOY)
All Praise to You, My God, This Night, 449
As Men of Old Their First Fruits Brought, 639
Because I Have Been Given Much, 605
Come, Ye Thankful People, Come, 637
Count Your Blessings, 644
Doxology, 253 (5, 27, 449)
For the Beauty of the Earth, 44
For the Fruit of All Creation, 643
Let All Things Now Living, 640
My Tribute, 153
Now Thank We All Our God, 638
Praise and Thanksgiving, 645

Praise Him! Praise Him, 227
Sing to the Lord of Harvest, 641
Thanksgiving/Thanks-living, 642
We Gather Together, 636

TITHE
(see: STEWARDSHIP)

TRINITY
(see also: HOLY SPIRIT)
All Creatures of Our God and King, 27
Christ Is Made the Sure Foundation, 356
Come, Thou Almighty King, 247
Creator God, Creating Still, 51
Doxology, 253 (5, 27, 449)
Eternal Father, Strong to Save, 69
Father, I Adore You, 256
Father, Son, Holy Spirit, 250
Glorify Thy Name, 249
Glory Be to the Father, 252
God, Our Father, We Adore Thee, 248
Grace, Love, and Fellowship, 661
Holy, Holy, 254
Holy, Holy, Holy, 2
Holy Is the Lord, 9
Holy Is the Lord (Schubert), 666
Make Room Within My Heart, O God, 491
O God, Almighty Father, 258
Of the Father's Love Begotten, 251
Praise the Father, 257

TRUST
(see: FAITH AND TRUST)

VICTORY
(see also: JOY)
A Mighty Fortress Is Our God, 8
Be Strong in the Lord, 476
Because He Lives, 407
Christ the Lord Is Risen Today, 159
Easter People, Raise Your Voices, 360
Faith Is the Victory, 413
For All the Saints, 355
He Is Risen! He Is Risen, 166
He Leadeth Me! O Blessed Thought, 52
I Will Sing of My Redeemer, 575
Jerusalem, the Golden, 527
Lead On, O King Eternal, 621
Majestic Sweetness Sits Enthroned, 219
Name of All Majesty, 207

Onward, Christian Soldiers, 493
Praise the Lord! Ye Heavens, Adore
  Him, 36
Soon and Very Soon, 192
Stand Up, Stand Up for Jesus
  (Geibel), 487
Stand Up, Stand Up for Jesus
  (Webb), 485
Standing on the Promises, 335
The Day of Resurrection, 164
The Strife Is O'er, 172
There Is Power in the Blood, 132
Thine Is the Glory, 163
This Is the Threefold Truth, 408
'Tis Finished! The Messiah Dies,
  148
'Tis the Church Triumphant
  Singing, 218
To God Be the Glory, 4

Victory in Jesus, 426
We Have Heard the Joyful Sound
  (Jesus Saves), 581
We Have Heard the Joyful Sound
  (Limpsfield), 584
We Praise You, O God, Our
  Redeemer, 19
We Welcome Glad Easter, 168
What If It Were Today, 195
When in Our Music God is
  Glorified, 435
When We All Get to Heaven, 514

VOCATION-CALLING
(see: COMMITMENT AND
  CONSECRATION; DISCIPLE-
  SHIP; MINISTRY, CHRISTIAN;
  SERVANTHOOD)

WITNESSING
(see: EVANGELISM; MISSION)

WORD OF GOD
(see: BIBLE)

WORSHIP
(see: JESUS CHRIST-LORDSHIP;
  PRAISE ANDADORATION-GOD
  THE FATHER; PRAISE AND
  ADORATION-JESUS CHRIST;
  THANKFULNESS AND
  THANKSGIVING)

Authors, Composers, & Sources Index

Abe, Yuji 190
Ackley, Alfred H. (1887-1960) 533
Adams, Sarah F. (1805-1848) 458
Adkins, Donna (1940-) 249
Ahnfelt, Oscar (1813-1882) 66
Akers, Doris (1922-) 243
Alexander, Cecil Frances (1818-1895) 46, 166, 293
Alexander, James W. (1804-1859) 137
Alford, Henry (1810-1871) 637
Alford, Janie (1887-1986) 171
Allen, Chester G. (1838-1878) 227
Allen, David Jonathan 213, 313, 499
Allen, Dennis C. (1952-) 642
Allen, George N. (1812-1877) 456, 475
Allen, Richard (1760-1831) 211
Allen, Tom (1958-) 377
Andrae, Reba Jones (1939-) 578
Andrews, Mark (1875-1939) 32
Angell, Warren M. (1907-) 100
Antes, John (1740-1811) 235
Arne, Thomas A. (1710-1778) 353, 358, 481
Asuncion, Francisca (1927-) 459
Atkins, George 379
Atkinson, Frederick C. (1841-1897) 245

Babcock, Maltbie D. (1858-1901) 43
Bach, Johann Sebastian (1685-1750) 114, 137
Bain, J. L. (c.1860-1925) 523
Baker, Henry (1835-1910) 373, 494
Baker, Henry W. (1821-1877) 251, 619
Baker, Margaret R. (1922-) 593
Baker, Richard D. (1927-) 324, 482
Baker, Theodore (1851-1934) 78, 636, 647
Ball, Diane (1941-) 53
Ballinger, Bruce T. (1945-) 361
Baring-Gould, Sabine (1834-1924) 493
Barnard, Charlotte A. (1830-1869) 602
Barnby, Joseph (1838-1896) 221, 512, 609
Bartlett, E. M. (1885-1941) 426
Bartlett, Jr., E. (Gene) M. (1918-1988) 566, 573
Bateman, Christian H. (1813-1889) 231
Bates, Katharine Lee (1859-1929) 630
Batya, Naomi (1961-) 234
Baughen, Michael A. (1930-) 207
Baxter, Lydia (1809-1874) 576

Beck, John Ness (1930-1987) 486
Beethoven, Ludwig van (1770-1827) 7, 47, 585
Benjamin, Linda L. Stassen (1951-) 214
Bennard, George (1873-1958) 141
Bennett, Sanford F. (1836-1889) 515
Bennett, W. Sterndale (1816-1875) 14
Benson, Louis F. (1855-1930) 120
Bernard of Cluny 527
Bevan, Emma F. (1827-1909) 563
Bigelow, James 582
Bilhorn, Peter P. (1865-1936) 537
Black, James M. (1856-1938) 516
Blakley, Duane (1937-) 508
Blanchard, Ferdinand Q. (1876-1966) 262
Blandy, E. W. 288
Blankenship, Lyle Mark (1943-) 3, 111, 112, 167, 218, 250, 251, 341, 357, 367, 380, 440, 465, 523, 532, 577, 663
Bliss, Philip P. (1838-1876) 175, 261, 314, 332, 410, 575, 606
Boberg, Carl (1859-1940) 10
Bock, Fred (1939-) 383
Bode, John E. (1816-1874) 276
Bohemian Brethren's Kirchengesänge (1566) 20
Bonar, Horatius (1808-1889) 270, 272, 339, 551
Bonner, Carey (1859-1938) 31
Book of Psalms, The (1871) 21
Booth, Josiah (1852-1930) 584
Bork, Lester 626
Borop, Niles A. (1956-) 388
Bourgeois, Louis (1510-1561) 5, 253
Bowman, Norman (1939-) 663
Bowring, John (1792-1872) 554
Bradbury, William B. (1816-1868) 52, 61, 148, 260, 307, 344, 406, 445
Brahms, Johannes (1833-1897) 383
Braman, Barry (1947-) 549
Breck, Carrie E. (1855-1934) 519
Bridgers, Luther B. (1884-1948) 425
Bridges, Matthew (1800-1894) 161
Bridges, Robert (1844-1930) 221
Broadwood, Lucy (1858-1929) 120
Bromehead, Joseph (1747-1826) 517
Brooks, Phillips (1835-1893) 86
Brorson, H. A. (1694-1764) 649

Brown, Ann
  (See Ann Brown Sims)
Brown-LeDoux, Joanne (1956-) 548
Buchanan, Annabel Morris (1888-1983) 371, 510, 517
Buck, Carlton C. (1907-) 510
Budry, Edmond Louis (1854-1932) 163
Buell, Harriet E. (1834-1910) 555
Burroughs, Bob L. (1937-) 166, 511
Burroughs, Esther M. (1937-) 511
Burton, John, Sr. (1773-1822) 260
Butler, A. L. (1933-) 392, 500, 531, 590
Byrne, Mary E. (1880-1931) 60

Calkin, John B. (1827-1905) 98
Cameron, Catherine (1927-) 47
Campbell, Thomas (1777-1844) 147
Capell, Evone Wood (1918-) 264
Carmichael, Ralph (1927-) 321
Carr, Benjamin (1768-1831) 231
Carter, R. Kelso (1849-1928) 335
Cason, Don (1954-) 610
Caswall, Edward (1814-1878) 221, 225
Cennick, John (1718-1755) 199
Challinor, Frederic A. (1866-1952) 129
Chandler, John (1806-1876) 414
Chaplin, Marian Wood (1914-) 239, 532
Chapman, J. Wilbur (1859-1918) 185, 193
Chisholm, Thomas O. (1866-1960) 54, 282
Christian Harmony (1805) (Jeremiah Ingalls) 211
Christian Lyre, The (1831) (Leavitt) 471, 591
Christiansen, Avis M. B. (1895-) 149
Christierson, Frank von (1900-) 639
Christopher, Keith (1958-) 657
Clark, John 305
Clarkson, E. Margaret (1915-) 496, 565
Clay, Crystal Davis (1957-) 454
Clayton, Norman J. (1903-) 345
Clephane, Elizabeth C. (1830-1869) 291
Cloninger, Claire (1942-) 178
Coelho, Terrye
  (See Strom, Terrye Coelho)
Coffin, Henry Sloane (1877-1954) 76
Coggins, Ross C. (1927-) 582

Collection of Psalm and
  Hymn Tunes (1851, Greatorex) 252, 414
Colvin, Thomas Stevenson (1925-) 110, 501
Conder, Josiah (1789-1855) 289
Conkey, Ithamar (1815-1867) 554
Conte, Paolo (1891-1966) 209
Conty, Sophie (1961-) 234
Converse, Charles C. (1832-1918) 182
Cook, George Harrison (1864-1946) 424
Cook, Joseph Simpson (1859-1933) 101
Cooke, Oliver (1873-1945) 155
Cory, Julia B. Cady (1882-1963) 19
Cotterill, Thomas (1779-1823) 165
Courtney, Ragan (1941-) 365
Cowper, William (1731-1800) 73, 142
Cox, Frances E. (1812-1897) 20
Croft, William (1678-1727) 51, 73, 74, 626
Croly, George (1780-1860) 245
Cropper, Margaret B. (1886-1980) 477
Crosby, Fanny J. (1820-1915) 4, 62, 122, 227, 280, 290, 308, 316, 334, 340, 464, 486, 528, 531, 544, 559, 615
Crotch, William (1775-1847) 30, 388, 623
Crouch, Andraé (1945-) 22, 133, 153, 192
Crowell, Grace Noll (1877-1969) 605
Crüger, Johann (1598-1662) 638
Cull, Robert M. (1949-) 499
Cummings, William H. (1831-1915) 88
Cushing, William O. (1823-1902) 428

Dailey, Anderson T. (1927-) 479
Danner, David (1951-) 343, 552, 646
Darwall, John (1731-1789) 197
Davis, Geron L. (1960-) 224
Davis, Katherine K. (1892-1980) 640
Davis, M. Vernon (1934-) 624
Davison, Fannie Estelle (1851-1887) 492
Daw, Carl P., Jr. (1944-) 523, 590
Dayyan, Daniel ben Judah 34
Dell, Michael G. (1959-) 299
DeVenter, Judson W. Van (See Van DeVenter, Judson W.)
Dix, William C. (1837-1898) 117, 118

Doane, William H. (1832-1915) 4, 280, 290, 308, 473, 559, 576, 615
Doddridge, Philip (1702-1751) 439
Dorsey, Thomas A. (1899-) 456
Doudney, Sarah (1841-1926) 497
Doving, Carl (1867-1937) 351
Douglas, Robert F. (1941-) 174
Drakestone, John 18
Draper, William H. (1855-1933) 27
Dubois, F. C. Théodore (1837-1924) 647
Duck, Ruth C. (1947-) 83
Dudley-Smith, Timothy (1926-) 40, 70, 81, 104, 154, 207, 268
Duffield, George, Jr. (1818-1888) 485, 487
Dunbar, C. R. 298
Duncan, David B. (1958-) 580
Dwight, Timothy (1752-1817) 354
Dyke, Henry van (see Van Dyke, Henry)
Dykes, John B. (1823-1876) 2, 69, 116, 225, 498, 505, 506, 551

Edgar, Mary S. (1889-1973) 500
Edmunds, Lidie H. 412
Elliott, Charlotte (1789-1871) 303, 307
Elliott, Emily E. S. (1836-1897) 121
Ellor, James (1819-1899) 200
Elvey, George J. (1816-1893) 161, 601, 628, 637
Emerson, Luther Orlando (1820-1915) 218, 643
English, Tina (1952-) 45
Evans, David (1874-1948) 60, 109, 231, 508
Everest, Charles W. (1814-1877) 494
Everett, Asa B. (1828-1875) 483
Ewing, Alexander C. (1830-1895) 527
Excell, Edwin O. (1851-1921) 330, 543, 644

Faber, Frederick W. (1814-1863) 11, 25, 352
Faircloth, Alta C. (1911-1983) 97
Farjeon, Eleanor (1881-1965) 48
Farquharson, Walter (1936-) 507
Farrell, Bob (1948-) 536
Fawcett, John (1740-1817) 387
Featherston, William R. (1846-1873) 210
Ferguson, John (1941-) 127
Fettke, Thomas Eugene (1941-) 37, 115, 178, 196, 359 476, 579, 661
Fillmore, James H. (1849-1936) 191, 301, 492

Fischer, William G. (1835-1912) 325, 572
Fishel, Donald (1950-) 170
Fisher, Albert C. (1886-1946) 431, 545
Forbis, Wesley L. (1930-) 401, 549, 646, 648
Fosdick, Harry Emerson (1878-1969) 395
Foster, Frederick W. (1760-1835) 378
Foundery Collection (1742) 33
Fox, Baynard L. (1932-1982) 553
Francis of Assisi (1182-1226) 27
Francis, Samuel Trevor (1834-1925) 409
Frazer, George W. (1830-1896) 248
Frazier, F. Philip (1892-1964) 49
Fry, Charles W. (1837-1882) 189
Funk, Joseph (1778-1862) 338

Gabriel, Charles H. (1856-1932) 65, 151, 242, 441, 452, 484, 520, 542, 547, 595
Gaither, Gloria (1942-) 174, 177, 194, 386, 407
Gaither, William J. (1936-) 177, 194, 386, 407
Gannett, William C. (1840-1923) 34
Gardiner, William (1770-1853) 402
Garo Christians 305
Garrett, Leslie N. (1943-) 359
Gaultney, Barbara Fowler (1935-1974) 59
Gauntlett, Henry John (1805-1876) 21, 257, 369
Geibel, Adam (1855-1933) 487
Geistliche Kirchengesäng (1599) 78
Geistliche Kirchengesäng (1623) 27
Genevan Psalter (1551 Edition) 5, 30, 253, 388, 623
Genuine Church Music (1832) (Joseph Funk) 338
Gerhardt, Paul (1607-1676) 123, 137
Gesangbuch der Herzogl, Wittenberg (1784) 130
Giardini, Felice de (1716-1796) 247
Gillard, Richard A. M. (1953-) 613
Gilmore, Joseph H. (1834-1918) 52
Gladden, Washington (1836-1918) 279
Gläser, Carl G. (1784-1829) 11, 216, 268
Good Pasteur, Ralph H. (1923-) 432
Gordon, Adoniram J. (1836-1895) 210
Govan, Ellis (1897-) 72
Grant, Sir Robert (1779-1838) 16

Grape, John T. (1835-1915) 134
Gray, Marie 420, 463
Greatorex, Henry W. (1813-1858) 252, 414
Greatorex, Walter (1877-1949) 81
Green, Fred Pratt (1903-) 357, 396, 402, 408, 435, 442, 643
Green, Joseph F. (1924-) 374
Greiter, Matthäus (1490-1500 or1552) 35
Grieg, Edvard Hagerup (1843-1907) 649
Grotenhuis, Dale (1931-) 222
Groves , Alexander (1842-1909) 263
Gruber, Franz X. (1787-1863) 91
Grundtvig, Nicolai F. S. (1783-1872) 351
Gurney, Dorothy F. (1858-1932) 512

Hall, Elvina M. (1820-1889) 134
Ham, Richard W. (1935-) 653, 654
Hanaoka, Nobuaki (1944-) 190
Hanby, Benjamin Russell (1833-1867) 124
Handel, George Frederick (1685-1759) 87, 163
Hankey, Katherine (1834-1911) 572
Hansen, Fred C. M. (1888-1965) 351
Harkness, Georgia (1891-1974) 585
Harris, John Roy (1891-1987) 209
Harris, Thoro (1873-1955) 391, 409, 429
Harrison, Ralph (1748-1810) 353, 358, 481
Hart, Joseph (1712-1768) 323
Hartsough, Lewis (1828-1919) 302
Hartsough, Palmer (1844-1932) 301
Hassler, Hans Leo (1562-1612) 137
Hastings, Thomas (1784-1872) 67, 219, 342, 453
Hatch, Edwin (1835-1889) 238, 241
Hatton, John (c.1710-1793) 13, 70, 587
Havergal, Frances R. (1836-1879) 58, 277, 283, 568, 606
Hawks, Annie S. (1836-1918) 450
Haydn, Franz Joseph (1732-1809) 262, 390, 398
Haydn, Johann Michael (1737-1806) 16, 589, 631
Hayes, Mark (1953-) 48, 105, 362, 562
Hayford, Jack W. (1934-) 215
Hays, William S. (1837-1907) 189
Heber, Reginald (1783-1826) 2

Hedge, Frederic H. (1805-1890) 8
Helmore, Thomas (1811-1890) 76
Helvering, Sandi Patti (1956-) 174, 536
Hemy, Henri F. (1818-1888) 123, 352
Henderson, Gerald S. 622
Hendrix, John D. (1935-) 663
Herbert, George (1593-1633) 28
Herrington, Leland H. (1941-) 233
Hewitt, Eliza E. (1851-1920) 430, 514, 600
Hine, Stuart W. K. (1899-) 10
Hoffman, Elisha A. (1839-1929) 136, 140, 333, 455, 582
Holden, Oliver (1765-1844) 202
Hopkins, Edward J. (1818-1901) 297
Hopkins, John Henry, Jr. (1820-1891) 113
Hopson, Hal H. (1933-) 171, 423
Houghton, Will H. (1887-1947) 560
How, William W. (1823-1897) 355, 609
Howe, Julia Ward (1819-1910) 633
Hoyle, Richard Birch (1875-1939) 163
Hoyt, May P. (late 19th century) 368
Huber, Jane M. Parker (1926-) 51
Hudson, Ralph E. (1843-1901) 139, 206, 298, 539
Huff, R. G. (1949-) 614
Hugg, George C. (1848-1907) 181
Hughes, John (1873-1932) 56, 395
Hull, Eleanor H. (1860-1935) 60
Hunter, William (1811-1877) 188
Husband, John J. (1760-1825) 469
Hussey, Jennie E. (1874-1958) 490
Hustad, Donald P. (1918-) 124
Hymns Ancient and Modern (1875) 509
Hymns for the Young (1836) 61

Ingalls, Jeremiah (1764-1838) 211
Ingham, Marie 460
Isáis, Juan M. (1926-) 222
Iverson, Daniel (1890-1977) 244

Jabusch, Willard F. (1930-) 127
Jackson, Robert (1840-1914) 241, 278, 363, 496
Jackson, Thomas A. (1931-) 390
James, William M. (1915-) 360
John of Damascus (-c.780) 164
Johnson, J. Rosamond (1873-1954) 627

Page, Anna Laura (1943-) 500
Palestrina, Giovanni P. da (1525-1594) 172
Palmer, Ray (1808-1887) 416
Paris, Twila (1958-) 213
Parker, Alice (1925-) 664
Parker, William H. (1845-1929) 129
Parks, Ralph 319, 382
Patti, Sandi (See Helvering, Sandi Patti)
Peace, Albert L. (1844-1912) 292
Perronet, Edward (1726-1792) 200, 201, 202
Perry, Michael A. (1942-) 257
Peterson, John W. (1921-) 422, 438, 565
Pethel, Stan (1950-) 152
Phelps, Sylvanus D. (1816-1895) 607
Pierpoint, Folliott S. (1835-1917) 44
Plumptre, Edward H. (1821-1891) 39
Pollard, Adelaide A. (1862-1934) 294
Poole, William C. (1875-1949) 65
Post, Marie J. (1919-1990) 645
Pott, Francis (1832-1909) 172
Pounds, Jessie B. (1861-1921) 151, 191
Praetorius, Michael (1571-1621) 78
Prentiss, Elizabeth P. (1818-1878) 473
Price, Charles P. (1920-) 506
Price, Geoffrey 258, 645
Price, Milburn (1938-) 392, 399, 588
Prichard, Rowland H. (1811-1887) 36, 77, 185, 535
Prudentius, Aurelius Clemens (348-413) 251
Psalms of David in Meter, The (1650) 523
Psalmodia Evangelica (1789) (Thomas Williams) 128, 173
Puckett, Martha (1927-) 90
Puckett, Paul E. (1923-) 90
Purifoy, John (1952-) 597

Quinn, James S. J. (1919-) 79

Rader, Paul (1879-1938) 534
Rambo, Joyce Reba (Dottie) (1934-) 196, 233
Rankin, Jeremiah E. (1828-1904) 451
Rawls, R. Maines (1916-) 287
Red, Buryl (1936-) 341, 365, 659
Redhead, Richard (1820-1901) 150
Redner, Lewis H. (1831-1908) 86
Reed, Edith M. G. (1885-1933) 106
Reinagle, Alexander R. (1799-1877) 385, 580

Reno, Delma B. (1916-1981) 232
Renville, Joseph R. (1779-1846) 49
Repository of Sacred Music, Part Second (1813) (Wyeth) 15, 507
Reyes, Gus (1953-) 186
Reynolds, William J. (1920-) 143, 305, 366, 418, 432, 567, 599
Rhodes, Sarah Betts (1829-1904) 50
Richardson, Paul A. (1951-) 369
Rinkart, Martin (1586-1649) 638
Rippon, John (1751-1836) 200, 201, 202, 338
Rist, Johann (1607-1667) 114
Roberts, Daniel C. (1841-1907) 629
Robinson, George W. (1838-1877) 336
Robinson, Robert (1735-1790) 15, 18
Root, George F. (1820-1895) 428, 592
Rosas, Carlos (1939-) 38
Rossetti, Christina G. (1830-1894) 109, 610
Rowe, James (1865-1933) 546
Rowley, Francis H. (1854-1952) 535, 537
Runyan, William M. (1870-1957) 54
Russell, Arthur Tozer (1806-1874) 114,
Russell, Anna B. (1862-1954) 434

Sacred Harp, The (1844) 18, 377, 604, 613
Sacred Melodies (1812) (William Gardiner) 16, 402, 589, 619, 631
Sammis, John H. (1846-1919) 447
Sandell-Berg, Caroline V. (1832-1903) 55, 66
Sankey, Ira D. (1840-1908) 413, 417
Saward, Michael J. (1932-) 362
Sawyer, L. Frank (1946-) 222
Schlesische Volkslieder (1842) 176
Scholfield, Jack P. (1882-1972) 540
Schop, Johann (c.1595-1667) 114
Schrader, Jack (1942-) 408
Schubert, Franz (1797-1828) 666
Schuler, George S. (1882-1973) 569
Schultz, Lawrence Edmond (1965-) 498
Schulz, Johann A.P. (1747-1800) 107
Schulz-Widmar, Russell (1944-) 509

Schumann, Robert A. (1810-1856) 299, 509, 568
Schütz, Johann J. (1640-1690) 20
Schwedler, Johann C. (1672-1730) 538
Schwoebel, David G. (1957-) 397
Scott, Robert Balgarnie Young (1899-1987) 623
Scott, Clara H. (1841-1897) 502
Scriven, Joseph M. (1819-1886) 182
Seabough, Ed E. (1932-) 488
Sears, Edmund H. (1810-1876) 93
Seddon, James Edward (1915-1983) 596
Seiss, Joseph Augustus (1823-1904) 176
Selection of Hymns (1787) (John Rippon) 338
Sellers, Ernest O. (1869-1952) 434
Sewell, Hampton H. (1874-1937) 436
Shea, George Beverly (1909-) 550
Shepherd, Thomas (1665-1739) 475
Sheppard, Franklin L. (1852-1930) 43, 529
Sherlock, Hugh B. (1905-) 391
Sherwin, William F. (1826-1888) 263, 368
Shimada, Katsushiko 190
Showalter, Anthony J. (1858-1924) 333
Shrubsole, William (1760-1806) 201
Shurtleff, Ernest W. (1862-1917) 621
Simmons, Houston (1956-) 443
Sims, Ann Brown (1908-1988) 655
Sims, W. Hines (1907-) 232, 655
Sinclair, Jerry (1943-) 223
Skillings, Otis (1935-) 384
Skoog, A. L. (1856-1934) 66
Slade, Mary B. C. (1826-1882) 483
Sleeper, William T. (1819-1904) 310, 322
Sleeth, Natalie A. (1930-1992) 660
Small, James G. (1817-1888) 183
Smart, Henry T. (1813-1879) 94, 164, 199, 360, 621
Smaw, Helen Sims (1935-) 373
Smith, Alfred B. (1916-) 422
Smith, Deborah D. (1958-) 12
Smith, H. Percy (1825-1898) 279, 364
Smith, Howard E. (1863-1918) 546
Smith, John Stafford (1750-1836) 635
Smith, Michael W. (1957-) 12, 29

Smith, Samuel F. (1808-1895) 634
Smith, Walter Chalmers (1824-1908) 6
Smith, William Farley (1941-) 192
Smyth, Harper G. (1873-1945) 564
Sosa, Nelson A. (1935-) 186
Sosa, Pablo D. (1933-) 167
Southern Harmony (William Walker) (1835) 68, 143, 323
Spaeth, Harriet Reynolds K. (1845-1925) 78
Spafford, Horatio G. (1828-1888) 410
Spohr, Louis (1784-1859) 46
Spratt, Ann B. (1829-) 270
Stainer, Sir John (1840-1901) 118, 512
Stanford, Charles V. (1852-1924) 435
Stanphill, Ira F. (1914-) 315
Starr, Richard 68, 228, 346
Stead, Louisa M.R. (c.1850-1917) 411
Stebbins, George C. (1846-1945) 183, 294, 310, 316, 322, 446
Steele, David Horatio (1950-) 115
Stennett, Samuel (1727-1795) 219, 521
Steuerlein, Johann (1546-1613) 389
Stephens, Wilhelmina D'A. (1889-) 602
Stites, Edgar Page (1836-1921) 417
Stockton, John H. (1813-1877) 140, 188, 317
Stone, Samuel J. (1839-1900) 350
Stowe, Everett M. 179
Stralsund Gesangbuch (1665) 14
Strattner, George C. (1644-1704) 461
Strom, Terrye Coelho (1952-) 256
Sullivan, Arthur S. (1842-1900) 493
Sumner, John B. (1838-1918) 555
Sweney, John R. (1837-1899) 122, 430, 528, 600

Tallis, Thomas (c.1505-1585) 449, 625
Terley, L. W. 265, 628
Teschner, Melchior (1584-1635) 126
Theodulph of Orleans (750-821) 126
Thesaurus Musicus (1744) 634
Thomas, Edith Lowell (1878-1970) 645
Thomas, Eugene 212, 215
Thompson, Will L. (1847-1909) 184, 312
Thomson, Mary Ann (1834-1923) 583

Threlfall, Jennette (1821-1880)
130
Thring, Godfrey (1823-1903)
161
Thrupp, Dorothy A. (1779-
1847) 61
Tindley, Charles A. (1851-1933)
522
Tomes, Aaron (1960-) 230
Toplady, Augustus M. (1740-
1778) 342
Tourjee, Lizzie S. (1858-1913)
25
Towner, Daniel B. (1850-1919)
138, 329, 447
Tredinnick, Nöel 207
Troeger, Thomas H. (1945-)
116, 226
Troutbeck, John (1832-1899)
114
Trueblood, David Elton (1900-)
618
Tucker, Francis Bland (1895-
1984) 229
Tullar, Grant Colfax (1869-
1950) 519

Udulutsch, Irvin M. (1920-) 258

Vail, Silas J. (1818-1884) 464
Van DeVenter, Judson W.
(1855-1939) 275, 444
Van Dyke, Henry (1852-1933) 7
Vaughan Williams, Ralph
(1872-1958) 27, 42, 79, 120,
229, 355, 396, 491, 639
Virginia Harmony (1831) 330
Wade, John Francis (*c.*1710-
1786) 89, 427
Walch, James (1837-1901) 583
Walford, William (1772-1850)
445
Walker, William (1809-1875)
(See *Southern Harmony*)

Wallace, William V. (1812-
1865) 154, 480
Walter, William H. (1825-1893)
83, 525
Walton, James G. (1821-1905)
123, 352
Ward, Samuel A. (1847-1903)
630
Ware, Henry Jr. (1794-1843)
505
Waring, Anna L. (1823-1910)
348
Warner, Anna B. (1820-1915)
344
Warner, Hugh 38, 186
Warren, George W. (1828-
1902) 596, 629
Watts, Isaac (1674-1748) 13, 35,
42, 68, 74, 87, 139, 144, 145,
358, 481, 524, 525, 587
Weaver, Mack 570
Webb, George J. (1803-1887)
485
Webbe, Samuel (1740-1816) 67
Weber, Carl Maria von (1786-
1826) 306
Webster, Joseph P. (1819-1875)
515
Weeden, Winfield S. (1847-
1908) 275, 444
Weissel, George (1590-1635)
128
Wesley, Charles (1707-1788)
33, 77, 88, 147, 148, 159,165,
180, 197, 199, 206, 208, 216,
306, 506, 589
Wesley, John (1703-1791) 35,
123
Wesley, Samuel S. (1810-1876)
272, 350
Wesleyan Sacred Harp (1854)
(William McDonald) 439
Whelpton, George (1847-1930)
658

White, Benjamin F. (1800-
1879) (See *Sacred Harp, The*)
Whitefield, George (1714-1770)
88
Whitfield, Frederick (1829-
1904) 217, 286
Whiting, William (1825-1878)
69
Whitney, Rae E. (1927-) 152,
548
Whittier, John Greenleaf
(1807-
1892) 267, 480
Whittle, Daniel W. (1840-1901)
337, 415, 467
Wilkes, John B. (1785-1869)
235
Williams, Aaron (1731-1776)
354, 400, 401
Williams, Clara T. (1858-1937)
539
Williams, David H. (1919-) 603
Williams, Peter (1722-1796) 56
Williams, Ralph Vaughan (see
Vaughan Williams, Ralph)
Williams, Thomas
(See *Psalmodia Evangelica*)
Williams, William (1717-1791)
56
Willis, Richard Storrs (1819-
1900) 93, 176
Wilson, Emily D. (1865-1942)
514
Wilson, Hugh (1766-1824) 145,
372
Wilson, Ira B. (1880-1950) 569
Wilson, John W. (1905-) 393
Winkworth, Catherine (1827-
1878) 14, 57, 128, 638
Witt, Christian F. (1660-1716)
21, 257, 369
Wolfe, Aaron R. (1821-1902)
375
Wolfe, Irving W. (1903-1977)
264

Wolfe, Lanny L. (1942-) 437
Wood, James H. (1921-) 377,
604, 613
Woolston, C. H. (1856-1927)
592
Work, Frederick J. (1879-1942)
156, 489
Work, John W., Jr. (1872-1925)
95, 156, 489
Work, John W., III, (1901-
1967)
95
Wren, Brian A. (1936-) 173,
370, 371, 393, 562
Wyeth, John (1770-1858) 15,
507 (*Repository of Sacred
Music, Part Second*)

Yamaguchi, Tokuo 179
Yates, John H. (1837-1900) 413
Yeary, Paul 265, 622, 641,
York, Terry W. (1949-) 3, 353,
397, 454, 642
Young, Carlton R. (1926-) 370
Young, Gordon (1919-) 665
Young, John Freeman (1820-
1885) 91
Young, Philip M. (1937-) 625

Zelley, Henry J. (1859-1942)
424
Zinzendorf, Nicolaus L. von
(1700-1760) 378
Zundel, John (1815-1882) 208,
248, 470

Medley Index (Sequenced)*

*If assistance is needed with modulations, consult the chart in the
Minister of Music, Organist, or Pianist Editions.

PRAISE AND ADORATION:
GOD THE SON (2)
Majesty, 215
O for a Thousand Tongues to Sing, 216
Oh, How I Love Jesus, 217

GOD THE HOLY SPIRIT
Breathe on Me, 238
Come, Holy Spirit, 239
Spirit, Now Live in Me, 240

GRACE
Wonderful Grace of Jesus, 328
Grace Greater than Our Sin, 329
Amazing Grace! How Sweet the Sound, 330

THE CHURCH'S MISSION
We Are Called to Be God's People, 390
Lord, Thy Church on Earth Is Seeking, 391
Stir Your Church, 392

FAITH AND HOPE
Have Faith in God, 405
The Solid Rock, 406
Because He Lives, 407

JOY AND TRIUMPH (1)
Heavenly Sunlight, 424
He Keeps Me Singing, 425
Victory in Jesus, 426

JOY AND TRIUMPH (2)
O Happy Day That Fixed MyChoice, 439
In the Presence of the Lord, 440
Since Jesus Came into My Heart, 441

PRAYER AND FELLOWSHIP
WITH GOD (1)
When We Walk with the Lord, 447
Take Time to Be Holy, 446
Sweet Hour of Prayer, 445
Just a Closer Walk with Thee, 448

PRAYER AND FELLOWSHIP
WITH GOD (2)
Tell It to Jesus, 451
He Is So Precious to Me, 452
How Sweet the Name of Jesus Sounds, 453

COMMITMENT (1)
Footsteps of Jesus, 483
Higher Ground, 484
Stand Up, Stand Up for Jesus,   485
Lord, Here Am I, 486

COMMITMENT (2)
The Master Hath Come, 497
O God, We Ask for Strength,   498
Open Our Eyes, Lord, 499 (play in D flat)

LIFE ETERNAL
When We All Get to Heaven,   514
There's a Land That Is Fairer than Day, 515
When the Roll Is Called Up Yonder, 516

TESTIMONY
Redeemed, 531
I Have Come from the Darkness, 532
He Lives, 533

EVANGELISM
People Need the Lord, 557
Rescue the Perishing, 559
Lead Me to Some Soul Today,   560
One by One, 561

MISSIONS
We Have Heard the Joyful Sound, 581
Send Me, O Lord, Send Me, 582
O Zion, Haste, 583

INVITATION/ACCEPTANCE
Jesus Calls You Now, 319
Turn Your Eyes upon Jesus, 320
The Savior Is Waiting, 321
Just a Closer Walk with Thee, 448

Use this space to list additional medleys

Suggested Medleys *(Non-sequenced)* *

PRAISE : GOD THE FATHER
How Majestic Is Your Name, 29
Glorify Thy Name, 249
Stand Up and Bless the Lord, 30
Majesty, 215
This Is My Father's World, 43

CREATION
Praise to the Lord, the Almighty, 14
Everything Was Made by God, 45
Creator God, Creating Still, 51
Creator of the Universe, 549
Fairest Lord Jesus, 176

PROMISES
Great Is Thy Faithfulness, 54
God Is So Good, 23
Standing on the Promises, 335
God Will Take Care of You, 64
Count Your Blessings, 644
My Tribute, 153

PROVIDENCE (1)
Savior, Like a Shepherd Lead Us, 61
All the Way My Savior Leads Me, 62
He Leadeth Me! O Blessed Thought, 52

PROVIDENCE (2)
O God, Our Help in Ages Past, 74
Guide Me, O Thou Great Jehovah, 56
Like a River Glorious, 58

BLOOD OF CHRIST
Nothing But the Blood, 135
I Know a Fount, 155
The Blood Will Never Lose Its Power, 133
And Can It Be, 147
Are You Washed in the Blood, 136

CROSS, SUFFERING, DEATH (1)
Alas, and Did My Savior Bleed, 145
The Old Rugged Cross, 141
"Man of Sorrows," What a Name, 175

CROSS, SUFFERING, DEATH (2)
Blessed Redeemer, 149
Jesus Paid It All, 134
O How He Loves You and Me, 146

CROSS, SUFFERING, DEATH (3)
A Purple Robe, 154
Worthy Is the Lamb, 157
And Can It Be, 147

FRIEND
The Great Physician, 188
The Lily of the Valley, 189
Jesus! What a Friend for Sinners, 185

ADORATION (1)
Holy, Holy, Holy, 2
Alleluia, 223
Holy, Holy, 254

ADORATION (2)
Fairest Lord Jesus, 176
I Love You, Lord, 212
My Jesus, I Love Thee, 210

ADORATION (3)
I've Come to Tell, 222
How I Love You, 230
My Jesus, I Love Thee, 210

PRAISE : GOD THE SON
His Name is Wonderful, 203
How Great Thou Art, 10
Glorify Thy Name, 249

JESUS' NAME (1)
O for a Thousand Tongues to Sing
(AZMON), 216
In the Name of the Lord, 174
Emmanuel, 82
Blessed Be the Name, 206

JESUS' NAME (2)
Oh, How I Love Jesus, 217
There's Something About That Name, 177
Bless That Wonderful Name, 236
Jesus Is the Sweetest Name I Know, 205
Glorious Is Thy Name, 204

JESUS' NAME (3)
All Hail the Power of Jesus' Name, 200
Bless His Holy Name, 22
We Have Come into His House, 361

MAJESTY
Majestic Sweetness, 219
How Majestic Is Your Name, 29
Glorify Thy Name, 249
Majesty, 215

CROSS OF CHRIST
Lift High the Cross, 294
Behold the Lamb, 233
At Calvary, 138
Worthy Is the Lamb, 157
I Will Sing the Wondrous Story
(WONDROUS STORY), 537

GRACE AND ASSURANCE (1)
Blessed Assurance, Jesus Is Mine, 334
I Am His, and He Is Mine, 336
Now I Belong to Jesus, 345

GRACE AND ASSURANCE (2)
Not What My Hands Have Done, 339
Forgiven, 341
Grace Greater than Our Sin (Refrain), 329

BIBLE
How Firm a Foundation, 338
Break Thou the Bread of Life, 263
Send Forth Your Word, 588
Wonderful Words of Life, 261

CHURCH
We Are God's People, 383
Lord, Thy Church on Earth Is Seeking, 391
Break Out, O Church of God, 401
'Tis the Church Triumphant Singing, 218

RETURN OF CHRIST
This Is the Threefold Truth, 408
Soon and Very Soon, 192
We Shall Behold Him, 196
One by One, 561

PRAYER AND FELLOWSHIP WITH GOD
I Must Tell Jesus, 455
I Need Thee Every Hour, 450
Precious Lord, Take My Hand, 456

DEDICATION
Jesus, I My Cross Have Taken, 471
More Love to Thee, O Christ, 473
Must Jesus Bear the Cross Alone, 475
Be Strong in the Lord, 476

COMMITMENT
Am I a Soldier of the Cross, 481
Open Our Eyes, Lord, 499
Jesu, Jesu, Fill Us with Your Love, 501

COURAGE
Stand Up, Stand Up for Jesus (WEBB), 485
Just a Closer Walk with Thee, 448
Be Strong in the Lord, 476
Take the Name of Jesus with You, 576

TESTIMONY
Since I Have Been Redeemed, 543
Redeemed, 531
Redeemed, How I Love to Proclaim It, 544

EVANGELISM AND MISSIONS (1)
Tell the Good News, 566
Set My Soul Afire, 573
Lord, Lay Some Soul upon My Heart, 570

EVANGELISM AND MISSIONS (2)
O Zion, Haste, 583
Jesus Shall Reign, 587
Hark, the Voice of Jesus Calling, 591

Use this space to list additional medleys

TUNE INDEXES

Hymn Keys Index

Key of A minor

O sacred Head, now wounded, 137

Key of A

Be strong in the Lord, 476
God, our Author and Creator, 590
God, the Father of Your people, 382
Lo, He comes with clouds descending, 199
Lord, Thy church on earth is seeking, 391
Once to every man and nation, 470
The King Is Coming, 194

Key of A♭

Alas, and did my Savior bleed (AVON), 145
Amen (DANISH), 650
Are You Washed in the Blood, 136
Arise, your light is come, 83
As with gladness men of old, 117
Because He Lives, 407
Because I have been given much, 605
Blessed Be the Name, 206
Brethren, we have met to worship, 379
Come, Christians, join to sing, 231
Deep in my heart there's a gladness, 541
Down at the cross, 140
God sent His Son, 407
Hail the day that sees Him rise, 165
Happy the home when God is there, 505
Hark, the voice of Jesus calling, 591
Have you been to Jesus, 136
He Keeps Me Singing, 425
Hosanna, loud hosanna, 130
How firm a foundation, 338

I am happy today, 421
I am Thine, O Lord, 290
I come to the garden alone, 187
I love to tell the story, 572
I need Thee every hour, 450
I stand amazed in the presence, 547
I will not be afraid, 72
I will sing of my Redeemer, 575
If you are tired of the load of your sin, 311
Immortal, invisible, God only wise, 6
In remembrance, 365
In the Garden, 187
Is your life a channel of blessing, 564
I've found a friend, O such a friend, 183
I've wandered far away from God, 309
Jesus calls us o'er the tumult, 293
Jesus is all the world to me, 184
Jesus Is the Song, 552
Jesus loves the little children, 592
Leaning on the Everlasting Arms, 333
Let Jesus Come into Your Heart, 311
Let Others See Jesus in You, 571
Lift every voice and sing, 627
Lord, as of old at Pentecost, 242
Lord, I'm Coming Home, 309
Lord Jesus, I long to be perfectly whole, 325
Lord, Send a Revival, 468
Lord, the light of Your love, 579
Lord, who across the ages, 624
Majestic sweetness sits enthroned, 219
Make Me a Channel of Blessing, 564

More about Jesus, 600
Must Jesus bear the cross alone, 475
My faith has found a resting place, 412
My Savior First of All, 528
My Savior is the Lord and King, 552
O day of God, draw nigh, 623
O for a thousand tongues to sing (AZMON), 216
O for a thousand tongues to sing (BLESSED NAME), 206
O God, we ask for strength, 498
O how He loves you and me, 146
O Love that wilt not let me go, 292
O say, can you see, 635
O That Will Be Glory, 520
O the deep, deep love of Jesus, 409
O worship the King, 16
Oh, How I Love Jesus, 217
Open my eyes, that I may see, 502
Out of my bondage, sorrow, and night, 310
Pass me not, O gentle Savior, 308
Pentecostal Power, 242
Precious Lord, take my hand, 456
Redeemed, how I love to proclaim it (REDEEMED), 544
Send a revival, O Christ, my Lord, 468
Shine, Jesus, Shine, 579
Since Jesus Came into My Heart, 441
Soldiers of Christ, in truth arrayed, 574
Sunshine in My Soul, 430
Take the name of Jesus with you, 576
The blood that Jesus shed for me, 133
The Blood Will Never Lose Its Power, 133

The church of Christ, in every age, 402
The Old Ship of Zion, 577
The Star-Spangled Banner, 635
There is a name I love to hear, 217
There is never a day so dreary, 434
There is sunshine in my soul, 430
There's within my heart a melody, 425
'Tis finished! The Messiah dies, 148
'Tis the old ship of Zion, 577
To God be the glory, 4
To worship, work, and witness, 389
We welcome glad Easter, 168
What a fellowship, what a joy divine, 333
What a wonderful change, 441
When all my labors and trials are o'er, 520
When my life work is ended, 528
When the Roll Is Called Up Yonder, 516
When the trumpet of the Lord shall sound, 516
While passing through this world, 571
Whiter Than Snow, 325
Who is He in yonder stall, 124
"Whosoever" Meaneth Me, 421
Why Do I Sing About Jesus, 541
Wonderful, Wonderful Jesus, 434
Your love, O God, has called us here, 509

Key of B♭

All glory, laud, and honor, 126
All hail the power of Jesus' name (DIADEM), 200
All hail the power of Jesus' name (MILES LANE), 201
All That Thrills My Soul, 429
America the Beautiful, 630
Angels, from the realms of glory, 94

Baptized in water, 362
Be not dismayed, 64
Come, we that love the Lord (FESTAL SONG), 525
Face to face with Christ, my Savior, 519
Father, we love You, 249
Glorify Thy Name, 249
God, our Father, we adore Thee, 248
God, who made the earth, 50
God Will Take Care of You, 64
God's Son has made me free, 649
He Included Me, 436
He Is Able to Deliver Thee, 24
He Lives, 533
How can I say thanks, 153
How Great Thou Art, 10
I am resolved, 301
I am so happy in Christ today, 436
I am weak, but Thou art strong, 448
I gave My life for thee, 606
I serve a risen Savior, 533
I was sinking deep in sin, 546
In the cross of Christ I glory, 554
It came upon the midnight clear, 93
I've found a friend who is all to me, 540
Just a Closer Walk with Thee, 448
Love divine, all loves excelling, 208
Love Is the Theme, 545
Love Lifted Me, 546
Majesty, 215
"Man of Sorrows," what a name, 175
Mine eyes have seen the glory, 633
My Tribute, 153
Name of all majesty, 207
O beautiful for spacious skies, 630
O God of love, O King of peace, 619
O God of prophets, known of old, 646

O Lord my God! when I in awesome wonder, 10
O Zion, haste, 583
Of the themes that men have known, 545
On a hill far away, 141
Our Father, which art in heaven, 462
Rescue the perishing, 559
Ring the bells of heaven, 428
Rock of Ages, cleft for me, 342
Saved, Saved, 540
Silent night, holy night, 91
Songs of praise the angels sang, 235
Stand up, stand up for Jesus (WEBB), 485
Standing on the promises, 335
The Bond of Love, 384
The Lord's Prayer, 462
The Old Rugged Cross, 141
There Is Power in the Blood, 132
There shall be showers of blessing, 467
There's a glad new song, 431
There's a wideness in God's mercy, 25
'Tis the grandest theme, 24
We are one in the bond of love, 384
What can I give Him, 610
When morning gilds the skies, 221
Who can cheer the heart like Jesus, 429
Would you be free from the burden of sin, 132

Key of C dorian

Here, O Lord, Your servants gather, 179

Key of C minor

Built on the Rock, 351
I want Jesus to walk with me, 465
Many and great, O God, 49
Sing hallelujah to the Lord, 214

Key of C

A mighty fortress is our God, 8
Amen (DRESDEN), 651
Amen (THREEFOLD 2), 653
Amen (THREEFOLD 3), 654
At Calvary, 138
Child in the manger, 105
Christ is alive, 173
Christ is made the sure
  foundation, 356
Christ the Lord is risen today,
  159
Christ, we do all adore Thee,
  647
Come, ye disconsolate, 67
Coming now to Thee, 466
Creator God, creating still, 51
Dear Lord, lead me day by
  day, 459
Easter people, raise your
  voices, 360
Emmanuel, 82
Eternal Father, strong to save,
  69
Father, Father, You are
  Jehovah, 250
Father, Son, Holy Spirit, 250
For God so loved the world,
  548
Go now in peace, 660
Go out and tell, 657
Go out in peace, 657
God, who touches earth with
  beauty, 500
Great is the Lord, 12
Have faith in God, 405
He is risen! He is risen, 166
He leadeth me! O blessed
  thought, 52
Holy, holy, 254
How Great Our Joy, 108
How I Love You, 230
How Majestic Is Your Name,
  29
I have come from the
  darkness, 532
I know that my Redeemer
  liveth, 191
I'm just a child, 488
In Christ, Our Liberty, 626
Jesus, how I love You, 230
Jesus is coming to earth again,
  195

Jesus is tenderly calling, 316
Jesus is the sweetest name I
  know, 205
Jesus, my Lord and Savior, 186
Lift high the cross, 594
Lord, Here Am I, 486
Low in the grave He lay, 160
Make Me a Blessing, 569
Master, Thou callest, 486
Morning has broken, 48
My Shepherd will supply my
  need, 68
O God, our help in ages past,
  74
O holy Dove of God
  descending, 240
O Lord, our Lord, how
  majestic, 29
O What a Wonder It Is, 548
Out in the highways and
  byways of life, 569
People need the Lord, 557
Rejoice, the Lord is King, 197
Send a Great Revival, 466
Send forth your Word, O God,
  588
Serve the Lord with gladness,
  495
Sing, Congregation, Sing, 397
Sing the wondrous love of
  Jesus, 514
Spirit, Now Live in Me, 240
Spirit of God, descend upon
  my heart, 245
Sweet hour of prayer, 445
Tell me the stories of Jesus,
  129
The day of resurrection, 164
The first day of the week, 357
The Lord bless you and keep
  you, 662
The majesty and glory of Your
  name, 37
The sky shall unfold, 196
There is a fountain, 142
This is the threefold truth, 408
Walking Along with Jesus, 186
We bind ourselves in
  freedom's chains, 626
We praise You, O God, our
  Redeemer, 19
We Shall Behold Him, 196
What If It Were Today, 195

When We All Get to Heaven,
  514
While by the sheep we
  watched, 108
"Whosoever Will," 314
With boldness in your speech,
  397
Wonderful grace of Jesus, 328
Years I spent in vanity and
  pride, 138

Key of D minor

Christmas has its cradle, 152
Grace to you and peace, 664
Let all mortal flesh keep
  silence, 80
O sing a song to God, 38
What wondrous love is this,
  143
When the church of Jesus, 396

Key of D

A purple robe, 154
A Servant of the Least, 628
A wonderful Savior is Jesus,
  340
All things bright and beautiful,
  46
All to Jesus I surrender, 275
Am I a soldier of the cross, 481
And God will raise you up, 71
As we gather around the table,
  367
Believers all, we bear the
  name, 399
Blessed assurance, Jesus is
  mine, 334
Break Thou the bread of life,
  263
Bring your sin to Him and
  confess, 319
Children of God, 479
Children of the heavenly
  Father, 55
Christ Receiveth Sinful Men,
  563
Come, Holy Spirit, Dove
  divine, 364
Come, let us reason, 313
Come, Thou Fount of every
  blessing (WARRENTON), 18
Dear Lord and Father of
  mankind, 267

Break forth, O beauteous heavenly light, 114
Break out, O Church of God, 401
Breathe on Me, 238
Bring ye all the tithes, 616
Come, Holy Spirit, 239
Come, Thou Fount of every blessing (NETTLETON), 15
Count Your Blessings, 644
Crown Him with many crowns, 161
Day by day, 66
Encamped along the hills of light, 413
Fairest Lord Jesus, 176
Faith Is the Victory, 413
Fill the earth with music, 614
Footsteps of Jesus, 483
Free from the law, O happy condition, 332
Freely, Freely, 273
Gloria Patri, 252
Glorious things of thee are spoken, 398
Glory be to the Father, 252
Go forth and tell, 596
Go to dark Gethsemane, 150
Go with God, 648
God forgave my sin in Jesus' name, 273
God, give us Christian homes, 504
God is so good, 23
God of our fathers, 629
God, our Father, You have led us, 454
Great is Thy faithfulness, 54
Great Redeemer, we adore Thee, 209
Have Thine own way, Lord, 294
Have You Been to Calvary, 324
Have you been to the cross, 324
Here, at Your table, Lord, 368
Holy Bible, Book of love, 264
Holy Ground, 224
Holy is the Lord (SCHUBERT), 666
Holy Spirit, breathe on me, 238

I am satisfied with Jesus, 472
I hear the Savior say, 134
I hear Thy welcome voice, 302
I heard the bells on Christmas day, 98
I know not why God's wondrous grace, 337
I love Thee, 211
I love You, Lord, 212
I must tell Jesus, 455
I saw the cross of Jesus, 286
I wandered in the shades of night, 444
I will sing the wondrous story (WONDROUS STORY), 537
Immortal Love, forever full, 480
In the lightning flash across the sky, 59
Jesus, Jesus, Jesus, 177
Jesus, our Lord and King, 363
Jesus Paid It All, 134
Jesus shall reign, 587
Just as I am (TABERNACLE), 303
Just as I am (WOODWORTH), 307
King of my life, I crown Thee now, 490
Lead Me to Calvary, 490
Let us break bread together, 366
Let your heart be broken, 611
Living Stones, 353
Lord, for the gift of children, 508
Lord, I want to be a Christian, 489
May God's grace go before you, 648
My faith looks up to Thee, 416
My Father is rich in houses and lands, 555
My Lord Is Near Me All the Time, 59
No, not despairingly, 270
O God of love, enable me, 580
O Lord, may church and home combine, 510
O Master, let me walk with Thee, 279
O perfect Love, 512
Of the Father's love begotten, 251

Onward, Christian soldiers, 493
Our God has built with living stones, 353
Praise Him, praise Him, all ye little children, 31
Redeemed, (ADA), 531
Satisfied, 539
Satisfied with Jesus, 472
Savior, teach me day by day, 461
Seek ye first, 478
Sing praise to God who reigns above, 20
Sunlight, 444
Surely Goodness and Mercy, 422
Sweetly, Lord, have we heard Thee calling, 483
Take up your cross, the Savior said, 494
Tell me the story of Jesus, 122
The church's one foundation, 350
The great Physician, 188
The strife is o'er, 172
There's Something About That Name, 177
Thine is the glory, 163
This is a day of new beginnings, 370
This is my Father's world, 43
This is the day, 359
To the work, 615
Trials dark on every hand, 522
Trust, Try, and Prove Me, 616
Up Calvary's mountain, 149
We are called to be God's people, 390
We are standing on holy ground, 224
We give Thee But Thine own, 609
We have come into His house, 361
We praise You with our minds, O Lord, 599
We stand united in the truth, 625
Were you there, 156
We've a story to tell, 586
When the Morning Comes, 522

When upon life's billows, 644
Ye Must Be Born Again, 322

Key of F
All day long, 463
All on the altar, 326
All praise to Thee, 229
All to Thee, 482
Alleluia, alleluia! Give thanks, 170
Amen (Threefold 1), 652
Angels we have heard on high, 100
As He gathered at His table, 369
As men of old their first fruits brought, 639
At the name of Jesus, 198
Away in a manger, 103
Blessed Savior, we adore Thee, 204
Blest be the tie, 387
Breathe on me, Breath of God, 241
Burn in me, Fire of God, 496
Carols sing, 90
Christ was born in a distant land, 566
Come, Thou Almighty King, 247
Come, Thou long-expected Jesus, 77
Come, ye thankful people, come, 637
Creator of the universe, 549
Dying with Jesus, by death reckoned mine, 415
Father, I adore You, 256
For the fruit of all creation, 643
For Thine is the kingdom, 659
Glorious Is Thy Name, 204
God, who stretched the spangled heavens, 47
Good Christian men, rejoice, 96
Grace, love, and peace abide, 655
Greater is He that is in me, 437
Guide me, O Thou great Jehovah, 56

Hark! the herald angels sing, 88
Hark to the story angels are telling, 97
Have you failed in your plan, 318
He Is Born, 112
Heaven Came Down, 438
Heavenly Sunlight, 424
His name is Wonderful, 203
Holy Bible, Book divine, 260
Holy, God is holy, 343
Holy Is His Name, 343
Holy Lord (Dona Nobis Pacem), 622
I can hear my Savior calling, 288
I have found a friend in Jesus, 189
I have heard the voice of Jesus, 482
I love Thy kingdom, Lord, 354
I sing the mighty power of God, 42
I'll Live for Him, 298
I'm so glad I'm a part of the family of God, 386
In the Presence of the Lord, 440
Jerusalem, my happy home, 517
Jesus, at Your holy table, 377
Jesus' hands were kind hands, 477
Jesus is Lord of all the earth, 170
Jesus, keep me near the cross, 280
Jesus, lover of my soul, 180
Jesus, my friend, is great, 190
Jesus, Thy boundless love to me, 123
Let all things now living, 640
Like a river glorious, 58
Living for Jesus, 282
Lo, how a Rose e'er blooming, 78
Lord, lay some soul upon my heart, 570
Lord, make our homes so loving, 511
Lord, speak to me, that I may speak, 568

Love came down at Christmas, 109
Mighty, God is Mighty, 343
Moment by Moment, 415
My country, 'tis of thee, 634
My hope is built on nothing less, 406
My Jesus, I love Thee, 210
My life, my love I give to Thee, 298
No, Not One, 181
Now thank we all our God, 638
O Christ, our hope, our heart's desire, 414
O God, Almighty Father, 258
O happy day that fixed my choice, 439
O land of rest, for thee I sigh, 608
O little town of Bethlehem, 86
O soul, are you weary and troubled, 320
O what a wonderful, wonderful day, 438
On Jordan's stormy banks, 521
One by one, 561
Our Savior's infant cries were heard, 116
Praise and thanksgiving, 645
Praise the Lord, the King of glory, 232
Praise the Lord who reigns above, 33
Praise the Lord! ye heavens, adore Him, 36
Praise to the Lord, the Almighty, 14
Rejoice in the Lord always, 433
Rejoice, ye pure in heart, 39
Set my soul afire, 573
Sing Hosannas, 97
Sing them over again to me, 261
Sister, let me be your servant, 613
So send I you, 565
Speak to my heart, 281
Spirit of the living God, 244
Stand up, stand up for Jesus (Geibel), 487

Take my life, and let it be consecrated (Hendon), 277
"Take up thy cross and follow Me," 285
Take time to be holy, 446
Tell the Good News, 566
That boy-child of Mary, 110
The Family of God, 386
The First Lord's Day, 162
The Lily of the Valley, 189
The love of Christ who died for me, 268
The Nail-Scarred Hand, 318
The Savior is waiting, 321
The Servant Song, 613
The Solid Rock, 406
There is a balm in Gilead, 269
There is joy, there is joy, 440
There's a Spirit in the air, 393
There's not a friend like the lowly Jesus, 181
They rolled a stone before the door, 162
This joy that I have, 443
Trust and Obey, 447
Turn Your Eyes upon Jesus, 320
Walking in sunlight, 424
We are God's people, 383
We are travellers on a journey, 613
We meet within this holy place, 376
We utter our cry, 631
We'll Work Till Jesus Comes, 608
What a friend we have in Jesus, 182
When I survey the wondrous cross, 144
When we walk with the Lord, 447
Where He Leads Me, 288
Wherever He Leads I'll Go, 285
Without Him, 300
Wonderful Words of Life, 261
Worthy of worship, 3

Key of G minor

Come, ye sinners, poor and needy, 323
I heard the voice of Jesus say, 551
If you will only let God guide you, 57
King of kings, 234
Look, ye saints! The sight is glorious, 169

Key of G

According to Thy gracious Word, 372
All hail the power of Jesus' name (Coronation), 202
All people that on earth do dwell, 5
All praise to You, my God, this night, 449
All the way my Savior leads me, 62
Alleluia, 223
Almighty Father, hear our prayer, 656
Amazing grace! How sweet the sound, 330
And can it be, 147
Are you weary, are you heavyhearted, 451
Ask ye what great thing I know, 538
Bless that wonderful Name, 236
Blessed be the God of Israel, 79
Christian hearts, in love united, 378
Close to Thee, 464
Come, all Christians, be committed, 604
Come, every soul by sin oppressed, 317
Come, we that love the Lord (Marching to Zion), 524
Doxology, 253, 5
Emptied of His glory, 178
Eternal God, may we be free, 299
Faith of our fathers, 352
For all the saints, 355
For He alone is worthy, 427
For the beauty of the earth, 44

Forgiven, 341
Gentle Mary laid her Child, 101
Go, tell it on the mountain, 95
God of grace and God of glory, 395
God, whose purpose is to kindle, 618
Grace Greater than Our Sin, 329
Grace to you, 663
He is Lord, 178
He Is So Precious to Me, 452
He Lifted Me, 542
Heavenly hosts in ceaseless worship, 40
Higher Ground, 484
Holy is the Lord, 9
How sweet the name of Jesus sounds, 453
I come with joy to meet my Lord, 371
I have a song I love to sing, 543
I heard an old, old story, 426
I must needs go home, 151
I will sing the wondrous story (Hyfrydol), 535
I will trust in the Lord, 420
I'm pressing on the upward way, 484
In loving-kindness Jesus came, 542
In the Family of God, 380
In the little village of Bethlehem, 102
In the Name of the Lord, 174
Infant holy, Infant lowly, 106
It's So Wonderful, 432
I've come to tell, 222
I've got peace like a river, 418
Jesus, I my cross have taken, 471
Jesus, my Lord, will love me forever, 345
Jesus, the very thought of Thee, 225
Jesus was a loving teacher, 602
Jesus! what a friend for sinners, 185
Joyful, joyful, we adore Thee, 7

Metrical Index of Tunes

SM = Short Meter, CM = Common Meter, LM = Long Meter

2.2.2.
DANISH, 650
THREEFOLD 1, 652
THREEFOLD 2, 653
THREEFOLD 3, 654

5.4.5.4.D.
ADELAIDE, 294
SAVIOR, 536

5.5.5.3.D.
BUNESSAN, 105, 362
BUNESSAN, 48 (5.5.5.4.D.)

6.4.6.4.D.
BREAD OF LIFE, 263, 368

6.4.6.4.6.6.6.4.
BETHANY, 458
SOMETHING FOR JESUS, 607

6.5.6.5.D.
AU CLAIR DE LA LUNE, 477
HOLINESS, 446
HOLY IS THE LORD, 666
SCHULZ, 107
WYE VALLEY (ABRIDGED), 198,
  611

6.5.6.5.D. WITH REFRAIN
ST. GERTRUDE, 493
WYE VALLEY, 58, 614

6.6.4.6.6.6.4.
AMERICA, 634
ITALIAN HYMN, 247

6.6.8.6.(S.M.)
DENNIS, 375, 387
FESTAL SONG, 83, 525
HILL, 357
OLD 134TH, 30, 388, 623
ST. ANDREW, 609
ST. THOMAS, 354, 400, 401
TRENTHAM, 241, 278, 363,
  496

6.6.8.6.(S.M.) WITH REFRAIN
LEDOUX, 548
MARCHING TO ZION, 524
MARION, 39, 226
WELCOME VOICE, 302

6.6.8.6.D.(S.M.D.)
DIADEMATA, 161, 601, 628
LEOMINSTER, 339
TERRA PATRIS, 43, 529

7.3.7.3.7.7.7.3.
JESUS SAVES, 581
LIMPSFIELD, 584

7.6.7.6.
JEWELL, 641

7.6.7.6. WITH REFRAIN
BALM IN GILEAD, 269
GO TELL IT, 95
GOTT VATER SEI
  GEPRIESEN, 258
HOLCOMB, 281
NEAR THE CROSS, 280
SOSA, 186

7.6.7.6.D.
ANGEL'S STORY, 276
AURELIA, 272, 350
ELLACOMBE, 130
EWING, 527
LANCASHIRE, 164, 621
NYLAND, 508
PASSION CHORALE, 137
SPOHR, 46
TEMPUS ADEST FLORIDUM,
  101
WEBB, 485
WHITFIELD, 286, 289, 348
WIE LIEBLICH IST DER
  MAIEN, 389

7.6.7.6.D. WITH REFRAIN
GEIBEL, 487
HANKEY, 572

7.7.7.7.
ALETTA, 260
INNOCENTS, 104
LAUDS, 393
MONKLAND, 235
POSEN, 461
SEYMOUR, 306
WOLFE, 264

7.7.7.7. WITH ALLELUIAS
ASCENSION, 165
EASTER HYMN, 159

7.7.7.7. WITH REFRAIN
CHINA, 344
COTTAGE GROVE, 459
GLORIA, 100
MCKAY, 578
NEUMEISTER, 563
TRUSTING JESUS, 417
YARBROUGH, 283

7.7.7.7.D.
EVERLASTING LOVE, 336
MARTYN, 180
ST. GEORGE'S WINDSOR,
  637

7.7.7.7.D. WITH REFRAIN
MENDELSSOHN, 88

7.7.7.7.7.
HENDON, 277, 538

7.7.7.7.7.7.
DIX, 44, 117
REDHEAD 76, 150
TOPLADY, 342

8.4.8.4.8.8.8.4.
AR HYD Y NOS, 218, 643

8.5.8.5.
BUTLER, 500

8.5.8.5. WITH REFRAIN
COMING HOME, 309

PASS ME NOT, 308

8.6.8.6.(C.M.)
ALTAR, 326
ARLINGTON, 353, 358, 481
AVON, 145, 372
AZMON, 11, 216, 268
CORONATION, 202
DIADEM, 200
HAYES, 562
LAND OF REST, 371, 510, 517
MAITLAND, 475
MANOAH, 414
MILES LANE, 201
NEW BRITAIN, 330
O LAND OF REST, 608
ORTONVILLE, 219, 453
SERENITY, 154, 480
ST. AGNES, 116, 225, 498, 505, 506
ST. ANNE, 51, 73, 74, 626
ST. PETER, 385, 580
VERMONT, 603

8.6.8.6.(C.M.) with Refrain
DUNCANNON, 490
EL NATHAN, 337
GOD CARES, 64
HUDSON, 139
LANDÅS, 412
LEILA, 570
MCAFEE, 295
OH, HOW I LOVE JESUS, 217
OLD-TIME POWER, 242
OTHELLO, 543
PROMISED LAND, 521
SPRINGBROOK, 162
STOCKTON, 317
SUNLIGHT IN MY SOUL, 444

8.6.8.6.D.(C.M.D.)
CAROL, 93
CLONMEL, 599
COTHEN, 646
EDGE, 399
FOREST GREEN, 42, 79, 491, 639
KINGSFOLD, 120
MATERNA, 630
NICHOLS, 376
PORTALES, 549
RESIGNATION, 68
TALLIS' ORDINAL, 625

VOX DILECTI, 551

8.6.8.6.D.(C.M.D.) with Refrain
SANKEY, 413

8.7.8.7.
BARNARD, 602
CLOSE TO THEE, 464
GALILEE, 293
RATHBUN, 554
STUTTGART, 21, 257, 369
WELLESLEY, 25

8.7.8.7. with Refrain
CLAY, 454
FACE TO FACE, 519
GLORIOUS NAME, 204
GREAT PHYSICIAN, 188
GREENSLEEVES, 118
HANSON PLACE, 518
HARRIS, 429
HEAVEN, 514
HYFRYDOL, 185
KETCHUM, 541
LORIANN, 482
MY REDEEMER, 575
MY SAVIOR'S LOVE, 547
PRECIOUS NAME, 576
RESTORATION, 323
ROUTH, 472
SATISFIED, 539
SHOWERS OF BLESSING, 467
SURRENDER, 275
TRUST IN JESUS, 411
WARRENTON, 18
WITHOUT HIM, 300
WONDROUS STORY, 537

8.7.8.7.D.
ALL THE WAY, 62
AUSTRIAN HYMN, 262, 390, 398
BEACH SPRING, 377, 604, 613
BEECHER, 208, 248, 470
BRADBURY, 61
CASSELL, 378
CENTRAL, 167
CHARLES, 232
CONVERSE, 182
ELLESDIE, 471, 591
FRIEND, 183
HARRIS, 391, 409

HARWELL, 40
HOLY MANNA, 379, 382, 618
HYFRYDOL, 36, 77, 535
HYMN TO JOY, 7, 47, 585
MADILL, 392
NALL AVENUE, 590
NETTLETON, 15, 507
REDENTORE, 209

8.7.8.7.D. with Refrain
STORY OF JESUS, 122

8.7.8.7.8.7.
CWM RHONDDA, 56, 395
LAUDA ANIMA (Andrews), 32
PICARDY, 80
REGENT SQUARE, 94, 199, 360
UNSER HERRSCHER, 356

8.7.8.7.8.8.7.
MIT FREUDEN ZART, 20
W ZLOBIE LEZY, 106

8.8.8.5.
DESMOND (KUM BA YAH), 319
JACOB'S LADDER, 474

8.8.8.6.
PROCLAMATION, 588
TABERNACLE, 303
YARMOUTH, 577
8.8.8.6. with Refrain
DUNBAR, 298
HE LIFTED ME, 542
SIMPSON, 552

8.8.8.8.(L.M.)
ALLELUIA, 223
CANONBURY, 299, 509, 568
DUKE STREET, 13, 70, 587
GERMANY, 402, 619
GIFT OF LOVE, 423
HAMBURG, 144, 374
MARYTON, 279, 364
MENDON, 574
OLD 100TH, 5
OLD 100TH (ALTERED), 253
OLIVE'S BROW, 148
QUEBEC, 373, 494

TALLIS' CANON, 449
TRURO, 128, 173
TRYGGARE KAN INGEN
  VARA, 55
WALTHAM, 98
WOODWORTH, 307

8.8.8.8.(L.M.) with Refrain
BLESSED NAME, 206
HAPPY DAY, 439
HE LEADETH ME, 52
HIGHER GROUND, 484
RHEA, 566
SOLID ROCK, 406
SWENEY, 600
VENI EMMANUEL, 76

8.8.8.8.D.(L.M.D.)
SWEET HOUR, 445

8.8.8.8.8.8.
MELITA, 69
OLD 113TH, 35
ST. CATHERINE, 123, 352

8.8.8.8.8.8. with Refrain
SAGINA, 147

9.8.9.8.
BEGINNINGS, 370

9.8.9.8. with Refrain
ADA, 531
HANNAH, 191
LEMMEL, 320
REDEEMED, 544
9.9.9.6.
LOIS, 240
WONDERFUL NAME, 236

9.9.9.9. with Refrain
FREELY, FREELY, 273
MOODY, 329
REDEEMER, 149
SWEET BY AND BY, 515

10.6.10.6.
BONNER, 31

10.6.10.6. with Refrain
HARPER MEMORIAL, 181
MCCRAY, 97
RESOLUTION, 301

10.7.10.7. with Refrain
I AM THINE, 290
SCHULER, 569

10.8.10.8. with Refrain
MCCONNELSVILLE, 311
REDEEMING LOVE, 431

10.9.10.9. with Refrain
ORWIGSBURG, 455
SHOWALTER, 333
SUNLIGHT, 424

10.10.10.8.
ASSAM, 305,

10.10.10.8. with Alleluias
SINE NOMINE, 229, 355

10.10.10.10.
BECK, 486,
CRUCIFER, 594
ELLERS, 297
EVENTIDE, 63
MORECAMBE, 245
NATIONAL HYMN, 629
NATIONAL HYMN
  (without trumpets), 596
SLANE, 60
WOODLANDS, 81

10.10.10.10. with Refrain
DELIVERANCE, 24
GLORY SONG, 520
LIVING, 282
WHITTLE, 415

10.10.11.11.
LYONS, 16, 589, 631

10.11.11.11. with Refrain
BINGHAMTON, 555
MACCABEUS, 163

11.8.11.8. with Refrain
KIRKPATRICK, 340
LUBBOCK, 318

11.9.11.9. with Refrain
RING THE BELLS, 428
WASHED IN THE BLOOD,
  136

11.10.11.10.
CONSOLATOR, 67
O PERFECT LOVE, 512

11.10.11.10. with Refrain
CHAPMAN, 193
FAITHFULNESS, 54
O STORE GUD, 10
TIDINGS, 583
TORONTO, 565

11.11. with Refrain
REVIVE US AGAIN, 469
ST. DENIO, 168

11.11.11.10.
I'D RATHER HAVE JESUS, 550
STRENGTH, 476

11.11.11.11.
FOUNDATION, 338
GORDON, 210
I LOVE THEE, 211
KING'S WESTON, 396
MUELLER, 103
PETHEL, 152
ST. DENIO, 6
WORTHY LAMB, 157

11.11.11.11. with Refrain
BLESSINGS, 644
FISCHER, 325
SCALES, 573
TO GOD BE THE GLORY, 4

12.11.12.11.D.
ASH GROVE, 497, 640

12.11.12.12.
KREMSER, 19, 636

Irregular
ACCLAMATIONS, 408
ACKLEY, 533
ADESTE FIDELIS, 89
ADESTE FIDELES (Refrain),
  427
ADORE THEE, 647
ALEXANDRIA, 624
ALL DAY LONG, 463
ALL THE WORLD, 28
ALL TO CHRIST, 134
ALLELUIA NO. 1, 170

ON EAGLE'S WINGS, 71
ONCE FOR ALL, 332
ONE BY ONE, 561
ONLY BELIEVE, 534
OPEN OUR EYES, 499
PARKER, 664
PARKS, 265
PATRICIA, 146
PEACE LIKE A RIVER, 418
PEOPLE NEED THE LORD,
 557
PLAINFIELD, 135
PLANO, 657
POWER IN THE BLOOD, 132
PRAISE YE, 665
PRECIOUS LORD, 456
PRECIOUS TO ME, 452
PROMISED ONE, 127
PROMISES, 335
PURER IN HEART, 492
RAPTURE, 540
RED, 365
REJOICE, 433
RESCUE, 559
REST (ELTON), 267
RESURRECTION, 407
RIDGECREST, 341
ROLL CALL, 516
ROSAS, 38
SAFETY, 546

SALLY TOWNSEND, 597
SALVATIONIST, 189
SCOTT, 502
SECOND COMING, 195
SEMINARY, 605
SEWELL, 436
SHINE, 579
SKILLINGS, 384
SOJOURNER, 465
SOLI DEO GLORIA, 37
SOON AND VERY SOON, 192
SPRING, 50
ST. CHRISTOPHER, 291
ST. LOUIS, 86
ST. MARGARET, 292
ST. THEODULPH, 126
STANPHILL, 315
STASSEN, 214
STEARNS, 663
STILLE NACHT, 91
STORIES OF JESUS, 129
SULLIVAN, 567
SUNSHINE, 430
SURABAJA, 582
SWEETEST NAME, 425
SYMPHONY, 383
TE VENGO, 222
THAT NAME, 177
THE BLOOD, 133
THE FIRST NOWELL, 85

THE LORD'S PRAYER, 659
THIS IS THE DAY, 359
THIS JOY, 443
THOMPSON, 312
THREEFOLD GIFTS, 442
TO THE LIGHT, 532
TOILING ON, 615
TOKYO, 179
TOMES, 230
TRAVIS AVENUE, 466
TRUETT, 238
TRUST AND OBEY, 447
TUCKER, 553
UNAFRAID, 72
VICTORY, 172
VILLE DU HAVRE, 410
WAY OF THE CROSS, 151
WE SHALL BEHOLD HIM, 196
WE WILL GLORIFY, 213
WERE YOU THERE, 156
WHELPTON, 658
WHEN I PRAY, 460
WHO IS HE, 124
WHOLE WORLD, 346
WHOSOEVER, 314
WONDERFUL GRACE, 328
WONDROUS LOVE, 143
WORDS OF LIFE, 261
WORSHIP HIM, 361

Hymn Tune Index

ACCLAMATIONS, Irregular 408

ACKLEY, Irregular 533

ADA, 9.8.9.8. with Refrain 531

ADELAIDE, 5.4.5.4.D. 294

ADESTE FIDELES, Irregular 89

ADESTE FIDELES (Refrain), Irregular 427

ADORE THEE, Irregular 647

ALETTA, 7.7.7.7. 260

ALEXANDRIA, Irregular 624

ALL DAY LONG, Irregular 463

ALL THE WAY, 8.7.8.7.D. 62

ALL THE WORLD, Irregular 28

ALL TO CHRIST, Irregular 134

ALLELUIA, 8.8.8.8.(L.M.) 223

ALLELUIA NO. 1, Irregular 170

ALMIGHTY FATHER, Irregular 656

ALTAR, 8.6.8.6.(C.M.) 326

AMERICA, 6.6.4.6.6.6.4. 634

AMSTERDAM, Irregular 33

ANGEL'S STORY, 7.6.7.6.D. 276

ANTIOCH, Irregular 87

AR HYD Y NOS, 8.4.8.4.8.8.8.4. 218, 643

ARLINGTON, 8.6.8.6.(C.M.) 353, 358, 481

ASCENSION, 7.7.7.7. with Alleluias 165

ASH GROVE, 12.11.12.11.D. 497, 640

ASSAM, 10.10.10.8. 305

ASSURANCE, Irregular 334

AU CLAIR DE LA LUNE, 6.5.6.5.D. 477

AURELIA, 7.6.7.6.D. 272, 350

AUSTRIAN HYMN, 8.7.8.7.D. 262, 390, 398

AVON, 8.6.8.6.(C.M.) 145, 372

AZMON, 8.6.8.6.(C.M.) 11, 216, 268

BAKER, Irregular 593

BALM IN GILEAD, 7.6.7.6. with Refrain 269

BARNARD, 8.7.8.7. 602

BATTLE HYMN, Irregular 633

BE GLORIFIED, Irregular 457

BEACH SPRING, 8.7.8.7.D. 377, 604, 613

BECK, 10.10.10.10. 486

BEECHER, 8.7.8.7.D. 208, 248, 470

BEGINNINGS, 9.8.9.8. 370

BEHOLD THE LAMB, Irregular 233

BENEDICTION, Irregular 662

BETHANY, 6.4.6.4.6.6.6.4. 458

BETHLEHEM SONG, Irregular 90

BINGHAMTON, 10.11.11.11. with Refrain 555

BLANTYRE, Irregular 110

BLESS HIS HOLY NAME, Irregular 22

BLESSED NAME, 8.8.8.8.(L.M.) with Refrain 206

BLESSINGS, 11.11.11.11. with Refrain 644

BLOTT EN DAG, Irregular 66

BONNER, 10.6.10.6. 31

BORN AGAIN, Irregular 322

BRADBURY, 8.7.8.7.D. 61

BREAD OF LIFE, 6.4.6.4.D. 263, 368

BREAK BREAD, Irregular 366

BROTHER JAMES' AIR, Irregular 523

BRYN CALFARIA, Irregular 169

BUNESSAN, 5.5.5.3.D. (5.5.5.4.D.) 48, 105, 362

BURROUGHS, Irregular 511

BUTLER, 8.5.8.5. 500

BY AND BY, Irregular 522

CALLING TODAY, Irregular 316

CALVARY, Irregular 138

CANDICE CHRISTOPHER, Irregular 45

CANE PEAK, Irregular 661

CANONBURY, 8.8.8.8.(L.M.) 299, 509, 568

CARMICHAEL, Irregular 321

CAROL, 8.6.8.6.D.(C.M.D.) 93

CASSELL, 8.7.8.7.D. 378

CASTLE, Irregular 610

CENTRAL, 8.7.8.7.D. 167

CHAPLIN, Irregular 239

CHAPMAN, 11.10.11.10. with Refrain 193

CHARLES, 8.7.8.7.D. 232

CHEREPONI, Irregular 501

CHILDREN, Irregular 592

CHILDREN OF GOD, Irregular 479

CHINA, 7.7.7.7. with Refrain 344

CHRIST AROSE, Irregular 160

CHRISTIAN HOME, Irregular 504

CLAY, 8.7.8.7. with Refrain 454

CLEANSING FOUNTAIN, Irregular 142

CLONMEL, 8.6.8.6.D.(C.M.D.) 599

CLOSE TO THEE, 8.7.8.7. 464

CLOSER WALK, Irregular 448

COBBS, Irregular 432

COLEMAN, Irregular 571

COME, LET US REASON, Irregular 313

COMING HOME, 8.5.8.5. with Refrain 309

CONSOLATOR, 11.10.11.10. 67

CONVERSE, 8.7.8.7.D. 182

CORONATION, 8.6.8.6.(C.M.) 202

COTHEN, 8.6.8.6.D.(C.M.D.) 646

COTTAGE GROVE, 7.7.7.7. with Refrain 459

CRUCIFER, 10.10.10.10. 594

CRUSADERS' HYMN (ST. ELIZABETH), Irregular 176

CWM RHONDDA, 8.7.8.7.8.7. 56, 395

DANISH, 2.2.2. 650

DARWALL, Irregular 197

DAYTON, Irregular 451

DELIVERANCE, 10.10.10.10. with Refrain 24

DENNIS, 6.6.8.6.(S.M.) 375, 387

DESMOND (KUM BA YAH),
8.8.8.5. 319
DIADEM, 8.6.8.6.(C.M.) 200
DIADEMATA,
6.6.8.6.D.(S.M.D.) 161, 601,
628
DIVINUM MYSTERIUM,
Irregular 251
DIX, 7.7.7.7.7.7. 44, 117
DONA NOBIS PACEM,
Irregular 622
DRESDEN, Irregular 651
DUKE STREET, 8.8.8.8.(L.M.)
13, 70, 587
DUNBAR, 8.8.8.6. with Refrain
298
DUNCANNON, 8.6.8.6.(C.M.)
with Refrain 490

EASTER HYMN, 7.7.7.7. with
Alleluias 159
EDGE, 8.6.8.6.D.(C.M.D.) 399
EIN' FESTE BURG, Irregular 8
EL NATHAN, 8.6.8.6.(C.M.)
with Refrain 337
ELIZABETH, Irregular 184
ELLACOMBE, 7.6.7.6.D. 130
ELLERS, 10.10.10.10. 297
ELLESDIE, 8.7.8.7.D. 471, 591
ELLSWORTH, Irregular 345
ENGELBERG, Irregular 435
ERMUNTRE DICH MEIN
SCHWACHER, Irregular 114
ES IST EIN ROS', Irregular 78
EUCLID, Irregular 564
EVENTIDE, 10.10.10.10. 63
EVERLASTING LOVE,
7.7.7.7.D. 336
EWING, 7.6.7.6.D. 527

FACE TO FACE, 8.7.8.7. with
Refrain 519
FAITHFULNESS, 11.10.11.10.
with Refrain 54
FALLS CREEK, Irregular 285
FAMILY, Irregular 380
FAMILY OF GOD, Irregular
386
FESTAL SONG, 6.6.8.6.(S.M.)
83, 525
FISCHER, 11.11.11.11. with
Refrain 325
FISHER, Irregular 545

FOOTSTEPS, Irregular 483
FOREST GREEN,
8.6.8.6.D.(C.M.D.) 42, 79,
491, 639
FOREST PARK, Irregular 59
FOUNDATION, 11.11.11.11.
338
FREE, Irregular 649
FREELY, FREELY, 9.9.9.9. with
Refrain 273
FRENCH CAROL, Irregular 111
FRIEND, 8.7.8.7.D. 183

GABRIEL, Irregular 65
GALILEE, 8.7.8.7. 293
GARDEN, Irregular 187
GARTAN, Irregular 109
GEIBEL, 7.6.7.6.D. with
Refrain 487
GERMANY, 8.8.8.8.(L.M.) 402,
619
GIFT OF LOVE, 8.8.8.8.(L.M.)
423
GIVING, Irregular 616
GLORIA, 7.7.7.7. with Refrain
100
GLORIA PATRI (Greatorex),
Irregular 252
GLORIFY THY NAME,
Irregular 249
GLORIOUS NAME, 8.7.8.7.
with Refrain 204
GLORY SONG, 10.10.10.10.
with Refrain 520
GLORY TO HIS NAME,
Irregular 140
GO NOW IN PEACE, Irregular
660
GO TELL IT, 7.6.7.6. with
Refrain 95
GO WITH GOD, Irregular 648
GOD CARES, 8.6.8.6.(C.M.)
with Refrain 64
GOD IS SO GOOD, Irregular
23
GOODNESS, Irregular 422
GORDON, 11.11.11.11. 210
GOTT VATER SEI GEPRIESEN,
7.6.7.6. with Refrain 258
GREAT IS THE LORD, Irregular
12
GREAT PHYSICIAN, 8.7.8.7.
with Refrain 188

GREATER IS HE, Irregular 437
GREENSLEEVES, 8.7.8.7. with
Refrain 118

HALLELUJAH, WHAT A
SAVIOR!, Irregular 175
HAMBURG, 8.8.8.8.(L.M.) 144,
374
HANKEY, 7.6.7.6.D. with
Refrain 572
HANNAH, 9.8.9.8. with
Refrain 191
HANSON PLACE, 8.7.8.7. with
Refrain 518
HAPPY DAY, 8.8.8.8.(L.M.)
with Refrain 439
HARPER MEMORIAL,
10.6.10.6. with Refrain 181
HARRIS, 8.7.8.7.D. 391, 409
HARRIS, 8.7.8.7. with Refrain
429
HARTFORD, Irregular 426
HARWELL, 8.7.8.7.D. 40
HAYES, 8.6.8.6.(C.M.) 562
HE IS LORD, Irregular 178
HE IS RISEN, Irregular 166
HE LEADETH ME,
8.8.8.8.(L.M.) with Refrain
52
HE LIFTED ME, 8.8.8.6. with
Refrain 542
HEAVEN, 8.7.8.7. with Refrain
514
HEAVEN CAME DOWN,
Irregular 438
HENDON, 7.7.7.7.7. 277, 538
HICKS, Irregular 343
HIGHER GROUND,
8.8.8.8.(L.M.) with Refrain
484
HILL, 6.6.8.6.(S.M.) 357
HOLCOMB, 7.6.7.6. with
Refrain 281
HOLINESS, 6.5.6.5.D. 446
HOLY GROUND, Irregular 224
HOLY, HOLY, Irregular 254
HOLY IS THE LORD,
6.5.6.5.D. 666
HOLY MANNA, 8.7.8.7.D.
379, 382, 618
HOW MAJESTIC, Irregular 29
HUDSON, 8.6.8.6.(C.M.) with
Refrain 139

HYFRYDOL, 8.7.8.7.D. 36, 77, 535
HYFRYDOL, 8.7.8.7. with Refrain 185
HYMN TO JOY, 8.7.8.7.D. 7, 47, 585

I AM THINE, 10.7.10.7. with Refrain 290
I KNOW A FOUNT, Irregular 155
I LOVE THEE, 11.11.11.11. 211
I LOVE YOU, LORD, Irregular 212
I SHALL KNOW HIM, Irregular 528
I WANT TO BE A CHRISTIAN, Irregular 489
I WILL TRUST, Irregular 420
I'D RATHER HAVE JESUS, 11.11.11.10. 550
IL EST NÉ, Irregular 112
IN DULCI JUBILO, Irregular 96
IN HIS TIME, Irregular 53
INNOCENTS, 7.7.7.7. 104
ITALIAN HYMN, 6.6.4.6.6.6.4. 247
IVERSON, Irregular 244

JACKSON, Irregular 250
JACOB'S LADDER, 8.8.8.5. 474
JANICE, Irregular 115
JESUS, I COME, Irregular 310
JESUS SAVES, 7.3.7.3.7.7.7.3. 581
JEWELL, 7.6.7.6. 641
JOYFUL SONG, Irregular 227
JUBILATE, Irregular 9
JUDSON, Irregular 3
JÜNGST, Irregular 108

KANTO, Irregular 190
KEDRON, Irregular 270
KENOSIS, Irregular 606
KETCHUM, 8.7.8.7. with Refrain 541
KING IS COMING, Irregular 194
KING OF KINGS, Irregular 234
KINGS OF ORIENT, Irregular 113

KING'S WESTON, 11.11.11.11. 396
KINGSFOLD, 8.6.8.6.D.(C.M.D.) 120
KIRKEN, Irregular 351
KIRKLAND, Irregular 488
KIRKPATRICK, 11.8.11.8. with Refrain 340
KNEEL, Irregular 440
KREMSER, 12.11.12.12. 19, 636

LACQUIPARLE, Irregular 49
LAFFERTY, Irregular 478
LANCASHIRE, 7.6.7.6.D. 164, 621
LAND OF REST, 8.6.8.6.(C.M.) 371, 510, 517
LAND_S, 8.6.8.6.(C.M.) with Refrain 412
LANGLEY, Irregular 287
LASST UNS ERFREUEN, Irregular 27
LAUDA ANIMA (Andrews), 8.7.8.7.8.7. 32
LAUDES DOMINI, Irregular 221
LAUDÅS, 7.7.7.7. 393
LEAD ME, Irregular 560
LEDOUX, 6.6.8.6. (S.M.) with Refrain 548
LEE, Irregular 495
LEILA, 8.6.8.6.(C.M.) with Refrain 570
LEMMEL, 9.8.9.8. with Refrain 320
LEOMINSTER, 6.6.8.6.D.(S.M.D.) 339
LEONI, Irregular 34
LIFT EVERY VOICE, Irregular 627
LIFT HIM UP, Irregular 220
LIMPSFIELD, 7.3.7.3.7.7.7.3. 584
LIVING, 10.10.10.10. with Refrain 282
LOBE DEN HERREN, Irregular 14
LOBET UND PREISET, Irregular 645
LOIS, 9.9.9.6. 240
LORDSHIP OF CHRIST, Irregular 296

LORIANN, 8.7.8.7. with Refrain 482
LOVELY NAME, Irregular 205
LUBBOCK, 11.8.11.8. with Refrain 318
LYONS, 10.10.11.11. 16, 589, 631

MACCABEUS, 10.11.11.11. with Refrain 163
MADILL, 8.7.8.7.D. 392
MADRID, Irregular 231
MAITLAND, 8.6.8.6.(C.M.) 475
MAJESTAS, Irregular 207
MAJESTY, Irregular 215
MALOTTE, Irregular 462
MANNA, Irregular 243
MANOAH, 8.6.8.6.(C.M.) 414
MARANATHA, Irregular 256
MARCHING TO ZION, 6.6.8.6.(S.M.) with Refrain 524
MARGARET, Irregular 121
MARIANNA, Irregular 642
MARION, 6.6.8.6.(S.M.) with Refrain 39, 226
MARTHA'S SONG, Irregular 171
MARTYN, 7.7.7.7.D. 180
MARYTON, 8.8.8.8.(L.M.) 279, 364
MATERNA, 8.6.8.6.D.(C.M.D.) 630
MATTHEWS, Irregular 468
MCAFEE, 8.6.8.6.(C.M.) with Refrain 295
MCCABE, Irregular 595
MCCONNELL, Irregular 421
MCCONNELSVILLE, 10.8.10.8. with Refrain 311
MCCRAY, 10.6.10.6. with Refrain 97
MCDANIEL, Irregular 441
MCGEE, Irregular 82
MCKAY, 7.7.7.7. with Refrain 578
MCKINNEY, Irregular 324
MELITA, 8.8.8.8.8.8. 69
MENDELSSOHN, 7.7.7.7.D. with Refrain 88
MENDON, 8.8.8.8.(L.M.) 574
MERIDIAN, Irregular 655

RING THE BELLS, 11.9.11.9.
with Refrain 428
ROLL CALL, Irregular 516
ROSAS, Irregular 38
ROUTH, 8.7.8.7. with Refrain
472

SAFETY, Irregular 546
SAGINA, 8.8.8.8.8.8. with
Refrain 147
SALLY TOWNSEND, Irregular
597
SALVATIONIST, Irregular 189
SANKEY, 8.6.8.6.D.(C.M.D.)
with Refrain 413
SATISFIED, 8.7.8.7. with
Refrain 539
SAVIOR, 5.4.5.4.D. 536
SCALES, 11.11.11.11. with
Refrain 573
SCHULER, 10.7.10.7. with
Refrain 569
SCHULZ, 6.5.6.5.D. 107
SCOTT, Irregular 502
SECOND COMING, Irregular
195
SEMINARY, Irregular 605
SERENITY, 8.6.8.6.(C.M.) 154,
480
SEWELL, Irregular 436
SEYMOUR, 7.7.7.7. 306
SHINE, Irregular 579
SHOWALTER, 10.9.10.9. with
Refrain 333
SHOWERS OF BLESSING,
8.7.8.7. with Refrain 467
SIMPSON, 8.8.8.6. with
Refrain 552
SINE NOMINE, 10.10.10.8.
with Alleluias 229, 355
SKILLINGS, Irregular 384
SLANE, 10.10.10.10. 60
SOJOURNER, Irregular 465
SOLI DEO GLORIA, Irregular
37
SOLID ROCK, 8.8.8.8.(L.M.)
with Refrain 406
SOMETHING FOR JESUS,
6.4.6.4.6.6.6.4. 607
SOON AND VERY SOON,
Irregular 192
SOSA, 7.6.7.6. with Refrain
186

SPOHR, 7.6.7.6.D. 46
SPRING, Irregular 50
SPRINGBROOK, 8.6.8.6.(C.M.)
with Refrain 162
ST. AGNES, 8.6.8.6.(C.M.) 116,
225, 498, 505, 506
ST. ANDREW, 6.6.8.6.(S.M.)
609
ST. ANNE, 8.6.8.6.(C.M.) 51,
73, 74, 626
ST. CATHERINE, 8.8.8.8.8.8.
123, 352
ST. CHRISTOPHER, Irregular
291
ST. DENIO, 11.11. with
Refrain 168 ST. DENIO,
11.11.11.11. 6
ST. GEORGE'S WINDSOR,
7.7.7.7.D. 637
ST. GERTRUDE, 6.5.6.5.D.
with Refrain 493
ST. LOUIS, Irregular 86
ST. MARGARET, Irregular 292
ST. PETER, 8.6.8.6.(C.M.) 385,
580
ST. THEODULPH, Irregular
126
ST. THOMAS, 6.6.8.6.(S.M.)
354, 400, 401
STANPHILL, Irregular 315
STASSEN, Irregular 214
STEARNS, Irregular 663
STILLE NACHT, Irregular 91
STOCKTON, 8.6.8.6.(C.M.)
with Refrain 317
STORIES OF JESUS, Irregular
129
STORY OF JESUS, 8.7.8.7.D.
with Refrain 122
STRENGTH, 11.11.11.10. 476
STUTTGART, 8.7.8.7. 21, 257,
369
SULLIVAN, Irregular 567
SUNLIGHT, 10.9.10.9. with
Refrain 424
SUNLIGHT IN MY SOUL,
8.6.8.6.(C.M.) with Refrain
444
SUNSHINE, Irregular 430
SURABAJA, Irregular 582
SURRENDER, 8.7.8.7. with
Refrain 275
SWEET BY AND BY, 9.9.9.9.

with Refrain 515
SWEET HOUR,
8.8.8.8.D.(L.M.D.) 445
SWEETEST NAME, Irregular
425
SWENEY, 8.8.8.8.(L.M.) with
Refrain 600
SYMPHONY, Irregular 383

TABERNACLE, 8.8.8.6. 303
TALLIS' CANON,
8.8.8.8.(L.M.) 449
TALLIS' ORDINAL,
8.6.8.6.D.(C.M.D.) 625
TE VENGO, Irregular 222
TEMPUS ADEST FLORIDUM,
7.6.7.6.D. 101
TERRA PATRIS,
6.6.8.6.D.(S.M.D.) 43, 529
THAT NAME, Irregular 177
THE BLOOD, Irregular 133
THE FIRST NOWELL, Irregular
85
THE LORD'S PRAYER,
Irregular 659
THIS IS THE DAY, Irregular
359
THIS JOY, Irregular 443
THOMPSON, Irregular 312
THREEFOLD 1, 2.2.2. 652
THREEFOLD 2, 2.2.2. 653
THREEFOLD 3, 2.2.2. 654
THREEFOLD GIFTS, Irregular
442
TIDINGS, 11.10.11.10. with
Refrain 583
TO GOD BE THE GLORY,
11.11.11.11. with Refrain
4
TO THE LIGHT, Irregular 532
TOILING ON, Irregular 615
TOKYO, Irregular 179
TOMES, Irregular 230
TOPLADY, 7.7.7.7.7.7. 342
TORONTO, 11.10.11.10. with
Refrain 565
TRAVIS AVENUE, Irregular
466
TRENTHAM, 6.6.8.6.(S.M.)
241, 278, 363, 496
TRUETT, Irregular 238
TRURO, 8.8.8.8.(L.M.) 128,
173

Bibliography

Adams, Raymond Wilson. "Hedge, Frederic Henry." *Dictionary of American Biography* 8 (1943): 498-99.

Allen, William Francis, Charles Pickard Ware, and Lucy McKim Garrison. *Slave Songs of the United States*. 1867. New York: Oak Publications, 1965.

Avery, Gordon, comp. *Companion to the Song Book of the Salvation Army*. London: Salvationist Publishing and Supplies, 1961.

Bailey, Albert Edward. *The Gospel in Hymns*. New York: Charles Scribner's Sons, 1950.

Baker, Theodore. *Baker's Biographical Dictionary of Musicians*. 5th ed. New York: G. Schirmer, Inc., 1958.

Barkley, John M., ed. *Handbook to the Church Hymnary*. 3rd ed. London: Oxford University Press, 1979.

Barr, Raymond A. "Schulz, J.A.P." *New Grove Dictionary of Music and Musicians* 16 (1980): 821-23.

Barrows, Cliff, and Donald Hustad. *Crusade Hymn Stories*. Carol Stream: Hope Publishing Company, 1967.

Bartlett, Emma-Jeanne. *Grace So Amazing*. Nashville: Broadman Press, 1989.

Baselt, Bernd, and Karl-Ernst Bergunder. "Will (Witt), Christian Friedrich." *New Grove Dictionary of Music and Musicians* 20 (1980): 465-66.

Bauman, Jackie. "In His Time: The story behind this beautiful song." *Aglow* (Sept./Oct. 1987): 26-27.

Bäumker, Wilhelm. *Das Katholische deutsche Kirchenlied*. 4 vols. Freiburg: Herdische Verlagshandlung, 1883-1911. Hidesheim: Georg Olms, 1962.

Belden, Henry M., and Arthur Palmer Hudson. *Folk Songs from North Carolina*. Durham: Duke University Press, 1952. Vol. 3 of *The Frank C. Brown Collection of North Carolina Folklore*.

Benson, Louis F. *The English Hymn*. Philadelphia: Presbyterian Board of Publication, 1915.

Bierley, Paul E. *Hallelujah Trombone*. Columbus: Integrity Press, 1982.

Blankenburg, Walter. "Hassler, Hans Leo." *New Grove Dictionary of Music and Musicians* 8 (1980): 294-97.

Blankenburg, Walter. "Praetorius, Michael." *New Grove Dictionary of Music and Musicians* 15 (1980): 188-92.

Blume, Friedrich. *Protestant Church Music: A History*. London: Victor Gollancz, 1975.

Bolwell, Robert, and Alice A. Graham. "Prentiss, Elizabeth Payson." *Dictionary of American Biography* 15 (1943): 188-89.

Boon, Brindley. Letter to Harry Eskew, 22 August 1989.

Brown, Sterling A. "Johnson, James Weldon." *Dictionary of American Biography* 10 (1943): 345-47.

Burrage, Henry S. *Baptist Hymn Writers and Their Hymns*. Portland: Brown, Thurston, and Company, 1888.

Burke, Emory Stevens, et al. *Companion to the Hymnal*. Nashville: Abingdon Press, 1970.

"Charles Albert Tindley." *Official Journal and Year Book of the Delaware Annual Conference of the Methodist Episcopal Church* (1934): 294-96.

Clarkson, Margaret E. *A Singing Heart*. Carol Stream: Hope Publishing Company, 1987.

Cockrell, Dale. "Hays, William Shakespeare." *New Grove Dictionary of American Music* 2 (1986): 357-58.

Colquhoun, Frank. *A Hymn Companion*. Wilton: Morehouse Barlow, 1985.

Colvin, Tom. *Fill Us with Your Love and Other Hymns from Africa*. Carol Stream: Agape, 1983.

Crawford, Richard. "Holden, Oliver." *New Grove Dictionary of American Music* 2 (1986): 408-09.

Crump, R.W. *The Complete Poems of Christina Rossetti*. Vol. 1. Baton Rouge: Louisiana State University Press, 1979.

Crump, R.W. *The Complete Poems of Christina Rossetti*. Vol. 2. Baton Rouge: Louisiana State University Press, 1986.

Daw, Carl P., Jr. *The Collected Hymns of Carl P. Daw, Jr.: A Year of Grace: Hymns for the Church Year*. Carol Stream: Hope Publishing Company, 1990.

Dearmer, Percy, comp. *Songs of Praise Discussed*. London: Oxford University Press, 1933.

Delaughter, Thomas J. "Ernest Orlando Sellers." *Theological Educator* XIV, 1 (Fall 1983): 3-9.

Dett, R. Nathaniel, ed. *Religious Folk-Songs of the Negro as Sung at Hampton Institute*. Hampton: Hampton Institute Press, 1927.

"Directions for Singing." *United Methodist Hymnal*. Nashville: United Methodist Publishing House, 1989.

Dooley, James Edward. "Thomas Hastings: American Church Musician." Diss. Florida State University, 1963.

"Dorsey, Thomas A." *The Music of Black Americans*. 2nd ed. New York: W.W. Norton, 1983.

"Dorsey, Thomas A." *The Gospel Sound: Good News and Bad Times*. rev. ed. New York: Limelight Editions, 1985.

Douen, E.O. *Clement Marot et le Psautier Huguenot*. Paris: L'Imprimerie Nationale, 1878-79.

Dox, Thurston J. "Wilson, Ira B." *American Oratorios and Cantatas* 2 (1986): 1100-24.

Dudley-Smith, Timothy. *Lift Every Heart*. Carol Stream: Hope Publishing Company, 1984.

Duffield, Samuel W. *English Hymns: Their Authors and History*. 3rd ed. New York: Funk and Wagnalls, 1888.

Eaton, Edward Dwight. "Rankin, Jeremiah Eames." *Dictionary of American Biography* 15 (1943): 374.

Ebert, Robert R. "The Reverend Elisha A. Hoffman: Ministry, Music and German Heritage." *Journal of German American Studies* 4, 13 (1978).

Ellinwood, Leonard, ed. *Dictionary of American Hymnology.* New York: University Music Editions, 1984.

Emurian, Ernest K. *Forty Stories of Famous Gospel Songs.* Grand Rapids: Baker Book House, 1959.

Eskew, Harry. "An Interview with Carl Daw." *The Hymn* 2, 40 (Apr. 1989): 24-29.

Eskew, Harry. "The Life and Work of William Walker." Thesis. New Orleans Baptist Theological Seminary, 1960.

Eskew, Harry. "William Walker and his *Southern Harmony.*" *Baptist History and Heritage* 4, 21 (Oct. 1986): 19-26.

Eslinger, Gary S., and Mark F. Daugherty. "Wilson, Ira B." *Sacred Music in Print.* 2nd ed. Philadelphia: Musicdata, 1985.

Fenner, Thomas P. *Religious Folk Songs of the Negro As Sung on the Plantations.* Hampton: The Institute Press, 1909.

Fisher, William Arms. *Seventy Negro Spirituals.* Boston: Oliver Ditson Company, 1926.

Franz Schubert Complete Works. (Breitkopf & Härtel Critical Edition of 1884-1897.) New York: Dover Publications, 1965.

Frere, W.H. *Hymns Ancient and Modern.* (hist. ed.) London: William Clowes and Sons, 1909.

Frost, Maurice. *English and Scottish Psalm and Hymn Tunes.* London: Oxford University Press, 1953.

Frost, Maurice. *Historical Companion to Hymns Ancient and Modern.* London: Parker and Company, 1962.

Garcia, William Burres. "Work, John Wesley." *New Grove Dictionary of American Music* 4 (1986):562-63.

Gealy, Fred D., Austin C. Lovelace, and Carlton R. Young. *Companion to the Hymnal.* Nashville: Abingdon Press, 1970.

Glass, James W. "The Sacred Art Song in the United States, 1869-1975." Diss. Southwestern Baptist Theological Seminary, 1976.

Glover, Raymond F. *A Commentary on New Hymns.* New York: The Church Hymnal Corporation, 1987.

Graziano, John. "Rosamond, J. Johnson." *New Grove Dictionary of American Music* 2 (1986): 583-84.

Grove, Sir George. *Grove's Dictionary of Music and Musicians.* ed. Eric Blom. 5th ed. Vol. 9. New York: St. Martin's Press, 1954.

Haeussler, Armin. *The Story of Our Hymns: The Handbook to the Hymnal of the Evangelical and Reformed Church.* St. Louis: Eden Publishing House, 1952.

Hall, Jacob Henry. *Biography of Gospel Song and Hymn Writers.* New York: Fleming H. Revell Company. 1914. New York: AMS Press, 1971.

Hammond, Paul Garnett. "Music in Urban Revivalism in the Northern United States, 1800-1835." Diss. The Southern Baptist Theological Seminary, 1974.

Hart, James. *The Oxford Companion to American Literature.* 5th ed. New York: Oxford University Press, 1983.

Hastings, Robert J. *Glorious Is Thy Name: B. B. McKinney; The Man and His Music.* Nashville: Broadman Press, 1986.

Hayden, Andrew J., and Robert F. Newton. *British Hymn Writers and Composers: A Check-List.* Croydon: The Hymn Society of Great Britain and Ireland, 1977.

Hewitt, Theodore Brown. *Paul Gerhardt as a Hymn Writer and His Influence on English Hymnody.* New Haven: Yale University Press, 1918. St. Louis: Concordia Publishing House, 1976.

Hillman, Joseph. *The Revivalist.* New York: Joseph Hillman, 1868.

Horder, W. Garrett. *The Hymn Lover.* 3rd ed. London: J. Curwen and Sons, 1905.

Houghton, Will H. *Wycliffe Biographical Dictionary of the Church.* Chicago: Moody Press, 1982.

Hughes, Charles W. *American Hymns Old and New: Notes on the Hymns and Biographies of the Authors and Composers.* New York: Columbia University Press, 1980.

Hustad, Donald P. *Dictionary-Handbook to Hymns for the Living Church.* Carol Stream: Hope Publishing Company, 1978.

Hymnody of the Church of the Nazarene. Kansas City: Lillenas Publishing Company, 1979.

Jackson, George Pullen. *White and Negro Spirituals.* New York: J.J. Augustin, 1943.

Jackson, George Pullen. *Spiritual Folk-Songs of Early America.* New York: J.J. Augustin, 1937.

Jessie Brown Pounds: Memorial Selections. Chicago: Disciples Publication Society, 1921.

Johnson, James Weldon. *Along This Way: The Autobiography of James Weldon Johnson.* New York: Viking Press, 1933.

"Johnson, John Rosamond." *The Music of Black Americans.* 2nd ed. New York: W.W. Norton, 1983.

Jones, Nettie Lou, and Saxe Adams, eds. *Songs for Children.* Nashville: Broadman Press, 1964, No. 86.

Jones, Ralph H. *Charles Albert Tindley: Prince of Preachers.* Nashville: Abingdon Press, 1982.

Julian, John, ed. *A Dictionary of Hymnology.* New York: Dover Publications, 1957.

Katherine K. Davis: A Memorial Retrospective. Boston: Galaxy Music Corporation, n.d.

Larson, Jens Peter. "Haydn, Franz Joseph." *New Grove Dictionary of Music and Musicians* 8 (1980): 328-407.

Levy, Eugene. *James Weldon Johnson: Black Leader, Black Voice.* Chicago and London: University of Chicago Press, 1973.

Liemohn, Edwin. *The Chorale Through Four Hundred Years of Musical Development as a Congregational Hymn.* Philadelphia: Muhlenberg Press, 1953.

Lillenas, Haldor. *Down Melody Lane*. Kansas City: Beacon Hill Press, 1953.

Loftis, Deborah C. "The Hymns of Georgia Harkness." *The Hymn* 4, 28 (Oct. 1977): 186-181.

Loftis, Deborah C. "Big Singing Day in Benton, Kentucky: A Study of the History, Ethnic Identity and Musical Style of *Southern Harmony* Singers." Diss. University of Kentucky, 1987.

Lomax, Alan. *The Folk Songs of North America in the English Language*. Garden City: Doubleday & Company, 1960.

Lorenz, Ellen Jane. *Glory Hallelujah! The Story of the Campmeeting Spiritual*. Nashville: Abingdon Press, 1978.

Lovell, John, Jr. *Black Song: The Forge and the Flame*. New York: The Macmillan Company, 1972.

Lowens, Irving. *Music and Musicians in Early America*. New York: W.W. Norton, 1964.

Luther, Martin. "Liturgy and Hymns." Vol. 53 of *Luther's Works*. Ed. Ulrich S. Leupold. Philadelphia: Fortress Press, 1965.

Martin, Hugh, ed. *The Baptist Hymn Book Companion*. London: Psalms and Hymns Trust, 1967.

Mason, Lowell. *The Modern Psalmist; A Collection of Church Music, . . .* Boston: J.H. Wilkins and R.B. Carter, 1839.

McCutchan, Robert Guy. *Hymn Tune Names: Their Sources and Significance*. New York and Nashville: Abingdon Press, 1957.

McCutchan, Robert G. *Our Hymnody*. New York and Nashville: Abingdon-Cokesbury Press, 1937.

Messenger, Ruth Ellis. *The Medieval Latin Hymn*. Washington: Capital Press, 1953.

Moffatt, James, and Millar Patrick, eds. *Handbook to the Church Hymnary with Supplement*. London: Oxford University Press, 1927.

Moore, Sydney H. *Sursum Corda, Being Studies of Some German Hymn Writers*. London: Independent Press, 1956.

Mordell, Albert. "Whittier, John Greenleaf." *Dictionary of American Biography* 20 (1943): 173-76.

Music, David W. "Wesley Hymns in Early American Hymnals and Tunebooks." *The Hymn* 39 (Oct. 1988): 37-42.

Neale, John Mason. *Collected Hymns, Sequences and Carols of John Mason Neale*. London, New York, and Toronto: Hodder and Stoughton, 1914.

Neil, Bob J. "Philip P. Bliss (1838-1876): Gospel Hymn Composer and Compiler." Diss. New Orleans Baptist Theological Seminary, 1977.

Odum, Howard W. and Guy B. Johnson. *Negro Workaday Songs*. New York: Negro Universities Press, 1969.

Oliver, Paul. "Dorsey, Thomas A(ndrew)." *New Grove Dictionary of American Music* 1 (1986): 648-49.

Osborne, Stanley L. *If Such Holy Song: The Story of the Hymns in The Hymn Book 1971*. Whitby: The Institute of Church Music, 1976.

Ottaway, Hugh. "Vaughan Williams, Ralph." *New Grove Dictionary of Music and Musicians* 19 (1980): 569-80.

Parry, K.L., ed. *Companion to Congregational Praise*. London: Independent Press, Limited, 1953.

Perkins, Dale David. "Ernest Orlando Sellers (1869-1952)." Martin Music Library, New Orleans Baptist Theological Seminary, 1969.

Pidoux, Pierre. *Le Psautier Huguenot du XVIe Siecle*. 2 vols. Basel: Edition Baerenreiter, 1962.

Poetical Works of Frances Ridley Havergal. New York and Chicago: Fleming H. Revell, 1884.

Porter, Ellen Jane Lorenz. "Portrait of a Patriarch." Martin Music Library, New Orleans Baptist Theological Seminary.

Porter, Ellen Jane. *Two Early American Tunes: Fraternal Friends?* New York: The Hymn Society of America, 1975.

Porter, Thomas H. "Ackley, Alfred Henry." *New Grove Dictionary of American Music* 1 (1986): 3.

Powell, Paul R. *Wherever He Leads I'll Go*. New Orleans: In Sight Press, 1974.

Prentiss, Elizabeth. *The Life and Letters of Elizabeth Prentiss*. New York: Anson D.F. Randolph & Company, 1882.

Price, Carl. "Hymn Patterns." *Religion in Life* (Summer, 1947): 431-42.

Randolph, Vance. *Ozark Folk Songs*. Columbia: Missouri State Historical Society, 1946-50.

Reed, Joel F. "Anthony J. Showalter (1858-1924): Southern Educator, Publisher, Composer." Diss. New Orleans Baptist Theological Seminary, 1975.

Reynolds, William J. *Companion to Baptist Hymnal*. Nashville: Broadman Press, 1976.

Reynolds, William J., comp. and Alta C. Faircloth, ed. *The Songs of B.B. McKinney*. Nashville: Broadman Press, 1974.

Reynolds, William J. *Songs of Glory*. Grand Rapids: Zondervan Books, 1990.

Reynolds, William J. *Hymns of our Faith*. Nashville: Broadman Press, 1964.

Riedel, Johannes. *The Lutheran Chorale: Its Basic Traditions*. Minneapolis: Augsburg Publishing House, 1967.

Rockwell, William W. "Prentiss, George Lewis." *Dictionary of American Biography* 15 (1943): 189-90.

Root, George F. *Story of a Musical Life*. New York: Da Capo Press, 1970.

Routley, Erik. *An English-Speaking Hymnal Guide*. Collegeville: The Liturgical Press, 1979.

Routley, Erik. *Hymns and Human Life*. London: J. Murray, 1952.

Routley, Erik. *The Music of Christian Hymns*. Chicago: GIA Publications, 1981.

Ryden, Ernest E. *The Story of Christian Hymnody*. Rock Island: Augustana Press, 1959.

Salazar, Veronica, "Rosas' Music Reflects Christian Unity." *West Side Sun* 27 Aug. 1987.

Sanchez, Diana, ed. *The Hymns of the United Methodist Hymnal*. Nashville: Abingdon Press, 1989.

Sankey, Ira D. *My Life and the Story of the Gospel Hymns*. New York: Harper and Brothers, 1906.

Schaff, Philip. *Christ in Song*. New York: Anson D.F. Randolph and Company, 1868.

Seroff, Doug. "Professor John Work II-Champion of Jubilee Music." *Gospel Arts Day Nashville: A Special Commemoration, Jubilee Hall, Fisk University, June 19, 1988*. Nashville: Nashville Gospel Ministries, 1988.

Sharp, Cecil J. *English Folk Songs from the Southern Appalachians*. Vol 2. London, New York, and Toronto: Oxford University Press, 1932.

Shea, George Beverly. *Then Sings My Soul*. Old Tappan: F.H. Revell Company, 1968.

Sleeth, Natalie. *Adventures for the Soul*. Carol Stream: Hope Publishing Company, 1987.

Smith, Wilbur M. *A Watchman on the Wall: the Life Story of Will H. Houghton*. Grand Rapids: Wm. B. Eerdmans Publishing Company, 1951.

Smoak, Alfred Merril, Jr. "William Walker's *Southern Harmony*." Thesis. The Southern Baptist Theological Seminary, 1975.

Smucker, David Joseph. "Philip Paul Bliss and the Musical, Cultural and Religious Sources of the Gospel Music Tradition in the United States, 1850-1876." Diss. Boston University Graduate School, 1981.

Southern, Eileen. "Dorsey, Thomas A." *Biographical Dictionary of Afro-American and African Musicians*. Westport and London: Greenwood Press, 1982.

Starr, Harris Elwood. "Payson, Edward." *Dictionary of American Biography* 14 (1943): 333-34.

Starr, Harris Elwood. "Dwight, Timothy." *Dictionary of American Biography* 5 (1943): 573-77.

Stebbins, George C. *Reminiscences and Gospel Hymn Stories*. New York: George H. Doran Company, 1924. New York: AMS Press, 1971.

Stevenson, Robert. *Protestant Church Music in America*. New York: W.W. Norton, 1966.

Stulken, Marilyn Kay. *Hymnal Companion to the Lutheran Book of Worship*. Philadelphia: Fortress Press, 1981.

Taylor, Cyril. *The Way to Heaven's Door*. London: Epworth Press, 1957.

Temperley, Nicholas. "Bennett, William Sterndale." *New Grove Dictionary of American Music and Musicians* 2 (1980):499-504.

Temperley, Nicholas. "Williams, Aaron." *New Grove Dictionary of Music and Musicians* 20 (1980): 432.

Temperley, Nicholas. "Webbe (i), Samuel." *New Grove Dictionary of Music and Musicians* 20 (1980): 238-40.

The Hymnal 1940 Companion. 3rd rev. ed. New York: The Church Pension Fund, 1951.

The Hymns and Ballads of Fred Pratt Green. Carol Stream: Hope Publishing Company, 1982.

Thomson, R.W., ed. *The Baptist Hymn Book Companion*. London: Psalms and Hymns Trust, 1967.

Tindley, E.T. *The Prince of Colored Preachers: The Remarkable Story of Charles Albert Tindley*. Muskegon: Patterson Press, 1942.

Wake, Arthur N. *Companion to Hymnbook for Christian Worship*. St. Louis: Bethany Press, 1970.

Ward, John Owen. *The Concise Oxford Dictionary of Music*. 2nd ed. London: Oxford University Press, 1964.

Watson, Richard, and Kenneth Trickett. *Companion to Hymns and Psalms*. Peterborough, England: Methodist Publishing House, 1988.

Watts, J. Wash. "Ernest Orlando Sellers." *Encyclopedia of Southern Baptists* II. Nashville: Broadman Press, 1959.

Weichlein, William J. *A Checklist of American Music Periodicals 1850-1900*. Detroit Studies in Music Bibliography 16. Detroit: Information Coordinators, 1970.

Wesley, John, "Directions for Singing." *The United Methodist Hymnal*. Nashville: United Methodist Publishing House, 1989.

Westrup, J.A., and F.L. Harrison. *The New College Encyclopedia of Music*. New York: W.W. Norton & Company, 1960.

Whittle, D.W., ed. *Memoirs of Philip P. Bliss*. New York: A.S. Barnes and Company, 1877.

Wiggins, Arch R. *Father of Salvation Army Music: Richard Slater*. London: Salvationist Publishing and Supplies, 1945.

Wilhoit, Melvin Ross. "A Guide to the Principal Authors and Composers of Gospel Song of the Nineteenth Century." Diss. The Southern Baptist Theological Seminary, 1982.

"Wilson, Ira B." *Sacred Music in Print*. 2nd ed. Philadelphia: Musicdata, 1985.

Wilson, John. "The Tune *Monkland* and John Antes." *The Hymn Society of Great Britain and Ireland Bulletin* 173 (Oct. 1987): 260-64.

Wilson, Robert S., and Mel R. Wilhoit. "Elisha Albright Hoffman." *The Hymn* 1, 35 (Jan. 1984): 35-39.

Wingard, Alan Burl. "The Life and Works of William Batchelder Bradbury, 1816-1868." Diss. The Southern Baptist Theological Seminary, 1973.

Words and Music. Videocassette. By George Shorney and Natalie Sleeth. Carol Stream: Hope Publishing Company, 1990.

York, Terry W. *Charles Hutchinson Gabriel (1856-1932): Composer, Author, and Editor in the Gospel Tradition*. Thesis. New Orleans Baptist Theological Seminary, 1985.

Young, Carlton R. "Wesley, John Benjamin." *Companion to the Hymnal*. Nashville: Abingdon Press, 1970.

Zahn, Johannes. *Die Melodien der Deutschen; Evangelischen Kirchenlieder, aus den Quellen; Geschopft und Mitgeteilt von Johannes Zahn*. Vol. 4. Reinheim: Druckerei Lokay, 1891. Hildesheim: Georg Olms Verlagsbuchhandlung, 1963.

Bibliography Notes

STAINED GLASS ART

THE WRITER

William L. Hendricks teaches at The Southern Baptist Theological Seminary in Louisville, Kentucky, where he is Professor of Christian Theology, Director of Seminary Graduate Studies, and Director for the Center of Religion and the Arts.

A native of Butte, Montana, he holds degrees from Oklahoma Baptist University, Shawnee, Oklahoma (B.A.); Southwestern Baptist Theological Seminary, Fort Worth, Texas (B.D., M.Div., Th.D.); University of Chicago (M.A., Ph.D.); with additional study at Southern Methodist University, Dallas, Texas; Union Theological Seminary, New York City; Texas Christian University, Fort Worth, Texas; The University of Tubingen, Germany; and Cambridge University (King's College), Cambridge, England.

Prior to his present position, Hendricks taught at Taiwan Baptist Seminary and Malaysia Baptist Seminary (1985), Golden Gate Baptist Theological Seminary (1978-84), The Southern Baptist Theological Seminary (January, 1981), and Southwestern Baptist Thelogical Seminary (1957-77).

He has served on the staffs of at least 10 churches in an interim capacity. In addition, he has had numerous articles published in Southern Baptist Convention publications and other scholastic journals, and has authored eight books, including *The Letters of John: Tapestries of Truth; The Doctrine of Man; A Theology for Children;* and *A Theology for Aging.* He has also traveled extensively abroad and throughout the United States as a speaker and lecturer.

Hendricks is past president of both the Southwest Region of the American Academy of Religion, and the Commission on Religious Studies in the Southwest. He is listed in *Who's Who in Religion* and the *Directory of American Scholars.*

He and his wife have one child, a son, and make their home in Louisville, Kentucky.

THE ARTIST

O. Dixon Waters is manager of design section II in the Church Programs and Services art department of the Southern Baptist Sunday School Board.

A native of Washington, D.C., he worked as a free-lance designer, production manager, and art director for various firms prior to coming to the Sunday School Board in 1968.

He and his wife have two daughters. A resident of suburban Nashville, he is a member of Forest Hills Baptist Church, where he teaches toddlers in Sunday School and serves on the church's public relations committee.

The Burning Bush

*T*HE bush that burned and was not consumed is a symbol of God's initiative in confronting humanity. It is a sign of revelation; it is the meeting place of God and humans. At the burning bush God gives to Moses the commission to lead Israel from Egyptian bondage. In fulfilling this commission, Moses (passing through the sea) brings about, under God's guidance, the definitive act of Israel's deliverance. It is at the burning bush that God reveals His commissioning command with the admonition "I am who I am" (Ex. 3:14, NIV). This term eventually becomes the word Jehovah, the name of God.

The burning bush looks backward to the leadership of God with Abraham, Isaac, and Jacob. The bush also looks forward in that Christian symbolism has seen a prefiguring of the incarnation in the welding of divine fire and an earthly bush in an enduring and indestructible union. The flames in the bush signify the presence of divine fire; the persistence of the bush signifies the endurance of God's calling and commissioning first of Moses, then of Christ. Some have even viewed the bush as a symbol of the church, called out of God, purged by fire, but persisting despite the flames of persecution.

Thus there are many layers of symbolism in the image of the burning bush. We have chosen it for this hymnal as a principle sign of God, the Father, who reveals Himself to establish a redemptive relationship with the world. It is God who calls and commissions. Israel is brought into being through the Exodus. The church comes into being through the Cross of Christ, God's elect one. In these affirmations the burning bush is related to the entire story of God's redemption. It is, therefore, a fitting representation of God, the Father, Jehovah.

The Burning Bush

God called to him from within the bush,... "Take off your sandals, for the place where you are standing is holy ground." EXODUS 3:4-5, NIV

The Creator's Hand

*T*HE Bible recognizes hands as the instruments of working, doing, making. In the only language and frame of reference people can understand, Scripture speaks of creation as the handwork of God (Psalms 8:3-4). The original act of making was creation; God set forth all potential and all created things that we see in the world around us. The world itself and the universe which embraces all the world comes from the creative hands of God.

Very early Christian visual representations of God show a hand emerging through the clouds from heaven. By using a part of the body for the whole (a figure of speech called metonomy) we are able to signify God and God's creative power without making a full-body picture of God, which is difficult to do without leaving the impression that God is only a human written in larger letters.

The visual presentation we use here of the hand of God involves two hands. The two hands are curved in a gesture of love and concern. They are the hands of God which symbolize power and love, creation with a redemptive impulse. The hands come from above and have just let loose a world which floats off into space following other planets, other worlds. The notion is at one and the same time a concept of vast space, of infinite power, of protective love.

The Creator's Hand

In the beginning God created the heavens and the earth.... God saw all that he had made, and it was very good. GENESIS 1:1, 31, NIV

In New Testament times the finger of God was an expression of God's power (Luke 11:20). It is by God's power the miracles of Christ were performed. It is significant to reflect that the power of redemption is also the power behind creation. This visual succeeds in expressing the divine power which comes down from God's dwelling place and provides a dwelling for all creation by making the universe and its multiple worlds. What is distinctive about this presentation is the softening of the hands of power by the gentle curving of the fingers to present the combined ideas of both power and love.

The Manger and Star

*J*ESUS' birth was heralded by the grandeur of God's heaven—symbolized by the star—and the humblest circumstances of earth—symbolized by the manger. It is a beautiful paradox that God's love has come to us in the person of Jesus, combining the heavenly and the earthly, the highest and the lowest.

The Manger and Star

For unto you is born this day in the city of David a Saviour, which is Christ the Lord. And this shall be a sign unto you; Ye shall find the babe wrapped in swaddling clothes, lying in a manger.
LUKE 2:11-12, KJV

The star is a symbol of heavenly light and of guidance. The biblical basis for the star is Matthew 2:2. Wise men (Magi) in the east saw a star guiding them to the place where the young child (Jesus) was. The star becomes the instrument by which the wise, the rich, and the powerful of earth come to recognize God's redemptive gift through the birth of the child. The rays of the star are extended to illustrate the heavenly radiance and to symbolize the significance of Christ's nativity for all the world. The coming of light in darkness is a sign of redemption and of God's Messiah (Isaiah 9:2). Light signifies clarity, the ability to see, to make one's way. Jesus' claim to be the light of the world (John 8:12) is an extension of the light of His nativity star, a pointer to the light at the beginning of creation and a light which comes to bring the new creation (John 1:1-14). The light begun at Bethlehem and with the nativity star will not be put out by the darkness.

The manger is a place where animals eat (the word *manger* is French for "to eat"). The biblical references for the manger are Luke 2:7, 12. The birth of Jesus was in an obscure place because "there was no room for them in the inn" (7, NIV). This event has been celebrated in song ("Away in a Manger") and art (P. Breugel's "The Arrival at Bethlehem"). The ox and ass are present in varied representations of Jesus' birth not just because there had to be animals to eat at the manger but because of the prophecy of Isaiah 1:3.

This visual representation of the manger and star gives a stark contrast of dark lines on a blue background highlighted by the brightness of the star in heaven and the figure of light which is the child in the manger. The implication is that in this contrast of the ancient light of heaven and the new born light on earth, the darkness is, indeed, passing away.

Loaves and Fishes

*T*HE life and ministry of Jesus is represented by the five loaves and two fish (John 6:9). These are an appropriate symbol of Jesus' ministry not only because of the miracle of the feeding of the

5,000, but also because the bread is a metaphor for Christ (John 6:35). The entire sixth chapter of John uses the miracle of the feeding of the 5,000 as an occasion for Jesus' discourse on himself as the bread of life. The church, the body of Christ, celebrates this metaphor of Jesus as the bread of life when we take the Lord's supper. (See the Cup and Bread on pages following.)

The fish also is a symbol of Christ and one of the earliest visual representations of the Christian community for Jesus. The acrostic ICHTHUS is the Greek word for fish and is taken from the first letters of the phrase or words "Jesus Christ Son of God Savior." There is a persistent legend that during times of persecution, Christians would identify themselves to one another by drawing in the sand with the toe of their sandal the two curved lines to symbolize a fish. This symbol has been brought back into wide usage among modern Christians who wear ICHTHUS pins, or use stickers bearing this sign on their possessions.

One allegorical interpretation of the number of the fishes and loaves indicates that the five loaves represent the five wounds in Jesus' body (hands, feet, side) and the two fish symbolize Jesus' two natures (divine and human). Such interpretations are extreme and read back meanings into the Bible which are not originally there. But these extended symbols can serve to remind us of theological and spiritual truths on which we may reflect. The feeding of the 5,000 provided a rich resource for Christian artists to represent this miracle (see a 14th century Italian drawing in Gertrude Grace Sill's *A Handbook of Symbols in Christian Art* [New York: Collier Books, 1975], p. 108).

The visual here shows two stylized fish among five lighter colored loaves of bread, reminiscent of the round flat bread used in the Middle East even today.

The Cross

*T*HE cross is the universal symbol of the Christian faith—a visual notation for the entire Christian event, the life and death of Jesus Christ. All four gospels give an account of Jesus' death by crucifixion. Paul's ministry was centered in the cross, which was the cause for glory, gratitude, and praise for him (Galatians 6:14). By way of extended symbol, the cross becomes a mark of Christian service and suffering (Mark 8:34, Galatians 6:12).

The Scriptures do not describe the specific shape of the cross. From the account of the crucifixion it may be assumed that the cross had a vertical piece and a horizonal piece. These two pieces may be seen as a symbol of the heavenly (the vertical) and the earthly (horizontal). It is probable that the vertical piece, which would need to have been strong enough to bear a person's weight, would already have been at the place of the crucifixion. That place was Golgotha, the place of the skull. The skull is itself a universal symbol of death. The most well-known shape of the cross in the western world is a Latin cross. There are several dozen types and styles of crosses in western visual signs. Protestants always use an empty cross, as opposed to Jesus on the cross (a crucifix), for theological reasons. The empty cross is both a reminder of Jesus' suffer-

Loaves and Fishes

"Here is a boy with five small barley loaves and two small fish, but how far will they go among so many?"
JOHN 6:9, NIV

The Cross

Jesus said, "It is finished." With that, he bowed his head and gave up his spirit.
JOHN 19:30, NIV

ing and a silent testimony to Jesus' resurrection. The cross was not widely used in Christian art until about the 5th century A.D. There are thousands of pictures of the crucifixion, one of the most notable of which is Grunewald's celebrated and graphic scene on the Isenheim Altar piece in Colmar, Germany.

The version of the cross shown here depicts a Latin cross. Shafts of glory and blessing radiate from the cross to bless all who look upon it (John 3:14). A possible interpretation of this version of the cross is that the shafts of blessing radiating from the cross, when viewed from the cross itself, are shards (sharp broken pieces) of sin and hatred which caused Christ's suffering on the cross (Isaiah 53:10). The cross is used in the hymnal more times than any other symbol.

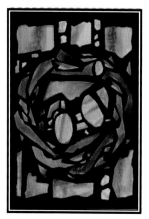

The Crown of Thorns and Nails

The soldiers twisted together a crown of thorns and put it on his head....
"Put your finger here; see my hands....
Stop doubting and believe."
JOHN 19:2; 20:27, NIV

The Crown of Thorns and Nails

ORDINARILY, a crown is a symbol of royalty, honor, or reward. Ancient heroes, athletes, and poets were given a crown of laurel leaves fashioned into a wreath as a reward for their labors. Faithful Christians are promised a crown of life (James 1:12, Revelation 2:10). The first Christian martyr was Stephen (Acts 6-7). The name Stephen means a crown. Christian iconography (assigning symbols to certain persons or ideas which will enable the viewer to know who the person or thing is) often assigns crowns to the depictions of martyrs.

The crown of thorns is an intense irony in that what was intended to be a sign of honor became an instrument of pain and humiliation. What was apparently an impulse of a mocking Roman soldier has become in Christian history a favored symbol of Christ's humiliation on our behalf. There is a picture of a marvelous 20th century wood carving in ebony depicting a Black Christ crowned with thorns. The pathos and sorrow of this contemporary art captures very ably the face of a fellow sufferer (*The Faces of Jesus* by Frederick Buechner and Lee Bolton [New York: Simon and Schuster, 1974], p. 173).

Other instruments of torture (there are five remembered in Christian art: the pillar on which Jesus was tied to be whipped, the whip, the crown of thorns, the nails of the cross, and the spear with which Christ's side was pierced) were the nails by which Jesus was fastened to the cross. Christian history usually depicts the nails more like modern rail spikes, for something of this size and strength would have been required to support the weight of a man.

The representation here places the brutish spikes within the rough circle of the crown of thorns as a composite image of the sufferings of Christ.

The Empty Tomb

THE definitive miracle that establishes the Christian faith is the resurrection of Jesus Christ. All of the gospels give accounts of the resurrection and Paul bases faith upon it (1 Corinthians 15). The major themes of religious art about the resurrection are: Christ rising from a burial place (see "The Resurrection" by Piero della

Francesca); Christ appearing to Mary Magdalene (see Albrecht Dürer's *Noli Me Tangere*, "Do Not Touch Me"); Christ at supper in Emmaus (see Caravaggio's "The Supper at Emmaus"); Christ appearing to the apostles with Thomas (Caravaggio's "Doubting Thomas"). Signs associated with the resurrection are: the resurrection banner (a red cross on a white field), the resurrection halo, the still visible wounds of Christ, and the empty tomb.

Matthew 27:60 speaks of Joseph of Arimathea placing Jesus' body in Joseph's own unused tomb and sealing it with a great stone. He "placed it in his own new tomb that he had cut out of the rock. He rolled a big stone in front of the entrance to the tomb and went away" (NIV). Matthew 28:2 tells of an Angel of the Lord rolling back the stone. The significance of the empty tomb is that Jesus Christ, by the power of God, was raised from the dead.

The hymnal artist, Dixon Waters, has given us a stark line drawing of a rocky open tomb. The vertical lines are broken only by the half circle curve of the stone rolled back from the door. The inner most door facing is a contrasting white, signifying the light and the power of life which emanates from the dark recess of death. In the hymnal it is an appropriate placement which puts the well-known Easter hymn "Christ the Lord Is Risen Today" on the page following this symbol. The resurrection is the occasion for all of our Alleluias.

The Empty Tomb

But Christ has indeed been raised from the dead, the firstfruits of those who have fallen asleep.
1 CORINTHIANS 15:20, NIV

The Dove Descending

*V*ISUAL images of spiritual beings and insights are hard to convey. Christian art has portrayed God, the Father and Creator, as a gigantic man (Michaelangelo on the Sistine Chapel) or as the Ancient of Days (William Blake). The Christian community uses figures for the divine because Jesus, the Son of God, became human. Since Christ took a human form, Christianity has not hesitated to portray Jesus Christ in a human way. This custom in Christian art is distinct from Judaism and Islam, which ordinarily do not use human figures in their religious art. But even Christianity is at a loss to know how to draw the Holy Spirit. Fortunately, there are two visual symbols for the Spirit in the New Testament, the tongues of fire and the dove.

The tongues of fire are taken from the experience of the earliest Christians at Pentecost (Acts 2). Behind this Christian experience is the use of fire in the Old Testament as a cleansing agent, especially in Isaiah's temple encounter with God (Isaiah 6). Moses' burning bush encounter with God also involved the flame of fire (see the first entry in this section).

The dove as a symbol of peace and safety is taken from the account of Noah (Genesis 8:8-12). The symbol of the dove as a metaphor for the Holy Spirit is taken from the accounts of Jesus' baptism (Matthew 3:13-17, Mark 1:9-11, Luke 3:21-22, and John 1:31-34). At Jesus' baptism, the dove descended on Him, a sign of the power and presence of God—the Holy Spirit. Christian depictions of the Spirit use the dove as a sign of the Holy Spirit. A third image which is sometimes used to indicate the Spirit is seven rays of light to indicate the gifts of the Spirit, and seven lamps to signify the presence of the Spirit (Revelation 4:5).

The Dove Descending

"All this I have spoken while still with you."
JOHN 14:25, NIV

"But when he, the Spirit of truth, comes, he will guide you into all truth."
JOHN 16:13, NIV

The symbol shown on the previous page has used both the descending dove and the seven rays (discernable even with the broken lines) to emphasize the Holy Spirit. The flapping motion of the wings indicates a dynamic movement of the Spirit rather than a static concept. A hymn expressing this vision of the Spirit, which due to limited space could not be included in the hymnal, is "Come Holy Spirit, Heavenly Dove."

Three in One

The grace of the Lord Jesus Christ, and the love of God, and the communion of the Holy Ghost, be with you all.
2 CORINTHIANS 13:14, KJV

Three in One

*T*HE two great mysteries of the Christian faith are the Incarnation and the Trinity. The Incarnation of God the Son who totally assumes human nature and becomes one person in two natures (divine and human) defies logic, but the incarnate Christ brings salvation. The threefold rhythm of God being Father, Son, and Holy Spirit is an exclusively Christian doctrine. This doctrine grows out of the doctrines of the divinity of Christ and of the personality of the Holy Spirit. All who believe in the absoluteness of the Father, the divinity of the Son, the personhood of the Holy Spirit are obliged to say something about the threefoldness of God.

Biblical basis for the trinity is found in the validation of the doctrines listed above. Specific passages used to draw the doctrine of the trinity have sometimes seemed forced (the plural "we, us" in Genesis 1 and 2; the appearance of the three visitors to Abraham and Sarah at Mamre, Genesis 18:2). Other references are circumstantial: the baptism of Jesus with the voice of the Father, the earthly form of the Son, and the presence of the Holy Spirit as a dove (see The Dove Ascending in the entry preceding). There are some specific references to all three persons of the trinity listed together (Matthew 28:19, 2 Corinthians 13:14).

Visual symbols for the trinity have been mostly geometric or abstract. Most frequent among visual symbols for the trinity used in manuscripts and architectural embellishments are: the equilateral triangle, the circle included in the triangle, the trefoil (like a three-leaf clover), the three intertwining arches, three small circles in a larger circle, or three equal interlocking circles. When human figures are used in Christian art to symbolize the trinity, we see either three identical human figures, or the Father holding up the arms of the Son on the cross and the Spirit hovering between them. There is an especially effective woodcarving of the latter threesome carved from one piece of wood by Tilman Reimenschneider in Jakobus Church in Rotenburg, Germany.

The figure for this entry is particularly appropriate. It is of three interlocking fish. The common eye serves as a unifying center and a symbol of oneness. Radiating from three sides are three bands of light providing an additional reference to the threesome in oneness.

Lamp and Bible

*T*WO elemental biblical metaphors are word and light. "Word" (Old Testament, *dabar*; New Testament, *logos*) is a term with wide meaning. The term "word" means an effective instrument of creating, the will of the Creator, the plan of creation, the organizing and energizing force of the universe. Word is the conveyor of meaning. Word is language, the primary means of communications. Given all of these in-depth definitions of the term "word," it is small wonder that the term is used both of Jesus Christ (John 1:1) and for the message God gives (Psalm 119:11 and some 23 times in Psalm 119). In post biblical days, Christians refer to the completed Bible as the Word of God. God communicates with His world in person and in precepts.

Light is a metaphor for truth, for illumination, for the ability to discern. To speak of God's Word as a lamp is to suggest that we are illumined (lighted up) and guided by God. Just as Jesus Christ is the primary reference for the term Word of God, so He is the primary reference for the Light of God (John 1:1-19, John 8:12). The Word is effective communication of God, including the Scriptures inspired of God. The Word is also the light, the lamp. Both book and lamp are containers for the Word of God so that God who created the world by word and light may also be seen as the God who redeems the world by word and light.

The open Bible is a sign of the effective power of God to speak from the words of the page, reflective of the heart of God, to the heart of humans. The lamp is a container of light which symbolizes sight and understanding. In the parable of the wise and foolish virgins, the careful keeping of the lamp and the wise use of its resources is a sign of readiness to receive Christ, the Bridegroom.

Artist Dixon Waters has given us a multilayered visual. There is an open Bible letting the Word into the world. There is a flaming lamp illuminating the Word and the readers. Behind both of these there is the light of God suggestively lined out in rays that are in the shape of the cross.

Lamp and Bible

Thy word is a lamp unto my feet,
and a light unto my path.
PSALM 119:105, KJV

All scripture is given by inspiration
of God, and is profitable for doctrine,
for reproof, for correction, for
instruction in righteousness."
2 TIMOTHY 3:16, KJV

Cross with Crown of Thorns

*T*HE hymnal artist has chosen the cross and the crown of thorns as a symbol for sins. These are depictions of the results of sin. The symbolism of the crown of thorns is seen in the art for an earlier entry (628), The Crown of Thorns and Nails. The symbolism of the cross is also depicted in the same section, The Cross (627).

Our discussion of this symbol concentrates on the combination of suffering and redemption, shame and glory. The portion of this symbol which is noteworthy is the band of pure white that shines behind the cross and the crown of thorns. In this band of pure white we find the elemental symbol of light and hope. The light and hope which stream from the cross both identify our sin and provide us with light to see how suffering can be redemptive and how shame can become glory. This transformation is accomplished by Christ because of his suffering and shame (humiliation) on the cross. A hymn which expresses this transformation is "I Lay My Sins on Jesus" (272).

John 1:9 is a central text about Jesus as the light who comes to highlight (illumine) persons in the world. The double meaning of this text is that by the light, which Jesus is and gives, humans can truly see who they are, since our sinfulness is revealed by this light. The second meaning is that Jesus provides that light and hope to all who believe that they many see their way out of the darkened con-

Cross with Crown of Thorns

For there is one God, and
one mediator between God
and men, the man Christ Jesus.
1 TIMOTHY 2:5, KJV

dition of sin. Our artist has combined both of these interpretations in the stark black hues of the cross and the outline of the crown of thorns. The background is a deep purple. It is only the light that relieves the picture and provides its contrast. It is only the light and hope streaming from the cross that provide spiritual light and hope.

It is fitting that Christian iconography (assigning pictures and visual forms to persons and things) does not have a symbol for sin itself. The serpent is the symbol for evil and for the evil one. Perhaps we do not want to glorify sin or the various sins by assigning them symbols. Or perhaps we recognize that the actuality of sin is so present that we do not need symbols to recognize it.

The Tree of Life

The Tree of Life
"I am the true vine, and my Father is the gardener."
JOHN 15:1, NIV

On either side of the river, was there the tree of life...and the leaves of the tree were for the healing of the nations.
REVELATION 22:2, KJV

TREES, in general, are symbols for life, the entire cosmos, and the cyclical process of natural renewal. Modern psychologists identify dreams of trees with growth. The biblical materials on trees is extraordinarily rich in its implications. There are two trees in the Garden of Eden. One is the tree of the knowledge of good and evil. Adam and Eve eat its fruit and commit sin. They are excluded from the garden so they will not eat the fruit of the tree of life and have to live forever in a fallen state under the painful conditions of human history. In a true biblical style of rounding out the purposes of God, we see in Revelation 22:1-2 the tree of life taken up into heaven, appearing in the Garden of God where it nourishes all life in God's eternal order. The healing power of the heavenly tree of life calls our attention back to the tree of Calvary, the cross, which redeems humankind. The Cross was sometimes portrayed as a cosmic tree which reached from heaven, penetrated hell, and whose arms were wide enough to save all the world. So by the tree of God we are saved and sustained.

Christian art refers to several trees. The fig tree was sometimes regarded as the tree of knowledge. The Cedar of Lebanon was seen as a token of prosperity and was also a symbol for Christ. The tree of Jesse (see the stained glass window version of Chartres Cathedral) was the family tree of Jesus on which the Old Testament ancestors (or heroes, kings, and prophets) are seen as branches leading up to the crown of the tree who is Christ. The branches of the grape vine are seen both as a symbol of Israel (a large cluster of grapes borne on a pole by two men is the symbol of modern Israel) and as a symbol of the union of Christ and believers.

This visual representation of the tree of life shows a flourishing tree with full foliage. Appropriately enough the top of the tree has a cross within a nimbus (a circle of light). The symbolism refers both to Christ, truly human, and to the people of God. Hymn 315, "Room at the Cross," suggests the symbolism of the cross as a shelter at which one may seek safety.

Hand Holding Hand

THE creation symbol speaks of the power and glory of God in making the world. The symbol of the hand holding a hand conveys the idea of God holding on to humanity, the crown of

God's creation. The hand is the extension of the body which works, which effects things, which does the will of the person. Hands are expressive. When open they indicate friendship, blessing, assurance. When closed in a fist they represent anger or wrath. The extended index finger, a particular sign associated with John the Baptist in Christian art, calls attention to another person or thing. The extended index finger raised on high points toward God and is a sign of witness and piety.

The symbol shown here is one of a human hand reaching up and the divine hand reaching down. The effect is theologically appropriate. Our times are in God's hand (Psalm 31:15). To be in the shelter of God's hand is to have salvation. To be delivered from the hands of wicked people is to be safe. One lifts up the hands to God for all of the divine blessings. Clean hands are a metaphor for righteousness. It is a thoroughly biblical metaphor to speak of the divine hands reaching down and of human hands reaching up. Our symbol here denotes a sense of peace, repose, and solidarity. God's hand is not grasping; humanity's hand is neither defiant nor struggling to be free. There is a confident togetherness.

The hands of our visual are especially appropriate as a commentary on John 10:28-29. These verses of assurance are dear to the heart of Baptist heritage which has stressed the divine initiative and holding power of God in the salvation event. Two hymns in the hymnal reinforce the notion of God's hands and human hands. These hymns are: "Not What My Hands Have Done," (339) and "He's Got the Whole World in His Hands," (346).

Hand Holding Hand

"I give them eternal life...no one can snatch them out of my hand.... no one can snatch them out of my Father's hand." JOHN 10:28-29, NIV

Christ Teaching

*J*ESUS taught in parables which were ways of reversing the order of things, of conveying a message about God in ordinary events, of saying things that invite further thought and interpretation. Our visual symbol of Jesus' teaching is a parable. Upon first glancing at the visual of Christ Teaching, one cannot readily make out what the shapes mean. On closer reflection it becomes apparent that one figure is standing surrounded by rows of other figures. The standing figure gestures with the right arm, a speaker's pose. There is a nimbus (halo) around the speaker's head. Rays of light radiate from the speaker. The title of the symbol "Christ Teaching" aids in our interpretation of the picture. The crowd is swirled around the teacher in a V-shaped arrangement. With that explanation the picture becomes clear. That God sent the Son to proclaim God's message to people is not easy to comprehend in either verbal or visual form. We must be patient with the mystery. We must probe the parable, of this picture, and of Jesus' teaching which gives a message about the kingdom of God.

The biblical reference in Ephesians 2:20 to a foundation suggests another metaphor: that of Christ as the chief cornerstone (See also 1 Peter 2:4-8 and hymns 353 and 356) upon which our faith is built. In the modern world, a cornerstone is usually an ornamental slab on which some message is written. In biblical days the cornerstone was the keystone on which a large portion of the weight rested. The symbol and the verse provide a double meaning. Jesus, who

Christ Teaching

Built on the foundation of the apostles and prophets, with Christ Jesus himself as the chief cornerstone. EPHESIANS 2:20, NIV

brings us the Word of God, both provides and becomes the foundation stone for God's community, the church.

Dove, Water, and Light

*T*HIS symbol provides a threefold reference to the Holy Spirit and to Christian baptism. One thinks instantly of the baptism of Jesus (Matthew 3:13-17) where the symbols of water, light, and the dove converge. Although light is not specifically mentioned in the passages referring to Jesus' baptism (Matthew 3:13-17, Mark 1:9-11, Luke 3:21-22, John 1:31-34), the opening of heaven expresses the notion of light. In the ancient world, lightning was seen as a means by which heaven was opened. The rays of light, growing wider as they descend from heaven to earth, are the artist's way of conveying the divine light. The dove is a symbol of the Holy Spirit (see The Dove Descending). The dove descending on the waters is a symbol of baptism and is reminiscent of the dove of peace returning to the Ark of Noah (Genesis. 8:10; cf. 1 Peter 3:20-22). One of the earliest Christian visual symbols for the church is the ark. The waters in the middle of this symbol (Dove, Water, and Light) are, appropriately, the ruffled waters which imply the threat and difficulty through which Christians and the church must pass. Baptism is itself a symbol of death, burial, and resurrection, both the resurrection of Christ and the resurrection of the believer who is born again in Christian commitment as well as raised up at the last day (Romans 6:1-4). Hymns 362 ("Baptized in Water") and 364 ("Come, Holy Spirit, Dove Divine") convey the words of the symbols. Note especially the first phrases of "Come, Holy Spirit, Dove Divine": *Come, Holy Spirit, Dove divine, On these baptismal waters shine.*

Baptism is the public profession of one's faith and the first act of obedience of the Christian life. The three symbols shown on this page and the preceding page are aptly arranged. The teaching of Jesus and the person of Jesus are the foundation of the people of God; baptism is the open profession of the people of God; and the supper is the remembrance of Jesus' death by the people of God.

Cup and Bread

*T*HE cup and bread are symbols of the Lord's Supper. These symbols are especially sacred to the family of God since Jesus identified these symbols and explained their meaning (1 Corinthians 11:24-25). The churches through the centuries have beautified these symbols almost to the point of making them innocuous. The chalice of Antioch in the Cloisters Museum in New York is an example of a beautified cup that romanticizes the reality of what the cup of Jesus' suffering meant historically. The Medieval quest for the Holy Grail was a visionary legend which sought the cup actually used at the Lord's Supper. Leonardo da Vinci's "Last Supper," perhaps the best known picture in western art made some attempts to return these symbols to a more simple depiction. In our century, Salvador Dali's "Last Supper" (The National Gallery) is a mystical version of the bread and cup. In Dali's painting, the light from heaven shines through the cup, filled with clear wine. The effect is that the blessing of salvation shines through the symbol of the blood of Christ to all believers. Just as we must not permit the cross to be domesticated until it is merely an object of prettiness which loses all contact with the reality of suffering, so we must not embellish the cup and bread until they lose the grim reality of Christ's sacrifice.

Artist Dixon Waters has given us a plain and unmistakable picture of the cup, surrounded by the two halves of a broken loaf of bread. Once more the visual impression is broken by the shafts of vertical light from heaven. It is a tragedy that theological verbal disputations over the meaning of the Supper have overshadowed these simple visual symbols of the sacrifice of Jesus Christ on behalf of the sins of the world. Pictures and poetry have expressed the event better than strident theological discourse.

Anchor, Cross, and Heart

*D*IXON Waters, following ancient iconography (assigning of a specific symbol to a special thing so as to permit easy recognition), has combined three symbols. They are the anchor, a symbol of hope; the cross, a symbol of faith; and the heart, a symbol of love. Faith, hope, and love are the essential gifts of the Spirit to the people of God (1 Corinthians 12-14, esp. 13:13). These gifts are classically known as the cardinal virtues of Christian living. We need to remember that these are indeed gifts from God and, like all gifts, are intended to be used by those who receive them.

The basic outline of our symbol is an anchor. The shaft and the horizontal bar at the top, plus the chain loop, form an Egyptian cross. The cross is a symbol of faith. We both put our faith in the cross as the means whereby we are saved and we are enabled to have faith by the one who died on the cross.

The anchor proper is a symbol of hope. The grappling hooks at the bottom of the cross serve to hold fast whatever is buffeted by the storms on the surface. This is a profound symbol of the peace hope gives to the people of God.

The heart attached to the anchor is a symbol of love. Jesus said the greatest commandment is to love God, our neighbor, and ourself (Matthew 22:37-40). In biblical times the heart was considered a symbol for thoughts, motivation, and desires (Proverbs 4:23). In the church's symbols, the heart stands as the organ of love, sentiment, and devotion. Uniting the two we have the idea of the heart as a symbol for motivation and dedication. A hymn which expresses the love of Christ to the believer is "O the Deep, Deep Love of Jesus" (409). A hymn which expresses the believers love for Christ is "My Jesus, I Love Thee" (211).

Cross and Family

*A*MONG the 17 articles of *The Baptist Faith and Message*, there is no article specifically addressed to the family. The topic, however, is appropriately addressed in the third section of the hymnal (The People of God). The selection of hymns on the family is placed, aptly enough, between Christian discipleship and life eternal ("Last Things," article X of *The Baptist Faith and Message*).

Anchor, Cross, and Heart

We have this hope as an anchor for the soul, firm and secure.
HEBREWS 6:19, NIV

And now these three remain: faith, hope and love. But the greatest of these is love.
1 CORINTHIANS 13:13, NIV

Cross and Family

Be...an example of the believers, in word, in conversation, in charity, in spirit, in faith, in purity.
1 TIMOTHY 4:12, KJV

The visual symbol of Home and Family is the Cross and Family. It is fitting to bring together representative persons of the family, clustering them around the cross, the primary symbol of the Christian faith. Several features about this picture are significant. One notices the encircling oval which surrounds the family, drawing them together. The smaller circle in the center, firmly attached to the cross, repeats the larger oval motif but also draws the members of the family into a unity of faith and belief. If one can imagine the outer oval holding out the threats to the family, giving a sense of solidarity, then one can see the inner circle drawing the family members together and uniting them in faith at the cross. One also notices the integration and placement of the family members. The mother and son are positioned on one side; the father and daughter on the other. The father rises somewhat above the mother, but the mother is to the forefront of the viewer. The artist has made every attempt to grant to each member, mother, father, son, and daughter a rightful place of honor in the family. This visual is an accurate portrayal of a true exegesis of Ephesians 5:21—6:4.

Book of Life and Lamb

Book of Life and Lamb

I am Alpha and Omega, the first and the last.
Revelation 1:11, KJV

And when he had taken the book, the...elders fell down before the Lamb...and they sung a new song, saying, Thou art worthy to take the book, and to open the seals thereof.
REVELATION 5:8-9, KJV

THIS visual is another threefold symbol. It has a lamb, an Alpha and Omega, and a book of life. The section which this symbol introduces is on eternal life and is counterpart to article X, "Last Things," in *The Baptist Faith and Message*. These three symbols are drawn from the Book of Revelation. Each has been used separately as an expression of the last things (eschatology). When combined, they form a powerful triad bearing witness to God, Christ, and the Spirit.

The Alpha and Omega are the first and last letters of the Greek alphabet and stand for the fact that God and Christ are the beginning and the end of all creation. These letters are a universally acknowledged symbol of the divine. In Revelation 1:11 it is not certain whether the reference is to God the Father or God the Son. Later the letters are applied to God in Revelation 21:6 and to Jesus in 22:13. The letters usually appear side by side. Our artist, in an effort to provide visual harmony and work all of the elements of this tripartite symbol into a small space, has placed the Alpha on top and the Omega in a logical sequence.

The lamb with the cross is a representation of Christ, God's sin offering. Standing on the Book of Life, the lamb is a symbol of judgment. Often in Scripture one of the divine persons is portrayed as an animal. The portrayal of God as an animal is called a theriomorphism (*therios*, animal; *morphe*, to have the form of). From the plaintive cry of John the Baptist in John's gospel, "Behold the Lamb of God, which taketh away the sin of the world," (John 1:29), to the worship of the lamb who is worthy (Revelation 5:6-14), we are reminded of God's Son who is our salvation.

The book with seven seals is a symbol of judgment. The artist's rendition seems to have eight horizontal seals, but the largest one of these nearest the viewer is to be seen as the end of the book, not as one of the seals. Each of the seals contains a judgment of God. The opening of the seals and the content of each section is detailed in Revelation 6 and 8:1-5. If one relates the seven seals to the seven lamps before the throne (Revelation 4:5), it is possible to relate the sealed book to the Spirit. We then would have the trinitarian symbol of: Alpha and Omega—the Father; the Lamb—the Son; and the book—the Holy Spirit.

Fish, Cross, Earth, and Sky

THIS composite visual comes at the beginning of a group of hymns which convey the idea of the testimony or witness of the people of God. Most of these selections in this section are from the perspective of personal piety. Many of the gospel songs contain "I" in the title. The corporate expressions of gratitude and praise are placed in the first section of the hymnal, the Glory of God.

The specific symbols in this picture refer primarily to the believer. The fish, rather than being the ICHTHUS of Christ, refers to Christians as fishers of men. The cross, rather than being the specific cross of Christ, is the cross that believers are called to bear (Matthew 16:24). The rainbow in the sky is symbolic of the promise of God that the earth will not again be destroyed by a flood (Genesis 8:13-14). The earth symbolizes the place of humanity's habitation and the arena for the individual's testimony and praise. The sky represents the dwelling of God whence our praise is directed.

Fish, Cross, Earth, and Sky
And he saith unto them, Follow me, and I will make you fishers of men.
MATTHEW 4:19, KJV

Cross and People

Cross and People
For thou...hast redeemed us to God by thy blood out of every kindred, and tongue, and people, and nation; and hast made us unto our God kings and priests: and we shall reign on the earth.
REVELATION 5:9-10, KJV

THE artist has superimposed on the cross a group of people representing ethnic diversity. By means of headdress, hair style, and subtle lines on the faces, Dixon Waters has brought the whole world around the cross. All the world belongs at the cross, which is one of three cosmic moments. A cosmic moment, by the intention of God, affects all that come before it and come after it. The cosmic moments are creation, cross, and consummation. The artist helps us see that the gospel is universal and the witness of the church must be to all the world. The familiar song "Jesus Loves the Little Children," is a well-known expression of the church's mission to all the world. Note the change in wording so as to be all inclusive.

The cross in our picture is highlighted by striations (lines or furrows) to highlight the diversity of the world's peoples. The cross is the universal symbol; humanity is the basic recipient of the benefits of Christ's cross. They are brought together, cross and people, in this asymmetrical, somewhat off-centered, representation. By making the cross uneven in proportion and off center at the bottom of the frame, the artist has given the cross and the picture a sense of fluidity and motion.

This hymnal is distinct from its predecessors in many ways. One of its distinctions is these iconic symbols. Another distinction is the intentional inclusion of ethnic hymns and gospel songs. A subcommittee on new materials sought world ethnic hymns for inclusion. One such example is the old negro spiritual "The Old Ship of Zion" (577). The words of this spiritual have an inclusivist message.

This section of the hymnal "Evangelism and Missions" is counterpart to section XI of The Baptist Faith and Message.

Cross and World

Cross and World

*I*T is a mistake to separate evangelism and missions. It might be possible to suggest that the "Cross and People" symbol stresses evangelism and the "Cross and World" symbol emphasizes missions. This is a distinction but not an essential difference. The Scripture connected with the "Cross and the World" is one we ordinarily associate with missions. Yet, it is the mission of the church to evangelize everywhere and the focus of evangelism is people, all people, everywhere. The terms mission and evangelism are rightly held together in the faith statement this hymnal reflects, and by the placement of these two visual expressions on the same page.

The cross over the world is an ancient symbol known as the "Cross of Triumph"—a symbol of the triumph of Christianity throughout the world. By the placement of this symbol in this particular location, the emphasis shifts from a past to an ongoing and future reference. That is, we must not see the cross as already having completely triumphed over the world. Rather, the cross becomes a source of power by which Christianity may triumph in every age and by which, eventually, all the world may be brought back to God. There is a double symbolism in this picture. The triune rays of light serve as an X-shaped radiance behind the cross atop the world, forming a St. Andrew's Cross. Andrew was the first apostle called by Christ and the first to be a missionary and evangelist, bringing his brother Simon Peter to Christ. The picture of the world is that of unity (the circle) in diversity (the various shapes within the circle). Isaac Watts familiar text "Jesus Shall Reign" (587), is a good hymn expression of the symbol "Cross and World."

Root, Seed, and Fruit

Root, Seed, and Fruit

*T*HE "Root, Seed, and Fruit" symbol depicts Nurture and Education. Illustrations of growth from nature, plant life, and agriculture abound in Scripture. The beginning of the Bible is in the Garden of Eden. The conclusion is in the Garden of Paradise. Jesus is called the seed of Jesse and of David, the awaited and expected fruit of these forebearers. Jesus used primarily agricultural parables. His parable of sowing the seed is a parable of the spreading of the kingdom. Jesus encourages the ministry of the disciples by the picture of ripened grain and its need for harvesting.

All parts of the germinating process are expressed in our picture. The roots of the germinating seed grow deep, like those of a tree planted by water. Such a tree is deep-rooted and cannot be moved. Older readers will remember the 19th century gospel song "I Shall Not Be Moved." The message of the song was taken from the tree planted near water which could not be moved.

The sprout of the seed gives evidence of future growth and success. In Mark 4:31, the small mustard seed is taken as a simile for the nurture of the kingdom of heaven and its rapid growth. The leaf in the picture expresses the idea of a healthy plant, one that will be productive, one that will give fruit. We are instinctively reminded of Jesus' metaphor of the vine and the branches (John15:111). This consummate metaphor speaks of the necessity and need for nurture and the production of fruit. "Come, All Christians, Be Committed" (604), is a hymn reflective of the need for Christian nurture and education. The visual is reflective of article XII of *The Baptist Faith and Message*.

Hourglass and Coins

*T*HIS visual shows an hourglass with coins running through it. It is a symbol of stewardship and service. Time and talent (originally a term for a unit of money) are brought together in this symbolic form. Ordinarily, one would expect sand, or in more extravagant times, gold dust, to be running through the hourglass. In this instance, coins are an unmistakable symbol which tie together time and money. The hourglass is often a negative symbol, a reminder of the brevity of life. Often it is held by a skeleton, symbolizing death. In our picture there is the negative sense of urgency, but there is also the positive reenforcements that we have time and money, and they are to be expended in the service of God. This powerful symbol of stewardship reminds us that time is money and that all we have belongs to God.

The biblical materials begin with the beginning of time and highlight the sabbath day as a time set aside for God. This sabbath principle is extended through the year of jubilee. The Christian sabbath is shifted to the first day by virtue of the resurrection. Finally, all time is brought under the divine control by the commitment of Christian stewardship (Romans 12:1 and 1 Corinthians 10:31).

Just as with time, so with money. The Old Testament principle of the tithe recognizes the need for returning to God a portion of our money. Jesus recognized the necessity of rendering to Caesar his due, but he also recognized the prior need to give God his due (Matthew 22:21). Particularly, Christ applauded the sacrificial gift of the widow's mite and taught, by his instructions to the rich young ruler (Matthew 19:21), that money must not stand between us and our Christian discipleship and stewardship (Matthew 19:22). There is a moving painting by George Frederick Watts (*The Bible and Its Painters*, p. 196) entitled "For He Had Great Possessions." It is an example of stewardship rejected. Our visual is an example of the possibility of stewardship and service. William How's hymn,"We Give Thee But Thine Own" (609), presents the challenge of stewardship and service in music.

Cross, Bible, and Pilgrim's Hat

*T*HIS visual, in the Section of hymns entitled "The Christian and the Social Order" represents the concerns addressed in article XVII of *The Baptist Faith and Message*. The flared out cross tied together by the two small concentric circles is reminiscent of the cross in the symbol "Cross and Family." Yet the flaring shaped at the ends of each arm of the cross works the distinctiveness of this cross. Since the cross is the primary symbol of the Christian faith, the artist has used it numerous times and in a variety of shapes, each somewhat different. This cross has three lined sections on each piece. These may be seen as a reference to the trinity. It is pos-

Hourglass and Coins

Every man according as he purposeth in his heart, so let him give; not grudgingly, or of necessity: for God loveth a cheerful giver.
2 CORINTHIANS 9:7, KJV

Cross, Bible, and Pilgrim's Hat

Where the Spirit of the Lord is, there is liberty....Stand fast therefore in the liberty wherewith Christ hath made us free....If the Son therefore shall make you free, ye shall be free indeed.
2 CORINTHIANS 3:17;
GALATIANS 5:1;
JOHN 8:36, KJV

sible that the flared ends of this cross indicate the expanded sense of liberty which religious freedom brings to any society.

The pilgrim's hat is readily recognized as such by its broad brim, high rounded crown, and embellishing square buckle on the band. Whereas the record of Plymouth Bay colony and the history of the established denominations are not as eloquent a witness for religious liberty as some other American colonies, nevertheless, the Pilgrim hat has become a symbol of American religious liberty. This symbol of Puritanism and religious liberty is brought to mind by the second stanza of the hymn "America the Beautiful" (630).

The Bible portrayed is a large, heavy tome, reflective of the family bibles in use in the American colonies. It is said that three books shaped frontier opinion and were to be found on the bookshelf of every home. These were the Bible, a hymn book, and Foxes' *Book of Martyrs*. This triad of figures makes a significant symbol for religious liberty.

Dove and Olive Branch

Dove and Olive Branch

Glory to God in the highest, and on earth peace, good will toward men.
LUKE 2:14, KJV

And they shall beat their swords into plowshears, and their spears into pruninghooks: nation shall not lift up a sword against nation, neither shall they learn war any more.
MICAH 4:3, KJV

*T*HE final visual symbol in the 1991 Baptist Hymnal, the first hymnal to provide extensive visual symbols, is entitled "Dove and Olive Branch." This visual conveys a visual representation of article XVI of *The Baptist Faith and Message*. The article is on peace and war. The biblical setting for the symbol is Genesis 8:6-13. The first return of the dove and the olive branch are the perennial symbols of peace. Even the political and secular societies of our time use the terms hawk and dove as metaphors for war and peace. The polarity of war and peace, hostility and friendship is a polarity with which all societies in every age have had to deal. This bifocal motif has called forth the best and the worst in humankind. Leo Tolstoy's famous novel *War and Peace* is a classic piece of literature expressing these perennial opposites.

Our artist has used the dove in several of these symbols, both as a symbol of the Holy Spirit and as, in this instance, a sign of peace. Just as the crosses in each of our visual symbols are different, so too, the doves are different. The dove is seen full front in flight. Behind is the sun, shining after the rain, the flood, the crisis. Below is the rainbow, the sign of peace between God and persons. The green olive branch indicates that plant life is growing and that the process of nature has returned to its productive stage. Absent is any hint of war or strife. This is the case, not because war and strife have permanently ceased. Rather, this final visual seeks to convey only the positive, the peace of God.